FEDERAL RULES OF CIVIL PROCEDURE

As Amended Through April 1, 2004

Together with:

FOUNDATION PRESS

NEW YORK, NEW YORK

2004

THOMSON

WEST

ISBN 1–58778–662–1

ISSN 1082–9024

Cover Photos: SUPREME COURT HISTORICAL SOCIETY and USDA Photos

TEXT IS PRINTED ON 10% POST CONSUMER RECYCLED PAPER

PREFACE

Welcome to the world of the Federal Rules of Civil Procedure. Here is a roadmap to the interior:

1. Federal Rules of Civil Procedure

This booklet begins with the Civil Rules themselves or, more exactly, with (i) the Table of Rules, which allows you to see the structure of the Federal Rules of Civil Procedure, (ii) the main corpus of Civil Rules 1–86, (iii) the Appendix of Forms, as prefaced by its own explanatory Introductory Statement, and (iv) the Supplemental Rules for Certain Admiralty and Maritime Claims.

The most important pointer on use of this portion of the booklet regards the history of amendments. After each amended Rule or Form appears a line listing by year the effective date of all amendments. Details of these amendments appear in and immediately after Federal Rule of Civil Procedure 86—there the booklet tells which particular subdivisions underwent amendment in each year, and it gives both an official citation to the amendatory order or statute and a reference to a readily available source containing any Advisory Committee's Notes. For example, you might want to know how Fed.R.Civ.P. 7(b) read when some 1980 case came down: Rule 7 closes with an indication of amendment in 1948, 1963, and 1983; referring to Rule 86 informs that 1948 and 1963 saw amendments to Rule 7(a) and that only the 1983 changes affected Rule 7(b); for 1983 in particular, the Supreme Court's amendatory order appears at 461 U.S. 1095, while the Advisory Committee's Notes appear at 97 F.R.D. 165; the latter source will tell you exactly how Rule 7(b) looked in 1980.

2. Civil Advisory Committee's Notes

This booklet in fact reprints the most significant of the Advisory Committee's Notes on amendments to the Federal Rules of Civil Procedure. These come right after the booklet's Civil Rules portion, with the primary organization of the Notes being by date of amendment. Thus, the Note on Rule 7(b) lies with the set of 1983 amendments. Each set of reprinted amendments has a separate entry in the thumb index on the booklet's back cover, permitting quick access.

The most important pointer on using this portion of the booklet regards the style of Advisory Committee's Notes. For each amendment, the Rule appears with its changes (new matter is in italics; omitted matter appears with a line through it) and then the following Note allows the Advisory Committee to explain the changes. All this enables you to reconstruct the former Rule. Using the same example, you can see that in 1980 Rule 7(b) lacked a subdivision (3), although its essence came through Rule 7(b)(2)'s former reference to "signing." Indeed, you have reconstructed Rule 7(b) as it existed from the beginning in 1938, and you can find the Advisory Committee's Note on that original Rule 7 in the set of Early Committee's Notes.

3. Federal Rules of Appellate Procedure

This booklet's next portion contains most of the Appellate Rules and Forms. The organization is similar to the booklet's treatment of the Civil Rules.

Also, you can trace the history of amendments in the same way, using the detailed information that appears after Federal Rule of Appellate Procedure 48.

4. Constitution and Procedural Statutes

This booklet next reprints selected provisions of the United States Constitution, title 28 of the United States Code, and other procedural statutes—all preceded by this portion's own table of contents. The editing effort centered on including those provisions most effectively considered in connection with the study of civil procedure. For example, the selection of "other procedural statutes" includes a few key federal statutes that lie outside title 28 (antitrust procedural provisions and civil rights statutes) and also illustrative state statutes in a few key procedural subjects (California's long-arm statute and New York's statute of limitations and jurisdiction, service, and venue provisions).

Title 28 is of course the centerpiece, and accordingly the booklet contains many of its sections. This systematization of statutes on the federal judiciary and judicial procedure comes from the Act of June 25, 1948, ch. 646, § 1, 62 Stat. 869 ("Act to revise, codify, and enact into law title 28 of the United States Code"). After each reprinted statutory section, the booklet lists all amending statutes since the 1948 Act.

5. Federal Rules of Evidence

This booklet sets out the complete Rules of Evidence for United States Courts and Magistrates. Although the Evidence Rules constitute a statute, the booklet presents them in a format similar to that of the Civil and Appellate Rules.

Again, you can trace the history of amendments in the same way, using the detailed information that appears after Federal Rule of Evidence 1103.

6. Sample Local Rules

PREFACE

This booklet finally presents, for illustrative purposes, the local rules of the United States District Court for the Northern District of New York.

7. General Comments

The foregoing descriptions evince an editing effort to select thoughtfully a collection of procedural provisions. Also, this preface and the closing consolidated index represent a similarly serious attempt to facilitate the collection's use. We nevertheless want to continue improving this booklet. That does not establish an easy goal, however, because users' widely varying desires are not always obvious. Accordingly, I sincerely request the users to send suggestions for improvement to me.

The booklet also reflects a dedication to keeping it up to date. The Court and Congress are surprisingly active in the procedural arena. We update the Civil Rules through the date shown on the booklet's title page. We update the various other provisions at least through the end of the preceding congressional session, which roughly corresponds to the beginning of the year that appears on the booklet's cover.

KEVIN M. CLERMONT
Flanagan Professor of Law
Myron Taylor Hall
Cornell Law School
Ithaca, NY 14853

P.S. Notwithstanding all the above, this booklet still gives you only the raw materials. To get into the immense body of legal doctrine adhering to these materials, you should consult the secondary literature. I especially recommend Charles Alan Wright's single-volume hornbook on Federal Courts and the multi-volume Federal Practice and Procedure by Professors Wright and Miller and others. To give you a sample, while also providing you with valuable background information on the Federal Rules that are the subject of the booklet, I close this preface with an excerpt from the former reference work, reprinted here with kind permission:

CHARLES ALAN WRIGHT & MARY KAY KANE, LAW OF FEDERAL COURTS

429–35, 764 (6th ed. 2002).

§ 62. The Federal Rules of Civil Procedure [1]

... An erratic conformity to state procedure, an anachronistic survival of the separation between law and equity, and a failure to

1. 4 Wright & Miller, Civil 2d §§ 1003–1008; Burbank, The Transformation of American Civil Procedure: The Example of Rule 11, 1989, 137 U.Pa.L.Rev. 1925;

take advantage of the possibilities of judicial rulemaking were hallmarks of the system [of federal procedure prior to 1938]. The last of these points, that procedure is better regulated by the courts than by legislative bodies, was seen to be the key to the problem. It is doubtful whether, as some have contended, the legislature lacks constitutional power to regulate procedure,[2] but it is certainly clear that this power can be delegated by the legislature to the courts.[3] It cannot be doubted that legislative regulation is less satisfactory than regulation by court-made rules.[4]

The fight for court-made rules of civil procedure for the federal courts began in 1911 when the American Bar Association, at the instigation of Thomas Shelton, adopted a resolution favoring such a system. For almost 20 years a bill to give the Supreme Court power to make such rules was introduced in every Congress, but never was passed, despite the gallant efforts of Mr. Shelton. In later years, in response to a suggestion by Chief Justice Taft,[5] the bill included a provision authorizing the Court to unify law and equity. Opposition to the bill was led by Senator Walsh of Montana, and was based in large measure on the fear that grant of the

Chandler, Some Major Advances in the Federal Judicial System, 1922–1947, 1963, 31 F.R.D. 307, 477–516; Clark, Two Decades of the Federal Civil Rules, 1958, 58 Col.L.Rev. 435; Clark, The Role of the Supreme Court in Federal Rule–Making, 1963, 46 J.Am.Jud.Soc. 250; Goodman, On the Fiftieth Anniversary of the Federal Rules of Civil Procedure: What Did the Drafters Intend?, 1987, 21 Suffolk U.L.Rev. 351; Holtzoff, Origin and Sources of the Federal Rules of Civil Procedure, 1955, 30 N.Y.U.L.Rev. 1057; Subrin, How Equity Conquered Common Law: The Federal Rules of Civil Procedure in Historical Perspective, 1987, 135 U.Pa.L.Rev. 909; Sunderland, The Grant of Rule–Making Power to the Supreme Court of the United States, 1934, 32 Mich.L.Rev. 1116; Tolman, Historical Beginnings of Procedural Reform, 1936, 22 A.B.A.J. 783; Toran, 'Tis A Gift To Be Simple: Aesthetics and Procedural Reform, 1990, 89 Mich.L.Rev. 352; Weinstein, The Ghost of Process Past: The Fiftieth Anniversary of the Federal Rules of Civil Procedure and Erie, 1988, 54 Brooklyn L.Rev. 1.

2. Compare Wigmore, Legislative Rules for Judicial Procedure are Void Constitutionally, 1928, 23 Ill.L.Rev. 276, with Kaplan & Greene, The Legislature's Relation to Judicial Rule–Making: An Appraisal of Winberry v. Salisbury, 1951, 65 Harv. L.Rev. 234.

Indeed Professor Whitten argues that separation-of-powers principles restrict the authority of the Court to make even "purely procedural" rules under a general delegation of rulemaking power if Congress has occupied the procedural field in question. Whitten, Separation of Powers Restrictions on Judicial Rulemaking: A Case Study of Federal Rule 4, 1988, 40 Me.L.Rev. 41.

3. See Mistretta v. U.S., 1989, 109 S.Ct. 647, 662–664, 488 U.S. 361, 386–390, 102 L.Ed.2d 714, and cases there cited. The principle was recognized as early as Wayman v. Southard, 1825, 10 Wheat. 1, 43, 6 L.Ed. 253.

4. 4 Wright & Miller, Civil 2d § 1001; Clark & Wright, The Judicial Council and the Rule–Making Power: A Dissent and a Protest, 1950, 1 Syracuse L.Rev. 346; Joiner & Miller, Rules of Practice and Procedure: A Study of Judicial Rule–Making, 1957, 55 Mich.L.Rev. 623; Levin & Amsterdam, Legislative Control over Judicial Rule–Making: A Problem in Constitutional Revision, 1958, 107 U.Pa.L.Rev. 1.

5. Taft, Three Needed Steps of Progress, 1922, 8 A.B.A.J. 34, 35; Taft, Possible and Needed Reforms in the Administration of Justice in Federal Courts, 1922, 8 A.B.A.J. 601, 604, 607.

rulemaking power would result in the rather simplified code practice of the western states being superseded by the involved practice that had developed in New York.[6] In 1930 Mr. Shelton died, and the American Bar Association lost interest, even to the point of abolishing its committee that had been pressing for this reform.

Senator Walsh was to have been appointed Attorney General in 1933, which would surely have ended, for the time at least, any hope of obtaining rulemaking power for the Supreme Court. He died, however, on the eve of his appointment, and the new Attorney General, Homer Cummings, assumed sponsorship of the bill authorizing the court to make procedural rules and to unite law and equity. So effective was his leadership that the bill was adopted unanimously by Congress in 1934 with very little discussion.[7]

It is a long step from a grant of rulemaking power to the adoption of effective rules. Indeed one familiar argument against rulemaking power is that it will not be exercised. For almost a year after the Enabling Act was passed the Supreme Court took no action with regard to it. The Department of Justice and the Conference of Senior Circuit Judges apparently contemplated that no more would be required than the drafting of uniform rules for actions at law to supplement the existing Equity Rules of 1912.[8]

That the reform was not so limited, that law and equity were merged under a single set of simple and effective rules, was due primarily to the efforts of William D. Mitchell, a former Attorney General of the United States, and Charles E. Clark, then Dean of the Yale Law School and later Chief Judge of the Court of Appeals for the Second Circuit. In January 1935, Dean Clark, in collaboration with James Wm. Moore, published a major article summarizing the history of federal procedure and predicting that reform would be a failure unless it included a merger of law and equity.[9] Aroused by this article, General Mitchell wrote Chief Justice Hughes, on February 9, 1935, setting forth powerfully and persuasively the need for the full reform.[10] Three months later the Chief

6. Walsh, Rule–Making Power on Law Side of Federal Practice, 1927, 13 A.B.A.J. 84. See Clark, Code Pleading, 2d ed. 1947, p. 35.

7. Act of June 19, 1934, c. 651, 48 Stat. 1064; 4 Wright & Miller, Civil 2d § 1003; Burbank, The Rules Enabling Act of 1934, 1982, 130 U.Pa.L.Rev. 1015. See Cummings, Immediate Problems of the Bar, 1934, 20 A.B.A.J. 212. The Enabling Act, as subsequently revised, is now 28 U.S.C.A. §§ 2072–2074.

8. Subrin, Charles E. Clark and His Procedural Outlook: The Disciplined Champion of Undisciplined Rules, in Judge Charles E. Clark, Petruck ed. 1991, p. 115.

9. Clark & Moore, A New Federal Civil Procedure: I. The Background, 1935, 44 Yale L.J. 387.

10. Subrin, note 8 above, at pp. 128–131. The letter appears in full in Mitchell, The Federal Rules of Civil Procedure, in David Dudley Field Centenary Essays, 1949, pp. 73, 76–78.

Justice, addressing the American Law Institute, made the dramatic announcement that the rules would not be limited to common-law cases, but would unify the procedure for cases in equity and actions at law "so as to secure one form of civil action and procedure for both." [11] A few weeks later the Court appointed an Advisory Committee of the most distinguished lawyers and law professors in the country to prepare and submit a draft of unified rules. General Mitchell was named by the Court as chairman, a post he filled with distinction until his death in 1955, and Dean Clark was designated as Reporter for the Committee.[12]

The Committee circulated three printed drafts for comment and criticism by the profession. The third draft, which was the Final Report of the Committee, was submitted to the Supreme Court in November 1937, and on December 20, 1937, the Court adopted the rules proposed by the Committee with some changes of its own.[13] The rules were submitted to Congress, as the Enabling Act required, and when Congress adjourned without any adverse legislation,[14] the rules became effective September 16, 1938.

Even the best system of court rules cannot remain static. Experience under the rules, and continued scholarly thinking about problems of procedure, will disclose places in which improvement is possible. Amendment will be necessary in other instances to remove unsound judicial glosses on the rules, or to codify desirable lines of decision. It is essential, therefore, that there be a continuing body charged with the responsibility of examining the rules in action and recommending change to the Court when this seems desirable.[15] The Advisory Committee that drafted the federal rules was reconstituted in 1942 to serve this function, and did so until its discharge in 1956. Various amendments were made by the Court, on the recommendation of that Committee, but the most significant was the set of amendments adopted in 1946, effective March 19,

11. Address of Chief Justice Hughes, 1935, 55 S.Ct. xxxv, xxxvii, 21 A.B.A.J. 340, 12 A.L.I.Proc. 54.

12. Order of June 3, 1935, 295 U.S. 774. For a full list of members of the committee, see 4 Wright & Miller, Civil 2d § 1003, pp. 21–24.

The contributions of Dean—later Judge—Clark are described in Smith, Judge Charles E. Clark and The Federal Rules of Civil Procedure, 1976, 85 Yale L.J. 914. See also Subrin, note 8 above.

13. Order of Dec. 20, 1937, 302 U.S. 783. Justice Brandeis dissented from adoption of the rules.

14. There was opposition to the rules in the Senate, but that body took no action, since the House of Representatives favored the rules, and concurrent action of both houses would have been required to delay or defeat adoption of the rules. See Chandler, Some Major Advances in the Federal Judicial System, 1922–1947, 1963, 31 F.R.D. 307, 505–512.

15. Clark, "Clarifying" Amendments to the Federal Rules, 1953, 14 Ohio St.L.J. 241; Wright, Rule 56(e): A Case Study on the Need for Amending the Federal Rules, 1956, 69 Harv.L.Rev. 839; Wright, Amendments to the Federal Rules: The Function of a Continuing Rules Committee, 1954, 7 Vand.L.Rev. 521.

1948, which reflected the results of a general study of the rules in operation.

The old Advisory Committee was discharged in 1956. In 1958 Congress amended the act creating the Judicial Conference to include among the duties of that body advising the Supreme Court with regard to necessary changes in the various rules the Court has power to make or amend.[16] An elaborate structure was created to assist the Judicial Conference, and ultimately the Court, in this task. There have been, as needed, advisory committees of practitioners, judges, and scholars for civil procedure, criminal procedure, appellate procedure, admiralty, bankruptcy, and evidence. These report to a standing Committee on Rules of Practice and Procedure and it in turn reports to the Judicial Conference.[17] The Judicial Conference transmits those recommendations it approves to the Supreme Court, for under this new plan, as under that in effect from 1934 to 1956, the Court retains ultimate responsibility for the adoption of amendments to the rules.

This new machinery led to significant amendments to the Civil Rules in 1961, 1963, 1966, 1970, 1980, and 1983. More recently there have been amendments almost every other year.

The success of the Federal Rules of Civil Procedure has been quite phenomenal. They provide for the federal courts a uniform procedure in civil actions. This in itself would be a fine accomplishment, but the rules go beyond this to create a uniform procedure that is flexible, simple, clear, and efficient. It may smack of hyperbole to say, as one commentator has, that the rules are "one of the greatest contributions to the free and unhampered administration of law and justice ever struck off by any group of men since the dawn of civilized law." [18] It is nevertheless true that the chorus of approval of the rules by judges, lawyers, and commentators had been, until very recently, unanimous, unstinted, and spontaneous.[19] In the last few years, however, there has been questioning and reexamination of the assumptions about the proper goals of procedure that are at the heart of the Civil Rules.[20] This questioning has been sparked particularly by what some think is abuse of the discovery procedures made available by the rules.

16. 28 U.S.C.A. § 331, as amended by Act of July 11, 1958, 72 Stat. 356. For discussion of this amendment prior to its adoption, see Symposium, 1957, 21 F.R.D. 117.

17. The work of the new committees is described by the chairman of the Judicial Conference's Standing Committee on Rules of Practice and Procedure in Maris, Federal Procedural Rule-Making: The Program of the Judicial Conference, 1961, 37 A.B.A.J. 772. Their members are listed in 4 Wright & Miller, Civil 2d § 1007.

18. Carey, In Favor of Uniformity, 1943, 3 F.R.D. 507, 18 Temp.L.Q. 145.

19. See 4 Wright & Miller, Civil 2d § 1008, and particularly n. 6.

20. Subrin, The New Era in American Civil Procedure, 1981, 67 A.B.A.J. 1648.

PREFACE

The impact of the rules has not been limited to the federal courts. The excellence of the rules is such that in more than half the states the rules have been adapted for state use virtually unchanged, and there is not a jurisdiction that has not revised its procedure in some way that reflects the influence of the federal rules.[22]

The Enabling Act declares that the rules are to regulate only "practice and procedure" and are not to "abridge, enlarge or modify any substantive rights." [23] Particular rules have been attacked as affecting matters of substance, but the Supreme Court, in a notable series of decisions, has upheld all such rules challenged before it.[24]

The success of the Civil Rules caused many to think that formulation of Federal Rules of Evidence would be desirable. An Advisory Committee on Rules of Evidence was created in 1965 and followed the methods of the committee that had drafted the Civil Rules in its work. Ultimately Federal Rules of Evidence became effective July 1, 1975, but their gestation period was as troubled as it was lengthy. ... [A] draft of Evidence Rules was promulgated by the Supreme Court in 1972, but they caused so much controversy that Congress passed a statute providing that they could not take effect until they were expressly approved by Act of Congress. Congress then made very substantial revisions in the rules as they had been promulgated by the Supreme Court before [enacting] them [as a statute,] to become effective in 1975.

22. A commentator has pointed out, however, that certain provisions in the Civil Rules respond to special problems of a federal system and of courts of constitutionally limited jurisdiction, and that those provisions ought not be blindly adopted by the states. Rowe, A Comment on the Federalism of the Federal Rules, 1979 Duke L.J. 843.

23. 28 U.S.C.A. § 2072(b). See Carrington, "Substance" and "Procedure" in the Rules Enabling Act, 1989 Duke L.J. 281.

24. Hanna v. Plumer, 1965, 85 S.Ct. 1136, 380 U.S. 460, 14 L.Ed.2d 8 (Rule 4(d)(1)); Cold Metal Process Co. v. United Engineering & Foundry Co., 1956, 76 S.Ct. 904, 351 U.S. 445, 100 L.Ed. 1311 (amended Rule 54(b)); Mississippi Pub. Co. v. Murphree, 1946, 66 S.Ct. 242, 326 U.S. 438, 90 L.Ed. 185 (Rule 4(f)); Sibbach v. Wilson & Co., 1941, 61 S.Ct. 422, 312 U.S. 1, 85 L.Ed. 479 (Rule 35(a)).

It has been argued, however, that the Court has been too permissive in upholding rules that do affect substantive rights, contrary to the Enabling Act. Ely, The Irrepressible Myth of Erie, 1974, 87 Harv.L.Rev. 693. Professor Ely's view is rejected, in the course of a thoughtful decision holding that Rule 25(a) is valid, in Boggs v. Blue Diamond Coal Co., D.C.Ky.1980, 497 F.Supp. 1105, 1118–1121, noted 1981, 11 Mem.St.U.L.Rev. 413.

It has also been argued that the Supreme Court has become increasingly fond of using the plain-meaning doctrine to interpret the Federal Rules. Moore, The Supreme Court's Role in Interpreting the Federal Rules of Civil Procedure, 1993, 44 Hastings L.J. 1039. The author argues that because of the Court's dual roles as rulemaker and rule interpreter, the determination of the proper interpretation and application of a rule should be informed by many considerations beyond the simple literal language of the rule.

PREFACE

The controversy over the Evidence Rules, and a similar furor over amendments to the Criminal Rules that the Supreme Court had approved in 1974, has led to some reappraisal of the rulemaking process.[27] The critics have not been directing themselves particularly to the Civil Rules, but insofar as the criticism goes to the methods that the rulemaking committees have used over the years, they must inevitably have an impact on future amendments of the Civil Rules. Legislation in 1988 amended the Enabling Act to respond to some of the arguments of the critics,[28] but the more important changes go to rules made by district courts and courts of appeals. Rulemaking by the Supreme Court for the federal courts generally is now subjected to closer public and congressional scrutiny, but is not changed in substance.[29]

Another threat to the integrity of the Civil Rules has come from the proliferation of local rules for particular districts. Although Rule 83 authorizes local rules, it had been expected that these would be few in number and confined to purely housekeeping matters. Instead the use of local rules has been extensive and they cover a great variety of important matters.[30] This in itself is a threat to uniformity of procedure throughout the country, the local rules often provide "a series of traps" [31] for lawyers from other districts, and the casual manner in which until recently the judges in a district have decided to adopt a rule or set of rules is in striking contrast to the care with which the Civil Rules themselves

27. Weinstein, Reform of Court Rule–Making Procedures, 1977 (shorter versions of this book appeared in 1977, 63 A.B.A.J. 47, and 1976, 76 Col.L.Rev. 905). See also Clinton, Rule 9 of the Federal Habeas Corpus Rules: A Case Study on the Need for Reform of the Rules Enabling Acts, 1977, 63 Iowa L.Rev. 15; Friedenthal, The Rulemaking Power of the Supreme Court: A Contemporary Crisis, 1975, 27 Stan.L.Rev. 673; Lesnick, The Federal Rule–Making Process: Time for Re-examination, 1975, 61 A.B.A.J. 579; Wright, Book Review, 1978, 9 St. Mary's L.J. 652.

28. Act of Nov. 19, 1988, Pub.L. 100–702, Title IV, 102 Stat. 4648.

29. Carrington, The New Order in Judicial Rulemaking, 1991, 75 Judicature 161; Mullenix, Hope Over Experience: Mandatory Informal Discovery and the Politics of Rulemaking, 1991, 69 N.C.L.Rev. 795.

It has been argued that recent controversies suggest that rulemaking should be reformed and follow what is done in modern administrative law. Walker, A Comprehensive Reform for Federal Civil Rulemaking, 1993, 61 Geo.Wash.L.Rev. 455.

30. 12 Wright, Miller & Marcus, Civil 2d § 3154. See also Coquilette, Squiers & Subrin, The Role of Local Rules, A.B.A.J., Jan. 1989, p. 62; Subrin, Federal Rules, Local Rules, and State Rules: Uniformity, Divergence, and Emerging Procedural Patterns, 1989, 137 U.Pa.L.Rev. 1999.

31. Woodham v. American Cystoscope Co. of Pelham, C.A.5th, 1964, 335 F.2d 551, 552.

The difficulty in finding out what local rules are in effect is illustrated by Doran v. U.S., C.A.1st, 1973, 475 F.2d 742, where the United States attorney had no knowledge of a local rule in effect for 20 years. See also U.S. v. Ferretti, C.A.3d, 1980, 635 F.2d 1089, in which the judges in the district were uncertain about the continued existence of a local rule.

are made and amended. Almost every study of experience with local rules has demonstrated how unsatisfactory it has been.[32]

The Supreme Court sought to provide a check when it ruled in 1960 that the power to make local rules is not to be used to introduce "basic procedural innovations,"[33] but it seemed to retreat from this when it later held that local rules reducing the size of civil juries from 12 to six did not fall afoul of that restriction.[34] Many local rules have been held invalid for this reason, or because they are inconsistent with the Civil Rules, an Act of Congress, or the Constitution,[35] but patently there are many other invalid local rules on the books that have escaped scrutiny in a contested case.[36]

Rule 83 was amended in 1985 to provide that local rules can be made only after appropriate public notice and an opportunity to comment, and to give the judicial council of the circuit power to abrogate any local rule of a district. These provisions were made statutory in 1988. The statutes also require each district court and court of appeals to appoint an advisory committee to study and make recommendations about the rules of the court[37] and they give the Judicial Conference of the United States power to modify or abrogate a rule adopted by any court other than a district court or the Supreme Court.[38] These changes, if they stood alone, could improve the local rulemaking process. But the Civil Justice Reform Act of 1990[39] has led to the adoption in many districts of

32. 12 Wright, Miller & Marcus, Civil 2d § 3152; Weinstein, note 27 above, at pp. 117–137; Roberts, The Myth of Uniformity in Federal Civil Procedure: Federal Civil Rule 83 and District Court Local Rulemaking Powers, 1985, 8 U.Puget Sound L.Rev. 537; Tobias, Civil Justice Reform and the Balkanization of Federal Civil Procedure, 1992, 24 Ariz.St.L.J. 1393, 1397–1401; Note, Rule 83 and the Local Federal Rules, 1967, 67 Col.L.Rev. 1251; Note, The Local Rules of Civil Procedure in the Federal District Courts—A Survey, 1966 Duke L.J. 1011.

But see Flanders, Local Rules in Federal District Courts: Usurpation, Legislation, or Information?, 1981, 14 Loy.L.A.L.Rev. 213; Flanders, In Praise of Local Rules, 1978, 62 Judicature 28.

33. Miner v. Atlass, 1960, 80 S.Ct. 1300, 1306, 363 U.S. 641, 650, 4 L.Ed.2d 1462.

34. Colgrove v. Battin, 1973, 93 S.Ct. 2448, 2456 n. 23, 413 U.S. 149, 163 n. 23, 37 L.Ed.2d 522.

35. See Frazier v. Heebe, 1987, 107 S.Ct. 2607, 482 U.S. 641, 96 L.Ed.2d 557; Carver v. Bunch, C.A.6th, 1991, 946 F.2d 451; Bailey v. Systems Innovation, Inc., C.A.3d, 1988, 852 F.2d 93; Carter v. Clark, C.A.5th, 1980, 616 F.2d 228; and cases cited in 12 Wright, Miller & Marcus, Civil 2d § 3153 nn. 77–79.

36. "[A]nother failure of rule 83 flows from the fact that occasions for judicially testing local rules have been and will continue to be infrequent. Given practical realities and economic constraints, few litigants will venture into battle over issues that seem so arcane." Roberts, note 32 above, at 546–547.

37. 28 U.S.C.A. §§ 2071, 2077(b). See also 28 U.S.C.A. § 332(d)(4).

38. 28 U.S.C.A. § 2071(c)(2).

39. 28 U.S.C.A. §§ 471–482, added by Act of Dec. 1, 1990, Pub.L. No. 101–650, 104 Stat. 5089.

procedures that vary among themselves and that are often inconsistent with the Federal Rules of Civil Procedure....

One of the most striking achievements in the federal rules from the first has been the simplified procedures they introduced for taking appeals. These matters were dealt with until 1968 by Civil Rules 73 to 76 and Criminal Rules 37 to 39. In that year the Federal Rules of Appellate Procedure were adopted, applicable to all cases, and the former civil and criminal provisions were repealed. The Appellate Rules incorporate in general the portions of the Civil Rules and Criminal Rules that they replaced but they also make uniform provision for a number of other matters of appellate practice that prior to 1968 were dealt with in varying ways by the rules of the eleven courts of appeals.

*

RULES OF CIVIL PROCEDURE FOR THE UNITED STATES DISTRICT COURTS

TABLE OF RULES

V. Depositions and Discovery—Continued

VI. Trials—Continued

XI. General Provisions—Continued

Form

RULES OF CIVIL PROCEDURE FOR THE UNITED STATES DISTRICT COURTS

I. SCOPE OF RULES—ONE FORM OF ACTION

Rule 1.

SCOPE AND PURPOSE OF RULES

These rules govern the procedure in the United States district courts in all suits of a civil nature whether cognizable as cases at law or in equity or in admiralty, with the exceptions stated in Rule 81. They shall be construed and administered to secure the just, speedy, and inexpensive determination of every action.

As amended 1949, 1966, 1993.

Rule 2.

ONE FORM OF ACTION

There shall be one form of action to be known as "civil action".

II. COMMENCEMENT OF ACTION; SERVICE OF PROCESS, PLEADINGS, MOTIONS, AND ORDERS

Rule 3.

COMMENCEMENT OF ACTION

A civil action is commenced by filing a complaint with the court.

Rule 4.

SUMMONS

(a) Form. The summons shall be signed by the clerk, bear the seal of the court, identify the court and the parties, be directed to the defendant, and state the name and address of the plaintiff's attorney or, if unrepresented, of the plaintiff. It shall also state the time within which the defendant must appear and defend, and notify the defendant that failure to do so will result in a judgment by default against the defendant for the relief demanded in the complaint. The court may allow a summons to be amended.

(b) Issuance. Upon or after filing the complaint, the plaintiff may present a summons to the clerk for signature and seal. If the summons is in proper form, the clerk shall sign, seal, and issue it to the plaintiff for service on the defendant. A summons, or a copy of the summons if addressed to multiple defendants, shall be issued for each defendant to be served.

(c) Service with Complaint; by Whom Made.

(1) A summons shall be served together with a copy of the complaint. The plaintiff is responsible for service of a summons and complaint within the time allowed under subdivision (m) and shall furnish the person effecting service with the necessary copies of the summons and complaint.

(2) Service may be effected by any person who is not a party and who is at least 18 years of age. At the request of the plaintiff, however, the court may direct that service be effected by a United States marshal, deputy United States marshal, or other person or officer specially appointed by the court for that purpose. Such an appointment must be made when the plaintiff is authorized to proceed in forma pauperis pursuant to 28 U.S.C. § 1915 or is authorized to proceed as a seaman under 28 U.S.C. § 1916.

(d) Waiver of Service; Duty to Save Costs of Service; Request to Waive.

(1) A defendant who waives service of a summons does not thereby waive any objection to the venue or to the jurisdiction of the court over the person of the defendant.

(2) An individual, corporation, or association that is subject to service under subdivision (e), (f), or (h) and that receives notice of an action in the manner provided in this paragraph has a duty to avoid unnecessary costs of serving the summons. To avoid costs, the plaintiff may notify such a defendant of the commencement of the action and request that the defendant waive service of a summons. The notice and request

(A) shall be in writing and shall be addressed directly to the defendant, if an individual, or else to an officer or managing or general agent (or other agent authorized by appointment or law to receive service of process) of a defendant subject to service under subdivision (h);

(B) shall be dispatched through first-class mail or other reliable means;

(C) shall be accompanied by a copy of the complaint and shall identify the court in which it has been filed;

(D) shall inform the defendant, by means of a text prescribed in an official form promulgated pursuant to Rule 84, of the consequences of compliance and of a failure to comply with the request;

(E) shall set forth the date on which the request is sent;

(F) shall allow the defendant a reasonable time to return the waiver, which shall be at least 30 days from the date on which the request is sent, or 60 days from that date if the defendant is addressed outside any judicial district of the United States; and

(G) shall provide the defendant with an extra copy of the notice and request, as well as a prepaid means of compliance in writing.

If a defendant located within the United States fails to comply with a request for waiver made by a plaintiff located within the United States, the court shall impose the costs subsequently incurred in effecting service on the defendant unless good cause for the failure be shown.

(3) A defendant that, before being served with process, timely returns a waiver so requested is not required to serve an answer to the complaint until 60 days after the date on which the request for waiver of service was sent, or 90 days after that date if the defendant was addressed outside any judicial district of the United States.

(4) When the plaintiff files a waiver of service with the court, the action shall proceed, except as provided in paragraph (3), as if a summons and complaint had been served at the time of filing the waiver, and no proof of service shall be required.

(5) The costs to be imposed on a defendant under paragraph (2) for failure to comply with a request to waive service of a summons shall include the costs subsequently incurred in effecting service under subdivision (e), (f), or (h), together with the costs, including a reasonable attorney's fee, of any motion required to collect the costs of service.

(e) Service upon Individuals Within a Judicial District of the United States. Unless otherwise provided by federal law, service upon an individual from whom a waiver has not been obtained and filed, other than an infant or an incompetent person, may be effected in any judicial district of the United States:

(1) pursuant to the law of the state in which the district court is located, or in which service is effected, for the service of a summons upon the defendant in an action brought in the courts of general jurisdiction of the State; or

(2) by delivering a copy of the summons and of the complaint to the individual personally or by leaving copies thereof at the individual's dwelling house or usual place of abode with some person of suitable age and discretion then residing therein or by delivering a copy of the summons and of the complaint to an agent authorized by appointment or by law to receive service of process.

(f) Service upon Individuals in a Foreign Country. Unless otherwise provided by federal law, service upon an individual from whom a waiver has not been obtained and filed, other than an infant or an incompetent person, may be effected in a place not within any judicial district of the United States:

(1) by any internationally agreed means reasonably calculated to give notice, such as those means authorized by the Hague Convention on the Service Abroad of Judicial and Extrajudicial Documents; or

(2) if there is no internationally agreed means of service or the applicable international agreement allows other means of service, provided that service is reasonably calculated to give notice:

(A) in the manner prescribed by the law of the foreign country for service in that country in an action in any of its courts of general jurisdiction; or

(B) as directed by the foreign authority in response to a letter rogatory or letter of request; or

(C) unless prohibited by the law of the foreign country, by

(i) delivery to the individual personally of a copy of the summons and the complaint; or

(ii) any form of mail requiring a signed receipt, to be addressed and dispatched by the clerk of the court to the party to be served; or

(3) by other means not prohibited by international agreement as may be directed by the court.

(g) Service upon Infants and Incompetent Persons. Service upon an infant or an incompetent person in a judicial district of the United States shall be effected in the manner prescribed by the law of the state in which the service is made for the service of summons or other like process upon any such defendant in an action brought in the courts of general jurisdiction of that state. Service upon an infant or an incompetent person in a place not within any judicial district of the United States shall be effected in the manner prescribed by paragraph (2)(A) or (2)(B) of subdivision (f) or by such means as the court may direct.

(h) Service upon Corporations and Associations. Unless otherwise provided by federal law, service upon a domestic or foreign corporation or upon a partnership or other unincorporated association that is subject to suit under a common name, and from which a waiver of service has not been obtained and filed, shall be effected:

(1) in a judicial district of the United States in the manner prescribed for individuals by subdivision (e)(1), or by delivering a copy of the summons and of the complaint to an officer, a managing or general agent, or to any other agent authorized by appointment or by law to receive service of process and, if the agent is one authorized by statute to receive service and the statute so requires, by also mailing a copy to the defendant, or

(2) in a place not within any judicial district of the United States in any manner prescribed for individuals by subdivision (f) except personal delivery as provided in paragraph (2)(C)(i) thereof.

(i) Serving the United States, Its Agencies, Corporations, Officers, or Employees.

(1) Service upon the United States shall be effected

(A) by delivering a copy of the summons and of the complaint to the United States attorney for the district in which the action is brought or to an assistant United States attorney or clerical employee designated by the United States attorney in a writing filed with the clerk of the court or by sending a copy of the summons and of the complaint by registered or certified mail addressed to the civil process clerk at the office of the United States attorney and

(B) by also sending a copy of the summons and of the complaint by registered or certified mail to the Attorney General of the United States at Washington, District of Columbia, and

(C) in any action attacking the validity of an order of an officer or agency of the United States not made a party, by also sending a copy of the summons and of the complaint by registered or certified mail to the officer or agency.

(2)(A) Service on an agency or corporation of the United States, or an officer or employee of the United States sued only in an official capacity, is effected by serving the United States in the manner prescribed by Rule 4(i)(1) and by also sending a copy of the summons and complaint by registered or certified mail to the officer, employee, agency, or corporation.

(B) Service on an officer or employee of the United States sued in an individual capacity for acts or omissions occurring in connection with the performance of duties on behalf of the United States—whether or not the officer or employee is sued also in an official capacity—is effected by serving the United States in the manner prescribed by Rule 4(i)(1) and by serving the officer or employee in the manner prescribed by Rule 4(e), (f), or (g).

(3) The court shall allow a reasonable time to serve process under Rule 4(i) for the purpose of curing the failure to serve:

(A) all persons required to be served in an action governed by Rule 4(i)(2)(A), if the plaintiff has served either the United States attorney or the Attorney General of the United States, or

(B) the United States in an action governed by Rule 4(i)(2)(B), if the plaintiff has served an officer or employee of the United States sued in an individual capacity.

(j) Service upon Foreign, State, or Local Governments.

(1) Service upon a foreign state or a political subdivision, agency, or instrumentality thereof shall be effected pursuant to 28 U.S.C. § 1608.

(2) Service upon a state, municipal corporation, or other governmental organization subject to suit shall be effected by delivering a copy of the summons and of the complaint to its chief executive officer or by serving the summons and complaint in the manner prescribed by the law of that state for the service of summons or other like process upon any such defendant.

(k) Territorial Limits of Effective Service.

(1) Service of a summons or filing a waiver of service is effective to establish jurisdiction over the person of a defendant

(A) who could be subjected to the jurisdiction of a court of general jurisdiction in the state in which the district court is located, or

(B) who is a party joined under Rule 14 or Rule 19 and is served at a place within a judicial district of the United States and not more than 100 miles from the place from which the summons issues, or

(C) who is subject to the federal interpleader jurisdiction under 28 U.S.C. § 1335, or

(D) when authorized by a statute of the United States.

(2) If the exercise of jurisdiction is consistent with the Constitution and laws of the United States, serving a summons or filing a waiver of service is also effective, with respect to claims arising under federal law, to establish personal jurisdiction over the person of any defendant who is not subject to the jurisdiction of the courts of general jurisdiction of any state.

(*l*) Proof of Service. If service is not waived, the person effecting service shall make proof thereof to the court. If service is made by a person other than a United States marshal or deputy United States marshal, the person shall make affidavit thereof. Proof of service in a place not within any judicial district of the United States shall, if effected under paragraph (1) of subdivision (f), be made pursuant to the applicable treaty or convention, and shall, if effected under paragraph (2) or (3) thereof, include a receipt signed by the addressee or other evidence of delivery to the addressee satisfactory to the court. Failure to make proof of service does not affect the validity of the service. The court may allow proof of service to be amended.

(m) Time Limit for Service. If service of the summons and complaint is not made upon a defendant within 120 days after the filing of the complaint, the court, upon motion or on its own initiative after notice to the plaintiff, shall dismiss the action without prejudice as to that defendant or direct that service be effected within a specified time; provided that if the plaintiff shows good cause for the failure, the court shall extend the time for service for an appropriate period. This subdivision does not apply to service in a foreign country pursuant to subdivision (f) or (j)(1).

(n) Seizure of Property; Service of Summons Not Feasible.

(1) If a statute of the United States so provides, the court may assert jurisdiction over property. Notice to claimants of the property shall then be sent in the manner provided by the statute or by service of a summons under this rule.

(2) Upon a showing that personal jurisdiction over a defendant cannot, in the district where the action is brought, be obtained with reasonable efforts by service of summons in any manner authorized by this rule, the court may assert jurisdiction over any of the defendant's assets found within the district by seizing the assets under the circumstances and in the manner provided by the law of the state in which the district court is located.

As amended 1963, 1966, 1980, 1983, 1987, 1993, 2000.

Rule 4.1.

SERVICE OF OTHER PROCESS

(a) Generally. Process other than a summons as provided in Rule 4 or subpoena as provided in Rule 45 shall be served by a United States marshal, a deputy United States marshal, or a person specially appointed for that purpose, who shall make proof of service as provided in Rule 4(*l*). The process may be served anywhere within the territorial limits of the state in which the district court is located, and, when authorized by a statute of the United States, beyond the territorial limits of that state.

(b) Enforcement of Orders: Commitment for Civil Contempt. An order of civil commitment of a person held to be in contempt of a decree or injunction issued to enforce the laws of the United States may be served and enforced in any district. Other orders in civil contempt proceedings shall be served in the state in which the court issuing the order to be enforced is located or elsewhere within the United States if not more than 100 miles from the place at which the order to be enforced was issued.

Added 1993.

Rule 5.

SERVING AND FILING OF PLEADINGS AND OTHER PAPERS

(a) Service: When Required. Except as otherwise provided in these rules, every order required by its terms to be served, every pleading subsequent to the original complaint unless the court otherwise orders because of numerous defendants, every paper relating to discovery required to be served upon a party unless the court otherwise orders, every written motion other than one which may be heard ex parte, and every written notice, appearance, demand, offer of judgment, designation of record on appeal, and similar paper shall be served upon each of the parties. No service need be made on parties in default for failure to appear except that pleadings asserting new or additional claims for relief against them shall be served upon them in the manner provided for service of summons in Rule 4.

In an action begun by seizure of property, in which no person need be or is named as defendant, any service required to be made prior to the filing of an answer, claim, or appearance shall be made upon the person having custody or possession of the property at the time of its seizure.

(b) Making Service.

(1) Service under Rules 5(a) and 77(d) on a party represented by an attorney is made on the attorney unless the court orders service on the party.

(2) Service under Rule 5(a) is made by:

(A) Delivering a copy to the person served by:

(i) handing it to the person;

(ii) leaving it at the person's office with a clerk or other person in charge, or if no one is in charge leaving it in a conspicuous place in the office; or

(iii) if the person has no office or the office is closed, leaving it at the person's dwelling house or usual place of abode with someone of suitable age and discretion residing there.

(B) Mailing a copy to the last known address of the person served. Service by mail is complete on mailing.

(C) If the person served has no known address, leaving a copy with the clerk of the court.

(D) Delivering a copy by any other means, including electronic means, consented to in writing by the person served. Service by electronic means is complete on transmission; service by other consented means is complete when the person making service delivers the copy to the agency designated to make delivery. If authorized by local rule, a party may make service under this subparagraph (D) through the court's transmission facilities.

(3) Service by electronic means under Rule 5(b)(2)(D) is not effective if the party making service learns that the attempted service did not reach the person to be served.

(c) Same: Numerous Defendants. In any action in which there are unusually large numbers of defendants, the court, upon motion or of its own initiative, may order that service of the pleadings of the defendants and replies thereto need not be made as between the defendants and that any cross-claim, counterclaim, or matter constituting an avoidance or affirmative defense contained therein shall be deemed to be denied or avoided by all other parties and that the filing of any such pleading and service thereof upon the plaintiff constitutes due notice of it to the parties. A copy of every such order shall be served upon the parties in such manner and form as the court directs.

(d) Filing; Certificate of Service. All papers after the complaint required to be served upon a party, together with a certificate of service, must be filed with the court within a reasonable time after service, but disclosures under Rule 26(a)(1) or (2) and the following discovery requests and responses must not be filed until they are used in the proceeding or the court orders filing: (i) depositions, (ii) interrogatories, (iii) requests for documents or to permit entry upon land, and (iv) requests for admission.

(e) Filing with the Court Defined. The filing of papers with the court as required by these rules shall be made by filing them with the clerk of court, except that the judge may permit the papers to be filed with the judge, in which event the judge shall note thereon the filing date and forthwith transmit them to the office of the clerk. A court may by local rule permit papers to be filed, signed, or verified by electronic means that are consistent with technical standards, if any, that the Judicial Conference of the United States establishes. A paper filed by electronic means in compliance with a local rule constitutes a written paper for the purpose of applying these rules. The clerk shall not refuse to accept for filing any paper presented for that purpose solely because it is not presented in proper form as required by these rules or any local rules or practices.

As amended 1963, 1970, 1980, 1987, 1991, 1993, 1996, 2000, 2001.

Rule 6.

TIME

(a) Computation. In computing any period of time prescribed or allowed by these rules, by the local rules of any district court, by order of court, or by any applicable statute, the day of the act, event, or default from which the designated period of time begins to run shall not be included. The last day of the period so computed shall be included, unless it is a Saturday, a Sunday, or a legal holiday, or, when the act to be done is the filing of a paper in court, a day on which weather or other conditions have made the office of the clerk of the district court inaccessible, in which event the period runs until the end of the next day which is not one of the aforementioned days. When the period of time prescribed or allowed is less than 11 days, intermediate Saturdays, Sundays, and legal holidays shall be excluded in the computation. As used in this rule and in Rule 77(c), "legal holiday" includes New Year's Day, Birthday of Martin Luther King, Jr., Washington's Birthday, Memorial Day, Independence Day, Labor Day, Columbus Day, Veterans Day, Thanksgiving Day, Christmas Day, and any other day appointed as a holiday by the President or the Congress of the United States, or by the state in which the district court is held.

(b) Enlargement. When by these rules or by a notice given thereunder or by order of court an act is required or allowed to be done at or within a specified time, the court for cause shown may at any time in its discretion (1) with or without motion or notice order the period enlarged if request therefor is made before the expiration of the period originally prescribed or as extended by a previous order, or (2) upon motion made after the expiration of the specified period permit the act to be done where the failure to act was the result of excusable neglect; but it may not extend the time for taking any action under Rules 50(b) and (c)(2), 52(b), 59(b), (d) and (e), and 60(b), except to the extent and under the conditions stated in them.

(c) Unaffected by Expiration of Term. Rescinded Feb. 28, 1966, eff. July 1, 1966.

(d) For Motions—Affidavits. A written motion, other than one which may be heard ex parte, and notice of the hearing thereof shall be served not later than 5 days before the time specified for the hearing, unless a different period is fixed by these rules or by order of the court. Such an order may for cause shown be made on ex parte application. When a motion is supported by affidavit, the affidavit shall be served with the motion; and, except as otherwise provided in Rule 59(c), opposing affidavits may be served not later than 1 day before the hearing, unless the court permits them to be served at some other time.

(e) Additional Time After Service Under Rule 5(b)(2)(B), (C), or (D). Whenever a party has the right or is required to do some act or take some proceedings within a prescribed period after the service of a notice or other paper upon the party and the notice or paper is served upon the party under Rule 5(b)(2)(B), (C), or (D), 3 days shall be added to the prescribed period.

As amended 1948, 1963, 1966, 1968, 1971, 1983, 1985, 1987, 1999, 2001.

III. PLEADINGS AND MOTIONS

Rule 7.

PLEADINGS ALLOWED; FORM OF MOTIONS

(a) Pleadings. There shall be a complaint and an answer; a reply to a counterclaim denominated as such; an answer to a cross-claim, if the answer contains a cross-claim; a third-party complaint, if a person who was not an original party is summoned under the provisions of Rule 14; and a third-party answer, if a third-party complaint is served. No other pleading shall be allowed, except that the court may order a reply to an answer or a third-party answer.

(b) Motions and Other Papers.

(1) An application to the court for an order shall be by motion which, unless made during a hearing or trial, shall be made in writing, shall state with particularity the grounds therefor, and shall set forth the relief or order sought. The requirement of writing is fulfilled if the motion is stated in a written notice of the hearing of the motion.

(2) The rules applicable to captions and other matters of form of pleadings apply to all motions and other papers provided for by these rules.

(3) All motions shall be signed in accordance with Rule 11.

(c) Demurrers, Pleas, etc., Abolished. Demurrers, pleas, and exceptions for insufficiency of a pleading shall not be used.

As amended 1948, 1963, 1983.

Rule 7.1.

DISCLOSURE STATEMENT

(a) Who Must File: Nongovernmental Corporate Party. A nongovernmental corporate party to an action or proceeding in a district court must file two copies of a statement that identifies any parent corporation and any publicly held corporation that owns 10% or more of its stock or states that there is no such corporation.

(b) Time for Filing; Supplemental Filing. A party must:

(1) file the Rule 7.1(a) statement with its first appearance, pleading, petition, motion, response, or other request addressed to the court, and

(2) promptly file a supplemental statement upon any change in the information that the statement requires.

Added 2002.

Rule 8.

GENERAL RULES OF PLEADING

(a) Claims for Relief. A pleading which sets forth a claim for relief, whether an original claim, counterclaim, cross-claim, or third-party claim, shall contain (1) a short and plain statement of the grounds upon which the court's jurisdiction depends, unless the court already has jurisdiction and the claim needs no new grounds of jurisdiction to support it, (2) a short and plain statement of the claim showing that the pleader is entitled to relief, and (3) a demand for judgment for the relief the pleader seeks. Relief in the alternative or of several different types may be demanded.

(b) Defenses; Form of Denials. A party shall state in short and plain terms the party's defenses to each claim asserted and shall admit or deny the averments upon which the adverse party relies. If a party is without knowledge or information sufficient to form a belief as to the truth of an averment, the party shall so state and this has the effect of a denial. Denials shall fairly meet the substance of the averments denied. When a pleader intends in good faith to deny only a part or a qualification of an averment, the pleader shall specify so much of it as is true and material and shall deny only the remainder. Unless the pleader intends in good faith to controvert all the averments of the preceding pleading, the pleader may make denials as specific denials of designated averments or paragraphs or may generally deny all the averments except such designated averments or paragraphs as the pleader expressly admits; but, when the pleader does so intend to controvert all its averments, including averments of the grounds upon which the court's jurisdiction depends, the pleader may do so by general denial subject to the obligations set forth in Rule 11.

(c) Affirmative Defenses. In pleading to a preceding pleading, a party shall set forth affirmatively accord and satisfaction, arbitration and award, assumption of risk, contributory negligence, discharge in bankruptcy, duress, estoppel, failure of consideration, fraud, illegality, injury by fellow servant, laches, license, payment, release, res judicata, statute of frauds, statute of limitations, waiver, and any other matter constituting an avoidance or affirmative defense. When a party has mistakenly designated a defense as a counterclaim or a counterclaim as a defense, the court on terms, if justice so requires, shall treat the pleading as if there had been a proper designation.

(d) Effect of Failure to Deny. Averments in a pleading to which a responsive pleading is required, other than those as to the amount of damage, are admitted when not denied in the responsive pleading. Averments in a pleading to which no responsive pleading is required or permitted shall be taken as denied or avoided.

(e) Pleading to Be Concise and Direct; Consistency.

(1) Each averment of a pleading shall be simple, concise, and direct. No technical forms of pleading or motions are required.

(2) A party may set forth two or more statements of a claim or defense alternately or hypothetically, either in one count or defense or in separate counts or defenses. When two or more statements are made in the alternative and one of them if made independently would be sufficient, the pleading is not made insufficient by the insufficiency of one or more of the alternative statements. A party

may also state as many separate claims or defenses as the party has regardless of consistency and whether based on legal, equitable, or maritime grounds. All statements shall be made subject to the obligations set forth in Rule 11.

(f) Construction of Pleadings. All pleadings shall be so construed as to do substantial justice.

As amended 1966, 1987.

Rule 9.

PLEADING SPECIAL MATTERS

(a) Capacity. It is not necessary to aver the capacity of a party to sue or be sued or the authority of a party to sue or be sued in a representative capacity or the legal existence of an organized association of persons that is made a party, except to the extent required to show the jurisdiction of the court. When a party desires to raise an issue as to the legal existence of any party or the capacity of any party to sue or be sued or the authority of a party to sue or be sued in a representative capacity, the party desiring to raise the issue shall do so by specific negative averment, which shall include such supporting particulars as are peculiarly within the pleader's knowledge.

(b) Fraud, Mistake, Condition of the Mind. In all averments of fraud or mistake, the circumstances constituting fraud or mistake shall be stated with particularity. Malice, intent, knowledge, and other condition of mind of a person may be averred generally.

(c) Conditions Precedent. In pleading the performance or occurrence of conditions precedent, it is sufficient to aver generally that all conditions precedent have been performed or have occurred. A denial of performance or occurrence shall be made specifically and with particularity.

(d) Official Document or Act. In pleading an official document or official act it is sufficient to aver that the document was issued or the act done in compliance with law.

(e) Judgment. In pleading a judgment or decision of a domestic or foreign court, judicial or quasi-judicial tribunal, or of a board or officer, it is sufficient to aver the judgment or decision without setting forth matter showing jurisdiction to render it.

(f) Time and Place. For the purpose of testing the sufficiency of a pleading, averments of time and place are material and shall be considered like all other averments of material matter.

(g) Special Damage. When items of special damage are claimed, they shall be specifically stated.

(h) Admiralty and Maritime Claims. A pleading or count setting forth a claim for relief within the admiralty and maritime jurisdiction that is also within the jurisdiction of the district court on some other ground may contain a statement identifying the claim as an admiralty or maritime claim for the purposes of Rules 14(c), 38(e), 82, and the Supplemental Rules for Certain Admiralty and Maritime Claims. If the claim is cognizable only in admiralty, it is an admiralty or maritime claim for those purposes whether so identified or not. The amendment of a pleading to add or withdraw an identifying statement is governed by the principles of Rule 15. A case that includes an admiralty or maritime claim within this subdivision is an admiralty case within 28 U.S.C. § 1292(a)(3).

As amended 1966, 1968, 1970, 1987, 1997.

Rule 10.

FORM OF PLEADINGS

(a) Caption; Names of Parties. Every pleading shall contain a caption setting forth the name of the court, the title of the action, the file number, and a designation as in Rule 7(a). In the complaint the title of the action shall include the names of all the parties, but in other pleadings it is sufficient to state the name of the first party on each side with an appropriate indication of other parties.

(b) Paragraphs; Separate Statements. All averments of claim or defense shall be made in numbered paragraphs, the contents of each of which shall be limited as far as practicable to a statement of a single set of circumstances; and a paragraph may be referred to by number in all succeeding pleadings. Each claim founded upon a separate transaction or occurrence and each defense other than denials shall be stated in a separate count or defense whenever a separation facilitates the clear presentation of the matters set forth.

(c) Adoption by Reference; Exhibits. Statements in a pleading may be adopted by reference in a different part of the same pleading or in another pleading or in any motion. A copy of any written instrument which is an exhibit to a pleading is a part thereof for all purposes.

Rule 11.

SIGNING OF PLEADINGS, MOTIONS, AND OTHER PAPERS; REPRESENTATIONS TO COURT; SANCTIONS

(a) Signature. Every pleading, written motion, and other paper shall be signed by at least one attorney of record in the attorney's individual name, or, if the party is not represented by an attorney, shall be signed by the party. Each paper shall state the signer's address and telephone number, if any. Except when otherwise specifically provided by rule or statute, pleadings need not be verified or accompanied by affidavit. An unsigned paper shall be stricken unless omission of the signature is corrected promptly after being called to the attention of the attorney or party.

(b) Representations to Court. By presenting to the court (whether by signing, filing, submitting, or later advocating) a pleading, written motion, or other paper, an attorney or unrepresented party is certifying that to the best of the person's knowledge, information, and belief, formed after an inquiry reasonable under the circumstances,—

(1) it is not being presented for any improper purpose, such as to harass or to cause unnecessary delay or needless increase in the cost of litigation;

(2) the claims, defenses, and other legal contentions therein are warranted by existing law or by a nonfrivolous argument for the extension, modification, or reversal of existing law or the establishment of new law;

(3) the allegations and other factual contentions have evidentiary support or, if specifically so identified, are likely to have evidentiary support after a reasonable opportunity for further investigation or discovery; and

(4) the denials of factual contentions are warranted on the evidence or, if specifically so identified, are reasonably based on a lack of information or belief.

(c) Sanctions. If, after notice and a reasonable opportunity to respond, the court determines that subdivision (b) has been violated, the court may, subject to the conditions stated below, impose an appropriate sanction upon the attorneys, law firms, or parties that have violated subdivision (b) or are responsible for the violation.

(1) *How Initiated.*

(A) *By Motion.* A motion for sanctions under this rule shall be made separately from other motions or requests and shall describe the specific conduct alleged to violate subdivision (b). It shall be served as provided in Rule 5, but shall not be filed with or presented to the court unless, within 21 days after service of the motion (or such other period as the court may prescribe), the challenged paper, claim, defense, contention, allegation, or denial is not withdrawn or appropriately corrected. If warranted, the court may award to the party prevailing on the motion the reasonable expenses and attorney's fees incurred in presenting or opposing the motion. Absent exceptional circumstances, a law firm shall be held jointly responsible for violations committed by its partners, associates, and employees.

(B) *On Court's Initiative.* On its own initiative, the court may enter an order describing the specific conduct that appears to violate subdivision (b) and directing an attorney, law firm, or party to show cause why it has not violated subdivision (b) with respect thereto.

(2) *Nature of Sanction; Limitations.* A sanction imposed for violation of this rule shall be limited to what is sufficient to deter repetition of such conduct or comparable conduct by others similarly situated. Subject to the limitations in subparagraphs (A) and (B), the sanction may consist of, or include, directives of a nonmonetary nature, an order to pay a penalty into court, or, if imposed on motion and warranted for effective deterrence, an order directing payment to the movant of some or all of the reasonable attorneys' fees and other expenses incurred as a direct result of the violation.

(A) Monetary sanctions may not be awarded against a represented party for a violation of subdivision (b)(2).

(B) Monetary sanctions may not be awarded on the court's initiative unless the court issues its order to show cause before a voluntary dismissal or settlement of the claims made by or against the party which is, or whose attorneys are, to be sanctioned.

(3) *Order.* When imposing sanctions, the court shall describe the conduct determined to constitute a violation of this rule and explain the basis for the sanction imposed.

(d) Inapplicability to Discovery. Subdivisions (a) through (c) of this rule do not apply to disclosures and discovery requests, responses, objections, and motions that are subject to the provisions of Rules 26 through 37.

As amended 1983, 1987, 1993.

Rule 12.

DEFENSES AND OBJECTIONS—WHEN AND HOW PRESENTED—BY PLEADING OR MOTION—MOTION FOR JUDGMENT ON THE PLEADINGS

(a) When Presented.

(1) Unless a different time is prescribed in a statute of the United States, a defendant shall serve an answer

(A) within 20 days after being served with the summons and complaint, or

(B) if service of the summons has been timely waived on request under Rule 4(d), within 60 days after the date when the request for waiver was sent, or within 90 days after that date if the defendant was addressed outside any judicial district of the United States.

(2) A party served with a pleading stating a cross-claim against that party shall serve an answer thereto within 20 days after being served. The plaintiff shall serve a reply to a counterclaim in the answer within 20 days after service of the answer, or, if a reply is ordered by the court, within 20 days after service of the order, unless the order otherwise directs.

(3)(A) The United States, an agency of the United States, or an officer or employee of the United States sued in an official capacity, shall serve an answer to the complaint or cross-claim—or a reply to a counterclaim—within 60 days after the United States attorney is served with the pleading asserting the claim.

(B) An officer or employee of the United States sued in an individual capacity for acts or omissions occurring in connection with the performance of duties on behalf of the United States shall serve an answer to the complaint or cross-claim—or a reply to a counterclaim—within 60 days after service on the officer or employee, or service on the United States attorney, whichever is later.

(4) Unless a different time is fixed by court order, the service of a motion permitted under this rule alters these periods of time as follows:

(A) if the court denies the motion or postpones its disposition until the trial on the merits, the responsive pleading shall be served within 10 days after notice of the court's action; or

(B) if the court grants a motion for a more definite statement, the responsive pleading shall be served within 10 days after the service of the more definite statement.

(b) How Presented. Every defense, in law or fact, to a claim for relief in any pleading, whether a claim, counterclaim, cross-claim, or third-party claim, shall be asserted in the responsive pleading thereto if one is required, except that the following defenses may at the option of the pleader be made by motion: (1) lack of jurisdiction over the subject matter, (2) lack of jurisdiction over the person, (3) improper venue, (4) insufficiency of process, (5) insufficiency of service of process, (6) failure to state a claim upon which relief can be granted, (7) failure to join a party under Rule 19. A motion making any of these defenses shall be made before pleading if a further pleading is permitted. No defense or objection is waived by being joined with one or more other defenses or objections in a responsive pleading or motion. If a pleading sets forth a claim for relief to which the adverse party is not required to serve a responsive pleading, the adverse party may assert at the trial any defense in law or fact to that claim for relief. If, on a motion asserting the defense numbered (6) to dismiss for failure of the pleading to state a claim upon which relief can be granted, matters outside the pleading are presented to and not excluded by the court, the motion shall be treated as one for summary judgment and disposed of as provided in Rule 56, and all parties shall be given reasonable opportunity to present all material made pertinent to such a motion by Rule 56.

(c) Motion for Judgment on the Pleadings. After the pleadings are closed but within such time as not to delay the trial, any party may move for judgment on the pleadings. If, on a motion for judgment on the pleadings, matters outside the pleadings are presented to and not excluded by the court, the motion shall be treated as one for summary judgment and disposed of as provided in Rule 56, and all parties shall be given reasonable opportunity to present all material made pertinent to such a motion by Rule 56.

(d) Preliminary Hearings. The defenses specifically enumerated (1)–(7) in subdivision (b) of this rule, whether made in a pleading or by motion, and the motion for judgment mentioned in subdivision (c) of this rule shall be heard and determined before trial on application of any party, unless the court orders that the hearing and determination thereof be deferred until the trial.

(e) Motion for More Definite Statement. If a pleading to which a responsive pleading is permitted is so vague or ambiguous that a party cannot reasonably be required to frame a responsive pleading, the party may move for a more definite statement before interposing a responsive pleading. The motion shall point out the defects complained of and the details desired. If the motion is granted and the order of the court is not obeyed within 10 days after notice of the order or within such other time as the court may fix, the court may strike the pleading to which the motion was directed or make such order as it deems just.

(f) Motion to Strike. Upon motion made by a party before responding to a pleading or, if no responsive pleading is permitted by these rules, upon motion made by a party within 20 days after the service of the pleading upon the party or upon the court's own initiative at any time, the court may order stricken from any pleading any insufficient defense or any redundant, immaterial, impertinent, or scandalous matter.

(g) Consolidation of Defenses in Motion. A party who makes a motion under this rule may join with it any other motions herein provided for and then available to the party. If a party makes a motion under this rule but omits therefrom any defense or objection then available to the party which this rule permits to be raised by motion, the party shall not thereafter make a motion based on the defense or objection so omitted, except a motion as provided in subdivision (h)(2) hereof on any of the grounds there stated.

(h) Waiver or Preservation of Certain Defenses.

(1) A defense of lack of jurisdiction over the person, improper venue, insufficiency of process, or insufficiency of service of process is waived (A) if omitted from a motion in the circumstances described in subdivision (g), or (B) if it is neither made by motion under this rule nor included in a responsive pleading or an amendment thereof permitted by Rule 15(a) to be made as a matter of course.

(2) A defense of failure to state a claim upon which relief can be granted, a defense of failure to join a party indispensable under Rule 19, and an objection of failure to state a legal defense to a claim may be made in any pleading permitted or ordered under Rule 7(a), or by motion for judgment on the pleadings, or at the trial on the merits.

(3) Whenever it appears by suggestion of the parties or otherwise that the court lacks jurisdiction of the subject matter, the court shall dismiss the action.

As amended 1948, 1963, 1966, 1987, 1993, 2000.

Rule 13.

COUNTERCLAIM AND CROSS-CLAIM

(a) Compulsory Counterclaims. A pleading shall state as a counterclaim any claim which at the time of serving the pleading the pleader has against any opposing party, if it arises out of the transaction or occurrence that is the subject matter of the opposing party's claim and does not require for its adjudication the presence of third parties of whom the court cannot acquire jurisdiction. But the pleader need not state the claim if (1) at the time the action was commenced the claim was the subject of another pending action, or (2) the opposing party brought suit upon the claim by attachment or other process by which the court did not acquire jurisdiction to render a personal judgment on that claim, and the pleader is not stating any counterclaim under this Rule 13.

(b) Permissive Counterclaims. A pleading may state as a counterclaim any claim against an opposing party not arising out of the transaction or occurrence that is the subject matter of the opposing party's claim.

(c) Counterclaim Exceeding Opposing Claim. A counterclaim may or may not diminish or defeat the recovery sought by the opposing party. It may claim relief exceeding in amount or different in kind from that sought in the pleading of the opposing party.

(d) Counterclaim Against the United States. These rules shall not be construed to enlarge beyond the limits now fixed by law the right to assert counterclaims or to claim credits against the United States or an officer or agency thereof.

(e) Counterclaim Maturing or Acquired After Pleading. A claim which either matured or was acquired by the pleader after serving a pleading may, with the permission of the court, be presented as a counterclaim by supplemental pleading.

(f) Omitted Counterclaim. When a pleader fails to set up a counterclaim through oversight, inadvertence, or excusable neglect, or when justice requires, the pleader may by leave of court set up the counterclaim by amendment.

(g) Cross-Claim Against Co-Party. A pleading may state as a cross-claim any claim by one party against a co-party arising out of the transaction or occurrence that is the subject matter either of the original action or of a counterclaim therein or relating to any property that is the subject matter of the original action. Such cross-claim may include a claim that the party against whom it is asserted is or may be liable to the cross-claimant for all or part of a claim asserted in the action against the cross-claimant.

(h) Joinder of Additional Parties. Persons other than those made parties to the original action may be made parties to a counterclaim or cross-claim in accordance with the provisions of Rules 19 and 20.

(i) Separate Trials; Separate Judgments. If the court orders separate trials as provided in Rule 42(b), judgment on a counterclaim or cross-claim may be rendered in accordance with the terms of Rule 54(b) when the court has jurisdiction so to do, even if the claims of the opposing party have been dismissed or otherwise disposed of.

As amended 1948, 1963, 1966, 1987.

Rule 14.

THIRD-PARTY PRACTICE

(a) When Defendant May Bring in Third Party. At any time after commencement of the action a defending party, as a third-party plaintiff, may cause a summons and complaint to be served upon a person not a party to the action who is or may be liable to the third-party plaintiff for all or part of the plaintiff's claim against the third-party plaintiff. The third-party plaintiff need not obtain leave to make the service if the third-party plaintiff files the third-party complaint not later than 10 days after serving the original answer. Otherwise the third-party plaintiff must obtain leave on motion upon notice to all parties to the action. The person served with the summons and third-party complaint, hereinafter called the third-party defendant, shall make any defenses to the third-party plaintiff's claim as provided in Rule 12 and any counterclaims against the third-party plaintiff and cross-claims against other third-party defendants as provided in Rule 13. The third-party defendant may assert against the plaintiff any defenses which the third-party plaintiff has to the plaintiff's claim. The third-party defendant may also assert any claim against the plaintiff arising out of the transaction or occurrence that is the subject matter of the plaintiff's claim against the third-party plaintiff. The plaintiff may assert any claim against the third-party defendant arising out of the transaction or occurrence that is the subject matter of the plaintiff's claim against the third-party plaintiff, and the third-party defendant thereupon shall assert any defenses as provided in Rule 12 and any counterclaims and cross-claims as provided in Rule 13. Any party may move to strike the third-party claim, or for its severance or separate trial. A third-party defendant may proceed under this rule against any person not a party to the action who is or may be liable to the third-party defendant for all or part of the claim made in the action against the third-party defendant. The third-party complaint, if within the admiralty and maritime jurisdiction, may be in rem against a vessel, cargo, or other property subject to admiralty or maritime process in rem, in which case references in this rule to the summons include the warrant of arrest, and references to the third-party plaintiff or defendant include, where appropriate, a person who asserts a right under Supplemental Rule C(6)(b)(i) in the property arrested.

(b) When Plaintiff May Bring in Third Party. When a counterclaim is asserted against a plaintiff, the plaintiff may cause a third party to be brought in under circumstances which under this rule would entitle a defendant to do so.

(c) Admiralty and Maritime Claims. When a plaintiff asserts an admiralty or maritime claim within the meaning of Rule 9(h), the defendant or person who asserts a right under Supplemental Rule C(6)(b)(i), as a third-party plaintiff, may bring in a third-party defendant who may be wholly or partly liable, either to the plaintiff or to the third-party plaintiff, by way of remedy over, contribution, or otherwise on account of the same transaction, occurrence, or series of transactions or occurrences. In such a case the third-party plaintiff may also demand judgment against the third-party defendant in favor of the plaintiff, in which event the third-party defendant shall make any defenses to the claim of the plaintiff as well as to that of the third-party plaintiff in the manner provided in Rule 12 and the action shall proceed as if the plaintiff had commenced it against the third-party defendant as well as the third-party plaintiff.

As amended 1948, 1963, 1966, 1987, 2000.

Rule 15.

AMENDED AND SUPPLEMENTAL PLEADINGS

(a) Amendments. A party may amend the party's pleading once as a matter of course at any time before a responsive pleading is served or, if the pleading is one to which no responsive pleading is permitted and the action has not been placed upon the trial calendar, the party may so amend it at any time within 20 days after it is served. Otherwise a party may amend the party's pleading only by leave of court or by written consent of the adverse party; and leave shall be freely given when justice so requires. A party shall plead in response to an amended pleading within the time remaining for response to the original pleading or within 10 days after service of the amended pleading, whichever period may be the longer, unless the court otherwise orders.

(b) Amendments to Conform to the Evidence. When issues not raised by the pleadings are tried by express or implied consent of the parties, they shall be treated in all respects as if they had been raised in the pleadings. Such amendment of the pleadings as may be necessary to cause them to conform to the evidence and to raise these issues may be made upon motion of any party at any time, even after judgment; but failure so to amend does not affect the result of the trial of these issues. If evidence is objected to at the trial on the ground that it is not within the issues made by the pleadings, the court may allow the pleadings to be amended and shall do so freely when the presentation of the merits of the action will be subserved thereby and the objecting party fails to satisfy the court that the admission of such evidence would prejudice the party in maintaining the party's action or defense upon the merits. The court may grant a continuance to enable the objecting party to meet such evidence.

(c) Relation Back of Amendments. An amendment of a pleading relates back to the date of the original pleading when

(1) relation back is permitted by the law that provides the statute of limitations applicable to the action, or

(2) the claim or defense asserted in the amended pleading arose out of the conduct, transaction, or occurrence set forth or attempted to be set forth in the original pleading, or

(3) the amendment changes the party or the naming of the party against whom a claim is asserted if the foregoing provision (2) is satisfied and, within the period provided by Rule 4(m) for service of the summons and complaint, the party to be brought in by amendment (A) has received such notice of the institution of the action that the party will not be prejudiced in maintaining a defense on the merits, and (B) knew or should have known that, but for a mistake concerning the identity of the proper party, the action would have been brought against the party.

The delivery or mailing of process to the United States Attorney, or United States Attorney's designee, or the Attorney General of the United States, or an agency or officer who would have been a proper defendant if named, satisfies the requirement of subparagraphs (A) and (B) of this paragraph (3) with respect to the United States or any agency or officer thereof to be brought into the action as a defendant.

(d) Supplemental Pleadings. Upon motion of a party the court may, upon reasonable notice and upon such terms as are just, permit the party to serve a supplemental pleading setting forth transactions or occurrences or events which have happened since the date of the pleading sought to be supplemented. Permission may be granted even though the original pleading is defective in its statement of a claim for relief or defense. If the court deems it advisable that the adverse party plead to the supplemental pleading, it shall so order, specifying the time therefor.

As amended 1963, 1966, 1987, 1991, 1993.

Rule 16.

PRETRIAL CONFERENCES; SCHEDULING; MANAGEMENT

(a) Pretrial Conferences; Objectives. In any action, the court may in its discretion direct the attorneys for the parties and any unrepresented parties to appear before it for a conference or conferences before trial for such purposes as

(1) expediting the disposition of the action;

(2) establishing early and continuing control so that the case will not be protracted because of lack of management;

(3) discouraging wasteful pretrial activities;

(4) improving the quality of the trial through more thorough preparation, and;

(5) facilitating the settlement of the case.

(b) Scheduling and Planning. Except in categories of actions exempted by district court rule as inappropriate, the district judge, or a magistrate judge when authorized by district court rule, shall, after receiving the report from the parties under Rule 26(f) or after consulting with the attorneys for the parties and any unrepresented parties by a scheduling conference, telephone, mail, or other suitable means, enter a scheduling order that limits the time

(1) to join other parties and to amend the pleadings;

(2) to file motions; and

(3) to complete discovery.

The scheduling order may also include

(4) modifications of the times for disclosures under Rules 26(a) and 26(e)(1) and of the extent of discovery to be permitted;

(5) the date or dates for conferences before trial, a final pretrial conference, and trial; and

(6) any other matters appropriate in the circumstances of the case.

The order shall issue as soon as practicable but in any event within 90 days after the appearance of a defendant and within 120 days after the complaint has been served on a defendant. A schedule shall not be modified except upon a showing of good cause and by leave of the district judge or, when authorized by local rule, by a magistrate judge.

(c) Subjects for Consideration at Pretrial Conferences. At any conference under this rule consideration may be given, and the court may take appropriate action, with respect to

(1) the formulation and simplification of the issues, including the elimination of frivolous claims or defenses;

(2) the necessity or desirability of amendments to the pleadings;

(3) the possibility of obtaining admissions of fact and of documents which will avoid unnecessary proof, stipulations regarding the authenticity of documents, and advance rulings from the court on the admissibility of evidence;

(4) the avoidance of unnecessary proof and of cumulative evidence, and limitations or restrictions on the use of testimony under Rule 702 of the Federal Rules of Evidence;

(5) the appropriateness and timing of summary adjudication under Rule 56;

(6) the control and scheduling of discovery, including orders affecting disclosures and discovery pursuant to Rule 26 and Rules 29 through 37;

(7) the identification of witnesses and documents, the need and schedule for filing and exchanging pretrial briefs, and the date or dates for further conferences and for trial;

(8) the advisability of referring matters to a magistrate judge or master;

(9) settlement and the use of special procedures to assist in resolving the dispute when authorized by statute or local rule;

(10) the form and substance of the pretrial order;

(11) the disposition of pending motions;

(12) the need for adopting special procedures for managing potentially difficult or protracted actions that may involve complex issues, multiple parties, difficult legal questions, or unusual proof problems;

(13) an order for a separate trial pursuant to Rule 42(b) with respect to a claim, counterclaim, cross-claim, or third-party claim, or with respect to any particular issue in the case;

(14) an order directing a party or parties to present evidence early in the trial with respect to a manageable issue that could, on the evidence, be the basis for a judgment as a matter

of law under Rule 50(a) or a judgment on partial findings under Rule 52(c);

(15) an order establishing a reasonable limit on the time allowed for presenting evidence; and

(16) such other matters as may facilitate the just, speedy, and inexpensive disposition of the action.

At least one of the attorneys for each party participating in any conference before trial shall have authority to enter into stipulations and to make admissions regarding all matters that the participants may reasonably anticipate may be discussed. If appropriate, the court may require that a party or its representative be present or reasonably available by telephone in order to consider possible settlement of the dispute.

(d) Final Pretrial Conference. Any final pretrial conference shall be held as close to the time of trial as reasonable under the circumstances. The participants at any such conference shall formulate a plan for trial, including a program for facilitating the admission of evidence. The conference shall be attended by at least one of the attorneys who will conduct the trial for each of the parties and by any unrepresented parties.

(e) Pretrial Orders. After any conference held pursuant to this rule, an order shall be entered reciting the action taken. This order shall control the subsequent course of the action unless modified by a subsequent order. The order following a final pretrial conference shall be modified only to prevent manifest injustice.

(f) Sanctions. If a party or party's attorney fails to obey a scheduling or pretrial order, or if no appearance is made on behalf of a party at a scheduling or pretrial conference, or if a party or party's attorney is substantially unprepared to participate in the conference, or if a party or party's attorney fails to participate in good faith, the judge, upon motion or the judge's own initiative, may make such orders with regard thereto as are just, and among others any of the orders provided in Rule 37(b)(2)(B), (C), (D). In lieu of or in addition to any other sanction, the judge shall require the party or the attorney representing the party or both to pay the reasonable expenses incurred because of any noncompliance with this rule, including attorney's fees, unless the judge finds that the noncompliance was substantially justified or that other circumstances make an award of expenses unjust.

As amended 1983, 1987, 1993.

IV. PARTIES

Rule 17.

PARTIES PLAINTIFF AND DEFENDANT; CAPACITY

(a) Real Party in Interest. Every action shall be prosecuted in the name of the real party in interest. An executor, administrator, guardian, bailee, trustee of an express trust, a party with whom or in whose name a contract has been made for the benefit of another, or a party authorized by statute may sue in that person's own name without joining the party for whose benefit the action is brought; and when a statute of the United States so provides, an action for the use or benefit of another shall be brought in the name of the United States. No action shall be dismissed on the ground that it is not prosecuted in the name of the real party in interest until a reasonable time has been allowed after objection for ratification of commencement of the action by, or joinder or substitution of, the real party in interest; and such ratification, joinder, or substitution shall have the same effect as if the action had been commenced in the name of the real party in interest.

(b) Capacity to Sue or Be Sued. The capacity of an individual, other than one acting in a representative capacity, to sue or be sued shall be determined by the law of the individual's domicile. The capacity of a corporation to sue or be sued shall be determined by the law under which it was organized. In all other cases capacity to sue or be sued shall be determined by the law of the state in which the district court is held, except (1) that a partnership or other unincorporated association, which has no such capacity by the law of such state, may sue or be sued in its common name for the purpose of enforcing for or against it a substantive right existing under the Constitution or laws of the United States, and (2) that the capacity of a receiver appointed by a court of the United States to sue or be sued in a court of the United States is governed by Title 28, U.S.C. §§ 754 and 959(a).

(c) Infants or Incompetent Persons. Whenever an infant or incompetent person has a representative, such as a general guardian, committee, conservator, or other like fiduciary, the representative may sue or defend on behalf of the infant or incompetent person. An infant or incompetent person who does not have a duly appointed representative may sue by a next friend or by a guardian ad litem. The court shall appoint a guardian ad litem for an infant or incompetent person not otherwise represented in an action or shall make such other order as it deems proper for the protection of the infant or incompetent person.

As amended 1948, 1949, 1966, 1987, 1988.

Rule 18.

JOINDER OF CLAIMS AND REMEDIES

(a) Joinder of Claims. A party asserting a claim to relief as an original claim, counterclaim, cross-claim, or third-party claim, may join, either as independent or as alternate claims, as many claims, legal, equitable, or maritime, as the party has against an opposing party.

(b) Joinder of Remedies; Fraudulent Conveyances. Whenever a claim is one heretofore cognizable only after another claim has been prosecuted to a conclusion, the two claims may be joined in a single action; but the court shall grant relief in that action only in accordance with the relative substantive rights of the parties. In particular, a plaintiff may state a claim for money and a claim to have set aside a conveyance fraudulent as to that plaintiff, without first having obtained a judgment establishing the claim for money.

As amended 1966, 1987.

Rule 19.

JOINDER OF PERSONS NEEDED FOR JUST ADJUDICATION

(a) Persons to Be Joined if Feasible. A person who is subject to service of process and whose joinder will not deprive the court of jurisdiction over the subject matter of the action shall be joined as a party in the action if (1) in the person's absence complete relief cannot be accorded among those already parties, or (2) the person claims an interest relating to the subject of the action and is so situated that the disposition of the action in the person's absence may (i) as a practical matter impair or impede the person's ability to protect that interest or (ii) leave any of the persons already parties subject to a substantial risk of incurring double, multiple, or otherwise inconsistent obligations by reason of the claimed interest. If the person has not been so joined, the court shall order that the person be made a party. If the person should join as a plaintiff but refuses to do so, the person may be made a defendant, or, in a proper case, an involuntary plaintiff. If the joined party objects to venue and joinder of that party would render the venue of the action improper, that party shall be dismissed from the action.

(b) Determination by Court Whenever Joinder Not Feasible. If a person as described in subdivision (a)(1)–(2) hereof cannot be made a party, the court shall determine whether in equity and good conscience the action should proceed among the parties before it, or should be dismissed, the absent person being thus regarded as indispensable. The factors to be considered by the court include: first, to what extent a judgment rendered in the person's absence might be prejudicial to the person or those already parties; second, the extent to which, by protective provisions in the judgment, by the shaping of relief, or other measures, the prejudice can be lessened or avoided; third, whether a judgment rendered in the person's absence will be adequate; fourth, whether the plaintiff will have an adequate remedy if the action is dismissed for nonjoinder.

(c) Pleading Reasons for Nonjoinder. A pleading asserting a claim for relief shall state the names, if known to the pleader, of any persons as described in subdivision (a)(1)–(2) hereof who are not joined, and the reasons why they are not joined.

(d) Exception of Class Actions. This rule is subject to the provisions of Rule 23.

As amended 1966, 1987.

Rule 20.

PERMISSIVE JOINDER OF PARTIES

(a) Permissive Joinder. All persons may join in one action as plaintiffs if they assert any right to relief jointly, severally, or in the alternative in respect of or arising out of the same transaction, occurrence, or series of transactions or occurrences and if any question of law or fact common to all these persons will arise in the action. All persons (and any vessel, cargo or other property subject to admiralty process in rem) may be joined in one action as defendants if there is asserted against them jointly, severally, or in the alternative, any right to relief in respect of or arising out of the same transaction, occurrence, or series of transactions or occurrences and if any question of law or fact common to all defendants will arise in the action. A plaintiff or defendant need not be interested in obtaining or defending against all the relief demanded. Judgment may be given for one or more of the plaintiffs according to their respective rights to relief, and against one or more defendants according to their respective liabilities.

(b) Separate Trials. The court may make such orders as will prevent a party from being embarrassed, delayed, or put to expense by the inclusion of a party against whom the party asserts no claim and who asserts no claim against the party, and may order separate trials or make other orders to prevent delay or prejudice.

As amended 1966, 1987.

Rule 21.

MISJOINDER AND NON-JOINDER OF PARTIES

Misjoinder of parties is not ground for dismissal of an action. Parties may be dropped or added by order of the court on motion of any party or of its own initiative at any stage of the action and on such terms as are just. Any claim against a party may be severed and proceeded with separately.

Rule 22.

INTERPLEADER

(1) Persons having claims against the plaintiff may be joined as defendants and required to interplead when their claims are such that the plaintiff is or may be exposed to double or multiple liability. It is not ground for objection to the joinder that the claims of the several claimants or the titles on which their claims depend do not have a common origin or are not identical but are adverse to and independent of one another, or that the plaintiff avers that the plaintiff is not liable in whole or in part to any or all of the claimants. A defendant exposed to similar liability may obtain such interpleader by way of cross-claim or counterclaim. The provisions of this rule supplement and do not in any way limit the joinder of parties permitted in Rule 20.

(2) The remedy herein provided is in addition to and in no way supersedes or limits the remedy provided by Title 28, U.S.C. §§ 1335, 1397, and 2361. Actions under those provisions shall be conducted in accordance with these rules.

As amended 1949, 1987.

Rule 23.

CLASS ACTIONS

(a) Prerequisites to a Class Action. One or more members of a class may sue or be sued as representative parties on behalf of all only if (1) the class is so numerous that joinder of all members is impracticable, (2) there are questions of law or fact common to the class, (3) the claims or defenses of the representative parties are typical of the claims or defenses of the class, and (4) the representative parties will fairly and adequately protect the interests of the class.

(b) Class Actions Maintainable. An action may be maintained as a class action if the prerequisites of subdivision (a) are satisfied, and in addition:

(1) the prosecution of separate actions by or against individual members of the class would create a risk of

(A) inconsistent or varying adjudications with respect to individual members of the class which would establish incompatible standards of conduct for the party opposing the class, or

(B) adjudications with respect to individual members of the class which would as a practical matter be dispositive of the interests of the other members not parties to the adjudications or substantially impair or impede their ability to protect their interests; or

(2) the party opposing the class has acted or refused to act on grounds generally applicable to the class, thereby making appropriate final injunctive relief or corresponding declaratory relief with respect to the class as a whole; or

(3) the court finds that the questions of law or fact common to the members of the class predominate over any questions affecting only individual members, and that a class action is superior to other available methods for the fair and efficient adjudication of the controversy. The matters pertinent to the findings include: (A) the interest of members of the class in individually controlling the prosecution or defense of separate actions; (B) the extent and nature of any litigation concerning the controversy already commenced by or against members of the class; (C) the desirability or undesirability of concentrating the litigation of the claims in the particular forum; (D) the difficulties likely to be encountered in the management of a class action.

(c) Determining by Order Whether to Certify a Class Action; Appointing Class Counsel; Notice and Membership in Class; Judgment; Multiple Classes and Subclasses.

(1)(A) When a person sues or is sued as a representative of a class, the court must—at an early practicable time—determine by order whether to certify the action as a class action.

(B) An order certifying a class action must define the class and the class claims, issues, or defenses, and must appoint class counsel under Rule 23(g).

(C) An order under Rule 23(c)(1) may be altered or amended before final judgment.

(2)(A) For any class certified under Rule 23(b)(1) or (2), the court may direct appropriate notice to the class.

(B) For any class certified under Rule 23(b)(3), the court must direct to class members the best notice practicable under the circumstances, including individual notice to all members who can be identified through reasonable effort. The notice must concisely and clearly state in plain, easily understood language:

- the nature of the action,
- the definition of the class certified,
- the class claims, issues, or defenses,
- that a class member may enter an appearance through counsel if the member so desires,
- that the court will exclude from the class any member who requests exclusion, stating when and how members may elect to be excluded, and
- the binding effect of a class judgment on class members under Rule 23(c)(3).

(3) The judgment in an action maintained as a class action under subdivision (b)(1) or (b)(2), whether or not favorable to the class, shall include and describe those whom the court finds to be members of the class. The judgment in an action maintained as a class action under subdivision (b)(3), whether or not favorable to the class, shall include and specify or describe those to whom the notice provided in subdivision (c)(2) was directed, and who have not requested exclusion, and whom the court finds to be members of the class.

(4) When appropriate (A) an action may be brought or maintained as a class action with respect to particular issues, or (B) a class may be divided into subclasses and each subclass treated as a class, and the provisions of this rule shall then be construed and applied accordingly.

(d) Orders in Conduct of Actions. In the conduct of actions to which this rule applies, the court may make appropriate orders: (1) determining the course of proceedings or prescribing measures to prevent undue repetition or complication in the presentation of evidence or argument; (2) requiring, for the protection of the members of the class or otherwise for the fair conduct of the action, that notice be given in such manner as the court may direct to some or all of the members of any step in the action, or of the proposed extent of the judgment, or of the opportunity of members to signify whether they consider the representation fair and adequate, to intervene and present claims or defenses, or otherwise to come into the action; (3) imposing conditions on the representative parties or on intervenors; (4) requiring that the pleadings be amended to eliminate therefrom allegations as to representation of absent persons, and that the action proceed accordingly; (5) dealing with similar procedural matters. The orders may be combined with an order under Rule 16, and may be altered or amended as may be desirable from time to time.

(e) Settlement, Voluntary Dismissal, or Compromise.

(1)(A) The court must approve any settlement, voluntary dismissal, or compromise of the claims, issues, or defenses of a certified class.

(B) The court must direct notice in a reasonable manner to all class members who would be bound by a proposed settlement, voluntary dismissal, or compromise.

(C) The court may approve a settlement, voluntary dismissal, or compromise that would bind class members only after a hearing and on finding that the settlement, voluntary dismissal, or compromise is fair, reasonable, and adequate.

(2) The parties seeking approval of a settlement, voluntary dismissal, or compromise under Rule 23(e)(1) must file a statement identifying any agreement made in connection with the proposed settlement, voluntary dismissal, or compromise.

(3) In an action previously certified as a class action under Rule 23(b)(3), the court may refuse to approve a settlement unless it affords a new opportunity to request exclusion to individual class members who had an earlier opportunity to request exclusion but did not do so.

(4)(A) Any class member may object to a proposed settlement, voluntary dismissal, or compromise that requires court approval under Rule 23(e)(1)(A).

(B) An objection made under Rule 23(e)(4)(A) may be withdrawn only with the court's approval.

(f) Appeals. A court of appeals may in its discretion permit an appeal from an order of a district court granting or denying class action certification under this rule if application is made to it within ten days after entry of the order. An appeal does not stay proceedings in the district court unless the district judge or the court of appeals so orders.

(g) Class Counsel.

(1) *Appointing Class Counsel.*

(A) Unless a statute provides otherwise, a court that certifies a class must appoint class counsel.

(B) An attorney appointed to serve as class counsel must fairly and adequately represent the interests of the class.

(C) In appointing class counsel, the court

(i) must consider:

- the work counsel has done in identifying or investigating potential claims in the action,

- counsel's experience in handling class actions, other complex litigation, and claims of the type asserted in the action,
- counsel's knowledge of the applicable law, and
- the resources counsel will commit to representing the class;

(ii) may consider any other matter pertinent to counsel's ability to fairly and adequately represent the interests of the class;

(iii) may direct potential class counsel to provide information on any subject pertinent to the appointment and to propose terms for attorney fees and nontaxable costs; and

(iv) may make further orders in connection with the appointment.

(2) *Appointment Procedure.*

(A) The court may designate interim counsel to act on behalf of the putative class before determining whether to certify the action as a class action.

(B) When there is one applicant for appointment as class counsel, the court may appoint that applicant only if the applicant is adequate under Rule 23(g)(1)(B) and (C). If more than one adequate applicant seeks appointment as class counsel, the court must appoint the applicant best able to represent the interests of the class.

(C) The order appointing class counsel may include provisions about the award of attorney fees or nontaxable costs under Rule 23(h).

(h) Attorney Fees Award. In an action certified as a class action, the court may award reasonable attorney fees and nontaxable costs authorized by law or by agreement of the parties as follows:

(1) *Motion for Award of Attorney Fees.* A claim for an award of attorney fees and nontaxable costs must be made by motion under Rule 54(d)(2), subject to the provisions of this subdivision, at a time set by the court. Notice of the motion must be served on all parties and, for motions by class counsel, directed to class members in a reasonable manner.

(2) *Objections to Motion.* A class member, or a party from whom payment is sought, may object to the motion.

(3) *Hearing and Findings.* The court may hold a hearing and must find the facts and state its conclusions of law on the motion under Rule 52(a).

(4) *Reference to Special Master or Magistrate Judge.* The court may refer issues related to the amount of the award to a special master or to a magistrate judge as provided in Rule 54(d)(2)(D).

As amended 1966, 1987, 1998, 2003.

Rule 23.1.

DERIVATIVE ACTIONS BY SHAREHOLDERS

In a derivative action brought by one or more shareholders or members to enforce a right of a corporation or of an unincorporated association, the corporation or association having failed to enforce a right which may properly be asserted by it, the complaint shall be verified and shall allege (1) that the plaintiff was a shareholder or member at the time of the transaction of which the plaintiff complains or that the plaintiff's share or membership thereafter devolved on the plaintiff by operation of law, and (2) that the action is not a collusive one to confer jurisdiction on a court of the United States which it would not otherwise have. The complaint shall also allege with particularity the efforts, if any, made by the plaintiff to obtain the action the plaintiff desires from the directors or comparable authority and, if necessary, from the shareholders or members, and the reasons for the plaintiff's failure to obtain the action or for not making the effort. The derivative action may not be maintained if it appears that the plaintiff does not fairly and adequately represent the interests of the shareholders or members similarly situated in enforcing the right of the corporation or association. The action shall not be dismissed or compromised without the approval of the court, and notice of the proposed dismissal or compromise shall be given to shareholders or members in such manner as the court directs.

Added 1966; as amended 1987.

Rule 23.2.

ACTIONS RELATING TO UNINCORPORATED ASSOCIATIONS

An action brought by or against the members of an unincorporated association as a class by naming certain members as representative parties may be maintained only if it appears that the representative parties will fairly and adequately protect the interests of the association and its members. In the conduct of the action the court may make appropriate orders corresponding with those described in Rule 23(d), and the procedure for dismissal or compromise of the action shall correspond with that provided in Rule 23(e).

Added 1966.

Rule 24.

INTERVENTION

(a) Intervention of Right. Upon timely application anyone shall be permitted to intervene in an action: (1) when a statute of the United States confers an unconditional right to intervene; or (2) when the applicant claims an interest relating to the property or transaction which is the subject of the action and the applicant is so situated that the disposition of the action may as a practical matter impair or impede the applicant's ability to protect that interest, unless the applicant's interest is adequately represented by existing parties.

(b) Permissive Intervention. Upon timely application anyone may be permitted to intervene in an action: (1) when a statute of the United States confers a conditional right to intervene; or (2) when an applicant's claim or defense and the main action have a question of law or fact in common. When a party to an action relies for ground of claim or defense upon any statute or executive order administered by a federal or state governmental officer or agency or upon any regulation, order, requirement or agreement issued or made pursuant to the statute or executive order, the officer or agency upon timely application may be permitted to intervene in the action. In exercising its discretion the court shall consider whether the intervention will unduly delay or prejudice the adjudication of the rights of the original parties.

(c) Procedure. A person desiring to intervene shall serve a motion to intervene upon the parties as provided in Rule 5. The motion shall state the grounds therefor and shall be accompanied by a pleading setting forth the claim or defense for which intervention is sought. The same procedure shall be followed when a statute of the United States gives a right to intervene. When the constitutionality of an act of Congress affecting the public interest is drawn in question in any action to which the United States or an officer, agency, or employee thereof is not a party, the court shall notify the Attorney General of the United States as provided in Title 28, U.S.C. § 2403. When the constitutionality of any statute of a State affecting the public interest is drawn in question in any action in which that State or any agency, officer, or employee thereof is not a party, the court shall notify the attorney general of the State as provided in Title 28, U.S.C. § 2403. A party challenging the constitutionality of legislation should call the attention of the court to its consequential duty, but failure to do so is not a waiver of any constitutional right otherwise timely asserted.

As amended 1948, 1949, 1963, 1966, 1987, 1991.

Rule 25.

SUBSTITUTION OF PARTIES

(a) Death.

(1) If a party dies and the claim is not thereby extinguished, the court may order substitution of the proper parties. The motion for substitution may be made by any party or by the successors or representatives of the deceased party and, together with the notice of hearing, shall be served on the parties as provided in Rule 5 and upon persons not parties in the manner provided in Rule 4 for the service of a summons, and may be served in any judicial district. Unless the motion for substitution is made not later than 90 days after the death is suggested upon the record by service of a statement of the fact of the death as provided herein for the service of the motion, the action shall be dismissed as to the deceased party.

(2) In the event of the death of one or more of the plaintiffs or of one or more of the defendants in an action in which the right sought to be enforced survives only to the surviving plaintiffs or only against the surviving defendants, the action does not abate. The death shall be suggested upon the record and the action shall proceed in favor of or against the surviving parties.

(b) Incompetency. If a party becomes incompetent, the court upon motion served as provided in subdivision (a) of this rule may allow the action to be continued by or against the party's representative.

(c) Transfer of Interest. In case of any transfer of interest, the action may be continued by or against the original party, unless the court upon motion directs the person to whom the interest is transferred to be substituted in the action or joined with the original party. Service of the motion shall be made as provided in subdivision (a) of this rule.

(d) Public Officers; Death or Separation from Office.

(1) When a public officer is a party to an action in an official capacity and during its pendency dies, resigns, or otherwise ceases to hold office, the action does not abate and the officer's successor is automatically substituted as a party. Proceedings following the substitution shall be in the name of the substituted party, but any misnomer not affecting the substantial rights of the parties shall be disregarded. An order of substitution may be entered at any time, but the omission to enter such an order shall not affect the substitution.

(2) A public officer who sues or is sued in an official capacity may be described as a party by the officer's official title rather than by name; but the court may require the officer's name to be added.

As amended 1949, 1961, 1963, 1987.

V. DEPOSITIONS AND DISCOVERY

Rule 26.

GENERAL PROVISIONS GOVERNING DISCOVERY; DUTY OF DISCLOSURE

(a) Required Disclosures; Methods to Discover Additional Matter.

(1) *Initial Disclosures.* Except in categories of proceedings specified in Rule 26(a)(1)(E), or to the extent otherwise stipulated or directed by order, a party must, without awaiting a discovery request, provide to other parties:

(A) the name and, if known, the address and telephone number of each individual likely to have discoverable information that the disclosing party may use to support its claims or defenses, unless solely for impeachment, identifying the subjects of the information;

(B) a copy of, or a description by category and location of, all documents, data compilations, and tangible things that are in the possession, custody, or control of the party and that the disclosing party may use to support its claims or defenses, unless solely for impeachment;

(C) a computation of any category of damages claimed by the disclosing party, making available for inspection and copying as under Rule 34 the documents or other evidentiary material, not privileged or protected from disclosure, on which such computation is based, including materials bearing on the nature and extent of injuries suffered; and

(D) for inspection and copying as under Rule 34 any insurance agreement under which any person carrying on an insurance business may be liable to satisfy part or all of a judgment which may be entered in the action or to indemnify or reimburse for payments made to satisfy the judgment.

(E) The following categories of proceedings are exempt from initial disclosure under Rule 26(a)(1):

(i) an action for review on an administrative record;

(ii) a petition for habeas corpus or other proceeding to challenge a criminal conviction or sentence;

(iii) an action brought without counsel by a person in custody of the United States, a state, or a state subdivision;

(iv) an action to enforce or quash an administrative summons or subpoena;

(v) an action by the United States to recover benefit payments;

(vi) an action by the United States to collect on a student loan guaranteed by the United States;

(vii) a proceeding ancillary to proceedings in other courts; and

(viii) an action to enforce an arbitration award.

These disclosures must be made at or within 14 days after the Rule 26(f) conference unless a different time is set by stipulation or court order, or unless a party objects during the conference that initial disclosures are not appropriate in the circumstances of the action and states the objection in the Rule 26(f) discovery plan. In ruling on the objection, the court must determine what disclosures—if any—are to be made, and set the time for disclosure. Any party first served or otherwise joined after the Rule 26(f) conference must make these disclosures within 30 days after being served or joined unless a different time is set by stipulation or court order. A party must make its initial disclosures based on the information then reasonably available to it and is not excused from making its disclosures because it has not fully completed its investigation of the case or because it challenges the sufficiency of another party's disclosures or because another party has not made its disclosures.

(2) *Disclosure of Expert Testimony.*

(A) In addition to the disclosures required by paragraph (1), a party shall disclose to other parties the identity of any person who may be used at trial to present evidence under Rules 702, 703, or 705 of the Federal Rules of Evidence.

(B) Except as otherwise stipulated or directed by the court, this disclosure shall, with respect to a witness who is retained or specially employed to provide expert testimony in the case or whose duties as an employee of the party regularly involve giving expert testimony, be accompanied by a written report prepared and signed by the witness. The report shall contain a complete statement of all opinions to be expressed and the basis and reasons therefor; the data or other information considered by the witness in forming the opinions; any exhibits to be used as a summary of or support for the opinions; the qualifications of the witness, including a list of all publications authored by the witness within the preceding ten years; the compensation to be paid for the study and testimony;

and a listing of any other cases in which the witness has testified as an expert at trial or by deposition within the preceding four years.

(C) These disclosures shall be made at the times and in the sequence directed by the court. In the absence of other directions from the court or stipulation by the parties, the disclosures shall be made at least 90 days before the trial date or the date the case is to be ready for trial or, if the evidence is intended solely to contradict or rebut evidence on the same subject matter identified by another party under paragraph (2)(B), within 30 days after the disclosure made by the other party. The parties shall supplement these disclosures when required under subdivision (e)(1).

(3) *Pretrial Disclosures.* In addition to the disclosures required by Rule 26(a)(1) and (2), a party must provide to other parties and promptly file with the court the following information regarding the evidence that it may present at trial other than solely for impeachment:

(A) the name and, if not previously provided, the address and telephone number of each witness, separately identifying those whom the party expects to present and those whom the party may call if the need arises;

(B) the designation of those witnesses whose testimony is expected to be presented by means of a deposition and, if not taken stenographically, a transcript of the pertinent portions of the deposition testimony; and

(C) an appropriate identification of each document or other exhibit, including summaries of other evidence, separately identifying those which the party expects to offer and those which the party may offer if the need arises.

Unless otherwise directed by the court, these disclosures must be made at least 30 days before trial. Within 14 days thereafter, unless a different time is specified by the court, a party may serve and promptly file a list disclosing (i) any objections to the use under Rule 32(a) of a deposition designated by another party under Rule 26(a)(3)(B), and (ii) any objection, together with the grounds therefor, that may be made to the admissibility of materials identified under Rule 26(a)(3)(C). Objections not so disclosed, other than objections under Rules 402 and 403 of the Federal Rules of Evidence, are waived unless excused by the court for good cause.

(4) *Form of Disclosures.* Unless the court orders otherwise, all disclosures under Rules 26(a)(1) through (3) must be made in writing, signed, and served.

(5) *Methods to Discover Additional Matter.* Parties may obtain discovery by one or more of the following methods: depositions upon oral examination or written questions; written interrogato-

ries; production of documents or things or permission to enter upon land or other property under Rule 34 or 45(a)(1)(C), for inspection and other purposes; physical and mental examinations; and requests for admission.

(b) Discovery Scope and Limits. Unless otherwise limited by order of the court in accordance with these rules, the scope of discovery is as follows:

(1) *In General.* Parties may obtain discovery regarding any matter, not privileged, that is relevant to the claim or defense of any party, including the existence, description, nature, custody, condition, and location of any books, documents, or other tangible things and the identity and location of persons having knowledge of any discoverable matter. For good cause, the court may order discovery of any matter relevant to the subject matter involved in the action. Relevant information need not be admissible at the trial if the discovery appears reasonably calculated to lead to the discovery of admissible evidence. All discovery is subject to the limitations imposed by Rule 26(b)(2)(i), (ii), and (iii).

(2) *Limitations.* By order, the court may alter the limits in these rules on the number of depositions and interrogatories or the length of depositions under Rule 30. By order or local rule, the court may also limit the number of requests under Rule 36. The frequency or extent of use of the discovery methods otherwise permitted under these rules and by any local rule shall be limited by the court if it determines that: (i) the discovery sought is unreasonably cumulative or duplicative, or is obtainable from some other source that is more convenient, less burdensome, or less expensive; (ii) the party seeking discovery has had ample opportunity by discovery in the action to obtain the information sought; or (iii) the burden or expense of the proposed discovery outweighs its likely benefit, taking into account the needs of the case, the amount in controversy, the parties' resources, the importance of the issues at stake in the litigation, and the importance of the proposed discovery in resolving the issues. The court may act upon its own initiative after reasonable notice or pursuant to a motion under Rule 26(c).

(3) *Trial Preparation: Materials.* Subject to the provisions of subdivision (b)(4) of this rule, a party may obtain discovery of documents and tangible things otherwise discoverable under subdivision (b)(1) of this rule and prepared in anticipation of litigation or for trial by or for another party or by or for that other party's representative (including the other party's attorney, consultant, surety, indemnitor, insurer, or

agent) only upon a showing that the party seeking discovery has substantial need of the materials in the preparation of the party's case and that the party is unable without undue hardship to obtain the substantial equivalent of the materials by other means. In ordering discovery of such materials when the required showing has been made, the court shall protect against disclosure of the mental impressions, conclusions, opinions, or legal theories of an attorney or other representative of a party concerning the litigation.

A party may obtain without the required showing a statement concerning the action or its subject matter previously made by that party. Upon request, a person not a party may obtain without the required showing a statement concerning the action or its subject matter previously made by that person. If the request is refused, the person may move for a court order. The provisions of Rule 37(a)(4) apply to the award of expenses incurred in relation to the motion. For purposes of this paragraph, a statement previously made is (A) a written statement signed or otherwise adopted or approved by the person making it, or (B) a stenographic, mechanical, electrical, or other recording, or a transcription thereof, which is a substantially verbatim recital of an oral statement by the person making it and contemporaneously recorded.

(4) *Trial Preparation: Experts.*

(A) A party may depose any person who has been identified as an expert whose opinions may be presented at trial. If a report from the expert is required under subdivision (a)(2)(B), the deposition shall not be conducted until after the report is provided.

(B) A party may, through interrogatories or by deposition, discover facts known or opinions held by an expert who has been retained or specially employed by another party in anticipation of litigation or preparation for trial and who is not expected to be called as a witness at trial only as provided in Rule 35(b) or upon a showing of exceptional circumstances under which it is impracticable for the party seeking discovery to obtain facts or opinions on the same subject by other means.

(C) Unless manifest injustice would result, (i) the court shall require that the party seeking discovery pay the expert a reasonable fee for time spent in responding to discovery under this subdivision; and (ii) with respect to discovery obtained under subdivision (b)(4)(B) of this rule the court shall require the party seeking discovery to pay the other party a fair portion of the fees and expenses reasonably incurred by the latter party in obtaining facts and opinions from the expert.

(5) *Claims of Privilege or Protection of Trial Preparation Materials.* When a party withholds information otherwise discoverable under these rules by claiming that it is privileged or subject to protection as trial preparation material, the party shall make the claim expressly and shall describe the nature of the documents, communications, or things not produced or disclosed in a manner that, without revealing information itself privileged or protected, will enable other parties to assess the applicability of the privilege or protection.

(c) Protective Orders. Upon motion by a party or by the person from whom discovery is sought, accompanied by a certification that the movant has in good faith conferred or attempted to confer with other affected parties in an effort to resolve the dispute without court action, and for good cause shown, the court in which the action is pending or alternatively, on matters relating to a deposition, the court in the district where the deposition is to be taken may make any order which justice requires to protect a party or person from annoyance, embarrassment, oppression, or undue burden or expense, including one or more of the following:

(1) that the disclosure or discovery not be had;

(2) that the disclosure or discovery may be had only on specified terms and conditions, including a designation of the time or place;

(3) that the discovery may be had only by a method of discovery other than that selected by the party seeking discovery;

(4) that certain matters not be inquired into, or that the scope of the disclosure or discovery be limited to certain matters;

(5) that discovery be conducted with no one present except persons designated by the court;

(6) that a deposition, after being sealed, be opened only by order of the court;

(7) that a trade secret or other confidential research, development, or commercial information not be revealed or be revealed only in a designated way; and

(8) that the parties simultaneously file specified documents or information enclosed in sealed envelopes to be opened as directed by the court.

If the motion for a protective order is denied in whole or in part, the court may, on such terms and conditions as are just, order that any party or other person provide or permit discovery. The provisions of Rule 37(a)(4) apply to the award of expenses incurred in relation to the motion.

(d) Timing and Sequence of Discovery. Except in categories of proceedings exempted from initial disclosure under Rule 26(a)(1)(E), or when authorized under these rules or by order or agreement of the parties, a party may not seek discovery from any source before the parties have conferred as required by Rule 26(f). Unless the court upon motion, for the convenience of parties and witnesses and in the interests of justice, orders otherwise, methods of discovery may be used in any sequence, and the fact that a party is conducting discovery, whether by deposition or otherwise, does not operate to delay any other party's discovery.

(e) Supplementation of Disclosures and Responses. A party who has made a disclosure under subdivision (a) or responded to a request for discovery with a disclosure or response is under a duty to supplement or correct the disclosure or response to include information thereafter acquired if ordered by the court or in the following circumstances:

(1) A party is under a duty to supplement at appropriate intervals its disclosures under subdivision (a) if the party learns that in some material respect the information disclosed is incomplete or incorrect and if the additional or corrective information has not otherwise been made known to the other parties during the discovery process or in writing. With respect to testimony of an expert from whom a report is required under subdivision (a)(2)(B) the duty extends both to information contained in the report and to information provided through a deposition of the expert, and any additions or other changes to this information shall be disclosed by the time the party's disclosures under Rule 26(a)(3) are due.

(2) A party is under a duty seasonably to amend a prior response to an interrogatory, request for production, or request for admission if the party learns that the response is in some material respect incomplete or incorrect and if the additional or corrective information has not otherwise been made known to the other parties during the discovery process or in writing.

(f) Conference of Parties; Planning for Discovery. Except in categories of proceedings exempted from initial disclosure under Rule 26(a)(1)(E) or when otherwise ordered, the parties must, as soon as practicable and in any event at least 21 days before a scheduling conference is held or a scheduling order is due under Rule 16(b), confer to consider the nature and basis of their claims and defenses and the possibilities for a prompt settlement or resolution of the case, to make or arrange for the disclosures required by Rule 26(a)(1), and to develop a proposed discovery plan that indicates the parties' views and proposals concerning:

(1) what changes should be made in the timing, form, or requirement for disclosures under Rule 26(a), including a statement as to when disclosures under Rule 26(a)(1) were made or will be made;

(2) the subjects on which discovery may be needed, when discovery should be completed, and whether discovery should be conducted in phases or be limited to or focused upon particular issues;

(3) what changes should be made in the limitations on discovery imposed under these rules or by local rule, and what other limitations should be imposed; and

(4) any other orders that should be entered by the court under Rule 26(c) or under Rule 16(b) and (c).

The attorneys of record and all unrepresented parties that have appeared in the case are jointly responsible for arranging the conference, for attempting in good faith to agree on the proposed discovery plan, and for submitting to the court within 14 days after the conference a written report outlining the plan. A court may order that the parties or attorneys attend the conference in person. If necessary to comply with its expedited schedule for Rule 16(b) conferences, a court may by local rule (i) require that the conference between the parties occur fewer than 21 days before the scheduling conference is held or a scheduling order is due under Rule 16(b), and (ii) require that the written report outlining the discovery plan be filed fewer than 14 days after the conference between the parties, or excuse the parties from submitting a written report and permit them to report orally on their discovery plan at the Rule 16(b) conference.

(g) Signing of Disclosures, Discovery Requests, Responses, and Objections.

(1) Every disclosure made pursuant to subdivision (a)(1) or subdivision (a)(3) shall be signed by at least one attorney of record in the attorney's individual name, whose address shall be stated. An unrepresented party shall sign the disclosure and state the party's address. The signature of the attorney or party constitutes a certification that to the best of the signer's knowledge, information, and belief, formed after a reasonable inquiry, the disclosure is complete and correct as of the time it is made.

(2) Every discovery request, response, or objection made by a party represented by an attorney shall be signed by at least one attorney of record in the attorney's individual name, whose address shall be stated. An unrepresented party shall sign the request,

response, or objection and state the party's address. The signature of the attorney or party constitutes a certification that to the best of the signer's knowledge, information, and belief, formed after a reasonable inquiry, the request, response, or objection is:

(A) consistent with these rules and warranted by existing law or a good faith argument for the extension, modification, or reversal of existing law;

(B) not interposed for any improper purpose, such as to harass or to cause unnecessary delay or needless increase in the cost of litigation; and

(C) not unreasonable or unduly burdensome or expensive, given the needs of the case, the discovery already had in the case, the amount in controversy, and the importance of the issues at stake in the litigation.

If a request, response, or objection is not signed, it shall be stricken unless it is signed promptly after the omission is called to the attention of the party making the request, response, or objection, and a party shall not be obligated to take any action with respect to it until it is signed.

(3) If without substantial justification a certification is made in violation of the rule, the court, upon motion or upon its own initiative, shall impose upon the person who made the certification, the party on whose behalf the disclosure, request, response, or objection is made, or both, an appropriate sanction, which may include an order to pay the amount of the reasonable expenses incurred because of the violation, including a reasonable attorney's fee.

As amended 1948, 1963, 1966, 1970, 1980, 1983, 1987, 1993, 2000.

Rule 27.

DEPOSITIONS BEFORE ACTION OR PENDING APPEAL

(a) Before Action.

(1) *Petition.* A person who desires to perpetuate testimony regarding any matter that may be cognizable in any court of the United States may file a verified petition in the United States district court in the district of the residence of any expected adverse party. The petition shall be entitled in the name of the petitioner and shall show: 1, that the petitioner expects to be a party to an action cognizable in a court of the United States but is presently unable to bring it or cause it to be brought, 2, the subject matter of the expected action and the petitioner's interest therein, 3, the facts which the petitioner desires to establish by the proposed

testimony and the reasons for desiring to perpetuate it, 4, the names or a description of the persons the petitioner expects will be adverse parties and their addresses so far as known, and 5, the names and addresses of the persons to be examined and the substance of the testimony which the petitioner expects to elicit from each, and shall ask for an order authorizing the petitioner to take the depositions of the persons to be examined named in the petition, for the purpose of perpetuating their testimony.

(2) *Notice and Service.* The petitioner shall thereafter serve a notice upon each person named in the petition as an expected adverse party, together with a copy of the petition, stating that the petitioner will apply to the court, at a time and place named therein, for the order described in the petition. At least 20 days before the date of hearing the notice shall be served either within or without the district or state in the manner provided in Rule 4(d) for service of summons; but if such service cannot with due diligence be made upon any expected adverse party named in the petition, the court may make such order as is just for service by publication or otherwise, and shall appoint, for persons not served in the manner provided in Rule 4(d), an attorney who shall represent them, and, in case they are not otherwise represented, shall cross-examine the deponent. If any expected adverse party is a minor or incompetent the provisions of Rule 17(c) apply.

(3) *Order and Examination.* If the court is satisfied that the perpetuation of the testimony may prevent a failure or delay of justice, it shall make an order designating or describing the persons whose depositions may be taken and specifying the subject matter of the examination and whether the depositions shall be taken upon oral examination or written interrogatories. The depositions may then be taken in accordance with these rules; and the court may make orders of the character provided for by Rules 34 and 35. For the purpose of applying these rules to depositions for perpetuating testimony, each reference therein to the court in which the action is pending shall be deemed to refer to the court in which the petition for such deposition was filed.

(4) *Use of Deposition.* If a deposition to perpetuate testimony is taken under these rules or if, although not so taken, it would be admissible in evidence in the courts of the state in which it is taken, it may be used in any action involving the same subject matter subsequently brought in a United States district court, in accordance with the provisions of Rule 32(a).

(b) Pending Appeal. If an appeal has been taken from a judgment of a district court or before the taking of an appeal if the time therefor has not expired, the district court in which the judgment was rendered may allow the taking of the depositions of witnesses to perpetuate their testimony for use in the event of further proceedings in the district court. In such case the party who desires to perpetuate the testimony may make a motion in the district court for leave to take the depositions, upon the same notice and service thereof as if the action was pending in the district court. The motion shall show (1) the names and addresses of persons to be examined and the substance of the testimony which the party expects to elicit from each; (2) the reasons for perpetuating their testimony. If the court finds that the perpetuation of the testimony is proper to avoid a failure or delay of justice, it may make an order allowing the depositions to be taken and may make orders of the character provided for by Rules 34 and 35, and thereupon the depositions may be taken and used in the same manner and under the same conditions as are prescribed in these rules for depositions taken in actions pending in the district court.

(c) Perpetuation by Action. This rule does not limit the power of a court to entertain an action to perpetuate testimony.

As amended 1948, 1949, 1971, 1987.

Rule 28.

PERSONS BEFORE WHOM DEPOSITIONS MAY BE TAKEN

(a) Within the United States. Within the United States or within a territory or insular possession subject to the jurisdiction of the United States, depositions shall be taken before an officer authorized to administer oaths by the laws of the United States or of the place where the examination is held, or before a person appointed by the court in which the action is pending. A person so appointed has power to administer oaths and take testimony. The term officer as used in Rules 30, 31 and 32 includes a person appointed by the court or designated by the parties under Rule 29.

(b) In Foreign Countries. Depositions may be taken in a foreign country (1) pursuant to any applicable treaty or convention, or (2) pursuant to a letter of request (whether or not captioned a letter rogatory), or (3) on notice before a person authorized to administer oaths in the place where the examination is held, either by the law thereof or by the law of the United States, or (4) before a person commissioned by the court, and a person so commissioned shall have the power by virtue of the commission to administer any necessary oath and take testimony. A commission or a letter of request shall be issued on application and notice and on terms that are just and appropriate. It is not requisite to the issuance of a commission or a letter of request that the taking of the deposition in any other manner is impracticable or inconvenient; and both a commission and a letter of request may be issued in proper cases. A notice or commission may designate the person before whom the deposition is to be taken either by name or descriptive title. A letter of request may be addressed "To the Appropriate Authority in [here name the country]." When a letter of request or any other device is used pursuant to any applicable treaty or convention, it shall be captioned in the form prescribed by that treaty or convention. Evidence obtained in response to a letter of request need not be excluded merely because it is not a verbatim transcript, because the testimony was not taken under oath, or because of any similar departure from the requirements for depositions taken within the United States under these rules.

(c) Disqualification for Interest. No deposition shall be taken before a person who is a relative or employee or attorney or counsel of any of the parties, or is a relative or employee of such attorney or counsel, or is financially interested in the action.

As amended 1948, 1963, 1980, 1987, 1993.

Rule 29.

STIPULATIONS REGARDING DISCOVERY PROCEDURE

Unless otherwise directed by the court, the parties may by written stipulation (1) provide that depositions may be taken before any person, at any time or place, upon any notice, and in any manner and when so taken may be used like other depositions, and (2) modify other procedures governing or limitations placed upon discovery, except that stipulations extending the time provided in Rules 33, 34, and 36 for responses to discovery may, if they would interfere with any time set for completion of discovery, for hearing of a motion, or for trial, be made only with the approval of the court.

As amended 1970, 1993.

Rule 30.

DEPOSITIONS UPON ORAL EXAMINATION

(a) When Depositions May Be Taken; When Leave Required.

(1) A party may take the testimony of any person, including a party, by deposition upon oral examination without leave of court except as provided in paragraph (2). The attendance of witnesses may be compelled by subpoena as provided in Rule 45.

(2) A party must obtain leave of court, which shall be granted to the extent consistent with the principles stated in Rule 26(b)(2),

if the person to be examined is confined in prison or if, without the written stipulation of the parties,

(A) a proposed deposition would result in more than ten depositions being taken under this rule or Rule 31 by the plaintiffs, or by the defendants, or by third-party defendants;

(B) the person to be examined already has been deposed in the case; or

(C) a party seeks to take a deposition before the time specified in Rule 26(d) unless the notice contains a certification, with supporting facts, that the person to be examined is expected to leave the United States and be unavailable for examination in this country unless deposed before that time.

(b) Notice of Examination: General Requirements; Method of Recording; Production of Documents and Things; Deposition of Organization; Deposition by Telephone.

(1) A party desiring to take the deposition of any person upon oral examination shall give reasonable notice in writing to every other party to the action. The notice shall state the time and place for taking the deposition and the name and address of each person to be examined, if known, and, if the name is not known, a general description sufficient to identify the person or the particular class or group to which the person belongs. If a subpoena duces tecum is to be served on the person to be examined, the designation of the materials to be produced as set forth in the subpoena shall be attached to, or included in, the notice.

(2) The party taking the deposition shall state in the notice the method by which the testimony shall be recorded. Unless the court orders otherwise, it may be recorded by sound, sound-and-visual, or stenographic means, and the party taking the deposition shall bear the cost of the recording. Any party may arrange for a transcription to be made from the recording of a deposition taken by nonstenographic means.

(3) With prior notice to the deponent and other parties, any party may designate another method to record the deponent's testimony in addition to the method specified by the person taking the deposition. The additional record or transcript shall be made at that party's expense unless the court otherwise orders.

(4) Unless otherwise agreed by the parties, a deposition shall be conducted before an officer appointed or designated under Rule 28 and shall begin with a statement on the record by the officer that includes (A) the officer's name and business address; (B) the date, time, and place of the deposition; (C) the name of the deponent; (D) the administration of the oath or affirmation to the

deponent; and (E) an identification of all persons present. If the deposition is recorded other than stenographically, the officer shall repeat items (A) through (C) at the beginning of each unit of recorded tape or other recording medium. The appearance or demeanor of deponents or attorneys shall not be distorted through camera or sound-recording techniques. At the end of the deposition, the officer shall state on the record that the deposition is complete and shall set forth any stipulations made by counsel concerning the custody of the transcript or recording and the exhibits, or concerning other pertinent matters.

(5) The notice to a party deponent may be accompanied by a request made in compliance with Rule 34 for the production of documents and tangible things at the taking of the deposition. The procedure of Rule 34 shall apply to the request.

(6) A party may in the party's notice and in a subpoena name as the deponent a public or private corporation or a partnership or association or governmental agency and describe with reasonable particularity the matters on which examination is requested. In that event, the organization so named shall designate one or more officers, directors, or managing agents, or other persons who consent to testify on its behalf, and may set forth, for each person designated, the matters on which the person will testify. A subpoena shall advise a non-party organization of its duty to make such a designation. The persons so designated shall testify as to matters known or reasonably available to the organization. This subdivision (b)(6) does not preclude taking a deposition by any other procedure authorized in these rules.

(7) The parties may stipulate in writing or the court may upon motion order that a deposition be taken by telephone or other remote electronic means. For the purposes of this rule and Rules 28(a), 37(a)(1), and 37(b)(1), a deposition taken by such means is taken in the district and at the place where the deponent is to answer questions.

(c) Examination and Cross-Examination; Record of Examination; Oath; Objections. Examination and cross-examination of witnesses may proceed as permitted at the trial under the provisions of the Federal Rules of Evidence except Rules 103 and 615. The officer before whom the deposition is to be taken shall put the witness on oath or affirmation and shall personally, or by someone acting under the officer's direction and in the officer's presence, record the testimony of the witness. The testimony shall be taken stenographically or recorded by any other method authorized by subdivision (b)(2) of this rule. All objections made at the time of the examination to the qualifications of the officer taking the deposition, to the manner of taking it, to the evidence presented, to the conduct of any party, or to any other aspect of the proceedings shall be noted by the officer upon the record of the deposition; but the examination shall proceed, with the testimony being taken subject to the objections. In lieu of participating in the oral examination, parties may serve written questions in a sealed envelope on the party taking the deposition and the party taking the deposition shall transmit them to the officer, who shall propound them to the witness and record the answers verbatim.

(d) Schedule and Duration; Motion to Terminate or Limit Examination.

(1) Any objection during a deposition must be stated concisely and in a non-argumentative and non-suggestive manner. A person may instruct a deponent not to answer only when necessary to preserve a privilege, to enforce a limitation directed by the court, or to present a motion under Rule 30(d)(4).

(2) Unless otherwise authorized by the court or stipulated by the parties, a deposition is limited to one day of seven hours. The court must allow additional time consistent with Rule 26(b)(2) if needed for a fair examination of the deponent or if the deponent or another person, or other circumstance, impedes or delays the examination.

(3) If the court finds that any impediment, delay, or other conduct has frustrated the fair examination of the deponent, it may impose upon the persons responsible an appropriate sanction, including the reasonable costs and attorney's fees incurred by any parties as a result thereof.

(4) At any time during a deposition, on motion of a party or of the deponent and upon a showing that the examination is being conducted in bad faith or in such manner as unreasonably to annoy, embarrass, or oppress the deponent or party, the court in which the action is pending or the court in the district where the deposition is being taken may order the officer conducting the examination to cease forthwith from taking the deposition, or may limit the scope and manner of the taking of the deposition as provided in Rule 26(c). If the order made terminates the examination, it may be resumed thereafter only upon the order of the court in which the action is pending. Upon demand of the objecting party or deponent, the taking of the deposition must be suspended for the time necessary to make a motion for an order. The provisions of Rule 37(a)(4) apply to the award of expenses incurred in relation to the motion.

(e) Review by Witness; Changes; Signing. If requested by the deponent or a party before completion of the deposition, the deponent shall have 30 days after being notified by the officer that the transcript or recording is available in which to review the transcript or recording and, if there are changes in form or substance, to sign a statement reciting such changes and the reasons given by the deponent for making them. The officer shall indicate in the certificate prescribed by subdivision (f)(1) whether any review was requested and, if so, shall append any changes made by the deponent during the period allowed.

(f) Certification and Delivery by Officer; Exhibits; Copies.

(1) The officer must certify that the witness was duly sworn by the officer and that the deposition is a true record of the testimony given by the witness. This certificate must be in writing and accompany the record of the deposition. Unless otherwise ordered by the court, the officer must securely seal the deposition in an envelope or package indorsed with the title of the action and marked "Deposition of [here insert name of witness]" and must promptly send it to the attorney who arranged for the transcript or recording, who must store it under conditions that will protect it against loss, destruction, tampering, or deterioration. Documents and things produced for inspection during the examination of the witness must, upon the request of a party, be marked for identification and annexed to the deposition and may be inspected and copied by any party, except that if the person producing the materials desires to retain them the person may (A) offer copies to be marked for identification and annexed to the deposition and to serve thereafter as originals if the person affords to all parties fair opportunity to verify the copies by comparison with the originals, or (B) offer the originals to be marked for identification, after giving to each party an opportunity to inspect and copy them, in which event the materials may then be used in the same manner as if annexed to the deposition. Any party may move for an order that the original be annexed to and returned with the deposition to the court, pending final disposition of the case.

(2) Unless otherwise ordered by the court or agreed by the parties, the officer shall retain stenographic notes of any deposition taken stenographically or a copy of the recording of any deposition taken by another method. Upon payment of reasonable charges therefor, the officer shall furnish a copy of the transcript or other recording of the deposition to any party or to the deponent.

(3) The party taking the deposition shall give prompt notice of its filing to all other parties.

(g) Failure to Attend or to Serve Subpoena; Expenses.

(1) If the party giving the notice of the taking of a deposition fails to attend and proceed therewith and another party attends in person or by attorney pursuant to the notice, the court may order the party giving the notice to pay to such other party the reason-

able expenses incurred by that party and that party's attorney in attending, including reasonable attorney's fees.

(2) If the party giving the notice of the taking of a deposition of a witness fails to serve a subpoena upon the witness and the witness because of such failure does not attend, and if another party attends in person or by attorney because that party expects the deposition of that witness to be taken, the court may order the party giving the notice to pay to such other party the reasonable expenses incurred by that party and that party's attorney in attending, including reasonable attorney's fees.

As amended 1963, 1970, 1971, 1975, 1980, 1987, 1993, 2000.

Rule 31.

DEPOSITIONS UPON WRITTEN QUESTIONS

(a) Serving Questions; Notice.

(1) A party may take the testimony of any person, including a party, by deposition upon written questions without leave of court except as provided in paragraph (2). The attendance of witnesses may be compelled by the use of subpoena as provided in Rule 45.

(2) A party must obtain leave of court, which shall be granted to the extent consistent with the principles stated in Rule 26(b)(2), if the person to be examined is confined in prison or if, without the written stipulation of the parties,

(A) a proposed deposition would result in more than ten depositions being taken under this rule or Rule 30 by the plaintiffs, or by the defendants, or by third-party defendants;

(B) the person to be examined has already been deposed in the case; or

(C) a party seeks to take a deposition before the time specified in Rule 26(d).

(3) A party desiring to take a deposition upon written questions shall serve them upon every other party with a notice stating (1) the name and address of the person who is to answer them, if known, and if the name is not known, a general description sufficient to identify the person or the particular class or group to which the person belongs, and (2) the name or descriptive title and address of the officer before whom the deposition is to be taken. A deposition upon written questions may be taken of a public or private corporation or a partnership or association or governmental agency in accordance with the provisions of Rule 30(b)(6).

(4) Within 14 days after the notice and written questions are served, a party may serve cross questions upon all other parties.

Within 7 days after being served with cross questions, a party may serve redirect questions upon all other parties. Within 7 days after being served with redirect questions, a party may serve recross questions upon all other parties. The court may for cause shown enlarge or shorten the time.

(b) Officer to Take Responses and Prepare Record. A copy of the notice and copies of all questions served shall be delivered by the party taking the deposition to the officer designated in the notice, who shall proceed promptly, in the manner provided by Rule 30(c), (e), and (f), to take the testimony of the witness in response to the questions and to prepare, certify, and file or mail the deposition, attaching thereto the copy of the notice and the questions received by the officer.

(c) Notice of Filing. When the deposition is filed the party taking it shall promptly give notice thereof to all other parties.

As amended 1970, 1987, 1993.

Rule 32.

USE OF DEPOSITIONS IN COURT PROCEEDINGS

(a) Use of Depositions. At the trial or upon the hearing of a motion or an interlocutory proceeding, any part or all of a deposition, so far as admissible under the rules of evidence applied as though the witness were then present and testifying, may be used against any party who was present or represented at the taking of the deposition or who had reasonable notice thereof, in accordance with any of the following provisions:

(1) Any deposition may be used by any party for the purpose of contradicting or impeaching the testimony of deponent as a witness, or for any other purpose permitted by the Federal Rules of Evidence.

(2) The deposition of a party or of anyone who at the time of taking the deposition was an officer, director, or managing agent, or a person designated under Rule 30(b)(6) or 31(a) to testify on behalf of a public or private corporation, partnership or association or governmental agency which is a party may be used by an adverse party for any purpose.

(3) The deposition of a witness, whether or not a party, may be used by any party for any purpose if the court finds:

(A) that the witness is dead; or

(B) that the witness is at a greater distance than 100 miles from the place of trial or hearing, or is out of the United States, unless it appears that the absence of the witness was procured by the party offering the deposition; or

(C) that the witness is unable to attend or testify because of age, illness, infirmity, or imprisonment; or

(D) that the party offering the deposition has been unable to procure the attendance of the witness by subpoena; or

(E) upon application and notice, that such exceptional circumstances exist as to make it desirable, in the interest of justice and with due regard to the importance of presenting the testimony of witnesses orally in open court, to allow the deposition to be used.

A deposition taken without leave of court pursuant to a notice under Rule 30(a)(2)(C) shall not be used against a party who demonstrates that, when served with the notice, it was unable through the exercise of diligence to obtain counsel to represent it at the taking of the deposition; nor shall a deposition be used against a party who, having received less than 11 days notice of a deposition, has promptly upon receiving such notice filed a motion for a protective order under Rule 26(c)(2) requesting that the deposition not be held or be held at a different time or place and such motion is pending at the time the deposition is held.

(4) If only part of a deposition is offered in evidence by a party, an adverse party may require the offeror to introduce any other part which ought in fairness to be considered with the part introduced, and any party may introduce any other parts.

Substitution of parties pursuant to Rule 25 does not affect the right to use depositions previously taken; and, when an action has been brought in any court of the United States or of any State and another action involving the same subject matter is afterward brought between the same parties or their representatives or successors in interest, all depositions lawfully taken and duly filed in the former action may be used in the latter as if originally taken therefor. A deposition previously taken may also be used as permitted by the Federal Rules of Evidence.

(b) Objections to Admissibility. Subject to the provisions of Rule 28(b) and subdivision (d)(3) of this rule, objection may be made at the trial or hearing to receiving in evidence any deposition or part thereof for any reason which would require the exclusion of the evidence if the witness were then present and testifying.

(c) Form of Presentation. Except as otherwise directed by the court, a party offering deposition testimony pursuant to this rule may offer it in stenographic or nonstenographic form, but, if in nonstenographic form, the party shall also provide the court with a transcript of the portions so offered. On request of any party in a case tried before a jury, deposition testimony offered other than for impeachment purposes shall be presented in nonstenographic form, if available, unless the court for good cause orders otherwise.

(d) Effect of Errors and Irregularities in Depositions.

(1) *As to Notice.* All errors and irregularities in the notice for taking a deposition are waived unless written objection is promptly served upon the party giving the notice.

(2) *As to Disqualification of Officer.* Objection to taking a deposition because of disqualification of the officer before whom it is to be taken is waived unless made before the taking of the deposition begins or as soon thereafter as the disqualification becomes known or could be discovered with reasonable diligence.

(3) *As to Taking of Deposition.*

(A) Objections to the competency of a witness or to the competency, relevancy, or materiality of testimony are not waived by failure to make them before or during the taking of the deposition, unless the ground of the objection is one which might have been obviated or removed if presented at that time.

(B) Errors and irregularities occurring at the oral examination in the manner of taking the deposition, in the form of the questions or answers, in the oath or affirmation, or in the conduct of parties, and errors of any kind which might be obviated, removed, or cured if promptly presented, are waived unless seasonable objection thereto is made at the taking of the deposition.

(C) Objections to the form of written questions submitted under Rule 31 are waived unless served in writing upon the party propounding them within the time allowed for serving the succeeding cross or other questions and within 5 days after service of the last questions authorized.

(4) *As to Completion and Return of Deposition.* Errors and irregularities in the manner in which the testimony is transcribed or the deposition is prepared, signed, certified, sealed, indorsed, transmitted, filed, or otherwise dealt with by the officer under Rules 30 and 31 are waived unless a motion to suppress the deposition or some part thereof is made with reasonable promptness after such defect is, or with due diligence might have been, ascertained.

As amended 1970, 1975, 1980, 1987, 1993.

Rule 33.

INTERROGATORIES TO PARTIES

(a) Availability. Without leave of court or written stipulation, any party may serve upon any other party written interrogatories, not exceeding 25 in number including all discrete subparts, to be answered by the party served or, if the party served is a public or private corporation or a partnership or association or governmental agency, by any officer or agent, who shall furnish such information as is available to the party. Leave to serve additional interrogatories shall be granted to the extent consistent with the principles of Rule 26(b)(2). Without leave of court or written stipulation, interrogatories may not be served before the time specified in Rule 26(d).

(b) Answers and Objections.

(1) Each interrogatory shall be answered separately and fully in writing under oath, unless it is objected to, in which event the objecting party shall state the reasons for objection and shall answer to the extent the interrogatory is not objectionable.

(2) The answers are to be signed by the person making them, and the objections signed by the attorney making them.

(3) The party upon whom the interrogatories have been served shall serve a copy of the answers, and objections if any, within 30 days after the service of the interrogatories. A shorter or longer time may be directed by the court or, in the absence of such an order, agreed to in writing by the parties subject to Rule 29.

(4) All grounds for an objection to an interrogatory shall be stated with specificity. Any ground not stated in a timely objection is waived unless the party's failure to object is excused by the court for good cause shown.

(5) The party submitting the interrogatories may move for an order under Rule 37(a) with respect to any objection to or other failure to answer an interrogatory.

(c) Scope; Use at Trial. Interrogatories may relate to any matters which can be inquired into under Rule 26(b)(1), and the answers may be used to the extent permitted by the rules of evidence.

An interrogatory otherwise proper is not necessarily objectionable merely because an answer to the interrogatory involves an opinion or contention that relates to fact or the application of law to fact, but the court may order that such an interrogatory need not be answered until after designated discovery has been completed or until a pre-trial conference or other later time.

(d) Option to Produce Business Records. Where the answer to an interrogatory may be derived or ascertained from the business records of the party upon whom the interrogatory has been served or from an examination, audit or inspection of such business records, including a compilation, abstract or summary thereof and the burden of deriving or ascertaining the answer is substantially the same for the party serving the interrogatory as for the party served, it is a sufficient answer to such interrogatory to specify the records from which the answer may be derived or ascertained and to afford to the party serving the interrogatory reasonable opportunity to examine, audit or inspect such records and to make copies, compilations, abstracts or summaries. A specification shall be in sufficient detail to permit the interrogating party to locate and to identify, as readily as can the party served, the records from which the answer may be ascertained.

As amended 1948, 1970, 1980, 1993.

Rule 34.

PRODUCTION OF DOCUMENTS AND THINGS AND ENTRY UPON LAND FOR INSPECTION AND OTHER PURPOSES

(a) Scope. Any party may serve on any other party a request (1) to produce and permit the party making the request, or someone acting on the requestor's behalf, to inspect and copy, any designated documents (including writings, drawings, graphs, charts, photographs, phono-records, and other data compilations from which information can be obtained, translated, if necessary, by the respondent through detection devices into reasonably usable form), or to inspect and copy, test, or sample any tangible things which constitute or contain matters within the scope of Rule 26(b) and which are in the possession, custody or control of the party upon whom the request is served; or (2) to permit entry upon designated land or other property in the possession or control of the party upon whom the request is served for the purpose of inspection and measuring, surveying, photographing, testing, or sampling the property or any designated object or operation thereon, within the scope of Rule 26(b).

(b) Procedure. The request shall set forth, either by individual item or by category, the items to be inspected, and describe each with reasonable particularity. The request shall specify a reasonable time, place, and manner of making the inspection and performing the related acts. Without leave of court or written stipulation, a request may not be served before the time specified in Rule 26(d).

The party upon whom the request is served shall serve a written response within 30 days after the service of the request. A shorter or longer time may be directed by the court or, in the absence of such an order, agreed to in writing by the parties, subject to Rule 29. The response shall state, with respect to each item or category, that inspection and related activities will be permitted as requested, unless the request is objected to, in which event the reasons for the objection shall be stated. If objection is made to part of an item or category, the part shall be specified and inspection permitted of the remaining parts. The party submitting the request may move for an order under Rule 37(a) with respect to any objection to or other failure to respond to the request or any part thereof, or any failure to permit inspection as requested.

A party who produces documents for inspection shall produce them as they are kept in the usual course of business or shall organize and label them to correspond with the categories in the request.

(c) Persons Not Parties. A person not a party to the action may be compelled to produce documents and things or to submit to an inspection as provided in Rule 45.

As amended 1948, 1970, 1980, 1987, 1991, 1993.

Rule 35.

PHYSICAL AND MENTAL EXAMINATION OF PERSONS

(a) Order for Examination. When the mental or physical condition (including the blood group) of a party, or of a person in the custody or under the legal control of a party, is in controversy, the court in which the action is pending may order the party to submit to a physical or mental examination by a suitably licensed or certified examiner or to produce for examination the person in the party's custody or legal control. The order may be made only on motion for good cause shown and upon notice to the person to be examined and to all parties and shall specify the time, place, manner, conditions, and scope of the examination and the person or persons by whom it is to be made.

(b) Report of Examiner.

(1) If requested by the party against whom an order is made under Rule 35(a) or the person examined, the party causing the examination to be made shall deliver to the requesting party a copy of the detailed written report of the examiner setting out the examiner's findings, including results of all tests made, diagnoses

and conclusions, together with like reports of all earlier examinations of the same condition. After delivery the party causing the examination shall be entitled upon request to receive from the party against whom the order is made a like report of any examination, previously or thereafter made, of the same condition, unless, in the case of a report of examination of a person not a party, the party shows that such party is unable to obtain it. The court on motion may make an order against a party requiring delivery of a report on such terms as are just, and if an examiner fails or refuses to make a report the court may exclude the examiner's testimony if offered at trial.

(2) By requesting and obtaining a report of the examination so ordered or by taking the deposition of the examiner, the party examined waives any privilege the party may have in that action or any other involving the same controversy, regarding the testimony of every other person who has examined or may thereafter examine the party in respect of the same mental or physical condition.

(3) This subdivision applies to examinations made by agreement of the parties, unless the agreement expressly provides otherwise. This subdivision does not preclude discovery of a report of an examiner or the taking of a deposition of the examiner in accordance with the provisions of any other rule.

As amended 1970, 1987, 1988, 1991.

Rule 36.

REQUESTS FOR ADMISSION

(a) Request for Admission. A party may serve upon any other party a written request for the admission, for purposes of the pending action only, of the truth of any matters within the scope of Rule 26(b)(1) set forth in the request that relate to statements or opinions of fact or of the application of law to fact, including the genuineness of any documents described in the request. Copies of documents shall be served with the request unless they have been or are otherwise furnished or made available for inspection and copying. Without leave of court or written stipulation, requests for admission may not be served before the time specified in Rule 26(d).

Each matter of which an admission is requested shall be separately set forth. The matter is admitted unless, within 30 days after service of the request, or within such shorter or longer time as the court may allow or as the parties may agree to in writing, subject to Rule 29, the party to whom the request is directed serves upon the party requesting the admission a written answer or objection addressed to the matter, signed by the party or by the party's attorney. If objection is made, the reasons therefor shall be stated. The answer shall specifically deny the matter or set forth in detail the reasons why the answering party cannot truthfully admit or deny the matter. A denial shall fairly meet the substance of the requested admission, and when good faith requires that a party qualify an answer or deny only a part of the matter of which an admission is requested, the party shall specify so much of it as is true and qualify or deny the remainder. An answering party may not give lack of information or knowledge as a reason for failure to admit or deny unless the party states that the party has made reasonable inquiry and that the information known or readily obtainable by the party is insufficient to enable the party to admit or deny. A party who considers that a matter of which an admission has been requested presents a genuine issue for trial may not, on that ground alone, object to the request; the party may, subject to the provisions of Rule 37(c), deny the matter or set forth reasons why the party cannot admit or deny it.

The party who has requested the admissions may move to determine the sufficiency of the answers or objections. Unless the court determines that an objection is justified, it shall order that an answer be served. If the court determines that an answer does not comply with the requirements of this rule, it may order either that the matter is admitted or that an amended answer be served. The court may, in lieu of these orders, determine that final disposition of the request be made at a pre-trial conference or at a designated time prior to trial. The provisions of Rule 37(a)(4) apply to the award of expenses incurred in relation to the motion.

(b) Effect of Admission. Any matter admitted under this rule is conclusively established unless the court on motion permits withdrawal or amendment of the admission. Subject to the provisions of Rule 16 governing amendment of a pre-trial order, the court may permit withdrawal or amendment when the presentation of the merits of the action will be subserved thereby and the party who obtained the admission fails to satisfy the court that withdrawal or amendment will prejudice that party in maintaining the action or defense on the merits. Any admission made by a party under this rule is for the purpose of the pending action only and is not an admission for any other purpose nor may it be used against the party in any other proceeding.

As amended 1948, 1970, 1987, 1993.

Rule 37.

FAILURE TO MAKE DISCLOSURE OR COOPERATE IN DISCOVERY; SANCTIONS

(a) Motion for Order Compelling Disclosure or Discovery. A party, upon reasonable notice to other parties and all persons affected thereby, may apply for an order compelling disclosure or discovery as follows:

(1) *Appropriate Court.* An application for an order to a party shall be made to the court in which the action is pending. An application for an order to a person who is not a party shall be made to the court in the district where the discovery is being, or is to be, taken.

(2) *Motion.*

(A) If a party fails to make a disclosure required by Rule 26(a), any other party may move to compel disclosure and for appropriate sanctions. The motion must include a certification that the movant has in good faith conferred or attempted to confer with the party not making the disclosure in an effort to secure the disclosure without court action.

(B) If a deponent fails to answer a question propounded or submitted under Rules 30 or 31, or a corporation or other entity fails to make a designation under Rule 30(b)(6) or 31(a), or a party fails to answer an interrogatory submitted under Rule 33, or if a party, in response to a request for inspection submitted under Rule 34, fails to respond that inspection will be permitted as requested or fails to permit inspection as requested, the discovering party may move for an order compelling an answer, or a designation, or an order compelling inspection in accordance with the request. The motion must include a certification that the movant has in good faith conferred or attempted to confer with the person or party failing to make the discovery in an effort to secure the information or material without court action. When taking a deposition on oral examination, the proponent of the question may complete or adjourn the examination before applying for an order.

(3) *Evasive or Incomplete Disclosure, Answer, or Response.* For purposes of this subdivision an evasive or incomplete disclosure, answer, or response is to be treated as a failure to disclose, answer, or respond.

(4) *Expenses and Sanctions.*

(A) If the motion is granted or if the disclosure or requested discovery is provided after the motion was filed, the court shall, after affording an opportunity to be heard, require the party or deponent whose conduct necessitated the motion or the party or attorney advising such conduct or both of them to pay to the moving party the reasonable expenses incurred in making the motion, including attorney's fees, unless the court finds that the motion was filed without the movant's first making a good faith effort to obtain the disclosure or discovery without court action, or that the opposing party's nondisclosure, response, or objection was substantially justified, or that other circumstances make an award of expenses unjust.

(B) If the motion is denied, the court may enter any protective order authorized under Rule 26(c) and shall, after affording an opportunity to be heard, require the moving party or the attorney filing the motion or both of them to pay to the party or deponent who opposed the motion the reasonable expenses incurred in opposing the motion, including attorney's fees, unless the court finds that the making of the motion was substantially justified or that other circumstances make an award of expenses unjust.

(C) If the motion is granted in part and denied in part, the court may enter any protective order authorized under Rule 26(c) and may, after affording an opportunity to be heard, apportion the reasonable expenses incurred in relation to the motion among the parties and persons in a just manner.

(b) Failure to Comply with Order.

(1) *Sanctions by Court in District Where Deposition Is Taken.* If a deponent fails to be sworn or to answer a question after being directed to do so by the court in the district in which the deposition is being taken, the failure may be considered a contempt of that court.

(2) *Sanctions by Court in Which Action Is Pending.* If a party or an officer, director, or managing agent of a party or a person designated under Rule 30(b)(6) or 31(a) to testify on behalf of a party fails to obey an order to provide or permit discovery, including an order made under subdivision (a) of this rule or Rule 35, or if a party fails to obey an order entered under Rule 26(f), the court in which the action is pending may make such orders in regard to the failure as are just, and among others the following:

(A) An order that the matters regarding which the order was made or any other designated facts shall be taken to be established for the purposes of the action in accordance with the claim of the party obtaining the order;

(B) An order refusing to allow the disobedient party to support or oppose designated claims or defenses, or prohibiting that party from introducing designated matters in evidence;

(C) An order striking out pleadings or parts thereof, or staying further proceedings until the order is obeyed, or dismissing the action or proceeding or any part thereof, or rendering a judgment by default against the disobedient party;

(D) In lieu of any of the foregoing orders or in addition thereto, an order treating as a contempt of court the failure to obey any orders except an order to submit to a physical or mental examination;

(E) Where a party has failed to comply with an order under Rule 35(a) requiring that party to produce another for examination, such orders as are listed in paragraphs (A), (B), and (C) of this subdivision, unless the party failing to comply shows that that party is unable to produce such person for examination.

In lieu of any of the foregoing orders or in addition thereto, the court shall require the party failing to obey the order or the attorney advising that party or both to pay the reasonable expenses, including attorney's fees, caused by the failure, unless the court finds that the failure was substantially justified or that other circumstances make an award of expenses unjust.

(c) Failure to Disclose; False or Misleading Disclosure; Refusal to Admit.

(1) A party that without substantial justification fails to disclose information required by Rule 26(a) or 26(e)(1), or to amend a prior response to discovery as required by Rule 26(e)(2), is not, unless such failure is harmless, permitted to use as evidence at a trial, at a hearing, or on a motion any witness or information not so disclosed. In addition to or in lieu of this sanction, the court, on motion and after affording an opportunity to be heard, may impose other appropriate sanctions. In addition to requiring payment of reasonable expenses, including attorney's fees, caused by the failure, these sanctions may include any of the actions authorized under Rule 37(b)(2)(A), (B), and (C) and may include informing the jury of the failure to make the disclosure.

(2) If a party fails to admit the genuineness of any document or the truth of any matter as requested under Rule 36, and if the party requesting the admissions thereafter proves the genuineness of the document or the truth of the matter, the requesting party may apply to the court for an order requiring the other party to pay the reasonable expenses incurred in making that proof, including reasonable attorney's fees. The court shall make the order unless

it finds that (A) the request was held objectionable pursuant to Rule 36(a), or (B) the admission sought was of no substantial importance, or (C) the party failing to admit had reasonable ground to believe that the party might prevail on the matter, or (D) there was other good reason for the failure to admit.

(d) Failure of Party to Attend at Own Deposition or Serve Answers to Interrogatories or Respond to Request for Inspection. If a party or an officer, director, or managing agent of a party or a person designated under Rule 30(b)(6) or 31(a) to testify on behalf of a party fails (1) to appear before the officer who is to take the deposition, after being served with a proper notice, or (2) to serve answers or objections to interrogatories submitted under Rule 33, after proper service of the interrogatories, or (3) to serve a written response to a request for inspection submitted under Rule 34, after proper service of the request, the court in which the action is pending on motion may make such orders in regard to the failure as are just, and among others it may take any action authorized under subparagraphs (A), (B), and (C) of subdivision (b)(2) of this rule. Any motion specifying a failure under clause (2) or (3) of this subdivision shall include a certification that the movant has in good faith conferred or attempted to confer with the party failing to answer or respond in an effort to obtain such answer or response without court action. In lieu of any order or in addition thereto, the court shall require the party failing to act or the attorney advising that party or both to pay the reasonable expenses, including attorney's fees, caused by the failure, unless the court finds that the failure was substantially justified or that other circumstances make an award of expenses unjust.

The failure to act described in this subdivision may not be excused on the ground that the discovery sought is objectionable unless the party failing to act has a pending motion for a protective order as provided by Rule 26(c).

(e) Subpoena of Person in Foreign Country. Abrogated Apr. 29, 1980, eff. Aug. 1, 1980.

(f) Expenses Against United States. Repealed by P.L. 96–481, eff. Oct. 1, 1981.

(g) Failure to Participate in the Framing of a Discovery Plan. If a party or a party's attorney fails to participate in good faith in the development and submission of a proposed discovery plan as required by Rule 26(f), the court may, after opportunity for hearing, require such party or attorney to pay to any other party the reasonable expenses, including attorney's fees, caused by the failure.

As amended 1949, 1970, 1980, 1981, 1987, 1993, 2000.

VI. TRIALS

Rule 38.

JURY TRIAL OF RIGHT

(a) Right Preserved. The right of trial by jury as declared by the Seventh Amendment to the Constitution or as given by a statute of the United States shall be preserved to the parties inviolate.

(b) Demand. Any party may demand a trial by jury of any issue triable of right by a jury by (1) serving upon the other parties a demand therefor in writing at any time after the commencement of the action and not later than 10 days after the service of the last pleading directed to such issue, and (2) filing the demand as required by Rule 5(d). Such demand may be indorsed upon a pleading of the party.

(c) Same: Specification of Issues. In the demand a party may specify the issues which the party wishes so tried; otherwise the party shall be deemed to have demanded trial by jury for all the issues so triable. If the party has demanded trial by jury for only some of the issues, any other party within 10 days after service of the demand or such lesser time as the court may order, may serve a demand for trial by jury of any other or all of the issues of fact in the action.

(d) Waiver. The failure of a party to serve and file a demand as required by this rule constitutes a waiver by the party of trial by jury. A demand for trial by jury made as herein provided may not be withdrawn without the consent of the parties.

(e) Admiralty and Maritime Claims. These rules shall not be construed to create a right to trial by jury of the issues in an admiralty or maritime claim within the meaning of Rule 9(h).

As amended 1966, 1987, 1993.

Rule 39.

TRIAL BY JURY OR BY THE COURT

(a) By Jury. When trial by jury has been demanded as provided in Rule 38, the action shall be designated upon the docket as a jury action. The trial of all issues so demanded shall be by jury, unless (1) the parties or their attorneys of record, by written stipulation filed with the court or by an oral stipulation made in open court and entered in the record, consent to trial by the court sitting without a jury or (2) the court upon motion or of its own initiative finds that a right of trial by jury of some or all of those issues does not exist under the Constitution or statutes of the United States.

(b) By the Court. Issues not demanded for trial by jury as provided in Rule 38 shall be tried by the court; but, notwithstanding the failure of a party to demand a jury in an action in which such a demand might have been made of right, the court in its discretion upon motion may order a trial by a jury of any or all issues.

(c) Advisory Jury and Trial by Consent. In all actions not triable of right by a jury the court upon motion or of its own initiative may try any issue with an advisory jury or, except in actions against the United States when a statute of the United States provides for trial without a jury, the court, with the consent of both parties, may order a trial with a jury whose verdict has the same effect as if trial by jury had been a matter of right.

Rule 40.

ASSIGNMENT OF CASES FOR TRIAL

The district courts shall provide by rule for the placing of actions upon the trial calendar (1) without request of the parties or (2) upon request of a party and notice to the other parties or (3) in such other manner as the courts deem expedient. Precedence shall be given to actions entitled thereto by any statute of the United States.

Rule 41.

DISMISSAL OF ACTIONS

(a) Voluntary Dismissal: Effect Thereof.

(1) *By Plaintiff; by Stipulation.* Subject to the provisions of Rule 23(e), of Rule 66, and of any statute of the United States, an action may be dismissed by the plaintiff without order of court (i) by filing a notice of dismissal at any time before service by the adverse party of an answer or of a motion for summary judgment, whichever first occurs, or (ii) by filing a stipulation of dismissal signed by all parties who have appeared in the action. Unless otherwise stated in the notice of dismissal or stipulation, the dismissal is without prejudice, except that a notice of dismissal operates as an adjudication upon the merits when filed by a plaintiff who has once dismissed in any court of the United States or of any state an action based on or including the same claim.

(2) *By Order of Court.* Except as provided in paragraph (1) of this subdivision of this rule, an action shall not be dismissed at the

plaintiff's instance save upon order of the court and upon such terms and conditions as the court deems proper. If a counterclaim has been pleaded by a defendant prior to the service upon the defendant of the plaintiff's motion to dismiss, the action shall not be dismissed against the defendant's objection unless the counterclaim can remain pending for independent adjudication by the court. Unless otherwise specified in the order, a dismissal under this paragraph is without prejudice.

(b) Involuntary Dismissal: Effect Thereof. For failure of the plaintiff to prosecute or to comply with these rules or any order of court, a defendant may move for dismissal of an action or of any claim against the defendant. Unless the court in its order for dismissal otherwise specifies, a dismissal under this subdivision and any dismissal not provided for in this rule, other than a dismissal for lack of jurisdiction, for improper venue, or for failure to join a party under Rule 19, operates as an adjudication upon the merits.

(c) Dismissal of Counterclaim, Cross-Claim, or Third-Party Claim. The provisions of this rule apply to the dismissal of any counterclaim, cross-claim, or third-party claim. A voluntary dismissal by the claimant alone pursuant to paragraph (1) of subdivision (a) of this rule shall be made before a responsive pleading is served or, if there is none, before the introduction of evidence at the trial or hearing.

(d) Costs of Previously Dismissed Action. If a plaintiff who has once dismissed an action in any court commences an action based upon or including the same claim against the same defendant, the court may make such order for the payment of costs of the action previously dismissed as it may deem proper and may stay the proceedings in the action until the plaintiff has complied with the order.

As amended 1948, 1963, 1966, 1968, 1987, 1991.

Rule 42.

CONSOLIDATION; SEPARATE TRIALS

(a) Consolidation. When actions involving a common question of law or fact are pending before the court, it may order a joint hearing or trial of any or all the matters in issue in the actions; it may order all the actions consolidated; and it may make such orders concerning proceedings therein as may tend to avoid unnecessary costs or delay.

(b) Separate Trials. The court, in furtherance of convenience or to avoid prejudice, or when separate trials will be conducive to expedition and economy, may order a separate trial of any claim, cross-claim, counterclaim, or third-party claim, or of any separate issue or of any number of claims, cross-claims, counterclaims, third-party claims, or issues, always preserving inviolate the right of trial by jury as declared by the Seventh Amendment to the Constitution or as given by a statute of the United States.

As amended 1966.

Rule 43.

TAKING OF TESTIMONY

(a) Form. In every trial, the testimony of witnesses shall be taken in open court, unless a federal law, these rules, the Federal Rules of Evidence, or other rules adopted by the Supreme Court provide otherwise. The court may, for good cause shown in compelling circumstances and upon appropriate safeguards, permit presentation of testimony in open court by contemporaneous transmission from a different location.

(b) Scope of Examination and Cross-Examination. Abrogated Dec. 18, 1972, and expressly approved by P.L. 93–595, eff. July 1, 1975.

(c) Record of Excluded Evidence. Abrogated Dec. 18, 1972, and expressly approved by P.L. 93–595, eff. July 1, 1975.

(d) Affirmation in Lieu of Oath. Whenever under these rules an oath is required to be taken, a solemn affirmation may be accepted in lieu thereof.

(e) Evidence on Motions. When a motion is based on facts not appearing of record the court may hear the matter on affidavits presented by the respective parties, but the court may direct that the matter be heard wholly or partly on oral testimony or deposition.

(f) Interpreters. The court may appoint an interpreter of its own selection and may fix the interpreter's reasonable compensation. The compensation shall be paid out of funds provided by law or by one or more of the parties as the court may direct, and may be taxed ultimately as costs, in the discretion of the court.

As amended 1966, 1975, 1987, 1996.

Rule 44.

PROOF OF OFFICIAL RECORD

(a) Authentication.

(1) *Domestic.* An official record kept within the United States, or any state, district, or commonwealth, or within a territory

subject to the administrative or judicial jurisdiction of the United States, or an entry therein, when admissible for any purpose, may be evidenced by an official publication thereof or by a copy attested by the officer having the legal custody of the record, or by the officer's deputy, and accompanied by a certificate that such officer has the custody. The certificate may be made by a judge of a court of record of the district or political subdivision in which the record is kept, authenticated by the seal of the court, or may be made by any public officer having a seal of office and having official duties in the district or political subdivision in which the record is kept, authenticated by the seal of the officer's office.

(2) *Foreign.* A foreign official record, or an entry therein, when admissible for any purpose, may be evidenced by an official publication thereof; or a copy thereof, attested by a person authorized to make the attestation, and accompanied by a final certification as to the genuineness of the signature and official position (i) of the attesting person, or (ii) of any foreign official whose certificate of genuineness of signature and official position relates to the attestation or is in a chain of certificates of genuineness of signature and official position relating to the attestation. A final certification may be made by a secretary of embassy or legation, consul general, consul, vice consul, or consular agent of the United States, or a diplomatic or consular official of the foreign country assigned or accredited to the United States. If reasonable opportunity has been given to all parties to investigate the authenticity and accuracy of the documents, the court may, for good cause shown, (i) admit an attested copy without final certification or (ii) permit the foreign official record to be evidenced by an attested summary with or without a final certification. The final certification is unnecessary if the record and the attestation are certified as provided in a treaty or convention to which the United States and the foreign country in which the official record is located are parties.

(b) Lack of Record. A written statement that after diligent search no record or entry of a specified tenor is found to exist in the records designated by the statement, authenticated as provided in subdivision (a)(1) of this rule in the case of a domestic record, or complying with the requirements of subdivision (a)(2) of this rule for a summary in the case of a foreign record, is admissible as evidence that the records contain no such record or entry.

(c) Other Proof. This rule does not prevent the proof of official records or of entry or lack of entry therein by any other method authorized by law.

As amended 1966, 1987, 1991.

Rule 44.1.

DETERMINATION OF FOREIGN LAW

A party who intends to raise an issue concerning the law of a foreign country shall give notice by pleadings or other reasonable written notice. The court, in determining foreign law, may consider any relevant material or source, including testimony, whether or not submitted by a party or admissible under the Federal Rules of Evidence. The court's determination shall be treated as a ruling on a question of law.

Added 1966; as amended 1975, 1987.

Rule 45.

SUBPOENA

(a) Form; Issuance.

(1) Every subpoena shall

(A) state the name of the court from which it is issued; and

(B) state the title of the action, the name of the court in which it is pending, and its civil action number; and

(C) command each person to whom it is directed to attend and give testimony or to produce and permit inspection and copying of designated books, documents or tangible things in the possession, custody or control of that person, or to permit inspection of premises, at a time and place therein specified; and

(D) set forth the text of subdivisions (c) and (d) of this rule.

A command to produce evidence or to permit inspection may be joined with a command to appear at trial or hearing or at deposition, or may be issued separately.

(2) A subpoena commanding attendance at a trial or hearing shall issue from the court for the district in which the hearing or trial is to be held. A subpoena for attendance at a deposition shall issue from the court for the district designated by the notice of deposition as the district in which the deposition is to be taken. If separate from a subpoena commanding the attendance of a person, a subpoena for production or inspection shall issue from the court for the district in which the production or inspection is to be made.

(3) The clerk shall issue a subpoena, signed but otherwise in blank, to a party requesting it, who shall complete it before service.

An attorney as officer of the court may also issue and sign a subpoena on behalf of

(A) a court in which the attorney is authorized to practice; or

(B) a court for a district in which a deposition or production is compelled by the subpoena, if the deposition or production pertains to an action pending in a court in which the attorney is authorized to practice.

(b) Service.

(1) A subpoena may be served by any person who is not a party and is not less than 18 years of age. Service of a subpoena upon a person named therein shall be made by delivering a copy thereof to such person and, if the person's attendance is commanded, by tendering to that person the fees for one day's attendance and the mileage allowed by law. When the subpoena is issued on behalf of the United States or an officer or agency thereof, fees and mileage need not be tendered. Prior notice of any commanded production of documents and things or inspection of premises before trial shall be served on each party in the manner prescribed by Rule 5(b).

(2) Subject to the provisions of clause (ii) of subparagraph (c)(3)(A) of this rule, a subpoena may be served at any place within the district of the court by which it is issued, or at any place without the district that is within 100 miles of the place of the deposition, hearing, trial, production, or inspection specified in the subpoena or at any place within the state where a state statute or rule of court permits service of a subpoena issued by a state court of general jurisdiction sitting in the place of the deposition, hearing, trial, production, or inspection specified in the subpoena. When a statute of the United States provides therefor, the court upon proper application and cause shown may authorize the service of a subpoena at any other place. A subpoena directed to a witness in a foreign country who is a national or resident of the United States shall issue under the circumstances and in the manner and be served as provided in Title 28, U.S.C. § 1783.

(3) Proof of service when necessary shall be made by filing with the clerk of the court by which the subpoena is issued a statement of the date and manner of service and of the names of the persons served, certified by the person who made the service.

(c) Protection of Persons Subject to Subpoenas.

(1) A party or an attorney responsible for the issuance and service of a subpoena shall take reasonable steps to avoid imposing undue burden or expense on a person subject to that subpoena. The court on behalf of which the subpoena was issued shall enforce this duty and impose upon the party or attorney in breach of this

duty an appropriate sanction, which may include, but is not limited to, lost earnings and a reasonable attorney's fee.

(2)(A) A person commanded to produce and permit inspection and copying of designated books, papers, documents or tangible things, or inspection of premises need not appear in person at the place of production or inspection unless commanded to appear for deposition, hearing or trial.

(B) Subject to paragraph (d)(2) of this rule, a person commanded to produce and permit inspection and copying may, within 14 days after service of the subpoena or before the time specified for compliance if such time is less than 14 days after service, serve upon the party or attorney designated in the subpoena written objection to inspection or copying of any or all of the designated materials or of the premises. If objection is made, the party serving the subpoena shall not be entitled to inspect and copy the materials or inspect the premises except pursuant to an order of the court by which the subpoena was issued. If objection has been made, the party serving the subpoena may, upon notice to the person commanded to produce, move at any time for an order to compel the production. Such an order to compel production shall protect any person who is not a party or an officer of a party from significant expense resulting from the inspection and copying commanded.

(3)(A) On timely motion, the court by which a subpoena was issued shall quash or modify the subpoena if it

(i) fails to allow reasonable time for compliance;

(ii) requires a person who is not a party or an officer of a party to travel to a place more than 100 miles from the place where that person resides, is employed or regularly transacts business in person, except that, subject to the provisions of clause (c)(3)(B)(iii) of this rule, such a person may in order to attend trial be commanded to travel from any such place within the state in which the trial is held, or

(iii) requires disclosure of privileged or other protected matter and no exception or waiver applies, or

(iv) subjects a person to undue burden.

(B) If a subpoena

(i) requires disclosure of a trade secret or other confidential research, development, or commercial information, or

(ii) requires disclosure of an unretained expert's opinion or information not describing specific events or occurrences in dispute and resulting from the expert's study made not at the request of any party, or

(iii) requires a person who is not a party or an officer of a party to incur substantial expense to travel more than 100 miles to attend trial,

the court may, to protect a person subject to or affected by the subpoena, quash or modify the subpoena or, if the party in whose behalf the subpoena is issued shows a substantial need for the testimony or material that cannot be otherwise met without undue hardship and assures that the person to whom the subpoena is addressed will be reasonably compensated, the court may order appearance or production only upon specified conditions.

(d) Duties in Responding to Subpoena.

(1) A person responding to a subpoena to produce documents shall produce them as they are kept in the usual course of business or shall organize and label them to correspond with the categories in the demand.

(2) When information subject to a subpoena is withheld on a claim that it is privileged or subject to protection as trial preparation materials, the claim shall be made expressly and shall be supported by a description of the nature of the documents, communications, or things not produced that is sufficient to enable the demanding party to contest the claim.

(e) Contempt. Failure by any person without adequate excuse to obey a subpoena served upon that person may be deemed a contempt of the court from which the subpoena issued. An adequate cause for failure to obey exists when a subpoena purports to require a non-party to attend or produce at a place not within the limits provided by clause (ii) of subparagraph (c)(3)(A).

As amended 1948, 1949, 1970, 1980, 1985, 1987, 1991.

Rule 46.

EXCEPTIONS UNNECESSARY

Formal exceptions to rulings or orders of the court are unnecessary; but for all purposes for which an exception has heretofore been necessary it is sufficient that a party, at the time the ruling or order of the court is made or sought, makes known to the court the action which the party desires the court to take or the party's objection to the action of the court and the grounds therefor; and, if a party has no opportunity to object to a ruling or order at the time it is made, the absence of an objection does not thereafter prejudice the party.

As amended 1987.

Rule 47.

SELECTION OF JURORS

(a) Examination of Jurors. The court may permit the parties or their attorneys to conduct the examination of prospective jurors or may itself conduct the examination. In the latter event, the court shall permit the parties or their attorneys to supplement the examination by such further inquiry as it deems proper or shall itself submit to the prospective jurors such additional questions of the parties or their attorneys as it deems proper.

(b) Peremptory Challenges. The court shall allow the number of peremptory challenges provided by 28 U.S.C. § 1870.

(c) Excuse. The court may for good cause excuse a juror from service during trial or deliberation.

As amended 1966, 1991.

Rule 48.

NUMBER OF JURORS—PARTICIPATION IN VERDICT

The court shall seat a jury of not fewer than six and not more than twelve members and all jurors shall participate in the verdict unless excused from service by the court pursuant to Rule 47(c). Unless the parties otherwise stipulate, (1) the verdict shall be unanimous and (2) no verdict shall be taken from a jury reduced in size to fewer than six members.

As amended 1991.

Rule 49.

SPECIAL VERDICTS AND INTERROGATORIES

(a) Special Verdicts. The court may require a jury to return only a special verdict in the form of a special written finding upon each issue of fact. In that event the court may submit to the jury written questions susceptible of categorical or other brief answer or may submit written forms of the several special findings which might properly be made under the pleadings and evidence; or it may use such other method of submitting the issues and requiring the written findings thereon as it deems most appropriate. The court shall give to the jury such explanation and instruction concerning the matter thus submitted as may be necessary to enable the jury to make its findings upon each issue. If in so doing the court omits any issue of fact raised by the pleadings or by the evidence, each party waives the right to a trial by jury of the issue so omitted unless before the jury retires the party demands its submission to the jury. As to an issue omitted without such demand the court may make a finding; or, if it fails to do so, it shall be deemed to have made a finding in accord with the judgment on the special verdict.

(b) General Verdict Accompanied by Answer to Interrogatories. The court may submit to the jury, together with appropriate forms for a general verdict, written interrogatories upon one or more issues of fact the decision of which is necessary to a verdict. The court shall give such explanation or instruction as may be necessary to enable the jury both to make answers to the interrogatories and to render a general verdict, and the court shall direct the jury both to make written answers and to render a general verdict. When the general verdict and the answers are harmonious, the appropriate judgment upon the verdict and answers shall be entered pursuant to Rule 58. When the answers are consistent with each other but one or more is inconsistent with the general verdict, judgment may be entered pursuant to Rule 58 in accordance with the answers, notwithstanding the general verdict, or the court may return the jury for further consideration of its answers and verdict or may order a new trial. When the answers are inconsistent with each other and one or more is likewise inconsistent with the general verdict, judgment shall not be entered, but the court shall return the jury for further consideration of its answers and verdict or shall order a new trial.

As amended 1963, 1987.

Rule 50.

JUDGMENT AS A MATTER OF LAW IN JURY TRIALS; ALTERNATIVE MOTION FOR NEW TRIAL; CONDITIONAL RULINGS

(a) Judgment as a Matter of Law.

(1) If during a trial by jury a party has been fully heard on an issue and there is no legally sufficient evidentiary basis for a reasonable jury to find for that party on that issue, the court may determine the issue against that party and may grant a motion for judgment as a matter of law against that party with respect to a claim or defense that cannot under the controlling law be maintained or defeated without a favorable finding on that issue.

(2) Motions for judgment as a matter of law may be made at any time before submission of the case to the jury. Such a motion shall specify the judgment sought and the law and the facts on which the moving party is entitled to the judgment.

(b) Renewing Motion for Judgment After Trial; Alternative Motion for New Trial. If, for any reason, the court does not grant a motion for judgment as a matter of law made at the close of all the evidence, the court is considered to have submitted the action to the jury subject to the court's later deciding the legal questions raised by the motion. The movant may renew its request for judgment as a matter of law by filing a motion no later than 10 days after entry of judgment—and may alternatively request a new trial or join a motion for a new trial under Rule 59. In ruling on a renewed motion, the court may:

(1) if a verdict was returned:

(A) allow the judgment to stand,

(B) order a new trial, or

(C) direct entry of judgment as a matter of law; or

(2) if no verdict was returned:

(A) order a new trial, or

(B) direct entry of judgment as a matter of law.

(c) Granting Renewed Motion for Judgment as a Matter of Law; Conditional Rulings; New Trial Motion.

(1) If the renewed motion for judgment as a matter of law is granted, the court shall also rule on the motion for a new trial, if any, by determining whether it should be granted if the judgment is thereafter vacated or reversed, and shall specify the grounds for granting or denying the motion for the new trial. If the motion for a new trial is thus conditionally granted, the order thereon does not affect the finality of the judgment. In case the motion for a new trial has been conditionally granted and the judgment is reversed on appeal, the new trial shall proceed unless the appellate court has otherwise ordered. In case the motion for a new trial has been conditionally denied, the appellee on appeal may assert error in that denial; and if the judgment is reversed on appeal, subsequent proceedings shall be in accordance with the order of the appellate court.

(2) Any motion for a new trial under Rule 59 by a party against whom judgment as a matter of law is rendered shall be filed no later than 10 days after entry of the judgment.

(d) Same: Denial of Motion for Judgment as a Matter of Law. If the motion for judgment as a matter of law is denied, the party who prevailed on that motion may, as appellee, assert grounds entitling the party to a new trial in the event the appellate court concludes that the trial court erred in denying the motion for judgment. If the appellate court reverses the judgment, nothing in this rule precludes it from determining that the appellee is entitled to a new trial, or from directing the trial court to determine whether a new trial shall be granted.

As amended 1963, 1987, 1991, 1993, 1995.

Rule 51.

INSTRUCTIONS TO JURY; OBJECTIONS; PRESERVING A CLAIM OF ERROR

(a) Requests.

(1) A party may, at the close of the evidence or at an earlier reasonable time that the court directs, file and furnish to every other party written requests that the court instruct the jury on the law as set forth in the requests.

(2) After the close of the evidence, a party may:

(A) file requests for instructions on issues that could not reasonably have been anticipated at an earlier time for requests set under Rule 51(a)(1), and

(B) with the court's permission file untimely requests for instructions on any issue.

(b) Instructions. The court:

(1) must inform the parties of its proposed instructions and proposed action on the requests before instructing the jury and before final jury arguments;

(2) must give the parties an opportunity to object on the record and out of the jury's hearing to the proposed instructions and actions on requests before the instructions and arguments are delivered; and

(3) may instruct the jury at any time after trial begins and before the jury is discharged.

(c) Objections.

(1) A party who objects to an instruction or the failure to give an instruction must do so on the record, stating distinctly the matter objected to and the grounds of the objection.

(2) An objection is timely if:

(A) a party that has been informed of an instruction or action on a request before the jury is instructed and before final jury arguments, as provided by Rule 51(b)(1), objects at the opportunity for objection required by Rule 51(b)(2); or

(B) a party that has not been informed of an instruction or action on a request before the time for objection provided under Rule 51(b)(2) objects promptly after learning that the instruction or request will be, or has been, given or refused.

(d) Assigning Error; Plain Error.

(1) A party may assign as error:

(A) an error in an instruction actually given if that party made a proper objection under Rule 51(c), or

(B) a failure to give an instruction if that party made a proper request under Rule 51(a), and—unless the court made a definitive ruling on the record rejecting the request—also made a proper objection under Rule 51(c).

(2) A court may consider a plain error in the instructions affecting substantial rights that has not been preserved as required by Rule 51(d)(1)(A) or (B).

As amended 1987, 2003.

Rule 52.

FINDINGS BY THE COURT; JUDGMENT ON PARTIAL FINDINGS

(a) Effect. In all actions tried upon the facts without a jury or with an advisory jury, the court shall find the facts specially and state separately its conclusions of law thereon, and judgment shall be entered pursuant to Rule 58; and in granting or refusing interlocutory injunctions the court shall similarly set forth the findings of fact and conclusions of law which constitute the grounds of its action. Requests for findings are not necessary for purposes of review. Findings of fact, whether based on oral or documentary evidence, shall not be set aside unless clearly erroneous, and due regard shall be given to the opportunity of the trial court to judge of the credibility of the witnesses. The findings of a master, to the extent that the court adopts them, shall be considered as the findings of the court. It will be sufficient if the findings of fact and conclusions of law are stated orally and recorded in open court following the close of the evidence or appear in an opinion or memorandum of decision filed by the court. Findings of fact and conclusions of law are unnecessary on decisions of motions under Rules 12 or 56 or any other motion except as provided in subdivision (c) of this rule.

(b) Amendment. On a party's motion filed no later than 10 days after entry of judgment, the court may amend its findings—or make additional findings—and may amend the judgment accordingly. The motion may accompany a motion for a new trial under Rule 59. When findings of fact are made in actions tried without a jury, the sufficiency of the evidence supporting the findings may be later questioned whether or not in the district court the party raising the question objected to the findings, moved to amend them, or moved for partial findings.

(c) Judgment on Partial Findings. If during a trial without a jury a party has been fully heard on an issue and the court finds against the party on that issue, the court may enter judgment as a matter of law against that party with respect to a claim or defense that cannot under the controlling law be maintained or defeated without a favorable finding on that issue, or the court may decline to render any judgment until the close of all the evidence. Such a judgment shall be supported by findings of fact and conclusions of law as required by subdivision (a) of this rule.

As amended 1948, 1963, 1983, 1985, 1991, 1993, 1995.

Rule 53.

MASTERS

(a) Appointment.

(1) Unless a statute provides otherwise, a court may appoint a master only to:

(A) perform duties consented to by the parties;

(B) hold trial proceedings and make or recommend findings of fact on issues to be decided by the court without a jury if appointment is warranted by

(i) some exceptional condition, or

(ii) the need to perform an accounting or resolve a difficult computation of damages; or

(C) address pretrial and post-trial matters that cannot be addressed effectively and timely by an available district judge or magistrate judge of the district.

(2) A master must not have a relationship to the parties, counsel, action, or court that would require disqualification of a judge under 28 U.S.C. § 455 unless the parties consent with the court's approval to appointment of a particular person after disclosure of any potential grounds for disqualification.

(3) In appointing a master, the court must consider the fairness of imposing the likely expenses on the parties and must protect against unreasonable expense or delay.

(b) Order Appointing Master.

(1) *Notice.* The court must give the parties notice and an opportunity to be heard before appointing a master. A party may suggest candidates for appointment.

(2) *Contents.* The order appointing a master must direct the master to proceed with all reasonable diligence and must state:

(A) the master's duties, including any investigation or enforcement duties, and any limits on the master's authority under Rule 53(c);

(B) the circumstances—if any—in which the master may communicate ex parte with the court or a party;

(C) the nature of the materials to be preserved and filed as the record of the master's activities;

(D) the time limits, method of filing the record, other procedures, and standards for reviewing the master's orders, findings, and recommendations; and

(E) the basis, terms, and procedure for fixing the master's compensation under Rule 53(h).

(3) *Entry of Order.* The court may enter the order appointing a master only after the master has filed an affidavit disclosing whether there is any ground for disqualification under 28 U.S.C. § 455 and, if a ground for disqualification is disclosed, after the parties have consented with the court's approval to waive the disqualification.

(4) *Amendment.* The order appointing a master may be amended at any time after notice to the parties, and an opportunity to be heard.

(c) Master's Authority. Unless the appointing order expressly directs otherwise, a master has authority to regulate all proceedings and take all appropriate measures to perform fairly and efficiently the assigned duties. The master may by order impose upon a party any noncontempt sanction provided by Rule 37 or 45, and may recommend a contempt sanction against a party and sanctions against a nonparty.

(d) Evidentiary Hearings. Unless the appointing order expressly directs otherwise, a master conducting an evidentiary hearing may exercise the power of the appointing court to compel, take, and record evidence.

(e) Master's Orders. A master who makes an order must file the order and promptly serve a copy on each party. The clerk must enter the order on the docket.

(f) Master's Reports. A master must report to the court as required by the order of appointment. The master must file the report and promptly serve a copy of the report on each party unless the court directs otherwise.

(g) Action on Master's Order, Report, or Recommendations.

(1) *Action.* In acting on a master's order, report, or recommendations, the court must afford an opportunity to be heard and may receive evidence, and may: adopt or affirm; modify; wholly or partly reject or reverse; or resubmit to the master with instructions.

(2) *Time to Object or Move.* A party may file objections to—or a motion to adopt or modify—the master's order, report, or recommendations no later than 20 days from the time the master's order, report, or recommendations are served, unless the court sets a different time.

(3) *Fact Findings.* The court must decide de novo all objections to findings of fact made or recommended by a master unless the parties stipulate with the court's consent that:

(A) the master's findings will be reviewed for clear error, or

(B) the findings of a master appointed under Rule 53(a)(1)(A) or (C) will be final.

(4) *Legal Conclusions.* The court must decide de novo all objections to conclusions of law made or recommended by a master.

(5) *Procedural Matters.* Unless the order of appointment establishes a different standard of review, the court may set aside a master's ruling on a procedural matter only for an abuse of discretion.

(h) Compensation.

(1) *Fixing Compensation.* The court must fix the master's compensation before or after judgment on the basis and terms stated in the order of appointment, but the court may set a new basis and terms after notice and an opportunity to be heard.

(2) *Payment.* The compensation fixed under Rule 53(h)(1) must be paid either:

(A) by a party or parties; or

(B) from a fund or subject matter of the action within the court's control.

(3) *Allocation.* The court must allocate payment of the master's compensation among the parties after considering the nature and amount of the controversy, the means of the parties, and the extent to which any party is more responsible than other parties for the reference to a master. An interim allocation may be amended to reflect a decision on the merits.

(i) Appointment of Magistrate Judge. A magistrate judge is subject to this rule only when the order referring a matter to the magistrate judge expressly provides that the reference is made under this rule.

As amended 1966, 1983, 1987, 1991, 1993, 2003.

VII. JUDGMENT

Rule 54.

JUDGMENTS; COSTS

(a) Definition; Form. "Judgment" as used in these rules includes a decree and any order from which an appeal lies. A judgment shall not contain a recital of pleadings, the report of a master, or the record of prior proceedings.

(b) Judgment upon Multiple Claims or Involving Multiple Parties. When more than one claim for relief is presented in an action, whether as a claim, counterclaim, cross-claim, or third-party claim, or when multiple parties are involved, the court may direct the entry of a final judgment as to one or more but fewer than all of the claims or parties only upon an express determination that there is no just reason for delay and upon an express direction for the entry of judgment. In the absence of such determination and direction, any order or other form of decision, however designated, which adjudicates fewer than all the claims or the rights and liabilities of fewer than all the parties shall not terminate the action as to any of the claims or parties, and the order or other form of decision is subject to revision at any time before the entry of judgment adjudicating all the claims and the rights and liabilities of all the parties.

(c) Demand for Judgment. A judgment by default shall not be different in kind from or exceed in amount that prayed for in the demand for judgment. Except as to a party against whom a judgment is entered by default, every final judgment shall grant the relief to which the party in whose favor it is rendered is entitled, even if the party has not demanded such relief in the party's pleadings.

(d) Costs; Attorneys' Fees.

(1) *Costs Other than Attorneys' Fees.* Except when express provision therefor is made either in a statute of the United States or in these rules, costs other than attorneys' fees shall be allowed as of course to the prevailing party unless the court otherwise directs; but costs against the United States, its officers, and agencies shall be imposed only to the extent permitted by law. Such costs may be taxed by the clerk on one day's notice. On motion served within 5 days thereafter, the action of the clerk may be reviewed by the court.

(2) *Attorneys' Fees.*

(A) Claims for attorneys' fees and related nontaxable expenses shall be made by motion unless the substantive law governing the action provides for the recovery of such fees as an element of damages to be proved at trial.

(B) Unless otherwise provided by statute or order of the court, the motion must be filed no later than 14 days after entry of judgment; must specify the judgment and the statute, rule, or other grounds entitling the moving party to the award; and must state the amount or provide a fair estimate of the amount sought. If directed by the court, the motion shall also disclose the terms of any agreement with respect to fees to be paid for the services for which claim is made.

(C) On request of a party or class member, the court shall afford an opportunity for adversary submissions with respect to the motion in accordance with Rule 43(e) or Rule 78. The court may determine issues of liability for fees before receiving submissions bearing on issues of evaluation of services for which liability is imposed by the court. The court shall find the facts and state its conclusions of law as provided in Rule 52(a).

(D) By local rule the court may establish special procedures by which issues relating to such fees may be resolved without extensive evidentiary hearings. In addition, the court may refer issues relating to the value of services to a special master under Rule 53 without regard to the provisions of Rule 53(a)(1) and may refer a motion for attorneys' fees to a magistrate judge under Rule 72(b) as if it were a dispositive pretrial matter.

(E) The provisions of subparagraphs (A) through (D) do not apply to claims for fees and expenses as sanctions for violations of these rules or under 28 U.S.C. § 1927.

As amended 1948, 1961, 1987, 1993, 2002, 2003.

Rule 55.

DEFAULT

(a) Entry. When a party against whom a judgment for affirmative relief is sought has failed to plead or otherwise defend as provided by these rules and that fact is made to appear by affidavit or otherwise, the clerk shall enter the party's default.

(b) Judgment. Judgment by default may be entered as follows:

(1) *By the Clerk.* When the plaintiff's claim against a defendant is for a sum certain or for a sum which can by computation be

made certain, the clerk upon request of the plaintiff and upon affidavit of the amount due shall enter judgment for that amount and costs against the defendant, if the defendant has been defaulted for failure to appear and is not an infant or incompetent person.

(2) *By the Court.* In all other cases the party entitled to a judgment by default shall apply to the court therefor; but no judgment by default shall be entered against an infant or incompetent person unless represented in the action by a general guardian, committee, conservator, or other such representative who has appeared therein. If the party against whom judgment by default is sought has appeared in the action, the party (or, if appearing by representative, the party's representative) shall be served with written notice of the application for judgment at least 3 days prior to the hearing on such application. If, in order to enable the court to enter judgment or to carry it into effect, it is necessary to take an account or to determine the amount of damages or to establish the truth of any averment by evidence or to make an investigation of any other matter, the court may conduct such hearings or order such references as it deems necessary and proper and shall accord a right of trial by jury to the parties when and as required by any statute of the United States.

(c) Setting Aside Default. For good cause shown the court may set aside an entry of default and, if a judgment by default has been entered, may likewise set it aside in accordance with Rule 60(b).

(d) Plaintiffs, Counterclaimants, Cross-Claimants. The provisions of this rule apply whether the party entitled to the judgment by default is a plaintiff, a third-party plaintiff, or a party who has pleaded a cross-claim or counterclaim. In all cases a judgment by default is subject to the limitations of Rule 54(c).

(e) Judgment Against the United States. No judgment by default shall be entered against the United States or an officer or agency thereof unless the claimant establishes a claim or right to relief by evidence satisfactory to the court.

As amended 1987.

Rule 56.

SUMMARY JUDGMENT

(a) For Claimant. A party seeking to recover upon a claim, counterclaim, or cross-claim or to obtain a declaratory judgment may, at any time after the expiration of 20 days from the commencement of the action or after service of a motion for summary judgment by the adverse party, move with or without supporting affidavits for a summary judgment in the party's favor upon all or any part thereof.

(b) For Defending Party. A party against whom a claim, counterclaim, or cross-claim is asserted or a declaratory judgment is sought may, at any time, move with or without supporting affidavits for a summary judgment in the party's favor as to all or any part thereof.

(c) Motion and Proceedings Thereon. The motion shall be served at least 10 days before the time fixed for the hearing. The adverse party prior to the day of hearing may serve opposing affidavits. The judgment sought shall be rendered forthwith if the pleadings, depositions, answers to interrogatories, and admissions on file, together with the affidavits, if any, show that there is no genuine issue as to any material fact and that the moving party is entitled to a judgment as a matter of law. A summary judgment, interlocutory in character, may be rendered on the issue of liability alone although there is a genuine issue as to the amount of damages.

(d) Case Not Fully Adjudicated on Motion. If on motion under this rule judgment is not rendered upon the whole case or for all the relief asked and a trial is necessary, the court at the hearing of the motion, by examining the pleadings and the evidence before it and by interrogating counsel, shall if practicable ascertain what material facts exist without substantial controversy and what material facts are actually and in good faith controverted. It shall thereupon make an order specifying the facts that appear without substantial controversy, including the extent to which the amount of damages or other relief is not in controversy, and directing such further proceedings in the action as are just. Upon the trial of the action the facts so specified shall be deemed established, and the trial shall be conducted accordingly.

(e) Form of Affidavits; Further Testimony; Defense Required. Supporting and opposing affidavits shall be made on personal knowledge, shall set forth such facts as would be admissible in evidence, and shall show affirmatively that the affiant is competent to testify to the matters stated therein. Sworn or certified copies of all papers or parts thereof referred to in an affidavit shall be attached thereto or served therewith. The court may permit affidavits to be supplemented or opposed by depositions, answers to interrogatories, or further affidavits. When a motion for summary judgment is made and supported as provided in this rule, an adverse party may not rest upon the mere allegations or denials of the adverse party's pleading, but the adverse party's response, by affidavits or as otherwise provided in this rule, must set forth specific facts showing that there is a genuine issue for trial. If the adverse party does not so respond, summary judgment, if appropriate, shall be entered against the adverse party.

(f) When Affidavits Are Unavailable. Should it appear from the affidavits of a party opposing the motion that the party cannot for reasons stated present by affidavit facts essential to justify the party's opposition, the court may refuse the application for judgment or may order a continuance to permit affidavits to be obtained or depositions to be taken or discovery to be had or may make such other order as is just.

(g) Affidavits Made in Bad Faith. Should it appear to the satisfaction of the court at any time that any of the affidavits presented pursuant to this rule are presented in bad faith or solely for the purpose of delay, the court shall forthwith order the party employing them to pay to the other party the amount of the reasonable expenses which the filing of the affidavits caused the other party to incur, including reasonable attorney's fees, and any offending party or attorney may be adjudged guilty of contempt.

As amended 1948, 1963, 1987.

Rule 57.

DECLARATORY JUDGMENTS

The procedure for obtaining a declaratory judgment pursuant to Title 28 U.S.C. § 2201, shall be in accordance with these rules, and the right to trial by jury may be demanded under the circumstances and in the manner provided in Rules 38 and 39. The existence of another adequate remedy does not preclude a judgment for declaratory relief in cases where it is appropriate. The court may order a speedy hearing of an action for a declaratory judgment and may advance it on the calendar.

As amended 1949.

Rule 58.

ENTRY OF JUDGMENT

(a) Separate Document.

(1) Every judgment and amended judgment must be set forth on a separate document, but a separate document is not required for an order disposing of a motion:

(A) for judgment under Rule 50(b);

(B) to amend or make additional findings of fact under Rule 52(b);

(C) for attorney fees under Rule 54;

(D) for a new trial, or to alter or amend the judgment, under Rule 59; or

(E) for relief under Rule 60.

(2) Subject to Rule 54(b):

(A) unless the court orders otherwise, the clerk must, without awaiting the court's direction, promptly prepare, sign, and enter the judgment when:

(i) the jury returns a general verdict,

(ii) the court awards only costs or a sum certain, or

(iii) the court denies all relief;

(B) the court must promptly approve the form of the judgment, which the clerk must promptly enter, when:

(i) the jury returns a special verdict or a general verdict accompanied by interrogatories, or

(ii) the court grants other relief not described in Rule 58(a)(2).

(b) Time of Entry. Judgment is entered for purposes of these rules:

(1) if Rule 58(a)(1) does not require a separate document, when it is entered in the civil docket under Rule 79(a), and

(2) if Rule 58(a)(1) requires a separate document, when it is entered in the civil docket under Rule 79(a) and when the earlier of these events occurs:

(A) when it is set forth on a separate document, or

(B) when 150 days have run from entry in the civil docket under Rule 79(a).

(c) Cost or Fee Awards.

(1) Entry of judgment may not be delayed, nor the time for appeal extended, in order to tax costs or award fees, except as provided in Rule 58(c)(2).

(2) When a timely motion for attorney fees is made under Rule 54(d)(2), the court may act before a notice of appeal has been filed and has become effective to order that the motion have the same effect under Federal Rule of Appellate Procedure 4(a)(4) as a timely motion under Rule 59.

(d) Request for Entry. A party may request that judgment be set forth on a separate document as required by Rule 58(a)(1).

As amended 1948, 1963, 1993, 2002.

Rule 59.

NEW TRIALS; AMENDMENT OF JUDGMENTS

(a) Grounds. A new trial may be granted to all or any of the parties and on all or part of the issues (1) in an action in which there has been a trial by jury, for any of the reasons for which new trials have heretofore been granted in actions at law in the courts of the United States; and (2) in an action tried without a jury, for any of the reasons for which rehearings have heretofore been granted in suits in equity in the courts of the United States. On a motion for a new trial in an action tried without a jury, the court may open the judgment if one has been entered, take additional testimony, amend findings of fact and conclusions of law or make new findings and conclusions, and direct the entry of a new judgment.

(b) Time for Motion. Any motion for a new trial shall be filed no later than 10 days after entry of the judgment.

(c) Time for Serving Affidavits. When a motion for new trial is based on affidavits, they shall be filed with the motion. The opposing party has 10 days after service to file opposing affidavits, but that period may be extended for up to 20 days, either by the court for good cause or by the parties' written stipulation. The court may permit reply affidavits.

(d) On Court's Initiative; Notice; Specifying Grounds. No later than 10 days after entry of judgment the court, on its own, may order a new trial for any reason that would justify granting one on a party's motion. After giving the parties notice and an opportunity to be heard, the court may grant a timely motion for a new trial for a reason not stated in the motion. When granting a new trial on its own initiative or for a reason not stated in a motion, the court shall specify the grounds in its order.

(e) Motion to Alter or Amend Judgment. Any motion to alter or amend a judgment shall be filed no later than 10 days after entry of the judgment.

As amended 1948, 1966, 1995.

Rule 60.

RELIEF FROM JUDGMENT OR ORDER

(a) Clerical Mistakes. Clerical mistakes in judgments, orders or other parts of the record and errors therein arising from oversight or omission may be corrected by the court at any time of its own initiative or on the motion of any party and after such notice, if any, as the court orders. During the pendency of an appeal, such mistakes may be so corrected before the appeal is docketed in the appellate court, and thereafter while the appeal is pending may be so corrected with leave of the appellate court.

(b) Mistakes; Inadvertence; Excusable Neglect; Newly Discovered Evidence; Fraud, etc. On motion and upon such terms as are just, the court may relieve a party or a party's legal representative from a final judgment, order, or proceeding for the following reasons: (1) mistake, inadvertence, surprise, or excusable neglect; (2) newly discovered evidence which by due diligence could not have been discovered in time to move for a new trial under Rule 59(b); (3) fraud (whether heretofore denominated intrinsic or extrinsic), misrepresentation, or other misconduct of an adverse party; (4) the judgment is void; (5) the judgment has been satisfied, released, or discharged, or a prior judgment upon which it is based has been reversed or otherwise vacated, or it is no longer equitable that the judgment should have prospective application; or (6) any other reason justifying relief from the operation of the judgment. The motion shall be made within a reasonable time, and for reasons (1), (2), and (3) not more than one year after the judgment, order, or proceeding was entered or taken. A motion under this subdivision (b) does not affect the finality of a judgment or suspend its operation. This rule does not limit the power of a court to entertain an independent action to relieve a party from a judgment, order, or proceeding, or to grant relief to a defendant not actually personally notified as provided in Title 28, U.S.C., § 1655, or to set aside a judgment for fraud upon the court. Writs of coram nobis, coram vobis, audita querela, and bills of review and bills in the nature of a bill of review, are abolished, and the procedure for obtaining any relief from a judgment shall be by motion as prescribed in these rules or by an independent action.

As amended 1948, 1949, 1987.

Rule 61.

HARMLESS ERROR

No error in either the admission or the exclusion of evidence and no error or defect in any ruling or order or in anything done or omitted by the court or by any of the parties is ground for granting a new trial or for setting aside a verdict or for vacating, modifying or otherwise disturbing a judgment or order, unless refusal to take such action appears to the court inconsistent with substantial justice. The court at every stage of the proceeding must disregard any error or defect in the proceeding which does not affect the substantial rights of the parties.

Rule 62.

STAY OF PROCEEDINGS TO ENFORCE A JUDGMENT

(a) Automatic Stay; Exceptions—Injunctions, Receiverships, and Patent Accountings. Except as stated herein, no execution shall issue upon a judgment nor shall proceedings be taken for its enforcement until the expiration of 10 days after its entry. Unless otherwise ordered by the court, an interlocutory or final judgment in an action for an injunction or in a receivership action, or a judgment or order directing an accounting in an action for infringement of letters patent, shall not be stayed during the period after its entry and until an appeal is taken or during the pendency of an appeal. The provisions of subdivision (c) of this rule govern the suspending, modifying, restoring, or granting of an injunction during the pendency of an appeal.

(b) Stay on Motion for New Trial or for Judgment. In its discretion and on such conditions for the security of the adverse party as are proper, the court may stay the execution of or any proceedings to enforce a judgment pending the disposition of a motion for a new trial or to alter or amend a judgment made pursuant to Rule 59, or of a motion for relief from a judgment or order made pursuant to Rule 60, or of a motion for judgment in accordance with a motion for a directed verdict made pursuant to Rule 50, or of a motion for amendment to the findings or for additional findings made pursuant to Rule 52(b).

(c) Injunction Pending Appeal. When an appeal is taken from an interlocutory or final judgment granting, dissolving, or denying an injunction, the court in its discretion may suspend, modify, restore, or grant an injunction during the pendency of the appeal upon such terms as to bond or otherwise as it considers proper for the security of the rights of the adverse party. If the judgment appealed from is rendered by a district court of three judges specially constituted pursuant to a statute of the United States, no such order shall be made except (1) by such court sitting in open court or (2) by the assent of all the judges of such court evidenced by their signatures to the order.

(d) Stay upon Appeal. When an appeal is taken the appellant by giving a supersedeas bond may obtain a stay subject to the exceptions contained in subdivision (a) of this rule. The bond may be given at or after the time of filing the notice of appeal or of procuring the order allowing the appeal, as the case may be. The stay is effective when the supersedeas bond is approved by the court.

(e) Stay in Favor of the United States or Agency Thereof. When an appeal is taken by the United States or an officer or agency thereof or by direction of any department of the Government of the United States and the operation or enforcement of the judgment is stayed, no bond, obligation, or other security shall be required from the appellant.

(f) Stay According to State Law. In any state in which a judgment is a lien upon the property of the judgment debtor and in which the judgment debtor is entitled to a stay of execution, a judgment debtor is entitled, in the district court held therein, to such stay as would be accorded the judgment debtor had the action been maintained in the courts of that state.

(g) Power of Appellate Court Not Limited. The provisions in this rule do not limit any power of an appellate court or of a judge or justice thereof to stay proceedings during the pendency of an appeal or to suspend, modify, restore, or grant an injunction during the pendency of an appeal or to make any order appropriate to preserve the status quo or the effectiveness of the judgment subsequently to be entered.

(h) Stay of Judgment as to Multiple Claims or Multiple Parties. When a court has ordered a final judgment under the conditions stated in Rule 54(b), the court may stay enforcement of that judgment until the entering of a subsequent judgment or judgments and may prescribe such conditions as are necessary to secure the benefit thereof to the party in whose favor the judgment is entered.

As amended 1948, 1949, 1961, 1987.

Rule 63.

INABILITY OF A JUDGE TO PROCEED

If a trial or hearing has been commenced and the judge is unable to proceed, any other judge may proceed with it upon certifying familiarity with the record and determining that the proceedings in the case may be completed without prejudice to the parties. In a hearing or trial without a jury, the successor judge shall at the request of a party recall any witness whose testimony is material and disputed and who is available to testify again without undue burden. The successor judge may also recall any other witness.

As amended 1987, 1991.

VIII. PROVISIONAL AND FINAL REMEDIES

Rule 64.

SEIZURE OF PERSON OR PROPERTY

At the commencement of and during the course of an action, all remedies providing for seizure of person or property for the purpose of securing satisfaction of the judgment ultimately to be entered in the action are available under the circumstances and in the manner provided by the law of the state in which the district court is held, existing at the time the remedy is sought, subject to the following qualifications: (1) any existing statute of the United States governs to the extent to which it is applicable; (2) the action in which any of the foregoing remedies is used shall be commenced and prosecuted or, if removed from a state court, shall be prosecuted after removal, pursuant to these rules. The remedies thus available include arrest, attachment, garnishment, replevin, sequestration, and other corresponding or equivalent remedies, however designated and regardless of whether by state procedure the remedy is ancillary to an action or must be obtained by an independent action.

Rule 65.

INJUNCTIONS

(a) Preliminary Injunction.

(1) *Notice.* No preliminary injunction shall be issued without notice to the adverse party.

(2) *Consolidation of Hearing with Trial on Merits.* Before or after the commencement of the hearing of an application for a preliminary injunction, the court may order the trial of the action on the merits to be advanced and consolidated with the hearing of the application. Even when this consolidation is not ordered, any evidence received upon an application for a preliminary injunction which would be admissible upon the trial on the merits becomes part of the record on the trial and need not be repeated upon the trial. This subdivision (a)(2) shall be so construed and applied as to save to the parties any rights they may have to trial by jury.

(b) Temporary Restraining Order; Notice; Hearing; Duration. A temporary restraining order may be granted without written or oral notice to the adverse party or that party's attorney only if (1) it clearly appears from specific facts shown by affidavit or by the verified complaint that immediate and irreparable injury, loss, or damage will result to the applicant before the adverse party or that party's attorney can be heard in opposition, and (2) the applicant's attorney certifies to the court in writing the efforts, if any, which have been made to give the notice and the reasons supporting the claim that notice should not be required. Every temporary restraining order granted without notice shall be indorsed with the date and hour of issuance; shall be filed forthwith in the clerk's office and entered of record; shall define the injury and state why it is irreparable and why the order was granted without notice; and shall expire by its terms within such time after entry, not to exceed 10 days, as the court fixes, unless within the time so fixed the order, for good cause shown, is extended for a like period or unless the party against whom the order is directed consents that it may be extended for a longer period. The reasons for the extension shall be entered of record. In case a temporary restraining order is granted without notice, the motion for a preliminary injunction shall be set down for hearing at the earliest possible time and takes precedence of all matters except older matters of the same character; and when the motion comes on for hearing the party who obtained the temporary restraining order shall proceed with the application for a preliminary injunction and, if the party does not do so, the court shall dissolve the temporary restraining order. On 2 days' notice to the party who obtained the temporary restraining order without notice or on such shorter notice to that party as the court may prescribe, the adverse party may appear and move its dissolution or modification and in that event the court shall proceed to hear and determine such motion as expeditiously as the ends of justice require.

(c) Security. No restraining order or preliminary injunction shall issue except upon the giving of security by the applicant, in such sum as the court deems proper, for the payment of such costs and damages as may be incurred or suffered by any party who is found to have been wrongfully enjoined or restrained. No such security shall be required of the United States or of an officer or agency thereof.

The provisions of Rule 65.1 apply to a surety upon a bond or undertaking under this rule.

(d) Form and Scope of Injunction or Restraining Order. Every order granting an injunction and every restraining order shall set forth the reasons for its issuance; shall be specific in terms; shall describe in reasonable detail, and not by reference to the complaint or other document, the act or acts sought to be restrained; and is binding only upon the parties to the action, their officers, agents, servants, employees, and attorneys, and upon those persons in active concert or participation with them who receive actual notice of the order by personal service or otherwise.

(e) Employer and Employee; Interpleader; Constitutional Cases. These rules do not modify any statute of the United States relating to temporary restraining orders and preliminary injunctions in actions affecting employer and employee; or the provisions of Title 28, U.S.C., § 2361, relating to preliminary injunctions in actions of interpleader or in the nature of interpleader; or Title 28, U.S.C., § 2284, relating to actions required by Act of Congress to be heard and determined by a district court of three judges.

(f) Copyright Impoundment. This rule applies to copyright impoundment proceedings.

As amended 1948, 1949, 1966, 1987, 2001.

Rule 65.1.

SECURITY: PROCEEDINGS AGAINST SURETIES

Whenever these rules, including the Supplemental Rules for Certain Admiralty and Marine Claims, require or permit the giving of security by a party, and security is given in the form of a bond or stipulation or other undertaking with one or more sureties, each surety submits to the jurisdiction of the court and irrevocably appoints the clerk of the court as the surety's agent upon whom any papers affecting the surety's liability on the bond or undertaking may be served. The surety's liability may be enforced on motion without the necessity of an independent action. The motion and such notice of the motion as the court prescribes may be served on the clerk of the court, who shall forthwith mail copies to the sureties if their addresses are known.

Added 1966; as amended 1987.

Rule 66.

RECEIVERS APPOINTED BY FEDERAL COURTS

An action wherein a receiver has been appointed shall not be dismissed except by order of the court. The practice in the administration of estates by receivers or by other similar officers appointed by the court shall be in accordance with the practice heretofore followed in the courts of the United States or as provided in rules promulgated by the district courts. In all other respects the action in which the appointment of a receiver is sought or which is brought by or against a receiver is governed by these rules.

As amended 1948, 1949.

Rule 67.

DEPOSIT IN COURT

In an action in which any part of the relief sought is a judgment for a sum of money or the disposition of a sum of money or the disposition of any other thing capable of delivery, a party, upon notice to every other party, and by leave of court, may deposit with the court all or any part of such sum or thing, whether or not that party claims all or any part of the sum or thing. The party making the deposit shall serve the order permitting deposit on the clerk of the court. Money paid into court under this rule shall be deposited and withdrawn in accordance with the provisions of Title 28, U.S.C., §§ 2041, and 2042; the Act of June 26, 1934, c. 756, § 23, as amended (48 Stat. 1236, 58 Stat. 845), U.S.C., Title 31, § 725v; or any like statute. The fund shall be deposited in an interest-bearing account or invested in an interest-bearing instrument approved by the court.

As amended 1949, 1983.

Rule 68.

OFFER OF JUDGMENT

At any time more than 10 days before the trial begins, a party defending against a claim may serve upon the adverse party an offer to allow judgment to be taken against the defending party for the money or property or to the effect specified in the offer, with costs then accrued. If within 10 days after the service of the offer the adverse party serves written notice that the offer is accepted, either party may then file the offer and notice of acceptance together with proof of service thereof and thereupon the clerk shall enter judgment. An offer not accepted shall be deemed withdrawn and evidence thereof is not admissible except in a proceeding to determine costs. If the judgment finally obtained by the offeree is not more favorable than the offer, the offeree must pay the costs incurred after the making of the offer. The fact that an offer is made but not accepted does not preclude a subsequent offer. When the liability of one party to another has been determined by verdict or order or judgment, but the amount or extent of the liability remains to be determined by further proceedings, the party adjudged liable may make an offer of judgment, which shall have the same effect as an offer made before trial if it is served within a reasonable time not less than 10 days prior to the commencement of hearings to determine the amount or extent of liability.

As amended 1948, 1966, 1987.

Rule 69.

EXECUTION

(a) In General. Process to enforce a judgment for the payment of money shall be a writ of execution, unless the court directs otherwise. The procedure on execution, in proceedings supplementary to and in aid of a judgment, and in proceedings on and in aid of execution shall be in accordance with the practice and procedure of the state in which the district court is held, existing at the time the remedy is sought, except that any statute of the United States governs to the extent that it is applicable. In aid of the judgment or execution, the judgment creditor or a successor in interest when that interest appears of record, may obtain discovery from any person, including the judgment debtor, in the manner provided in these rules or in the manner provided by the practice of the state in which the district court is held.

(b) Against Certain Public Officers. When a judgment has been entered against a collector or other officer of revenue under the circumstances stated in Title 28, U.S.C., § 2006, or against an officer of Congress in an action mentioned in the Act of March 3, 1875, c. 130, § 8 (18 Stat. 401), U.S.C., Title 2, § 118, and when the court has given the certificate of probable cause for the officer's act as provided in those statutes, execution shall not issue against the officer or the officer's property but the final judgment shall be satisfied as provided in such statutes.

As amended 1949, 1970, 1987.

Rule 70.

JUDGMENT FOR SPECIFIC ACTS; VESTING TITLE

If a judgment directs a party to execute a conveyance of land or to deliver deeds or other documents or to perform any other specific act and the party fails to comply within the time specified, the court may direct the act to be done at the cost of the disobedient party by some other person appointed by the court and the act when so done has like effect as if done by the party. On application of the party entitled to performance, the clerk shall issue a writ of attachment or sequestration against the property of the disobedient party to compel obedience to the judgment. The court may also in proper cases adjudge the party in contempt. If real or personal property is within the district, the court in lieu of directing a conveyance thereof may enter a judgment divesting the title of any party and vesting it in others and such judgment has the effect of a conveyance executed in due form of law. When any order or judgment is for the delivery of possession, the party in whose favor it is entered is entitled to a writ of execution or assistance upon application to the clerk.

Rule 71.

PROCESS IN BEHALF OF AND AGAINST PERSONS NOT PARTIES

When an order is made in favor of a person who is not a party to the action, that person may enforce obedience to the order by the same process as if a party; and, when obedience to an order may be lawfully enforced against a person who is not a party, that person is liable to the same process for enforcing obedience to the order as if a party.

As amended 1987.

IX. SPECIAL PROCEEDINGS

Rule 71A.

CONDEMNATION OF PROPERTY

(a) Applicability of Other Rules. The Rules of Civil Procedure for the United States District Courts govern the procedure for the condemnation of real and personal property under the power of eminent domain, except as otherwise provided in this rule.

(b) Joinder of Properties. The plaintiff may join in the same action one or more separate pieces of property, whether in the same or different ownership and whether or not sought for the same use.

(c) Complaint.

(1) *Caption.* The complaint shall contain a caption as provided in Rule 10(a), except that the plaintiff shall name as defendants the property, designated generally by kind, quantity, and location, and at least one of the owners of some part of or interest in the property.

(2) *Contents.* The complaint shall contain a short and plain statement of the authority for the taking, the use for which the property is to be taken, a description of the property sufficient for its identification, the interests to be acquired, and as to each separate piece of property a designation of the defendants who have been joined as owners thereof or of some interest therein. Upon the commencement of the action, the plaintiff need join as defendants only the persons having or claiming an interest in the property whose names are then known, but prior to any hearing involving the compensation to be paid for a piece of property, the

plaintiff shall add as defendants all persons having or claiming an interest in that property whose names can be ascertained by a reasonably diligent search of the records, considering the character and value of the property involved and the interests to be acquired, and also those whose names have otherwise been learned. All others may be made defendants under the designation "Unknown Owners." Process shall be served as provided in subdivision (d) of this rule upon all defendants, whether named as defendants at the time of the commencement of the action or subsequently added, and a defendant may answer as provided in subdivision (e) of this rule. The court meanwhile may order such distribution of a deposit as the facts warrant.

(3) *Filing.* In addition to filing the complaint with the court, the plaintiff shall furnish to the clerk at least one copy thereof for the use of the defendants and additional copies at the request of the clerk or of a defendant.

(d) Process.

(1) *Notice; Delivery.* Upon the filing of the complaint the plaintiff shall forthwith deliver to the clerk joint or several notices directed to the defendants named or designated in the complaint. Additional notices directed to defendants subsequently added shall be so delivered. The delivery of the notice and its service have the same effect as the delivery and service of the summons under Rule 4.

(2) *Same; Form.* Each notice shall state the court, the title of the action, the name of the defendant to whom it is directed, that the action is to condemn property, a description of the defendant's property sufficient for its identification, the interest to be taken, the authority for the taking, the uses for which the property is to be taken, that the defendant may serve upon the plaintiff's attorney an answer within 20 days after service of the notice, and that the failure so to serve an answer constitutes a consent to the taking and to the authority of the court to proceed to hear the action and to fix the compensation. The notice shall conclude with the name of the plaintiff's attorney and an address within the district in which action is brought where the attorney may be served. The notice need contain a description of no other property than that to be taken from the defendants to whom it is directed.

(3) *Service of Notice.*

(A) *Personal Service.* Personal service of the notice (but without copies of the complaint) shall be made in accordance with Rule 4 upon a defendant whose residence is known and who resides within the United States or a territory subject to the administrative or judicial jurisdiction of the United States.

(B) *Service by Publication.* Upon the filing of a certificate of the plaintiff's attorney stating that the attorney believes a defendant cannot be personally served, because after diligent inquiry within the state in which the complaint is filed the defendant's place of residence cannot be ascertained by the plaintiff or, if ascertained, that it is beyond the territorial limits of personal service as provided in this rule, service of the notice shall be made on this defendant by publication in a newspaper published in the county where the property is located, or if there is no such newspaper, then in a newspaper having a general circulation where the property is located, once a week for not less than three successive weeks. Prior to the last publication, a copy of the notice shall also be mailed to a defendant who cannot be personally served as provided in this rule but whose place of residence is then known. Unknown owners may be served by publication in like manner by a notice addressed to "Unknown Owners."

Service by publication is complete upon the date of the last publication. Proof of publication and mailing shall be made by certificate of the plaintiff's attorney, to which shall be attached a printed copy of the published notice with the name and dates of the newspaper marked thereon.

(4) *Return; Amendment.* Proof of service of the notice shall be made and amendment of the notice or proof of its service allowed in the manner provided for the return and amendment of the summons under Rule 4.

(e) Appearance or Answer. If a defendant has no objection or defense to the taking of the defendant's property, the defendant may serve a notice of appearance designating the property in which the defendant claims to be interested. Thereafter, the defendant shall receive notice of all proceedings affecting it. If a defendant has any objection or defense to the taking of the property, the defendant shall serve an answer within 20 days after the service of notice upon the defendant. The answer shall identify the property in which the defendant claims to have an interest, state the nature and extent of the interest claimed, and state all the defendant's objections and defenses to the taking of the property. A defendant waives all defenses and objections not so presented, but at the trial of the issue of just compensation, whether or not the defendant has previously appeared or answered, the defendant may present evidence as to the amount of the compensation to be paid for the property, and the defendant may share in the distribution of the award. No other pleading or motion asserting any additional defense or objection shall be allowed.

(f) Amendment of Pleadings. Without leave of court, the plaintiff may amend the complaint at any time before the trial of the issue of compensation and as many times as desired, but no amendment shall be made which will result in a dismissal forbidden by subdivision (i) of this rule. The plaintiff need not serve a copy of an amendment, but shall serve notice of the filing, as provided in Rule 5(b), upon any party affected thereby who has appeared and, in the manner provided in subdivision (d) of this rule, upon any party affected thereby who has not appeared. The plaintiff shall furnish to the clerk of the court for the use of the defendants at least one copy of each amendment and shall furnish additional copies on the request of the clerk or of a defendant. Within the time allowed by subdivision (e) of this rule a defendant may serve an answer to the amended pleading, in the form and manner and with the same effect as there provided.

(g) Substitution of Parties. If a defendant dies or becomes incompetent or transfers an interest after the defendant's joinder, the court may order substitution of the proper party upon motion and notice of hearing. If the motion and notice of hearing are to be served upon a person not already a party, service shall be made as provided in subdivision (d)(3) of this rule.

(h) Trial. If the action involves the exercise of the power of eminent domain under the law of the United States, any tribunal specially constituted by an Act of Congress governing the case for the trial of the issue of just compensation shall be the tribunal for the determination of that issue; but if there is no such specially constituted tribunal any party may have a trial by jury of the issue of just compensation by filing a demand therefor within the time allowed for answer or within such further time as the court may fix, unless the court in its discretion orders that, because of the character, location, or quantity of the property to be condemned, or for other reasons in the interest of justice, the issue of compensation shall be determined by a commission of three persons appointed by it.

In the event that a commission is appointed the court may direct that not more than two additional persons serve as alternate commissioners to hear the case and replace commissioners who, prior to the time when a decision is filed, are found by the court to be unable or disqualified to perform their duties. An alternate who does not replace a regular commissioner shall be discharged after the commission renders its final decision. Before appointing the members of the commission and alternates the court shall advise the parties of the identity and qualifications of each prospective commissioner and alternate and may permit the parties to examine each such designee. The parties shall not be permitted or required by the court to suggest nominees. Each party shall have the right to object for valid cause to the appointment of any person as a commissioner or alternate. If a commission is appointed it shall have the authority of a master provided in Rule 53(c) and proceedings before it shall be governed by the provisions of Rule 53(d). Its action and report shall be determined by a majority and its findings and report shall have the effect, and be dealt with by the court in accordance with the practice, prescribed in Rule 53(e), (f), and (g). Trial of all issues shall otherwise be by the court.

(i) Dismissal of Action.

(1) *As of Right.* If no hearing has begun to determine the compensation to be paid for a piece of property and the plaintiff has not acquired the title or a lesser interest in or taken possession, the plaintiff may dismiss the action as to that property, without an order of the court, by filing a notice of dismissal setting forth a brief description of the property as to which the action is dismissed.

(2) *By Stipulation.* Before the entry of any judgment vesting the plaintiff with title or a lesser interest in or possession of property, the action may be dismissed in whole or in part, without an order of the court, as to any property by filing a stipulation of dismissal by the plaintiff and the defendant affected thereby; and, if the parties so stipulate, the court may vacate any judgment that has been entered.

(3) *By Order of the Court.* At any time before compensation for a piece of property has been determined and paid and after motion and hearing, the court may dismiss the action as to that property, except that it shall not dismiss the action as to any part of the property of which the plaintiff has taken possession or in which the plaintiff has taken title or a lesser interest, but shall award just compensation for the possession, title or lesser interest so taken. The court at any time may drop a defendant unnecessarily or improperly joined.

(4) *Effect.* Except as otherwise provided in the notice, or stipulation of dismissal, or order of the court, any dismissal is without prejudice.

(j) Deposit and Its Distribution. The plaintiff shall deposit with the court any money required by law as a condition to the exercise of the power of eminent domain; and, although not so required, may make a deposit when permitted by statute. In such cases the court and attorneys shall expedite the proceedings for the distribution of the money so deposited and for the ascertainment and payment of just compensation. If the compensation finally awarded to any defendant exceeds the amount which has been paid to that defendant on distribution of the deposit, the court shall enter judgment against the plaintiff and in favor of that defendant for the deficiency. If the compensation finally awarded to any defendant is less than the amount which has been paid to that defendant, the court shall enter judgment against that defendant and in favor of the plaintiff for the overpayment.

(k) Condemnation Under a State's Power of Eminent Domain. The practice as herein prescribed governs in actions involving the exercise of the power of eminent domain under the law of a state, provided that if the state law makes provision for trial of any issue by jury, or for trial of the issue of compensation by jury or commission or both, that provision shall be followed.

(*l*) Costs. Costs are not subject to Rule 54(d).

Added 1951; as amended 1963, 1985, 1987, 1988, 1993, 2003.

Rule 72.

MAGISTRATE JUDGES; PRETRIAL ORDERS

(a) Nondispositive Matters. A magistrate judge to whom a pretrial matter not dispositive of a claim or defense of a party is referred to hear and determine shall promptly conduct such proceedings as are required and when appropriate enter into the record a written order setting forth the disposition of the matter. Within 10 days after being served with a copy of the magistrate judge's order, a party may serve and file objections to the order; a party may not thereafter assign as error a defect in the magistrate judge's order to which objection was not timely made. The district judge to whom the case is assigned shall consider such objections and shall modify or set aside any portion of the magistrate judge's order found to be clearly erroneous or contrary to law.

(b) Dispositive Motions and Prisoner Petitions. A magistrate judge assigned without consent of the parties to hear a pretrial matter dispositive of a claim or defense of a party or a prisoner petition challenging the conditions of confinement shall promptly conduct such proceedings as are required. A record shall be made of all evidentiary proceedings before the magistrate judge, and a record may be made of such other proceedings as the magistrate judge deems necessary. The magistrate judge shall enter into the record a recommendation for disposition of the matter, including proposed findings of fact when appropriate. The clerk shall forthwith mail copies to all parties.

A party objecting to the recommended disposition of the matter shall promptly arrange for the transcription of the record, or portions of it as all parties may agree upon or the magistrate judge deems sufficient, unless the district judge otherwise directs. Within 10 days after being served with a copy of the recommended disposition, a party may serve and file specific, written objections to the proposed findings and recommendations. A party may respond to another party's objections within 10 days after being served with a copy thereof. The district judge to whom the case is assigned shall make a de novo determination upon the record, or after additional evidence, of any portion of the magistrate judge's disposition to which specific written objection has been made in accordance with this rule. The district judge may accept, reject, or modify the recommended decision, receive further evidence, or recommit the matter to the magistrate judge with instructions.

Added 1983; as amended 1991, 1993.

Rule 73.

MAGISTRATE JUDGES; TRIAL BY CONSENT AND APPEAL

(a) Powers; Procedure. When specially designated to exercise such jurisdiction by local rule or order of the district court and when all parties consent thereto, a magistrate judge may exercise the authority provided by Title 28, U.S.C. § 636(c) and may conduct any or all proceedings, including a jury or nonjury trial, in a civil case. A record of the proceedings shall be made in accordance with the requirements of Title 28, U.S.C. § 636(c)(5).

(b) Consent. When a magistrate judge has been designated to exercise civil trial jurisdiction, the clerk shall give written notice to the parties of their opportunity to consent to the exercise by a magistrate judge of civil jurisdiction over the case, as authorized by Title 28, U.S.C. § 636(c). If, within the period specified by local rule, the parties agree to a magistrate judge's exercise of such authority, they shall execute and file a joint form of consent or separate forms of consent setting forth such election.

A district judge, magistrate judge, or other court official may again advise the parties of the availability of the magistrate judge, but, in so doing, shall also advise the parties that they are free to withhold consent without adverse substantive consequences. A district judge or magistrate judge shall not be informed of a party's response to the clerk's notification, unless all parties have consented to the referral of the matter to a magistrate judge.

The district judge, for good cause shown on the judge's own initiative, or under extraordinary circumstances shown by a party, may vacate a reference of a civil matter to a magistrate judge under this subdivision.

(c) Appeal. In accordance with Title 28, U.S.C. § 636(c)(3), appeal from a judgment entered upon direction of a magistrate judge in proceedings under this rule will lie to the court of appeals as it would from a judgment of the district court.

Added 1983; as amended 1987, 1993, 1997.

Rule 74.

METHOD OF APPEAL FROM MAGISTRATE JUDGE TO DISTRICT JUDGE UNDER TITLE 28, U.S.C. § 636(c)(4) AND RULE 73(d)

Abrogated 1997

Rule 75.

PROCEEDINGS ON APPEAL FROM MAGISTRATE JUDGE TO DISTRICT JUDGE UNDER RULE 73(d)

Abrogated 1997

Rule 76.

JUDGMENT OF THE DISTRICT JUDGE ON THE APPEAL UNDER RULE 73(d) AND COSTS

Abrogated 1997

X. DISTRICT COURTS AND CLERKS

Rule 77.

DISTRICT COURTS AND CLERKS

(a) District Courts Always Open. The district courts shall be deemed always open for the purpose of filing any pleading or other proper paper, of issuing and returning mesne and final process, and of making and directing all interlocutory motions, orders, and rules.

(b) Trials and Hearings; Orders in Chambers. All trials upon the merits shall be conducted in open court and so far as convenient in a regular court room. All other acts or proceedings may be done or conducted by a judge in chambers, without the attendance of the clerk or other court officials and at any place either within or without the district; but no hearing, other than one ex parte, shall be conducted outside the district without the consent of all parties affected thereby.

(c) Clerk's Office and Orders by Clerk. The clerk's office with the clerk or a deputy in attendance shall be open during business hours on all days except Saturdays, Sundays, and legal holidays, but a district court may provide by local rule or order that its clerk's office shall be open for specified hours on Saturdays or particular legal holidays other than New Year's Day, Birthday of

Martin Luther King, Jr., Washington's Birthday, Memorial Day, Independence Day, Labor Day, Columbus Day, Veterans Day, Thanksgiving Day, and Christmas Day. All motions and applications in the clerk's office for issuing mesne process, for issuing final process to enforce and execute judgments, for entering defaults or judgments by default, and for other proceedings which do not require allowance or order of the court are grantable of course by the clerk; but the clerk's action may be suspended or altered or rescinded by the court upon cause shown.

(d) Notice of Orders or Judgments. Immediately upon the entry of an order or judgment the clerk shall serve a notice of the entry in the manner provided for in Rule 5(b) upon each party who is not in default for failure to appear, and shall make a note in the docket of the service. Any party may in addition serve a notice of such entry in the manner provided in Rule 5(b) for the service of papers. Lack of notice of the entry by the clerk does not affect the time to appeal or relieve or authorize the court to relieve a party for failure to appeal within the time allowed, except as permitted in Rule 4(a) of the Federal Rules of Appellate Procedure.

As amended 1948, 1963, 1968, 1971, 1987, 1991, 2001.

Rule 78.

MOTION DAY

Unless local conditions make it impracticable, each district court shall establish regular times and places, at intervals sufficiently frequent for the prompt dispatch of business, at which motions requiring notice and hearing may be heard and disposed of; but the judge at any time or place and on such notice, if any, as the judge considers reasonable may make orders for the advancement, conduct, and hearing of actions.

To expedite its business, the court may make provision by rule or order for the submission and determination of motions without oral hearing upon brief written statements of reasons in support and opposition.

As amended 1987.

Rule 79.

BOOKS AND RECORDS KEPT BY THE CLERK AND ENTRIES THEREIN

(a) Civil Docket. The clerk shall keep a book known as "civil docket" of such form and style as may be prescribed by the Director of the Administrative Office of the United States Courts with the approval of the Judicial Conference of the United States, and shall enter therein each civil action to which these rules are made applicable. Actions shall be assigned consecutive file numbers. The file number of each action shall be noted on the folio of the docket whereon the first entry of the action is made. All papers filed with the clerk, all process issued and returns made thereon, all appearances, orders, verdicts, and judgments shall be entered chronologically in the civil docket on the folio assigned to the action and shall be marked with its file number. These entries shall be brief but shall show the nature of each paper filed or writ issued and the substance of each order or judgment of the court and of the returns showing execution of process. The entry of an order or judgment shall show the date the entry is made. When in an action trial by jury has been properly demanded or ordered the clerk shall enter the word "jury" on the folio assigned to that action.

(b) Civil Judgments and Orders. The clerk shall keep, in such form and manner as the Director of the Administrative Office of the United States Courts with the approval of the Judicial Conference of the United States may prescribe, a correct copy of every final judgment or appealable order, or order affecting title to or lien upon real or personal property, and any other order which the court may direct to be kept.

(c) Indices; Calendars. Suitable indices of the civil docket and of every civil judgment and order referred to in subdivision (b) of this rule shall be kept by the clerk under the direction of the court. There shall be prepared under the direction of the court calendars of all actions ready for trial, which shall distinguish "jury actions" from "court actions."

(d) Other Books and Records of the Clerk. The clerk shall also keep such other books and records as may be required from time to time by the Director of the Administrative Office of the United States Courts with the approval of the Judicial Conference of the United States.

As amended 1948, 1949, 1963.

Rule 80.

STENOGRAPHER; STENOGRAPHIC REPORT OR TRANSCRIPT AS EVIDENCE

(a) Stenographer. Abrogated Dec. 27, 1946, eff. Mar. 19, 1948.

(b) Official Stenographer. Abrogated Dec. 27, 1946, eff. Mar. 19, 1948.

(c) Stenographic Report or Transcript as Evidence. Whenever the testimony of a witness at a trial or hearing which was stenographically reported is admissible in evidence at a later trial, it may be proved by the transcript thereof duly certified by the person who reported the testimony.

As amended 1948.

XI. GENERAL PROVISIONS

Rule 81.

APPLICABILITY IN GENERAL

(a) To What Proceedings Applicable.

(1) These rules do not apply to prize proceedings in admiralty governed by Title 10, U.S.C. §§ 7651–7681. They do apply to proceedings in bankruptcy to the extent provided by the Federal Rules of Bankruptcy Procedure.

(2) These rules are applicable to proceedings for admission to citizenship, habeas corpus, and quo warranto, to the extent that the practice in such proceedings is not set forth in statutes of the United States, the Rules Governing Section 2254 Cases, or the Rules Governing Section 2255 Proceedings, and has heretofore conformed to the practice in civil actions.

(3) In proceedings under Title 9, U.S.C., relating to arbitration, or under the Act of May 20, 1926, ch. 347, § 9 (44 Stat. 585), U.S.C., Title 45, § 159, relating to boards of arbitration of railway labor disputes, these rules apply only to the extent that matters of procedure are not provided for in those statutes. These rules apply to proceedings to compel the giving of testimony or production of documents in accordance with a subpoena issued by an officer or agency of the United States under any statute of the United States except as otherwise provided by statute or by rules of the district court or by order of the court in the proceedings.

(4) These rules do not alter the method prescribed by the Act of February 18, 1922, c. 57, § 2 (42 Stat. 388), U.S.C., Title 7, § 292; or by the Act of June 10, 1930, c. 436, § 7 (46 Stat. 534), as amended, U.S.C., Title 7, § 499g(c), for instituting proceedings in the United States district courts to review orders of the Secretary of Agriculture; or prescribed by the Act of June 25, 1934, c. 742, § 2 (48 Stat. 1214), U.S.C., Title 15, § 522, for instituting proceedings to review orders of the Secretary of the Interior; or prescribed by the Act of February 22, 1935, c. 18, § 5 (49 Stat. 31), U.S.C., Title 15, § 715d(c), as extended, for instituting proceedings to review orders of petroleum control boards; but the conduct of such

proceedings in the district courts shall be made to conform to these rules as far as applicable.

(5) These rules do not alter the practice in the United States district courts prescribed in the Act of July 5, 1935, c. 372, §§ 9 and 10 (49 Stat. 453), as amended, U.S.C., Title 29, §§ 159 and 160, for beginning and conducting proceedings to enforce orders of the National Labor Relations Board; and in respects not covered by those statutes, the practice in the district courts shall conform to these rules so far as applicable.

(6) These rules apply to proceedings for enforcement or review of compensation orders under the Longshoremen's and Harbor Workers' Compensation Act, Act of March 4, 1927, c. 509, §§ 18, 21 (44 Stat. 1434, 1436), as amended, U.S.C., Title 33, §§ 918, 921, except to the extent that matters of procedure are provided for in that Act. The provisions for service by publication and for answer in proceedings to cancel certificates of citizenship under the Act of June 27, 1952, c. 477, Title III, c. 2, § 340 (66 Stat. 260), U.S.C., Title 8, § 1451, remain in effect.

(7) Abrogated Apr. 30, 1951, eff. Aug. 1, 1951.

(b) Scire Facias and Mandamus. The writs of scire facias and mandamus are abolished. Relief heretofore available by mandamus or scire facias may be obtained by appropriate action or by appropriate motion under the practice prescribed in these rules.

(c) Removed Actions. These rules apply to civil actions removed to the United States district courts from the state courts and govern procedure after removal. Repleading is not necessary unless the court so orders. In a removed action in which the defendant has not answered, the defendant shall answer or present the other defenses or objections available under these rules within 20 days after the receipt through service or otherwise of a copy of the initial pleading setting forth the claim for relief upon which the action or proceeding is based, or within 20 days after the service of summons upon such initial pleading, then filed, or within 5 days after the filing of the petition for removal, whichever period is longest. If at the time of removal all necessary pleadings have been served, a party entitled to trial by jury under Rule 38 shall be accorded it, if the party's demand therefor is served within 10 days after the petition for removal is filed if the party is the petitioner, or if not the petitioner within 10 days after service on the party of the notice of filing the petition. A party who, prior to removal, has made an express demand for trial by jury in accordance with state law, need not make a demand after removal. If state law applicable in the court from which the case is removed does not require the parties to make express demands in order to claim trial by jury, they need not make demands after removal unless the court directs that they do so within a specified time if they desire to claim trial by jury. The court may make this direction on its own motion and shall do so as a matter of course at the request of any party. The failure of a party to make demand as directed constitutes a waiver by that party of trial by jury.

(d) District of Columbia; Courts and Judges. Abrogated Dec. 29, 1948, eff. Oct. 20, 1949.

(e) Law Applicable. Whenever in these rules the law of the state in which the district court is held is made applicable, the law applied in the District of Columbia governs proceedings in the United States District Court for the District of Columbia. When the word "state" is used, it includes, if appropriate, the District of Columbia. When the term "statute of the United States" is used, it includes, so far as concerns proceedings in the United States District Court for the District of Columbia, any Act of Congress locally applicable to and in force in the District of Columbia. When the law of a state is referred to, the word "law" includes the statutes of that state and the state judicial decisions construing them.

(f) References to Officer of the United States. Under any rule in which reference is made to an officer or agency of the United States, the term "officer" includes a district director of internal revenue, a former district director or collector of internal revenue, or the personal representative of a deceased district director or collector of internal revenue.

As amended 1941, 1948, 1949, 1951, 1963, 1966, 1968, 1971, 1987, 2001, 2002.

Rule 82.

JURISDICTION AND VENUE UNAFFECTED

These rules shall not be construed to extend or limit the jurisdiction of the United States district courts or the venue of actions therein. An admiralty or maritime claim within the meaning of Rule 9(h) shall not be treated as a civil action for the purposes of Title 28, U.S.C. §§ 1391–1392.

As amended 1949, 1966, 2001.

Rule 83.

RULES BY DISTRICT COURTS; JUDGE'S DIRECTIVES

(a) Local Rules.

(1) Each district court, acting by a majority of its district judges, may, after giving appropriate public notice and an opportu-

nity for comment, make and amend rules governing its practice. A local rule shall be consistent with—but not duplicative of—Acts of Congress and rules adopted under 28 U.S.C. §§ 2072 and 2075, and shall conform to any uniform numbering system prescribed by the Judicial Conference of the United States. A local rule takes effect on the date specified by the district court and remains in effect unless amended by the court or abrogated by the judicial council of the circuit. Copies of rules and amendments shall, upon their promulgation, be furnished to the judicial council and the Administrative Office of the United States Courts and be made available to the public.

(2) A local rule imposing a requirement of form shall not be enforced in a manner that causes a party to lose rights because of a nonwillful failure to comply with the requirement.

(b) Procedures When There Is No Controlling Law. A judge may regulate practice in any manner consistent with federal law, rules adopted under 28 U.S.C. §§ 2072 and 2075, and local rules of the district. No sanction or other disadvantage may be imposed for noncompliance with any requirement not in federal law, federal rules, or the local district rules unless the alleged violator has been furnished in the particular case with actual notice of the requirement.

As amended 1985, 1995.

Rule 84.

FORMS

The forms contained in the Appendix of Forms are sufficient under the rules and are intended to indicate the simplicity and brevity of statement which the rules contemplate.

As amended 1948.

Rule 85.

TITLE

These rules may be known and cited as the Federal Rules of Civil Procedure.

Rule 86.

EFFECTIVE DATE

(a) [Effective Date of Original Rules]. These rules will take effect on the day which is 3 months subsequent to the adjournment of the second regular session of the 75th Congress, but if that day is prior to September 1, 1938, then these rules will take effect on September 1, 1938. They govern all proceedings in actions brought after they take effect and also all further proceedings in actions then pending, except to the extent that in the opinion of the court their application in a particular action pending when the rules take effect would not be feasible or would work injustice, in which event the former procedure applies.

[The order of the Supreme Court of December 20, 1937, adopted the rules, to be known as the Federal Rules of Civil Procedure. The Rules became effective on September 16, 1938. 302 U.S. 783, 308 U.S. 645; see 12A Wright, Miller, Kane & Marcus, Federal Practice and Procedure app. C.]

[Rule 81(a) was amended by the order of the Supreme Court of December 28, 1939, to be effective February 3, 1941. 308 U.S. 642; see 1 F.R.D. 79.]

(b) Effective Date of Amendments. The amendments adopted by the Supreme Court on December 27, 1946, and transmitted to the Attorney General on January 2, 1947, shall take effect on the day which is three months subsequent to the adjournment of the first regular session of the 80th Congress, but, if that day is prior to September 1, 1947, then these amendments shall take effect on September 1, 1947. They govern all proceedings in actions brought after they take effect and also all further proceedings in actions then pending, except to the extent that in the opinion of the court their application in a particular action pending when the amendments take effect would not be feasible or would work injustice, in which event the former procedure applies.

[Rules 6(b) and (c), 7(a), 12(a), (b), (c), (d), (e), (f), (g), and (h), 13(a), (g), and (i), 14(a), 17(b), 24(a) and (b), 26, 27(a) and (b), 28(a), 33, 34, 36(a), 41(a) and (b), 45(b) and (d), 52(a), 54(b), 56(a) and (c), 58, 59(b) and (e), 60 (a) and (b), 62(b) and (h), 65(c), 66, 68, 73, 75, 77(d), 79(a), (b), (c), and (d), 80(a) and (b), 81(a), (c), and (f), 84, and 86 and Forms 17, 20, 22, and 25 were amended by the order of the Supreme Court of December 27, 1946, to be effective March 19, 1948. 329 U.S. 839; cf. 5 F.R.D. 433.]

(c) Effective Date of Amendments. The amendments adopted by the Supreme Court on December 29, 1948, and transmitted to the Attorney General on December 31, 1948, shall take effect on the day following the adjournment of the first regular session of the 81st Congress.

[Rules 1, 17(b), 22(2), 24(c), 25(d), 27(a), 37(e), 45(e), 57, 60(b), 62(g), 65(e), 66, 67, 69(b), 72, 73, 74, 75, 76, 79(a), (b), and (d), 81(a), (c), (d), and (e), 82, and 86(c) and Forms 1, 19, 22, 23, and 27 were amended by the order of the Supreme Court of December 29, 1948, to be effective October 20, 1949. 335 U.S. 919; see 8 F.R.D. 591.]

[Rule 81(a) was amended, and Rule 71A and Forms 28 and 29 added, by the order of the Supreme Court of April 30, 1951, to be effective August 1, 1951. 341 U.S. 959; see 11 F.R.D. 213.]

(d) Effective Date of Amendments. The amendments adopted by the Supreme Court on April 17, 1961, and transmitted to the Congress on April 18, 1961, shall take effect on July 19, 1961. They govern all proceedings in actions brought after they take effect and also all further proceedings in actions then pending, except to the extent that in the opinion of the court their application in a particular action pending when the amendments take effect would not be feasible or would work injustice, in which event the former procedure applies.

[Rules 25(d), 54(b), 62(h), and 86(d) and Forms 2 and 19 were amended by the order of the Supreme Court of April 17, 1961, to be effective July 19, 1961. 368 U.S. 1009; see 12A Wright, Miller, Kane & Marcus, Federal Practice and Procedure app. C.]

(e) Effective Date of Amendments. The amendments adopted by the Supreme Court on January 21, 1963, and transmitted to the Congress on January 21, 1963, shall take effect on July 1, 1963. They govern all proceedings in actions brought after they take effect and also all further proceedings in actions then pending, except to the extent that in the opinion of the court their application in a particular action pending when the amendments take effect would not be feasible or would work injustice, in which event the former procedure applies.

[Rules 4(b), (d), (e), (f), and (i), 5(a), 6(a) and (b), 7(a), 12(a), 13(a), 14(a), 15(d), 24(c), 25(a), 26, 28(b), 30(f), 41(b), 49(b), 50(a), (b), (c), and (d), 52(a), 56(c) and (e), 58, 71A(d), 77(c) and (d), 79(a), 81(a), (c), and (f), and 86(e) and Forms 3, 4, 5, 6, 7, 8, 9, 10, 11, 12, 13, 16, 18, and 21 were amended, Form 22 eliminated, and Forms 22–A, 22–B, 30, 31, and 32 added, by the orders of the Supreme Court of January 21, 1963, and March 18, 1963, to be effective July 1, 1963. 374 U.S. 861; see 31 F.R.D. 587.]

As amended 1948, 1949, 1961, 1963.

[Rules 1, 4(f), 6(c), 8(e), 9(h), 12(b), (g), and (h), 13(h), 14(a) and (c), 15(c), 17(a), 18(a), 19, 20(a), 23, 24(a), 26, 38(e), 41(b), 42(b), 43(f), 44(a), (b), and (c), 47(b), 53(a) and (b), 59(d), 65(a), (b), and (c), 68, 73, 74, 75, 81(a), and 82 and Forms 2 and 15 were amended, and Rules 23.1, 23.2, 44.1, and 65.1 and Supplemental Rules A–F added, by the order of the Supreme Court of February 28, 1966, to be effective July 1, 1966. 383 U.S. 1029; see 39 F.R.D. 69.]

[Rules 6(b), 9(h), 41(a), 77(d), and 81(a) were amended, and former Rules 72–76 and Form 27 abrogated, by the order of the Supreme Court of December 4, 1967, to be effective July 1, 1968. 389 U.S. 1121; see 43 F.R.D. 163.]

[Rules 5(a), 9(h), 26, 29, 30, 31, 32, 33, 34, 35, 36, 37, 45(d), and 69(a) and Form 24 were amended by the order of the Supreme Court of March 30, 1970, to be effective July 1, 1970. 398 U.S. 977; see 48 F.R.D. 485.]

[Rules 6(a), 27(a), 30(b), 77(c), and 81(a) were amended by the order of the Supreme Court of March 1, 1971, to be effective July 1, 1971. 401 U.S. 1017; see 52 F.R.D. 79.]

[Rules 30(c), 32(c), 43(a), (b), and (c), and 44.1 were amended by the orders of the Supreme Court of November 20, 1972, and December 18, 1972. 419 U.S. 1133; see 56 F.R.D. 355. Those amendments were expressly approved by Congress January 2, 1975, Pub.L. 93–595, § 3, 88 Stat. 1949, to be effective July 1, 1975.]

[Rules 4(a) and (c), 5(d), 26(f), 28(a), 30(b) and (f), 32(a), 33(c), 34(b), 37(b), (e), and (g), and 45(d) and (e) were amended by the order of the Supreme Court of April 29, 1980, to be effective August 1, 1980. 446 U.S. 995; see 85 F.R.D. 521.]

[Rule 37(f) was repealed October 21, 1980, Pub.L. 96–481, Title II, § 205(a), 94 Stat. 2330, to be effective October 1, 1981.]

[Rule 4(a), (c), (d), (e), (g), and (j) was amended by the order of the Supreme Court of April 28, 1982, to be effective August 1, 1982. 456 U.S. 1013; see 93 F.R.D. 255. That amendment was suspended by Congress August 2, 1982, Pub.L. 97–227, 96 Stat. 246, effective August 1, 1982. See 94 F.R.D. 221. Rule 4(a), (c), (d), (e), (g), and (j) was then amended, and Form 18–A added, January 12, 1983, Pub.L. 97–462, 96 Stat. 2527, to be effective February 26, 1983. See 96 F.R.D. 75.]

[Rules 6(b), 7(b), 11, 16, 26(a), (b), and (g), 52(a), 53(a), (b), (c), and (f), and 67 were amended, and Rules 72–76 and Forms 33 and 34 added, by the order of the Supreme Court of April 28, 1983, to be effective August 1, 1983. 461 U.S. 1095; see 97 F.R.D. 165.]

[Rules 6(a), 45(d), 52(a), 71A(h), and 83, Form 18–A, and Supplemental Rules B(1), C(3), and E(4) were amended by the order of the Supreme Court of April 29, 1985, to be effective August 1, 1985. 471 U.S. 1153; see 105 F.R.D. 202.]

[Rules 51 and 77(c) were amended, and gender-specific language was neutralized in numerous Rules and Supplemental Rules, by the order of the Supreme Court of March 2, 1987, to be effective August 1, 1987. 480 U.S. 953; see 113 F.R.D. 189.]

[Technical corrections to Rules 17(a) and 71A(e) were made by the order of the Supreme Court of April 25, 1988, to be effective August 1, 1988. 485 U.S. 1043; see 119 F.R.D. 261.]

[Rule 35 was amended November 18, 1988, Pub.L. 100–690, Title VII, § 7047, 102 Stat. 4401. See 122 F.R.D. 276.]

[Rules 5(d) and (e), 15(c), 24(c), 34(c), 35, 41(b), 44(a), 45, 47(b) and (c), 48, 50, 52(a) and (c), 53(e), 63, 72(a), and 77(d) and Supplemental Rules C(3) and (5) and E(4), (5), and (9) were amended by the order of the Supreme Court of April 30, 1991, to be effective December 1, 1991. 500 U.S. 963; see 134 F.R.D. 525. A technical correction to Rule 15(c) was made December 9, 1991, Pub.L. 102–198, § 11(a), 105 Stat. 1626.]

[Rules 1, 4, 5(e), 11, 12(a), 15(c), 16(b) and (c), 26, 28(b), 29, 30(a), (b), (c), (d), (e), and (f), 31(a), 32(a) and (c), 33, 34(b), 36(a), 37(a), (c), (d), and (g), 38(b) and (d), 50(a), 52(c), 53(a), (b), and (f), 54(d), 58, 71A(d), 72, 73, 74(a) and (c), 75(b), and 76(a) and (c) and Forms 2, 33, and 34 were amended, Form 18–A abrogated, and Rule 4.1 and Forms 1A, 1B, 34A, and

35 added, by the order of the Supreme Court of April 22, 1993, to be effective December 1, 1993. 507 U.S. 1089; see 146 F.R.D. 401.]

[Rules 50(b) and (c), 52(b), 59(b), (c), (d), and (e), and 83 were amended by the order of the Supreme Court of April 27, 1995, to be effective December 1, 1995. 514 U.S. 1151; see 161 F.R.D. 149.]

[Rules 5(e) and 43(a) were amended by the order of the Supreme Court of April 23, 1996, to be effective December 1, 1996. 517 U.S. 1279; see 167 F.R.D. 209.]

[Rules 9(h) and 73(a), (c), and (d) and Forms 33 and 34 were amended, and Rules 74–76 abrogated, by the order of the Supreme Court of April 11, 1997, to be effective December 1, 1997. 520 U.S. 1305; see 171 F.R.D. 679.]

[Rule 23(f) was added by the order of the Supreme Court of April 24, 1998, to be effective December 1, 1998. 523 U.S. 1221; see 12A Wright, Miller, Kane & Marcus, Federal Practice and Procedure app. C.]

[Rule 6(b) and Form 2 were amended by the order of the Supreme Court of April 26, 1999, to be effective December 1, 1999. 526 U.S. 1183; see 185 F.R.D. 27.]

[Rules 4(i), 5(d), 12(a), 14(a) and (c), 26(a), (b), (d), and (f), 30(d) and (f), and 37(c) and Supplemental Rules B, C, and E were amended by the order of the Supreme Court of April 17, 2000, to be effective December 1, 2000. 529 U.S. 1155; see 192 F.R.D. 340.]

[Rules 5(b), 6(e), 65(f), 77(d), 81(a), and 82 were amended by the order of the Supreme Court of April 23, 2001, to be effective December 1, 2001. 532 U.S. 1085; see 200 F.R.D. 52.]

[Rules 54(d), 58, and 81(a) and Supplemental Rule C(3) and (6) were amended, and Rule 7.1 added, by the order of the Supreme Court of April 29, 2002, to be effective December 1, 2002. 535 U.S. 1147; see 207 F.R.D. 50.]

[Rules 23(c), (e), (g), and (h), 51, and 53 were amended, with technical changes to Rules 54(d) and 71A(h) and Forms 19, 31, and 32, by the order of the Supreme Court of March 27, 2003, to be effective December 1, 2003. ___ U.S. ___; see ___ F.R.D. ___.]

APPENDIX OF FORMS

(See Rule 84)

Introductory Statement [1938]

1. The following forms are intended for illustration only. They are limited in number. No attempt is made to furnish a manual of forms. Each form assumes the action to be brought in the Southern District of New York. If the district in which an action is brought has divisions, the division should be indicated in the caption.

2. Except where otherwise indicated each pleading, motion, and other paper should have a caption similar to that of the summons, with the designation of the particular paper substituted for the word "Summons". In the caption of the summons and in the caption of the complaint all parties must be named but in other pleadings and papers, it is sufficient to state the name of the first party on either side, with an appropriate indication of other parties. See Rules 4(b), 7(b)(2), and 10(a).

3. In Form 3 and the forms following, the words, "Allegation of jurisdiction", are used to indicate the appropriate allegation in Form 2.

4. Each pleading, motion, and other paper is to be signed in his individual name by at least one attorney of record (Rule 11). The attorney's name is to be followed by his address as indicated in Form 3. In forms following Form 3 the signature and address are not indicated.

5. If a party is not represented by an attorney, the signature and address of the party are required in place of those of the attorney.

Form 1.

SUMMONS

UNITED STATES DISTRICT COURT FOR THE
SOUTHERN DISTRICT OF NEW YORK

Civil Action, File Number ______

A. B., Plaintiff)
v.) *Summons*
C. D., Defendant)

To the above-named Defendant:

You are hereby summoned and required to serve upon _______, plaintiff's attorney, whose address is ___________________, an answer to the complaint which is herewith served upon you, within 20 [1] days after service of this summons upon you, exclusive of the day of service. If you fail to do so, judgment by default will be taken against you for the relief demanded in the complaint.

______________________________,
Clerk of Court.

[Seal of the U. S. District Court]

Dated ___________________

(This summons is issued pursuant to Rule 4 of the Federal Rules of Civil Procedure).

As amended 1949.

Form 1A.

NOTICE OF LAWSUIT AND REQUEST FOR WAIVER OF SERVICE OF SUMMONS

TO: ______________(A)______________
[as _______(B)_______ of _______(C)_______]

A lawsuit has been commenced against you (or the entity on whose behalf you are addressed). A copy of the complaint is attached to this notice. It has been filed in the United States District Court for the ____(D)____ and has been assigned docket number ____(E)____.

This is not a formal summons or notification from the court, but rather my request that you sign and return the enclosed waiver of service in order to save the cost of serving you with a judicial summons and an additional copy of the complaint. The cost of service will be avoided if I receive a signed copy of the waiver within ____(F)____ days after the date designated below as the date on which this Notice and Request is sent. I enclose a stamped and addressed envelope (or other means of cost-free return) for your use. An extra copy of the waiver is also attached for your records.

If you comply with this request and return the signed waiver, it will be filed with the court and no summons will be served on you.

[1] If the United States or an officer or agency thereof is a defendant, the time to be inserted as to it is 60 days.

The action will then proceed as if you had been served on the date the waiver is filed, except that you will not be obligated to answer the complaint before 60 days from the date designated below as the date on which this notice is sent (or before 90 days from that date if your address is not in any judicial district of the United States).

If you do not return the signed waiver within the time indicated, I will take appropriate steps to effect formal service in a manner authorized by the Federal Rules of Civil Procedure and will then, to the extent authorized by those Rules, ask the court to require you (or the party on whose behalf you are addressed) to pay the full costs of such service. In that connection, please read the statement concerning the duty of parties to waive the service of the summons, which is set forth on the reverse side (or at the foot) of the waiver form.

I affirm that this request is being sent to you on behalf of the plaintiff, this __ day of ______, ___.

____

Signature of Plaintiff's Attorney or Unrepresented Plaintiff

Added 1993.

Note

A—Name of individual defendant (or name of officer or agent of corporate defendant)

B—Title, or other relationship of individual to corporate defendant

C—Name of corporate defendant, if any

D—District

E—Docket number of action

F—Addressee must be given at least 30 days (60 days if located in foreign country) in which to return waiver

Form 1B.

WAIVER OF SERVICE OF SUMMONS

TO: (name of plaintiff's attorney or unrepresented plaintiff)

I acknowledge receipt of your request that I waive service of a summons in the action of (caption of action), which is case number (docket number) in the United States District Court for the (district). I have also received a copy of the complaint in the action, two copies of this instrument, and a means by which I can return the signed waiver to you without cost to me.

I agree to save the cost of service of a summons and an additional copy of the complaint in this lawsuit by not requiring that I (or the entity on whose behalf I am acting) be served with judicial process in the manner provided by Rule 4.

I (or the entity on whose behalf I am acting) will retain all defenses or objections to the lawsuit or to the jurisdiction or venue of the court except for objections based on a defect in the summons or in the service of the summons.

I understand that a judgment may be entered against me (or the party on whose behalf I am acting) if an answer or motion under Rule 12 is not served upon you within 60 days after (date request was sent), or within 90 days after that date if the request was sent outside the United States.

____________________ ____________________

Date *Signature*

Printed/typed name: ________

[as ________________]

[of ________________]

To be printed on reverse side of the waiver form or set forth at the foot of the form:

Duty to Avoid Unnecessary Costs of Service of Summons

Rule 4 of the Federal Rules of Civil Procedure requires certain parties to cooperate in saving unnecessary costs of service of the summons and complaint. A defendant located in the United States who, after being notified of an action and asked by a plaintiff located in the United States to waive service of a summons, fails to do so will be required to bear the cost of such service unless good cause be shown for its failure to sign and return the waiver.

It is not good cause for a failure to waive service that a party believes that the complaint is unfounded, or that the action has been brought in an improper place or in a court that lacks jurisdiction over the subject matter of the action or over its person or property. A party who waives service of the summons retains all defenses and objections (except any relating to the summons or to the service of the summons), and may later object to the jurisdiction of the court or to the place where the action has been brought.

A defendant who waives service must within the time specified on the waiver form serve on the plaintiff's attorney (or unrepresented plaintiff) a response to the complaint and must also file a signed copy of the response with the court. If the answer or motion is not served within this time, a default judgment may be taken against that defendant. By waiving service, a defendant is allowed more time to answer than if the summons had been actually served when the request for waiver of service was received.

Added 1993.

Form 2.

ALLEGATION OF JURISDICTION

(a) Jurisdiction founded on diversity of citizenship and amount.

Plaintiff is a [citizen of the State of Connecticut] [2] [corporation incorporated under the laws of the State of Connecticut having its principal place of business in the State of Connecticut] and defendant is a corporation incorporated under the laws of the State of New York having its principal place of business in a State other than the State of Connecticut. The matter in controversy exceeds, exclusive of interest and costs, the sum specified by 28 U.S.C. § 1332.

(b) Jurisdiction founded on the existence of a Federal question.

The action arises under [the Constitution of the United States, Article ___, Section ___]; [the ___ Amendment to the Constitution of the United States, Section ___]; [the Act of ___, ___ Stat. ___; U.S.C., Title ___, § ___]; [the Treaty of the United States (here describe the treaty)][3] as hereinafter more fully appears.

(c) Jurisdiction founded on the existence of a question arising under particular statutes.

The action arises under the Act of ___, ___ Stat. ___; U.S.C., Title ___, § ___, as hereinafter more fully appears.

(d) Jurisdiction founded on the admiralty or maritime character of the claim.

This is a case of admiralty and maritime jurisdiction, as hereinafter more fully appears. [If the pleader wishes to invoke the distinctively maritime procedures referred to in Rule 9(h), add the following or its substantial equivalent: This is an admiralty or maritime claim within the meaning of Rule 9(h).]

As amended 1961, 1966, 1993, 1999.

Note

1. Diversity of Citizenship. U.S.C., Title 28, § 1332 (Diversity of citizenship; amount in controversy; costs), as amended by PL 85–554, 72 Stat. 415, July 25, 1958, states in subsection (c) that "For the purposes of this section and section 1441 of this title [removable actions], a corporation shall be deemed a citizen of any State by which it has been incorporated and of the State where it has its principal place of business." Thus if the defendant corporation in Form 2(a) had its principal place of business in Connecticut, diversi-

[2] Form for natural person.

[3] Use the appropriate phrase or phrases. The general allegation of the existence of a Federal question is ineffective unless the matters constituting the claim for relief as set forth in the complaint raise a Federal question.

ty of citizenship would not exist. An allegation regarding the principal place of business of each corporate party must be made in addition to an allegation regarding its place of incorporation.

2. **Jurisdictional Amount.** U.S.C., Title 28, § 1331 (Federal question; amount in controversy; costs) and § 1332 (Diversity of citizenship; amount in controversy; costs), as amended by PL 85–554, 72 Stat. 415, July 25, 1958, require that the amount in controversy, exclusive of interest and costs, be in excess of $10,000. The allegation as to the amount in controversy may be omitted in any case where by law no jurisdictional amount is required. See, for example, U.S.C., Title 28, § 1338 (Patents, copyrights, trademarks, and unfair competition), § 1343 (Civil rights and elective franchise).

3. **Pleading Venue.** Since improper venue is a matter of defense, it is not necessary for plaintiff to include allegations showing the venue to be proper. See 1 Moore's Federal Practice, par. 0.140[1.–4.] (2d ed. 1959).

Form 3.

COMPLAINT ON A PROMISSORY NOTE

1. Allegation of jurisdiction.

2. Defendant on or about June 1, 1935, executed and delivered to plaintiff a promissory note [in the following words and figures: (here set out the note verbatim)]; [a copy of which is hereto annexed as Exhibit A]; [whereby defendant promised to pay to plaintiff or order on June 1, 1936 the sum of ______ dollars with interest thereon at the rate of six percent per annum].

3. Defendant owes to plaintiff the amount of said note and interest.

Wherefore plaintiff demands judgment against defendant for the sum of ______ dollars, interest, and costs.

Signed: ____________________
Attorney for Plaintiff.
Address: ____________________

As amended 1963.

Note

1. The pleader may use the material in one of the three sets of brackets. His choice will depend upon whether he desires to plead the document verbatim, or by exhibit, or according to its legal effect.

2. Under the rules free joinder of claims is permitted. See rules 8(e) and 18. Consequently the claims set forth in each and all of the following forms may be joined with this complaint or with each other. Ordinarily each claim should be stated in a separate division of the complaint, and the divisions should be designated as counts successively numbered. In particular the rules permit alternative and inconsistent pleading. See Form 10.

Form 4.

COMPLAINT ON AN ACCOUNT

1. Allegation of jurisdiction.

2. Defendant owes plaintiff ______ dollars according to the account hereto annexed as Exhibit A.

Wherefore (etc. as in Form 3).

As amended 1963.

Form 5.

COMPLAINT FOR GOODS SOLD AND DELIVERED

1. Allegation of jurisdiction.

2. Defendant owes plaintiff ______ dollars for goods sold and delivered by plaintiff to defendant between June 1, 1936 and December 1, 1936.

Wherefore (etc. as in Form 3).

As amended 1963.

Note

This form may be used where the action is for an agreed price or for the reasonable value of the goods.

Form 6.

COMPLAINT FOR MONEY LENT

1. Allegation of jurisdiction.

2. Defendant owes plaintiff ______ dollars for money lent by plaintiff to defendant on June 1, 1936.

Wherefore (etc. as in Form 3).

As amended 1963.

Form 7.

COMPLAINT FOR MONEY PAID BY MISTAKE

1. Allegation of jurisdiction.

2. Defendant owes plaintiff ______ dollars for money paid by plaintiff to defendant by mistake on June 1, 1936, under the following circumstances: [here state the circumstances with particularity—see Rule 9(b)].

Wherefore (etc. as in Form 3).

As amended 1963.

Form 8.

COMPLAINT FOR MONEY HAD AND RECEIVED

1. Allegation of jurisdiction.

2. Defendant owes plaintiff ______ dollars for money had and received from one G. H. on June 1, 1936, to be paid by defendant to plaintiff.

Wherefore (etc. as in Form 3).

As amended 1963.

Form 9.

COMPLAINT FOR NEGLIGENCE

1. Allegation of jurisdiction.

2. On June 1, 1936, in a public highway called Boylston Street in Boston, Massachusetts, defendant negligently drove a motor vehicle against plaintiff who was then crossing said highway.

3. As a result plaintiff was thrown down and had his leg broken and was otherwise injured, was prevented from transacting his business, suffered great pain of body and mind, and incurred expenses for medical attention and hospitalization in the sum of one thousand dollars.

Wherefore plaintiff demands judgment against defendant in the sum of ______ dollars and costs.

As amended 1963.

Note

Since contributory negligence is an affirmative defense, the complaint need contain no allegation of due care of plaintiff.

Form 10.

COMPLAINT FOR NEGLIGENCE WHERE PLAINTIFF IS UNABLE TO DETERMINE DEFINITELY WHETHER THE PERSON RESPONSIBLE IS C. D. OR E. F. OR WHETHER BOTH ARE RESPONSIBLE AND WHERE HIS EVIDENCE MAY JUSTIFY A FINDING OF WILFULNESS OR OF RECKLESSNESS OR OF NEGLIGENCE

A. B., Plaintiff)
v.) *Complaint*
C. D. and E. F., Defendants)

1. Allegation of jurisdiction.

2. On June 1, 1936, in a public highway called Boylston Street in Boston, Massachusetts, defendant C. D. or defendant E. F., or both defendants C. D. and E. F. wilfully or recklessly or negligently drove or caused to be driven a motor vehicle against plaintiff who was then crossing said highway.

3. As a result plaintiff was thrown down and had his leg broken and was otherwise injured, was prevented from transacting his business, suffered great pain of body and mind, and incurred expenses for medical attention and hospitalization in the sum of one thousand dollars.

Wherefore plaintiff demands judgment against C. D. or against E. F. or against both in the sum of ______ dollars and costs.

As amended 1963.

Form 11.

COMPLAINT FOR CONVERSION

1. Allegation of jurisdiction.

2. On or about December 1, 1936, defendant converted to his own use ten bonds of the ______ Company (here insert brief identification as by number and issue) of the value of ______ dollars, the property of plaintiff.

Wherefore plaintiff demands judgment against defendant in the sum of ______ dollars, interest, and costs.

As amended 1963.

Form 12.

COMPLAINT FOR SPECIFIC PERFORMANCE OF CONTRACT TO CONVEY LAND

1. Allegation of jurisdiction.

2. On or about December 1, 1936, plaintiff and defendant entered into an agreement in writing a copy of which is hereto annexed as Exhibit A.

3. In accord with the provisions of said agreement plaintiff tendered to defendant the purchase price and requested a conveyance of the land, but defendant refused to accept the tender and refused to make the conveyance.

4. Plaintiff now offers to pay the purchase price.

Wherefore plaintiff demands (1) that defendant be required specifically to perform said agreement, (2) damages in the sum of one thousand dollars, and (3) that if specific performance is not granted plaintiff have judgment against defendant in the sum of ______ dollars.

As amended 1963.

Note

Here, as in Form 3, plaintiff may set forth the contract verbatim in the complaint or plead it, as indicated, by exhibit, or plead it according to its legal effect. Furthermore, plaintiff may seek legal or equitable relief or both even though this was impossible under the system in operation before these rules.

Form 13.

COMPLAINT ON CLAIM FOR DEBT AND TO SET ASIDE FRAUDULENT CONVEYANCE UNDER RULE 18(b)

A. B., Plaintiff)
v.) *Complaint*
C. D. and E. F., Defendants)

1. Allegation of jurisdiction.

2. Defendant C. D. on or about ______ executed and delivered to plaintiff a promissory note [in the following words and figures: (here set out the note verbatim)]; [a copy of which is hereto annexed as Exhibit A]; [whereby defendant C. D. promised to pay to plaintiff or order on ______ the sum of five thousand dollars with interest thereon at the rate of __ percent. per annum].

3. Defendant C. D. owes to plaintiff the amount of said note and interest.

4. Defendant C. D. on or about _______ conveyed all his property, real and personal [or specify and describe] to defendant E. F. for the purpose of defrauding plaintiff and hindering and delaying the collection of the indebtedness evidenced by the note above referred to.

Wherefore plaintiff demands:

(1) That plaintiff have judgment against defendant C. D. for _______ dollars and interest; (2) that the aforesaid conveyance to defendant E. F. be declared void and the judgment herein be declared a lien on said property; (3) that plaintiff have judgment against the defendants for costs.

As amended 1963.

Form 14.

COMPLAINT FOR NEGLIGENCE UNDER FEDERAL EMPLOYERS' LIABILITY ACT

1. Allegation of jurisdiction.

2. During all the times herein mentioned defendant owned and operated in interstate commerce a railroad which passed through a tunnel located at _______ and known as Tunnel No. _______.

3. On or about June 1, 1936, defendant was repairing and enlarging the tunnel in order to protect interstate trains and passengers and freight from injury and in order to make the tunnel more conveniently usable for interstate commerce.

4. In the course of thus repairing and enlarging the tunnel on said day defendant employed plaintiff as one of its workmen, and negligently put plaintiff to work in a portion of the tunnel which defendant had left unprotected and unsupported.

5. By reason of defendant's negligence in thus putting plaintiff to work in that portion of the tunnel, plaintiff was, while so working pursuant to defendant's orders, struck and crushed by a rock, which fell from the unsupported portion of the tunnel, and was (here describe plaintiff's injuries).

6. Prior to these injuries, plaintiff was a strong, able-bodied man, capable of earning and actually earning _______ dollars per day. By these injuries he has been made incapable of any gainful activity, has suffered great physical and mental pain, and has incurred expense in the amount of _______ dollars for medicine, medical attendance, and hospitalization.

Wherefore plaintiff demands judgment against defendant in the sum of _______ dollars and costs.

Form 15.

COMPLAINT FOR DAMAGES UNDER MERCHANT MARINE ACT

1. Allegation of jurisdiction. [If the pleader wishes to invoke the distinctively maritime procedures referred to in Rule 9(h), add the following or its substantial equivalent: This is an admiralty or maritime claim within the meaning of Rule 9(h).]

2. During all the times herein mentioned defendant was the owner of the steamship ______ and used it in the transportation of freight for hire by water in interstate and foreign commerce.

3. During the first part of (month and year) at ______ plaintiff entered the employ of defendant as an able seaman on said steamship under seamen's articles of customary form for a voyage from ______ ports to the Orient and return at a wage of ______ dollars per month and found, which is equal to a wage of ______ dollars per month as a shore worker.

4. On June 1, 1936, said steamship was about ______ days out of the port of ______ and was being navigated by the master and crew on the return voyage to ______ ports. (Here describe weather conditions and the condition of the ship and state as in an ordinary complaint for personal injuries the negligent conduct of defendant.)

5. By reason of defendant's negligence in thus (brief statement of defendant's negligent conduct) and the unseaworthiness of said steamship, plaintiff was (here describe plaintiff's injuries).

6. Prior to these injuries, plaintiff was a strong, able-bodied man, capable of earning and actually earning ______ dollars per day. By these injuries he has been made incapable of any gainful activity; has suffered great physical and mental pain, and has incurred expense in the amount of ______ dollars for medicine, medical attendance, and hospitalization.

Wherefore plaintiff demands judgment against defendant in the sum of ______ dollars and costs.

As amended 1966.

Form 16.

COMPLAINT FOR INFRINGEMENT OF PATENT

1. Allegation of jurisdiction.

2. On May 16, 1934, United States Letters Patent No. ______ were duly and legally issued to plaintiff for an invention in an electric motor; and since that date plaintiff has been and still is the owner of those Letters Patent.

3. Defendant has for a long time past been and still is infringing those Letters Patent by making, selling, and using electric motors embodying the patented invention, and will continue to do so unless enjoined by this court.

4. Plaintiff has placed the required statutory notice on all electric motors manufactured and sold by him under said Letters Patent, and has given written notice to defendant of his said infringement.

Wherefore plaintiff demands a preliminary and final injunction against continued infringement, an accounting for damages, and an assessment of interest and costs against defendant.

As amended 1963.

Form 17.

COMPLAINT FOR INFRINGEMENT OF COPYRIGHT AND UNFAIR COMPETITION

1. Allegation of jurisdiction.

2. Prior to March, 1936, plaintiff, who then was and ever since has been a citizen of the United States, created and wrote an original book, entitled ______.

3. This book contains a large amount of material wholly original with plaintiff and is copyrightable subject matter under the laws of the United States.

4. Between March 2, 1936, and March 10, 1936, plaintiff complied in all respects with the Act of (give citation) and all other laws governing copyright, and secured the exclusive rights and privileges in and to the copyright of said book, and received from the Register of Copyrights a certificate of registration, dated and identified as follows: "March 10, 1936, Class ______, No. ______."

5. Since March 10, 1936, said book has been published by plaintiff and all copies of it made by plaintiff or under his authority or license have been printed, bound, and published in strict conformity with the provisions of the Act of ______ and all other laws governing copyright.

6. Since March 10, 1936, plaintiff has been and still is the sole proprietor of all rights, title, and interest in and to the copyright in said book.

7. After March 10, 1936, defendant infringed said copyright by publishing and placing upon the market a book entitled ______, which was copied largely from plaintiff's copyrighted book, entitled ______.

8. A copy of plaintiff's copyrighted book is hereto attached as "Exhibit 1"; and a copy of defendant's infringing book is hereto attached as "Exhibit 2."

9. Plaintiff has notified defendant that defendant has infringed the copyright of plaintiff, and defendant has continued to infringe the copyright.

10. After March 10, 1936, and continuously since about _______, defendant has been publishing, selling and otherwise marketing the book entitled _______, and has thereby been engaging in unfair trade practices and unfair competition against plaintiff to plaintiff's irreparable damage.

Wherefore plaintiff demands:

(1) That defendant, his agents, and servants be enjoined during the pendency of this action and permanently from infringing said copyright of said plaintiff in any manner, and from publishing, selling, marketing or otherwise disposing of any copies of the book entitled _______.

(2) That defendant be required to pay to plaintiff such damages as plaintiff has sustained in consequence of defendant's infringement of said copyright and said unfair trade practices and unfair competition and to account for

(a) all gains, profits and advantages derived by defendant by said trade practices and unfair competition and

(b) all gains, profits, and advantages derived by defendant by his infringement of plaintiff's copyright or such damages as to the court shall appear proper within the provisions of the copyright statutes, but not less than two hundred and fifty dollars.

(3) That defendant be required to deliver up to be impounded during the pendency of this action all copies of said book entitled _______ in his possession or under his control and to deliver up for destruction all infringing copies and all plates, molds, and other matter for making such infringing copies.

(4) That defendant pay to plaintiff the costs of this action and reasonable attorney's fees to be allowed to the plaintiff by the court.

(5) That plaintiff have such other and further relief as is just.

As amended 1948.

Form 18.

COMPLAINT FOR INTERPLEADER AND DECLARATORY RELIEF

1. Allegation of jurisdiction.

2. On or about June 1, 1935, plaintiff issued to G. H. a policy of life insurance whereby plaintiff promised to pay to K. L. as beneficiary the sum of ______ dollars upon the death of G. H. The policy required the payment by G. H. of a stipulated premium on June 1, 1936, and annually thereafter as a condition precedent to its continuance in force.

3. No part of the premium due June 1, 1936, was ever paid and the policy ceased to have any force or effect on July 1, 1936.

4. Thereafter, on September 1, 1936, G. H. and K. L. died as the result of a collision between a locomotive and the automobile in which G. H. and K. L. were riding.

5. Defendant C. D. is the duly appointed and acting executor of the will of G. H.; defendant E. F. is the duly appointed and acting executor of the will of K. L.; defendant X. Y. claims to have been duly designated as beneficiary of said policy in place of K. L.

6. Each of defendants, C. D., E. F., and X. Y. is claiming that the above-mentioned policy was in full force and effect at the time of the death of G. H.; each of them is claiming to be the only person entitled to receive payment of the amount of the policy and has made demand for payment thereof.

7. By reason of these conflicting claims of the defendants, plaintiff is in great doubt as to which defendant is entitled to be paid the amount of the policy, if it was in force at the death of G. H.

Wherefore plaintiff demands that the court adjudge:

(1) That none of the defendants is entitled to recover from plaintiff the amount of said policy or any part thereof.

(2) That each of the defendants be restrained from instituting any action against plaintiff for the recovery of the amount of said policy or any part thereof.

(3) That, if the court shall determine that said policy was in force at the death of G. H., the defendants be required to interplead and settle between themselves their rights to the money due under said policy, and that plaintiff be discharged from all liability in the premises except to the person whom the court shall adjudge entitled to the amount of said policy.

(4) That plaintiff recover its costs.

As amended 1963.

Form 18–A.

NOTICE AND ACKNOWLEDGMENT FOR SERVICE BY MAIL

Abrogated 1993

Form 19.

MOTION TO DISMISS, PRESENTING DEFENSES OF FAILURE TO STATE A CLAIM, OF LACK OF SERVICE OF PROCESS, OF IMPROPER VENUE, AND OF LACK OF JURISDICTION UNDER RULE 12(b)

The defendant moves the court as follows:

1. To dismiss the action because the complaint fails to state a claim against defendant upon which relief can be granted.

2. To dismiss the action or in lieu thereof to quash the return of service of summons on the grounds (a) that the defendant is a corporation organized under the laws of Delaware and was not and is not subject to service of process within the Southern District of New York, and (b) that the defendant has not been properly served with process in this action, all of which more clearly appears in the affidavits of M. N. and X. Y. hereto annexed as Exhibit A and Exhibit B, respectively.

3. To dismiss the action on the ground that it is in the wrong district because (a) the jurisdiction of this court is invoked solely on the ground that the action arises under the Constitution and laws of the United States and (b) the defendant is a corporation incorporated under the laws of the State of Delaware and is not licensed to do or doing business in the Southern District of New York, all of which more clearly appears in the affidavits of K. L. and V. W. hereto annexed as Exhibits C and D, respectively.

4. To dismiss the action on the ground that the court lacks jurisdiction because the amount actually in controversy is less than ten thousand dollars exclusive of interest and costs.

Signed: ____________________
Attorney for Defendant.
Address: ____________________

Notice of Motion

To:____________________
Attorney for Plaintiff.

____

Please take notice, that the undersigned will bring the above motion on for hearing before this Court at Room ______, United States Court House, Foley Square, City of New York, on the ______ day of ______, 20__, at 10 o'clock in the forenoon of that day or as soon thereafter as counsel can be heard.

Signed: ______________________
Attorney for Defendant.
Address: ______________________

As amended 1949, 1961, 2003.

Note

1. The above motion and notice of motion may be combined and denominated Notice of Motion. See Rule 7(b).

2. As to paragraph 3, see U.S.C., Title 28, § 1391 (Venue generally), subsections (b) and (c).

3. As to paragraph 4, see U.S.C., Title 28, § 1331 (Federal question; amount in controversy; costs), as amended by P.L. 85–554, 72 Stat. 415, July 25, 1958, requiring that the amount in controversy, exclusive of interest and costs, be in excess of $10,000.

Form 20.

ANSWER PRESENTING DEFENSES UNDER RULE 12(b)

First Defense

The complaint fails to state a claim against defendant upon which relief can be granted.

Second Defense

If defendant is indebted to plaintiffs for the goods mentioned in the complaint, he is indebted to them jointly with G. H. G. H. is alive; is a citizen of the State of New York and a resident of this district, is subject to the jurisdiction of this court, as to both service of process and venue; can be made a party without depriving this court of jurisdiction of the present parties, and has not been made a party.

Third Defense

Defendant admits the allegation contained in paragraphs 1 and 4 of the complaint; alleges that he is without knowledge or information sufficient to form a belief as to the truth of the allegations contained in paragraph 2 of the complaint; and denies each and every other allegation contained in the complaint.

Fourth Defense

The right of action set forth in the complaint did not accrue within six years next before the commencement of this action.

Counterclaim

(Here set forth any claim as a counterclaim in the manner in which a claim is pleaded in a complaint. No statement of the grounds on which the court's jurisdiction depends need be made unless the counterclaim requires independent grounds of jurisdiction.)

Cross-Claim Against Defendant M. N.

(Here set forth the claim constituting a cross-claim against defendant M. N. in the manner in which a claim is pleaded in a complaint. The statement of grounds upon which the court's jurisdiction depends need not be made unless the cross-claim requires independent grounds of jurisdiction.)

As amended 1948.

Note

The above form contains examples of certain defenses provided for in Rule 12(b). The first defense challenges the legal sufficiency of the complaint. It is a substitute for a general demurrer or a motion to dismiss.

The second defense embodies the old plea in abatement; the decision thereon, however, may well provide under Rules 19 and 21 for the citing in of the party rather than an abatement of the action.

The third defense is an answer on the merits.

The fourth defense is one of the affirmative defenses provided for in Rule 8(c).

The answer also includes a counterclaim and a cross-claim.

Form 21.

ANSWER TO COMPLAINT SET FORTH IN FORM 8, WITH COUNTERCLAIM FOR INTERPLEADER

Defense

Defendant admits the allegations stated in paragraph 1 of the complaint; and denies the allegations stated in paragraph 2 to the extent set forth in the counterclaim herein.

Counterclaim for Interpleader

1. Defendant received the sum of ______ dollars as a deposit from E. F.

2. Plaintiff has demanded the payment of such deposit to him by virtue of an assignment of it which he claims to have received from E. F.

3. E. F. has notified the defendant that he claims such deposit, that the purported assignment is not valid, and that he holds the defendant responsible for the deposit.

Wherefore defendant demands:

(1) That the court order E. F. to be made a party defendant to respond to the complaint and to this counterclaim.[4]

(2) That the court order the plaintiff and E. F. to interplead their respective claims.

(3) That the court adjudge whether the plaintiff or E. F. is entitled to the sum of money.

(4) That the court discharge defendant from all liability in the premises except to the person it shall adjudge entitled to the sum of money.

(5) That the court award to the defendant its costs and attorney's fees.

As amended 1963.

Form 22.

MOTION TO BRING IN THIRD–PARTY DEFENDANT

Eliminated 1963

Form 22–A.

SUMMONS AND COMPLAINT AGAINST THIRD–PARTY DEFENDANT

UNITED STATES DISTRICT COURT FOR THE SOUTHERN DISTRICT OF NEW YORK

Civil Action, File Number ______

A. B., Plaintiff	)	
v.	)	
C. D., Defendant and	)	
Third-Party Plaintiff	)	Summons
v.	)	
E. F., Third-Party	)	
Defendant	)	

To the above-named Third-Party Defendant:

You are hereby summoned and required to serve upon ______, plaintiff's attorney whose address is ______, and upon ______,

[4] Rule 13(h) provides for the court ordering parties to a counterclaim, but who are not parties to the original action, to be brought in as defendants.

who is attorney for C. D., defendant and third-party plaintiff, and whose address is ______, an answer to the third-party complaint which is herewith served upon you within 20 days after the service of this summons upon you exclusive of the day of service. If you fail to do so, judgment by default will be taken against you for the relief demanded in the third-party complaint. There is also served upon you herewith a copy of the complaint of the plaintiff which you may but are not required to answer.

____
Clerk of Court.

[Seal of District Court]

Dated __________

UNITED STATES DISTRICT COURT FOR THE SOUTHERN DISTRICT OF NEW YORK

Civil Action, File Number ______

A. B., Plaintiff	)	
v.	)	
C. D., Defendant and	)	
Third-Party Plaintiff	)	Third-Party Complaint
v.	)	
E. F., Third-Party	)	
Defendant	)	

1. Plaintiff A. B. has filed against defendant C. D. a complaint, a copy of which is hereto attached as "Exhibit A."

2. (Here state the grounds upon which C. D. is entitled to recover from E. F., all or part of what A. B. may recover from C. D. The statement should be framed as in an original complaint.)

Wherefore C. D. demands judgment against third-party defendant E. F. for all sums [5] that may be adjudged against defendant C. D. in favor of plaintiff A. B.

Signed: ____________________
Attorney for C. D., Third-Party Plaintiff.
Address: ____________________

Added 1963.

Form 22–B.

[5] Make appropriate change where C. D. is entitled to only partial recovery-over against E. F.

MOTION TO BRING IN THIRD–PARTY DEFENDANT

Defendant moves for leave, as third-party plaintiff, to cause to be served upon E. F. a summons and third-party complaint, copies of which are hereto attached as Exhibit X.

Signed: ____________________
Attorney for Defendant C.D.
Address: ____________________

Notice of Motion

(Contents the same as in Form 19. The notice should be addressed to all parties to the action.)

Exhibit X

(Contents the same as in Form 22–A.)

Added 1963.

Form 23.

MOTION TO INTERVENE AS A DEFENDANT UNDER RULE 24

(Based upon the complaint, Form 16)

United States District Court for the Southern District of New York

Civil Action, File Number ______

A. B., Plaintiff)
v.) *Motion to intervene as*
C. D., Defendant) *a defendant*
E. F., Applicant for Intervention)

E. F. moves for leave to intervene as a defendant in this action, in order to assert the defenses set forth in his proposed answer, of which a copy is hereto attached, on the ground that he is the manufacturer and vendor to the defendant, as well as to others, of the articles alleged in the complaint to be an infringement of plaintiff's patent, and as such has a defense to plaintiff's claim presenting both questions of law and of fact which are common to the main action.[6]

Signed: ________________________,

[6] For other grounds of intervention, either of right or in the discretion of the court, see Rule 24(a) and (b).

Attorney for E. F.,
Applicant for Intervention.

Address: ____________________.

Notice of Motion

(Contents the same as in Form 19)

United States District Court for the Southern District of New York

Civil Action, File Number ______

A. B., Plaintiff)
v.) *Intervener's answer*
C. D., Defendant)
E. F., Intervener)

First Defense

Intervener admits the allegations stated in paragraphs 1 and 4 of the complaint; denies the allegations in paragraph 3, and denies the allegations in paragraph 2 in so far as they assert the legality of the issuance of the Letters Patent to plaintiff.

Second Defense

Plaintiff is not the first inventor of the articles covered by the Letters Patent specified in his complaint, since articles substantially identical in character were previously patented in Letters Patent granted to intervener on January 5, 1920.

Signed: __________________,
Attorney for
E. F., Intervener.
Address: __________________.

As amended 1949.

Form 24.

REQUEST FOR PRODUCTION OF DOCUMENTS, ETC., UNDER RULE 34

Plaintiff A. B. requests defendant C. D. to respond within ______ days to the following requests:

(1) That defendant produce and permit plaintiff to inspect and to copy each of the following documents:

(Here list the documents either individually or by category and describe each of them.)

(Here state the time, place, and manner of making the inspection and performance of any related acts.)

(2) That defendant produce and permit plaintiff to inspect and to copy, test, or sample each of the following objects:

(Here list the objects either individually or by category and describe each of them.)

(Here state the time, place, and manner of making the inspection and performance of any related acts.)

(3) That defendant permit plaintiff to enter (here describe property to be entered) and to inspect and to photograph, test or sample (here describe the portion of the real property and the objects to be inspected).

(Here state the time, place, and manner of making the inspection and performance of any related acts.)

Signed: ____________________

Attorney for Plaintiff.

Address: ____________________

As amended 1970.

Form 25.

REQUEST FOR ADMISSION UNDER RULE 36

Plaintiff A. B. requests defendant C. D. within ______ days after service of this request to make the following admissions for the purpose of this action only and subject to all pertinent objections to admissibility which may be interposed at the trial:

1. That each of the following documents, exhibited with this request, is genuine.

(Here list the documents and describe each document.)

2. That each of the following statements is true.

(Here list the statements.)

Signed: ____________________,

Attorney for Plaintiff.

Address: ____________________

As amended 1948.

Form 26.

ALLEGATION OF REASON FOR OMITTING PARTY

When it is necessary, under Rule 19(c), for the pleader to set forth in his pleading the names of persons who ought to be made parties, but who are not so made, there should be an allegation such as the one set out below:

John Doe named in this complaint is not made a party to this action [because he is not subject to the jurisdiction of this court]; [because he cannot be made a party to this action without depriving this court of jurisdiction].

Form 27.

NOTICE OF APPEAL TO COURT OF APPEALS UNDER RULE 73(b)

Abrogated 1968

Form 28.

NOTICE: CONDEMNATION

United States District Court for the Southern District of New York

Civil Action, File Number ______

UNITED STATES OF AMERICA, Plaintiff	)	
v.	)	
1,000 ACRES OF LAND IN [here insert a general location as "City of ______" or "County of ______"], JOHN DOE ET AL., AND UNKNOWN OWNERS, Defendants	)	*Notice.*

To (here insert the names of the defendants to whom the notice is directed):

You are hereby notified that a complaint in condemnation has heretofore been filed in the office of the clerk of the United States District Court for the Southern District of New York, in the United States Court House in New York City, New York, for the taking (here state the interest to be acquired, as "an estate in fee simple") for use (here state briefly the use, "as a site for a post-office building") of the following described property in which you have or claim an interest.

> (Here insert brief description of the property in which the defendants, to whom the notice is directed, have or claim an interest.)

The authority for the taking is (here state briefly, as "the Act of ______, ______ Stat. ______, U.S.C., Title ______, § ______".)[7]

You are further notified that if you desire to present any objection or defense to the taking of your property you are required to serve your answer on the plaintiff's attorney at the address herein designated within twenty days after ______.[8]

Your answer shall identify the property in which you claim to have an interest, state the nature and extent of the interest you claim, and state all of your objections and defenses to the taking of your property. All defenses and objections not so presented are waived. And in case of your failure so to answer the complaint, judgment of condemnation of that part of the above-described property in which you have or claim an interest will be rendered.

But without answering, you may serve on the plaintiff's attorney a notice of appearance designating the property in which you claim to be interested. Thereafter you will receive notice of all proceedings affecting it. At the trial of the issue of just compensation, whether or not you have previously appeared or answered, you may present evidence as to the amount of the compensation to be paid for your property, and you may share in the distribution of the award.

____

United States Attorney.

Address ______________________

(Here state an address within the district where the United States Attorney may be served, as "United States Court House, New York, N. Y.")

Dated ____________

Added 1951.

Form 29.

COMPLAINT: CONDEMNATION

United States District Court for the Southern District of New York

Civil Action, File Number ______

[7] And where appropriate add a citation to any applicable Executive Order.

[8] Here insert the words "personal service of this notice upon you," if personal service is to be made pursuant to subdivision (d)(3)(i) of this rule [Rule 71A]; or, insert the date of the last publication of notice, if service by publication is to be made pursuant to subdivision (d)(3)(ii) of this rule.

UNITED STATES OF AMERICA, Plaintiff	)	
v.	)	
1,000 ACRES OF LAND IN [here insert a general	)	*Complaint.*
location as "City of ______" or	)	
"County of ______"], JOHN DOE ET AL.,	)	
AND UNKNOWN OWNERS, Defendants	)	

1. This is an action of a civil nature brought by the United States of America for the taking of property under the power of eminent domain and for the ascertainment and award of just compensation to the owners and parties in interest.[9]

2. The authority for the taking is (here state briefly, as "the Act of ______, ______ Stat. ______, U.S.C., Title ______, § ______").[10]

3. The use for which the property is to be taken is (here state briefly the use, "as a site for a post-office building").

4. The interest to be acquired in the property is (here state the interest as "an estate in fee simple").

5. The property so to be taken is (here set forth a description of the property sufficient for its identification) or (described in Exhibit A hereto attached and made a part hereof).

6. The persons known to the plaintiff to have or claim an interest in the property [11] are:

(Here set forth the names of such persons and the interests claimed.)[12]

7. In addition to the persons named, there are or may be others who have or may claim some interest in the property to be taken, whose names are unknown to the plaintiff and on diligent inquiry have not been ascertained. They are made parties to the action under the designation "Unknown Owners."

[9] If the plaintiff is not the United States, but is, for example, a corporation invoking the power of eminent domain delegated to it by the state, then this paragraph 1 of the complaint should be appropriately modified and should be preceded by a paragraph appropriately alleging federal jurisdiction for the action, such as diversity. See Form 2.

[10] And where appropriate add a citation to any applicable Executive Order.

[11] At the commencement of the action the plaintiff need name as defendants only the persons having or claiming an interest in the property whose names are then known, but prior to any hearing involving the compensation to be paid for a particular piece of property the plaintiff must add as defendants all persons having or claiming an interest in that property whose names can be ascertained by an appropriate search of the records and also those whose names have otherwise been learned. See Rule 71A(c)(2).

[12] The plaintiff should designate, as to each separate piece of property, the defendants who have been joined as owners thereof or of some interest therein. See Rule 71A(c)(2).

Wherefore the plaintiff demands judgment that the property be condemned and that just compensation for the taking be ascertained and awarded and for such other relief as may be lawful and proper.

____

United States Attorney.

Address ____________________

(Here state an address within the district where the United States Attorney may be served, as "United States Court House, New York, N. Y.").

Added 1951.

Form 30.

SUGGESTION OF DEATH UPON THE RECORD UNDER RULE 25(a)(1)

A. B. [describe as a party, or as executor, administrator, or other representative or successor of C. D., the deceased party] suggests upon the record, pursuant to Rule 25(a)(1), the death of C. D. [describe as party] during the pendency of this action.

Added 1963.

Form 31.

JUDGMENT ON JURY VERDICT

UNITED STATES DISTRICT COURT FOR THE SOUTHERN DISTRICT OF NEW YORK

Civil Action, File Number ______

A. B., Plaintiff)
v.) Judgment
C. D., Defendant)

This action came on for trial before the Court and a jury, Honorable John Marshall, District Judge, presiding, and the issues having been duly tried and the jury having duly rendered its verdict,

It is Ordered and Adjudged

[that the plaintiff A. B. recover of the defendant C. D. the sum of ______, with interest thereon at the rate of ______ per cent as provided by law, and his costs of action.]

[that the plaintiff take nothing, that the action be dismissed on the merits, and that the defendant C. D. recover of the plaintiff A. B. his costs of action.]

Dated at New York, New York, this ______ day of ______, 20__.

____

Clerk of Court.

Added 1963; as amended 2003.

Note

1. This Form is illustrative of the judgment to be entered upon the general verdict of a jury. It deals with the cases where there is a general jury verdict awarding the plaintiff money damages or finding for the defendant, but is adaptable to other situations of jury verdicts.

2. The clerk, unless the court otherwise orders, is required forthwith to prepare, sign, and enter the judgment upon a general jury verdict without awaiting any direction by the court. The form of the judgment upon a special verdict or a general verdict accompanied by answers to interrogatories shall be promptly approved by the court, and the clerk shall thereupon enter it. See Rule 58, as amended.

3. The Rules contemplate a simple judgment promptly entered. See Rule 54(a). Every judgment shall be set forth on a separate document. See Rule 58, as amended.

4. Attorneys are not to submit forms of judgment unless directed in exceptional cases to do so by the court. See Rule 58, as amended.

Form 32.

JUDGMENT ON DECISION BY THE COURT

UNITED STATES DISTRICT COURT FOR THE SOUTHERN DISTRICT OF NEW YORK

Civil Action, File Number ______

A. B., Plaintiff)
v.) Judgment
C. D., Defendant)

This action came on for [trial] [hearing] before the Court, Honorable John Marshall, District Judge, presiding, and the issues having been duly [tried] [heard] and a decision having been duly rendered,

It is Ordered and Adjudged

[that the plaintiff A. B. recover of the defendant C. D. the sum of ______, with interest thereon at the rate of ______ per cent as provided by law, and his costs of action.]

[that the plaintiff take nothing, that the action be dismissed on the merits, and that the defendant C. D. recover of the plaintiff A. B. his costs of action.]

Dated at New York, New York, this ______ day of ______, 20__.

____

Clerk of Court.

Added 1963; as amended 2003.

Note

1. This Form is illustrative of the judgment to be entered upon a decision of the court. It deals with the cases of decisions by the court awarding a party only money damages or costs, but is adaptable to other decisions by the court.

2. The clerk, unless the court otherwise orders, is required forthwith, without awaiting any direction by the court, to prepare, sign, and enter the judgment upon a decision by the court that a party shall recover only a sum certain or costs or that all relief shall be denied. The form of the judgment upon a decision by the court granting other relief shall be promptly approved by the court, and the clerk shall thereupon enter it. See Rule 58, as amended.

3. See also paragraphs 3–4 of the Explanatory Note to Form 31.

Form 33.

NOTICE OF AVAILABILITY OF MAGISTRATE JUDGE TO EXERCISE JURISDICTION

In accordance with the provisions of Title 28, U.S.C. § 636(c), you are hereby notified that a United States magistrate judge of this district court is available to exercise the court's jurisdiction and to conduct any or all proceedings in this case including a jury or nonjury trial, and entry of a final judgment. Exercise of this jurisdiction by a magistrate judge is, however, permitted only if all parties voluntarily consent.

You may, without adverse substantive consequences, withhold your consent, but this will prevent the court's jurisdiction from being exercised by a magistrate judge. If any party withholds consent, the identity of the parties consenting or withholding consent will not be communicated to any magistrate judge or to the district judge to whom the case has been assigned.

An appeal from a judgment entered by a magistrate judge may be taken directly to the United States court of appeals for this judicial circuit in the same manner as an appeal from any other judgment of a district court.

Copies of the Form for the "Consent to Jurisdiction by a United States Magistrate Judge" are available from the clerk of the court.

Added 1983; as amended 1993, 1997.

Form 34.

CONSENT TO EXERCISE OF JURISDICTION BY A UNITED STATES MAGISTRATE JUDGE

UNITED STATES DISTRICT COURT
______ DISTRICT OF ______

Plaintiff,	)	
vs.	)	Docket No. ______
Defendant.	)	

CONSENT TO JURISDICTION BY A UNITED STATES MAGISTRATE JUDGE

In accordance with the provisions of Title 28, U.S.C. § 636(c), the undersigned party or parties to the above-captioned civil matter hereby voluntarily consent to have a United States magistrate judge conduct any and all further proceedings in the case, including trial, and order the entry of a final judgment.

____________________ ____________________

Date *Signature*

Note: Return this form to the Clerk of the Court if you consent to jurisdiction by a magistrate judge. Do not send a copy of this form to any district judge or magistrate judge.

Added 1983; as amended 1993, 1997.

Form 34A.

ORDER OF REFERENCE

UNITED STATES DISTRICT COURT
______ DISTRICT OF ______

Plaintiff,	)	
vs.	)	Docket No. ______
Defendant.	)	

ORDER OF REFERENCE

IT IS HEREBY ORDERED that the above-captioned matter be referred to United States Magistrate Judge __________ for all further proceedings and entry of judgment in accordance with Title 28, U.S.C. § 636(c) and the consent of the parties.

____

U.S. District Judge

Added 1993.

Form 35.

REPORT OF PARTIES' PLANNING MEETING

[Caption and Names of Parties]

1. Pursuant to Fed.R.Civ.P. 26(f), a meeting was held on (date) at (place) and was attended by:

(name) for plaintiff(s)
(name) for defendant(s) (party name)
(name) for defendant(s) (party name)

2. **Pre–Discovery Disclosures.** The parties [have exchanged] [will exchange by (date)] the information required by [Fed.R.Civ.P. 26(a)(1)] [local rule ______].

3. **Discovery Plan.** The parties jointly propose to the court the following discovery plan: [Use separate paragraphs or subparagraphs as necessary if parties disagree.]

Discovery will be needed on the following subjects: (brief description of subjects on which discovery will be needed)

All discovery commenced in time to be completed by (date) . [Discovery on (issue for early discovery) to be completed by (date) .]

Maximum of ______ interrogatories by each party to any other party. [Responses due ______ days after service.]

Maximum of ______ requests for admission by each party to any other party. [Responses due ______ days after service.]

Maximum of ______ depositions by plaintiff(s) and ______ by defendant(s).

Each deposition [other than of ______] limited to maximum of ______ hours unless extended by agreement of parties.

Reports from retained experts under Rule 26(a)(2) due: from plaintiff(s) by (date) from defendant(s) by (date)

Supplementations under Rule 26(e) due (time(s) or interval(s)).

4. **Other Items.** [Use separate paragraphs or subparagraphs as necessary if parties disagree.]

The parties [request] [do not request] a conference with the court before entry of the scheduling order.

The parties request a pretrial conference in (month and year).

Plaintiff(s) should be allowed until (date) to join additional parties and until (date) to amend the pleadings.

Defendant(s) should be allowed until (date) to join additional parties and until (date) to amend the pleadings.

All potentially dispositive motions should be filed by (date).

Settlement [is likely] [is unlikely] [cannot be evaluated prior to (date)] [may be enhanced by use of the following alternative dispute resolution procedure: [__________].

Final lists of witnesses and exhibits under Rule 26(a)(3) should be due from plaintiff(s) by (date) from defendant(s) by (date)

Parties should have ______ days after service of final lists of witnesses and exhibits to list objections under Rule 26(a)(3).

The case should be ready for trial by (date) [and at this time is expected to take approximately (length of time)].

[Other matters.]

Date: ______

Added 1993.

*

SUPPLEMENTAL RULES FOR CERTAIN ADMIRALTY AND MARITIME CLAIMS

Adopted February 28, 1966, effective July 1, 1966

Rule A.

SCOPE OF RULES

These Supplemental Rules apply to the procedure in admiralty and maritime claims within the meaning of Rule 9(h) with respect to the following remedies:

(1) Maritime attachment and garnishment;

(2) Actions in rem;

(3) Possessory, petitory, and partition actions;

(4) Actions for exoneration from or limitation of liability.

These rules also apply to the procedure in statutory condemnation proceedings analogous to maritime actions in rem, whether within the admiralty and maritime jurisdiction or not. Except as otherwise provided, references in these Supplemental Rules to actions in rem include such analogous statutory condemnation proceedings.

The general Rules of Civil Procedure for the United States District Courts are also applicable to the foregoing proceedings except to the extent that they are inconsistent with these Supplemental Rules.

Rule B.

IN PERSONAM ACTIONS: ATTACHMENT AND GARNISHMENT

(1) When Available; Complaint, Affidavit, Judicial Authorization, and Process. In an in personam action:

(a) If a defendant is not found within the district, a verified complaint may contain a prayer for process to attach the defendant's tangible or intangible personal property—up to the amount sued for—in the hands of garnishees named in the process.

(b) The plaintiff or the plaintiff's attorney must sign and file with the complaint an affidavit stating that, to the affiant's knowledge, or on information and belief, the defendant cannot be found within the district. The court must review the complaint and affidavit and, if the conditions of this Rule B appear to exist, enter an order so stating and authorizing process of attachment and garnishment. The clerk may issue supplemental process enforcing the court's order upon application without further court order.

(c) If the plaintiff or the plaintiff's attorney certifies that exigent circumstances make court review impracticable, the clerk must issue the summons and process of attachment and garnishment. The plaintiff has the burden in any post-attachment hearing under Rule E(4)(f) to show that exigent circumstances existed.

(d)(i) If the property is a vessel or tangible property on board a vessel, the summons, process, and any supplemental process must be delivered to the marshal for service.

(ii) If the property is other tangible or intangible property, the summons, process, and any supplemental process must be delivered to a person or organization authorized to serve it, who may be (A) a marshal; (B) someone under contract with the United States; (C) someone specially appointed by the court for that purpose; or, (D) in an action brought by the United States, any officer or employee of the United States.

(e) The plaintiff may invoke state-law remedies under Rule 64 for seizure of person or property for the purpose of securing satisfaction of the judgment.

(2) Notice to Defendant. No default judgment may be entered except upon proof—which may be by affidavit—that:

(a) the complaint, summons, and process of attachment or garnishment have been served on the defendant in a manner authorized by Rule 4;

(b) the plaintiff or the garnishee has mailed to the defendant the complaint, summons, and process of attachment or garnishment, using any form of mail requiring a return receipt; or

(c) the plaintiff or the garnishee has tried diligently to give notice of the action to the defendant but could not do so.

(3) Answer.

(a) By Garnishee. The garnishee shall serve an answer, together with answers to any interrogatories served with the complaint, within 20 days after service of process upon the garnishee. Interrogatories to the garnishee may be served with the complaint without leave of court. If the garnishee refuses or neglects to

answer on oath as to the debts, credits, or effects of the defendant in the garnishee's hands, or any interrogatories concerning such debts, credits, and effects that may be propounded by the plaintiff, the court may award compulsory process against the garnishee. If the garnishee admits any debts, credits, or effects, they shall be held in the garnishee's hands or paid into the registry of the court, and shall be held in either case subject to the further order of the court.

(b) By Defendant. The defendant shall serve an answer within 30 days after process has been executed, whether by attachment of property or service on the garnishee.

As amended 1985, 1987, 2000.

Rule C.

IN REM ACTIONS: SPECIAL PROVISIONS

(1) When Available. An action in rem may be brought:

(a) To enforce any maritime lien;

(b) Whenever a statute of the United States provides for a maritime action in rem or a proceeding analogous thereto.

Except as otherwise provided by law a party who may proceed in rem may also, or in the alternative, proceed in personam against any person who may be liable.

Statutory provisions exempting vessels or other property owned or possessed by or operated by or for the United States from arrest or seizure are not affected by this rule. When a statute so provides, an action against the United States or an instrumentality thereof may proceed on in rem principles.

(2) Complaint. In an action in rem the complaint must:

(a) be verified;

(b) describe with reasonable particularity the property that is the subject of the action;

(c) in an admiralty and maritime proceeding, state that the property is within the district or will be within the district while the action is pending;

(d) in a forfeiture proceeding for violation of a federal statute, state:

(i) the place of seizure and whether it was on land or on navigable waters;

(ii) whether the property is within the district, and if the property is not within the district the statutory basis for the court's exercise of jurisdiction over the property; and

(iii) all allegations required by the statute under which the action is brought.

(3) Judicial Authorization and Process.

(a) Arrest Warrant.

(i) When the United States files a complaint demanding a forfeiture for violation of a federal statute, the clerk must promptly issue a summons and a warrant for the arrest of the vessel or other property without requiring a certification of exigent circumstances, but if the property is real property the United States must proceed under applicable statutory procedures.

(ii)(A) In other actions, the court must review the complaint and any supporting papers. If the conditions for an in rem action appear to exist, the court must issue an order directing the clerk to issue a warrant for the arrest of the vessel or other property that is the subject of the action.

(B) If the plaintiff or the plaintiff's attorney certifies that exigent circumstances make court review impracticable, the clerk must promptly issue a summons and a warrant for the arrest of the vessel or other property that is the subject of the action. The plaintiff has the burden in any post-arrest hearing under Rule E(4)(f) to show that exigent circumstances existed.

(b) Service.

(i) If the property that is the subject of the action is a vessel or tangible property on board a vessel, the warrant and any supplemental process must be delivered to the marshal for service.

(ii) If the property that is the subject of the action is other property, tangible or intangible, the warrant and any supplemental process must be delivered to a person or organization authorized to enforce it, who may be: (A) a marshal; (B) someone under contract with the United States; (C) someone specially appointed by the court for that purpose; or, (D) in an action brought by the United States, any officer or employee of the United States.

(c) Deposit in Court. If the property that is the subject of the action consists in whole or in part of freight, the proceeds of property sold, or other intangible property, the clerk must issue—in addition to the warrant—a summons directing any person controlling the property to show cause why it should not be deposited in court to abide the judgment.

(d) Supplemental Process. The clerk may upon application issue supplemental process to enforce the court's order without further court order.

(4) Notice. No notice other than execution of process is required when the property that is the subject of the action has been released under Rule E(5). If the property is not released within 10 days after execution, the plaintiff must promptly—or within the time that the court allows—give public notice of the action and arrest in a newspaper designated by court order and having general circulation in the district, but publication may be terminated if the property is released before publication is completed. The notice must specify the time under Rule C(6) to file a statement of interest in or right against the seized property and to answer. This rule does not affect the notice requirements in an action to foreclose a preferred ship mortgage under 46 U.S.C. § 31301 et seq., as amended.

(5) Ancillary Process. In any action in rem in which process has been served as provided by this rule, if any part of the property that is the subject of the action has not been brought within the control of the court because it has been removed or sold, or because it is intangible property in the hands of a person who has not been served with process, the court may, on motion, order any person having possession or control of such property or its proceeds to show cause why it should not be delivered into the custody of the marshal or other person or organization having a warrant for the arrest of the property, or paid into court to abide the judgment; and, after hearing, the court may enter such judgment as law and justice may require.

(6) Responsive Pleading; Interrogatories.

(a) Civil Forfeiture. In an in rem forfeiture action for violation of a federal statute:

(i) a person who asserts an interest in or right against the property that is the subject of the action must file a verified statement identifying the interest or right:

(A) within 30 days after the earlier of (1) the date of service of the Government's complaint or (2) completed publication of notice under Rule C(4), or

(B) within the time that the court allows;

(ii) an agent, bailee, or attorney must state the authority to file a statement of interest in or right against the property on behalf of another; and

(iii) a person who files a statement of interest in or right against the property must serve and file an answer within 20 days after filing the statement.

(b) Maritime Arrests and Other Proceedings. In an in rem action not governed by Rule C(6)(a):

(i) A person who asserts a right of possession or any ownership interest in the property that is the subject of the action must file a verified statement of right or interest:

(A) within 10 days after the earlier of (1) the execution of process, or (2) completed publication of notice under Rule C(4), or

(B) within the time that the court allows;

(ii) the statement of right or interest must describe the interest in the property that supports the person's demand for its restitution or right to defend the action;

(iii) an agent, bailee, or attorney must state the authority to file a statement of right or interest on behalf of another; and

(iv) a person who asserts a right of possession or any ownership interest must serve an answer within 20 days after filing the statement of interest or right.

(c) Interrogatories. Interrogatories may be served with the complaint in an in rem action without leave of court. Answers to the interrogatories must be served with the answer to the complaint.

As amended 1985, 1987, 1991, 2000, 2002.

Rule D.

POSSESSORY, PETITORY, AND PARTITION ACTIONS

In all actions for possession, partition, and to try title maintainable according to the course of the admiralty practice with respect to a vessel, in all actions so maintainable with respect to the possession of cargo or other maritime property, and in all actions by one or more part owners against the others to obtain security for the return of the vessel from any voyage undertaken without their consent, or by one or more part owners against the others to obtain possession of the vessel for any voyage on giving security for its safe return, the process shall be by a warrant of arrest of the vessel, cargo, or other property, and by notice in the manner provided by Rule B(2) to the adverse party or parties.

Rule E.

ACTIONS IN REM AND QUASI IN REM: GENERAL PROVISIONS

(1) Applicability. Except as otherwise provided, this rule applies to actions in personam with process of maritime attachment and garnishment, actions in rem, and petitory, possessory, and partition actions, supplementing Rules B, C, and D.

(2) Complaint; Security.

(a) Complaint. In actions to which this rule is applicable the complaint shall state the circumstances from which the claim arises with such particularity that the defendant or claimant will be able, without moving for a more definite statement, to commence an investigation of the facts and to frame a responsive pleading.

(b) Security for Costs. Subject to the provisions of Rule 54(d) and of relevant statutes, the court may, on the filing of the complaint or on the appearance of any defendant, claimant, or any other party, or at any later time, require the plaintiff, defendant, claimant, or other party to give security, or additional security, in such sum as the court shall direct to pay all costs and expenses that shall be awarded against the party by any interlocutory order or by the final judgment, or on appeal by any appellate court.

(3) Process.

(a) In admiralty and maritime proceedings process in rem or of maritime attachment and garnishment may be served only within the district.

(b) In forfeiture cases process in rem may be served within the district or outside the district when authorized by statute.

(c) Issuance and Delivery. Issuance and delivery of process in rem, or of maritime attachment and garnishment, shall be held in abeyance if the plaintiff so requests.

(4) Execution of Process; Marshal's Return; Custody of Property; Procedures for Release.

(a) In General. Upon issuance and delivery of the process, or, in the case of summons with process of attachment and garnishment, when it appears that the defendant cannot be found within the district, the marshal or other person or organization having a warrant shall forthwith execute the process in accordance with this subdivision (4), making due and prompt return.

(b) Tangible Property. If tangible property is to be attached or arrested, the marshal or other person or organization having the warrant shall take it into the marshal's possession for safe custody. If the character or situation of the property is such that the taking of actual possession is impracticable, the marshal or other person executing the process shall affix a copy thereof to the property in a conspicuous place and leave a copy of the complaint and process with the person having possession or the person's agent. In furtherance of the marshal's custody of any vessel the marshal is authorized to make a written request to the collector of customs not to grant clearance to such vessel until notified by the marshal or a deputy marshal or by the clerk that the vessel has been released in accordance with these rules.

(c) Intangible Property. If intangible property is to be attached or arrested the marshal or other person or organization having the warrant shall execute the process by leaving with the garnishee or other obligor a copy of the complaint and process requiring the garnishee or other obligor to answer as provided in Rules B(3)(a) and C(6); or the marshal may accept for payment into the registry of the court the amount owed to the extent of the amount claimed by the plaintiff with interest and costs, in which event the garnishee or other obligor shall not be required to answer unless alias process shall be served.

(d) Directions with Respect to Property in Custody. The marshal or other person or organization having the warrant may at any time apply to the court for directions with respect to property that has been attached or arrested, and shall give notice of such application to any or all of the parties as the court may direct.

(e) Expenses of Seizing and Keeping Property; Deposit. These rules do not alter the provisions of Title 28, U.S.C., § 1921, as amended, relative to the expenses of seizing and keeping property attached or arrested and to the requirement of deposits to cover such expenses.

(f) Procedure for Release from Arrest or Attachment. Whenever property is arrested or attached, any person claiming an interest in it shall be entitled to a prompt hearing at which the plaintiff shall be required to show why the arrest or attachment should not be vacated or other relief granted consistent with these rules. This subdivision shall have no application to suits for seamen's wages when process is issued upon a certification of sufficient cause filed pursuant to Title 46, U.S.C. §§ 603 and 604 or to actions by the United States for forfeitures for violation of any statute of the United States.

(5) Release of Property.

(a) Special Bond. Except in cases of seizures for forfeiture under any law of the United States, whenever process of maritime attachment and garnishment or process in rem is issued the execution of such process shall be stayed, or the property released, on the giving of security, to be approved by the court or clerk, or by stipulation of the parties, conditioned to answer the judgment of the court or of any appellate court. The parties may stipulate the amount and nature of such security. In the event of the inability or refusal of the parties so to stipulate the court shall fix the principal sum of the bond or stipulation at an amount sufficient to cover the amount of the plaintiff's claim fairly stated with accrued interest and costs; but the principal sum shall in no event exceed (i) twice the amount of the plaintiff's claim or (ii) the value of the property on due appraisement, whichever is smaller. The bond or

stipulation shall be conditioned for the payment of the principal sum and interest thereon at 6 per cent per annum.

(b) General Bond. The owner of any vessel may file a general bond or stipulation, with sufficient surety, to be approved by the court, conditioned to answer the judgment of such court in all or any actions that may be brought thereafter in such court in which the vessel is attached or arrested. Thereupon the execution of all such process against such vessel shall be stayed so long as the amount secured by such bond or stipulation is at least double the aggregate amount claimed by plaintiffs in all actions begun and pending in which such vessel has been attached or arrested. Judgments and remedies may be had on such bond or stipulation as if a special bond or stipulation had been filed in each of such actions. The district court may make necessary orders to carry this rule into effect, particularly as to the giving of proper notice of any action against or attachment of a vessel for which a general bond has been filed. Such bond or stipulation shall be indorsed by the clerk with a minute of the actions wherein process is so stayed. Further security may be required by the court at any time.

If a special bond or stipulation is given in a particular case, the liability on the general bond or stipulation shall cease as to that case.

(c) Release by Consent or Stipulation; Order of Court or Clerk; Costs. Any vessel, cargo, or other property in the custody of the marshal or other person or organization having the warrant may be released forthwith upon the marshal's acceptance and approval of a stipulation, bond, or other security, signed by the party on whose behalf the property is detained or the party's attorney and expressly authorizing such release, if all costs and charges of the court and its officers shall have first been paid. Otherwise no property in the custody of the marshal, other person or organization having the warrant, or other officer of the court shall be released without an order of the court; but such order may be entered as of course by the clerk, upon the giving of approved security as provided by law and these rules, or upon the dismissal or discontinuance of the action; but the marshal or other person or organization having the warrant shall not deliver any property so released until the costs and charges of the officers of the court shall first have been paid.

(d) Possessory, Petitory, and Partition Actions. The foregoing provisions of this subdivision (5) do not apply to petitory, possessory, and partition actions. In such cases the property arrested shall be released only by order of the court, on such terms and conditions and on the giving of such security as the court may require.

(6) Reduction or Impairment of Security. Whenever security is taken the court may, on motion and hearing, for good cause shown, reduce the amount of security given; and if the surety shall be or become insufficient, new or additional sureties may be required on motion and hearing.

(7) Security on Counterclaim.

(a) When a person who has given security for damages in the original action asserts a counterclaim that arises from the transaction or occurrence that is the subject of the original action, a plaintiff for whose benefit the security has been given must give security for damages demanded in the counterclaim unless the court, for cause shown, directs otherwise. Proceedings on the original claim must be stayed until this security is given, unless the court directs otherwise.

(b) The plaintiff is required to give security under Rule E(7)(a) when the United States or its corporate instrumentality counterclaims and would have been required to give security to respond in damages if a private party but is relieved by law from giving security.

(8) Restricted Appearance. An appearance to defend against an admiralty and maritime claim with respect to which there has issued process in rem, or process of attachment and garnishment, may be expressly restricted to the defense of such claim, and in that event is not an appearance for the purposes of any other claim with respect to which such process is not available or has not been served.

(9) Disposition of Property; Sales.

(a) Actions for Forfeitures. In any action in rem to enforce a forfeiture for violation of a statute of the United States the property shall be disposed of as provided by statute.

(b) Interlocutory Sales; Delivery.

(i) On application of a party, the marshal, or other person having custody of the property, the court may order all or part of the property sold—with the sales proceeds, or as much of them as will satisfy the judgment, paid into court to await further orders of the court—if:

(A) the attached or arrested property is perishable, or liable to deterioration, decay, or injury by being detained in custody pending the action;

(B) the expense of keeping the property is excessive or disproportionate; or

(C) there is an unreasonable delay in securing release of the property.

(ii) In the circumstances described in Rule E(9)(b)(i), the court, on motion by a defendant or a person filing a statement of interest or right under Rule C(6), may order that the property, rather than being sold, be delivered to the movant upon giving security under these rules.

(c) Sales; Proceeds. All sales of property shall be made by the marshal or a deputy marshal, or by other person or organization having the warrant, or by any other person assigned by the court where the marshal or other person or organization having the warrant is a party in interest; and the proceeds of sale shall be forthwith paid into the registry of the court to be disposed of according to law.

(10) Preservation of Property. When the owner or another person remains in possession of property attached or arrested under the provisions of Rule E(4)(b) that permit execution of process without taking actual possession, the court, on a party's motion or on its own, may enter any order necessary to preserve the property and to prevent its removal.

As amended 1985, 1987, 1991, 2000.

Rule F.

LIMITATION OF LIABILITY

(1) Time for Filing Complaint; Security. Not later than six months after receipt of a claim in writing, any vessel owner may file a complaint in the appropriate district court, as provided in subdivision (9) of this rule, for limitation of liability pursuant to statute. The owner (a) shall deposit with the court, for the benefit of claimants, a sum equal to the amount or value of the owner's interest in the vessel and pending freight, or approved security therefor, and in addition such sums, or approved security therefor, as the court may from time to time fix as necessary to carry out the provisions of the statutes as amended; or (b) at the owner's option shall transfer to a trustee to be appointed by the court, for the benefit of claimants, the owner's interest in the vessel and pending freight, together with such sums, or approved security therefor, as the court may from time to time fix as necessary to carry out the provisions of the statutes as amended. The plaintiff shall also give security for costs and, if the plaintiff elects to give security, for interest at the rate of 6 percent per annum from the date of the security.

(2) Complaint. The complaint shall set forth the facts on the basis of which the right to limit liability is asserted, and all facts necessary to enable the court to determine the amount to which the owner's liability shall be limited. The complaint may demand exoneration from as well as limitation of liability. It shall state the voyage, if any, on which the demands sought to be limited arose, with the date and place of its termination; the amount of all demands including all unsatisfied liens or claims of lien, in contract or in tort or otherwise, arising on that voyage, so far as known to the plaintiff, and what actions and proceedings, if any, are pending thereon; whether the vessel was damaged, lost, or abandoned, and, if so, when and where; the value of the vessel at the close of the voyage or, in case of wreck, the value of her wreckage, strippings, or proceeds, if any, and where and in whose possession they are; and the amount of any pending freight recovered or recoverable. If the plaintiff elects to transfer the plaintiff's interest in the vessel to a trustee, the complaint must further show any prior paramount liens thereon, and what voyages or trips, if any, she has made since the voyage or trip on which the claims sought to be limited arose, and any existing liens arising upon any such subsequent voyage or trip, with the amounts and causes thereof, and the names and addresses of the lienors, so far as known; and whether the vessel sustained any injury upon or by reason of such subsequent voyage or trip.

(3) Claims Against Owner; Injunction. Upon compliance by the owner with the requirements of subdivision (1) of this rule all claims and proceedings against the owner or the owner's property with respect to the matter in question shall cease. On application of the plaintiff the court shall enjoin the further prosecution of any action or proceeding against the plaintiff or the plaintiff's property with respect to any claim subject to limitation in the action.

(4) Notice to Claimants. Upon the owner's compliance with subdivision (1) of this rule the court shall issue a notice to all persons asserting claims with respect to which the complaint seeks limitation, admonishing them to file their respective claims with the clerk of the court and to serve on the attorneys for the plaintiff a copy thereof on or before a date to be named in the notice. The date so fixed shall not be less than 30 days after issuance of the notice. For cause shown, the court may enlarge the time within which claims may be filed. The notice shall be published in such newspaper or newspapers as the court may direct once a week for four successive weeks prior to the date fixed for the filing of claims. The plaintiff not later than the day of second publication shall also mail a copy of the notice to every person known to have made any claim against the vessel or the plaintiff arising out the voyage or trip on which the claims sought to be limited arose. In cases involving death a copy of such notice shall be mailed to the decedent at the decedent's last known address, and also to any person who shall be known to have made any claim on account of such death.

(5) Claims and Answer. Claims shall be filed and served on or before the date specified in the notice provided for in subdivision (4) of this rule. Each claim shall specify the facts upon which the claimant relies in support of the claim, the items thereof, and the dates on which the same accrued. If a claimant desires to contest either the right to exoneration from or the right to limitation of liability the claimant shall file and serve an answer to the complaint unless the claim has included an answer.

(6) Information to Be Given Claimants. Within 30 days after the date specified in the notice for filing claims, or within such time as the court thereafter may allow, the plaintiff shall mail to the attorney for each claimant (or if the claimant has no attorney to the claimant) a list setting forth (a) the name of each claimant, (b) the name and address of the claimant's attorney (if the claimant is known to have one), (c) the nature of the claim, i.e., whether property loss, property damage, death, personal injury, etc., and (d) the amount thereof.

(7) Insufficiency of Fund or Security. Any claimant may by motion demand that the funds deposited in court or the security given by the plaintiff be increased on the ground that they are less than the value of the plaintiff's interest in the vessel and pending freight. Thereupon the court shall cause due appraisement to be made of the value of the plaintiff's interest in the vessel and pending freight; and if the court finds that the deposit or security is either insufficient or excessive it shall order its increase or reduction. In like manner any claimant may demand that the deposit or security be increased on the ground that it is insufficient to carry out the provisions of the statutes relating to claims in respect of loss of life or bodily injury; and, after notice and hearing, the court may similarly order that the deposit or security be increased or reduced.

(8) Objections to Claims: Distribution of Fund. Any interested party may question or controvert any claim without filing an objection thereto. Upon determination of liability the fund deposited or secured, or the proceeds of the vessel and pending freight, shall be divided pro rata, subject to all relevant provisions of law, among the several claimants in proportion to the amounts of their respective claims, duly proved, saving, however, to all parties any priority to which they may be legally entitled.

(9) Venue; Transfer. The complaint shall be filed in any district in which the vessel has been attached or arrested to answer for any claim with respect to which the plaintiff seeks to limit liability; or, if the vessel has not been attached or arrested, then in any district in which the owner has been sued with respect to any such claim. When the vessel has not been attached or arrested to answer the matters aforesaid, and suit has not been commenced against the owner, the proceedings may be had in the district in which the vessel may be, but if the vessel is not within any district and no suit has been commenced in any district, then the complaint may be filed in any district. For the convenience of parties and witnesses, in the interest of justice, the court may transfer the action to any district; if venue is wrongly laid the court shall dismiss or, if it be in the interest of justice, transfer the action to any district in which it could have been brought. If the vessel shall have been sold, the proceeds shall represent the vessel for the purposes of these rules.

As amended 1987.

CERTAIN OF THE EARLY CIVIL ADVISORY COMMITTEE'S NOTES FROM 1938, 1948, AND 1961

Rule 4. Process

Advisory Committee's Note to Original Rule

Note to Subdivision (a). With the provision permitting additional summons upon request of the plaintiff, compare Equity Rule 14 (Alias Subpoena) and the last sentence of Equity Rule 12 (Issue of Subpoena—Time for Answer).

Note to Subdivision (b). This rule prescribes a form of summons which follows substantially the requirements stated in Equity Rules 12 (Issue of Subpoena—Time for Answer) and 7 (Process, Mesne and Final).

U.S.C., Title 28, § 721 [now § 1691] (Sealing and testing of writs) is substantially continued in so far as it applies to a summons, but its requirements as to teste of process are superseded. U.S.C., Title 28, § 722 [1946 ed.] (Teste of process, day of) is superseded.

See Rule 12(a) for a statement of the time within which the defendant is required to appear and defend.

Note to Subdivision (c). This Rule does not affect U.S.C., Title 28, § 503, as amended June 15, 1935 [1946 ed.] (Marshals; duties) and such statutes as the following in so far as they provide for service of process by a marshal, but modifies them in so far as they may imply service by a marshal only:

U.S.C., Title 15:

§ 5 (Bringing in additional parties) (Sherman Act)

§ 10 (Bringing in additional parties)

§ 25 (Restraining violations; procedure)

U.S.C., Title 28:

§ 45 [1946 ed.] (Practice and procedure in certain cases under the interstate commerce laws)

Compare Equity Rule 15 (Process, by Whom Served).

Note to Subdivision (d). Under this rule the complaint must always be served with the summons.

Paragraph (1). For an example of a statute providing for service upon an agent of an individual see U.S.C., Title 28, § 109 [now §§ 1400, 1694] (Patent cases).

Paragraph (3). This enumerates the officers and agents of a corporation or of a partnership or other unincorporated association upon whom service of process may be made, and permits service of process only upon the officers, managing or general agents, or agents authorized by appointment or by law, of the corporation, partnership or unincorporated association against which the action is brought. See *Christian v. International Ass'n of Machinists,* 7 F.(2d) 481 (D.C.Ky.,1925) and *Singleton v. Order of Railway Conductors of America,* 9 F.Supp. 417 (D.C.Ill.,1935). Compare

Operative Plasterers' and Cement Finishers' International Ass'n of the United States and Canada v. Case, 93 F.(2d) 56 (App.D.C.,1937).

For a statute authorizing service upon a specified agent and requiring mailing to the defendant, see U.S.C., Title 6, § 7 (Surety companies as sureties; appointment of agents; service of process).

Paragraphs (4) and (5) provide a uniform and comprehensive method of service for all actions against the United States or an officer or agency thereof. For statutes providing for such service, see U.S.C., Title 7, §§ 217 (Proceedings for suspension of orders), 499k (Injunctions; application of injunction laws governing orders of Interstate Commerce Commission), 608c(15)(B) (Court review of ruling of Secretary of Agriculture), and 855 (making § 608c(15)(B) applicable to orders of the Secretary of Agriculture as to handlers of anti-hog-cholera serum and hog-cholera virus); U.S.C., Title 26, § 1569 (Bill in chancery to clear title to realty on which the United States has a lien for taxes); U.S.C., Title 28, §§ 45 [1946 ed.] (District Courts; practice and procedure in certain cases under the interstate commerce laws), 763 [1946 ed.] (Petition in suit against the United States; service; appearance by district attorney), 766 [now § 2409] (Partition suits where United States is tenant in common or joint tenant), 902 [now § 2410] (Foreclosure of mortgages or other liens on property in which the United States has an interest). These and similar statutes are modified in so far as they prescribe a different method of service or dispense with the service of a summons.

For the Equity Rule on service, see Equity Rule 13 (Manner of Serving Subpoena).

Note to Subdivision (e). The provisions for the service of a summons or of notice or of an order in lieu of summons contained in U.S.C., Title 8, § 405 (Cancellation of certificates of citizenship fraudulently or illegally procured) (service by publication in accordance with state law); U.S.C., Title 28, § 118 [now § 1655] (Absent defendants in suits to enforce liens); U.S.C., Title 35, § 72a (Jurisdiction of District Court of United States for the District of Columbia in certain equity suits where adverse parties reside elsewhere) (service by publication against parties residing in foreign countries); U.S.C., Title 38, § 445 (Action against the United States on a veteran's contract of insurance) (parties not inhabitants of or not found within the district may be served with an order of the court, personally or by publication) and similar statutes are continued by this rule. Title 24, § 378 of the Code of the District of Columbia (Publication against non-resident; those absent for six months; unknown heirs or devisees; for divorce or in rem; actual service beyond District) is continued by this rule.

Note to Subdivision (f). This rule enlarges to some extent the present rule as to where service may be made. It does not, however, enlarge the jurisdiction of the district courts.

U.S.C., Title 28, §§ 113 [now § 1392] (Suits in States containing more than one district) (where there are two or more defendants residing in different districts), 115 [1946 ed.] (Suits of a local nature), 116 [now § 1392] (Property in different districts in same state), 838 [1946 ed.] (Executions run in all districts of state); U.S.C., Title 47, § 13 (Action for damages against a railroad or telegraph company whose officer or agent in control of a telegraph line refuses or fails to operate such line in a certain manner—"upon any agent of the company found in such state"); U.S.C., Title 49, § 321(c) (Requiring designation of a process agent by interstate motor carriers and in case of failure so to do, service may be made upon any agent in the state) and similar statutes, allowing the running of process throughout a state, are substantially continued.

U.S.C., Title 15, §§ 5 (Bringing in additional parties) (Sherman Act), 25 (Restraining violations; procedure); U.S.C., Title 28, §§ 44 [now § 2321] (Procedure in certain cases under interstate commerce laws; service of processes of court), 117 [now §§ 754, 1692] (Property in different states in same circuit; jurisdiction of receiver), 839 [now § 2413] (Executions; run in every State and Territory) and similar statutes, providing for the running of process beyond the territorial limits of a state, are expressly continued.

Note to Subdivision (g). With the second sentence compare Equity Rule 15 (Process, by Whom Served).

Note to Subdivision (h). This rule substantially continues U.S.C., Title 28, § 767 [1946 ed.] (Amendment of process).

Rule 7. Pleadings Allowed; Form of Motions

Advisory Committee's Note to Original Rule

1. A provision designating pleadings and defining a motion is common in the state practice acts. See Ill.Rev.Stat. (1937) ch. 110, § 156 (Designation and order of pleadings); 2 Minn.Stat. (Mason, 1927) § 9246 (Definition of motion); and N.Y.C.P.A. (1937) § 113 (Definition of motion). Equity Rules 18 (Pleadings—Technical Forms Abrogated), 29 (Defenses—How Presented), and 33 (Testing Sufficiency of Defense) abolished technical forms of pleading, demurrers, and pleas, and exceptions for insufficiency of an answer.

2. *Note to Subdivision (a).* This preserves the substance of Equity Rule 31 (Reply—When Required—When Cause at Issue). Compare the English practice, English Rules Under the Judicature Act (The Annual Practice, 1937) O. 23, r. r. 1, 2 (Reply to counterclaim; amended, 1933, to be subject to the rules applicable to defenses, O. 21). See O. 21, r. r. 1–14; O. 27, r. 13 (When pleadings deemed denied and put in issue). Under the codes the pleadings are generally limited. A reply is sometimes required to an affirmative defense in the answer. 1 Colo.Stat.Ann. (1935) § 66; Ore.Code Ann. (1930) §§ 1–614, 1–616. In other jurisdictions no reply is necessary to an affirmative defense in the answer, but a reply may be ordered by the court. N.C.Code Ann. (1935) § 525; 1 S.D.Comp.Laws (1929) § 2357. A reply to a counterclaim is usually required. Ark.Civ.Code (Crawford, 1934) §§ 123–125; Wis.Stat. (1935) §§ 263.20, 263.21. U.S.C., Title 28, § 45 [1946 ed.] (District courts; practice and procedure in certain cases) is modified in so far as it may dispense with a reply to a counterclaim.

For amendment of pleadings, see Rule 15 dealing with amended and supplemental pleadings.

3. All statutes which use the words "petition", "bill of complaint", "plea", "demurrer", and other such terminology are modified in form by this rule.

(a) Pleadings. There shall be a complaint and an answer; and there shall be a reply~~, if the answer contains~~ *to* a counterclaim denominated as such; an answer to a cross-claim, if the answer contains a cross-claim; a third-party complaint, if leave is given under Rule 14 to summon a person who was not an original party; and there shall be a third-party answer, if a third-party complaint

New matter is shown in italics; matter to be omitted is lined through

is served. No other pleading shall be allowed, except that the court may order a reply to an answer or a third-party answer.

Advisory Committee's Note to 1948 Amendment

This amendment eliminates any question as to whether the compulsory reply, where a counterclaim is pleaded, is a reply only to the counterclaim or is a general reply to the answer containing the counterclaim. See Commentary, *Scope of Reply Where Defendant Has Pleaded Counterclaim,* 1939, 1 Fed.Rules Serv. 672; *Fort Chartres and Ivy Landing Drainage and Levee District No. Five v. Thompson,* E.D.Ill.1945, 8 Fed.Rules Serv. 13.32, Case 1.

Rule 12. Defenses and Objections—When and How Presented—By Pleading or Motion—Motion for Judgment on Pleadings

Advisory Committee's Note to Original Rule

Note to Subdivision (a). 1. Compare Equity Rules 12 (Issue of Subpoena—Time for Answer) and 31 (Reply—When Required—When Cause at Issue); 4 Mont.Rev. Codes Ann. (1935) §§ 9107, 9158; N.Y.C.P.A. (1937) § 263; N.Y.R.C.P. (1937) Rules 109–111.

2. U.S.C., Title 28, § 763 [1946 ed.] (Petition in action against United States; service; appearance by district attorney) provides that the United States as a defendant shall have 60 days within which to answer or otherwise defend. This and other statutes which provide 60 days for the United States or an officer or agency thereof to answer or otherwise defend are continued by this rule. In so far as any statutes not excepted in Rule 81 provide a different time for a defendant to defend, such statutes are modified. See U.S.C., Title 28, § 45 [1946 ed.] (District courts; practice and procedure in certain cases under the interstate commerce laws) (30 days).

3. Compare the last sentence of Equity Rule 29 (Defenses—How Presented) and N.Y.C.P.A (1937) § 283. See Rule 15(a) for time within which to plead to an amended pleading.

Note to Subdivisions (b) and (d). 1. See generally Equity Rules 29 (Defenses—How Presented), 33 (Testing Sufficiency of Defense), 43 (Defect of Parties—Resisting Objection), and 44 (Defect of Parties—Tardy Objection); N.Y.C.P.A. (1937) §§ 277–280; N.Y.R.C.P. (1937) Rules 106–112; English Rules Under the Judicature Act (The Annual Practice, 1937) O. 25, r. r. 1–4; Clark, Code Pleading (1928) pp. 371–381.

2. For provisions authorizing defenses to be made in the answer or reply see English Rules Under the Judicature Act (The Annual Practice, 1937) O. 25, r. r. 1–4; 1 Miss.Code Ann. (1930) §§ 378, 379. Compare Equity Rule 29 (Defenses—How Presented); U.S.C., Title 28, § 45 [1946 ed.] (District Courts; practice and procedure in certain cases under the interstate commerce laws). U.S.C., Title 28, § 45, [1946 ed.] substantially continued by this rule, provides: "No replication need be filed to the answer, and objections to the sufficiency of the petition or answer as not setting forth a cause of action or defense must be taken at the final hearing or by motion to dismiss the petition based on said grounds, which motion may be made at any time before answer is filed." Compare Calif.Code Civ.Proc. (Deering, 1937) § 433; 4 Nev.Comp.Laws (Hillyer, 1929) § 8600. For provisions that the defendant may demur and answer at the same time, see Calif.Code Civ.Proc. (Deering, 1937) § 431; 4 Nev.Comp.Laws (Hillyer, 1929) § 8598.

---

3. Equity Rule 29 (Defenses—How Presented) abolished demurrers and provided that defenses in point of law arising on the face of the bill should be made by motion to dismiss or in the answer, with further provision that every such point of law going to the whole or material part of the cause or causes stated might be called up and disposed of before final hearing "at the discretion of the court." Likewise many state practices have abolished the demurrer, or retain it only to attack substantial and not formal defects. See 6 Tenn.Code Ann. (Williams, 1934) § 8784; Ala.Code Ann. (Michie, 1928) § 9479; 2 Mass.Gen.Laws (Ter.Ed., 1932) ch. 231, §§ 15–18; Kansas Gen.Stat.Ann. (1935) §§ 60–705, 60–706.

Note to Subdivision (c). Compare Equity Rule 33 (Testing Sufficiency of Defense); N.Y.R.C.P. (1937) Rules 111 and 112.

Note to Subdivisions (e) and (f). Compare Equity Rules 20 (Further and Particular Statement in Pleading May Be Required) and 21 (Scandal and Impertinence); English Rules Under the Judicature Act (The Annual Practice, 1937) O. 19, r. r. 7, 7a, 7b, 8; 4 Mont.Rev.Codes Ann. (1935) §§ 9166, 9167; N.Y.C.P.A. (1937) § 247; N.Y.R.C.P. (1937) Rules 103, 115, 116, 117; Wyo.Rev.Stat.Ann. (Courtright, 1931) §§ 89–1033, 89–1034.

Note to Subdivision (g). Compare Rules of the District Court of the United States for the District of Columbia (1937), Equity Rule 11; N.M. Rules of Pleading, Practice and Procedure, 38 N.M.Rep. vii [105–408] (1934); Wash.Gen.Rules of the Superior Courts, 1 Wash.Rev.Stat.Ann. (Remington, 1932) p. 160, Rule VI(e) and (f).

Note to Subdivision (h). Compare Calif.Code Civ.Proc. (Deering, 1937) § 434; 2 Minn.Stat. (Mason, 1927) § 9252; N.Y.C.P.A. (1937) §§ 278 and 279; Wash.Gen. Rules of the Superior Courts, 1 Wash.Rev.Stat.Ann. (Remington, 1932) p. 160, Rule VI(e). This rule continues U.S.C., Title 28, § 80 [now §§ 1359, 1447, 1919] (Dismissal or remand) (of action over which district court lacks jurisdiction), while U.S.C., Title 28, § 399 [now § 1653] (Amendments to show diverse citizenship) is continued by Rule 15.

(a) When Presented. A defendant shall serve his answer within 20 days after the service of the summons and complaint upon him, unless the court directs otherwise when service of process is made pursuant to Rule 4(e). A party served with a pleading stating a cross-claim against him shall serve an answer thereto within 20 days after the service upon him. The plaintiff shall serve his reply to a counterclaim in the answer within 20 days after service of the answer or, if a reply is ordered by the court, within 20 days after service of the order, unless the order otherwise directs. The United States or an officer or agency thereof shall serve an answer to the complaint or to a cross-claim, or a reply to a counterclaim, within 60 days after the service upon the United States attorney of the pleading in which the claim is asserted. The service of ~~any~~ *a* motion ~~provided for in~~ *permitted under* this rule alters ~~the time fixed by these rules for serving any required responsive pleading~~ *these periods of time* as follows, unless a different time is fixed by order of the court: (1) if the court denies the motion or postpones its disposition until the trial on the merits, the responsive pleading ~~may~~ *shall* be served within 10 days after notice of the court's action; (2) if the court grants a motion for a more definite statement ~~or for a bill of particulars,~~ the responsive pleading ~~may~~ *shall* be served within ~~ten~~ *10* days after the service of the more definite statement ~~or bill of particulars~~. ~~In either case the time for service of the responsive pleading shall be not less than remains of the time which would have been allowed under these rules if the motion had not been made.~~

(b) How Presented. Every defense, in law or fact, to a claim for relief in any pleading, whether a claim, counterclaim, cross-claim, or third-party claim, shall be asserted in the responsive pleading thereto if one is required, except that the following defenses may at the option of the pleader be made by motion: (1) lack of jurisdiction over the subject matter, (2) lack of jurisdiction over the person, (3) improper venue, (4) insufficiency of process, (5) insufficiency of service of process, (6) failure to state a claim upon which relief can be granted, *(7) failure to join an indispensable party.* A motion making any of these defenses shall be made before pleading if a further pleading is permitted. No defense or objection is waived by being joined with one or more other defenses or objections in a responsive pleading or motion. If a pleading sets forth a claim for relief to which the adverse party is not required to serve a responsive pleading, he may assert at the trial any defense in law or fact to that claim for relief. *If, on a motion asserting the defense numbered (6) to dismiss for failure of the pleading to state a claim upon which relief can be granted, matters outside the pleading are presented to and not excluded by the court, the motion shall be treated as one for summary judgment and disposed of as provided in Rule 56, and all parties shall be given reasonable opportunity to present all material made pertinent to such a motion by Rule 56.*

(c) Motion for Judgment on the Pleadings. After the pleadings are closed but within such time as not to delay the trial, any party may move for judgment on the pleadings. *If, on a motion for judgment on the pleadings, matters outside the pleadings are presented to and not excluded by the court, the motion shall be treated as one for summary judgment and disposed of as provided in Rule 56, and all parties shall be given reasonable opportunity to present all material made pertinent to such a motion by Rule 56.*

(d) Preliminary Hearings. The defenses specifically enumerated (1)-~~(6)~~ *(7)* in subdivision (b) of this rule, whether made in a pleading or by motion, and the motion for judgment mentioned in subdivision (c) of this rule shall be heard and determined before trial on application of any party, unless the court orders that the hearing and determination thereof be deferred until the trial.

New matter is shown in italics; matter to be omitted is lined through

(e) Motion for More Definite Statement ~~or for Bill of Particulars~~. ~~Before responding to a pleading or, if no responsive pleading is permitted by these rules, within 20 days after the service of the pleading upon him, a party may move for a more definite statement or for a bill of particulars of any matter which is not averred with sufficient definiteness or particularity to enable him properly to prepare his responsive pleading or to prepare for trial.~~ *If a pleading to which a responsive pleading is permitted is so vague or ambiguous that a party cannot reasonably be required to frame a responsive pleading, he may move for a more definite statement before interposing his responsive pleading.* The motion shall point out the defects complained of and the details desired. If the motion is granted and the order of the court is not obeyed within 10 days after notice of the order or within such other time as the court may fix, the court may strike the pleading to which the motion was directed or make such order as it deems just. ~~A bill of particulars becomes part of the pleading which it supplements.~~

(f) Motion to Strike. Upon motion made by a party before responding to a pleading or, if no responsive pleading is permitted by these rules, upon motion made by a party within 20 days after the service of the pleading upon him or upon the court's own initiative at any time, the court may order *stricken from any pleading any insufficient defense or* any redundant, immaterial, impertinent, or scandalous matter ~~stricken from any pleading~~.

(g) Consolidation of ~~Motions~~ *Defenses*. A party who makes a motion under this rule may join with it the other motions herein provided for and then available to him. If a party makes a motion under this rule and does not include therein all defenses and objections then available to him which this rule permits to be raised by motion, he shall not thereafter make a motion based on any of the defenses or objections so omitted, except ~~that prior to making any other motions under this rule he may make a motion in which are joined all the defenses numbered (1) to (5) in subdivision (b) of this rule which he cares to assert~~ *as provided in subdivision (h) of this rule.*

(h) Waiver of Defenses. A party waives all defenses and objections which he does not present either by motion as hereinbefore provided or, if he has made no motion, in his answer or reply, except (1) that the defense of failure to state a claim upon which relief can be granted, *the defense of failure to join an indispensable party,* and the objection of failure to state a legal defense to a claim may also be made by a later pleading, if one is permitted, or by motion for judgment on the pleadings or at the trial on the merits, and except (2) that, whenever it appears by suggestion of the

New matter is shown in italics; matter to be omitted is lined through

parties or otherwise that the court lacks jurisdiction of the subject matter, the court shall dismiss the action. The objection or defense, if made at the trial, shall be disposed of as provided in Rule 15(b) in the light of any evidence that may have been received.

Advisory Committee's Note to 1948 Amendment

Subdivision (a). Various minor alterations in language have been made to improve the statement of the rule. All references to bills of particulars have been stricken in accordance with changes made in subdivision (e).

Subdivision (b). The addition of defense (7), "failure to join an indispensable party", cures an omission in the rules, which are silent as to the mode of raising such failure. See Commentary, *Manner of Raising Objection of Non-Joinder of Indispensable Party,* 1940, 2 Fed.Rules Serv. 658 and, 1942, 5 Fed.Rules Serv. 820. In one case, *United States v. Metropolitan Life Ins. Co.,* E.D.Pa.1941, 36 F.Supp. 399, the failure to join an indispensable party was raised under Rule 12(c).

Rule 12(b)(6), permitting a motion to dismiss for failure of the complaint to state a claim on which relief can be granted, is substantially the same as the old demurrer for failure of a pleading to state a cause of action. Some courts have held that as the rule by its terms refers to statements in the complaint, extraneous matter on affidavits, depositions or otherwise, may not be introduced in support of the motion, or to resist it. On the other hand, in many cases the district courts have permitted the introduction of such material. When these cases have reached circuit courts of appeals in situations where the extraneous material so received shows that there is no genuine issue as to any material question of fact and that on the undisputed facts as disclosed by the affidavits or depositions, one party or the other is entitled to judgment as a matter of law, the circuit courts, properly enough, have been reluctant to dispose of the case merely on the face of the pleading, and in the interest of prompt disposition of the action have made a final disposition of it. In dealing with such situations the Second Circuit has made the sound suggestion that whatever its label or original basis, the motion may be treated as a motion for summary judgment and disposed of as such. *Samara v. United States,* C.C.A.2d, 1942, 129 F.2d 594, cert. den., 1942, 317 U.S. 686, 63 S.Ct. 258; *Boro Hall Corp. v. General Motors Corp.,* C.C.A.2d, 1942, 124 F.2d 822, cert. den., 1943, 317 U.S. 695, 63 S.Ct. 436. See also *Kithcart v. Metropolitan Life Ins. Co.,* C.C.A.8th, 1945, 150 F.2d 997, aff'g 62 F.Supp. 93.

It has also been suggested that this practice could be justified on the ground that the federal rules permit "speaking" motions. The Committee entertains the view that on motion under Rule 12(b)(6) to dismiss for failure of the complaint to state a good claim, the trial court should have authority to permit the introduction of extraneous matter, such as may be offered on a motion for summary judgment, and if it does not exclude such matter the motion should then be treated as a motion for summary judgment and disposed of in the manner and on the conditions stated in Rule 56 relating to summary judgments, and, of course, in such a situation, when the case reaches the circuit court of appeals, that court should treat the motion in the same way. The Committee believes that such practice, however, should be tied to the summary judgment rule. The term "speaking motion" is not mentioned in the rules, and if there is such a thing its limitations are undefined. Where extraneous matter is received, by tying further proceedings to the summary judgment rule the courts have a definite basis in the rules for disposing of the motion.

The Committee emphasizes particularly the fact that the summary judgment rule does not permit a case to be disposed of by judgment on the merits on affidavits, which disclose a conflict on a material issue of fact, and unless this practice is tied to the summary judgment rule, the extent to which a court, on the introduction of such extraneous matter, may resolve questions of fact on conflicting proof would be left uncertain.

The decisions dealing with this general situation may be generally grouped as follows: (1) cases dealing with the use of affidavits and other extraneous material on motions; (2) cases reversing judgments to prevent final determination on mere pleading allegations alone.

Under group (1) are: *Boro Hall Corp. v. General Motors Corp.*, C.C.A.2d, 1942, 124 F.2d 822, cert. den., 1943, 317 U.S. 695, 63 S.Ct. 436; *Gallup v. Caldwell,* C.C.A.3d, 1941, 120 F.2d 90; *Central Mexico Light & Power Co. v. Munch,* C.C.A.2d, 1940, 116 F.2d 85; *National Labor Relations Board v. Montgomery Ward & Co.,* App.D.C.1944, 79 U.S.App.D.C. 200, 144 F.2d 528, cert. den., 1944, 65 S.Ct. 134; *Urquhart v. American-La France Foamite Corp.,* App.D.C.1944, 79 U.S.App.D.C. 219, 144 F.2d 542; *Samara v. United States,* C.C.A.2d, 1942, 129 F.2d 594; *Cohen v. American Window Glass Co.,* C.C.A.2d, 1942, 126 F.2d 111; *Sperry Products Inc. v. Association of American Railroads,* C.C.A.2d, 1942, 132 F.2d 408; *Joint Council Dining Car Employees Local 370 v. Delaware, Lackawanna and Western R. Co.,* C.C.A.2d, 1946, 157 F.2d 417; *Weeks v. Bareco Oil Co.,* C.C.A.7th, 1941, 125 F.2d 84; *Carroll v. Morrison Hotel Corp.,* C.C.A.7th, 1945, 149 F.2d 404; *Victory v. Manning,* C.C.A.3rd, 1942, 128 F.2d 415; *Locals No. 1470, No. 1469, and No. 1512 of International Longshoremen's Association v. Southern Pacific Co.,* C.C.A.5th, 1942, 131 F.2d 605; *Lucking v. Delano,* C.C.A.6th, 1942, 129 F.2d 283; *San Francisco Lodge No. 68 of International Association of Machinists v. Forrestal,* N.D.Cal.1944, 58 F.Supp. 466; *Benson v. Export Equipment Corp.,* N.Mex.1945, 164 P.2d 380, construing New Mexico rule identical with Rule 12(b)(6); *F.E. Myers & Bros. Co. v. Gould Pumps, Inc.*, W.D.N.Y.1946, 9 Fed.Rules Serv. 12b.33, Case 2, 5 F.R.D. 132. Cf. *Kohler v. Jacobs,* C.C.A.5th, 1943, 138 F.2d 440; *Cohen v. United States,* C.C.A.8th, 1942, 129 F.2d 733.

Under group (2) are: *Sparks v. England,* C.C.A.8th, 1940, 113 F.2d 579; *Continental Collieries, Inc. v. Shober,* C.C.A.3d, 1942, 130 F.2d 631; *Downey v. Palmer,* C.C.A.2d, 1940, 114 F.2d 116; *DeLoach v. Crowley's Inc.*, C.C.A.5th, 1942, 128 F.2d 378; *Leimer v. State Mutual Life Assurance Co. of Worcester, Mass.,* C.C.A.8th, 1940, 108 F.2d 302; *Rossiter v. Vogel,* C.C.A.2d, 1943, 134 F.2d 908, compare s.c., C.C.A.2d, 1945, 148 F.2d 292; *Karl Kiefer Machine Co. v. United States Bottlers Machinery Co.,* C.C.A.7th, 1940, 113 F.2d 356; *Chicago Metallic Mfg. Co. v. Edward Katzinger Co.,* C.C.A.7th, 1941, 123 F.2d 518; *Louisiana Farmers' Protective Union, Inc. v. Great Atlantic & Pacific Tea Co. of America, Inc.,* C.C.A.8th, 1942, 131 F.2d 419; *Publicity Bldg. Realty Corp. v. Hannegan,* C.C.A.8th, 1943, 139 F.2d 583; *Dioguardi v. Durning,* C.C.A.2d, 1944, 139 F.2d 774; *Package Closure Corp. v. Sealright Co., Inc.,* C.C.A.2d, 1944, 141 F.2d 972; *Tahir Erk v. Glenn L. Martin Co.,* C.C.A.4th, 1941, 116 F.2d 865; *Bell v. Preferred Life Assurance Society of Montgomery, Ala.,* 1943, 320 U.S. 238, 64 S.Ct. 5.

The addition at the end of subdivision (b) makes it clear that on a motion under Rule 12(b)(6) extraneous material may not be considered if the court excludes it, but that if the court does not exclude such material the motion shall be treated as a motion for summary judgment and disposed of as provided in Rule 56. It will also be observed that if a motion under Rule 12(b)(6) is thus converted into a summary judgment motion, the amendment insures that both parties shall be given a reasonable opportunity to submit affidavits and extraneous proofs to avoid taking a party by surprise through the conversion of the motion into a motion for summary judgment. In this manner and to this extent the amendment regularizes the practice above described. As the courts are already dealing with cases in this way, the effect of this amendment is really only to define the practice carefully and apply the requirements of the summary judgment rule in the disposition of the motion.

Subdivision (c). The sentence appended to subdivision (c) performs the same function and is grounded on the same reasons as the corresponding sentence added in subdivision (b).

Subdivision (d). The change here was made necessary because of the addition of defense (7) in subdivision (b).

Subdivision (e). References in this subdivision to a bill of particulars have been deleted, and the motion provided for is confined to one for a more definite statement, to be obtained only in cases where the movant cannot reasonably be required to frame an answer or other responsive pleading to the pleading in question. With respect to preparations for trial, the party is properly relegated to the various methods of examination and discovery provided in the rules for that purpose. *Slusher v. Jones,* E.D.Ky.1943, 7 Fed.Rules Serv. 12e.231, Case 5, 3 F.R.D. 168; *Best Foods, Inc. v. General Mills, Inc.,* D.Del.1943, 7 Fed.Rules Serv. 12e.231, Case 7, 3 F.R.D. 275; *Braden v. Callaway,* E.D.Tenn.1943, 8 Fed.Rules Serv. 12e.231, Case 1 ("... most courts ... conclude that the definiteness required is only such as will be sufficient for the party to prepare responsive pleadings"). Accordingly, the reference to the 20 day time limit has also been eliminated, since the purpose of this present provision is to state a time period where the motion for a bill is made for the purpose or preparing for trial.

Rule 12(e) as originally drawn has been the subject of more judicial rulings than any other part of the rules, and has been much criticized by commentators, judges and members of the bar. See general discussion and cases cited in 1 *Moore's Federal Practice,* 1938, Cum.Supplement § 12.07, under "Page 657"; also, Holtzoff, *New Federal Procedure and the Courts,* 1940, 35–41. And compare vote of Second Circuit Conference of Circuit and District Judges, June 1940, recommending the abolition of the bill of particulars; *Sun Valley Mfg. Co. v. Mylish,* E.D.Pa.1944, 8 Fed.Rules Serv. 12e.231, Case 6 ("Our experience ... has demonstrated not only that 'the office of the bill of particulars is fast becoming obsolete' ... but that in view of the adequate discovery procedure available under the Rules, motions for bills of particulars should be abolished altogether."); *Walling v. American Steamship Co.,* W.D.N.Y.1945, 4 F.R.D. 355, 8 Fed.Rules Serv. 12e.244, Case 8 ("... the adoption of the rule was ill advised. It has led to confusion, duplication and delay.") The tendency of some courts freely to grant extended bills of particulars has served to neutralize any helpful benefits derived from Rule 8, and has overlooked the intended use of the rules on depositions and discovery. The words "or to prepare for trial"—eliminated by the proposed amendment—have sometimes been seized upon as grounds for compulsory statement in the opposing pleading of all the details which the movant would have to meet at the trial. On the other hand, many courts have in effect read these words out of the rule. See *Walling v. Alabama Pipe Co.,* W.D.Mo.1942, 3 F.R.D. 159, 6 Fed.Rules Serv. 12e.244, Case 7; *Fleming v. Mason & Dixon Lines, Inc.,* E.D.Tenn.1941, 42 F.Supp. 230; *Kellogg Co. v. National Biscuit Co.,* D.N.J. 1941, 38 F.Supp. 643; *Brown v. H.L. Green Co.,* S.D.N.Y.1943, 7 Fed.Rules Serv. 12e.231, Case 6; *Pedersen v. Standard Accident Ins. Co.,* W.D.Mo.1945, 8 Fed.Rules Serv. 12e.231, Case 8; *Bowles v. Ohse,* D.Neb.1945, 4 F.R.D. 403, 9 Fed.Rules Serv. 12e.231, Case 1; *Klages v. Cohen,* E.D.N.Y.1945, 9 Fed.Rules Serv. 8a.25, Case 4; *Bowles v. Lawrence,* D.Mass.1945, 8 Fed.Rules Serv. 12e.231, Case 19; *McKinney Tool & Mfg. Co. v. Hoyt,* N.D.Ohio 1945, 9 Fed.Rules Serv. 12e.235, Case 1; *Bowles v. Jack,* D.Minn.1945, 5 F.R.D. 1, 9 Fed.Rules Serv. 12e.244, Case 9. And it has been urged from the bench that the phrase be stricken. *Poole v. White,* N.D.W.Va. 1941, 5 Fed.Rules Serv. 12e.231, Case 4, 2 F.R.D. 40. See also *Bowles v. Gabel,* W.D.Mo.1946, 9 Fed.Rules Serv. 12e.244, Case 10 ("The courts have never favored that portion of the rules which undertook to justify a motion of this kind for the purpose of aiding counsel in preparing his case for trial.").

Subdivision (f). This amendment affords a specific method of raising the insufficiency of a defense, a matter which has troubled some courts, although attack has been permitted in one way or another. See *Dysart v. Remington–Rand, Inc.*, D.Conn.1939, 31 F.Supp. 296; *Eastman Kodak Co. v. McAuley,* S.D.N.Y.1941, 4 Fed.Rules Serv. 12f.21, Case 8, 2 F.R.D. 21; *Schenley Distillers Corp. v. Renken,* E.D.S.C.1940, 34 F.Supp. 678; *Yale Transport Corp. v. Yellow Truck & Coach Mfg. Co.,* S.D.N.Y.1944, 3 F.R.D. 440; *United States v. Turner Milk Co.,* N.D.Ill.1941, 4 Fed.Rules Serv. 12b.51, Case 3, 1 F.R.D. 643; *Teiger v. Stephan Oderwald, Inc.,* S.D.N.Y.1940, 31 F.Supp. 626; *Teplitsky v. Pennsylvania R. Co.,* N.D.Ill.1941, 38 F.Supp. 535; *Gallagher v. Carroll,* E.D.N.Y.1939, 27 F.Supp. 568; *United States v. Palmer,* S.D.N.Y.1939, 28 F.Supp. 936. And see *Indemnity Ins. Co. of North America v. Pan American Airways, Inc.,* S.D.N.Y.1944, 58 F.Supp. 338; Commentary, *Modes of Attacking Insufficient Defenses in the Answer,* 1939, 1 Fed.Rules Serv. 669, 1940, 2 Fed.Rules Serv. 640.

Subdivision (g). The change in title conforms with the companion provision in subdivision (h).

The alteration of the "except" clause requires that other than provided in subdivision (h) a party who resorts to a motion to raise defenses specified in the rule, must include in one motion all that are then available to him. Under the original rule defenses which could be raised by motion were divided into two groups which could be the subjects of two successive motions.

Subdivision (h). The addition of the phrase relating to indispensable parties is one of necessity.

Rule 13. Counterclaim and Cross-Claim

Advisory Committee's Note to Original Rule

1. This is substantially Equity Rule 30 (Answer—Contents—Counterclaim), broadened to include legal as well as equitable counterclaims.

2. Compare the English practice, English Rules Under the Judicature Act (The Annual Practice, 1937) O. 19, r. r. 2 and 3, and O. 21, r. r. 10–17; *Beddall v. Maitland,* L.R. 17 Ch.Div. 174, 181, 182 (1881).

3. Certain states have also adopted almost unrestricted provisions concerning both the subject matter of and the parties to a counterclaim. This seems to be the modern tendency. Ark.Civ.Code (Crawford, 1934) §§ 117 (as amended) and 118; N.J.Comp.Stat., (2 Cum.Supp. 1911–1924) tit. 163, § 288; N.Y.C.P.A. (1937) §§ 262, 266, 267 (all as amended, Laws of 1936, ch. 324), 268, 269, and 271; Wis.Stat. (1935) § 263.14(1)(c).

4. Most codes do not expressly provide for a counterclaim in the reply. Clark, *Code Pleading* (1928), p. 486. Ky.Codes (Carroll, 1932) Civ.Pract. § 98 does provide, however, for such counterclaim.

5. The provisions of this rule respecting counterclaims are subject to Rule 82 (Jurisdiction and Venue Unaffected). For a discussion of federal jurisdiction and venue in regard to counterclaims and cross-claims, see Shulman and Jaegerman, *Some Jurisdictional Limitations in Federal Procedure* (1936), 45 Yale L.J. 393, 410 *et seq.*

6. This rule does not affect such statutes of the United States as U.S.C., Title 28, § 41(1) [now §§ 1331, 1332, 1341, 1342, 1345, 1354, 1359] (United States as

plaintiff; civil suits at common law and in equity), relating to assigned claims in actions based on diversity of citizenship.

7. If the action proceeds to judgment without the interposition of a counterclaim as required by subdivision (a) of this rule, the counterclaim is barred. See *American Mills Co. v. American Surety Co.*, 260 U.S. 360, 43 S.Ct. 149, 67 L.Ed. 306 (1922); *Marconi Wireless Telegraph Co. v. National Electric Signalling Co.*, 206 Fed. 295 (E.D.N.Y., 1913); Hopkins, *Federal Equity Rules* (8th ed., 1933), p. 213; Simkins, *Federal Practice* (1934), p. 663.

8. For allowance of credits against the United States see U.S.C., Title 26, §§ 1672–1673 (Suits for refunds of internal revenue taxes—limitations); U.S.C., Title 28, §§ 774 [now § 2406] (Suits by United States against individuals; credits), 775 [1946 ed.] (Suits under postal laws; credits); U.S.C., Title 31, § 227 (Offsets against judgments and claims against United States).

(a) Compulsory Counterclaims. A pleading shall state as a counterclaim any claim~~, not the subject of a pending action,~~ which at the time of ~~filing~~ *serving* the pleading the pleader has against any opposing party, if it arises out of the transaction or occurrence that is the subject matter of the opposing party's claim and does not require for its adjudication the presence of third parties of whom the court cannot acquire jurisdiction, *except that such a claim need not be so stated if at the time the action was commenced the claim was the subject of another pending action.*

(g) Cross-Claim Against Co-Party. A pleading may state as a cross-claim any claim by one party against a co-party arising out of the transaction or occurrence that is the subject matter either of the original action or of a counterclaim therein *or relating to any property that is the subject matter of the original action.* Such cross-claim may include a claim that the party against whom it is asserted is or may be liable to the cross-claimant for all or part of a claim asserted in the action against the cross-claimant.

(i) Separate Trials; Separate Judgments. If the court orders separate trials as provided in Rule 42(b), judgment on a counterclaim or cross-claim may be rendered *in accordance with the terms of Rule 54(b)* when the court has jurisdiction so to do, even if the claims of the opposing party have been dismissed or otherwise disposed of.

Advisory Committee's Note to 1948 Amendment

Subdivision (a). The use of the word "filing" was inadvertent. The word "serving" conforms with subdivision (e) and with usage generally throughout the rules.

The removal of the phrase "not the subject of a pending action" and the addition of the new clause at the end of the subdivision is designed to eliminate the ambiguity noted in *Prudential Insurance Co. of America v. Saxe*, App.D.C.1943, 77

New matter is shown in italics; matter to be omitted is lined through

U.S.App.D.C. 144, 134 F.2d 16, 33–34, cert. den., 1943, 319 U.S. 745, 63 S.Ct. 1033. The rewording of the subdivision in this respect insures against an undesirable possibility presented under the original rule whereby a party having a claim which would be the subject of a compulsory counterclaim could avoid stating it as such by bringing an independent action in another court after the commencement of the federal action but before serving his pleading in the federal action.

Subdivision (g). The amendment is to care for a situation such as where a second mortgagee is made defendant in a foreclosure proceeding and wishes to file a cross-complaint against the mortgagor in order to secure a personal judgment for the indebtedness and foreclose his lien. A claim of this sort by the second mortgagee may not necessarily arise out of the transaction or occurrence that is the subject matter of the original action under the terms of Rule 13(g).

Subdivision (i). The change clarifies the interdependence of Rules 13(i) and 54(b).

Rule 15. Amended and Supplemental Pleadings

Advisory Committee's Note to Original Rule

See generally for the present federal practice, Equity Rules 19 (Amendments Generally), 28 (Amendment of Bill as of Course), 32 (Answer to Amended Bill), 34 (Supplemental Pleading), and 35 (Bills of Revivor and Supplemental Bills—Form); U.S.C., Title 28, §§ 399 [now § 1653] (Amendments to show diverse citizenship) and 777 [1946 ed.] (Defects of form; amendments). See English Rules Under the Judicature Act (The Annual Practice, 1937) O. 28, r. r. 1–13; O. 20, r. 4; O. 24, r. r. 1–3.

Note to Subdivision (a). The right to serve an amended pleading once as of course is common. 4 Mont.Rev.Codes Ann. (1935) § 9186; 1 Ore.Code Ann. (1930) § 1–904; 1 S.C.Code (Michie, 1932) § 493; English Rules Under the Judicature Act (The Annual Practice, 1937) O. 28, r. 2. Provision for amendment of pleading before trial, by leave of court, is in almost every code. If there is no statute the power of the court to grant leave is said to be inherent. Clark, *Code Pleading* (1928), pp. 498, 509.

Note to Subdivision (b). Compare Equity Rule 19 (Amendments Generally) and code provisions which allow an amendment "at any time in furtherance of justice," (e.g., Ark.Civ.Code (Crawford, 1934) § 155) and which allow an amendment of pleadings to conform to the evidence, where the adverse party has not been misled and prejudiced (e.g., N.M. Stat.Ann. (Courtright, 1929) §§ 105–601, 105–602).

Note to Subdivision (c). "Relation back" is a well recognized doctrine of recent and now more frequent application. Compare Ala.Code Ann. (Michie, 1928) § 9513; Ill.Rev.Stat. (1937) ch. 110, § 170(2); 2 Wash.Rev.Stat.Ann. (Remington, 1932) § 308–3(4). See U.S.C., Title 28, § 399 [now § 1653] (Amendments to show diverse citizenship) for a provision for "relation back".

Note to Subdivision (d). This is an adaptation of Equity Rule 34 (Supplemental Pleading).

Rule 16. Pre–Trial Procedure; Formulating Issues

Advisory Committee's Note to Original Rule

1. Similar rules of pre-trial procedure are now in force in Boston, Cleveland, Detroit, and Los Angeles, and a rule substantially like this one has been proposed for

the urban centers of New York state. For a discussion of the successful operation of pre-trial procedure in relieving the congested condition of trial calendars of the courts in such cities and for the proposed New York plan, see *A Proposal for Minimizing Calendar Delay in Jury Cases* (Dec. 1936—published by The New York Law Society); *Pre-Trial Procedure and Administration,* Third Annual Report of the Judicial Council of the State of New York (1937), pages 207–243; *Report of the Commission on the Administration of Justice in New York State* (1934), pp. (288)–(290). See also *Pre-trial Procedure in the Wayne Circuit Court, Detroit, Michigan,* Sixth Annual Report of the Judicial Council of Michigan (1936), pp. 63–75; and Sunderland, *The Theory and Practice of Pre-Trial Procedure* (Dec. 1937) 36 Mich.L.Rev. 215–226, 21 J.Am.Jud.Soc. 125. Compare the English procedure known as the "summons for directions", English Rules Under the Judicature Act (The Annual Practice, 1937) O. 38a; and a similar procedure in New Jersey, N.J.Comp.Stat. (2 Cum.Supp. 1911–1924) tit. 163, § 293, (Supp. 1925–1930) tit. 163, § 347a, N.J.Supreme Court Rules, 2 N.J.Misc.Rep. (1924) 1230, Rules 94, 92, 93, 95 (the last three as amended 1933, 11 N.J.Misc.Rep. (1933) 955).

2. Compare the similar procedure under rule 56(d) (Summary Judgment—Case Not Fully Adjudicated on Motion). Rule 12(g) (Consolidation of Motions), by requiring to some extent the consolidation of motions dealing with matters preliminary to trial, is a step in the same direction. In connection with clause (5) of this rule, see Rules 53(b) (Masters; Reference) and 53(e)(3) (Master's Report: In Jury Actions).

Rule 19. Necessary Joinder of Parties

Advisory Committee's Note to Original Rule

Note to Subdivision (a). The first sentence with verbal differences (e.g., "united" interest for "joint" interest) is to be found in Equity Rule 37 (Parties Generally—Intervention). Such compulsory joinder provisions are common. Compare Alaska Comp.Laws (1933) § 3392 (containing in same sentence a "class suit" provision); Wyo.Rev.Stat.Ann. (Courtright, 1931) § 89–515 (immediately followed by "class suit" provisions, § 89–516). See also Equity Rule 42 (Joint and Several Demands). For example of a proper case for involuntary plaintiff, see *Independent Wireless Telegraph Co. v. Radio Corp. of America,* 269 U.S. 459, 46 S.Ct. 166, 70 L.Ed. 357 (1926).

The joinder provisions of this rule are subject to Rule 82 (Jurisdiction and Venue Unaffected).

Note to Subdivision (b). For the substance of this rule see Equity Rule 39 (Absence of Persons who Would be Proper Parties) and U.S.C., Title 28, § 111 [now § 1391] (When part of several defendants cannot be served); *Camp v. Gress,* 250 U.S. 308, 39 S.Ct. 478, 63 L.Ed. 997 (1919). See also the second and third sentences of Equity Rule 37 (Parties Generally—Intervention).

Note to Subdivision (c). For the substance of this rule see the fourth subdivision of Equity Rule 25 (Bill of Complaint—Contents).

Rule 23. Class Actions

Advisory Committee's Note to Original Rule

Note to Subdivision (a). This is a substantial restatement of Equity Rule 38 (Representatives of Class) as that rule has been construed. It applies to all actions, whether formerly denominated legal or equitable. For a general analysis of class actions, effect of judgment, and requisites of jurisdiction see Moore, *Federal Rules of Civil Procedure: Some Problems Raised by the Preliminary Draft,* 25 Georgetown L.J. 551, 570 *et seq.* (1937); Moore and Cohn, *Federal Class Actions,* 32 Ill.L.Rev. 307 (1937); Moore and Cohn, *Federal Class Actions—Jurisdiction and Effect of Judgment,* 32 Ill.L.Rev. 555–567 (1938); Lesar, *Class Suits and the Federal Rules,* 22 Minn.L.Rev. 34 (1937); *cf.* Arnold and James, *Cases on Trials, Judgments and Appeals* (1936) 175; and see Blume, *Jurisdictional Amount in Representative Suits,* 15 Minn.L.Rev. 501 (1931).

The general test of Equity Rule 38 (Representatives of Class) that the question should be "one of common or general interest to many persons constituting a class so numerous as to make it impracticable to bring them all before the court," is a common test. For states which require the two elements of a common or general interest *and* numerous persons, as provided for in Equity Rule 38, see Del.Ch.Rule 113; Fla.Comp.Gen.Laws Ann. (Supp., 1936) § 4918(7); Georgia Code (1933) § 37–1002, and see English Rules Under the Judicature Act (The Annual Practice, 1937) O. 16, r. 9. For statutory provisions providing for class actions when the question is one of common or general interest *or* when the parties are numerous, see Ala.Code Ann. (Michie, 1928) § 5701; 2 Ind.Stat.Ann. (Burns, 1933) § 2–220; N.Y.C.P.A. (1937) § 195; Wis.Stat. (1935) § 260.12. These statutes have, however, been uniformly construed as though phrased in the conjunctive. See *Garfein v. Stiglitz,* 260 Ky. 430, 86 S.W.(2d) 155 (1935). The rule adopts the test of Equity Rule 38, but defines what constitutes a "common or general interest". Compare with code provisions which make the action dependent upon the propriety of joinder of the parties. See Blume, *The "Common Questions" Principle in the Code Provision for Representative Suits,* 30 Mich.L.Rev. 878 (1932). For discussion of what constitutes "numerous persons" see Wheaton, *Representative Suits Involving Numerous Litigants,* 19 Corn.L.Q. 399 (1934); Note, 36 Harv.L.Rev. 89 (1922).

Clause (1). Joint, Common, or Secondary Right. This clause is illustrated in actions brought by or against representatives of an unincorporated association. See *Oster v. Brotherhood of Locomotive Firemen and Enginemen,* 271 Pa. 419, 114 Atl. 377 (1921); *Pickett v. Walsh,* 192 Mass 572, 78 N.E. 753, 6 L.R.A.(N.S.) 1067 (1906); *Colt v. Hicks,* 97 Ind.App. 177, 179 N.E. 335 (1932). Compare Rule 17(b) as to when an unincorporated association has capacity to sue or be sued in its common name; *United Mine Workers of America v. Coronado Coal Co.,* 259 U.S. 344, 42 S.Ct. 570, 66 L.Ed. 975, 27 A.L.R. 762 (1922) (an unincorporated association was sued as an entity for the purpose of enforcing against it a federal substantive right); Moore, *Federal Rules of Civil Procedure: Some Problems Raised by the Preliminary Draft,* 25 Georgetown L.J. 551, 566 (for discussion of jurisdictional requisites when an unincorporated association sues or is sued in its common name and jurisdiction is founded upon diversity of citizenship). For an action brought by representatives of one group against representatives of another group for distribution of a fund held by an unincorporated association, see *Smith v. Swormstedt,* 16 How. 288, 14 L.Ed. 942 (U.S., 1853). Compare *Christopher, et al. v. Brusselback,* 302 U.S. 500, 58 S.Ct. 350, 82 L.Ed. 388 (1938).

For an action to enforce rights held in common by policyholders against the corporate issuer of the policies, see *Supreme Tribe of Ben Hur v. Cauble,* 255 U.S. 356, 41 S.Ct. 338, 65 L.Ed. 673 (1921). See also *Terry v. Little,* 101 U.S. 216, 25 L.Ed. 864 (1880); *John A. Roebling's Sons Co. v. Kinnicutt,* 248 Fed. 596 (D.C.N.Y., 1917) dealing with the right held in common by creditors to enforce the statutory liability of stockholders.

Typical of a secondary action is a suit by stockholders to enforce a corporate right. For discussion of the general nature of these actions see *Ashwander v. Tennessee Valley Authority,* 297 U.S. 288, 56 S.Ct. 466, 80 L.Ed. 688 (1936); Glenn,

The Stockholder's Suit—Corporate and Individual Grievances, 33 Yale L.J. 580 (1924); McLaughlin, *Capacity of Plaintiff–Stockholder to Terminate a Stockholder's Suit,* 46 Yale L.J. 421 (1937). See also Subdivision (b) of this rule which deals with Shareholder's Action; note, 15 Minn.L.Rev. 453 (1931).

Clause (2). A creditor's action for liquidation or reorganization of a corporation is illustrative of this clause. An action by a stockholder against certain named defendants as representatives of numerous claimants presents a situation converse to the creditor's action.

Clause (3). See *Everglades Drainage League v. Napoleon Broward Drainage Dist.,* 253 Fed. 246 (D.C.Fla., 1918); *Gramling v. Maxwell,* 52 F.2d 256 (D.C.N.C., 1931), approved in 30 Mich.L.Rev. 624 (1932); *Skinner v. Mitchell,* 108 Kan. 861, 197 Pac. 569 (1921); *Duke of Bedford v. Ellis* (1901) A.C. 1, for class actions when there were numerous persons and there was only a question of law or fact common to them; and see Blume, *The "Common Questions" Principle in the Code Provision for Representative Suits,* 30 Mich.L.Rev. 878 (1932).

Note to Subdivision (b). This is Equity Rule 27 (Stockholder's Bill) with verbal changes. See also *Hawes v. Oakland,* 104 U.S. 450, 26 L.Ed. 827 (1882) and former Equity Rule 94, promulgated January 23, 1882, 104 U.S. IX.

Note to Subdivision (c). See McLaughlin, *Capacity of Plaintiff–Stockholder to Terminate a Stockholder's Suit,* 46 Yale L.J. 421 (1937).

Rule 50. Motion for a Directed Verdict

Advisory Committee's Note to Original Rule

Note to Subdivision (a). The present federal rule is changed to the extent that the formality of an express reservation of rights against waiver is no longer necessary. See *Sampliner v. Motion Picture Patents Co.,* 254 U.S. 233, 41 S.Ct. 79, 65 L.Ed. 240 (1920); *Union Indemnity Co. v. United States,* 74 F.(2d) 645 (C.C.A.6th, 1935). The requirement that specific grounds for the motion for a directed verdict must be stated settles a conflict in the federal cases. See Simkins, *Federal Practice* (1934) § 189.

Note to Subdivision (b). For comparable state practice upheld under the conformity act, see *Baltimore and Carolina Line v. Redman,* 295 U.S. 654, 55 S.Ct. 890, 79 L.Ed. 1636 (1935); compare *Slocum v. New York Life Ins. Co.,* 228 U.S. 364, 33 S.Ct. 523, 57 L.Ed. 879, Ann.Cas.1914D, 1029 (1913).

See *Northern Ry. Co. v. Page,* 274 U.S. 65, 47 S.Ct. 491, 71 L.Ed. 929 (1927), following the Massachusetts practice of alternative verdicts, explained in Thorndike, *Trial by Jury in United States Courts,* 26 Harv.L.Rev. 732 (1913). See also Thayer, *Judicial Administration,* 63 U. of Pa.L.Rev. 585, 600–601, and note 32 (1915); Scott, *Trial by Jury and the Reform of Civil Procedure,* 31 Harv.L.Rev. 669, 685 (1918); Comment, 34 Mich.L.Rev. 93, 98 (1935).

Rule 54. Judgments; Costs

Advisory Committee's Note to Original Rule

Note to Subdivision (a). The second sentence is derived substantially from Equity Rule 71 (Form of Decree).

Note to Subdivision (b). This provides for the separate judgment of equity and code practice. See Wis.Stat. (1935) § 270.54; Compare N.Y.C.P.A. (1937) § 476.

Note to Subdivision (c). For the limitation on default contained in the first sentence, see 2 N.D.Comp.Laws Ann. (1913) § 7680; N.Y.C.P.A. (1937) § 479. Compare English Rules Under the Judicature Act (The Annual Practice, 1937) O. 13, r. r. 3–12. The remainder is a usual code provision. It makes clear that a judgment should give the relief to which a party is entitled, regardless of whether it is legal or equitable or both. This necessarily includes the deficiency judgment in foreclosure cases formerly provided for by Equity Rule 10 (Decree for Deficiency in Foreclosures, Etc.).

Note to Subdivision (d). For the present rule in common law actions, see *Ex parte Peterson,* 253 U.S. 300, 40 S.Ct. 543, 64 L.Ed. 919 (1920); Payne, *Costs in Common Law Actions in the Federal Courts* (1935), 21 Va.L.Rev. 397.

The provisions as to costs in actions in forma pauperis contained in U.S.C., Title 28, §§ 832–836 [now § 1915] are unaffected by this rule. Other sections of U.S.C., Title 28, which are unaffected by this rule are: §§ 815 [1946 ed.] (Costs; plaintiff not entitled to, when), 821 [now § 1928] (Costs; infringement of patent; disclaimer), 825 [1946 ed.] (Costs; several actions), 829 [now § 1927] (Costs; attorney liable for, when), and 830 [now § 1920] (Costs; bill of; taxation).

The provisions of the following and similar statutes as to costs against the United States and its officers and agencies are specifically continued:

U.S.C., Title 15, §§ 77v(a), 78aa, 79y (Securities and Exchange Commission)

U.S.C., Title 16, § 825p (Federal Power Commission)

U.S.C., Title 26, §§ 1569(d) and 1645(d) (Internal revenue actions)

U.S.C., Title 26, § 1670(b)(2) (Reimbursement of costs of recovery against revenue officers)

U.S.C., Title 28, § 817 [1946 ed.] (Internal revenue actions)

U.S.C., Title 28, § 836 [now § 1915] (United States—actions in forma pauperis)

U.S.C., Title 28, § 842 [now § 2006] (Actions against revenue officers)

U.S.C., Title 28, § 870 [now § 2408] (United States—in certain cases)

U.S.C., Title 28, § 906 [1946 ed.] (United States—foreclosure actions)

U.S.C., Title 47, § 401 (Communications Commission)

The provisions of the following and similar statutes as to costs are unaffected:

U.S.C., Title 7, § 210(f) (Actions for damages based on an order of the Secretary of Agriculture under Stockyards Act)

U.S.C., Title 7, § 499g(c) (Appeals from reparations orders of Secretary of Agriculture under Perishable Commodities Act)

U.S.C., Title 8, § 45 (Action against district attorneys in certain cases)

U.S.C., Title 15, § 15 (Actions for injuries due to violation of antitrust laws)

U.S.C., Title 15, § 72 (Actions for violation of law forbidding importation or sale of articles at less than market value or wholesale prices)

U.S.C., Title 15, § 77k (Actions by persons acquiring securities registered with untrue statements under Securities Act of 1933)

U.S.C., Title 15, § 78i(e) (Certain actions under the Securities Exchange Act of 1934)

U.S.C., Title 15, § 78r (Similar to 78i(e))

U.S.C., Title 15, § 96 (Infringement of trade-mark—damages)

U.S.C., Title 15, § 99 (Infringement of trade-mark—injunctions)

U.S.C., Title 15, § 124 (Infringement of trade-mark—damages)

U.S.C., Title 19, § 274 (Certain actions under customs law)

U.S.C., Title 30, § 32 (Action to determine right to possession of mineral lands in certain cases)

U.S.C., Title 31, §§ 232 and 234 (Action for making false claims upon United States)

U.S.C., Title 33, § 926 (Actions under Harbor Workers' Compensation Act)

U.S.C., Title 35, § 67 (Infringement of patent—damages)

U.S.C., Title 35, § 69 (Infringement of patent—pleading and proof)

U.S.C., Title 35, § 71 (Infringement of patent—when specification too broad)

U.S.C., Title 45, § 153p (Actions for non-compliance with an order of National R.R. Adjustment Board for payment of money)

U.S.C., Title 46, § 38 (Action for penalty for failure to register vessel)

U.S.C., Title 46, § 829 (Action based on non-compliance with an order of Maritime Commission for payment of money)

U.S.C., Title 46, § 941 (Certain actions under Ship Mortgage Act)

U.S.C., Title 46, § 1227 (Actions for damages for violation of certain provisions of the Merchant Marine Act, 1936)

U.S.C., Title 47, § 206 (Actions for certain violations of Communications Act of 1934)

U.S.C., Title 49, § 16(2) (Action based on non-compliance with an order of I.C.C. for payment of money)

(b) ~~**Judgment at Various Stages.** When more than one claim for relief is presented in an action, the court at any stage, upon a determination of the issues material to a particular claim and all counterclaims arising out of the transaction or occurrence which is the subject matter of the claim, may enter a judgment disposing of such claim. The judgment shall terminate the action with respect to the claim so disposed of and the action shall proceed as to the remaining claims. In case a separate judgment is so entered, the court by order may stay its enforcement until the entering of a subsequent judgment or judgments and may prescribe such conditions as are necessary to secure the benefit thereof to the party in whose favor the judgment is entered.~~ ***Judgment Upon Multiple Claims.*** *When more than one claim for relief is presented in an action, whether as a claim, counterclaim, cross-claim, or third-party claim, the court may direct the entry of a final judgment upon one or more but less than all of the claims only upon an* *express determination that there is no just reason for delay and upon an express direction for the entry of judgment. In the absence of such determination and direction, any order or other form of decision, however designated, which adjudicates less than all the claims shall not terminate the action as to any of the claims, and the order or other form of decision is subject to revision at any time before the entry of judgment adjudicating all the claims.*

Advisory Committee's Note to 1948 Amendment

The historic rule in the federal courts has always prohibited piecemeal disposal of litigation and permitted appeals only from final judgments except in those special instances covered by statute. *Hohorst v. Hamburg-American Packet Co.,* 1893, 148 U.S. 262, 13 S.Ct. 590; *Rexford v. Brunswick-Balke-Collender Co.,* 1913, 228 U.S. 339, 33 S.Ct. 515; *Collins v. Miller,* 1920, 252 U.S. 364, 40 S.Ct. 347. Rule 54(b) was originally adopted in view of the wide scope and possible content of the newly created "civil action" in order to avoid the possible injustice of a delay in judgment of a distinctly separate claim to await adjudication of the entire case. It was not designed to overturn the settled federal rule stated above, which, indeed, has more recently been reiterated in *Catlin v. United States,* 1945, 324 U.S. 229, 65 S.Ct. 631. See also *United States v. Florian,* 1941, 312 U.S. 656, 61 S.Ct. 713, rev'g, and restoring the first opinion in, *Florian v. United States,* C.C.A.7th, 1940, 114 F.2d 990; *Reeves v. Beardall,* 1942, 316 U.S. 283, 62 S.Ct. 1085.

Unfortunately, this was not always understood, and some confusion ensued. Hence situations arose where district courts made a piecemeal disposition of an action and entered what the parties thought amounted to a judgment, although a trial remained to be had on other claims similar or identical with those disposed of. In the interim the parties did not know their ultimate rights, and accordingly took an appeal, thus putting the finality of the partial judgment in question. While most appellate courts have reached a result generally in accord with the intent of the rule, yet there have been divergent precedents and division of views which have served to render the issues more clouded to the parties appellant. It hardly seems a case where multiplicity of precedents will tend to remove the problem from debate. The problem is presented and discussed in the following cases: *Atwater v. North American Coal Corp.,* C.C.A.2d, 1940, 111 F.2d 125; *Rosenblum v. Dingfelder,* C.C.A.2d, 1940, 111 F.2d 406; *Audi-Vision, Inc. v. RCA Mfg. Co., Inc.,* C.C.A.2d, 1943, 136 F.2d 621; *Zalkind v. Scheinman,* C.C.A.2d, 1943, 139 F.2d 895; *Oppenheimer v. F.J. Young & Co., Inc.,* C.C.A.2d, 1944, 144 F.2d 387; *Libbey-Owens-Ford Glass Co. v. Sylvania Industrial Corp.,* C.C.A.2d, 1946, 154 F.2d 814, cert. den., 1946, 66 S.Ct. 1353; *Zarati Steamship Co. v. Park Bridge Corp.,* C.C.A.2d, 1946, 154 F.2d 377; *Baltimore and Ohio R. Co. v. United Fuel Gas Co.,* C.C.A.4th, 1946, 154 F.2d 545; *Jefferson Electric Co. v. Sola Electric Co.,* C.C.A.7th, 1941, 122 F.2d 124; *Leonard v. Socony-Vacuum Oil Co.,* C.C.A.7th, 1942, 130 F.2d 535; *Markham v. Kasper,* C.C.A.7th, 1945, 152 F.2d 270; *Hanney v. Franklin Fire Ins. Co. of Philadelphia,* C.C.A.9th, 1944, 142 F.2d 864; *Toomey v. Toomey,* App.D.C.1945, 80 U.S.App.D.C. 77, 149 F.2d 19.

In view of the difficulty thus disclosed, the Advisory Committee in its two preliminary drafts of proposed amendments attempted to redefine the original rule with particular stress upon the interlocutory nature of partial judgments which did not adjudicate all claims arising out of a single transaction or occurrence. This attempt appeared to meet with almost universal approval from those of the profession commenting upon it, although there were, of course, helpful suggestions for additional changes in language or clarification of detail. But *cf.* Circuit Judge

Frank's dissenting opinion in *Libbey-Owens-Ford Glass Co. v. Sylvania Industrial Corp., supra,* n. 21 of the dissenting opinion. The Committee, however, became convinced on careful study of its own proposals that the seeds of ambiguity still remained, and that it had not completely solved the problem of piecemeal appeals. After extended consideration, it concluded that a retention of the older federal rule was desirable, and that this rule needed only the exercise of a discretionary power to afford a remedy in the infrequent harsh case to provide a simple, definite, workable rule. This is afforded by amended Rule 54(b). It re-establishes an ancient policy with clarity and precision. For the possibility of staying execution where not all claims are disposed of under Rule 54(b), see amended Rule 62(h).

(b) Judgment Upon Multiple Claims *or Involving Multiple Parties.* When more than one claim for relief is presented in an action, whether as a claim, counterclaim, cross-claim, or third-party claim, *or when multiple parties are involved,* the court may direct the entry of a final judgment ~~upon~~ *as to* one or more but ~~less~~ *fewer* than all of the claims *or parties* only upon an express determination that there is no just reason for delay and upon an express direction for the entry of judgment. In the absence of such determination and direction, any order or other form of decision, however designated, which adjudicates ~~less~~ *fewer* than all the claims *or the rights and liabilities of fewer than all the parties* shall not terminate the action as to any of the claims *or parties,* and the order or other form of decision is subject to revision at any time before the entry of judgment adjudicating all the claims *and the rights and liabilities of all the parties.*

Advisory Committee's Note to 1961 Amendment

This rule permitting appeal, upon the trial court's determination of "no just reason for delay," from a judgment upon one or more but fewer than all the claims in an action, has generally been given a sympathetic construction by the courts and its validity is settled. *Reeves v. Beardall,* 316 U.S. 283 (1942); *Sears, Roebuck & Co. v. Mackey,* 351 U.S. 427 (1956); *Cold Metal Process Co. v. United Engineering & Foundry Co.,* 351 U.S. 445 (1956).

A serious difficulty has, however, arisen because the rule speaks of claims but nowhere mentions parties. A line of cases has developed in the circuits consistently holding the rule to be inapplicable to the dismissal, even with the requisite trial court determination, of one or more but fewer than all defendants jointly charged in an action, *i.e.,* charged with various forms of concerted or related wrongdoing or related liability. See *Mull v. Ackerman,* 279 F.2d 25 (2d Cir.1960); *Richards v. Smith,* 276 F.2d 652 (5th Cir.1960); *Hardy v. Bankers Life & Cas. Co.,* 222 F.2d 827 (7th Cir.1955); *Steiner v. 20th Century-Fox Film Corp.,* 220 F.2d 105 (9th Cir.1955). For purposes of Rule 54(b) it was arguable that there were as many "claims" as there were parties defendant and that the rule in its present text applied where fewer than all of the parties were dismissed, *cf. United Artists Corp. v. Masterpiece Productions, Inc.,* 221 F.2d 213, 215 (2d Cir.1955); *Bowling Machines, Inc. v. First Nat. Bank,* 283 F.2d 39 (1st Cir.1960); but the Courts of Appeals are now committed to an opposite view.

The danger of hardship through delay of appeal until the whole action is concluded may be at least as serious in the multiple-parties situations as in multiple-claims cases, see *Pabellon v. Grace Line, Inc.,* 191 F.2d 169, 179 (2d Cir.1951), *cert. denied,* 342 U.S. 893 (1951), and courts and commentators have urged that Rule 54(b) be changed to take in the former. See *Reagan v. Traders & General Ins. Co.,* 255 F.2d 845 (5th Cir.1958); *Meadows v. Greyhound Corp.,* 235 F.2d 233 (5th Cir.1956); *Steiner v. 20th Century-Fox Film Corp., supra;* 6 *Moore's Federal Practice* ¶ 54.34[2] (2d ed. 1953); 3 Barron & Holtzoff, *Federal Practice & Procedure* § 1193.2 (Wright ed. 1958); *Developments in the Law—Multiparty Litigation,* 71 Harv.L.Rev. 874, 981 (1958); Note, 62 Yale L.J. 263, 271 (1953); Ill.Ann.Stat. ch. 110, § 50(2) (Smith-Hurd 1956). The amendment accomplishes this purpose by referring explicitly to parties.

There has been some recent indication that interlocutory appeal under the provisions of 28 U.S.C. § 1292(b), added in 1958, may now be available for the multiple-parties cases here considered. See *Jaftex Corp. v. Randolph Mills, Inc.,* 282 F.2d 508 (2d Cir.1960). The Rule 54(b) procedure seems preferable for those cases, and § 1292(b) should be held inapplicable to them when the rule is enlarged as here proposed. See *Luckenbach Steamship Co., Inc., v. H. Muehlstein & Co., Inc.,* 280 F.2d 755, 757 (2d Cir.1960); 1 Barron & Holtzoff, *supra,* § 58.1, p. 321 (Wright ed. 1960).

Rule 56. Summary Judgment

Advisory Committee's Note to Original Rule

This rule is applicable to all actions, including those against the United States or an officer or agency thereof.

Summary judgment procedure is a method for promptly disposing of actions in which there is no genuine issue as to any material fact. It has been extensively used in England for more than 50 years and has been adopted in a number of American states. New York, for example, has made great use of it. During the first nine years after its adoption there, the records of New York county alone show 5,600 applications for summary judgments. *Report of the Commission on the Administration of Justice in New York State* (1934), p. 383. See also Third Annual Report of the Judicial Council of the State of New York (1937), p. 30.

In England it was first employed only in cases of liquidated claims, but there has been a steady enlargement of the scope of the remedy until it is now used in actions to recover land or chattels and in all other actions at law, for liquidated or unliquidated claims, except for a few designated torts and breach of promise of marriage. English Rules Under the Judicature Act (The Annual Practice, 1937) O. 3, r. 6; Orders 14, 14A, and 15; see also O. 32, r. 6, authorizing an application for judgment at any time upon admissions. In Michigan (3 Comp.Laws (1929) § 14260) and Illinois (Ill.Rev.Stat. (1937) ch. 110, §§ 181, 259.15, 259.16), it is not limited to liquidated demands. New York (N.Y.R.C.P. (1937) Rule 113; see also Rule 107) has brought so many classes of actions under the operation of the rule that the Commission on Administration of Justice in New York State (1934) recommend that all restrictions be removed and that the remedy be available "in any action" (p. 287). For the history and nature of the summary judgment procedure and citations of state statutes, see Clark and Samenow, *The Summary Judgment* (1929), 38 Yale L.J. 423.

Note to Subdivision (d). See Rule 16 (Pre-Trial Procedure; Formulating Issues) and the Note thereto.

Note to Subdivisions (e) and (f). These are similar to rules in Michigan. Mich.Court Rules Ann. (Searl, 1933) Rule 30.

(a) For Claimant. A party seeking to recover upon a claim, counterclaim, or cross-claim or to obtain a declaratory judgment may, at any time after the ~~pleading in answer thereto has been served,~~ *expiration of 20 days from the commencement of the action or after service of a motion for summary judgment by the adverse party*, move with or without supporting affidavits for summary judgment in his favor upon all or any part thereof.

(c) Motion and Proceedings Thereon. The motion shall be served at least 10 days before the time ~~specified~~ *fixed* for the hearing. The adverse party prior to the day of hearing may serve opposing affidavits. The judgment sought shall be rendered forthwith if the pleadings, depositions, and admissions on file, together with the affidavits, if any, show that, ~~except as to the amount of damages,~~ there is no genuine issue as to any material fact and that the moving party is entitled to a judgment as a matter of law. *A summary judgment, interlocutory in character, may be rendered on the issue of liability alone although there is a genuine issue as to the amount of damages.*

Advisory Committee's Note to 1948 Amendment

Subdivision (a). The amendment allows a claimant to move for a summary judgment at any time after the expiration of 20 days from the commencement of the action or after service of a motion for summary judgment by the adverse party. This will normally operate to permit an earlier motion by the claimant than under the original rule, where the phrase "at any time after the pleading in answer thereto has been served" operates to prevent a claimant from moving for summary judgment, even in a case clearly proper for its exercise, until a former answer has been filed. Thus in *Peoples Bank v. Federal Reserve Bank of San Francisco,* N.D.Cal. 1944, 58 F.Supp. 25, the plaintiff's counter-motion for a summary judgment was stricken as premature, because the defendant had not filed an answer. Since Rule 12(a) allows at least 20 days for an answer, that time plus the 10 days required in Rule 56(c) means that under original Rule 56(a) a minimum period of 30 days necessarily has to elapse in every case before the claimant can be heard on his right to a summary judgment. An extension of time by the court or the service of preliminary motions of any kind will prolong that period even further. In many cases this merely represents unnecessary delay. See *United States v. Adler's Creamery, Inc.*, C.C.A.2d, 1939, 107 F.2d 987. The changes are in the interest of more expeditious litigation. The 20-day period, as provided, gives the defendant an opportunity to secure counsel and determine a course of action. But in a case where the defendant himself serves a motion for summary judgment within that time, there is no reason to restrict the plaintiff and the amended rule so provides.

Subdivision (c). The amendment of Rule 56(c), by the addition of the final sentence, resolves a doubt expressed in *Sartor v. Arkansas Natural Gas Corp.*, 1944, 321 U.S. 620, 64 S.Ct. 724. See also Commentary, *Summary Judgment as to*

New matter is shown in italics; matter to be omitted is lined through

Damages, 1944, 7 Fed.Rules Serv. 974; *Madeirense Do Brasil S/A v. Stulman-Emrick Lumber Co.*, C.C.A.2d, 1945, 147 F.2d 399, cert. den., 1945, 325 U.S. 861, 65 S.Ct. 1201. It makes clear that although the question of recovery depends on the amount of damages, the summary judgment rule is applicable and summary judgment may be granted in a proper case. If the case is not fully adjudicated it may be dealt with as provided in subdivision (d) of Rule 56, and the right to summary recovery determined by a preliminary order, interlocutory in character, and the precise amount of recovery left for trial.

Subdivision (d). Rule 54(a) defines "judgment" as including a decree and "any order from which an appeal lies." Subdivision (d) of Rule 56 indicates clearly, however, that a partial summary "judgment" is not a final judgment, and, therefore, that it is not appealable, unless in the particular case some statute allows an appeal from the interlocutory order involved. The partial summary judgment is merely a pre-trial adjudication that certain issues shall be deemed established for the trial of the case. This adjudication is more nearly akin to the preliminary order under Rule 16, and likewise serves the purpose of speeding up litigation by eliminating before trial matters wherein there is no genuine issue of fact. See *Leonard v. Socony-Vacuum Oil Co.*, C.C.A.7th, 1942, 130 F.2d 535; *Biggins v. Oltmer Iron Works*, C.C.A.7th, 1946, 154 F.2d 214; 3 *Moore's Federal Practice*, 1938, 3190–3192. Since interlocutory appeals are not allowed, except where specifically provided by statute, see 3 *Moore, op. cit. supra*, 3155–3156, this interpretation is in line with that policy, *Leonard v. Socony-Vacuum Oil Co., supra*. See also *Audi Vision Inc. v. RCA Mfg. Co.*, C.C.A.2d, 1943, 136 F.2d 621; *Toomey v. Toomey*, App.D.C.1945, 80 U.S.App. D.C. 77, 149 F.2d 19; *Biggins v. Oltmer Iron Works, supra*; *Catlin v. United States*, 1945, 324 U.S. 229, 65 S.Ct. 631.

*

CERTAIN OF THE AMENDMENTS OF FEDERAL RULES OF CIVIL PROCEDURE ADOPTED BY THE SUPREME COURT OF THE UNITED STATES ON JANUARY 21, 1963, EFFECTIVE JULY 1, 1963, WITH ADVISORY COMMITTEE'S NOTES THEREON

[*Amendments here omitted: Changes in Rule 86 and Forms 3, 4, 5, 6, 7, 8, 9, 10, 11, 12, 13, 16, 18, and 21; elimination of Form 22; and addition of new Forms 22–A, 22–B, 30, 31, and 32.*]

Rule 4. Process

(b) Same: Form. The summons shall be signed by the clerk, be under the seal of the court, contain the name of the court and the names of the parties, be directed to the defendant, state the name and address of the plaintiff's attorney, if any, otherwise the plaintiff's address, and the time within which these rules require the defendant to appear and defend, and shall notify him that in case of his failure to do so judgment by default will be rendered against him for the relief demanded in the complaint. *When, under Rule 4(e), service is made pursuant to a statute or rule of court of a state, the summons, or notice, or order in lieu of summons shall correspond as nearly as may be to that required by the statute or rule.*

(d) Summons: Personal Service.

(4) Upon the United States, by delivering a copy of the summons and of the complaint to the United States attorney for the district in which the action is brought or to an assistant United States attorney or clerical employee designated by the United States attorney in a writing filed with the clerk of the court and by sending a copy of the summons and of the complaint by registered *or certified* mail to the Attorney General of the United States at Washington, District of Columbia, and in any action attacking the validity of an order of an officer or agency of the United States not made a party, by also sending a copy of the summons and of the complaint by registered *or certified* mail to such officer or agency.

(7) Upon a defendant of any class referred to in paragraph (1) or (3) of this subdivision of this rule, it is also sufficient if the summons and complaint are served in the manner prescribed by

---

New matter is shown in italics; matter to be omitted is lined through

any statute of the United States or in the manner prescribed by the law of the state in which the ~~service is made~~ *district court is held* for the service of summons or other like process upon any such defendant in an action brought in the courts of general jurisdiction of that state.

(e) Same: ~~Other Service~~ *Service Upon Party Not Inhabitant of or Found Within State.* Whenever a statute of the United States or an order of court *thereunder* provides for service of a summons, or of a notice, or of an order in lieu of summons upon a party not an inhabitant of or found within the state *in which the district court is held,* service ~~shall~~ *may* be made under the circumstances and in the manner prescribed by the statute~~, rule,~~ or order~~.~~*, or, if there is no provision therein prescribing the manner of service, in a manner stated in this rule. Whenever a statute or rule of court of the state in which the district court is held provides (1) for service of a summons, or of a notice, or of an order in lieu of summons upon a party not an inhabitant of or found within the state, or (2) for service upon or notice to him to appear and respond or defend in an action by reason of the attachment or garnishment or similar seizure of his property located within the state, service may in either case be made under the circumstances and in the manner prescribed in the statute or rule.*

(f) Territorial Limits of Effective Service. All process other than a subpoena may be served anywhere within the territorial limits of the state in which the district court is held, and, when *authorized by* a statute of the United States *or by these rules,* ~~so provides,~~ beyond the territorial limits of that state. *In addition, persons who are brought in as parties pursuant to Rule 13(h) or Rule 14, or as additional parties to a pending action pursuant to Rule 19, may be served in the manner stated in paragraphs (1)–(6) of subdivision (d) of this rule at all places outside the state but within the United States that are not more than 100 miles from the place in which the action is commenced, or to which it is assigned or transferred for trial; and persons required to respond to an order of commitment for civil contempt may be served at the same places.* A subpoena may be served within the territorial limits provided in Rule 45.

*(i) Alternative Provisions for Service in a Foreign Country.**

(1) Manner. When the federal or state law referred to in subdivision (e) of this rule authorizes service upon a party not an

* This subdivision was developed collaboratively by the Commission and Advisory Committee on International Rules of Judicial Procedure, a statutory organization established pursuant to Act of September 2, 1958, 72 Stat. 1743, and the Advisory Committee on Civil Rules.

inhabitant of or found within the state in which the district court is held, and service is to be effected upon the party in a foreign country, it is also sufficient if service of the summons and complaint is made: (A) in the manner prescribed by the law of the foreign country for service in that country in an action in any of its courts of general jurisdiction, or (B) as directed by the foreign authority in response to a letter rogatory, when service in either case is reasonably calculated to give actual notice; or (C) upon an individual, by delivery to him personally, and upon a corporation or partnership or association, by delivery to an officer, a managing or general agent; or (D) by any form of mail, requiring a signed receipt, to be addressed and dispatched by the clerk of the court to the party to be served; or (E) as directed by order of the court. Service under (C) or (E) above may be made by any person who is not a party and is not less than 18 years of age or who is designated by order of the district court or by the foreign court. On request, the clerk shall deliver the summons to the plaintiff for transmission to the person or the foreign court or officer who will make the service.

(2) Return. Proof of service may be made as prescribed by subdivision (g) of this rule, or by the law of the foreign country, or by order of the court. When service is made pursuant to subparagraph (1)(D) of this subdivision, proof of service shall include a receipt signed by the addressee or other evidence of delivery to the addressee satisfactory to the court.

Advisory Committee's Note

Subdivision (b). Under amended subdivision (e) of this rule, an action may be commenced against a nonresident of the State in which the district court is held by complying with State procedures. Frequently the form of the summons or notice required in these cases by State law differs from the Federal form of summons described in present subdivision (b) and exemplified in Form 1. To avoid confusion, the amendment of subdivision (b) states that a form of summons or notice, corresponding "as nearly as may be" to the State form, shall be employed. See also a corresponding amendment of Rule 12(a) with regard to the time to answer.

Subdivision (d)(4). This paragraph, governing service upon the United States, is amended to allow the use of certified mail as an alternative to registered mail for sending copies of the papers to the Attorney General or to a United States officer or agency. *Cf.* N.J. Rule 4:5–2. See also the amendment of Rule 30(f)(1).

Subdivision (d)(7). Formerly a question was raised whether this paragraph, in the context of the rule as a whole, authorized service in original Federal actions pursuant to State statutes permitting service on a State official as a means of bringing a nonresident motorist defendant into court. It was argued in *McCoy v. Siler,* 205 F.2d 498, 501–2 (3d Cir.) (concurring opinion), *cert. denied,* 346 U.S. 872, 74 S.Ct. 120, 98 L.Ed. 380 (1953), that the effective service in those cases occurred not when the State official was served but when notice was given to the defendant outside the State, and that subdivision (f) (Territorial limits of effective service), as then worded, did not authorize out-of-State service. This contention found little support. A considerable number of cases held the service to be good, either by fixing upon the service on the official within the State as the effective service, thus satisfying the wording of subdivision (f) as it then stood, see *Holbrook v. Cafiero,* 18 F.R.D. 218 (D.Md.1955); *Pasternack v. Dalo,* 17 F.R.D. 420 (W.D.Pa.1955); *cf. Super Prods. Corp. v. Parkin,* 20 F.R.D. 377 (S.D.N.Y.1957), or by reading paragraph (7) as not limited by subdivision (f). See *Giffin v. Ensign,* 234 F.2d 307 (3d Cir.1956); 2 *Moore's Federal Practice,* ¶ 4.19 (2d ed. 1948); 1 Barron & Holtzoff, *Federal Practice & Procedure* § 182.1 (Wright ed. 1960); Comment, 27 U. of Chi.L.Rev. 751 (1960). See also *Olberding v. Illinois Central R. R.,* 201 F.2d 582 (6th Cir.), *rev'd on other grounds,* 346 U.S. 338, 74 S.Ct. 83, 98 L.Ed. 39 (1953); *Feinsinger v. Bard,* 195 F.2d 45 (7th Cir. 1952).

An important and growing class of State statutes base personal jurisdiction over nonresidents on the doing of acts or on other contacts within the State, and permit notice to be given the defendant outside the State without any requirement of service on a local State official. See, *e.g.,* Ill.Ann.Stat., c. 110, §§ 16, 17 (Smith-Hurd 1956); Wis.Stat. § 262.06 (1959). This service, employed in original Federal actions pursuant to paragraph (7), has also been held proper. See *Farr & Co. v. Cia. Intercontinental de Nav. de Cuba,* 243 F.2d 342 (2d Cir. 1957); *Kappus v. Western Hills Oil, Inc.,* 24 F.R.D. 123 (E.D.Wis.1959); *Star v. Rogalny,* 162 F.Supp. 181 (E.D.Ill.1957). It has also been held that the clause of paragraph (7) which permits service "in the manner prescribed by the law of the state," etc., is not limited by subdivision (c) requiring that service of all process be made by certain designated persons. See *Farr & Co. v. Cia. Intercontinental de Nav. de Cuba, supra. But cf. Sappia v. Lauro Lines,* 130 F.Supp. 810 (S.D.N.Y.1955).

The salutary results of these cases are intended to be preserved. See paragraph (7), with a clarified reference to State law, and amended subdivisions (e) and (f).

Subdivision (e). For the general relation between subdivisions (d) and (e), see 2 Moore, *supra,* ¶ 4.32.

The amendment of the first sentence inserting the word "thereunder" supports the original intention that the "order of court" must be authorized by a specific United States statute. See 1 Barron & Holtzoff, *supra,* at 731. The clause added at the end of the first sentence expressly adopts the view taken by commentators that, if no manner of service is prescribed in the statute or order, the service may be made in a manner stated in Rule 4. See 2 Moore, *supra,* ¶ 4.32, at 1004; Smit, *International Aspects of Federal Civil Procedure,* 61 Colum.L.Rev. 1031, 1036–39 (1961). *But see* Commentary, 5 Fed. Rules Serv. 791 (1942).

Examples of the statutes to which the first sentence relates are 28 U.S.C. § 2361 (Interpleader; process and procedure); 28 U.S.C. § 1655 (Lien enforcement; absent defendants).

The second sentence, added by amendment, expressly allows resort in original Federal actions to the procedures provided by State law for effecting service on nonresident parties (as well as on domiciliaries not found within the State). See, as illustrative, the discussion under amended subdivision (d)(7) of service pursuant to State nonresident motorist statutes and other comparable State statutes. Of particular interest is the change brought about by the reference in this sentence to State procedures for commencing actions against nonresidents by attachment and the like, accompanied by notice. Although an action commenced in a State court by attachment may be removed to the Federal court if ordinary conditions for removal are satisfied, see 28 U.S.C. § 1450; *Rorick v. Devon Syndicate, Ltd.,* 307 U.S. 299, 59 S.Ct. 877, 83 L.Ed. 1303 (1939); Clark v. Wells, 203 U.S. 164, 27 S.Ct. 43, 51 L.Ed. 138 (1906), there has heretofore been no provision recognized by the courts for commencing an original Federal civil action by attachment. See Currie, *Attachment and Garnishment in the Federal Courts,* 59 Mich.L.Rev. 337 (1961), arguing that this result came about through historical anomaly. Rule 64, which refers to attachment, garnishment, and similar procedures under State law, furnishes only provisional remedies in actions otherwise validly commenced. See *Big Vein Coal Co. v. Read,* 229 U.S. 31, 33 S.Ct. 694, 57 L.Ed. 1053 (1913); *Davis v. Ensign-Bickford Co.,* 139 F.2d 624 (8th Cir. 1944); 7 *Moore's Federal Practice* ¶ 64.05 (2d ed. 1954); 3 Barron & Holtzoff, *Federal Practice & Procedure* § 1423 (Wright ed. 1958); *but cf.* Note, 13 So.Calif.L.Rev. 361 (1940). The amendment will now permit the institution of original Federal actions against nonresidents through the use of familiar State procedures by which property of these defendants is brought within the custody of the court and some appropriate service is made upon them.

The necessity of satisfying subject-matter jurisdictional requirements and requirements of venue will limit the practical utilization of these methods of effecting service. Within those limits, however, there appears to be no reason for denying plaintiffs means of commencing actions in Federal courts which are generally available in the State courts. See 1 Barron & Holtzoff, *supra,* at 374–80; Nordbye, *Comments on Proposed Amendments to Rules of Civil Procedure for the United States District Courts,* 18 F.R.D. 105, 106 (1956); Note, 34 Corn.L.Q. 103 (1948); Note, 13 So.Calif.L.Rev. 361 (1940).

If the circumstances of a particular case satisfy the applicable Federal law (first sentence of Rule 4(e), as amended) and the applicable State law (second sentence), the party seeking to make the service may proceed under the Federal or the State law, at his option.

See also amended Rule 13(a), and the Advisory Committee's Note thereto.

Subdivision (f). The first sentence is amended to assure the effectiveness of service outside the territorial limits of the State in all the cases in which any of the rules authorize service beyond those boundaries. Besides the preceding provisions of Rule 4, see Rule 71A(d)(3). In addition, the new second sentence of the subdivision permits effective service within a limited area outside the State in certain special situations, namely, to bring in additional parties to a counterclaim or cross-claim (Rule 13(h)), impleaded parties (Rule 14), and indispensable or conditionally necessary parties to a pending action (Rule 19); and to secure compliance with an order of commitment for civil contempt. In those situations effective service can be made at points not more than 100 miles distant from the courthouse in which the action is commenced, or to which it is assigned or transferred for trial.

The bringing in of parties under the 100-mile provision in the limited situations enumerated is designed to promote the objective of enabling the court to determine entire controversies. In the light of present-day facilities for communication and travel, the territorial range of the service allowed, analogous to that which applies to the service of a subpoena under Rule 45(e)(1), can hardly work hardship on the parties summoned. The provision will be especially useful in metropolitan areas spanning more than one State. Any requirements of subject-matter jurisdiction and venue will still have to be satisfied as to the parties brought in, although these requirements will be eased in some instances when the parties can be regarded as "ancillary." See *Pennsylvania R.R. v. Erie Avenue Warehouse Co.,* 5 F.R. Serv. 2d 14a.62, Case 2 (3d Cir. 1962); *Dery v. Wyer,* 265 F.2d 804 (2d Cir. 1959); *United Artists Corp. v. Masterpiece Productions, Inc.,* 221 F.2d 213 (2d Cir. 1955); *Lesnik v. Public Industrials Corp.,* 144 F.2d 968 (2d Cir. 1944); *Vaughn v. Terminal Transp. Co.,* 162 F.Supp. 647 (E.D.Tenn.1957); and compare the fifth paragraph of the Advisory Committee's Note to Rule 4(e), as amended. The amendment is but a moderate extension of the territorial reach of Federal process and has ample practical justification. See 2 Moore, *supra,* § 4.01[13] (Supp.1960); 1 Barron & Holtzoff, *supra,* § 184; Note, 51 Nw.U.L.Rev. 354 (1956). *But cf.* Nordbye, *Com-*

ments on Proposed Amendments to Rules of Civil Procedure for the United States District Courts, 18 F.R.D. 105, 106 (1956).

As to the need for enlarging the territorial area in which orders of commitment for civil contempt may be served, see *Graber v. Graber,* 93 F.Supp. 281 (D.D.C.1950); *Teele Soap Mfg. Co. v. Pine Tree Products Co., Inc.,* 8 F.Supp. 546 (D.N.H.1934); *Mitchell v. Dexter,* 244 Fed. 926 (1st Cir.1917); *In re Graves,* 29 Fed. 60 (N.D.Iowa 1886).

As to the Court's power to amend subdivisions (e) and (f) as here set forth, see *Mississippi Pub. Corp. v. Murphree,* 326 U.S. 438, 66 S.Ct. 242, 90 L.Ed. 185 (1946).

Subdivision (i). The continual increase of civil litigation having international elements makes it advisable to consolidate, amplify, and clarify the provisions governing service upon parties in foreign countries. See generally Jones, *International Judicial Assistance: Procedural Chaos and a Program for Reform,* 62 Yale L.J. 515 (1953); Longley, *Serving Process, Subpoenas and Other Documents in Foreign Territory,* Proc.A.B.A., Sec.Int'l & Comp.L. 34 (1959); Smit, *International Aspects of Federal Civil Procedure,* 61 Colum.L.Rev. 1031 (1961).

As indicated in the opening lines of new subdivision (i), referring to the provisions of subdivision (e), the authority for effecting foreign service must be found in a statute of the United States or a statute or rule of court of the State in which the district court is held providing in terms or upon proper interpretation for service abroad upon persons not inhabitants of or found within the State. See the Advisory Committee's Note to amended Rule 4(d)(7) and Rule 4(e). For examples of Federal and State statutes expressly authorizing such service, see 8 U.S.C. § 1451(b); 35 U.S.C. §§ 146, 293; Me.Rev.Stat., ch. 22, § 70 (Supp.1961); Minn. Stat.Ann. § 303.13 (1947); N.Y.Veh. & Tfc. Law § 253. Several decisions have construed statutes to permit service in foreign countries, although the matter is not expressly mentioned in the statutes. See, *e.g., Chapman v. Superior Court,* 162 Cal.App.2d 421, 328 P.2d 23 (Dist.Ct.App.1958); *Sperry v. Fliegers,* 194 Misc. 438, 86 N.Y.S.2d 830 (Sup.Ct.1949); *Ewing v. Thompson,* 233 N.C. 564, 65 S.E.2d 17 (1951); *Rushing v. Bush,* 260 S.W.2d 900 (Tex.Ct.Civ.App.1953). Federal and State statutes authorizing service on nonresidents in such terms as to warrant the interpretation that service abroad is permissible include 15 U.S.C. §§ 77v(a), 78aa, 79y; 28 U.S.C. § 1655; 38 U.S.C. § 784(a); Ill.Ann.Stat., c. 110, §§ 16, 17 (Smith-Hurd 1956); Wis.Stat. § 262.06 (1959).

Under subdivisions (e) and (i), when authority to make foreign service is found in a Federal statute or statute or rule of court of a State, it is always sufficient to carry out the service in the manner indicated therein. Subdivision (i) introduces considerable further flexibility by permitting the foreign service and the return thereof to be carried out in any of a number of other alternative ways that are also declared to be sufficient. Other aspects of foreign service continue to be governed by the other provisions of Rule 4. Thus, for example, subdivision (i) effects no change in the form of the summons, or the issuance of separate or additional summons, or the amendment of service.

Service of process beyond the territorial limits of the United States may involve difficulties not encountered in the case of domestic service. Service abroad may be considered by a foreign country to require the performance of judicial, and therefore "sovereign," acts within its territory, which that country may conceive to be offensive to its policy or contrary to its law. See Jones, *supra,* at 537. For example, a person not qualified to serve process according to the law of the foreign country may find himself subject to sanctions if he attempts service therein. See Inter-American Juridical Committee, *Report on Uniformity of Legislation on International Cooperation in Judicial Procedures* 20 (1952). The enforcement of a judgment in the foreign country in which the service was made may be embarrassed or prevented if the service did not comport with the law of that country. See *ibid.*

One of the purposes of subdivision (i) is to allow accommodation to the policies and procedures of the foreign country. It is emphasized, however, that the attitudes of foreign countries vary considerably and that the question of recognition of United States judgments abroad is complex. Accordingly, if enforcement is to be sought in the country of service, the foreign law should be examined before a choice is made among the methods of service allowed by subdivision (i).

Subdivision (i)(1). Subparagraph (a) of paragraph (1), permitting service by the method prescribed by the law of the foreign country for service on a person in that country in a civil action in any of its courts of general jurisdiction, provides an alternative that is likely to create least objection in the place of service and also is likely to enhance the possibilities of securing ultimate enforcement of the judgment abroad. See *Report on Uniformity of Legislation on International Cooperation in Judicial Procedures, supra.*

In certain foreign countries service in aid of litigation pending in other countries can lawfully be accomplished only upon request to the foreign court, which in turn directs the service to be made. In many countries this has long been a customary way of accomplishing the service. See *In re Letters Rogatory out of First Civil Court of City of Mexico,* 261 Fed. 652 (S.D.N.Y.1919); Jones, *supra,* at 543; Comment, 44 Colum.L.Rev. 72 (1944); Note, 58 Yale L.J. 1193 (1949). Subparagraph (B) of paragraph (1), referring to a letter rogatory, validates this method. A proviso, applicable to this subparagraph and the preceding one, requires, as a safeguard, that the service made shall be reasonably calculated to give actual notice of the proceedings to the party. See *Milliken v. Meyer,* 311 U.S. 457, 61 S.Ct. 339, 85 L.Ed. 278 (1940).

Subparagraph (C) of paragraph (1), permitting foreign service by personal delivery on individuals and corporations, partnerships, and associations, provides for a manner of service that is not only traditionally preferred, but also is most likely to lead to actual notice. Explicit provision for this manner of service was thought desirable because a number of Federal and State statutes permitting foreign service do not specifically provide for service by personal delivery abroad, see *e.g.,* 35 U.S.C. §§ 146, 293; 46 U.S.C. § 1292; Calif.Ins.Code § 1612; N.Y.Veh. & Tfc. Law § 253, and it also may be unavailable under the law of the country in which the service is made.

Subparagraph (D) of paragraph (1), permitting service by certain types of mail, affords a manner of service that is inexpensive and expeditious, and requires a minimum of activity within the foreign country. Several statutes specifically provide for service in a foreign country by mail, *e.g.,* Hawaii Rev. Laws §§ 230–31, 230–32 (1955); Minn.Stat.Ann. § 303.13 (1947); N.Y.Civ.Prac. Act, § 229–b; N.Y.Veh. & Tfc. Law § 253, and it has been sanctioned by the courts even in the absence of statutory provision specifying that form of service. *Zurini v. United States,* 189 F.2d 722 (8th Cir. 1951); *United States v. Cardillo,* 135 F.Supp. 798 (W.D.Pa.1955); *Autogiro Co. v. Kay Gyroplanes, Ltd.,* 55 F.Supp. 919 (D.D.C.1944). Since the reliability of postal service may vary from country to country, service by mail is proper only when it is addressed to the party to be served and a form of mail requiring a signed receipt is used. An additional safeguard is provided by the requirement that the mailing be attended to by the clerk of the court. See also the provisions of paragraph (2) of this subdivision (i) regarding proof of service by mail.

Under the applicable law it may be necessary, when the defendant is an infant or incompetent person, to deliver the summons and complaint to a guardian, committee, or similar fiduciary. In such a case it would be advisable to make service under subparagraph (A), (B), or (E).

Subparagraph (E) of paragraph (1) adds flexibility by permitting the court by order to tailor the manner of service to fit the necessities of a particular case or the peculiar requirements of the law of the country in which the service is to be made. A similar provision appears in a number of statutes, *e.g.,* 35 U.S.C. §§ 146, 293; 38 U.S.C. § 784(a); 46 U.S.C. § 1292.

The next-to-last sentence of paragraph (1) permits service under (C) and (E) to be made by any person who is not a party and is not less than 18 years of age or who is designated by court order or by the foreign court. *Cf.* Rule 45(c); N.Y.Civ.Prac. Act §§ 233, 235. This alternative increases the possibility that the plaintiff will be able to find a process server who can proceed unimpeded in the foreign country; it also may improve the chances of enforcing the judgment in the country of service. Especially is this alternative valuable when authority for the foreign service is found in a statute or rule of court that limits the group of eligible process servers to designated officials or special appointees who, because directly connected with another "sovereign," may be particularly offensive to the foreign country. See generally Smit, *supra,* at 1040–41. When recourse is had to subparagraph (A) or (B) the identity of the process server always will be determined by the law of the foreign country in which the service is made.

The last sentence of paragraph (1) sets forth an alternative manner for the issuance and transmission of the summons for service. After obtaining the summons from the clerk, the plaintiff must ascertain the best manner of delivering the summons and complaint to the person, court, or officer who will make the service. Thus the clerk is not burdened with the task of determining who is permitted to serve process under the law of a particular country or the appropriate governmental or nongovernmental channel for forwarding a letter rogatory. Under (D), however, the papers must always be posted by the clerk.

Subdivision (i)(2). When service is made in a foreign country, paragraph (2) permits methods for proof of service in addition to those prescribed by subdivision (g). Proof of service in accordance with the law of the foreign country is permitted because foreign process servers, unaccustomed to the form or the requirement of return of service prevalent in the United States, have on occasion been unwilling to execute the affidavit required by Rule 4(g). See Jones, *supra,* at 537; Longley, *supra,* at 35. As a corollary of the alternate manner of service in subdivision (i)(1)(E), proof of service as directed by order of the court is permitted. The special provision for proof of service by mail is intended as an additional safeguard when that method is used. On the type of evidence of delivery that may be satisfactory to a court in lieu of a signed receipt, see *Aero Associates, Inc. v. La Metropolitana,* 183 F.Supp. 357 (S.D.N.Y.1960).

Rule 5. Service and Filing of Pleadings and Other Papers

(a) Service: When Required. *Except as otherwise provided in these rules,* ~~E~~*e*very order required by its terms to be served, every pleading subsequent to the original complaint unless the court otherwise orders because of numerous defendants, every written motion other than one which may be heard ex parte, and every written notice, appearance, demand, offer of judgment, designation of record on appeal, and similar paper shall be served upon each of the parties. ~~affected thereby, but n~~*N*o service need be made on parties in default for failure to appear except that pleadings asserting new or additional claims for relief against them shall be served upon them in the manner provided for service of summons in Rule 4.

Advisory Committee's Note

The words "affected thereby," stricken out by the amendment, introduced a problem of interpretation. See 1 Barron & Holtzoff, *Federal Practice & Procedure* 760–61 (Wright ed. 1960). The amendment eliminates this difficulty and promotes full exchange of information among the parties by requiring service of papers on all the parties to the action, except as otherwise provided in the rules. See also subdivision (c) of Rule 5. So, for example, a third-party defendant is required to serve his answer to the third-party complaint not only upon the defendant but also upon the plaintiff. See amended Form 22–A and the Advisory Committee's Note thereto.

As to the method of serving papers upon a party whose address is unknown, see Rule 5(b).

Rule 6. Time

(a) Computation. In computing any period of time prescribed or allowed by these rules, *by the local rules of any district court,* by order of court, or by any applicable statute, the day of the act, event, or default ~~after~~ *from* which the designated period of time begins to run ~~is~~ *shall* not ~~to~~ be included. The last day of the period so computed ~~is to~~ *shall* be included, unless it is *a Saturday,* a Sunday, or a legal holiday, in which event the period runs until the end of the next day which is ~~neither~~ *not a Saturday,* a Sunday, ~~nor~~ *or* a *legal* holiday. When the period of time prescribed or allowed is less than 7 days, intermediate *Saturdays,* Sundays, and *legal* holidays shall be excluded in the computation. ~~A half holiday shall be considered as other days and not as a holiday.~~ *As used in this rule and in rule 77(c), "legal holiday" includes New Year's Day, Washington's Birthday, Memorial Day, Independence Day, Labor Day, Veterans Day, Thanksgiving Day, Christmas Day, and any other day appointed as a holiday by the President or the Congress of the United States, or by the state in which the district court is held.*

(b) Enlargement. When by these rules or by a notice given thereunder or by order of court an act is required or allowed to be done at or within a specified time, the court for cause shown may at any time in its discretion (1) with or without motion or notice order the period enlarged if request therefor is made before the expiration of the period originally prescribed or as extended by a previous order or (2) upon motion made after the expiration of the specified period permit the act to be done where the failure to act was the result of excusable neglect; but it may not extend the time for taking any action under Rules ~~25,~~ 50(b), 52(b), 59(b), (d) and (e),

60(b), and 73(a) and (g), except to the extent and under the conditions stated in them.

Advisory Committee's Note

Subdivision (a). This amendment is related to the amendment of Rule 77(c) changing the regulation of the days on which the clerk's office shall be open.

The wording of the first sentence of Rule 6(a) is clarified and the subdivision is made expressly applicable to computing periods of time set forth in local rules.

Saturday is to be treated in the same way as Sunday or a "legal holiday" in that it is not to be included when it falls on the last day of a computed period, nor counted as an intermediate day when the period is less than 7 days. "Legal holiday" is defined for purposes of this subdivision and amended Rule 77(c). Compare the definition of "holiday" in 11 U.S.C. § 1(18); also 5 U.S.C. § 86a; Executive Order No. 10358, "Observance of Holidays," June 9, 1952, 17 Fed.Reg. 5269. In the light of these changes the last sentence of the present subdivision, dealing with half holidays, is eliminated.

With Saturdays and State holidays made "dies non" in certain cases by the amended subdivision, computation of the usual 5-day notice of motion or the 2-day notice to dissolve or modify a temporary restraining order may work out so as to cause embarrassing delay in urgent cases. The delay can be obviated by applying to the court to shorten the time, see Rules 6(d) and 65(b).

Subdivision (b). The prohibition against extending the time for taking action under Rule 25 (Substitution of parties) is eliminated. The only limitation of time provided for in amended Rule 25 is the 90-day period following a suggestion upon the record of the death of a party within which to make a motion to substitute the proper parties for the deceased party. See Rule 25(a) (1), as amended, and the Advisory Committee's Note thereto. It is intended that the court shall have discretion to enlarge that period.

Rule 7. Pleadings Allowed; Form of Motions

(a) Pleadings. There shall be a complaint and an answer; ~~and there shall be~~ a reply to a counterclaim denominated as such; an answer to a cross-claim, if the answer contains a cross-claim; a third-party complaint, if ~~leave is given under Rule 14 to summon~~ a person who was not an original party *is summoned under the provisions of Rule 14;* and ~~there shall be~~ a third-party answer, if a third-party complaint is served. No other pleading shall be allowed, except that the court may order a reply to an answer or a third-party answer.

Advisory Committee's Note

Certain redundant words are eliminated and the subdivision is modified to reflect the amendment of Rule 14(a) which in certain cases eliminates the requirement of obtaining leave to bring in a third-party defendant.

Rule 12. Defenses and Objections—When and How Presented—By Pleading or Motion—Motion for Judgment on Pleadings

(a) When Presented. A defendant shall serve his answer within 20 days after the service of the summons and complaint upon him, ~~unless the court directs otherwise when service is made pursuant to Rule 4(e)~~ *except when service is made under Rule 4(e) and a different time is prescribed in the order of court under the statute of the United States or in the statute or rule of court of the state.* A party served with a pleading stating a cross-claim against him shall serve an answer thereto within 20 days after the service upon him. The plaintiff shall serve his reply to a counterclaim in the answer within 20 days after service of the answer or, if a reply is ordered by the court, within 20 days after service of the order, unless the order otherwise directs. The United States or an officer or agency thereof shall serve an answer to the complaint or to a cross-claim, or a reply to a counterclaim, within 60 days after the service upon the United States attorney of the pleading in which the claim is asserted. The service of a motion permitted under this rule alters these periods of time as follows, unless a different time is fixed by order of the court: (1) if the court denies the motion or postpones its disposition until the trial on the merits, the responsive pleading shall be served within 10 days after notice of the court's action; (2) if the court grants a motion for a more definite statement the responsive pleading shall be served within 10 days after the service of the more definite statement.

Advisory Committee's Note

This amendment conforms to the amendment of Rule 4(e). See also the Advisory Committee's Note to amended Rule 4(b).

Rule 13. Counterclaim and Cross-Claim

(a) Compulsory Counterclaims. A pleading shall state as a counterclaim any claim which at the time of serving the pleading the pleader has against any opposing party, if it arises out of the transaction or occurrence that is the subject matter of the opposing party's claim and does not require for its adjudication the presence of third parties of whom the court cannot acquire jurisdiction~~,~~. ~~except that such a claim need not be so stated~~ *But the pleader need not state the claim* if *(1)* at the time the action was commenced the claim was the subject of another pending action~~.~~, *or (2) the opposing party brought suit upon his claim by attachment or other process by which the court did not acquire jurisdiction to render a personal judgment on that claim, and the pleader is not stating any counterclaim under this Rule 13.*

New matter is shown in italics; matter to be omitted is lined through

Advisory Committee's Note

When a defendant, if he desires to defend his interest in property, is obliged to come in and litigate in a court to whose jurisdiction he could not ordinarily be subjected, fairness suggests that he should not be required to assert counterclaims, but should rather be permitted to do so at his election. If, however, he does elect to assert a counterclaim, it seems fair to require him to assert any other which is compulsory within the meaning of Rule 13(a). Clause (2), added by amendment to Rule 13(a), carries out this idea. It will apply to various cases described in Rule 4(e), as amended, where service is effected through attachment or other process by which the court does not acquire jurisdiction to render a personal judgment against the defendant. Clause (2) will also apply to actions commenced in State courts jurisdictionally grounded on attachment or the like, and removed to the Federal courts.

Rule 14. Third-Party Practice

(a) When Defendant May Bring in Third Party. ~~Before the service of his answer~~ *At any time after commencement of the action* a defendant, ~~may move ex parte or, after the service of his answer, on notice to the plaintiff for leave~~ as a third-party plaintiff, ~~to serve~~ *may cause* a summons and complaint *to be served* upon a person not a party to the action who is or may be liable to him for all or part of the plaintiff's claim against him. *The third-party plaintiff need not obtain leave to make the service if he files the third-party complaint not later than 10 days after he serves his original answer. Otherwise he must obtain leave on motion upon notice to all parties to the action.* ~~If the motion is granted and the summons and complaint are served, t~~*T*he person ~~so~~ served *with the summons and third-party complaint,* hereinafter called the third-party defendant, shall make his defenses to the third-party plaintiff's claim as provided in Rule 12 and his counterclaims against the third-party plaintiff and cross-claims against other third-party defendants as provided in Rule 13. The third-party defendant may assert against the plaintiff any defenses which the third-party plaintiff has to the plaintiff's claim. The third-party defendant may also assert any claim against the plaintiff arising out of the transaction or occurrence that is the subject matter of the plaintiff's claim against the third-party plaintiff. The plaintiff may assert any claim against the third-party defendant arising out of the transaction or occurrence that is the subject matter of the plaintiff's claim against the third-party plaintiff, and the third-party defendant thereupon shall assert his defenses as provided in Rule 12 and his counterclaims and cross-claims as provided in Rule 13. *Any party may move to strike the third-party claim, or for its severance or separate trial.* A third-party defendant may proceed under this rule against any person not a party to the action who is or may be liable to him for all or part of the claim made in the action against the third-party defendant.

Advisory Committee's Note

Under the amendment of the initial sentences of the subdivision, a defendant as third-party plaintiff may freely and without leave of court bring in a third-party defendant if he files the third-party complaint not later than 10 days after he serves his original answer. When the impleader comes so early in the case, there is little value in requiring a preliminary ruling by the court on the propriety of the impleader.

After the third-party defendant is brought in, the court has discretion to strike the third-party claim if it is obviously unmeritorious and can only delay or prejudice the disposition of the plaintiff's claim, or to sever the third-party claim or accord it separate trial if confusion or prejudice would otherwise result. This discretion, applicable not merely to the cases covered by the amendment where the third-party defendant is brought in without leave, but to all impleaders under the rule, is emphasized in the next-to-last sentence of the subdivision, added by amendment.

In dispensing with leave of court for an impleader filed not later than 10 days after serving the answer, but retaining the leave requirement for impleaders sought to be effected thereafter, the amended subdivision takes a moderate position on the lines urged by some commentators, see Note, 43 Minn.L.Rev. 115 (1958); *cf.* Pa.R.Civ.P. 2252–53 (60 days after service on the defendant); Minn.R.Civ.P. 14.01 (45 days). Other commentators would dispense with the requirement of leave regardless of the time when impleader is effected, and would rely on subsequent action by the court to dismiss the impleader if it would unduly delay or complicate the litigation or would be otherwise objectionable. See 1A Barron & Holtzoff, *Federal Practice & Procedure* 649–50 (Wright ed. 1960); Comment, 58 Colum.L.Rev. 532, 546 (1958); *cf.* N.Y.Civ.Prac.Act § 193–a; Me.R.Civ.P. 14. The amended subdivision preserves the value of a preliminary screening, through the leave procedure, of impleaders attempted after the 10–day period.

The amendment applies also when an impleader is initiated by a third-party defendant against a person who may be liable to him, as provided in the last sentence of the subdivision.

Rule 15. Amended and Supplemental Pleadings

(d) Supplemental Pleadings. Upon motion of a party the court may, upon reasonable notice and upon such terms as are just, permit him to serve a supplemental pleading setting forth transactions or occurrences or events which have happened since the date of the pleading sought to be supplemented. *Permission may be granted even though the original pleading is defective in its statement of a claim for relief or defense.* If the court deems it advisable that the adverse party plead ~~thereto~~ *to the supplemental pleading,* it shall so order, specifying the time therefor.

Advisory Committee's Note

Rule 15(d) is intended to give the court broad discretion in allowing a supplemental pleading. However, some cases, opposed by other cases and criticized by the commentators, have taken the rigid and formalistic view that where the original complaint fails to state a claim upon which relief can be granted, leave to serve a supplemental complaint must be denied. See *Bonner v. Elizabeth Arden, Inc.,* 177 F.2d 703 (2d Cir. 1949); *Bowles v. Senderowitz,* 65 F.Supp. 548 (E.D.Pa.), *rev'd on*

New matter is shown in italics; matter to be omitted is lined through

other grounds, 158 F.2d 435 (3d Cir.1946), *cert. denied, Senderowitz v. Fleming,* 330 U.S. 848, 67 S.Ct. 1091, 91 L.Ed. 1292 (1947); *cf. LaSalle Nat. Bank v. 222 East Chestnut St. Corp.,* 267 F.2d 247 (7th Cir.), *cert. denied,* 361 U.S. 836, 80 S.Ct. 88, 4 L.Ed.2d 77 (1959). *But see Camilla Cotton Oil Co. v. Spencer Kellogg & Sons,* 257 F.2d 162 (5th Cir. 1958); *Genuth v. National Biscuit Co.,* 81 F.Supp. 213 (S.D.N.Y. 1948), *app. dism.,* 177 F.2d 962 (2d Cir. 1949); 3 *Moore's Federal Practice* ¶ 15.01[5] (Supp.1960); 1A Barron & Holtzoff, *Federal Practice & Procedure* 820–21 (Wright ed. 1960). Thus plaintiffs have sometimes been needlessly remitted to the difficulties of commencing a new action even though events occurring after the commencement of the original action have made clear the right to relief.

Under the amendment the court has discretion to permit a supplemental pleading despite the fact that the original pleading is defective. As in other situations where a supplemental pleading is offered, the court is to determine in the light of the particular circumstances whether filing should be permitted, and if so, upon what terms. The amendment does not attempt to deal with such questions as the relation of the statute of limitations to supplemental pleadings, the operation of the doctrine of laches, or the availability of other defenses. All these questions are for decision in accordance with the principles applicable to supplemental pleadings generally. *Cf. Blau v. Lamb,* 191 F.Supp. 906 (S.D.N.Y.1961); *Lendonsol Amusement Corp. v. B. & Q. Assoc., Inc.,* 23 F.R.Serv. 15d.3, Case 1 (D.Mass.1957).

Rule 24. Intervention

(c) Procedure. A person desiring to intervene shall serve a motion to intervene upon ~~all~~ *the* parties ~~affected thereby~~ *as provided in Rule 5.* The motion shall state the grounds therefor and shall be accompanied by a pleading setting forth the claim or defense for which intervention is sought. The same procedure shall be followed when a statute of the United States gives a right to intervene. When the constitutionality of an act of Congress affecting the public interest is drawn in question in any action to which the United States or an officer, agency, or employee thereof is not a party, the court shall notify the Attorney General of the United States as provided in Title 28, U.S.C., § 2403.

Advisory Committee's Note

This amendment conforms to the amendment of Rule 5(a). See the Advisory Committee's Note to that amendment.

Rule 25. Substitution of Parties

(a) Death.

(1) If a party dies and the claim is not thereby extinguished, the court ~~within 2 years after the death~~ may order substitution of the proper parties. ~~If substitution is not so made, the action shall be dismissed as to the deceased party.~~ The motion for substitution my be made by *any party or by* the successors or representatives of the deceased party ~~or by any~~

New matter is shown in italics; matter to be omitted is lined through

~~party~~ and, together with the notice of hearing, shall be served on the parties as provided in Rule 5 and upon persons not parties in the manner provided in Rule 4 for the service of a summons, and may be served in any judicial district. *Unless the motion for substitution is made not later than 90 days after the death is suggested upon the record by service of a statement of the fact of the death as provided herein for the service of the motion, the action shall be dismissed as to the deceased party.*

Advisory Committee's Note

Present Rule 25(a)(1), together with present Rule 6(b), results in an inflexible requirement that an action be dismissed as to a deceased party if substitution is not carried out within a fixed period measured from the time of the death. The hardships and inequities of this unyielding requirement plainly appear from the cases. See, *e. g., Anderson v. Yungkau,* 329 U.S. 482, 67 S.Ct. 428, 91 L.Ed. 436 (1947); *Iovino v. Waterson,* 274 F.2d 41 (1959), *cert. denied, Carlin v. Sovino,* 362 U.S. 949, 80 S.Ct. 860, 4 L.Ed.2d 867 (1960); *Perry v. Allen,* 239 F.2d 107 (5th Cir. 1956); *Starnes v. Pennsylvania R. R.,* 26 F.R.D. 625 (E.D.N.Y.), *aff'd per curiam,* 295 F.2d 704 (2d Cir. 1961), *cert. denied,* 369 U.S. 813, 82 S.Ct. 688, 7 L.Ed.2d 612 (1962); *Zdanok v. Glidden Co.,* 28 F.R.D. 346 (S.D.N.Y.1961). See also 4 *Moore's Federal Practice* ¶ 25.01[9] (Supp.1960); 2 Barron & Holtzoff, *Federal Practice & Procedure,* § 621, at 420–21 (Wright ed. 1961).

The amended rule establishes a time limit for the motion to substitute based not upon the time of the death, but rather upon the time information of the death is provided by means of a suggestion of death upon the record, *i. e.* service of a statement of the fact of the death. *Cf.* Ill.Ann.Stat., c. 110, § 54(2) (Smith-Hurd 1956). The motion may not be made later than 90 days after the service of the statement unless the period is extended pursuant to Rule 6(b), as amended. See the Advisory Committee's Note to amended Rule 6(b). See also the new Official Form 30.

A motion to substitute may be made by any party or by the representative of the deceased party without awaiting the suggestion of death. Indeed, the motion will usually be so made. If a party or the representative of the deceased party desires to limit the time within which another may make the motion, he may do so by suggesting the death upon the record.

A motion to substitute made within the prescribed time will ordinarily be granted, but under the permissive language of the first sentence of the amended rule ("the court may order") it may be denied by the court in the exercise of a sound discretion if made long after the death—as can occur if the suggestion of death is not made or is delayed—and circumstances have arisen rendering it unfair to allow substitution. *Cf. Anderson v. Yungkau, supra,* 329 U.S. at 485, 486, 67 S.Ct. at 430, 431, 91 L.Ed. 436, where it was noted under the present rule that settlement and distribution of the estate of a deceased defendant might be so far advanced as to warrant denial of a motion for substitution even though made within the time limit prescribed by that rule. Accordingly, a party interested in securing substitution under the amended rule should not assume that he can rest indefinitely awaiting the suggestion of death before he makes his motion to substitute.

Rule 26. Depositions Pending Action

(e) Objections to Admissibility. Subject to the provisions of Rules *28(b) and* 32(c), objection may be made at the trial or hearing to receiving in evidence any deposition or part thereof for any reason which would require the exclusion of the evidence if the witness were then present and testifying.

Advisory Committee's Note

This amendment conforms to the amendment of Rule 28(b). See the next-to-last paragraph of the Advisory Committee's Note to that amendment.

Rule 28. Persons Before Whom Depositions May Be Taken

(b) In Foreign Countries.* In a foreign ~~state or~~ country, depositions ~~shall~~ *may* be taken (1) on notice before a ~~secretary of embassy or legation, consul general, consul, vice consul, or consular agent of the United States~~ *person authorized to administer oaths in the place in which the examination is held, either by the law thereof or by the law of the United States,* or (2) before ~~such~~ *a* person ~~or officer as may be appointed by commission~~ *commissioned by the court, and a person so commissioned shall have the power by virtue of his commission to administer any necessary oath and take testimony,* or *(3)* ~~under~~ *pursuant to a* letters rogatory. A commission or *a* letters rogatory shall be issued ~~only when necessary or convenient,~~ on application and notice~~,~~ and on ~~such~~ terms ~~and with such directions as~~ *that* are just and appropriate. *It is not requisite to the issuance of a commission or a letter rogatory that the taking of the deposition in any other manner is impracticable or inconvenient; and both a commission and a letter rogatory may be issued in proper cases.* ~~Officers may be designated in notices or commissions~~ *A notice or commission may designate the person before whom the deposition is to be taken* either by name or descriptive title. ~~and~~ *A* letters rogatory may be addressed "To the Appropriate ~~Judicial~~ Authority in [here name the country]." *Evidence obtained in response to a letter rogatory need not be excluded merely for the reason that it is not a verbatim transcript or that the testimony was not taken under oath or for any similar departure from the requirements for depositions taken within the United States under these rules.*

Advisory Committee's Note

The amendment of clause (1) is designed to facilitate depositions in foreign countries by enlarging the class of persons before whom the depositions may be taken on notice. The class is no longer confined, as at present, to a secretary of

* The amendments of this subdivision and of Rule 26(e) were developed collaboratively by the Commission and Advisory Committee on International Rules of Judicial Procedure, a statutory organization established pursuant to Act of September 2, 1958, 72 Stat. 1743, and the Advisory Committee on Civil Rules.

embassy or legation, consul general, consul, vice consul, or consular agent of the United States. In a country that regards the taking of testimony by a foreign official in aid of litigation pending in a court of another country as an infringement upon its sovereignty, it will be expedient to notice depositions before officers of the country in which the examination is taken. See generally *Symposium Letters Rogatory* (Grossman ed. 1956); Doyle, *Taking Evidence by Deposition and Letters Rogatory and Obtaining Documents in Foreign Territory,* Proc.A.B.A., Sec. Int'l & Comp.L. 37 (1959); Heilpern, *Procuring Evidence Abroad,* 14 Tul.L.Rev. 29 (1939); Jones, *International Judicial Assistance: Procedural Chaos and a Program for Reform,* 62 Yale L.J. 515, 526–29 (1953); Smit, *International Aspects of Federal Civil Procedure,* 61 Colum.L.Rev. 1031, 1056–58 (1961).

Clause (2) of amended subdivision (b), like the corresponding provision of subdivision (a) dealing with depositions taken in the United States, makes it clear that the appointment of a person by commission in itself confers power upon him to administer any necessary oath.

It has been held that a letter rogatory will not be issued unless the use of a notice or commission is shown to be impossible or impractical. See, *e. g., United States v. Matles,* 154 F.Supp. 574 (E.D.N.Y.1957); *The Edmund Fanning,* 89 F.Supp. 282 (E.D.N.Y.1950); *Branyan v. Koninklijke Luchtvaart Maatschappij,* 13 F.R.D. 425 (S.D.N.Y.1953). See also *Ali Akber Kiachif v. Philco International Corp.,* 10 F.R.D. 277 (S.D.N.Y.1950). The intent of the fourth sentence of the amended subdivision is to overcome this judicial antipathy and to permit a sound choice between depositions under a letter rogatory and on notice or by commission in the light of all the circumstances. In a case in which the foreign country will compel a witness to attend or testify in aid of a letter rogatory but not in aid of a commission, a letter rogatory may be preferred on the ground that it is less expensive to execute, even if there is plainly no need for compulsive process. A letter rogatory may also be preferred when it cannot be demonstrated that a witness will be recalcitrant or when the witness states that he is willing to testify voluntarily, but the contingency exists that he will change his mind at the last moment. In the latter case, it may be advisable to issue both a commission and a letter rogatory, the latter to be executed if the former fails. The choice between a letter rogatory and a commission may be conditioned by other factors, including the nature and extent of the assistance that the foreign country will give to the execution of either.

In executing a letter rogatory the courts of other countries may be expected to follow their customary procedure for taking testimony. See *United States v. Paraffin Wax, 2255 Bags,* 23 F.R.D. 289 (E.D.N.Y.1959). In many noncommon-law countries the judge questions the witness, sometimes without first administering an oath, the attorneys put any supplemental questions either to the witness or through the judge, and the judge dictates a summary of the testimony, which the witness acknowledges as correct. See Jones, *supra,* at 530–32; Doyle, *supra,* at 39–41. The last sentence of the amended subdivision provides, contrary to the implications of some authority, that evidence recorded in such a fashion need not be excluded on that account. See *The Mandu,* 11 F.Supp. 845 (E.D.N.Y.1935). *But cf. Nelson v. United States,* 17 Fed.Cas. 1340 (No. 10,116) (C.C.D.Pa.1816); *Winthrop v. Union Ins. Co.,* 30 Fed.Cas. 376 (No. 17,901) (C.C.D.Pa.1807). The specific reference to the lack of an oath or a verbatim transcript is intended to be illustrative. Whether or to what degree the value or weight of the evidence may be affected by the method of taking or recording the testimony is left for determination according to the circumstances of the particular case, *cf. Uebersee Finanz-Korporation, A. G. v. Brownell,* 121 F.Supp. 420 (D.D.C.1954); *Danisch v. Guardian Life Ins. Co.,*19 F.R.D. 235 (S.D.N.Y.1956); the testimony may indeed be so devoid of substance or probative value as to warrant its exclusion altogether.

Some foreign countries are hostile to allowing a deposition to be taken in their country, especially by notice or commission, or to lending assistance in the taking of a deposition. Thus compliance with the terms of amended subdivision (b) may not in all cases ensure completion of a deposition abroad. Examination of the law and policy of the particular foreign country in advance of attempting a deposition is therefore advisable. See 4 *Moore's Federal Practice* ¶¶ 28.05–28.08 (2d ed. 1950).

Rule 30. Depositions Upon Oral Examination

(f) Certification and Filing by Officer; Copies; Notice of Filing.

(1) The officer shall certify on the deposition that the witness was duly sworn by him and that the deposition is a true record of the testimony given by the witness. He shall then securely seal the deposition in an envelope indorsed with the title of the action and marked "Deposition of [here insert name of witness]" and shall promptly file it with the court in which the action is pending or send it by registered *or certified* mail to the clerk thereof for filing.

Advisory Committee's Note

This amendment corresponds to the change in Rule 4(d)(4). See the Advisory Committee's Note to that amendment.

Rule 41. Dismissal of Actions

(b) Involuntary Dismissal: Effect Thereof. For failure of the plaintiff to prosecute or to comply with these rules or any order of court, a defendant may move for dismissal of an action or of any claim against him. After the plaintiff, *in an action tried by the court without a jury,* has completed the presentation of his evidence the defendant, without waiving his right to offer evidence in the event the motion is not granted, may move for a dismissal on the ground that upon the facts and the law the plaintiff has shown no right to relief. ~~In an action tried by the court without a jury t~~*T*he court as trier of the facts may then determine them and render judgment against the plaintiff or may decline to render any judgment until the close of all the evidence. If the court renders judgment on the merits against the plaintiff, the court shall make findings as provided in Rule 52(a). Unless the court in its order for dismissal otherwise specifies, a dismissal under this subdivision and any dismissal not provided for in this rule, other than a dismissal for lack of jurisdiction or for improper venue *or for lack of an indispensable party,* operates as an adjudication upon the merits.

Advisory Committee's Note

Under the present text of the second sentence of this subdivision, the motion for dismissal at the close of the plaintiff's evidence may be made in a case tried to a jury as well as in a case tried without a jury. But, when made in a jury-tried case, this motion overlaps the motion for a directed verdict under Rule 50(a), which is also available in the same situation. It has been held that the standard to be applied in deciding the Rule 41(b) motion at the close of the plaintiff's evidence in a jury-tried case is the same as that used upon a motion for a directed verdict made at the same stage; and, just as the court need not make findings pursuant to Rule 52(a) when it directs a verdict, so in a jury-tried case it may omit these findings in granting the Rule 41(b) motion. See generally *O'Brien v. Westinghouse Electric Corp.,* 293 F.2d 1, 5–10 (3d Cir. 1961).

As indicated by the discussion in the *O'Brien* case, the overlap has caused confusion. Accordingly, the second and third sentences of Rule 41(b) are amended to provide that the motion for dismissal at the close of the plaintiff's evidence shall apply only to non-jury cases (including cases tried with an advisory jury). Hereafter the correct motion in jury-tried cases will be the motion for a directed verdict. This involves no change of substance. It should be noted that the court upon a motion for a directed verdict may in appropriate circumstances deny that motion and grant instead a new trial, or a voluntary dismissal without prejudice under Rule 41(a)(2). See 6 *Moore's Federal Practice* ¶ 59.08[5] (2d ed. 1954); *cf. Cone v. West Virginia Pulp & Paper Co.,* 330 U.S. 212, 217, 67 S.Ct. 752, 91 L.Ed. 849 (1947).

The first sentence of Rule 41(b), providing for dismissal for failure to prosecute or to comply with the Rules or any order of court, and the general provisions of the last sentence remain applicable in jury as well as non-jury cases.

The amendment of the last sentence of Rule 41(b) indicates that a dismissal for lack of an indispensable party does not operate as an adjudication on the merits. Such a dismissal does not bar a new action, for it is based merely "on a plaintiff's failure to comply with a precondition requisite to the Court's going forward to determine the merits of his substantive claim." See *Costello v. United States,* 365 U.S. 265, 284–288, 81 S.Ct. 534, 5 L.Ed.2d 551 & n. 5 (1961); *Mallow v. Hinde,* 12 Wheat. (25 U.S.) 193, 6 L.Ed. 599 (1827); Clark, *Code Pleading* 602 (2d ed. 1947); *Restatement of Judgments* § 49, comm. a, b (1942). This amendment corrects an omission from the rule and is consistent with an earlier amendment, effective in 1948, adding "the defense of failure to join an indispensable party" to clause (1) of Rule 12(h).

Rule 49. Special Verdicts and Interrogatories

(b) General Verdict Accompanied by Answer to Interrogatories. The court may submit to the jury, together with appropriate forms for a general verdict, written interrogatories upon one or more issues of fact the decision of which is necessary to a verdict. The court shall give such explanation or instruction as may be necessary to enable the jury both to make answers to the interrogatories and to render a general verdict, and the court shall direct the jury both to make written answers and to render a general verdict. When the general verdict and the answers are harmonious, ~~the court shall direct the entry of~~ the appropriate judgment upon the verdict and answers *shall be entered pursuant to Rule 58.* When the answers are consistent with each other but one or more is inconsistent with the general verdict, ~~the court may direct the entry of~~ judgment *may be entered pursuant to Rule 58* in accordance with the answers, notwithstanding the general verdict, or *the court* may return the jury for further consideration of its answers and verdict or may order a new trial. When the answers are inconsistent with each other and one or more is likewise inconsistent with the general verdict, ~~the court shall not direct the entry of~~ judgment *shall not be entered,* but *the court* ~~may~~ *shall* return the jury for further consideration of its answers and verdict or ~~may~~ *shall* order a new trial.

Advisory Committee's Note

This amendment conforms to the amendment of Rule 58. See the Advisory Committee's Note to Rule 58, as amended.

Rule 50. Motion for a Directed Verdict *and for Judgment Notwithstanding the Verdict*

(a) *Motion for Directed Verdict:* **When Made~~.~~*;* Effect.** A party who moves for a directed verdict at the close of the evidence offered by an opponent may offer evidence in the event that the motion is not granted, without having reserved the right so to do and to the same extent as if the motion had not been made. A motion for a directed verdict which is not granted is not a waiver of trial by jury even though all parties to the action have moved for directed verdicts. A motion for a directed verdict shall state the specific grounds therefor. *The order of the court granting a motion for a directed verdict is effective without any assent of the jury.*

(b) ~~**Reservation of Decision on Motion.**~~ *Motion for Judgment Notwithstanding the Verdict.* Whenever a motion for a directed verdict made at the close of all the evidence is denied or for any reason is not granted, the court is deemed to have submitted the action to the jury subject to a later determination of the legal questions raised by the motion. ~~Within 10 days after the reception of a verdict~~ *Not later than 10 days after entry of judgment,* a party who has moved for a directed verdict may move to have the verdict and any judgment entered thereon set aside and to have judgment entered in accordance with his motion for a directed verdict; or if a verdict was not returned such party, within 10 days after the jury has been discharged, may move for judgment in accordance with his motion for a directed verdict. A motion for a new trial may be joined with this motion, or a new trial may be prayed for in the alternative. If a verdict was returned the court may allow the judgment to stand or may reopen the judgment and either order a new trial or direct the entry of judgment as if the requested verdict had been directed. If no verdict was returned the court may direct the entry of judgment as if the requested verdict had been directed or may order a new trial.

(c) Same: Conditional Rulings on Grant of Motion.

(1) If the motion for judgment notwithstanding the verdict, provided for in subdivision (b) of this rule, is granted, the court shall also rule on the motion for a new trial, if any, by determining whether it should be granted if the judgment is thereafter vacated or reversed, and shall specify the grounds for granting or denying the motion for the new trial. If the motion for a new trial is thus conditionally granted, the order thereon does not affect the finality of the judgment. In case the motion for a new trial has been conditionally granted and the judgment is reversed on appeal, the new trial shall proceed unless the appellate court has otherwise ordered. In case the motion for a new trial has been conditionally denied, the appellee on appeal may assert error in that denial; and if the judgment is reversed on appeal, subsequent proceedings shall be in accordance with the order of the appellate court.

(2) The party whose verdict has been set aside on motion for judgment notwithstanding the verdict may serve a motion for a new trial pursuant to Rule 59 not later than 10 days after entry of the judgment notwithstanding the verdict.

(d) Same: Denial of Motion. If the motion for judgment notwithstanding the verdict is denied, the party who prevailed on that motion may, as appellee, assert grounds entitling him to a new trial in the event the appellate court concludes that the trial court erred in denying the motion for judgment notwithstanding the verdict. If the appellate court reverses the judgment, nothing in this rule precludes it from determining that the appellee is entitled to a new trial, or from directing the trial court to determine whether a new trial shall be granted.

Advisory Committee's Note

Subdivision (a). The practice, after the court has granted a motion for a directed verdict, of requiring the jury to express assent to a verdict they did not reach by their own deliberations serves no useful purpose and may give offense to the members of the jury. See 2B Barron & Holtzoff, *Federal Practice & Procedure* § 1072, at 367 (Wright ed. 1961); Blume, *Origin and Development of the Directed Verdict,* 48 Mich.L.Rev. 555, 582–85, 589–90 (1950). The final sentence of the subdivision, added by amendment, provides that the court's order granting a motion for a directed verdict is effective in itself, and that no action need be taken by the foreman or other members of the jury. See Ariz.R.Civ.P. 50(c); *cf.* Fed.R.Crim.P. 29(a). No change is intended in the standard to be applied in deciding the motion. To assure this interpretation, and in the interest of simplicity, the traditional term, "directed verdict," is retained.

Subdivision (b). A motion for judgment notwithstanding the verdict will not lie unless it was preceded by a motion for a directed verdict made at the close of all the evidence.

The amendment of the second sentence of this subdivision sets the time limit for making the motion for judgment n. o. v. at 10 days after the entry of judgment, rather than 10 days after the reception of the verdict. Thus the time provision is made consistent with that contained in Rule 59(b) (time for motion for new trial) and Rule 52(b) (time for motion to amend findings by the court).

Subdivision (c) deals with the situation where a party joins a motion for a new trial with his motion for judgment n. o. v., or prays for a new trial in the alternative, and the motion for judgment n. o. v. is granted. The procedure to be followed in making rulings on the motion for the new trial, and the consequences of the rulings thereon, were partly set out in *Montgomery Ward & Co. v. Duncan,* 311 U.S. 243, 253, 61 S.Ct. 189, 85 L.Ed. 147 (1940), and have been further elaborated in later cases. See *Cone v. West Virginia Pulp & Paper Co.,* 330 U.S. 212, 67 S.Ct. 752, 91 L.Ed. 849 (1947); *Globe Liquor Co., Inc. v. San Roman,* 332 U.S. 571, 68 S.Ct. 246, 92 L.Ed. 177 (1948); *Fountain v. Filson,* 336 U.S. 681, 69 S.Ct. 754, 93 L.Ed. 971 (1949); *Johnson v. New York, N. H. & H. R. R. Co.,* 344 U.S. 48, 73 S.Ct. 125, 97 L.Ed. 77 (1952). However, courts as well as counsel have often misunderstood the procedure, and it will be helpful to summarize the proper practice in the text of the rule. The amendments do not alter the effects of a jury verdict or the scope of appellate review.

In the situation mentioned, *subdivision (c)(1)* requires that the court make a "conditional" ruling on the new-trial motion, *i. e.,* a ruling which goes on the assumption that the motion for judgment n. o. v. was erroneously granted and will be reversed or vacated; and the court is required to state its grounds for the conditional ruling. Subdivision (c)(1) then spells out the consequences of a reversal of the judgment in the light of the conditional ruling on the new-trial motion.

If the motion for new trial has been conditionally granted, and the judgment is reversed, "the new trial shall proceed unless the appellate court has otherwise ordered." The party against whom the judgment n. o. v. was entered below may, as appellant, besides seeking to overthrow that judgment, also attack the conditional grant of the new trial. And the appellate court, if it reverses the judgment n. o. v., may in an appropriate case also reverse the conditional grant of the new trial and direct that judgment be entered on the verdict. See *Bailey v. Slentz,* 189 F.2d 406 (10th Cir. 1951); *Moist Cold Refrigerator Co. v. Lou Johnson Co.,* 249 F.2d 246 (9th Cir. 1957), *cert. denied,* 356 U.S. 968, 78 S.Ct. 1008, 2 L.Ed.2d 1074 (1958); *Peters v. Smith,* 221 F.2d 721 (3d Cir. 1955); *Dailey v. Timmer,* 292 F.2d 824 (3d Cir. 1961), explaining *Lind v. Schenley Industries, Inc.,* 278 F.2d 79 (3d Cir.), *cert. denied,* 364 U.S. 835, 81 S.Ct. 58, 5 L.Ed.2d 60 (1960); *Cox v. Pennsylvania R. R.,* 120 A.2d 214 (D.C.Mun.Ct.App.1956); 3 Barron & Holtzoff, *Federal Practice & Procedure* § 1302.1 at 346–47 (Wright ed. 1958); 6 *Moore's Federal Practice* ¶ 59.16 at 3915 n. 8a (2d ed. 1954).

If the motion for a new trial has been conditionally denied, and the judgment is reversed, "subsequent proceedings shall be in accordance with the order of the appellate court." The party in whose favor judgment n. o. v. was entered below may, as appellee, besides seeking to uphold that judgment, also urge on the appellate court that the trial court committed error in conditionally denying the new trial. The appellee may assert this error in his brief, without taking a cross-appeal. *Cf. Patterson v. Pennsylvania R. R.,* 238 F.2d 645, 650 (6th Cir. 1956); *Hughes v. St. Louis Nat. L. Baseball Club, Inc.,* 359 Mo. 993, 997, 224 S.W.2d 989, 992 (1949). If the appellate court concludes that the judgment cannot stand, but accepts the appellee's contention that there was error in the conditional denial of the new trial, it may order a new trial in lieu of directing the entry of judgment upon the verdict.

Subdivision (c)(2), which also deals with the situation where the trial court has granted the motion for judgment n. o. v., states that the verdict-winner may apply to the trial court for a new trial pursuant to Rule 59 after the judgment n. o. v. has been entered against him. In arguing to the trial court in opposition to the motion for judgment n. o. v., the verdict-winner may, and often will, contend that he is entitled, at the least, to a new trial, and the court has a range of discretion to grant a new trial or (where plaintiff won the verdict) to order a dismissal of the action without prejudice instead of granting judgment n. o. v. See *Cone v. West Virginia Pulp & Paper Co., supra,* 330 U.S. at 217, 218, 67 S.Ct. at 755, 756, 91 L.Ed. 849. Subdivision (c)(2) is a reminder that the verdict-winner is entitled, even after entry of judgment n. o. v. against him, to move for a new trial in the usual course. If in these circumstances the motion is granted, the judgment is superseded.

In some unusual circumstances, however, the grant of the new-trial motion may be only conditional, and the judgment will not be superseded. See the situation in *Tribble v. Bruin,* 279 F.2d 424 (4th Cir. 1960) (upon a verdict for plaintiff, defendant moves for and obtains judgment n. o. v.; plaintiff moves for a new trial on the ground of inadequate damages; trial court might properly have granted plaintiff's motion, conditional upon reversal of the judgment n. o. v.).

Even if the verdict-winner makes no motion for a new trial, he is entitled upon his appeal from the judgment n. o. v. not only to urge that that judgment should be reversed and judgment entered upon the verdict, but that errors were committed during the trial which at the least entitle him to a new trial.

Subdivision (d) deals with the situation where judgment has been entered on the jury verdict, the motion for judgment n. o. v. and any motion for a new trial having been denied by the trial court. The verdict-winner, as appellee, besides seeking to uphold the judgment, may urge upon the appellate court that in case the trial court is found to have erred in entering judgment on the verdict, there are grounds for granting him a new trial instead of directing the entry of judgment for his opponent. In appropriate cases the appellate court is not precluded from itself directing that a new trial be had. See *Weade v. Dichmann, Wright & Pugh, Inc.,* 337 U.S. 801, 69 S.Ct. 1326, 93 L.Ed. 1704 (1949). Nor is it precluded in proper cases from remanding the case for a determination by the trial court as to whether a new trial should be granted. The latter course is advisable where the grounds urged are suitable for the exercise of trial court discretion.

Subdivision (d) does not attempt a regulation of all aspects of the procedure where the motion for judgment n. o. v. and any accompanying motion for a new trial are denied, since the problems have not been fully canvassed in the decisions and the procedure is in some respects still in a formative stage. It is, however, designed to give guidance on certain important features of the practice.

Rule 52. Findings by the Court

(a) Effect. In all actions tried upon the facts without a jury or with an advisory jury, the court shall find the facts specially and state separately its conclusions of law thereon, and ~~direct the entry of the appropriate~~ judgment *shall be entered pursuant to Rule 58;* and in granting or refusing interlocutory injunctions the court shall similarly set forth the findings of fact and conclusions of law which constitute the grounds of its action. Requests for findings are not necessary for purposes of review. Findings of fact shall not be set aside unless clearly erroneous, and due regard shall be given to the opportunity of the trial court to judge of the credibility of the witnesses. The findings of a master, to the extent that the court adopts them, shall be considered as the findings of the court. If an opinion or memorandum of decision is filed, it will be sufficient if the findings of fact and conclusions of law appear therein. Findings of fact and conclusions of law are unnecessary on decisions of motions under Rules 12 or 56 or any other motion except as provided in Rule 41(b).

Advisory Committee's Note

This amendment conforms to the amendment of Rule 58. See the Advisory Committee's Note to Rule 58, as amended.

Rule 56. Summary Judgment

(c) Motion and Proceedings Thereon. The motion shall be served at least 10 days before the time fixed for the hearing. The adverse party prior to the day of hearing may serve opposing affidavits. The judgment sought shall be rendered forthwith if the pleadings, depositions, *answers to interrogatories,* and admissions on file, together with the affidavits, if any, show that there is no genuine issue as to any material fact and that the moving party is entitled to a judgment as a matter of law. A summary judgment, interlocutory in character, may be rendered on the issue of liability alone although there is a genuine issue as to the amount of damages.

(e) Form of Affidavits; Further Testimony*; Defense Required.* Supporting and opposing affidavits shall be made on personal knowledge, shall set forth such facts as would be admissible in evidence, and shall show affirmatively that the affiant is competent to testify to the matters stated therein. Sworn or certified copies of all papers or parts thereof referred to in an affidavit shall be attached thereto or served therewith. The court may permit affidavits to be supplemented or opposed by depositions, *answers to interrogatories,* or ~~by~~ further affidavits. *When a motion for summary judgment is made and supported as provided in this rule, an adverse party may not rest upon the mere allegations or denials of his pleading, but his response, by affidavits or as otherwise provided in this rule, must set forth specific facts showing that there is a genuine issue for trial. If he does not so respond, summary judgment, if appropriate, shall be entered against him.*

New matter is shown in italics; matter to be omitted is lined through

Advisory Committee's Note

Subdivision (c). By the amendment "answers to interrogatories" are included among the materials which may be considered on motion for summary judgment. The phrase was inadvertently omitted from the rule, see 3 Barron & Holtzoff, *Federal Practice & Procedure* 159–60 (Wright ed. 1958), and the courts have generally reached by interpretation the result which will hereafter be required by the text of the amended rule. See Annot., 74 A.L.R.2d 984 (1960).

Subdivision (e). The words "answers to interrogatories" are added in the third sentence of this subdivision to conform to the amendment of subdivision (c).

The last two sentences are added to overcome a line of cases, chiefly in the Third Circuit, which has impaired the utility of the summary judgment device. A typical case is as follows: A party supports his motion for summary judgment by affidavits or other evidentiary matter sufficient to show that there is no genuine issue as to a material fact. The adverse party, in opposing the motion, does not produce any evidentiary matter, or produces some but not enough to establish that there is a genuine issue for trial. Instead, the adverse party rests on averments of his pleadings which on their face present an issue. In this situation Third Circuit cases have taken the view that summary judgment must be denied, at least if the averments are "well-pleaded," and not supposititious, conclusory, or ultimate. See *Frederick Hart & Co., Inc. v. Recordgraph Corp.,* 169 F.2d 580 (3d Cir. 1948); *United States ex rel. Kolton v. Halpern,* 260 F.2d 590 (3d Cir. 1958); *United States ex rel. Nobles v. Ivey Bros. Constr. Co., Inc.,* 191 F.Supp. 383 (D.Del.1961); *Jamison v. Pennsylvania Salt Mfg. Co.,* 22 F.R.D. 238 (W.D.Pa.1958); *Bunny Bear, Inc. v. Dennis Mitchell Industries,* 139 F.Supp. 542 (E.D.Pa.1956); *Levy v. Equitable Life Assur. Society,* 18 F.R.D. 164 (E.D.Pa.1955).

The very mission of the summary judgment procedure is to pierce the pleadings and to assess the proof in order to see whether there is a genuine need for trial. The Third Circuit doctrine, which permits the pleadings themselves to stand in the way of granting an otherwise justified summary judgment, is incompatible with the basic purpose of the rule. See 6 *Moore's Federal Practice* 2069 (2d ed. 1953); 3 Barron & Holtzoff, *supra,* § 1235.1.

It is hoped that the amendment will contribute to the more effective utilization of the salutary device of summary judgment.

The amendment is not intended to derogate from the solemnity of the pleadings. Rather it recognizes that, despite the best efforts of counsel to make his pleadings accurate, they may be overwhelmingly contradicted by the proof available to his adversary.

Nor is the amendment designed to affect the ordinary standards applicable to the summary judgment motion. So, for example: Where an issue as to a material fact cannot be resolved without observation of the demeanor of witnesses in order to evaluate their credibility, summary judgment is not appropriate. Where the evidentiary matter in support of the motion does not establish the absence of a genuine issue, summary judgment must be denied even if no opposing evidentiary matter is presented. And summary judgment may be inappropriate where the party opposing it shows under subdivision (f) that he cannot at the time present facts essential to justify his opposition.

Rule 58. Entry of Judgment

~~Unless the court otherwise directs and subject to the provisions of Rule 54(b), judgment upon the verdict of a jury shall be entered~~

~~forthwith by the clerk; but the court shall direct the appropriate judgment to be entered upon a special verdict or upon a general verdict accompanied by answers to interrogatories returned by a jury pursuant to Rule 40. When the court directs that a party recover only money or costs or that all relief be denied, the clerk shall enter judgment forthwith upon receipt by him of the direction; but when the court directs entry of judgment for other relief, the judge shall promptly settle or approve the form of the judgment and direct that it be entered by the clerk. The notation of a judgment in the civil docket as provided by Rule 79(a) constitutes the entry of the judgment; and the judgment is not effective before such entry. The entry of the judgment shall not be delayed for the taxing of costs.~~

Subject to the provisions of Rule 54(b): (1) upon a general verdict of a jury, or upon a decision by the court that a party shall recover only a sum certain or costs or that all relief shall be denied, the clerk, unless the court otherwise orders, shall forthwith prepare, sign, and enter the judgment without awaiting any direction by the court; (2) upon a decision by the court granting other relief, or upon a special verdict or a general verdict accompanied by answers to interrogatories, the court shall promptly approve the form of the judgment, and the clerk shall thereupon enter it. Every judgment shall be set forth on a separate document. A judgment is effective only when so set forth and when entered as provided in Rule 79(a). Entry of the judgment shall not be delayed for the taxing of costs. Attorneys shall not submit forms of judgment except upon direction of the court, and these directions shall not be given as a matter of course.

Advisory Committee's Note

Under the present rule a distinction has sometimes been made between judgments on general jury verdicts, on the one hand, and, on the other, judgments upon decisions of the court that a party shall recover only money or costs or that all relief shall be denied. In the first situation, it is clear that the clerk should enter the judgment without awaiting a direction by the court unless the court otherwise orders. In the second situation it was intended that the clerk should similarly enter the judgment forthwith upon the court's decision; but because of the separate listing in the rule, and the use of the phrase "upon receipt . . . of the direction," the rule has sometimes been interpreted as requiring the clerk to await a separate direction of the court. All these judgments are usually uncomplicated, and should be handled in the same way. The amended rule accordingly deals with them as a single group in clause (1) (substituting the expression "only a sum certain" for the present expression "only money"), and requires the clerk to prepare, sign, and enter them forthwith, without awaiting court direction, unless the court makes a contrary order. (The clerk's duty is ministerial and may be performed by a deputy clerk in the name of the clerk. See 28 U.S.C. § 956; *cf. Gilbertson v. United States,* 168 Fed. 672 (7th Cir. 1909).) The more complicated judgments described in clause (2) must be approved by the court before they are entered.

New matter is shown in italics; matter to be omitted is lined through

Rule 58 is designed to encourage all reasonable speed in formulating and entering the judgment when the case has been decided. Participation by the attorneys through the submission of forms of judgment involves needless expenditure of time and effort and promotes delay, except in special cases where counsel's assistance can be of real value. See *Matteson v. United States,* 240 F.2d 517, 518–19 (2d Cir. 1956). Accordingly, the amended rule provides that attorneys shall not submit forms of judgment unless directed to do so by the court. This applies to the judgments mentioned in clause (2) as well as clause (1).

Hitherto some difficulty has arisen, chiefly where the court has written an opinion or memorandum containing some apparently directive or dispositive words, *e.g.,* "the plaintiff's motion [for summary judgment] is granted," see *United States v. F. & M. Schaefer Brewing Co.,* 356 U.S. 227, 229, 78 S.Ct. 674, 2 L.Ed.2d 721 (1958). Clerks on occasion have viewed these opinions or memoranda as being in themselves a sufficient basis for entering judgment in the civil docket as provided by Rule 79(a). However, where the opinion or memorandum has not contained all the elements of a judgment, or where the judge has later signed a formal judgment, it has become a matter of doubt whether the purported entry of judgment was effective, starting the time running for post-verdict motions and for the purpose of appeal. See *id.*; and *compare Blanchard v. Commonwealth Oil Co.,* 294 F.2d 834 (5th Cir. 1961); *United States v. Higginson,* 238 F.2d 439 (1st Cir. 1956); *Danzig v. Virgin Isle Hotel, Inc.,* 278 F.2d 580 (3d Cir. 1960); *Sears v. Austin,* 282 F.2d 340 (9th Cir. 1960), *with Matteson v. United States, supra; Erstling v. Southern Bell Tel. & Tel. Co.,* 255 F.2d 93 (5th Cir. 1958); *Barta v. Oglala Sioux Tribe,* 259 F.2d 553 (8th Cir. 1958), *cert. denied,* 358 U.S. 932, 79 S.Ct. 320, 3 L.Ed.2d 304 (1959); *Beacon Fed. S. & L. Assn. v. Federal Home L. Bank Bd.,* 266 F.2d 246 (7th Cir.), *cert. denied,* 361 U.S. 823, 80 S.Ct. 70, 4 L.Ed.2d 67 (1959); *Ram v. Paramount Film D. Corp.,* 278 F.2d 191 (4th Cir. 1960).

The amended rule eliminates these uncertainties by requiring that there be a judgment set out on a separate document—distinct from any opinion or memorandum—which provides the basis for the entry of judgment. That judgments shall be on separate documents is also indicated in Rule 79(b); and see General Rule 10 of the U. S. District Courts for the Eastern and Southern Districts of New York; *Ram v. Paramount Film D. Corp., supra,* at 194.

See the amendment of Rule 79(a) and the new specimen forms of judgment, Forms 31 and 32.

See also Rule 55(b)(1) and (2) covering the subject of judgments by default.

Rule 71A. Condemnation of Property

(d) Process.

(3) Service of Notice. (i) Personal service. Personal service of the notice (but without copies of the complaint) shall be made in accordance with Rule 4(c) and (d) upon a defendant who resides within the United States or its territories or insular possessions and whose residence is known. ~~The provisions of Rule 4(f) shall not be applicable.~~

Advisory Committee's Note

This amendment conforms to the amendment of Rule 4(f).

New matter is shown in italics; matter to be omitted is lined through

Rule 77. District Courts and Clerks

(c) Clerk's Office and Orders by Clerk. The clerk's office with the clerk or a deputy in attendance shall be open during business hours on all days except *Saturdays,* Sundays, and legal holidays~~.~~*, but a district court may provide by local rule or order that its clerk's office shall be open for specified hours on Saturdays or particular legal holidays other than New Year's Day, Washington's Birthday, Memorial Day, Independence Day, Labor Day, Veterans Day, Thanksgiving Day, and Christmas Day.* All motions and applications in the clerk's office for issuing mesne process, for issuing final process to enforce and execute judgments, for entering defaults or judgments by default, and for other proceedings which do not require allowance or order of the court are grantable of course by the clerk; but his action may be suspended or altered or rescinded by the court upon cause shown.

(d) Notice of Orders or Judgments. Immediately upon the entry of an order or judgment the clerk shall serve a notice of the entry by mail in the manner provided for in Rule 5 upon ~~every~~ *each* party ~~affected thereby~~ who is not in default for failure to appear, and shall make a note in the docket of the mailing. Such mailing is sufficient notice for all purposes for which notice of the entry of an order is required by these rules; but any party may in addition serve a notice of such entry in the manner provided in Rule 5 for the service of papers. Lack of notice of the entry by the clerk does not affect the time to appeal or relieve or authorize the court to relieve a party for failure to appeal within the time allowed, except as permitted in Rule 73(a).

Advisory Committee's Note

Subdivision (c). The amendment authorizes closing of the clerk's office on Saturday as far as civil business is concerned. However, a district court may require its clerk's office to remain open for specified hours on Saturdays or "legal holidays" other than those enumerated. ("Legal holiday" is defined in Rule 6(a), as amended.) The clerk's offices of many district courts have customarily remained open on some of the days appointed as holidays by State law. This practice could be continued by local rule or order.

Subdivision (d). This amendment conforms to the amendment of Rule 5(a). See the Advisory Committee's Note to that amendment.

Rule 79. Books and Records Kept by the Clerk and Entries Therein

(a) Civil Docket. The clerk shall keep a book known as "civil docket" of such form and style as may be prescribed by the Director of the Administrative Office of the United States Courts with the approval of the Judicial Conference of the United States, and shall enter therein each civil action to which these rules are made applicable. Actions shall be assigned consecutive file numbers. The file number of each action shall be noted on the folio of the docket whereon the first entry of the action is made. All papers filed with the clerk, all process issued and returns made thereon, all appearances, orders, verdicts, and judgments shall be ~~noted~~ *entered* chronologically in the civil docket on the folio assigned to the action and shall be marked with its file number. These ~~notations~~ *entries* shall be brief but shall show the nature of each paper filed or writ issued and the substance of each order or judgment of the court and of the returns showing execution of process. The ~~notation~~ *entry* of an order or judgment shall show the date the ~~notation~~ *entry* is made. When in an action trial by jury has been properly demanded or ordered the clerk shall enter the word "jury" on the folio assigned to that action.

Advisory Committee's Note

The terminology is clarified without any change of the prescribed practice. See amended Rule 58, and the Advisory Committee's Note thereto.

Rule 81. Applicability in General

(a) To What Proceedings Applicable.

(4) These rules do not alter the method prescribed by the Act of February 18, 1922, c. 57, § 2 (42 Stat. 388), U.S.C., Title 7, § 292; or by the Act of June 10, 1930, c. 436, § 7 (46 Stat. 534), as amended, U.S.C., Title 7, § 499g(c), for instituting proceedings in the United States district courts to review orders of the Secretary of Agriculture; or prescribed by the Act of June 25, 1934, c. 742, § 2 (48 Stat. 1214), U.S.C., Title 15, § 522, for instituting proceedings to review orders of the Secretary of ~~Commerce~~ *the Interior*; or prescribed by the Act of February 22, 1935, c. 18, § 5 (49 Stat. 31), U.S.C., Title 15, § 715d(c), as extended, for instituting proceedings to review orders of petroleum control boards; but the conduct of such proceedings in the district courts shall be made to conform to these rules so far as applicable.

(6) These rules apply to proceedings for enforcement or review of compensation orders under the Longshoremen's and Harbor Workers' Compensation Act, Act of March 4, 1927, c. 509, §§ 18, 21 (44 Stat. 1434, 1436), as amended, U.S.C., Title 33, §§ 918, 921, except to the extent that matters of procedure are provided for in that Act. The provisions for service by publication and for answer in proceedings to cancel certificates of citizenship under the ~~Act of October 14, 1940, c. 876, § 338 (54 Stat. 1158), U.S.C., Title 8,~~

New matter is shown in italics; matter to be omitted is lined through

~~§ 738,~~ *Act of June 27, 1952, c. 477, Title III, c. 2, § 340 (66 Stat. 260), U.S.C., Title 8, § 1451,* remain in effect.

(c) Removed Actions. These rules apply to civil actions removed to the United States district courts from the state courts and govern procedure after removal. Repleading is not necessary unless the court so orders. In a removed action in which the defendant has not answered, he shall answer or present the other defenses or objections available to him under these rules within 20 days after the receipt through service or otherwise of a copy of the initial pleading setting forth the claim for relief upon which the action or proceeding is based, or within 20 days after the service of summons upon such initial pleading, then filed, or within 5 days after the filing of the petition for removal, whichever period is longest. If at the time of removal all necessary pleadings have been served, a party entitled to trial by jury under Rule 38 shall be accorded it, if his demand therefor is served within 10 days after the petition for removal is filed if he is the petitioner, or if he is not the petitioner within 10 days after service on him of the notice of filing the petition. *A party who, prior to removal, has made an express demand for trial by jury in accordance with state law, need not make a demand after removal. If state law applicable in the court from which the case is removed does not require the parties to make express demands in order to claim trial by jury, they need not make demands after removal unless the court directs that they do so within a specified time if they desire to claim trial by jury. The court may make this direction on its own motion and shall do so as a matter of course at the request of any party. The failure of a party to make demand as directed constitutes a waiver by him of trial by jury.*

(f) References to Officer of the United States. Under any rule in which reference is made to an officer or agency of the United States, the term "officer" includes a ~~collector~~ *district director* of internal revenue, a former *district director or* collector of internal revenue, or the personal representative of a deceased *district director or* collector of internal revenue.

Advisory Committee's Note

Subdivision (a)(4). This change reflects the transfer of functions from the Secretary of Commerce to the Secretary of the Interior made by 1939 Reorganization Plan No. II, § 4(e), 53 Stat. 1433.

Subdivision (a)(6). The proper current reference is to the 1952 statute superseding the 1940 statute.

Subdivision (c). Most of the cases have held that a party who has made a proper express demand for jury trial in the State court is not required to renew the demand after removal of the action. *Zakoscielny v. Waterman Steamship Corp.*, 16

F.R.D. 314 (D.Md.1954); *Talley v. American Bakeries Co.*, 15 F.R.D. 391 (E.D.Tenn. 1954); *Rehrer v. Service Trucking Co.*, 15 F.R.D. 113 (D.Del.1953); 5 *Moore's Federal Practice* ¶ 38.39[3] (2d ed. 1951); 1 Barron & Holtzoff, *Federal Practice & Procedure* § 132 (Wright ed. 1960). But there is some authority to the contrary. *Petsel v. Chicago, B. & Q. R. Co.*, 101 F.Supp. 1006 (S.D.Iowa 1951); *Nelson v. American Nat. Bank & Trust Co.*, 9 F.R.D. 680 (E.D.Tenn.1950). The amendment adopts the preponderant view.

In order still further to avoid unintended waivers of jury trial, the amendment provides that where by State law applicable in the court from which the case is removed a party is entitled to jury trial without making an express demand, he need not make a demand after removal. However, the district court for calendar or other purposes may on its own motion direct the parties to state whether they demand a jury, and the court must make such a direction upon the request of any party. Under the amendment a district court may find it convenient to establish a routine practice of giving these directions to the parties in appropriate cases.

Subdivision (f). The amendment recognizes the change of nomenclature made by Treasury Dept. Order 150–26(2), 18 Fed.Reg. 3499 (1953).

As to a special problem arising under Rule 25 (Substitution of parties) in actions for refund of taxes, see the Advisory Committee's Note to the amendment of Rule 25(d), effective July 19, 1961; and 4 *Moore's Federal Practice* ¶ 25.09 at 531 (2d ed. 1950).

*

CERTAIN OF THE AMENDMENTS OF FEDERAL RULES OF CIVIL PROCEDURE ADOPTED BY THE SUPREME COURT OF THE UNITED STATES ON FEBRUARY 28, 1966, EFFECTIVE JULY 1, 1966, WITH ADVISORY COMMITTEE'S NOTES THEREON

[*Amendments here omitted: Changes in Rules 4, 6, 8, 14, 26, 38, 41, 42, 43, 44, 47, 53, 68, 73, 74, 75, and 81 and Forms 2 and 15; and addition of new Rule 65.1 and Supplemental Rules A, B, C, D, E, and F for Certain Admiralty and Maritime Claims.*]

Rule 1.

SCOPE OF RULES

These rules govern the procedure in the United States district courts in all suits of a civil nature whether cognizable as cases at law or in equity *or in admiralty*, with the exceptions stated in Rule 81. They shall be construed to secure the just, speedy, and inexpensive determination of every action.

Advisory Committee's Note

This is the fundamental change necessary to effect unification of the civil and admiralty procedure. Just as the 1938 rules abolished the distinction between actions at law and suits in equity, this change would abolish the distinction between civil actions and suits in admiralty. See also Rule 81.

Rule 9.

PLEADING SPECIAL MATTERS

(h) Admiralty and Maritime Claims. A pleading or count setting forth a claim for relief within the admiralty and maritime jurisdiction that is also within the jurisdiction of the district court on some other ground may contain a statement identifying the claim as an admiralty or maritime claim for the purposes of Rules 14(c), 26(a), 38(e), 73(h), 82, and the Supplemental Rules for Certain Admiralty and Maritime Claims. If the claim is cognizable only in admiralty it is an admiralty or maritime claim for those purposes whether so identified or not. The amendment of a pleading to add or withdraw an identifying statement is governed by the principles of Rule 15.

New matter is shown in italics; matter to be omitted is lined through

Advisory Committee's Note

Certain distinctive features of the admiralty practice must be preserved for what are now suits in admiralty. This raises the question: After unification, when a single form of action is established, how will the counterpart of the present suit in admiralty be identifiable? In part the question is easily answered. Some claims for relief can only be suits in admiralty, either because the admiralty jurisdiction is exclusive or because no nonmaritime ground of federal jurisdiction exists. Many claims, however, are cognizable by the district courts whether asserted in admiralty or in a civil action, assuming the existence of a nonmaritime ground of jurisdiction. Thus at present the pleader has power to determine procedural consequences by the way in which he exercises the classic privilege given by the saving-to-suitors clause (28 U.S.C. § 1333) or by equivalent statutory provisions. For example, a longshoreman's claim for personal injuries suffered by reason of the unseaworthiness of a vessel may be asserted in a suit in admiralty or, if diversity of citizenship exists, in a civil action. One of the important procedural consequences is that in the civil action either party may demand a jury trial, while in the suit in admiralty there is no right to jury trial except as provided by statute.

It is no part of the purpose of unification to inject a right to jury trial into those admiralty cases in which that right is not provided by statute. Similarly, as will be more specifically noted below, there is no disposition to change the present law as to interlocutory appeals in admiralty, or as to the venue of suits in admiralty; and, of course, there is no disposition to inject into the civil practice as it now is the distinctively maritime remedies (maritime attachment and garnishment, actions in rem, possessory, petitory, and partition actions and limitation of liability). The unified rules must therefore provide some device for preserving the present power of the pleader to determine whether these historically maritime procedures shall be applicable to his claim or not; the pleader must be afforded some means of designating his claim as the counterpart of the present suit in admiralty, where its character as such is not clear.

The problem is different from the similar one concerning the identification of claims that were formerly suits in equity. While that problem is not free from complexities, it is broadly true that the modern counterpart of the suit in equity is distinguishable from the former action at law by the character of the relief sought. This mode of identification is possible in only a limited category of admiralty cases. In large numbers of cases the relief sought in admiralty is simple money damages, indistinguishable from the remedy afforded by the common law. This is true, for example, in the case of the longshoreman's action for personal injuries stated above. After unification has abolished the distinction between civil actions and suits in admiralty, the complaint in such an action would be almost completely ambiguous as to the pleader's intentions regarding the procedure invoked. The allegation of diversity of citizenship might be regarded as a clue indicating an intention to proceed as at present under the saving-to-suitors clause; but this, too, would be ambiguous if there were also reference to the admiralty jurisdiction, and the pleader ought not to be required to forego mention of all available jurisdictional grounds.

Other methods of solving the problem were carefully explored, but the Advisory Committee concluded that the preferable solution is to allow the pleader who now has power to determine procedural consequences by filing a suit in admiralty to exercise that power under unification, for the limited instances in which procedural differences will remain, by a simple statement in his pleading to the effect that the claim is an admiralty or maritime claim.

The choice made by the pleader in identifying or in failing to identify his claim as an admiralty or maritime claim is not an irrevocable election. The rule provides that the amendment of a pleading to add or withdraw an identifying statement is subject to the principles of Rule 15.

Rule 12.

DEFENSES AND OBJECTIONS—WHEN AND HOW PRESENTED—BY PLEADING OR MOTION—MOTION FOR JUDGMENT ON THE PLEADINGS

(b) How Presented. Every defense, in law or fact, to a claim for relief in any pleading, whether a claim, counterclaim, cross-claim, or third-party claim, shall be asserted in the responsive pleading thereto if one is required, except that the following defenses may at the option of the pleader be made by motion: (1) lack of jurisdiction over the subject matter, (2) lack of jurisdiction over the person, (3) improper venue, (4) insufficiency of process, (5) insufficiency of service of process, (6) failure to state a claim upon which relief can be granted, (7) failure to join ~~an indispensable~~ *a* party *under Rule 19*. A motion making any of these defenses shall be made before pleading if a further pleading is permitted. No defense or objection is waived by being joined with one or more other defenses or objections in a responsive pleading or motion. If a pleading sets forth a claim for relief to which the adverse party is not required to serve a responsive pleading, he may assert at the trial any defense in law or fact to that claim for relief. If, on a motion asserting the defense numbered (6) to dismiss for failure of the pleading to state a claim upon which relief can be granted, matters outside the pleading are presented to and not excluded by the court, the motion shall be treated as one for summary judgment and disposed of as provided in Rule 56, and all parties shall be given reasonable opportunity to present all material made pertinent to such a motion by Rule 56.

(g) Consolidation of Defenses *in Motion*. A party who makes a motion under this rule may join with it any other motions herein provided for and then available to him. If a party makes a motion under this rule but ~~does not include therein all defenses and objections~~ *omits therefrom any defense or objection* then available to him which this rule permits to be raised by motion, he shall not thereafter make a motion based on ~~any of the defenses or objections~~ *the defense or objection* so omitted, except *a motion* as provided in subdivision (h)*(2)* ~~of this rule~~ *hereof on any of the grounds there stated*.

(h) Waiver or Preservation of Certain Defenses. ~~A party waives all defenses and objections which he does not present either by motion as hereinbefore provided or, if he has made no motion, in~~

New matter is shown in italics; matter to be omitted is lined through

~~his answer or reply, except (1) that the defense of failure to state a claim upon which relief can be granted, the defense of failure to join an indispensable party, and the objection of failure to state a legal defense to a claim may also be made by a later pleading, if one is permitted, or by motion for judgment on the pleadings or at the trial on the merits, and except (2) that, whenever it appears by suggestion of the parties or otherwise that the court lacks jurisdiction of the subject matter, the court shall dismiss the action. The objection or defense, if made at the trial, shall be disposed of as provided in Rule 15(b) in the light of any evidence that may have been received.~~ *(1) A defense of lack of jurisdiction over the person, improper venue, insufficiency of process, or insufficiency of service of process is waived (A) if omitted from a motion in the circumstances described in subdivision (g), or (B) if it is neither made by motion under this rule nor included in a responsive pleading or an amendment thereof permitted by Rule 15(a) to be made as a matter of course.*

(2) A defense of failure to state a claim upon which relief can be granted, a defense of failure to join a party indispensable under Rule 19, and an objection of failure to state a legal defense to a claim may be made in any pleading permitted or ordered under Rule 7(a), or by motion for judgment on the pleadings, or at the trial on the merits.

(3) Whenever it appears by suggestion of the parties or otherwise that the court lacks jurisdiction of the subject matter, the court shall dismiss the action.

Advisory Committee's Note

Subdivision (b)(7). The terminology of this subdivision is changed to accord with the amendment of Rule 19. See the Advisory Committee's Note to Rule 19, as amended, especially the third paragraph therein before the caption "Subdivision (c)."

Subdivision (g). Subdivision (g) has forbidden a defendant who makes a preanswer motion under this rule from making a further motion presenting any defense or objection which was available to him at the time he made the first motion and which he could have included, but did not in fact include therein. Thus if the defendant moves before answer to dismiss the complaint for failure to state a claim, he is barred from making a further motion presenting the defense of improper venue, if that defense was available to him when he made his original motion. Amended subdivision (g) is to the same effect. This required consolidation of defenses and objections in a Rule 12 motion is salutary in that it works against piecemeal consideration of a case. For exceptions to the requirement of consolidation, see the last clause of subdivision (g), referring to new subdivision (h)(2).

Subdivision (h). The question has arisen whether an omitted defense which cannot be made the basis of a second motion may nevertheless be pleaded in the answer. Subdivision (h) called for waiver of "* * * defenses and objections which he [defendant] does not present * * * by motion * * * or, if he has made no motion,

---

New matter is shown in italics; matter to be omitted is lined through

in his answer * * *." If the clause "if he has made no motion," was read literally, it seemed that the omitted defense was waived and could not be pleaded in the answer. On the other hand, the clause might be read as adding nothing of substance to the preceding words; in that event it appeared that a defense was not waived by reason of being omitted from the motion and might be set up in the answer. The decisions were divided. Favoring waiver, see *Keefe v. Derounian,* 6 F.R.D. 11 (N.D.Ill.1946); *Elbinger v. Precision Metal Workers Corp.,* 18 F.R.D. 467 (E.D.Wis.1956); see also *Rensing v. Turner Aviation Corp.,* 166 F.Supp. 790 (N.D.Ill.1958); *P. Beiersdorf & Co. v. Duke Laboratories, Inc.,* 10 F.R.D. 282 (S.D.N.Y.1950); *Neset v. Christensen,* 92 F.Supp. 78 (E.D.N.Y.1950). Opposing waiver, see *Phillips v. Baker,* 121 F.2d 752 (9th Cir.1941); *Crum v. Graham,* 32 F.R.D. 173 (D.Mont.1963) (regretfully following the Phillips case); see also *Birnbaum v. Birrell,* 9 F.R.D. 72 (S.D.N.Y.1948); *Johnson v. Joseph Schlitz Brewing Co.,* 33 F.Supp. 176 (E.D.Tenn.1940); *cf. Carter v. American Bus Lines, Inc.,* 22 F.R.D. 323 (D.Neb.1958).

Amended subdivision (h)(1)(A) eliminates the ambiguity and states that certain specified defenses which were available to a party when he made a preanswer motion, but which he omitted from the motion, are waived. The specified defenses are lack of jurisdiction over the person, improper venue, insufficiency of process, and insufficiency of service of process (see Rule 12(b)(2)–(5)). A party who by motion invites the court to pass upon a threshold defense should bring forward all the specified defenses he then has and thus allow the court to do a reasonably complete job. The waiver reinforces the policy of subdivision (g) forbidding successive motions.

By amended subdivision (h)(1)(B), the specified defenses, even if not waived by the operation of (A), are waived by the failure to raise them by a motion under Rule 12 or in the responsive pleading or any amendment thereof to which the party is entitled as a matter of course. The specified defenses are of such a character that they should not be delayed and brought up for the first time by means of an application to the court to amend the responsive pleading.

Since the language of the subdivisions is made clear, the party is put on fair notice of the effect of his actions and omissions and can guard himself against unintended waiver. It is to be noted that while the defenses specified in subdivision (h)(1) are subject to waiver as there provided, the more substantial defenses of failure to state a claim upon which relief can be granted, failure to join a party indispensible under Rule 19, and failure to state a legal defense to a claim (see Rule 12(b)(6), (7), (f)), as well as the defense of lack of jurisdiction over the subject matter (see Rule 12(b)(1)), are expressly preserved against waiver by amended subdivision (h)(2) and (3).

Rule 13.

COUNTERCLAIM AND CROSS-CLAIM

(h) ~~**Additional Parties May Be Brought in**~~ *Joinder of Additional Parties.* ~~When the presence of parties other than those to the original action is required for the granting of complete relief in the determination of a counterclaim or cross-claim, the court shall order them to be brought in as defendants as provided in these rules, if jurisdiction of them can be obtained and their joinder will not deprive the court of jurisdiction of the action.~~ *Persons other than those made parties to the original action may be made*

New matter is shown in italics; matter to be omitted is lined through

parties to a counterclaim or cross-claim in accordance with the provisions of Rules 19 and 20.

Advisory Committee's Note

Rule 13(h), dealing with the joinder of additional parties to a counterclaim or cross-claim, has partaken of some of the textual difficulties of Rule 19 on necessary joinder of parties. See Advisory Committee's Note to Rule 19, as amended; *cf.* 3 *Moore's Federal Practice* ¶ 13.39 (2d ed. 1963), and Supp. thereto; 1A Barron & Holtzoff, *Federal Practice and Procedure* § 399 (Wright ed. 1960). Rule 13(h) has also been inadequate in failing to call attention to the fact that a party pleading a counterclaim or cross-claim may join additional persons when the conditions for permissive joinder of parties under Rule 20 are satisfied.

The amendment of Rule 13(h) supplies the latter omission by expressly referring to Rule 20, as amended, and also incorporates by direct reference the revised criteria and procedures of Rule 19, as amended. Hereafter, for the purpose of determining who must or may be joined as additional parties to a counterclaim or cross-claim, the party pleading the claim is to be regarded as a plaintiff and the additional parties as plaintiffs or defendants as the case may be, and amended Rules 19 and 20 are to be applied in the usual fashion. See also Rules 13(a) (compulsory counterclaims) and 22 (interpleader).

The amendment of Rule 13(h), like the amendment of Rule 19, does not attempt to regulate Federal jurisdiction or venue. See Rule 82. It should be noted, however, that in some situations the decisional law has recognized "ancillary" Federal jurisdiction over counterclaims and cross-claims and "ancillary" venue as to parties to these claims.

Rule 15.

AMENDED AND SUPPLEMENTAL PLEADINGS

(c) Relation Back of Amendments. Whenever the claim or defense asserted in the amended pleading arose out of the conduct, transaction, or occurrence set forth or attempted to be set forth in the original pleading, the amendment relates back to the date of the original pleading. *An amendment changing the party against whom a claim is asserted relates back if the foregoing provision is satisfied and, within the period provided by law for commencing the action against him, the party to be brought in by amendment (1) has received such notice of the institution of the action that he will not be prejudiced in maintaining his defense on the merits, and (2) knew or should have known that, but for a mistake concerning the identity of the proper party, the action would have been brought against him.*

The delivery or mailing of process to the United States Attorney, or his designee, or the Attorney General of the United States, or an agency or officer who would have been a proper defendant if named, satisfies the requirement of clauses (1) and (2) hereof with respect to the United States or any agency or officer thereof to be brought into the action as a defendant.

New matter is shown in italics; matter to be omitted is lined through

Advisory Committee's Note

Rule 15(c) is amplified to state more clearly when an amendment of a pleading changing the party against whom a claim is asserted (including an amendment to correct a misnomer or misdescription of a defendant) shall "relate back" to the date of the original pleading.

The problem has arisen most acutely in certain actions by private parties against officers or agencies of the United States. Thus an individual denied social security benefits by the Secretary of Health, Education, and Welfare may secure review of the decision by bringing a civil action against that officer within sixty days. 42 U.S.C. § 405(g) (Supp. III, 1962). In several recent cases the claimants instituted timely action but mistakenly named as defendant the United States, the Department of HEW, the "Federal Security Administration" (a nonexistent agency), and a Secretary who had retired from the office nineteen days before. Discovering their mistakes, the claimants moved to amend their complaints to name the proper defendant; by this time the statutory sixty-day period had expired. The motions were denied on the ground that the amendment "would amount to the commencement of a new proceeding and would not relate back in time so as to avoid the statutory provision * * * that suit be brought within sixty days. * * *" *Cohn v. Federal Security Adm.*, 199 F.Supp. 884, 885 (W.D.N.Y.1961); see also *Cunningham v. United States,* 199 F.Supp. 541 (W.D.Mo.1958); *Hall v. Department of HEW,* 199 F.Supp. 833 (S.D.Tex.1960); *Sandridge v. Folsom, Secretary of HEW,* 200 F.Supp. 25 (M.D.Tenn.1959). [The Secretary of Health, Education, and Welfare has approved certain ameliorative regulations under 42 U.S.C. § 405(g). See 29 Fed.Reg. 8209 (June 30, 1964); Jacoby, *The Effect of Recent Changes in the Law of "Nonstatutory" Judicial Review,* 53 Geo.L.J. 19, 42–43 (1964); see also *Simmons v. United States Dept. HEW,* 328 F.2d 86 (3d Cir.1964).]

Analysis in terms of "new proceeding" is traceable to *Davis v. L. L. Cohen & Co.,* 268 U.S. 638 (1925), and *Mellon v. Arkansas Land & Lumber Co.,* 275 U.S. 460 (1928), but those cases antedate the adoption of the rules which import different criteria for determining when an amendment is to "relate back". As lower courts have continued to rely on the *Davis* and *Mellon* cases despite the contrary intent of the rules, clarification of Rule 15(c) is considered advisable.

Relation back is intimately connected with the policy of the statute of limitations. The policy of the statute limiting the time for suit against the Secretary of HEW would not have been offended by allowing relation back in the situations described above. For the government was put on notice of the claim within the stated period—in the particular instances, by means of the initial delivery of process to a responsible government official (see Rule 4(d)(4) and (5)). In these circumstances, characterization of the amendment as a new proceeding is not responsive to the reality, but is merely question-begging; and to deny relation back is to defeat unjustly the claimant's opportunity to prove his case. See the full discussion by Byse, *Suing the "Wrong" Defendant in Judicial Review of Federal Administrative Action: Proposals for Reform,* 77 Harv.L.Rev. 40 (1963); see also Ill.Civ.P.Act § 46(4).

Much the same question arises in other types of actions against the government (see Byse, *supra,* at 45 n. 15). In actions between private parties, the problem of relation back of amendments changing defendants has generally been better handled by the courts, but incorrect criteria have sometimes been applied, leading sporadically to doubtful results. See 1A Barron & Holtzoff, *Federal Practice & Procedure* § 451 (Wright ed. 1960); 1 *id.* § 186 (1960); 2 *id.* § 543 (1961); 3 *Moore's Federal Practice* ¶ 15.15 (Cum.Supp.1962); Annot., *Change in Party After Statute of Limitations Has Run,* 8 A.L.R.2d 6 (1949). Rule 15(c) has been amplified to provide a general solution. An amendment changing the party against whom a claim is asserted relates back if the amendment satisfies the usual condition of Rule 15(c) of "arising out of the conduct * * * set forth * * * in the original pleading," and if, within the applicable limitations period, the party brought in by amendment, *first,* received such notice of the institution of the action—the notice need not be formal—that he would not be prejudiced in defending the action, and, *second,* knew or should have known that the action would have been brought against him initially had there not been a mistake concerning the identity of the proper party. Revised Rule 15(c) goes on to provide specifically in the government cases that the *first* and *second* requirements are satisfied when the government has been notified in the manner there described (see Rule 4(d)(4) and (5)). As applied to the government cases, revised Rule 15(c) further advances the objectives of the 1961 amendment of Rule 25(d) (substitution of public officers).

The relation back of amendments changing plaintiffs is not expressly treated in revised Rule 15(c) since the problem is generally easier. Again the chief consideration of policy is that of the statute of limitations, and the attitude taken in revised Rule 15(c) toward change of defendants extends by analogy to amendments changing plaintiffs. Also relevant is the amendment of Rule 17(a) (real party in interest). To avoid forfeitures of just claims, revised Rule 17(a) would provide that no action shall be dismissed on the ground that it is not prosecuted in the name of the real party in interest until a reasonable time has been allowed for correction of the defect in the manner there stated.

Rule 17.

PARTIES PLAINTIFF AND DEFENDANT; CAPACITY

(a) Real Party in Interest. Every action shall be prosecuted in the name of the real party in interest~~;~~*.* ~~but a~~*A*n executor, administrator, guardian, *bailee,* trustee of an express trust, a party with whom or in whose name a contract has been made for the benefit of another, or a party authorized by statute may sue in his own name without joining with him the party for whose benefit the action is brought; and when a statute of the United States so provides, an action for the use or benefit of another shall be brought in the name of the United States. *No action shall be dismissed on the ground that it is not prosecuted in the name of the real party in interest until a reasonable time has been allowed after objection for ratification of commencement of the action by, or joinder or substitution of, the real party in interest; and such ratification, joinder, or substitution shall have the same effect as if the action had been commenced in the name of the real party in interest.*

Advisory Committee's Note

The minor change in the text of the rule is designed to make it clear that the specific instances enumerated are not exceptions to, but illustrations of, the rule. These illustrations, of course, carry no negative implication to the effect that there are not other instances of recognition as the real party in interest of one whose standing as such may be in doubt. The enumeration is simply of cases in which

---

New matter is shown in italics; matter to be omitted is lined through

there might be substantial doubt as to the issue but for the specific enumeration. There are other potentially arguable cases that are not excluded by the enumeration. For example, the enumeration states that the promisee in a contract for the benefit of a third party may sue as real party in interest; it does not say, because it is obvious, that the third-party beneficiary may sue (when the applicable law gives him that right.)

The rule adds to the illustrative list of real parties in interest a bailee—meaning, of course, a bailee suing on behalf of the bailor with respect to the property bailed. (When the possessor of property other than the owner sues for an invasion of the possessory interest he is the real party in interest.) The word "bailee" is added primarily to preserve the admiralty practice whereby the owner of a vessel as bailee of the cargo, or the master of the vessel as bailee of both vessel and cargo, sues for damage to either property interest or both. But there is no reason to limit such a provision to maritime situations. The owner of a warehouse in which household furniture is stored is equally entitled to sue on behalf of the numerous owners of the furniture stored. *Cf. Gulf Oil Corp. v. Gilbert,* 330 U.S. 501 (1947).

The provision that no action shall be dismissed on the ground that it is not prosecuted in the name of the real party in interest until a reasonable time has been allowed, after the objection has been raised, for ratification, substitution, etc., is added simply in the interests of justice. In its origin the rule concerning the real party in interest was permissive in purpose: it was designed to *allow* an assignee to sue in his own name. That having been accomplished, the modern function of the rule in its negative aspect is simply to protect the defendant against a subsequent action by the party actually entitled to recover, and to insure generally that the judgment will have its proper effect as res judicata.

This provision keeps pace with the law as it is actually developing. Modern decisions are inclined to be lenient when an honest mistake has been made in choosing the party in whose name the action is to be filed—in both maritime and nonmaritime cases. See *Levinson v. Deupree,* 345 U.S. 648 (1953); *Link Aviation, Inc. v. Downs,* 325 F.2d 613 (D.C.Cir.1963). The provision should not be misunderstood or distorted. It is intended to prevent forfeiture when determination of the proper party to sue is difficult or when an understandable mistake has been made. It does not mean, for example, that, following an airplane crash in which all aboard were killed, an action may be filed in the name of John Doe (a fictitious person), as personal representative of Richard Roe (another fictitious person), in the hope that at a later time the attorney filing the action may substitute the real name of the real personal representative of a real victim, and have the benefit of suspension of the limitation period. It does not even mean, when an action is filed by the personal representative of John Smith, of Buffalo, in the good faith belief that he was aboard the flight, that upon discovery that Smith is alive and well, having missed the fatal flight, the representative of James Brown, of San Francisco, an actual victim, can be substituted to take advantage of the suspension of the limitation period. It is, in cases of this sort, intended to insure against forfeiture and injustice—in short, to codify in broad terms the salutary principle of *Levinson v. Deupree,* 345 U.S. 648 (1953), and *Link Aviation, Inc. v. Downs,* 325 F.2d 613 (D.C.Cir.1963).

Rule 18.

JOINDER OF CLAIMS AND REMEDIES

(a) Joinder of Claims. ~~The plaintiff in his complaint or in a reply setting forth a counterclaim may join either as independent or~~

~~as alternate claims as many claims either legal or equitable or both as he may have against an opposing party. There may be a like joinder of claims when there are multiple parties if the requirements of Rules 19, 20, and 22 are satisfied. There may be a like joinder of cross-claims or third-party claims if the requirements of Rule 13 and 14 respectively are satisfied.~~ *A party asserting a claim to relief as an original claim, counterclaim, cross-claim, or third-party claim, may join, either as independent or as alternate claims, as many claims, legal, equitable, or maritime, as he has against an opposing party.*

Advisory Committee's Note

The rules "proceed upon the theory that no inconvenience can result from the joinder of any two or more matters in the pleadings, but only from trying two or more matters together which have little or nothing in common." Sunderland, *The New Federal Rules,* 45 W.Va.L.Q. 5, 13 (1938); see Clark, *Code Pleading,* 58 (2d ed. 1947). Accordingly, Rule 18(a) has permitted a party to plead multiple claims of all types against an opposing party, subject to the court's power to direct an appropriate procedure for trying the claims. See Rules 42(b), 20(b), 21.

The liberal policy regarding joinder of claims in the pleadings extends to cases with multiple parties. However, the language used in the second sentence of Rule 18(a)—"if the requirements of Rules 19 [necessary joinder of parties], 20 [permissive joinder of parties], and 22 [interpleader] are satisfied"—has led some courts to infer that the rules regulating joinder of parties are intended to carry back to Rule 18(a) and to impose some special limits on joinder of claims in multiparty cases. In particular, Rule 20(a) has been read as restricting the operation of Rule 18(a) in certain situations in which a number of parties have been permissively joined in an action. In *Federal Housing Admr. v. Christianson,* 26 F.Supp. 419 (D.Conn.1939), the indorsee of two notes sued the three co-makers of one note, and sought to join in the action a count on a second note which had been made by two of the three defendants. There was no doubt about the propriety of the joinder of the three parties defendant, for a right to relief was being asserted against all three defendants which arose out of a single "transaction" (the first note) and a question of fact or law "common" to all three defendants would arise in the action. See the text of Rule 20(a). The court, however, refused to allow the joinder of the count on the second note, on the ground that this right to relief, assumed to arise from a distinct transaction, did not involve a question common to all the defendants but only two of them. For analysis of the *Christianson* case and other authorities, see 2 Barron & Holtzoff, *Federal Practice & Procedure,* § 533.1 (Wright ed. 1961); 3 *Moore's Federal Practice* ¶ 18.04[3] (2d ed. 1963).

If the court's view is followed, it becomes necessary to enter at the pleading stage into speculations about the exact relation between the claim sought to be joined against fewer than all the defendants properly joined in the action, and the claims asserted against all the defendants. *Cf.* Wright, *Joinder of Claims and Parties Under Modern Pleading Rules,* 36 Minn.L.Rev. 580, 605–06 (1952). Thus if it could be found in the *Christianson* situation that the claim on the second note arose out of the same transaction as the claim on the first or out of a transaction forming part of a "series," and that any question of fact or law with respect to the second note also arose with regard to the first, it would be held that the claim on the second note could be joined in the complaint. See 2 Barron & Holtzoff, *supra,* at 199; see also *id.* at 198 n. 60.4; *cf.* 3 *Moore's Federal Practice, supra,* at 1811. Such pleading niceties provide a basis for delaying and wasteful maneuver. It is more compatible with the design of the rules to allow the claim to be joined in the pleading, leaving the question of possible separate trial of that claim to be later decided. See 2 Barron & Holtzoff, *supra,* § 533.1; Wright, *supra,* 36 Minn.L.Rev. at 604–11; *Developments in the Law—Multiparty Litigation in the Federal Courts,* 71 Harv. 874, 970–71 (1958); Commentary, *Relation Between Joinder of Parties and Joinder of Claims,* 5 F.R.Serv. 822 (1942). It is instructive to note that the court in the *Christianson* case, while holding that the claim on the second note could not be joined as a matter of pleading, held open the possibility that both claims would later be consolidated for trial under Rule 42(a). See 26 F.Supp. 419.

Rule 18(a) is now amended not only to overcome the *Christianson* decision and similar authority, but also to state clearly, as a comprehensive proposition, that a party asserting a claim (an original claim, counterclaim, cross-claim, or third-party claim) may join as many claims as he has against an opposing party. See *Noland Co., Inc. v. Graver Tank & Mfg. Co.,* 301 F.2d 43, 49–51 (4th Cir.1962); but *cf. C. W. Humphrey Co. v. Security Alum. Co.,* 31 F.R.D. 41 (E.D.Mich.1962). This permitted joinder of claims is not affected by the fact there are multiple parties in the action. The joinder of parties is governed by other rules operating independently.

It is emphasized that amended Rule 18(a) deals only with pleading. As already indicated, a claim properly joined as a matter of pleading need not be proceeded with together with the other claims if fairness or convenience justifies separate treatment.

Amended Rule 18(a), like the rule prior to amendment, does not purport to deal with questions of jurisdiction or venue which may arise with respect to claims properly joined as a matter of pleading. See Rule 82.

See also the amendment of Rule 20(a) and the Advisory Committee's Note thereto.

Free joinder of claims and remedies is one of the basic purposes of unification of the admiralty and civil procedure. The amendment accordingly provides for the inclusion in the rule of maritime claims as well as those which are legal and equitable in character.

~~Rule 19.~~

~~NECESSARY JOINDER OF PARTIES~~

~~**(a) Necessary Joinder.** Subject to the provisions of Rule 23 and of subdivision (b) of this rule, persons having a joint interest shall be made parties and be joined on the same side as plaintiffs or defendants. When a person who should join as a plaintiff refuses to do so, he may be made a defendant or, in proper cases, an involuntary plaintiff.~~

~~**(b) Effect of Failure to Join.** When persons who are not indispensable, but who ought to be parties if complete relief is to be accorded between those already parties, have not been made parties and are subject to the jurisdiction of the court as to both service of process and venue and can be made parties without depriving the court of jurisdiction of the parties before it, the court shall order them summoned to appear in the action. The court in its discre-~~

~~tion may proceed in the action without making such persons parties, if its jurisdiction over them as to either service of process or venue can be acquired only by their consent or voluntary appearance or if, though they are subject to its jurisdiction, their joinder would deprive the court of jurisdiction of the parties before it, but the judgment rendered therein does not affect the rights or liabilities of absent persons.~~

~~**(c) Same: Names of Omitted Persons and Reasons for Non-Joinder to be Pleaded.** In any pleading in which relief is asked, the pleader shall set forth the names, if known to him, of persons who ought to be parties if complete relief is to be accorded between those already parties, but who are not joined, and shall state why they are omitted.~~

Rule 19.

JOINDER OF PERSONS NEEDED FOR JUST ADJUDICATION

(a) Persons to be Joined if Feasible. A person who is subject to service of process and whose joinder will not deprive the court of jurisdiction over the subject matter of the action shall be joined as a party in the action if (1) in his absence complete relief cannot be accorded among those already parties, or (2) he claims an interest relating to the subject of the action and is so situated that the disposition of the action in his absence may (i) as a practical matter impair or impede his ability to protect that interest or (ii) leave any of the persons already parties subject to a substantial risk of incurring double, multiple, or otherwise inconsistent obligations by reason of his claimed interest. If he has not been so joined, the court shall order that he be made a party. If he should join as a plaintiff but refuses to do so, he may be made a defendant, or, in a proper case, an involuntary plaintiff. If the joined party objects to venue and his joinder would render the venue of the action improper, he shall be dismissed from the action.

(b) Determination by Court Whenever Joinder Not Feasible. If a person as described in subdivision (a)(1)–(2) hereof cannot be made a party, the court shall determine whether in equity and good conscience the action should proceed among the parties before it, or should be dismissed, the absent person being thus regarded as indispensable. The factors to be considered by the court include: first, to what extent a judgment rendered in the person's absence might be prejudicial to him, or those already parties; second, the extent to which, by protective provisions in the judgment, by the shaping of relief, or other measures, the prejudice can be lessened or avoided; third, whether a judgment rendered in the person's ab-

sence will be adequate; fourth, whether the plaintiff will have an adequate remedy if the action is dismissed for nonjoinder.

(c) Pleading Reasons for Nonjoinder. A pleading asserting a claim for relief shall state the names, if known to the pleader, of any persons as described in subdivision (a)(1)–(2) hereof who are not joined, and the reasons why they are not joined.

(d) Exception of Class Actions. This rule is subject to the provisions of Rule 23.

Advisory Committee's Note

General Considerations

Whenever feasible, the persons materially interested in the subject of an action—see the more detailed description of these persons in the discussion of new subdivision (a) below—should be joined as parties so that they may be heard and a complete disposition made. When this comprehensive joinder cannot be accomplished—a situation which may be encountered in Federal courts because of limitations on service of process, subject matter jurisdiction, and venue—the case should be examined pragmatically and a choice made between the alternatives of proceeding with the action in the absence of particular interested persons, and dismissing the action.

Even if the court is mistaken in its decision to proceed in the absence of an interested person, it does not by that token deprive itself of the power to adjudicate as between the parties already before it through proper service of process. But the court can make a legally binding adjudication only between the parties actually joined in the action. It is true that an adjudication between the parties before the court may on occasion adversely affect the absent person as a practical matter, or leave a party exposed to a later inconsistent recovery by the absent person. These are factors which should be considered in deciding whether the action should proceed, or should rather be dismissed; but they do not themselves negate the court's power to adjudicate as between the parties who have been joined.

Defects in the Original Rule

The foregoing propositions were well understood in the older equity practice, see Hazard, *Indispensable Party: The Historical Origin of a Procedural Phantom,* 61 Colum.L.Rev. 1254 (1961), and Rule 19 could be and often was applied in consonance with them. But experience showed that the rule was defective in its phrasing and did not point clearly to the proper basis of decision.

Textual defects. (1) The expression "persons * * * who ought to be parties if complete relief is to be accorded between those already parties," appearing in original subdivision (b), was apparently intended as a description of the persons whom it would be desirable to join in the action, all questions of feasibility of joinder being put to one side; but it was not adequately descriptive of those persons.

(2) The word "indispensable," appearing in original subdivision (b), was apparently intended as an inclusive reference to the interested persons in whose absence it would be advisable, all factors having been considered, to dismiss the action. Yet the sentence implied that there might be interested persons, not "indispensable," in whose absence the action ought also to be dismissed. Further, it seemed at least superficially plausible to equate the word "indispensable" with the expression "having a joint interest," appearing in subdivision (a). See *United States v. Washington Inst. of Tech., Inc.,* 138 F.2d 25, 26 (3d Cir.1943); *cf. Chidester v. City of*

Newark, 162 F.2d 598 (3d Cir.1947). But persons holding an interest technically "joint" are not always so related to an action that it would be unwise to proceed without joining all of them, whereas persons holding an interest not technically "joint" may have this relation to an action. See Reed, *Compulsory Joinder of Parties in Civil Actions,* 55 Mich.L.Rev. 327, 356 ff., 483 (1957).

(3) The use of "indispensable" and "joint interest" in the context of original Rule 19 directed attention to the technical or abstract character of the rights or obligations of the persons whose joinder was in question, and correspondingly distracted attention from the pragmatic considerations which should be controlling.

(4) The original rule, in dealing with the feasibility of joining a person as a party to the action, besides referring to whether the person was "subject to the jurisdiction of the court as to both service of process and venue," spoke of whether the person could be made a party "without depriving the court of jurisdiction of the parties before it." The second quoted expression used "jurisdiction" in the sense of the competence of the court over the subject matter of the action, and in this sense the expression was apt. However, by a familiar confusion, the expression seems to have suggested to some that the absence from the lawsuit of a person who was "indispensable" or "who ought to be [a] part[y]" itself deprived the court of the power to adjudicate as between the parties already joined. See *Samuel Goldwyn, Inc. v. United Artists Corp.,* 113 F.2d 703, 707 (3d Cir. 1940); *McArthur v. Rosenbaum Co. of Pittsburgh,* 180 F.2d 617, 621 (3d Cir. 1949); *cf. Calcote v. Texas Pac. Coal & Oil Co.,* 157 F.2d 216 (5th Cir. 1946), *cert. denied,* 329 U.S. 782 (1946), noted in 56 Yale L.J. 1088 (1947); Reed, *supra,* 55 Mich.L.Rev. at 332–34.

Failure to point to correct basis of decision. The original rule did not state affirmatively what factors were relevant in deciding whether the action should proceed or be dismissed when joinder of interested persons was infeasible. In some instances courts did not undertake the relevant inquiry or were misled by the "jurisdiction" fallacy. In other instances there was undue preoccupation with abstract classifications of rights or obligations, as against consideration of the particular consequences of proceeding with the action and the ways by which these consequences might be ameliorated by the shaping of final relief or other precautions.

Although these difficulties cannot be said to have been general, analysis of the cases showed that there was good reason for attempting to strengthen the rule. The literature also indicated how the rule should be reformed. See Reed, *supra* (discussion of the important case of *Shields v. Barrow,* 17 How. (58 U.S.) 130 (1854), appears at 55 Mich.L.Rev., p. 340 ff.); Hazard, *supra*; N.Y. Temporary Comm. on Courts, *First Preliminary Report,* Legis.Doc. 1957, No. 6(b), pp. 28, 233; N.Y. Judicial Council, *Twelfth Ann.Rep.,* Legis.Doc. 1946, No. 17, p. 163; Joint Comm. on Michigan Procedural Revision, *Final Report,* Pt. III, p. 69 (1960); Note, *Indispensable Parties in the Federal Courts,* 65 Harv.L.Rev. 1050 (1952); *Developments in the Law—Multiparty Litigation in the Federal Courts,* 71 Harv.L.Rev. 874, 879 (1958); Mich.Gen. Court Rules, R. 205 (effective Jan. 1, 1963); N.Y.Civ.Prac. Law & Rules, § 1001 (effective Sept. 1, 1963).

The Amended Rule

New *subdivision (a)* defines the persons whose joinder in the action is desirable. Clause (1) stresses the desirability of joining those persons in whose absence the court would be obliged to grant partial or "hollow" rather than complete relief to the parties before the court. The interests that are being furthered here are not only those of the parties, but also that of the public in avoiding repeated lawsuits on the same essential subject matter. Clause (2)(i) recognizes the importance of protecting the person whose joinder is in question against the practical prejudice to him which may arise through a disposition of the action in his absence. Clause (2)(ii) recognizes the need for considering whether a party may be left, after the adjudication, in a position where a person not joined can subject him to a double or otherwise inconsistent liability. See Reed, *supra,* 55 Mich.L.Rev. at 330, 338; Note, *supra,* 65 Harv.L.Rev. at 1052–57; *Developments in the Law, supra,* 71 Harv.L.Rev. at 881–85.

The subdivision (a) definition of persons to be joined is not couched in terms of the abstract nature of their interests—"joint," "united," "separable," or the like. See N.Y. Temporary Comm. on Courts, *First Preliminary Report, supra; Developments in the Law, supra,* at 880. It should be noted particularly, however, that the description is not at variance with the settled authorities holding that a tortfeasor with the usual "joint-and-several" liability is merely a permissive party to an action against another with like liability. See 3 *Moore's Federal Practice,* § 2153 (2d ed. 1963); 2 Barron & Holtzoff, *Federal Practice & Procedure* § 513.8 (Wright ed. 1961). Joinder of these tortfeasors continues to be regulated by Rule 20; compare Rule 14 on third-party practice.

If a person as described in subdivision (a)(1)–(2) is amenable to service of process and his joinder would not deprive the court of jurisdiction in the sense of competence over the action, he should be joined as a party; and if he has not been joined, the court should order him to be brought into the action. If a party joined has a valid objection to the venue and chooses to assert it, he will be dismissed from the action.

Subdivision (b). When a person as described in subdivision (a)(1)–(2) cannot be made a party, the court is to determine whether in equity and good conscience the action should proceed among the parties already before it, or should be dismissed. That this decision is to be made in the light of pragmatic considerations has often been acknowledged by the courts. See *Roos v. Texas Co.,* 23 F.2d 171 (2d Cir. 1927), *cert. denied,* 277 U.S. 587 (1928); *Niles-Bement-Pond Co. v. Iron Moulders' Union,* 254 U.S. 77, 80 (1920). The subdivision sets out four relevant considerations drawn from the experience revealed in the decided cases. The factors are to a certain extent overlapping, and they are not intended to exclude other considerations which may be applicable in particular situations.

The *first factor* brings in a consideration of what a judgment in the action would mean to the absentee. Would the absentee by adversely affected in a practical sense, and if so, would the prejudice be immediate and serious, or remote and minor? The possible collateral consequences of the judgment upon the parties already joined are also to be appraised. Would any party be exposed to a fresh action by the absentee, and if so, how serious is the threat? See the elaborate discussion in Reed, *supra; cf. A. L. Smith Iron Co. v. Dickson,* 141 F.2d 3 (2d Cir. 1944); *Caldwell Mfg. Co. v. Unique Balance Co.,* 18 F.R.D. 258 (S.D.N.Y.1955).

The *second factor* calls attention to the measures by which prejudice may be averted or lessened. The "shaping of relief" is a familiar expedient to this end. See, *e. g.,* the award of money damages in lieu of specific relief where the latter might affect an absentee adversely. *Ward v. Deavers,* 203 F.2d 72 (D.C.Cir. 1953); *Miller & Lux, Inc. v. Nickel,* 141 F.Supp. 41 (N.D.Calif.1956). On the use of "protective provisions," see *Roos v. Texas Co., supra; Atwood v. Rhode Island Hosp. Trust Co.,* 275 Fed. 513, 519 (1st Cir. 1921), *cert. denied,* 257 U.S. 661 (1922); *cf. Stumpf v. Fidelity Gas Co.,* 294 F.2d 886 (9th Cir. 1961); and the general statement in *National Licorice Co. v. Labor Board,* 309 U.S. 350, 363 (1940).

Sometimes the party is himself able to take measures to avoid prejudice. Thus a defendant faced with a prospect of a second suit by an absentee may be in a position to bring the latter into the action by defensive interpleader. See *Hudson v. Newell,* 172 F.2d 848, 852, *mod.,* 176 F.2d 546 (5th Cir. 1949); *Gauss v. Kirk,* 198 F.2d 83, 86 (D.C.Cir. 1952); *Abel v. Brayton Flying Service, Inc.,* 248 F.2d 713, 716 (5th Cir. 1957) (suggestion of possibility of counterclaim under Rule 13(h)); *cf. Parker Rust-Proof Co. v. Western Union Tel. Co.,* 105 F.2d 976 (2d Cir. 1939), *cert. denied,* 308 U.S. 597 (1939). So also the absentee may sometimes be able to avert prejudice to himself by voluntarily appearing in the action or intervening on an ancillary basis. See *Developments in the Law, supra,* 71 Harv.L.Rev. at 882; Annot., *Intervention or Subsequent Joinder of Parties as Affecting Jurisdiction of Federal Court Based on Diversity of Citizenship,* 134 A.L.R. 335 (1941); *Johnson v. Middleton,* 175 F.2d 535 (7th Cir. 1949); *Kentucky Nat. Gas Corp. v. Duggins,* 165 F.2d 1011 (6th Cir. 1948); *McComb v. McCormack,* 159 F.2d 219 (5th Cir. 1947). The court should consider whether this, in turn, would impose undue hardship on the absentee. (For the possibility of the court's informing an absentee of the pendency of the action, see comment under subdivision (c) below.)

The *third factor*—whether an "adequate" judgment can be rendered in the absence of a given person—calls attention to the extent of the relief that can be accorded among the parties joined. It meshes with the other factors, especially the "shaping of relief" mentioned under the second factor. *Cf. Kroese v. General Steel Castings Corp.,* 179 F.2d 760 (3d Cir. 1949), *cert. denied,* 339 U.S. 983 (1950).

The *fourth factor,* looking to the practical effects of a dismissal, indicates that the court should consider whether there is any assurance that the plaintiff, if dismissed, could sue effectively in another forum where better joinder would be possible. See *Fitzgerald v. Haynes,* 241 F.2d 417, 420 (3d Cir. 1957); *Fouke v. Schenewerk,* 197 F.2d 234, 236 (5th Cir. 1952); *cf. Warfield v. Marks,* 190 F.2d 178 (5th Cir. 1951).

The subdivision uses the word "indispensable" only in a conclusory sense, that is, a person is "regarded as indispensable" when he cannot be made a party and, upon consideration of the factors above-mentioned, it is determined that in his absence it would be preferable to dismiss the action, rather than to retain it.

A person may be added as a party at any stage of the action on motion or on the court's initiative (see Rule 21); and a motion to dismiss, on the ground that a person has not been joined and justice requires that the action should not proceed in his absence, may be made as late as the trial on the merits (see Rule 12(h)(2), as amended; *cf.* Rule 12(b)(7), as amended). However, when the moving party is seeking dismissal in order to protect himself against a later suit by the absent person (subdivision (a)(2)(ii)), and is not seeking vicariously to protect the absent person against a prejudicial judgment (subdivision (a)(2)(i)), his undue delay in making the motion can properly be counted against him as a reason for denying the motion. A joinder question should be decided with reasonable promptness, but decision may properly be deferred if adequate information is not available at the time. Thus the relationship of an absent person to the action, and the practical effects of an adjudication upon him and others, may not be sufficiently revealed at the pleading state; in such a case it would be appropriate to defer decision until the action was further advanced. *Cf.* Rule 12(d).

The amended rule makes no special provision for the problem arising in suits against subordinate Federal officials where it has often been set up as a defense that some superior officer must be joined. Frequently this defense has been accompanied by or intermingled with defenses of sovereign immunity or lack of consent of the United States to suit. So far as the issue of joinder can be isolated from the rest, the new subdivision seems better adapted to handle it than the predecessor provision. See the discussion in *Johnson v. Kirkland,* 290 F.2d 440, 446–47 (5th Cir. 1961) (stressing the practical orientation of the decisions); *Shaughnessy v. Pedreiro,* 349 U.S. 48, 54 (1955). Recent legislation, P.L. 87–748, 76 Stat. 744, approved October 5, 1962, adding §§ 1361, 1391(e) to Title 28, U.S.C., vests original jurisdiction in the district courts over actions in the nature of mandamus to compel officials of the United States to perform their legal duties, and extends the range of service of process and liberalizes venue in these actions. If, then, it is found that a particular official should be joined in the action, the legislation will make it easy to bring him in.

Subdivision (c) parallels the predecessor subdivision (c) of Rule 19. In some situations it may be desirable to advise a person who has not been joined of the fact that the action is pending, and in particular cases the court in its discretion may itself convey this information by directing a letter or other informal notice to the absentee.

Subdivision (d) repeats the exception contained in the first clause of the predecessor subdivision (a).

Rule 20.

PERMISSIVE JOINDER OF PARTIES

(a) Permissive Joinder. All persons may join in one action as plaintiffs if they assert any right to relief jointly, severally, or in the alternative in respect of or arising out of the same transaction, occurrence, or series of transactions or occurrences and if any question of law or fact common to all ~~of them~~ *these persons* will arise in the action. All persons *(and any vessel, cargo or other property subject to admiralty process in rem)* may be joined in one action as defendants if there is asserted against them jointly, severally, or in the alternative, any right to relief in respect of or arising out of the same transaction, occurrence, or series of transactions or occurrences and if any question of law or fact common to all ~~of them~~ *defendants* will arise in the action. A plaintiff or defendant need not be interested in obtaining or defending against all the relief demanded. Judgment may be given for one or more of the plaintiffs according to their respective rights to relief, and against one or more defendants according to their respective liabilities.

Advisory Committee's Note

See the amendment of Rule 18(a) and the Advisory Committee's Note thereto. It has been thought that a lack of clarity in the antecedent of the word "them," as it appeared in two places in Rule 20(a), contributed to the view, taken by some courts, that this rule limited the joinder of claims in certain situations of permissive party-joinder. Although the amendment of Rule 18(a) should make clear that this view is untenable, it has been considered advisable to amend Rule 20(a) to eliminate any ambiguity. See 2 Barron & Holtzoff, *Federal Practice & Procedure* 202 (Wright ed. 1961).

A basic purpose of unification of admiralty and civil procedure is to reduce barriers to joinder; hence the reference to "any vessel," etc.

New matter is shown in italics; matter to be omitted is lined through

~~Rule 23.~~

~~CLASS ACTIONS~~

~~**(a) Representation.** If persons constituting a class are so numerous as to make it impracticable to bring them all before the court, such of them, one or more, as will fairly insure the adequate representation of all may, on behalf of all, sue or be sued, when the character of the right sought to be enforced for or against the class is~~

~~(1) joint or common, or secondary in the sense that the owner of a primary right refuses to enforce that right and a member of the class thereby becomes entitled to enforce it;~~

~~(2) several, and the object of the action is the adjudication of claims which do or may affect specific property involved in the action; or~~

~~(3) several, and there is a common question of law or fact affecting the several rights and a common relief is sought.~~

~~**(b) Secondary Action by Shareholders.** In an action brought to enforce a secondary right on the part of one or more shareholders in an association, incorporated or unincorporated, because the association refuses to enforce rights which may properly be asserted by it, the complaint shall be verified by oath and shall aver (1) that the plaintiff was a shareholder at the time of the transaction of which he complains or that his share thereafter devolved on him by operation of law and (2) that the action is not a collusive one to confer on a court of the United States jurisdiction of any action of which it would not otherwise have jurisdiction. The complaint shall also set forth with particularity the efforts of the plaintiff to secure from the managing directors or trustees and, if necessary, from the shareholders such action as he desires, and the reasons for his failure to obtain such action or the reasons for not making such effort.~~

~~**(c) Dismissal or Compromise.** A class action shall not be dismissed or compromised without the approval of the court. If the right sought to be enforced is one defined in paragraph (1) of subdivision (a) of this rule notice of the proposed dismissal or compromise shall be given to all members of the class in such manner as the court directs. If the right is one defined in paragraphs (2) or (3) of subdivision (a) notice shall be given only if the court requires it.~~

Rule 23.

CLASS ACTIONS

(a) Prerequisites to a Class Action. One or more members of a class may sue or be sued as representative parties on behalf of all only if (1) the class is so numerous that joinder of all members is impracticable, (2) there are questions of law or fact common to the class, (3) the claims or defenses of the representative parties are typical of the claims or defenses of the class, and (4) the representative parties will fairly and adequately protect the interests of the class.

(b) Class Actions Maintainable. An action may be maintained as a class action if the prerequisites of subdivision (a) are satisfied, and in addition:

(1) the prosecution of separate actions by or against individual members of the class would create a risk of

(A) inconsistent or varying adjudications with respect to individual members of the class which would establish incompatible standards of conduct for the party opposing the class, or

(B) adjudications with respect to individual members of the class which would as a practical matter be dispositive of the interests of the other members not parties to the adjudications or substantially impair or impede their ability to protect their interests; or

(2) the party opposing the class has acted or refused to act on grounds generally applicable to the class, thereby making appropriate final injunctive relief or corresponding declaratory relief with respect to the class as a whole; or

(3) the court finds that the questions of law or fact common to the members of the class predominate over any questions affecting only individual members, and that a class action is superior to other available methods for the fair and efficient adjudication of the controversy. The matters pertinent to the findings include: (A) the interest of members of the class in individually controlling the prosecution or defense of separate actions; (B) the extent and nature of any litigation concerning the controversy already commenced by or against members of the class; (C) the desirability or undesirability of concentrating the litigation of the claims in the particular forum; (D) the difficulties likely to be encountered in the management of a class action.

(c) Determination by Order Whether Class Action to be Maintained; Notice; Judgment; Actions Conducted Partially as Class Actions.

New matter is shown in italics; matter to be omitted is lined through

(1) As soon as practicable after the commencement of an action brought as a class action, the court shall determine by order whether it is to be so maintained. An order under this subdivision may be conditional, and may be altered or amended before the decision on the merits.

(2) In any class action maintained under subdivision (b)(3), the court shall direct to the members of the class the best notice practicable under the circumstances, including individual notice to all members who can be identified through reasonable effort. The notice shall advise each member that (A) the court will exclude him from the class if he so requests by a specified date; (B) the judgment, whether favorable or not, will include all members who do not request exclusion; and (C) any member who does not request exclusion may, if he desires, enter an appearance through his counsel.

(3) The judgment in an action maintained as a class action under subdivision (b)(1) or (b)(2), whether or not favorable to the class, shall include and describe those whom the court finds to be members of the class. The judgment in an action maintained as a class action under subdivision (b)(3), whether or not favorable to the class, shall include and specify or describe those to whom the notice provided in subdivision (c)(2) was directed, and who have not requested exclusion, and whom the court finds to be members of the class.

(4) When appropriate (A) an action may be brought or maintained as a class action with respect to particular issues, or (B) a class may be divided into subclasses and each subclass treated as a class, and the provisions of this rule shall then be construed and applied accordingly.

(d) Orders in Conduct of Actions. In the conduct of actions to which this rule applies, the court may make appropriate orders: (1) determining the course of proceedings or prescribing measures to prevent undue repetition or complication in the presentation of evidence or argument; (2) requiring, for the protection of the members of the class or otherwise for the fair conduct of the action, that notice be given in such manner as the court may direct to some or all of the members of any step in the action, or of the proposed extent of the judgment, or of the opportunity of members to signify whether they consider the representation fair and adequate, to intervene and present claims or defenses, or otherwise to come into the action; (3) imposing conditions on the representative parties or on intervenors; (4) requiring that the pleadings be amended to eliminate therefrom allegations as to representation of absent persons, and that the action proceed accordingly; (5) dealing with similar procedural matters. The orders may be combined with an order under Rule 16,

New matter is shown in italics; matter to be omitted is lined through

and may be altered or amended as may be desirable form time to time.

(e) Dismissal or Compromise. A class action shall not be dismissed or compromised without the approval of the court, and notice of the proposed dismissal or compromise shall be given to all members of the class in such manner as the court directs.

Advisory Committee's Note

Difficulties with the original rule. The categories of class actions in the original rule were defined in terms of the abstract nature of the rights involved: the so-called "true" category was defined as involving "joint, common, or secondary rights"; the "hybrid" category, as involving "several" rights related to "specific property"; the "spurious" category, as involving "several" rights affected by a common question and related to common relief. It was thought that the definitions accurately described the situations amenable to the class-suit device, and also would indicate the proper extent of the judgment in each category, which would in turn help to determine the *res judicata* effect of the judgment if questioned in a later action. Thus the judgments in "true" and "hybrid" class actions would extend to the class (although in somewhat different ways); the judgment in a "spurious" class action would extend only to the parties including intervenors. See Moore, *Federal Rules of Civil Procedure: Some Problems Raised by the Preliminary Draft,* 25 Geo.L.J. 551, 570–76 (1937).

In practice the terms "joint," "common," etc., which were used as the basis of the Rule 23 classification proved obscure and uncertain. See Chafee, *Some Problems of Equity* 245–46, 256–57 (1950); Kalven & Rosenfield, *The Contemporary Function of the Class Suit,* 8 U. of Chi.L.Rev. 684, 707 & n. 73 (1941); Keeffe, Levy & Donovan, *Lee Defeats Ben Hur,* 33 Corn.L.Q. 327, 329–36 (1948); *Developments in the Law: Multiparty Litigation in the Federal Courts,* 71 Harv.L.Rev. 874, 931 (1958); Advisory Committee's Note to Rule 19, as amended. The courts had considerable difficulty with these terms. See, *e. g., Gullo v. Veterans' Coop. H. Assn.,* 13 F.R.D. 11 (D.D.C.1952); *Shipley v. Pittsburgh & L. E. R. Co.,* 70 F.Supp. 870 (W.D.Pa.1947); *Deckert v. Independence Shares Corp.,* 27 F.Supp. 763 (E.D.Pa. 1939), *rev'd,* 108 F.2d 51 (3d Cir. 1939), *rev'd,* 311 U.S. 282 (1940), *on remand,* 39 F.Supp. 592 (E.D.Pa.1941), *rev'd sub nom. Pennsylvania Co. for Ins. on Lives v. Deckert,* 123 F.2d 979 (3d Cir. 1941) (see Chafee, *supra,* at 264–65).

Nor did the rule provide an adequate guide to the proper extent of the judgments in class actions. First, we find instances of the courts classifying actions as "true" or intimating that the judgments would be decisive for the class where these results seemed appropriate but were reached by dint of depriving the word "several" of coherent meaning. See, *e. g., System Federation No. 91 v. Reed,* 180 F.2d 991 (6th Cir. 1950); *Wilson v. City of Paducah,* 100 F.Supp. 116 (W.D.Ky.1951); *Citizens Banking Co. v. Monticello State Bank,* 143 F.2d 261 (8th Cir. 1944); *Redmond v. Commerce Trust Co.,* 144 F.2d 140 (8th Cir. 1944), *cert. denied,* 323 U.S. 776 (1944); *United States v. American Optical Co.,* 97 F.Supp. 66 (N.D.Ill.1951); *National Hairdressers' & C. Assn. v. Philad Co.,* 34 F.Supp. 264 (D.Del.1940); 41 F.Supp. 701 (D.Del.1940), *aff'd mem.,* 129 F.2d 1020 (3d Cir. 1942). Second, we find cases classified by the courts as "spurious" in which, on a realistic view, it would seem fitting for the judgments to extend to the class. See, *e. g., Knapp v. Bankers Sec. Corp.,* 17 F.R.D. 245 (E.D.Pa.1954), *aff'd,* 230 F.2d 717 (3d Cir. 1956); *Giesecke v. Denver Tramway Corp.,* 81 F.Supp. 957 (D.Del.1949); *York v. Guaranty Trust Co.,* 143 F.2d 503 (2d Cir. 1944), *rev'd on grounds not here relevant,* 326 U.S. 99 (1945) (see Chafee, *supra,* at 208); *cf. Webster Eisenlohr, Inc. v. Kalodner,* 145 F.2d 316,

320 (3d Cir. 1944), *cert. denied,* 325 U.S. 867 (1945). But *cf.* the early decisions, *Duke of Bedford v. Ellis,* [1901] A.C. 1; *Sheffield Waterworks v. Yeomans,* L.R. 2 Ch.App. 8 (1866); *Brown v. Vermuden,* 1 Ch.Cas. 272, 22 Eng.Rep. 796 (1676).

The "spurious" action envisaged by original Rule 23 was in any event an anomaly because, although denominated a "class" action and pleaded as such, it was supposed not to adjudicate the rights or liabilities of any person not a party. It was believed to be an advantage of the "spurious" category that it would invite decisions that a member of the "class" could, like a member of the class in a "true" or "hybrid" action, intervene on an ancillary basis without being required to show an independent basis of Federal jurisdiction, and have the benefit of the date of the commencement of the action for purposes of the statute of limitations. See 3 *Moore's Federal Practice* ¶¶ 23.10[1], 23.12 (2d ed. 1963). These results were attained in some instances but not in others. On the statute of limitations, see *Union Carbide & Carbon Corp. v. Nisley,* 300 F.2d 561 (10th Cir. 1961), *pet. cert. dism.,* 371 U.S. 801 (1963); but *cf. P. W. Husserl, Inc. v. Newman,* 25 F.R.D. 264 (S.D.N.Y.1960); *Athas v. Day,* 161 F.Supp. 916 (D.Colo.1958). On ancillary intervention, see *Amen v. Black,* 234 F.2d 12 (10th Cir. 1956), *cert. granted,* 352 U.S. 888 (1956), *dism. on stip.,* 355 U.S. 600 (1958); but *cf. Wagner v. Kemper,* 13 F.R.D. 128 (W.D.Mo.1952). The results, however, can hardly depend upon the mere appearance of a "spurious" category in the rule; they should turn on more basic considerations. See discussion of subdivision (c)(1) below.

Finally, the original rule did not squarely address itself to the question of the measures that might be taken during the course of the action to assure procedural fairness, particularly giving notice to members of the class, which may in turn be related in some instances to the extension of the judgment to the class. See Chafee, *supra,* at 230–31; Keeffe, Levy & Donovan, *supra; Developments in the Law, supra,* 71 Harv.L.Rev. at 937–38; Note, *Binding Effect of Class Actions,* 67 Harv.L.Rev. 1059, 1062–65 (1954); Note, *Federal Class Actions: A Suggested Revision of Rule 23,* 46 Colum.L.Rev. 818, 833–36 (1946); Mich.Gen.Court R. 208.4 (effective Jan. 1, 1963); Idaho R.Civ.P. 23(d); Minn.R.Civ.P. 23.04; N.Dak.R.Civ.P. 23(d).

The amended rule describes in more practical terms the occasions for maintaining class action; provides that all class actions maintained to the end as such will result in judgments including those whom the court finds to be members of the class, whether or not the judgment is favorable to the class; and refers to the measures which can be taken to assure the fair conduct of these actions.

Subdivision (a) states the prerequisites for maintaining any class action in terms of the numerousness of the class making joinder of the members impracticable, the existence of questions common to the class, and the desired qualifications of the representative parties. See Weinstein, *Revision of Procedure: Some Problems in Class Actions,* 9 Buffalo L.Rev. 433, 458–59 (1960); 2 Barron & Holtzoff, *Federal Practice & Procedure* § 562, at 265, § 572, at 351–52 (Wright ed. 1961). These are necessary but not sufficient conditions for a class action. See *e. g., Giordano v. Radio Corp. of Am.,* 183 F.2d 558, 560 (3d Cir. 1950); *Zachman v. Erwin,* 186 F.Supp. 681 (S.D.Tex.1959); *Baim & Blank, Inc. v. Warren-Connelly Co., Inc.,* 19 F.R.D. 108 (S.D.N.Y.1956). Subdivision (b) describes the additional elements which in varying situations justify the use of a class action.

Subdivision (b)(1). The difficulties which would be likely to arise if resort were had to separate actions by or against the individual members of the class here furnish the reasons for, and the principal key to, the propriety and value of utilizing the class-action device. The considerations stated under clauses (A) and (B) are comparable to certain of the elements which define the persons whose joinder in an action is desirable as stated in Rule 19(a), as amended. See amended Rule

19(a)(2)(i) and (ii), and the Advisory Committee's Note thereto; Hazard, *Indispensable Party: The Historical Origin of a Procedural Phantom,* 61 Colum.L.Rev. 1254, 1259–60 (1961); *cf.* 3 Moore, *supra,* ¶ 23.08, at 3435.

Clause (A): One person may have rights against, or be under duties toward, numerous persons constituting a class, and be so positioned that conflicting or varying adjudications in lawsuits with individual members of the class might establish incompatible standards to govern his conduct. The class action device can be used effectively to obviate the actual or virtual dilemma which would thus confront the party opposing the class. The matter has been stated thus: "The felt necessity for a class action is greatest when the courts are called upon to order or sanction the alteration of the status quo in circumstances such that a large number of persons are in a position to call on a single person to alter the status quo, or to complain if it is altered, and the possibility exists that [the] actor might be called upon to act in inconsistent ways." Louisell & Hazard, *Pleading and Procedure: State and Federal* 719 (1962); see *Supreme Tribe of Ben-Hur v. Cauble,* 255 U.S. 356, 366–67 (1921). To illustrate: Separate actions by individuals against a municipality to declare a bond issue invalid or condition or limit it, to prevent or limit the making of a particular appropriation or to compel or invalidate an assessment, might create a risk of inconsistent or varying determinations. In the same way, individual litigations of the rights and duties of riparian owners, or of landowners' rights and duties respecting a claimed nuisance, could create a possibility of incompatible adjudications. Actions by or against a class provide a ready and fair means of achieving unitary adjudication. See *Maricopa County Mun. Water Con. Dist. v. Looney,* 219 F.2d 529 (9th Cir. 1955); *Rank v. Krug,* 142 F.Supp. 1, 154–59 (S.D.Calif.1956), *on app., State of California v. Rank,* 293 F.2d 340, 348 (9th Cir. 1961); *Gart v. Cole,* 263 F.2d 244 (2d Cir. 1959), *cert. denied,* 359 U.S. 978 (1959); *cf. Martinez v. Maverick Cty. Water Con. & Imp. Dist.,* 219 F.2d 666 (5th Cir. 1955); 3 Moore, *supra,* ¶ 23.11[2], at 3458–59.

Clause (B): This clause takes in situations where the judgment in a nonclass action by or against an individual member of the class, while not technically concluding the other members, might do so as a practical matter. The vice of an individual action would lie in the fact that the other members of the class, thus practically concluded, would have had no representation in the lawsuit. In an action by policy holders against a fraternal benefit association attacking a financial reorganization of the society, it would hardly have been practical, if indeed it would have been possible, to confine the effects of a validation of the reorganization to the individual plaintiffs. Consequently a class action was called for with adequate representation of all members of the class. See *Supreme Tribe of Ben-Hur v. Cauble,* 255 U.S. 356 (1921); *Waybright v. Columbian Mut. Life Ins. Co.,* 30 F.Supp. 885 (W.D.Tenn.1939); *cf. Smith v. Swormstedt,* 16 How. (57 U.S.) 288 (1853). For much the same reason actions by shareholders to compel the declaration of a dividend, the proper recognition and handling of redemption or pre-emption rights, or the like (or actions by the corporation for corresponding declaration of rights), should ordinarily be conducted as class actions, although the matter has been much obscured by the insistence that each shareholder has an individual claim. See *Knapp v. Bankers Securities Corp.* 17 F.R.D. 245 (E.D.Pa.1954), *aff'd,* 230 F.2d 717 (3d Cir. 1956); *Giesecke v. Denver Tramway Corp.,* 81 F.Supp. 957 (D.Del.1949); *Zahn v. Transamerica Corp.,* 162 F.2d 36 (3d Cir. 1947); *Speed v. Transamerica Corp.,* 100 F.Supp. 461 (D.Del.1951); *Sobel v. Whittier Corp.,* 95 F.Supp. 643 (E.D.Mich.1951), *app. dism.,* 195 F.2d 361 (6th Cir. 1952); *Goldberg v. Whittier Corp.,* 111 F.Supp. 382 (E.D.Mich.1953); *Dann v. Studebaker-Packard Corp.,* 288 F.2d 201 (6th Cir. 1961); *Edgerton v. Armour & Co.,* 94 F.Supp. 549 (S.D.Calif.1950); *Ames v. Mengel Co.,* 190 F.2d 344 (2d Cir. 1951). (These shareholders' actions are to be distinguished from derivative actions by shareholders dealt with in new Rule 23.1). The same reasoning applies to an action which charges a breach of trust by an indenture trustee or other fiduciary similarly affecting the members of a large class of security holders or other beneficiaries, and which requires an accounting or like measures to restore the subject of the trust. See *Boesenberg v. Chicago T. & T. Co.,* 128 F.2d 245 (7th Cir. 1942); *Citizens Banking Co. v. Monticello State Bank,* 143 F.2d 261 (8th Cir. 1944); *Redmond v. Commerce Trust Co.* 144 F.2d 140 (8th Cir. 1944), *cert. denied,* 323 U.S. 776 (1944); *cf. York v. Guaranty Trust Co.,* 143 F.2d 503 (2d Cir. 1944), *rev'd on grounds not here relevant,* 326 U.S. 99 (1945).

In various situations an adjudication as to one or more members of the class will necessarily or probably have an adverse practical effect on the interests of other members who should therefore be represented in the lawsuit. This is plainly the case when claims are made by numerous persons against a fund insufficient to satisfy all claims. A class action by or against representative members to settle the validity of the claims as a whole, or in groups, followed by separate proof of the amount of each valid claim and proportionate distribution of the fund, meets the problem. *Cf. Dickinson v. Burnham,* 197 F.2d 973 (2d Cir. 1952), *cert. denied,* 344 U.S. 875 (1952); 3 Moore, *supra,* at ¶ 23.09. The same reasoning applies to an action by a creditor to set aside a fraudulent conveyance by the debtor and to appropriate the property to his claim, when the debtor's assets are insufficient to pay all creditors' claims. See *Heffernan v. Bennett & Armour,* 110 Cal.App.2d 564, 243 P.2d 846 (1952); *cf. City & County of San Francisco v. Market Street Ry.,* 95 Cal.App.2d 648, 213 P.2d 780 (1950). Similar problems, however, can arise in the absence of a fund either present or potential. A negative or mandatory injunction secured by one of a numerous class may disable the opposing party from performing claimed duties toward the other members of the class or materially affect his ability to do so. An adjudication as to movie "clearances and runs" nominally affecting only one exhibitor would often have practical effects on all the exhibitors in the same territorial area. *Cf. United States v. Paramount Pictures, Inc.,* 66 F.Supp. 323, 341–46 (S.D.N.Y.1946); 334 U.S. 131, 144–48 (1948). Assuming a sufficiently numerous class of exhibitors, a class action would be advisable. (Here representation of subclasses of exhibitors could become necessary; see subdivision (c)(3)(B).)

Subdivision (b)(2). This subdivision is intended to reach situations where a party has taken action or refused to take action with respect to a class, and final relief of an injunctive nature or of a corresponding declaratory nature, settling the legality of the behavior with respect to the class as a whole, is appropriate. Declaratory relief "corresponds" to injunctive relief when as a practical matter it affords injunctive relief or serves as a basis for later injunctive relief. The subdivision does not extend to cases in which the appropriate final relief relates exclusively or predominantly to money damages. Action or inaction is directed to a class within the meaning of this subdivision even if it has taken effect or is threatened only as to one or a few members of the class, provided it is based on grounds which have general application to the class.

Illustrative are various actions in the civil-rights field where a party is charged with discriminating unlawfully against a class, usually one whose members are incapable of specific enumeration. See *Potts v. Flax,* 313 F.2d 284 (5th Cir. 1963); *Bailey v. Patterson,* 323 F.2d 201 (5th Cir. 1963), *cert. denied,* 377 U.S. 972 (1964); *Brunson v. Board of Trustees of School District No. 1, Clarendon Cty., S. C.,* 311 F.2d 107 (4th Cir. 1962), *cert. denied,* 373 U.S. 933 (1963); *Green v. School Bd. of Roanoke, Va.,* 304 F.2d 118 (4th Cir. 1962); *Orleans Parish School Bd. v. Bush,* 242 F.2d 156 (5th Cir. 1957), *cert. denied,* 354 U.S. 921 (1957); *Mannings v. Board of Public Inst. of Hillsborough County, Fla.,* 277 F.2d 370 (5th Cir. 1960); *Northcross v. Board of Ed. of City of Memphis,* 302 F.2d 818 (6th Cir. 1962), *cert. denied,* 370 U.S. 944 (1962); *Frasier v. Board of Trustees of Univ. of N. C.,* 134 F.Supp. 589

(M.D.N.C.1955, 3-judge court), *aff'd,* 350 U.S. 979 (1956). Subdivision (b)(2) is not limited to civil-rights cases. Thus an action looking to specific or declaratory relief could be brought by a numerous class of purchasers, say retailers of a given description, against a seller alleged to have undertaken to sell to that class at prices higher than those set for other purchasers, say retailers of another description, when the applicable law forbids such a pricing differential. So also a patentee of a machine, charged with selling or licensing the machine on condition that purchasers or licensees also purchase or obtain licenses to use an ancillary unpatented machine, could be sued on a class basis by a numerous group of purchasers or licensees, or by a numerous group of competing sellers or licensors of the unpatented machine, to test the legality of the "tying" condition.

Subdivision (b)(3). In the situations to which this subdivision relates, class-action treatment is not as clearly called for as in those described above, but it may nevertheless be convenient and desirable depending upon the particular facts. Subdivision (b)(3) encompasses those cases in which a class action would achieve economies of time, effort, and expense, and promote uniformity of decision as to persons similarly situated, without sacrificing procedural fairness or bringing about other undesirable results. *Cf.* Chafee, *supra,* at 201.

The court is required to find, as a condition of holding that a class action may be maintained under this subdivision, that the questions common to the class predominate over the questions affecting individual members. It is only where this predominance exists that economies can be achieved by means of the class-action device. In this view, a fraud perpetrated on numerous persons by the use of similar misrepresentations may be an appealing situation for a class action, and it may remain so despite the need, if liability is found, for separate determination of the damages suffered by individuals within the class. On the other hand, although having some common core, a fraud case may be unsuited for treatment as a class action if there was material variation in the representations made or in the kinds or degrees of reliance by the persons to whom they were addressed. See *Oppenheimer v. F. J. Young & Co., Inc.,* 144 F.2d 387 (2d Cir. 1944); *Miller v. National City Bank of N. Y.,* 166 F.2d 723 (2d Cir. 1948); and for like problems in other contexts, see *Hughes v. Encyclopaedia Britannica,* 199 F.2d 295 (7th Cir. 1952); *Sturgeon v. Great Lakes Steel Corp.,* 143 F.2d 819 (6th Cir. 1944). A "mass accident" resulting in injuries to numerous persons is ordinarily not appropriate for a class action because of the likelihood that significant questions, not only of damages but of liability and defenses to liability, would be present, affecting the individuals in different ways. In these circumstances an action conducted nominally as a class action would degenerate in practice into multiple lawsuits separately tried. See *Pennsylvania R. R. v. United States,* 111 F.Supp. 80 (D.N.J.1953); *cf.* Weinstein, *supra,* 9 Buffalo L.Rev. at 469. Private damage claims by numerous individuals arising out of concerted antitrust violations may or may not involve predominating common questions. See *Union Carbide & Carbon Corp. v. Nisley,* 300 F.2d 561 (10th Cir. 1961), *pet. cert. dism.,* 371 U.S. 801 (1963); *cf. Weeks v. Bareco Oil Co.,* 125 F.2d 84 (7th Cir. 1941); *Kainz v. Anheuser-Busch, Inc.,* 194 F.2d 737 (7th Cir. 1952); *Hess v. Anderson, Clayton & Co.,* 20 F.R.D. 466 (S.D.Calif.1957).

That common questions predominate is not itself sufficient to justify a class action under subdivision (b)(3), for another method of handling the litigious situation may be available which has greater practical advantages. Thus one or more actions agreed to by the parties as test or model actions may be preferable to a class action; or it may prove feasible and preferable to consolidate actions. *Cf.* Weinstein, *supra,* 9 Buffalo L.Rev. at 438–54. Even when a number of separate actions are proceeding simultaneously, experience shows that the burdens on the parties and the courts can sometimes be reduced by arrangements for avoiding repetitious discovery or the like. Currently the Coordinating Committee on Multiple Litigation in the United States District Courts (a subcommittee of the Committee on Trial Practice and Technique of the Judicial Conference of the United States) is charged with developing methods for expediting such massive litigation. To reinforce the point that the court with the aid of the parties ought to assess the relative advantages of alternative procedures for handling the total controversy, subdivision (b)(3) requires, as a further condition of maintaining the class action, that the court shall find that that procedure is "superior" to the others in the particular circumstances.

Factors (A)–(D) are listed, non-exhaustively, as pertinent to the findings. The court is to consider the interests of individual members of the class in controlling their own litigations and carrying them on as they see fit. See *Weeks v. Bareco Oil Co.*, 125 F.2d 84, 88–90, 93–94 (7th Cir.1941) (anti-trust action); see also *Pentland v. Dravo Corp.*, 152 F.2d 851 (3d Cir.1945), and Chafee, *supra,* at 273–75, regarding policy of Fair Labor Standards Act of 1938, § 16(b), 29 U.S.C. § 216(b), prior to amendment by Portal-to-Portal Act of 1947, § 5(a). [The present provisions of 29 U.S.C. § 216(b) are not intended to be affected by Rule 23, as amended.] In this connection the court should inform itself of any litigation actually pending by or against the individuals. The interests of individuals in conducting separate lawsuits may be so strong as to call for denial of a class action. On the other hand, these interests may be theoretic rather than practical: the class may have a high degree of cohesion and prosecution of the action through representatives would be quite unobjectionable, or the amounts at stake for individuals may be so small that separate suits would be impracticable. The burden that separate suits would impose on the party opposing the class, or upon the court calendars, may also fairly be considered. (See the discussion, under subdivision (c)(2) below, of the right of members to be excluded from the class upon their request.)

Also pertinent is the question of the desirability of concentrating the trial of the claims in the particular forum by means of a class action, in contrast to allowing the claims to be litigated separately in forums to which they would ordinarily be brought. Finally, the court should consider the problems of management which are likely to arise in the conduct of a class action.

Subdivision (c)(1). In order to give clear definition to the action, this provision requires the court to determine, as early in the proceedings as may be practicable, whether an action brought as a class action is to be so maintained. The determination depends in each case on satisfaction of the terms of subdivision (a) and the relevant provisions of subdivision (b).

An order embodying a determination can be conditional; the court may rule, for example, that a class action may be maintained only if the representation is improved through intervention of additional parties of a stated type. A determination once made can be altered or amended before the decision on the merits if, upon full development of the facts, the original determination appears unsound. A negative determination means that the action should be stripped of its character as a class action. See subdivision (d)(4). Although an action thus becomes a nonclass action, the court may still be receptive to interventions before the decision on the merits so that the litigation may cover as many interests as can be conveniently handled; the questions whether the intervenors in the nonclass action shall be permitted to claim "ancillary" jurisdiction or the benefit of the date of the commencement of the action for purposes of the statute of limitations are to be decided by reference to the laws governing jurisdiction and limitations as they apply in particular contexts.

Whether the court should require notice to be given to members of the class of its intention to make a determination, or of the order embodying it, is left to the court's discretion under subdivision (d)(2).

Subdivision (c)(2) makes special provision for class actions maintained under subdivision (b)(3). As noted in the discussion of the latter subdivision, the interests of the individuals in pursuing their own litigations may be so strong here as to warrant denial of a class action altogether. Even when a class action is maintained under subdivision (b)(3), this individual interest is respected. Thus the court is required to direct notice to the members of the class of the right of each member to be excluded from the class upon his request. A member who does not request exclusion may, if he wishes, enter an appearance in the action through his counsel; whether or not he does so, the judgment in the action will embrace him.

The notice, setting forth the alternatives open to the members of the class, is to be the best practicable under the circumstances, and shall include individual notice to the members who can be identified through reasonable effort. (For further discussion of this notice, see the statement under subdivision (d)(2) below.)

Subdivision (c)(3). The judgment in a class action maintained as such to the end will embrace the class, that is, in a class action under subdivision (b)(1) or (b)(2), those found by the court to be class members; in a class action under subdivision (b)(3), those to whom the notice prescribed by subdivision (c)(2) was directed, excepting those who requested exclusion or who are ultimately found by the court not to be members of the class. The judgment has this scope whether it is favorable or unfavorable to the class. In a (b)(1) or (b)(2) action the judgment "describes" the members of the class, but need not specify the individual members; in a (b)(3) action the judgment "specifies" the individual members who have been identified and describes the others.

Compare subdivision (c)(4) as to actions conducted as class actions only with respect to particular issues. Where the class-action character of the lawsuit is based solely on the existence of a "limited fund," the judgment, while extending to all claims of class members against the fund, has ordinarily left unaffected the personal claims of nonappearing members against the debtor. See 3 Moore, *supra,* ¶ 23.11[4].

Hitherto, in a few actions conducted as "spurious" class actions and thus nominally designed to extend only to parties and others intervening *before* the determination of liability, courts have held or intimated that class members might be permitted to intervene *after* a decision on the merits favorable to their interests, in order to secure the benefits of the decision for themselves, although they would presumably be unaffected by an unfavorable decision. See, as to the propriety of this so-called "one-way" intervention in "spurious" actions, the conflicting views expressed in *Union Carbide & Carbon Corp. v. Nisley,* 300 F.2d 561 (10th Cir.1961), *pet. cert. dism.,* 371 U.S. 801 (1963); *York v. Guaranty Trust Co.,* 143 F.2d 503, 529 (2d Cir.1944), *rev'd on grounds not here relevant,* 326 U.S. 99 (1945); *Pentland v. Dravo Corp.,* 152 F.2d 851, 856 (3d Cir.1945); *Speed v. Transamerica Corp.,* 100 F.Supp. 461, 463 (D.Del.1951); *State Wholesale Grocers v. Great Atl. & Pac. Tea Co.,* 24 F.R.D. 510 (N.D.Ill.1959); *Alabama Ind. Serv. Stat. Assn. v. Shell Pet. Corp.,* 28 F.Supp. 386, 390 (N.D.Ala.1939); *Tolliver v. Cudahy Packing Co.,* 39 F.Supp. 337, 339 (E.D.Tenn.1941); Kalven & Rosenfield, *supra,* 8 U. of Chi.L.Rev. 684 (1941); Comment, 53 Nw.U.L.Rev. 627, 632–33 (1958); *Developments in the Law, supra,* 71 Harv.L.Rev. at 935; 2 Barron & Holtzoff, *supra,* § 568; but *cf. Lockwood v. Hercules Powder Co.,* 7 F.R.D. 24, 28–29 (W.D.Mo.1947); *Abram v. San Joaquin Cotton Oil Co.,* 46 F.Supp. 969, 976–77 (S.D.Calif.1942); Chafee, *supra,* at 280, 285; 3 Moore, *supra,* ¶ 23.12, at 3476. Under proposed subdivision (c)(3), one-way intervention is excluded; the action will have been early determined to be a class or nonclass action, and in the former case the judgment, whether or not favorable, will include the class, as above stated.

Although thus declaring that the judgment in a class action includes the class, as defined, subdivision (c)(3) does not disturb the recognized principle that the court conducting the action cannot predetermine the *res judicata* effect of the judgment; this can be tested only in a subsequent action. See Restatement, *Judgments* § 86, comment (h), § 116 (1942). The court, however, in framing the judgment in any suit brought as a class action, must decide what its extent or coverage shall be, and if the matter is carefully considered, questions of *res judicata* are less likely to be raised at a later time and if raised will be more satisfactorily answered. See Chafee, *supra,* at 294; Weinstein, *supra,* 9 Buffalo L.Rev. at 460.

Subdivision (c)(4). This provision recognizes that an action may be maintained as a class action as to particular issues only. For example, in a fraud or similar case the action may retain its "class" character only through the adjudication of liability to the class; the members of the class may thereafter be required to come in individually and prove the amounts of their respective claims.

Two or more classes may be represented in a single action. Where a class is found to include subclasses divergent in interest, the class may be divided correspondingly, and each subclass treated as a class.

Subdivision (d) is concerned with the fair and efficient conduct of the action and lists some types of orders which may be appropriate.

The court should consider how the proceedings are to be arranged in sequence, and what measures should be taken to simplify the proof and argument. See subdivision (d)(1). The orders resulting from this consideration, like the others referred to in subdivision (d), may be combined with a pretrial order under Rule 16, and are subject to modification as the case proceeds.

Subdivision (d)(2) sets out a non-exhaustive list of possible occasions for orders requiring notice to the class. Such notice is not a novel conception. For example, in "limited fund" cases, members of the class have been notified to present individual claims after the basic class decision. Notice has gone to members of a class so that they might express any opposition to the representation, see *United States v. American Optical Co.,* 97 F.Supp. 66 (N.D.Ill.1951), and 1950–51 CCH Trade Cases 64573–74 (¶ 62869); *cf. Weeks v. Bareco Oil Co.,* 125 F.2d 84, 94 (7th Cir.1941), and notice may encourage interventions to improve the representation of the class. *Cf. Oppenheimer v. F.J. Young & Co.,* 144 F.2d 387 (2d Cir.1944). Notice has been used to poll members on a proposed modification of a consent decree. See record in *Sam Fox Publishing Co. v. United States,* 366 U.S. 683 (1961).

Subdivision (d)(2) does not require notice at any stage, but rather calls attention to its availability and invokes the court's discretion. In the degree that there is cohesiveness or unity in the class and the representation is effective, the need for notice to the class will tend toward a minimum. These indicators suggest that notice under subdivision (d)(2) may be particularly useful and advisable in certain class actions maintained under subdivision (b)(3), for example, to permit members of the class to object to the representation. Indeed, under subdivision (c)(2), notice must be ordered, and is not merely discretionary, to give the members in a subdivision (b)(3) class action an opportunity to secure exclusion from the class. This mandatory notice pursuant to subdivision (c)(2), together with any discretionary notice which the court may find it advisable to give under subdivision (d)(2), is designed to fulfill requirements of due process to which the class action procedure is of course subject. See *Hansberry v. Lee,* 311 U.S. 32 (1940); *Mullane v. Central Hanover Bank & Trust Co.,* 339 U.S. 306 (1950); *cf. Dickinson v. Burnham,* 197 F.2d 973, 979 (2d Cir.1952), and studies cited at 979 n. 4; see also *All American*

Airways, Inc. v. Eldered, 209 F.2d 247, 249 (2d Cir.1954); *Gart v. Cole,* 263 F.2d 244, 248–49 (2d Cir.1959), *cert. denied,* 359 U.S. 978 (1959).

Notice to members of the class, whenever employed under amended Rule 23, should be accommodated to the particular purpose but need not comply with the formalities for service of process. See Chafee, *supra,* at 230–31; *Brendle v. Smith,* 7 F.R.D. 119 (S.D.N.Y.1946). The fact that notice is given at one stage of the action does not mean that it must be given at subsequent stages. Notice is available fundamentally "for the protection of the members of the class or otherwise for the fair conduct of the action" and should not be used merely as a device for the undesirable solicitation of claims. See the discussion in *Cherner v. Transitron Electronic Corp.,* 201 F.Supp. 934 (D.Mass.1962); *Hormel v. United States,* 17 F.R.D. 303 (S.D.N.Y.1955).

In appropriate cases the court should notify interested government agencies of the pendency of the action or of particular steps therein.

Subdivision (d)(3) reflects the possibility of conditioning the maintenance of a class action, *e. g.,* on the strengthening of the representation, see subdivision (c)(1) above; and recognizes that the imposition of conditions on intervenors may be required for the proper and efficient conduct of the action.

As to orders under subdivision (d)(4), see subdivision (c)(1) above.

Subdivision (e) requires approval of the court, after notice, for the dismissal or compromise of any class action.

Rule 23.1 [New].

DERIVATIVE ACTIONS BY SHAREHOLDERS

In a derivative action brought by one or more shareholders or members to enforce a right of a corporation or of an unincorporated association, the corporation or association having failed to enforce a right which may properly be asserted by it, the complaint shall be verified and shall allege (1) that the plaintiff was a shareholder or member at the time of the transaction of which he complains or that his share or membership thereafter devolved on him by operation of law, and (2) that the action is not a collusive one to confer jurisdiction on a court of the United States which it would not otherwise have. The complaint shall also allege with particularity the efforts, if any, made by the plaintiff to obtain the action he desires from the directors or comparable authority and, if necessary, from the shareholders or members, and the reasons for his failure to obtain the action or for not making the effort. The derivative action may not be maintained if it appears that the plaintiff does not fairly and adequately represent the interests of the shareholders or members similarly situated in enforcing the right of the corporation or association. The action shall not be dismissed or compromised without the approval of the court, and notice of the proposed dismissal or compromise shall be given to shareholders or members in such manner as the court directs.

Advisory Committee's Note

A derivative action by a shareholder of a corporation or by a member of an unincorporated association has distinctive aspects which require the special provisions set forth in the new rule. The next-to-the-last sentence recognizes that the question of adequacy of representation may arise when the plaintiff is one of a group of shareholders or members. *Cf.* 3 *Moore's Federal Practice* ¶ 23.08 (2d ed.1963).

The court has inherent power to provide for the conduct of the proceedings in a derivative action, including the power to determine the course of the proceedings and require that any appropriate notice be given to shareholders or members.

Rule 23.2 [New].

ACTIONS RELATING TO UNINCORPORATED ASSOCIATIONS

An action brought by or against the members of an unincorporated association as a class by naming certain members as representative parties may be maintained only if it appears that the representative parties will fairly and adequately protect the interests of the association and its members. In the conduct of the action the court may make appropriate orders corresponding with those described in Rule 23(d), and the procedure for dismissal or compromise of the action shall correspond with that provided in Rule 23(e).

Advisory Committee's Note

Although an action by or against representatives of the membership of an unincorporated association has often been viewed as a class action, the real or main purpose of this characterization has been to give "entity treatment" to the association when for formal reasons it cannot sue or be sued as a jural person under Rule 17(b). See Louisell & Hazard, *Pleading and Procedure: State and Federal* 718 (1962); 3 *Moore's Federal Practice* ¶ 23.08 (2d ed.1963); Story, J. in *West v. Randall,* 29 Fed.Cas. 718, 722–23, No. 17,424 (C.C.D.R.I.1820); and, for examples, *Gibbs v. Buck,* 307 U.S. 66 (1939); *Tunstall v. Brotherhood of Locomotive F. & E.,* 148 F.2d 403 (4th Cir.1945); *Oskoian v. Canuel,* 269 F.2d 311 (1st Cir.1959). Rule 23.2 deals separately with these actions, referring where appropriate to Rule 23.

Rule 24.

INTERVENTION

(a) Intervention of Right. Upon timely application anyone shall be permitted to intervene in an action: (1) when a statute of the United States confers an unconditional right to intervene; or (2) when the ~~representation of the applicant's interest by existing parties is or may be inadequate and the applicant is or may be bound by a judgment in the action; or (3) when the applicant is so situated as to be adversely affected by a distribution or other disposition of property which is in the custody or subject to the control or disposition of the court or an officer thereof.~~ *applicant*

New matter is shown in italics; matter to be omitted is lined through

claims an interest relating to the property or transaction which is the subject of the action and he is so situated that the disposition of the action may as a practical matter impair or impede his ability to protect that interest, unless the applicant's interest is adequately represented by existing parties.

Advisory Committee's Note

In attempting to overcome certain difficulties which have arisen in the application of present Rule 24(a)(2) and (3), this amendment draws upon the revision of the related Rules 19 (joinder of persons needed for just adjudication) and 23 (class actions), and the reasoning underlying that revision.

Rule 24(a)(3) as amended in 1948 provided for intervention of right where the applicant established that he would be adversely affected by the distribution or disposition of property involved in an action to which he had not been made a party. Significantly, some decided cases virtually disregarded the language of this provision. Thus Professor Moore states: "The concept of a fund has been applied so loosely that it is possible for a court to find a fund in almost any in personam action." 4 *Moore's Federal Practice,* ¶ 24.09[3], at 55 (2d ed. 1962), and see, *e.g., Formulabs, Inc. v. Hartley Pen Co.,* 275 F.2d 52 (9th Cir.1960). This development was quite natural, for Rule 24(a)(3) was unduly restricted. If an absentee would be substantially affected in a practical sense by the determination made in an action, he should, as a general rule, be entitled to intervene, and his right to do so should not depend on whether there is a fund to be distributed or otherwise disposed of. Intervention of right is here seen to be a kind of counterpart to Rule 19(a)(2)(i) on joinder of persons needed for a just adjudication: where, upon motion of a party in an action, an absentee should be joined so that he may protect his interest which as a practical matter may be substantially impaired by the disposition of the action, he ought to have a right to intervene in the action on his own motion. See Louisell & Hazard, *Pleading and Procedure: State and Federal* 749–50 (1962).

The general purpose of original Rule 24(a)(2) was to entitle an absentee, purportedly represented by a party, to intervene in the action if he could establish with fair probability that the representation was inadequate. Thus, where an action is being prosecuted or defended by a trustee, a beneficiary of the trust should have a right to intervene if he can show that the trustee's representation of his interest probably is inadequate; similarly a member of a class should have the right to intervene in a class action if he can show the inadequacy of the representation of his interest by the representative parties before the court.

Original Rule 24(a)(2), however, made it a condition of intervention that "the applicant is or may be bound by a judgment in the action," and this created difficulties with intervention in class actions. If the "bound" language was read literally in the sense of res judicata, it could defeat intervention in some meritorious cases. A member of a class to whom a judgment in a class action extended by its terms (see Rule 23(c)(3), as amended) might be entitled to show in a later action, when the judgment in the class action was claimed to operate as res judicata against him, that the "representative" in the class action had not in fact adequately represented him. If he could make this showing, the class-action judgment might be held not to bind him. See *Hansberry v. Lee,* 311 U.S. 32 (1940). If a class member sought to intervene in the class action proper, while it was still pending, on grounds of inadequacy of representation, he could be met with the argument: if the representation was in fact inadequate, he would not be "bound" by the judgment when it was subsequently asserted against him as res judicata, hence he was not entitled to intervene; if the representation was in fact adequate, there was no occasion or ground for intervention. See *Sam Fox Publishing Co. v. United States*, 366 U.S. 683 (1961); *cf. Sulphen Estates, Inc. v. United States*, 342 U.S. 19 (1951). This reasoning might be linguistically justified by original Rule 24(a)(2); but it could lead to poor results. Compare the discussion in *International M. & I. Corp. v. Von Clemm*, 301 F.2d 857 (2d Cir.1962); *Atlantic Refining Co. v. Standard Oil Co.*, 304 F.2d 387 (D.C.Cir.1962). A class member who claims that his "representative" does not adequately represent him, and is able to establish that proposition with sufficient probability should not be put to the risk of having a judgment entered in the action which by its terms extends to him, and be obliged to test the validity of the judgment as applied to his interest by a later collateral attack. Rather he should, as a general rule, be entitled to intervene in the action.

The amendment provides that an applicant is entitled to intervene in an action when his position is comparable to that of a person under Rule 19(a)(2)(i), as amended, unless his interest is already adequately represented in the action by existing parties. The Rule 19(a)(2)(i) criterion imports practical considerations, and the deletion of the "bound" language similarly frees the rule from undue preoccupation with strict considerations of res judicata.

The representation whose adequacy comes into question under the amended rule is not confined to formal representation like that provided by a trustee for his beneficiary or a representative party in a class action for a member of the class. A party to an action may provide practical representation to the absentee seeking intervention although no such formal relationship exists between them, and the adequacy of this practical representation will then have to be weighed. See *International M. & I. Corp. v. Von Clemm*, and *Atlantic Refining Co. v. Standard Oil Co.*, both supra; *Wolpe v. Poretsky*, 144 F.2d 505 (D.C.Cir.1944), cert. denied, 323 U.S. 777 (1944); *cf. Ford Motor Co. v. Bisanz Bros.*, 249 F.2d 22 (8th Cir.1957); and generally Annot., 84 A.L.R.2d 1412 (1962).

An intervention of right under the amended rule may be subject to appropriate conditions or restrictions responsive among other things to the requirements of efficient conduct of the proceedings.

Rule 44.1 [New].

DETERMINATION OF FOREIGN LAW *

A party who intends to raise an issue concerning the law of a foreign country shall give notice in his pleadings or other reasonable written notice. The court, in determining foreign law, may consider any relevant material or source, including testimony, whether or not submitted by a party or admissible under Rule 43. The court's determination shall be treated as a ruling on a question of law.

Advisory Committee's Note

Rule 44.1 is added by amendment to furnish Federal courts with a uniform and effective procedure for raising and determining an issue concerning the law of a foreign country.

* This rule was developed collaboratively by the Advisory Committee on Civil Rules, the Commission and Advisory Committee on International Rules of Judicial Procedure (see Act of Sept. 2, 1958, 72 Stat. 1743), and the Columbia Law School Project on International Procedure.

To avoid unfair surprise, the *first sentence* of the new rule requires that a party who intends to raise an issue of foreign law shall give notice thereof. The uncertainty under Rule 8(a) about whether foreign law must be pleaded—*compare Siegelman v. Cunard White Star, Ltd.*, 221 F.2d 189 (2d Cir.1955), and *Pedersen v. United States*, 191 F.Supp. 95 (D.Guam 1961) *with Harrison v. United Fruit Co.*, 143 F.Supp. 598 (S.D.N.Y.1956)—is eliminated by the provision that the notice shall be "written" and "reasonable." It may, but need not be, incorporated in the pleadings. In some situations the pertinence of foreign law is apparent from the outset; accordingly the necessary investigation of that law will have been accomplished by the party at the pleading stage, and the notice can be given conveniently in the pleadings. In other situations the pertinence of foreign law may remain doubtful until the case is further developed. A requirement that notice of foreign law be given only through the medium of the pleadings would tend in the latter instances to force the party to engage in a peculiarly burdensome type of investigation which might turn out to be unnecessary; and correspondingly the adversary would be forced into a possibly wasteful investigation. The liberal provisions for amendment of the pleadings afford help if the pleadings are used as the medium of giving notice of the foreign law; but it seems best to permit a written notice to be given outside of and later than the pleadings, provided the notice is reasonable.

The new rule does not attempt to set any definite limit on the party's time for giving the notice of an issue of foreign law; in some cases the issue may not become apparent until the trial, and notice then given may still be reasonable. The stage which the case has reached at the time of the notice, the reason proffered by the party for his failure to give earlier notice, and the importance to the case as a whole of the issue of foreign law sought to be raised, are among the factors which the court should consider in deciding a question of the reasonableness of a notice. If notice is given by one party it need not be repeated by any other and serves as a basis for presentation of material on the foreign law by all parties.

The *second sentence* of the new rule describes the materials to which the court may resort in determining an issue of foreign law. Heretofore the district courts, applying Rule 43(a), have looked in certain cases to State law to find the rules of evidence by which the content of foreign-country law is to be established. The State laws vary; some embody procedures which are inefficient, time consuming, and expensive. See, generally, Nussbaum, *Proving the Law of Foreign Countries*, 3 Am.J.Comp.L. 60 (1954). In all events the ordinary rules of evidence are often inapposite to the problem of determining foreign law and have in the past prevented examination of material which could have provided a proper basis for the determination. The new rule permits consideration by the court of any relevant material, including testimony, without regard to its admissibility under Rule 43. *Cf.* N.Y.Civ. Prac.Law & Rules, R. 4511 (effective Sept. 1, 1963); 2 Va.Code Ann. tit. 8, § 8–273; 2 W.Va.Code Ann. § 5711.

In further recognition of the peculiar nature of the issue of foreign law, the new rule provides that in determining this law the court is not limited by material presented by the parties; it may engage in its own research and consider any relevant material thus found. The court may have at its disposal better foreign law materials than counsel have presented, or may wish to reexamine and amplify material that has been presented by counsel in partisan fashion or in insufficient detail. On the other hand, the court is free to insist on a complete presentation by counsel.

There is no requirement that the court give formal notice to the parties of its intention to engage in its own research on an issue of foreign law which has been raised by them, or of its intention to raise and determine independently an issue not raised by them. Ordinarily the court should inform the parties of material it has found diverging substantially from the material which they have presented; and in general the court should give the parties an opportunity to analyze and counter new points upon which it proposes to rely. See Schlesinger, *Comparative Law* 142 (2d ed. 1959); Wyzanski, *A Trial Judge's Freedom and Responsibility*, 65 Harv.L.Rev. 1281, 1296 (1952); *cf. Siegelman v. Cunard White Star, Ltd., supra*, 221 F.2d at 197. To require, however, that the court give formal notice from time to time as it proceeds with its study of the foreign law would add an element of undesirable rigidity to the procedure for determining issues of foreign law.

The new rule refrains from imposing an obligation on the court to take "judicial notice" of foreign law because this would put an extreme burden on the court in many cases; and it avoids use of the concept of "judicial notice" in any form because of the uncertain meaning of that concept as applied to foreign law. See, *e.g.*, Stern, *Foreign Law in the Courts: Judicial Notice and Proof*, 45 Calif.L.Rev. 23, 43 (1957). Rather the rule provides flexible procedures for presenting and utilizing material on issues of foreign law by which a sound result can be achieved with fairness to the parties.

Under the *third sentence*, the court's determination of an issue of foreign law is to be treated as a ruling on a question of "law," not "fact," so that appellate review will not be narrowly confined by the "clearly erroneous" standard of Rule 52(a). *Cf.* Uniform Judicial Notice of Foreign Law Act § 3; Note, 72 Harv.L.Rev. 318 (1958).

The new rule parallels Article IV of the Uniform Interstate and International Procedure Act, approved by the Commissioners on Uniform State Laws in 1962, except that section 4.03 of Article IV states that "[t]he court, not the jury" shall determine foreign law. The new rule does not address itself to this problem, since the rules refrain from allocating functions as between the court and the jury. See Rule 38(a). It has long been thought, however, that the jury is not the appropriate body to determine issues of foreign law. See, *e.g.*, Story, *Conflict of Laws* § 638 (1st ed. 1834, 8th ed. 1883); 1 Greenleaf, *Evidence* § 486 (1st ed. 1842, 16th ed. 1899); 4 Wigmore, *Evidence* § 2558 (1st ed. 1905); 9 *id.* § 2558 (3d ed. 1940). The majority of the States have committed such issues to determination by the court. See Article 5 of the Uniform Judicial Notice of Foreign Law Act, adopted by twenty-six states, 9A U.L.A. 318 (1957) (Supp.1961, at 134); N.Y.Civ.Prac.Law & Rules, R. 4511 (effective Sept. 1, 1963); Wigmore, *loc. cit.* And Federal courts that have considered the problem in recent years have reached the same conclusion without reliance on statute. See *Jansson v. Swedish American Line*, 185 F.2d 212, 216 (1st Cir. 1950); *Bank of Nova Scotia v. San Miguel*, 196 F.2d 950, 957 n. 6 (1st Cir.1952); *Liechti v. Roche*, 198 F.2d 174 (5th Cir.1952); *Daniel Lumber Co. v. Empresas Hondurenas, S.A.*, 215 F.2d 465 (5th Cir.1954).

Rule 59.

NEW TRIALS; AMENDMENT OF JUDGMENTS

(d) On Initiative of Court. Not later than 10 days after entry of judgment the court of its own initiative may order a new trial for any reason for which it might have granted a new trial on motion of a party~~, and in the order shall specify the grounds therefor~~. *After giving the parties notice and an opportunity to be heard on the matter, the court may grant a motion for a new trial, timely served, for a reason not stated in the motion. In either case, the court shall specify in the order the grounds therefor.*

New matter is shown in italics; matter to be omitted is lined through

Advisory Committee's Note

By narrow interpretation of Rule 59(b) and (d), it has been held that the trial court is without power to grant a motion for a new trial, timely served, by an order made more than 10 days after the entry of judgment, based upon a ground not stated in the motion but perceived and relied on by the trial court *sua sponte. Freid v. McGrath*, 133 F.2d 350 (D.C.Cir.1942); *National Farmers Union Auto. & Cas. Co. v. Wood*, 207 F.2d 659 (10th Cir.1953); *Bailey v. Slentz*, 189 F.2d 406 (10th Cir.1951); *Marshall's U.S. Auto Supply, Inc. v. Cashman*, 111 F.2d 140 (10th Cir.1940), *cert. denied*, 311 U.S. 667 (1940); but see *Steinberg v. Indemnity Ins. Co.*, 36 F.R.D. 253 (E.D.La.1964).

The result is undesirable. Just as the court has power under Rule 59(d) to grant a new trial of its own initiative within the 10 days, so it should have power, when an effective new trial motion has been made and is pending, to decide it on grounds thought meritorious by the court although not advanced in the motion. The second sentence added by amendment to Rule 59(d) confirms the court's power in the latter situation, with provision that the parties be afforded a hearing before the power is exercised. See 6 *Moore's Federal Practice* ¶ 59.09[2] (2d ed. 1953).

In considering whether a given ground has or has not been advanced in the motion made by the party, it should be borne in mind that the particularity called for in stating the grounds for a new-trial motion is the same as that required for all motions by Rule 7(b)(1). The latter rule does not require ritualistic detail but rather a fair indication to court and counsel of the substance of the grounds relied on. See *Lebeck v. William A. Jarvis Co.*, 250 F.2d 285 (3d Cir.1957); *Tsai v. Rosenthal*, 297 F.2d 614 (8th Cir.1961); *General Motors Corp. v. Perry*, 303 F.2d 544 (7th Cir.1962); *cf. Grimm v. California Spray-Chemical Corp.*, 264 F.2d 145 (9th Cir.1959); *Cooper v. Midwest Feed Products Co.*, 271 F.2d 177 (8th Cir.1959).

Rule 65.

INJUNCTIONS

(a) Preliminary~~; Notice~~ *Injunction.*

(1) Notice. No preliminary injunction shall be issued without notice to the adverse party.

(2) Consolidation of Hearing With Trial on Merits. Before or after the commencement of the hearing of an application for a preliminary injunction, the court may order the trial of the action on the merits to be advanced and consolidated with the hearing of the application. Even when this consolidation is not ordered, any evidence received upon an application for a preliminary injunction which would be admissible upon the trial on the merits becomes part of the record on the trial and need not be repeated upon the trial. This subdivision (a)(2) shall be so construed and applied as to save to the parties any rights they may have to trial by jury.

(b) Temporary Restraining Order; Notice; Hearing; Duration. ~~No~~ *A* temporary restraining order ~~shall~~ *may* be granted without *written or oral* notice to the adverse party *or his attorney* ~~unless~~ *only if (1)* it clearly appears from specific facts shown by affidavit or by the verified complaint that immediate and irreparable injury, loss, or damage will result to the applicant before ~~notice can be served and a hearing had thereon.~~ *the adverse party or his attorney can be heard in opposition, and (2) the applicant's attorney certifies to the court in writing the efforts, if any, which have been made to give the notice and the reasons supporting his claim that notice should not be required.* Every temporary restraining order granted without notice shall be indorsed with the date and hour of issuance; shall be filed forthwith in the clerk's office and entered of record; shall define the injury and state why it is irreparable and why the order was granted without notice; and shall expire by its terms within such time after entry, not to exceed 10 days, as the court fixes, unless within the time so fixed the order, for good cause shown, is extended for a like period or unless the party against whom the order is directed consents that it may be extended for a longer period. The reasons for the extension shall be entered of record. In case a temporary restraining order is granted without notice, the motion for a preliminary injunction shall be set down for hearing at the earliest possible time and takes precedence of all matters except older matters of the same character; and when the motion comes on for hearing the party who obtained the temporary restraining order shall proceed with the application for a preliminary injunction and, if he does not do so, the court shall dissolve the temporary restraining order. On 2 days' notice to the party who obtained the temporary restraining order without notice or on such shorter notice to that party as the court may prescribe, the adverse party may appear and move its dissolution or modification and in that event the court shall proceed to hear and determine such motion as expeditiously as the ends of justice require.

(c) Security. No restraining order or preliminary injunction shall issue except upon the giving of security by the applicant, in such sum as the court deems proper, for the payment of such costs and damages as may be incurred or suffered by any party who is found to have been wrongfully enjoined or restrained. No such security shall be required of the United States or of an officer or agency thereof.

~~A surety upon a bond or undertaking under this rule submits himself to the jurisdiction of the court and irrevocably appoints the clerk of the court as his agent upon whom any papers affecting his liability on the bond or undertaking may be served. His liability may be enforced on motion without the necessity of an independent action. The motion and such notice of the motion as the court prescribes may be served on the clerk of the court who shall forthwith mail copies to the persons giving the security if their~~

New matter is shown in italics; matter to be omitted is lined through

~~addresses are known.~~ *The provisions of Rule 65.1 apply to a surety upon a bond or undertaking under this rule.*

Advisory Committee's Note

Subdivision (a)(2). This new subdivision provides express authority for consolidating the hearing of an application for a preliminary injunction with the trial on the merits. The authority can be exercised with particular profit when it appears that a substantial part of the evidence offered on the application will be relevant to the merits and will be presented in such form as to qualify for admission on the trial proper. Repetition of evidence is thereby avoided. The fact that the proceedings have been consolidated should cause no delay in the disposition of the application for the preliminary injunction, for the evidence will be directed in the first instance to that relief, and the preliminary injunction, if justified by the proof, may be issued in the course of the consolidated proceedings. Furthermore, to consolidate the proceeding will tend to expedite the final disposition of the action. It is believed that consolidation can be usefully availed of in many cases.

The subdivision further provides that even when consolidation is not ordered, evidence received in connection with an application for a preliminary injunction which would be admissible on the trial on the merits forms part of the trial record. This evidence need not be repeated on the trial. On the other hand, repetition is not altogether prohibited. That would be impractical and unwise. For example, a witness testifying comprehensively on the trial who has previously testified upon the application for a preliminary injunction might sometimes be hamstrung in telling his story if he could not go over some part of his prior testimony to connect it with his present testimony. So also, some repetition of testimony may be called for where the trial is conducted by a judge who did not hear the application for the preliminary injunction. In general, however, repetition can be avoided with an increase of efficiency in the conduct of the case and without any distortion of the presentation of evidence by the parties.

Since an application for a preliminary injunction may be made in an action in which, with respect to all or part of the merits, there is a right to trial by jury, it is appropriate to add the caution appearing in the last sentence of the subdivision. In such a case the jury will have to hear all the evidence bearing on its verdict, even if some part of the evidence has already been heard by the judge alone on the application for the preliminary injunction.

The subdivision is believed to reflect the substance of the best current practice and introduces no novel conception.

Subdivision (b). In view of the possibly drastic consequences of a temporary restraining order, the opposition should be heard, if feasible, before the order is granted. Many judges have properly insisted that, when time does not permit of formal notice of the application to the adverse party, some expedient, such as telephonic notice to the attorney for the adverse party, be resorted to if this can reasonably be done. On occasion, however, temporary restraining orders have been issued without any notice when it was feasible for some fair, although informal, notice to be given. See the emphatic criticisms in *Pennsylvania Rd. Co. v. Transport Workers Union*, 278 F.2d 693, 694 (3d Cir.1960); *Arvida Corp. v. Sugarman*, 259 F.2d 428, 429 (2d Cir.1958); *Lummus Co. v. Commonwealth Oil Ref. Co., Inc.*, 297 F.2d 80, 83 (2d Cir.1961), *cert. denied*, 368 U.S. 986 (1962).

Heretofore the first sentence of subdivision (b), in referring to a notice "served" on the "adverse party" on which a "hearing" could be held, perhaps invited the interpretation that the order might be granted without notice if the circumstances did not permit of a formal hearing on the basis of a formal notice. The subdivision is amended to make it plain that informal notice, which may be communicated to the attorney rather than the adverse party, is to be preferred to no notice at all.

Before notice can be dispensed with, the applicant's counsel must give his certificate as to any efforts made to give notice and the reasons why notice should not be required. This certificate is in addition to the requirement of an affidavit or verified complaint setting forth the facts as to the irreparable injury which would result before the opposition could be heard.

The amended subdivision continues to recognize that a temporary restraining order may be issued without any notice when the circumstances warrant.

Subdivision (c). Original Rules 65 and 73 contained substantially identical provisions for summary proceedings against sureties on bonds required or permitted by the rules. There was fragmentary coverage of the same subject in the Admiralty Rules. Clearly, a single comprehensive rule is required, and is incorporated as Rule 65.1.

Rule 82.

JURISDICTION AND VENUE UNAFFECTED

These rules shall not be construed to extend or limit the jurisdiction of the United States district courts or the venue of actions therein. *An admiralty or maritime claim within the meaning of Rule 9(h) shall not be treated as a civil action for the purposes of Title 28, U.S.C., §§ 1391–93.*

Advisory Committee's Note

Title 28, U.S.C., § 1391(b) provides: "A civil action wherein jurisdiction is not founded solely on diversity of citizenship may be brought only in the judicial district where all defendants reside, except as otherwise provided by law." This provision cannot appropriately be applied to what were formerly suits in admiralty. The rationale of decisions holding it inapplicable rests largely on the use of the term "civil action": i.e., a suit in admiralty is not a "civil action" within the statute. By virtue of the amendment to Rule 1, the provisions of Rule 2 convert suits in admiralty into civil actions. The added sentence is necessary to avoid an undesirable change in existing law with respect to venue.

CERTAIN OF THE AMENDMENTS OF FEDERAL RULES OF CIVIL PROCEDURE ADOPTED BY THE SUPREME COURT OF THE UNITED STATES ON MARCH 30, 1970, EFFECTIVE JULY 1, 1970, WITH ADVISORY COMMITTEE'S NOTES THEREON

[*Amendments here omitted: Changes in Form 24.*]

Advisory Committee's Explanatory Statement Concerning Amendments of the Discovery Rules

This statement is intended to serve as a general introduction to the amendments of Rules 26–37, concerning discovery, as well as related amendments of other rules. A separate note of customary scope is appended to amendments proposed for each rule. This statement provides a framework for the consideration of individual rule changes.

Changes in the Discovery Rules

The discovery rules, as adopted in 1938, were a striking and imaginative departure from tradition. It was expected from the outset that they would be important, but experience has shown them to play an even larger role than was initially foreseen. Although the discovery rules have been amended since 1938, the changes were relatively few and narrowly focused, made in order to remedy specific defects. The amendments now proposed reflect the first comprehensive review of the discovery rules undertaken since 1938. These amendments make substantial changes in the discovery rules. Those summarized here are among the more important changes.

Scope of Discovery. New provisions are made and existing provisions changed affecting the scope of discovery: (1) The contents of insurance policies are made discoverable (Rule 26(b)(2)). (2) A showing of good cause is no longer required for discovery of documents and things and entry upon land (Rule 34). However, a showing of need is required for discovery of "trial preparation" materials other than a party's discovery of his own statement and a witness' discovery of his own statement; and protection is afforded against disclosure in such documents of mental impressions, conclusions, opinions, or legal theories concerning the litigation (Rule 26(b)(3)). (3) Provision is made for discovery with respect to experts retained for trial preparation, and particularly those experts who will be called to testify at trial (Rule 26(b)(4)). (4) It is provided that interrogatories and requests for admission are not objectionable simply because they relate to matters of opinion or contention, subject of course to the supervisory power of the court (Rules 33(b), 36(a)). (5) Medical examination is made available as to certain nonparties (Rule 35(a)).

Mechanics of Discovery. A variety of changes are made in the mechanics of the discovery process, affecting the sequence and timing of discovery, the respective obligations of the parties with respect to requests, responses, and motions for court orders, and the related powers of the court to enforce discovery requests and to protect against their abusive use. A new provision eliminates the automatic grant of priority in discovery to one side (Rule 26(d)). Another provides that a party is not under a duty to supplement his responses to requests for discovery, except as specified (Rule 26(e)).

Other changes in the mechanics of discovery are designed to encourage extrajudicial discovery with a minimum of court intervention. Among these are the following: (1) The requirement that a plaintiff seek leave of court for early discovery requests is eliminated or reduced, and motions for a court order under Rule 34 are made unnecessary. Motions under Rule 35 are continued. (2) Answers and objections are to be served together and an enlargement of the time for response is provided. (3) The party seeking discovery, rather than the objecting party, is made responsible for invoking judicial determination of discovery disputes not resolved by the parties. (4) Judicial sanctions are tightened with respect to unjustified insistence upon or objection to discovery. These changes bring Rules 33, 34, and 36 substantially into line with the procedure now provided for depositions.

Failure to amend Rule 35 in the same way is based upon two considerations. First, the Columbia Survey (described below) finds that only about 5 percent of medical examinations require court motions, of which about half result in court orders. Second and of greater importance, the interest of the person to be examined in the privacy of his person was recently stressed by the Supreme Court in *Schlagenhauf v. Holder*, 379 U.S. 104 (1964). The court emphasized the trial judge's responsibility to assure that the medical examination was justified, particularly as to its scope.

Rearrangement of Rules. A limited rearrangement of the discovery rules has been made, whereby certain provisions are transferred from one rule to another. The reasons for this rearrangement are discussed below in a separate section of this statement, and the details are set out in a table at the end of this statement.

Optional Procedures. In two instances, new optional procedures have been made available. A new procedure is provided to a party seeking to take the deposition of a corporation or other organization (Rule 30(b)(6)). A party on whom interrogatories have been served requesting information derivable from his business records may under specified circumstances produce the records rather than give answers (Rule 33(c)).

Other Changes. This summary of changes is by no means exhaustive. Various changes have been made in order to improve, tighten, or clarify particular provisions, to resolve conflicts in the case law, and to improve language. All changes, whether mentioned here or not, are discussed in the appropriate note for each rule.

A Field Survey of Discovery Practice

Despite widespread acceptance of discovery as an essential part of litigation, disputes have inevitably arisen concerning the values claimed for discovery and abuses alleged to exist. Many disputes about discovery relate to particular rule provisions or court decisions and can be studied in traditional fashion with a view to specific amendment. Since discovery is in large measure extrajudicial, however, even these disputes may be enlightened by a study of discovery "in the field." And some of the larger questions concerning discovery can be pursued only by a study of its operation at the law office level and in unreported cases.

The Committee, therefore, invited the Project for Effective Justice of Columbia Law School to conduct a field survey of discovery. Funds were obtained from the Ford Foundation and the Walter E. Meyer Research Institute of Law, Inc. The survey was carried on under the direction of Prof. Maurice Rosenberg of Columbia Law School. The Project for Effective Justice has submitted a report to the Committee entitled "Field Survey of Federal Pretrial Discovery" (hereafter referred to as the Columbia Survey). The Committee is deeply grateful for the benefit of this extensive undertaking and is most appreciative of the cooperation of the Project and the funding organizations. The Committee is particularly grateful to Professor Rosenberg who not only directed the survey but has given much time in order to assist the Committee in assessing the results.

The Columbia Survey concludes, in general, that there is no empirical evidence to warrant a fundamental change in the philosophy of the discovery rules. No widespread or profound failings are disclosed in the scope or availability of discovery. The costs of discovery do not appear to be oppressive, as a general matter, either in relation to ability to pay or to the stakes of the litigation. Discovery frequently provides evidence that would not otherwise be available to the parties and thereby makes for a fairer trial or settlement. On the other hand, no positive evidence is found that discovery promotes settlement.

More specific findings of the Columbia Survey are described in other Committee notes, in relation to particular rule provisions and amendments. Those interested in more detailed information may obtain it from the Project for Effective Justice.

Rearrangement of the Discovery Rules

The present discovery rules are structured entirely in terms of individual discovery devices, except for Rule 27 which deals with perpetuation of testimony, and Rule 37 which provides sanctions to enforce discovery. Thus, Rules 26 and 28 to 32 are in terms addressed only to the taking of a deposition of a party or third person. Rules 33 to 36 then deal in succession with four additional discovery devices: Written interrogatories to parties, production for inspection of documents and things, physical or mental examination and requests for admission.

Under the rules as promulgated in 1938, therefore, each of the discovery devices was separate and self-contained. A defect of this arrangement is that there is no natural location in the discovery rules for provisions generally applicable to all discovery or to several discovery devices. From 1938 until the present, a few amendments have applied a discovery provision to several rules. For example, in 1948, the scope of deposition discovery in Rule 26(b) and the provision for protective orders in Rule 30(b) were incorporated by reference in Rules 33 and 34. The arrangement was adequate so long as there were few provisions governing discovery generally and these provisions were relatively simple.

As will be seen, however, a series of amendments are now proposed which govern most or all of the discovery devices. Proposals of a similar nature will probably be made in the future. Under these circumstances, it is very desirable, even necessary, that the discovery rules contain one rule addressing itself to discovery generally.

Rule 26 is obviously the most appropriate rule for this purpose. One of its subdivisions, Rule 26(b), in terms governs only scope of deposition discovery, but it has been expressly incorporated by reference in Rules 33 and 34 and is treated by courts as setting a general standard. By means of a transfer to Rule 26 of the provisions for protective orders now contained in Rule 30(b), and a transfer from Rule 26 of provisions addressed exclusively to depositions, Rule 26 is converted into a rule concerned with discovery generally. It becomes a convenient vehicle for the inclusion of new provisions dealing with the scope, timing, and regulation of discovery. Few additional transfers are needed. See table showing rearrangement of rules, set out below.

There are, to be sure, disadvantages in transferring any provision from one rule to another. Familiarity with the present pattern, reinforced by the references made by prior court decisions and the various secondary writings about the rules, is not lightly to be sacrificed. Revision of treatises and other reference works is burdensome and costly. Moreover, many States have adopted the existing pattern as a model for their rules.

On the other hand, the amendments now proposed will in any event require revision of texts and reference works as well as reconsideration by States following the Federal model. If these amendments are to be incorporated in an understandable way, a rule with general discovery provisions is needed. As will be seen, the proposed rearrangement produces a more coherent and intelligible pattern for the discovery rules taken as a whole. The difficulties described are those encountered whenever statutes are reexamined and revised. Failure to rearrange the discovery rules now would freeze the present scheme, making future change even more difficult.

Table Showing Rearrangement of Rules

Existing Rule No.	*New Rule No.*
26(a)	30(a), 31(a)
26(c)	30(c)
26(d)	32(a)
26(e)	32(b)
26(f)	32(c)
30(a)	30(b)
30(b)	26(c)
32	32(d)

Rule 5. Service and Filing of Pleadings and Other Papers

(a) Service: When Required. Except as otherwise provided in these rules, every order required by its terms to be served, every pleading subsequent to the original complaint unless the court otherwise orders because of numerous defendants, *every paper relating to discovery required to be served upon a party unless the*

New matter is shown in italics; matter to be omitted is lined through

court otherwise orders, every written motion other than one which may be heard ex parte, and every written notice, appearance, demand, offer of judgment, designation of record on appeal, and similar paper shall be served upon each of the parties. No service need be made on parties in default for failure to appear except that pleadings asserting new or additional claims for relief against them shall be served upon them in the manner provided for service of summons in Rule 4.

In an action begun by seizure of property, in which no person need be or is named as defendant, any service required to be made prior to the filing of an answer, claim, or appearance shall be made upon the person having custody or possession of the property at the time of the seizure.

Advisory Committee's Note

The amendment makes clear that all papers relating to discovery which are required to be served on any party must be served on all parties, unless the court orders otherwise. The present language expressly includes notices and demands, but it is not explicit as to answers or responses as provided in Rules 33, 34, and 36. Discovery papers may be voluminous or the parties numerous, and the court is empowered to vary the requirement if in a given case it proves needlessly onerous.

In actions begun by seizure of property, service will at times have to be made before the absent owner of the property has filed an appearance. For example, a prompt deposition may be needed in a maritime action in rem. See Rules 30(a) and 30(b)(2) and the related notes. A provision is added authorizing service on the person having custody or possession of the property at the time of its seizure.

Rule 9. Pleading Special Matters

(h) Admiralty and Maritime Claims. A pleading or count setting forth a claim for relief within the admiralty and maritime jurisdiction that is also within the jurisdiction of the district court on some other ground may contain a statement identifying the claim as an admiralty or maritime claim for the purposes of Rules 14(c), ~~26(a),~~ 38(e), 82, and the Supplemental Rules for Certain Admiralty and Maritime Claims. If the claim is cognizable only in admiralty it is an admiralty or maritime claim for those purposes whether so identified or not. The amendment of a pleading to add or withdraw an identifying statement is governed by the principles of Rule 15. The reference in Title 28, U.S.C., § 1292(a)(3), to admiralty cases shall be construed to mean admiralty and maritime claims within the meaning of this subdivision (h).

Advisory Committee's Note

The reference to Rule 26(a) is deleted, in light of the transfer of that subdivision to Rule 30(a) and the elimination of the de bene esse procedure therefrom. See the Advisory Committee's note to Rule 30(a).

Rule 26. ~~Depositions Pending Action~~ *General Provisions Governing Discovery*

~~**(a) When Depositions May Be Taken.** Any party may take the testimony of any person, including a party, by deposition upon oral examination or written interrogatories for the purpose of discovery or for use as evidence in the action or for both purposes. After commencement of the action the deposition may be taken without leave of court, except that leave, granted with or without notice, must be obtained if notice of the taking is served by the plaintiff within 20 days after commencement of the action. The attendance of witnesses may be compelled by the use of subpoena as provided in Rule 45. Depositions shall be taken only in accordance with these rules, except that in admiralty and maritime claims within the meaning of Rule 9(h) depositions may also be taken under and used in accordance with sections 863, 864, and 865 of the Revised Statutes (see note preceding 28 U.S.C. § 1781). The deposition of a person confined in prison may be taken only by leave of court on such terms as the court prescribes.~~

(a) Discovery Methods. Parties may obtain discovery by one or more of the following methods: depositions upon oral examination or written questions; written interrogatories; production of documents or things or permission to enter upon land or other property, for inspection and other purposes; physical and mental examinations; and requests for admission. Unless the court orders otherwise under subdivision (c) of this rule, the frequency of use of these methods is not limited.

(b) Scope of ~~Examination~~ *Discovery.* Unless otherwise ~~ordered by~~ *limited by order of* the court ~~as provided by Rule 30(b) or (d), the deponent may be examined~~ *in accordance with these rules, the scope of discovery is as follows:*

(1) In General. Parties may obtain discovery regarding any matter, not privileged, which is relevant to the subject matter involved in the pending action, whether it relates to the claim or defense of the ~~examining~~ party *seeking discovery* or to the claim or defense of any other party, including the existence, description, nature, custody, condition and location of any books, documents, or other tangible things and the identity and location of persons having knowledge of *any discoverable matter* ~~relevant facts.~~ It is not ground for objection that the ~~testimony~~ *information sought* will be inadmissible at the trial if the ~~testimony~~ *information* sought appears reasonably calculated to lead to the discovery of admissible evidence.

New matter is shown in italics; matter to be omitted is lined through

(2) Insurance Agreements. A party may obtain discovery of the existence and contents of any insurance agreement under which any person carrying on an insurance business may be liable to satisfy part or all of a judgment which may be entered in the action or to indemnify or reimburse for payments made to satisfy the judgment. Information concerning the insurance agreement is not by reason of disclosure admissible in evidence at trial. For purposes of this paragraph, an application for insurance shall not be treated as part of an insurance agreement.

(3) Trial Preparation: Materials. Subject to the provisions of subdivision (b)(4) of this rule, a party may obtain discovery of documents and tangible things otherwise discoverable under subdivision (b)(1) of this rule and prepared in anticipation of litigation or for trial by or for another party or by or for that other party's representative (including his attorney, consultant, surety, indemnitor, insurer, or agent) only upon a showing that the party seeking discovery has substantial need of the materials in the preparation of his case and that he is unable without undue hardship to obtain the substantial equivalent of the materials by other means. In ordering discovery of such materials when the required showing has been made, the court shall protect against disclosure of the mental impressions, conclusions, opinions, or legal theories of an attorney or other representative of a party concerning the litigation.

A party may obtain without the required showing a statement concerning the action or its subject matter previously made by that party. Upon request, a person not a party may obtain without the required showing a statement concerning the action or its subject matter previously made by that person. If the request is refused, the person may move for a court order. The provisions of Rule 37(a)(4) apply to the award of expenses incurred in relation to the motion. For purposes of this paragraph, a statement previously made is (A) a written statement signed or otherwise adopted or approved by the person making it, or (B) a stenographic, mechanical, electrical, or other recording, or a transcription thereof, which is a substantially verbatim recital of an oral statement by the person making it and contemporaneously recorded.

(4) Trial Preparation: Experts. Discovery of facts known and opinions held by experts, otherwise discoverable under the provisions of subdivision (b)(1) of this rule and acquired or developed in anticipation of litigation or for trial, may be obtained only as follows:

(A)(i) A party may through interrogatories require any other party to identify each person whom the other party expects to call as an expert witness at trial, to state the subject matter on which the

expert is expected to testify, and to state the substance of the facts and opinions to which the expert is expected to testify and a summary of the grounds for each opinion. (ii) Upon motion the court may order further discovery by other means, subject to such restrictions as to scope and such provisions, pursuant to subdivision (b)(4)(C) of this rule, concerning fees and expenses as the court may deem appropriate.

(B) A party may discover facts known or opinions held by an expert who has been retained or specially employed by another party in anticipation of litigation or preparation for trial and who is not expected to be called as a witness at trial, only as provided in Rule 35(b) or upon a showing of exceptional circumstances under which it is impracticable for the party seeking discovery to obtain facts or opinions on the same subject by other means.

(C) Unless manifest injustice would result, (i) the court shall require that the party seeking discovery pay the expert a reasonable fee for time spent in responding to discovery under subdivisions (b)(4)(A)(ii) and (b)(4)(B) of this rule; and (ii) with respect to discovery obtained under subdivision (b)(4)(A)(ii) of this rule the court may require, and with respect to discovery obtained under subdivision (b)(4)(B) of this rule the court shall require, the party seeking discovery to pay the other party a fair portion of the fees and expenses reasonably incurred by the latter party in obtaining facts and opinions from the expert.

~~**(c) Examination and Cross Examination.** Examination and cross examination of deponents may proceed as permitted at the trial under the provisions of Rule 43(b).~~

~~**(d) Use of Depositions.** At the trial or upon the hearing of a motion or an interlocutory proceeding, any part or all of a deposition, so far as admissible under the rules of evidence, may be used against any party who was present or represented at the taking of the deposition or who had due notice thereof, in accordance with any one of the following provisions:~~

~~(1) Any deposition may be used by any party for the purpose of contradicting or impeaching the testimony of deponent as a witness.~~

~~(2) The deposition of a party or of any one who at the time of taking the deposition was an officer, director, or managing agent of a public or private corporation, partnership, or association which is a party may be used by an adverse party for any purpose.~~

~~(3) The deposition of a witness, whether or not a party, may be used by any party for any purpose if the court finds: 1, that the witness is dead; or 2, that the witness is at a greater distance than~~

~~100 miles from the place of trial or hearing, or is out of the United States, unless it appears that the absence of the witness was procured by the party offering the deposition; or 3, that the witness is unable to attend or testify because of age, sickness, infirmity, or imprisonment; or 4, that the party offering the deposition has been unable to procure the attendance of the witness by subpoena; or 5, upon application and notice, that such exceptional circumstances exist as to make it desirable, in the interest of justice and with due regard to the importance of presenting the testimony of witnesses orally in open court, to allow the deposition to be used.~~

~~(4) If only part of a deposition is offered in evidence by a party, an adverse party may require him to introduce all of it which is relevant to the part introduced, and any party may introduce any other parts.~~

~~Substitution of parties does not affect the right to use depositions previously taken; and, when an action in any court of the United States or of any state has been dismissed and another action involving the same subject matter is afterward brought between the same parties or their representatives or successors in interest, all depositions lawfully taken and duly filed in the former action may be used in the latter as if originally taken therefor.~~

~~**(e) Objections to Admissibility.** Subject to the provisions of Rules 28(b) and 32(c) objection may be made at the trial or hearing to receiving in evidence any deposition or part thereof for any reason which would require the exclusion of the evidence if the witness were then present and testifying.~~

~~**(f) Effect of Taking or Using Depositions.** A party shall not be deemed to make a person his own witness for any purpose by taking his deposition. The introduction in evidence of the deposition or any part thereof for any purpose other than that of contradicting or impeaching the deponent makes the deponent the witness of the party introducing the deposition, but this shall not apply to the use by an adverse party of a deposition as described in paragraph (2) of subdivision (d) of this rule. At the trial or hearing any party may rebut any relevant evidence contained in a deposition whether introduced by him or by any other party.~~

(c) Protective Orders. Upon motion by a party or by the person from whom discovery is sought, and for good cause shown, the court in which the action is pending or alternatively, on matters relating to a deposition, the court in the district where the deposition is to be taken may make any order which justice requires to protect a party or person from annoyance, embarrassment, oppression, or undue burden or expense, including one or more of the following: (1) that

the discovery not be had; (2) that the discovery may be had only on specified terms and conditions, including a designation of the time or place; (3) that the discovery may be had only by a method of discovery other than that selected by the party seeking discovery; (4) that certain matters not be inquired into, or that the scope of the discovery be limited to certain matters; (5) that discovery be conducted with no one present except persons designated by the court; (6) that a deposition after being sealed be opened only by order of the court; (7) that a trade secret or other confidential research, development, or commercial information not be disclosed or be disclosed only in a designated way; (8) that the parties simultaneously file specified documents or information enclosed in sealed envelopes to be opened as directed by the court.

If the motion for a protective order is denied in whole or in part, the court may, on such terms and conditions as are just, order that any party or person provide or permit discovery. The provisions of Rule 37(a)(4) apply to the award of expenses incurred in relation to the motion.

(d) Sequence and Timing of Discovery. Unless the court upon motion, for the convenience of parties and witnesses and in the interests of justice, orders otherwise, methods of discovery may be used in any sequence and the fact that a party is conducting discovery, whether by deposition or otherwise, shall not operate to delay any other party's discovery.

(e) Supplementation of Responses. A party who has responded to a request for discovery with a response that was complete when made is under no duty to supplement his response to include information thereafter acquired, except as follows:

(1) A party is under a duty seasonably to supplement his response with respect to any question directly addressed to (A) the identity and location of persons having knowledge of discoverable matters, and (B) the identity of each person expected to be called as an expert witness at trial, the subject matter on which he is expected to testify, and the substance of his testimony.

(2) A party is under a duty seasonably to amend a prior response if he obtains information upon the basis of which (A) he knows that the response was incorrect when made, or (B) he knows that the response though correct when made is no longer true and the circumstances are such that a failure to amend the response is in substance a knowing concealment.

(3) A duty to supplement responses may be imposed by order of the court, agreement of the parties, or at any time prior to trial through new requests for supplementation of prior responses.

Advisory Committee's Note

A limited rearrangement of the discovery rules is made, whereby certain rule provisions are transferred, as follows: Existing Rule 26(a) is transferred to Rules 30(a) and 31(a). Existing Rule 26(c) is transferred to Rule 30(c). Existing Rules 26(d), (e), and (f) are transferred to Rule 32. Revisions of the transferred provisions, if any, are discussed in the notes appended to Rules 30, 31, and 32. In addition, Rule 30(b) is transferred to Rule 26(c). The purpose of this rearrangement is to establish Rule 26 as a rule governing discovery in general. (The reasons are set out in the Advisory Committee's explanatory statement.)

Subdivision (a)—Discovery Devices. This is a new subdivision listing all of the discovery devices provided in the discovery rules and establishing the relationship between the general provisions of Rule 26 and the specific rules for particular discovery devices. The provision that the frequency of use of these methods is not limited confirms existing law. It incorporates in general form a provision now found in Rule 33.

Subdivision (b)—Scope of Discovery. This subdivision is recast to cover the scope of discovery generally. It regulates the discovery obtainable through any of the discovery devices listed in Rule 26(a).

All provisions as to scope of discovery are subject to the initial qualification that the court may limit discovery in accordance with these rules. Rule 26(c) (transferred from 30(b)) confers broad powers on the courts to regulate or prevent discovery even though the materials sought are within the scope of 26(b), and these powers have always been freely exercised. For example, a party's income tax return is generally held not privileged, 2A Barron & Holtzoff, *Federal Practice and Procedure,* § 651.2 (Wright ed. 1961), and yet courts have recognized that interests in privacy may call for a measure of extra protection. *E.g., Wiesenberger v. W. E. Hutton & Co.*, 35 F.R.D. 556 (S.D.N.Y.1964). Similarly, the courts have in appropriate circumstances protected materials that are primarily of an impeaching character. These two types of materials merely illustrate the many situations, not capable of governance by precise rule, in which courts must exercise judgment. The new subsections in Rule 26(b) do not change existing law with respect to such situations.

Subdivision (b)(1)—In General. The language is changed to provide for the scope of discovery in general terms. The existing subdivision, although in terms applicable only to depositions, is incorporated by reference in existing Rules 33 and 34. Since decisions as to relevance to the subject matter of the action are made for discovery purposes well in advance of trial, a flexible treatment of relevance is required and the making of discovery, whether voluntary or under court order, is not a concession or determination of relevance for purposes of trial. *Cf.* 4 *Moore's Federal Practice* ¶ 26–16[1] (2d ed. 1966).

Subdivision (b)(2)—Insurance Policies. Both the cases and commentators are sharply in conflict on the question whether defendant's liability insurance coverage is subject to discovery in the usual situation when the insurance coverage is not itself admissible and does not bear on another issue in the case. Examples of Federal cases requiring disclosure and supporting comments: *Cook v. Welty,* 253 F.Supp. 875 (D.D.C.1966) (cases cited); *Johanek v. Aberle,* 27 F.R.D. 272 (D.Mont. 1961); Williams, *Discovery of Dollar Limits in Liability Policies in Automobile Tort Cases,* 10 Ala.L.Rev. 355 (1958); Thode, *Some Reflections on the 1957 Amendments to the Texas Rules,* 37 Tex.L.Rev. 33, 40–42 (1958). Examples of Federal cases refusing disclosure and supporting comments: *Bisserier v. Manning,* 207 F.Supp. 476 (D.N.J.1962); *Cooper v. Stender,* 30 F.R.D. 389 (E.D.Tenn.1962); Frank, *Discovery and Insurance, Coverage* 1959 Ins.L.J. 281; Fournier, *Pre-Trial Discovery of Insurance Coverage and Limits,* 28 Ford.L.Rev. 215 (1959).

The division in reported cases is close. State decisions based on provisions similar to the federal rules are similarly divided. See cases collected in 2A Barron & Holtzoff, *Federal Practice and Procedure* § 647.1, nn. 45.5, 45.6 (Wright ed. 1961). It appears to be difficult if not impossible to obtain appellate review of the issue. Resolution by rule amendment is indicated. The question is essentially procedural in that it bears upon preparation for trial and settlement before trial, and courts confronting the question, however they have decided it, have generally treated it as procedural and governed by the rules.

The amendment resolves this issue in favor of disclosure. Most of the decisions denying discovery, some explicitly, reason from the text of Rule 26(b) that it permits discovery only of matters which will be admissible in evidence or appear reasonably calculated to lead to such evidence; they avoid considerations of policy, regarding them as foreclosed. See *Bisserier v. Manning, supra.* Some note also that facts about a defendant's financial status are not discoverable as such, prior to judgment with execution unsatisfied, and fear that, if courts hold insurance coverage discoverable, they must extend the principle to other aspects of the defendant's financial status. The cases favoring disclosure rely heavily on the practical significance of insurance in the decisions lawyers make about settlement and trial preparation. In *Clauss v. Danker,* 264 F.Supp. 246 (S.D.N.Y.1967), the court held that the rules forbid disclosure but called for an amendment to permit it.

Disclosure of insurance coverage will enable counsel for both sides to make the same realistic appraisal of the case, so that settlement and litigation strategy are based on knowledge and not speculation. It will conduce to settlement and avoid protracted litigation in some cases, though in others it may have an opposite effect. The amendment is limited to insurance coverage, which should be distinguished from any other facts concerning defendant's financial status (1) because insurance is an asset created specifically to satisfy the claim; (2) because the insurance company ordinarily controls the litigation; (3) because information about coverage is available only from defendant or his insurer; and (4) because disclosure does not involve a significant invasion of privacy.

Disclosure is required when the insurer "may be liable" on part or all of the judgment. Thus, an insurance company must disclose even when it contests liability under the policy, and such disclosure does not constitute a waiver of its claim. It is immaterial whether the liability is to satisfy the judgment directly or merely to indemnify or reimburse another after he pays the judgment.

The provision applies only to persons "carrying on an insurance business" and thus covers insurance companies and not the ordinary business concern that enters into a contract of indemnification. *Cf.* N.Y.Ins.Law § 41. Thus, the provision makes no change in existing law on discovery of indemnity agreements other than insurance agreements by persons carrying on an insurance business. Similarly, the provision does not cover the business concern that creates a reserve fund for purposes of self-insurance.

For some purposes other than discovery, an application for insurance is treated as a part of the insurance agreement. The provision makes clear that, for discovery purposes, the application is not to be so treated. The insurance application may contain personal and financial information concerning the insured, discovery of which is beyond the purpose of this provision.

In no instance does disclosure make the facts concerning insurance coverage admissible in evidence.

Subdivision (b)(3)—Trial Preparation: Materials. Some of the most controversial and vexing problems to emerge from the discovery rules have arisen out of requests for the production of documents or things prepared in anticipation of litigation or for trial. The existing rules make no explicit provision for such materials. Yet, two verbally distinct doctrines have developed, each conferring a qualified immunity on these materials—the "good cause" requirement in Rule 34 (now generally held applicable to discovery of documents via deposition under Rule 45 and interrogatories under Rule 33) and the work-product doctrine of *Hickman v. Taylor,* 329 U.S. 495 (1947). Both demand a showing of justification before production can be had, the one of "good cause" and the other variously described in the *Hickman* case: "necessity or justification," "denial * * * would unduly prejudice the preparation of petitioner's case," or "cause hardship or injustice" 329 U.S. at 509–510.

In deciding the *Hickman* case, the Supreme Court appears to have expressed a preference in 1947 for an approach to the problem of trial preparation materials by judicial decision rather than by rule. Sufficient experience has accumulated, however, with lower court applications of the *Hickman* decision to warrant a reappraisal.

The major difficulties visible in the existing case law are (1) confusion and disagreement as to whether "good cause" is made out by a showing of relevance and lack of privilege, or requires an additional showing of necessity, (2) confusion and disagreement as to the scope of the *Hickman* work-product doctrine, particularly whether it extends beyond work actually performed by lawyers, and (3) the resulting difficulty of relating the "good cause" required by Rule 34 and the "necessity or justification" of the work-product doctrine, so that their respective roles and the distinctions between them are understood.

Basic Standard.—Since Rule 34 in terms requires a showing of "good cause" for the production of all documents and things, whether or not trial preparation is involved, courts have felt that a single formula is called for and have differed over whether a showing of relevance and lack of privilege is enough or whether more must be shown. When the facts of the cases are studied, however, a distinction emerges based upon the type of materials. With respect to documents not obtained or prepared with an eye to litigation, the decisions, while not uniform, reflect a strong and increasing tendency to relate "good cause" to a showing that the documents are relevant to the subject matter of the action. *E.g., Connecticut Mutual Life Ins. Co. v. Shields*, 17 F.R.D. 273 (S.D.N.Y.1959), with cases cited; *Houdry Process Corp. v. Commonwealth Oil Refining Co.*, 24 F.R.D. 58 (S.D.N.Y. 1955); see *Bell v. Commercial Ins. Co.*, 280 F.2d 514, 517 (3d Cir.1960). When the party whose documents are sought shows that the request for production is unduly burdensome or oppressive, courts have denied discovery for lack of "good cause", although they might just as easily have based their decision on the protective provisions of existing Rule 30(b) (new Rule 26(c)). *E.g., Lauer v. Tankrederi*, 39 F.R.D. 334 (E.D.Pa.1966).

As to trial-preparation materials, however, the courts are increasingly interpreting "good cause" as requiring more than relevance. When lawyers have prepared or obtained the materials for trial, all courts require more than relevance; so much is clearly commanded by *Hickman*. But even as to the preparatory work of nonlawyers, while some courts ignore work-product and equate "good cause" with relevance, *e.g., Brown v. New York, N.H. & H.R.R.*, 17 F.R.D. 324 (S.D.N.Y.1955), the more recent trend is to read "good cause" as requiring inquiry into the importance of and need for the materials, as well as into alternative sources for securing the same information. In *Guilford Nat'l Bank v. Southern Ry.*, 297 F.2d 921 (4th Cir.1962), statements of witnesses obtained by claim agents were held not discoverable because both parties had had equal access to the witnesses at about the same time, shortly after the collision in question. The decision was based solely on Rule 34 and "good cause"; the court declined to rule on whether the statements were work-product. The court's treatment of "good cause" is quoted at length and with approval in *Schlagenhauf v. Holder*, 379 U.S. 104, 117–118 (1964). See also *Mitchell v. Bass*, 252 F.2d 513 (8th Cir.1958); *Hauger v. Chicago, R.I. & Pac. R.R.*, 216 F.2d 501 (7th Cir.1954); *Burke v. United States*, 32 F.R.D. 213 (E.D.N.Y.1963). While the opinions dealing with "good cause" do not often draw an explicit distinction between trial preparation materials and other materials, in fact an overwhelming proportion of the cases in which a special showing is required are cases involving trial preparation materials.

The rules are amended by eliminating the general requirement of "good cause" from Rule 34 but retaining a requirement of a special showing for trial preparation materials in this subdivision. The required showing is expressed, not in terms of "good cause" whose generality has tended to encourage confusion and controversy, but in terms of the elements of the special showing to be made: substantial need of the materials in the preparation of the case and inability without undue hardship to obtain the substantial equivalent of the materials by other means.

These changes conform to the holdings of the cases, when viewed in light of their facts. Apart from trial preparation, the fact that the materials sought are documentary does not in and of itself require a special showing beyond relevance and absence of privilege. The protective provisions are of course available, and if the party from whom production is sought raises a special issue of privacy (as with respect to income tax returns or grand jury minutes) or points to evidence primarily impeaching, or can show serious burden or expense, the court will exercise its traditional power to decide whether to issue a protective order. On the other hand, the requirement of a special showing for discovery of trial preparation materials reflects the view that each side's informal evaluation of its case should be protected, that each side should be encouraged to prepare independently, and that one side should not automatically have the benefit of the detailed preparatory work of the other side. See Field and McKusick, *Maine Civil Practice* 264 (1959).

Elimination of a "good cause" requirement from Rule 34 and the establishment of a requirement of a special showing in this subdivision will eliminate the confusion caused by having two verbally distinct requirements of justification that the courts have been unable to distinguish clearly. Moreover, the language of the subdivision suggests the factors which the courts should consider in determining whether the requisite showing has been made. The importance of the materials sought to the party seeking them in preparation of his case and the difficulty he will have obtaining them by other means are factors noted in the *Hickman* case. The courts should also consider the likelihood that the party, even if he obtains the information by independent means, will not have the substantial equivalent of the documents the production of which he seeks.

Consideration of these factors may well lead the court to distinguish between witness statements taken by an investigator, on the one hand, and other parts of the investigative file, on the other. The court in *Southern Ry. v. Lanham,* 403 F.2d 119 (5th Cir.1968), while it naturally addressed itself to the "good cause" requirements of Rule 34, set forth as controlling considerations the factors contained in the language of this subdivision. The analysis of the court suggests circumstances under which witness statements will be discoverable. The witness may have given a fresh and contemporaneous account in a written statement while he is available to the party seeking discovery only a substantial time thereafter. *Lanham, supra* at 127–128; *Guilford, supra* at 926. Or he may be reluctant or hostile, *Lanham, supra* at 128–129; *Brookshire v. Pennsylvania R.R.*, 14 F.R.D. 154 (N.D.Ohio 1953); *Diamond v. Mohawk Rubber Co.,* 33 F.R.D. 264 (D.Colo.1963). Or he may have a lapse of memory. *Tannenbaum v. Walker,* 16 F.R.D. 570 (E.D.Pa.1954). Or he may probably be deviating from his prior statement. *Cf. Hauger v. Chicago, R.I. & Pac. R.R.,* 216 F.2d 501 (7th Cir.1954). On the other hand, a much stronger showing is needed to obtain evaluative materials in an investigator's reports. *Lanham, supra* at 131–133; *Pickett v. L. R. Ryan, Inc.*, 237 F.Supp. 198 (E.D.S.C.1965).

Materials assembled in the ordinary course of business, or pursuant to public requirements unrelated to litigation, or for other nonlitigation purposes are not under the qualified immunity provided by this subdivision. *Goosman v. A. Duie Pyle, Inc.*, 320 F.2d 45 (4th Cir.1963); *cf. United States v. New York Foreign Trade Zone Operators, Inc.*, 304 F.2d 792 (2d Cir.1962). No change is made in the existing doctrine, noted in the *Hickman* case, that one party may discover relevant facts known or available to the other party, even though such facts are contained in a document which is not itself discoverable.

Treatment of Lawyers; Special Protection of Mental Impressions, Conclusions, Opinions, and Legal Theories Concerning the Litigation.—The courts are divided as to whether the work-product doctrine extends to the preparatory work only of lawyers. The *Hickman* case left this issue open since the statements in that case were taken by a lawyer. As to courts of appeals, *compare Alltmont v. United States,* 177 F.2d 971, 976 (3d Cir.1949), *cert. denied,* 339 U.S. 967 (1950) (*Hickman* applied to statements obtained by FBI agents on theory it should apply to "all statements of prospective witnesses which a party has obtained for his trial counsel's use"), with *Southern Ry. v. Campbell,* 309 F.2d 569 (5th Cir.1962) (statements taken by claim agents not work-product), and *Guilford Nat'l Bank v. Southern Ry.,* 297 F.2d 921 (4th Cir.1962) (avoiding issue of work-product as to claim agents, deciding case instead under Rule 34 "good cause"). Similarly, the district courts are divided on statements obtained by claim agents, *compare, e.g., Brown v. New York, N.H. & H. R.R.*, 17 F.R.D. 324 (S.D.N.Y 1955) with *Hanke v. Milwaukee Electric Ry. & Transp. Co.,* 7 F.R.D. 540 (E.D.Wis.1947); investigators, *compare Burke v. United States*, 32 F.R.D. 213 (E.D.N.Y.1963) with *Snyder v. United States*, 20 F.R.D. 7 (E.D.N.Y.1956); and insurers, *compare Gottlieb v. Bresler*, 24 F.R.D. 371 (D.D.C.1959) with *Burns v. Mulder*, 20 F.R.D. 605 (E.D.Pa.1957). See 4 *Moore's Federal Practice* ¶ 26.23[8.1] (2d ed. 1966); 2A Barron & Holtzoff, *Federal Practice and Procedure* § 652.2 (Wright ed. 1961).

A complication is introduced by the use made by courts of the "good cause" requirement of Rule 34, as described above. A court may conclude that trial preparation materials are not work-product because not the result of lawyer's work and yet hold that they are not producible because "good cause" has not been shown. *Cf. Guilford Nat'l Bank v. Southern Ry.*, 297 F.2d 921 (4th Cir.1962), cited and described above. When the decisions on "good cause" are taken into account, the weight of authority affords protection of the preparatory work of both lawyers and nonlawyers (though not necessarily to the same extent) by requiring more than a showing of relevance to secure production.

Subdivision (b)(3) reflects the trend of the cases by requiring a special showing, not merely as to materials prepared by an attorney, but also as to materials prepared in anticipation of litigation or preparation for trial by or for a party or any representative acting on his behalf. The subdivision then goes on to protect against disclosure the mental impressions, conclusions, opinions, or legal theories concerning the litigation of an attorney or other representative of a party. The *Hickman* opinion drew special attention to the need for protecting an attorney against discovery of memoranda prepared from recollection of oral interviews. The courts have steadfastly safeguarded against disclosure of lawyers' mental impressions and legal theories, as well as mental impressions and subjective evaluations of investigators and claim-agents. In enforcing this provision of the subdivision, the courts will sometimes find it necessary to order disclosure of a document but with portions deleted.

Rules 33 and 36 have been revised in order to permit discovery calling for opinions, contentions, and admissions relating not only to fact but also to the application of law to fact. Under those rules, a party and his attorney or other representative may be required to disclose, to some extent, mental impressions, opinions, or conclusions. But documents or parts of documents containing these matters are protected against discovery by this subdivision. Even though a party may ultimately have to disclose in response to interrogatories or requests to admit, he is entitled to keep confidential documents containing such matters prepared for internal use.

Party's Right to Own Statement.—An exception to the requirement of this subdivision enables a party to secure production of his own statement without any special showing. The cases are divided. *Compare, e. g., Safeway Stores, Inc. v. Reynolds*, 176 F.2d 476 (D.C.Cir.1949); *Shupe v. Pennsylvania R. R.*, 19 F.R.D. 144 (W.D.Pa.1956); with *e. g., New York Central R. R. v. Carr*, 251 F.2d 433 (4th Cir.1957); *Belback v. Wilson Freight Forwarding Co.*, 40 F.R.D. 16 (W.D.Pa.1966).

Courts which treat a party's statement as though it were that of any witness overlook the fact that the party's statement is, without more, admissible in evidence. Ordinarily, a party gives a statement without insisting on a copy because he does not yet have a lawyer and does not understand the legal consequences of his actions. Thus, the statement is given at a time when he functions at a disadvantage. Discrepancies between his trial testimony and earlier statement may result from lapse of memory or ordinary inaccuracy; a written statement produced for the first time at trial may give such discrepancies a prominence which they do not deserve. In appropriate cases the court may order a party to be deposed before his statement is produced. *E.g., Smith v. Central Linen Service Co.*, 39 F.R.D. 15 (D.Md.1966); *McCoy v. General Motors Corp.*, 33 F.R.D. 354 (W.D.Pa.1963).

Commentators strongly support the view that a party be able to secure his statement without a showing. 4 *Moore's Federal Practice* ¶ 26.23[8.4] (2d ed. 1966); 2A Barron & Holtzoff, *Federal Practice and Procedure* § 652.3 (Wright ed. 1961); see also Note, *Developments in the Law—Discovery*, 74 Harv.L.Rev. 940, 1039 (1961). The following states have by statute or rule taken the same position: *Statutes:* Fla.Stat.Ann. § 92.33; Ga.Code Ann. § 38–2109(b); La.Stat.Ann.R.S. 13:3732; Mass.Gen.Laws Ann. c. 271, § 44; Minn.Stat.Ann. § 602.01; N.Y.C.P.L.R. § 3101(e). *Rules:* Mo.R.C.P. 56.01(a); N.Dak.R.C.P. 34(b); Wyo.R.C.P. 34(b); *cf.* Mich.G.C.R. 306.2.

In order to clarify and tighten the provision on statements by a party, the term "statement" is defined. The definition is adapted from 18 U.S.C. § 3500(e) (Jencks Act). The statement of a party may of course be that of plaintiff or defendant, and it may be that of an individual or of a corporation or other organization.

Witness' Right to Own Statement.—A second exception to the requirement of this subdivision permits a non-party witness to obtain a copy of his own statement without any special showing. Many, though not all, of the considerations supporting a party's right to obtain his statement apply also to the non-party witness. Insurance companies are increasingly recognizing that a witness is entitled to a copy of his statement and are modifying their regular practice accordingly.

Subdivision (b)(4)—Trial Preparation: Experts. This is a new provision dealing with discovery of information (including facts and opinions) obtained by a party from an expert retained by that party in relation to litigation or obtained by the expert and not yet transmitted to the party. The subdivision deals separately with those experts whom the party expects to call as trial witnesses and with those experts who have been retained or specially employed by the party but who are not expected to be witnesses. It should be noted that the subdivision does not address itself to the expert whose information was not acquired in preparation for trial but rather because he was an actor or viewer with respect to transactions or occurrences that are part of the subject matter of the lawsuit. Such an expert should be treated as an ordinary witness.

Subsection (b)(4)(A) deals with discovery of information obtained by or through experts who will be called as witnesses at trial. The provision is responsive to problems suggested by a relatively recent line of authorities. Many of these cases present intricate and difficult issues as to which expert testimony is likely to be determinative. Prominent among them are food and drug, patent, and condemnation cases. See, *e. g., United States v. Nysco Laboratories, Inc.*, 26 F.R.D. 159, 162 (E.D.N.Y.1960) (food and drug); *E. I. du Pont de Nemours & Co. v. Phillips Petroleum Co.*, 24 F.R.D. 416, 421 (D.Del.1959) (patent); *Cold Metal Process Co. v. Aluminum Co. of America*, 7 F.R.D. 425 (N.D.Ohio 1947), aff'd, *Sachs v. Aluminum Co. of America*, 167 F.2d 570 (6th Cir.1948) (same); *United States v. 50.34 Acres of Land*, 13 F.R.D. 19 (E.D.N.Y.1952) (condemnation).

In cases of this character, a prohibition against discovery of information held by expert witnesses produces in acute form the very evils that discovery has been created to prevent. Effective cross-examination of an expert witness requires advance preparation. The lawyer even with the help of his own experts frequently cannot anticipate the particular approach his adversary's expert will take or the data on which he will base his judgment on the stand. McGlothlin, *Some Practical Problems in Proof of Economic, Scientific, and Technical Facts*, 23 F.R.D. 467, 478 (1958). A California study of discovery and pretrial in condemnation cases notes that the only substitute for discovery of experts' valuation materials is "lengthy—and often fruitless—cross-examination during trial," and recommends pretrial exchange of such material. Calif.Law Rev.Comm'n, *Discovery in Eminent Domain Proceedings* 707–710 (Jan.1963). Similarly, effective rebuttal requires advance knowledge of the line of testimony of the other side. If the latter is foreclosed by a rule against discovery, then the narrowing of issues and elimination of surprise which discovery normally produces are frustrated.

These considerations appear to account for the broadening of discovery against experts in the cases cited where expert testimony was central to the case. In some instances, the opinions are explicit in relating expanded discovery to improved cross-examination and rebuttal at trial. *Franks v. National Dairy Products Corp.*, 41 F.R.D. 234 (W.D.Tex.1966); *United States v. 23.76 Acres*, 32 F.R.D. 593 (D.Md. 1963); see also an unpublished opinion of Judge Hincks, quoted in *United States v. 48 Jars, etc.*, 23 F.R.D. 192, 198 (D.D.C.1958). On the other hand, the need for new provision is shown by the many cases in which discovery of expert trial witnesses is needed for effective cross-examination and rebuttal, and yet courts apply the traditional doctrine and refuse disclosure. *E.g., United States v. Certain Parcels of Land*, 25 F.R.D. 192 (N.D.Cal.1959); *United States v. Certain Acres*, 18 F.R.D. 98 (M.D.Ga.1955).

Although the trial problems flowing from lack of discovery of expert witnesses are most acute and noteworthy when the case turns largely on experts, the same problems are encountered when a single expert testifies. Thus, subdivision (b)(4)(A) draws no line between complex and simple cases, or between cases with many experts and those with but one. It establishes by rule substantially the procedure adopted by decision of the court in *Knighton v. Villian & Fassio*, 39 F.R.D. 11 (D.Md.1965). For a full analysis of the problem and strong recommendations to the same effect, see Friedenthal, *Discovery and Use of an Adverse Party's Expert Information*, 14 Stan.L.Rev. 455, 485–488 (1962); Long, *Discovery and Experts under the Federal Rules of Civil Procedure*, 38 F.R.D. 111 (1965).

Past judicial restrictions on discovery of an adversary's expert, particularly as to his opinions, reflect the fear that one side will benefit unduly from the other's better preparation. The procedure established in subsection (b)(4)(A) holds the risk to a minimum. Discovery is limited to trial witnesses, and may be obtained only at a time when the parties know who their expert witnesses will be. A party must as a practical matter prepare his own case in advance of that time, for he can hardly hope to build his case out of his opponent's experts.

Subdivision (b)(4)(A) provides for discovery of an expert who is to testify at the trial. A party can require one who intends to use the expert to state the substance of the testimony that the expert is expected to give. The court may order further discovery, and it has ample power to regulate its timing and scope and to prevent abuse. Ordinarily, the order for further discovery shall compensate the expert for his time, and may compensate the party who intends to use the expert for past expenses reasonably incurred in obtaining facts or opinions from the expert. Those provisions are likely to discourage abusive practices.

Subdivision (b)(4)(B) deals with an expert who has been retained or specially employed by the party in anticipation of litigation or preparation for trial (thus excluding an expert who is simply a general employee of the party not specially employed on the case), but who is not expected to be called as a witness. Under its provisions, a party may discover facts known or opinions held by such an expert only on a showing of exceptional circumstances under which it is impracticable for the party seeking discovery to obtain facts or opinions on the same subject by other means.

Subdivision (b)(4)(B) is concerned only with experts retained or specially consulted in relation to trial preparation. Thus the subdivision precludes discovery against experts who were informally consulted in preparation for trial, but not retained or specially employed. As an ancillary procedure, a party may on a proper showing require the other party to name experts retained or specially employed, but not those informally consulted.

These new provisions of subdivision (b)(4) repudiate the few decisions that have held an expert's information privileged simply because of his status as an expert, *e. g., American Oil Co. v. Pennsylvania Petroleum Products Co.*, 23 F.R.D. 680, 685–686 (D.R.I.1959). See Louisell, *Modern California Discovery* 315–316 (1963). They also reject as ill-considered the decisions which have sought to bring expert information within the work-product doctrine. See *United States v. McKay*, 372 F.2d 174, 176–177 (5th Cir.1967). The provisions adopt a form of the more recently developed doctrine of "unfairness". See *e. g., United States v. 23.76 Acres of Land*, 32 F.R.D. 593, 597 (D.Md.1963); Louisell, *supra*, at 317–318; 4 *Moore's Federal Practice* ¶ 26.24 (2d ed. 1966).

Under subdivision (b)(4)(C), the court is directed or authorized to issue protective orders, including an order that the expert be paid a reasonable fee for time spent in responding to discovery, and that the party whose expert is made subject to discovery be paid a fair portion of the fees and expenses that the party incurred in obtaining information from the expert. The court may issue the latter order as a condition of discovery, or it may delay the order until after discovery is completed. These provisions for fees and expenses meet the objection that it is unfair to permit one side to obtain without cost the benefit of an expert's work for which the other side has paid, often a substantial sum. *E. g., Lewis v. United Air Lines Transp. Corp.*, 32 F.Supp. 21 (W.D.Pa.1940); *Walsh v. Reynolds Metal Co.*, 15 F.R.D. 376 (D.N.J.1954). On the other hand, a party may not obtain discovery simply by offering to pay fees and expenses. *Cf. Boynton v. R. J. Reynolds Tobacco Co.*, 36 F.Supp. 593 (D.Mass.1941).

In instances of discovery under subdivision (b)(4)(B), the court is directed to award fees and expenses to the other party, since the information is of direct value to the discovering party's preparation of his case. In ordering discovery under (b)(4)(A)(ii), the court has discretion whether to award fees and expenses to the other party; its decision should depend upon whether the discovering party is simply learning about the other party's case or is going beyond this to develop his own case. Even in cases where the court is directed to issue a protective order, it may decline to do so if it finds that manifest injustice would result. Thus, the court can protect, when necessary and appropriate, the interests of an indigent party.

Subdivision (c)—Protective Orders. The provisions of existing Rule 30(b) are transferred to this subdivision (c), as part of the rearrangement of Rule 26. The language has been changed to give it application to discovery generally. The subdivision recognizes the power of the court in the district where a deposition is being taken to make protective orders. Such power is needed when the deposition is being taken far from the court where the action is pending. The court in the district where the deposition is being taken may, and frequently will, remit the deponent or party to the court where the action is pending.

In addition, drafting changes are made to carry out and clarify the sense of the rule. Insertions are made to avoid any possible implication that a protective order does not extend to "time" as well as to "place" or may not safeguard against "undue burden or expense."

The new reference to trade secrets and other confidential commercial information reflects existing law. The courts have not given trade secrets automatic and complete immunity against disclosure, but have in each case weighed their claim to privacy against the need for disclosure. Frequently, they have been afforded a limited protection. See, *e.g., Covey Oil Co. v. Continental Oil Co.*, 340 F.2d 993 (10th Cir.1965); *Julius M. Ames Co. v. Bostitch, Inc.*, 235 F.Supp. 856 (S.D.N.Y. 1964).

The subdivision contains new matter relating to sanctions. When a motion for a protective order is made and the court is disposed to deny it, the court may go a step further and issue an order to provide or permit discovery. This will bring the sanctions of Rule 37(b) directly into play. Since the court has heard the contentions of all interested persons, an affirmative order is justified. See Rosenberg, *Sanctions to Effectuate Pretrial Discovery*, 58 Col.L.Rev. 480, 492–493 (1958). In addition, the court may require the payment of expenses incurred in relation to the motion.

Subdivision (d)—Sequence and Priority. This new provision is concerned with the sequence in which parties may proceed with discovery and with related problems of timing. The principal effects of the new provision are first, to eliminate any fixed priority in the sequence of discovery, and second, to make clear and explicit the court's power to establish priority by an order issued in a particular case.

A priority rule developed by some courts, which confers priority on the party who first serves notice of taking a deposition, is unsatisfactory in several important respects:

First, this priority rule permits a party to establish a priority running to all depositions as to which he has given earlier notice. Since he can on a given day serve notice of taking many depositions he is in a position to delay his adversary's taking of depositions for an inordinate time. Some courts have ruled that deposition priority also permits a party to delay his answers to interrogatories and production of documents. *E.g., E. I. du Pont de Nemours & Co. v. Phillips Petroleum Co.*, 23 F.R.D. 237 (D.Del.1959); *but cf. Sturdevant v. Sears, Roebuck & Co.*, 32 F.R.D. 426 (W.D.Mo.1963).

Second, since notice is the key to priority, if both parties wish to take depositions first a race results. See *Caldwell-Clements, Inc. v. McGraw-Hill Pub. Co.*, 11 F.R.D. 156 (S.D.N.Y.1951) (description of tactics used by parties). But the existing rules on notice of deposition create a race with runners starting from different positions. The plaintiff may not give notice without leave of court until 20 days after commencement of the action, whereas the defendant may serve notice at any time after commencement. Thus, a careful and prompt defendant can almost always secure priority. This advantage of defendants is fortuitous, because the purpose of requiring plaintiff to wait 20 days is to afford defendant an opportunity to obtain counsel, not to confer priority.

Third, although courts have ordered a change in the normal sequence of discovery on a number of occasions, *e. g., Kaeppler v. James H. Matthews & Co.*, 200 F.Supp. 229 (E.D.Pa.1961); *Park & Tilford Distillers Corp. v. Distillers Co.*, 19 F.R.D. 169 (S.D.N.Y.1956), and have at all times avowed discretion to vary the usual priority, most commentators are agreed that courts in fact grant relief only for "the most obviously compelling reasons." 2A Barron & Holtzoff, *Federal Practice and Procedure* 44–47 (Wright ed. 1961); see also Younger, *Priority of Pretrial Examination in the Federal Courts—A Comment*, 34 N.Y.U.L.Rev. 1271 (1959); Freund, *The Pleading and Pretrial of an Antitrust Claim*, 46 Corn.L.Q. 555, 564 (1964). Discontent with the fairness of actual practice has been evinced by other observers. Comment, 59 Yale L.J. 117, 134–136 (1949); Yudkin, *Some Refinements in Federal discovery Procedure*, 11 Fed.B.J. 289, 296–297 (1951); *Developments in the Law-Discovery*, 74 Harv.L.Rev. 940, 954–958 (1961).

Despite these difficulties, some courts have adhered to the priority rule, presumably because it provides a test which is easily understood and applied by the parties without much court intervention. It thus permits deposition discovery to function extrajudicially, which the rules provide for and the courts desire. For these same reasons, courts are reluctant to make numerous exceptions to the rule.

The Columbia Survey makes clear that the problem of priority does not affect litigants generally. It found that most litigants do not move quickly to obtain discovery. In over half of the cases, both parties waited at least 50 days. During the first 20 days after commencement of the action—the period when defendant might assure his priority by noticing depositions—16 percent of the defendants acted to obtain discovery. A race could not have occurred in more than 16 percent of the cases and it undoubtedly occurred in fewer. On the other hand, five times as many defendants as plaintiffs served notice of deposition during the first 19 days. To the same effect, see Comment, *Tactical Use and Abuse of Depositions Under the Federal Rules*, 59 Yale L.J. 117, 134 (1949).

These findings do not mean, however, that the priority rule is satisfactory or that a problem of priority does not exist. The court decisions show that parties do battle on this issue and carry their disputes to court. The statistics show that these court cases are not typical. By the same token, they reveal that more extensive exercise of judicial discretion to vary the priority will not bring a flood of litigation, and that a change in the priority rule will in fact affect only a small fraction of the cases.

It is contended by some that there is no need to alter the existing priority practice. In support, it is urged that there is no evidence that injustices in fact result from present practice and that, in any event, the courts can and do promulgate local rules, as in New York, to deal with local situations and issue orders to avoid possible injustice in particular cases.

Subdivision (d) is based on the contrary view that the rule of priority based on notice is unsatisfactory and unfair in its operation. Subdivision (d) follows an approach adapted from Civil Rule 4 of the District Court for the Southern District of New York. That rule provides that starting 40 days after commencement of the action, unless otherwise ordered by the court, the fact that one party is taking a deposition shall not prevent another party from doing so "concurrently." In practice, the depositions are not usually taken simultaneously; rather, the parties work out arrangements for alternation in the taking of depositions. One party may take a complete deposition and then the other, or, if the depositions are extensive, one party deposes for a set time, and then the other. See *Caldwell-Clements, Inc. v. McGraw-Hill Pub. Co.*, 11 F.R.D. 156 (S.D.N.Y.1951).

In principle, one party's initiation of discovery should not wait upon the other's completion, unless delay is dictated by special considerations. Clearly the principle is feasible with respect to all methods of discovery other than depositions. And the experience of the Southern District of New York shows that the principle can be applied to depositions as well. The courts have not had an increase in motion business on this matter. Once it is clear to lawyers that they bargain on an equal footing, they are usually able to arrange for an orderly succession of depositions without judicial intervention. Professor Moore has called attention to Civil Rule 4 and suggested that it may usefully be extended to other areas. 4 *Moore's Federal Practice* 1154 (2d ed. 1966).

The court may upon motion and by order grant priority in a particular case. But a local court rule purporting to confer priority in certain classes of cases would be inconsistent with this subdivision and thus void.

Subdivision (e)—Supplementation of Responses. The rules do not now state whether interrogatories (and questions at deposition as well as requests for inspection and admissions) impose a "continuing burden" on the responding party to supplement his answers if he obtains new information. The issue is acute when new information renders substantially incomplete or inaccurate an answer which was complete and accurate when made. It is essential that the rules provide an answer to this question. The parties can adjust to a rule either way, once they know what it is. See 4 *Moore's Federal Practice* ¶ 33.25[4] (2d ed. 1966).

Arguments can be made both ways. Imposition of a continuing burden reduces the proliferation of additional sets of interrogatories. Some courts have adopted local rules establishing such a burden. *E.g.*, E.D.Pa.R. 20(f), quoted in *Taggart v. Vermont Transp. Co.*, 32 F.R.D. 587 (E.D.Pa.1963); D.Me.R.15(c). Others have imposed the burden by decision. *E.g., Chenault v. Nebraska Farm Products, Inc.*, 9 F.R.D. 529, 533 (D.Nebr.1949). On the other hand, there are serious objections to the burden, especially in protracted cases. Although the party signs the answers, it is his lawyer who understands their significance and bears the responsibility to bring answers up to date. In a complex case all sorts of information reaches the party, who little understands its bearing on answers previously given to interrogatories. In practice, therefore, the lawyer under a continuing burden must periodically recheck all interrogatories and canvass all new information. But a full set of new answers may no longer be needed by the interrogating party. Some issues will have been dropped from the case, some questions are now seen as unimportant, and other questions must in any event by reformulated. See *Novick v. Pennsylvania R. R.*, 18 F.R.D. 296, 298 (W.D.Pa.1955).

Subdivision (e) provides that a party is not under a continuing burden except as expressly provided. *Cf.* Note, 68 Harv.L.Rev. 673, 677 (1955). An exception is made as to the identity of persons having knowledge of discoverable matters, because of the obvious importance to each side of knowing all witnesses and because information about witnesses routinely comes to each lawyer's attention. Many of the decisions on the issue of a continuing burden have in fact concerned the identity of witnesses. An exception is also made as to expert trial witnesses in order to carry out the provisions of Rule 26(b)(4). See *Diversified Products Corp. v. Sports Center Co.*, 42 F.R.D. 3 (D.Md.1967).

Another exception is made for the situation in which a party, or more frequently his lawyer, obtains actual knowledge that a prior response is incorrect. This exception does not impose a duty to check the accuracy of prior responses, but it prevents knowing concealment by a party or attorney. Finally, a duty to supplement may be imposed by order of the court in a particular case (including an order resulting from a pretrial conference) or by agreement of the parties. A party may of course make a new discovery request which requires supplementation of prior responses.

The duty will normally be enforced, in those limited instances where it is imposed, through sanctions imposed by the trial court, including exclusion of evidence, continuance, or other action, as the court may deem appropriate.

Rule 29. Stipulations Regarding ~~the Taking of Depositions~~ *Discovery Procedure*

Unless the court orders otherwise, ~~If the parties so stipulate in writing,~~ *the parties may by written stipulation (1) provide that* depositions may be taken before any person, at any time or place, upon any notice, and in any manner and when so taken may be used like other depositions~~.~~, *and (2) modify the procedures provided by these rules for other methods of discovery, except that stipulations extending the time provided in Rules 33, 34, and 36 for responses to discovery may be made only with the approval of the court.*

Advisory Committee's Note

There is no provision for stipulations varying the procedures by which methods of discovery other than depositions are governed. It is common practice for parties to agree on such variations, and the amendment recognizes such agreements and provides a formal mechanism in the rules for giving them effect. Any stipulation varying the procedures may be superseded by court order, and stipulations extending the time for response to discovery under Rules 33, 34, and 36 require court approval.

Rule 30. Depositions Upon Oral Examination

(a) When Depositions May Be Taken. After commencement of the action, any party may take the testimony of any person, including a party, by deposition upon oral examination. Leave of court, granted with or without notice, must be obtained only if the plaintiff seeks to take a deposition prior to the expiration of 30 days after service of the summons and complaint upon any defendant or service made under Rule 4(e), except that leave is not required (1) if a defendant has served a notice of taking deposition or otherwise sought discovery, or (2) if special notice is given as provided in subdivision (b)(2) of this rule. The attendance of witnesses may be compelled by subpoena as provided in Rule 45. The deposition of a

person confined in prison may be taken only by leave of court on such terms as the court prescribes.

~~**(a)**~~*(b) Notice of Examination:* ~~**Time and Place**~~ *General Requirements; Special Notice; Non-Stenographic Recording; Production of Documents and Things; Deposition of Organization.*

(1) A party desiring to take the deposition of any person upon oral examination shall give reasonable notice in writing to every other party to the action. The notice shall state the time and place for taking the deposition and the name and address of each person to be examined, if known, and, if the name is not known, a general description sufficient to identify him or the particular class or group to which he belongs. *If a subpoena duces tecum is to be served on the person to be examined, a designation of the materials to be produced as set forth in the subpoena shall be attached to or included in the notice.*

(2) Leave of court is not required for the taking of a deposition by plaintiff if the notice (A) states that the person to be examined is about to go out of the district where the action is pending and more than 100 miles from the place of trial, or is about to go out of the United States, or is bound on a voyage to sea, and will be unavailable for examination unless his deposition is taken before expiration of the 30-day period, and (B) sets forth facts to support the statement. The plaintiff's attorney shall sign the notice, and his signature constitutes a certification by him that to the best of his knowledge, information, and belief the statement and supporting facts are true. The sanctions provided by Rule 11 are applicable to the certification.

If a party shows that when he was served with notice under this subdivision (b)(2) he was unable through the exercise of diligence to obtain counsel to represent him at the taking of the deposition, the deposition may not be used against him.

(3) ~~On motion of any party upon whom the notice is served, the~~ *The* court may for cause shown enlarge or shorten the time~~.~~ *for taking the deposition.*

(4) The court may upon motion order that the testimony at a deposition be recorded by other than stenographic means, in which event the order shall designate the manner of recording, preserving, and filing the deposition, and may include other provisions to assure that the recorded testimony will be accurate and trustworthy. If the order is made, a party may nevertheless arrange to have a stenographic transcription made at his own expense.

(5) The notice to a party deponent may be accompanied by a request made in compliance with Rule 34 for the production of

documents and tangible things at the taking of the deposition. The procedure of Rule 34 shall apply to the request.

(6) A party may in his notice name as the deponent a public or private corporation or a partnership or association or governmental agency and designate with reasonable particularity the matters on which examination is requested. The organization so named shall designate one or more officers, directors, or managing agents, or other persons who consent to testify on its behalf, and may set forth, for each person designated, the matters on which he will testify. The persons so designated shall testify as to matters known or reasonably available to the organization. This subdivision (b)(6) does not preclude taking a deposition by any other procedure authorized in these rules.

~~**(b) Orders for the Protection of Parties and Deponents.** After notice is served for taking a deposition by oral examination, upon motion seasonably made by any party or by the person to be examined and upon notice and for good cause shown, the court in which the action is pending may make an order that the deposition shall not be taken, or that it may be taken only at some designated place other than that stated in the notice, or that it may be taken only on written interrogatories, or that certain matters shall not be inquired into, or that the scope of the examination shall be limited to certain matters, or that the examination shall be held with no one present except the parties to the action and their officers or counsel, or that after being sealed the deposition shall be opened only by order of the court, or that secret processes, developments, or research need not be disclosed, or that the parties shall simultaneously file specified documents or information enclosed in sealed envelopes to be opened as directed by the court; or the court may make any other order which justice requires to protect the party or witness from annoyance, embarrassment, or oppression.~~

(c) *Examination and Cross-Examination;* **Record of Examination; Oath; Objections.** *Examination and cross-examination of witnesses may proceed as permitted at the trial under the provisions of Rule 43(b).* The officer before whom the deposition is to be taken shall put the witness on oath and shall personally, or by some one acting under his direction and in his presence, record the testimony of the witness. The testimony shall be taken stenographically *or recorded by any other means ordered in accordance with subdivision (b)(4) of this rule.* ~~and~~ *If requested by one of the parties, the testimony shall be* transcribed ~~unless the parties agree otherwise~~.

All objections made at the time of the examination to the qualifications of the officer taking the deposition, or to the manner of taking it, or to the evidence presented, or to the conduct of any party, and any other objection to the proceedings, shall be noted by the officer upon the deposition. Evidence objected to shall be taken subject to the objections. In lieu of participating in the oral examination, parties ~~served with notice of taking a deposition~~ may ~~transmit~~ *serve* written ~~interrogatories~~ *questions in a sealed envelope on the party taking the deposition and he shall transmit them* to the officer, who shall propound them to the witness and record the answers verbatim.

(d) Motion To Terminate or Limit Examination. At any time during the taking of the deposition, on motion of ~~any~~ *a* party or of the deponent and upon a showing that the examination is being conducted in bad faith or in such manner as unreasonably to annoy, embarrass, or oppress the deponent or party, the court in which the action is pending or the court in the district where the deposition is being taken may order the officer conducting the examination to cease forthwith from taking the deposition, or may limit the scope and manner of the taking of the deposition as provided in ~~subdivision (b)~~ *Rule 26(c).* If the order made terminates the examination, it shall be resumed thereafter only upon the order of the court in which the action is pending. Upon demand of the objecting party or deponent, the taking of the deposition shall be suspended for the time necessary to make a motion for an order. ~~In granting or refusing such order the court may impose upon either party or upon the witness the requirement to pay such costs or expenses as the court may deem reasonable.~~ *The provisions of Rule 37(a)(4) apply to the award of expenses incurred in relation to the motion.*

(e) Submission to Witness; Changes; Signing. When the testimony is fully transcribed the deposition shall be submitted to the witness for examination and shall be read to or by him, unless such examination and reading are waived by the witness and by the parties. Any changes in form or substance which the witness desires to make shall be entered upon the deposition by the officer with a statement of the reasons given by the witness for making them. The deposition shall then be signed by the witness, unless the parties by stipulation waive the signing or the witness is ill or cannot be found or refuses to sign. If the deposition is not signed by the witness *within 30 days of its submission to him,* the officer shall sign it and state on the record the fact of the waiver or of the illness or absence of the witness or the fact of the refusal to sign together with the reason, if any, given therefor; and the deposition may then be used as fully as though signed, unless on a motion to suppress under Rule 32(d)*(4)* the court holds that the reasons given

New matter is shown in italics; matter to be omitted is lined through

for the refusal to sign require rejection of the deposition in whole or in part.

(f) Certification and Filing by Officer; *Exhibits;* Copies; Notice of Filing.

(1) The officer shall certify on the deposition that the witness was duly sworn by him and that the deposition is a true record of the testimony given by the witness. He shall then securely seal the deposition in an envelope indorsed with the title of the action and marked "Deposition of [here insert name of witness]" and shall promptly file it with the court in which the action is pending or send it by registered or certified mail to the clerk thereof for filing.

Documents and things produced for inspection during the examination of the witness, shall, upon the request of a party, be marked for identification and annexed to and returned with the deposition, and may be inspected and copied by any party, except that (A) the person producing the materials may substitute copies to be marked for identification, if he affords to all parties fair opportunity to verify the copies by comparison with the originals, and (B) if the person producing the materials requests their return, the officer shall mark them, give each party an opportunity to inspect and copy them, and return them to the person producing them, and the materials, may then be used in the same manner as if annexed to and returned with the deposition. Any party may move for an order that the original be annexed to and returned with the deposition to the court, pending final disposition of the case.

(2) Upon payment of reasonable charges therefor, the officer shall furnish a copy of the deposition to any party or to the deponent.

(3) The party taking the deposition shall give prompt notice of its filing to all other parties.

(g) Failure To Attend or To Serve Subpoena; Expenses.

(1) If the party giving the notice of the taking of a deposition fails to attend and proceed therewith and another party attends in person or by attorney pursuant to the notice, the court may order the party giving the notice to pay to such other party the ~~amount of the~~ reasonable expenses incurred by him and his attorney in ~~so~~ attending, including reasonable attorney's fees.

(2) If the party giving the notice of the taking of a deposition of a witness fails to serve a subpoena upon him and the witness because of such failure does not attend, and if another party attends in person or by attorney because he expects the deposition of that witness to be taken, the court may order the party giving the notice to pay to such other party the ~~amount of the~~ reasonable

expenses incurred by him and his attorney in ~~so~~ attending, including reasonable attorney's fees.

Advisory Committee's Note

Subdivision (a). This subdivision contains the provisions of the existing Rule 26(a), transferred here as part of the rearrangement relating to Rule 26. Existing Rule 30(a) is transferred to 30(b). Changes in language have been made to conform to the new arrangement.

This subdivision is further revised in regard to the requirement of leave of court for taking a deposition. The present procedure, requiring a plaintiff to obtain leave of court if he serves notice of taking a deposition within 20 days after commencement of the action, is changed in several respects. First, leave is required by reference to the time the deposition is to be taken rather than the date of serving notice of taking. Second, the 20–day period is extended to 30 days and runs from the service of summons and complaint on any defendant, rather than the commencement of the action. *Cf.* Ill.S.Ct.R. 19–1, S—H Ill.Ann.Stat. § 101.19–1. Third, leave is not required beyond the time that defendant initiates discovery, thus showing that he has retained counsel. As under the present practice, a party not afforded a reasonable opportunity to appear at a deposition, because he has not yet been served with process, is protected against use of the deposition at trial against him. See Rule 32(a), transferred from 26(d). Moreover, he can later redepose the witness if he so desires.

The purpose of requiring the plaintiff to obtain leave of court is, as stated by the Advisory Committee that proposed the present language of Rule 26(a), to protect "a defendant who has not had an opportunity to retain counsel and inform himself as to the nature of the suit." Note to 1948 amendment of Rule 26(a), quoted in 3A Barron & Holtzoff, *Federal Practice and Procedure* 455–456 (Wright ed. 1958). In order to assure defendant of this opportunity, the period is lengthened to 30 days. This protection, however, is relevant to the time of taking the deposition, not to the time that notice is served. Similarly, the protective period should run from the service of process rather than the filing of the complaint with the court. As stated in the note to Rule 26(d), the courts have used the service of notice as a convenient reference point for assigning priority in taking depositions, but with the elimination of priority in new Rule 26(d) the reference point is no longer needed. The new procedure is consistent in principle with the provisions of Rules 33, 34, and 36 as revised.

Plaintiff is excused from obtaining leave even during the initial 30-day period if he gives the special notice provided in subdivision (b)(2). The required notice must state that the person to be examined is about to go out of the district where the action is pending and more than 100 miles from the place of trial, or out of the United States, or on a voyage to sea, and will be unavailable for examination unless deposed within the 30-day period. These events occur most often in maritime litigation, when seamen are transferred from one port to another or are about to go to sea. Yet, there are analogous situations in nonmaritime litigation, and although the maritime problems are more common, a rule limited to claims in the admiralty and maritime jurisdiction is not justified.

In the recent unification of the civil and admiralty rules, this problem was temporarily met through addition in Rule 26(a) of a provision that depositions de bene esse may continue to be taken as to admiralty and maritime claims within the meaning of Rule 9(h). It was recognized at the time that "a uniform rule applicable alike to what are now civil actions and suits in admiralty" was clearly preferable, but the de bene esse procedure was adopted "for the time being at least." See

Advisory Committee's note in *Report of the Judicial Conference: Proposed Amendments to Rules of Civil Procedure* 43–44 (1966).

The changes in Rule 30(a) and the new Rule 30(b)(2) provide a formula applicable to ordinary civil as well as maritime claims. They replace the provision for depositions de bene esse. They authorize an early deposition without leave of court where the witness is about to depart and, unless his deposition is promptly taken, (1) it will be impossible or very difficult to depose him before trial or (2) his deposition can later be taken but only with substantially increased effort and expense. *Cf.* S. S. Hai Chang, 1966 A.M.C. 2239 (S.D.N.Y.1966), in which the deposing party is required to prepay expenses and counsel fees of the other party's lawyer when the action is pending in New York and depositions are to be taken on the West Coast. Defendant is protected by a provision that the deposition cannot be used against him if he was unable through exercise of diligence to obtain counsel to represent him.

The distance of 100 miles from place of trial is derived from the de bene esse provision and also conforms to the reach of a subpoena of the trial court, as provided in Rule 45(e). See also S.D.N.Y.Civ.R. 5(a). Some parts of the de bene esse provision are omitted from Rule 30(b)(2). Modern deposition practice adequately covers the witness who lives more than 100 miles away from place of trial. If a witness is aged or infirm, leave of court can be obtained.

Subdivision (b). Existing Rule 30(b) on protective orders has been transferred to Rule 26(c), and existing Rule 30(a) relating to the notice of taking deposition has been transferred to this subdivision. Because new material has been added, subsection numbers have been inserted.

Subdivision (b)(1). If a subpoena duces tecum is to be served, a copy thereof or a designation of the materials to be produced must accompany the notice. Each party is thereby enabled to prepare for the deposition more effectively.

Subdivision (b)(2). This subdivision is discussed in the note to subdivision (a), to which it relates.

Subdivision (b)(3). This provision is derived from existing Rule 30(a), with a minor change of language.

Subdivision (b)(4). In order to facilitate less expensive procedures, provision is made for the recording of testimony by other than stenographic means—*e.g.*, by mechanical, electronic, or photographic means. Because these methods give rise to problems of accuracy and trustworthiness, the party taking the deposition is required to apply for a court order. The order is to specify how the testimony is to be recorded, preserved, and filed, and it may contain whatever additional safeguards the court deems necessary.

Subdivision (b)(5). A provision is added to enable a party, through service of notice, to require another party to produce documents or things at the taking of his deposition. This may now be done as to a nonparty deponent through use of a subpoena duces tecum as authorized by Rule 45, but some courts have held that documents may be secured from a party only under Rule 34. See 2A Barron & Holtzoff, *Federal Practice and Procedure* § 644.1 n. 83.2, § 792 n. 16 (Wright ed. 1961). With the elimination of "good cause" from Rule 34, the reason for this restrictive doctrine has disappeared. *Cf.* N.Y.C.P.L.R. § 3111.

Whether production of documents or things should be obtained directly under rule 34 or at the deposition under this rule will depend on the nature and volume of the documents or things. Both methods are made available. When the documents are few and simple, and closely related to the oral examination, ability to proceed via this rule will facilitate discovery. If the discovering party insists on examining many and complex documents at the taking of the deposition, thereby causing undue burdens on others, the latter may, under Rules 26(c) or 30(d), apply for a court order that the examining party proceed via Rule 34 alone.

Subdivision (b)(6). A new provision is added, whereby a party may name a corporation, partnership, association, or governmental agency as the deponent and designate the matters on which he requests examination, and the organization shall then name one or more of its officers, directors, or managing agents, or other persons consenting to appear and testify on its behalf with respect to matters known or reasonably available to the organization. *Cf.* Alberta Sup.Ct. R. 255. The organization may designate persons other than officers, directors, and managing agents, but only with their consent. Thus, an employee or agent who has an independent or conflicting interest in the litigation—for example, in a personal injury case—can refuse to testify on behalf of the organization.

This procedure supplements the existing practice whereby the examining party designates the corporate official to be deposed. Thus, if the examining party believes that certain officials who have not testified pursuant to this subdivision have added information, he may depose them. On the other hand, a court's decision whether to issue a protective order may take account of the availability and use made of the procedures provided in this subdivision.

The new procedure should be viewed as an added facility for discovery, one which may be advantageous to both sides as well as an improvement in the deposition process. It will reduce the difficulties now encountered in determining, prior to the taking of a deposition, whether a particular employee or agent is a "managing agent." See Note, *Discovery Against Corporations Under the Federal Rules,* 47 Iowa L.Rev. 1006–1016 (1962). It will curb the "bandying" by which officers or managing agents of a corporation are deposed in turn but each disclaims knowledge of facts that are clearly known to persons in the organization and thereby to it. *Cf. Haney v. Woodward & Lothrop, Inc.,* 330 F.2d 940, 944 (4th Cir.1964). The provision should also assist organizations which find that an unnecessarily large number of their officers and agents are being deposed by a party uncertain of who in the organization has knowledge. Some courts have held that under the existing rules a corporation should not be burdened with choosing which person is to appear for it. *E.g., United States v. Gahagan Dredging Corp.,* 24 F.R.D. 328, 329 (S.D.N.Y. 1958). This burden is not essentially different from that of answering interrogatories under Rule 33, and is in any case lighter than that of an examining party ignorant of who in the corporation has knowledge.

Subdivision (c). A new sentence is inserted at the beginning, representing the transfer of existing Rule 26(c) to this subdivision. Another addition conforms to the new provision in subdivision (b)(4).

The present rule provides that transcription shall be carried out unless all parties waive it. In view of the many depositions taken from which nothing useful is discovered, the revised language provides that transcription is to be performed if any party requests it. The fact of the request is relevant to the exercise of the court's discretion in determining who shall pay for transcription.

Parties choosing to serve written questions rather than participate personally in an oral deposition are directed to serve their questions on the party taking the deposition, since the officer is often not identified in advance. Confidentiality is preserved, since the questions may be served in a sealed envelope.

Subdivision (d). The assessment of expenses incurred in relation to motions made under this subdivision (d) is made subject to the provisions of Rule 37(a). The standards for assessment of expenses are more fully set out in Rule 37(a), and these standards should apply to the essentially similar motions of this subdivision.

Subdivision (e). The provision relating to the refusal of a witness to sign his deposition is tightened through insertion of a 30-day time period.

Subdivision (f)(1). A provision is added which codifies in a flexible way the procedure for handling exhibits related to the deposition and at the same time assures each party that he may inspect and copy documents and things produced by a nonparty witness in response to a subpoena duces tecum. As a general rule and in the absence of agreement to the contrary or order of the court, exhibits produced without objection are to be annexed to and returned with the deposition, but a witness may substitute copies for purposes of marking and he may obtain return of the exhibits. The right of the parties to inspect exhibits for identification and to make copies is assured. *Cf.* N.Y.C.P.L.R. § 3116(c).

Rule 31. Depositions ~~of Witnesses~~ Upon Written ~~Interrogatories~~ *Questions*

(a) Serving ~~Interrogatories~~ *Questions*; Notice. *After commencement of the action, any party may take the testimony of any person, including a party, by deposition upon written questions. The attendance of witnesses may be compelled by the use of subpoena as provided in Rule 45. The deposition of a person confined in prison may be taken only by leave of court on such terms as the court prescribes.*

A party desiring to take ~~the~~ *a* deposition ~~of any person~~ upon written ~~interrogatories~~ *questions* shall serve them upon every other party with a notice stating *(1)* the name and address of the person who is to answer them, *if known, and if the name is not known, a general description sufficient to identify him or the particular class or group to which he belongs,* and *(2)* the name or descriptive title and address of the officer before whom the deposition is to be taken. *A deposition upon written questions may be taken of a public or private corporation or a partnership or association or governmental agency in accordance with the provisions of Rule 30(b)(6).*

Within ~~10~~ *30* days ~~thereafter~~ *after the notice and written questions are served,* a party ~~so served~~ may serve cross ~~interrogatories~~ *questions* upon ~~the party proposing to take the deposition.~~ *all other parties.* Within ~~5~~ *10* days ~~thereafter the latter~~ *after being served with cross questions, a party* may serve redirect ~~interrogatories~~ *questions* upon *all other parties.* ~~a party who has served cross interrogatories.~~ Within ~~3~~ *10* days after being served with redirect ~~interrogatories~~ *questions,* a party may serve recross ~~interrogatories~~ *questions* upon *all other parties.* ~~the party proposing to take the deposition.~~ *The court may for cause shown enlarge or shorten the time.*

(b) Officer To Take Responses and Prepare Record. A copy of the notice and copies of all ~~interrogatories~~ *questions* served

New matter is shown in italics; matter to be omitted is lined through

shall be delivered by the party taking the deposition to the officer designated in the notice, who shall proceed promptly, in the manner provided by Rule 30(c), (e), and (f), to take the testimony of the witness in response to the ~~interrogatories~~ *questions* and to prepare, certify, and file or mail the deposition, attaching thereto the copy of the notice and the ~~interrogatories~~ *questions* received by him.

(c) Notice of Filing. When the deposition is filed the party taking it shall promptly give notice thereof to all other parties.

~~**(d) Orders for the Protection of Parties and Deponents.** After the service of interrogatories and prior to the taking of the testimony of the deponent, the court in which the action is pending, on motion promptly made by a party or a deponent, upon notice and good cause shown, may make any order specified in Rule 30 which is appropriate and just or an order that the deposition shall not be taken before the officer designated in the notice or that it shall not be taken except upon oral examination.~~

Advisory Committee's Note

Confusion is created by the use of the same terminology to describe both the taking of a deposition upon "written interrogatories" pursuant to this rule and the serving of "written interrogatories" upon parties pursuant to Rule 33. The distinction between these two modes of discovery will be more readily and clearly grasped through substitution of the word "questions" for "interrogatories" throughout this rule.

Subdivision (a). A new paragraph is inserted at the beginning of this subdivision to conform to the rearrangement of provisions in Rules 26(a), 30(a), and 30(b).

The revised subdivision permits designation of the deponent by general description or by class or group. This conforms to the practice for depositions on oral examination.

The new procedure provided in Rule 30(b)(6) for taking the deposition of a corporation or other organization through persons designated by the organization is incorporated by reference.

The service of all questions, including cross, redirect, and recross, is to be made on all parties. This will inform the parties and enable them to participate fully in the procedure.

The time allowed for service of cross, redirect, and recross questions has been extended. Experience with the existing time limits shows them to be unrealistically short. No special restriction is placed on the time for serving the notice of taking the deposition and the first set of questions. Since no party is required to serve cross questions less than 30 days after the notice and questions are served, the defendant has sufficient time to obtain counsel. The court may for cause shown enlarge or shorten the time.

Subdivision (d). Since new Rule 26(c) provides for protective orders with respect to all discovery, and expressly provides that the court may order that one discovery device be used in place of another, subdivision (d) is eliminated as unnecessary.

Rule 32. ~~Effect of Errors and Irregularities in Depositions~~ *Use of Depositions in Court Proceedings*

[*Special Note:* The provisions of Rule 32(a), (b), and (c) set out below represent the transfer of Rules 26(d), (e), and (f) with a few amendments. To enable the reader to distinguish easily between transferred material and amendments of material, the provisions are presented within brackets and in roman type as they have heretofore appeared in Rule 26, with line deletions and italics representing the changes made.]

[~~(d)~~ *(a)* **Use of Depositions.** At the trial or upon the hearing of a motion or an interlocutory proceeding, any part or all of a deposition, so far as admissible under the rules of evidence *applied as though the witness were then present and testifying,* may be used against any party who was present or represented at the taking of the deposition or who had ~~due~~ *reasonable* notice thereof, in accordance with any ~~one~~ of the following provisions:

(1) Any deposition may be used by any party for the purpose of contradicting or impeaching the testimony of deponent as a witness.

(2) The deposition of a party or of any one who at the time of taking the deposition was an officer, director, or managing agent, *or a person designated under Rule 30(b)(6) or 31(a) to testify on behalf* of a public or private corporation, partnership or association *or governmental agency* which is a party may be used by an adverse party for any purpose.

(3) The deposition of a witness, whether or not a party, may be used by any party for any purpose if the court finds: ~~1,~~ *(A)* that the witness is dead; or ~~2,~~ *(B)* that the witness is at a greater distance than 100 miles from the place of trial or hearing, or is out of the United States, unless it appears that the absence of the witness was procured by the party offering the deposition; or ~~3,~~ *(C)* that the witness is unable to attend or testify because of age, *illness* ~~sickness~~, infirmity, or imprisonment; or ~~4,~~ *(D)* that the party offering the deposition has been unable to procure the attendance of the witness by subpoena; or ~~5,~~ *(E)* upon application and notice, that such exceptional circumstances exist as to make it desirable, in the interest of justice and with due regard to the importance of presenting the testimony of witnesses orally in open court, to allow the deposition to be used.

(4) If only part of a deposition is offered in evidence by a party, an adverse party may require him to introduce ~~all of it which is relevant to~~ *any other part which ought in fairness to be considered*

with the part introduced, and any party may introduce any other parts.

Substitution of parties *pursuant to Rule 25* does not affect the right to use depositions previously taken; and, when an action in any court of the United States or of any state has been dismissed and another action involving the same subject matter is afterward brought between the same parties or their representatives or successors in interest, all depositions lawfully taken and duly filed in the former action may be used in the latter as if originally taken therefor.

~~**(e)**~~ *(b)* **Objections to Admissibility.** Subject to the provisions of Rules 28(b) and ~~32(c)~~ *subdivision (d)(3) of this rule,* objection may be made at the trial or hearing to receiving in evidence any deposition or part thereof for any reason which would require the exclusion of the evidence if the witness were then present and testifying.

~~**(f)**~~ *(c)* **Effect of Taking or Using Depositions.** A party ~~shall~~ *does* not ~~be deemed to~~ make a person his own witness for any purpose by taking his deposition. The introduction in evidence of the deposition or any part thereof for any purpose other than that of contradicting or impeaching the deponent makes the deponent the witness of the party introducing the deposition, but this shall not apply to the use by an adverse party of a deposition *under* ~~as described in paragraph (2) of subdivision (d)~~ *subdivision (a)(2)* of this rule. At the trial or hearing any party may rebut any relevant evidence contained in a deposition whether introduced by him or by any other party.]

(d) Effect of Errors and Irregularities in Depositions.

~~**(a)**~~ *(1) As to Notice.* All errors and irregularities in the notice for taking a deposition are waived unless written objection is promptly served upon the party giving the notice.

~~**(b)**~~ *(2) As to Disqualification of Officer.* Objection to taking a deposition because of disqualification of the officer before whom it is to be taken is waived unless made before the taking of the deposition begins or as soon thereafter as the disqualification becomes known or could be discovered with reasonable diligence.

~~**(c)**~~ *(3) As to Taking of Deposition.*

~~(1)~~ *(A)* Objections to the competency of a witness or to the competency, relevancy, or materiality of testimony are not waived by failure to make them before or during the taking of the deposition, unless the ground of the objection is one which might have been obviated or removed if presented at that time.

New matter is shown in italics; matter to be omitted is lined through

~~(2)~~ *(B)* Errors and irregularities occurring at the oral examination in the manner of taking the deposition, in the form of the questions or answers, in the oath or affirmation, or in the conduct of parties and errors of any kind which might be obviated, removed, or cured if promptly presented, are waived unless seasonable objection thereto is made at the taking of the deposition.

~~(3)~~ *(C)* Objections to the form of written ~~interrogatories~~ *questions* submitted under Rule 31 are waived unless served in writing upon the party propounding them within the time allowed for serving the succeeding cross or other ~~interrogatories~~ *questions* and within ~~3~~ *5* days after service of the last ~~interrogatories~~ *questions* authorized.

~~(d)~~ *(4) As to Completion and Return of Deposition.* Errors and irregularities in the manner in which the testimony is transcribed or the deposition is prepared, signed, certified, sealed, indorsed, transmitted, filed, or otherwise dealt with by the officer under Rules 30 and 31 are waived unless a motion to suppress the deposition or some part thereof is made with reasonable promptness after such defect is, or with due diligence might have been, ascertained.

Advisory Committee's Note

As part of the rearrangement of the discovery rules, existing subdivisions (d), (e), and (f) of Rule 26 are transferred to Rule 32 as new subdivisions (a), (b), and (c). The provisions of Rule 32 are retained as subdivision (d) of Rule 32 with appropriate changes in the lettering and numbering of subheadings. The new rule is given a suitable new title. A beneficial byproduct of the rearrangement is that provisions which are naturally related to one another are placed in one rule.

A change is made in new Rule 32(a), whereby it is made clear that the rules of evidence are to be applied to depositions offered at trial as though the deponent were then present and testifying at trial. This eliminates the possibility of certain technical hearsay objections which are based, not on the contents of deponent's testimony, but on his absence from court. The language of present Rule 26(d) does not appear to authorize these technical objections, but it is not entirely clear. Note present Rule 26(e), transferred to Rule 32(b); see 2A Barron & Holtzoff, *Federal Practice and Procedure* 164–166 (Wright ed. 1961).

An addition in Rule 32(a)(2) provides for use of a deposition of a person designated by a corporation or other organization, which is a party, to testify on its behalf. This complements the new procedure for taking the deposition of a corporation or other organization provided in Rules 30(b)(6) and 31(a). The addition is appropriate, since the deposition is in substance and effect that of the corporation or other organization which is a party.

A change is made in the standard under which a party offering part of a deposition in evidence may be required to introduce additional parts of the deposition. The new standard is contained in a proposal made by the Advisory Committee on Rules of Evidence. See Rule 1–07 and accompanying Note, Preliminary Draft of Proposed Rules of Evidence for the United States District Courts and Magistrates 21–22 (March, 1969).

References to other rules are changed to conform to the rearrangement, and minor verbal changes have been made for clarification. The time for objecting to written questions served under Rule 31 is slightly extended.

Rule 33. Interrogatories to Parties

(a) Availability; Procedures for Use. Any party may serve upon any ~~adverse~~ *other* party written interrogatories to be answered by the party served or, if the party served is a public or private corporation or a partnership or association *or governmental agency,* by any officer or agent, who shall furnish such information as is available to the party. Interrogatories may, *without leave of court,* be served *upon the plaintiff* after commencement of the action *and upon any other party with or after service of the summons and complaint upon that party.* ~~and without leave of court, except that, if service is made by the plaintiff within 10 days after such commencement, leave of court granted with or without notice must first be obtained. The interrogatories~~

Each interrogatory shall be answered separately and fully in writing under oath~~.~~, *unless it is objected to, in which event the reasons for objection shall be stated in lieu of an answer.* The answers ~~shall~~ *are to* be signed by the person making them~~;~~, and *the objections signed by the attorney making them.* ~~t~~*T*he party upon whom the interrogatories have been served shall serve a copy of the answers, *and objections if any,* ~~on the party submitting the interrogatories within 15 days after the service of the interrogatories, unless the court, on motion and notice and for good cause shown, enlarges or shortens the time.~~ *within 30 days after the service of the interrogatories, except that a defendant may serve answers or objections within 45 days after service of the summons and complaint upon that defendant. The court may allow a shorter or longer time.* ~~Within 10 days after service of interrogatories a party may serve written objections thereto together with a notice of hearing the objections at the earliest practicable time. Answers to interrogatories to which objection is made shall be deferred until the objections are determined.~~ *The party submitting the interrogatories may move for an order under Rule 37(a) with respect to any objection to or other failure to answer an interrogatory.*

(b) Scope; Use at Trial. Interrogatories may relate to any matters which can be inquired into under Rule 26(b), and the answers may be used to the ~~same~~ extent *permitted by the rules of evidence.* ~~as provided in Rule 26(d) for the use of the deposition of a party. Interrogatories may be served after a deposition has been taken, and a deposition may be sought after interrogatories have been answered, but the court, on motion of the deponent or the~~

New matter is shown in italics; matter to be omitted is lined through

~~party interrogated, may make such protective order as justice may require. The number of interrogatories or of sets of interrogatories to be served is not limited except as justice requires to protect the party from annoyance, expense, embarrassment, or oppression. The provisions of Rule 30(b) are applicable for the protection of the party from whom answers to interrogatories are sought under this rule.~~

An interrogatory otherwise proper is not necessarily objectionable merely because an answer to the interrogatory involves an opinion or contention that relates to fact or the application of law to fact, but the court may order that such an interrogatory need not be answered until after designated discovery has been completed or until a pre-trial conference or other later time.

(c) Option to Produce Business Records. Where the answer to an interrogatory may be derived or ascertained from the business records of the party upon whom the interrogatory has been served or from an examination, audit or inspection of such business records, or from a compilation, abstract or summary based thereon, and the burden of deriving or ascertaining the answer is substantially the same for the party serving the interrogatory as for the party served, it is a sufficient answer to such interrogatory to specify the records from which the answer may be derived or ascertained and to afford to the party serving the interrogatory reasonable opportunity to examine, audit or inspect such records and to make copies, compilations, abstracts or summaries.

Advisory Committee's Note

Subdivision (a). The mechanics of the operation of Rule 33 are substantially revised by the proposed amendment, with a view to reducing court intervention. There is general agreement that interrogatories spawn a greater percentage of objections and motions than any other discovery device. The Columbia Survey shows that, although half of the litigants resorted to depositions and about one-third used interrogatories, about 65 percent of the objections were made with respect to interrogatories and 26 percent related to depositions. See also Speck, *The Use of Discovery in United States District Courts,* 60 Yale L.J. 1132, 1144, 1151 (1951); Note, 36 Minn.L.Rev. 364, 379 (1952).

The procedures now provided in Rule 33 seem calculated to encourage objections and court motions. The time periods now allowed for responding to interrogatories—15 days for answers and 10 days for objections—are too short. The Columbia Survey shows that tardy response to interrogatories is common, virtually expected. The same was reported in Speck, *supra,* 60 Yale L.J. 1132, 1144. The time pressures tend to encourage objections as a means of gaining time to answer.

The time for objections is even shorter than for answers, and the party runs the risk that if he fails to object in time he may have waived his objections. *E.g., Cleminshaw v. Beech Aircraft Corp.,* 21 F.R.D 300 (D.Del.1957); see 4 *Moore's Federal Practice,* ¶ 33.27 (2d ed. 1966); 2A Barron & Holtzoff, *Federal Practice and Procedure* 372–373 (Wright ed. 1961). It often seems easier to object than to seek an extension of time. Unlike Rules 30(d) and 37(a), Rule 33 imposes no sanction of expenses on a party whose objections are clearly unjustified.

Rule 33 assures that the objections will lead directly to court, through its requirement that they be served with a notice of hearing. Although this procedure does not preclude an out-of-court resolution of the dispute, the procedure tends to discourage informal negotiations. If answers are served and they are thought inadequate, the interrogating party may move under Rule 37(a) for an order compelling adequate answers. There is no assurance that the hearing on objections and that on inadequate answers will be heard together.

The amendment improves the procedure of Rule 33 in the following respects:

(1) The time allowed for response is increased to 30 days and this time period applies to both answers and objections, but a defendant need not respond in less than 45 days after service of the summons and complaint upon him. As is true under existing law, the responding party who believes that some parts or all of the interrogatories are objectionable may choose to seek a protective order under new Rule 26(c) or may serve objections under this rule. Unless he applies for a protective order, he is required to serve answers or objections in response to the interrogatories, subject to the sanctions provided in Rule 37(d). Answers and objections are served together, so that a response to each interrogatory is encouraged, and any failure to respond is easily noted.

(2) In view of the enlarged time permitted for response, it is no longer necessary to require leave of court for service of interrogatories. The purpose of this requirement—that defendant have time to obtain counsel before a response must be made—is adequately fulfilled by the requirement that interrogatories be served upon a party with or after service of the summons and complaint upon him.

Some would urge that the plaintiff nevertheless not be permitted to serve interrogatories with the complaint. They fear that a routine practice might be invited, whereby form interrogatories would accompany most complaints. More fundamentally, they feel that, since very general complaints are permitted in present-day pleading, it is fair that the defendant have a right to take the lead in serving interrogatories. (These views apply also to Rule 36.) The amendment of Rule 33 rejects these views, in favor of allowing both parties to go forward with discovery, each free to obtain the information he needs respecting the case.

(3) If objections are made, the burden is on the interrogating party to move under Rule 37(a) for a court order compelling answers, in the course of which the court will pass on the objections. The change in the burden of going forward does not alter the existing obligation of an objecting party to justify his objections. *E.g., Pressley v. Boehlke,* 33 F.R.D. 316 (W.D.N.C. 1963). If the discovering party asserts that an answer is incomplete or evasive, again he may look to Rule 37(a) for relief, and he should add this assertion to his motion to overrule objections. There is no requirement that the parties consult informally concerning their differences, but the new procedure should encourage consultation, and the court may by local rule require it.

The proposed changes are similar in approach to those adopted by California in 1961. See Calif.Code Civ.Proc. § 2030(a). The experience of the Los Angeles Superior Court is informally reported as showing that the California amendment resulted in a significant reduction in court motions concerning interrogatories. Rhode Island takes a similar approach. See R. 33, R.I.R. Civ.Proc. Official Draft, p. 74 (Boston Law Book Co.).

A change is made in subdivision (a) which is not related to the sequence of procedures. The restriction to "adverse" parties is eliminated. The courts have generally construed this restriction as precluding interrogatories unless an issue between the parties is disclosed by the pleadings—even though the parties may have conflicting interests. *E.g., Mozeika v. Kaufman Construction Co.,* 25 F.R.D. 233 (E.D.Pa.1960) (plaintiff and third-party defendant); *Biddle v. Hutchinson,* 24 F.R.D. 256 (M.D.Pa.1959) (codefendants). The resulting distinctions have often been highly technical. In *Schlagenhauf v. Holder,* 379 U.S. 104 (1964), the Supreme Court rejected a contention that examination under Rule 35 could be had only against an "opposing" party, as not in keeping "with the aims of a liberal, nontechnical application of the Federal Rules." 379 U.S. at 116. Eliminating the requirement of "adverse" parties from Rule 33 brings it into line with all other discovery rules.

A second change in subdivision (a) is the addition of the term "governmental agency" to the listing of organizations whose answers are to be made by any officer or agent of the organization. This does not involve any change in existing law. Compare the similar listing in Rule 30(b)(6).

The duty of a party to supplement his answers to interrogatories is governed by a new provision in Rule 26(e).

Subdivision (b). There are numerous and conflicting decisions on the question whether and to what extent interrogatories are limited to matters "of fact," or may elicit opinions, contentions, and legal conclusions. *Compare, e.g., Payer, Hewitt & Co. v. Bellanca Corp.,* 26 F.R.D. 219 (D.Del.1960) (opinions bad); *Zinsky v. New York Central R. R.,* 36 F.R.D. 680 (N.D.Ohio 1964) (factual opinion or contention good, but legal theory bad); *United States v. Carter Products, Inc.,* 28 F.R.D. 373 (S.D.N.Y.1961) (factual contentions and legal theories bad) *with Taylor v. Sound Steamship Lines, Inc.,* 100 F.Supp. 388 (D.Conn.1951) (opinions good); *Bynum v. United States,* 36 F.R.D. 14 (E.D.La.1964) (contentions as to facts constituting negligence good). For lists of the many conflicting authorities, see 4 *Moore's Federal Practice* ¶ 33.17 (2d ed. 1966); 2A Barron & Holtzoff, *Federal Practice and Procedure* § 768 (Wright ed. 1961).

Rule 33 is amended to provide that an interrogatory is not objectionable merely because it calls for an opinion or contention that relates to fact or the application of law to fact. Efforts to draw sharp lines between facts and opinions have invariably been unsuccessful, and the clear trend of the cases is to permit "factual" opinions. As to requests for opinions or contentions that call for the application of law to fact, they can be most useful in narrowing and sharpening the issues, which is a major purpose of discovery. See *Diversified Products Corp. v. Sports Center Co.,* 42 F.R.D. 3 (D.Md.1967); Moore, *supra;* Field & McKusick, *Maine Civil Practice* § 26.18 (1959). On the other hand, under the new language interrogatories may not extend to issues of "pure law," *i.e.,* legal issues unrelated to the facts of the case. *Cf. United States v. Maryland & Va. Milk Producers Assn., Inc.,* 22 F.R.D. 300 (D.D.C.1958).

Since interrogatories involving mixed questions of law and fact may create disputes between the parties which are best resolved after much or all of the other discovery has been completed, the court is expressly authorized to defer an answer. Likewise, the court may delay determination until pretrial conference, if it believes that the dispute is best resolved in the presence of the judge.

The principal question raised with respect to the cases permitting such interrogatories is whether they reintroduce undesirable aspects of the prior pleading practice, whereby parties were chained to misconceived contentions or theories, and ultimate determination on the merits was frustrated. See James, *The Revival of Bills of Particulars under the Federal Rules,* 71 Harv.L.Rev. 1473 (1958). But there are few if any instances in the recorded cases demonstrating that such frustration has occurred. The general rule governing the use of answers to interrogatories is that under ordinary circumstances they do not limit proof. See, *e.g., McElroy v. United Air Lines, Inc.*, 21 F.R.D. 100 (W.D.Mo.1967); *Pressley v. Boehlke,* 33 F.R.D. 316, 317 (W.D.N.C.1963). Although in exceptional circumstances reliance on an answer may cause such prejudice that the court will hold the answering party bound to his answer, *e.g., Zielinski v. Philadelphia Piers, Inc.*, 139 F.Supp. 408 (E.D.Pa. 1956), the interrogating party will ordinarily not be entitled to rely on the unchanging character of the answers he receives and cannot base prejudice on such reliance. The rule does not affect the power of a court to permit withdrawal or amendment of answers to interrogatories.

The use of answers to interrogatories at trial is made subject to the rules of evidence. The provisions governing use of depositions, to which Rule 33 presently refers, are not entirely apposite to answers to interrogatories, since deposition practice contemplates that all parties will ordinarily participate through cross-examination. See 4 *Moore's Federal Practice* ¶ 33.29[1] (2d ed. 1966).

Certain provisions are deleted from subdivision (b) because they are fully covered by new Rule 26(c) providing for protective orders and Rules 26(a) and 26(d). The language of the subdivision is thus simplified without any change of substance.

Subdivision (c). This is a new subdivision, adapted from Calif.Code Civ.Proc. § 2030(c), relating especially to interrogatories which require a party to engage in burdensome or expensive research into his own business records in order to give an answer. The subdivision gives the party an option to make the records available and place the burden of research on the party who seeks the information. "This provision, without undermining the liberal scope of interrogatory discovery, places the burden of discovery upon its potential benefitee," Louisell, *Modern California Discovery,* 124–125 (1963), and alleviates a problem which in the past has troubled Federal courts. See Speck, *The Use of Discovery in United States District Courts,* 60 Yale L.J. 1132, 1142–1144 (1951). The interrogating party is protected against abusive use of this provision through the requirement that the burden of ascertaining the answer be substantially the same for both sides. A respondent may not impose on an interrogating party a mass of records as to which research is feasible only for one familiar with the records. At the same time, the respondent unable to invoke this subdivision does not on that account lose the protection available to him under new Rule 26(c) against oppressive or unduly burdensome or expensive interrogatories. And even when the respondent successfully invokes the subdivision, the court is not deprived of its usual power, in appropriate cases, to require that the interrogating party reimburse the respondent for the expense of assembling his records and making them intelligible.

~~Rule 34. Discovery and Production of Documents and Things for Inspection, Copying, or Photographing~~

~~Upon motion of any party showing good cause therefor and upon notice to all other parties, and subject to the provisions of Rule 30(b), the court in which an action is pending may (1) order any party to produce and permit the inspection and copying or photographing, by or on behalf of the moving party, of any designated documents, papers, books, accounts, letters, photographs, objects, or tangible things, not privileged, which constitute or contain evidence relating to any of the matters within the scope of the examination permitted by Rule 26(b) and which are in his~~

~~possession, custody, or control; or (2) order any party to permit entry upon designated land or other property in his possession or control for the purpose of inspecting, measuring, surveying, or photographing the property or any designated object or operation thereon within the scope of the examination permitted by Rule 26(b). The order shall specify the time, place, and manner of making the inspection and taking the copies and photographs and may prescribe such terms and conditions as are just.~~

Rule 34. Production of Documents and Things and Entry Upon Land for Inspection and Other Purposes

(a) Scope. Any party may serve on any other party a request (1) to produce and permit the party making the request, or someone acting on his behalf, to inspect and copy, any designated documents (including writings, drawings, graphs, charts, photographs, phono-records, and other data compilations from which information can be obtained, translated, if necessary, by the respondent through detection devices into reasonable usable form), or to inspect and copy, test, or sample any tangible things which constitute or contain matters within the scope of Rule 26(b) and which are in the possession, custody or control of the party upon whom the request is served; or (2) to permit entry upon designated land or other property in the possession or control of the party upon whom the request is served for the purpose of inspection and measuring, surveying, photographing, testing, or sampling the property or any designated objection or operation thereon, within the scope of Rule 26(b).

(b) Procedure. The request may, without leave of court, be served upon the plaintiff after commencement of the action and upon any other party with or after service of the summons and complaint upon that party. The request shall set forth the items to be inspected either by individual item or by category, and describe each item and category with reasonable particularity. The request shall specify a reasonable time, place, and manner of making the inspection and performing the related acts.

The party upon whom the request is served shall serve a written response within 30 days after the service of the request, except that a defendant may serve a response within 45 days after service of the summons and complaint upon that defendant. The court may allow a shorter or longer time. The response shall state, with respect to each item or category, that inspection and related activities will be permitted as requested, unless the request is objected to, in which event the reasons for objection shall be stated. If objection is made to part of an item or category, the part shall be specified. The party submitting the request may move for an order under Rule 37(a) with respect to any objection to or other failure to respond to the request or any part thereof, or any failure to permit inspection as requested.

(c) Persons Not Parties. This rule does not preclude an independent action against a person not a party for production of documents and things and permission to enter upon land.

Advisory Committee's Note

Rule 34 is revised to accomplish the following major changes in the existing rule: (1) to eliminate the requirement of good cause; (2) to have the rule operate extrajudicially; (3) to include testing and sampling as well as inspecting or photographing tangible things; and (4) to make clear that the rule does not preclude an independent action for analogous discovery against persons not parties.

Subdivision (a). Good cause is eliminated because it has furnished an uncertain and erratic protection to the parties from whom production is sought and is now rendered unnecessary by virtue of the more specific provisions added to Rule 26(b) relating to materials assembled in preparation for trial and to experts retained or consulted by parties.

The good cause requirement was originally inserted in Rule 34 as a general protective provision in the absence of experience with the specific problems that would arise thereunder. As the note to Rule 26(b)(3) on trial preparation materials makes clear, good cause has been applied differently to varying classes of documents, though not without confusion. It has often been said in court opinions that good cause requires a consideration of need for the materials and of alternative means of obtaining them, *i. e.*, something more than relevance and lack of privilege. But the overwhelming proportion of the cases in which the formula of good cause has been applied to require a special showing are those involving trial preparation. In practice, the courts have not treated documents as having a special immunity to discovery simply because of their being documents. Protection may be afforded to claims of privacy or secrecy or of undue burden or expense under what is now Rule 26(c) (previously Rule 30(b)). To be sure, an appraisal of "undue" burden inevitably entails consideration of the needs of the party seeking discovery. With special provisions added to govern trial preparation materials and experts, there is no longer any occasion to retain the requirement of good cause.

The revision of Rule 34 to have it operate extrajudicially, rather than by court order, is to a large extent a reflection of existing law office practice. The Columbia Survey shows that of the litigants seeking inspection of documents or things, only about 25 percent filed motions for court orders. This minor fraction nevertheless accounted for a significant number of motions. About half of these motions were uncontested and in almost all instances the party seeking production ultimately prevailed. Although an extrajudicial procedure will not drastically alter existing practice under Rule 34—it will conform to it in most cases—it has the potential of saving court time in a substantial though proportionately small number of cases tried annually.

The inclusion of testing and sampling of tangible things and objects or operations on land reflects a need frequently encountered by parties in preparation for trial. If the operation of a particular machine is the basis of a claim for negligent injury, it will often be necessary to test its operating parts or to sample and test the products it is producing. *Cf.* Mich.Gen.Ct.R. 310.1(1) (1963) (testing authorized).

The inclusive description of "documents" is revised to accord with changing technology. It makes clear that Rule 34 applies to electronic data compilations from which information can be obtained only with the use of detection devices, and that when the data can as a practical matter be made usable by the discovering party only through respondent's devices, respondent may be required to use his devices to translate the data into usable form. In many instances, this means that respondent will have to supply a print-out of computer data. The burden thus placed on respondent will vary from case to case, and the courts have ample power under Rule 26(c) to protect respondent against undue burden or expense, either by restricting discovery or requiring that the discovering party pay costs. Similarly, if the discovering party needs to check the electronic source itself, the court may protect respondent with respect to preservation of his records, confidentiality of nondiscoverable matters, and costs.

Subdivision (b). The procedure provided in Rule 34 is essentially the same as that in Rule 33, as amended, and the discussion in the note appended to that rule is relevant to Rule 34 as well. Problems peculiar to Rule 34 relate to the specific arrangements that must be worked out for inspection and related acts of copying, photographing, testing, or sampling. The rule provides that a request for inspection shall set forth the items to be inspected either by item or category, describing each with reasonable particularity, and shall specify a reasonable time, place, and manner of making the inspection.

Subdivision (c). Rule 34 as revised continues to apply only to parties. Comments from the bar make clear that in the preparation of cases for trial it is occasionally necessary to enter land or inspect large tangible things in the possession of a person not a party, and that some courts have dismissed independent actions in the nature of bills in equity for such discovery on the ground that Rule 34 is preemptive. While an ideal solution to this problem is to provide for discovery against persons not parties in Rule 34, both the jurisdictional and procedural problems are very complex. For the present, this subdivision makes clear that Rule 34 does not preclude independent actions for discovery against persons not parties.

Rule 35. Physical and Mental Examination of Persons

(a) Order for Examination. ~~In an action in which~~ *When* the mental or physical condition *(including the blood group)* of a party, *or of a person in the custody or under the legal control of a party,* is in controversy, the court in which the action is pending may order ~~him~~ *the party* to submit to a physical or mental examination by a physician *or to produce for examination the person in his custody or legal control.* The order may be made only on motion for good cause shown and upon notice to the ~~party~~ *person* to be examined and to all ~~other~~ parties and shall specify the time, place, manner, conditions, and scope of the examination and the person or persons by whom it is to be made.

(b) Report of *Examining Physician* ~~**Findings**~~**.**

(1) If requested by the *party against whom an order is made under Rule 35(a) or the* person examined, the party causing the examination to be made shall deliver to him a copy of a detailed written report of the examining physician setting out his findings, *including results of all tests made, diagnoses* and conclusions~~.~~, *together with like reports of all earlier examinations of the same condition.* After ~~such request and~~ delivery the party causing the

New matter is shown in italics; matter to be omitted is lined through

examination ~~to be made~~ shall be entitled upon request to receive from the party ~~examined~~ *against whom the order is made* a like report of any examination, previously or thereafter made, of the same ~~mental or physical~~ condition~~.~~, *unless, in the case of a report of examination of a person not a party, the party shows that he is unable to obtain it.* ~~If the party examined refuses to deliver such report t~~*T*he court on motion ~~and notice~~ may make an order *against a party* requiring delivery of a *report* on such terms as are just, and if a physician fails or refuses to make ~~such~~ a report the court may exclude his testimony if offered at the trial.

(2) By requesting and obtaining a report of the examination so ordered or by taking the deposition of the examiner, the party examined waives any privilege he may have in that action or any other involving the same controversy, regarding the testimony of every other person who has examined or may thereafter examine him in respect of the same mental or physical condition.

(3) This subdivision applies to examinations made by agreement of the parties, unless the agreement expressly provides otherwise. This subdivision does not preclude discovery of a report of an examining physician or the taking of a deposition of the physician in accordance with the provisions of any other rule.

Advisory Committee's Note

Subdivision (a). Rule 35(a) has hitherto provided only for an order requiring a party to submit to an examination. It is desirable to extend the rule to provide for an order against the party for examination of a person in his custody or under his legal control. As appears from the provisions of amended Rule 37(b)(2) and the comment under that rule, an order to "produce" the third person imposes only an obligation to use good faith efforts to produce the person.

The amendment will settle beyond doubt that a parent or guardian suing to recover for injuries to a minor may be ordered to produce the minor for examination. Further, the amendment expressly includes blood examination within the kinds of examinations that can be ordered under the rule. See *Beach v. Beach,* 114 F.2d 479 (D.C.Cir.1940). Provisions similar to the amendment have been adopted in at least 10 States: Calif.Code Civ.Proc. § 2032; Ida.R.Civ.P. 35; Ill. S–H Ann. c. 110A, § 215; Md.R.P. 420; Mich.Gen.Ct.R. 311; Minn.R.Civ.P. 35; Mo.Vern.Ann.R.Civ.P. 60.01; N.Dak.R.Civ.P. 35; N.Y.C.P.L. § 3121; Wyo.R.Civ.R. 35.

The amendment makes no change in the requirements of Rule 35 that, before a court order may issue, the relevant physical or mental condition must be shown to be "in controversy" and "good cause" must be shown for the examination. Thus, the amendment has no effect on the recent decision of the Supreme Court in *Schlagenhauf v. Holder,* 379 U.S. 104 (1964), stressing the importance of these requirements and applying them to the facts of the case. The amendment makes no reference to employees of a party. Provisions relating to employees in the State statutes and rules cited above appear to have been virtually unused.

Subdivision (b)(1). This subdivision is amended to correct an imbalance in Rule 35(b)(1) as heretofore written. Under that text, a party causing a Rule 35(a) examination to be made is required to furnish to the party examined, on request, a copy of the examining physician's report. If he delivers this copy, he is in turn entitled to receive from the party examined reports of all examinations of the same condition previously or later made. But the rule has not in terms entitled the examined party to receive from the party causing the Rule 35(a) examination any reports of earlier examinations of the same condition to which the latter may have access. The amendment cures this defect. See La.Stat.Ann., Civ.Proc. art. 1495 (1960); Utah R.Civ.P. 35(c).

The amendment specifies that the written report of the examining physician includes results of all tests made, such as results of X-rays and cardiograms. It also embodies changes required by the broadening of Rule 35(a) to take in persons who are not parties.

Subdivision (b)(3). This new subdivision removes any possible doubt that reports of examination may be obtained although no order for examination has been made under Rule 35(a). Examinations are very frequently made by agreement, and sometimes before the party examined has an attorney. The courts have uniformly ordered that reports be supplied, see 4 *Moore's Federal Practice* ¶ 35.06, n. 1 (2d ed. 1966); 2A Barron & Holtzoff, *Federal Practice and Procedure* § 823, n. 22 (Wright ed. 1961), and it appears best to fill the technical gap in the present rule.

The subdivision also makes clear that reports of examining physicians are discoverable not only under Rule 35(b) but under other rules as well. To be sure, if the report is privileged, then discovery is not permissible under any rule other than Rule 35(b) and it is permissible under Rule 35(b) only if the party requests a copy of the report of examination made by the other party's doctor. *Sher v. De Haven,* 199 F.2d 777 (D.C.Cir.1952), *cert. denied* 345 U.S. 936 (1953). But if the report is unprivileged and is subject to discovery under the provisions of rules other than Rule 35(b)—such as Rules 34 or 26(b)(3) or (4)—discovery should not depend upon whether the person examined demands a copy of the report. Although a few cases have suggested the contrary, *e. g., Galloway v. National Dairy Products Corp.,* 24 F.R.D. 362 (E.D.Pa.1959), the better considered district court decisions hold that Rule 35(b) is not preemptive. *E. g., Leszynski v. Russ,* 29 F.R.D. 10, 12 (D.Md.1961) and cases cited. The question was recently given full consideration in *Buffington v. Wood,* 351 F.2d 292 (3d Cir.1965), holding that Rule 35(b) is not preemptive.

Rule 36. *Requests for* Admission ~~of Facts and of Genuineness of Documents~~

(a) Request for Admission. ~~After commencement of an action a party may serve upon any other party a written request for the admission by the latter of the genuineness of any relevant documents described in and exhibited with the request or of the truth of any relevant matters of fact set forth in the request. If a plaintiff desires to serve a request within 10 days after commencement of the action leave of court, granted with or without notice, must be obtained. Copies of the documents shall be served with the request unless copies have already been furnished.~~ *A party may serve upon any other party a written request for the admission, for purposes of the pending action only, of the truth of any matters within the scope of Rule 26(b) set forth in the request that relate to statements or opinions of fact or of the application of law to fact,*

New matter is shown in italics; matter to be omitted is lined through

including the genuineness of any documents described in the request. Copies of documents shall be served with the request unless they have been or are otherwise furnished or made available for inspection and copying. The request may, without leave of court, be served upon the plaintiff after commencement of the action and upon any other party with or after service of the summons and complaint upon that party.

Each ~~of the matters~~ *matter* of which an admission is requested *shall be separately set forth.* ~~shall be deemed~~ *The matter is* admitted unless, within ~~a period designated in the request, not less than 10~~ *30* days after service ~~thereof~~ *of the request,* or within such shorter or longer time as the court may allow ~~on motion and notice~~, the party to whom the request is directed serves upon the party requesting the admission ~~either (1) a sworn statement denying~~ *a written answer or objection addressed to the matter, signed by the party or by his attorney, but, unless the court shortens the time, a defendant shall not be required to serve answers or objections before the expiration of 45 days after service of the summons and complaint upon him. If objection is made, the reasons therefor shall be stated. The answer shall* specifically *deny* the ~~matters of which an admission is requested~~ *matter* or ~~setting~~ *set* forth in detail the reasons why ~~he~~ *the answering party* cannot truthfully admit or deny ~~those matters~~ *the matter.* ~~or (2) written objections on the ground that some or all of the requested admissions are privileged or irrelevant or that the request is otherwise improper in whole or in part, together with a notice of hearing the objections at the earliest practicable time. If written objections to a part of the request are made, the remainder of the request shall be answered within the period designated in the request.~~ A denial shall fairly meet the substance of the requested admission, and when good faith requires that a party *qualify his answer or* deny only a part ~~or a qualification~~ of ~~a~~ *the* matter of which an admission is requested, he shall specify so much of it as is true and *qualify or* deny ~~only~~ the remainder. *An answering party may not give lack of information or knowledge as a reason for failure to admit or deny unless he states that he has made reasonable inquiry and that the information known or readily obtainable by him is insufficient to enable him to admit or deny. A party who considers that a matter of which an admission has been requested presents a genuine issue for trial may not, on that ground alone, object to the request; he may, subject to the provisions of Rule 37(c), deny the matter or set forth reasons why he cannot admit or deny it.*

The party who has requested the admissions may move to determine the sufficiency of the answers or objections. Unless the court determines that an objection is justified, it shall order that an

---

New matter is shown in italics; matter to be omitted is lined through

answer be served. If the court determines that an answer does not comply with the requirements of this rule, it may order either that the matter is admitted or that an amended answer be served. The court may, in lieu of these orders, determine that final disposition of the request be made at a pre-trial conference or at a designated time prior to trial. The provisions of Rule 37(a)(4) apply to the award of expenses incurred in relation to the motion.

(b) Effect of Admission. *Any matter admitted under this rule is conclusively established unless the court on motion permits withdrawal or amendment of the admission. Subject to the provisions of Rule 16 governing amendment of a pre-trial order, the court may permit withdrawal or amendment when the presentation of the merits of the action will be subserved thereby and the party who obtained the admission fails to satisfy the court that withdrawal or amendment will prejudice him in maintaining his action or defense on the merits.* Any admission made by a party ~~pursuant to such request~~ *under this rule* is for the purpose of the pending action only and ~~neither constitutes~~ *is not* an admission by him for any other other purpose nor may *it* be used against him in any other proceeding.

Advisory Committee's Note

Rule 36 serves two vital purposes, both of which are designed to reduce trial time. Admissions are sought, first to facilitate proof with respect to issues that cannot be eliminated from the case, and secondly, to narrow the issues by eliminating those that can be. The changes made in the rule are designed to serve these purposes more effectively. Certain disagreements in the courts about the proper scope of the rule are resolved. In addition, the procedural operation of the rule is brought into line with other discovery procedures, and the binding effect of an admission is clarified. See generally Finman, *The Request for Admissions in Federal Civil Procedure*, 71 Yale L.J. 371 (1962).

Subdivision (a). As revised, the subdivision provides that a request may be made to admit any matters within the scope of Rule 26(b) that relate to statements or opinions of fact or of the application of law to fact. It thereby eliminates the requirement that the matters be "of fact." This change resolves conflicts in the court decisions as to whether a request to admit matters of "opinion" and matters involving "mixed law and fact" is proper under the rule. As to "opinion," *compare, e. g., Jackson Bluff Corp. v. Marcelle,* 20 F.R.D. 139 (E.D.N.Y.1957); *California v. The S. S. Jules Fribourg,* 19 F.R.D. 432 (N.D.Calif.1955), *with e. g., Photon, Inc. v. Harris Intertype, Inc.*, 28 F.R.D. 327 (D.Mass.1961); *Hise v. Lockwood Grader Corp.*, 153 F.Supp. 276 (D.Nebr.1957). As to "mixed law and fact" the majority of courts sustain objections, *e. g., Minnesota Mining and Mfg. Co. v. Norton Co.,* 36 F.R.D. 1 (N.D.Ohio 1964), but *McSparran v. Hanigan*, 225 F.Supp. 628 (E.D.Pa.1963) is to the contrary.

Not only is it difficult as a practical matter to separate "fact" from "opinion," see 4 *Moore's Federal Practice* ¶ 36.04 (2d ed. 1966); *cf.* 2A Barron & Holtzoff, *Federal Practice and Procedure* 317 (Wright ed. 1961), but an admission on a matter of opinion may facilitate proof or narrow the issues or both. An admission of a matter involving the application of law to fact may, in a given case, even more clearly narrow the issues. For example, an admission that an employee acted in the scope of his employment may remove a major issue from the trial. In *McSparran v. Hanigan, supra,* plaintiff admitted that "the premises on which said accident occurred, were occupied or under the control" of one of the defendants, 225 F.Supp. at 636. This admission, involving law as well as fact, removed one of the issues from the lawsuit and thereby reduced the proof required at trial. The amended provision does not authorize requests for admissions of law unrelated to the facts of the case.

Requests for admission involving the application of law to fact may create disputes between the parties which are best resolved in the presence of the judge after much or all of the other discovery has been completed. Power is therefore expressly conferred upon the court to defer decision until a pretrial conference is held or until a designated time prior to trial. On the other hand, the court should not automatically defer decision; in many instances, the importance of the admission lies in enabling the requesting party to avoid the burdensome accumulation of proof prior to the pretrial conference.

Courts have also divided on whether an answering party may properly object to request for admission as to matters which that party regards as "in dispute." *Compare, e. g., Syracuse Broadcasting Corp. v. Newhouse,* 271 F.2d 910, 917 (2d Cir.1959); *Driver v. Gindy Mfg. Corp.*, 24 F.R.D. 473 (E.D.Pa.1959); *with, e. g., McGonigle v. Baxter*, 27 F.R.D. 504 (E.D.Pa.1961); *United States v. Ehbauer*, 13 F.R.D. 462 (W.D.Mo.1952). The proper response in such cases is an answer. The very purpose of the request is to ascertain whether the answering party is prepared to admit or regards the matter as presenting a genuine issue for trial. In his answer, the party may deny, or he may give as his reason for inability to admit or deny the existence of a genuine issue. The party runs no risk of sanctions if the matter is genuinely in issue, since Rule 37(c) provides a sanction of costs only when there are no good reasons for a failure to admit.

On the other hand, requests to admit may be so voluminous and so framed that the answering party finds the task of identifying what is in dispute and what is not unduly burdensome. If so, the responding party may obtain a protective order under Rule 26(c). Some of the decisions sustaining objections on "disputability" grounds could have been justified by the burdensome character of the requests. See, *e. g., Syracuse Broadcasting Corp. v. Newhouse, supra.*

Another sharp split of authority exists on the question whether a party may base his answer on lack of information or knowledge without seeking out additional information. One line of cases has held that a party may answer on the basis of such knowledge as he has at the time he answers. *E. g., Jackson Buff Corp. v. Marcelle,* 20 F.R.D. 139 (E.D.N.Y.1957); *Sladek v. General Motors Corp.*, 16 F.R.D. 104 (S.D.Iowa 1954). A larger group of cases, supported by commentators, has taken the view that if the responding party lacks knowledge, he must inform himself in reasonable fashion. *E. g., Hise v. Lockwood Grader Corp.*, 153 F.Supp. 276 (D.Nebr.1957); *E. H. Tate Co. v. Jiffy Enterprises, Inc.*, 16 F.R.D. 571 (E.D.Pa.1954); Finman, *supra*, 71 Yale L.J. 371, 404–409; 4 *Moore's Federal Practice* ¶ 36.04 (2d ed. 1966); 2A Barron & Holtzoff, *Federal Practice and Procedure* 509 (Wright ed. 1961).

The rule as revised adopts the majority view, as in keeping with a basic principle of the discovery rules that a reasonable burden may be imposed on the parties when its discharge will facilitate preparation for trial and ease the trial process. It has been argued against this view that one side should not have the burden of "proving" the other side's case. The revised rule requires only that the answering party make reasonable inquiry and secure such knowledge and information as are readily obtainable by him. In most instances, the investigation will be necessary either to his own case or to preparation for rebuttal. Even when it is not, the information may be close enough at hand to be "readily obtainable." Rule 36 requires only that the party state that he has taken these steps. The sanction for failure of a party to inform himself before he answers lies in the award of costs after trial, as provided in Rule 37(c).

The requirement that the answer to a request for admission be sworn is deleted, in favor of a provision that the answer be signed by the party or by his attorney. The provisions of Rule 36 make it clear that admissions function very much as pleadings do. Thus, when a party admits in part and denies in part, his admission is for purposes of the pending action only and may not be used against him in any other proceeding. The broadening of the rule to encompass mixed questions of law and fact reinforces this feature. Rule 36 does not lack a sanction for false answers; Rule 37(c) furnishes an appropriate deterrent.

The existing language describing the available grounds for objection to a request for admission is eliminated as neither necessary nor helpful. The statement that objection may be made to any request which is "improper" adds nothing to the provisions that the party serve an answer or objection addressed to each matter and that he state his reasons for any objection. None of the other discovery rules sets forth grounds for objection, except so far as all are subject to the general provisions of Rule 26.

Changes are made in the sequence of procedures in Rule 36 so that they conform to the new procedures in Rules 33 and 34. The major changes are as follows:

(1) The normal time for response to a request for admissions is lengthened from 10 to 30 days, conforming more closely to prevailing practice. A defendant need not respond, however, in less than 45 days after service of the summons and complaint upon him. The court may lengthen or shorten the time when special situations require it.

(2) The present requirement that the plaintiff wait 10 days to serve requests without leave of court is eliminated. The revised provision accords with those in Rules 33 and 34.

(3) The requirement that the objecting party move automatically for a hearing on his objection is eliminated, and the burden is on the requesting party to move for an order. The change in the burden of going forward does not modify present law on burden of persuasion. The award of expenses incurred in relation to the motion is made subject to the comprehensive provisions of Rule 37(a)(4).

(4) A problem peculiar to Rule 36 arises if the responding party serves answers that are not in conformity with the requirements of the rule—for example, a denial is not "specific," or the explanation of inability to admit or deny is not "in detail." Rule 36 now makes no provision for court scrutiny of such answers before trial, and it seems to contemplate that defective answers bring about admissions just as effectively as if no answer had been served. Some cases have so held. *E. g., Southern Ry. Co. v. Crosby*, 201 F.2d 878 (4th Cir.1953); *United States v. Laney*, 96 F.Supp. 482 (E.D.S.C.1951).

Giving a defective answer the automatic effect of an admission may cause unfair surprise. A responding party who purported to deny or to be unable to admit or deny will for the first time at trial confront the contention that he has made a binding admission. Since it is not always easy to know whether a denial is "specific" or an explanation is "in detail," neither party can know how the court will rule at trial and whether proof must be prepared. Some courts, therefore, have entertained motions to rule on defective answers. They have at times ordered that amended answers be served, when the defects were technical, and at other times have declared that the matter was admitted. *E. g., Woods v. Stewart,* 171 F.2d 544 (5th Cir.1948); *SEC v. Kaye, Real & Co.*, 122 F.Supp. 639 (S.D.N.Y.1954); *Sieb's Hatcheries, Inc. v. Lindley*, 13 F.R.D. 113 (W.D.Ark.1952). The rule as revised conforms to the latter practice.

Subdivision (b). The rule does not now indicate the extent to which a party is bound by his admission. Some courts view admissions as the equivalent of sworn testimony. *E. g., Ark-Tenn Distributing Corp. v. Breidt*, 209 F.2d 359 (3d Cir.1954); *United States v. Lemons*, 125 F.Supp. 686 (W.D.Ark.1954); 4 *Moore's Federal Practice* ¶ 36.08 (2d ed. 1966 Supp.). At least in some jurisdictions a party may rebut his own testimony, *e. g., Alamo v. Del Rosario*, 98 F.2d 328 (D.C.Cir.1938), and by analogy an admission made pursuant to Rule 36 may likewise be thought rebuttable. The courts in *Ark-Tenn* and *Lemons, supra,* reasoned in this way, although the results reached may be supported on different grounds. In *McSparran v. Hanigan*, 225 F.Supp. 628, 636–637 (E.D.Pa.1963), the court held that an admission is conclusively binding, though noting the confusion created by prior decisions.

The new provisions give an admission a conclusively binding effect, for purposes only of the pending action, unless the admission is withdrawn or amended. In form and substance a Rule 36 admission is comparable to an admission in pleadings or a stipulation drafted by counsel for use at trial, rather than to an evidentiary admission of a party. Louisell, *Modern California Discovery* § 8.07 (1963); 2A Barron & Holtzoff, *Federal Practice and Procedure* § 838 (Wright ed. 1961). Unless the party securing an admission can depend on its binding effect, he cannot safely avoid the expense of preparing to prove the very matters on which he has secured the admission, and the purpose of the rule is defeated. Field & McKusick, *Maine Civil Practice* § 36.4 (1959); Finman, *supra,* 71 Yale L.J. 371, 418–426; Comment, 56 Nw.U.L.Rev. 679, 682–683 (1961).

Provision is made for withdrawal or amendment of an admission. This provision emphasizes the importance of having the action resolved on the merits, while at the same time assuring each party that justified reliance on an admission in preparation for trial will not operate to his prejudice. *Cf. Moosman v. Joseph P. Blitz, Inc.*, 358 F.2d 686 (2d Cir.1966).

Rule 37. ~~Refusal~~ *Failure* to Make Discovery: ~~Consequences~~ *Sanctions*

~~**(a) Refusal to Answer.** If a party or other deponent refuses to answer any question propounded upon oral examination, the examination shall be completed on other matters or adjourned, as the proponent of the question may prefer. Thereafter, on reasonable notice to all persons affected thereby, he may apply to the court in the district where the deposition is taken for an order compelling an answer. Upon the refusal of a deponent to answer any interrogatory submitted under Rule 31 or upon the refusal of a party to answer any interrogatory submitted under Rule 33, the proponent of the question may on like notice make like application for such an order. If the motion is granted and if the court finds that the refusal was without substantial justification the court shall require the refusing party or deponent and the party or attorney~~

~~advising the refusal or either of them to pay to the examining party the amount of the reasonable expenses incurred in obtaining the order, including reasonable attorney's fees. If the motion is denied and if the court finds that the motion was made without substantial justification, the court shall require the examining party or the attorney advising the motion or both of them to pay to the refusing party or witness the amount of the reasonable expenses incurred in opposing the motion, including reasonable attorney's fees.~~

(a) Motion for Order Compelling Discovery. A party, upon reasonable notice to other parties and all persons affected thereby, may apply for an order compelling discovery as follows:

(1) Appropriate Court. An application for an order to a party may be made to the court in which the action is pending, or, on matters relating to a deposition, to the court in the district where the deposition is being taken. An application for an order to a deponent who is not a party shall be made to the court in the district where the deposition is being taken.

(2) Motion. If a deponent fails to answer a question propounded or submitted under Rule 30 or 31, or a corporation or other entity fails to make a designation under Rule 30(b)(6) or 31(a), or a party fails to answer an interrogatory submitted under Rule 33, or if a party, in response to a request for inspection submitted under Rule 34, fails to respond that inspection will be permitted as requested or fails to permit inspection as requested, the discovering party may move for an order compelling an answer, or a designation, or an order compelling inspection in accordance with the request. When taking a deposition on oral examination, the proponent of the question may complete or adjourn the examination before he applies for an order.

If the court denies the motion in whole or in part, it may make such protective order as it would have been empowered to make on a motion made pursuant to Rule 26(c).

(3) Evasive or Incomplete Answer. For purposes of this subdivision an evasive or incomplete answer is to be treated as a failure to answer.

(4) Award of Expenses of Motion. If the motion is granted, the court shall, after opportunity for hearing, require the party or deponent whose conduct necessitated the motion or the party or attorney advising such conduct or both of them to pay to the moving party the reasonable expenses incurred in obtaining the order, including attorney's fees, unless the court finds that the opposition to the motion was substantially justified or that other circumstances make an award of expenses unjust.

If the motion is denied, the court shall, after opportunity for hearing, require the moving party or the attorney advising the motion or both of them to pay the party or deponent who opposed the motion the reasonable expenses incurred in opposing the motion, including attorney's fees, unless the court finds that the making of the motion was substantially justified or that other circumstances make an award of expenses unjust.

If the motion is granted in part and denied in part, the court may apportion the reasonable expenses incurred in relation to the motion among the parties and persons in a just manner.

(b) Failure to Comply With Order.

(1) ~~**Contempt**~~ *Sanctions by Court in District Where Deposition is Taken.* If a ~~party or other~~ *deponent* ~~witness refuses~~ *fails* to be sworn or ~~refuses~~ to answer ~~any~~ *a* question after being directed to do so by the court in the district in which the deposition is being taken, the ~~refusal~~ *failure* may be considered a contempt of that court.

(2) ~~**Other Consequences**~~ *Sanctions by Court in Which Action is Pending.* If ~~any~~ *a* party or an officer, *director,* or managing agent of a party *or a person designated under Rule 30(b)(6) or 31(a) to testify on behalf of a party* ~~refuses~~ *fails* to obey an order *to provide or permit discovery, including an order* made under subdivision (a) of this rule ~~requiring him to answer designated questions, or an order made under Rule 34 to produce any document or other thing for inspection, copying, or photographing or to permit it to be done, or to permit entry upon land or other property, or an order made under~~ *or* Rule 35 ~~requiring him to submit to a physical or mental examination~~, the court *in which the action is pending* may make such orders in regard to the ~~refusal~~ *failure* as are just, and among others the following:

~~(i)~~*(A)* An order that the matters regarding which the ~~questions were asked, or the character or description of the thing or land, or the contents of the paper, or the physical or mental condition of the party,~~ *order was made* or any other designated facts shall be taken to be established for the purposes of the action in accordance with the claim of the party obtaining the order;

~~(ii)~~*(B)* An order refusing to allow the disobedient party to support or oppose designated claims or defenses, or prohibiting him from introducing *designated matters* in evidence ~~designated documents or things or items of testimony, or from introducing evidence of physical or mental condition~~;

~~(iii)~~*(C)* An order striking out pleadings or parts thereof, or staying further proceedings until the order is obeyed, or dismissing

New matter is shown in italics; matter to be omitted is lined through

the action or proceeding or any part thereof, or rendering a judgment by default against the disobedient party;

~~(iv)~~*(D)* In lieu of any of the foregoing orders or in addition thereto, an order ~~directing the arrest of any party or agent of a party for disobeying~~ *treating as a contempt of court the failure to obey* any ~~of such~~ orders except an order to submit to a physical or mental examination~~.~~*;*

(E) Where a party has failed to comply with an order under Rule 35(a) requiring him to produce another for examination, such orders as are listed in paragraphs (A), (B), and (C) of this subdivision, unless the party failing to comply shows that he is unable to produce such person for examination.

In lieu of any of the foregoing orders or in addition thereto, the court shall require the party failing to obey the order or the attorney advising him or both to pay the reasonable expenses, including attorney's fees, caused by the failure, unless the court finds that the failure was substantially justified or that other circumstances make an award of expenses unjust.

(c) Expenses on ~~Refusal~~ *Failure* **To Admit.** If a party ~~after being served with request under Rule 36,~~ *fails* to admit the genuineness of any documents or the truth of any matter~~s of fact~~ *as requested under Rule 36,* ~~serves a sworn denial thereof~~ and if the party requesting the admissions thereafter proves the genuineness of ~~any such~~ *the* document or the truth of ~~any such~~ *the* matter ~~of fact~~, he may apply to the court for an order requiring the other party to pay him the reasonable expenses incurred in making ~~such~~ *that* proof, including reasonable attorney's fees. ~~Unless the court finds that there were good reasons for the denial or that the admissions sought were of no substantial importance, the order shall be made.~~ *The court shall make the order unless it finds that (1) the request was held objectionable pursuant to Rule 36(a), or (2) the admission sought was of no substantial importance, or (3) the party failing to admit had reasonable ground to believe that he might prevail on the matter, or (4) there was other good reason for the failure to admit.*

(d) Failure of Party To Attend *at Own Deposition* **or Serve Answers** *to Interrogatories or Respond to Request for Inspection.* If a party or an officer, *director,* or managing agent of a party *or a person designated under Rule 30(b)(6) or 31(a) to testify on behalf of a party* ~~wilfully~~ fails *(1)* to appear before the officer who is to take his deposition, after being served with a proper notice, or ~~fails~~ *(2)* to serve answers *or objections* to interrogatories submitted under Rule 33, after proper service of ~~such~~ *the* interrogatories, *or (3) to serve a written response to a request for inspection submitted under Rule 34,*

New matter is shown in italics; matter to be omitted is lined through

after proper service of the request, the court *in which the action is pending* on motion ~~and notice~~ may ~~strike out all or any part of any pleading of that party, or dismiss the action or proceeding or any part thereof, or enter a judgment by default against that party.~~ *make such orders in regard to the failure as are just, and among others it may take any action authorized under paragraph (A), (B), and (C) of subdivision (b)(2) of this rule. In lieu of any order or in addition thereto, the court shall require the party failing to act or the attorney advising him or both to pay the reasonable expenses, including attorney's fees, caused by the failure, unless the court finds that the failure was substantially justified or that other circumstances make an award of expenses unjust.*

The failure to act described in this subdivision may not be excused on the ground that the discovery sought is objectionable unless the party failing to act has applied for a protective order as provided by Rule 26(c).

(e) ~~**Failure To Respond to Letters Rogatory.**~~ *Subpoena of Person in Foreign Country.* A subpoena may be issued as provided in Title 28 U.S.C. § 1783, under the circumstances and conditions therein stated.

(f) Expenses Against United States. ~~Expenses and attorney's fees are not to be imposed upon~~ *Except to the extent permitted by statute, expenses and fees may not be awarded against* the United States under this rule.

Advisory Committee's Note

Rule 37 provides generally for sanctions against parties or persons unjustifiably resisting discovery. Experience has brought to light a number of defects in the language of the rule as well as instances in which it is not serving the purposes for which it was designed. See Rosenberg, *Sanctions to Effectuate Pretrial Discovery,* 58 Col.L.Rev. 480 (1958). In addition, changes being made in other discovery rules require conforming amendments to Rule 37.

Rule 37 sometimes refers to a "failure" to afford discovery and at other times to a "refusal" to do so. Taking note of this dual terminology, courts have imported into "refusal" a requirement of "wilfullness." See *Roth v. Paramount Pictures Corp.*, 8 F.R.D. 31 (W.D.Pa.1948); *Campbell v. Johnson*, 101 F.Supp. 705, 707 (S.D.N.Y.1951). In *Societe Internationale v. Rogers*, 357 U.S. 197 (1958), the Supreme Court concluded that the rather random use of these two terms in Rule 37 showed no design to use them with consistently distinctive meanings, that "refused" in Rule 37(b)(2) meant simply a failure to comply, and that wilfullness was relevant only to the selection of sanctions, if any, to be imposed. Nevertheless, after the decision in *Societe,* the court in *Hinson v. Michigan Mutual Liability Co.*, 275 F.2d 537 (5th Cir.1960) once again ruled that "refusal" required wilfullness. Substitution of "failure" for "refusal" throughout Rule 37 should eliminate this confusion and bring the rule into harmony with the *Societe Internationale* decision. See Rosenberg, *supra*, 58 Col.L.Rev. 480, 489–490 (1958).

Subdivision (a). Rule 37(a) provides relief to a party seeking discovery against one who, with or without stated objections, fails to afford the discovery sought. It has always fully served this function in relation to depositions, but the amendments being made to Rules 33 and 34 give Rule 37(a) added scope and importance. Under existing Rule 33, a party objecting to interrogatories must make a motion for court hearing on his objections. The changes now made in Rules 33 and 37(a) make it clear that the interrogating party must move to compel answers, and the motion is provided for in Rule 37(a). Existing Rule 34, since it requires a court order prior to production of documents or things or permission to enter on land, has no relation to Rule 37(a). Amendments of Rules 34 and 37(a) create a procedure similar to that provided for Rule 33.

Subdivision (a)(1). This is a new provision making clear to which court a party may apply for an order compelling discovery. Existing Rule 37(a) refers only to the court in which the deposition is being taken; nevertheless, it has been held that the court where the action is pending has "inherent power" to compel a party deponent to answer. *Lincoln Laboratories, Inc. v. Savage Laboratories, Inc.*, 27 F.R.D. 476 (D.Del.1961). In relation to Rule 33 interrogatories and Rule 34 requests for inspection, the court where the action is pending is the appropriate enforcing tribunal. The new provision eliminates the need to resort to inherent power by spelling out the respective roles of the court where the action is pending and the court where the deposition is taken. In some instances, two courts are available to a party seeking to compel answers from a party deponent. The party seeking discovery may choose the court to which he will apply, but the court has power to remit the party to the other court as a more appropriate forum.

Subdivision (a)(2). This subdivision contains the substance of existing provisions of Rule 37(a) authorizing motions to compel answers to questions put at depositions and to interrogatories. New provisions authorize motions for orders compelling designation under Rules 30(b) (6) and 31(a) and compelling inspection in accordance with a request made under Rule 34. If the court denies a motion, in whole or part, it may accompany the denial with issuance of a protective order. Compare the converse provision in Rule 26(c).

Subdivision (a)(3). This new provision makes clear that an evasive or incomplete answer is to be considered, for purposes of subdivision (a), a failure to answer. The courts have consistently held that they have the power to compel adequate answers. *E.g., Cone Mills Corp. v. Joseph Bancroft & Sons Co.*, 33 F.R.D. 318 (D.Del.1963). This power is recognized and incorporated into the rule.

Subdivision (a)(4). This subdivision amends the provisions for award of expenses, including reasonable attorney's fees, to the prevailing party or person when a motion is made for an order compelling discovery. At present, an award of expenses is made only if the losing party or person is found to have acted without substantial justification. The change requires that expenses be awarded unless the conduct of the losing party or person is found to have been substantially justified. The test of "substantial justification" remains, but the change in language is intended to encourage judges to be more alert to abuses occurring in the discovery process.

On many occasions, to be sure, the dispute over discovery between the parties is genuine, though ultimately resolved one way or the other by the court. In such cases, the losing party is substantially justified in carrying the matter to court. But the rules should deter the abuse implicit in carrying or forcing a discovery dispute to court when no genuine dispute exists. And the potential or actual imposition of expenses is virtually the sole formal sanction in the rules to deter a party from pressing to a court hearing frivolous requests for or objections to discovery.

The present provision of Rule 37(a) that the court shall require payment if it finds that the defeated party acted without "substantial justification" may appear adequate, but in fact it has been little used. Only a handful of reported cases include an award of expenses, and the Columbia Survey found that in only one instance out of about 50 motions decided under Rule 37(a) did the court award expenses. It appears that the courts do not utilize the most important available sanction to deter abusive resort to the judiciary.

The proposed change provides in effect that expenses should ordinarily be awarded unless a court finds that the losing party acted justifiably in carrying his point to court. At the same time, a necessary flexibility is maintained, since the court retains the power to find that other circumstances make an award of expenses unjust—as where, the prevailing party also acted unjustifiably. The amendment does not significantly narrow the discretion of the court, but rather presses the court to address itself to abusive practices. The present provision that expenses may be imposed upon either the party or his attorney or both is unchanged. But it is not contemplated that expenses will be imposed upon the attorney merely because the party is indigent.

Subdivision (b). This subdivision deals with sanctions for failure to comply with a court order. The present captions for subsections (1) and (2) entitled, "Contempt" and "Other Consequences," respectively, are confusing. One of the consequences listed in (2) is the arrest of the party, representing the exercise of the contempt power. The contents of the subsections show that the first authorizes the sanction of contempt (and no other) by the court in which the deposition is taken, whereas the second subsection authorizes a variety of sanctions, including contempt, which may be imposed by the court in which the action is pending. The captions of the subsections are changed to reflect their contents.

The scope of Rule 37(b)(2) is broadened by extending it to include any order "to provide or permit discovery," including orders issued under Rules 37(a) and 35. Various rules authorize orders for discovery—*e.g.*, Rule 35(b)(1), Rule 26(c) as revised, Rule 37(d). See Rosenberg, *supra,* 58 Col.L.Rev. 480, 484–486. Rule 37(b)(2) should provide comprehensively for enforcement of all these orders. *Cf. Societe Internationale v. Rogers,* 357 U.S. 197, 207 (1958). On the other hand, the reference to Rule 34 is deleted to conform to the changed procedure in that rule.

A new subsection (E) provides that sanctions which have been available against a party for failure to comply with an order under Rule 35(a) to submit to examination will now be available against him for his failure to comply with a Rule 35(a) order to produce a third person for examination, unless he shows that he is unable to produce the person. In this context, "unable" means in effect "unable in good faith." See *Societe Internationale v. Rogers,* 357 U.S. 197 (1958).

Subdivision (b)(2) is amplified to provide for payment of reasonable expenses caused by the failure to obey the order. Although Rules 37(b)(2) and 37(d) have been silent as to award of expenses, courts have nevertheless ordered them on occasion. *E.g., United Sheeplined Clothing Co. v. Arctic Fur Cap Corp.,* 165 F.Supp. 193 (S.D.N.Y.1958); *Austin Theatre, Inc. v. Warner Bros. Pictures, Inc.,* 22 F.R.D. 302 (S.D.N.Y.1958). The provision places the burden on the disobedient party to avoid expenses by showing that his failure is justified or that special circumstances make an award of expenses unjust. Allocating the burden in this way conforms to the changed provisions as to expenses in Rule 37(a), and is particularly appropriate when a court order is disobeyed.

An added reference to directors of a party is similar to a change made in subdivision (d) and is explained in the note to that subdivision. The added reference to persons designated by a party under Rules 30(b)(6) or 31(a) to testify on behalf of the party carries out the new procedure in those rules for taking a deposition of a corporation or other organization.

Subdivision (c). Rule 37(c) provides a sanction for the enforcement of Rule 36 dealing with requests for admission. Rule 36 provides the mechanism whereby a party may obtain from another party in appropriate instances either (1) an admission, or (2) a sworn and specific denial, or (3) a sworn statement "setting forth in detail the reasons why he cannot truthfully admit or deny." If the party obtains the second or third of these responses, in proper form, Rule 36 does not provide for a pretrial hearing on whether the response is warranted by the evidence thus far accumulated. Instead, Rule 37(c) is intended to provide posttrial relief in the form of a requirement that the party improperly refusing the admission pay the expenses of the other side in making the necessary proof at trial.

Rule 37(c), as now written, addresses itself in terms only to the sworn denial and is silent with respect to the statement of reasons for an inability to admit or deny. There is no apparent basis for this distinction, since the sanction provided in Rule 37(c) should deter all unjustified failures to admit. This omission in the rule has caused confused and diverse treatment in the courts. One court has held that if a party gives inadequate reasons, he should be treated before trial as having denied the request, so that Rule 37(c) may apply. *Bertha Bldg. Corp. v. National Theatres Corp.,* 15 F.R.D. 339 (E.D.N.Y.1954). Another has held that the party should be treated as having admitted the request. *Heng Hsin Co. v. Stern, Morgenthau & Co.,* 20 Fed.Rules Serv. 36a.52, Case 1 (S.D.N.Y. Dec. 10, 1954). Still another has ordered a new response, without indicating what the outcome should be if the new response were inadequate. *United States Plywood Corp. v. Hudson Lumber Co.,* 127 F.Supp. 489, 497–498 (S.D.N.Y.1954). See generally Finman, *The Request for Admissions in Federal Civil Procedure,* 71 Yale L.J. 371, 426–430 (1962). The amendment eliminates this defect in Rule 37(c) by bringing within its scope all failures to admit.

Additional provisions in Rule 37(c) protect a party from having to pay expenses if the request for admission was held objectionable under Rule 36(a) or if the party failing to admit had reasonable ground to believe that he might prevail on the matter. The latter provision emphasizes that the true test under Rule 37(c) is not whether a party prevailed at trial but whether he acted reasonably in believing that he might prevail.

Subdivision (d). The scope of subdivision (d) is broadened to include responses to requests for inspection under Rule 34, thereby conforming to the new procedures of Rule 34.

Two related changes are made in subdivision (d): the permissible sanctions are broadened to include such orders "as are just"; and the requirement that the failure to appear or respond be "wilful" is eliminated. Although Rule 37(d) in terms provides for only three sanctions, all rather severe, the courts have interpreted it as permitting softer sanctions than those which it sets forth. *E.g., Gill v. Stolow,* 240 F.2d 669 (2d Cir.1957); *Saltzman v. Birrell,* 156 F.Supp. 538 (S.D.N.Y.1957); 2A Barron & Holtzoff, *Federal Practice and Procedure* 554–557 (Wright ed. 1961). The rule is changed to provide the greater flexibility as to sanctions which the cases show is needed.

The resulting flexibility as to sanctions eliminates any need to retain the requirement that the failure to appear or respond be "wilful." The concept of "wilful failure" is at best subtle and difficult, and the cases do not supply a bright line. Many courts have imposed sanctions without referring to wilfullness. *E.g., Milewski v. Schneider Transportation Co.,* 238 F.2d 397 (6th Cir.1956); *Dictograph Products, Inc. v. Kentworth Corp.,* 7 F.R.D. 543 (W.D.Ky.1947). In addition, in view of the possibility of light sanctions, even a negligent failure should come within Rule 37(d). If default is caused by counsel's ignorance of Federal practice, *cf. Dunn v. Pa. R. R.*, 96 F.Supp. 597 (N.D.Ohio 1951), or by his preoccupation with another aspect of the case, *cf. Maurer-Neuer, Inc. v. United Packinghouse Workers,* 26 F.R.D. 139 (D.Kans.1960), dismissal of the action and default judgment are not justified, but the imposition of expenses and fees may well be. "Wilfullness" continues to play a role, along with various other factors, in the choice of sanctions. Thus, the scheme conforms to Rule 37(b) as construed by the Supreme Court in *Societe Internationale v. Rogers,* 357 U.S. 197, 208 (1958).

A provision is added to make clear that a party may not properly remain completely silent even when he regards a notice to take his deposition or a set of interrogatories or requests to inspect as improper and objectionable. If he desires not to appear or not to respond, he must apply for a protective order. The cases are divided on whether a protective order must be sought. Compare *Collins v. Wayland,* 139 F.2d 677 (9th Cir.1944), *cert. den.* 322 U.S. 744; *Bourgeois v. El Paso Natural Gas Co.,* 20 F.R.D. 358 (S.D.N.Y.1957); *Loosley v. Stone,* 15 F.R.D. 373 (S.D.Ill. 1954), with *Scarlatos v. Kulukundis,* 21 F.R.D. 185 (S.D.N.Y.1957); *Ross v. True Temper Corp.,* 11 F.R.D. 307 (N.D.Ohio 1951). Compare also Rosenberg, *supra,* 58 Col.L.Rev. 480, 496 (1958) with 2A Barron & Holtzoff, *Federal Practice and Procedure* 530–531 (Wright ed. 1961). The party from whom discovery is sought is afforded, through Rule 26(c), a fair and effective procedure whereby he can challenge the request made. At the same time, the total non-compliance with which Rule 37(d) is concerned may impose severe inconvenience or hardship on the discovering party and substantially delay the discovery process. *Cf.* 2B Barron & Holtzoff, *Federal Practice and Procedure* 306–307 (Wright ed. 1961) (response to a subpoena).

The failure of an officer or managing agent of a party to make discovery as required by present Rule 37(d) is treated as the failure of the party. The rule as revised provides similar treatment for a director of a party. There is slight warrant for the present distinction between officers and managing agents on the one hand and directors on the other. Although the legal power over a director to compel his making discovery may not be as great as over officers or managing agents, *Campbell v. General Motors Corp.,* 13 F.R.D. 331 (S.D.N.Y.1952), the practical differences are negligible. That a director's interests are normally aligned with those of his corporation is shown by the provisions of old Rule 26(d)(2), transferred to 32(a)(2) (deposition of director of party may be used at trial by an adverse party for any purpose) and of Rule 43(b) (director of party may be treated at trial as a hostile witness on direct examination by any adverse party). Moreover, in those rare instances when a corporation is unable through good faith efforts to compel a director to make discovery, it is unlikely that the court will impose sanctions. *Cf. Societe Internationale v. Rogers,* 357 U.S. 197 (1958).

Subdivision (e). The change in the caption conforms to the language of 28 U.S.C. § 1783, as amended in 1964.

Subdivision (f). Until recently, costs of a civil action could be awarded against the United States only when expressly provided by Act of Congress, and such provision was rarely made. See H.R.Rep.No.1535, 89th Cong., 2d Sess., 2–3 (1966). To avoid any conflict with this doctrine, Rule 37(f) has provided that expenses and attorney's fees may not be imposed upon the United States under Rule 37. See 2A Barron & Holtzoff, *Federal Practice and Procedure* 857 (Wright ed. 1961).

A major change in the law was made in 1966, 80 Stat. 308, 28 U.S.C. § 2412 (1966), whereby a judgment for costs may ordinarily be awarded to the prevailing party in any civil action brought by or against the United States. Costs are not to include the fees and expenses of attorneys. In light of this legislative development,

Rule 37(f) is amended to permit the award of expenses and fees against the United States under Rule 37, but only to the extent permitted by statute. The amendment brings Rule 37(f) into line with present and future statutory provisions.

Rule 45. Subpoena

(d) Subpoena for Taking Depositions; Place of Examination.

(1) Proof of service of a notice to take a deposition as provided in Rules ~~30(a)~~ *30(b)* and 31(a) constitutes a sufficient authorization for issuance by the clerk of the district court for the district in which the deposition is to be taken of subpoenas for the persons named or described therein. The subpoena may command the person to whom it is directed to produce *and permit inspection and copying of* designated books, papers, documents, or tangible things which constitute or contain ~~evidence relating to any of the~~ matters within the scope of the examination permitted by Rule 26(b), but in that event the subpoena will be subject to the provisions ~~of subdivision (b)~~ of Rule ~~30~~ *26(c)* and subdivision (b) of this ~~Rule 45~~ *rule.*

The person to whom the subpoena is directed may, within 10 days after the service thereof or on or before the time specified in the subpoena for compliance if such time is less than 10 days after service, serve upon the attorney designated in the subpoena written objection to inspection or copying of any or all of the designated materials. If objection is made, the party serving the subpoena shall not be entitled to inspect and copy the materials, except pursuant to an order of the court from which the subpoena was issued. The party serving the subpoena may, if objection has been made, move upon notice to the deponent for an order at any time before or during the taking of the deposition.

Advisory Committee's Note

At present, when a subpoena duces tecum is issued to a deponent, he is required to produce the listed materials at the deposition, but is under no clear compulsion to permit their inspection and copying. This results in confusion and uncertainty before the time the deposition is taken, with no mechanism provided whereby the court can resolve the matter. Rule 45(d)(1), as revised, makes clear that the subpoena authorizes inspection and copying of the materials produced. The deponent is afforded full protection since he can object, thereby forcing the party serving the subpoena to obtain a court order if he wishes to inspect and copy. The procedure is thus analogous to that provided in Rule 34.

The changed references to other rules conform to changes made in those rules. The deletion of words in the clause describing the proper scope of the subpoena conforms to a change made in the language of Rule 34. The reference to Rule 26(b) is unchanged but encompasses new matter in that subdivision. The changes make it clear that the scope of discovery through a subpoena is the same as that applicable to Rule 34 and the other discovery rules.

Rule 69. Execution

(a) In General. Process to enforce a judgment for the payment of money shall be a writ of execution, unless the court directs otherwise. The procedure on execution, in proceedings supplementary to and in aid of a judgment, and in proceedings on and in aid of execution shall be in accordance with the practice and procedure of the state in which the district court is held, existing at the time the remedy is sought, except that any statute of the United States governs to the extent that it is applicable. In aid of the judgment or execution, the judgment creditor or his successor in interest when that interest appears of record, may ~~examine~~ *obtain discovery from* any person, including the judgment debtor, in the manner provided in these rules ~~for taking depositions~~ or in the manner provided by the practice of the state in which the district court is held.

Advisory Committee's Note

The amendment assures that, in aid of execution on a judgment, all discovery procedures provided in the rules are available and not just discovery via the taking of a deposition. Under the present language, one court has held that Rule 34 discovery is unavailable to the judgment creditor. *M. Lowenstein & Sons, Inc. v. American Underwear Mfg. Co.,* 11 F.R.D. 172 (E.D.Pa.1951). Notwithstanding the language, and relying heavily on legislative history referring to Rule 33, the Fifth Circuit has held that a judgment creditor may invoke Rule 33 interrogatories. *United States v. McWhirter,* 376 F.2d 102 (5th Cir.1967). But the court's reasoning does not extend to discovery except as provided in Rules 26–33. One commentator suggests that the existing language might properly be stretched to all discovery, 7 *Moore's Federal Practice* ¶69.05[1] (2d ed. 1966), but another believes that a rules amendment is needed. 3 Barron & Holtzoff, *Federal Practice and Procedure* 1484 (Wright ed. 1958). Both commentators and the court in *McWhirter* are clear that, as a matter of policy, Rule 69 should authorize the use of all discovery devices provided in the rules.

AMENDMENTS OF FEDERAL RULES OF CIVIL PROCEDURE ADOPTED BY THE SUPREME COURT OF THE UNITED STATES ON APRIL 29, 1980, EFFECTIVE AUGUST 1, 1980, WITH ADVISORY COMMITTEE'S NOTES THEREON

Rule 4. Process

(a) Summons: Issuance. Upon the filing of the complaint the clerk shall forthwith issue a summons and deliver it for service to the marshal or to ~~a~~ *any other* person ~~specially appointed~~ *authorized by Rule 4(c)* to serve it. Upon request of the plaintiff separate or additional summons shall issue against any defendants.

(c) By Whom Served. Service of ~~all~~ process shall be made by a United States marshal, by his deputy, or by some person specially appointed by the court for that purpose, except that a subpoena may be served as provided in Rule 45. Special appointments to serve process shall be made freely. ~~when substantial savings in travel fees will result.~~ *Service of process may also be made by a person authorized to serve process in an action brought in the courts of general jurisdiction of the state in which the district court is held or in which service is made.*

Advisory Committee's Note

Subdivision (a). This is a technical amendment to conform this subdivision with the amendment of subdivision (c).

Subdivision (c). The purpose of this amendment is to authorize service of process to be made by any person who is authorized to make service in actions in the courts of general jurisdiction of the state in which the district court is held or in which service is made.

There is a troublesome ambiguity in Rule 4. Rule 4(c) directs that all process is to be served by the marshal, by his deputy, or by a person specially appointed by the court. But Rule 4(d)(7) authorizes service in certain cases "in the manner prescribed by the law of the state in which the district court is held. . . ." And Rule 4(e), which authorizes service beyond the state and service in *quasi in rem* cases when state law permits such service, directs that "service may be made . . . under the circumstances and in the manner prescribed in the [state] statute or rule." State statutes and rules of the kind referred to in Rule 4(d)(7) and Rule 4(e) commonly designate the persons who are to make the service provided for, *e.g.,* a sheriff or a plaintiff. When that is so, may the persons so designated by state law make service, or is service in all cases to be made by a marshal or by one specially appointed under present Rule 4(c)? The commentators have noted the ambiguity and have suggested the desirability of an amendment. See 2 *Moore's Federal*

Practice ¶4.08 (1974); Wright & Miller, *Federal Practice and Procedure: Civil* § 1092 (1969). And the ambiguity has given rise to unfortunate results. See *United States for the use of Tanos v. St. Paul Mercury Ins. Co.,* 361 F.2d 838 (5th Cir.1966); *Veeck v. Commodity Enterprises, Inc.,* 487 F.2d 423 (9th Cir.1973).

The ambiguity can be resolved by specific amendments to Rules 4(d)(7) and 4(e), but the Committee is of the view that there is no reason why Rule 4(c) should not generally authorize service of process in all cases by anyone authorized to make service in the courts of general jurisdiction of the state in which the district court is held or in which service is made. The marshal continues to be the obvious, always effective officer for service of process.

Rule 5. Service and Filing of Pleadings and Other Papers

(d) Filing. All papers after the complaint required to be served upon a party shall be filed with the court either before service or within a reasonable time thereafter~~.~~, *but the court may on motion of a party or on its own initiative order that depositions upon oral examination and interrogatories, requests for documents, requests for admission, and answers and responses thereto not be filed unless on order of the court or for use in the proceeding.*

Advisory Committee's Note

Subdivision (d). By the terms of this rule and Rule 30(f)(1) discovery materials must be promptly filed, although it often happens that no use is made of the materials after they are filed. Because the copies required for filing are an added expense and the large volume of discovery filings presents serious problems of storage in some districts, the Committee in 1978 first proposed that discovery materials not be filed unless on order of the court or for use in the proceedings. But such materials are sometimes of interest to those who may have no access to them except by a requirement of filing, such as members of a class, litigants similarly situated, or the public generally. Accordingly, this amendment and a change in Rule 30(f)(1) continue the requirement of filing but make it subject to an order of the court that discovery materials not be filed unless filing is requested by the court or is effected by parties who wish to use the materials in the proceeding.

Rule 26. General Provisions Governing Discovery

(f) Discovery Conference. At any time after commencement of an action the court may direct the attorneys for the parties to appear before it for a conference on the subject of discovery. The court shall do so upon motion by the attorney for any party if the motion includes:

(1) A statement of the issues as they then appear;

(2) A proposed plan and schedule of discovery;

(3) Any limitations proposed to be placed on discovery;

(4) Any other proposed orders with respect to discovery; and

(5) A statement showing that the attorney making the motion has made a reasonable effort to reach agreement with opposing attorneys on the matters set forth in the motion. Each party and his attorney are under a duty to participate in good faith in the framing of a discovery plan if a plan is proposed by the attorney for any party. Notice of the motion shall be served on all parties. Objections or additions to matters set forth in the motion shall be served not later than 10 days after service of the motion.

Following the discovery conference, the court shall enter an order tentatively identifying the issues for discovery purposes, establishing a plan and schedule for discovery, setting limitations on discovery, if any; and determining such other matters, including the allocation of expenses, as are necessary for the proper management of discovery in the action. An order may be altered or amended whenever justice so requires.

Subject to the right of a party who properly moves for a discovery conference to prompt convening of the conference, the court may combine the discovery conference with a pretrial conference authorized by Rule 16.

Advisory Committee's Note

Subdivision (f). This subdivision is new. There has been widespread criticism of abuse of discovery. The Committee has considered a number of proposals to eliminate abuse, including a change in Rule 26(b)(1) with respect to the scope of discovery and a change in Rule 33(a) to limit the number of questions that can be asked by interrogatories to parties.

The Committee believes that abuse of discovery, while very serious in certain cases, is not so general as to require such basic changes in the rules that govern discovery in all cases. A very recent study of discovery in selected metropolitan districts tends to support its belief. P. Connolly, E. Holleman, & M. Kuhlman, *Judicial Controls and the Civil Litigative Process: Discovery* (Federal Judicial Center, 1978). In the judgment of the Committee abuse can best be prevented by intervention by the court as soon as abuse is threatened.

To this end this subdivision provides that counsel who has attempted without success to effect with opposing counsel a reasonable program or plan for discovery is entitled to the assistance of the court.

It is not contemplated that requests for discovery conferences will be made routinely. A relatively narrow discovery dispute should be resolved by resort to Rules 26(c) or 37(a), and if it appears that a request for a conference is in fact grounded in such a dispute, the court may refer counsel to those rules. If the court is persuaded that a request is frivolous or vexatious, it can strike it. See Rules 11 and 7(b)(2).

A number of courts routinely consider discovery matters in preliminary pretrial conferences held shortly after the pleadings are closed. This subdivision does not interfere with such a practice. It authorizes the court to combine a discovery conference with a pretrial conference under Rule 16 if a pretrial conference is held sufficiently early to prevent or curb abuse.

Rule 28. Persons Before Whom Depositions May Be Taken

(a) Within the United States. Within the United States or within a territory or insular possession subject to the ~~dominion~~ *jurisdiction* of the United States, depositions shall be taken before an officer authorized to administer oaths by the laws of the United States or of the place where the examination is held, or before a person appointed by the court in which the action is pending. A person so appointed has power to administer oaths and take testimony. *The term officer as used in Rules 30, 31 and 32 includes a person appointed by the court or designated by the parties under Rule 29.*

Advisory Committee's Note

The amendments are clarifying.

Rule 30. Depositions Upon Oral Examination

(b) Notice of Examination: General Requirements; Special Notice; Non-Stenographic Recording; Production of Documents and Things; Deposition of Organization~~.~~; *Deposition by Telephone.*

(4) *The parties may stipulate in writing or* [~~T~~]*t*he court may upon motion order that the testimony at a deposition be recorded by other than stenographic means~~,~~. ~~in which event~~ [~~t~~]*The stipulation or* order shall designate *the person before whom the deposition shall be taken,* the manner of recording, preserving and filing the deposition, and may include other provisions to assure that the recorded testimony will be accurate and trustworthy. ~~If the order is made, a~~ *A* party may ~~nevertheless~~ arrange to have a stenographic transcription made at his own expense. *Any objections under subdivision (c), any changes made by the witness, his signature identifying the deposition as his own or the statement of the officer that is required if the witness does not sign, as provided in subdivision (e), and the certification of the officer required by subdivision (f) shall be set forth in a writing to accompany a deposition recorded by non-stenographic means.*

(7) The parties may stipulate in writing or the court may upon motion order that a deposition be taken by telephone. For the purposes of this rule and Rules 28(a), 37(a)(1), 37(b)(1) and 45(d), a deposition taken by telephone is taken in the district and at the place where the deponent is to answer questions propounded to him.

(f) Certification and Filing by Officer; Exhibits; Copies; Notice of Filing.

(1) The officer shall certify on the deposition that the witness was duly sworn by him and that the deposition is a true record of

New matter is shown in italics; matter to be omitted is lined through

the testimony given by the witness. *Unless otherwise ordered by the court,* [~~H~~]*he* shall then securely seal the deposition in an envelope indorsed with the title of the action and marked "Deposition of [here insert name of witness]" and shall promptly file it with the court in which the action is pending or send it by registered or certified mail to the clerk thereof for filing.

Documents and things produced for inspection during the examination of the witness, shall, upon the request of a party, be marked for identification and annexed to ~~and returned with~~ the deposition and may be inspected and copied by any party, except that ~~(A)~~ *if* the person producing the materials *desires to retain them he* may ~~substitute~~ *(A) offer* copies to be marked for identification *and annexed to the deposition and to serve thereafter as originals* if he affords to all parties fair opportunity to verify the copies by comparison with the originals, ~~and~~ *or* (B) ~~if the person producing the materials requests their return, the officer shall mark them, give~~ *offer the originals to be marked for identification, after giving to* each party an opportunity to inspect and copy them, ~~and return them to the person producing them, and~~ *in which event* the materials may then be used in the same manner as if annexed to ~~and returned with~~ the deposition. Any party may move for an order that the original be annexed to and returned with the deposition to the court, pending final disposition of the case.

Advisory Committee's Note

Subdivision (b)(4). It has been proposed that electronic recording of depositions be authorized as a matter of course, subject to the right of a party to seek an order that a deposition be recorded by stenographic means. The Committee is not satisfied that a case has been made for a reversal of present practice. The amendment is made to encourage parties to agree to the use of electronic recording of depositions so that conflicting claims with respect to the potential of electronic recording for reducing costs of depositions can be appraised in the light of greater experience. The provision that the parties may stipulate that depositions may be recorded by other than stenographic means seems implicit in Rule 29. The amendment makes it explicit. The provision that the stipulation or order shall designate the person before whom the deposition is to be taken is added to encourage the naming of the recording technician as that person, eliminating the necessity of the presence of one whose only function is to administer the oath. See Rules 28(a) and 29.

Subdivision (b)(7). Depositions by telephone are now authorized by Rule 29 upon stipulation of the parties. The amendment authorizes that method by order of the court. The final sentence is added to make it clear that when a deposition is taken by telephone it is taken in the district and at the place where the witness is to answer the questions rather than that where the questions are propounded.

Subdivision (f)(1). For the reasons set out in the Note following the amendment of Rule 5(d), the court may wish to permit the parties to retain depositions unless they are to be used in the action. The amendment of the first paragraph permits the court to so order.

The amendment of the second paragraph is clarifying. The purpose of the paragraph is to permit a person who produces materials at a deposition to offer copies for marking and annexation to the deposition. Such copies are a "substitute" for the originals, which are not to be marked and which can thereafter be used or even disposed of by the person who produces them. In the light of that purpose, the former language of the paragraph had been justly termed "opaque." Wright & Miller, *Federal Practice and Procedure: Civil* § 2114.

Rule 32. Use of Depositions in Court Proceedings

(a) Use of Depositions. At the trial or upon the hearing of a motion or an interlocutory proceeding, any part or all of a deposition, so far as admissible under the rules of evidence applied as though the witness were then present and testifying, may be used against any party who was present or represented at the taking of the deposition or who had reasonable notice thereof, in accordance with any of the following provisions:

(1) Any deposition may be used by any party for the purpose of contradicting or impeaching the testimony of deponent as a witness~~.~~, *or for any other purpose permitted by the Federal Rules of Evidence.*

(4) If only part of a deposition is offered in evidence by a party, an adverse party may require him to introduce any other part which ought in fairness to be considered with the part introduced, and any party may introduce any other parts.

Substitution of parties pursuant to Rule 25 does not affect the right to use depositions previously taken; and when an action *has been brought* in any court of the United States or of any State ~~has been dismissed~~ and another action involving the same subject matter is afterward brought between the same parties or their representatives or successors in interest, all depositions lawfully taken and duly filed in the former action may be used in the latter as if originally taken therefor. *A deposition previously taken may also be used as permitted by the Federal Rules of Evidence.*

Advisory Committee's Note

Subdivision (a)(1). Rule 801(d) of the Federal Rules of Evidence permits a prior inconsistent statement of a witness in a deposition to be used as substantive evidence. And Rule 801(d)(2) makes the statement of an agent or servant admissible against the principal under the circumstances described in the Rule. The language of the present subdivision is, therefore, too narrow.

Subdivision (a)(4). The requirement that a prior action must have been dismissed before depositions taken for use in it can be used in a subsequent action was doubtless an oversight, and the courts have ignored it. See Wright & Miller, *Federal Practice and Procedure: Civil* § 2150. The final sentence is added to reflect the fact that the Federal Rules of Evidence permit a broader use of depositions previously taken under certain circumstances. For example, Rule 804(b)(1) of the Federal Rules of Evidence provides that if a witness is unavailable, as that term is defined by the rule, his deposition in any earlier proceeding can be used against a party to the prior proceeding who had an opportunity and similar motive to develop the testimony of the witness.

Rule 33. Interrogatories to Parties

(c) Option to Produce Business Records. Where the answer to an interrogatory may be derived or ascertained from the business records of the party upon whom the interrogatory has been served or from an examination, audit or inspection of such business records, ~~or from~~ *including* a compilation, abstract or summary ~~based thereon~~ *thereof*, and the burden of deriving or ascertaining the answer is substantially the same for the party serving the interrogatory as for the party served, it is a sufficient answer to such interrogatory to specify the records from which the answer may be derived or ascertained and to afford to the party serving the interrogatory reasonable opportunity to examine, audit or inspect such records and to make copies, compilations, abstracts or summaries. *A specification shall be in sufficient detail to permit the interrogating party to locate and to identify, as readily as can the party served, the records from which the answer may be ascertained.*

Advisory Committee's Note

Subdivision (c). The Committee is advised that parties upon whom interrogatories are served have occasionally responded by directing the interrogating party to a mass of business records or by offering to make all of their records available, justifying the response by the option provided by this subdivision. Such practices are an abuse of the option. A party who is permitted by the terms of this subdivision to offer records for inspection in lieu of answering an interrogatory should offer them in a manner that permits the same direct and economical access that is available to the party. If the information sought exists in the form of compilations, abstracts or summaries then available to the responding party, those should be made available to the interrogating party. The final sentence is added to make it clear that a responding party has the duty to specify, by category and location, the records from which answers to interrogatories can be derived.

Rule 34. Production of Documents and Things and Entry Upon Land For Inspection and Other Purposes

(b) Procedure. The request may, without leave of court, be served upon the plaintiff after commencement of the action and upon any other party with or after service of the summons and complaint upon that party. The request shall set forth the items to be inspected either by individual item or by category, and describe each item and category with reasonable particularity. The request shall specify a reasonable time, place, and manner of making the inspection and performing the related acts.

New matter is shown in italics; matter to be omitted is lined through

The party upon whom the request is served shall serve a written response within 30 days after the service of the request, except that a defendant may serve a response within 45 days after service of the summons and complaint upon that defendant. The court may allow a shorter or longer time. The response shall state, with respect to each item or category, that inspection and related activities will be permitted as requested, unless the request is objected to, in which event the reasons for objection shall be stated. If objection is made to part of an item or category, the part shall be specified. The party submitting the request may move for an order under Rule 37(a) with respect to any objection to or other failure to respond to the request or any part thereof, or any failure to permit inspection as requested.

A party who produces documents for inspection shall produce them as they are kept in the usual course of business or shall organize and label them to correspond with the categories in the request.

Advisory Committee's Note

Subdivision (b). The Committee is advised that, "It is apparently not rare for parties deliberately to mix critical documents with others in the hope of obscuring significance." *Report of the Special Committee for the Study of Discovery Abuse, Section of Litigation of the American Bar Association* (1977) 22. The sentence added by this subdivision follows the recommendation of the *Report.*

Rule 37. Failure to Make *or Cooperate in* Discovery: Sanctions

(b) Failure to Comply with Order.

(2) Sanctions by Court in Which Action is Pending. If a party or an officer, director, or managing agent of a party or a person designated under Rule 30(b)(6) or 31(a) to testify on behalf of a party fails to obey an order to provide or permit discovery, including an order made under subdivision (a) of this rule or Rule 35, *or if a party fails to obey an order entered under Rule 26(f),* the court in which the action is pending may make such orders in regard to the failure as are just, and among others the following:

(A) An order that the matters regarding which the order was made or any other designated facts shall be taken to be established for the purposes of the action in accordance with the claim of the party obtaining the order;

(B) An order refusing to allow the disobedient party to support or oppose designated claims or defenses, or prohibiting him from introducing designated matters in evidence;

New matter is shown in italics; matter to be omitted is lined through

(C) An order striking out pleadings or parts thereof, or staying further proceedings until the order is obeyed, or dismissing the action or proceeding or any part thereof, or rendering a judgment by default against the disobedient party;

(D) In lieu of any of the foregoing orders or in addition thereto, an order treating as a contempt of court the failure to obey any orders except an order to submit to a physical or mental examination;

(E) Where a party has failed to comply with an order under Rule 35(a) requiring him to produce another for examination, such orders as are listed in paragraphs (A), (B), and (C) of this subdivision, unless the party failing to comply shows that he is unable to produce such person for examination.

In lieu of any of the foregoing orders or in addition thereto, the court shall require the party failing to obey the order or the attorney advising him or both to pay the reasonable expenses, including attorney's fees, caused by the failure, unless the court finds that the failure was substantially justified or that other circumstances make an award of expenses unjust.

[(e) Subpoena of Person in Foreign Country.] ~~A subpoena may be issued as provided in Title 28 U.S.C. § 1783, under the circumstances and conditions therein stated.~~

(g) Failure to Participate in the Framing of a Discovery Plan. If a party or his attorney fails to participate in good faith in the framing of a discovery plan by agreement as is required by Rule 26(f), the court may, after opportunity for hearing, require such party or his attorney to pay to any other party the reasonable expenses, including attorney's fees, caused by the failure.

Advisory Committee's Note

Subdivision (b)(2). New Rule 26(f) provides that if a discovery conference is held, at its close the court shall enter an order respecting the subsequent conduct of discovery. The amendment provides that the sanctions available for violation of other court orders respecting discovery are available for violation of the discovery conference order.

Subdivision (e). Subdivision (e) is stricken. Title 28, U.S.C. § 1783 no longer refers to sanctions. The subdivision otherwise duplicates Rule 45(e)(2).

Subdivision (g). New Rule 26(f) imposes a duty on parties to participate in good faith in the framing of a discovery plan by agreement upon the request of any party. This subdivision authorizes the court to award to parties who participate in good faith in an attempt to frame a discovery plan the expenses incurred in the attempt if any party or his attorney fails to participate in good faith and thereby causes additional expense.

* * *

Failure of United States to Participate in Good Faith in Discovery. Rule 37 authorizes the court to direct that parties or attorneys who fail to participate in good faith in the discovery process pay the expenses, including attorneys' fees, incurred by other parties as a result of that failure. Since attorneys' fees cannot ordinarily be awarded against the United States (28 U.S.C. § 2412), there is often no practical remedy for the misconduct of its officers and attorneys. However, in the case of a government attorney who fails to participate in good faith in discovery, nothing prevents a court in an appropriate case from giving written notification of that fact to the Attorney General of the United States and other appropriate heads of offices or agencies thereof.

Rule 45. Subpoena

(d) Subpoena for Taking Depositions; Place of Examination.

(1) Proof of service of a notice to take a deposition as provided in Rules 30(b) and 31(a) constitutes a sufficient authorization for the issuance by the clerk of the district court for the district in which the deposition is to be taken of subpoenas for the persons named or described therein. *Proof of service may be made by filing with the clerk of the district court for the district in which the deposition is to be taken a copy of the notice together with a statement of the date and manner of service and of the names of the persons served, certified by the person who made service.* The subpoena may command the person to whom it is directed to produce and permit inspection and copying of designated books, papers, documents, or tangible things which constitute or contain matters within the scope of the examination permitted by Rule 26(b), but in that event the subpoena will be subject to the provisions of Rule 26(c) and subdivision (b) of this rule.

The person to whom the subpoena is directed may, within 10 days after the service thereof or on or before the time specified in the subpoena for compliance if such time is less than 10 days after service, serve upon the attorney designated in the subpoena written objection to inspection or copying of any or all of the designated materials. If objection is made, the party serving the subpoena shall not be entitled to inspect and copy the materials except pursuant to an order of the court from which the subpoena was issued. The party serving the subpoena may, if objection has been made, move upon notice to the deponent for an order at any time before or during the taking of the deposition.

(e) Subpoena for a Hearing or Trial.

(1) At the request of any party subpoenas for attendance at a hearing or trial shall be issued by the clerk of the district court for the district in which the hearing or trial is held. A subpoena requiring the attendance of a witness at a hearing or trial may be

served at any place within the district, or at any place without the district that is within 100 miles of the place of the hearing or trial specified in the subpoena~~;~~*, or at a place within the state where a state statute or rule of court permits service of a subpoena issued by a state court of general jurisdiction sitting in the place where the district court is held.* ~~and,~~ *W*~~w~~hen a statute of the United States provides therefor, the court upon proper application and cause shown may authorize the service of a subpoena at any other place.

Advisory Committee's Note

Subdivision (d)(1). The amendment defines the term "proof of service" as used in the first sentence of the present subdivision. For want of a definition, the district court clerks have been obliged to fashion their own, with results that vary from district to district. All that seems required is a simple certification on a copy of the notice to take a deposition that the notice has been served on every other party to the action. That is the proof of service required by Rule 25(d) of both the Federal Rules of Appellate Procedure and the Supreme Court Rules.

Subdivision (e)(1). The amendment makes the reach of a subpoena of a district court at least as extensive as that of the state courts of general jurisdiction in the state in which the district court is held. Under the present rule the reach of a district court subpoena is often greater, since it extends throughout the district. No reason appears why it should be less, as it sometimes is because of the accident of district lines. Restrictions upon the reach of subpoenas are imposed to prevent undue inconvenience to witnesses. State statutes and rules of court are quite likely to reflect the varying degrees of difficulty and expense attendant upon local travel.

*

CERTAIN OF THE AMENDMENTS OF FEDERAL RULES OF CIVIL PROCEDURE ADOPTED BY THE SUPREME COURT OF THE UNITED STATES ON APRIL 28, 1983, EFFECTIVE AUGUST 1, 1983, WITH ADVISORY COMMITTEE'S NOTES THEREON

[*Amendments here omitted: Addition of new Forms 33 and 34.*]

Rule 6. Time

(b) Enlargement. When by these rules or by a notice given thereunder or by order of court an act is required or allowed to be done at or within a specified time, the court for cause shown may at any time in its discretion (1) with or without motion or notice order the period enlarged if request therefor is made before the expiration of the period originally prescribed or as extended by a previous order, or (2) upon motion made after the expiration of the specified period permit the act to be done where the failure to act was the result of excusable neglect; but it may not extend the time for taking any action under Rules 50(b) *and (c)(2)*, 52(b), 59(b), (d) and (e), 60(b), *and 74(a)*, except to the extent and under the conditions stated in them.

Advisory Committee's Note

Subdivision (b). The amendment confers finality upon the judgments of magistrates by foreclosing enlargement of the time for appeal except as provided in new Rule 74(a) (20 day period for demonstration of excusable neglect).

Rule 7. Pleadings Allowed; Form of Motions

(b) Motions and Other Papers.

(2) The rules applicable to captions~~, signing,~~ and other matters of form of pleadings apply to all motions and other papers provided for by these rules.

(3) All motions shall be signed in accordance with Rule 11.

Advisory Committee's Note

One of the reasons sanctions against improper motion practice have been employed infrequently is the lack of clarity of Rule 7. That rule has stated only generally that the pleading requirements relating to captions, signing, and other matters of form also apply to motions and other papers. The addition of Rule 7(b)(3) makes explicit the applicability of the signing requirement and the sanctions of Rule 11, which have been amplified.

Rule 11. Signing of Pleadings, *Motions, and Other Papers; Sanctions*

Every pleading, *motion, and other paper* of a party represented by an attorney shall be signed by at least one attorney of record in his individual name, whose address shall be stated. A party who is not represented by an attorney shall sign his pleading, *motion, or other paper* and state his address. Except when otherwise specifically provided by rule or statute, pleadings need not be verified or accompanied by affidavit. The rule in equity that the averments of an answer under oath must be overcome by the testimony of two witnesses or of one witness sustained by corroborating circumstances is abolished. The signature of an attorney *or party* constitutes a certificate by him that he has read the pleading, *motion, or other paper*; that to the best of his knowledge, information, and belief ~~there is good ground to support it; and that it is not interposed for delay~~ *formed after reasonable inquiry it is well grounded in fact and is warranted by existing law or a good faith argument for the extension, modification, or reversal of existing law, and that it is not interposed for any improper purpose, such as to harass or to cause unnecessary delay or needless increase in the cost of litigation.* If a pleading, *motion, or other paper* is not signed, *it shall be stricken unless it is signed promptly after the omission is called to the attention of the pleader or movant.* ~~or is signed with intent to defeat the purpose of this rule; it may be stricken as sham and false and the action may proceed as though the pleading had not been served. For a wilful violation of this rule an attorney may be subjected to appropriate disciplinary action. Similar action may be taken if scandalous or indecent matter is inserted.~~ *If a pleading, motion, or other paper is signed in violation of this rule, the court, upon motion or upon its own initiative, shall impose upon the person who signed it, a represented party, or both, an appropriate sanction, which may include an order to pay to the other party or parties the amount of the reasonable expenses incurred because of the filing of the pleading, motion, or other paper, including a reasonable attorney's fee.*

Advisory Committee's Note

Since its original promulgation, Rule 11 has provided for the striking of pleadings and the imposition of disciplinary sanctions to check abuses in the signing of pleadings. Its provisions have always applied to motions and other papers by virtue of incorporation by reference in Rule 7(b)(2). The amendment and the addition of Rule 7(b)(3) expressly confirms this applicability.

New matter is shown in italics; matter to be omitted is lined through

Experience shows that in practice Rule 11 has not been effective in deterring abuses. See 6 Wright & Miller, *Federal Practice and Procedure: Civil* § 1334 (1971). There has been considerable confusion as to (1) the circumstances that should trigger striking a pleading or motion or taking disciplinary action, (2) the standard of conduct expected of attorneys who sign pleadings and motions, and (3) the range of available and appropriate sanctions. See Rodes, Ripple & Mooney, *Sanctions Imposable for Violations of the Federal Rules of Civil Procedure* 64–65, Federal Judicial Center (1981). The new language is intended to reduce the reluctance of courts to impose sanctions, see Moore, *Federal Practice* ¶ 7.05, at 1547, by emphasizing the responsibilities of the attorney and reenforcing those obligations by the imposition of sanctions.

The amended rule attempts to deal with the problem by building upon and expanding the equitable doctrine permitting the court to award expenses, including attorney's fees, to a litigant whose opponent acts in bad faith in instituting or conducting litigation. See, *e.g., Roadway Express, Inc. v. Piper,* 447 U.S. 752 (1980); *Hall v. Cole,* 412 U.S. 1, 5 (1973). Greater attention by the district courts to pleading and motion abuses and the imposition of sanctions when appropriate, should discourage dilatory or abusive tactics and help to streamline the litigation process by lessening frivolous claims or defenses.

The expanded nature of the lawyer's certification in the fifth sentence of amended Rule 11 recognizes that the litigation process may be abused for purposes other than delay. See, *e.g., Browning Debenture Holders' Committee v. DASA Corp.,* 560 F.2d 1078 (2d Cir.1977).

The words "good ground to support" the pleading in the original rule were interpreted to have both factual and legal elements. See, *e.g., Heart Disease Research Foundation v. General Motors Corp.,* 15 Fed.R.Serv.2d 1517, 1519 (S.D.N.Y.1972). They have been replaced by a standard of conduct that is more focused.

The new language stresses the need for some prefiling inquiry into both the facts and the law to satisfy the affirmative duty imposed by the rule. The standard is one of reasonableness under the circumstances. See *Kinee v. Abraham Lincoln Fed. Sav. & Loan Ass'n,* 365 F.Supp. 975 (E.D.Pa.1973). This standard is more stringent than the original good-faith formula and thus it is expected that a greater range of circumstances will trigger its violation. See *Nemeroff v. Abelson,* 620 F.2d 339 (2d Cir.1980).

The rule is not intended to chill an attorney's enthusiasm or creativity in pursuing factual or legal theories. The court is expected to avoid using the wisdom of hindsight and should test the signer's conduct by inquiring what was reasonable to believe at the time the pleading, motion, or other paper was submitted. Thus, what constitutes a reasonable inquiry may depend on such factors as how much time for investigation was available to the signer; whether he had to rely on a client for information as to the facts underlying the pleading, motion, or other paper; whether the pleading, motion, or other paper was based on a plausible view of the law; or whether he depended on forwarding counsel or another member of the bar.

The rule does not require a party or an attorney to disclose privileged communications or work product in order to show that the signing of the pleading, motion, or other paper is substantially justified. The provisions of Rule 26(c), including appropriate orders after *in camera* inspection by the court, remain available to protect a party claiming privilege or work product protection.

Amended Rule 11 continues to apply to anyone who signs a pleading, motion, or other paper. Although the standard is the same for unrepresented parties, who are obliged themselves to sign the pleadings, the court has sufficient discretion to take account of the special circumstances that often arise in *pro se* situations. See *Haines v. Kerner,* 404 U.S. 519 (1972).

The provision in the original rule for striking pleadings and motions as sham and false has been deleted. The passage has rarely been utilized, and decisions thereunder have tended to confuse the issue of attorney honesty with the merits of the action. See generally Risinger, *Honesty in Pleading and its Enforcement: Some "Striking" Problems with Fed.R.Civ.P. 11,* 61 Minn.L.Rev. 1 (1976). Motions under this provision generally present issues better dealt with under Rules 8, 12, or 56. See *Murchison v. Kirby,* 27 F.R.D. 14 (S.D.N.Y. 1961); 5 Wright & Miller, *Federal Practice and Procedure: Civil* § 1334 (1969).

The former reference to the inclusion of scandalous or indecent matter, which is itself strong indication that an improper purpose underlies the pleading, motion, or other paper, also has been deleted as unnecessary. Such matter may be stricken under Rule 12(f) as well as dealt with under the more general language of amended Rule 11.

The text of the amended rule seeks to dispel apprehensions that efforts to obtain enforcement will be fruitless by insuring that the rule will be applied when properly invoked. The word "sanctions" in the caption, for example, stresses a deterrent orientation in dealing with improper pleadings, motions or other papers. This corresponds to the approach in imposing sanctions for discovery abuses. See *National Hockey League v. Metropolitan Hockey Club,* 427 U.S. 639 (1976) (per curiam). And the words "shall impose" in the last sentence focus the court's attention on the need to impose sanctions for pleading and motion abuses. The court, however, retains the necessary flexibility to deal appropriately with violations of the rule. It has discretion to tailor sanctions to the particular facts of the case, with which it should be well acquainted.

The reference in the former text to wilfulness as a prerequisite to disciplinary action has been deleted. However, in considering the nature and severity of the sanctions to be imposed, the court should take account of the state of the attorney's or party's actual or presumed knowledge when the pleading or other paper was signed. Thus, for example, when a party is not represented by counsel, the absence of legal advice is an appropriate factor to be considered.

Courts currently appear to believe they may impose sanctions on their own motion. See *North American Trading Corp. v. Zale Corp.,* 73 F.R.D. 293 (S.D.N.Y. 1979). Authority to do so has been made explicit in order to overcome the traditional reluctance of courts to intervene unless requested by one of the parties. The detection and punishment of a violation of the signing requirement, encouraged by the amended rule, is part of the court's responsibility for securing the system's effective operation.

If the duty imposed by the rule is violated, the court should have the discretion to impose sanctions on either the attorney, the party the signing attorney represents, or both, or on an unrepresented party who signed the pleading, and the new rule so provides. Although Rule 11 has been silent on the point, courts have claimed the power to impose sanctions on an attorney personally, either by imposing costs or employing the contempt technique. See 5 Wright & Miller, *Federal Practice and Procedure: Civil* § 1334 (1969); 2A Moore, *Federal Practice* ¶ 11.02, at 2104 n. 8. This power has been used infrequently. The amended rule should eliminate any doubt as to the propriety of assessing sanctions against the attorney.

Even though it is the attorney whose signature violates the rule, it may be appropriate under the circumstances of the case to impose a sanction on the client. See *Browning Debenture Holders' Committee v. DASA Corp., supra.* This modification brings Rule 11 in line with practice under Rule 37, which allows sanctions for abuses during discovery to be imposed upon the party, the attorney, or both.

A party seeking sanctions should give notice to the court and the offending party promptly upon discovering a basis for doing so. The time when sanctions are to be imposed rests in the discretion of the trial judge. However, it is anticipated that in the case of pleadings the sanctions issue under Rule 11 normally will be determined at the end of the litigation, and in the case of motions at the time when the motion is decided or shortly thereafter. The procedure obviously must comport with due process requirements. The particular format to be followed should depend on the circumstances of the situation and the severity of the sanction under consideration. In many situations the judge's participation in the proceedings provides him with full knowledge of the relevant facts and little further inquiry will be necessary.

To assure that the efficiencies achieved through more effective operation of the pleading regimen will not be offset by the cost of satellite litigation over the imposition of sanctions, the court must to the extent possible limit the scope of sanction proceedings to the record. Thus, discovery should be conducted only by leave of the court, and then only in extraordinary circumstances.

Although the encompassing reference to "other papers" in new Rule 11 literally includes discovery papers, the certification requirement in that context is governed by proposed new Rule 26(g). Discovery motions, however, fall within the ambit of Rule 11.

Rule 16. *Pretrial Conferences; Scheduling; Management* ~~Pre-Trial Procedure; Formulating Issues~~

(a) Pretrial Conferences; Objectives. In any action, the court may in its discretion direct the attorneys for the parties *and any unrepresented parties* to appear before it for a conference *or conferences before trial* ~~to consider~~ *for such purposes as*

(1) expediting the disposition of the action;

(2) establishing early and continuing control so that the case will not be protracted because of lack of management;

(3) discouraging wasteful pretrial activities;

(4) improving the quality of the trial through more thorough preparation, and;

(5) facilitating the settlement of the case.

(b) Scheduling and Planning. Except in categories of actions exempted by district court rule as inappropriate, the judge, or a magistrate when authorized by district court rule, shall, after consulting with the attorneys for the parties and any unrepresented parties, by a scheduling conference, telephone, mail, or other suitable means, enter a scheduling order that limits the time

(1) to join other parties and to amend the pleadings;

(2) to file and hear motions; and

(3) to complete discovery.

The scheduling order also may include

(4) the date or dates for conferences before trial, a final pretrial conference, and trial; and

(5) any other matters appropriate in the circumstances of the case.

The order shall issue as soon as practicable but in no event more than 120 days after filing of the complaint. A schedule shall not be modified except by leave of the judge or a magistrate when authorized by district court rule upon a showing of good cause.

(c) Subjects to Be Discussed at Pretrial Conferences. The participants at any conference under this rule may consider and take action with respect to

(1) the *formulation and* simplification of the issues, *including the elimination of frivolous claims or defenses*;

(2) the necessity or desirability of amendments to the pleadings;

(3) the possibility of obtaining admissions of fact and of documents which will avoid unnecessary proof, *stipulations regarding the authenticity of documents, and advance rulings from the court on the admissibility of evidence*;

(4) the avoidance of unnecessary proof and of cumulative evidence;

(5)~~(4)~~ the ~~limitation of the number of expert~~ *identification of* witnesses *and documents, the need and schedule for filing and exchanging pretrial briefs, and the date or dates for further conferences and for trial*;

(6)~~(5)~~ the advisability of ~~a preliminary reference of~~ referring ~~issues~~ *matters* to a *magistrate or* master ~~for findings to be used as evidence when the trial is to be by jury~~;

(7) the possibility of settlement or the use of extrajudicial procedures to resolve the dispute;

(8) the form and substance of the pretrial order;

(9) the disposition of pending motions;

(10) the need for adopting special procedures for managing potentially difficult or protracted actions that may involve complex issues, multiple parties, difficult legal questions, or unusual proof problems; and

(11)~~(6)~~ such other matters as may aid in the disposition of the action.

New matter is shown in italics; matter to be omitted is lined through

At least one of the attorneys for each party participating in any conference before trial shall have authority to enter into stipulations and to make admissions regarding all matters that the participants may reasonably anticipate may be discussed.

(d) Final Pretrial Conference. Any final pretrial conference shall be held as close to the time of trial as reasonable under the circumstances. The participants at any such conference shall formulate a plan for trial, including a program for facilitating the admission of evidence. The conference shall be attended by at least one of the attorneys who will conduct the trial for each of the parties and by any unrepresented parties.

(e) Pretrial Orders. After any conference held pursuant to this rule, an order shall be entered reciting the action taken. This order shall control the subsequent course of the action unless modified by a subsequent order. The order following a final pretrial conference shall be modified only to prevent manifest injustice.

(f) Sanctions. If a party or party's attorney fails to obey a scheduling or pretrial order, or if no appearance is made on behalf of a party at a scheduling or pretrial conference, or if a party or party's attorney is substantially unprepared to participate in the conference, or if a party or party's attorney fails to participate in good faith, the judge, upon motion or his own initiative, may make such orders with regard thereto as are just, and among others any of the orders provided in Rule 37(b)(2)(B), (C), (D). In lieu of or in addition to any other sanction, the judge shall require the party or the attorney representing him or both to pay the reasonable expenses incurred because of any noncompliance with this rule, including attorney's fees, unless the judge finds that the noncompliance was substantially justified or that other circumstances make an award of expenses unjust.

~~The court shall make an order which recites the action taken at the conference, the amendments allowed to the pleadings, and the agreements made by the parties as to any of the matters considered, and which limits the issues for trial to those not disposed of by admissions or agreements of counsel; and such order when entered controls the subsequent course of the action, unless modified at the trial to prevent manifest injustice. The court in its discretion may establish by rule a pretrial calendar on which actions may be placed for consideration as above provided and may either confine the calendar to jury actions or to non-jury actions or extend it to all actions.~~

Advisory Committee's Note

Introduction

Rule 16 has not been amended since the Federal Rules were promulgated in 1938. In many respects, the rule has been a success. For example, there is evidence

New matter is shown in italics; matter to be omitted is lined through

that pretrial conferences may improve the quality of justice rendered in the federal courts by sharpening the preparation and presentation of cases, tending to eliminate trial surprise, and improving, as well as facilitating, the settlement process. See 6 Wright & Miller, *Federal Practice and Procedure: Civil* § 1522 (1971). However, in other respects particularly with regard to case management, the rule has not always been as helpful as it might have been. Thus there has been a widespread feeling that amendment is necessary to encourage pretrial management that meets the needs of modern litigation. See *Report of the National Commission for the Review of Antitrust Laws and Procedures* (1979).

Major criticism of Rule 16 has centered on the fact that its application can result in over-regulation of some cases and under-regulation of others. In simple, run-of-the-mill cases, attorneys have found pretrial requirements burdensome. It is claimed that over-administration leads to a series of mini-trials that result in a waste of an attorney's time and needless expense to a client. Pollack, *Pretrial Procedures More Effectively Handled,* 65 F.R.D. 475 (1974). This is especially likely to be true when pretrial proceedings occur long before trial. At the other end of the spectrum, the discretionary character of Rule 16 and its orientation toward a single conference late in the pretrial process has led to under-administration of complex or protracted cases. Without judicial guidance beginning shortly after institution, these cases often become mired in discovery.

Four sources of criticism of pretrial have been identified. First, conferences often are seen as a mere exchange of legalistic contentions without any real analysis of the particular case. Second, the result frequently is nothing but a formal agreement on minutiae. Third, the conferences are seen as unnecessary and time-consuming in cases that will be settled before trial. Fourth, the meetings can be ceremonial and ritualistic, having little effect on the trial and being of minimal value, particularly when the attorneys attending the sessions are not the ones who will try the case or lack authority to enter into binding stipulations. See generally *McCargo v. Hedrick*, 545 F.2d 393 (4th Cir. 1976); Pollack, *Pretrial Procedures More Effectively Handled*, 65 F.R.D. 475 (1974); Rosenberg, *The Pretrial Conference and Effective Justice* 45 (1964).

There also have been difficulties with the pretrial orders that issue following Rule 16 conferences. When an order is entered far in advance of trial, some issues may not be properly formulated. Counsel naturally are cautious and often try to preserve as many options as possible. If the judge who tries the case did not conduct the conference, he could find it difficult to determine exactly what was agreed to at the conference. But any insistence on a detailed order may be too burdensome, depending on the nature or posture of the case.

Given the significant changes in federal civil litigation since 1938 that are not reflected in Rule 16, it has been extensively rewritten and expanded to meet the challenges of modern litigation. Empirical studies reveal that when a trial judge intervenes personally at an early stage to assume judicial control over a case and to schedule dates for completion by the parties of the principal pretrial steps, the case is disposed of by settlement or trial more efficiently and with less cost and delay than when the parties are left to their own devices. Flanders, *Case Management and Court Management in United States District Courts* 17, Federal Judicial Center (1977). Thus, the rule mandates a pretrial scheduling order. However, although scheduling and pretrial conferences are encouraged in appropriate cases, they are not mandated.

Discussion

Subdivision (a); Pretrial Conferences; Objectives. The amended rule makes scheduling and case management an express goal of pretrial procedure. This is done in Rule 16(a) by shifting the emphasis away from a conference focused solely on the trial and toward a process of judicial management that embraces the entire pretrial phase, especially motions and discovery. In addition, the amendment explicitly recognizes some of the objectives of pretrial conferences and the powers that many courts already have assumed. Rule 16 thus will be a more accurate reflection of actual practice.

Subdivision (b); Scheduling and Planning. The most significant change in Rule 16 is the mandatory scheduling order described in Rule 16(b), which is based in part on Wisconsin Civil Procedure Rule 802.10. The idea of scheduling orders is not new. It has been used by many federal courts. See, *e.g.*, Southern District of Indiana, Local Rule 19.

Although a mandatory scheduling order encourages the court to become involved in case management early in the litigation, it represents a degree of judicial involvement that is not warranted in many cases. Thus, subdivision (b) permits each district court to promulgate a local rule under Rule 83 exempting certain categories of cases in which the burdens of scheduling orders exceed the administrative efficiencies that would be gained. See Eastern District of Virginia, Local Rule 12(1). Logical candidates for this treatment include social security disability matters, habeas corpus petitions, forfeitures, and reviews of certain administrative actions.

A scheduling conference may be requested either by the judge, a magistrate when authorized by district court rule, or a party within 120 days after the summons and complaint are filed. If a scheduling conference is not arranged within that time and the case is not exempted by local rule, a scheduling order must be issued under Rule 16(b), after some communication with the parties, which may be by telephone or mail rather than in person. The use of the term "judge" in subdivision (b) reflects the Advisory Committee's judgment that it is preferable that this task should be handled by a district judge rather than a magistrate, except when the magistrate is acting under 28 U.S.C. § 636(c). While personal supervision by the trial judge is preferred, the rule, in recognition of the impracticality or difficulty of complying with such a requirement in some districts, authorizes a district by local rule to delegate the duties to a magistrate. In order to formulate a practicable scheduling order, the judge, or a magistrate when authorized by district court rule, and attorneys are required to develop a timetable for the matters listed in Rule 16(b)(1)–(3). As indicated in Rule 16(b)(4)–(5), the order may also deal with a wide range of other matters. The rule is phrased permissively as to clauses (4) and (5), however, because scheduling these items at an early point may not be feasible or appropriate. Even though subdivision (b) relates only to scheduling, there is no reason why some of the procedural matters listed in Rule 16(c) cannot be addressed at the same time, at least when a scheduling conference is held.

Item (1) assures that at some point both the parties and the pleadings will be fixed, by setting a time within which joinder of parties shall be completed and the pleadings amended.

Item (2) requires setting time limits for interposing various motions that otherwise might be used as stalling techniques.

Item (3) deals with the problem of procrastination and delay by attorneys in a context in which scheduling is especially important—discovery. Scheduling the completion of discovery can serve some of the same functions as the conference described in Rule 26(f).

Item (4) refers to setting dates for conferences and for trial. Scheduling multiple pretrial conferences may well be desirable if the case is complex and the court believes that a more elaborate pretrial structure, such as that described in the

Manual for Complex Litigation, should be employed. On the other hand, only one pretrial conference may be necessary in an uncomplicated case.

As long as the case is not exempted by local rule, the court must issue a written scheduling order even if no scheduling conference is called. The order, like pretrial orders under the former rule and those under new Rule 16(c), normally will "control the subsequent course of the action." See Rule 16(e). After consultation with the attorneys for the parties and any unrepresented parties—a formal motion is not necessary—the court may modify the schedule on a showing of good cause if it cannot reasonably be met despite the diligence of the party seeking the extension. Since the scheduling order is entered early in the litigation, this standard seems more appropriate than a "manifest injustice" or "substantial hardship" test. Otherwise, a fear that extensions will not be granted may encourage counsel to request the longest possible periods for completing pleading, joinder, and discovery. Moreover, changes in the court's calendar sometimes will oblige the judge or magistrate when authorized by district court rule to modify the scheduling order.

The district courts undoubtedly will develop several prototype scheduling orders for different types of cases. In addition, when no formal conference is held, the court may obtain scheduling information by telephone, mail, or otherwise. In many instances this will result in a scheduling order better suited to the individual case than a standard order, without taking the time that would be required by a formal conference.

Rule 16(b) assures that the judge will take some early control over the litigation, even when its character does not warrant holding a scheduling conference. Despite the fact that the process of preparing a scheduling order does not always bring the attorneys and judge together, the fixing of time limits serves

> to stimulate litigants to narrow the areas of inquiry and advocacy to those they believe are truly relevant and material. Time limits not only compress the amount of time for litigation, they should also reduce the amount of resources invested in litigation. Litigants are forced to establish discovery priorities and thus to do the most important work first.

Report of the National Commission for the Review of Antitrust Laws and Procedures 28 (1979).

Thus, except in exempted cases, the judge or a magistrate when authorized by district court rule will have taken some action in every case within 120 days after the complaint is filed that notifies the attorneys that the case *will* be moving toward trial. Subdivision (b) is reenforced by subdivision (f), which makes it clear that the sanctions for violating a scheduling order are the same as those for violating a pretrial order.

Subdivision (c); Subjects to be Discussed at Pretrial Conferences. This subdivision expands upon the list of things that may be discussed at a pretrial conference that appeared in original Rule 16. The intention is to encourage better planning and management of litigation. Increased judicial control during the pretrial process accelerates the processing and termination of cases. Flanders, *Case Management and Court Management in United States District Courts,* Federal Judicial Center (1977). See also *Report of the National Commission for the Review of Antitrust Laws and Procedures* (1979).

The reference in Rule 16(c)(1) to "formulation" is intended to clarify and confirm the court's power to identify the litigable issues. It has been added in the hope of promoting efficiency and conserving judicial resources by identifying the real issues prior to trial, thereby saving time and expense for everyone. See generally *Meadow Gold Prods. Co. v. Wright,* 278 F.2d 867 (D.C. Cir. 1960). The notion is emphasized by expressly authorizing the elimination of frivolous claims or defenses at a pretrial conference. There is no reason to require that this await a formal motion for summary judgment. Nor is there any reason for the court to wait for the parties to initiate the process called for in Rule 16(c)(1).

The timing of any attempt at issue formulation is a matter of judicial discretion. In relatively simple cases it may not be necessary or may take the form of a stipulation between counsel or a request by the court that counsel work together to draft a proposed order.

Counsel bear a substantial responsibility for assisting the court in identifying the factual issues worthy of trial. If counsel fail to identify an issue for the court, the right to have the issue tried is waived. Although an order specifying the issues is intended to be binding, it may be amended at trial to avoid manifest injustice. See Rule 16(e). However, the rule's effectiveness depends on the court employing its discretion sparingly.

Clause (6) acknowledges the widespread availability and use of magistrates. The corresponding provision in the original rule referred only to masters and limited the function of the reference to the making of "findings to be used as evidence" in a case to be tried to a jury. The new text is not limited and broadens the potential use of a magistrate to that permitted by the Magistrate's Act.

Clause (7) explicitly recognizes that it has become commonplace to discuss settlement at pretrial conferences. Since it obviously eases crowded court dockets and results in savings to the litigants and the judicial system, settlement should be facilitated at as early a stage of the litigation as possible. Although it is not the purpose of Rule 16(b)(7) to impose settlement negotiations on unwilling litigants, it is believed that providing a neutral forum for discussing the subject might foster it. See Moore's *Federal Practice* ¶ 16.17; 6 Wright & Miller, *Federal Practice and Procedure: Civil* § 1522 (1971). For instance, a judge to whom a case has been assigned may arrange, on his own motion or at a party's request, to have settlement conferences handled by another member of the court or by a magistrate. The rule does not make settlement conferences mandatory because they would be a waste of time in many cases. See Flanders, *Case Management and Court Management in the United States District Courts,* 39, Federal Judicial Center (1977). Requests for a conference from a party indicating a willingness to talk settlement normally should be honored, unless thought to be frivolous or dilatory.

A settlement conference is appropriate at any time. It may be held in conjunction with a pretrial or discovery conference, although various objectives of pretrial management, such as moving the case toward trial, may not always be compatible with settlement negotiations, and thus a separate settlement conference may be desirable. See 6 Wright & Miller, *Federal Practice and Procedure: Civil* § 1522, at p. 571 (1971).

In addition to settlement, Rule 16(c)(7) refers to exploring the use of procedures other than litigation to resolve the dispute. This includes urging the litigants to employ adjudicatory techniques outside the courthouse. See, for example, the experiment described in Green, Marks & Olson, *Settling Large Case Litigation: An Alternative Approach,* 11 Loyola of L.A.L.Rev. 493 (1978).

Rule 16(c)(10) authorizes the use of special pretrial procedures to expedite the adjudication of potentially difficult or protracted cases. Some district courts obviously have done so for many years. See Rubin, *The Managed Calendar: Some Pragmatic Suggestions About Achieving the Just, Speedy and Inexpensive Determination of Civil Cases in Federal Courts,* 4 Just.Sys.J. 135 (1976). Clause 10 provides an explicit authorization for such procedures and encourages their use. No particular techniques have been described; the Committee felt that flexibility and experience are the keys to efficient management of complex cases. Extensive guidance is offered in such documents as the *Manual for Complex Litigation.*

The rule simply identifies characteristics that make a case a strong candidate for special treatment. The four mentioned are illustrative, not exhaustive, and overlap to some degree. But experience has shown that one or more of them will be present in every protracted or difficult case and it seems desirable to set them out. See Kendig, *Procedures for Management of Non-Routine Cases,* 3 Hofstra L.Rev. 701 (1975).

The last sentence of subdivision (c) is new. See Wisconsin Civil Procedure Rule 802.11(2). It has been added to meet one of the criticisms of the present practice described earlier and insure proper preconference preparation so that the meeting is more than a ceremonial or ritualistic event. The reference to "authority" is not intended to insist upon the ability to settle the litigation. Nor should the rule be read to encourage the judge conducting the conference to compel attorneys to enter into stipulations or to make admissions that they consider to be unreasonable, that touch on matters that could not normally have been anticipated to arise at the conference, or on subjects of a dimension that normally require prior consultation with and approval from the client.

Subdivision (d); Final Pretrial Conference. This provision has been added to make it clear that the time between any final pretrial conference (which in a simple case may be the *only* pretrial conference) and trial should be as short as possible to be certain that the litigants make substantial progress with the case and avoid the inefficiency of having that preparation repeated when there is a delay between the last pretrial conference and trial. An optimum time of 10 days to two weeks has been suggested by one federal judge. Rubin, *The Managed Calendar: Some Pragmatic Suggestions About Achieving the Just, Speedy and Inexpensive Determination of Civil Cases in Federal Courts,* 4 Just.Sys.J. 135, 141 (1976). The Committee, however, concluded that it would be inappropriate to fix a precise time in the rule, given the numerous variables that could bear on the matter. Thus the timing has been left to the court's discretion.

At least one of the attorneys who will conduct the trial for each party must be present at the final pretrial conference. At this late date there should be no doubt as to which attorney or attorneys this will be. Since the agreements and stipulations made at this final conference will control the trial, the presence of lawyers who will be involved in it is especially useful to assist the judge in structuring the case, and to lead to a more effective trial.

Subdivision (e); Pretrial Orders. Rule 16(e) does not substantially change the portion of the original rule dealing with pretrial orders. The purpose of an order is to guide the course of the litigation and the language of the original rule making that clear has been retained. No compelling reason has been found for major revision, especially since this portion of the rule has been interpreted and clarified by over forty years of judicial decisions with comparatively little difficulty. See 6 Wright & Miller, *Federal Practice and Procedure: Civil* §§ 1521–30 (1971). Changes in language therefore have been kept to a minimum to avoid confusion.

Since the amended rule encourages more extensive pretrial management than did the original, two or more conferences may be held in many cases. The language of Rule 16(e) recognizes this possibility and the corresponding need to issue more than one pretrial order in a single case.

Once formulated, pretrial orders should not be changed lightly; but total inflexibility is undesirable. See, *e.g., Clark v. Pennsylvania R.R. Co.,* 328 F.2d 591 (2d Cir. 1964). The exact words used to describe the standard for amending the pretrial order probably are less important than the meaning given them in practice.

By not imposing any limitation on the ability to modify a pretrial order, the rule reflects the reality that in any process of continuous management what is done at one conference may have to be altered at the next. In the case of the final pretrial order, however, a more stringent standard is called for and the words "to prevent manifest injustice," which appeared in the original rule, have been retained. They have the virtue of familiarity and adequately describe the restraint the trial judge should exercise.

Many local rules make the plaintiff's attorney responsible for drafting a proposed pretrial order, either before or after the conference. Others allow the court to appoint any of the attorneys to perform the task, and others leave it to the court. See Note, *Pretrial Conference: A Critical Examination of Local Rules Adopted by Federal District Courts,* 64 Va.L.Rev. 467 (1978). Rule 16 has never addressed this matter. Since there is no consensus about which method of drafting the order works best and there is no reason to believe that nationwide uniformity is needed, the rule has been left silent on the point. See *Handbook for Effective Pretrial Procedure,* 37 F.R.D. 225 (1964).

Subdivision (f); Sanctions. Original Rule 16 did not mention the sanctions that might be imposed for failing to comply with the rule. However, courts have not hesitated to enforce it by appropriate measures. See, *e.g., Link v. Wabash R. Co.,* 370 U.S. 628 (1962) (district court's dismissal under Rule 41(b) after plaintiff's attorney failed to appear at a pretrial conference upheld); *Admiral Theatre Corp. v. Douglas Theatre,* 585 F.2d 877 (8th Cir. 1978) (district court has discretion to exclude exhibits or refuse to permit the testimony of a witness not listed prior to trial in contravention of its pretrial order).

To reflect that existing practice, and to obviate dependence upon Rule 41(b) or the court's inherent power to regulate litigation, *cf. Societe Internationale Pour Participations Industrielles et Commerciales, S.A. v. Rogers,* 357 U.S. 197 (1958), Rule 16(f) expressly provides for imposing sanctions on disobedient or recalcitrant parties, their attorneys, or both in four types of situations. Rodes, Ripple & Mooney, *Sanctions Imposable for Violations of the Federal Rules of Civil Procedure* 65–67, 80–84, Federal Judicial Center (1981). Furthermore, explicit reference to sanctions reenforces the rule's intention to encourage forceful judicial management.

Rule 16(f) incorporates portions of Rule 37(b)(2), which prescribes sanctions for failing to make discovery. This should facilitate application of Rule 16(f), since courts and lawyers already are familiar with the Rule 37 standards. Among the sanctions authorized by the new subdivision are: preclusion order, striking a pleading, staying the proceeding, default judgment, contempt, and charging a party, his attorney, or both with the expenses, including attorney's fees, caused by noncompliance. The contempt sanction, however, is only available for a violation of a court order. The references in Rule 16(f) are not exhaustive.

As is true under Rule 37(b)(2), the imposition of sanctions may be sought by either the court or a party. In addition, the court has discretion to impose whichever sanction it feels is appropriate under the circumstances. Its action is reviewable under the abuse-of-discretion standard. See *National Hockey League v. Metropolitan Hockey Club, Inc.,* 427 U.S. 639 (1976).

Rule 26. General Provisions Governing Discovery

(a) Discovery Methods. Parties may obtain discovery by one or more of the following methods: depositions upon oral examination or written questions; written interrogatories; production of documents or things or permission to enter upon land or other property, for inspection and other purposes; physical and mental examinations; and requests for admission. ~~Unless the court orders otherwise under subdivision (c) of this rule, the frequency of use of these methods is not limited.~~

(b) ~~**Scope of Discovery**~~ *Discovery Scope and Limits.* Unless other wise limited by order of the court in accordance with these rules, the scope of discovery is as follows:

(1) In General. Parties may obtain discovery regarding any matter, not privileged, which is relevant to the subject matter involved in the pending action, whether it relates to the claim or defense of the party seeking discovery or to the claim or defense of any other party, including the existence, description, nature, custody, condition and location of any books, documents, or other tangible things and the identity and location of persons having knowledge of any discoverable matter. It is not ground for objection that the information sought will be inadmissible at the trial if the information sought appears reasonably calculated to lead the discovery of admissible evidence.

The frequency or extent of use of the discovery methods set forth in subdivision (a) shall be limited by the court if it determines that: (i) the discovery sought is unreasonably cumulative or duplicative, or is obtainable from some other source that is more convenient, less burdensome, or less expensive; (ii) the party seeking discovery has had ample opportunity by discovery in the action to obtain the information sought; or (iii) the discovery is unduly burdensome or expensive, taking into account the needs of the case, the amount in controversy, limitations on the parties' resources, and the importance of the issues at stake in the litigation. The court may act upon its own initiative after reasonable notice or pursuant to a motion under subdivision (c).

(g) Signing of Discovery Requests, Responses, and Objections. Every request for discovery or response or objection thereto made by a party represented by an attorney shall be signed by at least one attorney of record in his individual name, whose address shall be stated. A party who is not represented by an attorney shall sign the request, response, or objection and state his address. The signature of the attorney or party constitutes a certification that he has read the request, response, or objection, and that to the best of his knowledge, information, and belief formed after a reasonable inquiry it is: (1) consistent with these rules and warranted by existing law or a good faith argument for the extension, modification, or reversal of existing law; (2) not interposed for any improper purpose, such as to harass or to cause unnecessary delay or needless

---

New matter is shown in italics; matter to be omitted is lined through

increase in the cost of litigation; and (3) not unreasonable or unduly burdensome or expensive, given the needs of the case, the discovery already had in the case, the amount in controversy, and the importance of the issues at stake in the litigation. If a request, response, or objection is not signed, it shall be stricken unless it is signed promptly after the omission is called to the attention of the party making the request, response or objection and a party shall not be obligated to take any action with respect to it until it is signed.

If a certification is made in violation of the rule, the court, upon motion or upon its own initiative, shall impose upon the person who made the certification, the party on whose behalf the request, response, or objection is made, or both, an appropriate sanction, which may include an order to pay the amount of the reasonable expenses incurred because of the violation, including a reasonable attorney's fee.

Advisory Committee's Note

Excessive discovery and evasion or resistance to reasonable discovery requests pose significant problems. Recent studies have made some attempt to determine the sources and extent of the difficulties. See Brazil, *Civil Discovery: Lawyers' Views of its Effectiveness, Principal Problems and Abuses,* American Bar Foundation (1980); Connolly, Holleman & Kuhlman, *Judicial Controls and the Civil Litigative Process: Discovery,* Federal Judicial Center (1978); Ellington, *A Study of Sanctions for Discovery Abuse,* Department of Justice (1979); Schroeder & Frank, *The Proposed Changes in the Discovery Rules,* 1978 Ariz.St.L.J. 475.

The purpose of discovery is to provide a mechanism for making relevant information available to the litigants. "Mutual knowledge of all the relevant facts gathered by both parties is essential to proper litigation." *Hickman v. Taylor,* 329 U.S. 495, 507 (1947). Thus the spirit of the rules is violated when advocates attempt to use discovery tools as tactical weapons rather than to expose the facts and illuminate the issues by overuse of discovery or unnecessary use of defensive weapons or evasive responses. All of this results in excessively costly and time-consuming activities that are disproportionate to the nature of the case, the amount involved, or the issues or values at stake.

Given our adversary tradition and the current discovery rules, is it not surprising that there are many opportunities, if not incentives, for attorneys to engage in discovery that, although authorized by the broad, permissive terms of the rules, nevertheless results in delay. See Brazil, *The Adversary Character of Civil Discovery: A Critique and Proposals for Change,* 31 Vand.L.Rev. 1259 (1978). As a result, it has been said that the rules have "not infrequently [been] exploited to the disadvantage of justice." *Herbert v. Lando,* 441 U.S. 153, 179 (1979) (Powell, J., concurring). These practices impose costs on an already overburdened system and impede the fundamental goal of the "just, speedy, and inexpensive determination of every action." Fed.R.Civ.P. 1.

Subdivision (a); Discovery Methods. The deletion of the last sentence of Rule 26(a)(1), which provided that unless the court ordered otherwise under Rule 26(c) "the frequency of use" of the various discovery methods was not to be limited, is an attempt to address the problem of duplicative, redundant, and excessive discovery and to reduce it. The amendment, in conjunction with the changes in Rule 26(b)(1), is designed to encourage district judges to identify instances of needless discovery and to limit the use of the various discovery devices accordingly. The question may be raised by one of the parties, typically on a motion for a protective order, or by the court on its own initiative. It is entirely appropriate to consider a limitation on the frequency of use of discovery at a discovery conference under Rule 26(f) or at any other pretrial conference authorized by these rules. In considering the discovery needs of a particular case, the court should consider the factors described in Rule 26(b)(1).

Subdivision (b); Discovery Scope and Limits. Rule 26(b)(1) has been amended to add a sentence to deal with the problem of over-discovery. The objective is to guard against redundant or disproportionate discovery by giving the court authority to reduce the amount of discovery that may be directed to matters that are otherwise proper subjects of inquiry. The new sentence is intended to encourage judges to be more aggressive in identifying and discouraging discovery overuse. The grounds mentioned in the amended rule for limiting discovery reflect the existing practice of many courts in issuing protective orders under Rule 26(c). See, *e.g., Carlson Cos. v. Sperry & Hutchinson Co.,* 374 F.Supp. 1080 (D.Minn.1974); *Dolgow v. Anderson,* 53 F.R.D. 661 (E.D.N.Y.1971); *Mitchell v. American Tobacco Co.,* 33 F.R.D. 262 (M.D.Pa.1963); *Welty v. Clute,* 1 F.R.D. 446 (W.D.N.Y.1941). On the whole, however, district judges have been reluctant to limit the use of the discovery devices. See, *e.g., Apco Oil Co. v. Certified Transp., Inc.,* 46 F.R.D. 428 (W.D.Mo. 1969). See generally 8 Wright & Miller, *Federal Practice and Procedure: Civil* §§ 2036, 2037, 2039, 2040 (1970).

The first element of the standard, Rule 26(b)(1)(i), is designed to minimize redundancy in discovery and encourage attorneys to be sensitive to the comparative costs of different methods of securing information. Subdivision (b)(1)(ii) also seeks to reduce repetitiveness and to oblige lawyers to think through their discovery activities in advance so that full utilization is made of each deposition, document request, or set of interrogatories. The elements of Rule 26(b)(1)(iii) address the problem of discovery that is disproportionate to the individual lawsuit as measured by such matters as its nature and complexity, the importance of the issues at stake in a case seeking damages, the limitations on a financially weak litigant to withstand extensive opposition to a discovery program or to respond to discovery requests, and the significance of the substantive issues, as measured in philosophic, social, or institutional terms. Thus the rule recognizes that many cases in public policy spheres, such as employment practices, free speech, and other matters, may have importance far beyond the monetary amount involved. The court must apply the standards in an even-handed manner that will prevent use of discovery to wage a war of attrition or as a device to coerce a party, whether financially weak or affluent.

The rule contemplates greater judicial involvement in the discovery process and thus acknowledges the reality that it cannot always operate on a self-regulating basis. See Connolly, Holleman & Kuhlman, *Judicial Controls and the Civil Litigative Process: Discovery* 77, Federal Judicial Center (1978). In an appropriate case the court could restrict the number of depositions, interrogatories, or the scope of a production request. But the court must be careful not to deprive a party of discovery that is reasonably necessary to afford a fair opportunity to develop and prepare the case.

The court may act on motion, or its own initiative. It is entirely appropriate to resort to the amended rule in conjunction with a discovery conference under Rule 26(f) or one of the other pretrial conferences authorized by the rules.

Subdivision (g); Signing of Discovery Requests, Responses, and Objections. Rule 26(g) imposes an affirmative duty to engage in pretrial discovery in a responsible manner that is consistent with the spirit and purposes of Rules 26 through 37. In addition, Rule 26(g) is designed to curb discovery abuse by explicitly encouraging the imposition of sanctions. The subdivision provides a deterrent to both excessive discovery and evasion by imposing a certification requirement that obliges each attorney to stop and think about the legitimacy of a discovery request, a response thereto, or an objection. The term "response" includes answers to interrogatories and to requests to admit as well as responses to production requests.

If primary responsibility for conducting discovery is to continue to rest with the litigants, they must be obliged to act responsibly and avoid abuse. With this in mind, Rule 26(g), which parallels the amendments to Rule 11, requires an attorney or unrepresented party to sign each discovery request, response, or objection. Motions relating to discovery are governed by Rule 11. However, since a discovery request, response, or objection usually deals with more specific subject matter than motions or papers, the elements that must be certified in connection with the former are spelled out more completely. The signature is a certification of the elements set forth in Rule 26(g).

Although the certification duty requires the lawyer to pause and consider the reasonableness of his request, response, or objection, it is not meant to discourage or restrict necessary and legitimate discovery. The rule simply requires that the attorney make a reasonable inquiry into the factual basis of his response, request, or objection.

The duty to make a "reasonable inquiry" is satisfied if the investigation undertaken by the attorney and the conclusions drawn therefrom are reasonable under the circumstances. It is an objective standard similar to the one imposed by Rule 11. See the Advisory Committee Note to Rule 11. See also *Kinee v. Abraham Lincoln Fed. Sav. & Loan Ass'n,* 365 F.Supp. 975 (E.D.Pa.1973). In making the inquiry, the attorney may rely on assertions by the client and on communications with other counsel in the case as long as that reliance is appropriate under the circumstances. Ultimately, what is reasonable is a matter for the court to decide on the totality of the circumstances.

Rule 26(g) does not require the signing attorney to certify the truthfulness of the client's factual responses to a discovery request. Rather, the signature certifies that the lawyer has made a reasonable effort to assure that the client has provided all the information and documents available to him that are responsive to the discovery demand. Thus, the lawyer's certification under Rule 26(g) should be distinguished from other signature requirements in the rules, such as those in Rules 30(e) and 33.

Nor does the rule require a party or an attorney to disclose privileged communications or work product in order to show that a discovery request, response, or objection is substantially justified. The provisions of Rule 26(c), including appropriate orders after *in camera* inspection by the court, remain available to protect a party claiming privilege or work product protection.

The signing requirement means that every discovery request, response, or objection should be grounded on a theory that is reasonable under the precedents or a good faith belief as to what should be the law. This standard is heavily dependent on the circumstances of each case. The certification speaks as of the time it is made. The duty to supplement discovery responses continues to be governed by Rule 26(e).

Concern about discovery abuse has led to widespread recognition that there is a need for more aggressive judicial control and supervision. *ACF Industries, Inc. v. EEOC,* 439 U.S. 1081 (1979) (certiorari denied) (Powell, J., dissenting). Sanctions to deter discovery abuse would be more effective if they were diligently applied "not merely to penalize those whose conduct may be deemed to warrant such a sanction, but to deter those who might be tempted to such conduct in the absence of such a deterrent." *National Hockey League v. Metropolitan Hockey Club,* 427 U.S. 639, 643 (1976). See also Note, *The Emerging Deterrence Orientation in the Imposition of Discovery Sanctions,* 91 Harv.L.Rev. 1033 (1978). Thus the premise of Rule 26(g) is that imposing sanctions on attorneys who fail to meet the rule's standards will significantly reduce abuse by imposing disadvantages therefor.

Because of the asserted reluctance to impose sanctions on attorneys who abuse the discovery rules, see Brazil, *Civil Discovery: Lawyers' Views of its Effectiveness, Principal Problems and Abuses,* American Bar Foundation (1980); Ellington, *A Study of Sanctions for Discovery Abuse,* Department of Justice (1979), Rule 26(g) makes explicit the authority judges now have to impose appropriate sanctions and requires them to use it. This authority derives from Rule 37, 28 U.S.C. § 1927, and the court's inherent power. See *Roadway Express, Inc. v. Piper,* 447 U.S. 752 (1980); *Martin v. Bell Helicopter Co.,* 85 F.R.D. 654, 661–62 (D.Col.1980); Note, *Sanctions Imposed by Courts on Attorneys Who Abuse the Judicial Process,* 44 U.Chi.L.Rev. 619 (1977). The new rule mandates that sanctions be imposed on attorneys who fail to meet the standards established in the first portion of Rule 26(g). The nature of the sanction is a matter of judicial discretion to be exercised in light of the particular circumstances. The court may take into account any failure by the party seeking sanctions to invoke protection under Rule 26(c) at an early stage in the litigation.

The sanctioning process must comport with due process requirements. The kind of notice and hearing required will depend on the facts of the case and the severity of the sanction being considered. To prevent the proliferation of the sanction procedure and to avoid multiple hearings, discovery in any sanction proceeding normally should be permitted only when it is clearly required by the interests of justice. In most cases the court will be aware of the circumstances and only a brief hearing should be necessary.

Rule 52. Findings by the Court

(a) Effect. In all actions tried upon the facts without a jury or with an advisory jury, the court shall find the facts specially and state separately its conclusions of law thereon, and judgment shall be entered pursuant to Rule 58; and in granting or refusing interlocutory injunctions the court shall similarly set forth the findings of fact and conclusions of law which constitute the grounds of its action. Requests for findings are not necessary for purposes of review. Findings of fact shall not be set aside unless clearly erroneous, and due regard shall be given to the opportunity of the trial court to judge of the credibility of the witnesses. The findings of a master, to the extent that the court adopts them, shall be considered as the findings of the court. ~~If an opinion or memorandum of decision is filed, it~~ *It* will be sufficient if the findings of fact and conclusions of law *are stated orally and recorded in open court following the close of the evidence or* appear ~~therein~~ *in an opinion or memorandum of decision filed by the court.* Findings of fact and conclusions of law are unnecessary on decisions of motions under Rules 12 or 56 or any other motion except as provided in Rule 41(b).

New matter is shown in italics; matter to be omitted is lined through

Advisory Committee's Note

Rule 52(a) has been amended to revise its penultimate sentence to provide explicitly that the district judge may make the findings of fact and conclusions of law required in nonjury cases orally. Nothing in the prior text of the rule forbids this practice, which is widely utilized by district judges. See Christensen, *A Modest Proposal for Immeasurable Improvement,* 64 A.B.A.J. 693 (1978). The objective is to lighten the burden on the trial court in preparing findings in nonjury cases. In addition, the amendment should reduce the number of published district court opinions that embrace written findings.

Rule 53. Masters

(a) Appointment and Compensation. ~~Each district court with the concurrence of a majority of all the judges thereof may appoint one or more standing masters for its district, and~~ *T*he court in which any action is pending may appoint a special master therein. As used in these rules the word "master" includes a referee, an auditor, an examiner, ~~a commissioner,~~ and an assessor. The compensation to be allowed to a master shall be fixed by the court, and shall be charged upon such of the parties or paid out of any fund or subject matter of the action, which is in the custody and control of the court as the court may direct*; provided that this provision for compensation shall not apply when a United States magistrate is designated to serve as a master pursuant to Title 28, U.S.C. § 636(b)(2).* The master shall not retain his report as security for his compensation; but when the party ordered to pay the compensation allowed by the court does not pay it after notice and within the time prescribed by the court, the master is entitled to a writ of execution against the delinquent party.

(b) Reference. A reference to a master shall be the exception and not the rule. In actions to be tried by a jury, a reference shall be made only when the issues are complicated; in actions to be tried without a jury, save in matters of account and of difficult computation of damages, a reference shall be made only upon a showing that some exceptional condition requires it. *Upon the consent of the parties, a magistrate may be designated to serve as a special master without regard to the provisions of this subdivision.*

(c) Powers. The order of reference to the master may specify or limit his powers and may direct him to report only upon particular issues or to do or perform particular acts or to receive and report evidence only and may fix the time and place for beginning and closing the hearings and for the filing of the master's report. Subject to the specifications and limitations stated in the order, the master has and shall exercise the power to regulate all proceedings in every hearing before him and to do all acts and take all measures necessary or proper for the efficient performance of his duties under the order. He may require the production before him of evidence upon all matters embraced in the reference, including the production of all books, papers, vouchers, documents, and writings applicable thereto. He may rule upon the admissibility of evidence unless otherwise directed by the order of reference and has the authority to put witnesses on oath and may himself examine them and may call the parties to the action and examine them upon oath. When a party so requests, the master shall make a record of the evidence offered and excluded in the same manner and subject to the same limitations as provided in ~~Rule 43(e)~~ *the Federal Rules of Evidence* for a court sitting without a jury.

(f) A magistrate is subject to this rule only when the order referring a matter to the magistrate expressly provides that the reference is made under this Rule.

Advisory Committee's Note

Subdivision (a). The creation of full-time magistrates, who serve at government expense and have no nonjudicial duties competing for their time, eliminates the need to appoint standing masters. Thus the prior provision in Rule 53(a) authorizing the appointment of standing masters is deleted. Additionally, the definition of "master" in subdivision (a) now eliminates the superseded office of commissioner.

The term "special master" is retained in Rule 53 in order to maintain conformity with 28 U.S.C. § 636(b)(2), authorizing a judge to designate a magistrate "to serve as a special master pursuant to the applicable provisions of this title and the Federal Rules of Civil Procedure for the United States District Courts." Obviously, when a magistrate serves as a special master, the provisions for compensation of masters are inapplicable, and the amendment to subdivision (a) so provides.

Although the existence of magistrates may make the appointment of outside masters unnecessary in many instances, see, *e.g., Gautreaux v. Chicago Housing Authority,* 384 F.Supp. 37 (N.D.Ill.1974), mandamus denied *sub nom., Chicago Housing Authority v. Austin,* 511 F.2d 82 (7th Cir. 1975); *Avco Corp. v. American Tel. & Tel. Co.,* 68 F.R.D. 532 (S.D.Ohio 1975), such masters may prove useful when some special expertise is desired or when a magistrate is unavailable for lengthy and detailed supervision of a case.

Subdivision (b). The provisions of 28 U.S.C. § 636(b)(2) not only permit magistrates to serve as masters under Rule 53(b) but also eliminate the exceptional condition requirement of Rule 53(b) when the reference is made with the consent of the parties. The amendment to subdivision (b) brings Rule 53 into harmony with the statute by exempting magistrates, appointed with the consent of the parties, from the general requirement that some exceptional condition requires the reference. It should be noted that subdivision (b) does not address the question, raised in recent decisional law and commentary, as to whether the exceptional condition requirement is applicable when *private masters* who are not magistrates are appointed with the consent of the parties. See Silberman, *Masters and Magistrates Part II: The American Analogue,* 50 N.Y.U.L.Rev. 1297, 1354 (1975).

Subdivision (c). The amendment recognizes the abrogation of Federal Rule 43(c) by the Federal Rules of Evidence.

Subdivision (f). The new subdivision responds to confusion flowing from the dual authority for references of pretrial matters to magistrates. Such references can be made, with or without the consent of the parties, pursuant to Rule 53 or under 28 U.S.C. § 636(b)(1)(A) and (b)(1)(B). There are a number of distinctions between references made under the statute and under the rule. For example, under the statute nondispositive pretrial matters may be referred to a magistrate, without consent, for final determination with reconsideration by the district judge if the magistrate's order is clearly erroneous or contrary to law. Under the rule, however, the appointment of a master, without consent of the parties, to supervise discovery would require some exceptional condition (Rule 53(b)) and would subject the proceedings to the report procedures of Rule 53(e). If an order of reference does not clearly articulate the source of the court's authority the resulting proceedings could be subject to attack on grounds of the magistrate's noncompliance with the provisions of Rule 53. This subdivision therefore establishes a presumption that the limitations of Rule 53 are not applicable unless the reference is specifically made subject to Rule 53.

A magistrate serving as a special master under 28 U.S.C. § 636(b)(2) is governed by the provisions of Rule 53, with the exceptional condition requirement lifted in the case of a consensual reference.

Rule 67. Deposit in Court

In an action in which any part of the relief sought is a judgment for a sum of money or the disposition of a sum of money or the disposition of any other thing capable of delivery, a party, upon notice to every other party, and by leave of court, may deposit with the court all or any part of such sum or thing~~.~~, *whether or not that party claims all or any part of the sum or thing. The party making the deposit shall serve the order permitting deposit on the clerk of the court.* Money paid into court under this rule shall be deposited and withdrawn in accordance with the provisions of Title 28, U.S.C., §§ 2041, and 2042; the Act of June 26, 1934, c. 756, § 23, as amended (48 Stat. 1236, 58 Stat. 845), U.S.C., Title 31, § 725v; or any like statute. *The fund shall be deposited in an interest-bearing account or invested in an interest-bearing instrument approved by the court.*

Advisory Committee's Note

Rule 67 has been amended in three ways. The first change is the addition of the clause in the first sentence. Some courts have construed the present rule to permit deposit only when the party making it claims no interest in the fund or thing deposited. *E.g., Blasin-Stern v. Beech-Nut Life Savers Corp.,* 429 F.Supp. 533 (D.Puerto Rico 1975); *Dinkins v. General Aniline & Film Corp.,* 214 F.Supp. 281 (S.D.N.Y.1963). However, there are situations in which a litigant may wish to be relieved of responsibility for a sum or thing, but continue to claim an interest in all or part of it. In these cases the deposit-in-court procedure should be available; in addition to the advantages to the party making the deposit, the procedure gives other litigants assurance that any judgment will be collectable. The amendment is intended to accomplish that.

The second change is the addition of a requirement that the order of deposit be served on the clerk of the court in which the sum or thing is to be deposited. This is simply to assure that the clerk knows what is being deposited and what his responsibilities are with respect to the deposit. The latter point is particularly important since the rule as amended contemplates that deposits will be placed in interest-bearing accounts; the clerk must know what treatment has been ordered for the particular deposit.

The third change is to require that any money be deposited in an interest-bearing account or instrument approved by the court.

Rule 72. Magistrates; Pretrial Matters

(a) Nondispositive Matters. A magistrate to whom a pretrial matter not dispositive of a claim or defense of a party is referred to hear and determine shall promptly conduct such proceedings as are required and when appropriate enter into the record a written order setting forth the disposition of the matter. The district judge to whom the case is assigned shall consider objections made by the parties, provided they are served and filed within 10 days after the entry of the order, and shall modify or set aside any portion of the magistrate's order found to be clearly erroneous or contrary to law.

(b) Dispositive Motions and Prisoner Petitions. A magistrate assigned without consent of the parties to hear a pretrial matter dispositive of a claim or defense of a party or a prisoner petition challenging the conditions of confinement shall promptly conduct such proceedings as are required. A record shall be made of all evidentiary proceedings before the magistrate, and a record may be made of such other proceedings as the magistrate deems necessary. The magistrate shall enter into the record a recommendation for disposition of the matter, including proposed findings of fact when appropriate. The clerk shall forthwith mail copies to all parties.

A party objecting to the recommended disposition of the matter shall promptly arrange for the transcription of the record, or portions of it as all parties may agree upon or the magistrate deems sufficient, unless the district judge otherwise directs. Within 10 days after being served with a copy of the recommended disposition, a party may serve and file specific, written objections to the proposed findings and recommendations. A party may respond to another party's objections within 10 days after being served with a copy thereof. The district judge to whom the case is assigned shall make a de novo determination upon the record, or after additional evidence, of any portion of the magistrate's disposition to which specific written objection has been made in accordance with this rule. The district judge may accept, reject, or modify the recommended decision, receive further evidence, or recommit the matter to the magistrate with instructions.

Advisory Committee's Note

Subdivision (a). This subdivision addresses court-ordered referrals of non-dispositive matters under 28 U.S.C. § 636(b)(1)(A). The rule calls for a written order of the magistrate's disposition to preserve the record and facilitate review. An oral order read into the record by the magistrate will satisfy this requirement.

No specific procedures or timetables for raising objections to the magistrate's rulings on nondispositive matters are set forth in the Magistrates Act. The rule fixes a 10-day period in order to avoid uncertainty and provide uniformity that will eliminate the confusion that might arise if different periods were prescribed by local rule in different districts. It also is contemplated that a party who is successful before the magistrate will be afforded an opportunity to respond to objections raised to the magistrate's ruling.

The last sentence of subdivision (a) specifies that reconsideration of a magistrate's order, as provided for in the Magistrates Act, shall be by the district judge to whom the case is assigned. This rule does not restrict experimentation by the district courts under 28 U.S.C. § 636(b)(3) involving references of matters other than pretrial matters, such as appointment of counsel, taking of default judgments, and acceptance of jury verdicts when the judge is unavailable.

Subdivision (b). This subdivision governs court-ordered referrals of dispositive pretrial matters and prisoner petitions challenging conditions of confinement, pursuant to statutory authorization in 28 U.S.C. § 636(b)(1)(B). This rule does not extend to habeas corpus petitions, which are covered by the specific rules relating to proceedings under Sections 2254 and 2255 of Title 28.

This rule implements the statutory procedures for making objections to the magistrate's proposed findings and recommendations. The 10-day period, as specified in the statute, is subject to Rule 6(e) which provides for an additional 3-day period when service is made by mail. Although no specific provision appears in the Magistrates Act, the rule specifies a 10-day period for a party to respond to objections to the magistrate's recommendation.

Implementing the statutory requirements, the rule requires the district judge to whom the case is assigned to make a de novo determination of those portions of the report, findings, or recommendations to which timely objection is made. The term "de novo" signifies that the magistrate's findings are not protected by the clearly erroneous doctrine, but does not indicate that a second evidentiary hearing is required. See *United States v. Raddatz,* 417 U.S. 667 (1980). See also Silberman, *Masters and Magistrates Part II: The American Analogue,* 50 N.Y.U.L.Rev. 1297, 1367 (1975). When no timely objection is filed, the court need only satisfy itself that there is no clear error on the face of the record in order to accept the recommendation. See *Campbell v. United States Dist. Court,* 501 F.2d 196, 206 (9th Cir.1974), cert. denied, 419 U.S. 879, quoted in House Report No. 94–1609, 94th Cong. 2d Sess. (1976) at 3. Compare *Park Motor Mart, Inc. v. Ford Motor Co.,* 616 F.2d 603 (1st Cir.1980). Failure to make timely objection to the magistrate's report prior to its adoption by the district judge may constitute a waiver of appellate review of the district judge's order. See *United States v. Walters,* 638 F.2d 947 (6th Cir.1981).

Rule 73. Magistrates; Trial by Consent and Appeal Options

(a) Powers; Procedure. When specially designated to exercise such jurisdiction by local rule or order of the district court and when all parties consent thereto, a magistrate may exercise the authority provided by Title 28, U.S.C. § 636(c) and may conduct any or all proceedings, including a jury or nonjury trial, in a civil case. A record of the proceedings shall be made in accordance with the requirements of Title 28, U.S.C. § 636(c)(7).

(b) Consent. When a magistrate has been designated to exercise civil trial jurisdiction, the clerk shall give written notice to the parties of their opportunity to consent to the exercise by a magistrate of civil jurisdiction over the case, as authorized by Title 28, U.S.C. § 636(c). If, within the period specified by local rule, the parties agree to a magistrate's exercise of such authority, they shall execute and file a joint form of consent or separate forms of consent setting forth such election.

No district judge, magistrate, or other court official shall attempt to persuade or induce a party to consent to a reference of a civil matter to a magistrate under this rule, nor shall a district judge or magistrate be informed of a party's response to the clerk's notification, unless all parties have consented to the referral of the matter to a magistrate.

The district judge, for good cause shown on his own motion or under extraordinary circumstances shown by a party, may vacate a reference of a civil matter to a magistrate under this subdivision.

(c) Normal Appeal Route. In accordance with Title 28, U.S.C. § 636(c)(3), unless the parties otherwise agree to the optional appeal route provided for in subdivision (d) of this rule, appeal from a judgment entered upon direction of a magistrate in proceedings under this rule will lie to the court of appeals as it would from a judgment of the district court.

(d) Optional Appeal Route. In accordance with Title 28, U.S.C. § 636(c)(4), at the time of reference to a magistrate, the parties may consent to appeal on the record to a judge of the district court and thereafter, by petition only, to the court of appeals.

Advisory Committee's Note

Subdivision (a). This subdivision implements the broad authority of the 1979 amendments to the Magistrates Act, 28 U.S.C. § 636(c), which permit a magistrate to sit in lieu of a district judge and exercise civil jurisdiction over a case, when the parties consent. See McCabe, *The Federal Magistrate Act of 1979,* 16 Harv.J.Legis. 343, 364–79 (1979). In order to exercise this jurisdiction, a magistrate must be specially designated under 28 U.S.C. § 636(c)(1) by the district court or courts he serves. The only exception to a magistrate's exercise of civil jurisdiction, which includes the power to conduct jury and nonjury trials and decide dispositive motions, is the contempt power. A hearing on contempt is to be conducted by the district judge upon certification of the facts and an order to show cause by the magistrate. See 28 U.S.C. § 639(e). In view of 28 U.S.C. § 636(c)(1) and this rule, it is unnecessary to amend Rule 58 to provide that the decision of a magistrate is a "decision by the court" for the purposes of that rule and a "final decision of the district court" for purposes of 28 U.S.C. § 1291 governing appeals.

Subdivision (b). This subdivision implements the blind consent provision of 28 U.S.C. § 636(c)(2) and is designed to ensure that neither the judge nor the magistrate attempts to induce a party to consent to reference of a civil matter under this rule to a magistrate. See House Rep. No. 96–444, 96th Cong. 1st Sess. 8 (1979).

The rule opts for a uniform approach in implementing the consent provision by directing the clerk to notify the parties of their opportunity to elect to proceed before a magistrate and by requiring the execution and filing of a consent form or forms setting forth the election. However, flexibility at the local level is preserved in that local rules will determine how notice shall be communicated to the parties, and local rules will specify the time period within which an election must be made.

The last paragraph of subdivision (b) reiterates the provision in 28 U.S.C. § 636(c)(6) for vacating a reference to the magistrate.

Subdivision (c). Under 28 U.S.C. § 636(c)(3), the normal route of appeal from the judgment of a magistrate—the only route that will be available unless the parties otherwise agree in advance—is an appeal by the aggrieved party "directly to the appropriate United States court of appeals from the judgment of the magistrate in the same manner as an appeal from any other judgment of a district court." The quoted statutory language indicates Congress' intent that the same procedures and standards of appealability that govern appeals from district court judgments govern appeals from magistrates' judgments.

Subdivision (d). 28 U.S.C. § 636(c)(4) offers parties who consent to the exercise of civil jurisdiction by a magistrate an alternative appeal route to that provided in subdivision (c) of this rule. This optional appellate route was provided by Congress in recognition of the fact that not all civil cases warrant the same appellate treatment. In cases where the amount in controversy is not great and there are no difficult questions of law to be resolved, the parties may desire to avoid the expense and delay of appeal to the court of appeals by electing an appeal to the district judge. See McCabe, *The Federal Magistrate Act of 1979,* 16 Harv.J.Legis. 343, 388 (1979). This subdivision provides that the parties may elect the optional appeal route at the time of reference to a magistrate. To this end, the notice by the clerk under subdivision (b) of this rule shall explain the appeal option and the corollary restriction on review by the court of appeals. This approach will avoid later claims of lack of consent to the avenue of appeal. The choice of the alternative appeal route to the judge of the district court should be made by the parties in their forms of consent. Special appellate rules to govern appeals from a magistrate to a district judge appear in new Rules 74 through 76.

Rule 74. Method of Appeal from Magistrate to District Judge under Title 28, U.S.C. § 636(c)(4) and Rule 73(d)

(a) When Taken. When the parties have elected under Rule 73(d) to proceed by appeal to a district judge from an appealable decision made by a magistrate under the consent provisions of Title 28, U.S.C. § 636(c)(4), an appeal may be taken from the decision of a magistrate by filing with the clerk of the district court a notice of appeal within 30 days of the date of entry of the judgment appealed from; but if the United States or an officer or agency thereof is a party, the notice of appeal may be filed by any party within 60 days of such entry. If a timely notice of appeal is filed by a party, any other party may file a notice of appeal within 14 days thereafter, or within the time otherwise prescribed by this subdivision, whichever period last expires.

The running of the time for filing a notice of appeal is terminated as to all parties by the timely filing of any of the following

New matter is shown in italics; matter to be omitted is lined through

motions with the magistrate by any party, and the full time for appeal from the judgment entered by the magistrate commences to run anew from entry of any of the following orders: (1) granting or denying a motion for judgment under Rule 50(b); (2) granting or denying a motion under Rule 52(b) to amend or make additional findings of fact, whether or not an alteration of the judgment would be required if the motion is granted; (3) granting or denying a motion under Rule 59 to alter or amend the judgment; (4) denying a motion for a new trial under Rule 59.

An interlocutory decision or order by a magistrate which, if made by a judge of the district court, could be appealed under any provision of law, may be appealed to a judge of the district court by filing a notice of appeal within 15 days after entry of the decision or order, provided the parties have elected to appeal to a judge of the district court under Rule 73(d). An appeal of such interlocutory decision or order shall not stay the proceedings before the magistrate unless the magistrate or judge shall so order.

Upon a showing of excusable neglect, the magistrate may extend the time for filing a notice of appeal upon motion filed not later than 20 days after the expiration of the time otherwise prescribed by this rule.

(b) Notice of Appeal; Service. The notice of appeal shall specify the party or parties taking the appeal, designate the judgment, order or part thereof appealed from, and state that the appeal is to a judge of the district court. The clerk shall mail copies of the notice to all other parties and note the date of mailing in the civil docket.

(c) Stay Pending Appeal. Upon a showing that the magistrate has refused or otherwise failed to stay the judgment pending appeal to the district judge under Rule 73(d), the appellant may make application for a stay to the district judge with reasonable notice to all parties. The stay may be conditioned upon the filing in the district court of a bond or other appropriate security.

(d) Dismissal. For failure to comply with these rules or any local rule or order, the district judge may take such action as is deemed appropriate, including dismissal of the appeal. The district judge also may dismiss the appeal upon the filing of a stipulation signed by all parties, or upon motion and notice by the appellant.

Advisory Committee's Note

Subdivision (a). This rule governs appeals from decisions of magistrates exercising consensual civil jurisdiction under Rule 73 when the parties elect to appeal to a judge of the district court under subdivision (d) of that rule. Congress specified that such an appeal would be "on the record to a judge of the district court in the same manner as on an appeal from a judgment of the district court to a court of appeals." See 28 U.S.C. § 636(c)(4). Presumably, Congress intended that the district court follow the same general procedures, including the "clearly erroneous" factual review standard of Civil Rule 52(a), that a court of appeals follows in reviewing a judgment of the district court. However, Congress also provided that "whenever possible" the local rules of the district court shall endeavor to make appeals expeditious and inexpensive. See 28 U.S.C. § 636(c)(4). Since the Federal Rules of Appellate Procedure are designed to cover appeals from a single judge to a three-member appeal tribunal, some modifications have proved desirable in assuring an expeditious appeal from a magistrate to a single district judge. Rules 74 through 76 provide this set of rules governing appeals from magistrates' exercise of consensual jurisdiction.

The time limits in subdivision (a) generally conform to those in Appellate Rule 4(a), except that the period in which a party may move for leave to file a late notice of appeal on grounds of excusable neglect is 20 days, rather than the 30-day period provided for in the Appellate Rules.

The term "appealable decision" as used in this rule embraces the "final decision" concept of 28 U.S.C. § 1291 and permits an appeal from a magistrate to a district judge in those situations in which an appeal from a district judge to the court of appeals would lie. That term, along with the specific provision in the rule permitting appeals of certain interlocutory orders, incorporates by reference the provisions of 28 U.S.C. § 1292 and adopts, by analogy to Section 1292(b), a certification procedure for otherwise unappealable orders "where the order is based on a controlling question of law as to which there is substantial ground for difference of opinion and an immediate appeal from the order may materially advance the ultimate termination of the litigation." Although no specific certification procedure is set forth, the rule contemplates that a magistrate may certify such an order for appeal, and the district judge, in his discretion, may allow the appeal. In the interest of expediting the trial, interlocutory appeals of any kind will not stay the proceedings unless the magistrate or district judge finds that the nature of the appeal or its relation to the remaining proceedings requires a stay.

Subdivision (b). The provisions governing the content and service of the notice of appeal conform substantially to Rules 3(c) and 3(d) of the Federal Rules of Appellate Procedure.

Subdivision (c). This subdivision represents a simplified version of Rule 8 of the Federal Rules of Appellate Procedure. Under this subdivision, the district judge is in the position of an appellate judge under Rule 8 of the Appellate Rules when the judge below has refused a stay under Rule 62.

In proceedings under 28 U.S.C. § 636(c), an application for a stay of the judgment under Rule 62 initially will be made to the magistrate. The district judge under this rule may hear an application for a stay of the judgment upon a showing that the magistrate has refused to stay the judgment pending appeal to the district judge.

Subdivision (d). The provisions governing dismissal are similar to Rule 3(a) (failure to prosecute) and Rule 42(a) (voluntary dismissal) of the Federal Rules of Appellate Procedure.

Rule 75. Proceedings on Appeal from Magistrate to District Judge under Rule 73(d)

(a) Applicability. In proceedings under Title 28, U.S.C. § 636(c), when the parties have previously elected under Rule 73(d) to appeal to a district judge rather than to the court of appeals, this rule shall govern the proceedings on appeal.

(b) Record on Appeal.

(1) Composition. The original papers and exhibits filed with the clerk of the district court, the transcript of the proceedings, if any, and the docket entries shall constitute the record on appeal. In lieu of this record the parties, within 10 days after the filing of the notice of appeal, may file a joint statement of the case showing how the issues presented by the appeal arose and were decided by the magistrate, and setting forth only so many of the facts averred and proved or sought to be proved as are essential to a decision of the issues presented.

(2) Transcript. Within 10 days after filing the notice of appeal the appellant shall make arrangements for the production of a transcript of such parts of the proceedings as he deems necessary. Unless the entire transcript is to be included, the appellant, within the time provided above, shall serve on the appellee and file with the court a description of the parts of the transcript which he intends to present on the appeal. If the appellee deems a transcript of other parts of the proceedings to be necessary, within 10 days after the service of the statement of the appellant, he shall serve on the appellant and file with the court a designation of additional parts to be included. The appellant shall promptly make arrangements for the inclusion of all such parts unless the magistrate, upon motion, exempts the appellant from providing certain parts, in which case the appellee may provide for their transcription.

(3) Statement in Lieu of Transcript. If no record of the proceedings is available for transcription, the parties shall, within 10 days after the filing of the notice of appeal, file a statement of the evidence from the best available means to be submitted in lieu of the transcript. If the parties cannot agree they shall submit a statement of their differences to the magistrate for settlement.

(c) Time for Filing Briefs. Unless a local rule or court order otherwise provides, the following time limits for filing briefs shall apply.

(1) The appellant shall serve and file his brief within 20 days after the filing of the transcript, statement of the case, or statement of the evidence.

(2) The appellee shall serve and file his brief within 20 days after service of the brief of the appellant.

(3) The appellant may serve and file a reply brief within 10 days after service of the brief of the appellee.

(4) If the appellee has filed a cross-appeal, he may file a reply brief limited to the issues on the cross-appeal within 10 days after service of the reply brief of the appellant.

(d) Length and Form of Briefs. Briefs may be typewritten. The length and form of briefs shall be governed by local rule.

(e) Oral Argument. The opportunity for the parties to be heard on oral argument shall be governed by local rule.

Advisory Committee's Note

Subdivision (a). 28 U.S.C. § 636(c)(4) provides that whenever possible the local rules of the district court shall endeavor to make appeals from the magistrate to the district judge expeditious and inexpensive. The provisions of this rule are directed to that end in simplifying the record on appeal and permitting typewritten briefs. The availability of oral argument and the length and form of briefs are matters appropriately left to local rule.

Subdivision (b). The provisions governing the composition of the record and the transcript are adapted from Rule 10 of the Federal Rules of Appellate Procedure. The language requiring the appellant to "make arrangements for the production of a transcript" is broad enough to require the party to order a transcript from the court reporter or to make arrangements to transcribe a taped record of the proceedings. The magistrate is to settle any differences regarding the extent of the transcript and to require the appellant to provide for transcription of any additional portions designated by the appellee that are material to the issues on appeal. Naturally, the rule is subject to the operation of 28 U.S.C. § 1915 in the case of a party who is unable to pay such costs.

Although it is not anticipated that an appeal will often be taken from a hearing or trial of which no record was made, the parties do have the option to forego a record in routine matters under 28 U.S.C. § 636(c)(7). In such cases a statement of the evidence will be prepared by the parties (or by the magistrate if the parties cannot agree) from the best available means, including the recollections and notes of the parties and the magistrate.

Subdivision (c). Although the parties, with agreement of the court, can dispense with the filing of briefs, a schedule for the serving and filing of briefs will often be necessary. In lieu of the elaborate provisions of Rules 28 through 32 of the Federal Rules of Appellate Procedure, this rule adopts a simplified approach for the filing and serving of briefs in order to achieve an inexpensive and expeditious appeal from a magistrate's judgment to a district judge. The timing of the appellant's initial brief is tied to the filing of the transcript or statement, instead of the filing of the record (Appellate Rule 31(a)) or the docketing of the appeal, because the rest of the record is already in the hands of the district court clerk and need not be transmitted. This rule does not require payment of a filing fee. Thus the filing of the transcript or statement is all that remains of the traditional concepts of filing the record and docketing the appeal.

The introductory clause of the rule recognizes the desirability of allowing local and individual variations in the filing of briefs, and the numbered clauses prescribe shorter periods than the corresponding intervals allowed by Appellate Rule 31(a). The provision allowing a reply brief for an appellee who has filed a cross-appeal is taken from Appellate Rule 28(c).

Subdivision (d). The use of typewritten briefs is urged as a means of minimizing costs and of expediting appeals from the magistrate to the district judge. The form and length of briefs should be addressed as a matter of local rule in order to avoid resort to the more elaborate provisions of the Federal Rules of Appellate Procedure.

Subdivision (e). The availability of oral argument has been left as a matter for local rule.

Rule 76. Judgment of the District Judge on the Appeal under Rule 73(d) and Costs

(a) Entry of Judgment. When the parties have elected under Rule 73(d) to appeal from a judgment of the magistrate to a district judge, the clerk shall prepare, sign, and enter judgment in accordance with the order or decision of the district judge following an appeal from a judgment of the magistrate, unless the district judge directs otherwise. The clerk shall mail to all parties a copy of the order or decision of the district judge.

(b) Stay of Judgments. The decision of the district judge shall be stayed for 10 days during which time a party may petition the district judge for rehearing, and a timely petition shall stay the decision of the district judge pending disposition of a petition for rehearing. Upon the motion of a party, the decision of the district judge may be stayed in order to allow a party to petition the court of appeals for leave to appeal.

(c) Costs. Except as otherwise provided by law or ordered by the district judge, costs shall be taxed against the losing party; if a judgment of the magistrate is affirmed in part or reversed in part, or is vacated, costs shall be allowed only as ordered by the district judge. The cost of the transcript, if necessary for the determination of the appeal, and the premiums paid for bonds to preserve rights pending appeal shall be taxed as costs by the clerk.

Advisory Committee's Note

Subdivision (a). This subdivision, adapted from Rule 36 of the Federal Rules of Appellate Procedure, directs the clerk to enter judgment in accordance with the order or decision of the district judge affirming, reversing, or modifying the judgment of the magistrate and to mail copies of the order or decision to all parties.

Subdivision (b). This subdivision, adapted from Rule 41 of the Federal Rules of Appellate Procedure, stays the effect of the district judge's decision on an appeal from a judgment of the magistrate. The availability of a rehearing by the district judge is contemplated (see Appellate Rule 40), but no particular form of petition is specified by the rule. The initial 10-day stay and the stay pending disposition of a timely petition for rehearing operate automatically upon the magistrate and all parties. Any other stay is at the discretion of the district judge.

Subdivision (c). This provision for costs on appeal is adapted from Rule 39 of the Federal Rules of Appellate Procedure to achieve the inexpensive appellate process envisioned from district judge review of magistrate action. No filing fee is required since a single clerk's office handles the file throughout, and no bond for costs is required. Ordinarily the only costs will be the costs of the transcript and the premium for any supersedeas bond.

CERTAIN OF THE AMENDMENTS OF FEDERAL RULES OF CIVIL PROCEDURE ADOPTED BY THE SUPREME COURT OF THE UNITED STATES ON APRIL 29, 1985, EFFECTIVE AUGUST 1, 1985, WITH ADVISORY COMMITTEE'S NOTES THEREON

[*Amendments here omitted: Changes in Rule 71A, Form 18–A, and Supplemental Rules B, C, and E.*]

Rule 6. Time

(a) Computation. In computing any period of time prescribed or allowed by these rules, by the local rules of any district court, by order of court, or by any applicable statute, the day of the act, event, or default from which the designated period of time begins to run shall not be included. The last day of the period so computed shall be included, unless it is a Saturday, a Sunday, or a legal holiday, *or, when the act to be done is the filing of a paper in court, a day on which weather or other conditions have made the office of the clerk of the district court inaccessible,* in which event the period runs until the end of the next day which is not ~~a Saturday, a Sunday, or a legal holiday~~ *one of the aforementioned days.* When the period of time prescribed or allowed is less than ~~7~~ *11* days, intermediate Saturdays, Sundays, and legal holidays shall be excluded in the computation. As used in this rule and in Rule 77(c), "legal holiday" includes New Year's Day, *Birthday of Martin Luther King, Jr.,* Washington's Birthday, Memorial Day, Independence Day, Labor Day, Columbus Day, Veterans Day, Thanksgiving Day, Christmas Day, and any other day appointed as a holiday by the President or the Congress of the United States, or by the state in which the district court is held.

Advisory Committee's Note

Rule 6(a) is amended to acknowledge that weather conditions or other events may render the clerk's office inaccessible one or more days. Parties who are obliged to file something with the court during that period should not be penalized if they cannot do so. The amendment conforms to changes made in Federal Rule of Criminal Procedure 45(a), effective August 1, 1982.

The Rule also is amended to extend the exclusion of intermediate Saturdays, Sundays, and legal holidays to the computation of time periods less than 11 days. Under the current version of the Rule, parties bringing motions under rules with

New matter is shown in italics; matter to be omitted is lined through

10-day periods could have as few as 5 working days to prepare their motions. This hardship would be especially acute in the case of Rules 50(b) and (c)(2), 52(b), and 59(b), (d), and (e), which may not be enlarged at the discretion of the court. See Rule 6(b). If the exclusion of Saturdays, Sundays, and legal holidays will operate to cause excessive delay in urgent cases, the delay can be obviated by applying to the court to shorten the time. See Rule 6(b).

The Birthday of Martin Luther King, Jr., which becomes a legal holiday effective in 1986, has been added to the list of legal holidays enumerated in the Rule.

Rule 45. Subpoena

(d) Subpoena for Taking Depositions; Place of Examination.

(2) ~~A resident of the district in which the deposition is to be taken may be required to attend an examination only in the county wherein he resides or is employed or transacts his business in person, or at such other convenient place as is fixed by an order of court. A nonresident of the district may be required to attend only in the county wherein he is served with a subpoena, or within 40 miles from the place of service, or at such other convenient place as is fixed by an order of court.~~ *A person to whom a subpoena for the taking of a deposition is directed may be required to attend at any place within 100 miles from the place where that person resides, is employed or transacts business in person, or is served, or at such other convenient place as is fixed by an order of court.*

Advisory Committee's Note

Present Rule 45(d)(2) has two sentences setting forth the territorial scope of deposition subpoenas. The first sentence is directed to depositions taken in the judicial district in which the deponent resides; the second sentence addresses situations in which the deponent is not a resident of the district in which the deposition is to take place. The Rule, as currently constituted, creates anomalous situations that often cause logistical problems in conducting litigation.

The first sentence of the present Rule states that a deponent may be required to attend only in the *county* wherein that person resides or is employed or transacts business in person, that is, where the person lives or works. Under this provision a deponent can be compelled, without court order, to travel from one end of that person's home county to the other, no matter how far that may be. The second sentence of the Rule is somewhat more flexible, stating that someone who does not reside in the district in which the deposition is to be taken can be required to attend in the county where the person is served with the subpoena, *or* within 40 miles from the place of service.

Under today's conditions there is no sound reason for distinguishing between residents of the district or county in which a deposition is to be taken and nonresidents, and the Rule is amended to provide that any person may be subpoenaed to attend a deposition within a specified radius from that person's residence, place of business, or where the person was served. The 40-mile radius has been increased to 100 miles.

Rule 52. Findings by the Court

(a) Effect. In all actions tried upon the facts without a jury or with an advisory jury, the court shall find the facts specially and state separately its conclusions of law thereon, and judgment shall be entered pursuant to Rule 58; and in granting or refusing interlocutory injunctions the court shall similarly set forth the findings of fact and conclusions of law which constitute the grounds of its action. Requests for findings are not necessary for purposes of review. Findings of fact, *whether based on oral or documentary evidence,* shall not be set aside unless clearly erroneous, and due regard shall be given to the opportunity of the trial court to judge of the credibility of the witnesses. The findings of a master, to the extent that the court adopts them, shall be considered as the findings of the court. It will be sufficient if the findings of fact and conclusions of law are stated orally and recorded in open court following the close of the evidence or appear in an opinion or memorandum of decision filed by the court. Findings of fact and conclusions of law are unnecessary on decisions of motions under Rules 12 or 56 or any other motion except as provided in Rule 41(b).

Advisory Committee's Note

Rule 52(a) has been amended (1) to avoid continued confusion and conflicts among the circuits as to the standard of appellate review of findings of fact by the court, (2) to eliminate the disparity between the standard of review as literally stated in Rule 52(a) and the practice of some courts of appeals, and (3) to promote nationwide uniformity. See Note, *Rule 52(a): Appellate Review of Findings of Fact Based on Documentary or Undisputed Evidence,* 49 Va.L.Rev. 506, 536 (1963).

Some courts of appeal have stated that when a trial court's findings do not rest on demeanor evidence and evaluation of a witness' credibility, there is no reason to defer to the trial court's findings and the appellate court more readily can find them to be clearly erroneous. See, *e.g.*, *Marcum v. United States*, 621 F.2d 142, 144–45 (5th Cir. 1980). Others go further, holding that appellate review may be had without application of the "clearly erroneous" test since the appellate court is in as good a position as the trial court to review a purely documentary record. See, *e.g.*, *Atari, Inc. v. North American Philips Consumer Electronics Corp.*, 672 F.2d 607, 614 (7th Cir.), *cert. denied*, 459 U.S. 880 (1982); *Lydle v. United States*, 635 F.2d 763, 765 n. 1 (6th Cir. 1981); *Swanson v. Baker Indus., Inc.*, 615 F.2d 479, 483 (8th Cir. 1980); *Taylor v. Lombard*, 606 F.2d 371, 372 (2d Cir. 1979), *cert. denied*, 445 U.S. 946 (1980); *Jack Kahn Music Co. v. Baldwin Piano & Organ Co.*, 604 F.2d 755, 758 (2d Cir. 1979); *John R. Thompson Co. v. United States*, 477 F.2d 164, 167 (7th Cir. 1973).

A third group has adopted the view that the "clearly erroneous" rule applies in all nonjury cases even when findings are based solely on documentary evidence or on inferences from undisputed facts. See, *e.g.*, *Maxwell v. Sumner*, 673 F.2d 1031, 1036 (9th Cir.), *cert. denied*, 459 U.S. 976 (1982); *United States v. Texas Education Agency*, 647 F.2d 504, 506–07 (5th Cir. 1981), *cert. denied*, 454 U.S. 1143 (1982);

Constructora Maza, Inc. v. Banco de Ponce, 616 F.2d 573, 576 (1st Cir. 1980); *In re Sierra Trading Corp.*, 482 F.2d 333, 337 (10th Cir. 1973); *Case v. Morrisette*, 475 F.2d 1300, 1306–07 (D.C. Cir. 1973).

The commentators also disagree as to the proper interpretation of the Rule. *Compare* Wright, *The Doubtful Omniscience of Appellate Courts*, 41 Minn. L. Rev. 751, 769–70 (1957) (language and intent of Rule support view that "clearly erroneous" test should apply to all forms of evidence), *and* 9 C. Wright & A. Miller, *Federal Practice and Procedure: Civil* § 2587, at 740 (1971) (language of the Rule is clear), *with* 5A J. Moore, *Federal Practice* ¶ 52.04, at 2687–88 (2d ed. 1982) (Rule as written supports broader review of findings based on non-demeanor testimony).

The Supreme Court has not clearly resolved the issue. See *Bose Corp. v. Consumers Union of United States, Inc.*, 104 S.Ct. 1949, 1958 (1984); *Pullman Standard v. Swint*, 456 U.S. 273, 293 (1982); *United States v. General Motors Corp.*, 384 U.S. 127, 141 n. 16 (1966); *United States v. United States Gypsum Co.*, 333 U.S. 364, 394–96 (1948).

The principal argument advanced in favor of a more searching appellate review of findings by the district court based solely on documentary evidence is that the rationale of Rule 52(a) does not apply when the findings do not rest on the trial court's assessment of credibility of the witnesses but on an evaluation of documentary proof and the drawing of inferences from it, thus eliminating the need for any special deference to the trial court's findings. These considerations are outweighed by the public interest in the stability and judicial economy that would be promoted by recognizing that the trial court, not the appellate tribunal, should be the finder of the facts. To permit courts of appeals to share more actively in the fact-finding function would tend to undermine the legitimacy of the district courts in the eyes of litigants, multiply appeals by encouraging appellate retrial of some factual issues, and needlessly reallocate judicial authority.

Rule 83. Rules by District Courts

Each district court by action of a majority of the judges thereof may from time to time, *after giving appropriate public notice and an opportunity to comment,* make and amend rules governing its practice not inconsistent with these rules. *A local rule so adopted shall take effect upon the date specified by the district court and shall remain in effect unless amended by the district court or abrogated by the judicial council of the circuit in which the district is located.* Copies of rules and amendments so made by any district court shall upon their promulgation be furnished to the ~~Supreme Court of the United States~~ *judicial council and the Administrative Office of the United States Courts and be made available to the public.* In all cases not provided for by rule, the district ~~courts~~ *judges and magistrates* may regulate their practice in any manner not inconsistent with these rules *or those of the district in which they act.*

Advisory Committee's Note

Rule 83, which has not been amended since the Federal Rules were promulgated in 1938, permits each district to adopt local rules not inconsistent with the Federal

Rules by a majority of the judges. The only other requirement is that copies be furnished to the Supreme Court.

The widespread adoption of local rules and the modest procedural prerequisites for their promulgation have led many commentators to question the soundness of the process as well as the validity of some rules. See 12 C. Wright & A. Miller, *Federal Practice and Procedure: Civil* § 3152, at 217 (1973); Caballero, *Is There an Over-Exercise of Local Rule-Making Powers by the United States District Courts?*, 24 Fed. Bar News 325 (1977). Although the desirability of local rules for promoting uniform practice within a district is widely accepted, several commentators also have suggested reforms to increase the quality, simplicity, and uniformity of the local rules. See Note, *Rule 83 and the Local Federal Rules*, 67 Colum. L. Rev. 1251 (1967), and Comment, *The Local Rules of Civil Procedure in the Federal District Courts—A Survey*, 1966 Duke L.J. 1011.

The amended Rule attempts, without impairing the procedural validity of existing local rules, to enhance the local rulemaking process by requiring appropriate public notice of proposed rules and an opportunity to comment on them. Although some district courts apparently consult the local bar before promulgating rules, many do not, which has led to criticism of a process that has district judges consulting only with each other. See 12 C. Wright & A. Miller, *supra*, § 3152, at 217; Blair, *The New Local Rules for Federal Practice in Iowa*, 23 Drake L. Rev. 517 (1974). The new language subjects local rulemaking to scrutiny similar to that accompanying the Federal Rules, administrative rulemaking, and legislation. It attempts to assure that the expert advice of practitioners and scholars is made available to the district court before local rules are promulgated. See Weinstein, *Reform of Court Rule-Making Procedures* 84–87, 127–37, 151 (1977).

The amended Rule does not detail the procedure for giving notice and an opportunity to be heard since conditions vary from district to district. Thus, there is no explicit requirement for a public hearing, although a district may consider that procedure appropriate in all or some rulemaking situations. See generally, Weinstein, *supra*, at 117–37, 151. The new Rule does not foreclose any other form of consultation. For example, it can be accomplished through the mechanism of an "Advisory Committee" similar to that employed by the Supreme Court in connection with the Federal Rules themselves.

The amended Rule provides that a local rule will take effect upon the date specified by the district court and will remain in effect unless amended by the district court or abrogated by the judicial council. The effectiveness of a local rule should not be deferred until approved by the judicial council because that might unduly delay promulgation of a local rule that should become effective immediately, especially since some councils do not meet frequently. Similarly, it was thought that to delay a local rule's effectiveness for a fixed period of time would be arbitrary and that to require the judicial council to abrogate a local rule within a specified time would be inconsistent with its power under 28 U.S.C. § 332 (1976) to nullify a local rule at any time. The expectation is that the judicial council will examine all local rules, including those currently in effect, with an eye toward determining whether they are valid and consistent with the Federal Rules, promote inter-district uniformity and efficiency, and do not undermine the basic objectives of the Federal Rules.

The amended Rule requires copies of local rules to be sent upon their promulgation to the judicial council and the Administrative Office of the United States Courts rather than to the Supreme Court. The Supreme Court was the appropriate filing place in 1938, when Rule 83 originally was promulgated, but the establishment of the Administrative Office makes it a more logical place to develop a centralized file of local rules. This procedure is consistent with both the Criminal and the

Appellate Rules. See Fed. R. Crim. P. 57(a); Fed. R. App. P. 47. The Administrative Office also will be able to provide improved utilization of the file because of its recent development of a Local Rules Index.

The practice pursued by some judges of issuing standing orders has been controversial, particularly among members of the practicing bar. The last sentence in Rule 83 has been amended to make certain that standing orders are not inconsistent with the Federal Rules or any local district court rules. Beyond that, it is hoped that each district will adopt procedures, perhaps by local rule, for promulgating and reviewing single-judge standing orders.

CERTAIN OF THE AMENDMENTS OF FEDERAL RULES OF CIVIL PROCEDURE ADOPTED BY THE SUPREME COURT OF THE UNITED STATES ON APRIL 30, 1991, EFFECTIVE DECEMBER 1, 1991, WITH ADVISORY COMMITTEE'S NOTES THEREON

[*Amendments here omitted: Changes in Supplemental Rules C and E.*]

Rule 5. Service and Filing of Pleadings and Other Papers

(d) Filing*; Certificate of Service.* All papers after the complaint required to be served upon a party, *together with a certificate of service,* shall be filed with the court ~~either before service or~~ within a reasonable time ~~there~~after *service,* but the court may on motion of a party or on its own initiative order that depositions upon oral examination and interrogatories, requests for documents, requests for admission, and answers and responses thereto not be filed unless on order of the court or for use in the proceeding.

(e) Filing with the Court Defined. The filing of ~~pleadings and other~~ papers with the court as required by these rules shall be made by filing them with the clerk of the court, except that the judge may permit the papers to be filed with the judge, in which event the judge shall note thereon the filing date and forthwith transmit them to the office of the clerk. *Papers may be filed by facsimile transmission if permitted by rules of the district court, provided that the rules are authorized by and consistent with standards established by the Judicial Conference of the United States. The clerk shall not refuse to accept for filing any paper presented for that purpose solely because it is not presented in proper form as required by these rules or any local rules or practices.*

Advisory Committee's Note

Subdivision (d). This subdivision is amended to require that the person making service under the rule certify that service has been effected. Such a requirement has generally been imposed by local rule.

Having such information on file may be useful for many purposes, including proof of service if an issue arises concerning the effectiveness of the service. The certificate will generally specify the date as well as the manner of service, but parties employing private delivery services may sometimes be unable to specify the date of delivery. In the latter circumstance, a specification of the date of transmission of the paper to the delivery service may be sufficient for the purposes of this rule.

Subdivision (e). The words "pleading and other" are stricken as unnecessary. Pleadings are papers within the meaning of the rule. The revision also accommodates the development of the use of facsimile transmission for filing.

Several local district rules have directed the office of the clerk to refuse to accept for filing papers not conforming to certain requirements of form imposed by local rules or practice. This is not a suitable role for the office of the clerk, and the practice exposes litigants to the hazards of time bars; for these reasons, such rules are proscribed by this revision. The enforcement of these rules and of the local rules is a role for a judicial officer. A clerk may of course advise a party or counsel that a particular instrument is not in proper form, and may be directed to so inform the court.

Rule 15. Amended and Supplemental Pleadings

(c) Relation Back of Amendments. *An amendment of a pleading relates back to the date of the original pleading when*

(1) relation back is permitted by the law that provides the statute of limitations applicable to the action, or

(2) ~~Whenever~~ the claim or defense asserted in the amended pleading arose out of the conduct, transaction, or occurrence set forth or attempted to be set forth in the original pleading, ~~the amendment relates back to the date of the original pleading.~~ *or*

(3) ~~An~~ *the* amendment ~~changing~~ *changes* the party *or the naming of the party* against whom a claim is asserted ~~relates back~~ if the foregoing provision *(2)* is satisfied and, within the period provided by ~~law~~ *Rule 4(m)* for ~~commencing the action against~~ *service of the summons and complaint,* the party to be brought in by amendment~~, that party~~ (~~1~~ *A*) has received such notice of the institution of the action that the party will not be prejudiced in maintaining a defense on the merits, and (~~2~~ *B*) knew or should have known that, but for a mistake concerning the identity of the proper party, the action would have been brought against the party.

The delivery or mailing of process to the United States Attorney, or United States Attorney's designee, or the Attorney General of the United States, or an agency or officer who would have been a proper defendant if named, satisfies the requirement of ~~clauses~~ *subparagraphs* (~~1~~ *A*) and (~~2~~ *B*) ~~here~~of *this paragraph (3)* with respect to the United States or any agency or officer thereof to be brought into the action as a defendant.

New matter is shown in italics; matter to be omitted is lined through

Advisory Committee's Note

The rule has been revised to prevent parties against whom claims are made from taking unjust advantage of otherwise inconsequential pleading errors to sustain a limitations defense.

Paragraph (c)(1). This provision is new. It is intended to make it clear that the rule does not apply to preclude any relation back that may be permitted under the applicable limitations law. Generally, the applicable limitations law will be state law. If federal jurisdiction is based on the citizenship of the parties, the primary reference is the law of the state in which the district court sits. *Walker v. Armco Steel Corp.,* 446 U.S. 740 (1980). If federal jurisdiction is based on a federal question, the reference may be to the law of the state governing relations between the parties. *E.g., Board of Regents v. Tomanio,* 446 U.S. 478 (1980). In some circumstances, the controlling limitations law may be federal law. *E.g., West v. Conrail, Inc.,* 107 S.Ct. 1538 (1987). Cf. *Burlington Northern R. Co. v. Woods,* 480 U.S. 1 (1987); *Stewart Organization v. Ricoh,* 108 S.Ct. 2239 (1988). Whatever may be the controlling body of limitations law, if that law affords a more forgiving principle of relation back than the one provided in this rule, it should be available to save the claim. Accord, *Marshall v. Mulrenin,* 508 F.2d 39 (1st Cir.1974). If *Schiavone v. Fortune,* 106 S.Ct. 2379 (1986) implies the contrary, this paragraph is intended to make a material change in the rule.

Paragraph (c)(3). This paragraph has been revised to change the result in *Schiavone v. Fortune, supra,* with respect to the problem of a misnamed defendant. An intended defendant who is notified of an action within the period allowed by Rule 4(m) for service of a summons and complaint may not under the revised rule defeat the action on account of a defect in the pleading with respect to the defendant's name, provided that the requirements of clauses (A) and (B) have been met. If the notice requirement is met within the Rule 4(m) period, a complaint may be amended at any time to correct a formal defect such as a misnomer or misidentification. On the basis of the text of the former rule, the Court reached a result in *Schiavone v. Fortune* that was inconsistent with the liberal pleading practices secured by Rule 8. See Bauer, Schiavone: *An Un–Fortune–ate Illustration of the Supreme Court's Role as Interpreter of the Federal Rules of Civil Procedure,* 63 Notre Dame L.Rev. 720 (1988); Brussack, *Outrageous Fortune: The Case for Amending Rule 15(c) Again,* 61 S.Cal.L.Rev. 671 (1988); Lewis, *The Excessive History of Federal Rule 15(c) and Its Lessons for Civil Rules Revision,* 86 Mich.L.Rev. 1507 (1987).

In allowing a name-correcting amendment within the time allowed by Rule 4(m), this rule allows not only the 120 days specified in that rule, but also any additional time resulting from any extension ordered by the court pursuant to that rule, as may be granted, for example, if the defendant is a fugitive from service of the summons.

This revision, together with the revision of Rule 4(i) with respect to the failure of a plaintiff in an action against the United States to effect timely service on all the appropriate officials, is intended to produce results contrary to those reached in *Gardner v. Gartman,* 880 F.2d 797 (4th Cir.1989), *Rys v. U.S. Postal Service,* 886 F.2d 443 (1st Cir.1989), *Martin's Food & Liquor, Inc. v. U.S. Dept. of Agriculture,* 702 F.Supp. 215 (N.D.Ill.1988). *But cf. Montgomery v. United States Postal Service,* 867 F.2d 900 (5th Cir.1989), *Warren v. Department of the Army,* 867 F.2d 1156 (8th Cir.1989); *Miles v. Department of the Army,* 881 F.2d 777 (9th Cir.1989), *Barsten v. Department of the Interior,* 896 F.2d 422 (9th Cir.1990); *Brown v. Georgia Dept. of Revenue,* 881 F.2d 1018 (11th Cir.1989).

Rule 24. Intervention

(c) Procedure. A person desiring to intervene shall serve a motion to intervene upon the parties as provided in Rule 5. The motion shall state the grounds therefor and shall be accompanied by a pleading setting forth the claim or defense for which intervention is sought. The same procedure shall be followed when a statute of the United States gives a right to intervene. When the constitutionality of an act of Congress affecting the public interest is drawn in question in any action in which the United States or an officer, agency, or employee thereof is not a party, the court shall notify the Attorney General of the United States as provided in Title 28, U.S.C. § 2403. *When the constitutionality of any statute of a State affecting the public interest is drawn in question in any action in which that State or any agency, officer, or employee thereof is not a party, the court shall notify the attorney general of the State as provided in Title 28, U.S.C. § 2403. A party challenging the constitutionality of legislation should call the attention of the court to its consequential duty, but failure to do so is not a waiver of any constitutional right otherwise timely asserted.*

Advisory Committee's Note

Language is added to bring Rule 24(c) into conformity with the statute cited, resolving some confusion reflected in district court rules. As the text provides, counsel challenging the constitutionality of legislation in an action in which the appropriate government is not a party should call the attention of the court to its duty to notify the appropriate governmental officers. The statute imposes the burden of notification on the court, not the party making the constitutional challenge, partly in order to protect against any possible waiver of constitutional rights by parties inattentive to the need for notice. For this reason, the failure of a party to call the court's attention to the matter cannot be treated as a waiver.

Rule 34. Production of Documents and Things and Entry Upon Land for Inspection and Other Purposes

(c) Persons Not Parties. ~~This rule does not preclude an independent action against a person not a party for production of documents and things and permission to enter upon land~~ *A person not a party to the action may be compelled to produce documents and things or to submit to an inspection as provided in Rule 45.*

Advisory Committee's Note

This amendment reflects the change effected by revision of Rule 45 to provide for subpoenas to compel non-parties to produce documents and things and to submit to inspections of premises. The deletion of the text of the former paragraph is not intended to preclude an independent action for production of documents or things or for permission to enter upon land, but such actions may no longer be necessary in light of this revision.

Rule 35. Physical and Mental Examinations of Persons

(a) Order for Examination. When the mental or physical condition (including the blood group) of a party or of a person in the custody or under the legal control of a party, is in controversy, the court in which the action is pending may order the party to submit to a physical ~~examination by a physician,~~ or mental examination by a ~~physician or psychologist~~ *suitably licensed or certified examiner* or to produce for examination the person in the party's custody or legal control. The order may be made only on motion for good cause shown and upon notice to the person to be examined and to all parties and shall specify the time, place, manner, conditions, and scope of the examination and the person or persons by whom it is to be made.

(b) Report of ~~Examining Physician or Psychologist~~ *Examiner*.

(1) If requested by the party against whom an order is made under Rule 35(a) or the person examined, the party causing the examination to be made shall deliver to the requesting party a copy of the detailed written report of the ~~examining physician or psychologist~~ *examiner* setting out the ~~physician's~~ *examiner's* findings, including results of all tests made, diagnoses and conclusions, together with like reports of all earlier examinations of the same condition. After delivery the party causing the examination shall be entitled upon request to receive from the party against whom the order is made a like report of any examination, previously or thereafter made, of the same condition, unless, in the case of a report of examination of a person not a party, the party shows that the party is unable to obtain it. The court on motion may make an order against a party requiring delivery of a report on such terms as are just, and if a*n* ~~physician or psychologist~~ *examiner* fails or refuses to make a report the court may exclude the ~~physician~~ *examiner's* testimony if offered at trial.

(3) This subdivision applies to examinations made by agreement of the parties, unless the agreement expressly provides otherwise. This subdivision does not preclude discovery of a report of an ~~examining physician or psychologist~~ *examiner* or the taking of a deposition of the ~~physician psychologist~~ *examiner* in accordance with the provisions of any other rule.

~~**(c) Definitions.** For the purpose of this rule, a psychologist is a psychologist licensed or certified by a State or the District of Columbia.~~

New matter is shown in italics; matter to be omitted is lined through

Advisory Committee's Note

The revision authorizes the court to require physical or mental examinations conducted by any person who is suitably licensed or certified.

The rule was revised in 1988 by Congressional enactment to authorize mental examinations by licensed clinical psychologists. This revision extends that amendment to include other certified or licensed professionals, such as dentists or occupational therapists, who are not physicians or clinical psychologists, but who may be well-qualified to give valuable testimony about the physical or mental condition that is the subject of dispute.

The requirement that the examiner be *suitably* licensed or certified is a new requirement. The court is thus expressly authorized to assess the credentials of the examiner to assure that no person is subjected to a court-ordered examination by an examiner whose testimony would be of such limited value that it would be unjust to require the person to undergo the invasion of privacy associated with the examination. This authority is not wholly new, for under the former rule, the court retained discretion to refuse to order an examination, or to restrict an examination. 8 Wright & Miller, Federal Practice & Procedure § 2234 (1986 Supp.). The revision is intended to encourage the exercise of this discretion, especially with respect to examinations by persons having narrow qualifications.

The court's responsibility to determine the suitability of the examiner's qualifications applies even to a proposed examination by a physician. If the proposed examination and testimony calls for an expertise that the proposed examiner does not have, it should not be ordered, even if the proposed examiner is a physician. The rule does not, however, require that the license or certificate be conferred by the jurisdiction in which the examination is conducted.

Rule 41. Dismissal of Actions

(b) Involuntary Dismissal: Effect Thereof. For failure of the plaintiff to prosecute or to comply with these rules or any order of court, a defendant may move for dismissal of an action or of any claim against the defendant. ~~After the plaintiff, in an action tried by the court without a jury, has completed the presentation of evidence, the defendant, without waiving the right to offer evidence in the event the motion is not granted, may move for a dismissal on the ground that upon the facts and the law the plaintiff has shown no right to relief. The court as trier of the facts may then determine them and render judgment against the plaintiff or may decline to render any judgment until the close of all the evidence. If the court renders judgment on the merits against the plaintiff, the court shall make findings as provided in Rule 52(a).~~ Unless the court in its order for dismissal otherwise specifies, a dismissal under this subdivision and any dismissal not provided for in this rule, other than a dismissal for lack of jurisdiction, for improper venue, or for failure to join a party under Rule 19, operates as an adjudication upon the merits.

Advisory Committee's Note

Language is deleted that authorized the use of this rule as a means of terminating a non-jury action on the merits when the plaintiff has failed to carry a burden of proof in presenting the plaintiff's case. The device is replaced by the new provisions of Rule 52(c), which authorize entry of judgment against the defendant as well as the plaintiff, and earlier than the close of the case of the party against whom judgment is rendered. A motion to dismiss under Rule 41 on the ground that a plaintiff's evidence is legally insufficient should now be treated as a motion for judgment on partial findings as provided in Rule 52(c).

Rule 44. Proof of Official Record

(a) Authentication.

(1) Domestic. An official record kept within the United States, or any state, district, *or* commonwealth, ~~territory, or insular possession thereof,~~ or within ~~the Panama Canal Zone, the Trust Territory of the Pacific Islands, or the Ryukyu Islands~~ *a territory subject to the administrative or judicial jurisdiction of the United States,* or an entry therein, when admissible for any purpose, may be evidenced by an official publication thereof or by a copy attested by the officer having the legal custody of the record, or by the officer's deputy, and accompanied by a certificate that such officer has the custody. The certificate may be made by a judge of a court of record of the district or political subdivision in which the record is kept, authenticated by the seal of the court, or may be made by any public officer having a seal of office and having official duties in the district or political subdivision in which the record is kept, authenticated by the seal of the officer's office.

(2) Foreign. A foreign official record, or an entry therein, when admissible for any purpose, may be evidenced by an official publication thereof; or a copy thereof, attested by a person authorized to make the attestation, and accompanied by a final certification as to the genuineness of the signature and official position (i) of the attesting person, or (ii) of any foreign official whose certificate of genuineness of signature and official position relates to the attestation or is in a chain of certificates of genuineness of signature and official position relating to the attestation. A final certification may be made by a secretary of embassy or legation, consul general, vice consul, or consular agent of the United States, or a diplomatic or consular official of the foreign country assigned or accredited to the United States. If reasonable opportunity has been given to all parties to investigate the authenticity and accuracy of the documents, the court may, for good cause shown, (i) admit an attested copy without final certification or (ii) permit the foreign official record to be evidenced by an attested summary with or without a final certification. *The final certification is unnecessary if the record and the attestation are certified as provided in a treaty or convention to which the United States and the foreign country in which the official record is located are parties.*

New matter is shown in italics; matter to be omitted is lined through

Advisory Committee's Note

The amendment to paragraph (a)(1) strikes the references to specific territories, two of which are no longer subject to the jurisdiction of the United States, and adds a generic term to describe governments having a relationship with the United States such that their official records should be treated as domestic records.

The amendment to paragraph (a)(2) adds a sentence to dispense with the final certification by diplomatic officers when the United States and the foreign country where the record is located are parties to a treaty or convention that abolishes or displaces the requirement. In that event the treaty or convention is to be followed. This changes the former procedure for authenticating foreign official records only with respect to records from countries that are parties to the Hague Convention Abolishing the Requirement of Legalization for Foreign Public Documents. Moreover, it does not affect the former practice of attesting the records, but only changes the method of certifying the attestation.

The Hague Public Documents Convention provides that the requirement of a final certification is abolished and replaced with a model *apostille,* which is to be issued by officials of the country where the records are located. See Hague Public Documents Convention, Arts. 2–4. The *apostille* certifies the signature, official position, and seal of the attesting officer. The authority who issues the *apostille* must maintain a register or card index showing the serial number of the *apostille* and other relevant information recorded on it. A foreign court can then check the serial number and information on the *apostille* with the issuing authority in order to guard against the use of fraudulent *apostilles.* This system provides a reliable method for maintaining the integrity of the authentication process, and the *apostille* can be accorded greater weight than the normal authentication procedure because foreign officials are more likely to know the precise capacity under their law of the attesting officer than would an American official. See generally Comment, *The United States and the Hague Convention Abolishing the Requirement of Legalization for Foreign Public Documents,* 11 Harv. Int'l L.J. 476, 482, 488 (1970).

Rule 45. Subpoena

(a) ~~For Attendance of Witnesses;~~ Form; Issuance.

(1) Every subpoena shall ~~be issued by the clerk under the seal of the court, shall~~

(A) state the name of the court *from which it is issued;* and

(B) state the title of the action, *the name of the court in which it is pending, and its civil action number;* and

(C) command each person to whom it is directed to attend and give testimony *or to produce and permit inspection and copying of designated books, documents or tangible things in the possession, custody or control of that person, or to permit inspection of premises,* at a time and place therein specified*; and*

(D) set forth the text of subdivisions (c) and (d) of this rule.

A command to produce evidence or to permit inspection may be joined with a command to appear at trial or hearing or at deposition, or may be issued separately.

(2) A subpoena commanding attendance at a trial or hearing shall issue from the court for the district in which the hearing or trial is to be held. A subpoena for attendance at a deposition shall issue from the court for the district designated by the notice of deposition as the district in which the deposition is to be taken. If separate from a subpoena commanding the attendance of a person, a subpoena for production or inspection shall issue from the court for the district in which the production or inspection is to be made.

(3) The clerk shall issue a subpoena, ~~or a subpoena for the production of documentary evidence,~~ signed ~~and sealed~~ but otherwise in blank, to a party requesting it, who shall ~~fill~~ *complete* it ~~in~~ before service. *An attorney as officer of the court may also issue and sign a subpoena on behalf of*

(A) a court in which the attorney is authorized to practice; or

(B) a court for a district in which a deposition or production is compelled by the subpoena, if the deposition or production pertains to an action pending in a court in which the attorney is authorized to practice.

(b) ~~For Production of Documentary Evidence.~~ ~~A subpoena may also command the person to whom it is directed to produce the books, papers, documents, or tangible things designated therein; but the court, upon motion made promptly and in any event at or before the time specified in the subpoena for compliance therewith, may (1) quash or modify the subpoena if it is unreasonable or oppressive or (2) condition denial of the motion upon the advancement by the person in whose behalf the subpoena is issued of the reasonable cost of producing the books, papers, documents, or tangible things.~~

~~(c)~~ Service.

(1) A subpoena may be served by ~~the marshal, a deputy marshal, or by~~ any person who is not a party and is not less than 18 years of age. Service of a subpoena upon a person named therein shall be made by delivering a copy thereof to such person and, *if the person's attendance is commanded,* by tendering to that person the fees for one day's attendance and the mileage allowed by law. When the subpoena is issued on behalf of the United States or an officer or agency thereof, fees and mileage need not be tendered. *Prior notice of any commanded production of documents and things*

New matter is shown in italics; matter to be omitted is lined through

or inspection of premises before trial shall be served on each party in the manner prescribed by Rule 5(b).

~~**(d) Subpoena for Taking Depositions; Place of Examination.**~~

~~(1) Proof of service of a notice to take a deposition as provided in Rules 30(b) and 31(a) constitutes a sufficient authorization for the issuance by the clerk of the district court for the district in which the deposition is to be taken of subpoenas for the persons named or described therein. Proof of service may be made by filing with the clerk of the district court for the district in which the deposition is to be taken a copy of the notice together with a statement of the date and manner of service and of the names of the persons served, certified by the person who made service. The subpoena may command the person to whom it is directed to produce and permit inspection and copying of designated books, papers, documents, or tangible things which constitute or contain matters within the scope of the examination permitted by Rule 26(b), but in that event the subpoena will be subject to the provisions of Rule 26(c) and subdivision (b) of this rule.~~

~~The person to whom the subpoena is directed may, within 10 days after the service thereof or on or before the time specified in the subpoena for compliance if such time is less than 10 days after service, serve upon the attorney designated in the subpoena written objection to inspection or copying of any or all of the designated materials. If objection is made, the party serving the subpoena shall not be entitled to inspect and copy the materials except pursuant to an order of the court from which the subpoena was issued. The party serving the subpoena may, if objection has been made, move upon notice to the deponent for an order at any time before or during the taking of the deposition.~~

~~(2) A person to whom a subpoena for the taking of a deposition is directed may be required to attend at any place within 100 miles from the place where that person resides, is employed or transacts business in person, or is served, or at such other convenient place as is fixed by an order of court.~~

~~**(e) Subpoena for a Hearing or Trial.**~~

~~(1) At the request of any party subpoenas for attendance at a hearing or trial shall be issued by the clerk of the district court for the district in which the hearing or trial is held.~~

(2) Subject to the provisions of clause (ii) of subparagraph (c)(3)(A) of this rule, ~~A~~ *a* subpoena ~~requiring the attendance of a witness at a hearing or trial~~ may be served at any place within the district *of the court by which it is issued*, or at any place without the

district that is within 100 miles of the place of the *deposition,* hearing, ~~or~~ trial, *production, or inspection* specified in the subpoena or at any place within the state where a state statute or rule of court permits service of a subpoena issued by a state court of general jurisdiction sitting in the place ~~where the district court is held~~ *of the deposition, hearing, trial, production or inspection specified in the subpoena.* When a statute of the United States provides therefor, the court upon proper application and cause shown may authorize the service of a subpoena at any other place.

~~(2)~~ A subpoena directed to a witness in a foreign country *who is a national or resident of the United States* shall issue under the circumstances and in the manner and be served as provided in Title 28, U.S.C. § 1783.

(3) Proof of service when necessary shall be made by filing with the clerk of the court by which the subpoena is issued a statement of the date and manner of service and of the names of the persons served, certified by the person who made the service.

(c) Protection of Persons Subject to Subpoenas.

(1) A party or an attorney responsible for the issuance and service of a subpoena shall take reasonable steps to avoid imposing undue burden or expense on a person subject to that subpoena. The court on behalf of which the subpoena was issued shall enforce this duty and impose upon the party or attorney in breach of this duty an appropriate sanction, which may include, but is not limited to, lost earnings and a reasonable attorney's fee.

(2)(A) A person commanded to produce and permit inspection and copying of designated books, papers, documents or tangible things or inspection of premises need not appear in person at the place of production or inspection unless commanded to appear for deposition, hearing or trial.

(B) Subject to paragraph (d)(2) of this rule, a person commanded to produce and permit inspection and copying may, within 14 days after service of the subpoena or before the time specified for compliance if such time is less than 14 days after service, serve upon the party or attorney designated in the subpoena written objection to inspection or copying of any or all of the designated materials or of the premises. If objection is made, the party serving the subpoena shall not be entitled to inspect and copy the materials or inspect the premises except pursuant to an order of the court by which the subpoena was issued. If objection has been made, the party serving the subpoena may, upon notice to the person commanded to produce, move at any time for an order to compel the production. Such an order to compel production shall protect any person who is not a

party or an officer of a party from significant expense resulting from the inspection and copying commanded.

(3)(A) On timely motion, the court by which a subpoena was issued shall quash or modify the subpoena if it

(i) fails to allow reasonable time for compliance;

(ii) requires a person who is not a party or an officer of a party to travel to a place more than 100 miles from the place where that person resides, is employed or regularly transacts business in person, except that, subject to the provisions of clause (c)(3)(B)(iii) of this rule, such a person may in order to attend trial be commanded to travel from any such place within the state in which the trial is held, or

(iii) requires disclosure of privileged or other protected matter and no exception or waiver applies, or

(iv) subjects a person to undue burden.

(B) If a subpoena

(i) requires disclosure of a trade secret or other confidential research, development, or commercial information, or

(ii) requires disclosure of an unretained expert's opinion or information not describing specific events or occurrences in dispute and resulting from the expert's study made not at the request of any party, or

(iii) requires a person who is not a party or an officer of a party to incur substantial expense to travel more than 100 miles to attend trial,

the court may, to protect a person subject to or affected by the subpoena, quash or modify the subpoena or, if the party in whose behalf the subpoena is issued shows a substantial need for the testimony or material that cannot be otherwise met without undue hardship and assures that the person to whom the subpoena is addressed will be reasonably compensated, the court may order appearance or production only upon specified conditions.

(d) Duties in Responding to Subpoena.

(1) A person responding to a subpoena to produce documents shall produce them as they are kept in the usual course of business or shall organize and label them to correspond with the categories in the demand.

(2) When information subject to a subpoena is withheld on a claim that it is privileged or subject to protection as trial preparation materials, the claim shall be made expressly and shall be supported by a description of the nature of the documents, communi-

cations, or things not produced that is sufficient to enable the demanding party to contest the claim.

(~~f~~*e*) Contempt. Failure by any person without adequate excuse to obey a subpoena served upon that person may be deemed a contempt of the court from which the subpoena issued. *An adequate cause for failure to obey exists when a subpoena purports to require a non-party to attend or produce at a place not within the limits provided by clause (ii) of subparagraph (c)(3)(A).*

Advisory Committee's Note

Purposes of Revision. The purposes of this revision are (1) to clarify and enlarge the protections afforded persons who are required to assist the court by giving information or evidence; (2) to facilitate access outside the deposition procedure provided by Rule 30 to documents and other information in the possession of persons who are not parties; (3) to facilitate service of subpoenas for depositions or productions of evidence at places distant from the district in which an action is proceeding; (4) to enable the court to compel a witness found within the state in which the court sits to attend trial; (5) to clarify the organization of the text of the rule.

Subdivision (a). This subdivision is amended in seven significant respects.

First, Paragraph (a)(3) modifies the requirement that a subpoena be issued by the clerk of court. Provision is made for the issuance of subpoenas by attorneys as officers of the court. This revision perhaps culminates an evolution. Subpoenas were long issued by specific order of the court. As this became a burden to the court, general orders were made authorizing clerks to issue subpoenas on request. Since 1948, they have been issued in blank by the clerk of any federal court to any lawyer, the clerk serving as stationer to the bar. In allowing counsel to issue the subpoena, the rule is merely a recognition of present reality.

Although the subpoena is in a sense the command of the attorney who completes the form, defiance of a subpoena is nevertheless an act in defiance of a court order and exposes the defiant witness to contempt sanctions. In *ICC v. Brimson,* 154 U.S. 447 (1894), the Court upheld a statute directing federal courts to issue subpoenas to compel testimony before the ICC. In *CAB v. Hermann,* 353 U.S. 322 (1957), the Court approved as established practice the issuance of administrative subpoenas as a matter of absolute agency right. And in *NLRB v. Warren Co.,* 350 U.S. 107 (1955), the Court held that the lower court had no discretion to withhold sanctions against a contemnor who violated such subpoenas. The 1948 revision of Rule 45 put the attorney in a position similar to that of the administrative agency, as a public officer entitled to use the court's contempt power to investigate facts in dispute. Two courts of appeals have touched on the issue and have described lawyer-issued subpoenas as mandates of the court. *Waste Conversion, Inc. v. Rollins Environmental Services (NJ), Inc.,* 893 F.2d 605 (3d Cir.1990); *Fisher v. Marubeni Cotton Corp.,* 526 F.2d 1338, 1340 (8th Cir.1975). Cf. *Young v. United States ex rel. Vuitton et Fils S.A.,* 481 U.S. 787, 821 (1987) (Scalia, J., concurring). This revision makes the rule explicit that the attorney acts as an officer of the court in issuing and signing subpoenas.

Necessarily accompanying the evolution of this power of the lawyer as officer of the court is the development of increased responsibility and liability for the misuse of this power. The latter development is reflected in the provisions of subdivision

(c) of this rule, and also in the requirement imposed by paragraph (3) of this subdivision that the attorney issuing a subpoena must sign it.

Second, Paragraph (a)(3) authorizes attorneys in distant districts to serve as officers authorized to issue commands in the name of the court. Any attorney permitted to represent a client in a federal court, even one admitted pro haec vice, has the same authority as a clerk to issue a subpoena from any federal court for the district in which the subpoena is served and enforced. In authorizing attorneys to issue subpoenas from distant courts, the amended rule effectively authorizes service of a subpoena anywhere in the United States by an attorney representing any party. This change is intended to ease the administrative burdens of inter-district law practice. The former rule resulted in delay and expense caused by the need to secure forms from clerks' offices some distance from the place at which the action proceeds. This change does not enlarge the burden on the witness.

Pursuant to Paragraph (a)(2), a subpoena for a deposition must still issue from the court in which the deposition or production would be compelled. Accordingly, a motion to quash such a subpoena if it overbears the limits of the subpoena power must, as under the previous rule, be presented to the court for the district in which the deposition would occur. Likewise, the court in whose name the subpoena is issued is responsible for its enforcement.

Third, in order to relieve attorneys of the need to secure an appropriate seal to affix to a subpoena issued as an officer of a distant court, the requirement that a subpoena be under seal is abolished by the provisions of Paragraph (a)(1).

Fourth, Paragraph (a)(1) authorizes the issuance of a subpoena to compel a non-party to produce evidence independent of any deposition. This revision spares the necessity of a deposition of the custodian of evidentiary material required to be produced. A party seeking additional production from a person subject to such a subpoena may serve an additional subpoena requiring additional production at the same time and place.

Fifth, Paragraph (a)(2) makes clear that the person subject to the subpoena is required to produce materials in that person's control whether or not the materials are located within the district or within the territory within which the subpoena can be served. The non-party witness is subject to the same scope of discovery under this rule as that person would be as a party to whom a request is addressed pursuant to Rule 34.

Sixth, Paragraph (a)(1) requires that the subpoena include a statement of the rights and duties of witnesses by setting forth in full the text of the new subdivisions (c) and (d).

Seventh, the revised rule authorizes the issuance of a subpoena to compel the inspection of premises in the possession of a non-party. Rule 34 has authorized such inspections of premises in the possession of a party as discovery compelled under Rule 37, but prior practice required an independent proceeding to secure such relief ancillary to the federal proceeding when the premises were not in the possession of a party. Practice in some states has long authorized such use of a subpoena for this purpose without apparent adverse consequence.

Subdivision (b). Paragraph (b)(1) retains the text of the former subdivision (c) with minor changes.

The reference to the United States marshal and deputy marshal is deleted because of the infrequency of the use of these officers for this purpose. Inasmuch as these officers meet the age requirement, they may still be used if available.

A provision requiring service of prior notice pursuant to Rule 5 of compulsory pretrial production or inspection has been added to paragraph (b)(1). The purpose of such notice is to afford other parties an opportunity to object to the production or inspection, or to serve a demand for additional documents or things. Such additional notice is not needed with respect to a deposition because of the requirement of notice imposed by Rule 30 or 31. But when production or inspection is sought independently of a deposition, other parties may need notice in order to monitor the discovery and in order to pursue access to any information that may or should be produced.

Paragraph (b)(2) retains language formerly set forth in subdivision (e) and extends its application to subpoenas for depositions or production.

Paragraph (b)(3) retains language formerly set forth in paragraph (d)(1) and extends its applications to subpoenas for trial or hearing or production.

Subdivision (c). This provision is new and states the rights of witnesses. It is not intended to diminish rights conferred by Rules 26–37 or any other authority.

Paragraph (c)(1) gives specific application to the principle stated in Rule 26(g) and specifies liability for earnings lost by a non-party witness as a result of a misuse of the subpoena. No change in existing law is thereby effected. Abuse of a subpoena is an actionable tort, *Board of Ed. v. Farmingdale Classroom Teach. Ass'n,* 38 N.Y.2d 397, 380 N.Y.S.2d 635, 343 N.E.2d 278 (1975), and the duty of the attorney to the non-party is also embodied in Model Rule of Professional Conduct 4.4. The liability of the attorney is correlative to the expanded power of the attorney to issue subpoenas. The liability may include the cost of fees to collect attorneys' fees owed as a result of a breach of this duty.

Paragraph (c)(2) retains language from the former subdivision (b) and paragraph (d)(1). The 10–day period for response to a subpoena is extended to 14 days to avoid the complex calculations associated with short time periods under Rule 6 and to allow a bit more time for such objections to be made.

A non-party required to produce documents or materials is protected against significant expense resulting from involuntary assistance to the court. This provision applies, for example, to a non-party required to provide a list of class members. The court is not required to fix the costs in advance of production, although this will often be the most satisfactory accommodation to protect the party seeking discovery from excessive costs. In some instances, it may be preferable to leave uncertain costs to be determined after the materials have been produced, provided that the risk of uncertainty is fully disclosed to the discovering party. See, *e.g., United States v. Columbia Broadcasting Systems, Inc.,* 666 F.2d 364 (9th Cir.1982).

Paragraph (c)(3) explicitly authorizes the quashing of a subpoena as a means of protecting a witness from misuse of the subpoena power. It replaces and enlarges on the former subdivision (b) of this rule and tracks the provisions of Rule 26(c). While largely repetitious, this rule is addressed to the witness who may read it on the subpoena, where it is required to be printed by the revised paragraph (a)(1) of this rule.

Subparagraph (c)(3)(A) identifies those circumstances in which a subpoena must be quashed or modified. It restates the former provisions with respect to the limits of mandatory travel that are set forth in the former paragraphs (d)(2) and (e)(1), with one important change. Under the revised rule, a federal court can compel a witness to come from any place in the state to attend trial, whether or not the local state law so provides. This extension is subject to the qualification provided in the next paragraph, which authorizes the court to condition enforcement of a subpoena compelling a non-party witness to bear substantial expense to attend trial. The traveling non-party witness may be entitled to reasonable compensation for the time and effort entailed.

Clause (c)(3)(A)(iv) requires the court to protect all persons from undue burden imposed by the use of the subpoena power. Illustratively, it might be unduly burdensome to compel an adversary to attend trial as a witness if the adversary is known to have no personal knowledge of matters in dispute, especially so if the adversary would be required to incur substantial travel burdens.

Subparagraph (c)(3)(B) identifies circumstances in which a subpoena should be quashed unless the party serving the subpoena shows a substantial need and the court can devise an appropriate accommodation to protect the interests of the witness. An additional circumstance in which such action is required is a request for costly production of documents; that situation is expressly governed by subparagraph (b)(2)(B).

Clause (c)(3)(B)(i) authorizes the court to quash, modify, or condition a subpoena to protect the person subject to or affected by the subpoena from unnecessary or unduly harmful disclosures of confidential information. It corresponds to Rule 26(c)(7).

Clause (c)(3)(B)(ii) provides appropriate protection for the intellectual property of the non-party witness; it does not apply to the expert retained by a party, whose information is subject to the provisions of Rule 26(b)(4). A growing problem has been the use of subpoenas to compel the giving of evidence and information by unretained experts. Experts are not exempt from the duty to give evidence, even if they cannot be compelled to prepare themselves to give effective testimony, *e.g., Carter–Wallace, Inc. v. Otte,* 474 F.2d 529 (2d Cir.1972), but compulsion to give evidence may threaten the intellectual property of experts denied the opportunity to bargain for the value of their services. See generally Maurer, *Compelling the Expert Witness: Fairness and Utility Under the Federal Rules of Civil Procedure,* 19 Ga.L.Rev. 71 (1984); Note, *Discovery and Testimony of Unretained Experts,* 1987 Duke L.J. 140. Arguably the compulsion to testify can be regarded as a "taking" of intellectual property. The rule establishes the right of such persons to withhold their expertise, at least unless the party seeking it makes the kind of showing required for a conditional denial of a motion to quash as provided in the final sentence of subparagraph (c)(3)(B); that requirement is the same as that necessary to secure work product under Rule 26(b)(3) and gives assurance of reasonable compensation. The Rule thus approves the accommodation of competing interests exemplified in *United States v. Columbia Broadcasting Systems Inc.,* 666 F.2d 364 (9th Cir.1982). See also *Wright v. Jeep Corporation,* 547 F.Supp. 871 (E.D.Mich. 1982).

As stated in *Kaufman v. Edelstein,* 539 F.2d 811, 822 (2d Cir.1976), the district court's discretion in these matters should be informed by "the degree to which the expert is being called because of his knowledge of facts relevant to the case rather than in order to give opinion testimony; the difference between testifying to a previously formed or expressed opinion and forming a new one; the possibility that, for other reasons, the witness is a unique expert; the extent to which the calling party is able to show the unlikelihood that any comparable witness will willingly testify; and the degree to which the witness is able to show that he has been oppressed by having continually to testify. . . ."

Clause (c)(3)(B)(iii) protects non-party witnesses who may be burdened to perform the duty to travel in order to provide testimony at trial. The provision requires the court to condition a subpoena requiring travel of more than 100 miles on reasonable compensation.

Subdivision (d). This provision is new. Paragraph (d)(1) extends to non-parties the duty imposed on parties by the last paragraph of Rule 34(b), which was added in 1980.

Paragraph (d)(2) is new and corresponds to the new Rule 26(b)(5). Its purpose is to provide a party whose discovery is constrained by a claim of privilege or work product protection with information sufficient to evaluate such a claim and to resist if it seems unjustified. The person claiming a privilege or protection cannot decide the limits of that party's own entitlement.

A party receiving a discovery request who asserts a privilege or protection but fails to disclose that claim is at risk of waiving the privilege or protection. A person claiming a privilege or protection who fails to provide adequate information about the privilege or protection claim to the party seeking the information is subject to an order to show cause why the person should not be held in contempt under subdivision (e). Motions for such orders and responses to motions are subject to the sanctions provisions of Rules 7 and 11.

A person served a subpoena that is too broad may be faced with a burdensome task to provide full information regarding all that person's claims to privilege or work product protection. Such a person is entitled to protection that may be secured through an objection made pursuant to paragraph (c)(2).

Subdivision (e). This provision retains most of the language of the former subdivision (f).

"Adequate cause" for a failure to obey a subpoena remains undefined. In at least some circumstances, a non-party might be guilty of contempt for refusing to obey a subpoena even though the subpoena manifestly overreaches the appropriate limits of the subpoena power. *E.g., Walker v. City of Birmingham,* 388 U.S. 307 (1967). But, because the command of the subpoena is not in fact one uttered by a judicial officer, contempt should be very sparingly applied when the non-party witness has been overborne by a party or attorney. The language added to subdivision (f) is intended to assure that result where a non-party has been commanded, on the signature of an attorney, to travel greater distances than can be compelled pursuant to this rule.

Rule 47. *Selection of* Jurors

(b) ~~**Alternate Jurors.** The court may direct that not more than six jurors in addition to the regular jury be called and impanelled to sit as alternate jurors. Alternate jurors in the order in which they are called shall replace jurors who, prior to the time the jury retires to consider its verdict, become or are found to be unable or disqualified to perform their duties. Alternate jurors shall be drawn in the same manner, shall have the same qualifications, shall be subject to the same examination and challenges, shall take the same oath, and shall have the same functions, powers, facilities, and privileges as the regular jurors. An alternate juror who does not replace a regular juror shall be discharged after the jury retires to consider its verdict. Each side is entitled to 1 peremptory challenge in addition to those otherwise allowed by law if 1 or 2 alternate jurors are to be impanelled, 2 peremptory challenges if 3 or 4 alternate jurors are to be impanelled, and 3~~

~~peremptory challenges if 5 or 6 alternate jurors are to be impanelled. The additional peremptory challenges may be used against an alternate juror only, and the other peremptory challenges allowed by law shall not be used against an alternate juror.~~

Peremptory Challenges. *The court shall allow the number of peremptory challenges provided by 28 U.S.C. § 1870.*

(c) Excuse. *The court may for good cause excuse a juror from service during trial or deliberation.*

Advisory Committee's Note

Subdivision (b). The former provision for alternate jurors is stricken and the institution of the alternate juror abolished.

The former rule reflected the long-standing assumption that a jury would consist of exactly twelve members. It provided for additional jurors to be used as substitutes for jurors who are for any reason excused or disqualified from service after the commencement of the trial. Additional jurors were traditionally designated at the outset of the trial, and excused at the close of the evidence if they had not been promoted to full service on account of the elimination of one of the original jurors.

The use of alternate jurors has been a source of dissatisfaction with the jury system because of the burden it places on alternates who are required to listen to the evidence but denied the satisfaction of participating in its evaluation.

Subdivision (c). This provision makes it clear that the court may in appropriate circumstances excuse a juror during the jury deliberations without causing a mistrial. Sickness, family emergency or juror misconduct that might occasion a mistrial are examples of appropriate grounds for excusing a juror. It is not grounds for the dismissal of a juror that the juror refuses to join with fellow jurors in reaching a unanimous verdict.

Rule 48. ~~Juries of Less Than Twelve—Majority Verdict~~ *Number of Jurors—Participation in Verdict*

~~The parties may stipulate that the jury shall consist of any number less than twelve or that a verdict or a finding of a stated majority of the jurors shall be taken as the verdict or finding of the jury.~~

The court shall seat a jury of not fewer than six and not more than twelve members and all jurors shall participate in the verdict unless excused from service by the court pursuant to Rule 47(c). Unless the parties otherwise stipulate, (1) the verdict shall be unanimous and (2) no verdict shall be taken from a jury reduced in size to fewer than six members.

Advisory Committee's Note

The former rule was rendered obsolete by the adoption in many districts of local rules establishing six as the standard size for a civil jury.

It appears that the minimum size of a jury consistent with the Seventh Amendment is six. *Cf. Ballew v. Georgia,* 435 U.S. 223 (1978) (holding that a conviction based on a jury of less than six is a denial of due process of law). If the parties agree to trial before a smaller jury, a verdict can be taken, but the parties should not other than in exceptional circumstances be encouraged to waive the right to a jury of six, not only because of the constitutional stature of the right, but also because smaller juries are more erratic and less effective in serving to distribute responsibility for the exercise of judicial power.

Because the institution of the alternate juror has been abolished by the proposed revision of Rule 47, it will ordinarily be prudent and necessary, in order to provide for sickness or disability among jurors, to seat more than six jurors. The use of jurors in excess of six increases the representativeness of the jury and harms no interest of a party. *Ray v. Parkside Surgery Center,* 13 F.R.Serv. 585 (6th Cir.1989).

If the court takes the precaution of seating a jury larger than six, an illness occurring during the deliberation period will not result in a mistrial, as it did formerly, because all seated jurors will participate in the verdict and a sufficient number will remain to render a unanimous verdict of six or more.

In exceptional circumstances, as where a jury suffers depletions during trial and deliberation that are greater than can reasonably be expected, the parties may agree to be bound by a verdict rendered by fewer than six jurors. The court should not, however, rely upon the availability of such an agreement, for the use of juries smaller than six is problematic for reasons fully explained in *Ballew v. Georgia,* supra.

Rule 50. ~~Motion for a Directed Verdict and for~~ Judgment ~~Notwithstanding the Verdict~~ *as a Matter of Law in Actions Tried by Jury; Alternative Motion for New Trial; Conditional Rulings*

(a) ~~**Motion for Directed Verdict: When Made; Effect.** A party who moves for a directed verdict at the close of the evidence offered by an opponent may offer evidence in the event that the motion is not granted, without having reserved the right so to do and to the same extent as if the motion had not been made. A motion for a directed verdict which is not granted is not a waiver of trial by jury even though all parties to the action have moved for directed verdicts. A motion for a directed verdict shall state the specific grounds therefor. The order of the court granting a motion for a directed verdict is effective without any assent of the jury.~~

Judgment as a Matter of Law.

(1) If during a trial by jury a party has been fully heard with respect to an issue and there is no legally sufficient evidentiary basis for a reasonable jury to have found for that party with respect to that issue, the court may grant a motion for judgment as a matter of law against that party on any claim, counterclaim, cross-claim, or third

party claim that cannot under the controlling law be maintained without a favorable finding on that issue.

(2) Motions for judgment as a matter of law may be made at any time before submission of the case to the jury. Such a motion shall specify the judgment sought and the law and the facts on which the moving party is entitled to the judgment.

(b) *Renewal of Motion for Judgment After Trial; Alternative* Motion for *New Trial* ~~Judgment Notwithstanding the Verdict~~. Whenever a motion for a ~~directed verdict~~ *judgment as a matter of law* made at the close of all the evidence is denied or for any reason is not granted, the court is deemed to have submitted the action to the jury subject to a later determination of the legal questions raised by the motion. *Such a motion may be renewed by service and filing* ~~N~~*n*ot later than 10 days after entry of judgment~~, a party who has moved for a directed verdict may move to have the verdict and any judgment entered thereon set aside and to have judgment entered in accordance with the party's motion for a directed verdict; or if a verdict was not returned such party, within 10 days after the jury has been discharged, may move for judgment in accordance with the party's motion for a directed verdict~~. A motion for a new trial *under Rule 59* may be joined with *a renewal of the* ~~this~~ motion *for judgment as a matter of law,* or a new trial may be ~~prayed for~~ *requested* in the alternative. If a verdict was returned, the court may, *in disposing of the renewed motion,* allow the judgment to stand or may reopen the judgment and either order a new trial or direct the entry of judgment as *a matter of law* ~~if the requested verdict had been directed~~. If no verdict was returned, the court may, *in disposing of the renewed motion,* direct the entry of judgment as *a matter of law* ~~if the requested verdict had been directed~~ or may order a new trial.

(c) Same: Conditional Rulings on Grant of Motion *for Judgment as a Matter of Law.*

(1) If the *renewed* motion for judgment ~~notwithstanding the verdict, provided for in subdivision (b) of this rule,~~ *as a matter of law* is granted, the court shall also rule on the motion for a new trial, if any, by determining whether it should be granted if the judgment is thereafter vacated or reversed, and shall specify the grounds for granting or denying the motion for the new trial. If the motion for a new trial is thus conditionally granted, the order thereon does not affect the finality of the judgment. In case the motion for a new trial has been conditionally granted and the judgment is reversed on appeal, the new trial shall proceed unless the appellate court has otherwise ordered. In case the motion for a new trial has been conditionally denied, the appellee on appeal may

assert error in that denial; and if the judgment is reversed on appeal, subsequent proceedings shall be in accordance with the order of the appellate court.

(2) The party ~~whose verdict has been set aside on motion for judgment notwithstanding the verdict~~ *against whom judgment as a matter of law has been rendered* may serve a motion for a new trial pursuant to Rule 59 not later than 10 days after entry of the judgment ~~notwithstanding the verdict~~.

(d) Same: Denial of Motion *for Judgment as a Matter of Law*. If the motion for judgment ~~notwithstanding the verdict~~ *as a matter of law* is denied, the party who prevailed on that motion may, as appellee, assert grounds entitling the party to a new trial in the event the appellate court concludes that the trial court erred in denying the motion for judgment ~~notwithstanding the verdict~~. If the appellate court reverses the judgment, nothing in this rule precludes it from determining that the appellee is entitled to a new trial, or from directing the trial court to determine whether a new trial shall be granted.

Advisory Committee's Note

Subdivision (a). The revision of this subdivision aims to facilitate the exercise by the court of its responsibility to assure the fidelity of its judgment to the controlling law, a responsibility imposed by the Due Process Clause of the Fifth Amendment. *Cf. Galloway v. United States,* 319 U.S. 372 (1943).

The revision abandons the familiar terminology of *direction of verdict* for several reasons. The term is misleading as a description of the relationship between judge and jury. It is also freighted with anachronisms some of which are the subject of the text of former subdivision (a) of this rule that is deleted in this revision. Thus, it should not be necessary to state in the text of this rule that a motion made pursuant to it is not a waiver of the right to jury trial, and only the antiquities of directed verdict practice suggest that it might have been. The term "judgment as a matter of law" is an almost equally familiar term and appears in the text of Rule 56; its use in Rule 50 calls attention to the relationship between the two rules. Finally, the change enables the rule to refer to preverdict and post-verdict motions with a terminology that does not conceal the common identity of two motions made at different times in the proceeding.

If a motion is denominated a motion for directed verdict or for judgment notwithstanding the verdict, the party's error is merely formal. Such a motion should be treated as a motion for judgment as a matter of law in accordance with this rule.

Paragraph (a)(1) articulates the standard for the granting of a motion for judgment as a matter of law. It effects no change in the existing standard. That existing standard was not expressed in the former rule, but was articulated in long-standing case law. *See generally* Cooper, *Directions for Directed Verdicts: A Compass for Federal Courts,* 55 Minn.L.Rev. 903 (1971). The expressed standard makes clear that action taken under the rule is a performance of the court's duty to assure enforcement of the controlling law and is not an intrusion on any responsibility for factual determinations conferred on the jury by the Seventh Amendment or any other provision of federal law. Because this standard is also used as a reference point for entry of summary judgment under 56(a), it serves to link the two related provisions.

The revision authorizes the court to perform its duty to enter judgment as a matter of law at any time during the trial, as soon as it is apparent that either party is unable to carry a burden of proof that is essential to that party's case. Thus, the second sentence of paragraph (a)(1) authorizes the court to consider a motion for judgment as a matter of law as soon as a party has completed a presentation on a fact essential to that party's case. Such early action is appropriate when economy and expedition will be served. In no event, however, should the court enter judgment against a party who has not been apprised of the materiality of the dispositive fact and been afforded an opportunity to present any available evidence bearing on that fact. In order further to facilitate the exercise of the authority provided by this rule, Rule 16 is also revised to encourage the court to schedule an order of trial that proceeds first with a presentation on an issue that is likely to be dispositive, if such an issue is identified in the course of pretrial. Such scheduling can be appropriate where the court is uncertain whether favorable action should be taken under Rule 56. Thus, the revision affords the court the alternative of denying a motion for summary judgment while scheduling a separate trial of the issue under Rule 42(b) or scheduling the trial to begin with a presentation on that essential fact which the opposing party seems unlikely to be able to maintain.

Paragraph (a)(2) retains the requirement that a motion for judgment be made prior to the close of the trial, subject to renewal after a jury verdict has been rendered. The purpose of this requirement is to assure the responding party an opportunity to cure any deficiency in that party's proof that may have been overlooked until called to the party's attention by a late motion for judgment. Cf. *Farley Transp. Co. v. Santa Fe Trail Transp. Co.,* 786 F.2d 1342 (9th Cir.1986) ("If the moving party is then permitted to make a later attack on the evidence through a motion for judgment notwithstanding the verdict or an appeal, the opposing party may be prejudiced by having lost the opportunity to present additional evidence before the case was submitted to the jury"); *Benson v. Allphin,* 786 F.2d 268 (7th Cir.1986) ("the motion for directed verdict at the close of all the evidence provides the nonmovant an opportunity to do what he can to remedy the deficiencies in his case . . ."); *McLaughlin v. The Fellows Gear Shaper Co.,* 786 F.2d 592 (3d Cir.1986) (per Adams, J., dissenting: "This Rule serves important practical purposes in ensuring that neither party is precluded from presenting the most persuasive case possible and in preventing unfair surprise after a matter has been submitted to the jury"). At one time, this requirement was held to be of constitutional stature, being compelled by the Seventh Amendment. Cf. *Slocum v. New York Insurance Co.,* 228 U.S. 364 (1913). But cf. *Baltimore & Carolina Line v. Redman,* 295 U.S. 654 (1935).

The second sentence of paragraph (a)(2) does impose a requirement that the moving party articulate the basis on which a judgment as a matter of law might be rendered. The articulation is necessary to achieve the purpose of the requirement that the motion be made before the case is submitted to the jury, so that the responding party may seek to correct any overlooked deficiencies in the proof. The revision thus alters the result in cases in which courts have used various techniques to avoid the requirement that a motion for a directed verdict be made as a predicate to a motion for judgment notwithstanding the verdict. E.g., *Benson v. Allphin,* 786 F.2d 268 (7th Cir.1986) ("this circuit has allowed something less than a formal motion for directed verdict to preserve a party's right to move for judgment notwithstanding the verdict"). *See generally* 9 Wright & Miller, Federal Practice and Procedure § 2537 (1971 and Supp.). The information required with the motion may be supplied by explicit reference to materials and argument previously supplied to the court.

This subdivision deals only with the entry of judgment and not with the resolution of particular factual issues as a matter of law. The court may, as before, properly refuse to instruct a jury to decide an issue if a reasonable jury could on the evidence presented decide that issue in only one way.

Subdivision (b). This provision retains the concept of the former rule that the post-verdict motion is a renewal of an earlier motion made at the close of the evidence. One purpose of this concept was to avoid any question arising under the Seventh Amendment. *Montgomery Ward & Co. v. Duncan,* 311 U.S. 243 (1940). It remains useful as a means of defining the appropriate issue posed by the post-verdict motion. A post-trial motion for judgment can be granted only on grounds advanced in the pre-verdict motion. *E.g., Kutner Buick, Inc. v. American Motors Corp.,* 868 F.2d 614 (3d Cir.1989).

Often it appears to the court or to the moving party that a motion for judgment as a matter of law made at the close of the evidence should be reserved for a post-verdict decision. This is so because a jury verdict for the moving party moots the issue and because a preverdict ruling gambles that a reversal may result in a new trial that might have been avoided. For these reasons, the court may often wisely decline to rule on a motion for judgment as a matter of law made at the close of the evidence, and it is not inappropriate for the moving party to suggest such a postponement of the ruling until after the verdict has been rendered.

In ruling on such a motion, the court should disregard any jury determination for which there is no legally sufficient evidentiary basis enabling a reasonable jury to make it. The court may then decide such issues as a matter of law and enter judgment if all other material issues have been decided by the jury on the basis of legally sufficient evidence, or by the court as a matter of law.

The revised rule is intended for use in this manner with Rule 49. Thus, the court may combine facts established as a matter of law either before trial under Rule 56 or at trial on the basis of the evidence presented with other facts determined by the jury under instructions provided under Rule 49 to support a proper judgment under this rule.

This provision also retains the former requirement that a post-trial motion under the rule must be made within 10 days after entry of a contrary judgment. The renewed motion must be served and filed as provided by Rule 5. A purpose of this requirement is to meet the requirements of F.R.App.P. 4(a)(4).

Subdivision (c). Revision of this subdivision conforms the language to the change in diction set forth in subdivision (a) of this revised rule.

Subdivision (d). Revision of this subdivision conforms the language to that of the previous subdivisions.

Rule 52. Findings by the Court; *Judgment on Partial Findings*

(a) Effect. In all actions tried upon the facts without a jury or with an advisory jury, the court shall find the facts specially and state separately its conclusions of law thereon, and judgment shall be entered pursuant to Rule 58; and in granting or refusing interlocutory injunctions the court shall similarly set forth the findings of fact and conclusions of law which constitute the grounds of its action. Requests for findings are not necessary for purposes of review. Findings of fact, whether based on oral or documentary evidence, shall not be set aside unless clearly erroneous, and due regard shall be given to the opportunity of the trial court to judge of the credibility of the witnesses. The findings of a master, to the extent that the court adopts them, shall be considered as the findings of the court. It will be sufficient if the findings of fact and conclusions of law are stated orally and recorded in open court following the close of the evidence or appear in an opinion or memorandum of decision filed by the court. Findings of fact and conclusions of law are unnecessary on decisions of motions under Rule 12 or 56 or any other motion except as provided in ~~Rule 41(b)~~ *subdivision (c) of this rule.*

(c) Judgment on Partial Findings. *If during a trial without a jury a party has been fully heard with respect to an issue and the court finds against the party on that issue, the court may enter judgment as a matter of law against that party on any claim, counterclaim, cross-claim or third-party claim that cannot under the controlling law be maintained or defeated without a favorable finding on that issue, or the court may decline to render any judgment until the close of all the evidence. Such a judgment shall be supported by findings of fact and conclusions of law as required by subdivision (a) of this rule.*

Advisory Committee's Note

Subdivision (c) is added. It parallels the revised Rule 50(a), but is applicable to non-jury trials. It authorizes the court to enter judgment at any time that it can appropriately make a dispositive finding of fact on the evidence.

The new subdivision replaces part of Rule 41(b), which formerly authorized a dismissal at the close of the plaintiff's case if the plaintiff had failed to carry an essential burden of proof. Accordingly, the reference to Rule 41 formerly made in subdivision (a) of this rule is deleted.

As under the former Rule 41(b), the court retains discretion to enter no judgment prior to the close of the evidence.

Judgment entered under this rule differs from a summary judgment under Rule 56 in the nature of the evaluation made by the court. A judgment on partial findings is made after the court has heard all the evidence bearing on the crucial issue of fact, and the finding is reversible only if the appellate court finds it to be "clearly erroneous." A summary judgment, in contrast, is made on the basis of facts established on account of the absence of contrary evidence or presumptions; such establishments of fact are rulings on questions of law as provided in Rule 56(a) and are not shielded by the "clear error" standard of review.

Rule 53. Masters

(e) Report.

(1) Contents and Filing. The master shall prepare a report upon the matters submitted to the master by the order of reference and, if required to make findings of fact and conclusions of law, the master shall set them forth in the report. The master shall file the report with the clerk of the court and *serve on all parties notice of the filing. I*~~i~~n an action to be tried without a jury, unless otherwise directed by the order of reference, *the master* shall file with ~~it~~ *the report* a transcript of the proceedings and of the evidence and the original exhibits. ~~The clerk shall forthwith mail to all parties notice of the filing.~~ *Unless otherwise directed by the order of reference, the master shall serve a copy of the report on each party.*

Advisory Committee's Note

The purpose of the revision is to expedite proceedings before a master. The former rule required only a filing of the master's report, with the clerk then notifying the parties of the filing. To receive a copy, a party would then be required to secure it from the clerk. By transmitting directly to the parties, the master can save some efforts of counsel. Some local rules have previously required such action by the master.

Rule 63. ~~Disability~~ *Inability* of a Judge *to Proceed*

If ~~by reason of death, sickness or other disability, a judge before whom an action has been tried~~ *a trial or hearing has been commenced and the judge* is unable to ~~perform the duties to be performed by the court under these rules~~ *proceed,* ~~after a verdict is returned or findings of fact and conclusions of law are filed, then~~ any other judge ~~regularly sitting in or assigned to the court in which the action was tried~~ may ~~perform those duties;~~ *proceed with it* ~~but if such other judge is satisfied that such other judge cannot perform those duties because such other judge did not preside at the trial or for any other reason, such other judge may in such other judge's discretion grant a new trial~~ *upon certifying familiarity with the record and determining that the proceedings in the case may be completed without prejudice to the parties. In a hearing or trial without a jury, the successor judge shall at the request of a party recall any witness whose testimony is material and disputed and who is available to testify again without undue burden. The successor judge may also recall any other witness.*

Advisory Committee's Note

The revision substantially displaces the former rule. The former rule was limited to the disability of the judge, and made no provision for disqualification or

---

New matter is shown in italics; matter to be omitted is lined through

possible other reasons for the withdrawal of the judge during proceedings. In making provision for other circumstances, the revision is not intended to encourage judges to discontinue participation in a trial for any but compelling reasons. Cf. *United States v. Lane,* 708 F.2d 1394, 1395–1397 (9th Cir.1983). Manifestly, a substitution should not be made for the personal convenience of the court, and the reasons for a substitution should be stated on the record.

The former rule made no provision for the withdrawal of the judge during the trial, but was limited to disqualification after trial. Several courts concluded that the text of the former rule prohibited substitution of a new judge prior to the points described in the rule, thus requiring a new trial, whether or not a fair disposition was within reach of a substitute judge. *E.g., Whalen v. Ford Motor Credit Co.,* 684 F.2d 272 (4th Cir.1982, en banc), *cert. denied,* 459 U.S. 910 (1982) (jury trial); *Arrow–Hart, Inc. v. Philip Carey Co.,* 552 F.2d 711 (6th Cir.1977) (non-jury trial). *See generally* Comment, *The Case of the Dead Judge: Fed.R.Civ.P. 63: Whalen v. Ford Motor Credit Co.,* 67 Minn.L.Rev. 827 (1983).

The increasing length of federal trials has made it likely that the number of trials interrupted by the disability of the judge will increase. An efficient mechanism for completing these cases without unfairness is needed to prevent unnecessary expense and delay. To avoid the injustice that may result if the substitute judge proceeds despite unfamiliarity with the action, the new Rule provides, in language similar to Federal Rule of Criminal Procedure 25(a), that the successor judge must certify familiarity with the record and determine that the case may be completed before that judge without prejudice to the parties. This will necessarily require that there be available a transcript or a videotape of the proceedings prior to substitution. If there has been a long but incomplete jury trial, the prompt availability of the transcript or videotape is crucial to the effective use of this rule, for the jury cannot long be held while an extensive transcript is prepared without prejudice to one or all parties.

The revised text authorizes the substitute judge to make a finding of fact at a bench trial based on evidence heard by a different judge. This may be appropriate in limited circumstances. First, if a witness has become unavailable, the testimony recorded at trial can be considered by the successor judge pursuant to F.R.Ev. 804, being equivalent to a recorded deposition available for use at trial pursuant to Rule 32. For this purpose, a witness who is no longer subject to a subpoena to compel testimony at trial is unavailable. Secondly, the successor judge may determine that particular testimony is not material or is not disputed, and so need not be reheard. The propriety of proceeding in this manner may be marginally affected by the availability of a videotape record; a judge who has reviewed a trial on videotape may be entitled to greater confidence in his or her ability to proceed.

The court would, however, risk error to determine the credibility of a witness not seen or heard who is available to be recalled. Cf. *Anderson v. City of Bessemer City NC,* 470 U.S. 564, 575 (1985); *Marshall v. Jerrico Inc.,* 446 U.S. 238, 242 (1980). See also *United States v. Raddatz,* 447 U.S. 667 (1980).

Rule 72. Magistrates; Pretrial Orders

(a) Nondispositive Matters. A magistrate to whom a pretrial matter not dispositive of a claim or defense of a party is referred to hear and determine shall promptly conduct such proceedings as are required and when appropriate enter into the record a written order setting forth the disposition of the matter.

Within 10 days after being served with a copy of the magistrate's order, a party may serve and file objections to the order; a party may not thereafter assign as error a defect in the magistrate's order to which objection was not timely made. The district judge to whom the case is assigned shall consider *such* objections ~~made by the parties, provided they are served and filed within 10 days after entry of the order,~~ and shall modify or set aside any portion of the magistrate's order found to be clearly erroneous or contrary to law.

Advisory Committee's Note

This amendment is intended to eliminate a discrepancy in measuring the 10 days for serving and filing objections to a magistrate's action under subdivisions (a) and (b) of this Rule. The rule as promulgated in 1983 required objections to the magistrate's handling of nondispositive matters to be served and filed within 10 days of entry of the order, but required objections to dispositive motions to be made within 10 days of being served with a copy of the recommended disposition. Subdivision (a) is here amended to conform to subdivision (b) to avoid any confusion or technical defaults, particularly in connection with magistrate orders that rule on both dispositive and nondispositive matters.

The amendment is also intended to assure that objections to magistrate's orders that are not timely made shall not be considered. *Compare* Rule 51.

Rule 77. District Courts and Clerks

(d) Notice of Order or Judgments. Immediately upon the entry of an order or judgment the clerk shall serve a notice of the entry by mail in the manner provided for in Rule 5 upon each party who is not in default for failure to appear, and shall make a note in the docket of the mailing. ~~Such mailing is sufficient notice for all purposes for which notice of the entry of an order is required by these rules; but a~~*A*ny party may in addition serve a notice of such entry in the manner provided in Rule 5 for the service of papers. Lack of notice of the entry by the clerk does not affect the time to appeal or relieve or authorize the court to relieve a party for failure to appeal within the time allowed, except as permitted in Rule 4(a) of the Federal Rules of Appellate Procedure.

Advisory Committee's Note

This revision is a companion to the concurrent amendment to Rule 4 of the Federal Rules of Appellate Procedure. The purpose of the revisions is to permit district courts to ease strict sanctions now imposed on appellants whose notices of appeal are filed late because of their failure to receive notice of entry of a judgment. See, e.g. *Tucker v. Commonwealth Land Title Ins. Co.*, 800 F.2d 1054 (11th Cir.1986); *Ashby Enterprises, Ltd. v. Weitzman, Dym & Associates*, 780 F.2d 1043 (D.C.Cir.1986); *In re OPM Leasing Services, Inc.*, 769 F.2d 911 (2d Cir.1985); *Spika v. Village of Lombard, Ill.*, 763 F.2d 282 (7th Cir.1985); *Hall v. Community Mental Health Center of Beaver County*, 772 F.2d 42 (3d Cir.1985); *Wilson v. Atwood v. Stark*, 725 F.2d 255 (5th Cir. en banc), *cert. dismissed*, 105 S.Ct. 17 (1984); *Case v. BASF Wyandotte*, 737 F.2d 1034 (Fed.Cir.1984), *cert. denied*, 105 S.Ct. 386 (1984);

Hensley v. Chesapeake & Ohio R.R. Co., 651 F.2d 226 (4th Cir.1981); *Buckeye Cellulose Corp. v. Electric Construction Co.,* 569 F.2d 1036 (8th Cir.1978).

Failure to receive notice may have increased in frequency with the growth in the caseload in the clerks' offices. The present strict rule imposes a duty on counsel to maintain contact with the court while a case is under submission. Such contact is more difficult to maintain if counsel is outside the district, as is increasingly common, and can be a burden to the court as well as counsel.

The effect of the revisions is to place a burden on prevailing parties who desire certainty that the time for appeal is running. Such parties can take the initiative to assure that their adversaries receive effective notice. An appropriate procedure for such notice is provided in Rule 5.

The revised rule lightens the responsibility but not the workload of the clerk's offices, for the duty of that office to give notice of entry of judgment must be maintained.

CERTAIN OF THE AMENDMENTS OF FEDERAL RULES OF CIVIL PROCEDURE ADOPTED BY THE SUPREME COURT OF THE UNITED STATES ON APRIL 22, 1993, EFFECTIVE DECEMBER 1, 1993, WITH ADVISORY COMMITTEE'S NOTES THEREON

[*Amendments here omitted: Changes in Forms 2, 33, and 34; abrogation of Form 18–A; and addition of new Forms 1A, 1B, 34A, and 35.*]

Rule 1. Scope *and Purpose* of Rules

These rules govern the procedure in the United States district courts in all suits of a civil nature whether cognizable as cases at law or in equity or in admiralty, with the exceptions stated in Rule 81. They shall be construed *and administered* to secure the just, speedy, and inexpensive determination of every action.

Advisory Committee's Note

The purpose of this revision, adding the words "and administered" to the second sentence, is to recognize the affirmative duty of the court to exercise the authority conferred by these rules to ensure that civil litigation is resolved not only fairly, but also without undue cost or delay. As officers of the court, attorneys share this responsibility with the judge to whom the case is assigned.

Rule 4. ~~Process~~ *Summons*

(a) ~~**Summons: Issuance.** Upon the filing of the complaint the clerk shall forthwith issue a summons and deliver the summons to the plaintiff or the plaintiff's attorney, who shall be responsible for prompt service of the summons and a copy of the complaint. Upon request of the plaintiff separate or additional summons shall issue against any defendants.~~

~~**(b) Same:**~~ **Form.** The summons shall be signed by the clerk, ~~be under~~ *bear* the seal of the court, ~~contain the name of~~ *identify* the court and ~~the names of~~ the parties, be directed to the defendant, *and* state the name and address of the plaintiff's attorney~~, if any, otherwise the plaintiff's address~~ *or, if unrepresented, of the plaintiff*~~, and~~. *It shall also state* the time within which ~~these rules require~~ the defendant ~~to~~ *must* appear and defend, and ~~shall~~

notify the defendant that ~~in case of the defendant's~~ failure to do so *will result in a* judgment by default ~~will be rendered~~ against the defendant for the relief demanded in the complaint. ~~When, under Rule 4(e), service is made pursuant to a statute or rule of court of a state, the summons, or notice, or order in lieu of summons shall correspond as nearly as may be to that required by the statute or rule.~~ *The court may allow a summons to be amended.*

(b) Issuance. *Upon or after filing the complaint, the plaintiff may present a summons to the clerk for signature and seal. If the summons is in proper form, the clerk shall sign, seal, and issue it to the plaintiff for service on the defendant. A summons, or a copy of the summons if addressed to multiple defendants, shall be issued for each defendant to be served.*

(c) Service *with Complaint; by Whom Made.*

(1) ~~Process, other than a subpoena or a summons and complaint, shall be served by a United States marshal or deputy United States marshal, or by a person specially appointed for that purpose.~~ *A summons shall be served together with a copy of the complaint. The plaintiff is responsible for service of a summons and complaint within the time allowed under subdivision (m) and shall furnish the person effecting service with the necessary copies of the summons and complaint.*

(2) ~~(A) A summons and complaint shall, except as provided in subparagraphs (B) and (C) of this paragraph, be served~~ *Service may be effected* by any person who is not a party and *who* is ~~not less than~~ *at least* 18 years of age. *At the request of the plaintiff, however, the court may direct that service be effected by a United States marshal, deputy United States marshal, or other person or officer specially appointed by the court for that purpose. Such an appointment must be made when the plaintiff is*

~~(B) A summons and complaint shall, at the request of the party seeking service or such party's attorney, be served by a United States marshal or deputy United States marshal, or by a person specially appointed by the court for that purpose, only~~

~~(i) on behalf of a party~~ authorized to proceed in forma pauperis pursuant to ~~Title~~ 28~~,~~ U.S.C. § 1915~~,~~ or ~~of a seaman~~ *is* authorized to proceed *as a seaman* under ~~Title~~ 28~~,~~ U.S.C. § 1916~~,~~.

~~(ii) on behalf of the United States or an officer or agency of the United States, or~~

~~(iii) pursuant to an order issued by the court stating that a United States marshal or deputy United States~~

~~marshal, or a person specially appointed for that purpose, is required to serve the summons and complaint in order that service be properly effected in that particular action.~~

~~(C) A summons and complaint may be served upon a defendant of any class referred to in paragraph (1) or (3) of subdivision (d) of this rule~~

~~(i) pursuant to the law of the State in which the district court is held for the service of summons or other like process upon such defendant in an action brought in the courts of general jurisdiction of that State, or~~

~~(ii) by mailing a copy of the summons and of the complaint (by first class mail, postage prepaid) to the person to be served, together with two copies of a notice and acknowledgment conforming substantially to form 18–A and a return envelope, postage prepaid, addressed to the sender. If no acknowledgment of service under this subdivision of this rule is received by the sender within 20 days after the date of mailing, service of such summons and complaint shall be made under subparagraph (A) or (B) of this paragraph in the manner prescribed by subdivision (d)(1) or (d)(3).~~

~~(D) Unless good cause is shown for not doing so the court shall order the payment of the costs of personal service by the person served if such person does not complete and return within 20 days after mailing, the notice and acknowledgment of receipt of summons.~~

~~(E) The notice and acknowledgment of receipt of summons and complaint shall be executed under oath or affirmation.~~

~~(3) The court shall freely make special appointments to serve summonses and complaints under paragraph (2)(B) of this subdivision of this rule and all other process under paragraph (1) of this subdivision of this rule.~~

(d) ~~**Summons and Complaint: Person to be Served.**~~ ***Waiver of Service; Duty to Save Costs of Service; Request to Waive.*** ~~The summons and complaint shall be served together. The plaintiff shall furnish the person making service with such copies as are necessary. Service shall be made as follows:~~

(1) A defendant who waives service of a summons does not thereby waive any objection to the venue or to the jurisdiction of the court over the person of the defendant.

(2) An individual, corporation, or association that is subject to service under subdivision (e), (f), or (h) and that receives

notice of an action in the manner provided in this paragraph has a duty to avoid unnecessary costs of serving the summons. To avoid costs, the plaintiff may notify such a defendant of the commencement of the action and request that the defendant waive service of a summons. The notice and request

(A) shall be in writing and shall be addressed directly to the defendant, if an individual, or else to an officer or managing or general agent (or other agent authorized by appointment or law to receive service of process) of a defendant subject to service under subdivision (h);

(B) shall be dispatched through first-class mail or other reliable means;

(C) shall be accompanied by a copy of the complaint and shall identify the court in which it has been filed;

(D) shall inform the defendant, by means of a text prescribed in an official form promulgated pursuant to Rule 84, of the consequences of compliance and of a failure to comply with the request;

(E) shall set forth the date on which the request is sent;

(F) shall allow the defendant a reasonable time to return the waiver, which shall be at least 30 days from the date on which the request is sent, or 60 days from that date if the defendant is addressed outside any judicial district of the United States; and

(G) shall provide the defendant with an extra copy of the notice and request, as well as a prepaid means of compliance in writing.

If a defendant located within the United States fails to comply with a request for waiver made by a plaintiff located within the United States, the court shall impose the costs subsequently incurred in effecting service on the defendant unless good cause for the failure be shown.

(3) A defendant that, before being served with process, timely returns a waiver so requested is not required to serve an answer to the complaint until 60 days after the date on which the request for waiver of service was sent, or 90 days after that date if the defendant was addressed outside any judicial district of the United States.

(4) When the plaintiff files a waiver of service with the court, the action shall proceed, except as provided in paragraph (3), as if a summons and complaint had been served at the time of filing the waiver, and no proof of service shall be required.

(5) The costs to be imposed on a defendant under paragraph (2) for failure to comply with a request to waive service of a summons shall include the costs subsequently incurred in effecting service under subdivision (e), (f), or (h), together with the costs, including a reasonable attorney's fee, of any motion required to collect the costs of service.

(e~~1~~) ***Service Upon Individuals Within a Judicial District of the United States.*** *Unless otherwise provided by federal law, service* ~~U~~*u*pon an individual *from whom a waiver has not been obtained and filed,* other than an infant or an incompetent person, *may be effected in any judicial district of the United States:*

(1) pursuant to the law of the state in which the district court is located, or in which service is effected, for the service of a summons upon the defendant in an action brought in the courts of general jurisdiction of the State; or

(2) by delivering a copy of the summons and of the complaint to the individual personally or by leaving copies thereof at the individual's dwelling house or usual place of abode with some person of suitable age and discretion then residing therein or by delivering a copy of the summons and of the complaint to an agent authorized by appointment or by law to receive service of process.

(f) Service Upon Individuals in a Foreign Country. *Unless otherwise provided by federal law, service upon an individual from whom a waiver has not been obtained and filed, other than an infant or an incompetent person, may be effected in a place not within any judicial district of the United States:*

(1) by any internationally agreed means reasonably calculated to give notice, such as those means authorized by the Hague Convention on the Service Abroad of Judicial and Extrajudicial Documents; or

(2) if there is no internationally agreed means of service or the applicable international agreement allows other means of service, provided that service is reasonably calculated to give notice:

(A) in the manner prescribed by the law of the foreign country for service in that country in an action in any of its courts of general jurisdiction; or

(B) as directed by the foreign authority in response to a letter rogatory or letter of request; or

(C) unless prohibited by the law of the foreign country, by

(i) delivery to the individual personally of a copy of the summons and the complaint; or

(ii) any form of mail requiring a signed receipt, to be addressed and dispatched by the clerk of the court to the party to be served; or

(3) by other means not prohibited by international agreement as may be directed by the court.

(*g*~~2~~) *Service Upon Infants and Incompetent Persons.* *Service u*~~U~~pon an infant or an incompetent person~~, by serving the summons and complaint~~ *in a judicial district of the United States shall be effected* in the manner prescribed by the law of the state in which the service is made for the service of summons or other like process upon any such defendant in an action brought in the courts of general jurisdiction of that state. *Service upon an infant or an incompetent person in a place not within any judicial district of the United States shall be effected in the manner prescribed by paragraph (2)(A) or (2)(B) of subdivision (f) or by such means as the court may direct.*

(*h*~~3~~) *Service Upon Corporations and Associations.* *Unless otherwise provided by federal law, service u*~~U~~pon a domestic or foreign corporation or upon a partnership or other unincorporated association ~~which~~ *that* is subject to suit under a common name, *and from which a waiver of service has not been obtained and filed, shall be effected:*

(1) in a judicial district of the United States in the manner prescribed for individuals by subdivision (e)(1), or by delivering a copy of the summons and of the complaint to an officer, a managing or general agent, or to any other agent authorized by appointment or by law to receive service of process and, if the agent is one authorized by statute to receive service and the statute so requires, by also mailing a copy to the defendant~~.~~*, or*

(2) in a place not within any judicial district of the United States in any manner prescribed for individuals by subdivision (f) except personal delivery as provided in paragraph (2)(C)(i) thereof.

(*i*4) *Service Upon the United States, and Its Agencies, Corporations, or Officers.*

(1) Service u~~U~~pon the United States~~,~~ *shall be effected*

(A) by delivering a copy of the summons and of the complaint to the United States attorney for the district in which the action is brought or to an assistant United States attorney or clerical employee designated by the

New matter is shown in italics; matter to be omitted is lined through

United States attorney in a writing filed with the clerk of the court *or by sending a copy of the summons and of the complaint by registered or certified mail addressed to the civil process clerk at the office of the United States attorney* and

(B) by *also* sending a copy of the summons and of the complaint by registered or certified mail to the Attorney General of the United States at Washington, District of Columbia, and

(C) in any action attacking the validity of an order of an officer or agency of the United States not made a party, by also sending a copy of the summons and of the complaint by registered or certified mail to ~~such~~ *the* officer or agency.

(~~5~~*2) Service* ~~U~~*u*pon an officer, ~~or~~ agency, *or corporation* of the United States~~,~~ *shall be effected* by serving the United States *in the manner prescribed by paragraph (1) of this subdivision* and by *also* sending a copy of the summons and of the complaint by registered or certified mail to ~~such~~ *the* officer, ~~or~~ agency, *or corporation.* ~~If the agency is a corporation the copy shall be delivered as provided in paragraph (3) of this subdivision of this rule.~~

(3) The court shall allow a reasonable time for service of process under this subdivision for the purpose of curing the failure to serve multiple officers, agencies, or corporations of the United States if the plaintiff has effected service on either the United States attorney or the Attorney General of the United States.

(*j*~~6~~) *Service Upon Foreign, State, or Local Governments.*

(1) Service upon a foreign state or a political subdivision, agency, or instrumentality thereof shall be effected pursuant to 28 U.S.C. § 1608.

(2) Service u~~U~~pon a state, ~~or~~ municipal corporation, or other governmental organization ~~thereof~~ subject to suit~~,~~ *shall be effected* by delivering a copy of the summons and of the complaint to ~~the~~ *its* chief executive officer ~~thereof~~ or by serving the summons and complaint in the manner prescribed by the law of that state for the service of summons or other like process upon any such defendant.

~~**(e) Summons: Service Upon Party Not Inhabitant of or Found Within State.** Whenever a statute of the United States or an order of court thereunder provides for service of a summons, or of a notice, or of an order in lieu of summons upon a party not an~~

New matter is shown in italics; matter to be omitted is lined through

~~inhabitant of or found within the state in which the district court is held, service may be made under the circumstances and in the manner prescribed by the statute or order, or, if there is no provision therein prescribing the manner of service, in a manner stated in this rule. Whenever a statute or rule of court of the state in which the district court is held provides (1) for service of a summons, or of a notice, or of an order in lieu of summons upon a party not an inhabitant of or found within the state, or (2) for service upon or notice to such a party to appear and respond or defend in an action by reason of the attachment or garnishment or similar seizure of the party's property located within the state, service may in either case be made under the circumstances and in the manner prescribed in the statute or rule.~~

(~~f~~*k*) Territorial Limits of Effective Service. ~~All process other than a subpoena may be served anywhere within the territorial limits of the state in which the district court is held, and, when authorized by a statute of the United States or by these rules, beyond the territorial limits of that state. In addition, persons who are brought in as parties pursuant to Rule 14, or as additional parties to a pending action or a counterclaim or cross claim therein pursuant to Rule 19, may be served in the manner stated in paragraphs (1)–(6) of subdivision (d) of this rule at all places outside the state but within the United States that are not more than 100 miles from the place in which the action is commenced, or to which it is assigned or transferred for trial; and persons required to respond to an order of commitment for civil contempt may be served at the same places. A subpoena may be served within the territorial limits provided in Rule 45.~~

(1) Service of a summons or filing a waiver of service is effective to establish jurisdiction over the person of a defendant

(A) who could be subjected to the jurisdiction of a court of general jurisdiction in the state in which the district court is located, or

(B) who is a party joined under Rule 14 or Rule 19 and is served at a place within a judicial district of the United States and not more than 100 miles from the place from which the summons issues, or

(C) who is subject to the federal interpleader jurisdiction under 28 U.S.C. § 1335, or

(D) when authorized by a statute of the United States.

(2) If the exercise of jurisdiction is consistent with the Constitution and laws of the United States, serving a summons or filing a waiver of service is also effective, with respect to

---

New matter is shown in italics; matter to be omitted is lined through

claims arising under federal law, to establish personal jurisdiction over the person of any defendant who is not subject to the jurisdiction of the courts of general jurisdiction of any state.

(~~g~~*l*) ~~Return.~~ *Proof of Service.* *If service is not waived, t*~~T~~he person ~~serving the process~~ *effecting service* shall make proof ~~of service~~ thereof to the court ~~promptly and in any event within the time during which the person served must respond to the process~~. If service is made by a person other than a United States marshal or deputy United States marshal, ~~such~~ *the* person shall make affidavit thereof. *Proof of service in a place not within any judicial district of the United States shall, if effected under paragraph (1) of subdivision (f), be made pursuant to the applicable treaty or convention, and shall, if effected under paragraph (2) or (3) thereof, include a receipt signed by the addressee or other evidence of delivery to the addressee satisfactory to the court.* ~~If service is made under subdivision (c)(2)(C)(ii) of this rule, return shall be made by the sender's filing with the court the acknowledgment received pursuant to such subdivision.~~ Failure to make proof of service does not affect the validity of the service. *The court may allow proof of service to be amended.*

~~**(h) Amendment.** At any time in its discretion and upon such terms as it deems just, the court may allow any process or proof of service thereof to be amended, unless it clearly appears that material prejudice would result to the substantial rights of the party against whom the process issued.~~

~~**(i) Alternative Provisions for Service in a Foreign Country.**~~

~~(1) Manner. When the federal or state law referred to in subdivision (e) of this rule authorizes service upon a party not an inhabitant of or found within the state in which the district court is held, and service is to be effected upon the party in a foreign country, it is also sufficient if service of the summons and complaint is made: (A) in the manner prescribed by the law of the foreign country for service in that country in an action in any of its courts of general jurisdiction; or (B) as directed by the foreign authority in response to a letter rogatory, when service in either case is reasonably calculated to give actual notice; or (C) upon an individual, by delivery to the individual personally, and upon a corporation or partnership or association, by delivery to an officer, a managing or general agent; or (D) by any form of mail, requiring a signed receipt, to be addressed and dispatched by the clerk of the court to the party to be served; or (E) as directed by order of the court. Service under (C) or (E) above may be made by any person who~~

~~is not a party and is not less than 18 years of age or who is designated by order of the district court or by the foreign court. On request, the clerk shall deliver the summons to the plaintiff for transmission to the person or the foreign court or officer who will make the service.~~

~~(2) Return. Proof of service may be made as prescribed by subdivision (g) of this rule, or by the law of the foreign country, or by order of the court. When service is made pursuant to subparagraph (1)(D) of this subdivision, proof of service shall include a receipt signed by the addressee or other evidence of delivery to the addressee satisfactory to the court.~~

(~~j~~*m*) ~~Summons:~~ Time Limit for Service. If ~~a~~ service of the summons and complaint is not made upon a defendant within 120 days after the filing of the complaint ~~and the party on whose behalf such service was required cannot show good cause why such service was not made within that period~~, the *court* ~~action shall be dismissed as to that defendant without prejudice~~, upon ~~the court's~~ *motion or on its* own initiative ~~with~~ *after* notice to ~~such party or upon motion~~ *the plaintiff, shall dismiss the action without prejudice as to that defendant or direct that service be effected within a specified time; provided that if the plaintiff shows good cause for the failure, the court shall extend the time for service for an appropriate period.* This subdivision ~~shall~~ *does* not apply to service in a foreign country pursuant to subdivision (~~i~~*f*) *or (j)(1)* ~~of this rule~~.

(n) Seizure of Property; Service of Summons Not Feasible.

(1) If a statute of the United States so provides, the court may assert jurisdiction over property. Notice to claimants of the property shall then be sent in the manner provided by the statute or by service of a summons under this rule.

(2) Upon a showing that personal jurisdiction over a defendant cannot, in the district where the action is brought, be obtained with reasonable efforts by service of summons in any manner authorized by this rule, the court may assert jurisdiction over any of the defendant's assets found within the district by seizing the assets under the circumstances and in the manner provided by the law of the state in which the district court is located.

Advisory Committee's Note

SPECIAL NOTE: Mindful of the constraints of the Rules Enabling Act, the Committee calls the attention of the Supreme Court and Congress to new subdivision (k)(2). Should this limited extension of service be disapproved, the Committee nevertheless recommends adoption of the balance of the rule, with subdivision (k)(1) becoming simply subdivision (k). The Committee Notes would be revised to eliminate references to subdivision (k)(2).

Purposes of Revision. The general purpose of this revision is to facilitate the service of the summons and complaint. The revised rule explicitly authorizes a means for service of the summons and complaint on any defendant. While the methods of service so authorized always provide appropriate notice to persons against whom claims are made, effective service under this rule does not assure that personal jurisdiction has been established over the defendant served.

First, the revised rule authorizes the use of any means of service provided by the law not only of the forum state, but also of the state in which a defendant is served, unless the defendant is a minor or incompetent.

Second, the revised rule clarifies and enhances the cost-saving practice of securing the assent of the defendant to dispense with actual service of the summons and complaint. This practice was introduced to the rule in 1983 by an act of Congress authorizing "service-by-mail," a procedure that effects economic service with cooperation of the defendant. Defendants that magnify costs of service by requiring expensive service not necessary to achieve full notice of an action brought against them are required to bear the wasteful costs. This provision is made available in actions against defendants who cannot be served in the districts in which the actions are brought.

Third, the revision reduces the hazard of commencing an action against the United States or its officers, agencies, and corporations. A party failing to effect service on all the offices of the United States as required by the rule is assured adequate time to cure defects in service.

Fourth, the revision calls attention to the important effect of the Hague Convention and other treaties bearing on service of documents in foreign countries and favors the use of internationally agreed means of service. In some respects, these treaties have facilitated service in foreign countries but are not fully known to the bar.

Finally, the revised rule extends the reach of federal courts to impose jurisdiction over the person of all defendants against whom federal law claims are made and who can be constitutionally subjected to the jurisdiction of the courts of the United States. The present territorial limits on the effectiveness of service to subject a defendant to the jurisdiction of the court over the defendant's person are retained for all actions in which there is a state in which personal jurisdiction can be asserted consistently with state law and the Fourteenth Amendment. A new provision enables district courts to exercise jurisdiction, if permissible under the Constitution and not precluded by statute, when a federal claim is made against a defendant not subject to the jurisdiction of any single state.

The revised rule is reorganized to make its provisions more accessible to those not familiar with all of them. Additional subdivisions in this rule allow for more captions; several overlaps among subdivisions are eliminated; and several disconnected provisions are removed, to be relocated in a new Rule 4.1.

The Caption of the Rule. Prior to this revision, Rule 4 was entitled "Process" and applied to the service of not only the summons but also other process as well, although these are not covered by the revised rule. Service of process in eminent domain proceedings is governed by Rule 71A. Service of a subpoena is governed by Rule 45, and service of papers such as orders, motions, notices, pleadings, and other documents is governed by Rule 5.

The revised rule is entitled "Summons" and applies only to that form of legal process. Unless service of the summons is waived, a summons must be served whenever a person is joined as a party against whom a claim is made. Those few provisions of the former rule which relate specifically to service of process other than a summons are relocated in Rule 4.1 in order to simplify the text of this rule.

Subdivision (a). Revised subdivision (a) contains most of the language of the former subdivision (b). The second sentence of the former subdivision (b) has been stricken, so that the federal court summons will be the same in all cases. Few states now employ distinctive requirements of form for a summons and the applicability of such a requirement in federal court can only serve as a trap for an unwary party or attorney. A sentence is added to this subdivision authorizing an amendment of a summons. This sentence replaces the rarely used former subdivision 4(h). *See* 4A Wright & Miller, *Federal Practice and Procedure* § 1131 (2d ed. 1987).

Subdivision (b). Revised subdivision (b) replaces the former subdivision (a). The revised text makes clear that the responsibility for filling in the summons falls on the plaintiff, not the clerk of the court. If there are multiple defendants, the plaintiff may secure issuance of a summons for each defendant, or may serve copies of a single original bearing the names of multiple defendants if the addressee of the summons is effectively identified.

Subdivision (c). Paragraph (1) of revised subdivision (c) retains language from the former subdivision (d)(1). Paragraph (2) retains language from the former subdivision (a), and adds an appropriate caution regarding the time limit for service set forth in subdivision (m).

The 1983 revision of Rule 4 relieved the marshals' offices of much of the burden of serving the summons. Subdivision (c) eliminates the requirement for service by the marshal's office in actions in which the party seeking service is the United States. The United States, like other civil litigants, is now permitted to designate any person who is 18 years of age and not a party to serve its summons.

The court remains obligated to appoint a marshal, a deputy, or some other person to effect service of a summons in two classes of cases specified by statute: actions brought *in forma pauperis* or by a seaman. 28 U.S.C. §§ 1915, 1916. The court also retains discretion to appoint a process server on motion of a party. If a law enforcement presence appears to be necessary or advisable to keep the peace, the court should appoint a marshal or deputy or other official person to make the service. The Department of Justice may also call upon the Marshals Service to perform services in actions brought by the United States. 28 U.S.C. § 651.

Subdivision (d). This text is new, but is substantially derived from the former subdivisions (c)(2)(C) and (D), added to the rule by Congress in 1983. The aims of the provision are to eliminate the costs of service of a summons on many parties and to foster cooperation among adversaries and counsel. The rule operates to impose upon the defendant those costs that could have been avoided if the defendant had cooperated reasonably in the manner prescribed. This device is useful in dealing with defendants who are furtive, who reside in places not easily reached by process servers, or who are outside the United States and can be served only at substantial and unnecessary expense. Illustratively, there is no useful purpose achieved by requiring a plaintiff to comply with all the formalities of service in a foreign country, including costs of translation, when suing a defendant manufacturer, fluent in English, whose products are widely distributed in the United States. *See Bankston v. Toyota Motor Corp.,* 889 F.2d 172 (8th Cir.1989).

The former text described this process as service-by-mail. This language misled some plaintiffs into thinking that service could be effected by mail without the affirmative cooperation of the defendant. *E.g., Gulley v. Mayo Foundation,* 886 F.2d

161 (8th Cir.1989). It is more accurate to describe the communication sent to the defendant as a request for a waiver of formal service.

The request for waiver of service may be sent only to defendants subject to service under subdivision (e), (f), or (h). The United States is not expected to waive service for the reason that its mail receiving facilities are inadequate to assure that the notice is actually received by the correct person in the Department of Justice. The same principle is applied to agencies, corporations, and officers of the United States and to other governments and entities subject to service under subdivision (j). Moreover, there are policy reasons why governmental entities should not be confronted with the potential for bearing costs of service in cases in which they ultimately prevail. Infants or incompetent persons likewise are not called upon to waive service because, due to their presumed inability to understand the request and its consequences, they must generally be served through fiduciaries.

It was unclear whether the former rule authorized mailing of a request for "acknowledgement of service" to defendants outside the forum state. *See* 1 R. Casad, *Jurisdiction in Civil Actions* (2d Ed.) 5–29, 30 (1991) and cases cited. But, as Professor Casad observed, there was no reason not to employ this device in an effort to obtain service outside the state, and there are many instances in which it was in fact so used, with respect both to defendants within the United States and to defendants in other countries.

The opportunity for waiver has distinct advantages to a foreign defendant. By waiving service, the defendant can reduce the costs that may ultimately be taxed against it if unsuccessful in the lawsuit, including the sometimes substantial expense of translation that may be wholly unnecessary for defendants fluent in English. Moreover, a foreign defendant that waives service is afforded substantially more time to defend against the action than if it had been formally served: under Rule 12, a defendant ordinarily has only 20 days after service in which to file its answer or raise objections by motion, but by signing a waiver it is allowed 90 days after the date the request for waiver was mailed in which to submit its defenses. Because of the additional time needed for mailing and the unreliability of some foreign mail services, a period of 60 days (rather than the 30 days required for domestic transmissions) is provided for a return of a waiver sent to a foreign country.

It is hoped that, since transmission of the notice and waiver forms is a private nonjudicial act, does not purport to effect service, and is not accompanied by any summons or directive from a court, use of the procedure will not offend foreign sovereignties, even those that have withheld their assent to formal service by mail or have objected to the "service-by-mail" provisions of the former rule. Unless the addressee consents, receipt of the request under the revised rule does not give rise to any obligation to answer the lawsuit, does not provide a basis for default judgment, and does not suspend the statute of limitations in those states where the period continues to run until service. Nor are there any adverse consequences to a foreign defendant, since the provisions for shifting the expense of service to a defendant that declines to waive service apply only if the plaintiff and defendant are both located in the United States.

With respect to a defendant located in a foreign country like the United Kingdom, which accepts documents in English, whose Central Authority acts promptly in effecting service, and whose policies discourage its residents from waiving formal service, there will be little reason for a plaintiff to send the notice and request under subdivision (d) rather than use convention methods. On the other hand, the procedure offers significant potential benefits to a plaintiff when suing a defendant that, though fluent in English, is located in a country where, as a condition to formal service under a convention, documents must be translated into another language or where formal service will be otherwise costly or time-consuming.

Paragraph (1) is explicit that a timely waiver of service of a summons does not prejudice the right of a defendant to object by means of a motion authorized by Rule 12(b)(2) to the absence of jurisdiction over the defendant's person, or to assert other defenses that may be available. The only issues eliminated are those involving the sufficiency of the summons or the sufficiency of the method by which it is served.

Paragraph (2) states what the present rule implies: the defendant has a duty to avoid costs associated with the service of a summons not needed to inform the defendant regarding the commencement of an action. The text of the rule also sets forth the requirements for a Notice and Request for Waiver sufficient to put the cost-shifting provision in place. These requirements are illustrated in Forms 1A and 1B, which replace the former Form 18–A.

Paragraph (2)(A) is explicit that a request for waiver of service by a corporate defendant must be addressed to a person qualified to receive service. The general mail rooms of large organizations cannot be required to identify the appropriate individual recipient for an institutional summons.

Paragraph (2)(B) permits the use of alternatives to the United States mails in sending the Notice and Request. While private messenger services or electronic communications may be more expensive than the mail, they may be equally reliable and on occasion more convenient to the parties. Especially with respect to transmissions to foreign countries, alternative means may be desirable, for in some countries facsimile transmission is the most efficient and economical means of communication. If electronic means such as facsimile transmission are employed, the sender should maintain a record of the transmission to assure proof of transmission if receipt is denied, but a party receiving such a transmission has a duty to cooperate and cannot avoid liability for the resulting cost of formal service if the transmission is prevented at the point of receipt.

A defendant failing to comply with a request for waiver shall be given an opportunity to show good cause for the failure, but sufficient cause should be rare. It is not a good cause for failure to waive service that the claim is unjust or that the court lacks jurisdiction. Sufficient cause not to shift the cost of service would exist, however, if the defendant did not receive the request or was insufficiently literate in English to understand it. It should be noted that the provisions for shifting the cost of service apply only if the plaintiff and the defendant are both located in the United States, and accordingly a foreign defendant need not show "good cause" for its failure to waive service.

Paragraph (3) extends the time for answer if, before being served with process, the defendant waives formal service. The extension is intended to serve as an inducement to waive service and to assure that a defendant will not gain any delay by declining to waive service and thereby causing the additional time needed to effect service. By waiving service, a defendant is not called upon to respond to the complaint until 60 days from the date the notice was sent to it—90 days if the notice was sent to a foreign country—rather than within the 20 day period from date of service specified in Rule 12.

Paragraph (4) clarifies the effective date of service when service is waived; the provision is needed to resolve an issue arising when applicable law requires service of process to toll the statute of limitations. *E.g., Morse v. Elmira Country Club,* 752 F.2d 35 (2d Cir.1984). *Cf. Walker v. Armco Steel Corp.,* 446 U.S. 740 (1980).

The provisions in former subdivision (c)(2)(C)(ii) of this rule may have been misleading to some parties. Some plaintiffs, not reading the rule carefully, supposed that receipt by the defendant of the mailed complaint had the effect both of establishing the jurisdiction of the court over the defendant's person and of tolling the statute of limitations in actions in which service of the summons is required to toll the limitations period. The revised rule is clear that, if the waiver is not returned and filed, the limitations period under such a law is not tolled and the action will not otherwise proceed until formal service of process is effected.

Some state limitations laws may toll an otherwise applicable statute at the time when the defendant receives notice of the action. Nevertheless, the device of requested waiver of service is not suitable if a limitations period which is about to expire is not tolled by filing the action. Unless there is ample time, the plaintiff should proceed directly to the formal methods for service identified in subdivisions (e), (f), or (h).

The procedure of requesting waiver of service should also not be used if the time for service under subdivision (m) will expire before the date on which the waiver must be returned. While a plaintiff has been allowed additional time for service in that situation, *e.g., Prather v. Raymond Constr. Co.,* 570 F.Supp. 278 (N.D.Ga.1983), the court could refuse a request for additional time unless the defendant appears to have evaded service pursuant to subdivision (e) or (h). It may be noted that the presumptive time limit for service under subdivision (m) does not apply to service in a foreign country.

Paragraph (5) is a cost-shifting provision retained from the former rule. The costs that may be imposed on the defendant could include, for example, the cost of the time of a process server required to make contact with a defendant residing in a guarded apartment house or residential development. The paragraph is explicit that the costs of enforcing the cost-shifting provision are themselves recoverable from a defendant who fails to return the waiver. In the absence of such a provision, the purpose of the rule would be frustrated by the cost of its enforcement, which is likely to be high in relation to the small benefit secured by the plaintiff.

Some plaintiffs may send a notice and request for waiver and, without waiting for return of the waiver, also proceed with efforts to effect formal service on the defendant. To discourage this practice, the cost-shifting provisions in paragraphs (2) and (5) are limited to costs of effecting service incurred after the time expires for the defendant to return the waiver. Moreover, by returning the waiver within the time allowed and before being served with process, a defendant receives the benefit of the longer period for responding to the complaint afforded for waivers under paragraph (3).

Subdivision (e). This subdivision replaces former subdivisions (c)(2)(C)(i) and (d)(1). It provides a means for service of summons on individuals within a judicial district of the United States. Together with subdivision (f), it provides for service on persons anywhere, subject to constitutional and statutory constraints.

Service of the summons under this subdivision does not conclusively establish the jurisdiction of the court over the person of the defendant. A defendant may assert the territorial limits of the court's reach set forth in subdivision (k), including the constitutional limitations that may be imposed by the Due Process Clause of the Fifth Amendment.

Paragraph (1) authorizes service in any judicial district in conformity with state law. This paragraph sets forth the language of former subdivision (c)(2)(C)(i), which authorized the use of the law of the state in which the district court sits, but adds as an alternative the use of the law of the state in which the service is effected.

Paragraph (2) retains the text of the former subdivision (d)(1) and authorizes the use of the familiar methods of personal or abode service or service on an authorized agent in any judicial district.

To conform to these provisions, the former subdivision (e) bearing on proceedings against parties not found within the state is stricken. Likewise stricken is the first sentence of the former subdivision (f), which had restricted the authority of the federal process server to the state in which the district court sits.

Subdivision (f). This subdivision provides for service on individuals who are in a foreign country, replacing the former subdivision (i) that was added to Rule 4 in 1963. Reflecting the pattern of Rule 4 in incorporating state law limitations on the exercise of jurisdiction over persons, the former subdivision (i) limited service outside the United States to cases in which extraterritorial service was authorized by state or federal law. The new rule eliminates the requirement of explicit authorization. On occasion, service in a foreign country was held to be improper for lack of statutory authority. *E.g., Martens v. Winder,* 341 F.2d 197 (9th Cir.), *cert. denied,* 382 U.S. 937 (1965). This authority, however, was found to exist by implication. *E.g., SEC v. VTR, Inc.,* 39 F.R.D. 19 (S.D.N.Y.1966). Given the substantial increase in the number of international transactions and events that are the subject of litigation in federal courts, it is appropriate to infer a general legislative authority to effect service on defendants in a foreign country.

A secondary effect of this provision for foreign service of a federal summons is to facilitate the use of federal long-arm law in actions brought to enforce the federal law against defendants who cannot be served under any state law but who can be constitutionally subjected to the jurisdiction of the federal court. Such a provision is set forth in paragraph (2) of subdivision (k) of this rule, applicable only to persons not subject to the territorial jurisdiction of any particular state.

Paragraph (1) gives effect to the Hague Convention on the Service Abroad of Judicial and Extrajudicial Documents, which entered into force for the United States on February 10, 1969. See 28 U.S.C.A., Fed.R.Civ.P. 4 (Supp.1986). This Convention is an important means of dealing with problems of service in a foreign country. *See generally* 1 B. Ristau, *International Judicial Assistance* §§ 4–1–1 to 4–5–2 (1990). Use of the Convention procedures, when available, is mandatory if documents must be transmitted abroad to effect service. *See Volkswagenwerk Aktiengesellschaft v. Schlunk,* 486 U.S. 694 (1988) (noting that voluntary use of these procedures may be desirable even when service could constitutionally be effected in another manner); J. Weis, *The Federal Rules and the Hague Conventions: Concerns of Conformity and Comity,* 50 *U.Pitt.L.Rev.* 903 (1989). Therefore, this paragraph provides that, when service is to be effected outside a judicial district of the United States, the methods of service appropriate under an applicable treaty shall be employed if available and if the treaty so requires.

The Hague Convention furnishes safeguards against the abridgment of rights of parties through inadequate notice. Article 15 provides for verification of actual notice or a demonstration that process was served by a method prescribed by the internal laws of the foreign state before a default judgment may be entered. Article 16 of the Convention also enables the judge to extend the time for appeal after judgment if the defendant shows a lack of adequate notice either to defend or to appeal the judgment, or has disclosed a prima facie case on the merits.

The Hague Convention does not specify a time within which a foreign country's Central Authority must effect service, but Article 15 does provide that alternate methods may be used if a Central Authority does not respond within six months. Generally, a Central Authority can be expected to respond much more quickly than that limit might permit, but there have been occasions when the signatory state was dilatory or refused to cooperate for substantive reasons. In such cases, resort may be had to the provision set forth in subdivision (f)(3).

Two minor changes in the text reflect the Hague Convention. First, the term "letter of request" has been added. Although these words are synonymous with "letter rogatory," "letter of request" is preferred in modern usage. The provision should not be interpreted to authorize use of a letter of request when there is in fact no treaty obligation on the receiving country to honor such a request from this country or when the United States does not extend diplomatic recognition to the foreign nation. Second, the passage formerly found in subdivision (i)(1)(B), "when service in either case is reasonably calculated to give actual notice," has been relocated.

Paragraph (2) provides alternative methods for use when internationally agreed methods are not intended to be exclusive, or where there is no international agreement applicable. It contains most of the language formerly set forth in subdivision (i) of the rule. Service by methods that would violate foreign law is not generally authorized. Subparagraphs (A) and (B) prescribe the more appropriate methods for conforming to local practice or using a local authority. Subparagraph (C) prescribes other methods authorized by the former rule.

Paragraph (3) authorizes the court to approve other methods of service not prohibited by international agreements. The Hague Convention, for example, authorizes special forms of service in cases of urgency if convention methods will not permit service within the time required by the circumstances. Other circumstances that might justify the use of additional methods include the failure of the foreign country's Central Authority to effect service within the six-month period provided by the Convention, or the refusal of the Central Authority to serve a complaint seeking punitive damages or to enforce the antitrust laws of the United States. In such cases, the court may direct a special method of service not explicitly authorized by international agreement if not prohibited by the agreement. Inasmuch as our Constitution requires that reasonable notice be given, an earnest effort should be made to devise a method of communication that is consistent with due process and minimizes offense to foreign law. A court may in some instances specially authorize use of ordinary mail. *Cf. Levin v. Ruby Trading Corp.*, 248 F.Supp. 537 (S.D.N.Y. 1965).

Subdivision (g). This subdivision retains the text of former subdivision (d)(2). Provision is made for service upon an infant or incompetent person in a foreign country.

Subdivision (h). This subdivision retains the text of former subdivision (d)(3), with changes reflecting those made in subdivision (e). It also contains the provisions for service on a corporation or association in a foreign country, as formerly found in subdivision (i).

Frequent use should be made of the Notice and Request procedure set forth in subdivision (d) in actions against corporations. Care must be taken, however, to address the request to an individual officer or authorized agent of the corporation. It is not effective use of the Notice and Request procedure if the mail is sent undirected to the mail room of the organization.

Subdivision (i). This subdivision retains much of the text of former subdivisions (d)(4) and (d)(5). Paragraph (1) provides for service of a summons on the United States; it amends former subdivision (d)(4) to permit the United States attorney to be served by registered or certified mail. The rule does not authorize the use of the Notice and Request procedure of revised subdivision (d) when the United States is the defendant. To assure proper handling of mail in the United

States attorney's office, the authorized mail service must be specifically addressed to the civil process clerk of the office of the United States attorney.

Paragraph (2) replaces former subdivision (d)(5). Paragraph (3) saves the plaintiff from the hazard of losing a substantive right because of failure to comply with the complex requirements of multiple service under this subdivision. That risk has proved to be more than nominal. *E.g., Whale v. United States,* 792 F.2d 951 (9th Cir.1986). This provision should be read in connection with the provisions of subdivision (c) of Rule 15 to preclude the loss of substantive rights against the United States or its agencies, corporations, or officers resulting from a plaintiff's failure to correctly identify and serve all the persons who should be named or served.

Subdivision (j). This subdivision retains the text of former subdivision (d)(6) without material change. The waiver-of-service provision is also inapplicable to actions against governments subject to service pursuant to this subdivision.

The revision adds a new paragraph (1) referring to the statute governing service of a summons on a foreign state and its political subdivisions, agencies, and instrumentalities, the Foreign Sovereign Immunities Act of 1976, 28 U.S.C. § 1608. The caption of the subdivision reflects that change.

Subdivision (k). This subdivision replaces the former subdivision (f), with no change in the title. Paragraph (1) retains the substance of the former rule in explicitly authorizing the exercise of personal jurisdiction over persons who can be reached under state long-arm law, the "100–mile bulge" provision added in 1963, or the federal interpleader act. Paragraph (1)(D) is new, but merely calls attention to federal legislation that may provide for nationwide or even world-wide service of process in cases arising under particular federal laws. Congress has provided for nationwide service of process and full exercise of territorial jurisdiction by all district courts with respect to specified federal actions. *See* 1 R. Casad, *Jurisdiction in Civil Actions* (2d Ed.) chap. 5 (1991).

Paragraph (2) is new. It authorizes the exercise of territorial jurisdiction over the person of any defendant against whom is made a claim arising under any federal law if that person is subject to personal jurisdiction in no state. This addition is a companion to the amendments made in revised subdivisions (e) and (f).

This paragraph corrects a gap in the enforcement of federal law. Under the former rule, a problem was presented when the defendant was a non-resident of the United States having contacts with the United States sufficient to justify the application of United States law and to satisfy federal standards of forum selection, but having insufficient contact with any single state to support jurisdiction under state long-arm legislation or meet the requirements of the Fourteenth Amendment limitation on state court territorial jurisdiction. In such cases, the defendant was shielded from the enforcement of federal law by the fortuity of a favorable limitation on the power of state courts, which was incorporated into the federal practice by the former rule. In this respect, the revision responds to the suggestion of the Supreme Court made in *Omni Capital Int'l v. Rudolf Wolff & Co., Ltd.,* 484 U.S. 97, 111 (1987).

There remain constitutional limitations on the exercise of territorial jurisdiction by federal courts over persons outside the United States. These restrictions arise from the Fifth Amendment rather than from the Fourteenth Amendment, which limits state-court reach and which was incorporated into federal practice by the reference to state law in the text of the former subdivision (e) that is deleted by this revision. The Fifth Amendment requires that any defendant have affiliating contacts with the United States sufficient to justify the exercise of personal jurisdiction over that party. *Cf. Wells Fargo & Co. v. Wells Fargo Express Co.,* 556 F.2d 406, 418 (9th Cir.1977). There also may be a further Fifth Amendment constraint in that a plaintiff's forum selection might be so inconvenient to a defendant that it would be a denial of "fair play and substantial justice" required by the due process clause, even though the defendant had significant affiliating contacts with the United States. *See DeJames v. Magnificent Carriers,* 654 F.2d 280, 286 n.3 (3rd Cir.), *cert. denied,* 454 U.S. 1085 (1981). *Compare World–Wide Volkswagen Corp. v. Woodson,* 444 U.S. 286, 293–294 (1980); *Insurance Corp. of Ireland v. Compagnie des Bauxites de Guinee,* 456 U.S. 694, 702–03 (1982); *Burger King Corp. v. Rudzewicz,* 471 U.S. 462, 476–78 (1985); *Asahi Metal Indus. v. Superior Court of Cal., Solano County,* 480 U.S. 102, 108–13 (1987). *See generally* R. Lusardi, *Nationwide Service of Process: Due Process Limitations on the Power of the Sovereign,* 33 *Vill.L.Rev.* 1 (1988).

This provision does not affect the operation of federal venue legislation. *See generally* 28 U.S.C. § 1391. Nor does it affect the operation of federal law providing for the change of venue. 28 U.S.C. §§ 1404, 1406. The availability of transfer for fairness and convenience under § 1404 should preclude most conflicts between the full exercise of territorial jurisdiction permitted by this rule and the Fifth Amendment requirement of "fair play and substantial justice."

The district court should be especially scrupulous to protect aliens who reside in a foreign country from forum selections so onerous that injustice could result. "[G]reat care and reserve should be exercised when extending our notions of personal jurisdiction into the international field." *Asahi Metal Indus. v. Superior Court of Cal., Solano County,* 480 U.S. 102, 115 (1987), quoting *United States v. First Nat'l City Bank,* 379 U.S. 378, 404 (1965) (Harlan, J., dissenting).

This narrow extension of the federal reach applies only if a claim is made against the defendant under federal law. It does not establish personal jurisdiction if the only claims are those arising under state law or the law of another country, even though there might be diversity or alienage subject matter jurisdiction as to such claims. If, however, personal jurisdiction is established under this paragraph with respect to a federal claim, then 28 U.S.C. § 1367(a) provides supplemental jurisdiction over related claims against that defendant, subject to the court's discretion to decline exercise of that jurisdiction under 28 U.S.C. § 1367(c).

Subdivision (l). This subdivision assembles in one place all the provisions of the present rule bearing on proof of service. No material change in the rule is effected. The provision that proof of service can be amended by leave of court is retained from the former subdivision (h). *See generally* 4A Wright & Miller, *Federal Practice and Procedure* § 1132 (2d ed. 1987).

Subdivision (m). This subdivision retains much of the language of the present subdivision (j).

The new subdivision explicitly provides that the court shall allow additional time if there is good cause for the plaintiff's failure to effect service in the prescribed 120 days, and authorizes the court to relieve a plaintiff of the consequences of an application of this subdivision even if there is no good cause shown. Such relief formerly was afforded in some cases, partly in reliance on Rule 6(b). Relief may be justified, for example, if the applicable statute of limitations would bar the refiled action, or if the defendant is evading service or conceals a defect in attempted service. *E.g., Ditkof v. Owens–Illinois, Inc.,* 114 F.R.D. 104 (E.D.Mich.1987). A specific instance of good cause is set forth in paragraph (3) of this rule, which provides for extensions if necessary to correct oversights in compliance with the requirements of multiple service in actions against the United States or its officers, agencies, and corporations. The district court should also take care to protect *pro se* plaintiffs from consequences of confusion or delay attending the resolution of an *in forma pauperis* petition. *Robinson v. America's Best Contacts & Eyeglasses,* 876 F.2d 596 (7th Cir.1989).

The 1983 revision of this subdivision referred to the "party on whose behalf such service was required," rather than to the "plaintiff," a term used generically elsewhere in this rule to refer to any party initiating a claim against a person who is not a party to the action. To simplify the text, the revision returns to the usual practice in the rule of referring simply to the plaintiff even though its principles apply with equal force to defendants who may assert claims against non-parties under Rules 13(h), 14, 19, 20, or 21.

Subdivision (n). This subdivision provides for in rem and quasi-in-rem jurisdiction. Paragraph (1) incorporates any requirements of 28 U.S.C. § 1655 or similar provisions bearing on seizures or liens.

Paragraph (2) provides for other uses of quasi-in-rem jurisdiction but limits its use to exigent circumstances. Provisional remedies may be employed as a means to secure jurisdiction over the property of a defendant whose person is not within reach of the court, but occasions for the use of this provision should be rare, as where the defendant is a fugitive or assets are in imminent danger of disappearing. Until 1963, it was not possible under Rule 4 to assert jurisdiction in a federal court over the property of a defendant not personally served. The 1963 amendment to subdivision (e) authorized the use of state law procedures authorizing seizures of assets as a basis for jurisdiction. Given the liberal availability of long-arm jurisdiction, the exercise of power quasi-in-rem has become almost an anachronism. Circumstances too spare to affiliate the defendant to the forum state sufficiently to support long-arm jurisdiction over the defendant's person are also inadequate to support seizure of the defendant's assets fortuitously found within the state. *Shaffer v. Heitner,* 433 U.S. 186 (1977).

Rule 4.1. Service of Other Process

(a) Generally. *Process other than a summons as provided in Rule 4 or subpoena as provided in Rule 45 shall be served by a United States marshal, a deputy United States marshal, or a person specially appointed for that purpose, who shall make proof of service as provided in Rule 4(l). The process may be served anywhere within the territorial limits of the state in which the district court is located, and, when authorized by a statute of the United States, beyond the territorial limits of that state.*

(b) Enforcement of Orders: Commitment for Civil Contempt. *An order of civil commitment of a person held to be in contempt of a decree or injunction issued to enforce the laws of the United States may be served and enforced in any district. Other orders in civil contempt proceedings shall be served in the state in which the court issuing the order to be enforced is located or elsewhere within the United States if not more than 100 miles from the place at which the order to be enforced was issued.*

Advisory Committee's Note

This is a new rule. Its purpose is to separate those few provisions of the former Rule 4 bearing on matters other than service of a summons to allow greater textual clarity in Rule 4. Subdivision (a) contains no new language.

New matter is shown in italics; matter to be omitted is lined through

Subdivision (b) replaces the final clause of the penultimate sentence of the former subdivision 4(f), a clause added to the rule in 1963. The new rule provides for nationwide service of orders of civil commitment enforcing decrees of injunctions issued to compel compliance with federal law. The rule makes no change in the practice with respect to the enforcement of injunctions or decrees not involving the enforcement of federally-created rights.

Service of process is not required to notify a party of a decree or injunction, or of an order that the party show cause why that party should not be held in contempt of such an order. With respect to a party who has once been served with a summons, the service of the decree or injunction itself or of an order to show cause can be made pursuant to Rule 5. Thus, for example, an injunction may be served on a party through that person's attorney. *Chagas v. United States,* 369 F.2d 643 (5th Cir.1966). The same is true for service of an order to show cause. *Waffenschmidt v. Mackay,* 763 F.2d 711 (5th Cir.1985).

The new rule does not affect the reach of the court to impose criminal contempt sanctions. Nationwide enforcement of federal decrees and injunctions is already available with respect to criminal contempt: a federal court may effect the arrest of a criminal contemnor anywhere in the United States, 28 U.S.C. § 3041, and a contemnor when arrested may be subject to removal to the district in which punishment may be imposed. Fed.R.Crim.P. 40. Thus, the present law permits criminal contempt enforcement against a contemnor wherever that person may be found.

The effect of the revision is to provide a choice of civil or criminal contempt sanctions in those situations to which it applies. Contempt proceedings, whether civil or criminal, must be brought in the court that was allegedly defied by a contumacious act. *Ex parte Bradley,* 74 U.S. 366 (1869). This is so even if the offensive conduct or inaction occurred outside the district of the court in which the enforcement proceeding must be conducted. *E.g., McCourtney v. United States,* 291 Fed. 497 (8th Cir.), *cert. denied,* 263 U.S. 714 (1923). For this purpose, the rule as before does not distinguish between parties and other persons subject to contempt sanctions by reason of their relation or connection to parties.

Rule 5. Service and Filing of Pleadings and Other Papers

(e) Filing with the Court Defined. The filing of papers with the court as required by these rules shall be made by filing them with the clerk of the court, except that the judge may permit the papers to be filed with the judge, in which event the judge shall note thereon the filing date and forthwith transmit them to the office of the clerk. ~~Papers may be filed by facsimile transmission if permitted by rules of the district court, provided that the rules~~ *A court may, by local rule, permit papers to be filed by facsimile or other electronic means if such means* are authorized by and consistent with standards established by the Judicial Conference of the United States. The clerk shall not refuse to accept for filing any paper presented for that purpose solely because it is not presented in proper form as required by these rules or any local rules or practices.

New matter is shown in italics; matter to be omitted is lined through

Advisory Committee's Note

This is a technical amendment, using the broader language of Rule 25 of the Federal Rules of Appellate Procedure. The district court—and the bankruptcy court by virtue of a cross-reference in Bankruptcy Rule 7005—can, by local rule, permit filing not only by facsimile transmissions but also by other electronic means, subject to standards approved by the Judicial Conference.

Rule 11. Signing of Pleadings, Motions, and Other Papers; *Representations to Court;* Sanctions

(a) Signature. Every pleading, *written* motion, and other paper ~~of a party represented by an attorney~~ shall be signed by at least one attorney of record in the attorney's individual name, *or, if the party is not represented by an attorney, shall be signed by the party.* ~~whose address shall be stated. A party who is not represented by an attorney shall sign the party's pleading, motion, or other paper and state the party's address.~~ *Each paper shall state the signer's address and telephone number, if any.* Except when otherwise specifically provided by rule or statute, pleadings need not be verified or accompanied by affidavit. ~~The rule in equity that the averments of an answer under oath must be overcome by the testimony of two witnesses or of one witness sustained by corroborating circumstances is abolished. The signature of an attorney or party constitutes a certificate by the signer that the signer has read the pleading, motion, or other paper; that to the best of the signer's knowledge, information, and belief formed after reasonable inquiry it is well grounded in fact and is warranted by existing law or a good faith argument for the extension, modification, or reversal of existing law, and that it is not interposed for any improper purpose, such as to harass or to cause unnecessary delay or needless increase in the cost of litigation. If a pleading, motion, or other~~ *An unsigned* paper ~~is not signed, it~~ shall be stricken unless ~~it is signed promptly after the~~ omission *of the signature* is *corrected promptly after being* called to the attention of the ~~pleader or movant~~ *attorney or party.*

(b) Representations to Court. ~~If a pleading, motion, or other paper is signed in violation of this rule, the court, upon motion or upon its own initiative, shall impose upon the person who signed it, a represented party, or both, an appropriate sanction, which may include an order to pay to the other party or parties the amount of the reasonable expenses incurred because of the filing of the pleading, motion, or other paper, including a reasonable attorney's fee.~~ *By presenting to the court (whether by signing, filing, submitting, or later advocating) a pleading, written motion, or other paper, an attorney or unrepresented party is certifying that to the best of the person's knowledge, information, and*

New matter is shown in italics; matter to be omitted is lined through

belief, formed after an inquiry reasonable under the circumstances,—

(1) it is not being presented for any improper purpose, such as to harass or to cause unnecessary delay or needless increase in the cost of litigation;

(2) the claims, defenses, and other legal contentions therein are warranted by existing law or by a nonfrivolous argument for the extension, modification, or reversal of existing law or the establishment of new law;

(3) the allegations and other factual contentions have evidentiary support or, if specifically so identified, are likely to have evidentiary support after a reasonable opportunity for further investigation or discovery; and

(4) the denials of factual contentions are warranted on the evidence or, if specifically so identified, are reasonably based on a lack of information or belief.

(c) Sanctions. *If, after notice and a reasonable opportunity to respond, the court determines that subdivision (b) has been violated, the court may, subject to the conditions stated below, impose an appropriate sanction upon the attorneys, law firms, or parties that have violated subdivision (b) or are responsible for the violation.*

(1) How Initiated.

(A) By Motion. A motion for sanctions under this rule shall be made separately from other motions or requests and shall describe the specific conduct alleged to violate subdivision (b). It shall be served as provided in Rule 5, but shall not be filed with or presented to the court unless, within 21 days after service of the motion (or such other period as the court may prescribe), the challenged paper, claim, defense, contention, allegation, or denial is not withdrawn or appropriately corrected. If warranted, the court may award to the party prevailing on the motion the reasonable expenses and attorney's fees incurred in presenting or opposing the motion. Absent exceptional circumstances, a law firm shall be held jointly responsible for violations committed by its partners, associates, and employees.

(B) On Court's Initiative. On its own initiative, the court may enter an order describing the specific conduct that appears to violate subdivision (b) and directing an attorney, law firm, or party to show cause why it has not violated subdivision (b) with respect thereto.

(2) Nature of Sanction; Limitations. A sanction imposed for violation of this rule shall be limited to what is sufficient to deter repetition of such conduct or comparable conduct by others similarly situated. Subject to the limitations in subparagraphs (A) and (B), the sanction may consist of, or include, directives of a nonmonetary nature, an order to pay a penalty into court, or, if imposed on motion and warranted for effective deterrence, an order directing payment to the movant of some or all of the reasonable attorneys' fees and other expenses incurred as a direct result of the violation.

(A) Monetary sanctions may not be awarded against a represented party for a violation of subdivision (b)(2).

(B) Monetary sanctions may not be awarded on the court's initiative unless the court issues its order to show cause before a voluntary dismissal or settlement of the claims made by or against the party which is, or whose attorneys are, to be sanctioned.

(3) Order. When imposing sanctions, the court shall describe the conduct determined to constitute a violation of this rule and explain the basis for the sanction imposed.

(d) Inapplicability to Discovery. *Subdivisions (a) through (c) of this rule do not apply to disclosures and discovery requests, responses, objections, and motions that are subject to the provisions of Rules 26 through 37.*

Advisory Committee's Note

Purpose of revision. This revision is intended to remedy problems that have arisen in the interpretation and application of the 1983 revision of the rule. For empirical examination of experience under the 1983 rule, see, *e.g.*, New York State Bar Committee on Federal Courts, *Sanctions and Attorneys' Fees* (1987); T. Willging, *The Rule 11 Sanctioning Process* (1989); American Judicature Society, *Report of the Third Circuit Task Force on Federal Rule of Civil Procedure 11* (S. Burbank ed., 1989); E. Wiggins, T. Willging, and D. Stienstra, *Report on Rule 11* (Federal Judicial Center 1991). For book-length analyses of the case law, see G. Joseph, *Sanctions: The Federal Law of Litigation Abuse* (1989); J. Solovy, *The Federal Law of Sanctions* (1991); G. Vairo, *Rule 11 Sanctions: Case Law Perspectives and Preventive Measures* (1991).

The rule retains the principle that attorneys and pro se litigants have an obligation to the court to refrain from conduct that frustrates the aims of Rule 1. The revision broadens the scope of this obligation, but places greater constraints on the imposition of sanctions and should reduce the number of motions for sanctions presented to the court. New subdivision (d) removes from the ambit of this rule all discovery requests, responses, objections, and motions subject to the provisions of Rule 26 through 37.

Subdivision (a). Retained in this subdivision are the provisions requiring signatures on pleadings, written motions, and other papers. Unsigned papers are to be received by the Clerk, but then are to be stricken if the omission of the signature is not corrected promptly after being called to the attention of the attorney or pro se litigant. Correction can be made by signing the paper on file or by submitting a duplicate that contains the signature. A court may require by local rule that papers contain additional identifying information regarding the parties or attorneys, such as telephone numbers to facilitate facsimile transmissions, though, as for omission of a signature, the paper should not be rejected for failure to provide such information.

The sentence in the former rule relating to the effect of answers under oath is no longer needed and has been eliminated. The provision in the former rule that signing a paper constitutes a certificate that it has been read by the signer also has been eliminated as unnecessary. The obligations imposed under subdivision (b) obviously require that a pleading, written motion, or other paper be read before it is filed or submitted to the court.

Subdivisions (b) and (c). These subdivisions restate the provisions requiring attorneys and pro se litigants to conduct a reasonable inquiry into the law and facts before signing pleadings, written motions, and other documents, and prescribing sanctions for violation of these obligations. The revision in part expands the responsibilities of litigants to the court, while providing greater constraints and flexibility in dealing with infractions of the rule. The rule continues to require litigants to "stop-and-think" before initially making legal or factual contentions. It also, however, emphasizes the duty of candor by subjecting litigants to potential sanctions for insisting upon a position after it is no longer tenable and by generally providing protection against sanctions if they withdraw or correct contentions after a potential violation is called to their attention.

The rule applies only to assertions contained in papers filed with or submitted to the court. It does not cover matters arising for the first time during oral presentations to the court, when counsel may make statements that would not have been made if there had been more time for study and reflection. However, a litigant's obligations with respect to the contents of these papers are not measured solely as of the time they are filed with or submitted to the court, but include reaffirming to the court and advocating positions contained in those pleadings and motions after learning that they cease to have any merit. For example, an attorney who during a pretrial conference insists on a claim or defense should be viewed as "presenting to the court" that contention and would be subject to the obligations of subdivision (b) measured as of that time. Similarly, if after a notice of removal is filed, a party urges in federal court the allegations of a pleading filed in state court (whether as claims, defenses, or in disputes regarding removal or remand), it would be viewed as "presenting"—and hence certifying to the district court under Rule 11—those allegations.

The certification with respect to allegations and other factual contentions is revised in recognition that sometimes a litigant may have good reason to believe that a fact is true or false but may need discovery, formal or informal, from opposing parties or third persons to gather and confirm the evidentiary basis for the allegation. Tolerance of factual contentions in initial pleadings by plaintiffs or defendants when specifically identified as made on information and belief does not relieve litigants from the obligation to conduct an appropriate investigation into the facts that is reasonable under the circumstances; it is not a license to join parties, make claims, or present defenses without any factual basis or justification. Moreover, if evidentiary support is not obtained after a reasonable opportunity for further investigation or discovery, the party has a duty under the rule not to persist with that contention. Subdivision (b) does not require a formal amendment to pleadings for which evidentiary support is not obtained, but rather calls upon a litigant not thereafter to advocate such claims or defenses.

The certification is that there is (or likely will be) "evidentiary support" for the allegation, not that the party will prevail with respect to its contention regarding the fact. That summary judgment is rendered against a party does not necessarily mean, for purposes of this certification, that it had no evidentiary support for its position. On the other hand, if a party has evidence with respect to a contention that would suffice to defeat a motion for summary judgment based thereon, it would have sufficient "evidentiary support" for purposes of Rule 11.

Denials of factual contentions involve somewhat different considerations. Often, of course, a denial is premised upon the existence of evidence contradicting the alleged fact. At other times a denial is permissible because, after an appropriate investigation, a party has no information concerning the matter or, indeed, has a reasonable basis for doubting the credibility of the only evidence relevant to the matter. A party should not deny an allegation it knows to be true; but it is not required, simply because it lacks contradictory evidence, to admit an allegation that it believes is not true.

The changes in subdivisions (b)(3) and (b)(4) will serve to equalize the burden of the rule upon plaintiffs and defendants, who under Rule 8(b) are in effect allowed to deny allegations by stating that from their initial investigation they lack sufficient information to form a belief as to the truth of the allegation. If, after further investigation or discovery, a denial is no longer warranted, the defendant should not continue to insist on that denial. While sometimes helpful, formal amendment of the pleadings to withdraw an allegation or denial is not required by subdivision (b).

Arguments for extensions, modifications, or reversals of existing law or for creation of new law do not violate subdivision (b)(2) provided they are "nonfrivolous." This establishes an objective standard, intended to eliminate any "empty-head pure-heart" justification for patently frivolous arguments. However, the extent to which a litigant has researched the issues and found some support for its theories even in minority opinions, in law review articles, or through consultation with other attorneys should certainly be taken into account in determining whether paragraph (2) has been violated. Although arguments for a change of law are not required to be specifically so identified, a contention that is so identified should be viewed with greater tolerance under the rule.

The court has available a variety of possible sanctions to impose for violations, such as striking the offending paper; issuing an admonition, reprimand, or censure; requiring participation in seminars or other educational programs; ordering a fine payable to the court; referring the matter to disciplinary authorities (or, in the case of government attorneys, to the Attorney General, Inspector General, or agency head), etc. *See Manual for Complex Litigation, Second,* § 42.3. The rule does not attempt to enumerate the factors a court should consider in deciding whether to impose a sanction or what sanctions would be appropriate in the circumstances; but, for emphasis, it does specifically note that a sanction may be nonmonetary as well as monetary. Whether the improper conduct was willful, or negligent; whether it was part of a pattern of activity, or an isolated event; whether it infected the entire pleading, or only one particular count or defense; whether the person has engaged in similar conduct in other litigation; whether it was intended to injure; what effect it had on the litigation process in time or expense; whether the responsible person is trained in the law; what amount, given the financial resources of the responsible person, is needed to deter that person from repetition in the same case; what amount is needed to deter similar activity by other litigants: all of these may in a particular case be proper considerations. The court has significant discretion in determining what sanctions, if any, should be imposed for a violation, subject to the principle that the sanctions should not be more severe than reasonably necessary to deter repetition of the conduct by the offending person or comparable conduct by similarly situated persons.

Since the purpose of Rule 11 sanctions is to deter rather than to compensate, the rule provides that, if a monetary sanction is imposed, it should ordinarily be paid into court as a penalty. However, under unusual circumstances, particularly for (b)(1) violations, deterrence may be ineffective unless the sanction not only requires the person violating the rule to make a monetary payment, but also directs that some or all of this payment be made to those injured by the violation. Accordingly, the rule authorizes the court, if requested in a motion and if so warranted, to award attorney's fees to another party. Any such award to another party, however, should not exceed the expenses and attorneys' fees for the services directly and unavoidably caused by the violation of the certification requirement. If, for example, a wholly unsupportable count were included in a multi-count complaint or counterclaim for the purpose of needlessly increasing the cost of litigation to an impecunious adversary, any award of expenses should be limited to those directly caused by inclusion of the improper count, and not those resulting from the filing of the complaint or answer itself. The award should not provide compensation for services that could have been avoided by an earlier disclosure of evidence or an earlier challenge to the groundless claims or defenses. Moreover, partial reimbursement of fees may constitute a sufficient deterrent with respect to violations by persons having modest financial resources. In cases brought under statutes providing for fees to be awarded to prevailing parties, the court should not employ cost-shifting under this rule in a manner that would be inconsistent with the standards that govern the statutory award of fees, such as stated in *Christiansburg Garment Co. v. EEOC,* 434 U.S. 412 (1978).

The sanction should be imposed on the persons—whether attorneys, law firms, or parties—who have violated the rule or who may be determined to be responsible for the violation. The person signing, filing, submitting, or advocating a document has a nondelegable responsibility to the court, and in most situations is the person to be sanctioned for a violation. Absent exceptional circumstances, a law firm is to be held also responsible when, as a result of a motion under subdivision (c)(1)(A), one of its partners, associates, or employees is determined to have violated the rule. Since such a motion may be filed only if the offending paper is not withdrawn or corrected within 21 days after service of the motion, it is appropriate that the law firm ordinarily be viewed as jointly responsible under established principles of agency. This provision is designed to remove the restrictions of the former rule. *Cf. Pavelic & LeFlore v. Marvel Entertainment Group,* 493 U.S. 120 (1989) (1983 version of Rule 11 does not permit sanctions against law firm of attorney signing groundless complaint).

The revision permits the court to consider whether other attorneys in the firm, co-counsel, other law firms, or the party itself should be held accountable for their part in causing a violation. When appropriate, the court can make an additional inquiry in order to determine whether the sanction should be imposed on such persons, firms, or parties either in addition to or, in unusual circumstances, instead of the person actually making the presentation to the court. For example, such an inquiry may be appropriate in cases involving governmental agencies or other institutional parties that frequently impose substantial restrictions on the discretion of individual attorneys employed by it.

Sanctions that involve monetary awards (such as a fine or an award of attorney's fees) may not be imposed on a represented party for causing a violation of subdivision (b)(2), involving frivolous contentions of law. Monetary responsibility for such violations is more properly placed solely on the party's attorneys. With this limitation, the rule should not be subject to attack under the Rules Enabling Act.

See Willy v. Coastal Corp., 503 U.S. 131 (1992); *Business Guides, Inc. v. Chromatic Communications Enter. Inc.*, 498 U.S. 533 (1991). This restriction does not limit the court's power to impose sanctions or remedial orders that may have collateral financial consequences upon a party, such as dismissal of a claim, preclusion of a defense, or preparation of amended pleadings.

Explicit provision is made for litigants to be provided notice of the alleged violation and an opportunity to respond before sanctions are imposed. Whether the matter should be decided solely on the basis of written submissions or should be scheduled for oral argument (or, indeed, for evidentiary presentation) will depend on the circumstances. If the court imposes a sanction, it must, unless waived, indicate its reasons in a written order or on the record; the court should not ordinarily have to explain its denial of a motion for sanctions. Whether a violation has occurred and what sanctions, if any, to impose for a violation are matters committed to the discretion of the trial court; accordingly, as under current law, the standard for appellate review of these decisions will be for abuse of discretion. *See Cooter & Gell v. Hartmarx Corp.*, 496 U.S. 384 (1990) (noting, however, that an abuse would be established if the court based its ruling on an erroneous view of the law or on a clearly erroneous assessment of the evidence).

The revision leaves for resolution on a case-by-case basis, considering the particular circumstances involved, the question as to when a motion for violation of Rule 11 should be served and when, if filed, it should be decided. Ordinarily the motion should be served promptly after the inappropriate paper is filed, and, if delayed too long, may be viewed as untimely. In other circumstances, it should not be served until the other party has had a reasonable opportunity for discovery. Given the "safe harbor" provisions discussed below, a party cannot delay serving its Rule 11 motion until conclusion of the case (or judicial rejection of the offending contention).

Rule 11 motions should not be made or threatened for minor, inconsequential violations of the standards prescribed by subdivision (b). They should not be employed as a discovery device or to test the legal sufficiency or efficacy of allegations in the pleadings; other motions are available for those purposes. Nor should Rule 11 motions be prepared to emphasize the merits of a party's position, to exact an unjust settlement, to intimidate an adversary into withdrawing contentions that are fairly debatable, to increase the costs of litigation, to create a conflict of interest between attorney and client, or to seek disclosure of matters otherwise protected by the attorney-client privilege or the work-product doctrine. As under the prior rule, the court may defer its ruling (or its decision as to the identity of the persons to be sanctioned) until final resolution of the case in order to avoid immediate conflicts of interest and to reduce the disruption created if a disclosure of attorney-client communications is needed to determine whether a violation occurred or to identify the person responsible for the violation.

The rule provides that requests for sanctions must be made as a separate motion, *i.e.*, not simply included as an additional prayer for relief contained in another motion. The motion for sanctions is not, however, to be filed until at least 21 days (or such other period as the court may set) after being served. If, during this period, the alleged violation is corrected, as by withdrawing (whether formally or informally) some allegation or contention, the motion should not be filed with the court. These provisions are intended to provide a type of "safe harbor" against motions under Rule 11 in that a party will not be subject to sanctions on the basis of another party's motion unless, after receiving the motion, it refuses to withdraw that position or to acknowledge candidly that it does not currently have evidence to support a specified allegation. Under the former rule, parties were sometimes reluctant to abandon a questionable contention lest that be viewed as evidence of a violation of Rule 11; under the revision, the timely withdrawal of a contention will protect a party against a motion for sanctions.

To stress the seriousness of a motion for sanctions and to define precisely the conduct claimed to violate the rule, the revision provides that the "safe harbor" period begins to run only upon service of the motion. In most cases, however, counsel should be expected to give informal notice to the other party, whether in person or by a telephone call or letter, of a potential violation before proceeding to prepare and serve a Rule 11 motion.

As under former Rule 11, the filing of a motion for sanctions is itself subject to the requirements of the rule and can lead to sanctions. However, service of a cross motion under Rule 11 should rarely be needed since under the revision the court may award to the person who prevails on a motion under Rule 11—whether the movant or the target of the motion—reasonable expenses, including attorney's fees, incurred in presenting or opposing the motion.

The power of the court to act on its own initiative is retained, but with the condition that this be done through a show cause order. This procedure provides the person with notice and an opportunity to respond. The revision provides that a monetary sanction imposed after a court-initiated show cause order be limited to a penalty payable to the court and that it be imposed only if the show cause order is issued before any voluntary dismissal or an agreement of the parties to settle the claims made by or against the litigant. Parties settling a case should not be subsequently faced with an unexpected order from the court leading to monetary sanctions that might have affected their willingness to settle or voluntarily dismiss a case. Since show cause orders will ordinarily be issued only in situations that are akin to a contempt of court, the rule does not provide a "safe harbor" to a litigant for withdrawing a claim, defense, etc., after a show cause order has been issued on the court's own initiative. Such corrective action, however, should be taken into account in deciding what—if any—sanction to impose if, after consideration of the litigant's response, the court concludes that a violation has occurred.

Subdivision (d). Rules 26(g) and 37 establish certification standards and sanctions that apply to discovery disclosures, requests, responses, objections, and motions. It is appropriate that Rules 26 through 37, which are specially designed for the discovery process, govern such documents and conduct rather than the more general provisions of Rule 11. Subdivision (d) has been added to accomplish this result.

Rule 11 is not the exclusive source for control of improper presentations of claims, defenses, or contentions. It does not supplant statutes permitting awards of attorney's fees to prevailing parties or alter the principles governing such awards. It does not inhibit the court in punishing for contempt, in exercising its inherent powers, or in imposing sanctions, awarding expenses, or directing remedial action authorized under other rules or under 28 U.S.C. § 1927. *See Chambers v. NASCO,* 501 U.S. 32 (1991). *Chambers* cautions, however, against reliance upon inherent powers if appropriate sanctions can be imposed under provisions such as Rule 11, and the procedures specified in Rule 11—notice, opportunity to respond, and findings—should ordinarily be employed when imposing a sanction under the court's inherent powers. Finally, it should be noted that Rule 11 does not preclude a party from initiating an independent action for malicious prosecution or abuse of process.

Rule 12. Defenses and Objections—When and How Presented—By Pleading or Motion—Motion for Judgment on the Pleadings

(a) When Presented.

(1) Unless a different time is prescribed in a statute of the United States, a ~~A~~ defendant shall serve an answer

(A) within 20 days after *being served with* ~~the service of~~ the summons and complaint ~~upon that defendant~~, *or*

(B) if service of the summons has been timely waived on request under Rule 4(d), within 60 days after the date when the request for waiver was sent, or within 90 days after that date if the defendant was addressed outside any judicial district of the United States ~~except when service is made under Rule 4(e) and a different time is prescribed in the order of court under the statute of the United States or in the statute or rule of court of the state~~.

(2) A party served with a pleading stating a cross-claim against that party shall serve an answer thereto within 20 days after ~~the service upon that party~~ *being served.* The plaintiff shall serve a reply to a counterclaim in the answer within 20 days after service of the answer, or, if a reply is ordered by the court, within 20 days after service of the order, unless the order otherwise directs.

(3) The United States or an officer or agency thereof shall serve an answer to the complaint or to a cross-claim, or a reply to a counterclaim, within 60 days after the service upon the United States attorney of the pleading in which the claim is asserted.

(4) Unless a different time is fixed by court order, t~~T~~he service of a motion permitted under this rule alters these periods of time as follows~~, unless a different time is fixed by order of the court~~:

(~~1~~*A*) if the court denies the motion or postpones its disposition until the trial on the merits, the responsive pleading shall be served within 10 days after notice of the court's action; *or*

(~~2~~*B*) if the court grants a motion for a more definite statement, the responsive pleading shall be served within 10 days after the service of the more definite statement.

Advisory Committee's Note

Subdivision (a) is divided into paragraphs for greater clarity, and paragraph (1)(B) is added to reflect amendments to Rule 4. Consistent with Rule 4(d)(3), a defendant that timely waives service is allowed 60 days from the date the request was mailed in which to respond to the complaint, with an additional 30 days afforded if the request was sent out of the country. Service is timely waived if the waiver is returned within the time specified in the request (30 days after the request was mailed, or 60 days if mailed out of the country) and before being formally served with process. Sometimes a plaintiff may attempt to serve a defendant with process while also sending the defendant a request for waiver of service; if the defendant executes the waiver of service within the time specified and before being served with process, it should have the longer time to respond afforded by waiving service.

The date of sending the request is to be inserted by the plaintiff on the face of the request for waiver and on the waiver itself. This date is used to measure the return day for the waiver form, so that the plaintiff can know on a day certain whether formal service of process will be necessary; it is also a useful date to measure the time for answer when service is waived. The defendant who returns the waiver is given additional time for answer in order to assure that it loses nothing by waiving service of process.

Rule 15. Amended and Supplemental Pleadings

(c) Relation Back of Amendments. An amendment of a pleading relates back to the date of the original pleading when

(1) relation back is permitted by the law that provides the statute of limitations applicable to the action, or

(2) the claim or defense asserted in the amended pleading arose out of the conduct, transaction, or occurrence set forth or attempted to be set forth in the original pleading, or

(3) the amendment changes the party or the naming of the party against whom a claim is asserted if the foregoing provision (2) is satisfied and, within the period provided by Rule 4(~~j~~*m*) for service of the summons and complaint, the party to be brought in by amendment (A) has received such notice of the institution of the action that the party will not be prejudiced in maintaining a defense on the merits, and (B) knew or should have known that, but for a mistake concerning the identity of the proper party, the action would have been brought against the party.

The delivery or mailing of process to the United States Attorney, or United States Attorney's designee, or the Attorney General of the United States, or an agency or officer who would have been a proper defendant if named, satisfies the requirement of subparagraphs (A) and (B) of this paragraph (3) with respect to the United States or any agency or officer thereof to be brought into the action as a defendant.

New matter is shown in italics; matter to be omitted is lined through

Advisory Committee's Note

The amendment conforms the cross reference to Rule 4 to the revision of that rule.

Rule 16. Pretrial Conferences; Scheduling; Management

(b) Scheduling and Planning. Except in categories of actions exempted by district court rule as inappropriate, the *district* judge, or a magistrate *judge* when authorized by district court rule, shall, *after receiving the report from the parties under Rule 26(f) or* after consulting with the attorneys for the parties and any unrepresented parties~~,~~ by a scheduling conference, telephone, mail, or other suitable means, enter a scheduling order that limits the time

(1) to join other parties and to amend the pleadings;

(2) to file ~~and hear~~ motions; and

(3) to complete discovery.

The scheduling order may also include

(4) modifications of the times for disclosures under Rules 26(a) and 26(e)(1) and of the extent of discovery to be permitted;

(~~4~~*5*) the date or dates for conferences before trial, a final pretrial conference, and trial; and

(~~5~~*6*) any other matters appropriate in the circumstances of the case.

The order shall issue as soon as practicable but in ~~no~~ *any* event ~~more than 120~~ *within 90* days after ~~filing of the complaint~~ *the appearance of a defendant and within 120 days after the complaint has been served on a defendant.* A schedule shall not be modified except *upon a showing of good cause and* by leave of the *district* judge or, *when authorized by local rule, by* a magistrate *judge* ~~when authorized by district court rule upon a showing of good cause~~.

(c) Subjects ~~to be Discussed~~ *for Consideration* at Pretrial Conferences. ~~The participants a~~*A*t any conference under this rule ~~may consider and take action~~ *consideration may be given, and the court may take appropriate action,* with respect to

(1) the formulation and simplification of the issues, including the elimination of frivolous claims or defenses;

(2) the necessity or desirability of amendments to the pleadings;

(3) the possibility of obtaining admissions of fact and of documents which will avoid unnecessary proof, stipulations regarding the authenticity of documents, and advance rulings from the court on the admissibility of evidence;

New matter is shown in italics; matter to be omitted is lined through

(4) the avoidance of unnecessary proof and of cumulative evidence, *and limitations or restrictions on the use of testimony under Rule 702 of the Federal Rules of Evidence*;

(5) the appropriateness and timing of summary adjudication under Rule 56;

(6) the control and scheduling of discovery, including orders affecting disclosures and discovery pursuant to Rule 26 and Rules 29 through 37;

(~~5~~*7*) the identification of witnesses and documents, the need and schedule for filing and exchanging pretrial briefs, and the date or dates for further conferences and for trial;

(~~6~~*8*) the advisability of referring matters to a magistrate *judge* or master;

(~~7~~*9*) ~~the possibility of~~ settlement ~~or~~ *and* the use of ~~extrajudicial~~ *special* procedures to ~~resolve~~ *assist in resolving* the dispute *when authorized by statute or local rule*;

(~~8~~*10*) the form and substance of the pretrial order;

(~~9~~*11*) the disposition of pending motions;

(1~~0~~*2*) the need for adopting special procedures for managing potentially difficult or protracted actions that may involve complex issues, multiple parties, difficult legal questions, or unusual proof problems;

(13) an order for a separate trial pursuant to Rule 42(b) with respect to a claim, counterclaim, cross-claim, or third-party claim, or with respect to any particular issue in the case;

(14) an order directing a party or parties to present evidence early in the trial with respect to a manageable issue that could, on the evidence, be the basis for a judgment as a matter of law under Rule 50(a) or a judgment on partial findings under Rule 52(c);

(15) an order establishing a reasonable limit on the time allowed for presenting evidence; and

(1~~1~~*6*) such other matters as may ~~aid in~~ *facilitate* the *just, speedy, and inexpensive* disposition of the action.

At least one of the attorneys for each party participating in any conference before trial shall have authority to enter into stipulations and to make admissions regarding all matters that the participants may reasonably anticipate may be discussed. *If appropriate, the court may require that a party or its representative be present or reasonably available by telephone in order to consider possible settlement of the dispute.*

Advisory Committee's Note

Subdivision (b). One purpose of this amendment is to provide a more appropriate deadline for the initial scheduling order required by the rule. The former rule directed that the order be entered within 120 days from the filing of the complaint. This requirement has created problems because Rule 4(m) allows 120 days for service and ordinarily at least one defendant should be available to participate in the process of formulating the scheduling order. The revision provides that the order is to be entered within 90 days after the date a defendant first appears (whether by answer or by a motion under Rule 12) or, if earlier (as may occur in some actions against the United States or if service is waived under Rule 4), within 120 days after service of the complaint on a defendant. The longer time provided by the revision is not intended to encourage unnecessary delays in entering the scheduling order. Indeed, in most cases the order can and should be entered at a much earlier date. Rather, the additional time is intended to alleviate problems in multi-defendant cases and should ordinarily be adequate to enable participation by all defendants initially named in the action.

In many cases the scheduling order can and should be entered before this deadline. However, when setting a scheduling conference, the court should take into account the effect this setting will have in establishing deadlines for the parties to meet under revised Rule 26(f) and to exchange information under revised Rule 26(a)(1). While the parties are expected to stipulate to additional time for making their disclosures when warranted by the circumstances, a scheduling conference held before defendants have had time to learn much about the case may result in diminishing the value of the Rule 26(f) meeting, the parties' proposed discovery plan, and indeed the conference itself.

New paragraph (4) has been added to highlight that it will frequently be desirable for the scheduling order to include provisions relating to the timing of disclosures under Rule 26(a). While the initial disclosures required by Rule 26(a)(1) will ordinarily have been made before entry of the scheduling order, the timing and sequence for disclosure of expert testimony and of the witnesses and exhibits to be used at trial should be tailored to the circumstances of the case and is a matter that should be considered at the initial scheduling conference. Similarly, the scheduling order might contain provisions modifying the extent of discovery (*e.g.*, number and length of depositions) otherwise permitted under these rules or by a local rule.

The report from the attorneys concerning their meeting and proposed discovery plan, as required by revised Rule 26(f), should be submitted to the court before the scheduling order is entered. Their proposals, particularly regarding matters on which they agree, should be of substantial value to the court in setting the timing and limitations on discovery and should reduce the time of the court needed to conduct a meaningful conference under Rule 16(b). As under the prior rule, while a scheduling order is mandated, a scheduling conference is not. However, in view of the benefits to be derived from the litigants and a judicial officer meeting in person, a Rule 16(b) conference should, to the extent practicable, be held in all cases that will involve discovery.

This subdivision, as well as subdivision (c)(8), also is revised to reflect the new title of United States Magistrate Judges pursuant to the Judicial Improvements Act of 1990.

Subdivision (c). The primary purposes of the changes in subdivision (c) are to call attention to the opportunities for structuring of trial under Rules 42, 50, and 52 and to eliminate questions that have occasionally been raised regarding the authority of the court to make appropriate orders designed either to facilitate settlement or to provide for an efficient and economical trial. The prefatory language of this subdivision is revised to clarify the court's power to enter appropriate orders at a conference notwithstanding the objection of a party. Of course settlement is dependent upon agreement by the parties and, indeed, a conference is most effective and productive when the parties participate in a spirit of cooperation and mindful of their responsibilities under Rule 1.

Paragraph (4) is revised to clarify that in advance of trial the court may address the need for, and possible limitations on, the use of expert testimony under Rule 702 of the Federal Rules of Evidence. Even when proposed expert testimony might be admissible under the standards of Rules 403 and 702 of the evidence rules, the court may preclude or limit such testimony if the cost to the litigants—which may include the cost to adversaries of securing testimony on the same subjects by other experts—would be unduly expensive given the needs of the case and the other evidence available at trial.

Paragraph (5) is added (and the remaining paragraphs renumbered) in recognition that use of Rule 56 to avoid or reduce the scope of trial is a topic that can, and often should, be considered at a pretrial conference. Renumbered paragraph (11) enables the court to rule on pending motions for summary adjudication that are ripe for decision at the time of the conference. Often, however, the potential use of Rule 56 is a matter that arises from discussions during a conference. The court may then call for motions to be filed.

Paragraph (6) is added to emphasize that a major objective of pretrial conferences should be to consider appropriate controls on the extent and timing of discovery. In many cases the court should also specify the times and sequence for disclosure of written reports from experts under revised Rule 26(a)(2)(B) and perhaps direct changes in the types of experts from whom written reports are required. Consideration should also be given to possible changes in the timing or form of the disclosure of trial witnesses and documents under Rule 26(a)(3).

Paragraph (9) is revised to describe more accurately the various procedures that, in addition to traditional settlement conferences, may be helpful in settling litigation. Even if a case cannot immediately be settled, the judge and attorneys can explore possible use of alternative procedures such as mini-trials, summary jury trials, mediation, neutral evaluation, and nonbinding arbitration that can lead to consensual resolution of the dispute without a full trial on the merits. The rule acknowledges the presence of statutes and local rules or plans that may authorize use of some of these procedures even when not agreed to by the parties. See 28 U.S.C. §§ 473(a)(6), 473(b)(4), 651–58; Section 104(b)(2), Pub.L. 101–650. The rule does not attempt to resolve questions as to the extent a court would be authorized to require such proceedings as an exercise of its inherent powers.

The amendment of paragraph (9) should be read in conjunction with the sentence added to the end of subdivision (c), authorizing the court to direct that, in appropriate cases, a responsible representative of the parties be present or available by telephone during a conference in order to discuss possible settlement of the case. The sentence refers to participation by a party or its representative. Whether this would be the individual party, an officer of a corporate party, a representative from an insurance carrier, or someone else would depend on the circumstances. Particularly in litigation in which governmental agencies or large amounts of money are involved, there may be no one with on-the-spot settlement authority, and the most that should be expected is access to a person who would have a major role in submitting a recommendation to the body or board with ultimate decision-making responsibility. The selection of the appropriate representative should ordinarily be left to the party and its counsel. Finally, it should be noted that the unwillingness of a party to be available, even by telephone, for a settlement conference may be a clear signal that the time and expense involved in pursuing settlement is likely to be unproductive and that personal participation by the parties should not be required.

The explicit authorization in the rule to require personal participation in the manner stated is not intended to limit the reasonable exercise of the court's inherent powers, *e.g.*, *G. Heileman Brewing Co. v. Joseph Oat Corp.*, 871 F.2d 648 (7th Cir.1989), or its power to require party participation under the Civil Justice Reform Act of 1990. See 28 U.S.C. § 473(b)(5) (civil justice expense and delay reduction plans adopted by district courts may include requirement that representatives "with authority to bind [parties] in settlement discussions" be available during settlement conferences).

New paragraphs (13) and (14) are added to call attention to the opportunities for structuring of trial under Rule 42 and under revised Rules 50 and 52.

Paragraph (15) is also new. It supplements the power of the court to limit the extent of evidence under Rules 403 and 611(a) of the Federal Rules of Evidence, which typically would be invoked as a result of developments during trial. Limits on the length of trial established at a conference in advance of trial can provide the parties with a better opportunity to determine priorities and exercise selectivity in presenting evidence than when limits are imposed during trial. Any such limits must be reasonable under the circumstances, and ordinarily the court should impose them only after receiving appropriate submissions from the parties outlining the nature of the testimony expected to be presented through various witnesses, and the expected duration of direct and cross-examination.

Rule 26. General Provisions Governing Discovery; *Duty of Disclosure*

(a) ***Required Disclosures;*** **~~Discovery~~ Methods** ***to Discover Additional Matter.***

(1) Initial Disclosures. Except to the extent otherwise stipulated or directed by order or local rule, a party shall, without awaiting a discovery request, provide to other parties:

(A) the name and, if known, the address and telephone number of each individual likely to have discoverable information relevant to disputed facts alleged with particularity in the pleadings, identifying the subjects of the information;

(B) a copy of, or a description by category and location of, all documents, data compilations, and tangible things in the possession, custody, or control of the party that are relevant to disputed facts alleged with particularity in the pleadings;

(C) a computation of any category of damages claimed by the disclosing party, making available for inspection and copying as under Rule 34 the documents or other evidentiary material, not privileged or protected from disclosure, on which such computation is based, including materials bearing on the nature and extent of injuries suffered; and

(D) for inspection and copying as under Rule 34 any insurance agreement under which any person carrying on an insurance business may be liable to satisfy part or all of a judgment which may be entered in the action or to indemnify or reimburse for payments made to satisfy the judgment.

Unless otherwise stipulated or directed by the court, these disclosures shall be made at or within 10 days after the meeting of the parties under subdivision (f). A party shall make its initial disclosures based on the information then reasonably available to it and is not excused from making its disclosures because it has not fully completed its investigation of the case or because it challenges the sufficiency of another party's disclosures or because another party has not made its disclosures.

(2) Disclosure of Expert Testimony.

(A) In addition to the disclosures required by paragraph (1), a party shall disclose to other parties the identity of any person who may be used at trial to present evidence under Rules 702, 703, or 705 of the Federal Rules of Evidence.

(B) Except as otherwise stipulated or directed by the court, this disclosure shall, with respect to a witness who is retained or specially employed to provide expert testimony in the case or whose duties as an employee of the party regularly involve giving expert testimony, be accompanied by a written report prepared and signed by the witness. The report shall contain a complete statement of all opinions to be expressed and the basis and reasons therefor; the data or other information considered by the witness in forming the opinions; any exhibits to be used as a summary of or support for the opinions; the qualifications of the witness, including a list of all publications authored by the witness within the preceding ten years; the compensation to be paid for the study and testimony; and a listing of any other cases in which the witness has testified as an expert at trial or by deposition within the preceding four years.

(C) These disclosures shall be made at the times and in the sequence directed by the court. In the absence of other directions from the court or stipulation by the parties, the disclosures shall be made at least 90 days before the trial date or the date the case is to be ready for trial or, if the evidence is intended solely to contradict or rebut evidence on the same subject matter identified by another

party under paragraph (2)(B), within 30 days after the disclosure made by the other party. The parties shall supplement these disclosures when required under subdivision (e)(1).

(3) Pretrial Disclosures. In addition to the disclosures required in the preceding paragraphs, a party shall provide to other parties the following information regarding the evidence that it may present at trial other than solely for impeachment purposes:

(A) the name and, if not previously provided, the address and telephone number of each witness, separately identifying those whom the party expects to present and those whom the party may call if the need arises;

(B) the designation of those witnesses whose testimony is expected to be presented by means of a deposition and, if not taken stenographically, a transcript of the pertinent portions of the deposition testimony; and

(C) an appropriate identification of each document or other exhibit, including summaries of other evidence, separately identifying those which the party expects to offer and those which the party may offer if the need arises.

Unless otherwise directed by the court, these disclosures shall be made at least 30 days before trial. Within 14 days thereafter, unless a different time is specified by the court, a party may serve and file a list disclosing (i) any objections to the use under Rule 32(a) of a deposition designated by another party under subparagraph (B) and (ii) any objection, together with the grounds therefor, that may be made to the admissibility of materials identified under subparagraph (C). Objections not so disclosed, other than objections under Rules 402 and 403 of the Federal Rules of Evidence, shall be deemed waived unless excused by the court for good cause shown.

(4) Form of Disclosures; Filing. Unless otherwise directed by order or local rule, all disclosures under paragraphs (1) through (3) shall be made in writing, signed, served, and promptly filed with the court.

(5) Methods to Discover Additional Matter. Parties may obtain discovery by one or more of the following methods: depositions upon oral examination or written questions; written interrogatories; production of documents or things or permission to enter upon land or other property *under Rule 34 or 45(a)(1)(C)*, for inspection and other purposes; physical and mental examinations; and requests for admission.

(b) Discovery Scope and Limits. Unless otherwise limited by order of the court in accordance with these rules, the scope of discovery is as follows:

(1) In General. Parties may obtain discovery regarding any matter, not privileged, which is relevant to the subject matter involved in the pending action, whether it relates to the claim or defense of the party seeking discovery or to the claim or defense of any other party, including the existence, description, nature, custody, condition, and location of any books, documents, or other tangible things and the identity and location of persons having knowledge of any discoverable matter. ~~It is not a ground for objection that t~~*T*he information sought *need not be* ~~will be in~~admissible at the trial if the information sought appears reasonably calculated to lead to the discovery of admissible evidence.

(2) Limitations. By order or by local rule, the court may alter the limits in these rules on the number of depositions and interrogatories and may also limit the length of depositions under Rule 30 and the number of requests under Rule 36. The frequency or extent of use of the discovery methods ~~set forth in subdivision (a)~~ *otherwise permitted under these rules and by any local rule* shall be limited by the court if it determines that: (i) the discovery sought is unreasonably cumulative or duplicative, or is obtainable from some other source that is more convenient, less burdensome, or less expensive; (ii) the party seeking discovery has had ample opportunity by discovery in the action to obtain the information sought; or (iii) ~~the discovery is unduly burdensome or expensive~~ *the burden or expense of the proposed discovery outweighs its likely benefit*, taking into account the needs of the case, the amount in controversy, ~~limitations on~~ the parties' resources, ~~and~~ the importance of the issues at stake in the litigation, *and the importance of the proposed discovery in resolving the issues.* The court may act upon its own initiative after reasonable notice or pursuant to a motion under subdivision (c).

~~(2) Insurance Agreements. A party may obtain discovery of the existence and contents of any insurance agreement under which any person carrying on an insurance business may be liable to satisfy part or all of a judgment which may be entered in the action or to indemnify or reimburse for payments made to satisfy the judgment. Information concerning the insurance agreement is not by reason of disclosure admissible in evidence at trial. For purposes of this paragraph, an~~

~~application for insurance shall not be treated as part of an insurance agreement.~~

(4) Trial Preparation: Experts. ~~Discovery of facts known and opinions held by experts, otherwise discoverable under the provisions of subdivision (b)(1) of this rule and acquired or developed in anticipation of litigation or for trial, may be obtained only as follows.~~

(A)~~(i)~~ A party may ~~through interrogatories require any other party to identify each person whom the other party expects to call as an expert witness at trial, to state the subject matter on which the expert is expected to testify, and to state the substance of the facts and opinions to which the expert is expected to testify and a summary of the grounds for each opinion. (ii) Upon motion, the court may order further discovery by other means, subject to such restrictions as to scope and such provisions, pursuant to subdivision (b)(4)(C) of this rule, concerning fees and expenses as the court may deem appropriate.~~ *depose any person who has been identified as an expert whose opinions may be presented at trial. If a report from the expert is required under subdivision (a)(2)(B), the deposition shall not be conducted until after the report is provided.*

(B) A party may*, through interrogatories or by deposition,* discover facts known or opinions held by an expert who has been retained or specially employed by another party in anticipation of litigation or preparation for trial and who is not expected to be called as a witness at trial~~,~~ only as provided in Rule 35(b) or upon a showing of exceptional circumstances under which it is impracticable for the party seeking discovery to obtain facts or opinions on the same subject by other means.

(C) Unless manifest injustice would result, (i) the court shall require that the party seeking discovery pay the expert a reasonable fee for time spent in responding to discovery under *this* subdivision~~s (b)(4)(A)(ii) and (b)(4)(B) of this rule~~; and (ii) with respect to discovery obtained under ~~subdivision (b)(4)(A)(ii) of this rule the court may require, and with respect to discovery obtained under~~ subdivision (b)(4)(B) of this rule the court shall require~~,~~ the party seeking discovery to pay the other party a fair portion of the fees and expenses reasonably incurred by the latter party in obtaining facts and opinions from the expert.

---

(5) Claims of Privilege or Protection of Trial Preparation Materials. When a party withholds information otherwise discoverable under these rules by claiming that it is privileged or subject to protection as trial preparation material, the party shall make the claim expressly and shall describe the nature of the documents, communications, or things not produced or disclosed in a manner that, without revealing information itself privileged or protected, will enable other parties to assess the applicability of the privilege or protection.

(c) Protective Orders. Upon motion by a party or by the person from whom discovery is sought, *accompanied by a certification that the movant has in good faith conferred or attempted to confer with other affected parties in an effort to resolve the dispute without court action,* and for good cause shown, the court in which the action is pending or alternatively, on matters relating to a deposition, the court in the district where the deposition is to be taken may make any order which justice requires to protect a party or person from annoyance, embarrassment, oppression, or undue burden or expense, including one or more of the following:

(1) that the *disclosure or* discovery not be had;

(2) that the *disclosure or* discovery may be had only on specified terms and conditions, including a designation of the time or place;

(3) that the discovery may be had only by a method of discovery other than that selected by the party seeking discovery;

(4) that certain matters not be inquired into, or that the scope of the *disclosure or* discovery be limited to certain matters;

(5) that discovery be conducted with no one present except persons designated by the court;

(6) that a deposition, after being sealed, be opened only by order of the court;

(7) that a trade secret or other confidential research, development, or commercial information not be ~~disclosed~~ *revealed* or be ~~disclosed~~ *revealed* only in a designated way; *and*

(8) that the parties simultaneously file specified documents or information enclosed in sealed envelopes to be opened as directed by the court.

If the motion for a protective order is denied in whole or in part, the court may, on such terms and conditions as are just, order that any party or *other* person provide or permit discovery. The

New matter is shown in italics; matter to be omitted is lined through

provisions of Rule 37(a)(4) apply to the award of expenses incurred in relation to the motion.

(d) ~~Sequence and~~ Timing *and Sequence* of Discovery. *Except when authorized under these rules or by local rule, order, or agreement of the parties, a party may not seek discovery from any source before the parties have met and conferred as required by subdivision (f).* Unless the court upon motion, for the convenience of parties and witnesses and in the interests of justice, orders otherwise, methods of discovery may be used in any sequence, and the fact that a party is conducting discovery, whether by deposition or otherwise, shall not operate to delay any other party's discovery.

(e) Supplementation of *Disclosures and* Responses. A party who has *made a disclosure under subdivision (a) or* responded to a request for discovery with a *disclosure or* response ~~that was complete when made~~ is under ~~no~~ *a* duty to supplement *or correct* the *disclosure or* response to include information thereafter acquired~~, except as follows~~ *if ordered by the court or in the following circumstances*:

(1) A party is under a duty ~~seasonably~~ to supplement ~~the response with respect to any question directly addressed to (A) the identity and location of persons having knowledge of discoverable matters, and (B) the identity of each person expected to be called as an expert witness at trial, the subject matter on which the person is expected to testify, and the substance of the person's testimony.~~ *at appropriate intervals its disclosures under subdivision (a) if the party learns that in some material respect the information disclosed is incomplete or incorrect and if the additional or corrective information has not otherwise been made known to the other parties during the discovery process or in writing. With respect to testimony of an expert from whom a report is required under subdivision (a)(2)(B) the duty extends both to information contained in the report and to information provided through a deposition of the expert, and any additions or other changes to this information shall be disclosed by the time the party's disclosures under Rule 26(a)(3) are due.*

(2) A party is under a duty seasonably to amend a prior response *to an interrogatory, request for production, or request for admission* if the party *learns* ~~obtains information upon the basis of which (A) the party knows~~ that the response ~~was incorrect when made, or (B) the party knows that the response though correct when made is no longer true and the circumstances are such that a failure to amend the response is in substance a knowing concealment~~ *is in some material respect*

New matter is shown in italics; matter to be omitted is lined through

incomplete or incorrect and if the additional or corrective information has not otherwise been made known to the other parties during the discovery process or in writing.

~~(3) A duty to supplement responses may be imposed by order of the court, agreement of the parties, or at any time prior to trial through new requests for supplementation of prior responses.~~

(f) ***Meeting of Parties; Planning for Discovery*** ~~**Conference.**~~ ~~At any time after commencement of an action the court may direct the attorneys for the parties to appear before it for a conference on the subject of discovery. The court shall do so upon motion by the attorney for any party if the motion includes~~ *Except in actions exempted by local rule or when otherwise ordered, the parties shall, as soon as practicable and in any event at least 14 days before a scheduling conference is held or a scheduling order is due under Rule 16(b), meet to discuss the nature and basis of their claims and defenses and the possibilities for a prompt settlement or resolution of the case, to make or arrange for the disclosures required by subdivision (a)(1), and to develop a proposed discovery plan. The plan shall indicate the parties' views and proposals concerning*:

(1) ~~A statement of the issues as they then appear;~~ *what changes should be made in the timing, form, or requirement for disclosures under subdivision (a) or local rule, including a statement as to when disclosures under subdivision (a)(1) were made or will be made;*

(2) ~~A proposed plan and schedule of discovery;~~ *the subjects on which discovery may be needed, when discovery should be completed, and whether discovery should be conducted in phases or be limited to or focused upon particular issues;*

(3) ~~Any limitations proposed to be placed on discovery;~~ *what changes should be made in the limitations on discovery imposed under these rules or by local rule, and what other limitations should be imposed; and*

(4) ~~A~~*a*ny other ~~proposed~~ orders ~~with respect to discovery~~ *that should be entered by the court under subdivision (c) or under Rule 16(b) and (c).*~~; and~~

~~(5) A statement showing that the attorney making the motion has made a reasonable effort to reach agreement with opposing attorneys on the matters set forth in the motion. Each party and each party's attorney are under a duty to participate in good faith in the framing of a discovery plan if a plan is proposed by the attorney for any party. Notice of the~~

~~motion shall be served on all parties. Objections or additions to matters set forth in the motion shall be served not later than 10 days after service of the motion.~~

The attorneys of record and all unrepresented parties that have appeared in the case are jointly responsible for arranging and being present or represented at the meeting, for attempting in good faith to agree on the proposed discovery plan, and for submitting to the court within 10 days after the meeting a written report outlining the plan. ~~Following the discovery conference, the court shall enter an order tentatively identifying the issues for discovery purposes, establishing a plan and schedule for discovery, setting limitations on discovery, if any; and determining such other matters, including the allocation of expenses, as are necessary for the proper management of discovery in the action. An order may be altered or amended whenever justice so requires.~~

~~Subject to the right of a party who properly moves for a discovery conference to prompt convening of the conference, the court may combine the discovery conference with a pretrial conference authorized by Rule 16.~~

(g) Signing of *Disclosures,* Discovery Requests, Responses, and Objections.

(1) Every disclosure made pursuant to subdivision (a)(1) or subdivision (a)(3) shall be signed by at least one attorney of record in the attorney's individual name, whose address shall be stated. An unrepresented party shall sign the disclosure and state the party's address. The signature of the attorney or party constitutes a certification that to the best of the signer's knowledge, information, and belief, formed after a reasonable inquiry, the disclosure is complete and correct as of the time it is made.

(2) Every *discovery* request, ~~for discovery or~~ response, or objection ~~thereto~~ made by a party represented by an attorney shall be signed by at least one attorney of record in the attorney's individual name, whose address shall be stated. A*n* *unrepresented* party ~~who is not represented by an attorney~~ shall sign the request, response, or objection and state the party's address. The signature of the attorney or party constitutes a certification ~~that the signer has read the request, response, or objection, and~~ that to the best of the signer's knowledge, information, and belief, formed after a reasonable inquiry, ~~it~~ *the request, response, or objection* is:

(~~1~~*A*) consistent with these rules and warranted by existing law or a good faith argument for the extension, modification, or reversal of existing law;

(~~2~~*B*) not interposed for any improper purpose, such as to harass or to cause unnecessary delay or needless increase in the cost of litigation; and

(~~3~~*C*) not unreasonable or unduly burdensome or expensive, given the needs of the case, the discovery already had in the case, the amount in controversy, and the importance of the issues at stake in the litigation.

If a request, response, or objection is not signed, it shall be stricken unless it is signed promptly after the omission is called to the attention of the party making the request, response, or objection, and a party shall not be obligated to take any action with respect to it until it is signed.

(3) If *without substantial justification* a certification is made in violation of the rule, the court, upon motion or upon its own initiative, shall impose upon the person who made the certification, the party on whose behalf the *disclosure,* request, response, or objection is made, or both, an appropriate sanction, which may include an order to pay the amount of the reasonable expenses incurred because of the violation, including a reasonable attorney's fee.

Advisory Committee's Note

Subdivision (a). Through the addition of paragraphs (1)–(4), this subdivision imposes on parties a duty to disclose, without awaiting formal discovery requests, certain basic information that is needed in most cases to prepare for trial or make an informed decision about settlement. The rule requires all parties (1) early in the case to exchange information regarding potential witnesses, documentary evidence, damages, and insurance, (2) at an appropriate time during the discovery period to identify expert witnesses and provide a detailed written statement of the testimony that may be offered at trial through specially retained experts, and (3) as the trial date approaches to identify the particular evidence that may be offered at trial. The enumeration in Rule 26(a) of items to be disclosed does not prevent a court from requiring by order or local rule that the parties disclose additional information without a discovery request. Nor are parties precluded from using traditional discovery methods to obtain further information regarding these matters, as for example asking an expert during a deposition about testimony given in other litigation beyond the four-year period specified in Rule 26(a)(2)(B).

A major purpose of the revision is to accelerate the exchange of basic information about the case and to eliminate the paper work involved in requesting such information, and the rule should be applied in a manner to achieve those objectives. The concepts of imposing a duty of disclosure were set forth in Brazil, *The Adversary Character of Civil Discovery: A Critique and Proposals for Change,* 31 *Vand.L.Rev.* 1348 (1978), and Schwarzer, *The Federal Rules, the Adversary Process, and Discovery Reform,* 50 *U.Pitt.L.Rev.* 703, 721–23 (1989).

The rule is based upon the experience of district courts that have required disclosure of some of this information through local rules, court-approved standard interrogatories, and standing orders. Most have required pretrial disclosure of the kind of information described in Rule 26(a)(3). Many have required written reports from experts containing information like that specified in Rule 26(a)(2)(B). While far more limited, the experience of the few state and federal courts that have required pre-discovery exchange of core information such as is contemplated in Rule 26(a)(1) indicates that savings in time and expense can be achieved, particularly if the litigants meet and discuss the issues in the case as a predicate for this exchange and if a judge supports the process, as by using the results to guide further proceedings in the case. Courts in Canada and the United Kingdom have for many years required disclosure of certain information without awaiting a request from an adversary.

Paragraph (1). As the functional equivalent of court-ordered interrogatories, this paragraph requires early disclosure, without need for any request, of four types of information that have been customarily secured early in litigation through formal discovery. The introductory clause permits the court, by local rule, to exempt all or particular types of cases from these disclosure requirement[s] or to modify the nature of the information to be disclosed. It is expected that courts would, for example, exempt cases like Social Security reviews and government collection cases in which discovery would not be appropriate or would be unlikely. By order the court may eliminate or modify the disclosure requirements in a particular case, and similarly the parties, unless precluded by order or local rule, can stipulate to elimination or modification of the requirements for that case. The disclosure obligations specified in paragraph (1) will not be appropriate for all cases, and it is expected that changes in these obligations will be made by the court or parties when the circumstances warrant.

Authorization of these local variations is, in large measure, included in order to accommodate the Civil Justice Reform Act of 1990, which implicitly directs districts to experiment during the study period with differing procedures to reduce the time and expense of civil litigation. The civil justice delay and expense reduction plans adopted by the courts under the Act differ as to the type, form, and timing of disclosures required. Section 105(c)(1) of the Act calls for a report by the Judicial Conference to Congress by December 31, 1995, comparing experience in twenty of these courts; and section 105(c)(2)(B) contemplates that some changes in the Rules may then be needed. While these studies may indicate the desirability of further changes in Rule 26(a)(1), these changes probably could not become effective before December 1998 at the earliest. In the meantime, the present revision puts in place a series of disclosure obligations that, unless a court acts affirmatively to impose other requirements or indeed to reject all such requirements for the present, are designed to eliminate certain discovery, help focus the discovery that is needed, and facilitate preparation for trial or settlement.

Subparagraph (A) requires identification of all persons who, based on the investigation conducted thus far, are likely to have discoverable information relevant to the factual disputes between the parties. All persons with such information should be disclosed, whether or not their testimony will be supportive of the position of the disclosing party. As officers of the court, counsel are expected to disclose the identity of those persons who may be used by them as witnesses or who, if their potential testimony were known, might reasonably be expected to be deposed or called as a witness by any of the other parties. Indicating briefly the general topics on which such persons have information should not be burdensome, and will assist other parties in deciding which depositions will actually be needed.

Subparagraph (B) is included as a substitute for the inquiries routinely made about the existence and location of documents and other tangible things in the possession, custody, or control of the disclosing party. Although, unlike subdivision (a)(3)(C), an itemized listing of each exhibit is not required, the disclosure should describe and categorize, to the extent identified during the initial investigation, the nature and location of potentially relevant documents and records, including computerized data and other electronically-recorded information, sufficiently to enable opposing parties (1) to make an informed decision concerning which documents might need to be examined, at least initially, and (2) to frame their document requests in a manner likely to avoid squabbles resulting from the wording of the requests. As with potential witnesses, the requirement for disclosure of documents applies to all potentially relevant items then known to the party, whether or not supportive of its contentions in the case.

Unlike subparagraphs (C) and (D), subparagraph (B) does not require production of any documents. Of course, in cases involving few documents a disclosing party may prefer to provide copies of the documents rather than describe them, and the rule is written to afford this option to the disclosing party. If, as will be more typical, only the description is provided, the other parties are expected to obtain the documents desired by proceeding under Rule 34 or through informal requests. The disclosing party does not, by describing documents under subparagraph (B), waive its right to object to production on the basis of privilege or work product protection, or to assert that the documents are not sufficiently relevant to justify the burden or expense of production.

The initial disclosure requirements of subparagraphs (A) and (B) are limited to identification of potential evidence "relevant to disputed facts alleged with particularity in the pleadings." There is no need for a party to identify potential evidence with respect to allegations that are admitted. Broad, vague, and conclusory allegations sometimes tolerated in notice pleading—for example, the assertion that a product with many component parts is defective in some unspecified manner—should not impose upon responding parties the obligation at that point to search for and identify all persons possibly involved in, or all documents affecting, the design, manufacture, and assembly of the product. The greater the specificity and clarity of the allegations in the pleadings, the more complete should be the listing of potential witnesses and types of documentary evidence. Although paragraphs (1)(A) and (1)(B) by their terms refer to the factual disputes defined in the pleadings, the rule contemplates that these issues would be informally refined and clarified during the meeting of the parties under subdivision (f) and that the disclosure obligations would be adjusted in the light of these discussions. The disclosure requirements should, in short, be applied with common sense in light of the principles of Rule 1, keeping in mind the salutary purposes that the rule is intended to accomplish. The litigants should not indulge in gamesmanship with respect to the disclosure obligations.

Subparagraph (C) imposes a burden of disclosure that includes the functional equivalent of a standing Request for Production under Rule 34. A party claiming damages or other monetary relief must, in addition to disclosing the calculation of such damages, make available the supporting documents for inspection and copying as if a request for such materials had been made under Rule 34. This obligation applies only with respect to documents then reasonably available to it and not privileged or protected as work product. Likewise, a party would not be expected to provide a calculation of damages which, as in many patent infringement actions, depends on information in the possession of another party or person.

Subparagraph (D) replaces subdivision (b)(2) of Rule 26, and provides that liability insurance policies be made available for inspection and copying. The last two sentences of that subdivision have been omitted as unnecessary, not to signify any change of law. The disclosure of insurance information does not thereby render such information admissible in evidence. See Rule 411, Federal Rules of Evidence. Nor does subparagraph (D) require disclosure of applications for insurance, though in particular cases such information may be discoverable in accordance with revised subdivision (a)(5).

Unless the court directs a different time, the disclosures required by subdivision (a)(1) are to be made at or within 10 days after the meeting of the parties under subdivision (f). One of the purposes of this meeting is to refine the factual disputes with respect to which disclosures should be made under paragraphs (1)(A) and (1)(B), particularly if an answer has not been filed by a defendant, or, indeed, to afford the parties an opportunity to modify by stipulation the timing or scope of these obligations. The time of this meeting is generally left to the parties provided it is held at least 14 days before a scheduling conference is held or before a scheduling order is due under Rule 16(b). In cases in which no scheduling conference is held, this will mean that the meeting must ordinarily be held within 75 days after a defendant has first appeared in the case and hence that the initial disclosures would be due no later than 85 days after the first appearance of a defendant.

Before making its disclosures, a party has the obligation under subdivision (g)(1) to make a reasonable inquiry into the facts of the case. The rule does not demand an exhaustive investigation at this stage of the case, but one that is reasonable under the circumstances, focusing on the facts that are alleged with particularity in the pleadings. The type of investigation that can be expected at this point will vary based upon such factors as the number and complexity of the issues; the location, nature, number, and availability of potentially relevant witnesses and documents; the extent of past working relationships between the attorney and the client, particularly in handling related or similar litigation; and of course how long the party has to conduct an investigation, either before or after filing of the case. As provided in the last sentence of subdivision (a)(1), a party is not excused from the duty of disclosure merely because its investigation is incomplete. The party should make its initial disclosures based on the pleadings and the information then reasonably available to it. As its investigation continues and as the issues in the pleadings are clarified, it should supplement its disclosures as required by subdivision (e)(1). A party is not relieved from its obligation of disclosure merely because another party has not made its disclosures or has made an inadequate disclosure.

It will often be desirable, particularly if the claims made in the complaint are broadly stated, for the parties to have their Rule 26(f) meeting early in the case, perhaps before a defendant has answered the complaint or had time to conduct other than a cursory investigation. In such circumstances, in order to facilitate more meaningful and useful initial disclosures, they can and should stipulate to a period of more than 10 days after the meeting in which to make these disclosures, at least for defendants who had no advance notice of the potential litigation. A stipulation at an early meeting affording such a defendant at least 60 days after receiving the complaint in which to make its disclosures under subdivision (a)(1)—a period that is two weeks longer than the time formerly specified for responding to interrogatories served with a complaint—should be adequate and appropriate in most cases.

Paragraph (2). This paragraph imposes an additional duty to disclose information regarding expert testimony sufficiently in advance of trial that opposing parties have a reasonable opportunity to prepare for effective cross examination and perhaps arrange for expert testimony from other witnesses. Normally the court should prescribe a time for these disclosures in a scheduling order under Rule 16(b), and in most cases the party with the burden of proof on an issue should disclose its expert testimony on that issue before other parties are required to make their disclosures with respect to that issue. In the absence of such a direction, the disclosures are to be made by all parties at least 90 days before the trial date or the date by which the case is to be ready for trial, except that an additional 30 days is allowed (unless the court specifies another time) for disclosure of expert testimony to be used solely to contradict or rebut the testimony that may be presented by another party's expert. For a discussion of procedures that have been used to enhance the reliability of expert testimony, see M. Graham, *Expert Witness Testimony and the Federal Rules of Evidence: Insuring Adequate Assurance of Trustworthiness,* 1986 *U.Ill.L.Rev.* 90.

Paragraph (2)(B) requires that persons retained or specially employed to provide expert testimony, or whose duties as an employee of the party regularly involve the giving of expert testimony, must prepare a detailed and complete written report, stating the testimony the witness is expected to present during direct examination, together with the reasons therefor. The information disclosed under the former rule in answering interrogatories about the "substance" of expert testimony was frequently so sketchy and vague that it rarely dispensed with the need to depose the expert and often was even of little help in preparing for a deposition of the witness. Revised Rule 37(c)(1) provides an incentive for full disclosure; namely, that a party will not ordinarily be permitted to use on direct examination any expert testimony not so disclosed. Rule 26(a)(2)(B) does not preclude counsel from providing assistance to experts in preparing the reports, and indeed, with experts such as automobile mechanics, this assistance may be needed. Nevertheless, the report, which is intended to set forth the substance of the direct examination, should be written in a manner that reflects the testimony to be given by the witness and it must be signed by the witness.

The report is to disclose the data and other information considered by the expert and any exhibits or charts that summarize or support the expert's opinions. Given this obligation of disclosure, litigants should no longer be able to argue that materials furnished to their experts to be used in forming their opinions—whether or not ultimately relied upon by the expert—are privileged or otherwise protected from disclosure when such persons are testifying or being deposed.

Revised subdivision (b)(4)(A) authorizes the deposition of expert witnesses. Since depositions of experts required to prepare a written report may be taken only after the report has been has been served, the length of the deposition of such experts should be reduced, and in many cases the report may eliminate the need for a deposition. Revised subdivision (e)(1) requires disclosure of any material changes made in the opinions of an expert from whom a report is required, whether the changes are in the written report or in testimony given at a deposition.

For convenience, this rule and revised Rule 30 continue to use the term "expert" to refer to those persons who will testify under Rule 702 of the Federal Rules of Evidence with respect to scientific, technical, and other specialized matters. The requirement of a written report in paragraph (2)(B), however, applies only to those experts who are retained or specially employed to provide such testimony in the case or whose duties as an employee of a party regularly involve the giving of such testimony. A treating physician, for example, can be deposed or called to testify at trial without any requirement for a written report. By local rule, order, or written stipulation, the requirement of a written report may be waived for particular experts or imposed upon additional persons who will provide opinions under Rule 702.

Paragraph (3). This paragraph imposes an additional duty to disclose, without any request, information customarily needed in final preparation for trial. These disclosures are to be made in accordance with schedules adopted by the court under Rule 16(b) or by special order. If no such schedule is directed by the court, the disclosures are to be made at least 30 days before commencement of the trial. By its terms, rule 26(a)(3) does not require disclosure of evidence to be used solely for impeachment purposes; however, disclosure of such evidence—as well as other items relating to conduct of trial—may be required by local rule or a pretrial order.

Subparagraph (A) requires the parties to designate the persons whose testimony they may present as substantive evidence at trial, whether in person or by deposition. Those who will probably be called as witnesses should be listed separately from those who are not likely to be called but who are being listed in order to preserve the right to do so if needed because of developments during trial. Revised Rule 37(c)(1) provides that only persons so listed may be used at trial to present substantive evidence. This restriction does not apply unless the omission was "without substantial justification" and hence would not bar an unlisted witness if the need for such testimony is based upon developments during trial that could not reasonably have been anticipated—*e.g.*, a change of testimony.

Listing a witness does not obligate the party to secure the attendance of the person at trial, but should preclude the party from objecting if the person is called to testify by another party who did not list the person as a witness.

Subparagraph (B) requires the party to indicate which of these potential witnesses will be presented by deposition at trial. A party expecting to use at trial a deposition not recorded by stenographic means is required by revised Rule 32 to provide the court with a transcript of the pertinent portions of such depositions. This rule requires that copies of the transcript of a nonstenographic deposition be provided to other parties in advance of trial for verification, an obvious concern since counsel often utilize their own personnel to prepare transcripts from audio or video tapes. By order or local rule, the court may require that parties designate the particular portions of stenographic depositions to be used at trial.

Subparagraph (C) requires disclosure of exhibits, including summaries (whether to be offered in lieu of other documentary evidence or to be used as an aid in understanding such evidence), that may be offered as substantive evidence. The rule requires a separate listing of each such exhibit, though it should permit voluminous items of a similar or standardized character to be described by meaningful categories. For example, unless the court has otherwise directed, a series of vouchers might be shown collectively as a single exhibit with their starting and ending dates. As with witnesses, the exhibits that will probably be offered are to be listed separately from those which are unlikely to be offered but which are listed in order to preserve the right to do so if needed because of developments during trial. Under revised Rule 37(c)(1) the court can permit use of unlisted documents the need for which could not reasonably have been anticipated in advance of trial.

Upon receipt of these final pretrial disclosures, other parties have 14 days (unless a different time is specified by the court) to disclose any objections they wish to preserve to the usability of the deposition testimony or to the admissibility of the documentary evidence (other than under Rules 402 and 403 of the Federal Rules of Evidence). Similar provisions have become commonplace either in pretrial orders or by local rules, and significantly expedite the presentation of evidence at trial, as well as eliminate the need to have available witnesses to provide "foundation" testimony for most items of documentary evidence. The listing of a potential objection does not constitute the making of that objection or require the court to rule on the objection; rather, it preserves the right of the party to make the objection when and as appropriate during trial. The court may, however, elect to treat the listing as a motion "in limine" and rule upon the objections in advance of trial to the extent appropriate.

The time specified in the rule for the final pretrial disclosures is relatively close to the trial date. The objective is to eliminate the time and expense in making these disclosures of evidence and objections in those cases that settle shortly before trial, while affording a reasonable time for final preparation for trial in those cases that do not settle. In many cases, it will be desirable for the court in a scheduling or pretrial order to set an earlier time for disclosures of evidence and provide more time for disclosing potential objections.

Paragraph (4). This paragraph prescribes the form of disclosures. A signed written statement is required, reminding the parties and counsel of the solemnity of the obligations imposed; and the signature on the initial or pretrial disclosure is a certification under subdivision (g)(1) that it is complete and correct as of the time when made. Consistent with Rule 5(d), these disclosures are to be filed with the court unless otherwise directed. It is anticipated that many courts will direct that expert reports required under paragraph (2)(B) not be filed until needed in connection with a motion or for trial.

Paragraph (5). This paragraph is revised to take note of the availability of revised Rule 45 for inspection from non-parties of documents and premises without the need for a deposition.

Subdivision (b). This subdivision is revised in several respects. First, former paragraph (1) is subdivided into two paragraphs for ease of reference and to avoid renumbering of paragraphs (3) and (4). Textual changes are then made in new paragraph (2) to enable the court to keep tighter rein on the extent of discovery. The information explosion of recent decades has greatly increased both the potential cost of wide-ranging discovery and the potential for discovery to be used as an instrument for delay or oppression. Amendments to Rules 30, 31, and 33 place presumptive limits on the number of depositions and interrogatories, subject to leave of court to pursue additional discovery. The revisions in Rule 26(b)(2) are intended to provide the court with broader discretion to impose additional restrictions on the scope and extent of discovery and to authorize courts that develop case tracking systems based on the complexity of cases to increase or decrease by local rule the presumptive number of depositions and interrogatories allowed in particular types or classifications of cases. The revision also dispels any doubt as to the power of the court to impose limitations on the length of depositions under Rule 30 or on the number of requests for admission under Rule 36.

Second, former paragraph (2), relating to insurance, has been relocated as part of the required initial disclosures under subdivision (a)(1)(D), and revised to provide for disclosure of the policy itself.

Third, paragraph (4)(A) is revised to provide that experts who are expected to be witnesses will be subject to deposition prior to trial, conforming the norm stated in the rule to the actual practice followed in most courts, in which depositions of experts have become standard. Concerns regarding the expense of such depositions should be mitigated by the fact that the expert's fees for the deposition will ordinarily be borne by the party taking the deposition. The requirement under subdivision (a)(2)(B) of a complete and detailed report of the expected testimony of certain forensic experts may, moreover, eliminate the need for some such depositions or at least reduce the length of the depositions. Accordingly, the deposition of an expert required by subdivision (a)(2)(B) to provide a written report may be taken only after the report has been served.

Paragraph (4)(C), bearing on compensation of experts, is revised to take account of the changes in paragraph (4)(A).

Paragraph (5) is a new provision. A party must notify other parties if it is withholding materials otherwise subject to disclosure under the rule or pursuant to a discovery request because it is asserting a claim of privilege or work product protection. To withhold materials without such notice is contrary to the rule, subjects the party to sanctions under Rule 37(b)(2), and may be viewed as a waiver of the privilege or protection.

The party must also provide sufficient information to enable other parties to evaluate the applicability of the claimed privilege or protection. Although the person from whom the discovery is sought decides whether to claim a privilege or protection, the court ultimately decides whether, if this claim is challenged, the privilege or protection applies. Providing information pertinent to the applicability of the privilege or protection should reduce the need for in camera examination of the documents.

The rule does not attempt to define for each case what information must be provided when a party asserts a claim of privilege or work product protection. Details concerning time, persons, general subject matter, etc., may be appropriate if only a few items are withheld, but may be unduly burdensome when voluminous documents are claimed to be privileged or protected, particularly if the items can be described by categories. A party can seek relief through a protective order under subdivision (c) if compliance with the requirement for providing this information would be an unreasonable burden. In rare circumstances some of the pertinent information affecting applicability of the claim, such as the identity of the client, may itself be privileged; the rule provides that such information need not be disclosed.

The obligation to provide pertinent information concerning withheld privileged materials applies only to items "otherwise discoverable." If a broad discovery request is made—for example, for all documents of a particular type during a twenty year period—and the responding party believes in good faith that production of documents for more than the past three years would be unduly burdensome, it should make its objection to the breadth of the request and, with respect to the documents generated in that three year period, produce the unprivileged documents and describe those withheld under the claim of privilege. If the court later rules that documents for a seven year period are properly discoverable, the documents for the additional four years should then be either produced (if not privileged) or described (if claimed to be privileged).

Subdivision (c). The revision requires that before filing a motion for a protective order the movant must confer—either in person or by telephone—with the other affected parties in a good faith effort to resolve the discovery dispute without the need for court intervention. If the movant is unable to get opposing parties even to discuss the matter, the efforts in attempting to arrange such a conference should be indicated in the certificate.

Subdivision (d). This subdivision is revised to provide that formal discovery—as distinguished from interviews of potential witnesses and other informal discovery—not commence until the parties have met and conferred as required by subdivision (f). Discovery can begin earlier if authorized under Rule 30(a)(2)(C) (deposition of person about to leave the country) or by local rule, order, or stipulation. This will be appropriate in some cases, such as those involving requests for a preliminary injunction or motions challenging personal jurisdiction. If a local rule exempts any types of cases in which discovery may be needed from the requirement of a meeting under Rule 26(f), it should specify when discovery may commence in those cases.

The meeting of counsel is to take place as soon as practicable and in any event at least 14 days before the date of the scheduling conference under Rule 16(b) or the date a scheduling order is due under Rule 16(b). The court can assure that discovery is not unduly delayed either by entering a special order or by setting the case for a scheduling conference.

Subdivision (e). This subdivision is revised to provide that the requirement for supplementation applies to all disclosures required by subdivisions (a)(1)–(3). Like the former rule, the duty, while imposed on a "party," applies whether the corrective information is learned by the client or by the attorney. Supplementations need not be made as each new item of information is learned but should be made at appropriate intervals during the discovery period, and with special promptness as the trial date approaches. It may be useful for the scheduling order to specify the time or times when supplementations should be made.

The revision also clarifies that the obligation to supplement responses to formal discovery requests applies to interrogatories, requests for production, and requests for admissions, but not ordinarily to deposition testimony. However, with respect to experts from whom a written report is required under subdivision (a)(2)(B), changes in the opinions expressed by the expert whether in the report or at a subsequent deposition are subject to a duty of supplemental disclosure under subdivision (e)(1).

The obligation to supplement disclosures and discovery responses applies whenever a party learns that its prior disclosures or responses are in some material respect incomplete or incorrect. There is, however, no obligation to provide supplemental or corrective information that has been otherwise made known to the parties in writing or during the discovery process, as when a witness not previously disclosed is identified during the taking of a deposition or when an expert during a deposition corrects information contained in an earlier report.

Subdivision (f). This subdivision was added in 1980 to provide a party threatened with abusive discovery with a special means for obtaining judicial intervention other than through discrete motions under Rules 26(c) and 37(a). The amendment envisioned a two-step process: first, the parties would attempt to frame a mutually agreeable plan; second, the court would hold a "discovery conference" and then enter an order establishing a schedule and limitations for the conduct of discovery. It was contemplated that the procedure, an elective one triggered on request of a party, would be used in special cases rather than as a routine matter. As expected, the device has been used only sparingly in most courts, and judicial controls over the discovery process have ordinarily been imposed through scheduling orders under Rule 16(b) or through rulings on discovery motions.

The provisions relating to a conference with the court are removed from subdivision (f). This change does not signal any lessening of the importance of judicial supervision. Indeed, there is a greater need for early judicial involvement to consider the scope and timing of the disclosure requirements of Rule 26(a) and the presumptive limits on discovery imposed under these rules or by local rules. Rather, the change is made because the provisions addressing the use of conferences with the court to control discovery are more properly included in Rule 16, which is being revised to highlight the court's powers regarding the discovery process.

The desirability of some judicial control of discovery can hardly be doubted. Rule 16, as revised, requires that the court set a time for completion of discovery and authorizes various other orders affecting the scope, timing, and extent of discovery and disclosures. Before entering such orders, the court should consider the views of the parties, preferably by means of a conference, but at the least through written submissions. Moreover, it is desirable that the parties' proposals regarding discovery be developed through a process where they meet in person, informally explore the nature and basis of the issues, and discuss how discovery can be conducted most efficiently and economically.

As noted above, former subdivision (f) envisioned the development of proposed discovery plans as an optional procedure to be used in relatively few cases. The revised rule directs that in all cases not exempted by local rule or special order the litigants must meet in person and plan for discovery. Following this meeting, the parties submit to the court their proposals for a discovery plan and can begin formal discovery. Their report will assist the court in seeing that the timing and scope of disclosures under revised Rule 26(a) and the limitations on the extent of discovery under these rules and local rules are tailored to the circumstances of the particular case.

To assure that the court has the litigants' proposals before deciding on a scheduling order and that the commencement of discovery is not delayed unduly, the rule provides that the meeting of the parties take place as soon as practicable and in any event at least 14 days before a scheduling conference is held or before a scheduling order is due under Rule 16(b). (Rule 16(b) requires that a scheduling order be entered within 90 days after the first appearance of a defendant or, if earlier, within 120 days after the complaint has been served on any defendant.) The obligation to participate in the planning process is imposed on all parties that have appeared in the case, including defendants who, because of a pending Rule 12 motion, may not have yet filed an answer in the case. Each such party should attend the meeting, either through one of its attorneys or in person if unrepresented. If more parties are joined or appear after the initial meeting, an additional meeting may be desirable.

Subdivision (f) describes certain matters that should be accomplished at the meeting and included in the proposed discovery plan. This listing does not exclude consideration of other subjects, such as the time when any dispositive motions should be filed and when the case should be ready for trial.

The parties are directed under subdivision (a)(1) to make the disclosures required by that subdivision at or within 10 days after this meeting. In many cases the parties should use the meeting to exchange, discuss, and clarify their respective disclosures. In other cases, it may be more useful if the disclosures are delayed until after the parties have discussed at the meeting the claims and defenses in order to define the issues with respect to which the initial disclosures should be made. As discussed in the Notes to subdivision (a)(1), the parties may also need to consider whether a stipulation extending this 10–day period would be appropriate, as when a defendant would otherwise have less than 60 days after being served in which to make its initial disclosure. The parties should also discuss at the meeting what additional information, although not subject to the disclosure requirements, can be made available informally without the necessity for formal discovery requests.

The report is to be submitted to the court within 10 days after the meeting and should not be difficult to prepare. In most cases counsel should be able to agree that one of them will be responsible for its preparation and submission to the court. Form 35 has been added in the Appendix to the Rules, both to illustrate the type of report that is contemplated and to serve as a checklist for the meeting.

The litigants are expected to attempt in good faith to agree on the contents of the proposed discovery plan. If they cannot agree on all aspects of the plan, their report to the court should indicate the competing proposals of the parties on those items, as well as the matters on which they agree. Unfortunately, there may be cases in which, because of disagreements about time or place or for other reasons, the meeting is not attended by all parties or, indeed, no meeting takes place. In such situations, the report—or reports—should describe the circumstances and the court may need to consider sanctions under Rule 37(g).

By local rule or special order, the court can exempt particular cases or types of cases from the meet-and-confer requirement of subdivision (f). In general this should include any types of cases which are exempted by local rule from the requirement for a scheduling order under Rule 16(b), such as cases in which there will be no discovery (*e.g.*, bankruptcy appeals and reviews of social security determinations). In addition, the court may want to exempt cases in which discovery is rarely needed (*e.g.*, government collection cases and proceedings to enforce administrative summonses) or in which a meeting of the parties might be impracticable (*e.g.*, actions by unrepresented prisoners). Note that if a court exempts from the requirements for a meeting any types of cases in which discovery may be needed, it should indicate when discovery may commence in those cases.

Subdivision (g). Paragraph (1) is added to require signatures on disclosures, a requirement that parallels the provisions of paragraph (2) with respect to discovery requests, responses, and objections. The provisions of paragraph (3) have been modified to be consistent with Rules 37(a)(4) and 37(c)(1); in combination, these rules establish sanctions for violation of the rules regarding disclosures and discovery matters. Amended Rule 11 no longer applies to such violations.

Rule 28. Persons Before Whom Depositions May Be Taken

(b) In Foreign Countries. ~~In a foreign country, d~~*D*epositions may be taken *in a foreign country* (1) *pursuant to any applicable treaty or convention, or (2) pursuant to a letter of request (whether or not captioned a letter rogatory), or (3)* on notice before a person authorized to administer oaths in the place ~~in which~~ *where* the examination is held, either by the law thereof or by the law of the United States, or (~~2~~*4*) before a person commissioned by the court, and a person so commissioned shall have the power by virtue of the commission to administer any necessary oath and take testimony~~, or (3) pursuant to a letter rogatory~~. A commission or a letter ~~rogatory~~ *of request* shall be issued on application and notice and on terms that are just and appropriate. It is not requisite to the issuance of a commission or a letter ~~rogatory~~ *of request* that the taking of the deposition in any other manner is impracticable or inconvenient; and both a commission and a letter ~~rogatory~~ *of request* may be issued in proper cases. A notice or commission may designate the person before whom the deposition is to be taken either by name or descriptive title. A letter ~~rogatory~~ *of request* may be addressed "To the Appropriate Authority in [here name the country]." *When a letter of request or any other device is used pursuant to any applicable treaty or convention, it shall be captioned in the form prescribed by that treaty or convention.* Evidence obtained in response to a letter ~~rogatory~~ *of request* need not be excluded merely ~~for the reason that~~ *because* it is not a verbatim transcript, *because* ~~or that~~ the testimony was not taken under oath, or ~~for~~ *because of* any similar departure from the requirements for depositions taken within the United States under these rules.

Advisory Committee's Note

This revision is intended to make effective use of the Hague Convention on the Taking of Evidence Abroad in Civil or Commercial Matters, and of any similar treaties that the United States may enter into in the future which provide proce-

New matter is shown in italics; matter to be omitted is lined through

dures for taking depositions abroad. The party taking the deposition is ordinarily obliged to conform to an applicable treaty or convention if an effective deposition can be taken by such internationally approved means, even though a verbatim transcript is not available or testimony cannot be taken under oath. For a discussion of the impact of such treaties upon the discovery process, and of the application of principles of comity upon discovery in countries not signatories to a convention, see *Société Nationale Industrielle Aérospatiale v. United States District Court,* 482 U.S. 522 (1987).

The term "letter of request" has been substituted in the rule for the term "letter rogatory" because it is the primary method provided by the Hague Convention. A letter rogatory is essentially a form of letter of request. There are several other minor changes that are designed merely to carry out the intent of the other alterations.

Rule 29. Stipulations Regarding Discovery Procedure

Unless ~~the court orders~~ otherwise *directed by the court,* the parties may by written stipulation (1) provide that depositions may be taken before any person, at any time or place, upon any notice, and in any manner and when so taken may be used like other depositions, and (2) modify ~~the procedures provided by these rules for other methods of~~ *other procedures governing or limitations placed upon* discovery, except that stipulations extending the time provided in Rules 33, 34, and 36 for responses to discovery may, *if they would interfere with any time set for completion of discovery, for hearing of a motion, or for trial,* be made only with the approval of the court.

Advisory Committee's Note

This rule is revised to give greater opportunity for litigants to agree upon modifications to the procedures governing discovery or to limitations upon discovery. Counsel are encouraged to agree on less expensive and time-consuming methods to obtain information, as through voluntary exchange of documents, use of interviews in lieu of depositions, etc. Likewise, when more depositions or interrogatories are needed than allowed under these rules or when more time is needed to complete a deposition than allowed under a local rule, they can, by agreeing to the additional discovery, eliminate the need for a special motion addressed to the court.

Under the revised rule, the litigants ordinarily are not required to obtain the court's approval of these stipulations. By order or local rule, the court can, however, direct that its approval be obtained for particular types of stipulations; and, in any event, approval must be obtained if a stipulation to extend the 30–day period for responding to interrogatories, requests for production, or requests for admissions would interfere with dates set by the court for completing discovery, for hearing of a motion, or for trial.

Rule 30. Depositions Upon Oral Examination

(a) When Depositions May Be Taken*; When Leave Required.*

(1) ~~After commencement of the action, any~~ party may take the testimony of any person, including a party, by deposition upon oral examination *without leave of court except as provided in paragraph (2)*. ~~Leave of court, granted with or without notice, must be obtained only if the plaintiff seeks to take a deposition prior to the expiration of 30 days after service of the summons and complaint upon any defendant or service made under Rule 4(e), except that leave is not required (1) if a defendant has served a notice of taking deposition or otherwise sought discovery, or (2) if special notice is given as provided in subdivision (b)(2) of this rule.~~ The attendance of witnesses may be compelled by subpoena as provided in Rule 45. ~~The deposition of a person confined in prison may be taken only by leave of court on such terms as the court prescribes.~~

(2) A party must obtain leave of court, which shall be granted to the extent consistent with the principles stated in Rule 26(b)(2), if the person to be examined is confined in prison or if, without the written stipulation of the parties,

(A) a proposed deposition would result in more than ten depositions being taken under this rule or Rule 31 by the plaintiffs, or by the defendants, or by third-party defendants;

(B) the person to be examined already has been deposed in the case; or

(C) a party seeks to take a deposition before the time specified in Rule 26(d) unless the notice contains a certification, with supporting facts, that the person to be examined is expected to leave the United States and be unavailable for examination in this country unless deposed before that time.

(b) Notice of Examination: General Requirements; ~~Special Notice; Non-Stenographic~~ *Method of* Recording; Production of Documents and Things; Deposition of Organization; Deposition by Telephone.

(1) A party desiring to take the deposition of any person upon oral examination shall give reasonable notice in writing to every other party to the action. The notice shall state the time and place for taking the deposition and the name and

New matter is shown in italics; matter to be omitted is lined through

address of each person to be examined, if known, and, if the name is not known, a general description sufficient to identify the person or the particular class or group to which the person belongs. If a subpoena duces tecum is to be served on the person to be examined, the designation of the materials to be produced as set forth in the subpoena shall be attached to, or included in, the notice.

(2) ~~Leave of court is not required for the taking of a deposition by the plaintiff if the notice (A) states that the person to be examined is about to go out of the district where the action is pending and more than 100 miles from the place of trial, or is about to go out of the United States, or is bound on a voyage to sea, and will be unavailable for examination unless the person's deposition is taken before expiration of the 30-day period, and (B) sets forth facts to support the statement. The plaintiff's attorney shall sign the notice, and the attorney's signature constitutes a certification by the attorney that to the best of the attorney's knowledge, information, and belief the statement and supporting facts are true. The sanctions provided by Rule 11 are applicable to the certification.~~

~~If a party shows that when the party was served with notice under this subdivision (b)(2) the party was unable through the exercise of diligence to obtain counsel to represent the party at the taking of the deposition, the deposition may not be used against the party.~~

The party taking the deposition shall state in the notice the method by which the testimony shall be recorded. Unless the court orders otherwise, it may be recorded by sound, sound-and-visual, or stenographic means, and the party taking the deposition shall bear the cost of the recording. Any party may arrange for a transcription to be made from the recording of a deposition taken by nonstenographic means.

(3) ~~The court may for cause shown enlarge or shorten the time for taking the deposition.~~ *With prior notice to the deponent and other parties, any party may designate another method to record the deponent's testimony in addition to the method specified by the person taking the deposition. The additional record or transcript shall be made at that party's expense unless the court otherwise orders.*

(4) ~~The parties may stipulate in writing or the court may upon motion order that the testimony at a deposition be recorded by other than stenographic means. The stipulation or order shall designate the person before whom the deposition shall be taken, the manner of recording, preserving and filing~~

New matter is shown in italics; matter to be omitted is lined through

~~the deposition, and may include other provisions to assure that the recorded testimony will be accurate and trustworthy. A party may arrange to have a stenographic transcription made at the party's own expense. Any objections under subdivision (c), any changes made by the witness, the witness' signature identifying the deposition as the witness' own or the statement of the officer that is required if the witness does not sign, as provided in subdivision (e), and the certification of the officer required by subdivision (f) shall be set forth in a writing to accompany a deposition recorded by non-stenographic means.~~ *Unless otherwise agreed by the parties, a deposition shall be conducted before an officer appointed or designated under Rule 28 and shall begin with a statement on the record by the officer that includes (A) the officer's name and business address; (B) the date, time, and place of the deposition; (C) the name of the deponent; (D) the administration of the oath or affirmation to the deponent; and (E) an identification of all persons present. If the deposition is recorded other than stenographically, the officer shall repeat items (A) through (C) at the beginning of each unit of recorded tape or other recording medium. The appearance or demeanor of deponents or attorneys shall not be distorted through camera or sound-recording techniques. At the end of the deposition, the officer shall state on the record that the deposition is complete and shall set forth any stipulations made by counsel concerning the custody of the transcript or recording and the exhibits, or concerning other pertinent matters.*

(7) The parties may stipulate in writing or the court may upon motion order that a deposition be taken by telephone *or other remote electronic means.* For the purposes of this rule and Rules 28(a), 37(a)(1), *and* 37(b)(1)~~, and 45(d)~~, a deposition taken by ~~telephone~~ *such means* is taken in the district and at the place where the deponent is to answer questions ~~propounded to the deponent~~.

(c) Examination and Cross–Examination; Record of Examination; Oath; Objections. Examination and cross-examination of witnesses may proceed as permitted at the trial under the provisions of the Federal Rules of Evidence *except Rules 103 and 615.* The officer before whom the deposition is to be taken shall put the witness on oath *or affirmation* and shall personally, or by someone acting under the officer's direction and in the officer's presence, record the testimony of the witness. The testimony shall be taken stenographically or recorded by any other ~~means ordered in accordance with~~ *method authorized by* subdivision (b)(~~4~~*2*) of this rule. ~~If requested by one of the parties the testimony shall be~~

New matter is shown in italics; matter to be omitted is lined through

~~transcribed.~~ All objections made at the time of the examination to the qualifications of the officer taking the deposition, ~~or~~ to the manner of taking it, ~~or~~ to the evidence presented, ~~or~~ to the conduct of any party, ~~and any other objection to~~ *or to any other aspect of* the proceedings~~,~~ shall be noted by the officer upon *the record of* the deposition~~. Evidence objected to shall be~~*; but the examination shall proceed, with the testimony being* taken subject to the objections. In lieu of participating in the oral examination, parties may serve written questions in a sealed envelope on the party taking the deposition and the party taking the deposition shall transmit them to the officer, who shall propound them to the witness and record the answers verbatim.

(d) *Schedule and Duration;* Motion to Terminate or Limit Examination.

(1) Any objection to evidence during a deposition shall be stated concisely and in a non-argumentative and non-suggestive manner. A party may instruct a deponent not to answer only when necessary to preserve a privilege, to enforce a limitation on evidence directed by the court, or to present a motion under paragraph (3).

(2) By order or local rule, the court may limit the time permitted for the conduct of a deposition, but shall allow additional time consistent with Rule 26(b)(2) if needed for a fair examination of the deponent or if the deponent or another party impedes or delays the examination. If the court finds such an impediment, delay, or other conduct that has frustrated the fair examination of the deponent, it may impose upon the persons responsible an appropriate sanction, including the reasonable costs and attorney's fees incurred by any parties as a result thereof.

(3) At any time during ~~the taking of the~~ *a* deposition, on motion of a party or of the deponent and upon a showing that the examination is being conducted in bad faith or in such manner as unreasonably to annoy, embarrass, or oppress the deponent or party, the court in which the action is pending or the court in the district where the deposition is being taken may order the officer conducting the examination to cease forthwith from taking the deposition, or may limit the scope and manner of the taking of the deposition as provided in Rule 26(c). If the order made terminates the examination, it shall be resumed thereafter only upon the order of the court in which the action is pending. Upon demand of the objecting party or deponent, the taking of the deposition shall be suspended for the time necessary to make a motion for an order.

The provisions of Rule 37(a)(4) apply to the award of expenses incurred in relation to the motion.

(e) ~~Submission to~~ *Review by* Witness; Changes; Signing. ~~When the testimony is fully transcribed, the deposition shall be submitted to the witness for examination and shall be read to or by the witness, unless such examination and reading are waived by the witness and by the parties. Any changes in form or substance which the witness desires to make shall be entered upon the deposition by the officer with a statement of the reasons given by the witness for making them. The deposition shall then be signed by the witness, unless the parties by stipulation waive the signing or the witness is ill or cannot be found or refuses to sign. If the deposition is not signed by the witness within 30 days of its submission to the witness, the officer shall sign it and state on the record the fact of the waiver or of the illness or absence of the witness or the fact of the refusal to sign, together with the reason, if any, given therefor; and the deposition may then be used as fully as though signed unless on a motion to suppress under Rule 32(d)(4) the court holds that the reasons given for the refusal to sign require rejection of the deposition in whole or in part.~~ *If requested by the deponent or a party before completion of the deposition, the deponent shall have 30 days after being notified by the officer that the transcript or recording is available in which to review the transcript or recording and, if there are changes in form or substance, to sign a statement reciting such changes and the reasons given by the deponent for making them. The officer shall indicate in the certificate prescribed by subdivision (f)(1) whether any review was requested and, if so, shall append any changes made by the deponent during the period allowed.*

(f) Certification and Filing by Officer; Exhibits; Copies; Notice of Filing.

(1) The officer shall certify ~~on the deposition~~ that the witness was duly sworn by the officer and that the deposition is a true record of the testimony given by the witness. *This certificate shall be in writing and accompany the record of the deposition.* Unless otherwise ordered by the court, the officer shall ~~then~~ securely seal the deposition in an envelope *or package* indorsed with the title of the action and marked "Deposition of [here insert name of witness]" and shall promptly file it with the court in which the action is pending ~~or send it by registered or certified mail to the clerk thereof for filing~~ *or send it to the attorney who arranged for the transcript or recording, who shall store it under conditions that will protect it against loss, destruction, tampering, or deterioration.* Docu-

New matter is shown in italics; matter to be omitted is lined through

ments and things produced for inspection during the examination of the witness, shall, upon the request of a party, be marked for identification and annexed to the deposition and may be inspected and copied by any party, except that if the person producing the materials desires to retain them the person may (A) offer copies to be marked for identification and annexed to the deposition and to serve thereafter as originals if the person affords to all parties fair opportunity to verify the copies by comparison with the originals, or (B) offer the originals to be marked for identification, after giving to each party an opportunity to inspect and copy them, in which event the materials may then be used in the same manner as if annexed to the deposition. Any party may move for an order that the original be annexed to and returned with the deposition to the court, pending final disposition of the case.

(2) *Unless otherwise ordered by the court or agreed by the parties, the officer shall retain stenographic notes of any deposition taken stenographically or a copy of the recording of any deposition taken by another method.* Upon payment of reasonable charges therefor, the officer shall furnish a copy of the *transcript or other recording of the* deposition to any party or to the deponent.

Advisory Committee's Note

Subdivision (a). Paragraph (1) retains the first and third sentences from the former subdivision (a) without significant modification. The second and fourth sentences are relocated.

Paragraph (2) collects all provisions bearing on requirements of leave of court to take a deposition.

Paragraph (2)(A) is new. It provides a limit on the number of depositions the parties may take, absent leave of court or stipulation with the other parties. One aim of this revision is to assure judicial review under the standards stated in Rule 26(b)(2) before any side will be allowed to take more than ten depositions in a case without agreement of the other parties. A second objective is to emphasize that counsel have a professional obligation to develop a mutual cost-effective plan for discovery in the case. Leave to take additional depositions should be granted when consistent with the principles of Rule 26(b)(2), and in some cases the ten-per-side limit should be reduced in accordance with those same principles. Consideration should ordinarily be given at the planning meeting of the parties under Rule 26(f) and at the time of a scheduling conference under Rule 16(b) as to enlargements or reductions in the number of depositions, eliminating the need for special motions.

A deposition under Rule 30(b)(6) should, for purposes of this limit, be treated as a single deposition even though more than one person may be designated to testify.

In multi-party cases, the parties on any side are expected to confer and agree as to which depositions are most needed, given the presumptive limit on the number of depositions they can take without leave of court. If these disputes cannot be amicably resolved, the court can be requested to resolve the dispute or permit additional depositions.

Paragraph (2)(B) is new. It requires leave of court if any witness is to be deposed in the action more than once. This requirement does not apply when a deposition is temporarily recessed for convenience of counsel or the deponent or to enable additional materials to be gathered before resuming the deposition. If significant travel costs would be incurred to resume the deposition, the parties should consider the feasibility of conducting the balance of the examination by telephonic means.

Paragraph (2)(C) revises the second sentence of the former subdivision (a) as to when depositions may be taken. Consistent with the changes made in Rule 26(d), providing that formal discovery ordinarily not commence until after the litigants have met and conferred as directed in revised Rule 26(f), the rule requires leave of court or agreement of the parties if a deposition is to be taken before that time (except when a witness is about to leave the country).

Subdivision (b). The primary change in subdivision (b) is that parties will be authorized to record deposition testimony by nonstenographic means without first having to obtain permission of the court or agreement from other counsel.

Former subdivision (b)(2) is partly relocated in subdivision (a)(2)(C) of this rule. The latter two sentences of the first paragraph are deleted, in part because they are redundant to Rule 26(g) and in part because Rule 11 no longer applies to discovery requests. The second paragraph of the former subdivision (b)(2), relating to use of depositions at trial where a party was unable to obtain counsel in time for an accelerated deposition, is relocated in Rule 32.

New paragraph (2) confers on the party taking the deposition the choice of the method of recording, without the need to obtain prior court approval for one taken other than stenographically. A party choosing to record a deposition only by videotape or audiotape should understand that a transcript will be required by Rule 26(a)(3)(B) and Rule 32(c) if the deposition is later to be offered as evidence at trial or on a dispositive motion under Rule 56. Objections to the nonstenographic recording of a deposition, when warranted by the circumstances, can be presented to the court under Rule 26(c).

Paragraph (3) provides that other parties may arrange, at their own expense, for the recording of a deposition by a means (stenographic, visual, or sound) in addition to the method designated by the person noticing the deposition. The former provisions of this paragraph, relating to the court's power to change the date of a deposition, have been eliminated as redundant in view of Rule 26(c)(2).

Revised paragraph (4) requires that all depositions be recorded by an officer designated or appointed under Rule 28 and contains special provisions designed to provide basic safeguards to assure the utility and integrity of recordings taken other than stenographically.

Paragraph (7) is revised to authorize the taking of a deposition not only by telephone but also by other remote electronic means, such as satellite television, when agreed to by the parties or authorized by the court.

Subdivision (c). Minor changes are made in this subdivision to reflect those made in subdivision (b) and to complement the new provisions of subdivision (d)(1), aimed at reducing the number of interruptions during depositions.

In addition, the revision addresses a recurring problem as to whether other potential deponents can attend a deposition. Courts have disagreed, some holding that witnesses should be excluded through invocation of Rule 615 of the evidence rules, and others holding that witnesses may attend unless excluded by an order under Rule 26(c)(5). The revision provides that other witnesses are not automatically excluded from a deposition simply by the request of a party. Exclusion, however, can be ordered under Rule 26(c)(5) when appropriate; and, if exclusion is ordered, consideration should be given as to whether the excluded witnesses likewise should be precluded from reading, or being otherwise informed about, the testimony given in the earlier depositions. The revision addresses only the matter of attendance by potential deponents, and does not attempt to resolve issues concerning attendance by others, such as members of the public or press.

Subdivision (d). The first sentence of new paragraph (1) provides that any objections during a deposition must be made concisely and in a nonargumentative and non-suggestive manner. Depositions frequently have been unduly prolonged, if not unfairly frustrated, by lengthy objections and colloquy, often suggesting how the deponent should respond. While objections may, under the revised rule, be made during a deposition, they ordinarily should be limited to those that under Rule 32(d)(3) might be waived if not made at that time, *i.e.*, objections on grounds that might be immediately obviated, removed, or cured, such as to the form of a question or the responsiveness of an answer. Under Rule 32(b), other objections can, even without the so-called "usual stipulation" preserving objections, be raised for the first time at trial and therefore should be kept to a minimum during a deposition.

Directions to a deponent not to answer a question can be even more disruptive than objections. The second sentence of new paragraph (1) prohibits such directions except in the three circumstances indicated: to claim a privilege or protection against disclosure (*e.g.*, as work product), to enforce a court directive limiting the scope or length of permissible discovery, or to suspend a deposition to enable presentation of a motion under paragraph (3).

Paragraph (2) is added to this subdivision to dispel any doubts regarding the power of the court by order or local rule to establish limits on the length of depositions. The rule also explicitly authorizes the court to impose the cost resulting from obstructive tactics that unreasonably prolong a deposition on the person engaged in such obstruction. This sanction may be imposed on a non-party witness as well as a party or attorney, but is otherwise congruent with Rule 26(g).

It is anticipated that limits on the length of depositions prescribed by local rules would be presumptive only, subject to modification by the court or by agreement of the parties. Such modifications typically should be discussed by the parties in their meeting under Rule 26(f) and included in the scheduling order required by Rule 16(b). Additional time, moreover, should be allowed under the revised rule when justified under the principles stated in Rule 26(b)(2). To reduce the number of special motions, local rules should ordinarily permit—and indeed encourage—the parties to agree to additional time, as when, during the taking of a deposition, it becomes clear that some additional examination is needed.

Paragraph (3) authorizes appropriate sanctions not only when a deposition is unreasonably prolonged, but also when an attorney engages in other practices that improperly frustrate the fair examination of the deponent, such as making improper objections or giving directions not to answer prohibited by paragraph (1). In general, counsel should not engage in any conduct during a deposition that would not be allowed in the presence of a judicial officer. The making of an excessive number of unnecessary objections may itself constitute sanctionable conduct, as may the refusal of an attorney to agree with other counsel on a fair apportionment of the time allowed for examination of a deponent or a refusal to agree to a reasonable request for some additional time to complete a deposition, when that is permitted by the local rule or order.

Subdivision (e). Various changes are made in this subdivision to reduce problems sometimes encountered when depositions are taken stenographically. Reporters frequently have difficulties obtaining signatures—and the return of depositions—

from deponents. Under the revision pre-filing review by the deponent is required only if requested before the deposition is completed. If review is requested, the deponent will be allowed 30 days to review the transcript or recording and to indicate any changes in form or substance. Signature of the deponent will be required only if review is requested and changes are made.

Subdivision (f). Minor changes are made in this subdivision to reflect those made in subdivision (b). In courts which direct that depositions not be automatically filed, the reporter can transmit the transcript or recording to the attorney taking the deposition (or ordering the transcript or record), who then becomes custodian for the court of the original record of the deposition. Pursuant to subdivision (f)(2), as under the prior rule, any other party is entitled to secure a copy of the deposition from the officer designated to take the deposition; accordingly, unless ordered or agreed, the officer must retain a copy of the recording or the stenographic notes.

Rule 31. Depositions Upon Written Questions

(a) Serving Questions; Notice.

(1) ~~After commencement of the action, any~~ party may take the testimony of any person, including a party, by deposition upon written questions *without leave of court except as provided in paragraph (2)*. The attendance of witnesses may be compelled by the use of subpoena as provided in Rule 45. ~~The deposition of a person confined in prison may be taken only by leave of court on such terms as the court prescribes.~~

(2) A party must obtain leave of court, which shall be granted to the extent consistent with the principles stated in Rule 26(b)(2), if the person to be examined is confined in prison or if, without the written stipulation of the parties,

(A) a proposed deposition would result in more than ten depositions being taken under this rule or Rule 30 by the plaintiffs, or by the defendants, or by third-party defendants;

(B) the person to be examined has already been deposed in the case; or

(C) a party seeks to take a deposition before the time specified in Rule 26(d).

(3) A party desiring to take a deposition upon written questions shall serve them upon every other party with a notice stating (1) the name and address of the person who is to answer them, if known, and if the name is not known, a general description sufficient to identify the person or the particular class or group to which the person belongs, and (2) the name or descriptive title and address of the officer before whom the deposition is to be taken. A deposition upon written questions may be taken of a public or private corporation or a

partnership or association or governmental agency in accordance with the provisions of Rule 30(b)(6).

(4) Within ~~30~~*14* days after the notice and written questions are served, a party may serve cross questions upon all other parties. Within ~~10~~*7* days after being served with cross questions, a party may serve redirect questions upon all other parties. Within ~~10~~*7* days after being served with redirect questions, a party may serve recross questions upon all other parties. The court may for cause shown enlarge or shorten the time.

Advisory Committee's Note

Subdivision (a). The first paragraph of subdivision (a) is divided into two subparagraphs, with provisions comparable to those made in the revision of Rule 30. Changes are made in the former third paragraph, numbered in the revision as paragraph (4), to reduce the total time for developing cross-examination, redirect, and recross questions from 50 days to 28 days.

Rule 32. Use of Depositions in Court Proceedings

(a) Use of Depositions.

(3) The deposition of a witness, whether or not a party, may be used by any party for any purpose if the court finds:

(A) that the witness is dead; or

(B) that the witness is at a greater distance than 100 miles from the place of trial or hearing, or is out of the United States, unless it appears that the absence of the witness was procured by the party offering the deposition; or

(C) that the witness is unable to attend or testify because of age, illness, infirmity, or imprisonment; or

(D) that the party offering the deposition has been unable to procure the attendance of the witness by subpoena; or

(E) upon application and notice, that such exceptional circumstances exist as to make it desirable, in the interest of justice and with due regard to the importance of presenting the testimony of witnesses orally in open court, to allow the deposition to be used.

A deposition taken without leave of court pursuant to a notice under Rule 30(a)(2)(C) shall not be used against a party who demonstrates that, when served with the notice, it was unable through the exercise of diligence to obtain counsel to represent it at the taking of the deposition; nor shall a deposition be used against a party who, having received less than 11 days notice of a deposition, has promptly upon receiving such notice filed a motion for a protective order under Rule 26(c)(2) requesting that the deposition not be held or be held at a different time or place and such motion is pending at the time the deposition is held.

(c) Form of Presentation. *Except as otherwise directed by the court, a party offering deposition testimony pursuant to this rule may offer it in stenographic or nonstenographic form, but, if in nonstenographic form, the party shall also provide the court with a transcript of the portions so offered. On request of any party in a case tried before a jury, deposition testimony offered other than for impeachment purposes shall be presented in nonstenographic form, if available, unless the court for good cause orders otherwise.*

Advisory Committee's Note

Subdivision (a). The last sentence of revised subdivision (a) not only includes the substance of the provisions formerly contained in the second paragraph of Rule 30(b)(2), but adds a provision to deal with the situation when a party, receiving minimal notice of a proposed deposition, is unable to obtain a court ruling on its motion for a protective order seeking to delay or change the place of the deposition. Ordinarily a party does not obtain protection merely by the filing of a motion for a protective order under Rule 26(c); any protection is dependent upon the court's ruling. Under the revision, a party receiving less than 11 days notice of a deposition can, provided its motion for a protective order is filed promptly, be spared the risks resulting from nonattendance at the deposition held before its motion is ruled upon. Although the revision of Rule 32(a) covers only the risk that the deposition could be used against the non-appearing movant, it should also follow that, when the proposed deponent is the movant, the deponent would have "just cause" for failing to appear for purposes of Rule 37(d)(1). Inclusion of this provision is not intended to signify that 11 days' notice is the minimum advance notice for all depositions or that greater than 10 days should necessarily be deemed sufficient in all situations.

Subdivision (c). This new subdivision, inserted at the location of a subdivision previously abrogated, is included in view of the increased opportunities for video-recording and audio-recording of depositions under revised Rule 30(b). Under this rule a party may offer deposition testimony in any of the forms authorized under Rule 30(b) but, if offering it in a nonstenographic form, must provide the court with a transcript of the portions so offered. On request of any party in a jury trial, deposition testimony offered other than for impeachment purposes is to be presented in a nonstenographic form if available, unless the court directs otherwise. Note that under Rule 26(a)(3)(B) a party expecting to use nonstenographic deposition testimony as substantive evidence is required to provide other parties with a transcript in advance of trial.

Rule 33. Interrogatories to Parties

(a) Availability~~; Procedures for Use~~. *Without leave of court or written stipulation, a*~~A~~ny party may serve upon any other party written interrogatories, *not exceeding 25 in number including all discrete subparts,* to be answered by the party served or, if the party served is a public or private corporation or a partnership or association or governmental agency, by any officer or agent, who shall furnish such information as is available to the party. *Leave to serve additional interrogatories shall be granted to the extent consistent with the principles of Rule 26(b)(2). Without leave of court or written stipulation, i*~~I~~nterrogatories may~~, without leave of court,~~ *not* be served ~~upon the plaintiff after commencement of the action and upon any other party with or after service of the summons and complaint upon that party~~ *before the time specified in Rule 26(d).*

(b) Answers and Objections.

(1) Each interrogatory shall be answered separately and fully in writing under oath, unless it is objected to, in which event *the objecting party shall state* the reasons for objection ~~shall be stated in lieu of an answer~~ *and shall answer to the extent the interrogatory is not objectionable.*

(2) The answers are to be signed by the person making them, and the objections signed by the attorney making them.

(3) The party upon whom the interrogatories have been served shall serve a copy of the answers, and objections if any, within 30 days after the service of the interrogatories~~, except that a defendant may serve answers or objections within 45 days after service of the summons and complaint upon that defendant~~. ~~The court may allow a~~*A* shorter or longer time *may be directed by the court or, in the absence of such an order, agreed to in writing by the parties subject to Rule 29.*

(4) All grounds for an objection to an interrogatory shall be stated with specificity. Any ground not stated in a timely objection is waived unless the party's failure to object is excused by the court for good cause shown.

(5) The party submitting the interrogatories may move for an order under Rule 37(a) with respect to any objection to or other failure to answer an interrogatory.

(~~b~~*c*) Scope; Use at Trial. Interrogatories may relate to any matters which can be inquired into under Rule 26(b)*(1)*, and the answers may be used to the extent permitted by the rules of evidence.

An interrogatory otherwise proper is not necessarily objectionable merely because an answer to the interrogatory involves an opinion or contention that relates to fact or the application of law to fact, but the court may order that such an interrogatory need not be answered until after designated discovery has been completed or until a pre-trial conference or other later time.

New matter is shown in italics; matter to be omitted is lined through

(~~c~~*d*) Option to Produce Business Records.

Advisory Committee's Note

Purpose of Revision. The purpose of this revision is to reduce the frequency and increase the efficiency of interrogatory practice. The revision is based on experience with local rules. For ease of reference, subdivision (a) is divided into two subdivisions and the remaining subdivisions renumbered.

Subdivision (a). Revision of this subdivision limits interrogatory practice. Because Rule 26(a)(1)–(3) requires disclosure of much of the information previously obtained by this form of discovery, there should be less occasion to use it. Experience in over half of the district courts has confirmed that limitations on the number of interrogatories are useful and manageable. Moreover, because the device can be costly and may be used as a means of harassment, it is desirable to subject its use to the control of the court consistent with the principles stated in Rule 26(b)(2), particularly in multi-party cases where it has not been unusual for the same interrogatory to be propounded to a party by more than one of its adversaries.

Each party is allowed to serve 25 interrogatories upon any other party, but must secure leave of court (or a stipulation from the opposing party) to serve a larger number. Parties cannot evade this presumptive limitation through the device of joining as "subparts" questions that seek information about discrete separate subjects. However, a question asking about communications of a particular type should be treated as a single interrogatory even though it requests that the time, place, persons present, and contents be stated separately for each such communication.

As with the number of depositions authorized by Rule 30, leave to serve additional interrogatories is to be allowed when consistent with Rule 26(b)(2). The aim is not to prevent needed discovery, but to provide judicial scrutiny before parties make potentially excessive use of this discovery device. In many cases it will be appropriate for the court to permit a larger number of interrogatories in the scheduling order entered under Rule 16(b).

Unless leave of court is obtained, interrogatories may not be served prior to the meeting of the parties under Rule 26(f).

When a case with outstanding interrogatories exceeding the number permitted by this rule is removed to federal court, the interrogating party must seek leave allowing the additional interrogatories, specify which twenty-five are to be answered, or resubmit interrogatories that comply with the rule. Moreover, under Rule 26(d), the time for response would be measured from the date of the parties' meeting under Rule 26(f). See Rule 81(c), providing that these rules govern procedures after removal.

Subdivision (b). A separate subdivision is made of the former second paragraph of subdivision (a). Language is added to paragraph (1) of this subdivision to emphasize the duty of the responding party to provide full answers to the extent not objectionable. If, for example, an interrogatory seeking information about numerous facilities or products is deemed objectionable, but an interrogatory seeking information about a lesser number of facilities or products would not have been objectionable, the interrogatory should be answered with respect to the latter even though an objection is raised as to the balance of the facilities or products. Similarly, the fact that additional time may be needed to respond to some questions (or to some aspects of questions) should not justify a delay in responding to those questions (or other aspects of questions) that can be answered within the prescribed time.

Paragraph (4) is added to make clear that objections must be specifically justified, and that unstated or untimely grounds for objection ordinarily are waived. Note also the provisions of revised Rule 26(b)(5), which require a responding party to indicate when it is withholding information under a claim of privilege or as trial preparation materials.

These provisions should be read in light of Rule 26(g), authorizing the court to impose sanctions on a party and attorney making an unfounded objection to an interrogatory.

Subdivisions (c) and (d). The provisions of former subdivisions (b) and (c) are renumbered.

Rule 34. Production of Documents and Things and Entry Upon Land for Inspection and Other Purposes

(b) Procedure. ~~The request may, without leave of court, be served upon the plaintiff after commencement of the action and upon any other party with or after service of the summons and complaint upon that party.~~ The request shall set forth, *either by individual item or by category,* the items to be inspected ~~either by individual item or by category~~, and describe each ~~item and category~~ with reasonable particularity. The request shall specify a reasonable time, place, and manner of making the inspection and performing the related acts. *Without leave of court or written stipulation, a request may not be served before the time specified in Rule 26(d).*

The party upon whom the request is served shall serve a written response within 30 days after the service of the request~~, except that a defendant may serve a response within 45 days after service of the summons and complaint upon that defendant~~. ~~The court may allow a~~*A* shorter or longer time *may be directed by the court or, in the absence of such an order, agreed to in writing by the parties, subject to Rule 29.* The response shall state, with respect to each item or category, that inspection and related activities will be permitted as requested, unless the request is objected to, in which event the reasons for the objection shall be stated. If objection is made to part of an item or category, the part shall be specified *and inspection permitted of the remaining parts.* The party submitting the request may move for an order under Rule 37(a) with respect to any objection to or other failure to respond to the request or any part thereof, or any failure to permit inspection as requested.

A party who produces documents for inspection shall produce them as they are kept in the usual course of business or shall organize and label them to correspond with the categories in the request.

New matter is shown in italics; matter to be omitted is lined through

Advisory Committee's Note

The rule is revised to reflect the change made by Rule 26(d), preventing a party from seeking formal discovery prior to the meeting of the parties required by Rule 26(f). Also, like a change made in Rule 33, the rule is modified to make clear that, if a request for production is objectionable only in part, production should be afforded with respect to the unobjectionable portions.

When a case with outstanding requests for production is removed to federal court, the time for response would be measured from the date of the parties' meeting. See Rule 81(c), providing that these rules govern procedures after removal.

Rule 36. Requests for Admission

(a) Request for Admission. A party may serve upon any other party a written request for the admission, for purposes of the pending action only, of the truth of any matters within the scope of Rule 26(b)*(1)* set forth in the request that relate to statements or opinions of fact or of the application of law to fact, including the genuineness of any documents described in the request. Copies of documents shall be served with the request unless they have been or are otherwise furnished or made available for inspection and copying. ~~The request may, without leave of court, be served upon the plaintiff after commencement of the action and upon any other party with or after service of the summons and complaint upon that party.~~ *Without leave of court or written stipulation, requests for admission may not be served before the time specified in Rule 26(d).*

Each matter of which an admission is requested shall be separately set forth. The matter is admitted unless, within 30 days after service of the request, or within such shorter or longer time as the court may allow *or as the parties may agree to in writing, subject to Rule 29*, the party to whom the request is directed serves upon the party requesting the admission a written answer or objection addressed to the matter, signed by the party or by the party's attorney~~, but, unless the court shortens the time, a defendant shall not be required to serve answers or objections before the expiration of 45 days after service of the summons and complaint upon that defendant~~. If objection is made, the reasons therefor shall be stated. The answer shall specifically deny the matter or set forth in detail the reasons why the answering party cannot truthfully admit or deny the matter. A denial shall fairly meet the substance of the requested admission, and when good faith requires that a party qualify an answer or deny only a part of the matter of which an admission is requested, the party shall specify so much of it as is true and qualify or deny the remainder. An answering party may not give lack of information or knowledge as a reason for failure to admit or deny unless the party states that the party has made reasonable inquiry and that the information known or readily obtainable by the party is insufficient to enable the party to admit or deny. A party who considers that a matter of which an admission has been requested presents a genuine issue for trial may not, on that ground alone, object to the request; the party may, subject to the provisions of Rule 37(c), deny the matter or set forth reasons why the party cannot admit or deny it.

Advisory Committee's Note

The rule is revised to reflect the change made by Rule 26(d), preventing a party from seeking formal discovery until after the meeting of the parties required by Rule 26(f).

Rule 37. Failure to Make *Disclosure* or Cooperate in Discovery: Sanctions

(a) Motion for Order Compelling *Disclosure or* Discovery. A party, upon reasonable notice to other parties and all persons affected thereby, may apply for an order compelling *disclosure or* discovery as follows:

(1) Appropriate Court. An application for an order to a party ~~may~~ *shall* be made to the court in which the action is pending~~, or, on matters relating to a deposition, to the court in the district where the deposition is being taken~~. An application for an order to a ~~deponent~~ *person* who is not a party shall be made to the court in the district where the ~~deposition is being taken~~ *discovery is being, or is to be, taken.*

(2) Motion.

(A) If a party fails to make a disclosure required by Rule 26(a), any other party may move to compel disclosure and for appropriate sanctions. The motion must include a certification that the movant has in good faith conferred or attempted to confer with the party not making the disclosure in an effort to secure the disclosure without court action.

(B) If a deponent fails to answer a question propounded or submitted under Rules 30 or 31, or a corporation or other entity fails to make a designation under Rule 30(b)(6) or 31(a), or a party fails to answer an interrogatory submitted under Rule 33, or if a party, in response to a request for inspection submitted under Rule 34, fails to respond that inspection will be permitted as requested or fails to permit inspection as requested, the discovering party may move for an order compelling an answer, or a designation, or an order compelling inspection in accor-

dance with the request. *The motion must include a certification that the movant has in good faith conferred or attempted to confer with the person or party failing to make the discovery in an effort to secure the information or material without court action.* When taking a deposition on oral examination, the proponent of the question may complete or adjourn the examination before applying for an order.

~~If the court denies the motion in whole or in part, it may make such protective order as it would have been empowered to make on a motion made pursuant to Rule 26(c).~~

(3) Evasive or Incomplete *Disclosure,* Answer, *or Response.* For purposes of this subdivision an evasive or incomplete *disclosure,* answer, *or response* is to be treated as a failure to *disclose,* answer, *or respond.*

(4) ~~Award of~~ Expenses ~~of Motion~~ *and Sanctions.*

(A) If the motion is granted *or if the disclosure or requested discovery is provided after the motion was filed,* the court shall, after *affording an* opportunity ~~for hearing,~~ *to be heard,* require the party or deponent whose conduct necessitated the motion or the party or attorney advising such conduct or both of them to pay to the moving party the reasonable expenses incurred in ~~obtaining the order~~ *making the motion,* including attorney's fees, unless the court finds that the *motion was filed without the movant's first making a good faith effort to obtain the disclosure or discovery without court action, or that the* ~~opposition to the motion~~ *opposing party's nondisclosure, response, or objection* was substantially justified, or that other circumstances make an award of expenses unjust.

(B) If the motion is denied, the court *may enter any protective order authorized under Rule 26(c) and* shall, after *affording an* opportunity ~~for hearing,~~ *to be heard,* require the moving party or the attorney ~~advising~~ *filing* the motion or both of them to pay to the party or deponent who opposed the motion the reasonable expenses incurred in opposing the motion, including attorney's fees, unless the court finds that the making of the motion was substantially justified or that other circumstances make an award of expenses unjust.

(C) If the motion is granted in part and denied in part, the court *may enter any protective order authorized under Rule 26(c) and* may, *after affording an opportunity*

New matter is shown in italics; matter to be omitted is lined through

to be heard, apportion the reasonable expenses incurred in relation to the motion among the parties and persons in a just manner.

(c) ~~Expenses on~~ Failure to *Disclose; False or Misleading Disclosure; Refusal to* Admit.

(1) A party that without substantial justification fails to disclose information required by Rule 26(a) or 26(e)(1) shall not, unless such failure is harmless, be permitted to use as evidence at a trial, at a hearing, or on a motion any witness or information not so disclosed. In addition to or in lieu of this sanction, the court, on motion and after affording an opportunity to be heard, may impose other appropriate sanctions. In addition to requiring payment of reasonable expenses, including attorney's fees, caused by the failure, these sanctions may include any of the actions authorized under subparagraphs (A), (B), and (C) of subdivision (b)(2) of this rule and may include informing the jury of the failure to make the disclosure.

(2) If a party fails to admit the genuineness of any document or the truth of any matter as requested under Rule 36, and if the party requesting the admissions thereafter proves the genuineness of the document or the truth of the matter, the requesting party may apply to the court for an order requiring the other party to pay the reasonable expenses incurred in making that proof, including reasonable attorney's fees. The court shall make the order unless it finds that (~~1~~*A*) the request was held objectionable pursuant to Rule 36(a), or (~~2~~*B*) the admission sought was of no substantial importance, or (~~3~~*C*) the party failing to admit had reasonable ground to believe that the party might prevail on the matter, or (~~4~~*D*) there was other good reason for the failure to admit.

(d) Failure of Party to Attend at Own Deposition or Serve Answers to Interrogatories or Respond to Request for Inspection. If a party or an officer, director, or managing agent of a party or a person designated under Rule 30(b)(6) or 31(a) to testify on behalf of a party fails (1) to appear before the officer who is to take the deposition, after being served with a proper notice, or (2) to serve answers or objections to interrogatories submitted under Rule 33, after proper service of the interrogatories, or (3) to serve a written response to a request for inspection submitted under Rule 34, after proper service of the request, the court in which the action is pending on motion may make such orders in regard to the failure as are just, and among others it may take any action authorized under *sub*paragraphs (A), (B), and (C) of subdivision (b)(2) of this rule. *Any motion specifying a failure under*

New matter is shown in italics; matter to be omitted is lined through

clause (2) or (3) of this subdivision shall include a certification that the movant has in good faith conferred or attempted to confer with the party failing to answer or respond in an effort to obtain such answer or response without court action. In lieu of any order or in addition thereto, the court shall require the party failing to act or the attorney advising that party or both to pay the reasonable expenses, including attorney's fees, caused by the failure unless the court finds that the failure was substantially justified or that other circumstances make an award of expenses unjust.

The failure to act described in this subdivision may not be excused on the ground that the discovery sought is objectionable unless the party failing to act has ~~applied~~ *a pending motion* for a protective order as provided by Rule 26(c).

(g) Failure to Participate in the Framing of a Discovery Plan. If a party or a party's attorney fails to participate in good faith in the *development and submission* ~~framing~~ of a *proposed* discovery plan ~~by agreement~~ as ~~is~~ required by Rule 26(f), the court may, after opportunity for hearing, require such party or attorney to pay to any other party the reasonable expenses, including attorney's fees, caused by the failure.

Advisory Committee's Note

Subdivision (a). This subdivision is revised to reflect the revision of Rule 26(a), requiring disclosure of matters without a discovery request.

Pursuant to new subdivision (a)(2)(A), a party dissatisfied with the disclosure made by an opposing party may under this rule move for an order to compel disclosure. In providing for such a motion, the revised rule parallels the provisions of the former rule dealing with failures to answer particular interrogatories. Such a motion may be needed when the information to be disclosed might be helpful to the party seeking the disclosure but not to the party required to make the disclosure. If the party required to make the disclosure would need the material to support its own contentions, the more effective enforcement of the disclosure requirement will be to exclude the evidence not disclosed, as provided in subdivision (c)(1) of this revised rule.

Language is included in the new paragraph and added to the subparagraph (B) that requires litigants to seek to resolve discovery disputes by informal means before filing a motion with the court. This requirement is based on successful experience with similar local rules of court promulgated pursuant to Rule 83.

The last sentence of paragraph (2) is moved into paragraph (4).

Under revised paragraph (3), evasive or incomplete disclosures and responses to interrogatories and production requests are treated as failures to disclose or respond. Interrogatories and requests for production should not be read or interpreted in an artificially restrictive or hypertechnical manner to avoid disclosure of information fairly covered by the discovery request, and to do so is subject to appropriate sanctions under subdivision (a).

Revised paragraph (4) is divided into three subparagraphs for ease of reference, and in each the phrase "after opportunity for hearing" is changed to "after affording an opportunity to be heard'' to make clear that the court can consider such questions on written submissions as well as on oral hearings.

Subparagraph (A) is revised to cover the situation where information that should have been produced without a motion to compel is produced after the motion is filed but before it is brought on for hearing. The rule also is revised to provide that a party should not be awarded its expenses for filing a motion that could have been avoided by conferring with opposing counsel.

Subparagraph (C) is revised to include the provision that formerly was contained in subdivision (a)(2) and to include the same requirement of an opportunity to be heard that is specified in subparagraphs (A) and (B).

Subdivision (c). The revision provides a self-executing sanction for failure to make a disclosure required by Rule 26(a), without need for a motion under subdivision (a)(2)(A).

Paragraph (1) prevents a party from using as evidence any witnesses or information that, without substantial justification, has not been disclosed as required by Rules 26(a) and 26(e)(1). This automatic sanction provides a strong inducement for disclosure of material that the disclosing party would expect to use as evidence, whether at a trial, at a hearing, or on a motion, such as one under Rule 56. As disclosure of evidence offered solely for impeachment purposes is not required under those rules, this preclusion sanction likewise does not apply to that evidence.

Limiting the automatic sanction to violations ''without substantial justification,'' coupled with the exception for violations that are ''harmless,'' is needed to avoid unduly harsh penalties in a variety of situations: *e.g.,* the inadvertent omission from a Rule 26(a)(1)(A) disclosure of the name of a potential witness known to all parties; the failure to list as a trial witness a person so listed by another party; or the lack of knowledge of a pro se litigant of the requirement to make disclosures. In the latter situation, however, exclusion would be proper if the requirement for disclosure had been called to the litigant's attention by either the court or another party.

Preclusion of evidence is not an effective incentive to compel disclosure of information that, being supportive of the position of the opposing party, might advantageously be concealed by the disclosing party. However, the rule provides the court with a wide range of other sanctions—such as declaring specified facts to be established, preventing contradictory evidence, or, like spoliation of evidence, allowing the jury to be informed of the fact of nondisclosure—that, though not self-executing, can be imposed when found to be warranted after a hearing. The failure to identify a witness or document in a disclosure statement would be admissible under the Federal Rules of Evidence under the same principles that allow a party's interrogatory answers to be offered against it.

Subdivision (d). This subdivision is revised to require that, where a party fails to file any response to interrogatories or a Rule 34 request, the discovering party should informally seek to obtain such responses before filing a motion for sanctions.

The last sentence of this subdivision is revised to clarify that it is the pendency of a motion for protective order that may be urged as an excuse for a violation of subdivision (d). If a party's motion has been denied, the party cannot argue that its subsequent failure to comply would be justified. In this connection, it should be noted that the filing of a motion under Rule 26(c) is not self-executing—the relief authorized under that rule depends on obtaining the court's order to that effect.

Subdivision (g). This subdivision is modified to conform to the revision of Rule 26(f).

Rule 38. Jury Trial of Right

(b) Demand. Any party may demand a trial by jury of any issue triable of right by a jury by *(1)* serving upon the other parties a demand therefor in writing at any time after the commencement of the action and not later than 10 days after the service of the last pleading directed to such issue, *and (2) filing the demand as required by Rule 5(d).* Such demand may be indorsed upon a pleading of the party.

(d) Waiver. The failure of a party to serve *and file* a demand as required by this rule ~~and to file it as required by Rule 5(d)~~ constitutes a waiver by the party of trial by jury. A demand for trial by jury made as herein provided may not be withdrawn without the consent of the parties.

Advisory Committee's Note

Language requiring the filing of a jury demand as provided in subdivision (d) is added to subdivision (b) to eliminate an apparent ambiguity between the two subdivisions. For proper scheduling of cases, it is important that jury demands not only be served on other parties, but also be filed with the court.

Rule 50. Judgment as a Matter of Law in Actions Tried by Jury; Alternative Motion for New Trial; Conditional Rulings

(a) Judgment as a Matter of Law.

(1) If during a trial by jury a party has been fully heard *on* ~~with respect to~~ an issue and there is no legally sufficient evidentiary basis for a reasonable jury to ~~have found~~ *find* for that party *on* ~~with respect to~~ that issue, the court may *determine the issue against that party and may* grant a motion for judgment as a matter of law against that party ~~on any~~ *with respect to a* claim~~, counterclaim, cross-claim, or third party claim~~ *or defense* that cannot under the controlling law be maintained *or defeated* without a favorable finding on that issue.

Advisory Committee's Note

This technical amendment corrects an ambiguity in the text of the 1991 revision of the rule, which, as indicated in the Notes, was not intended to change the existing standards under which "directed verdicts" could be granted. This amendment makes clear that judgments as a matter of law in jury trials may be entered against both plaintiffs and defendants and with respect to issues or defenses that may not be wholly dispositive of a claim or defense.

Rule 52. Findings by the Court; Judgment on Partial Findings

(c) Judgment on Partial Findings. If during a trial without a jury a party has been fully heard *on* ~~with respect to~~ an issue and the court finds against the party on that issue, the court may enter judgment as a matter of law against that party ~~on any~~ *with respect to a* claim~~, counterclaim, cross-claim, or third-party claim~~ *or defense* that cannot under the controlling law be maintained or defeated without a favorable finding on that issue, or the court may decline to render any judgment until the close of all the evidence. Such a judgment shall be supported by findings of fact and conclusions of law as required by subdivision (a) of this rule.

Advisory Committee's Note

This technical amendment corrects an ambiguity in the text of the 1991 revision of the rule, similar to the revision being made to Rule 50. This amendment makes clear that judgments as a matter of law in nonjury trials may be entered against both plaintiffs and defendants and with respect to issues or defenses that may not be wholly dispositive of a claim or defense.

Rule 53. Masters

(a) Appointment and Compensation. The court in which any action is pending may appoint a special master therein. As used in these rules, the word "master" includes a referee, an auditor, an examiner, and an assessor. The compensation to be allowed to a master shall be fixed by the court, and shall be charged upon such of the parties or paid out of any fund or subject matter of the action, which is in the custody and control of the court as the court may direct; provided that this provision for compensation shall not apply when a United States magistrate *judge* is designated to serve as a master ~~pursuant to Title 28, U.S.C. § 636(b)(2)~~. The master shall not retain the master's report as security for the master's compensation; but when the party ordered to pay the compensation allowed by the court does not pay it after notice and within the time prescribed by the court, the master is entitled to a writ of execution against the delinquent party.

(b) Reference. A reference to a master shall be the exception and not the rule. In actions to be tried by a jury, a reference shall be made only when the issues are complicated; in actions to be tried without a jury, save in matters of account and of difficult computation of damages, a reference shall be made only upon a showing that some exceptional condition requires it. Upon the consent of the parties, a magistrate *judge* may be designated to serve as a special master without regard to the provisions of this subdivision.

(f) *Application to Magistrate Judge.* A magistrate *judge* is subject to this rule only when the order referring a matter to the magistrate *judge* expressly provides that the reference is made under this rule.

Advisory Committee's Note

This revision is made to conform the rule to changes made by the Judicial Improvements Act of 1990.

Rule 54. Judgments; Costs

(d) Costs*; Attorneys' Fees.*

(1) Costs Other than Attorneys' Fees. Except when express provision therefor is made either in a statute of the United States or in these rules, costs *other than attorneys' fees* shall be allowed as of course to the prevailing party unless the court otherwise directs; but costs against the United States, its officers, and agencies shall be imposed only to the extent permitted by law. *Such c*~~C~~osts may be taxed by the clerk on one day's notice. On motion served within 5 days thereafter, the action of the clerk may be reviewed by the court.

(2) Attorneys' Fees.

(A) Claims for attorneys' fees and related nontaxable expenses shall be made by motion unless the substantive law governing the action provides for the recovery of such fees as an element of damages to be proved at trial.

(B) Unless otherwise provided by statute or order of the court, the motion must be filed and served no later than 14 days after entry of judgment; must specify the judgment and the statute, rule, or other grounds entitling the moving party to the award; and must state the amount or provide a fair estimate of the amount sought. If directed by the court, the motion shall also disclose the terms of any agreement with respect to fees to be paid for the services for which claim is made.

(C) On request of a party or class member, the court shall afford an opportunity for adversary submissions with respect to the motion in accordance with Rule 43(e) or Rule 78. The court may determine issues of liability for fees before receiving submissions bearing on issues of evaluation of services for which liability is imposed by the court. The court shall find the facts and state its conclusions of law as

provided in Rule 52(a), and a judgment shall be set forth in a separate document as provided in Rule 58.

(D) By local rule the court may establish special procedures by which issues relating to such fees may be resolved without extensive evidentiary hearings. In addition, the court may refer issues relating to the value of services to a special master under Rule 53 without regard to the provisions of subdivision (b) thereof and may refer a motion for attorneys' fees to a magistrate judge under Rule 72(b) as if it were a dispositive pretrial matter.

(E) The provisions of subparagraphs (A) through (D) do not apply to claims for fees and expenses as sanctions for violations of these rules or under 28 U.S.C. § 1927.

Advisory Committee's Note

Subdivision (d). This revision adds paragraph (2) to this subdivision to provide for a frequently recurring form of litigation not initially contemplated by the rules—disputes over the amount of attorneys' fees to be awarded in the large number of actions in which prevailing parties may be entitled to such awards or in which the court must determine the fees to be paid from a common fund. This revision seeks to harmonize and clarify procedures that have been developed through case law and local rules.

Paragraph (1). Former subdivision (d), providing for taxation of costs by the clerk, is renumbered as paragraph (1) and revised to exclude applications for attorneys' fees.

Paragraph (2). This new paragraph establishes a procedure for presenting claims for attorneys' fees, whether or not denominated as "costs." It applies also to requests for reimbursement of expenses, not taxable as costs, when recoverable under governing law incident to the award of fees. *Cf. West Virginia Univ. Hosp. v. Casey,* ___ U.S. ___ (1991), holding, prior to the Civil Rights Act of 1991, that expert witness fees were not recoverable under 42 U.S.C. § 1988. As noted in subparagraph (A), it does not, however, apply to fees recoverable as an element of damages, as when sought under the terms of a contract; such damages typically are to be claimed in a pleading and may involve issues to be resolved by a jury. Nor, as provided in subparagraph (E), does it apply to awards of fees as sanctions authorized or mandated under these rules or under 28 U.S.C. § 1927.

Subparagraph (B) provides a deadline for motions for attorneys' fees—14 days after final judgment unless the court or a statute specifies some other time. One purpose of this provision is to assure that the opposing party is informed of the claim before the time for appeal has elapsed. Prior law did not prescribe any specific time limit on claims for attorneys' fees. *White v. New Hampshire Dep't of Employment Sec.,* 455 U.S. 445 (1982). In many nonjury cases the court will want to consider attorneys' fee issues immediately after rendering its judgment on the merits of the case. Note that the time for making claims is specifically stated in some legislation, such as the Equal Access to Justice Act, 28 U.S.C. § 2412(d)(1)(B) (30–day filing period).

Prompt filing affords an opportunity for the court to resolve fee disputes shortly after trial, while the services performed are freshly in mind. It also enables the court in appropriate circumstances to make its ruling on a fee request in time for any appellate review of a dispute over fees to proceed at the same time as review on the merits of the case.

Filing a motion for fees under this subdivision does not affect the finality or the appealability of a judgment, though revised Rule 58 provides a mechanism by which prior to appeal the court can suspend the finality to resolve a motion for fees. If an appeal on the merits of the case is taken, the court may rule on the claim for fees, may defer its ruling on the motion, or may deny the motion without prejudice, directing under subdivision (d)(2)(B) a new period for filing after the appeal has been resolved. A notice of appeal does not extend the time for filing a fee claim based on the initial judgment, but the court under subdivision (d)(2)(B) may effectively extend the period by permitting claims to be filed after resolution of the appeal. A new period for filing will automatically begin if a new judgment is entered following a reversal or remand by the appellate court or the granting of a motion under Rule 59.

The rule does not require that the motion be supported at the time of filing with the evidentiary material bearing on the fees. This material must of course be submitted in due course, according to such schedule as the court may direct in light of the circumstances of the case. What is required is the filing of a motion sufficient to alert the adversary and the court that there is a claim for fees and the amount of such fees (or a fair estimate).

If directed by the court, the moving party is also required to disclose any fee agreement, including those between attorney and client, between attorneys sharing a fee to be awarded, and between adversaries made in partial settlement of a dispute where the settlement must be implemented by court action as may be required by Rules 23(e) and 23.1 or other like provisions. With respect to the fee arrangements requiring court approval, the court may also by local rule require disclosure immediately after such arrangements are agreed to. *E.g.*, Rule 5 of United States District Court for the Eastern District of New York; *cf. In re "Agent Orange" Product Liability Litigation (MDL 381),* 611 F.Supp. 1452, 1464 (E.D.N.Y.1985).

In the settlement of class actions resulting in a common fund from which fees will be sought, courts frequently have required that claims for fees be presented in advance of hearings to consider approval of the proposed settlement. The rule does not affect this practice, as it permits the court to require submissions of fee claims in advance of entry of judgment.

Subparagraph (C) assures the parties of an opportunity to make an appropriate presentation with respect to issues involving the evaluation of legal services. In some cases, an evidentiary hearing may be needed, but this is not required in every case. The amount of time to be allowed for the preparation of submissions both in support of and in opposition to awards should be tailored to the particular case.

The court is explicitly authorized to make a determination of the liability for fees before receiving submissions by the parties bearing on the amount of an award. This option may be appropriate in actions in which the liability issue is doubtful and the evaluation issues are numerous and complex.

The court may order disclosure of additional information, such as that bearing on prevailing local rates or on the appropriateness of particular services for which compensation is sought.

On rare occasions, the court may determine that discovery under Rules 26–37 would be useful to the parties. *Compare* Rules Governing Section 2254 Cases in the U.S. District Courts, Rule 6. *See* Note, *Determining the Reasonableness of Attorneys' Fees—the Discoverability of Billing Records,* 64 *B.U.L.Rev.* 241 (1984). In complex fee disputes, the court may use case management techniques to limit the scope of the dispute or to facilitate the settlement of fee award disputes.

Fee awards should be made in the form of a separate judgment under Rule 58 since such awards are subject to review in the court of appeals. To facilitate review, the paragraph provides that the court set forth its findings and conclusions as under Rule 52(a), though in most cases this explanation could be quite brief.

Subparagraph (D) explicitly authorizes the court to establish procedures facilitating the efficient and fair resolution of fee claims. A local rule, for example, might call for matters to be presented through affidavits, or might provide for issuance of proposed findings by the court, which would be treated as accepted by the parties unless objected to within a specified time. A court might also consider establishing a schedule reflecting customary fees or factors affecting fees within the community, as implicitly suggested by Justice O'Connor in *Pennsylvania v. Delaware Valley Citizens' Council,* 483 U.S. 711, 733 (1987) (O'Connor, J., concurring) (how particular markets compensate for contingency). *Cf. Thompson v. Kennickell,* 710 F.Supp. 1 (D.D.C.1989) (use of findings in other cases to promote consistency). The parties, of course, should be permitted to show that in the circumstances of the case such a schedule should not be applied or that different hourly rates would be appropriate.

The rule also explicitly permits, without need for a local rule, the court to refer issues regarding the amount of a fee award in a particular case to a master under Rule 53. The district judge may designate a magistrate judge to act as a master for this purpose or may refer a motion for attorneys' fees to a magistrate judge for proposed findings and recommendations under Rule 72(b). This authorization eliminates any controversy as to whether such references are permitted under Rule 53(b) as "matters of account and of difficult computation of damages" and whether motions for attorneys' fees can be treated as the equivalent of a dispositive pretrial matter that can be referred to a magistrate judge. For consistency and efficiency, all such matters might be referred to the same magistrate judge.

Subparagraph (E) excludes from this rule the award of fees as sanctions under these rules or under 28 U.S.C. § 1927.

Rule 58. Entry of Judgment

Subject to the provisions of Rule 54(b): (1) upon a general verdict of a jury, or upon a decision by the court that a party shall recover only a sum certain or costs or that all relief shall be denied, the clerk, unless the court otherwise orders, shall forthwith prepare, sign, and enter the judgment without awaiting any direction by the court; (2) upon a decision by the court granting other relief, or upon a special verdict or a general verdict accompanied by answers to interrogatories, the court shall promptly approve the form of the judgment, and the clerk shall thereupon enter it. Every judgment shall be set forth on a separate document. A judgment is effective only when so set forth and when entered as provided in Rule 79(a). Entry of the judgment shall not be delayed ~~for the taxing of costs~~, *nor the time for appeal extended, in order to tax costs or award fees, except that, when a timely motion for attorneys' fees is made under Rule 54(d)(2), the court, before a notice of appeal has been filed and has become effective, may order that the motion have the same effect under Rule 4(a)(4) of the Federal Rules of Appellate Procedure as a timely motion under Rule 59.* Attor-

New matter is shown in italics; matter to be omitted is lined through

neys shall not submit forms of judgment except upon direction of the court, and these directions shall not be given as a matter of course.

Advisory Committee's Note

Ordinarily the pendency or post-judgment filing of a claim for attorney's fees will not affect the time for appeal from the underlying judgment. *See Budinich v. Becton Dickinson & Co.,* 486 U.S. 196 (1988). Particularly if the claim for fees involves substantial issues or is likely to be affected by the appellate decision, the district court may prefer to defer consideration of the claim for fees until after the appeal is resolved. However, in many cases it may be more efficient to decide fee questions before an appeal is taken so that appeals relating to the fee award can be heard at the same time as appeals relating to the merits of the case. This revision permits, but does not require, the court to delay the finality of the judgment for appellate purposes under revised Fed.R.App.P. 4(a) until the fee dispute is decided. To accomplish this result requires entry of an order by the district court before the time a notice of appeal becomes effective for appellate purposes. If the order is entered, the motion for attorney's fees is treated in the same manner as a timely motion under Rule 59.

Rule 71A. Condemnation of Property

(d) Process.

(3) Service of Notice.

(~~i~~*A*) Personal Service. Personal service of the notice (but without copies of the complaint) shall be made in accordance with Rule 4~~(c) and (d)~~ upon a defendant *whose residence is known and* who resides within the United States or ~~its territories or insular possessions and whose residence is known~~ *a territory subject to the administrative or judicial jurisdiction of the United States.*

(~~ii~~*B*) Service by Publication.

(4) Return; Amendment. Proof of service of the notice shall be made and amendment of the notice or proof of its service allowed in the manner provided for the return and amendment of the summons under Rule 4~~(g) and (h)~~.

Advisory Committee's Note

The references to the subdivisions of Rule 4 are deleted in light of the revision of that rule.

Rule 72. Magistrates *Judges*; Pretrial Orders

(a) Nondispositive Matters. A magistrate *judge* to whom a pretrial matter not dispositive of a claim or defense of a party is referred to hear and determine shall promptly conduct such proceedings as are required and when appropriate enter into the record a written order setting forth the disposition of the matter. Within 10 days after being served with a copy of the magistrate~~'s~~ *judge's* order, a party may serve and file objections to the order; a party may not thereafter assign as error a defect in the magistrate~~'s~~ *judge's* order to which objection was not timely made. The district judge to whom the case is assigned shall consider such objections and shall modify or set aside any portion of the magistrate~~'s~~ *judge's* order found to be clearly erroneous or contrary to law.

(b) Dispositive Motions and Prisoner Petitions. A magistrate *judge* assigned without consent of the parties to hear a pretrial matter dispositive of a claim or defense of a party or a prisoner petition challenging the conditions of confinement shall promptly conduct such proceedings as are required. A record shall be made of all evidentiary proceedings before the magistrate *judge,* and a record may be made of such other proceedings as the magistrate *judge* deems necessary. The magistrate *judge* shall enter into the record a recommendation for disposition of the matter, including proposed findings of fact when appropriate. The clerk shall forthwith mail copies to all parties.

A party objecting to the recommended disposition of the matter shall promptly arrange for the transcription of the record, or portions of it as all parties may agree upon or the magistrate *judge* deems sufficient, unless the district judge otherwise directs. Within 10 days after being served with a copy of the recommended disposition, a party may serve and file specific, written objections to the proposed findings and recommendations. A party may respond to another party's objections within 10 days after being served with a copy thereof. The district judge to whom the case is assigned shall make a de novo determination upon the record, or after additional evidence, of any portion of the magistrate~~'s~~ *judge's* disposition to which specific written objection has been made in accordance with this rule. The district judge may accept, reject, or modify the recommended decision, receive further evidence, or recommit the matter to the magistrate *judge* with instructions.

Advisory Committee's Note

This revision is made to conform the rule to changes made by the Judicial Improvements Act of 1990.

Rule 73. Magistrates *Judges*; Trial by Consent and Appeal Options

(a) Powers; Procedure. When specially designated to exercise such jurisdiction by local rule or order of the district court and when all parties consent thereto, a magistrate *judge* may exercise the authority provided by Title 28, U.S.C. § 636(c) and may conduct any or all proceedings, including a jury or nonjury trial, in a civil case. A record of the proceedings shall be made in accordance with the requirements of Title 28, U.S.C. § 636(c)(7).

(b) Consent. When a magistrate *judge* has been designated to exercise civil trial jurisdiction, the clerk shall give written notice to the parties of their opportunity to consent to the exercise by a magistrate *judge* of civil jurisdiction over the case, as authorized by Title 28, U.S.C. § 636(c). If, within the period specified by local rule, the parties agree to a magistrate~~'s~~ *judge's* exercise of such authority, they shall execute and file a joint form of consent or separate forms of consent setting forth such election.

~~No~~ *A* district judge, magistrate *judge,* or other court official ~~shall attempt to persuade or induce a party to consent to a reference of a civil matter to a magistrate under this rule, nor shall~~ *may again advise the parties of the availability of the magistrate judge, but, in so doing, shall also advise the parties that they are free to withhold consent without adverse substantive consequences.* ~~a~~*A* district judge or magistrate *judge shall not* be informed of a party's response to the clerk's notification, unless all parties have consented to the referral of the matter to a magistrate *judge.*

The district judge, for good cause shown on the judge's ~~motion~~ *own initiative,* or under extraordinary circumstances shown by a party, may vacate a reference of a civil matter to a magistrate *judge* under this subdivision.

(c) Normal Appeal Route. In accordance with Title 28, U.S.C. § 636(c)(3), unless the parties otherwise agree to the optional appeal route provided for in subdivision (d) of this rule, appeal from a judgment entered upon direction of a magistrate *judge* in proceedings under this rule will lie to the court of appeals as it would from a judgment of the district court.

(d) Optional Appeal Route. In accordance with Title 28, U.S.C. § 636(c)(4), at the time of reference to a magistrate *judge,* the parties may consent to appeal on the record to a *district* judge of the ~~district~~ court and thereafter, by petition only, to the court of appeals.

Advisory Committee's Note

This revision is made to conform the rule to changes made by the Judicial Improvements Act of 1990. The Act requires that, when being reminded of the availability of a magistrate judge, the parties be advised that withholding of consent will have no "adverse substantive consequences." They may, however, be advised if the withholding of consent will have the adverse procedural consequence of a potential delay in trial.

New matter is shown in italics; matter to be omitted is lined through

Rule 74. Method of Appeal From Magistrate *Judge* to District Judge Under Title 28, U.S.C. § 636(c)(4) and Rule 73(d)

(a) When Taken. When the parties have elected under Rule 73(d) to proceed by appeal to a district judge from an appealable decision made by a magistrate *judge* under the consent provisions of Title 28, U.S.C. § 636(c)(4), an appeal may be taken from the decision of a magistrate *judge* by filing with the clerk of the district court a notice of appeal within 30 days of the date of entry of the judgment appealed from; but if the United States or an officer or agency thereof is a party, the notice of appeal may be filed by any party within 60 days of such entry. If a timely notice of appeal is filed by a party, any other party may file a notice of appeal within 14 days thereafter, or within the time otherwise prescribed by this subdivision, whichever period last expires.

The running of the time for filing a notice of appeal is terminated as to all parties by the timely filing of any of the following motions with the magistrate *judge* by any party, and the full time for appeal from the judgment entered by the magistrate *judge* commences to run anew from entry of any of the following orders: (1) granting or denying a motion for judgment under Rule 50(b); (2) granting or denying a motion under Rule 52(b) to amend or make additional findings of fact, whether or not an alteration of the judgment would be required if the motion is granted; (3) granting or denying a motion under Rule 59 to alter or amend the judgment; (4) denying a motion for a new trial under Rule 59.

An interlocutory decision or order by a magistrate *judge* which, if made by a *district* judge ~~of the district court~~, could be appealed under any provision of law, may be appealed to a *district* judge ~~of the district court~~ by filing a notice of appeal within 15 days after entry of the decision or order, provided the parties have elected to appeal to a *district* judge ~~of the district court~~ under Rule 73(d). An appeal of such interlocutory decision or order shall not stay the proceedings before the magistrate *judge* unless the magistrate *judge* or *district* judge shall so order.

Upon a showing of excusable neglect, the magistrate *judge* may extend the time for filing a notice of appeal upon motion filed not later than 20 days after the expiration of the time otherwise prescribed by this rule.

(c) Stay Pending Appeal. Upon a showing that the magistrate *judge* has refused or otherwise failed to stay the judgment pending appeal to the district judge under Rule 73(d), the appellant

New matter is shown in italics; matter to be omitted is lined through

may make application for a stay to the district judge with reasonable notice to all parties. The stay may be conditioned upon the filing in the district court of a bond or other appropriate security.

Advisory Committee's Note

This revision is made to conform the rule to changes made by the Judicial Improvements Act of 1990.

Rule 75. Proceedings on Appeal From Magistrate *Judge* to District Judge Under Rule 73(d)

(b) Record on Appeal.

(1) Composition. The original papers and exhibits filed with the clerk of the district court, the transcript of the proceedings, if any, and the docket entries shall constitute the record on appeal. In lieu of this record the parties, within 10 days after the filing of the notice of appeal, may file a joint statement of the case showing how the issues presented by the appeal arose and were decided by the magistrate *judge,* and setting forth only so many of the facts averred and proved or sought to be proved as are essential to a decision of the issues presented.

(2) Transcript. Within 10 days after filing the notice of appeal the appellant shall make arrangements for the production of a transcript of such parts of the proceedings as the appellant deems necessary. Unless the entire transcript is to be included, the appellant, within the time provided above, shall serve on the appellee and file with the court a description of the parts of the transcript which the appellant intends to present on the appeal. If the appellee deems a transcript of other parts of the proceedings to be necessary, within 10 days after the service of the statement of the appellant, the appellee shall serve on the appellant and file with the court a designation of additional parts to be included. The appellant shall promptly make arrangements for the inclusion of all such parts unless the magistrate *judge,* upon motion, exempts the appellant from providing certain parts, in which case the appellee may provide for their transcription.

(3) Statement in Lieu of Transcript. If no record of the proceedings is available for transcription, the parties shall, within 10 days after the filing of the notice of appeal, file a statement of the evidence from the best available means to be submitted in lieu of the transcript. If the parties cannot agree they shall submit a statement of their differences to the magistrate *judge* for settlement.

Advisory Committee's Note

This revision is made to conform the rule to changes made by the Judicial Improvements Act of 1990.

Rule 76. Judgment of the District Judge on the Appeal Under Rule 73(d) and Costs

(a) Entry of Judgment. When the parties have elected under Rule 73(d) to appeal from a judgment of the magistrate *judge* to a district judge, the clerk shall prepare, sign, and enter judgment in accordance with the order or decision of the district judge following an appeal from a judgment of the magistrate *judge,* unless the district judge directs otherwise. The clerk shall mail to all parties a copy of the order or decision of the district judge.

(c) Costs. Except as otherwise provided by law or ordered by the district judge, costs shall be taxed against the losing party; if a judgment of the magistrate *judge* is affirmed in part or reversed in part, or is vacated, costs shall be allowed only as ordered by the district judge. The cost of the transcript, if necessary for the determination of the appeal, and the premiums paid for bonds to preserve rights pending appeal shall be taxed as costs by the clerk.

Advisory Committee's Note

This revision is made to conform the rule to changes made by the Judicial Improvements Act of 1990.

CERTAIN OF THE AMENDMENTS OF FEDERAL RULES OF CIVIL PROCEDURE ADOPTED BY THE SUPREME COURT OF THE UNITED STATES ON APRIL 17, 2000, EFFECTIVE DECEMBER 1, 2000, WITH ADVISORY COMMITTEE'S NOTES THEREON

[*Amendments here omitted: Changes in Supplemental Rules B, C, and E.*]

Rule 4. Summons

(i) Serv*ing*~~ce Upon~~ the United States, ~~and~~ Its Agencies, Corporations, ~~or~~ Officers, *or Employees*.

(2)(A) Service ~~upon~~ *on* an ~~officer,~~ agency~~;~~ or corporation of the United States, *or an officer or employee of the United States sued only in an official capacity,* ~~shall be~~ *is* effected by serving the United States in the manner prescribed by ~~paragraph (1) of this subdivision~~ *Rule 4(i)(1)* and by also sending a copy of the summons and ~~of the~~ complaint by registered or certified mail to the officer, *employee,* agency, or corporation.

(B) Service on an officer or employee of the United States sued in an individual capacity for acts or omissions occurring in connection with the performance of duties on behalf of the United States—whether or not the officer or employee is sued also in an official capacity—is effected by serving the United States in the manner prescribed by Rule 4(i)(1) and by serving the officer or employee in the manner prescribed by Rule 4(e), (f), or (g).

(3) The court shall allow a reasonable time ~~for~~ *to* serv*e*~~ice of~~ process under ~~this subdivision~~ *Rule 4(i)* for the purpose of curing the failure to serve:

(A) all persons required to be served in an action governed by Rule 4(i)(2)(A), ~~multiple officers. agencies, or corporations of the United States~~ if the plaintiff has ~~effected service on~~ *served* either the United States attorney or the Attorney General of the United States, *or*

(B) the United States in an action governed by Rule 4(i)(2)(B), if the plaintiff has served an officer or employee of the United States sued in an individual capacity.

New matter is shown in italics; matter to be omitted is lined through

Advisory Committee's Note

Paragraph (2)(B) is added to Rule 4(i) to require service on the United States when a United States officer or employee is sued in an individual capacity for acts or omissions occurring in connection with duties performed on behalf of the United States. Decided cases provide uncertain guidance on the question whether the United States must be served in such actions. *See Vaccaro v. Dobre*, 81 F.3d 854, 856–857 (9th Cir. 1996); *Armstrong v. Sears*, 33 F.3d 182, 185–187 (2d Cir. 1994); *Ecclesiastical Order of the Ism of Am v. Chasin*, 845 F.2d 113, 116 (6th Cir.1988); *Light v. Wolf*, 816 F.2d 746 (D.C. Cir. 1987); *see also Simpkins v. District of Columbia*, 108 F.3d 366, 368–369 (D.C.Cir. 1997). Service on the United States will help to protect the interest of the individual defendant in securing representation by the United States, and will expedite the process of determining whether the United States will provide representation. It has been understood that the individual defendant must be served as an individual defendant, a requirement that is made explicit. Invocation of the individual service provisions of subdivisions (e), (f), and (g) invokes also the waiver-of-service provisions of subdivision (d).

Paragraph 2(B) reaches service when an officer or employee of the United States is sued in an individual capacity "for acts or omissions occurring in connection with the performance of duties on behalf of the United States." This phrase has been chosen as a functional phrase that can be applied without the occasionally distracting associations of such phrases as "scope of employment," "color of office," or "arising out of the employment." Many actions are brought against individual federal officers or employees of the United States for acts or omissions that have no connection whatever to their governmental roles. There is no reason to require service on the United States in these actions. The connection to federal employment that requires service on the United States must be determined as a practical matter, considering whether the individual defendant has reasonable grounds to look to the United States for assistance and whether the United States has reasonable grounds for demanding formal notice of the action.

An action against a former officer or employee of the United States is covered by paragraph (2)(B) in the same way as an action against a present officer or employee. Termination of the relationship between the individual defendant and the United States does not reduce the need to serve the United States.

Paragraph (3) is amended to ensure that failure to serve the United States in an action governed by paragraph 2(B) does not defeat an action. This protection is adopted because there will be cases in which the plaintiff reasonably fails to appreciate the need to serve the United States. There is no requirement, however, that the plaintiff show that the failure to serve the United States was reasonable. A reasonable time to effect service on the United States must be allowed after the failure is pointed out. An additional change ensures that if the United States or United States attorney is served in an action governed by paragraph 2(A), additional time is to be allowed even though no officer, employee, agency, or corporation of the United States was served.

Rule 5. Serv*ing*~~ice~~ and Filing of Pleadings and Other Papers

(d) Filing; Certificate of Service. All papers after the complaint required to be served upon a party, together with a certificate of service, ~~shall~~ *must* be filed with the court within a reasonable time after service, but *disclosures under Rule 26(a)(1) or (2)* *and the following discovery requests and responses must not be filed until they are used in the proceeding or the court orders filing: (i) depositions, (ii) interrogatories, (iii) requests for documents or to permit entry upon land, and (iv) requests for admission* ~~the court may on motion of a party or on its own initiative order that depositions upon oral examination and interrogatories, requests for documents, requests for admission, and answers and responses thereto not be filed unless on order of the court or for use in the proceeding~~.

Advisory Committee's Note

Subdivision (d). Rule 5(d) is amended to provide that disclosures under Rule 26(a)(1) and (2), and discovery requests and responses under Rules 30, 31, 33, 34, and 36 must not be filed until they are used in the action. "Discovery requests" includes deposition notices and "discovery responses" includes objections. The rule supersedes and invalidates local rules that forbid, permit, or require filing of these materials before they are used in the action. The former Rule 26(a)(4) requirement that disclosures under Rule 26(a)(1) and (2) be filed has been removed. Disclosures under Rule 26(a)(3), however, must be promptly filed as provided in Rule 26(a)(3). Filings in connection with Rule 35 examinations, which involve a motion proceeding when the parties do not agree, are unaffected by these amendments.

Recognizing the costs imposed on parties and courts by required filing of discovery materials that are never used in an action, Rule 5(d) was amended in 1980 to authorize court orders that excuse filing. Since then, many districts have adopted local rules that excuse or forbid filing. In 1989 the Judicial Conference Local Rules Project concluded that these local rules were inconsistent with Rule 5(d), but urged the Advisory Committee to consider amending the rule. *Local Rules Project* at 92 (1989). The Judicial Conference of the Ninth Circuit gave the Committee similar advice in 1997. The reality of nonfiling reflected in these local rules has even been assumed in drafting the national rules. In 1993, Rule 30(f)(1) was amended to direct that the officer presiding at a deposition file it with the court or send it to the attorney who arranged for the transcript or recording. The Committee Note explained that this alternative to filing was designed for "courts which direct that depositions not be automatically filed." Rule 30(f)(1) has been amended to conform to this change in Rule 5(d).

Although this amendment is based on widespread experience with local rules, and confirms the results directed by these local rules, it is designed to supersede and invalidate local rules. There is no apparent reason to have different filing rules in different districts. Even if districts vary in present capacities to store filed materials that are not used in an action, there is little reason to continue expending court resources for this purpose. These costs and burdens would likely change as parties make increased use of audio-and videotaped depositions. Equipment to facilitate review and reproduction of such discovery materials may prove costly to acquire, maintain, and operate.

The amended rule provides that discovery materials and disclosures under Rule 26(a)(1) and (a)(2) must not be filed until they are "used in the proceeding." This phrase is meant to refer to proceedings in court. This filing requirement is not triggered by "use" of discovery materials in other discovery activities, such as depositions. In connection with proceedings in court, however, the rule is to be interpreted broadly; any use of discovery materials in court in connection with a motion, a pretrial conference under Rule 16, or otherwise, should be interpreted as use in the proceeding.

Once discovery or disclosure materials are used in the proceeding, the filing requirements of Rule 5(d) should apply to them. But because the filing requirement applies only with regard to materials that are used, only those parts of voluminous materials that are actually used need be filed. Any party would be free to file other pertinent portions of materials that are so used. *See* Fed. R. Evid. 106; *cf.* Rule 32(a)(4). If the parties are unduly sparing in their submissions, the court may order further filings. By local rule, a court could provide appropriate direction regarding the filing of discovery materials, such as depositions, that are used in proceedings.

"Shall" is replaced by "must" under the program to conform amended rules to current style conventions when there is no ambiguity.

Rule 12. Defenses and Objections—When and How Presented—By Pleading or Motion—Motion for Judgment on the Pleadings

(a) When Presented.

(3)*(A)* The United States, *an agency of the United States,* or an officer or ~~agency thereof~~ *employee of the United States sued in an official capacity,* shall serve an answer to the complaint or ~~to a~~ cross-claim~~,~~ — or a reply to a counterclaim~~,~~ — within 60 days after ~~the service upon~~ the United States attorney *is served with* of the pleading ~~in which~~ *asserting* the claim ~~is asserted~~.

(B) An officer or employee of the United States sued in an individual capacity for acts or omissions occurring in connection with the performance of duties on behalf of the United States shall serve an answer to the complaint or cross-claim—or a reply to a counterclaim—within 60 days after service on the officer or employee, or service on the United States attorney, whichever is later.

Advisory Committee's Note

Rule 12(a)(3)(B) is added to complement the addition of Rule 4(i)(2)(B). The purposes that underlie the requirement that service be made on the United States in an action that asserts individual liability of a United States officer or employee for acts occurring in connection with the performance of duties on behalf of the United States also require that the time to answer be extended to 60 days. Time is needed for the United States to determine whether to provide representation to the defendant officer or employee. If the United States provides representation, the need for an extended answer period is the same as in actions against the United States, a United States agency, or a United States officer sued in an official capacity.

An action against a former officer or employee of the United States is covered by subparagraph (3)(B) in the same way as an action against a present officer or employee. Termination of the relationship between the individual defendant and the United States does not reduce the need for additional time to answer.

Rule 14. Third–Party Practice

(a) When Defendant May Bring in Third Party. At any time after commencement of the action a defending party, as a third-party plaintiff, may cause a summons and complaint to be served upon a person not a party to the action who is or may be liable to the third-party plaintiff for all or part of the plaintiff's claim against the third-party plaintiff. The third-party plaintiff need not obtain leave to make the service if the third-party plaintiff files the third-party complaint not later than 10 days after serving the original answer. Otherwise the third-party plaintiff must obtain leave on motion upon notice to all parties to the action. The person served with the summons and third-party complaint, hereinafter called the third-party defendant, shall make any defenses to the third-party plaintiff's claim as provided in Rule 12 and any counterclaims against the third-party plaintiff and cross-claims against other third-party defendants as provided in Rule 13. The third-party defendant may assert against the plaintiff any defenses which the third-party plaintiff has to the plaintiff's claim. The third-party defendant may also assert any claim against the plaintiff arising out of the transaction or occurrence that is the subject matter of the plaintiff's claim against the third-party plaintiff. The plaintiff may assert any claim against the third-party defendant arising out of the transaction or occurrence that is the subject matter of the plaintiff's claim against the third-party plaintiff, and the third-party defendant thereupon shall assert any defenses as provided in Rule 12 and any counterclaims and cross-claims as provided in Rule 13. Any party may move to strike the third-party claim, or for its severance or separate trial. A third-party defendant may proceed under this rule against any person not a party to the action who is or may be liable to the third-party defendant for all or part of the claim made in the action against the third-party defendant. The third-party complaint, if within the admiralty and maritime jurisdiction, may be in rem against a vessel, cargo, or other property subject to admiralty or maritime process in rem, in which case references in this rule to the summons include the warrant of arrest, and references to the third-party plaintiff or defendant include, where appropriate, ~~the claimant of~~ *a person who asserts a right under Supplemental Rule C(6)(b)(i) in* the property arrested.

(c) Admiralty and Maritime Claims. When a plaintiff asserts an admiralty or maritime claim within the meaning of Rule 9(h), the defendant or ~~claimant~~ *person who asserts a right under Supplemental Rule C(6)(b)(i)*, as a third-party plaintiff, may bring in a third-party defendant who may be wholly or partly liable,

New matter is shown in italics; matter to be omitted is lined through

either to the plaintiff or to the third-party plaintiff, by way of remedy over, contribution, or otherwise on account of the same transaction, occurrence, or series of transactions or occurrences. In such a case the third-party plaintiff may also demand judgment against the third-party defendant in favor of the plaintiff, in which event the third-party defendant shall make any defenses to the claim of the plaintiff as well as to that of the third-party plaintiff in the manner provided in Rule 12 and the action shall proceed as if the plaintiff had commenced it against the third-party defendant as well as the third-party plaintiff.

Advisory Committee's Note

Subdivisions (a) and (c) are amended to reflect revisions in Supplemental Rule C(6).

Rule 26. General Provisions Governing Discovery; Duty of Disclosure

(a) Required Disclosures; Methods to Discover Additional Matter.

(1) *Initial Disclosures.* Except *in categories of proceedings specified in Rule 26(a)(1)(E), or* to the extent otherwise stipulated or directed by order ~~or local rule~~, a party ~~shall~~ *must*, without awaiting a discovery request, provide to other parties:

(A) the name and, if known, the address and telephone number of each individual likely to have discoverable information *that the disclosing party may use to support its claims or defenses, unless solely for impeachment* ~~relevant to disputed facts alleged with particularity in the pleadings~~, identifying the subjects of the information;

(B) a copy of, or a description by category and location of, all documents, data compilations, and tangible things *that are* in the possession, custody, or control of the party *and that the disclosing party may use to support its claims or defenses, unless solely for impeachment* ~~that are relevant to disputed facts alleged with particularity in the pleadings~~;

(C) a computation of any category of damages claimed by the disclosing party, making available for inspection and copying as under Rule 34 the documents or other evidentiary material, not privileged or protected from disclosure, on which such computation is based, including materials bearing on the nature and extent of injuries suffered; and

(D) for inspection and copying as under Rule 34 any insurance agreement under which any person carrying on an

New matter is shown in italics; matter to be omitted is lined through

insurance business may be liable to satisfy part or all of a judgment which may be entered in the action or to indemnify or reimburse for payments made to satisfy the judgment.

(E) The following categories of proceedings are exempt from initial disclosure under Rule 26(a)(1):

(i) an action for review on an administrative record;

(ii) a petition for habeas corpus or other proceeding to challenge a criminal conviction or sentence;

(iii) an action brought without counsel by a person in custody of the United States, a state, or a state subdivision;

(iv) an action to enforce or quash an administrative summons or subpoena;

(v) an action by the United States to recover benefit payments;

(vi) an action by the United States to collect on a student loan guaranteed by the United States;

(vii) a proceeding ancillary to proceedings in other courts; and

(viii) an action to enforce an arbitration award.

~~Unless otherwise stipulated or directed by the court,~~ *T*~~t~~hese disclosures *must* ~~shall~~ be made at or within *14* ~~10~~ days after the *Rule 26(f) conference* ~~meeting of the parties under subdivision (f).~~ *unless a different time is set by stipulation or court order, or unless a party objects during the conference that initial disclosures are not appropriate in the circumstances of the action and states the objection in the Rule 26(f) discovery plan. In ruling on the objection, the court must determine what disclosures—if any—are to be made, and set the time for disclosure. Any party first served or otherwise joined after the Rule 26(f) conference must make these disclosures within 30 days after being served or joined unless a different time is set by stipulation or court order.* A party *must* ~~shall~~ make its initial disclosures based on the information then reasonably available to it and is not excused from making its disclosures because it has not fully completed its investigation of the case or because it challenges the sufficiency of another party's disclosures or because another party has not made its disclosures.

(3) *Pretrial Disclosures.* In addition to the disclosures required *by Rule 26(a)(1) and (2)* ~~in the preceding paragraphs~~, a party ~~shall~~ *must* provide to other parties *and promptly file with the court* the following information regarding the evidence that it may present at trial other than solely for impeachment ~~purposes~~:

New matter is shown in italics; matter to be omitted is lined through

(A) the name and, if not previously provided, the address and telephone number of each witness, separately identifying those whom the party expects to present and those whom the party may call if the need arises;

(B) the designation of those witnesses whose testimony is expected to be presented by means of a deposition and, if not taken stenographically, a transcript of the pertinent portions of the deposition testimony; and

(C) an appropriate identification of each document or other exhibit, including summaries of other evidence, separately identifying those which the party expects to offer and those which the party may offer if the need arises.

Unless otherwise directed by the court, these disclosures ~~shall~~ *must* be made at least 30 days before trial. Within 14 days thereafter, unless a different time is specified by the court, a party may serve and *promptly* file a list disclosing (i) any objections to the use under Rule 32(a) of a deposition designated by another party under ~~subparagraph (B)~~ *Rule 26(a)(3)(B),* and (ii) any objection, together with the grounds therefor, that may be made to the admissibility of materials identified under ~~subparagraph (C)~~ *Rule 26(a)(3)(C).* Objections not so disclosed, other than objections under Rules 402 and 403 of the Federal Rules of Evidence, ~~shall be deemed~~ *are* waived unless excused by the court for good cause ~~shown~~.

(4) *Form of Disclosures*~~; Filing~~. Unless *the court orders* otherwise ~~directed by order or local rule~~, all disclosures under ~~paragraphs~~ *Rules 26(a)*(1) through (3) *must* ~~shall~~ be made in writing, signed, *and* served.~~, and promptly filed with the court.~~

(b) Discovery Scope and Limits. Unless otherwise limited by order of the court in accordance with these rules. the scope of discovery is as follows:

(1) *In General.* Parties may obtain discovery regarding any matter, not privileged, *that* ~~which~~ is relevant to ~~the subject matter involved in the pending action, whether it relates to~~ the claim or defense of ~~the party seeking discovery or to the claim or defense of~~ any ~~other~~ party, including the existence, description, nature, custody, condition, and location of any books, documents, or other tangible things and the identity and location of persons having knowledge of any discoverable matter. *For good cause, the court may order discovery of any matter relevant to the subject matter involved in the action. Relevant* ~~The~~ information ~~sought~~ need not be admissible at the trial if the *discovery* ~~information sought~~ appears reasonably calculated to lead to the discovery of admissible evidence. *All discovery is*

subject to the limitations imposed by Rule 26(b)(2)(i), (ii), and (iii).

(2) *Limitations.* By order ~~or by local rule~~, the court may alter the limits in these rules on the number of depositions and interrogatories, *or* ~~and may also limit~~ the length of depositions under Rule 30. ~~and~~ *By order or local rule, the court may also limit* the number of requests under Rule 36. The frequency or extent of use of the discovery methods otherwise permitted under these rules and by any local rule shall be limited by the court if it determines that: (i) the discovery sought is unreasonably cumulative or duplicative, or is obtainable from some other source that is more convenient, less burdensome, or less expensive; (ii) the party seeking discovery has had ample opportunity by discovery in the action to obtain the information sought; or (iii) the burden or expense of the proposed discovery outweighs its likely benefit, taking into account the needs of the case, the amount in controversy, the parties' resources, the importance of the issues at stake in the litigation, and the importance of the proposed discovery in resolving the issues. The court may act upon its own initiative after reasonable notice or pursuant to a motion under ~~subdivision~~ *Rule 26*(c).

(d) Timing and Sequence of Discovery. Except *in categories of proceedings exempted from initial disclosure under Rule 26(a)(1)(E), or* when authorized under these rules or by ~~local rule,~~ order~~,~~ or agreement of the parties, a party may not seek discovery from any source before the parties have ~~met and~~ conferred as required by ~~subdivision~~ *Rule 26*(f). Unless the court upon motion, for the convenience of parties and witnesses and in the interests of justice, orders otherwise, methods of discovery may be used in any sequence, and the fact that a party is conducting discovery, whether by deposition or otherwise, ~~shall~~ *does* not operate to delay any other party's discovery.

(f) Conference ~~Meeting~~ of Parties; Planning for Discovery. Except in *categories of proceedings* ~~actions~~ exempted *from initial disclosure under Rule 26(a)(1)(E)* ~~by local rule~~ or when otherwise ordered, the parties ~~shall~~ *must,* as soon as practicable and in any event at least *21* ~~14~~ days before a scheduling conference is held or a scheduling order is due under Rule 16(b), *confer* ~~meet~~ to *consider* ~~discuss~~ the nature and basis of their claims and defenses and the possibilities for a prompt settlement or resolution of the case, to make or arrange for the disclosures required by ~~subdivision~~ *Rule 26*(a)(1), and to develop a proposed discovery plan~~. The plan shall~~ *that* indicates the parties' views and proposals concerning:

(1) what changes should be made in the timing, form, or requirement for disclosures under ~~subdivision~~ *Rule 26*(a) ~~or local rule~~, including a statement as to when disclosures under ~~subdivision~~ *Rule 26*(a)(1) were made or will be made;

(2) the subjects on which discovery may be needed, when discovery should be completed, and whether discovery should be conducted in phases or be limited to or focused upon particular issues;

(3) what changes should be made in the limitations on discovery imposed under these rules or by local rule, and what other limitations should be imposed; and

(4) any other orders that should be entered by the court under ~~subdivision~~ *Rule 26*(c) or under Rule 16(b) and (c).

The attorneys of record and all unrepresented parties that have appeared in the case are jointly responsible for arranging *the conference* ~~and being present or represented at the meeting~~, for attempting in good faith to agree on the proposed discovery plan, and for submitting to the court within *14*~~10~~ days after the *conference* ~~meeting~~ a written report outlining the plan. *A court may order that the parties or attorneys attend the conference in person. If necessary to comply with its expedited schedule for Rule 16(b) conferences, a court may by local rule (i) require that the conference between the parties occur fewer than 21 days before the scheduling conference is held or a scheduling order is due under Rule 16(b), and (ii) require that the written report outlining the discovery plan be filed fewer than 14 days after the conference between the parties, or excuse the parties from submitting a written report and permit them to report orally on their discovery plan at the Rule 16(b) conference.*

Advisory Committee's Note

Purposes of amendments. The Rule 26(a)(1) initial disclosure provisions are amended to establish a nationally uniform practice. The scope of the disclosure obligation is narrowed to cover only information that the disclosing party may use to support its position. In addition, the rule exempts specified categories of proceedings from initial disclosure, and permits a party who contends that disclosure is not appropriate in the circumstances of the case to present its objections to the court, which must then determine whether disclosure should be made. Related changes are made in Rules 26(d) and (f).

The initial disclosure requirements added by the 1993 amendments permitted local rules directing that disclosure would not be required or altering its operation. The inclusion of the "opt out" provision reflected the strong opposition to initial disclosure felt in some districts, and permitted experimentation with differing disclosure rules in those districts that were favorable to disclosure. The local option also recognized that—partly in response to the first publication in 1991 of a proposed disclosure rule—many districts had adopted a variety of disclosure programs under the aegis of the Civil Justice Reform Act. It was hoped that developing experience under a variety of disclosure systems would support eventual refinement of a uniform national disclosure practice. In addition, there was hope that local experience could identify categories of actions in which disclosure is not useful.

A striking array of local regimes in fact emerged for disclosure and related features introduced in 1993. *See* D. Stienstra. *Implementation of Disclosure in United States District Courts, With Specific Attention to Courts' Responses to Selected Amendments to Federal Rule of Civil Procedure 26* (Federal Judicial Center, March 30, 1998) (describing and categorizing local regimes). In its final report to Congress on the CJRA experience, the Judicial Conference recommended reexamination of the need for national uniformity, particularly in regard to initial disclosure. Judicial Conference, *Alternative Proposals for Reduction of Cost and Delay: Assessment of Principles, Guidelines and Techniques,* 175 F.R.D. 62, 98 (1997).

At the Committee's request, the Federal Judicial Center undertook a survey in 1997 to develop information on current disclosure and discovery practices. *See* T. Willging, J. Shapard, D. Stienstra & D. Miletich, *Discovery and Disclosure Practice, Problems, and Proposals for Change* (Federal Judicial Center, 1997). In addition, the Committee convened two conferences on discovery involving lawyers from around the country and received reports and recommendations on possible discovery amendments from a number of bar groups. Papers and other proceedings from the second conference are published in 39 Boston Col. L. Rev. 517–840 (1998).

The Committee has discerned widespread support for national uniformity. Many lawyers have experienced difficulty in coping with divergent disclosure and other practices as they move from one district to another. Lawyers surveyed by the Federal Judicial Center ranked adoption of a uniform national disclosure rule second among proposed rule changes (behind increased availability of judges to resolve discovery disputes) as a means to reduce litigation expenses without interfering with fair outcomes. *Discovery and Disclosure Practice, supra,* at 44–45. National uniformity is also a central purpose of the Rules Enabling Act of 1934, as amended, 28 U.S.C. §§ 2072–2077.

These amendments restore national uniformity to disclosure practice. Uniformity is also restored to other aspects of discovery by deleting most of the provisions authorizing local rules that vary the number of permitted discovery events or the length of depositions. Local rule options are also deleted from Rules 26(d) and (f).

Subdivision(a)(1). The amendments remove the authority to alter or opt out of the national disclosure requirements by local rule, invalidating not only formal local rules but also informal "standing" orders of an individual judge or court that purport to create exemptions from—or limit or expand—the disclosure provided under the national rule. *See* Rule 83. Case-specific orders remain proper, however, and are expressly required if a party objects that initial disclosure is not appropriate in the circumstances of the action. Specified categories of proceedings are excluded from initial disclosure under subdivision (a)(1)(E). In addition, the parties can stipulate to forgo disclosure, as was true before. But even in a case excluded by subdivision (a)(1)(E) or in which the parties stipulate to bypass disclosure, the court can order exchange of similar information in managing the action under Rule 16.

The initial disclosure obligation of subdivisions (a)(1)(A) and (B) has been narrowed to identification of witnesses and documents that the disclosing party may use to support its claims or defenses. "Use" includes any use at a pretrial conference, to support a motion, or at trial. The disclosure obligation is also triggered by intended use in discovery, apart from use to respond to a discovery request; use of a document to question a witness during a deposition is a common example. The disclosure obligation attaches both to witnesses and documents a party intends to use and also to witnesses and to documents the party intends to use if—in the language of Rule 26(a)(3)—"the need arises."

A party is no longer obligated to disclose witnesses or documents, whether favorable or unfavorable, that it does not intend to use. The obligation to disclose information the party may use connects directly to the exclusion sanction of Rule 37(c)(1). Because the disclosure obligation is limited to material that the party may use, it is no longer tied to particularized allegations in the pleadings. Subdivision (e)(1), which is unchanged, requires supplementation if information later acquired would have been subject to the disclosure requirement. As case preparation continues, a party must supplement its disclosures when it determines that it may use a witness or document that it did not previously intend to use.

The disclosure obligation applies to "claims and defenses," and therefore requires a party to disclose information it may use to support its denial or rebuttal of the allegations, claim, or defense of another party. It thereby bolsters the requirements of Rule 11(b)(4), which authorizes denials "warranted on the evidence," and disclosure should include the identity of any witness or document that the disclosing party may use to support such denials.

Subdivision (a)(3) presently excuses pretrial disclosure of information solely for impeachment. Impeachment information is similarly excluded from the initial disclosure requirement.

Subdivisions (a)(1)(C) and (D) are not changed. Should a case be exempted from initial disclosure by Rule 26(a)(1)(E) or by agreement or order, the insurance information described by subparagraph (D) should be subject to discovery, as it would have been under the principles of former Rule 26(b)(2), which was added in 1970 and deleted in 1993 as redundant in light of the new initial disclosure obligation.

New subdivision (a)(1)(E) excludes eight specified categories of proceedings from initial disclosure. The objective of this listing is to identify cases in which there is likely to be little or no discovery, or in which initial disclosure appears unlikely to contribute to the effective development of the case. The list was developed after a review of the categories excluded by local rules in various districts from the operation of Rule 16(b) and the conference requirements of subdivision (f). Subdivision (a)(1)(E) refers to categories of "proceedings" rather than categories of "actions" because some might not properly be labeled "actions." Case designations made by the parties or the clerk's office at the time of filing do not control application of the exemptions. The descriptions in the rule are generic and are intended to be administered by the parties—and, when needed, the courts—with the flexibility needed to adapt to gradual evolution in the types of proceedings that fall within these general categories. The exclusion of an action for review on an administrative record, for example, is intended to reach a proceeding that is framed as an "appeal" based solely on an administrative record. The exclusion should not apply to a proceeding in a form that commonly permits admission of new evidence to supplement the record. Item (vii), excluding a proceeding ancillary to proceedings in other courts, does not refer to bankruptcy proceedings; application of the Civil Rules to bankruptcy proceedings is determined by the Bankruptcy Rules.

Subdivision (a)(1)(E) is likely to exempt a substantial proportion of the cases in most districts from the initial disclosure requirement. Based on 1996 and 1997 case filing statistics, Federal Judicial Center staff estimate that, nationwide, these categories total approximately one-third of all civil filings.

The categories of proceedings listed in subdivision (a)(1)(E) are also exempted from the subdivision (f) conference requirement and from the subdivision (d) moratorium on discovery. Although there is no restriction on commencement of discovery in these cases, it is not expected that this opportunity will often lead to abuse since there is likely to be little or no discovery in most such cases. Should a defendant need more time to respond to discovery requests filed at the beginning of an exempted action, it can seek relief by motion under Rule 26(c) if the plaintiff is unwilling to defer the due date by agreement.

Subdivision (a)(1)(E)'s enumeration of exempt categories is exclusive. Although a case-specific order can alter or excuse initial disclosure, local rules or "standing" orders that purport to create general exemptions are invalid. *See* Rule 83.

The time for initial disclosure is extended to 14 days after the subdivision (f) conference unless the court orders otherwise. This change is integrated with corresponding changes requiring that the subdivision (f) conference be held 21 days before the Rule 16(b) scheduling conference or scheduling order, and that the report on the subdivision (f) conference be submitted to the court 14 days after the meeting. These changes provide a more orderly opportunity for the parties to review the disclosures, and for the court to consider the report. In many instances, the subdivision (f) conference and the effective preparation of the case would benefit from disclosure before the conference, and earlier disclosure is encouraged.

The presumptive disclosure date does not apply if a party objects to initial disclosure during the subdivision (f) conference and states its objection in the subdivision (f) discovery plan. The right to object to initial disclosure is not intended to afford parties an opportunity to "opt out" of disclosure unilaterally. It does provide an opportunity for an objecting party to present to the court its position that disclosure would be "inappropriate in the circumstances of the action." Making the objection permits the objecting party to present the question to the judge before any party is required to make disclosure. The court must then rule on the objection and determine what disclosures—if any—should be made. Ordinarily, this determination would be included in the Rule 16(b) scheduling order, but the court could handle the matter in a different fashion. Even when circumstances warrant suspending some disclosure obligations, others—such as the damages and insurance information called for by subdivisions (a)(1)(C) and (D)—may continue to be appropriate.

The presumptive disclosure date is also inapplicable to a party who is "first served or otherwise joined" after the subdivision (f) conference. This phrase refers to the date of service of a claim on a party in a defensive posture (such as a defendant or third-party defendant), and the date of joinder of a party added as a claimant or an intervenor. Absent court order or stipulation, a new party has 30 days in which to make its initial disclosures. But it is expected that later-added parties will ordinarily be treated the same as the original parties when the original parties have stipulated to forgo initial disclosure, or the court has ordered disclosure in a modified form.

Subdivision (a)(3). The amendment to Rule 5(d) forbids filing disclosures under subdivisions (a)(1) and (a)(2) until they are used in the proceeding, and this change is reflected in an amendment to subdivision (a)(4). Disclosures under subdivision (a)(3), however, may be important to the court in connection with the final pretrial conference or otherwise in preparing for trial. The requirement that objections to certain matters be filed points up the court's need to be provided with these materials. Accordingly, the requirement that subdivision (a)(3) materials be filed has been moved from subdivision (a)(4) to subdivision (a)(3), and it has also been made clear that they—and any objections—should be filed "promptly."

Subdivision (a)(4). The filing requirement has been removed from this subdivision. Rule 5(d) has been amended to provide that disclosures under subdivisions (a)(1) and (a)(2) must not be filed until used in the proceeding. Subdivision (a)(3) has been amended to require that the disclosures it directs, and objections to them, be filed promptly. Subdivision (a)(4) continues to require that all disclosures under subdivisions (a)(1), (a)(2), and (a)(3) be in writing, signed, and served.

"Shall" is replaced by "must" under the program to conform amended rules to current style conventions when there is no ambiguity.

Subdivision (b)(1). In 1978, the Committee published for comment a proposed amendment, suggested by the Section of Litigation of the American Bar Association, to refine the scope of discovery by deleting the "subject matter" language. This proposal was withdrawn, and the Committee has since then made other changes in the discovery rules to address concerns about overbroad discovery. Concerns about costs and delay of discovery have persisted nonetheless, and other bar groups have repeatedly renewed similar proposals for amendment to this subdivision to delete the "subject matter" language. Nearly one-third of the lawyers surveyed in 1997 by the Federal Judicial Center endorsed narrowing the scope of discovery as a means of reducing litigation expense without interfering with fair case resolutions. *Discovery and Disclosure Practice, supra*, at 44–45 (1997). The Committee has heard that in some instances, particularly cases involving large quantities of discovery, parties seek to justify discovery requests that sweep far beyond the claims and defenses of the parties on the ground that they nevertheless have a bearing on the "subject matter" involved in the action.

The amendments proposed for subdivision (b)(1) include one element of these earlier proposals but also differ from these proposals in significant ways. The similarity is that the amendments describe the scope of party-controlled discovery in terms of matter relevant to the claim or defense of any party. The court, however, retains authority to order discovery of any matter relevant to the subject matter involved in the action for good cause. The amendment is designed to involve the court more actively in regulating the breadth of sweeping or contentious discovery. The Committee has been informed repeatedly by lawyers that involvement of the court in managing discovery is an important method of controlling problems of inappropriately broad discovery. Increasing the availability of judicial officers to resolve discovery disputes and increasing court management of discovery were both strongly endorsed by the attorneys surveyed by the Federal Judicial Center. *See Discovery and Disclosure Practice, supra*, at 44. Under the amended provisions, if there is an objection that discovery goes beyond material relevant to the parties' claims or defenses, the court would become involved to determine whether the discovery is relevant to the claims or defenses and, if not, whether good cause exists for authorizing it so long as it is relevant to the subject matter of the action. The good-cause standard warranting broader discovery is meant to be flexible.

The Committee intends that the parties and the court focus on the actual claims and defenses involved in the action. The dividing line between information relevant to the claims and defenses and that relevant only to the subject matter of the action cannot be defined with precision. A variety of types of information not directly pertinent to the incident in suit could be relevant to the claims or defenses raised in a given action. For example, other incidents of the same type, or involving the same product, could be properly discoverable under the revised standard. Information about organizational arrangements or filing systems of a party could be discoverable if likely to yield or lead to the discovery of admissible information. Similarly, information that could be used to impeach a likely witness, although not otherwise relevant to the claims or defenses, might be properly discoverable. In each instance, the determination whether such information is discoverable because it is relevant to the claims or defenses depends on the circumstances of the pending action.

The rule change signals to the court that it has the authority to confine discovery to the claims and defenses asserted in the pleadings, and signals to the parties that they have no entitlement to discovery to develop new claims or defenses that are not already identified in the pleadings. In general, it is hoped that reasonable lawyers can cooperate to manage discovery without the need for judicial intervention. When judicial intervention is invoked, the actual scope of discovery should be determined according to the reasonable needs of the action. The court may permit broader discovery in a particular case depending on the circumstances of the case, the nature of the claims and defenses, and the scope of the discovery requested.

The amendments also modify the provision regarding discovery of information not admissible in evidence. As added in 1946, this sentence was designed to make clear that otherwise relevant material could not be withheld because it was hearsay or otherwise inadmissible. The Committee was concerned that the "reasonably calculated to lead to the discovery of admissible evidence" standard set forth in this sentence might swallow any other limitation on the scope of discovery. Accordingly, this sentence has been amended to clarify that information must be relevant to be discoverable, even though inadmissible, and that discovery of such material is permitted if reasonably calculated to lead to the discovery of admissible evidence. As used here, "relevant" means within the scope of discovery as defined in this subdivision, and it would include information relevant to the subject matter involved in the action if the court has ordered discovery to that limit based on a showing of good cause.

Finally, a sentence has been added calling attention to the limitations of subdivision (b)(2)(i), (ii), and (iii). These limitations apply to discovery that is otherwise within the scope of subdivision (b)(1). The Committee has been told repeatedly that courts have not implemented these limitations with the vigor that was contemplated. *See 8 Federal Practice & Procedure* § 2008.1 at 121. This otherwise redundant cross-reference has been added to emphasize the need for active judicial use of subdivision (b)(2) to control excessive discovery. *Cf. Crawford-El v. Britton*, 118 S. Ct. 1584, 1597 (1998) (quoting Rule 26(b)(2)(iii) and stating that "Rule 26 vests the trial judge with broad discretion to tailor discovery narrowly").

Subdivision (b)(2). Rules 30, 31, and 33 establish presumptive national limits on the numbers of depositions and interrogatories. New Rule 30(d)(2) establishes a presumptive limit on the length of depositions. Subdivision (b)(2) is amended to remove the previous permission for local rules that establish different presumptive limits on these discovery activities. There is no reason to believe that unique circumstances justify varying these nationally-applicable presumptive limits in certain districts. The limits can be modified by court order or agreement in an individual action, but "standing" orders imposing different presumptive limits are not authorized. Because there is no national rule limiting the number of Rule 36 requests for admissions, the rule continues to authorize local rules that impose numerical limits on them. This change is not intended to interfere with differentiated case management in districts that use this technique by case-specific order as part of their Rule 16 process.

Subdivision (d). The amendments remove the prior authority to exempt cases by local rule from the moratorium on discovery before the subdivision (f) conference, but the categories of proceedings exempted from initial disclosure under subdivision (a)(1)(E) are excluded from subdivision (d). The parties may agree to disregard the moratorium where it applies, and the court may so order in a case, out "standing" orders altering the moratorium are not authorized.

Subdivision (f). As in subdivision (d), the amendments remove the prior authority to exempt cases by local rule from the conference requirement. The Committee has been informed that the addition of the conference was one of the most successful changes made in the 1993 amendments, and it therefore has determined to apply the conference requirement nationwide. The categories of proceedings exempted from initial disclosure under subdivision (a)(1)(E) are exempted from the conference requirement for the reasons that warrant exclusion from initial disclosure. The court may order that the conference need not occur in a case where otherwise required, or that it occur in a case otherwise exempted by subdivision (a)(1)(E). "Standing" orders altering the conference requirement for categories of cases are not authorized.

The rule is amended to require only a "conference" of the parties, rather than a "meeting." There are important benefits to face-to-face discussion of the topics to be covered in the conference, and those benefits may be lost if other means of conferring were routinely used when face-to-face meetings would not impose burdens. Nevertheless, geographic conditions in some districts may exact costs far out of proportion to these benefits. The amendment allows the court by case-specific order to require a face-to-face meeting, but "standing" orders so requiring are not authorized.

As noted concerning the amendments to subdivision (a)(1), the time for the conference has been changed to at least 21 days before the Rule 16 scheduling conference, and the time for the report is changed to no more than 14 days after the Rule 26(f) conference. This should ensure that the court will have the report well in advance of the scheduling conference or the entry of the scheduling order.

Since Rule 16 was amended in 1983 to mandate some case management activities in all courts, it has included deadlines for Completing these tasks to ensure that all courts do so within a reasonable time. Rule 26(f) was fit into this scheme when it was adopted in 1993. It was never intended, however, that the national requirements that certain activities be completed by a certain time should delay case management in districts that move much faster than the national rules direct, and the rule is therefore amended to permit such a court to adopt a local rule that shortens the period specified for the completion of these tasks.

"Shall" is replaced by "must," "does," or an active verb under the program to conform amended rules to current style conventions when there is no ambiguity.

Rule 30. Depositions upon Oral Examination

(d) Schedule and Duration; Motion to Terminate or Limit Examination.

(1) Any objection ~~to evidence~~ during a deposition ~~shall~~ *must* be stated concisely and in a non-argumentative and non-suggestive manner. A *person* ~~party~~ may instruct a deponent not to answer only when necessary to preserve a privilege, to enforce a limitation ~~on evidence~~ directed by the court, or to present a motion under ~~paragraph~~ *Rule 30(d)(4*~~3~~*)*.

(2) *Unless otherwise authorized by the court or stipulated by the parties, a deposition is limited to one day of seven hours.* ~~By order or local rule, t~~*T*he court ~~may limit the time permitted for the conduct of a deposition, but shall~~ *must* allow additional time consistent with Rule 26(b)(2) if needed for a fair examination of the deponent or if the deponent or another *person* ~~party,~~ *or other circumstance,* impedes or delays the examination.

New matter is shown in italics; matter to be omitted is lined through

(3) If the court finds *that any* ~~such an~~ impediment, delay, or other conduct ~~that~~ has frustrated the fair examination of the deponent, it may impose upon the persons responsible an appropriate sanction, including the reasonable costs and attorney's fees incurred by any parties as a result thereof.

(*4*~~3~~) At any time during a deposition, on motion of a party or of the deponent and upon a showing that the examination is being conducted in bad faith or in such manner as unreasonably to annoy, embarrass, or oppress the deponent or party, the court in which the action is pending or the court in the district where the deposition is being taken may order the officer conducting the examination to cease forthwith from taking the deposition, or may limit the scope and manner of the taking of the deposition as provided in Rule 26(c). If the order made terminates the examination, it ~~shall~~ *may* be resumed thereafter only upon the order of the court in which the action is pending. Upon demand of the objecting party or deponent, the taking of the deposition ~~shall~~ *must* be suspended for the time necessary to make a motion for an order. The provisions of Rule 37(a)(4) apply to the award of expenses incurred in relation to the motion.

(f) Certification and *Delivery* ~~Filing~~ by Officer; Exhibits; Copies.~~; Notice of Filing.~~

(1) The officer ~~shall~~ *must* certify that the witness was duly sworn by the officer and that the deposition is a true record of the testimony given by the witness. This certificate ~~shall~~ *must* be in writing and accompany the record of the deposition. Unless otherwise ordered by the court, the officer ~~shall~~ *must* securely seal the deposition in an envelope or package indorsed with the title of the action and marked "Deposition of [here insert name of witness]" and ~~shall~~ *must* promptly ~~file it with the court in which the action is pending or~~ send it to the attorney who arranged for the transcript or recording, who ~~shall~~ *must* store it under conditions that will protect it against loss, destruction, tampering, or deterioration. Documents and things produced for inspection during the examination of the witness~~,~~ ~~shall~~ *must,* upon the request of a party, be marked for identification and annexed to the deposition and may be inspected and copied by any party, except that if the person producing the materials desires to retain them the person may (A) offer copies to be marked for identification and annexed to the deposition and to serve thereafter as originals if the person affords to all parties fair opportunity to verify the copies by comparison with the originals, or (B) offer the originals to be marked for identification, after giving to each party an opportunity to inspect and copy them, in which event the materials may then be used in

the same manner as if annexed to the deposition. Any party may move for an order that the original be annexed to and returned with the deposition to the court, pending final disposition of the case.

Advisory Committee's Note

Subdivision (d). Paragraph (1) has been amended to clarify the terms regarding behavior during depositions. The references to objections "to evidence" and limitations "on evidence" have been removed to avoid disputes about what is "evidence" and whether an objection is to, or a limitation is on, discovery instead. It is intended that the rule apply to any objection to a question or other issue arising during a deposition, and to any limitation imposed by the court in connection with a deposition, which might relate to duration or other matters.

The current rule places limitations on instructions that a witness not answer only when the instruction is made by a "party." Similar limitations should apply with regard to anyone who might purport to instruct a witness not to answer a question. Accordingly, the rule is amended to apply the limitation to instructions by any person. The amendment is not intended to confer new authority on nonparties to instruct witnesses to refuse to answer deposition questions. The amendment makes it clear that, whatever the legitimacy of giving such instructions, the nonparty is subject to the same limitations as parties.

Paragraph (2) imposes a presumptive durational limitation of one day of seven hours for any deposition. The Committee has been informed that overlong depositions can result in undue costs and delays in some circumstances. This limitation contemplates that there will be reasonable breaks during the day for lunch and other reasons, and that the only time to be counted is the time occupied by the actual deposition. For purposes of this durational limit, the deposition of each person designated under Rule 30(b)(6) should be considered a separate deposition. The presumptive duration may be extended, or otherwise altered, by agreement. Absent agreement, a court order is needed. The party seeking a court order to extend the examination, or otherwise alter the limitations, is expected to show good cause to justify such an order.

Parties considering extending the time for a deposition—and courts asked to order an extension—might consider a variety of factors. For example, if the witness needs an interpreter, that may prolong the examination. If the examination will cover events occurring over a long period of time, that may justify allowing additional time. In cases in which the witness will be questioned about numerous or lengthy documents, it is often desirable for the interrogating party to send copies of the documents to the witness sufficiently in advance of the deposition so that the witness can become familiar with them. Should the witness nevertheless not read the documents in advance, thereby prolonging the deposition, a court could consider that a reason for extending the time limit. If the examination reveals that documents have been requested but not produced, that may justify further examination once production has occurred. In multi-party cases, the need for each party to examine the witness may warrant additional time, although duplicative questioning should be avoided and parties with similar interests should strive to designate one lawyer to question about areas of common interest. Similarly, should the lawyer for the witness want to examine the witness, that may require additional time. Finally, with regard to expert witnesses, there may more often be a need for additional time—even after the submission of the report required by Rule 26(a)(2)—for full exploration of the theories upon which the witness relies.

It is expected that in most instances the parties and the witness will make reasonable accommodations to avoid the need for resort to the court. The limitation is phrased in terms of a single day on the assumption that ordinarily a single day would be preferable to a deposition extending over multiple days; if alternative arrangements would better suit the parties, they may agree to them. It is also assumed that there will be reasonable breaks during the day. Preoccupation with timing is to be avoided.

The rule directs the court to allow additional time where consistent with Rule 26(b)(2) if needed for a fair examination of the deponent. In addition, if the deponent or another person impedes or delays the examination, the court must authorize extra time. The amendment makes clear that additional time should also be allowed where the examination is impeded by an "other circumstance," which might include a power outage, a health emergency, or other event.

In keeping with the amendment to Rule 26(b)(2), the provision added in 1993 granting authority to adopt a local rule limiting the time permitted for depositions has been removed. The court may enter a case-specific order directing shorter depositions for all depositions in a case or with regard to a specific witness. The court may also order that a deposition be taken for limited periods on several days.

Paragraph (3) includes sanctions provisions formerly included in paragraph (2). It authorizes the court to impose an appropriate sanction on any person responsible for an impediment that frustrated the fair examination of the deponent. This could include the deponent, any party, or any other person involved in the deposition. If the impediment or delay results from an "other circumstance" under paragraph (2), ordinarily no sanction would be appropriate.

Former paragraph (3) has been renumbered (4) but is otherwise unchanged.

Subdivision (f)(1). This subdivision is amended because Rule 5(d) has been amended to direct that discovery materials, including depositions, ordinarily should not be filed. The rule already has provisions directing that the lawyer who arranged for the transcript or recording preserve the deposition. Rule 5(d) provides that, once the deposition is used in the proceeding, the attorney must file it with the court.

"Shall" is replaced by "must" or "may" under the program to conform amended rules to current style conventions when there is no ambiguity.

Rule 37. Failure to Make Disclosure or Cooperate in Discovery; Sanctions

(c) Failure to Disclose; False or Misleading Disclosure; Refusal to Admit.

(1) A party that without substantial justification fails to disclose information required by Rule 26(a) or 26(e)(1), *or to amend a prior response to discovery as required by Rule 26(e)(2),* ~~shall~~ *is* not, unless such failure is harmless, ~~be~~ permitted to use as evidence at a trial, at a hearing, or on a motion any witness or information not so disclosed. In addition to or in lieu of this sanction, the court, on motion and after affording an opportunity to be heard, may impose other appropriate sanctions. In addition to requiring payment of reasonable expenses, including attorney's fees, caused by the failure, these sanctions may include any of the actions authorized

New matter is shown in italics; matter to be omitted is lined through

under ~~subparagraphs~~ *Rule 37(b)(2)*(A), (B), and (C) ~~of subdivision (b)(2) of this rule~~ and may include informing the jury of the failure to make the disclosure.

Advisory Committee's Note

Subdivision (c)(1). When this subdivision was added in 1993 to direct exclusion of materials not disclosed as required, the duty to supplement discovery responses pursuant to Rule 26(e)(2) was omitted. In the face of this omission, courts may rely on inherent power to sanction for failure to supplement as required by Rule 26(e)(2), *see 8 Federal Practice & Procedure* § 2050 at 607–09, but that is an uncertain and unregulated ground for imposing sanctions. There is no obvious occasion for a Rule 37(a) motion in connection with failure to supplement, and ordinarily only Rule 37(c)(1) exists as rule-based authority for sanctions if this supplementation obligation is violated.

The amendment explicitly adds failure to comply with Rule 26(e)(2) as a ground for sanctions under Rule 37(c)(1), including exclusion of withheld materials. The rule provides that this sanction power only applies when the failure to supplement was "without substantial justification." Even if the failure was not substantially justified, a party should be allowed to use the material that was not disclosed if the lack of earlier notice was harmless.

"Shall" is replaced by "is" under the program to conform amended rules to current style conventions when there is no ambiguity.

CERTAIN OF THE AMENDMENTS OF FEDERAL RULES OF CIVIL PROCEDURE ADOPTED BY THE SUPREME COURT OF THE UNITED STATES ON MARCH 27, 2003, EFFECTIVE DECEMBER 1, 2003, WITH ADVISORY COMMITTEE'S NOTES THEREON

[*Amendments here omitted: Changes in Rules 54 and 71A and Forms 19, 31, and 32.*]

Rule 23. Class Actions

(c) Determin*ing*~~ation~~ by Order Whether *to Certify a* Class Action ~~to Be Maintained~~; *Appointing Class Counsel;* Notice *and Membership in Class*; Judgment; ~~Actions Conducted Partially as Class Actions~~ *Multiple Classes and Subclasses*.

(1)(A) ~~As soon as practicable after the commencement of an action brought as a class action, the court shall determine by order whether it is to be so maintained.~~ *When a person sues or is sued as a representative of a class, the court must—at an early practicable time—determine by order whether to certify the action as a class action.*

(B) An order certifying a class action must define the class and the class claims, issues, or defenses, and must appoint class counsel under Rule 23(g).

(C) An order under ~~this subdivision~~ *Rule 23(c)(1)* ~~may be conditional, and~~ may be altered or amended before ~~the decision on the merits~~ *final judgment.*

(2)*(A) For any class certified under Rule 23(b)(1) or (2), the court may direct appropriate notice to the class.*

(B) For ~~In~~ any class ~~action maintained~~ *certified* under ~~subdivision~~ *Rule 23*(b)(3), the court ~~shall~~ *must* direct to *class* ~~the~~ members ~~of the class~~ the best notice practicable under the circumstances, including individual notice to all members who can be identified through reasonable effort. *The notice must concisely and clearly state in plain, easily understood language:*

- *the nature of the action,*
- *the definition of the class certified,*

New material is shown in italics; matter to be omitted is lined through

- *the class claims, issues, or defenses,*
- *that a class member may enter an appearance through counsel if the member so desires,*
- *that the court will exclude from the class any member who requests exclusion, stating when and how members may elect to be excluded, and*
- *the binding effect of a class judgment on class members under Rule 23(c)(3).*

~~The notice shall advise each member that (A) the court will exclude the member from the class if the member so requests by a specified date; (B) the judgment, whether favorable or not, will include all members who do not request exclusion; and (C) any member who does not request exclusion may, if the member desires, enter an appearance through counsel.~~

(3) The judgment in an action maintained as a class action under subdivision (b)(1) or (b)(2), whether or not favorable to the class, shall include and describe those whom the court finds to be members of the class. The judgment in an action maintained as a class action under subdivision (b)(3), whether or not favorable to the class, shall include and specify or describe those to whom the notice provided in subdivision (c)(2) was directed, and who have not requested exclusion, and whom the court finds to be members of the class.

(4) When appropriate (A) an action may be brought or maintained as a class action with respect to particular issues, or (B) a class may be divided into subclasses and each subclass treated as a class, and the provisions of this rule shall then be construed and applied accordingly.

(e) *Settlement, Voluntary* Dismissal, or Compromise. ~~A class action shall not be dismissed or compromised without the approval of the court, and notice of the proposed dismissal or compromise shall be given to all members of the class in such manner as the court directs.~~

(1)(A) The court must approve any settlement, voluntary dismissal, or compromise of the claims, issues, or defenses of a certified class.

(B) The court must direct notice in a reasonable manner to all class members who would be bound by a proposed settlement, voluntary dismissal, or compromise.

(C) The court may approve a settlement, voluntary dismissal, or compromise that would bind class members only after a hearing and

on finding that the settlement, voluntary dismissal, or compromise is fair, reasonable, and adequate.

(2) The parties seeking approval of a settlement, voluntary dismissal, or compromise under Rule 23(e)(1) must file a statement identifying any agreement made in connection with the proposed settlement, voluntary dismissal, or compromise.

(3) In an action previously certified as a class action under Rule 23(b)(3), the court may refuse to approve a settlement unless it affords a new opportunity to request exclusion to individual class members who had an earlier opportunity to request exclusion but did not do so.

(4)(A) Any class member may object to a proposed settlement, voluntary dismissal, or compromise that requires court approval under Rule 23(e)(1)(A).

(B) An objection made under Rule 23(e)(4)(A) may be withdrawn only with the court's approval.

(g) Class Counsel.

(1) Appointing Class Counsel.

(A) Unless a statute provides otherwise, a court that certifies a class must appoint class counsel.

(B) An attorney appointed to serve as class counsel must fairly and adequately represent the interests of the class.

(C) In appointing class counsel, the court

(i) must consider:

- *the work counsel has done in identifying or investigating potential claims in the action,*
- *counsel's experience in handling class actions, other complex litigation, and claims of the type asserted in the action,*
- *counsel's knowledge of the applicable law, and*
- *the resources counsel will commit to representing the class;*

(ii) may consider any other matter pertinent to counsel's ability to fairly and adequately represent the interests of the class;

(iii) may direct potential class counsel to provide information on any subject pertinent to the appointment and to propose terms for attorney fees and nontaxable costs; and

(iv) may make further orders in connection with the appointment.

(2) Appointment Procedure.

(A) The court may designate interim counsel to act on behalf of the putative class before determining whether to certify the action as a class action.

(B) When there is one applicant for appointment as class counsel, the court may appoint that applicant only if the applicant is adequate under Rule 23(g)(1)(B) and (C). If more than one adequate applicant seeks appointment as class counsel, the court must appoint the applicant best able to represent the interests of the class.

(C) The order appointing class counsel may include provisions about the award of attorney fees or nontaxable costs under Rule 23(h).

(h) Attorney Fees Award. *In an action certified as a class action, the court may award reasonable attorney fees and nontaxable costs authorized by law or by agreement of the parties as follows:*

(1) Motion for Award of Attorney Fees. A claim for an award of attorney fees and nontaxable costs must be made by motion under Rule 54(d)(2), subject to the provisions of this subdivision, at a time set by the court. Notice of the motion must be served on all parties and, for motions by class counsel, directed to class members in a reasonable manner.

(2) Objections to Motion. A class member, or a party from whom payment is sought, may object to the motion.

(3) Hearing and Findings. The court may hold a hearing and must find the facts and state its conclusions of law on the motion under Rule 52(a).

(4) Reference to Special Master or Magistrate Judge. The court may refer issues related to the amount of the award to a special master or to a magistrate judge as provided in Rule 54(d)(2)(D).

Advisory Committee's Note

Subdivision (c). Subdivision (c) is amended in several respects. The requirement that the court determine whether to certify a class "as soon as practicable after commencement of an action" is replaced by requiring determination "at an early practicable time." The notice provisions are substantially revised.

Paragraph (1). Subdivision (c)(1)(A) is changed to require that the determination whether to certify a class be made "at an early practicable time." The "as soon as practicable" exaction neither reflects prevailing practice nor captures the many valid reasons that may justify deferring the initial certification decision. See Willging, Hooper & Niemic, *Empirical Study of Class Actions in Four Federal District Courts: Final Report to the Advisory Committee on Civil Rules 26–36* (Federal Judicial Center 1996).

Time may be needed to gather information necessary to make the certification decision. Although an evaluation of the probable outcome on the merits is not properly part of the certification decision, discovery in aid of the certification decision often includes information required to identify the nature of the issues that actually will be presented at trial. In this sense it is appropriate to conduct controlled discovery into the "merits," limited to those aspects relevant to making the certification decision on an informed basis. Active judicial supervision may be required to achieve the most effective balance that expedites an informed certification determination without forcing an artificial and ultimately wasteful division between "certification discovery" and "merits discovery." A critical need is to determine how the case will be tried. An increasing number of courts require a party requesting class certification to present a "trial plan" that describes the issues likely to be presented at trial and tests whether they are susceptible of class-wide proof. See Manual For Complex Litigation Third, § 21.213, p. 44; § 30.11, p. 214; § 30.12, p. 215.

Other considerations may affect the timing of the certification decision. The party opposing the class may prefer to win dismissal or summary judgment as to the individual plaintiffs without certification and without binding the class that might have been certified. Time may be needed to explore designation of class counsel under Rule 23(g), recognizing that in many cases the need to progress toward the certification determination may require designation of interim counsel under Rule 23(g)(2)(A).

Although many circumstances may justify deferring the certification decision, active management may be necessary to ensure that the certification decision is not unjustifiably delayed.

Subdivision (c)(1)(C) reflects two amendments. The provision that a class certification "may be conditional" is deleted. A court that is not satisfied that the requirements of Rule 23 have been met should refuse certification until they have been met. The provision that permits alteration or amendment of an order granting or denying class certification is amended to set the cut-off point at final judgment rather than "the decision on the merits." This change avoids the possible ambiguity in referring to "the decision on the merits." Following a determination of liability, for example, proceedings to define the remedy may demonstrate the need to amend the class definition or subdivide the class. In this setting the final judgment concept is pragmatic. It is not the same as the concept used for appeal purposes, but it should be flexible, particularly in protracted litigation.

The authority to amend an order under Rule 23(c)(1) before final judgment does not restore the practice of "one-way intervention" that was rejected by the 1966 revision of Rule 23. A determination of liability after certification, however, may show a need to amend the class definition. Decertification may be warranted after further proceedings.

If the definition of a class certified under Rule 23(b)(3) is altered to include members who have not been afforded notice and an opportunity to request exclusion, notice—including an opportunity to request exclusion—must be directed to the new class members under Rule 23(c)(2)(B).

Paragraph (2). The first change made in Rule 23(c)(2) is to call attention to the court's authority—already established in part by Rule 23(d)(2)—to direct notice of certification to a Rule 23(b)(1) or (b)(2) class. The present rule expressly requires notice only in actions certified under Rule 23(b)(3). Members of classes certified under Rules 23(b)(1) or (b)(2) have interests that may deserve protection by notice.

The authority to direct notice to class members in a (b)(1) or (b)(2) class action should be exercised with care. For several reasons, there may be less need for notice than in a (b)(3) class action. There is no right to request exclusion from a (b)(1) or (b)(2) class. The characteristics of the class may reduce the need for formal notice. The cost of providing notice, moreover, could easily cripple actions that do not seek damages. The court may decide not to direct notice after balancing the risk that notice costs may deter the pursuit of class relief against the benefits of notice.

When the court does direct certification notice in a (b)(1) or (b)(2) class action, the discretion and flexibility established by subdivision (c)(2)(A) extend to the method of giving notice. Notice facilitates the opportunity to participate. Notice calculated to reach a significant number of class members often will protect the interests of all. Informal methods may prove effective. A simple posting in a place visited by many class members, directing attention to a source of more detailed information, may suffice. The court should consider the costs of notice in relation to the probable reach of inexpensive methods.

If a Rule 23(b)(3) class is certified in conjunction with a (b)(2) class, the (c)(2)(B) notice requirements must be satisfied as to the (b)(3) class.

The direction that class-certification notice be couched in plain, easily understood language is a reminder of the need to work unremittingly at the difficult task of communicating with class members. It is difficult to provide information about most class actions that is both accurate and easily understood by class members who are not themselves lawyers. Factual uncertainty, legal complexity, and the complication of class-action procedure raise the barriers high. The Federal Judicial Center has created illustrative clear-notice forms that provide a helpful starting point for actions similar to those described in the forms.

Subdivision (e). Subdivision (e) is amended to strengthen the process of reviewing proposed class-action settlements. Settlement may be a desirable means of resolving a class action. But court review and approval are essential to assure adequate representation of class members who have not participated in shaping the settlement.

Paragraph (1). Subdivision (e)(1)(A) expressly recognizes the power of a class representative to settle class claims, issues, or defenses.

Rule 23(e)(1)(A) resolves the ambiguity in former Rule 23(e)'s reference to dismissal or compromise of "a class action." That language could be—and at times was—read to require court approval of settlements with putative class representatives that resolved only individual claims. See Manual for Complex Litigation Third, § 30.41. The new rule requires approval only if the claims, issues, or defenses of a certified class are resolved by a settlement, voluntary dismissal, or compromise.

Subdivision (e)(1)(B) carries forward the notice requirement of present Rule 23(e) when the settlement binds the class through claim or issue preclusion; notice is not required when the settlement binds only the individual class representatives. Notice of a settlement binding on the class is required either when the settlement follows class certification or when the decisions on certification and settlement proceed simultaneously.

Reasonable settlement notice may require individual notice in the manner required by Rule 23(c)(2)(B) for certification notice to a Rule 23(b)(3) class. Individual notice is appropriate, for example, if class members are required to take action—such as filing claims—to participate in the judgment, or if the court orders a settlement opt-out opportunity under Rule 23(e)(3).

Subdivision (e)(1)(C) confirms and mandates the already common practice of holding hearings as part of the process of approving settlement, voluntary dismissal, or compromise that would bind members of a class.

Subdivision (e)(1)(C) states the standard for approving a proposed settlement that would bind class members. The settlement must be fair, reasonable, and adequate. A helpful review of many factors that may deserve consideration is provided by *In re: Prudential Ins. Co. America Sales Practice Litigation Agent Actions*, 148 F.3d 283, 316–324 (3d Cir. 1998). Further guidance can be found in the Manual for Complex Litigation.

The court must make findings that support the conclusion that the settlement is fair, reasonable, and adequate. The findings must be set out in sufficient detail to explain to class members and the appellate court the factors that bear on applying the standard.

Settlement review also may provide an occasion to review the cogency of the initial class definition. The terms of the settlement themselves, or objections, may reveal divergent interests of class members and demonstrate the need to redefine the class or to designate subclasses. Redefinition of a class certified under Rule 23(b)(3) may require notice to new class members under Rule 23(c)(2)(B). See Rule 23(c)(1)(C).

Paragraph (2). Subdivision (e)(2) requires parties seeking approval of a settlement, voluntary dismissal, or compromise under Rule 23(e)(1) to file a statement identifying any agreement made in connection with the settlement. This provision does not change the basic requirement that the parties disclose all terms of the settlement or compromise that the court must approve under Rule 23(e)(1). It aims instead at related undertakings that, although seemingly separate, may have influenced the terms of the settlement by trading away possible advantages for the class in return for advantages for others. Doubts should be resolved in favor of identification.

Further inquiry into the agreements identified by the parties should not become the occasion for discovery by the parties or objectors. The court may direct the parties to provide to the court or other parties a summary or copy of the full terms of any agreement identified by the parties. The court also may direct the parties to provide a summary or copy of any agreement not identified by the parties that the court considers relevant to its review of a proposed settlement. In exercising discretion under this rule, the court may act in steps, calling first for a summary of any agreement that may have affected the settlement and then for a complete version if the summary does not provide an adequate basis for review. A direction to disclose a summary or copy of an agreement may raise concerns of confidentiality. Some agreements may include information that merits protection against general disclosure. And the court must provide an opportunity to claim work-product or other protections.

Paragraph (3). Subdivision (e)(3) authorizes the court to refuse to approve a settlement unless the settlement affords class members a new opportunity to request exclusion from a class certified under Rule 23(b)(3) after settlement terms are known. An agreement by the parties themselves to permit class members to elect exclusion at this point by the settlement agreement may be one factor supporting approval of the settlement. Often there is an opportunity to opt out at this point because the class is certified and settlement is reached in circumstances that lead to simultaneous notice of certification and notice of settlement. In these cases, the basic opportunity to elect exclusion applies without further complication. In some cases, particularly if settlement appears imminent at the time of certification, it may be possible to achieve equivalent protection by deferring notice and the opportunity to elect exclusion until actual settlement terms are known. This approach avoids the cost and potential confusion of providing two notices and makes the single notice more meaningful. But notice should not be delayed unduly after certification in the hope of settlement.

Rule 23(e)(3) authorizes the court to refuse to approve a settlement unless the settlement affords a new opportunity to elect exclusion in a case that settles after a certification decision if the earlier opportunity to elect exclusion provided with the certification notice has expired by the time of the settlement notice. A decision to remain in the class is likely to be more carefully considered and is better informed when settlement terms are known.

The opportunity to request exclusion from a proposed settlement is limited to members of a (b)(3) class. Exclusion may be requested only by individual class members; no class member may purport to opt out other class members by way of another class action.

The decision whether to approve a settlement that does not allow a new opportunity to elect exclusion is confided to the court's discretion. The court may make this decision before directing notice to the class under Rule 23(e)(1)(B) or after the Rule 23(e)(1)(C) hearing. Many factors may influence the court's decision. Among these are changes in the information available to class members since expiration of the first opportunity to request exclusion, and the nature of the individual class members' claims.

The terms set for permitting a new opportunity to elect exclusion from the proposed settlement of a Rule 23(b)(3) class action may address concerns of potential misuse. The court might direct, for example, that class members who elect exclusion are bound by rulings on the merits made before the settlement was proposed for approval. Still other terms or conditions may be appropriate.

Paragraph (4). Subdivision (e)(4) confirms the right of class members to object to a proposed settlement, voluntary dismissal, or compromise. The right is defined in relation to a disposition that, because it would bind the class, requires court approval under subdivision (e)(1)(C).

Subdivision (e)(4)(B) requires court approval for withdrawal of objections made under subdivision (e)(4)(A). Review follows automatically if the objections are withdrawn on terms that lead to modification of the settlement with the class. Review also is required if the objector formally withdraws the objections. If the objector simply abandons pursuit of the objection, the court may inquire into the circumstances.

Approval under paragraph (4)(B) may be given or denied with little need for further inquiry if the objection and the disposition go only to a protest that the individual treatment afforded the objector under the proposed settlement is unfair because of factors that distinguish the objector from other class members. Different considerations may apply if the objector has protested that the proposed settlement is not fair, reasonable, or adequate on grounds that apply generally to a class or subclass. Such objections, which purport to represent class-wide interests, may augment the opportunity for obstruction or delay. If such objections are surrendered on terms that do not affect the class settlement or the objector's participation in the class settlement, the court often can approve withdrawal of the objections without elaborate inquiry.

Once an objector appeals, control of the proceeding lies in the court of appeals. The court of appeals may undertake review and approval of a settlement with the objector, perhaps as part of appeal settlement procedures, or may remand to the district court to take advantage of the district court's familiarity with the action and settlement.

Subdivision (g). Subdivision (g) is new. It responds to the reality that the selection and activity of class counsel are often critically important to the successful handling of a class action. Until now, courts have scrutinized proposed class counsel as well as the class representative under Rule 23(a)(4). This experience has recognized the importance of judicial evaluation of the proposed lawyer for the class, and this new subdivision builds on that experience rather than introducing an entirely new element into the class certification process. Rule 23(a)(4) will continue to call for scrutiny of the proposed class representative, while this subdivision will guide the court in assessing proposed class counsel as part of the certification decision. This subdivision recognizes the importance of class counsel, states the obligation to represent the interests of the class, and provides a framework for selection of class counsel. The procedure and standards for appointment vary depending on whether there are multiple applicants to be class counsel. The new subdivision also provides a method by which the court may make directions from the outset about the potential fee award to class counsel in the event the action is successful.

Paragraph (1) sets out the basic requirement that class counsel be appointed if a class is certified and articulates the obligation of class counsel to represent the interests of the class, as opposed to the potentially conflicting interests of individual class members. It also sets out the factors the court should consider in assessing proposed class counsel.

Paragraph (1)(A) requires that the court appoint class counsel to represent the class. Class counsel must be appointed for all classes, including each subclass that the court certifies to represent divergent interests.

Paragraph (1)(A) does not apply if "a statute provides otherwise." This recognizes that provisions of the Private Securities Litigation Reform Act of 1995, Pub. L. No. 104–67, 109 Stat. 737 (1995) (codified in various sections of 15 U.S.C.), contain directives that bear on selection of a lead plaintiff and the retention of counsel. This subdivision does not purport to supersede or to affect the interpretation of those provisions, or any similar provisions of other legislation.

Paragraph (1)(B) recognizes that the primary responsibility of class counsel, resulting from appointment as class counsel, is to represent the best interests of the class. The rule thus establishes the obligation of class counsel, an obligation that may be different from the customary obligations of counsel to individual clients. Appointment as class counsel means that the primary obligation of counsel is to the class rather than to any individual members of it. The class representatives do not have an unfettered right to "fire" class counsel. In the same vein, the class representatives cannot command class counsel to accept or reject a settlement proposal. To the contrary, class counsel must determine whether seeking the court's approval of a settlement would be in the best interests of the class as a whole.

Paragraph (1)(C) articulates the basic responsibility of the court to appoint class counsel who will provide the adequate representation called for by paragraph (1)(B). It identifies criteria that must be considered and invites the court to consider any other pertinent matters. Although couched in terms of the court's duty, the listing also informs counsel seeking appointment about the topics that should be addressed in an application for appointment or in the motion for class certification.

The court may direct potential class counsel to provide additional information about the topics mentioned in paragraph (1)(C) or about any other relevant topic. For example, the court may direct applicants to inform the court concerning any agreements about a prospective award of attorney fees or nontaxable costs, as such agreements may sometimes be significant in the selection of class counsel. The court might also direct that potential class counsel indicate how parallel litigation might be coordinated or consolidated with the action before the court.

The court may also direct counsel to propose terms for a potential award of attorney fees and nontaxable costs. Attorney fee awards are an important feature of class action practice, and attention to this subject from the outset may often be a productive technique. Paragraph (2)(C) therefore authorizes the court to provide directions about attorney fees and costs when appointing class counsel. Because there will be numerous class actions in which this information is not likely to be useful, the court need not consider it in all class actions.

Some information relevant to class counsel appointment may involve matters that include adversary preparation in a way that should be shielded from disclosure to other parties. An appropriate protective order may be necessary to preserve confidentiality.

In evaluating prospective class counsel, the court should weigh all pertinent factors. No single factor should necessarily be determinative in a given case. For example, the resources counsel will commit to the case must be appropriate to its needs, but the court should be careful not to limit consideration to lawyers with the greatest resources.

If, after review of all applicants, the court concludes that none would be satisfactory class counsel, it may deny class certification, reject all applications, recommend that an application be modified, invite new applications, or make any other appropriate order regarding selection and appointment of class counsel.

Paragraph (2). This paragraph sets out the procedure that should be followed in appointing class counsel. Although it affords substantial flexibility, it provides the framework for appointment of class counsel in all class actions. For counsel who filed the action, the materials submitted in support of the motion for class certification may suffice to justify appointment so long as the information described in paragraph (g)(1)(C) is included. If there are other applicants, they ordinarily would file a formal application detailing their suitability for the position.

In a plaintiff class action the court usually would appoint as class counsel only an attorney or attorneys who have sought appointment. Different considerations may apply in defendant class actions.

The rule states that the court should appoint "class counsel." In many instances, the applicant will be an individual attorney. In other cases, however, an entire firm, or perhaps numerous attorneys who are not otherwise affiliated but are collaborating on the action will apply. No rule of thumb exists to determine when such arrangements are appropriate; the court should be alert to the need for adequate staffing of the case, but also to the risk of overstaffing or an ungainly counsel structure.

Paragraph (2)(A) authorizes the court to designate interim counsel during the pre-certification period if necessary to protect the interests of the putative class. Rule 23(c)(1)(B) directs that the order certifying the class include appointment of class counsel. Before class certification, however, it will usually be important for an attorney to take action to prepare for the certification decision. The amendment to Rule 23(c)(1) recognizes that some discovery is often necessary for that determination. It also may be important to make or respond to motions before certification. Settlement may be discussed before certification. Ordinarily, such work is handled by the lawyer who filed the action. In some cases, however, there may be rivalry or uncertainty that makes formal designation of interim counsel appropriate. Rule 23(g)(2)(A) authorizes the court to designate interim counsel to act on behalf of the putative class before the certification decision is made. Failure to make the formal designation does not prevent the attorney who filed the action from proceeding in it. Whether or not formally designated interim counsel, an attorney who acts on behalf of the class before certification must act in the best interests of the class as a whole.

For example, an attorney who negotiates a pre-certification settlement must seek a settlement that is fair, reasonable, and adequate for the class.

Rule 23(c)(1) provides that the court should decide whether to certify the class "at an early practicable time," and directs that class counsel should be appointed in the order certifying the class. In some cases, it may be appropriate for the court to allow a reasonable period after commencement of the action for filing applications to serve as class counsel. The primary ground for deferring appointment would be that there is reason to anticipate competing applications to serve as class counsel. Examples might include instances in which more than one class action has been filed, or in which other attorneys have filed individual actions on behalf of putative class members. The purpose of facilitating competing applications in such a case is to afford the best possible representation for the class. Another possible reason for deferring appointment would be that the initial applicant was found inadequate, but it seems appropriate to permit additional applications rather than deny class certification.

Paragraph (2)(B) states the basic standard the court should use in deciding whether to certify the class and appoint class counsel in the single applicant situation—that the applicant be able to provide the representation called for by paragraph (1)(B) in light of the factors identified in paragraph (1)(C).

If there are multiple adequate applicants, paragraph (2)(B) directs the court to select the class counsel best able to represent the interests of the class. This decision should also be made using the factors outlined in paragraph (1)(C), but in the multiple applicant situation the court is to go beyond scrutinizing the adequacy of counsel and make a comparison of the strengths of the various applicants. As with the decision whether to appoint the sole applicant for the position, no single factor should be dispositive in selecting class counsel in cases in which there are multiple applicants. The fact that a given attorney filed the instance action, for example, might not weigh heavily in the decision if that lawyer had not done significant work identifying or investigating claims. Depending on the nature of the case, one important consideration might be the applicant's existing attorney-client relationship with the proposed class representative.

Paragraph (2)(C) builds on the appointment process by authorizing the court to include provisions regarding attorney fees in the order appointing class counsel. Courts may find it desirable to adopt guidelines for fees or nontaxable costs, or to direct class counsel to report to the court at regular intervals on the efforts undertaken in the action, to facilitate the court's later determination of a reasonable attorney fee.

Subdivision (h). Subdivision (h) is new. Fee awards are a powerful influence on the way attorneys initiate, develop, and conclude class actions. Class action attorney fee awards have heretofore been handled, along with all other attorney fee awards, under Rule 54(d)(2), but that rule is not addressed to the particular concerns of class actions. This subdivision is designed to work in tandem with new subdivision (g) on appointment of class counsel, which may afford an opportunity for the court to provide an early framework for an eventual fee award, or for monitoring the work of class counsel during the pendency of the action.

Subdivision (h) applies to "an action certified as a class action." This includes cases in which there is a simultaneous proposal for class certification and settlement even though technically the class may not be certified unless the court approves the settlement pursuant to review under Rule 23(e). When a settlement is proposed for Rule 23(e) approval, either after certification or with a request for certification, notice to class members about class counsel's fee motion would ordinarily accompany the notice to the class about the settlement proposal itself.

This subdivision does not undertake to create new grounds for an award of attorney fees or nontaxable costs. Instead, it applies when such awards are authorized by law or by agreement of the parties. Against that background, it provides a format for all awards of attorney fees and nontaxable costs in connection with a class action, not only the award to class counsel. In some situations, there may be a basis for making an award to other counsel whose work produced a beneficial result for the class, such as attorneys who acted for the class before certification but were not appointed class counsel, or attorneys who represented objectors to a proposed settlement under Rule 23(e) or to the fee motion of class counsel. Other situations in which fee awards are authorized by law or by agreement of the parties may exist.

This subdivision authorizes an award of "reasonable" attorney fees and nontaxable costs. This is the customary term for measurement of fee awards in cases in which counsel may obtain an award of fees under the "common fund" theory that applies in many class actions, and is used in many fee-shifting statutes. Depending on the circumstances, courts have approached the determination of what is reasonable in different ways. In particular, there is some variation among courts about whether in "common fund" cases the court should use the lodestar or a percentage method of determining what fee is reasonable. The rule does not attempt to resolve the question whether the lodestar or percentage approach should be viewed as preferable.

Active judicial involvement in measuring fee awards is singularly important to the proper operation of the class-action process. Continued reliance on caselaw development of fee-award measures does not diminish the court's responsibility. In a class action, the district court must ensure that the amount and mode of payment of attorney fees are fair and proper whether the fees come from a common fund or are otherwise paid. Even in the absence of objections, the court bears this responsibility.

Courts discharging this responsibility have looked to a variety of factors. One fundamental focus is the result actually achieved for class members, a basic consideration in any case in which fees are sought on the basis of a benefit achieved for class members. The Private Securities Litigation Reform Act of 1995 explicitly makes this factor a cap for a fee award in actions to which it applies. See 15 U.S.C. §§ 77z–1(a)(6); 78u–4(a)(6) (fee award should not exceed a "reasonable percentage of the amount of any damages and prejudgment interest actually paid to the class"). For a percentage approach to fee measurement, results achieved is the basic starting point.

In many instances, the court may need to proceed with care in assessing the value conferred on class members. Settlement regimes that provide for future payments, for example, may not result in significant actual payments to class members. In this connection, the court may need to scrutinize the manner and operation of any applicable claims procedure. In some cases, it may be appropriate to defer some portion of the fee award until actual payouts to class members are known. Settlement involving nonmonetary provisions for class members also deserve careful scrutiny to ensure that these provisions have actual value to the class. On occasion the court's Rule 23(e) review will provide a solid basis for this sort of evaluation, but in any event it is also important to assessing the fee award for the class.

At the same time, it is important to recognize that in some class actions the monetary relief obtained is not the sole determinant of an appropriate attorney fees award. Cf. *Blanchard v. Bergeron*, 489 U.S. 87, 95 (1989) (cautioning in an individual case against an "undesirable emphasis" on "the importance of the recovery of damages in civil rights litigation" that might "shortchange efforts to seek effective injunctive or declaratory relief").

Any directions or orders made by the court in connection with appointing class counsel under Rule 23(g) should weigh heavily in making a fee award under this subdivision.

Courts have also given weight to agreements among the parties regarding the fee motion, and to agreements between class counsel and others about the fees claimed by the motion. Rule 54(d)(2)(B) provides: "If directed by the court, the motion shall also disclose the terms of any agreement with respect to fees to be paid for the services for which claim is made." The agreement by a settling party not to oppose a fee application up to a certain amount, for example, is worthy of consideration, but the court remains responsible to determine a reasonable fee. "Side agreements" regarding fees provide at least perspective pertinent to an appropriate fee award.

In addition, courts may take account of the fees charged by class counsel or other attorneys for representing individual claimants or objectors in the case. In determining a fee for class counsel, the court's objective is to ensure an overall fee that is fair for counsel and equitable within the class. In some circumstances individual fee agreements between class counsel and class members might have provisions inconsistent with those goals, and the court might determine that adjustments in the class fee award were necessary as a result.

Finally, it is important to scrutinize separately the application for an award covering nontaxable costs. If costs were addressed in the order appointing class counsel, those directives should be a presumptive starting point in determining what is an appropriate award.

Paragraph (1). Any claim for an award of attorney fees must be sought by motion under Rule 54(d)(2), which invokes the provisions for timing of appeal in Rule 58 and Appellate Rule 4. Owing to the distinctive features of class action fee motions, however, the provisions of this subdivision control disposition of fee motions in class actions, while Rule 54(d)(2) applies to matters not addressed in this subdivision.

The court should direct when the fee motion must be filed. For motions by class counsel in cases subject to court review of a proposed settlement under Rule 23(e), it would be important to require the filing of at least the initial motion in time for inclusion of information about the motion in the notice to the class about the proposed settlement that is required by Rule 23(e). In cases litigated to judgment, the court might also order class counsel's motion to be filed promptly so that notice to the class under this subdivision (h) can be given.

Besides service of the motion on all parties, notice of class counsel's motion for attorney fees must be "directed to the class in a reasonable manner." Because members of the class have an interest in the arrangements for payment of class counsel whether that payment comes from the class fund or is made directly by another party, notice is required in all instances. In cases in which settlement approval is contemplated under Rule 23(e), notice of class counsel's fee motion should be combined with notice of the proposed settlement, and the provision regarding notice to the class is parallel to the requirements for notice under Rule 23(e). In adjudicated class actions, the court may calibrate the notice to avoid undue expense.

Paragraph (2). A class member and any party from whom payment is sought may object to the fee motion. Other parties—for example, nonsettling defendants—may not object because they lack a sufficient interest in the amount the court awards. The rule does not specify a time limit for making an objection. In setting the date objections are due, the court should provide sufficient time after the full fee motion is on file to enable potential objectors to examine the motion.

The court may allow an objector discovery relevant to the objections. In determining whether to allow discovery, the court should weigh the need for the information against the cost and delay that would attend discovery. See Rule 26(b)(2). One factor in determining whether to authorize discovery is the completeness of the material submitted in support of the fee motion, which depends in part on the fee measurement standard applicable to the case. If the motion provides thorough information, the burden should be on the objector to justify discovery to obtain further information.

Paragraph (3). Whether or not there are formal objections, the court must determine whether a fee award is justified and, if so, set a reasonable fee. The rule does not require a formal hearing in all cases. The form and extent of a hearing depend on the circumstances of the case. The rule does require findings and conclusions under Rule 52(a).

Paragraph (4). By incorporating Rule 54(d)(2), this provision gives the court broad authority to obtain assistance in determining the appropriate amount to award. In deciding whether to direct submission of such questions to a special master or magistrate judge, the court should give appropriate consideration to the cost and delay that such a process might entail.

~~Rule 51~~

~~INSTRUCTIONS TO JURY: OBJECTION~~

~~At the close of the evidence or at such earlier time during the trial as the court reasonably directs, any party may file written requests that the court instruct the jury on the law as set forth in the requests. The court shall inform counsel of its proposed action upon the requests prior to their arguments to the jury. The court, at its election, may instruct the jury before or after argument, or both. No party may assign as error the giving or the failure to give an instruction unless that party objects thereto before the jury retires to consider its verdict, stating distinctly the matter objected to and the grounds of the objection. Opportunity shall be given to make the objection out of the hearing of the jury.~~

Rule 51. Instructions to Jury; Objections; Preserving a Claim of Error

(a) Requests.

(1) A party may, at the close of the evidence or at an earlier reasonable time that the court directs, file and furnish to every other party written requests that the court instruct the jury on the law as set forth in the requests.

(2) After the close of the evidence, a party may:

(A) file requests for instructions on issues that could not reasonably have been anticipated at an earlier time for requests set under Rule 51(a)(1), and

(B) with the court's permission file untimely requests for instructions on any issue.

(b) Instructions. *The court:*

(1) must inform the parties of its proposed instructions and proposed action on the requests before instructing the jury and before final jury arguments;

(2) must give the parties an opportunity to object on the record and out of the jury's hearing to the proposed instructions and actions on requests before the instructions and arguments are delivered; and

(3) may instruct the jury at any time after trial begins and before the jury is discharged.

(c) Objections.

(1) A party who objects to an instruction or the failure to give an instruction must do so on the record, stating distinctly the matter objected to and the grounds of the objection.

(2) An objection is timely if:

(A) a party that has been informed of an instruction or action on a request before the jury is instructed and before final jury arguments, as provided by Rule 51(b)(1), objects at the opportunity for objection required by Rule 51(b)(2); or

(B) a party that has not been informed of an instruction or action on a request before the time for objection provided under Rule 51(b)(2) objects promptly after learning that the instruction or request will be, or has been, given or refused.

(d) Assigning Error; Plain Error.

(1) A party may assign as error:

(A) an error in an instruction actually given if that party made a proper objection under Rule 51(c), or

(B) a failure to give an instruction if that party made a proper request under Rule 51(a), and—unless the court made a definitive ruling on the record rejecting the request—also made a proper objection under Rule 51(c).

(2) A court may consider a plain error in the instructions affecting substantial rights that has not been preserved as required by Rule 51(d)(1)(A) or (B).

Advisory Committee's Note

Rule 51 is revised to capture many of the interpretations that have emerged in practice. The revisions in text will make uniform the conclusions reached by a majority of decisions on each point. Additions also are made to cover some practices that cannot now be anchored in the text of Rule 51.

Scope. Rule 51 governs instructions to the trial jury on the law that governs the verdict. A variety of other instructions cannot practicably be brought within Rule 51. Among these instructions are preliminary instructions to a venire, and cautionary or limiting instructions delivered in immediate response to events at trial.

Requests. Subdivision (a) governs requests. Apart from the plain error doctrine recognized in subdivision (d)(2), a court is not obliged to instruct the jury on issues raised by the evidence unless a party requests an instruction. The revised rule recognizes the court's authority to direct that requests be submitted before trial.

The close-of-the-evidence deadline may come before trial is completed on all potential issues. Trial may be formally bifurcated or may be sequenced in some less formal manner. The close of the evidence is measured by the occurrence of two events: completion of all intended evidence on an identified phase of the trial and impending submission to the jury with instructions.

The risk in directing a pretrial request deadline is that trial evidence may raise new issues or reshape issues the parties thought they had understood. Courts need not insist on pretrial requests in all cases. Even if the request time is set before trial or early in the trial, subdivision (a)(2)(A) permits requests after the close of the evidence to address issues that could not reasonably have been anticipated at the earlier time for requests set by the court.

Subdivision (a)(2)(B) expressly recognizes the court's discretion to act on an untimely request. The most important consideration in exercising the discretion confirmed by subdivision (a)(2)(B) is the importance of the issue to the case—the closer the issue lies to the "plain error" that would be recognized under subdivision (d)(2), the better the reason to give an instruction. The cogency of the reason for failing to make a timely request also should be considered. To be considered under subdivision (a)(2)(B) a request should be made before final instructions and before final jury arguments. What is a "final" instruction and argument depends on the sequence of submitting the case to the jury. If separate portions of the case are submitted to the jury in sequence, the final arguments and final instructions are those made on submitting to the jury the portion of the case addressed by the arguments and instructions.

Instructions. Subdivision (b)(1) requires the court to inform the parties, before instructing the jury and before final jury arguments related to the instruction, of the proposed instructions as well as the proposed action on instruction requests. The time limit is addressed to final jury arguments to reflect the practice that allows interim arguments during trial in complex cases; it may not be feasible to develop final instructions before such interim arguments. It is enough that counsel know of the intended instructions before making final arguments addressed to the issue. If the trial is sequenced or bifurcated, the final arguments addressed to an issue may occur before the close of the entire trial.

Subdivision (b)(2) complements subdivision (b)(1) by carrying forward the opportunity to object established by present Rule 51. It makes explicit the opportunity to object on the record, ensuring a clear memorial of the objection.

Subdivision (b)(3) reflects common practice by authorizing instructions at any time after trial begins and before the jury is discharged.

Objections. Subdivision (c) states the right to object to an instruction or the failure to give an instruction. It carries forward the formula of present Rule 51 requiring that the objection state distinctly the matter objected to and the grounds of the objection, and makes explicit the requirement that the objection be made on the record. The provisions on the time to object make clear that it is timely to object promptly after learning of an instruction or action on a request when the court has not provided advance information as required by subdivision (b)(1). The need to repeat a request by way of objection is continued by new subdivision (d)(1)(B) except where the court made a definitive ruling on the record.

Preserving a claim of error and plain error. Many cases hold that a proper request for a jury instruction is not alone enough to preserve the right to appeal failure to give the instruction. The request must be renewed by objection. This doctrine is appropriate when the court may not have sufficiently focused on the request, or may believe that the request has been granted in substance although in different words. But this doctrine may also prove a trap for the unwary who fail to add an objection after the court has made it clear that the request has been considered and rejected on the merits. Subdivision (d)(1)(B) establishes authority to review the failure to grant a timely request, despite a failure to add an objection, when the court has made a definitive ruling on the record rejecting the request.

Many circuits have recognized that an error not preserved under Rule 51 may be reviewed in exceptional circumstances. The language adopted to capture these decisions in subdivision (d)(2) is borrowed from Criminal Rule 52. Although the language is the same, the context of civil litigation often differs from the context of criminal prosecution; actual application of the plain-error standard takes account of the differences. The Supreme Court has summarized application of Criminal Rule 52 as involving four elements: (1) there must be an error; (2) the error must be plain; (3) the error must affect substantial rights; and (4) the error must seriously affect the fairness, integrity, or public reputation of judicial proceedings. *Johnson v. U.S.*, 520 U.S. 461, 466–467, 469–470 (1997). (The Johnson case quoted the fourth element from its decision in a civil action, *U.S. v. Atkinson*, 297 U.S. 157, 160 (1936): "In exceptional circumstances, especially in criminal cases, appellate courts, in the public interest, may, of their own motion, notice errors to which no exception has been taken, if the errors are obvious, or if they otherwise substantially affect the fairness, integrity, or public reputation of judicial proceedings.")

The court's duty to give correct jury instructions in a civil action is shaped by at least four factors.

The factor most directly implied by a "plain" error rule is the obviousness of the mistake. The importance of the error is a second major factor. The costs of correcting an error reflect a third factor that is affected by a variety of circumstances. In a case that seems close to the fundamental error line, account also may be taken of the impact a verdict may have on nonparties.

~~Rule 53~~

~~MASTERS~~

~~**(a) Appointment and Compensation.** The court in which any action is pending may appoint a special master therein. As used in these rules, the word "master" includes a referee, an auditor, an examiner, and an assessor. The compensation to be allowed to a master shall be fixed by the court, and shall be charged upon such of the parties or paid out of any fund or subject matter of the action, which is in the custody and control of the court as the court may direct; provided that this provision for compensation shall not~~

New material is shown in italics; matter to be omitted is lined through

~~apply when a United States magistrate judge is designated to serve as a master. The master shall not retain the master's report as security for the master's compensation; but when the party ordered to pay the compensation allowed by the court does not pay it after notice and within the time prescribed by the court, the master is entitled to a writ of execution against the delinquent party.~~

~~**(b) Reference.** A reference to a master shall be the exception and not the rule. In actions to be tried by a jury, a reference shall be made only when the issues are complicated; in actions to be tried without a jury, save in matters of account and of difficult computation of damages, a reference shall be made only upon a showing that some exceptional condition requires it. Upon the consent of the parties, a magistrate judge may be designated to serve as a special master without regard to the provisions of this subdivision.~~

~~**(c) Powers.** The order of reference to the master may specify or limit the master's powers and may direct the master to report only upon particular issues or to do or perform particular acts or to receive and report evidence only and may fix the time and place for beginning and closing the hearings and for the filing of the master's report. Subject to the specifications and limitations stated in the order, the master has and shall exercise the power to regulate all proceedings in every hearing before the master and to do all acts and take all measures necessary or proper for the efficient performance of the master's duties under the order. The master may require the production before the master of evidence upon all matters embraced in the reference, including the production of all books, papers, vouchers, documents, and writings applicable thereto. The master may rule upon the admissibility of evidence unless otherwise directed by the order of reference and has the authority to put witnesses on oath and may examine them and may call the parties to the action and examine them upon oath. When a party so requests, the master shall make a record of the evidence offered and excluded in the same manner and subject to the same limitations as provided in the Federal Rules of Evidence for a court sitting without a jury.~~

~~**(d) Proceedings.**~~

~~(1) Meetings. When a reference is made, the clerk shall forthwith furnish the master with a copy of the order of reference. Upon receipt thereof unless the order of reference otherwise provides, the master shall forthwith set a time and place for the first meeting of the parties or their attorneys to be held within 20 days after the date of the order of reference and shall notify the parties or their attorneys. It is the duty of the master to proceed with all reasonable diligence. Either party, on notice to the parties and master,~~

~~may apply to the court for an order requiring the master to speed the proceedings and to make the report. If a party fails to appear at the time and place appointed, the master may proceed ex parte or, in the master's discretion, adjourn the proceedings to a future day, giving notice to the absent party of the adjournment.~~

~~(2) Witnesses. The parties may procure the attendance of witnesses before the master by the issuance and service of subpoenas as provided in Rule 45. If without adequate excuse a witness fails to appear or give evidence, the witness may be punished as for a contempt and be subjected to the consequences, penalties, and remedies provided in Rules 37 and 45.~~

~~(3) Statement of Accounts. When matters of accounting are in issue before the master, the master may prescribe the form in which the accounts shall be submitted and in any proper case may require or receive in evidence a statement by a certified public accountant who is called as a witness. Upon objection of a party to any of the items thus submitted or upon a showing that the form of statement is insufficient, the master may require a different form of statement to be furnished, or the accounts or specific items thereof to be proved by oral examination of the accounting parties or upon written interrogatories or in such other manner as the master directs.~~

~~**(e) Report.**~~

~~(1) Contents and Filing. The master shall prepare a report upon the matters submitted to the master by the order of reference and, if required to make findings of fact and conclusions of law, the master shall set them forth in the report. The master shall file the report with the clerk of the court and serve on all parties notice of the filing. In an action to be tried without a jury, unless otherwise directed by the order of reference, the master shall file with the report a transcript of the proceedings and of the evidence and the original exhibits. Unless otherwise directed by the order of reference, the master shall serve a copy of the report on each party.~~

~~(2) In Non–Jury Actions. In an action to be tried without a jury the court shall accept the master's findings of fact unless clearly erroneous. Within 10 days after being served with notice of the filing of the report any party may serve written objections thereto upon the other parties. Application to the court for action upon the report and upon objections thereto shall be by motion and upon notice as prescribed in Rule 6(d). The court after hearing may adopt the report or may modify it or may reject it in whole or in part or may receive further evidence or may recommit it with instructions.~~

~~(3) In Jury Actions. In an action to be tried by a jury the master shall not be directed to report the evidence. The master's findings upon the issues submitted to the master are admissible as evidence of the matters found and may be read to the jury, subject to the ruling of the court upon any objections in point of law which may be made to the report.~~

~~(4) Stipulation as to Findings. The effect of a master's report is the same whether or not the parties have consented to the reference; but, when the parties stipulate that a master's findings of fact shall be final, only questions of law arising upon the report shall thereafter be considered.~~

~~(5) Draft Report. Before filing the master's report a master may submit a draft thereof to counsel for all parties for the purpose of receiving their suggestions.~~

~~**(f) Application to Magistrate Judge.** A magistrate judge is subject to this rule only when the order referring a matter to the magistrate judge expressly provides that the reference is made under this rule.~~

Rule 53. Masters

(a) Appointment.

(1) Unless a statute provides otherwise, a court may appoint a master only to:

(A) perform duties consented to by the parties;

(B) hold trial proceedings and make or recommend findings of fact on issues to be decided by the court without a jury if appointment is warranted by

(i) some exceptional condition, or

(ii) the need to perform an accounting or resolve a difficult computation of damages; or

(C) address pretrial and post-trial matters that cannot be addressed effectively and timely by an available district judge or magistrate judge of the district.

(2) A master must not have a relationship to the parties, counsel, action, or court that would require disqualification of a judge under 28 U.S.C. § 455 unless the parties consent with the court's approval to appointment of a particular person after disclosure of any potential grounds for disqualification.

(3) In appointing a master, the court must consider the fairness of imposing the likely expenses on the parties and must protect against unreasonable expense or delay.

(b) Order Appointing Master.

(1) Notice. The court must give the parties notice and an opportunity to be heard before appointing a master. A party may suggest candidates for appointment.

(2) Contents. The order appointing a master must direct the master to proceed with all reasonable diligence and must state:

(A) the master's duties, including any investigation or enforcement duties, and any limits on the master's authority under Rule 53(c);

(B) the circumstances—if any—in which the master may communicate ex parte with the court or a party;

(C) the nature of the materials to be preserved and filed as the record of the master's activities;

(D) the time limits, method of filing the record, other procedures, and standards for reviewing the master's orders, findings, and recommendations; and

(E) the basis, terms, and procedure for fixing the master's compensation under Rule 53(h).

(3) Entry of Order. The court may enter the order appointing a master only after the master has filed an affidavit disclosing whether there is any ground for disqualification under 28 U.S.C. § 455 and, if a ground for disqualification is disclosed, after the parties have consented with the court's approval to waive the disqualification.

(4) Amendment. The order appointing a master may be amended at any time after notice to the parties, and an opportunity to be heard.

(c) Master's Authority. *Unless the appointing order expressly directs otherwise, a master has authority to regulate all proceedings and take all appropriate measures to perform fairly and efficiently the assigned duties. The master may by order impose upon a party any noncontempt sanction provided by Rule 37 or 45, and may recommend a contempt sanction against a party and sanctions against a nonparty.*

(d) Evidentiary Hearings. *Unless the appointing order expressly directs otherwise, a master conducting an evidentiary hearing may exercise the power of the appointing court to compel, take, and record evidence.*

(e) Master's Orders. *A master who makes an order must file the order and promptly serve a copy on each party. The clerk must enter the order on the docket.*

(f) Master's Reports. *A master must report to the court as required by the order of appointment. The master must file the report and promptly serve a copy of the report on each party unless the court directs otherwise.*

(g) Action on Master's Order, Report, or Recommendations.

(1) Action. In acting on a master's order, report, or recommendations, the court must afford an opportunity to be heard and may receive evidence, and may: adopt or affirm; modify; wholly or partly reject or reverse; or resubmit to the master with instructions.

(2) Time to Object or Move. A party may file objections to—or a motion to adopt or modify—the master's order, report, or recommmendations no later than 20 days from the time the master's order, report, or recommendations are served, unless the court sets a different time.

(3) Fact Findings. The court must decide de novo all objections to findings of fact made or recommended by a master unless the parties stipulate with the court's consent that:

(A) the master's findings will be reviewed for clear error, or

(B) the findings of a master appointed under Rule 53(a)(1)(A) or (C) will be final.

(4) Legal Conclusions. The court must decide de novo all objections to conclusions of law made or recommended by a master.

(5) Procedural Matters. Unless the order of appointment establishes a different standard of review, the court may set aside a master's ruling on a procedural matter only for an abuse of discretion.

(h) Compensation.

(1) Fixing Compensation. The court must fix the master's compensation before or after judgment on the basis and terms stated in the order of appointment, but the court may set a new basis and terms after notice and an opportunity to be heard.

(2) Payment. The compensation fixed under Rule 53(h)(1) must be paid either:

(A) by a party or parties; or

(B) from a fund or subject matter of the action within the court's control.

(3) Allocation. The court must allocate payment of the master's compensation among the parties after considering the nature and amount of the controversy, the means of the parties, and the extent to which any party is more responsible than other parties for the

reference to a master. An interim allocation may be amended to reflect a decision on the merits.

(i) Appointment of Magistrate Judge. *A magistrate judge is subject to this rule only when the order referring a matter to the magistrate judge expressly provides that the reference is made under this rule.*

Advisory Committee's Note

Rule 53 is revised extensively to reflect changing practices in using masters. From the beginning in 1938, Rule 53 focused primarily on special masters who perform trial functions. Since then, however, courts have gained experience with masters appointed to perform a variety of pretrial and post-trial functions. See Willging, Hooper, Leary, Miletich, Reagan, & Shapard, *Special Masters' Incidence and Activity* (Federal Judicial Center 2000). This revised Rule 53 recognizes that in appropriate circumstances masters may properly be appointed to perform these functions and regulates such appointments. Rule 53 continues to address trial masters as well, but permits appointment of a trial master in an action to be tried to a jury only if the parties consent. The new rule clarifies the provisions that govern the appointment and function of masters for all purposes. Rule 53(g) also changes the standard of review for findings of fact made or recommended by a master. The core of the original Rule 53 remains, including its prescription that appointment of a master must be the exception and not the rule.

Special masters are appointed in many circumstances outside the Civil Rules. Rule 53 applies only to proceedings that Rule 1 brings within its reach.

Subdivision (a)(1)

District judges bear primary responsibility for the work of their courts. A master should be appointed only in limited circumstances. Subdivision (a)(1) describes three different standards, relating to appointments by consent of the parties, appointments for trial duties, and appointments for pretrial or post-trial duties.

Consent Masters. Subparagraph (a)(1)(A) authorizes appointment of a master with the parties' consent. Party consent does not require that the court make the appointment; the court retains unfettered discretion to refuse appointment.

Trial Masters. Use of masters for the core functions of trial has been progressively limited. These limits are reflected in the provisions of subparagraph (a)(1)(B) that restrict appointments to exercise trial functions. The Supreme Court gave clear direction to this trend in *La Buy v. Howes Leather Co.*, 352 U.S. 249 (1957); earlier roots are sketched in *Los Angeles Brush Mfg. Corp. v. James*, 272 U.S. 701 (1927). As to nonjury trials, this trend has developed through elaboration of the "exceptional condition" requirement in present Rule 53(b). This phrase is retained, and will continue to have the same force as it has developed. Although the provision that a reference "shall be the exception and not the rule" is deleted, its meaning is embraced for this setting by the exceptional condition requirement.

Subparagraph (a)(1)(B)(ii) carries forward the approach of present Rule 53(b), which exempts from the "exceptional condition" requirement "matters of account and of difficult computation of damages." This approach is justified only as to essentially ministerial determinations that require mastery of much detailed information but that do not require extensive determinations of credibility. Evaluations of witness credibility should only be assigned to a trial master when justified by an exceptional condition.

The use of a trial master without party consent is abolished as to matters to be decided by a jury unless a statute provides for this practice.

Abolition of the direct power to appoint a trial master as to issues to be decided by a jury leaves the way free to appoint a trial master with the consent of all parties. A trial master should be appointed in a jury case, with consent of the parties and concurrence of the court, only if the parties waive jury trial with respect to the issues submitted to the master or if the master's findings are to be submitted to the jury as evidence in the manner provided by former Rule 53(e)(3). In no circumstance may a master be appointed to preside at a jury trial.

The central function of a trial master is to preside over an evidentiary hearing on the merits of the claims or defenses in the action. This function distinguishes the trial master from most functions of pretrial and post-trial masters. If any master is to be used for such matters as a preliminary injunction hearing or a determination of complex damages issues, for example, the master should be a trial master. The line, however, is not distinct. A pretrial master might well conduct an evidentiary hearing on a discovery dispute, and a post-trial master might conduct evidentiary hearings on questions of compliance.

Rule 53 has long provided authority to report the evidence without recommendations in nonjury trials. This authority is omitted from Rule 53(a)(1)(B). In some circumstances a master may be appointed under Rule 53(a)(1)(A) or (C) to take evidence and report without recommendations.

For nonjury cases, a master also may be appointed to assist the court in discharging trial duties other than conducting an evidentiary hearing.

Pretrial and Post-Trial Masters. Subparagraph (a)(1)(C) authorizes appointment of a master to address pretrial or post-trial matters. Appointment is limited to matters than cannot be addressed effectively and in a timely fashion by an available district judge or magistrate judge of the district. A master's pretrial or post-trial duties may include matters that could be addressed by a judge, such as reviewing discovery documents for privilege, or duties that might not be suitable for a judge. Some forms of settlement negotiations, investigations, or administration of an organization are familiar examples of duties that a judge might not feel free to undertake.

Magistrate Judges. Particular attention should be paid to the prospect that a magistrate judge may be available for special assignments. United States magistrate judges are authorized by statute to perform many pretrial functions in civil actions. 28 U.S.C. § 636(b)(1). Ordinarily a district judge who delegates these functions should refer them to a magistrate judge acting as magistrate judge.

There is statutory authority to appoint a magistrate judge as special master. 28 U.S.C. § 636(b)(2). In special circumstances, or when expressly authorized by a statute other than § 636(b)(2), it may be appropriate to appoint a magistrate judge as a master when needed to perform functions outside those listed in § 636(b)(1). There is no apparent reason to appoint a magistrate judge to perform as master duties that could be performed in the role of magistrate judge. Party consent is required for trial before a magistrate judge, moreover, and this requirement should not be undercut by resort to Rule 53 unless specifically authorized by statute; see 42 U.S.C. § 2000e–5(f)(5).

Pretrial Masters. The appointment of masters to participate in pretrial proceedings has developed extensively over the last two decades as some district courts have felt the need for additional help in managing complex litigation. This practice is not well regulated by present Rule 53, which focuses on masters as trial participants.

Rule 53 is amended to confirm the authority to appoint—and to regulate the use of—pretrial masters.

A pretrial master should be appointed only when the need is clear. Direct judicial performance of judicial functions may be particularly important in cases that involve important public issues or many parties. At the extreme, a broad delegation of pretrial responsibility as well as a delegation of trial responsibilities can run afoul of Article III.

A master also may be appointed to address matters that blur the divide between pretrial and trial functions. The court's responsibility to interpret patent claims as a matter of law, for example, may be greatly assisted by appointing a master who has expert knowledge of the field in which the patent operates. Review of the master's findings will be de novo under Rule 53(g)(4), but the advantages of initial determination by a master may make the process more effective and timely than disposition by the judge acting alone. Determination of foreign law may present comparable difficulties. The decision whether to appoint a master to address such matters is governed by subdivision (a)(1)(C), not the trial-master provisions of subdivision (a)(1)(B).

Post-Trial Masters. Courts have come to rely on masters to assist in framing and enforcing complex decrees. Present Rule 53 does not directly address this practice. Amended Rule 53 authorizes appointment of post-trial masters for these and similar purposes. The constraint of subdivision (a)(1)(C) limits this practice to cases in which the master's duties cannot be performed effectively and in a timely fashion by an available district judge or magistrate judge of the district.

Reliance on a master is appropriate when a complex decree requires complex policing, particularly when a party has proved resistant or intransigent. This practice has been recognized by the Supreme Court, see *Local 28, Sheet Metal Workers' Internat. Assn. v. EEOC*, 478 U.S. 421, 481–482 (1986). The master's role in enforcement may extend to investigation in ways that are quite unlike the traditional role of judicial officers in an adversary system.

Expert Witness Overlap. This rule does not address the difficulties that arise when a single person is appointed to perform overlapping roles as master and as court-appointed expert witness under Evidence Rule 706. Whatever combination of functions is involved, the Rule 53(a)(1)(B) limit that confines trial masters to issues to be decided by the court does not apply to a person who also is appointed as an expert witness under Evidence Rule 706.

Subdivision (a)(2) and (3)

Masters are subject to the Code of Conduct for United States Judges, with exceptions spelled out in the Code. Special care must be taken to ensure that there is no actual or apparent conflict of interest involving a master. The standard of disqualification is established by 28 U.S.C. § 455. The affidavit required by Rule 53(b)(3) provides an important source of information about possible grounds for disqualification, but careful inquiry should be made at the time of making the initial appointment. The disqualification standards established by § 455 are strict. Because a master is not a public judicial officer, it may be appropriate to permit the parties to consent to appointment of a particular person as master in circumstances that would require disqualification of a judge. The judge must be careful to ensure that no party feels any pressure to consent, but with such assurances—and with the judge's own determination that there is no troubling conflict of interests or disquieting appearance of impropriety—consent may justify an otherwise barred appointment.

One potential disqualification issue is peculiar to the master's role. It may happen that a master who is an attorney represents a client whose litigation is assigned to the judge who appointed the attorney as master. Other parties to the litigation may fear that the attorney-master will gain special respect from the judge. A flat prohibition on appearance before the appointing judge during the time of service as master, however, might in some circumstances unduly limit the opportunity to make a desirable appointment. These matters may be regulated to some extent by state rules of professional responsibility. The question of present conflicts, and the possibility of future conflicts, can be considered at the time of appointment. Depending on the circumstances, the judge may consider it appropriate to impose a non-appearance condition on the lawyer-master, and perhaps on the master's firm as well.

Subdivision (b)

The order appointing a pretrial master is vitally important in informing the master and the parties about the nature and extent of the master's duties and authority. Care must be taken to make the order as precise as possible. The parties must be given notice and opportunity to be heard on the question whether a master should be appointed and on the terms of the appointment. To the extent possible, the notice should describe the master's proposed duties, time to complete the duties, standards of review, and compensation. Often it will be useful to engage the parties in the process of identifying the master, inviting nominations, and reviewing potential candidates. Party involvement may be particularly useful if a pretrial master is expected to promote settlement.

The hearing requirement of Rule 53(b)(1) can be satisfied by an opportunity to make written submissions unless the circumstances require live testimony.

Rule 53(b)(2) requires precise designation of the master's duties and authority. Clear identification of any investigating or enforcement duties is particularly important. Clear delineation of topics for any reports or recommendations is also an important part of this process. And it is important to protect against delay by establishing a time schedule for performing the assigned duties. Early designation of the procedure for fixing the master's compensation also may provide useful guidance to the parties.

Ex parte communications between a master and the court present troubling questions. Ordinarily the order should prohibit such communications, assuring that the parties know where authority is lodged at each step of the proceedings. Prohibiting ex parte communications between master and court also can enhance the role of a settlement master by assuring the parties that settlement can be fostered by confidential revelations that will not be shared with the court. Yet there may be circumstances in which the master's role is enhanced by the opportunity for ex parte communications with the court. A master assigned to help coordinate multiple proceedings, for example, may benefit from off-the-record exchanges with the court about logistical matters. The rule does not directly regulate these matters. It requires only that the court exercise its discretion and address the topic in the order of appointment.

Similarly difficult questions surround ex parte communications between a master and the parties. Ex parte communications may be essential in seeking to advance settlement. Ex parte communications also may prove useful in other settings, as with in camera review of documents to resolve privilege questions. In most settings, however, ex parte communications with the parties should be discouraged or prohibited. The rule requires that the court address the topic in the order of appointment.

Subdivision (b)(2)(C) provides that the appointment order must state the nature of the materials to be preserved and filed as the record of the master's activities, and (b)(2)(D) requires that the order state the method of filing the record. It is not feasible to prescribe the nature of the record without regard to the nature of the master's duties. The records appropriate to discovery duties may be different from those appropriate to encouraging settlement, investigating possible violations of a complex decree, or making recommendations for trial findings. A basic requirement, however, is that the master must make and file a complete record of the evidence considered in making or recommending findings of fact on the basis of evidence. The order of appointment should routinely include this requirement unless the nature of the appointment precludes any prospect that the master will make or recommend evidence-based findings of fact. In some circumstances it may be appropriate for a party to file materials directly with the court as provided by Rule 5(e), but in many circumstances filing with the court may be inappropriate. Confidentiality is important with respect to many materials that may properly be considered by a master. Materials in the record can be transmitted to the court, and filed, in connection with review of a master's order, report, or recommendations under subdivisions (f) and (g). Independently of review proceedings, the court may direct filing of any materials that it wishes to make part of the public record.

The provision in subdivision (b)(2)(D) that the order must state the standards for reviewing the master's orders, findings, or recommendations is a reminder of the provisions of subdivision (g)(3) that recognize stipulations for review less searching than the presumptive requirement of de novo decision by the court. Subdivision (b)(2)(D) does not authorize the court to supersede the limits of subdivision (g)(3).

In setting the procedure for fixing the master's compensation, it is useful at the outset to establish specific guidelines to control total expense. The court has power under subdivision (h) to change the basis and terms for determining compensation after notice to the parties.

Subdivision (b)(3) permits entry of the order appointing a master only after the master has filed an affidavit disclosing whether there is any ground for disqualification under 28 U.S.C. § 455. If the affidavit discloses a possible ground for disqualification, the order can enter only if the court determines that there is no ground for disqualification or if the parties, knowing of the ground for disqualification, consent with the court's approval to waive the disqualification.

The provision in Rule 53(b)(4) for amending the order of appointment is as important as the provisions for the initial order. Anything that could be done in the initial order can be done by amendment. The hearing requirement can be satisfied by an opportunity to make written submissions unless the circumstances require live testimony.

Subdivision (c)

Subdivision (c) is a simplification of the provisions scattered throughout present Rule 53. It is intended to provide the broad and flexible authority necessary to discharge the master's responsibilities. The most important delineation of a master's authority and duties is provided by the Rule 53(b) appointing order.

Subdivision (d)

The subdivision (d) provisions for evidentiary hearings are reduced from the extensive provisions in current Rule 53. This simplification of the rule is not intended to diminish the authority that may be delegated to a master. Reliance is placed on the broad and general terms of subdivision (c).

Subdivision (e)

Subdivision (e) provides that a master's order must be filed and entered on the docket. It must be promptly served on the parties, a task ordinarily accomplished by mailing or other means as permitted by Rule 5(b). In some circumstances it may be appropriate to have the clerk's office assist the master in mailing the order to the parties.

Subdivision (f)

Subdivision (f) restates some of the provisions of present Rule 53(e)(1). The report is the master's primary means of communication with the court. The materials to be provided to support review of the report will depend on the nature of the report. The master should provide all portions of the record preserved under Rule 53(b)(2)(C) that the master deems relevant to the report. The parties may designate additional materials from the record, and may seek permission to supplement the record with evidence. The court may direct that additional materials from the record be provided and filed. Given the wide array of tasks that may be assigned to a pretrial master, there may be circumstances that justify sealing a report or review record against public access—a report on continuing or failed settlement efforts is the most likely example. A post-trial master may be assigned duties in formulating a decree that deserve similar protection. Such circumstances may even justify denying access to the report or review materials by the parties, although this step should be taken only for the most compelling reasons. Sealing is much less likely to be appropriate with respect to a trial master's report.

Before formally making an order, report, or recommendations, a master may find it helpful to circulate a draft to the parties for review and comment. The usefulness of this practice depends on the nature of the master's proposed action.

Subdivision (g)

The provisions of subdivision (g)(1), describing the court's powers to afford a hearing, take evidence, and act on a master's order, report, or recommendations are drawn from present Rule 53(e)(2), but are not limited, as present Rule 53(e)(2) is limited, to the report of a trial master in a nonjury action. The requirement that the court must afford an opportunity to be heard can be satisfied by taking written submissions when the court acts on the report without taking live testimony.

The subdivision (g)(2) time limits for objecting to—or seeking adoption or modification of—a master's order, report, or recommendations, are important. They are not jurisdictional. Although a court may properly refuse to entertain untimely review proceedings, the court may excuse the failure to seek timely review. The basic time period is lengthened to 20 days because the present 10–day period may be too short to permit thorough study and response to a complex report dealing with complex litigation. If no party asks the court to act on a master's report, the court is free to adopt the master's action or to disregard it at any relevant point in the proceedings.

Subdivision (g)(3) establishes the standards of review for a master's findings of fact or recommended findings of fact. The court must decide de novo all objections to findings of fact made or recommended by the master unless the parties stipulate, with the court's consent, that the findings will be reviewed for clear error or—with respect to a master appointed on the parties' consent or appointed to address pretrial or post-trial matters—that the findings will be final. Clear-error review is more likely to be appropriate with respect to findings that do not go to the merits of the underlying claims or defenses, such as findings of fact bearing on a privilege objection to a discovery request. Even if no objection is made, the court is free to decide the facts de novo; to review for clear error if an earlier approved stipulation provided clear-error review; or to withdraw its consent to a stipulation for clear-error review or finality, and then to decide de novo. If the court withdraws its consent to a stipulation for finality or clear-error review, it may reopen the opportunity to object.

Under Rule 53(g)(4), the court must decide de novo all objections to conclusions of law made or recommended by a master. As with findings of fact, the court also may decide conclusions of law de novo when no objection is made.

Apart from factual and legal questions, masters often make determinations that, when made by a trial court, would be treated as matters of procedural discretion. The court may set a standard for review of such matters in the order of appointment, and may amend the order to establish the standard. If no standard is set by the original or amended order appointing the master, review of procedural matters is for abuse of discretion. The subordinate role of the master means that the trial court's review for abuse of discretion may be more searching than the review that an appellate court makes of a trial court.

If a master makes a recommendation on any matter that does not fall within Rule 53(g)(3), (4), or (5), the court may act on the recommendation under Rule 53(g)(1).

Subdivision (h)

The need to pay compensation is a substantial reason for care in appointing private persons as masters.

Payment of the master's fees must be allocated among the parties and any property or subject-matter within the court's control. The amount in controversy and the means of the parties may provide some guidance in making the allocation. The nature of the dispute also may be important—parties pursuing matters of public interest, for example, may deserve special protection. A party whose unreasonable behavior has occasioned the need to appoint a master, on the other hand, may properly be charged all or a major portion of the master's fees. It may be proper to revise an interim allocation after decision on the merits. The revision need not await a decision that is final for purposes of appeal, but may be made to reflect disposition of a substantial portion of the case.

The basis and terms for fixing compensation should be stated in the order of appointment. The court retains power to alter the initial basis and terms, after notice and an opportunity to be heard, but should protect the parties against unfair surprise.

The provision of former Rule 53(a) that the "provision for compensation shall not apply when a United States Magistrate Judge is designated to serve as a master" is deleted as unnecessary. Other provisions of law preclude compensation.

Subdivision (i)

Rule 53(i) carries forward unchanged former Rule 53(f).

*

FEDERAL RULES OF APPELLATE PROCEDURE

(with some omissions)

TABLE OF RULES

Title I. Applicability of Rules

Title II. Appeal From a Judgment or Order of a District Court

Title III. Review of a Decision of the United States Tax Court [Omitted]

Title IV. Review or Enforcement of an Order of an Administrative Agency, Board, Commission, or Officer [Omitted]

Title V. Extraordinary Writs

Title VI. Habeas Corpus; Proceedings in Forma Pauperis

RULES OF APPELLATE PROCEDURE

Rule

Title VII. General Provisions

Appendix of Forms

FEDERAL RULES OF APPELLATE PROCEDURE

(with some omissions)

TITLE I. APPLICABILITY OF RULES

Rule 1.

SCOPE OF RULES; TITLE

(a) Scope of Rules.

(1) These rules govern procedure in the United States courts of appeals.

(2) When these rules provide for filing a motion or other document in the district court, the procedure must comply with the practice of the district court.

(b) [Abrogated.]

(c) Title. These rules are to be known as the Federal Rules of Appellate Procedure.

As amended 1979, 1989, 1994, 1998, 2002.

Rule 2.

SUSPENSION OF RULES

On its own or a party's motion, a court of appeals may—to expedite its decision or for other good cause—suspend any provision of these rules in a particular case and order proceedings as it directs, except as otherwise provided in Rule 26(b).

As amended 1998.

TITLE II. APPEAL FROM A JUDGMENT OR ORDER OF A DISTRICT COURT

Rule 3.

APPEAL AS OF RIGHT—HOW TAKEN

(a) Filing the Notice of Appeal.

(1) An appeal permitted by law as of right from a district court to a court of appeals may be taken only by filing a notice of appeal

with the district clerk within the time allowed by Rule 4. At the time of filing, the appellant must furnish the clerk with enough copies of the notice to enable the clerk to comply with Rule 3(d).

(2) An appellant's failure to take any step other than the timely filing of a notice of appeal does not affect the validity of the appeal, but is ground only for the court of appeals to act as it considers appropriate, including dismissing the appeal.

(3) An appeal from a judgment by a magistrate judge in a civil case is taken in the same way as an appeal from any other district court judgment.

(4) An appeal by permission under 28 U.S.C. § 1292(b) or an appeal in a bankruptcy case may be taken only in the manner prescribed by Rules 5 and 6, respectively.

(b) Joint or Consolidated Appeals.

(1) When two or more parties are entitled to appeal from a district-court judgment or order, and their interests make joinder practicable, they may file a joint notice of appeal. They may then proceed on appeal as a single appellant.

(2) When the parties have filed separate timely notices of appeal, the appeals may be joined or consolidated by the court of appeals.

(c) Contents of the Notice of Appeal.

(1) The notice of appeal must:

(A) specify the party or parties taking the appeal by naming each one in the caption or body of the notice, but an attorney representing more than one party may describe those parties with such terms as "all plaintiffs," "the defendants," "the plaintiffs A, B, et al.," or "all defendants except X";

(B) designate the judgment, order, or part thereof being appealed; and

(C) name the court to which the appeal is taken.

(2) A pro se notice of appeal is considered filed on behalf of the signer and the signer's spouse and minor children (if they are parties), unless the notice clearly indicates otherwise.

(3) In a class action, whether or not the class has been certified, the notice of appeal is sufficient if it names one person qualified to bring the appeal as representative of the class.

(4) An appeal must not be dismissed for informality of form or title of the notice of appeal, or for failure to name a party whose intent to appeal is otherwise clear from the notice.

(5) Form 1 in the Appendix of Forms is a suggested form of a notice of appeal.

(d) Serving the Notice of Appeal.

(1) The district clerk must serve notice of the filing of a notice of appeal by mailing a copy to each party's counsel of record—excluding the appellant's—or, if a party is proceeding pro se, to the party's last known address. When a defendant in a criminal case appeals, the clerk must also serve a copy of the notice of appeal on the defendant, either by personal service or by mail addressed to the defendant. The clerk must promptly send a copy of the notice of appeal and of the docket entries—and any later docket entries—to the clerk of the court of appeals named in the notice. The district clerk must note, on each copy, the date when the notice of appeal was filed.

(2) If an inmate confined in an institution files a notice of appeal in the manner provided by Rule 4(c), the district clerk must also note the date when the clerk docketed the notice.

(3) The district clerk's failure to serve notice does not affect the validity of the appeal. The clerk must note on the docket the names of the parties to whom the clerk mails copies, with the date of mailing. Service is sufficient despite the death of a party or the party's counsel.

(e) Payment of Fees. Upon filing a notice of appeal, the appellant must pay the district clerk all required fees. The district clerk receives the appellate docket fee on behalf of the court of appeals.

As amended 1979, 1986, 1989, 1993, 1994, 1998.

Rule 3.1.

APPEAL FROM A JUDGMENT OF A MAGISTRATE JUDGE IN A CIVIL CASE

Abrogated 1998

Rule 4.

APPEAL AS OF RIGHT—WHEN TAKEN

(a) Appeal in a Civil Case.

(1) *Time for Filing a Notice of Appeal.*

(A) In a civil case, except as provided in Rules 4(a)(1)(B), 4(a)(4), and 4(c), the notice of appeal required by Rule 3 must be filed with the district clerk within 30 days after the judgment or order appealed from is entered.

(B) When the United States or its officer or agency is a party, the notice of appeal may be filed by any party within 60 days after the judgment or order appealed from is entered.

(C) An appeal from an order granting or denying an application for a writ of error coram nobis is an appeal in a civil case for purposes of Rule 4(a).

(2) *Filing Before Entry of Judgment.* A notice of appeal filed after the court announces a decision or order—but before the entry of the judgment or order—is treated as filed on the date of and after the entry.

(3) *Multiple Appeals.* If one party timely files a notice of appeal, any other party may file a notice of appeal within 14 days after the date when the first notice was filed, or within the time otherwise prescribed by this Rule 4(a), whichever period ends later.

(4) *Effect of a Motion on a Notice of Appeal.*

(A) If a party timely files in the district court any of the following motions under the Federal Rules of Civil Procedure, the time to file an appeal runs for all parties from the entry of the order disposing of the last such remaining motion:

(i) for judgment under Rule 50(b);

(ii) to amend or make additional factual findings under Rule 52(b), whether or not granting the motion would alter the judgment;

(iii) for attorney's fees under Rule 54 if the district court extends the time to appeal under Rule 58;

(iv) to alter or amend the judgment under Rule 59;

(v) for a new trial under Rule 59; or

(vi) for relief under Rule 60 if the motion is filed no later than 10 days after the judgment is entered.

(B)(i) If a party files a notice of appeal after the court announces or enters a judgment—but before it disposes of any motion listed in Rule 4(a)(4)(A)—the notice becomes effective to appeal a judgment or order, in whole or in part, when the order disposing of the last such remaining motion is entered.

(ii) A party intending to challenge an order disposing of any motion listed in Rule 4(a)(4)(A), or a judgment altered or amended upon such a motion, must file a notice of appeal, or an amended notice of appeal—in compliance with Rule 3(c)—within the time prescribed by this Rule measured from the entry of the order disposing of the last such remaining motion.

(iii) No additional fee is required to file an amended notice.

(5) *Motion for Extension of Time.*

(A) The district court may extend the time to file a notice of appeal if:

(i) a party so moves no later than 30 days after the time prescribed by this Rule 4(a) expires; and

(ii) regardless of whether its motion is filed before or during the 30 days after the time prescribed by this Rule 4(a) expires, that party shows excusable neglect or good cause.

(B) A motion filed before the expiration of the time prescribed in Rule 4(a)(1) or (3) may be ex parte unless the court requires otherwise. If the motion is filed after the expiration of the prescribed time, notice must be given to the other parties in accordance with local rules.

(C) No extension under this Rule 4(a)(5) may exceed 30 days after the prescribed time or 10 days after the date when the order granting the motion is entered, whichever is later.

(6) *Reopening the Time to File an Appeal.* The district court may reopen the time to file an appeal for a period of 14 days after the date when its order to reopen is entered, but only if all the following conditions are satisfied:

(A) the motion is filed within 180 days after the judgment or order is entered or within 7 days after the moving party receives notice of the entry, whichever is earlier;

(B) the court finds that the moving party was entitled to notice of the entry of the judgment or order sought to be appealed but did not receive the notice from the district court or any party within 21 days after entry; and

(C) the court finds that no party would be prejudiced.

(7) *Entry Defined.*

(A) A judgment or order is entered for purposes of this Rule 4(a):

(i) if Federal Rule of Civil Procedure 58(a)(1) does not require a separate document, when the judgment or order is entered in the civil docket under Federal Rule of Civil Procedure 79(a); or

(ii) if Federal Rule of Civil Procedure 58(a)(1) requires a separate document, when the judgment or order is entered in the civil docket under Federal Rule of Civil Procedure 79(a) and when the earlier of these events occurs:

- the judgment or order is set forth on a separate document, or

- 150 days have run from entry of the judgment or order in the civil docket under Federal Rule of Civil Procedure 79(a).

(B) A failure to set forth a judgment or order on a separate document when required by Federal Rule of Civil Procedure 58(a)(1) does not affect the validity of an appeal from that judgment or order.

(b) Appeal in a Criminal Case.

(1) *Time for Filing a Notice of Appeal.*

(A) In a criminal case, a defendant's notice of appeal must be filed in the district court within 10 days after the later of:

(i) the entry of either the judgment or the order being appealed; or

(ii) the filing of the government's notice of appeal.

(B) When the government is entitled to appeal, its notice of appeal must be filed in the district court within 30 days after the later of:

(i) the entry of the judgment or order being appealed; or

(ii) the filing of a notice of appeal by any defendant.

(2) *Filing Before Entry of Judgment.* A notice of appeal filed after the court announces a decision, sentence, or order—but before the entry of the judgment or order—is treated as filed on the date of and after the entry.

(3) *Effect of a Motion on a Notice of Appeal.*

(A) If a defendant timely makes any of the following motions under the Federal Rules of Criminal Procedure, the notice of appeal from a judgment of conviction must be filed within 10 days after the entry of the order disposing of the last such remaining motion, or within 10 days after the entry of the judgment of conviction, whichever period ends later. This provision applies to a timely motion:

(i) for judgment of acquittal under Rule 29;

(ii) for a new trial under Rule 33, but if based on newly discovered evidence, only if the motion is made no later than 10 days after the entry of the judgment; or

(iii) for arrest of judgment under Rule 34.

(B) A notice of appeal filed after the court announces a decision, sentence, or order—but before it disposes of any of the motions referred to in Rule 4(b)(3)(A)—becomes effective upon the later of the following:

(i) the entry of the order disposing of the last such remaining motion; or

(ii) the entry of the judgment of conviction.

(C) A valid notice of appeal is effective—without amendment—to appeal from an order disposing of any of the motions referred to in Rule 4(b)(3)(A).

(4) *Motion for Extension of Time.* Upon a finding of excusable neglect or good cause, the district court may—before or after the time has expired, with or without motion and notice—extend the time to file a notice of appeal for a period not to exceed 30 days from the expiration of the time otherwise prescribed by this Rule 4(b).

(5) *Jurisdiction.* The filing of a notice of appeal under this Rule 4(b) does not divest a district court of jurisdiction to correct a sentence under Federal Rule of Criminal Procedure 35(a), nor does the filing of a motion under 35(a) affect the validity of a notice of appeal filed before entry of the order disposing of the motion. The filing of a motion under Federal Rule of Criminal Procedure 35(a) does not suspend the time for filing a notice of appeal from a judgment of conviction.

(6) *Entry Defined.* A judgment or order is entered for purposes of this Rule 4(b) when it is entered on the criminal docket.

(c) Appeal by an Inmate Confined in an Institution.

(1) If an inmate confined in an institution files a notice of appeal in either a civil or a criminal case, the notice is timely if it is deposited in the institution's internal mail system on or before the last day for filing. If an institution has a system designed for legal mail, the inmate must use that system to receive the benefit of this rule. Timely filing may be shown by a declaration in compliance with 28 U.S.C. § 1746 or by a notarized statement, either of which must set forth the date of deposit and state that first-class postage has been prepaid.

(2) If an inmate files the first notice of appeal in a civil case under this Rule 4(c), the 14–day period provided in Rule 4(a)(3) for another party to file a notice of appeal runs from the date when the district court dockets the first notice.

(3) When a defendant in a criminal case files a notice of appeal under this Rule 4(c), the 30–day period for the government to file its notice of appeal runs from the entry of the judgment or order appealed from or from the district court's docketing of the defendant's notice of appeal, whichever is later.

(d) Mistaken Filing in the Court of Appeals. If a notice of appeal in either a civil or a criminal case is mistakenly filed in the court of appeals, the clerk of that court must note on the notice the date when it was received and send it to the district clerk. The notice is then considered filed in the district court on the date so noted.

As amended 1979, 1988, 1991, 1993, 1995, 1998, 2002.

Rule 5.

APPEAL BY PERMISSION

(a) Petition for Permission to Appeal.

(1) To request permission to appeal when an appeal is within the court of appeals' discretion, a party must file a petition for permission to appeal. The petition must be filed with the circuit clerk with proof of service on all other parties to the district-court action.

(2) The petition must be filed within the time specified by the statute or rule authorizing the appeal or, if no such time is specified, within the time provided by Rule 4(a) for filing a notice of appeal.

(3) If a party cannot petition for appeal unless the district court first enters an order granting permission to do so or stating that the necessary conditions are met, the district court may amend its order, either on its own or in response to a party's motion, to include the required permission or statement. In that event, the time to petition runs from entry of the amended order.

(b) Contents of the Petition; Answer or Cross–Petition; Oral Argument.

(1) The petition must include the following:

(A) the facts necessary to understand the question presented;

(B) the question itself;

(C) the relief sought;

(D) the reasons why the appeal should be allowed and is authorized by a statute or rule; and

(E) an attached copy of:

(i) the order, decree, or judgment complained of and any related opinion or memorandum, and

(ii) any order stating the district court's permission to appeal or finding that the necessary conditions are met.

(2) A party may file an answer in opposition or a cross-petition within 7 days after the petition is served.

(3) The petition and answer will be submitted without oral argument unless the court of appeals orders otherwise.

(c) Form of Papers; Number of Copies. All papers must conform to Rule 32(c)(2). Except by the court's permission, a paper must not exceed 20 pages, exclusive of the disclosure statement, the proof of service, and the accompanying documents required by Rule 5(b)(1)(E). An original and 3 copies must be filed unless the court requires a different number by local rule or by order in a particular case.

(d) Grant of Permission; Fees; Cost Bond; Filing the Record.

(1) Within 10 days after the entry of the order granting permission to appeal, the appellant must:

(A) pay the district clerk all required fees; and

(B) file a cost bond if required under Rule 7.

(2) A notice of appeal need not be filed. The date when the order granting permission to appeal is entered serves as the date of the notice of appeal for calculating time under these rules.

(3) The district clerk must notify the circuit clerk once the petitioner has paid the fees. Upon receiving this notice, the circuit clerk must enter the appeal on the docket. The record must be forwarded and filed in accordance with Rules 11 and 12(c).

As amended 1979, 1994, 1998, 2002.

Rule 5.1.

APPEAL BY LEAVE UNDER 28 U.S.C. § 636(c)(5)

Abrogated 1998

Rule 6.

APPEAL IN A BANKRUPTCY CASE FROM A FINAL JUDGMENT, ORDER, OR DECREE OF A DISTRICT COURT OR BANKRUPTCY APPELLATE PANEL [OMITTED]

Rule 7.

BOND FOR COSTS ON APPEAL IN A CIVIL CASE

In a civil case, the district court may require an appellant to file a bond or provide other security in any form and amount necessary to ensure payment of costs on appeal. Rule 8(b) applies to a surety on a bond given under this rule.

As amended 1979, 1998.

Rule 8.

STAY OR INJUNCTION PENDING APPEAL

(a) Motion for Stay.

(1) *Initial Motion in the District Court.* A party must ordinarily move first in the district court for the following relief:

(A) a stay of the judgment or order of a district court pending appeal;

(B) approval of a supersedeas bond; or

(C) an order suspending, modifying, restoring, or granting an injunction while an appeal is pending.

(2) *Motion in the Court of Appeals; Conditions on Relief.* A motion for the relief mentioned in Rule 8(a)(1) may be made to the court of appeals or to one of its judges.

(A) The motion must:

(i) show that moving first in the district court would be impracticable; or

(ii) state that, a motion having been made, the district court denied the motion or failed to afford the relief requested and state any reasons given by the district court for its action.

(B) The motion must also include:

(i) the reasons for granting the relief requested and the facts relied on;

(ii) originals or copies of affidavits or other sworn statements supporting facts subject to dispute; and

(iii) relevant parts of the record.

(C) The moving party must give reasonable notice of the motion to all parties.

(D) A motion under this Rule 8(a)(2) must be filed with the circuit clerk and normally will be considered by a panel of the court. But in an exceptional case in which time requirements make that procedure impracticable, the motion may be made to and considered by a single judge.

(E) The court may condition relief on a party's filing a bond or other appropriate security in the district court.

(b) Proceeding Against a Surety. If a party gives security in the form of a bond or stipulation or other undertaking with one or more sureties, each surety submits to the jurisdiction of the district court and irrevocably appoints the district clerk as the surety's agent on whom any papers affecting the surety's liability on the bond or undertaking may be served. On motion, a surety's liability may be enforced in the district court without the necessity of an independent action. The motion and any notice that the district court prescribes may be served on the district clerk, who must promptly mail a copy to each surety whose address is known.

(c) Stay in a Criminal Case. Rule 38 of the Federal Rules of Criminal Procedure governs a stay in a criminal case.

As amended 1986, 1995, 1998.

Rule 9.

RELEASE IN A CRIMINAL CASE

(a) Release Before Judgment of Conviction.

(1) The district court must state in writing, or orally on the record, the reasons for an order regarding the release or detention of a defendant in a criminal case. A party appealing from the order must file with the court of appeals a copy of the district court's order and the court's statement of reasons as soon as practicable after filing the notice of appeal. An appellant who questions the factual basis for the district court's order must file a transcript of the release proceedings or an explanation of why a transcript was not obtained.

(2) After reasonable notice to the appellee, the court of appeals must promptly determine the appeal on the basis of the papers, affidavits, and parts of the record that the parties present or the court requires. Unless the court so orders, briefs need not be filed.

(3) The court of appeals or one of its judges may order the defendant's release pending the disposition of the appeal.

(b) Release After Judgment of Conviction. A party entitled to do so may obtain review of a district-court order regarding release after a judgment of conviction by filing a notice of appeal from that order in the district court, or by filing a motion in the court of appeals if the party has already filed a notice of appeal from the judgment of conviction. Both the order and the review are subject to Rule 9(a). The papers filed by the party seeking review must include a copy of the judgment of conviction.

(c) Criteria for Release. The court must make its decision regarding release in accordance with the applicable provisions of 18 U.S.C. §§ 3142, 3143, and 3145(c).

As amended 1972, 1984, 1994, 1998.

Rule 10.

THE RECORD ON APPEAL

(a) Composition of the Record on Appeal. The following items constitute the record on appeal:

(1) the original papers and exhibits filed in the district court;

(2) the transcript of proceedings, if any; and

(3) a certified copy of the docket entries prepared by the district clerk.

(b) The Transcript of Proceedings.

(1) *Appellant's Duty to Order.* Within 10 days after filing the notice of appeal or entry of an order disposing of the last timely remaining motion of a type specified in Rule 4(a)(4)(A), whichever is later, the appellant must do either of the following:

(A) order from the reporter a transcript of such parts of the proceedings not already on file as the appellant considers necessary, subject to a local rule of the court of appeals and with the following qualifications:

(i) the order must be in writing;

(ii) if the cost of the transcript is to be paid by the United States under the Criminal Justice Act, the order must so state; and

(iii) the appellant must, within the same period, file a copy of the order with the district clerk; or

(B) file a certificate stating that no transcript will be ordered.

(2) *Unsupported Finding or Conclusion.* If the appellant intends to urge on appeal that a finding or conclusion is unsupported by the evidence or is contrary to the evidence, the appellant must include in the record a transcript of all evidence relevant to that finding or conclusion.

(3) *Partial Transcript.* Unless the entire transcript is ordered:

(A) the appellant must—within the 10 days provided in Rule 10(b)(1)—file a statement of the issues that the appellant intends to present on the appeal and must serve on the appellee a copy of both the order or certificate and the statement;

(B) if the appellee considers it necessary to have a transcript of other parts of the proceedings, the appellee must, within 10 days after the service of the order or certificate and the statement of the issues, file and serve on the appellant a designation of additional parts to be ordered; and

(C) unless within 10 days after service of that designation the appellant has ordered all such parts, and has so notified the appellee, the appellee may within the following 10 days either order the parts or move in the district court for an order requiring the appellant to do so.

(4) *Payment.* At the time of ordering, a party must make satisfactory arrangements with the reporter for paying the cost of the transcript.

(c) Statement of the Evidence When the Proceedings Were Not Recorded or When a Transcript Is Unavailable. If the transcript of a hearing or trial is unavailable, the appellant may prepare a statement of the evidence or proceedings from the best available means, including the appellant's recollection. The statement must be served on the appellee, who may serve objections or proposed amendments within 10 days after being served. The statement and any objections or proposed amendments must then be submitted to the district court for settlement and approval. As settled and approved, the statement must be included by the district clerk in the record on appeal.

(d) Agreed Statement as the Record on Appeal. In place of the record on appeal as defined in Rule 10(a), the parties may prepare, sign, and submit to the district court a statement of the case showing how the issues presented by the appeal arose and were decided in the district court. The statement must set forth only those facts averred and proved or sought to be proved that are essential to the court's resolution of the issues. If the statement is truthful, it—together with any additions that the district court may consider necessary to a full presentation of the issues on appeal—must be approved by the district court and must then be certified to the court of appeals as the record on appeal. The district clerk must then send it to the circuit clerk within the time provided by Rule 11. A copy of the agreed statement may be filed in place of the appendix required by Rule 30.

(e) Correction or Modification of the Record.

(1) If any difference arises about whether the record truly discloses what occurred in the district court, the difference must be submitted to and settled by that court and the record conformed accordingly.

(2) If anything material to either party is omitted from or misstated in the record by error or accident, the omission or misstatement may be corrected and a supplemental record may be certified and forwarded:

(A) on stipulation of the parties;

(B) by the district court before or after the record has been forwarded; or

(C) by the court of appeals.

(3) All other questions as to the form and content of the record must be presented to the court of appeals.

As amended 1979, 1986, 1991, 1993, 1995, 1998.

Rule 11.

FORWARDING THE RECORD

(a) Appellant's Duty. An appellant filing a notice of appeal must comply with Rule 10(b) and must do whatever else is necessary to enable the clerk to assemble and forward the record. If there are multiple appeals from a judgment or order, the clerk must forward a single record.

(b) Duties of Reporter and District Clerk.

(1) *Reporter's Duty to Prepare and File a Transcript.* The reporter must prepare and file a transcript as follows:

(A) Upon receiving an order for a transcript, the reporter must enter at the foot of the order the date of its receipt and the expected completion date and send a copy, so endorsed, to the circuit clerk.

(B) If the transcript cannot be completed within 30 days of the reporter's receipt of the order, the reporter may request the circuit clerk to grant additional time to complete it. The clerk must note on the docket the action taken and notify the parties.

(C) When a transcript is complete, the reporter must file it with the district clerk and notify the circuit clerk of the filing.

(D) If the reporter fails to file the transcript on time, the circuit clerk must notify the district judge and do whatever else the court of appeals directs.

(2) *District Clerk's Duty to Forward.* When the record is complete, the district clerk must number the documents constituting the record and send them promptly to the circuit clerk together with a list of the documents correspondingly numbered and reasonably identified. Unless directed to do so by a party or the circuit clerk, the district clerk will not send to the court of appeals documents of unusual bulk or weight, physical exhibits other than documents, or other parts of the record designated for omission by local rule of the court of appeals. If the exhibits are unusually

bulky or heavy, a party must arrange with the clerks in advance for their transportation and receipt.

(c) Retaining the Record Temporarily in the District Court for Use in Preparing the Appeal. The parties may stipulate, or the district court on motion may order, that the district clerk retain the record temporarily for the parties to use in preparing the papers on appeal. In that event the district clerk must certify to the circuit clerk that the record on appeal is complete. Upon receipt of the appellee's brief, or earlier if the court orders or the parties agree, the appellant must request the district clerk to forward the record.

(d) [Abrogated.]

(e) Retaining the Record by Court Order.

(1) The court of appeals may, by order or local rule, provide that a certified copy of the docket entries be forwarded instead of the entire record. But a party may at any time during the appeal request that designated parts of the record be forwarded.

(2) The district court may order the record or some part of it retained if the court needs it while the appeal is pending, subject, however, to call by the court of appeals.

(3) If part or all of the record is ordered retained, the district clerk must send to the court of appeals a copy of the order and the docket entries together with the parts of the original record allowed by the district court and copies of any parts of the record designated by the parties.

(f) Retaining Parts of the Record in the District Court by Stipulation of the Parties. The parties may agree by written stipulation filed in the district court that designated parts of the record be retained in the district court subject to call by the court of appeals or request by a party. The parts of the record so designated remain a part of the record on appeal.

(g) Record for a Preliminary Motion in the Court of Appeals. If, before the record is forwarded, a party makes any of the following motions in the court of appeals:

- for dismissal;
- for release;
- for a stay pending appeal;
- for additional security on the bond on appeal or on a supersedeas bond; or
- for any other intermediate order—

the district clerk must send the court of appeals any parts of the record designated by any party.

As amended 1979, 1986, 1998.

Rule 12.

DOCKETING THE APPEAL; FILING A REPRESENTATION STATEMENT; FILING THE RECORD

(a) Docketing the Appeal. Upon receiving the copy of the notice of appeal and the docket entries from the district clerk under Rule 3(d), the circuit clerk must docket the appeal under the title of the district-court action and must identify the appellant, adding the appellant's name if necessary.

(b) Filing a Representation Statement. Unless the court of appeals designates another time, the attorney who filed the notice of appeal must, within 10 days after filing the notice, file a statement with the circuit clerk naming the parties that the attorney represents on appeal.

(c) Filing the Record, Partial Record, or Certificate. Upon receiving the record, partial record, or district clerk's certificate as provided in Rule 11, the circuit clerk must file it and immediately notify all parties of the filing date.

As amended 1979, 1986, 1993, 1998.

TITLE III. REVIEW OF A DECISION OF THE UNITED STATES TAX COURT [OMITTED]

TITLE IV. REVIEW OR ENFORCEMENT OF AN ORDER OF AN ADMINISTRATIVE AGENCY, BOARD, COMMISSION, OR OFFICER [OMITTED]

TITLE V. EXTRAORDINARY WRITS

Rule 21.

WRITS OF MANDAMUS AND PROHIBITION, AND OTHER EXTRAORDINARY WRITS

(a) Mandamus or Prohibition to a Court: Petition, Filing, Service, and Docketing.

(1) A party petitioning for a writ of mandamus or prohibition directed to a court must file a petition with the circuit clerk with

proof of service on all parties to the proceeding in the trial court. The party must also provide a copy to the trial-court judge. All parties to the proceeding in the trial court other than the petitioner are respondents for all purposes.

(2)(A) The petition must be titled "In re [name of petitioner]."

(B) The petition must state:

(i) the relief sought;

(ii) the issues presented;

(iii) the facts necessary to understand the issue presented by the petition; and

(iv) the reasons why the writ should issue.

(C) The petition must include a copy of any order or opinion or parts of the record that may be essential to understand the matters set forth in the petition.

(3) Upon receiving the prescribed docket fee, the clerk must docket the petition and submit it to the court.

(b) Denial; Order Directing Answer; Briefs; Precedence.

(1) The court may deny the petition without an answer. Otherwise, it must order the respondent, if any, to answer within a fixed time.

(2) The clerk must serve the order to respond on all persons directed to respond.

(3) Two or more respondents may answer jointly.

(4) The court of appeals may invite or order the trial-court judge to address the petition or may invite an amicus curiae to do so. The trial-court judge may request permission to address the petition but may not do so unless invited or ordered to do so by the court of appeals.

(5) If briefing or oral argument is required, the clerk must advise the parties, and when appropriate, the trial-court judge or amicus curiae.

(6) The proceeding must be given preference over ordinary civil cases.

(7) The circuit clerk must send a copy of the final disposition to the trial-court judge.

(c) Other Extraordinary Writs. An application for an extraordinary writ other than one provided for in Rule 21(a) must be made by filing a petition with the circuit clerk with proof of service on the respondents. Proceedings on the application must conform, so far as is practicable, to the procedures prescribed in Rule 21(a) and (b).

(d) Form of Papers; Number of Copies. All papers must conform to Rule 32(c)(2). Except by the court's permission, a paper must not exceed 30 pages, exclusive of the disclosure statement, the proof of service, and the accompanying documents required by Rule 21(a)(2)(C). An original and 3 copies must be filed unless the court requires the filing of a different number by local rule or by order in a particular case.

As amended 1994, 1996, 1998, 2002.

TITLE VI. HABEAS CORPUS; PROCEEDINGS IN FORMA PAUPERIS

Rule 22.

HABEAS CORPUS AND SECTION 2255 PROCEEDINGS

(a) Application for the Original Writ. An application for a writ of habeas corpus must be made to the appropriate district court. If made to a circuit judge, the application must be transferred to the appropriate district court. If a district court denies an application made or transferred to it, renewal of the application before a circuit judge is not permitted. The applicant may, under 28 U.S.C. § 2253, appeal to the court of appeals from the district court's order denying the application.

(b) Certificate of Appealability.

(1) In a habeas corpus proceeding in which the detention complained of arises from process issued by a state court, or in a 28 U.S.C. § 2255 proceeding, the applicant cannot take an appeal unless a circuit justice or a circuit or district judge issues a certificate of appealability under 28 U.S.C. § 2253(c). If an applicant files a notice of appeal, the district judge who rendered the judgment must either issue a certificate of appealability or state why a certificate should not issue. The district clerk must send the certificate or statement to the court of appeals with the notice of appeal and the file of the district-court proceedings. If the district judge has denied the certificate, the applicant may request a circuit judge to issue the certificate.

(2) A request addressed to the court of appeals may be considered by a circuit judge or judges, as the court prescribes. If no express request for a certificate is filed, the notice of appeal constitutes a request addressed to the judges of the court of appeals.

(3) A certificate of appealability is not required when a state or its representative or the United States or its representative appeals.

As amended 1996, 1998.

Rule 23.

CUSTODY OR RELEASE OF A PRISONER IN A HABEAS CORPUS PROCEEDING

(a) Transfer of Custody Pending Review. Pending review of a decision in a habeas corpus proceeding commenced before a court, justice, or judge of the United States for the release of a prisoner, the person having custody of the prisoner must not transfer custody to another unless a transfer is directed in accordance with this rule. When, upon application, a custodian shows the need for a transfer, the court, justice, or judge rendering the decision under review may authorize the transfer and substitute the successor custodian as a party.

(b) Detention or Release Pending Review of Decision Not to Release. While a decision not to release a prisoner is under review, the court or judge rendering the decision, or the court of appeals, or the Supreme Court, or a judge or justice of either court, may order that the prisoner be:

(1) detained in the custody from which release is sought;

(2) detained in other appropriate custody; or

(3) released on personal recognizance, with or without surety.

(c) Release Pending Review of Decision Ordering Release. While a decision ordering the release of a prisoner is under review, the prisoner must—unless the court or judge rendering the decision, or the court of appeals, or the Supreme Court, or a judge or justice of either court orders otherwise—be released on personal recognizance, with or without surety.

(d) Modification of the Initial Order on Custody. An initial order governing the prisoner's custody or release, including any recognizance or surety, continues in effect pending review unless for special reasons shown to the court of appeals or the Supreme Court, or to a judge or justice of either court, the order is modified or an independent order regarding custody, release, or surety is issued.

As amended 1986, 1998.

Rule 24.

PROCEEDING IN FORMA PAUPERIS

(a) Leave to Proceed In Forma Pauperis.

(1) *Motion in the District Court.* Except as stated in Rule 24(a)(3), a party to a district-court action who desires to appeal in forma pauperis must file a motion in the district court. The party must attach an affidavit that:

(A) shows in the detail prescribed by Form 4 of the Appendix of Forms, the party's inability to pay or to give security for fees and costs;

(B) claims an entitlement to redress; and

(C) states the issues that the party intends to present on appeal.

(2) *Action on the Motion.* If the district court grants the motion, the party may proceed on appeal without prepaying or giving security for fees and costs, unless a statute provides otherwise. If the district court denies the motion, it must state its reasons in writing.

(3) *Prior Approval.* A party who was permitted to proceed in forma pauperis in the district-court action, or who was determined to be financially unable to obtain an adequate defense in a criminal case, may proceed on appeal in forma pauperis without further authorization, unless:

(A) the district court—before or after the notice of appeal is filed—certifies that the appeal is not taken in good faith or finds that the party is not otherwise entitled to proceed in forma pauperis and states in writing its reasons for the certification or finding; or

(B) a statute provides otherwise.

(4) *Notice of District Court's Denial.* The district clerk must immediately notify the parties and the court of appeals when the district court does any of the following:

(A) denies a motion to proceed on appeal in forma pauperis;

(B) certifies that the appeal is not taken in good faith; or

(C) finds that the party is not otherwise entitled to proceed in forma pauperis.

(5) *Motion in the Court of Appeals.* A party may file a motion to proceed on appeal in forma pauperis in the court of appeals within 30 days after service of the notice prescribed in Rule

24(a)(4). The motion must include a copy of the affidavit filed in the district court and the district court's statement of reasons for its action. If no affidavit was filed in the district court, the party must include the affidavit prescribed by Rule 24(a)(1).

(b) Leave to Proceed In Forma Pauperis on Appeal or Review of an Administrative Agency Proceeding. When an appeal or review of a proceeding before an administrative agency, board, commission, or officer (including for the purpose of this rule the United States Tax Court) proceeds directly in a court of appeals, a party may file in the court of appeals a motion for leave to proceed on appeal in forma pauperis with an affidavit prescribed by Rule 24(a)(1).

(c) Leave to Use Original Record. A party allowed to proceed on appeal in forma pauperis may request that the appeal be heard on the original record without reproducing any part.

As amended 1979, 1986, 1998, 2002.

TITLE VII. GENERAL PROVISIONS

Rule 25.

FILING AND SERVICE

(a) Filing.

(1) *Filing with the Clerk.* A paper required or permitted to be filed in a court of appeals must be filed with the clerk.

(2) *Filing: Method and Timeliness.*

(A) In General. Filing may be accomplished by mail addressed to the clerk, but filing is not timely unless the clerk receives the papers within the time fixed for filing.

(B) A Brief or Appendix. A brief or appendix is timely filed, however, if on or before the last day for filing, it is:

(i) mailed to the clerk by First–Class Mail, or other class of mail that is at least as expeditious, postage prepaid; or

(ii) dispatched to a third-party commercial carrier for delivery to the clerk within 3 calendar days.

(C) Inmate Filing. A paper filed by an inmate confined in an institution is timely if deposited in the institution's internal mailing system on or before the last day for filing. If an institution has a system designed for legal mail, the inmate must use that system to receive the benefit of this rule. Timely filing may be shown by a declaration in compliance with 28 U.S.C. § 1746 or by a notarized statement, either of which must set forth the date of deposit and state that first-class postage has been prepaid.

(D) Electronic Filing. A court of appeals may by local rule permit papers to be filed, signed, or verified by electronic means that are consistent with technical standards, if any, that the Judicial Conference of the United States establishes. A paper filed by electronic means in compliance with a local rule constitutes a written paper for the purpose of applying these rules.

(3) *Filing a Motion with a Judge.* If a motion requests relief that may be granted by a single judge, the judge may permit the motion to be filed with the judge; the judge must note the filing date on the motion and give it to the clerk.

(4) *Clerk's Refusal of Documents.* The clerk must not refuse to accept for filing any paper presented for that purpose solely because it is not presented in proper form as required by these rules or by any local rule or practice.

(b) Service of All Papers Required. Unless a rule requires service by the clerk, a party must, at or before the time of filing a paper, serve a copy on the other parties to the appeal or review. Service on a party represented by counsel must be made on the party's counsel.

(c) Manner of Service.

(1) Service may be any of the following:

(A) personal, including delivery to a responsible person at the office of counsel;

(B) by mail;

(C) by third-party commercial carrier for delivery within 3 calendar days; or

(D) by electronic means, if the party being served consents in writing.

(2) If authorized by local rule, a party may use the court's transmission equipment to make electronic service under Rule 25(c)(1)(D).

(3) When reasonable considering such factors as the immediacy of the relief sought, distance, and cost, service on a party must be by a manner at least as expeditious as the manner used to file the paper with the court.

(4) Service by mail or by commercial carrier is complete on mailing or delivery to the carrier. Service by electronic means is complete on transmission, unless the party making service is notified that the paper was not received by the party served.

(d) Proof of Service.

(1) A paper presented for filing must contain either of the following:

(A) an acknowledgment of service by the person served; or

(B) proof of service consisting of a statement by the person who made service certifying:

(i) the date and manner of service;

(ii) the names of the persons served; and

(iii) their mail or electronic addresses, facsimile numbers, or the addresses of the places of delivery, as appropriate for the manner of service.

(2) When a brief or appendix is filed by mailing or dispatch in accordance with Rule 25(a)(2)(B), the proof of service must also state the date and manner by which the document was mailed or dispatched to the clerk.

(3) Proof of service may appear on or be affixed to the papers filed.

(e) Number of Copies. When these rules require the filing or furnishing of a number of copies, a court may require a different number by local rule or by order in a particular case.

As amended 1986, 1991, 1993, 1994, 1996, 1998, 2002.

Rule 26.

COMPUTING AND EXTENDING TIME

(a) Computing Time. The following rules apply in computing any period of time specified in these rules or in any local rule, court order, or applicable statute:

(1) Exclude the day of the act, event, or default that begins the period.

(2) Exclude intermediate Saturdays, Sundays, and legal holidays when the period is less than 11 days, unless stated in calendar days.

(3) Include the last day of the period unless it is a Saturday, Sunday, legal holiday, or—if the act to be done is filing a paper in court—a day on which the weather or other conditions make the clerk's office inaccessible.

(4) As used in this rule, "legal holiday" means New Year's Day, Martin Luther King, Jr.'s Birthday, Presidents' Day, Memorial Day, Independence Day, Labor Day, Columbus Day, Veterans' Day, Thanksgiving Day, Christmas Day, and any other day declared

a holiday by the President, Congress, or the state in which is located either the district court that rendered the challenged judgment or order, or the circuit clerk's principal office.

(b) Extending Time. For good cause, the court may extend the time prescribed by these rules or by its order to perform any act, or may permit an act to be done after that time expires. But the court may not extend the time to file:

(1) a notice of appeal (except as authorized in Rule 4) or a petition for permission to appeal; or

(2) a notice of appeal from or a petition to enjoin, set aside, suspend, modify, enforce, or otherwise review an order of an administrative agency, board, commission, or officer of the United States, unless specifically authorized by law.

(c) Additional Time After Service. When a party is required or permitted to act within a prescribed period after a paper is served on that party, 3 calendar days are added to the prescribed period unless the paper is delivered on the date of service stated in the proof of service. For purposes of this Rule 26(c), a paper that is served electronically is not treated as delivered on the date of service stated in the proof of service.

As amended 1971, 1986, 1989, 1991, 1996, 1998, 2002.

Rule 26.1.

CORPORATE DISCLOSURE STATEMENT

(a) Who Must File. Any nongovernmental corporate party to a proceeding in a court of appeals must file a statement that identifies any parent corporation and any publicly held corporation that owns 10% or more of its stock or states that there is no such corporation.

(b) Time for Filing; Supplemental Filing. A party must file the Rule 26.1(a) statement with the principal brief or upon filing a motion, response, petition, or answer in the court of appeals, whichever occurs first, unless a local rule requires earlier filing. Even if the statement has already been filed, the party's principal brief must include the statement before the table of contents. A party must supplement its statement whenever the information that must be disclosed under Rule 26.1(a) changes.

(c) Number of Copies. If the Rule 26.1(a) statement is filed before the principal brief, or if a supplemental statement is filed, the party must file an original and 3 copies unless the court requires a different number by local rule or by order in a particular case.

Added 1989; as amended 1991, 1994, 1998, 2002.

Rule 27.

MOTIONS

(a) In General.

(1) *Application for Relief.* An application for an order or other relief is made by motion unless these rules prescribe another form. A motion must be in writing unless the court permits otherwise.

(2) *Contents of a Motion.*

(A) Grounds and Relief Sought. A motion must state with particularity the grounds for the motion, the relief sought, and the legal argument necessary to support it.

(B) Accompanying Documents.

(i) Any affidavit or other paper necessary to support a motion must be served and filed with the motion.

(ii) An affidavit must contain only factual information, not legal argument.

(iii) A motion seeking substantive relief must include a copy of the trial court's opinion or agency's decision as a separate exhibit.

(C) Documents Barred or Not Required.

(i) A separate brief supporting or responding to a motion must not be filed.

(ii) A notice of motion is not required.

(iii) A proposed order is not required.

(3) *Response.*

(A) Time to File. Any party may file a response to a motion; Rule 27(a)(2) governs its contents. The response must be filed within 8 days after service of the motion unless the court shortens or extends the time. A motion authorized by Rules 8, 9, 18, or 41 may be granted before the 8–day period runs only if the court gives reasonable notice to the parties that it intends to act sooner.

(B) Request for Affirmative Relief. A response may include a motion for affirmative relief. The time to respond to the new motion, and to reply to that response, are governed by Rule 27(a)(3)(A) and (a)(4). The title of the response must alert the court to the request for relief.

(4) *Reply to Response.* Any reply to a response must be filed within 5 days after service of the response. A reply must not present matters that do not relate to the response.

(b) Disposition of a Motion for a Procedural Order. The court may act on a motion for a procedural order—including a motion under Rule 26(b)—at any time without awaiting a response, and may, by rule or by order in a particular case, authorize its clerk to act on specified types of procedural motions. A party adversely affected by the court's, or the clerk's, action may file a motion to reconsider, vacate, or modify that action. Timely opposition filed after the motion is granted in whole or in part does not constitute a request to reconsider, vacate, or modify the disposition; a motion requesting that relief must be filed.

(c) Power of a Single Judge to Entertain a Motion. A circuit judge may act alone on any motion, but may not dismiss or otherwise determine an appeal or other proceeding. A court of appeals may provide by rule or by order in a particular case that only the court may act on any motion or class of motions. The court may review the action of a single judge.

(d) Form of Papers; Page Limits; and Number of Copies.

(1) *Format.*

(A) Reproduction. A motion, response, or reply may be reproduced by any process that yields a clear black image on light paper. The paper must be opaque and unglazed. Only one side of the paper may be used.

(B) Cover. A cover is not required but there must be a caption that includes the case number, the name of the court, the title of the case, and a brief descriptive title indicating the purpose of the motion and identifying the party or parties for whom it is filed. If a cover is used, it must be white.

(C) Binding. The document must be bound in any manner that is secure, does not obscure the text, and permits the document to lie reasonably flat when open.

(D) Paper Size, Line Spacing, and Margins. The document must be on 8½ by 11 inch paper. The text must be double-spaced, but quotations more than two lines long may be indented and single-spaced. Headings and footnotes may be single-spaced. Margins must be at least one inch on all four sides. Page numbers may be placed in the margins, but no text may appear there.

(2) *Page Limits.* A motion or a response to a motion must not exceed 20 pages, exclusive of the corporate disclosure statement and accompanying documents authorized by Rule 27(a)(2)(B), unless the court permits or directs otherwise. A reply to a response must not exceed 10 pages.

(3) *Number of Copies.* An original and 3 copies must be filed unless the court requires a different number by local rule or by order in a particular case.

(e) Oral Argument. A motion will be decided without oral argument unless the court orders otherwise.

As amended 1979, 1989, 1994, 1998, 2002.

Rule 28.

BRIEFS

(a) Appellant's Brief. The appellant's brief must contain, under appropriate headings and in the order indicated:

(1) a corporate disclosure statement if required by Rule 26.1;

(2) a table of contents, with page references;

(3) a table of authorities—cases (alphabetically arranged), statutes, and other authorities—with references to the pages of the brief where they are cited;

(4) a jurisdictional statement, including:

(A) the basis for the district court's or agency's subject-matter jurisdiction, with citations to applicable statutory provisions and stating relevant facts establishing jurisdiction;

(B) the basis for the court of appeals' jurisdiction, with citations to applicable statutory provisions and stating relevant facts establishing jurisdiction;

(C) the filing dates establishing the timeliness of the appeal or petition for review; and

(D) an assertion that the appeal is from a final order or judgment that disposes of all parties' claims, or information establishing the court of appeals' jurisdiction on some other basis;

(5) a statement of the issues presented for review;

(6) a statement of the case briefly indicating the nature of the case, the course of proceedings, and the disposition below;

(7) a statement of facts relevant to the issues submitted for review with appropriate references to the record (see Rule 28(e));

(8) a summary of the argument, which must contain a succinct, clear, and accurate statement of the arguments made in the body of the brief, and which must not merely repeat the argument headings;

(9) the argument, which must contain:

(A) appellant's contentions and the reasons for them, with citations to the authorities and parts of the record on which the appellant relies; and

(B) for each issue, a concise statement of the applicable standard of review (which may appear in the discussion of the issue or under a separate heading placed before the discussion of the issues);

(10) a short conclusion stating the precise relief sought; and

(11) the certificate of compliance, if required by Rule 32(a)(7).

(b) Appellee's Brief. The appellee's brief must conform to the requirements of Rule 28(a)(1)–(9) and (11), except that none of the following need appear unless the appellee is dissatisfied with the appellant's statement:

(1) the jurisdictional statement;

(2) the statement of the issues;

(3) the statement of the case;

(4) the statement of the facts; and

(5) the statement of the standard of review.

(c) Reply Brief. The appellant may file a brief in reply to the appellee's brief. An appellee who has cross-appealed may file a brief in reply to the appellant's response to the issues presented by the cross-appeal. Unless the court permits, no further briefs may be filed. A reply brief must contain a table of contents, with page references, and a table of authorities—cases (alphabetically arranged), statutes, and other authorities—with references to the pages of the reply brief where they are cited.

(d) References to Parties. In briefs and at oral argument, counsel should minimize use of the terms "appellant" and "appellee." To make briefs clear, counsel should use the parties' actual names or the designations used in the lower court or agency proceeding, or such descriptive terms as "the employee," "the injured person," "the taxpayer," "the ship," "the stevedore."

(e) References to the Record. References to the parts of the record contained in the appendix filed with the appellant's brief must be to the pages of the appendix. If the appendix is prepared after the briefs are filed, a party referring to the record must follow one of the methods detailed in Rule 30(c). If the original record is used under Rule 30(f) and is not consecutively paginated, or if the brief refers to an unreproduced part of the record, any reference must be to the page of the original document. For example:

- Answer p. 7;
- Motion for Judgment p. 2;

- Transcript p. 231.

Only clear abbreviations may be used. A party referring to evidence whose admissibility is in controversy must cite the pages of the appendix or of the transcript at which the evidence was identified, offered, and received or rejected.

(f) Reproduction of Statutes, Rules, Regulations, etc. If the court's determination of the issues presented requires the study of statutes, rules, regulations, etc., the relevant parts must be set out in the brief or in an addendum at the end, or may be supplied to the court in pamphlet form.

(g) [Reserved.]

(h) Briefs in a Case Involving a Cross-Appeal. If a cross-appeal is filed, the party who files a notice of appeal first is the appellant for the purposes of this rule and Rules 30, 31, and 34. If notices are filed on the same day, the plaintiff in the proceeding below is the appellant. These designations may be modified by agreement of the parties or by court order. With respect to appellee's cross-appeal and response to appellant's brief, appellee's brief must conform to the requirements of Rule 28(a)(1)–(11). But an appellee who is satisfied with appellant's statement need not include a statement of the case or of the facts.

(i) Briefs in a Case Involving Multiple Appellants or Appellees. In a case involving more than one appellant or appellee, including consolidated cases, any number of appellants or appellees may join in a brief, and any party may adopt by reference a part of another's brief. Parties may also join in reply briefs.

(j) Citation of Supplemental Authorities. If pertinent and significant authorities come to a party's attention after the party's brief has been filed—or after oral argument but before decision—a party may promptly advise the circuit clerk by letter, with a copy to all other parties, setting forth the citations. The letter must state the reasons for the supplemental citations, referring either to the page of the brief or to a point argued orally. The body of the letter must not exceed 350 words. Any response must be made promptly and must be similarly limited.

As amended 1979, 1986, 1989, 1991, 1993, 1994, 1998, 2002.

Rule 29.

BRIEF OF AN AMICUS CURIAE

(a) When Permitted. The United States or its officer or agency, or a State, Territory, Commonwealth, or the District of Columbia may file an amicus-curiae brief without the consent of the parties or leave of court. Any other amicus curiae may file a brief only by leave of court or if the brief states that all parties have consented to its filing.

(b) Motion for Leave to File. The motion must be accompanied by the proposed brief and state:

(1) the movant's interest; and

(2) the reason why an amicus brief is desirable and why the matters asserted are relevant to the disposition of the case.

(c) Contents and Form. An amicus brief must comply with Rule 32. In addition to the requirements of Rule 32, the cover must identify the party or parties supported and indicate whether the brief supports affirmance or reversal. If an amicus curiae is a corporation, the brief must include a disclosure statement like that required of parties by Rule 26.1. An amicus brief need not comply with Rule 28, but must include the following:

(1) a table of contents, with page references;

(2) a table of authorities—cases (alphabetically arranged), statutes and other authorities—with references to the pages of the brief where they are cited;

(3) a concise statement of the identity of the amicus curiae, its interest in the case, and the source of its authority to file;

(4) an argument, which may be preceded by a summary and which need not include a statement of the applicable standard of review; and

(5) a certificate of compliance, if required by Rule 32(a)(7).

(d) Length. Except by the court's permission, an amicus brief may be no more than one-half the maximum length authorized by these rules for a party's principal brief. If the court grants a party permission to file a longer brief, that extension does not affect the length of an amicus brief.

(e) Time for Filing. An amicus curiae must file its brief, accompanied by a motion for filing when necessary, no later than 7 days after the principal brief of the party being supported is filed. An amicus curiae that does not support either party must file its brief no later than 7 days after the appellant's or petitioner's principal brief is filed. A court may grant leave for later filing, specifying the time within which an opposing party may answer.

(f) Reply Brief. Except by the court's permission, an amicus curiae may not file a reply brief.

(g) Oral Argument. An amicus curiae may participate in oral argument only with the court's permission.

As amended 1998.

Rule 30.

APPENDIX TO THE BRIEFS

(a) Appellant's Responsibility.

(1) *Contents of the Appendix.* The appellant must prepare and file an appendix to the briefs containing:

(A) the relevant docket entries in the proceeding below;

(B) the relevant portions of the pleadings, charge, findings, or opinion;

(C) the judgment, order, or decision in question; and

(D) other parts of the record to which the parties wish to direct the court's attention.

(2) *Excluded Material.* Memoranda of law in the district court should not be included in the appendix unless they have independent relevance. Parts of the record may be relied on by the court or the parties even though not included in the appendix.

(3) *Time to File; Number of Copies.* Unless filing is deferred under Rule 30(c), the appellant must file 10 copies of the appendix with the brief and must serve one copy on counsel for each party separately represented. An unrepresented party proceeding in forma pauperis must file 4 legible copies with the clerk, and one copy must be served on counsel for each separately represented party. The court may by local rule or by order in a particular case require the filing or service of a different number.

(b) All Parties' Responsibilities.

(1) *Determining the Contents of the Appendix.* The parties are encouraged to agree on the contents of the appendix. In the absence of an agreement, the appellant must, within 10 days after the record is filed, serve on the appellee a designation of the parts of the record the appellant intends to include in the appendix and a statement of the issues the appellant intends to present for review. The appellee may, within 10 days after receiving the designation, serve on the appellant a designation of additional parts to which it wishes to direct the court's attention. The appellant must include the designated parts in the appendix. The parties must not engage in unnecessary designation of parts of the record, because the entire record is available to the court. This paragraph applies also to a cross-appellant and a cross-appellee.

(2) *Costs of Appendix.* Unless the parties agree otherwise, the appellant must pay the cost of the appendix. If the appellant considers parts of the record designated by the appellee to be unnecessary, the appellant may advise the appellee, who must then

advance the cost of including those parts. The cost of the appendix is a taxable cost. But if any party causes unnecessary parts of the record to be included in the appendix, the court may impose the cost of those parts on that party. Each circuit must, by local rule, provide for sanctions against attorneys who unreasonably and vexatiously increase litigation costs by including unnecessary material in the appendix.

(c) Deferred Appendix.

(1) *Deferral Until After Briefs Are Filed.* The court may provide by rule for classes of cases or by order in a particular case that preparation of the appendix may be deferred until after the briefs have been filed and that the appendix may be filed 21 days after the appellee's brief is served. Even though the filing of the appendix may be deferred, Rule 30(b) applies; except that a party must designate the parts of the record it wants included in the appendix when it serves its brief, and need not include a statement of the issues presented.

(2) *References to the Record.*

(A) If the deferred appendix is used, the parties may cite in their briefs the pertinent pages of the record. When the appendix is prepared, the record pages cited in the briefs must be indicated by inserting record page numbers, in brackets, at places in the appendix where those pages of the record appear.

(B) A party who wants to refer directly to pages of the appendix may serve and file copies of the brief within the time required by Rule 31(a), containing appropriate references to pertinent pages of the record. In that event, within 14 days after the appendix is filed, the party must serve and file copies of the brief, containing references to the pages of the appendix in place of or in addition to the references to the pertinent pages of the record. Except for the correction of typographical errors, no other changes may be made to the brief.

(d) Format of the Appendix. The appendix must begin with a table of contents identifying the page at which each part begins. The relevant docket entries must follow the table of contents. Other parts of the record must follow chronologically. When pages from the transcript of proceedings are placed in the appendix, the transcript page numbers must be shown in brackets immediately before the included pages. Omissions in the text of papers or of the transcript must be indicated by asterisks. Immaterial formal matters (captions, subscriptions, acknowledgments, etc.) should be omitted.

(e) Reproduction of Exhibits. Exhibits designated for inclusion in the appendix may be reproduced in a separate volume, or volumes, suitably indexed. Four copies must be filed with the appendix, and one copy must be served on counsel for each separately represented party. If a transcript of a proceeding before an administrative agency, board, commission, or officer was used in a district-court action and has been designated for inclusion in the appendix, the transcript must be placed in the appendix as an exhibit.

(f) Appeal on the Original Record Without an Appendix. The court may, either by rule for all cases or classes of cases or by order in a particular case, dispense with the appendix and permit an appeal to proceed on the original record with any copies of the record, or relevant parts, that the court may order the parties to file.

As amended 1970, 1986, 1991, 1994, 1998.

Rule 31.

SERVING AND FILING BRIEFS

(a) Time to Serve and File a Brief.

(1) The appellant must serve and file a brief within 40 days after the record is filed. The appellee must serve and file a brief within 30 days after the appellant's brief is served. The appellant may serve and file a reply brief within 14 days after service of the appellee's brief but a reply brief must be filed at least 3 days before argument, unless the court, for good cause, allows a later filing.

(2) A court of appeals that routinely considers cases on the merits promptly after the briefs are filed may shorten the time to serve and file briefs, either by local rule or by order in a particular case.

(b) Number of Copies. Twenty-five copies of each brief must be filed with the clerk and 2 copies must be served on each unrepresented party and on counsel for each separately represented party. An unrepresented party proceeding in forma pauperis must file 4 legible copies with the clerk, and one copy must be served on each unrepresented party and on counsel for each separately represented party. The court may by local rule or by order in a particular case require the filing or service of a different number.

(c) Consequence of Failure to File. If an appellant fails to file a brief within the time provided by this rule, or within an extended time, an appellee may move to dismiss the appeal. An appellee who fails to file a brief will not be heard at oral argument unless the court grants permission.

As amended 1970, 1986, 1994, 1998, 2002.

Rule 32.

FORM OF BRIEFS, APPENDICES, AND OTHER PAPERS

(a) Form of a Brief.

(1) *Reproduction.*

(A) A brief may be reproduced by any process that yields a clear black image on light paper. The paper must be opaque and unglazed. Only one side of the paper may be used.

(B) Text must be reproduced with a clarity that equals or exceeds the output of a laser printer.

(C) Photographs, illustrations, and tables may be reproduced by any method that results in a good copy of the original; a glossy finish is acceptable if the original is glossy.

(2) *Cover.* Except for filings by unrepresented parties, the cover of the appellant's brief must be blue; the appellee's, red; an intervenor's or amicus curiae's, green; any reply brief, gray; and any supplemental brief, tan. The front cover of a brief must contain:

(A) the number of the case centered at the top;

(B) the name of the court;

(C) the title of the case (see Rule 12(a));

(D) the nature of the proceeding (e.g., Appeal, Petition for Review) and the name of the court, agency, or board below;

(E) the title of the brief, identifying the party or parties for whom the brief is filed; and

(F) the name, office address, and telephone number of counsel representing the party for whom the brief is filed.

(3) *Binding.* The brief must be bound in any manner that is secure, does not obscure the text, and permits the brief to lie reasonably flat when open.

(4) *Paper Size, Line Spacing, and Margins.* The brief must be on 8½ by 11 inch paper. The text must be double-spaced, but quotations more than two lines long may be indented and single-spaced. Headings and footnotes may be single-spaced. Margins must be at least one inch on all four sides. Page numbers may be placed in the margins, but no text may appear there.

(5) *Typeface.* Either a proportionally spaced or a monospaced face may be used.

(A) A proportionally spaced face must include serifs, but sans-serif type may be used in headings and captions. A proportionally spaced face must be 14–point or larger.

(B) A monospaced face may not contain more than 10½ characters per inch.

(6) *Type Styles.* A brief must be set in a plain, roman style, although italics or boldface may be used for emphasis. Case names must be italicized or underlined.

(7) *Length.*

(A) Page limitation. A principal brief may not exceed 30 pages, or a reply brief 15 pages, unless it complies with Rule 32(a)(7)(B) and (C).

(B) Type-volume limitation.

(i) A principal brief is acceptable if:

- it contains no more than 14,000 words; or
- it uses a monospaced face and contains no more than 1,300 lines of text.

(ii) A reply brief is acceptable if it contains no more than half of the type volume specified in Rule 32(a)(7)(B)(i).

(iii) Headings, footnotes, and quotations count toward the word and line limitations. The corporate disclosure statement, table of contents, table of citations, statement with respect to oral argument, any addendum containing statutes, rules or regulations, and any certificates of counsel do not count toward the limitation.

(C) Certificate of compliance.

(i) A brief submitted under Rule 32(a)(7)(B) must include a certificate by the attorney, or an unrepresented party, that the brief complies with the type-volume limitation. The person preparing the certificate may rely on the word or line count of the word-processing system used to prepare the brief. The certificate must state either:

- the number of words in the brief; or
- the number of lines of monospaced type in the brief.

(ii) Form 6 in the Appendix of Forms is a suggested form of a certificate of compliance. Use of Form 6 must be regarded as sufficient to meet the requirements of Rule 32(a)(7)(C)(i).

(b) Form of an Appendix. An appendix must comply with Rule 32(a)(1), (2), (3), and (4), with the following exceptions:

(1) The cover of a separately bound appendix must be white.

(2) An appendix may include a legible photocopy of any document found in the record or of a printed judicial or agency decision.

(3) When necessary to facilitate inclusion of odd-sized documents such as technical drawings, an appendix may be a size other than 8½ by 11 inches, and need not lie reasonably flat when opened.

(c) Form of Other Papers.

(1) *Motion.* The form of a motion is governed by Rule 27(d).

(2) *Other Papers.* Any other paper, including a petition for panel rehearing and a petition for hearing or rehearing en banc, and any response to such a petition, must be reproduced in the manner prescribed by Rule 32(a), with the following exceptions:

(A) A cover is not necessary if the caption and signature page of the paper together contain the information required by Rule 32(a)(2). If a cover is used, it must be white.

(B) Rule 32(a)(7) does not apply.

(d) Signature. Every brief, motion, or other paper filed with the court must be signed by the party filing the paper or, if the party is represented, by one of the party's attorneys.

(e) Local Variation. Every court of appeals must accept documents that comply with the form requirements of this rule. By local rule or order in a particular case a court of appeals may accept documents that do not meet all of the form requirements of this rule.

As amended 1998, 2002.

Rule 33.

APPEAL CONFERENCES

The court may direct the attorneys—and, when appropriate, the parties—to participate in one or more conferences to address any matter that may aid in disposing of the proceedings, including simplifying the issues and discussing settlement. A judge or other person designated by the court may preside over the conference, which may be conducted in person or by telephone. Before a settlement conference, the attorneys must consult with their clients and obtain as much authority as feasible to settle the case. The court may, as a result of the conference, enter an order controlling the course of the proceedings or implementing any settlement agreement.

As amended 1994, 1998.

Rule 34.

ORAL ARGUMENT

(a) In General.

(1) *Party's Statement.* Any party may file, or a court may require by local rule, a statement explaining why oral argument should, or need not, be permitted.

(2) *Standards.* Oral argument must be allowed in every case unless a panel of three judges who have examined the briefs and record unanimously agrees that oral argument is unnecessary for any of the following reasons:

(A) the appeal is frivolous;

(B) the dispositive issue or issues have been authoritatively decided; or

(C) the facts and legal arguments are adequately presented in the briefs and record, and the decisional process would not be significantly aided by oral argument.

(b) Notice of Argument; Postponement. The clerk must advise all parties whether oral argument will be scheduled, and, if so, the date, time, and place for it, and the time allowed for each side. A motion to postpone the argument or to allow longer argument must be filed reasonably in advance of the hearing date.

(c) Order and Contents of Argument. The appellant opens and concludes the argument. Counsel must not read at length from briefs, records, or authorities.

(d) Cross–Appeals and Separate Appeals. If there is a cross-appeal, Rule 28(h) determines which party is the appellant and which is the appellee for purposes of oral argument. Unless the court directs otherwise, a cross-appeal or separate appeal must be argued when the initial appeal is argued. Separate parties should avoid duplicative argument.

(e) Nonappearance of a Party. If the appellee fails to appear for argument, the court must hear appellant's argument. If the appellant fails to appear for argument, the court may hear the appellee's argument. If neither party appears, the case will be decided on the briefs, unless the court orders otherwise.

(f) Submission on Briefs. The parties may agree to submit a case for decision on the briefs, but the court may direct that the case be argued.

(g) Use of Physical Exhibits at Argument; Removal. Counsel intending to use physical exhibits other than documents at the argument must arrange to place them in the courtroom on the day of the argument before the court convenes. After the argument, counsel must remove the exhibits from the courtroom, unless the court directs otherwise. The clerk may destroy or dispose of the exhibits if counsel does not reclaim them within a reasonable time after the clerk gives notice to remove them.

As amended 1979, 1986, 1991, 1993, 1998.

Rule 35.

EN BANC DETERMINATION

(a) When Hearing or Rehearing En Banc May Be Ordered. A majority of the circuit judges who are in regular active service may order that an appeal or other proceeding be heard or reheard by the court of appeals en banc. An en banc hearing or rehearing is not favored and ordinarily will not be ordered unless:

(1) en banc consideration is necessary to secure or maintain uniformity of the court's decisions; or

(2) the proceeding involves a question of exceptional importance.

(b) Petition for Hearing or Rehearing En Banc. A party may petition for a hearing or rehearing en banc.

(1) The petition must begin with a statement that either:

(A) the panel decision conflicts with a decision of the United States Supreme Court or of the court to which the petition is addressed (with citation to the conflicting case or cases) and consideration by the full court is therefore necessary to secure and maintain uniformity of the court's decisions; or

(B) the proceeding involves one or more questions of exceptional importance, each of which must be concisely stated; for example, a petition may assert that a proceeding presents a question of exceptional importance if it involves an issue on which the panel decision conflicts with the authoritative decisions of other United States Courts of Appeals that have addressed the issue.

(2) Except by the court's permission, a petition for an en banc hearing or rehearing must not exceed 15 pages, excluding material not counted under Rule 32.

(3) For purposes of the page limit in Rule 35(b)(2), if a party files both a petition for panel rehearing and a petition for rehearing en banc, they are considered a single document even if they are filed separately, unless separate filing is required by local rule.

(c) Time for Petition for Hearing or Rehearing En Banc. A petition that an appeal be heard initially en banc must be filed by the date when the appellee's brief is due. A petition for a rehearing en banc must be filed within the time prescribed by Rule 40 for filing a petition for rehearing.

(d) Number of Copies. The number of copies to be filed must be prescribed by local rule and may be altered by order in a particular case.

(e) Response. No response may be filed to a petition for an en banc consideration unless the court orders a response.

(f) Call for a Vote. A vote need not be taken to determine whether the case will be heard or reheard en banc unless a judge calls for a vote.

As amended 1979, 1994, 1998.

Rule 36.

ENTRY OF JUDGMENT; NOTICE

(a) Entry. A judgment is entered when it is noted on the docket. The clerk must prepare, sign, and enter the judgment:

(1) after receiving the court's opinion—but if settlement of the judgment's form is required, after final settlement; or

(2) if a judgment is rendered without an opinion, as the court instructs.

(b) Notice. On the date when judgment is entered, the clerk must serve on all parties a copy of the opinion—or the judgment, if no opinion was written—and a notice of the date when the judgment was entered.

As amended 1998, 2002.

Rule 37.

INTEREST ON JUDGMENT

(a) When the Court Affirms. Unless the law provides otherwise, if a money judgment in a civil case is affirmed, whatever interest is allowed by law is payable from the date when the district court's judgment was entered.

(b) When the Court Reverses. If the court modifies or reverses a judgment with a direction that a money judgment be entered in the district court, the mandate must contain instructions about the allowance of interest.

As amended 1998.

Rule 38.

FRIVOLOUS APPEAL—DAMAGES AND COSTS

If a court of appeals determines that an appeal is frivolous, it may, after a separately filed motion or notice from the court and reasonable opportunity to respond, award just damages and single or double costs to the appellee.

As amended 1994, 1998.

Rule 39.

COSTS

(a) Against Whom Assessed. The following rules apply unless the law provides or the court orders otherwise:

(1) if an appeal is dismissed, costs are taxed against the appellant, unless the parties agree otherwise;

(2) if a judgment is affirmed, costs are taxed against the appellant;

(3) if a judgment is reversed, costs are taxed against the appellee;

(4) if a judgment is affirmed in part, reversed in part, modified, or vacated, costs are taxed only as the court orders.

(b) Costs For and Against the United States. Costs for or against the United States, its agency, or officer will be assessed under Rule 39(a) only if authorized by law.

(c) Costs of Copies. Each court of appeals must, by local rule, fix the maximum rate for taxing the cost of producing necessary copies of a brief or appendix, or copies of records authorized by Rule 30(f). The rate must not exceed that generally charged for such work in the area where the clerk's office is located and should encourage economical methods of copying.

(d) Bill of Costs: Objections; Insertion in Mandate.

(1) A party who wants costs taxed must—within 14 days after entry of judgment—file with the circuit clerk, with proof of service, an itemized and verified bill of costs.

(2) Objections must be filed within 10 days after service of the bill of costs, unless the court extends the time.

(3) The clerk must prepare and certify an itemized statement of costs for insertion in the mandate, but issuance of the mandate must not be delayed for taxing costs. If the mandate issues before costs are finally determined, the district clerk must—upon the

circuit clerk's request—add the statement of costs, or any amendment of it, to the mandate.

(e) Costs on Appeal Taxable in the District Court. The following costs on appeal are taxable in the district court for the benefit of the party entitled to costs under this rule:

(1) the preparation and transmission of the record;

(2) the reporter's transcript, if needed to determine the appeal;

(3) premiums paid for a supersedeas bond or other bond to preserve rights pending appeal; and

(4) the fee for filing the notice of appeal.

As amended 1979, 1986, 1998.

Rule 40.

PETITION FOR PANEL REHEARING

(a) Time to File; Contents; Answer; Action by the Court if Granted.

(1) *Time.* Unless the time is shortened or extended by order or local rule, a petition for panel rehearing may be filed within 14 days after entry of judgment. But in a civil case, if the United States or its officer or agency is a party, the time within which any party may seek rehearing is 45 days after entry of judgment, unless an order shortens or extends the time.

(2) *Contents.* The petition must state with particularity each point of law or fact that the petitioner believes the court has overlooked or misapprehended and must argue in support of the petition. Oral argument is not permitted.

(3) *Answer.* Unless the court requests, no answer to a petition for panel rehearing is permitted. But ordinarily rehearing will not be granted in the absence of such a request.

(4) *Action by the Court.* If a petition for panel rehearing is granted, the court may do any of the following:

(A) make a final disposition of the case without reargument;

(B) restore the case to the calendar for reargument or resubmission; or

(C) issue any other appropriate order.

(b) Form of Petition; Length. The petition must comply in form with Rule 32. Copies must be served and filed as Rule 31 prescribes. Unless the court permits or a local rule provides otherwise, a petition for panel rehearing must not exceed 15 pages.

As amended 1979, 1994, 1998.

Rule 41.

MANDATE: CONTENTS; ISSUANCE AND EFFECTIVE DATE; STAY

(a) Contents. Unless the court directs that a formal mandate issue, the mandate consists of a certified copy of the judgment, a copy of the court's opinion, if any, and any direction about costs.

(b) When Issued. The court's mandate must issue 7 calendar days after the time to file a petition for rehearing expires, or 7 calendar days after entry of an order denying a timely petition for panel rehearing, petition for rehearing en banc, or motion for stay of mandate, whichever is later. The court may shorten or extend the time.

(c) Effective Date. The mandate is effective when issued.

(d) Staying the Mandate.

(1) *On Petition for Rehearing or Motion.* The timely filing of a petition for panel rehearing, petition for rehearing en banc, or motion for stay of mandate, stays the mandate until disposition of the petition or motion, unless the court orders otherwise.

(2) *Pending Petition for Certiorari.*

(A) A party may move to stay the mandate pending the filing of a petition for a writ of certiorari in the Supreme Court. The motion must be served on all parties and must show that the certiorari petition would present a substantial question and that there is good cause for a stay.

(B) The stay must not exceed 90 days, unless the period is extended for good cause or unless the party who obtained the stay files a petition for the writ and so notifies the circuit clerk in writing within the period of the stay. In that case, the stay continues until the Supreme Court's final disposition.

(C) The court may require a bond or other security as a condition to granting or continuing a stay of the mandate.

(D) The court of appeals must issue the mandate immediately when a copy of a Supreme Court order denying the petition for writ of certiorari is filed.

As amended 1994, 1998, 2002.

Rule 42.

VOLUNTARY DISMISSAL

(a) Dismissal in the District Court. Before an appeal has been docketed by the circuit clerk, the district court may dismiss the appeal on the filing of a stipulation signed by all parties or on the appellant's motion with notice to all parties.

(b) Dismissal in the Court of Appeals. The circuit clerk may dismiss a docketed appeal if the parties file a signed dismissal agreement specifying how costs are to be paid and pay any fees that are due. But no mandate or other process may issue without a court order. An appeal may be dismissed on the appellant's motion on terms agreed to by the parties or fixed by the court.

As amended 1998.

Rule 43.

SUBSTITUTION OF PARTIES

(a) Death of a Party.

(1) *After Notice of Appeal Is Filed.* If a party dies after a notice of appeal has been filed or while a proceeding is pending in the court of appeals, the decedent's personal representative may be substituted as a party on motion filed with the circuit clerk by the representative or by any party. A party's motion must be served on the representative in accordance with Rule 25. If the decedent has no representative, any party may suggest the death on the record, and the court of appeals may then direct appropriate proceedings.

(2) *Before Notice of Appeal Is Filed—Potential Appellant.* If a party entitled to appeal dies before filing a notice of appeal, the decedent's personal representative—or, if there is no personal representative, the decedent's attorney of record—may file a notice of appeal within the time prescribed by these rules. After the notice of appeal is filed, substitution must be in accordance with Rule 43(a)(1).

(3) *Before Notice of Appeal Is Filed—Potential Appellee.* If a party against whom an appeal may be taken dies after entry of a judgment or order in the district court, but before a notice of appeal is filed, an appellant may proceed as if the death had not occurred. After the notice of appeal is filed, substitution must be in accordance with Rule 43(a)(1).

(b) Substitution for a Reason Other Than Death. If a party needs to be substituted for any reason other than death, the procedure prescribed in Rule 43(a) applies.

(c) Public Officer: Identification; Substitution.

(1) *Identification of Party.* A public officer who is a party to an appeal or other proceeding in an official capacity may be described as a party by the public officer's official title rather than by name. But the court may require the public officer's name to be added.

(2) *Automatic Substitution of Officeholder.* When a public officer who is a party to an appeal or other proceeding in an official capacity dies, resigns, or otherwise ceases to hold office, the action does not abate. The public officer's successor is automatically substituted as a party. Proceedings following the substitution are to be in the name of the substituted party, but any misnomer that does not affect the substantial rights of the parties may be disregarded. An order of substitution may be entered at any time, but failure to enter an order does not affect the substitution.

As amended 1986, 1998.

Rule 44.

CASE INVOLVING A CONSTITUTIONAL QUESTION WHEN THE UNITED STATES OR THE RELEVANT STATE IS NOT A PARTY

(a) Constitutional Challenge to Federal Statute. If a party questions the constitutionality of an Act of Congress in a proceeding in which the United States or its agency, officer, or employee is not a party in an official capacity, the questioning party must give written notice to the circuit clerk immediately upon the filing of the record or as soon as the question is raised in the court of appeals. The clerk must then certify that fact to the Attorney General.

(b) Constitutional Challenge to State Statute. If a party questions the constitutionality of a statute of a State in a proceeding in which that State or its agency, officer, or employee is not a party in an official capacity, the questioning party must give written notice to the circuit clerk immediately upon the filing of the record or as soon as the question is raised in the court of appeals. The clerk must then certify that fact to the attorney general of the State.

As amended 1998, 2002.

Rule 45.

CLERK'S DUTIES

(a) General Provisions.

(1) *Qualifications.* The circuit clerk must take the oath and post any bond required by law. Neither the clerk nor any deputy clerk may practice as an attorney or counselor in any court while in office.

(2) *When Court Is Open.* The court of appeals is always open for filing any paper, issuing and returning process, making a motion, and entering an order. The clerk's office with the clerk or a deputy in attendance must be open during business hours on all days except Saturdays, Sundays, and legal holidays. A court may provide by local rule or by order that the clerk's office be open for specified hours on Saturdays or on legal holidays other than New Year's Day, Martin Luther King, Jr.'s Birthday, Presidents' Day, Memorial Day, Independence Day, Labor Day, Columbus Day, Veterans' Day, Thanksgiving Day, and Christmas Day.

(b) Records.

(1) *The Docket.* The circuit clerk must maintain a docket and an index of all docketed cases in the manner prescribed by the Director of the Administrative Office of the United States Courts. The clerk must record all papers filed with the clerk and all process, orders, and judgments.

(2) *Calendar.* Under the court's direction, the clerk must prepare a calendar of cases awaiting argument. In placing cases on the calendar for argument, the clerk must give preference to appeals in criminal cases and to other proceedings and appeals entitled to preference by law.

(3) *Other Records.* The clerk must keep other books and records required by the Director of the Administrative Office of the United States Courts, with the approval of the Judicial Conference of the United States, or by the court.

(c) Notice of an Order or Judgment. Upon the entry of an order or judgment, the circuit clerk must immediately serve a notice of entry on each party, with a copy of any opinion, and must note the date of service on the docket. Service on a party represented by counsel must be made on counsel.

(d) Custody of Records and Papers. The circuit clerk has custody of the court's records and papers. Unless the court orders or instructs otherwise, the clerk must not permit an original record or paper to be taken from the clerk's office. Upon disposition of the case, original papers constituting the record on appeal or review must be returned to the court or agency from which they were received. The clerk must preserve a copy of any brief, appendix, or other paper that has been filed.

As amended 1971, 1986, 1998, 2002.

Rule 46.

ATTORNEYS

(a) Admission to the Bar.

(1) *Eligibility.* An attorney is eligible for admission to the bar of a court of appeals if that attorney is of good moral and professional character and is admitted to practice before the Supreme Court of the United States, the highest court of a state, another United States court of appeals, or a United States district court (including the district courts for Guam, the Northern Mariana Islands, and the Virgin Islands).

(2) *Application.* An applicant must file an application for admission, on a form approved by the court that contains the applicant's personal statement showing eligibility for membership. The applicant must subscribe to the following oath or affirmation:

> "I, ________________, do solemnly swear [or affirm] that I will conduct myself as an attorney and counselor of this court, uprightly and according to law; and that I will support the Constitution of the United States."

(3) *Admission Procedures.* On written or oral motion of a member of the court's bar, the court will act on the application. An applicant may be admitted by oral motion in open court. But, unless the court orders otherwise, an applicant need not appear before the court to be admitted. Upon admission, an applicant must pay the clerk the fee prescribed by local rule or court order.

(b) Suspension or Disbarment.

(1) *Standard.* A member of the court's bar is subject to suspension or disbarment by the court if the member:

(A) has been suspended or disbarred from practice in any other court; or

(B) is guilty of conduct unbecoming a member of the court's bar.

(2) *Procedure.* The member must be given an opportunity to show good cause, within the time prescribed by the court, why the member should not be suspended or disbarred.

(3) *Order.* The court must enter an appropriate order after the member responds and a hearing is held, if requested, or after the time prescribed for a response expires, if no response is made.

(c) Discipline. A court of appeals may discipline an attorney who practices before it for conduct unbecoming a member of the bar or for failure to comply with any court rule. First, however, the court must afford the attorney reasonable notice, an opportunity to show cause to the contrary, and, if requested, a hearing.

As amended 1986, 1998.

Rule 47.

LOCAL RULES BY COURTS OF APPEALS

(a) Local Rules.

(1) Each court of appeals acting by a majority of its judges in regular active service may, after giving appropriate public notice and opportunity for comment, make and amend rules governing its practice. A generally applicable direction to parties or lawyers regarding practice before a court must be in a local rule rather than an internal operating procedure or standing order. A local rule must be consistent with—but not duplicative of—Acts of Congress and rules adopted under 28 U.S.C. § 2072 and must conform to any uniform numbering system prescribed by the Judicial Conference of the United States. Each circuit clerk must send the Administrative Office of the United States Courts a copy of each local rule and internal operating procedure when it is promulgated or amended.

(2) A local rule imposing a requirement of form must not be enforced in a manner that causes a party to lose rights because of a nonwillful failure to comply with the requirement.

(b) Procedure When There Is No Controlling Law. A court of appeals may regulate practice in a particular case in any manner consistent with federal law, these rules, and local rules of the circuit. No sanction or other disadvantage may be imposed for noncompliance with any requirement not in federal law, federal rules, or the local circuit rules unless the alleged violator has been furnished in the particular case with actual notice of the requirement.

As amended 1995, 1998.

Rule 48.

MASTERS

(a) Appointment; Powers. A court of appeals may appoint a special master to hold hearings, if necessary, and to recommend factual findings and disposition in matters ancillary to proceedings in the court. Unless the order referring a matter to a master specifies or limits the master's powers, those powers include, but are not limited to, the following:

(1) regulating all aspects of a hearing;

(2) taking all appropriate action for the efficient performance of the master's duties under the order;

(3) requiring the production of evidence on all matters embraced in the reference; and

(4) administering oaths and examining witnesses and parties.

(b) Compensation. If the master is not a judge or court employee, the court must determine the master's compensation and whether the cost is to be charged to any party.

As amended 1994, 1998.

[The order of the Supreme Court of December 4, 1967, stated that the rules therein set forth, to be known as the Federal Rules of Appellate Procedure, "be, and they hereby are, prescribed, pursuant to sections 3771 and 3772 of Title 18, United States Code, and sections 2072 and 2075 of Title 28, United States Code, to govern the procedure in appeals to United States courts of appeals from the United States district courts, in the review by United States courts of appeals of decisions of the Tax Court of the United States, in proceedings in the United States courts of appeals for the review or enforcement of orders of administrative agencies, boards, commissions and officers, and in applications for writs or other relief which a United States court of appeals or judge thereof is competent to give."]

[The order of December 4, 1967, further stated that the Rules "shall take effect on July 1, 1968, and shall govern all proceedings in appeals and petitions for review or enforcement of orders thereafter brought and in all such proceedings then pending, except to the extent that in the opinion of the court of appeals their application in a particular proceeding then pending would not be feasible or would work injustice, in which case the former procedure may be followed." 389 U.S. 1063, 1065; see 43 F.R.D. 61.]

[Rules 30(a) and (c) and 31(a) were amended by the order of the Supreme Court of March 30, 1970, to be effective July 1, 1970. 398 U.S. 971; see 48 F.R.D. 481.]

[Rules 26(a) and 45(a) were amended by the order of the Supreme Court of March 1, 1971, to be effective July 1, 1971. 401 U.S. 1029; see 52 F.R.D. 84.]

[Rule 9(c) was amended by the order of the Supreme Court of April 24, 1972, to be effective October 1, 1972. 406 U.S. 1005; see 56 F.R.D. 181.]

[Rules 1(a), 3(c), (d), and (e), 4(a), 5(d), 6(d), 7, 10(b), 11(a), (b), (c), and (d), 12(a), (b), and (c), 13(a), 24(b), 27(b), 28(g) and (j), 34(a) and (b), 35(b) and (c), 39(c) and (d), and 40(a) and (b) were amended by the order of the Supreme Court of April 30, 1979, to be effective August 1, 1979. 441 U.S. 969; see 16A Wright, Miller & Cooper, Federal Practice and Procedure app. B.]

[Rule 9(c) was amended October 12, 1984, Pub.L. 98–473, Title II, § 210, 98 Stat. 1987.]

[Rules 19, 26(a), 28(c), 30(a) and (b), 39(c), and 45(a) and (b) were amended, and Rules 3.1, 5.1, and 15.1 added, by the order of the Supreme Court of March 10, 1986, to be effective July 1, 1986. That order also neutralized gender-specific language in numerous Rules. 475 U.S. 1153; see 109 F.R.D. 179.]

[Rule 4(b) was amended November 18, 1988, Pub.L. 100–690, Title VII, § 7111, 102 Stat. 4419.]

[Rules 1(a), 3(a), 6, 26(a), 27(a), and 28(g) were amended, and Rule 26.1 and Form 5 added, by the order of the Supreme Court of April 25, 1989, to be effective December 1, 1989. 490 U.S. 1125; see 124 F.R.D. 361.]

[Rules 4(a), 6, 10(c), 25(a), 26(a), 26.1, 28(a), (b), and (h), 30(b), and 34(d) were amended by the order of the Supreme Court of April 30, 1991, to be effective December 1, 1991. 500 U.S. 1007; see 134 F.R.D. 725.]

[Rules 3(c) and (d), 3.1, 4, 5.1(a), 6(b), 10(b), 12(b) and (c), 15(a) and (e), 25(a), 28(a) and (b), and 34(c) and Forms 1, 2, and 3 were amended by the order of the Supreme Court of April 22, 1993, to be effective December 1, 1993. 507 U.S. 1059; see 147 F.R.D. 287.]

[Rules 1(c), 3(a), 5(c), 5.1(c), 9, 13(a), 21(d), 25(a), (d), and (e), 26.1, 27(d), 28(a), (b), and (g), 30(a), 31(b), 33, 35(d), 38, 40(a), 41, and 48 were amended by the order of the Supreme Court of April 29, 1994, to be effective December 1, 1994. 511 U.S. 1155; see 154 F.R.D. 329.]

[Rules 4(a), 8(c), 10(a) and (b), and 47 were amended by the order of the Supreme Court of April 27, 1995, to be effective December 1, 1995. 514 U.S. 1137; see 161 F.R.D. 163.]

[Rule 22 was amended April 24, 1996, Pub.L. 104–132, Title I, § 103, 110 Stat. 1218.]

[Rules 21, 25(a), (c), and (d), and 26(c) were amended by the order of the Supreme Court of April 23, 1996, to be effective December 1, 1996. 517 U.S. 1255; see 167 F.R.D. 229.]

[Rules 3.1, 5, 5.1, 26.1, 27, 28, 29, 32, 35, and 41 and Form 4 were amended, and stylistic changes were made in all other Rules, by the order of the Supreme Court of April 24, 1998, to be effective December 1, 1998. 523 U.S. 1147; see 16A Wright, Miller & Cooper, Federal Practice and Procedure app. B.]

[Rules 1(b), 4(a) and (b), 5(c), 21(d), 24(a), 25(c) and (d), 26(a) and (c), 26.1, 27(a) and (d), 28(j), 31(b), 32(a), (c), (d), and (e), 36(b), 41(b), 44, and 45(c) were amended, and Form 6 added, by the order of the Supreme Court of April 29, 2002, to be effective December 1, 2002. 535 U.S. 1123; see 207 F.R.D. 655.]

[Forms 1, 2, 3, and 5 were amended by the order of the Supreme Court of March 27, 2003, to be effective December 1, 2003. ___ U.S. ___; see ___ F.R.D. ___.]

APPENDIX OF FORMS

Form 1.

NOTICE OF APPEAL TO A COURT OF APPEALS FROM A JUDGMENT OR ORDER OF A DISTRICT COURT

United States District Court for the . . . . .District of . . . .

File Number . . . .

A. B., Plaintiff)
v.) Notice of Appeal
C. D., Defendant)

Notice is hereby given that (here name all parties taking the appeal), (plaintiffs) (defendants) in the above named case,[1] hereby appeal to the United States Court of Appeals for the . . . . Circuit (from the final judgment) (from an order (describing it)) entered in this action on the . . . . . . day of . . . . , 20. . . .

(S) . . . .

Attorney for . . . .

. . . .

(Address)

As amended 1993, 2003.

FORMS 2–6 [Omitted]

1. See Rule 3(c) for permissible ways of identifying appellants.

TABLE OF CONTENTS

SELECTED PROVISIONS OF THE CONSTITUTION OF THE UNITED STATES

SELECTED PROVISIONS OF TITLE 28, UNITED STATES CODE

TABLE OF CONTENTS

TABLE OF CONTENTS

TABLE OF CONTENTS

TABLE OF CONTENTS

SELECTED PROVISIONS OF OTHER PROCEDURAL STATUTES

*

SELECTED PROVISIONS OF THE CONSTITUTION OF THE UNITED STATES

* * *

ARTICLE. I.

* * *

Section 8. The Congress shall have Power To lay and collect Taxes, Duties, Imposts and Excises, to pay the Debts and provide for the common Defence and general Welfare of the United States; but all Duties, Imposts and Excises shall be uniform throughout the United States;

To borrow Money on the credit of the United States;

To regulate Commerce with foreign Nations, and among the several States, and with the Indian Tribes;

To establish an uniform Rule of Naturalization, and uniform Laws on the subject of Bankruptcies throughout the United States;

To coin Money, regulate the Value thereof, and of foreign Coin, and fix the Standard of Weights and Measures;

To provide for the Punishment of counterfeiting the Securities and current Coin of the United States;

To establish Post Offices and post Roads;

To promote the Progress of Science and useful Arts, by securing for limited Times to Authors and Inventors the exclusive Right to their respective Writings and Discoveries;

To constitute Tribunals inferior to the supreme Court;

To define and punish Piracies and Felonies committed on the high Seas, and Offences against the Law of Nations;

To declare War, grant Letters of Marque and Reprisal, and make Rules concerning Captures on Land and Water;

To raise and support Armies, but no Appropriation of Money to that Use shall be for a longer Term than two Years;

To provide and maintain a Navy;

To make Rules for the Government and Regulation of the land and naval Forces;

To provide for calling forth the Militia to execute the Laws of the Union, suppress Insurrections and repel Invasions;

To provide for organizing, arming, and disciplining, the Militia, and for governing such Part of them as may be employed in the Service of the United States, reserving to the States respectively, the Appointment of the

Officers, and the Authority of training the Militia according to the discipline prescribed by Congress;

To exercise exclusive Legislation in all Cases whatsoever, over such District (not exceeding ten Miles square) as may, by Cession of particular States, and the Acceptance of Congress, become the Seat of the Government of the United States, and to exercise like Authority over all Places purchased by the Consent of the Legislature of the State in which the same shall be, for the Erection of Forts, Magazines, Arsenals, dock-Yards, and other needful Buildings;—And

To make all Laws which shall be necessary and proper for carrying into Execution the foregoing Powers, and all other Powers vested by this Constitution in the Government of the United States, or in any Department or Officer thereof.

* * *

ARTICLE. III.

Section 1. The judicial Power of the United States, shall be vested in one supreme Court, and in such inferior Courts as the Congress may from time to time ordain and establish. The Judges, both of the supreme and inferior Courts, shall hold their Offices during good Behaviour, and shall, at stated Times, receive for their Services, a Compensation, which shall not be diminished during their Continuance in Office.

Section 2. The judicial Power shall extend to all Cases, in Law and Equity, arising under this Constitution, the Laws of the United States, and Treaties made, or which shall be made, under their Authority;—to all Cases affecting Ambassadors, other public Ministers and Consuls;—to all Cases of admiralty and maritime Jurisdiction;—to Controversies to which the United States shall be a Party;—to Controversies between two or more States;—between a State and Citizens of another State;—between Citizens of different States;—between Citizens of the same State claiming Lands under Grants of different States, and between a State, or the Citizens thereof, and foreign States, Citizens or Subjects.

In all Cases affecting Ambassadors, other public Ministers and Consuls, and those in which a State shall be Party, the supreme Court shall have original Jurisdiction. In all the other Cases before mentioned, the supreme Court shall have appellate Jurisdiction, both as to Law and Fact, with such Exceptions, and under such Regulations as the Congress shall make.

The Trial of all Crimes, except in Cases of Impeachment, shall be by Jury; and such Trial shall be held in the State where the said Crimes shall have been committed; but when not committed within any State, the Trial shall be at such Place or Places as the Congress may by Law have directed.

* * *

ARTICLE. IV.

Section 1. Full Faith and Credit shall be given in each State to the public Acts, Records, and judicial Proceedings of every other State. And the Congress may by general Laws prescribe the Manner in which such Acts, Records and Proceedings shall be proved, and the Effect thereof.

Section 2. The Citizens of each State shall be entitled to all Privileges and Immunities of Citizens in the several States.

* * *

ARTICLE. VI.

* * *

This Constitution, and the Laws of the United States which shall be made in Pursuance thereof; and all Treaties made, or which shall be made, under the Authority of the United States, shall be the supreme Law of the Land; and the Judges in every State shall be bound thereby, any Thing in the Constitution or Laws of any State to the Contrary notwithstanding.

* * *

AMENDMENT. I.

[1791]

Congress shall make no law respecting an establishment of religion, or prohibiting the free exercise thereof; or abridging the freedom of speech, or of the press; or the right of the people peaceably to assemble, and to petition the Government for a redress of grievances.

AMENDMENT. IV.

The right of the people to be secure in their persons, houses, papers, and effects, against unreasonable searches and seizures, shall not be violated, and no Warrants shall issue, but upon probable cause, supported by Oath or affirmation, and particularly describing the place to be searched, and the persons or things to be seized.

AMENDMENT. V.

No person shall be held to answer for a capital, or otherwise infamous crime, unless on a presentment or indictment of a Grand Jury, except in cases arising in the land or naval forces, or in the Militia, when in actual service in time of War or public danger; nor shall any person be subject for the same offence to be twice put in jeopardy of life or limb; nor shall be compelled in any criminal case to be a witness against himself, nor be deprived of life, liberty, or property, without due process of law; nor shall private property be taken for public use, without just compensation.

AMENDMENT. VI.

In all criminal prosecutions, the accused shall enjoy the right to a speedy and public trial, by an impartial jury of the State and district wherein the crime shall have been committed, which district shall have been previously ascertained by law, and to be informed of the nature and cause of the accusation; to be confronted with the Witnesses against him; to have compulsory process for obtaining witnesses in his favor, and to have the Assistance of Counsel for his defence.

AMENDMENT. VII.

In suits at common law, where the value in controversy shall exceed twenty dollars, the right of trial by jury shall be preserved, and no fact tried by a jury, shall be otherwise re-examined in any Court of the United States, than according to the rules of the common law.

AMENDMENT. IX.

The enumeration in the Constitution, of certain rights, shall not be construed to deny or disparage others retained by the people.

AMENDMENT. X.

The powers not delegated to the United States by the Constitution, nor prohibited by it to the States, are reserved to the States respectively, or to the people.

AMENDMENT. XI.

[1795*]

The Judicial power of the United States shall not be construed to extend to any suit in law or equity, commenced or prosecuted against one of the United States by Citizens of another State, or by Citizens or Subjects of any Foreign State.

AMENDMENT. XIV.

[1868]

Section 1. All persons born or naturalized in the United States, and subject to the jurisdiction thereof, are citizens of the United States and of the State wherein they reside. No State shall make or enforce any law which shall abridge the privileges or immunities of citizens of the United States; nor shall any State deprive any person of life, liberty, or property, without due process of law; nor deny to any person within its jurisdiction the equal protection of the laws.

Section 2. Representatives shall be apportioned among the several States according to their respective numbers, counting the whole number of persons in each State, excluding Indians not taxed. But when the right to vote at any election for the choice of electors for President and Vice President of the United States, Representatives in Congress, the Executive and Judicial officers of a State, or the members of the Legislature thereof, is denied to any of the male inhabitants of such State, being twenty-one years of age, and citizens of the United States, or in any way abridged, except for participation in rebellion, or other crime, the basis of representation therein shall be reduced in the proportion which the number of such male citizens shall bear to the whole number of male citizens twenty-one years of age in such State.

Section 3. No person shall be a Senator or Representative in Congress, or elector of President and Vice President, or hold any office, civil or military, under the United States, or under any State, who, having previ-

* Official announcement of ratification was not made until January 8, 1798, in a message from the President to Congress.

ously taken an oath, as a member of Congress, or as an officer of the United States, or as a member of any State legislature, or as an executive or judicial officer of any State, to support the Constitution of the United States, shall have engaged in insurrection or rebellion against the same, or given aid or comfort to the enemies thereof. But Congress may by a vote of two-thirds of each House, remove such disability.

Section 4. The validity of the public debt of the United States, authorized by law, including debts incurred for payment of pensions and bounties for services in suppressing insurrection or rebellion, shall not be questioned. But neither the United States nor any State shall assume or pay any debt or obligation incurred in aid of insurrection or rebellion against the United States, or any claim for the loss or emancipation of any slave; but all such debts, obligations and claims shall be held illegal and void.

Section 5. The Congress shall have power to enforce, by appropriate legislation, the provisions of this article.

*

SELECTED PROVISIONS OF TITLE 28, UNITED STATES CODE

§ 1. Number of justices; quorum

The Supreme Court of the United States shall consist of a Chief Justice of the United States and eight associate justices, any six of whom shall constitute a quorum.

§ 2. Terms of court

The Supreme Court shall hold at the seat of government a term of court commencing on the first Monday in October of each year and may hold such adjourned or special terms as may be necessary.

§ 3. Vacancy in office of Chief Justice; disability

Whenever the Chief Justice is unable to perform the duties of his office or the office is vacant, his powers and duties shall devolve upon the associate justice next in precedence who is able to act, until such disability is removed or another Chief Justice is appointed and duly qualified.

§ 4. Precedence of associate justices

Associate justices shall have precedence according to the seniority of their commissions. Justices whose commissions bear the same date shall have precedence according to seniority in age.

§ 41. Number and composition of circuits

The thirteen judicial circuits of the United States are constituted as follows:

Circuits	*Composition*
District of Columbia	District of Columbia.
First	Maine, Massachusetts, New Hampshire, Puerto Rico, Rhode Island.
Second	Connecticut, New York, Vermont.
Third	Delaware, New Jersey, Pennsylvania, Virgin Islands.
Fourth	Maryland, North Carolina, South Carolina, Virginia, West Virginia.
Fifth	District of the Canal Zone, Louisiana, Mississippi, Texas.
Sixth	Kentucky, Michigan, Ohio, Tennessee.
Seventh	Illinois, Indiana, Wisconsin.
Eighth	Arkansas, Iowa, Minnesota, Missouri, Nebraska, North Dakota, South Dakota.
Ninth	Alaska, Arizona, California, Idaho, Montana, Nevada, Oregon, Washington, Guam, Hawaii.

Circuits	*Composition*
Tenth	Colorado, Kansas, New Mexico, Oklahoma, Utah, Wyoming.
Eleventh	Alabama, Florida, Georgia.
Federal	All Federal judicial districts.

As amended Oct. 31, 1951, c. 655, § 34, 65 Stat. 723; Oct. 14, 1980, Pub.L. 96–452, § 2, 94 Stat. 1994; Apr. 2, 1982, Pub.L. 97–164, Title I, § 101, 96 Stat. 25.

§ 42. Allotment of Supreme Court justices to circuits

The Chief Justice of the United States and the associate justices of the Supreme Court shall from time to time be allotted as circuit justices among the circuits by order of the Supreme Court. The Chief Justice may make such allotments in vacation.

A justice may be assigned to more than one circuit, and two or more justices may be assigned to the same circuit.

§ 43. Creation and composition of courts

(a) There shall be in each circuit a court of appeals, which shall be a court of record, known as the United States Court of Appeals for the circuit.

(b) Each court of appeals shall consist of the circuit judges of the circuit in regular active service. The circuit justice and justices or judges designated or assigned shall also be competent to sit as judges of the court.
As amended Nov. 13, 1963, Pub.L. 88–176, § 1(a), 77 Stat. 331.

§ 44. Appointment, tenure, residence and salary of circuit judges

(a) The President shall appoint, by and with the advice and consent of the Senate, circuit judges for the several circuits as follows:

Circuits	Number of Judges
District of Columbia	12
First	6
Second	13
Third	14
Fourth	15
Fifth	17
Sixth	16
Seventh	11
Eighth	11
Ninth	28
Tenth	12
Eleventh	12
Federal	12.

(b) Circuit judges shall hold office during good behavior.

(c) Except in the District of Columbia, each circuit judge shall be a resident of the circuit for which appointed at the time of his appointment and thereafter while in active service. While in active service, each circuit judge of the Federal judicial circuit appointed after the effective date of the Federal Courts Improvement Act of 1982, and the chief judge of the Federal judicial circuit, whenever appointed, shall reside within fifty miles of the District of Columbia. In each circuit (other than the Federal judicial) there shall be at least one circuit judge in regular active service appointed from the residents of each state in that circuit.

(d) Each circuit judge shall receive a salary at an annual rate determined under section 225 of the Federal Salary Act of 1967 (2 U.S.C. 351–361), as adjusted by section 461 of this title. Latest amendment Nov. 26, 1997, Pub.L. 105–119, Title III, § 307, 111 Stat. 2493.

§ 45. Chief judges; precedence of judges

(a)(1) The chief judge of the circuit shall be the circuit judge in regular active service who is senior in commission of those judges who—

(A) are sixty-four years of age or under;

(B) have served for one year or more as a circuit judge; and

(C) have not served previously as chief judge.

(2)(A) In any case in which no circuit judge meets the qualifications of paragraph (1), the youngest circuit judge in regular active service who is sixty-five years of age or over and who has served as circuit judge for one year or more shall act as the chief judge.

(B) In any case under subparagraph (A) in which there is no circuit judge in regular active service who has served as a circuit judge for one year or more, the circuit judge in regular active service who is senior in commission and who has not served previously as chief judge shall act as the chief judge.

(3)(A) Except as provided in subparagraph (C), the chief judge of the circuit appointed under paragraph (1) shall serve for a term of seven years and shall serve after expiration of such term until another judge is eligible under paragraph (1) to serve as chief judge of the circuit.

(B) Except as provided in subparagraph (C), a circuit judge acting as chief judge under subparagraph (A) or (B) of paragraph (2) shall serve until a judge has been appointed who meets the qualifications under paragraph (1).

(C) No circuit judge may serve or act as chief judge of the circuit after attaining the age of seventy years unless no other circuit judge is qualified to serve as chief judge of the circuit under paragraph (1) or is qualified to act as chief judge under paragraph (2).

(b) The chief judge shall have precedence and preside at any session of the court which he attends. Other circuit judges of the court in regular active service shall have precedence and preside according to the seniority of their commissions. Judges whose commissions bear the same date shall have precedence according to seniority in age. The circuit justice, however, shall have precedence over all the circuit judges and shall preside at any session which he attends.

(c) If the chief judge desires to be relieved of his duties as chief judge while retaining his active status as circuit judge, he may so certify to the Chief Justice of the United States, and thereafter the chief judge of the circuit shall be such other circuit judge who is qualified to serve or act as chief judge under subsection (a).

(d) If a chief judge is temporarily unable to perform his duties as such, they shall be performed by the circuit judge in active service, present in the circuit and able and qualified to act, who is next in precedence. As amended Oct. 31, 1951, c. 655, § 35, 65 Stat. 723; Aug. 6, 1958, Pub.L. 85–593, § 1, 72 Stat. 497; Apr. 2, 1982, Pub.L. 97–164, Title II, §§ 201, 204, 96 Stat. 51, 53.

§ 46. Assignment of judges; panels; hearings; quorum

(a) Circuit judges shall sit on the court and its panels in such order and at such times as the court directs.

(b) In each circuit the court may authorize the hearing and determination of cases and controversies by separate panels, each consisting of three judges, at lease a majority of whom shall be judges of that court, unless such judges cannot sit because recused or disqualified, or unless the chief judge of that court certifies that there is an emergency including, but not limited to, the unavailability of a judge of the court because of illness. Such panels shall sit at the times and places and hear the cases and controversies assigned as the court directs. The United States Court of Appeals for the Federal Circuit shall determine by rule a procedure for the rotation of judges from panel to panel to ensure that all of the judges sit on a representative cross section of the cases heard and, notwithstanding the first sentence of this subsection, may determine by rule the number of judges, not less than three, who constitute a panel.

(c) Cases and controversies shall be heard and determined by a court or panel of not more than three judges (except that the United States Court of Appeals for the Federal Circuit may sit in panels of more than three judges if its rules so provide), unless a hearing or rehearing before the court in banc is ordered by a majority of the circuit judges of the circuit who are in regular active service. A court in banc shall consist of all circuit judges in regular active service, or such number of judges as may be prescribed in accordance with section 6 of Public Law 95–486 (92 Stat. 1633), except that any senior circuit judge of the circuit shall be eligible (1) to participate, at his election and upon designation and assignment pursuant to section 294(c) of this title and the rules of the circuit, as a member of an in banc court reviewing a decision of a panel of which such judge was a member, or (2) to continue to participate in the decision of a case or controversy that was heard or reheard by the court in banc at a time when such judge was in regular active service.

(d) A majority of the number of judges authorized to constitute a court or panel thereof, as provided in paragraph (c), shall constitute a quorum.

As amended Nov. 13, 1963, Pub.L. 88–176, § 1(b), 77 Stat. 331; Oct. 20, 1978, Pub.L. 95–486, § 5(a), (b), 92 Stat. 1633; Apr. 2, 1982, Pub.L. 97–164, Title I, § 103, Title II, § 205, 96 Stat. 25, 53; Aug. 6, 1996, Pub.L. 104–175, § 1, 110 Stat. 1556.

§ 47. Disqualification of trial judge to hear appeal

No judge shall hear or determine an appeal from the decision of a case or issue tried by him.

§ 48. Terms of court

(a) The courts of appeals shall hold regular sessions at the places listed below, and at such other places within the respective circuit as each court may designate by rule.

Circuits	*Places*
District of Columbia	Washington.
First	Boston.
Second	New York.
Third	Philadelphia.
Fourth	Richmond, Asheville.
Fifth	New Orleans, Fort Worth, Jackson.
Sixth	Cincinnati.
Seventh	Chicago.
Eighth	St. Louis, Kansas City, Omaha, St. Paul.
Ninth	San Francisco, Los Angeles, Portland, Seattle.
Tenth	Denver, Wichita, Oklahoma City.
Eleventh	Atlanta, Jacksonville, Montgomery.
Federal	District of Columbia, and in any other place listed above as the court by rule directs.

(b) Each court of appeals may hold special sessions at any place within its circuit as the nature of the business may require, and upon such notice as the court orders. The court may transact any business at a special session which it might transact at a regular session.

(c) Any court of appeals may pretermit any regular session of court at any place for insufficient business or other good cause.

(d) The times and places of the sessions of the Court of Appeals for the Federal Circuit shall be prescribed with a view to securing reasonable opportunity to citizens to appear before the court with as little inconvenience and expense to citizens as is practicable. As amended Oct. 31, 1951, c. 655, § 36, 65 Stat. 723; Oct. 14, 1980, Pub.L. 96–452, § 4, 94 Stat. 1994; Apr. 2, 1982, Pub.L. 97–164, Title I, § 104, 96 Stat. 26; Oct. 29, 1992, Pub.L. 102–572, Title V, § 501, 106 Stat. 4512.

§ 132. Creation and composition of district courts

(a) There shall be in each judicial district a district court which shall be a court of record known as the United States District Court for the district.

(b) Each district court shall consist of the district judge or judges for the district in regular active service. Justices or judges designated or assigned shall be competent to sit as judges of the court.

(c) Except as otherwise provided by law, or rule or order of court, the judicial power of a district court with respect to any action, suit or proceeding may be exercised by a single judge, who may preside alone and hold a regular or special session of court at the same time other sessions are held by other judges. As amended Nov. 13, 1963, Pub.L. 88–176, § 2, 77 Stat. 331.

§ 133. Appointment and number of district judges

(a) The President shall appoint, by and with the advice and consent of the Senate, district judges for the several judicial districts, as follows:

Districts	Judges
Alabama:	
Northern	7
Middle	3
Southern	3
Alaska	3
Arizona	12
Arkansas:	
Eastern	5
Western	3
California:	
Northern	14
Eastern	6
Central	27
Southern	13
Colorado	7
Connecticut	8
Delaware	4
District of Columbia	15
Florida:	
Northern	4
Middle	15
Southern	17
Georgia:	
Northern	11
Middle	4
Southern	3
Hawaii	3
Idaho	2
Illinois:	

Districts	Judges
Northern	22
Central	4
Southern	4
Indiana:	
Northern	5
Southern	5
Iowa:	
Northern	2
Southern	3
Kansas	5
Kentucky:	
Eastern	5
Western	4
Eastern and Western *	1
Louisiana:	
Eastern	12
Middle	3
Western	7
Maine	3
Maryland	10
Massachusetts	13
Michigan:	
Eastern	15
Western	4
Minnesota	7
Mississippi:	
Northern	3
Southern	6
Missouri:	
Eastern	6
Western	5
Eastern and Western	2
Montana	3
Nebraska	3
Nevada	7
New Hampshire	3
New Jersey	17
New Mexico	6
New York:	
Northern	5
Southern	28
Eastern	15
Western	4
North Carolina:	
Eastern	4
Middle	4
Western	4
North Dakota	2

* A district judge may be appointed to serve in more than one district.—Ed.

Districts	Judges
Ohio:	
Northern	11
Southern	8
Oklahoma:	
Northern	3
Eastern	1
Western	6
Northern, Eastern, and Western	1
Oregon	6
Pennsylvania:	
Eastern	22
Middle	6
Western	10
Puerto Rico	7
Rhode Island	3
South Carolina	10
South Dakota	3
Tennessee:	
Eastern	5
Middle	4
Western	5
Texas:	
Northern	12
Southern	19
Eastern	7
Western	13
Utah	5
Vermont	2
Virginia:	
Eastern	11
Western	4
Washington:	
Eastern	4
Western	7
West Virginia:	
Northern	3
Southern	5
Wisconsin:	
Eastern	5
Western	2
Wyoming	3.

(b)(1) In any case in which a judge of the United States (other than a senior judge) assumes the duties of a full-time office of Federal judicial administration, the President shall appoint, by and with the advice and consent of the Senate, an additional judge for the court on which such judge serves. If the judge who assumes the duties of such full-time office leaves that office and resumes the duties as an active judge of the court, then the President shall not appoint a judge to fill the first vacancy which occurs thereafter in that court.

(2) For purposes of paragraph (1), the term "office of Federal judicial administration" means a position as Director of the Federal Judicial Center, Director of the Administrative Office of the United States Courts, or administrative assistant to the Chief Justice. Latest amendment Nov. 2, 2002, Pub.L. 107–273, Div. A, Title III, § 312, 116 Stat. 1786.

§ 134. Tenure and residence of district judges

(a) The district judges shall hold office during good behavior.

(b) Each district judge, except in the District of Columbia, the Southern District of New York, and the Eastern District of New York, shall reside in the district or one of the districts for which he is appointed. Each district judge of the Southern District of New York and the Eastern District of New York may reside within 20 miles of the district to which he or she is appointed.

(c) If the public interest and the nature of the business of a district court require that a district judge should maintain his adobe at or near a particular place for holding court in the district or within a particular part of the district the judicial council of the circuit may so declare and may make an appropriate order. If the district judges of such a district are unable to agree as to which of them shall maintain his adobe at or near the place or within the area specified in such an order the judicial council of the circuit may decide which of them shall do so. As amended Aug. 3, 1949, c. 387, § 2(b)(1), 63 Stat. 495; Feb. 10, 1954, c. 6, § 2(b)(13)(a), 68 Stat. 12; Mar. 18, 1959, Pub.L. 86–3, § 9(c), 73 Stat. 8; May 19, 1961, Pub.L. 87–36, § 2(e)(3), 75 Stat. 83; Sept. 12, 1966, Pub.L. 89–571, § 1, 80 Stat. 764; Dec. 18, 1971, Pub.L. 92–208, § 3(e), 85 Stat. 742; Oct. 19, 1996, Pub.L. 104–317, Title VI, § 607, 110 Stat. 3860.

§ 136. Chief judges; precedence of district judges

(a)(1) In any district having more than one district judge, the chief judge of the district shall be the district judge in regular active service who is senior in commission of those judges who—

(A) are sixty-four years of age or under;

(B) have served for one year or more as a district judge; and

(C) have not served previously as chief judge.

(2)(A) In any case in which no district judge meets the qualifications of paragraph (1), the youngest district judge in regular active service who is sixty-five years of age or over and who has served as district judge for one year or more shall act as the chief judge.

(B) In any case under subparagraph (A) in which there is no district judge in regular active service who has served as a district judge for one year or more, the district judge in regular active service who is senior in commission and who has not served previously as chief judge shall act as the chief judge.

(3)(A) Except as provided in subparagraph (C), the chief judge of the district appointed under paragraph (1) shall serve for a term of seven years and shall serve after expiration of such term until another judge is eligible under paragraph (1) to serve as chief judge of the district.

(B) Except as provided in subparagraph (C), a district judge acting as chief judge under subparagraph (A) or (B) of paragraph (2) shall serve until a judge has been appointed who meets the qualifications under paragraph (1).

(C) No district judge may serve or act as chief judge of the district after attaining the age of seventy years unless no other district judge is qualified to serve as chief judge of the district under paragraph (1) or is qualified to act as chief judge under paragraph (2).

(b) The chief judge shall have precedence and preside at any session which he attends.

Other district judges shall have precedence and preside according to the seniority of their commissions. Judges whose commissions bear the same date shall have precedence according to seniority in age.

(c) A judge who commission extends over more than one district shall be junior to all district judges except in the district in which he resided at the time he entered upon the duties of his office.

(d) If the chief judge desires to be relieved of his duties as chief judge while retaining his active status as district judge, he may so certify to the Chief Justice of the United States, and thereafter, the chief judge of the district shall be such other district judge who is qualified to serve or act as chief judge under subsection (a).

(e) If a chief judge is temporarily unable to perform his duties as such, they shall be performed by the district judge in active service, present in the district and able and qualified to act, who is next in precedence. As amended Oct. 31, 1951, c. 655, § 37, 65 Stat. 723; Aug. 6, 1958, Pub.L. 85–593, § 2, 72 Stat. 497; Apr. 2, 1982, Pub.L. 97–164, Title II, § 202, 96 Stat. 52.

§ 137. Division of business among district judges

The business of a court having more than one judge shall be divided among the judges as provided by the rules and orders of the court.

The chief judge of the district court shall be responsible for the observance of such rules and orders, and shall divide the business and assign the cases so far as such rules and orders do not otherwise prescribe.

If the district judges in any district are unable to agree upon the adoption of rules or orders for that purpose the judicial council of the circuit shall make the necessary orders.

§ 144. Bias or prejudice of judge

Whenever a party to any proceeding in a district court makes and files a timely and sufficient affidavit that the judge before whom the matter is pending has a personal bias or prejudice either against him or in favor of any adverse party, such judge shall proceed no further therein, but another judge shall be assigned to hear such proceeding.

The affidavit shall state the facts and the reasons for the belief that bias or prejudice exists, and shall be filed not less than ten days before the beginning of the term at which the proceeding is to be heard, or good cause shall be shown for failure to file it within such time. A party may file only one such affidavit in any case. It shall be accompanied by a certificate of counsel of record stating that it is made in good faith. As amended May 24, 1949, c. 139, § 65, 63 Stat. 99.

§ 331. Judicial Conference of the United States

The Chief Justice of the United States shall summon annually the chief judge of each judicial circuit, the chief judge of the Court of International Trade, and a district judge from each judicial circuit to a conference at such time and place in the United States as he may designate. He shall preside at such conference which shall be known as the Judicial Conference of the United States. Special sessions of the Conference may be called by the Chief Justice at such times and places as he may designate.

* * *

The Conference shall make a comprehensive survey of the condition of business in the courts of the United States and prepare plans for assignment of judges to or from circuits or districts where necessary. It shall also submit suggestions and recommendations to the various courts to promote uniformity of management procedures and the expeditious conduct of court business. The Conference is authorized to exercise the authority provided in chapter 16 of this title as the Conference, or through a standing committee. If the Conference elects to establish a standing committee, it shall be appointed by the Chief Justice and all petitions for review shall be reviewed by that committee. The Conference or the standing committee may hold hearings, take sworn testimony, issue subpoenas and subpoenas duces tecum, and make necessary and appropriate orders in the exercise of its authority. Subpoenas and subpoenas duces tecum shall be issued by the clerk of the Supreme Court or by the clerk of any court of appeals, at the direction of the Chief Justice or his designee and under the seal of the court, and shall be served in the manner provided in rule 45(c) of the Federal Rules of Civil Procedure for subpoenas and subpoenas duces tecum issued on behalf of the United States or an officer or any agency thereof. The Conference may also prescribe and modify rules for the exercise of the authority provided in chapter 16 of this title. All judicial officers and employees of the United States shall promptly carry into effect all orders of the Judicial Conference or the standing committee established pursuant to this section.

The Conference shall also carry on a continuous study of the operation and effect of the general rules of practice and procedure now or hereafter in use as prescribed by the Supreme Court for the other courts of the United States pursuant to law. Such changes in and additions to those rules as the Conference may deem desirable to promote simplicity in procedure, fairness in administration, the just determination of litigation, and the elimination of unjustifiable expense and delay shall be recommended by the Conference from time to time to the Supreme Court for its consideration and adoption, modification or rejection, in accordance with law.

The Judicial Conference shall review rules prescribed under section 2071 of this title by the courts, other than the Supreme Court and the district courts, for consistency with Federal law. The Judicial Conference may modify or abrogate any such rule so reviewed found inconsistent in the course of such a review.

* * *

The Chief Justice shall submit to Congress an annual report of the proceedings of the Judicial Conference and its recommendations for legislation. As amended July 9, 1956, c. 517, § 1(d), 70 Stat. 497; Aug. 28, 1957, Pub.L. 85–202, 71 Stat. 476; July 11, 1958, Pub.L. 85–513, 72 Stat. 356; Sept. 19, 1961, Pub.L. 87–253, §§ 1, 2, 75 Stat. 521; Oct. 15, 1980, Pub.L. 96–458, § 4, 94 Stat. 2040; Apr. 2, 1982, Pub.L. 97–164, Title I, § 111, 96 Stat. 29; Oct. 14, 1986, Pub.L. 99–466, § 1, 100 Stat. 1190; Nov. 19, 1988, Pub.L. 100–702, Title IV, § 402(b), 102 Stat. 4650; Oct. 19, 1996, Pub.L. 104–317, Title VI, § 601(a), 110 Stat. 3857; Nov. 2, 2002, Pub.L. 107–273, Div. C, Title I, § 11043(b), 116 Stat. 1855.

§ 332. Judicial councils of circuits

(a)(1) The chief judge of each judicial circuit shall call, at least twice in each year and at such places as he or she may designate, a meeting of the judicial council of the circuit, consisting of the chief judge of the circuit, who shall preside, and an equal number of circuit judges and district judges of the circuit, as such number is determined by majority vote of all such judges of the circuit in regular active service.

(2) Members of the council shall serve for terms established by a majority vote of all judges of the circuit in regular active service.

* * *

(d)(1) Each judicial council shall make all necessary and appropriate orders for the effective and expeditious administration of justice within its circuit. Any general order relating to practice and procedure shall be made or amended only after giving appropriate public notice and an opportunity for comment. Any such order so relating shall take effect upon the date specified by such judicial council. Copies of such orders so relating shall be furnished to the Judicial Conference and the Administrative Office of the United States Courts and be made available to the public. Each council is authorized to hold hearings, to take sworn testimony, and to issue subpoenas and subpoenas duces tecum. Subpoenas and subpoenas duces tecum shall be issued by the clerk of the court of appeals, at the direction of the chief judge of the circuit or his designee and under the seal of the court, and shall be served in the manner provided in rule 45(c) of the Federal

Rules of Civil Procedure for subpoenas and subpoenas duces tecum issued on behalf of the United States or an officer or agency thereof.

(2) All judicial officers and employees of the circuit shall promptly carry into effect all orders of the judicial council. In the case of failure to comply with an order made under this subsection or a subpoena issued under chapter 16 of this title, a judicial council or a special committee appointed under section 353 of this title may institute a contempt proceeding in any district court in which the judicial officer or employee of the circuit who fails to comply with the order made under this subsection shall be ordered to show cause before the court why he or she should not be held in contempt of court.

(3) Unless an impediment to the administration of justice is involved, regular business of the courts need not be referred to the council.

(4) Each judicial council shall periodically review the rules which are prescribed under section 2071 of this title by district courts within its circuit for consistency with rules prescribed under section 2072 of this title. Each council may modify or abrogate any such rule found inconsistent in the course of such a review.

* * *

As amended Nov. 13, 1963, Pub.L. 88–176, § 3, 77 Stat. 331; Jan. 5, 1971, Pub.L. 91–647, 84 Stat. 1907; Oct. 15, 1980, Pub.L. 96–458, § 2(a)–(d)(1), 94 Stat. 2035; Oct. 1, 1988, Pub.L. 100–459, Title IV, § 407, 102 Stat. 2213; Nov. 19, 1988, Pub.L. 100–702, Title IV, § 403(a)(2), (b), Title X, §§ 1018, 1020(a)(1), 102 Stat. 4651, 4670, 4671; Dec. 1, 1990, Pub.L. 101–650, Title III, §§ 323, 325(b)(1), Title IV, § 403, 104 Stat. 5120, 5121, 5124; Dec. 9, 1991, Pub.L. 102–198, § 1, 105 Stat. 1623; Oct. 19, 1996, Pub.L. 104–317, Title II, § 208, 110 Stat. 3851; Nov. 13, 2000, Pub.L. 106–518, Title II, § 205, Title III, § 306, 114 Stat. 2414, 2418; Dec. 21, 2000, Pub.L. 106–553, § 1(a)(2)[306], 114 Stat. 2762A–202; Nov. 2, 2002, Pub.L. 107–273, Div. C, Title I, § 11043(c), 116 Stat. 1855.

§ 333. Judicial conferences of circuits

The chief judge of each circuit may summon biennially, and may summon annually, the circuit, district, and bankruptcy judges of the circuit, in active service, to a conference at a time and place that he designates, for the purpose of considering the business of the courts and advising means of improving the administration of justice within such circuit. He may preside at such conference, which shall be known as the Judicial Conference of the circuit. The judges of the District Court of Guam, the District Court of the Virgin Islands, and the District Court of the Northern Mariana Islands may also be summoned biennially, and may be summoned annually, to the conferences of their respective circuits.

Every judge summoned may attend.

The court of appeals for each circuit shall provide by its rules for representation and active participation at such conference by members of the bar of such circuit. As amended Dec. 29, 1950, c. 1185, 64 Stat. 1128;

Oct. 31, 1951, c. 655, § 38, 65 Stat. 723; July 7, 1958, Pub.L. 85–508, § 12(e), 72 Stat. 348; Nov. 6, 1978, Pub.L. 95–598, Title II, § 210, 92 Stat. 2661; Dec. 1, 1990, Pub.L. 101–650, Title III, § 320, 104 Stat. 5117; Apr. 26, 1996, Pub.L. 104–134, Title I, § 305, 110 Stat. 1321–36.

§ 455. Disqualification of justice, judge, or magistrate

(a) Any justice, judge, or magistrate of the United States shall disqualify himself in any proceeding in which his impartiality might reasonably be questioned.

(b) He shall also disqualify himself in the following circumstances:

(1) Where he has a personal bias or prejudice concerning a party, or personal knowledge of disputed evidentiary facts concerning the proceeding;

(2) Where in private practice he served as lawyer in the matter in controversy, or a lawyer with whom he previously practiced law served during such association as a lawyer concerning the matter, or the judge or such lawyer has been a material witness concerning it;

(3) Where he has served in governmental employment and in such capacity participated as counsel, adviser or material witness concerning the proceeding or expressed an opinion concerning the merits of the particular case in controversy;

(4) He knows that he, individually or as a fiduciary, or his spouse or minor child residing in his household, has a financial interest in the subject matter in controversy or in a party to the proceeding, or any other interest that could be substantially affected by the outcome of the proceeding;

(5) He or his spouse, or a person within the third degree of relationship to either of them, or the spouse of such a person:

(i) Is a party to the proceeding, or an officer, director, or trustee of a party;

(ii) Is acting as a lawyer in the proceeding;

(iii) Is known by the judge to have an interest that could be substantially affected by the outcome of the proceeding;

(iv) Is to the judge's knowledge likely to be a material witness in the proceeding.

(c) A judge should inform himself about his personal and fiduciary financial interests, and make a reasonable effort to inform himself about the personal financial interests of his spouse and minor children residing in his household.

(d) For the purposes of this section the following words or phrases shall have the meaning indicated:

(1) "proceeding" includes pretrial, trial, appellate review, or other stages of litigation;

(2) the degree of relationship is calculated according to the civil law system;

(3) "fiduciary" includes such relationships as executor, administrator, trustee, and guardian;

(4) "financial interest" means ownership of a legal or equitable interest, however small, or a relationship as director, adviser, or other active participant in the affairs of a party, except that:

(i) Ownership in a mutual or common investment fund that holds securities is not a "financial interest" in such securities unless the judge participates in the management of the fund;

(ii) An office in an educational, religious, charitable, fraternal, or civic organization is not a "financial interest" in securities held by the organization;

(iii) The proprietary interest of a policyholder in a mutual insurance company, of a depositor in a mutual savings association, or a similar proprietary interest, is a "financial interest" in the organization only if the outcome of the proceeding could substantially affect the value of the interest;

(iv) Ownership of government securities is a "financial interest" in the issuer only if the outcome of the proceeding could substantially affect the value of the securities.

(e) No justice, judge, or magistrate shall accept from the parties to the proceeding a waiver of any ground for disqualification enumerated in subsection (b). Where the ground for disqualification arises only under subsection (a), waiver may be accepted provided it is preceded by a full disclosure on the record of the basis for disqualification.

(f) Notwithstanding the preceding provisions of this section, if any justice, judge, magistrate, or bankruptcy judge to whom a matter has been assigned would be disqualified, after substantial judicial time has been devoted to the matter, because of the appearance or discovery, after the matter was assigned to him or her, that he or she individually or as a fiduciary, or his or her spouse or minor child residing in his or her household, has a financial interest in a party (other than an interest that could be substantially affected by the outcome), disqualification is not required if the justice, judge, magistrate, bankruptcy judge, spouse or minor child, as the case may be, divests himself or herself of the interest that provides the grounds for the disqualification. As amended Dec. 5, 1974, Pub.L. 93–512, § 1, 88 Stat. 1609; Nov. 6, 1978, Pub.L. 95–598, Title II, § 214(a), (b), 92 Stat. 2661; Nov. 19, 1988, Pub.L. 100–702, Title X, § 1007, 102 Stat. 4667.

§ 636. Jurisdiction, powers, and temporary assignment

(a) Each United States magistrate serving under this chapter shall have within the territorial jurisdiction prescribed by his appointment—

(1) all powers and duties conferred or imposed upon United States commissioners by law or by the Rules of Criminal Procedure for the United States District Courts;

(2) the power to administer oaths and affirmations, issue orders pursuant to section 3142 of title 18 concerning release or detention of persons pending trial, and take acknowledgments, affidavits, and depositions;

(3) the power to conduct trials under section 3401, title 18, United States Code, in conformity with and subject to the limitations of that section;

(4) the power to enter a sentence for a petty offense; and

(5) the power to enter a sentence for a class A misdemeanor in a case in which the parties have consented.

(b)(1) Notwithstanding any provision of law to the contrary—

(A) a judge may designate a magistrate to hear and determine any pretrial matter pending before the court, except a motion for injunctive relief, for judgment on the pleadings, for summary judgment, to dismiss or quash an indictment or information made by the defendant, to suppress evidence in a criminal case, to dismiss or to permit maintenance of a class action, to dismiss for failure to state a claim upon which relief can be granted, and to involuntarily dismiss an action. A judge of the court may reconsider any pretrial matter under this subparagraph (A) where it has been shown that the magistrate's order is clearly erroneous or contrary to law.

(B) a judge may also designate a magistrate to conduct hearings, including evidentiary hearings, and to submit to a judge of the court proposed findings of fact and recommendations for the disposition, by a judge of the court, of any motion excepted in subparagraph (A), of applications for posttrial relief made by individuals convicted of criminal offenses and of prisoner petitions challenging conditions of confinement.

(C) the magistrate shall file his proposed findings and recommendations under subparagraph (B) with the court and a copy shall forthwith be mailed to all parties.

Within ten days after being served with a copy, any party may serve and file written objections to such proposed findings and recommendations as provided by rules of court. A judge of the court shall make a de novo determination of those portions of the report or specified proposed findings or recommendations to which objection is made. A judge of the court may accept, reject, or modify, in whole or in part, the findings or recommendations made by the magistrate. The judge may also receive further evidence or recommit the matter to the magistrate with instructions.

(2) A judge may designate a magistrate to serve as a special master pursuant to the applicable provisions of this title and the Federal Rules of Civil Procedure for the United States district courts. A judge may designate a magistrate to serve as a special master in any civil case, upon

consent of the parties, without regard to the provisions of rule 53(b) of the Federal Rules of Civil Procedure for the United States district courts.

(3) A magistrate may be assigned such additional duties as are not inconsistent with the Constitution and laws of the United States.

(4) Each district court shall establish rules pursuant to which the magistrates shall discharge their duties.

(c) Notwithstanding any provision of law to the contrary—

(1) Upon the consent of the parties, a full-time United States magistrate or a part-time United States magistrate who serves as a full-time judicial officer may conduct any or all proceedings in a jury or nonjury civil matter and order the entry of judgment in the case, when specially designated to exercise such jurisdiction by the district court or courts he serves. Upon the consent of the parties, pursuant to their specific written request, any other part-time magistrate may exercise such jurisdiction, if such magistrate meets the bar membership requirements set forth in section 631(b)(1) and the chief judge of the district court certifies that a full-time magistrate is not reasonably available in accordance with guidelines established by the judicial council of the circuit. When there is more than one judge of a district court, designation under this paragraph shall be by the concurrence of a majority of all the judges of such district court, and when there is no such concurrence, then by the chief judge.

(2) If a magistrate is designated to exercise civil jurisdiction under paragraph (1) of this subsection, the clerk of court shall, at the time the action is filed, notify the parties of the availability of a magistrate to exercise such jurisdiction. The decision of the parties shall be communicated to the clerk of court. Thereafter, either the district court judge or the magistrate may again advise the parties of the availability of the magistrate, but in so doing, shall also advise the parties that they are free to withhold consent without adverse substantive consequences. Rules of court for the reference of civil matters to magistrates shall include procedures to protect the voluntariness of the parties' consent.

(3) Upon entry of judgment in any case referred under paragraph (1) of this subsection, an aggrieved party may appeal directly to the appropriate United States court of appeals from the judgment of the magistrate in the same manner as an appeal from any other judgment of a district court. The consent of the parties allows a magistrate designated to exercise civil jurisdiction under paragraph (1) of this subsection to direct the entry of a judgment of the district court in accordance with the Federal Rules of Civil Procedure. Nothing in this paragraph shall be construed as a limitation of any party's right to seek review by the Supreme Court of the United States.

(4) The court may, for good cause shown on its own motion, or under extraordinary circumstances shown by any party, vacate a reference of a civil matter to a magistrate under this subsection.

(5) The magistrate shall, subject to guidelines of the Judicial Conference, determine whether the record taken pursuant to this section shall be taken by electronic sound recording, by a court reporter, or by other means.

(d) The practice and procedure for the trial of cases before officers serving under this chapter shall conform to rules promulgated by the Supreme Court pursuant to section 2072 of this title.

(e) Contempt Authority.—

(1) In general.—A United States magistrate judge serving under this chapter shall have within the territorial jurisdiction prescribed by the appointment of such magistrate judge the power to exercise contempt authority as set forth in this subsection.

(2) Summary criminal contempt authority.—A magistrate judge shall have the power to punish summarily by fine or imprisonment, or both, such contempt of the authority of such magistrate judge constituting misbehavior of any person in the magistrate judge's presence so as to obstruct the administration of justice. The order of contempt shall be issued under the Federal Rules of Criminal Procedure.

(3) Additional criminal contempt authority in civil consent and misdemeanor cases.—In any case in which a United States magistrate judge presides with the consent of the parties under subsection (c) of this section, and in any misdemeanor case proceeding before a magistrate judge under section 3401 of title 18, the magistrate judge shall have the power to punish, by fine or imprisonment, or both, criminal contempt constituting disobedience or resistance to the magistrate judge's lawful writ, process, order, rule, decree, or command. Disposition of such contempt shall be conducted upon notice and hearing under the Federal Rules of Criminal Procedure.

(4) Civil contempt authority in civil consent and misdemeanor cases.—In any case in which a United States magistrate judge presides with the consent of the parties under subsection (c) of this section, and in any misdemeanor case proceeding before a magistrate judge under section 3401 of title 18, the magistrate judge may exercise the civil contempt authority of the district court. This paragraph shall not be construed to limit the authority of a magistrate judge to order sanctions under any other statute, the Federal Rules of Civil Procedure, or the Federal Rules of Criminal Procedure.

(5) Criminal contempt penalties.—The sentence imposed by a magistrate judge for any criminal contempt provided for in paragraphs (2) and (3) shall not exceed the penalties for a Class C misdemeanor as set forth in sections 3581(b)(8) and 3571(b)(6) of title 18.

(6) Certification of other contempts to the district court.—Upon the commission of any such act—

(A) in any case in which a United States magistrate judge presides with the consent of the parties under subsection (c) of this section, or in any misdemeanor case proceeding before a magistrate judge under section 3401 of title 18, that may, in the opinion of the magistrate judge, constitute a serious criminal contempt punishable by penalties exceeding those set forth in paragraph (5) of this subsection, or

(B) in any other case or proceeding under subsection (a) or (b) of this section, or any other statute, where—

(i) the act committed in the magistrate judge's presence may, in the opinion of the magistrate judge, constitute a serious criminal contempt punishable by penalties exceeding those set forth in paragraph (5) of this subsection,

(ii) the act that constitutes a criminal contempt occurs outside the presence of the magistrate judge, or

(iii) the act constitutes a civil contempt,

the magistrate judge shall forthwith certify the facts to a district judge and may serve or cause to be served, upon any person whose behavior is brought into question under this paragraph, an order requiring such person to appear before a district judge upon a day certain to show cause why that person should not be adjudged in contempt by reason of the facts so certified. The district judge shall thereupon hear the evidence as to the act or conduct complained of and, if it is such as to warrant punishment, punish such person in the same manner and to the same extent as for a contempt committed before a district judge.

(7) Appeals of magistrate judge contempt orders.—The appeal of an order of contempt under this subsection shall be made to the court of appeals in cases proceeding under subsection (c) of this section. The appeal of any other order of contempt issued under this section shall be made to the district court.

* * *

As amended Oct. 17, 1968, Pub.L. 90–578, Title I, § 101, 82 Stat. 1113; Mar. 1, 1972, Pub.L. 92–239, § 2, 86 Stat. 47; Oct. 21, 1976, Pub.L. 94–577, § 1, 90 Stat. 2729; Oct. 28, 1977, Pub.L. 95–144, § 2, 91 Stat. 1220; Oct. 10, 1979, Pub.L. 96–82, § 2, 93 Stat. 643; Oct. 12, 1984, Pub.L. 98–473, Title II, § 208, 98 Stat. 1986; Nov. 8, 1984, Pub.L. 98–620, Title IV, § 402(29)(B), 98 Stat. 3359; Nov. 14, 1986, Pub.L. 99–651, Title II, § 201(a)(2), 100 Stat. 3647; Nov. 15, 1988, Pub.L. 100–659, § 4(c), 102 Stat. 3918; Nov. 18, 1988, Pub.L. 100–690, Title VII, § 7322, 102 Stat. 4467; Nov. 19, 1988, Pub.L. 100–702, Title IV, § 404(b)(1), Title X, § 1014, 102 Stat. 4651, 4669; Dec. 1, 1990, Pub.L. 101–650, Title III, § 308(a), 104 Stat. 5112; Oct. 19, 1996, Pub.L. 104–317, Title II, §§ 201, 202(b), 207, 110 Stat. 3848, 3849, 3850; Nov. 13, 2000, Pub.L. 106–518, Title II, §§ 202, 203(b), 114 Stat. 2412, 2414; Nov. 2, 2002, Pub.L. 107–273, Div. B, Title III, § 3002(b), 116 Stat. 1805.

§ 651. Authorization of alternative dispute resolution

(a) Definition.—For purposes of this chapter, an alternative dispute resolution process includes any process or procedure, other than an adjudication by a presiding judge, in which a neutral third party participates to assist in the resolution of issues in controversy, through processes such as early neutral evaluation, mediation, minitrial, and arbitration as provided in sections 654 through 658.

(b) Authority.—Each United States district court shall authorize, by local rule adopted under section 2071(a), the use of alternative dispute resolution processes in all civil actions, including adversary proceedings in bankruptcy, in accordance with this chapter, except that the use of arbitration may be authorized only as provided in section 654. Each United States district court shall devise and implement its own alternative dispute resolution program, by local rule adopted under section 2071(a), to encourage and promote the use of alternative dispute resolution in its district.

(c) Existing alternative dispute resolution programs.—In those courts where an alternative dispute resolution program is in place on the date of the enactment of the Alternative Dispute Resolution Act of 1998, the court shall examine the effectiveness of that program and adopt such improvements to the program as are consistent with the provisions and purposes of this chapter [§§ 651–658].

(d) Administration of alternative dispute resolution programs.—Each United States district court shall designate an employee, or a judicial officer, who is knowledgeable in alternative dispute resolution practices and processes to implement, administer, oversee, and evaluate the court's alternative dispute resolution program. Such person may also be responsible for recruiting, screening, and training attorneys to serve as neutrals and arbitrators in the court's alternative dispute resolution program.

(e) Title 9 not affected.—This chapter shall not affect title 9, United States Code.

(f) Program support.—The Federal Judicial Center and the Administrative Office of the United States Courts are authorized to assist the district courts in the establishment and improvement of alternative dispute resolution programs by identifying particular practices employed in successful programs and providing additional assistance as needed and appropriate. Added Nov. 19, 1988, Pub.L. 100–702, Title IX, § 901(a), 102 Stat. 4659; as amended Oct. 30, 1998, Pub.L. 105–315, § 3, 112 Stat. 2993.

§ 652. Jurisdiction

(a) Consideration of alternative dispute resolution in appropriate cases.—Notwithstanding any provision of law to the contrary and except as provided in subsections (b) and (c), each district court shall, by local rule adopted under section 2071(a), require that litigants in all civil cases consider the use of an alternative dispute resolution process at an appropriate stage in the litigation. Each district court shall provide litigants in all civil cases with at least one alternative dispute resolution process, including, but not limited to, mediation, early neutral evaluation, minitrial, and arbitration as authorized in sections 654 through 658. Any district court that elects to require the use of alternative dispute resolution in certain cases may do so only with respect to mediation, early neutral evaluation, and, if the parties consent, arbitration.

(b) Actions exempted from consideration of alternative dispute resolution.—Each district court may exempt from the requirements of this section specific cases or categories of cases in which use of alternative dispute resolution would not be appropriate. In defining these exemptions, each district court shall consult with members of the bar, including the United States Attorney for that district.

(c) Authority of the Attorney General.—Nothing in this section shall alter or conflict with the authority of the Attorney General to conduct litigation on behalf of the United States, with the authority of any Federal agency authorized to conduct litigation in the United States courts, or with any delegation of litigation authority by the Attorney General.

(d) Confidentiality provisions.—Until such time as rules are adopted under chapter 131 of this title [§§ 2071–2077] providing for the confidentiality of alternative dispute resolution processes under this chapter, each district court shall, by local rule adopted under section 2071(a), provide for the confidentiality of the alternative dispute resolution processes and to prohibit disclosure of confidential dispute resolution communications. Added Nov. 19, 1988, Pub.L. 100–702, Title IX, § 901(a), 102 Stat. 4659; as amended Oct. 30, 1998, Pub.L. 105–315, § 4, 112 Stat. 2994.

§ 653. Neutrals

(a) Panel of neutrals.—Each district court that authorizes the use of alternative dispute resolution processes shall adopt appropriate processes for making neutrals available for use by the parties for each category of process offered. Each district court shall promulgate its own procedures and criteria for the selection of neutrals on its panels.

(b) Qualifications and training.—Each person serving as a neutral in an alternative dispute resolution process should be qualified and trained to serve as a neutral in the appropriate alternative dispute resolution process. For this purpose, the district court may use, among others, magistrate judges who have been trained to serve as neutrals in alternative dispute resolution processes, professional neutrals from the private sector, and persons who have been trained to serve as neutrals in alternative dispute resolution processes. Until such time as rules are adopted under chapter 131 of this title relating to the disqualification of neutrals, each district court shall issue rules under section 2071(a) relating to the disqualification of neutrals (including, where appropriate, disqualification under section 455 of this title, other applicable law, and professional responsibility standards). Added Nov. 19, 1988, Pub.L. 100–702, Title IX, § 901(a), 102 Stat. 4660; as amended Oct. 30, 1998, Pub.L. 105–315, § 5, 112 Stat. 2995.

§ 654. Arbitration

(a) Referral of actions to arbitration.—Notwithstanding any provision of law to the contrary and except as provided in subsections (a), (b), and (c) of section 652 and subsection (d) of this section, a district court may allow the referral to arbitration of any civil action (including any adversary proceeding in bankruptcy) pending before it when the parties consent, except that referral to arbitration may not be made where—

(1) the action is based on an alleged violation of a right secured by the Constitution of the United States;

(2) jurisdiction is based in whole or in part on section 1343 of this title; or

(3) the relief sought consists of money damages in an amount greater than $150,000.

(b) Safeguards in consent cases.—Until such time as rules are adopted under chapter 131 of this title relating to procedures described in this subsection, the district court shall, by local rule adopted under section 2071(a), establish procedures to ensure that any civil action in which arbitration by consent is allowed under subsection (a)—

(1) consent to arbitration is freely and knowingly obtained; and

(2) no party or attorney is prejudiced for refusing to participate in arbitration.

(c) Presumptions.—For purposes of subsection (a)(3), a district court may presume damages are not in excess of $150,000 unless counsel certifies that damages exceed such amount.

(d) Existing programs.—Nothing in this chapter is deemed to affect any program in which arbitration is conducted pursuant to section title IX of the Judicial Improvements and Access to Justice Act (Public Law 100–702), as amended by section 1 of Public Law 105–53. Added Nov. 19, 1988, Pub.L. 100–702, Title IX, § 901(a), 102 Stat. 4660; as amended Oct. 30, 1998, Pub.L. 105–315, § 6, 112 Stat. 2995.

§ 655. Arbitrators

(a) Powers of arbitrators.—An arbitrator to whom an action is referred under section 654 shall have the power, within the judicial district of the district court which referred the action to arbitration—

(1) to conduct arbitration hearings;

(2) to administer oaths and affirmations; and

(3) to make awards.

(b) Standards for certification.—Each district court that authorizes arbitration shall establish standards for the certification of arbitrators and shall certify arbitrators to perform services in accordance with such standards and this chapter. The standards shall include provisions requiring that any arbitrator—

(1) shall take the oath or affirmation described in section 453; and

(2) shall be subject to the disqualification rules under section 455.

(c) Immunity.—All individuals serving as arbitrators in an alternative dispute resolution program under this chapter are performing quasi-judicial functions and are entitled to the immunities and protections that the law accords to persons serving in such capacity. Added Nov. 19, 1988,

Pub.L. 100–702, Title IX, § 901(a), 102 Stat. 4661; as amended Oct. 30, 1998, Pub.L. 105–315, § 7, 112 Stat. 2996.

§ 656. Subpoenas

Rule 45 of the Federal Rules of Civil Procedure (relating to subpoenas) applies to subpoenas for the attendance of witnesses and the production of documentary evidence at an arbitration hearing under this chapter. Added Nov. 19, 1988, Pub.L. 100–702, Title IX, § 901(a), 102 Stat. 4662; as amended Oct. 30, 1998, Pub.L. 105–315, § 8, 112 Stat. 2996.

§ 657. Arbitration award and judgment

(a) Filing and effect of arbitration award.—An arbitration award made by an arbitrator under this chapter, along with proof of service of such award on the other party by the prevailing party or by the plaintiff, shall be filed promptly after the arbitration hearing is concluded with the clerk of the district court that referred the case to arbitration. Such award shall be entered as the judgment of the court after the time has expired for requesting a trial de novo. The judgment so entered shall be subject to the same provisions of law and shall have the same force and effect as a judgment of the court in a civil action, except that the judgment shall not be subject to review in any other court by appeal or otherwise.

(b) Sealing of arbitration award.—The district court shall provide, by local rule adopted under section 2071(a), that the contents of any arbitration award made under this chapter shall not be made known to any judge who might be assigned to the case until the district court has entered final judgment in the action or the action has otherwise terminated.

(c) Trial de novo of arbitration awards.—

(1) Time for filing demand.—Within 30 days after the filing of an arbitration award with a district court under subsection (a), any party may file a written demand for a trial de novo in the district court.

(2) Action restored to court docket.—Upon a demand for a trial de novo, the action shall be restored to the docket of the court and treated for all purposes as if it had not been referred to arbitration.

(3) Exclusion of evidence of arbitration.—The court shall not admit at the trial de novo any evidence that there has been an arbitration proceeding, the nature or amount of any award, or any other matter concerning the conduct of the arbitration proceeding, unless—

(A) the evidence would otherwise be admissible in the court under the Federal Rules of Evidence; or

(B) the parties have otherwise stipulated. Added Nov. 19, 1988, Pub.L. 100–702, Title IX, § 901(a), 102 Stat. 4662; as amended Oct. 30, 1998, Pub.L. 105–315, § 9, 112 Stat. 2997.

§ 658. Compensation of arbitrators and neutrals

(a) Compensation.—The district court shall, subject to regulations approved by the Judicial Conference of the United States, establish the amount of compensation, if any, that each arbitrator or neutral shall receive for services rendered in each case under this chapter.

(b) Transportation allowances.—Under regulations prescribed by the Director of the Administrative Office of the United States Courts, a district court may reimburse arbitrators and other neutrals for actual transportation expenses necessarily incurred in the performance of duties under this chapter. Added Nov. 19, 1988, Pub.L. 100–702, Title IX, § 901(a), 102 Stat. 4662; as amended Oct. 30, 1998, Pub.L. 105–315, § 10, 112 Stat. 2997.

§ 1251. Original jurisdiction

(a) The Supreme Court shall have original and exclusive jurisdiction of all controversies between two or more States.

(b) The Supreme Court shall have original but not exclusive jurisdiction of:

(1) All actions or proceedings to which ambassadors, other public ministers, consuls, or vice consuls of foreign states are parties;

(2) All controversies between the United States and a State;

(3) All actions or proceedings by a State against the citizens of another State or against aliens. As amended Sept. 30, 1978, Pub.L. 95–393, § 8(b), 92 Stat. 810.

§ 1253. Direct appeals from decisions of three-judge courts

Except as otherwise provided by law, any party may appeal to the Supreme Court from an order granting or denying, after notice and hearing, an interlocutory or permanent injunction in any civil action, suit or proceeding required by any Act of Congress to be heard and determined by a district court of three judges.

§ 1254. Courts of appeals; certiorari; certified questions

Cases in the courts of appeals may be reviewed by the Supreme Court by the following methods:

(1) By writ of certiorari granted upon the petition of any party to any civil or criminal case, before or after rendition of judgment or decree;

(2) By certification at any time by a court of appeals of any question of law in any civil or criminal case as to which instructions are desired, and upon such certification the Supreme Court may give binding instructions or require the entire record to be sent up for decision of the entire matter in controversy. As amended June 27, 1988, Pub.L. 100–352, § 2, 102 Stat. 662.

§ 1257. State courts; certiorari

(a) Final judgments or decrees rendered by the highest court of a State in which a decision could be had, may be reviewed by the Supreme Court by writ of certiorari where the validity of a treaty or statute of the United States is drawn in question or where the validity of a statute of any State is drawn in question on the ground of its being repugnant to the Constitution, treaties, or laws of the United States, or where any title, right, privilege, or immunity is specially set up or claimed under the Constitution or the treaties or statutes of, or any commission held or authority exercised under, the United States.

(b) For the purposes of this section, the term "highest court of a State" includes the District of Columbia Court of Appeals. As amended July 29, 1970, Pub.L. 91–358, 84 Stat. 590; June 27, 1988, Pub.L. 100–352, § 3, 102 Stat. 662.

§ 1258. Supreme Court of Puerto Rico; certiorari

Final judgments or decrees rendered by the Supreme Court of the Commonwealth of Puerto Rico may be reviewed by the Supreme Court by writ of certiorari where the validity of a treaty or statute of the United States is drawn in question or where the validity of a statute of the Commonwealth of Puerto Rico is drawn in question on the ground of its being repugnant to the Constitution, treaties, or laws of the United States, or where any title, right, privilege, or immunity is specially set up or claimed under the Constitution or the treaties or statutes of, or any commission held or authority exercised under, the United States. Added Aug. 30, 1961, Pub.L. 87–189, § 1, 75 Stat. 417; as amended June 27, 1988, Pub.L. 100–352, § 4, 102 Stat. 662.

§ 1291. Final decisions of district courts

The courts of appeals (other than the United States Court of Appeals for the Federal Circuit) shall have jurisdiction of appeals from all final decisions of the district courts of the United States, the United States District Court for the District of the Canal Zone, the District Court of Guam, and the District Court of the Virgin Islands, except where a direct review may be had in the Supreme Court. The jurisdiction of the United States Court of Appeals for the Federal Circuit shall be limited to the jurisdiction described in sections 1292 (c) and (d) and 1295 of this title. As amended Oct. 31, 1951, c. 655, § 48, 65 Stat. 726; July 7, 1958, Pub.L. 85–508, § 12(e), 72 Stat. 348; Apr. 2, 1982, Pub.L. 97–164, Title I, § 124, 96 Stat. 36.

§ 1292. Interlocutory decisions

(a) Except as provided in subsections (c) and (d) of this section, the courts of appeals shall have jurisdiction of appeals from:

(1) Interlocutory orders of the district courts of the United States, the United States District Court for the District of the Canal Zone, the District Court of Guam, and the District Court of the Virgin Islands, or of the judges thereof, granting, continuing, modifying, refusing or dissolving injunctions, or refusing to dissolve or modify injunctions, except where a direct review may be had in the Supreme Court;

(2) Interlocutory orders appointing receivers, or refusing orders to wind up receiverships or to take steps to accomplish the purposes thereof, such as directing sales or other disposals of property;

(3) Interlocutory decrees of such district courts or the judges thereof determining the rights and liabilities of the parties to admiralty cases in which appeals from final decrees are allowed.

(b) When a district judge, in making in a civil action an order not otherwise appealable under this section, shall be of the opinion that such order involves a controlling question of law as to which there is substantial ground for difference of opinion and that an immediate appeal from the order may materially advance the ultimate termination of the litigation, he shall so state in writing in such order. The Court of Appeals which would have jurisdiction of an appeal of such action may thereupon, in its discretion, permit an appeal to be taken from such order, if application is made to it within ten days after the entry of the order: *Provided, however,* That application for an appeal hereunder shall not stay proceedings in the district court unless the district judge or the Court of Appeals or a judge thereof shall so order.

(c) The United States Court of Appeals for the Federal Circuit shall have exclusive jurisdiction—

(1) of an appeal from an interlocutory order or decree described in subsection (a) or (b) of this section in any case over which the court would have jurisdiction of an appeal under section 1295 of this title; and

(2) of an appeal from a judgment in a civil action for patent infringement which would otherwise be appealable to the United States Court of Appeals for the Federal Circuit and is final except for an accounting.

(d)(1) When the chief judge of the Court of International Trade issues an order under the provisions of section 256(b) of this title, or when any judge of the Court of International Trade, in issuing any other interlocutory order, includes in the order a statement that a controlling question of law is involved with respect to which there is a substantial ground for difference of opinion and that an immediate appeal from that order may materially advance the ultimate termination of the litigation, the United States Court of Appeals for the Federal Circuit may, in its discretion, permit an appeal to be taken from such order, if application is made to that Court within ten days after the entry of such order.

(2) When the chief judge of the United States Court of Federal Claims issues an order under section 798(b) of this title, or when any judge of the United States Court of Federal Claims, in issuing an interlocutory order, includes in the order a statement that a controlling question of law is involved with respect to which there is a substantial ground for difference of opinion and that an immediate appeal from that order may materially advance the ultimate termination of the litigation, the United States Court of Appeals for the Federal Circuit may, in its discretion, permit an appeal

to be taken from such order, if application is made to that Court within ten days after the entry of such order.

(3) Neither the application for nor the granting of an appeal under this subsection shall stay proceedings in the Court of International Trade or in the Court of Federal Claims, as the case may be, unless a stay is ordered by a judge of the Court of International Trade or of the Court of Federal Claims or by the United States Court of Appeals for the Federal Circuit or a judge of that court.

(4)(A) The United States Court of Appeals for the Federal Circuit shall have exclusive jurisdiction of an appeal from an interlocutory order of a district court of the United States, the District Court of Guam, the District Court of the Virgin Islands, or the District Court for the Northern Mariana Islands, granting or denying, in whole or in part, a motion to transfer an action to the United States Court of Federal Claims under section 1631 of this title.

(B) When a motion to transfer an action to the Court of Federal Claims is filed in a district court, no further proceedings shall be taken in the district court until 60 days after the court has ruled upon the motion. If an appeal is taken from the district court's grant or denial of the motion, proceedings shall be further stayed until the appeal has been decided by the Court of Appeals for the Federal Circuit. The stay of proceedings in the district court shall not bar the granting of preliminary or injunctive relief, where appropriate and where expedition is reasonably necessary. However, during the period in which proceedings are stayed as provided in this subparagraph, no transfer to the Court of Federal Claims pursuant to the motion shall be carried out.

(e) The Supreme Court may prescribe rules, in accordance with section 2072 of this title, to provide for an appeal of an interlocutory decision to the courts of appeals that is not otherwise provided for under subsection (a), (b), (c), or (d). As amended Oct. 31, 1951, c. 655, § 49, 65 Stat. 726; July 7, 1958, Pub.L. 85–508, § 12(e), 72 Stat. 348; Sept. 2, 1958, Pub.L. 85–919, 72 Stat. 1770; Apr. 2, 1982, Pub.L. 97–164, Title I, § 125, 96 Stat. 36; Nov. 8, 1984, Pub.L. 98–620, Title IV, § 412, 98 Stat. 3362; Nov. 19, 1988, Pub.L. 100–702, Title V, § 501, 102 Stat. 4652; Oct. 29, 1992, Pub.L. 102–572, Title I, § 101, Title IX, §§ 902(b), 906(c), 106 Stat. 4506, 4516, 4518.

§ 1295. Jurisdiction of the United States Court of Appeals for the Federal Circuit

(a) The United States Court of Appeals for the Federal Circuit shall have exclusive jurisdiction—

(1) of an appeal from a final decision of a district court of the United States, the United States District Court for the District of the Canal Zone, the District Court of Guam, the District Court of the Virgin Islands, or the District Court for the Northern Mariana Islands, if the jurisdiction of that court was based, in whole or in part, on section 1338 of this title, except that a case involving a claim arising

under any Act of Congress relating to copyrights, exclusive rights in mask works, or trademarks and no other claims under section 1338(a) shall be governed by sections 1291, 1292, and 1294 of this title;

(2) of an appeal from a final decision of a district court of the United States, the United States District Court for the District of the Canal Zone, the District Court of Guam, the District Court of the Virgin Islands, or the District Court for the Northern Mariana Islands, if the jurisdiction of that court was based, in whole or in part, on section 1346 of this title, except that jurisdiction of an appeal in a case brought in a district court under section 1346(a)(1), 1346(b), 1346(e), or 1346(f) of this title or under section 1346(a)(2) when the claim is founded upon an Act of Congress or a regulation of an executive department providing for internal revenue shall be governed by sections 1291, 1292, and 1294 of this title;

(3) of an appeal from a final decision of the United States Court of Federal Claims;

(4) of an appeal from a decision of—

(A) the Board of Patent Appeals and Interferences of the United States Patent and Trademark Office with respect to patent applications and interferences, at the instance of an applicant for a patent or any party to a patent interference, and any such appeal shall waive the right of such applicant or party to proceed under section 145 or 146 of title 35;

(B) the Under Secretary of Commerce for Intellectual Property and Director of the United States Patent and Trademark Office or the Trademark Trial and Appeal Board with respect to applications for registration of marks and other proceedings as provided in section 21 of the Trademark Act of 1946 (15 U.S.C. 1071); or

(C) a district court to which a case was directed pursuant to section 145, 146, or 154(b) of title 35;

(5) of an appeal from a final decision of the United States Court of International Trade;

(6) to review the final determinations of the United States International Trade Commission relating to unfair practices in import trade, made under section 337 of the Tariff Act of 1930 (19 U.S.C. 1337);

(7) to review, by appeal on questions of law only, findings of the Secretary of Commerce under U.S. note 6 to subchapter X of chapter 98 of the Harmonized Tariff Schedule of the United States (relating to importation of instruments or apparatus);

(8) of an appeal under section 71 of the Plant Variety Protection Act (7 U.S.C. 2461);

(9) of an appeal from a final order or final decision of the Merit Systems Protection Board, pursuant to sections 7703(b)(1) and 7703(d) of title 5;

(10) of an appeal from a final decision of an agency board of contract appeals pursuant to section 8(g)(1) of the Contract Disputes Act of 1978 (41 U.S.C. 607(g)(1));

(11) of an appeal under section 211 of the Economic Stabilization Act of 1970;

(12) of an appeal under section 5 of the Emergency Petroleum Allocation Act of 1973;

(13) of an appeal under section 506(c) of the Natural Gas Policy Act of 1978; and

(14) of an appeal under section 523 of the Energy Policy and Conservation Act.

(b) The head of any executive department or agency may, with the approval of the Attorney General, refer to the Court of Appeals for the Federal Circuit for judicial review any final decision rendered by a board of contract appeals pursuant to the terms of any contract with the United States awarded by that department or agency which the head of such department or agency has concluded is not entitled to finality pursuant to the review standards specified in section 10(b) of the Contract Disputes Act of 1978 (41 U.S.C. 609(b)). The head of each executive department or agency shall make any referral under this section within one hundred and twenty days after the receipt of a copy of the final appeal decision.

(c) The Court of Appeals for the Federal Circuit shall review the matter referred in accordance with the standards specified in section 10(b) of the Contract Disputes Act of 1978. The court shall proceed with judicial review on the administrative record made before the board of contract appeals on matters so referred as in other cases pending in such court, shall determine the issue of finality of the appeal decision, and shall, if appropriate, render judgment thereon, or remand the matter to any administrative or executive body or official with such direction as it may deem proper and just. Added Apr. 2, 1982, Pub.L. 97–164, Title I, § 127(a), 96 Stat. 37; as amended Nov. 8, 1984, Pub.L. 98–622, Title II, § 205(a), 98 Stat. 3388; Aug. 23, 1988, Pub.L. 100–418, Title I, § 1214(a)(3), 102 Stat. 1156; Nov. 19, 1988, Pub.L. 100–702, Title X, § 1020(a)(3), 102 Stat. 4671; Oct. 29, 1992, Pub.L. 102–572, Title I, § 102(c), Title IX, § 902(b)(1), 106 Stat. 4507, 4516; Nov. 29, 1999, Pub.L. 106–113, Div. B, § 1000(a)(9)[4402(b)(2), 4732(b)(14)], 113 Stat. 1501A–560, –584.

§ 1330. Actions against foreign states

(a) The district courts shall have original jurisdiction without regard to amount in controversy of any nonjury civil action against a foreign state as defined in section 1603(a) of this title as to any claim for relief in personam with respect to which the foreign state is not entitled to immunity either under sections 1605–1607 of this title or under any applicable international agreement.

(b) Personal jurisdiction over a foreign state shall exist as to every claim for relief over which the district courts have jurisdiction under subsection (a) where service has been made under section 1608 of this title.

(c) For purposes of subsection (b), an appearance by a foreign state does not confer personal jurisdiction with respect to any claim for relief not arising out of any transaction or occurrence enumerated in sections 1605–1607 of this title. Added Oct. 21, 1976, Pub.L. 94–583, § 2(a), 90 Stat. 2891.

§ 1331. Federal question

The district courts shall have original jurisdiction of all civil actions arising under the Constitution, laws, or treaties of the United States. As amended July 25, 1958, Pub.L. 85–554, § 1, 72 Stat. 415; Oct. 21, 1976, Pub.L. 94–574, § 2, 90 Stat. 2721; Dec. 1, 1980, Pub.L. 96–486, § 2(a), 94 Stat. 2369.

§ 1332. Diversity of citizenship; amount in controversy; costs

(a) The district courts shall have original jurisdiction of all civil actions where the matter in controversy exceeds the sum or value of $75,000, exclusive of interest and costs, and is between—

(1) citizens of different States;

(2) citizens of a State and citizens or subjects of a foreign state;

(3) citizens of different States and in which citizens or subjects of a foreign state are additional parties; and

(4) a foreign state, defined in section 1603(a) of this title, as plaintiff and citizens of a State or of different States.

For the purposes of this section, section 1335, and section 1441, an alien admitted to the United States for permanent residence shall be deemed a citizen of the State in which such alien is domiciled.

(b) Except when express provision therefor is otherwise made in a statute of the United States, where the plaintiff who files the case originally in the Federal courts is finally adjudged to be entitled to recover less than the sum or value of $75,000, computed without regard to any setoff or counterclaim to which the defendant may be adjudged to be entitled, and exclusive of interest and costs, the district court may deny costs to the plaintiff and, in addition, may impose costs on the plaintiff.

(c) For the purposes of this section and section 1441 of this title—

(1) a corporation shall be deemed to be a citizen of any State by which it has been incorporated and of the State where it has its principal place of business, except that in any direct action against the insurer of a policy or contract of liability insurance, whether incorporated or unincorporated, to which action the insured is not joined as a party-defendant, such insurer shall be deemed a citizen of the State of which the insured is a citizen, as well as of any State by which the insurer has been incorporated and of the State where it has its principal place of business; and

(2) the legal representative of the estate of a decedent shall be deemed to be a citizen only of the same State as the decedent, and the

legal representative of an infant or incompetent shall be deemed to be a citizen only of the same State as the infant or incompetent.

(d) The word "States", as used in this section, includes the Territories, the District of Columbia, and the Commonwealth of Puerto Rico. As amended July 26, 1956, c. 740, 70 Stat. 658; July 25, 1958, Pub.L. 85–554, § 2, 72 Stat. 415; Aug. 14, 1964, Pub.L. 88–439, § 1, 78 Stat. 445; Oct. 21, 1976, Pub.L. 94–583, § 3, 90 Stat. 2891; Nov. 19, 1988, Pub.L. 100–702, Title II, §§ 201–203, 102 Stat. 4646; Oct. 19, 1996, Pub.L. 104–317, Title II, § 205, 110 Stat. 3850.

§ 1333. Admiralty, maritime and prize cases

The district courts shall have original jurisdiction, exclusive of the courts of the States, of:

(1) Any civil case of admiralty or maritime jurisdiction, saving to suitors in all cases all other remedies to which they are otherwise entitled.

(2) Any prize brought into the United States and all proceedings for the condemnation of property taken as prize. As amended May 24, 1949, c. 139, § 79, 63 Stat. 101.

§ 1334. Bankruptcy cases and proceedings

(a) Except as provided in subsection (b) of this section, the district court shall have original and exclusive jurisdiction of all cases under title 11.

(b) Notwithstanding any Act of Congress that confers exclusive jurisdiction on a court or courts other than the district courts, the district courts shall have original but not exclusive jurisdiction of all civil proceedings arising under title 11, or arising in or related to cases under title 11.

(c)(1) Nothing in this section prevents a district court in the interest of justice, or in the interest of comity with State courts or respect for State law, from abstaining from hearing a particular proceeding arising under title 11 or arising in or related to a case under title 11.

(2) Upon timely motion of a party in a proceeding based upon a State law claim or State law cause of action, related to a case under title 11 but not arising under title 11 or arising in a case under title 11, with respect to which an action could not have been commenced in a court of the United States absent jurisdiction under this section, the district court shall abstain from hearing such proceeding if an action is commenced, and can be timely adjudicated, in a State forum of appropriate jurisdiction.

(d) Any decision to abstain or not to abstain made under this subsection (other than a decision not to abstain in a proceeding described in subsection (c)(2)) is not reviewable by appeal or otherwise by the court of appeals under section 158(d), 1291, or 1292 of this title or by the Supreme Court of the United States under section 1254 of this title. This subsection shall not be construed to limit the applicability of the stay provided for by section 362 of title 11, United States Code, as such section applies to an action affecting the property of the estate in bankruptcy.

(e) The district court in which a case under title 11 is commenced or is pending shall have exclusive jurisdiction of all of the property, wherever located, of the debtor as of the commencement of such case, and of property of the estate. As amended Nov. 6, 1978, Pub.L. 95–598, Title II, § 238(a), 92 Stat. 2667; July 10, 1984, Pub.L. 98–353, Title I, § 101(a), 98 Stat. 333; Oct. 27, 1986, Pub.L. 99–554, Title I, § 144(e), 100 Stat. 3096; Dec. 1, 1990, Pub.L. 101–650, Title III, § 309(b), 104 Stat. 5113; Oct. 22, 1994, Pub.L. 103–394, Title I, § 104(b), 108 Stat. 4109.

§ 1335. Interpleader

(a) The district courts shall have original jurisdiction of any civil action of interpleader or in the nature of interpleader filed by any person, firm, or corporation, association, or society having in his or its custody or possession money or property of the value of $500 or more, or having issued a note, bond, certificate, policy of insurance, or other instrument of value or amount of $500 or more, or providing for the delivery or payment or the loan of money or property of such amount or value, or being under any obligation written or unwritten to the amount of $500 or more, if

(1) Two or more adverse claimants, of diverse citizenship as defined in section 1332 of this title, are claiming or may claim to be entitled to such money or property, or to any one or more of the benefits arising by virtue of any note, bond, certificate, policy or other instrument, or arising by virtue of any such obligation; and if (2) the plaintiff has deposited such money or property or has paid the amount of or the loan or other value of such instrument or the amount due under such obligation into the registry of the court, there to abide the judgment of the court, or has given bond payable to the clerk of the court in such amount and with such surety as the court or judge may deem proper, conditioned upon the compliance by the plaintiff with the future order or judgment of the court with respect to the subject matter of the controversy.

(b) Such an action may be entertained although the titles or claims of the conflicting claimants do not have a common origin, or are not identical, but are adverse to and independent of one another.

§ 1337. Commerce and antitrust regulations; amount in controversy, costs

(a) The district courts shall have original jurisdiction of any civil action or proceeding arising under any Act of Congress regulating commerce or protecting trade and commerce against restraints and monopolies: *Provided, however,* That the district courts shall have original jurisdiction of an action brought under section 11706 or 14706 of title 49, only if the matter in controversy for each receipt or bill of lading exceeds $10,000, exclusive of interest and costs.

(b) Except when express provision therefor is otherwise made in a statute of the United States, where a plaintiff who files the case under section 11706 or 14706 of title 49, originally in the Federal courts is finally adjudged to be entitled to recover less than the sum or value of $10,000, computed without regard to any setoff or counterclaim to which the defendant may be adjudged to be entitled, and exclusive of any interest and costs, the district court may deny costs to the plaintiff and, in addition, may impose costs on the plaintiff.

(c) The district courts shall not have jurisdiction under this section of any matter within the exclusive jurisdiction of the Court of International Trade under chapter 95 of this title. As amended Oct. 20, 1978, Pub.L. 95–486, § 9(a), 92 Stat. 1633; Oct. 10, 1980, Pub.L. 96–417, Title V, § 505, 94 Stat. 1743; Jan. 12, 1983, Pub.L. 97–449, § 5(f), 96 Stat. 2442; Dec. 29, 1995, Pub.L. 104–88, Title III, § 305(a)(3), 109 Stat. 944.

§ 1338. Patents, plant variety protection, copyrights, mask works, designs, trademarks, and unfair competition

(a) The district courts shall have original jurisdiction of any civil action arising under any Act of Congress relating to patents, plant variety protection, copyrights and trademarks. Such jurisdiction shall be exclusive of the courts of the states in patent, plant variety protection and copyright cases.

(b) The district courts shall have original jurisdiction of any civil action asserting a claim of unfair competition when joined with a substantial and related claim under the copyright, patent, plant variety protection or trademark laws.

(c) Subsections (a) and (b) apply to exclusive rights in mask works under chapter 9 of title 17, and to exclusive rights in designs under chapter 13 of title 17, to the same extent as such subsections apply to copyrights. As amended Dec. 24, 1970, Pub.L. 91–577, Title III, § 143(b), 84 Stat. 1559; Nov. 19, 1988, Pub.L. 100–702, Title X, § 1020(a)(4), 102 Stat. 4671; Oct. 28, 1998, Pub.L. 105–304, Title V, § 503(b), 112 Stat. 2917; Nov. 29, 1999, Pub.L. 106–113, Div. B, § 1000(a)(9)[3009(1)], 113 Stat. 1501A–551.

§ 1339. Postal matters

The district courts shall have original jurisdiction of any civil action arising under any Act of Congress relating to the postal service.

§ 1340. Internal revenue; customs duties

The district courts shall have original jurisdiction of any civil action arising under any Act of Congress providing for internal revenue, or revenue from imports or tonnage except matters within the jurisdiction of the Court of International Trade. As amended Oct. 10, 1980, Pub.L. 96–417, Title V, § 501(21), 94 Stat. 1742.

§ 1341. Taxes by States

The district courts shall not enjoin, suspend or restrain the assessment, levy or collection of any tax under State law where a plain, speedy and efficient remedy may be had in the courts of such State.

§ 1342. Rate orders of State agencies

The district courts shall not enjoin, suspend or restrain the operation of, or compliance with, any order affecting rates chargeable by a public utility and made by a State administrative agency or a rate-making body of a State political subdivision, where:

(1) Jurisdiction is based solely on diversity of citizenship or repugnance of the order to the Federal Constitution; and,

(2) The order does not interfere with interstate commerce; and,

(3) The order has been made after reasonable notice and hearing; and,

(4) A plain, speedy and efficient remedy may be had in the courts of such State.

§ 1343. Civil rights and elective franchise

(a) The district courts shall have original jurisdiction of any civil action authorized by law to be commenced by any person:

(1) To recover damages for injury to his person or property, or because of the deprivation of any right or privilege of a citizen of the United States, by any act done in furtherance of any conspiracy mentioned in section 1985 of Title 42;

(2) To recover damages from any person who fails to prevent or to aid in preventing any wrongs mentioned in section 1985 of Title 42 which he had knowledge were about to occur and power to prevent;

(3) To redress the deprivation, under color of any State law, statute, ordinance, regulation, custom or usage, of any right, privilege or immunity secured by the Constitution of the United States or by any Act of Congress providing for equal rights of citizens or of all persons within the jurisdiction of the United States;

(4) To recover damages or to secure equitable or other relief under any Act of Congress providing for the protection of civil rights, including the right to vote.

(b) For purposes of this section—

(1) the District of Columbia shall be considered to be a State; and

(2) any Act of Congress applicable exclusively to the District of Columbia shall be considered to be a statute of the District of Columbia. As amended Sept. 3, 1954, c. 1263, § 42, 68 Stat. 1241; Sept. 9, 1957, Pub.L. 85–315, Part III, § 121, 71 Stat. 637; Dec. 29, 1979, Pub.L. 96–170, § 2, 93 Stat. 1284.

§ 1344. Election disputes

The district courts shall have original jurisdiction of any civil action to recover possession of any office, except that of elector of President or Vice President, United States Senator, Representative in or delegate to Congress, or member of a state legislature, authorized by law to be commenced, wherein it appears that the sole question touching the title to office arises out of denial of the right to vote, to any citizen offering to vote, on account of race, color or previous condition of servitude.

The jurisdiction under this section shall extend only so far as to determine the rights of the parties to office by reason of the denial of the right, guaranteed by the Constitution of the United States and secured by any law, to enforce the right of citizens of the United States to vote in all the States.

§ 1345. United States as plaintiff

Except as otherwise provided by Act of Congress, the district courts shall have original jurisdiction of all civil actions, suits or proceedings commenced by the United States, or by any agency or officer thereof expressly authorized to sue by Act of Congress.

§ 1346. United States as defendant

(a) The district courts shall have original jurisdiction, concurrent with the United States Court of Federal Claims, of:

(1) Any civil action against the United States for the recovery of any internal-revenue tax alleged to have been erroneously or illegally assessed or collected, or any penalty claimed to have been collected without authority or any sum alleged to have been excessive or in any manner wrongfully collected under the internal-revenue laws;

(2) Any other civil action or claim against the United States, not exceeding $10,000 in amount, founded either upon the Constitution, or any Act of Congress, or any regulation of an executive department, or upon any express or implied contract with the United States, or for liquidated or unliquidated damages in cases not sounding in tort, except that the district courts shall not have jurisdiction of any civil action or claim against the United States founded upon any express or implied contract with the United States or for liquidated or unliquidated damages in cases not sounding in tort which are subject to sections 8(g)(1) and 10(a)(1) of the Contract Disputes Act of 1978. For the purpose of this paragraph, an express or implied contract with the Army and Air Force Exchange Service, Navy Exchanges, Marine Corps Exchanges, Coast Guard Exchanges, or Exchange Councils of the National Aeronautics and Space Administration shall be considered an express or implied contract with the United States.

(b)(1) Subject to the provisions of chapter 171 of this title, the district courts, together with the United Stated District Court for the District of the Canal Zone and the District Court of the Virgin Islands, shall have exclusive jurisdiction of civil actions on claims against the United States, for money damages, accruing on and after January 1, 1945, for injury or loss of property, or personal injury or death caused by the negligent or wrongful act or omission of any employee of the government while acting within the scope of his office or employment, under circumstances where the United States, if a private person, would be liable to the claimant in accordance with the law of the place where the act or omission occurred.

(2) No person convicted of a felony who is incarcerated while awaiting sentencing or while serving a sentence may bring a civil action against the United States or an agency, officer, or employee of the Government, for mental or emotional injury suffered while in custody without a prior showing of physical injury.

(c) The jurisdiction conferred by this section includes jurisdiction of any set-off, counterclaim, or other claim or demand whatever on the part of the United States against any plaintiff commencing an action under this section.

(d) The district courts shall not have jurisdiction under this section of any civil action or claim for a pension.

(e) The district courts shall have original jurisdiction of any civil action against the United States provided in section 6226, 6228(a), 7426, or 7428 (in the case of the United States district court for the District of Columbia) or section 7429 of the Internal Revenue Code of 1954.

(f) The district courts shall have exclusive original jurisdiction of civil actions under section 2409a to quiet title to an estate or interest in real property in which an interest is claimed by the United States.

(g) Subject to the provisions of chapter 179, the district courts of the United States shall have exclusive jurisdiction over any civil action commenced under section 453(2) of title 3, by a covered employee under chapter 5 of such title. As amended Apr. 25, 1949, c. 92, § 2(a), 63 Stat. 62; May 24, 1949, c. 139, § 80(a, b), 63 Stat. 101; Oct. 31, 1951, c. 655, § 50(b), 65 Stat. 727; July 30, 1954, c. 648, § 1, 68 Stat. 589; July 7, 1958, Pub.L. 85–508, § 12(e), 72 Stat. 348; Aug. 30, 1964, Pub.L. 88–519, 78 Stat. 699; Nov. 2, 1966, Pub.L. 89–719, Title II, § 202(a), 80 Stat. 1148; July 23, 1970, Pub.L. 91–350, 84 Stat. 449; Oct. 25, 1972, Pub.L. 92–562, § 1, 86 Stat. 1176; Oct. 4, 1976, Pub.L. 94–455, Title XII, § 1204(c)(1), Title XIII, § 1306(b)(7), 90 Stat. 1697, 1719; Nov. 1, 1978, Pub.L. 95–563, § 14(a), 92 Stat. 2389; Apr. 2, 1982, Pub.L. 97–164, Title I, § 129, 96 Stat. 39; Sept. 3, 1982, Pub.L. 97–248, Title IV, § 402(c)(17), 96 Stat. 669; Oct. 29, 1992, Pub.L. 102–572, Title IX, § 902(b)(1), 106 Stat. 4516; Apr. 26, 1996, Pub.L. 104–134, Title I, § 806, 110 Stat. 1321–75; Oct. 26, 1996, Pub.L. 104–331, § 3(b)(1), 110 Stat. 4069.

§ 1350. Alien's action for tort

The district courts shall have original jurisdiction of any civil action by an alien for a tort only, committed in violation of the law of nations or a treaty of the United States.

§ 1351. Consuls, vice consuls, and members of a diplomatic mission as defendant

The district courts shall have original jurisdiction, exclusive of the courts of the States, of all civil actions and proceedings against—

(1) consuls or vice consuls of foreign states; or

(2) members of a mission or members of their families (as such terms are defined in section 2 of the Diplomatic Relations Act). As amended May 24, 1949, c. 139, § 80(c), 63 Stat. 101; Sept. 30, 1978, Pub.L. 95–393, § 8(a)(1), 92 Stat. 810.

§ 1359. Parties collusively joined or made

A district court shall not have jurisdiction of a civil action in which any party, by assignment or otherwise, has been improperly or collusively made or joined to invoke the jurisdiction of such court.

§ 1361. Action to compel an officer of the United States to perform his duty

The district courts shall have original jurisdiction of any action in the nature of mandamus to compel an officer or employee of the United States or any agency thereof to perform a duty owed to the plaintiff. Added Oct. 5, 1962, Pub.L. 87–748, § 1(a), 76 Stat. 744.

§ 1362. Indian tribes

The district courts shall have original jurisdiction of all civil actions, brought by any Indian tribe or band with a governing body duly recognized by the Secretary of the Interior, wherein the matter in controversy arises under the Constitution, laws, or treaties of the United States. Added Oct. 10, 1966, Pub.L. 89–635, § 1, 80 Stat. 880.

§ 1364. Direct actions against insurers of members of diplomatic missions and their families

(a) The district courts shall have original and exclusive jurisdiction, without regard to the amount in controversy, of any civil action commenced by any person against an insurer who by contract has insured an individual, who is, or was at the time of the tortious act or omission, a member of a mission (within the meaning of section 2(3) of the Diplomatic Relations Act (22 U.S.C. 254a(3))) or a member of the family of such a member of a mission, or an individual described in section 19 of the Convention on Privileges and Immunities of the United Nations of February 13, 1946, against liability for personal injury, death, or damage to property.

(b) Any direct action brought against an insurer under subsection (a) shall be tried without a jury, but shall not be subject to the defense that the insured is immune from suit, that the insured is an indispensable party, or in the absence of fraud or collusion, that the insured has violated a term of the contract, unless the contract was cancelled before the claim arose. Added Sept. 30, 1978, Pub.L. 95–393, § 7(a), 92 Stat. 809; as amended Aug. 24, 1982, Pub.L. 97–241, Title II, § 203(b)(4), 96 Stat. 291; Dec. 22, 1987, Pub.L. 100–204, Title I, § 138(a), 101 Stat. 1347.

§ 1366. Construction of references to laws of the United States or Acts of Congress

For the purposes of this chapter, references to laws of the United States or Acts of Congress do not include laws applicable exclusively to the

District of Columbia. Added July 29, 1970, Pub.L. 91–358, Title I, § 172(c)(1), 84 Stat. 590; as amended Nov. 2, 1978, Pub.L. 95–572, § 6(b)(1), 92 Stat. 2456; June 19, 1986, Pub.L. 99–336, § 6(a)(1)(C), 100 Stat. 639.

§ 1367. Supplemental jurisdiction

(a) Except as provided in subsections (b) and (c) or as expressly provided otherwise by Federal statute, in any civil action of which the district courts have original jurisdiction, the district courts shall have supplemental jurisdiction over all other claims that are so related to claims in the action within such original jurisdiction that they form part of the same case or controversy under Article III of the United States Constitution. Such supplemental jurisdiction shall include claims that involve the joinder or intervention of additional parties.

(b) In any civil action of which the district courts have original jurisdiction founded solely on section 1332 of this title, the district courts shall not have supplemental jurisdiction under subsection (a) over claims by plaintiffs against persons made parties under Rule 14, 19, 20, or 24 of the Federal Rules of Civil Procedure, or over claims by persons proposed to be joined as plaintiffs under Rule 19 of such rules, or seeking to intervene as plaintiffs under Rule 24 of such rules, when exercising supplemental jurisdiction over such claims would be inconsistent with the jurisdictional requirements of section 1332.

(c) The district courts may decline to exercise supplemental jurisdiction over a claim under subsection (a) if—

(1) the claim raises a novel or complex issue of State law,

(2) the claim substantially predominates over the claim or claims over which the district court has original jurisdiction,

(3) the district court has dismissed all claims over which it has original jurisdiction, or

(4) in exceptional circumstances, there are other compelling reasons for declining jurisdiction.

(d) The period of limitations for any claim asserted under subsection (a), and for any other claim in the same action that is voluntarily dismissed at the same time as or after the dismissal of the claim under subsection (a), shall be tolled while the claim is pending and for a period of 30 days after it is dismissed unless State law provides for a longer tolling period.

(e) As used in this section, the term "State" includes the District of Columbia, the Commonwealth of Puerto Rico, and any territory or possession of the United States. Added Dec. 1, 1990, Pub.L. 101–650, Title III, § 310(a), 104 Stat. 5113.

§ 1369. Multiparty, multiforum jurisdiction

(a) In General.—The district courts shall have original jurisdiction of any civil action involving minimal diversity between adverse parties that arises from a single accident, where at least 75 natural persons have died in the accident at a discrete location, if—

(1) a defendant resides in a State and a substantial part of the accident took place in another State or other location, regardless of whether that defendant is also a resident of the State where a substantial part of the accident took place;

(2) any two defendants reside in different States, regardless of whether such defendants are also residents of the same State or States; or

(3) substantial parts of the accident took place in different States.

(b) Limitation of Jurisdiction of District Courts.—The district court shall abstain from hearing any civil action described in subsection (a) in which—

(1) the substantial majority of all plaintiffs are citizens of a single State of which the primary defendants are also citizens; and

(2) the claims asserted will be governed primarily by the laws of that State.

(c) Special Rules and Definitions.—For purposes of this section—

(1) minimal diversity exists between adverse parties if any party is a citizen of a State and any adverse party is a citizen of another State, a citizen or subject of a foreign state, or a foreign state as defined in section 1603(a) of this title;

(2) a corporation is deemed to be a citizen of any State, and a citizen or subject of any foreign state, in which it is incorporated or has its principal place of business, and is deemed to be a resident of any State in which it is incorporated or licensed to do business or is doing business;

(3) the term "injury" means—

(A) physical harm to a natural person; and

(B) physical damage to or destruction of tangible property, but only if physical harm described in subparagraph (A) exists;

(4) the term "accident" means a sudden accident, or a natural event culminating in an accident, that results in death incurred at a discrete location by at least 75 natural persons; and

(5) the term "State" includes the District of Columbia, the Commonwealth of Puerto Rico, and any territory or possession of the United States.

(d) Intervening Parties.—In any action in a district court which is or could have been brought, in whole or in part, under this section, any person with a claim arising from the accident described in subsection (a) shall be permitted to intervene as a party plaintiff in the action, even if that person could not have brought an action in a district court as an original matter.

(e) Notification of Judicial Panel on Multidistrict Litigation.—A district court in which an action under this section is pending shall promptly notify the judicial panel on multidistrict litigation of the pendency of the action. Added Nov. 2, 2002, Pub.L. 107–273, Div. C, Title I, § 11020(b)(1), 116 Stat. 1826.

§ 1391. Venue generally

(a) A civil action wherein jurisdiction is founded only on diversity of citizenship may, except as otherwise provided by law, be brought only in (1) a judicial district where any defendant resides, if all defendants reside in the same State, (2) a judicial district in which a substantial part of the events or omissions giving rise to the claim occurred, or a substantial part of property that is the subject of the action is situated, or (3) a judicial district in which any defendant is subject to personal jurisdiction at the time the action is commenced, if there is no district in which the action may otherwise be brought.

(b) A civil action wherein jurisdiction is not founded solely on diversity of citizenship may, except as otherwise provided by law, be brought only in (1) a judicial district where any defendant resides, if all defendants reside in the same State, (2) a judicial district in which a substantial part of the events or omissions giving rise to the claim occurred, or a substantial part of property that is the subject of the action is situated, or (3) a judicial district in which any defendant may be found, if there is no district in which the action may otherwise be brought.

(c) For purposes of venue under this chapter, a defendant that is a corporation shall be deemed to reside in any judicial district in which it is subject to personal jurisdiction at the time the action is commenced. In a State which has more than one judicial district and in which a defendant that is a corporation is subject to personal jurisdiction at the time an action is commenced, such corporation shall be deemed to reside in any district in that State within which its contacts would be sufficient to subject it to personal jurisdiction if that district were a separate State, and, if there is no such district, the corporation shall be deemed to reside in the district within which it has the most significant contacts.

(d) An alien may be sued in any district.

(e) A civil action in which a defendant is an officer or employee of the United States or any agency thereof acting in his official capacity or under color of legal authority, or an agency of the United States, or the United States, may, except as otherwise provided by law, be brought in any judicial district in which (1) a defendant in the action resides, (2) a substantial part of the events or omissions giving rise to the claim occurred, or a substantial part of property that is the subject of the action is situated, or (3) the plaintiff resides if no real property is involved in the action. Additional persons may be joined as parties to any such action in accordance with the Federal Rules of Civil Procedure and with such other venue requirements as would be applicable if the United States or one of its officers, employees, or agencies were not a party.

The summons and complaint in such an action shall be served as provided by the Federal Rules of Civil Procedure except that the delivery of the summons and complaint to the officer or agency as required by the rules may be made by certified mail beyond the territorial limits of the district in which the action is brought.

(f) A civil action against a foreign state as defined in section 1603(a) of this title may be brought—

(1) in any judicial district in which a substantial part of the events or omissions giving rise to the claim occurred, or a substantial part of property that is the subject of the action is situated;

(2) in any judicial district in which the vessel or cargo of a foreign state is situated, if the claim is asserted under section 1605(b) of this title;

(3) in any judicial district in which the agency or instrumentality is licensed to do business or is doing business, if the action is brought against an agency or instrumentality of a foreign state as defined in section 1603(b) of this title; or

(4) in the United States District Court for the District of Columbia if the action is brought against a foreign state or political subdivision thereof.

(g) A civil action in which jurisdiction of the district court is based upon section 1369 of this title may be brought in any district in which any defendant resides or in which a substantial part of the accident giving rise to the action took place. As amended Oct. 5, 1962, Pub.L. 87–748, § 2, 76 Stat. 744; Dec. 23, 1963, Pub.L. 88–234, 77 Stat. 473; Nov. 2, 1966, Pub.L. 89–714, §§ 1, 2, 80 Stat. 1111; Oct. 21, 1976, Pub.L. 94–574, § 3, 90 Stat. 2721; Oct. 21, 1976, Pub.L. 94–583, § 5, 90 Stat. 2897; Nov. 19, 1988, Pub.L. 100–702, Title X, § 1013, 102 Stat. 4669; Dec. 1, 1990, Pub.L. 101–650, Title III, § 311, 104 Stat. 5114; Dec. 9, 1991, Pub.L. 102–198, § 3, 105 Stat. 1623; Oct. 29, 1992, Pub.L. 102–572, Title V, § 504, 106 Stat. 4513; Oct. 3, 1995, Pub.L. 104–34, § 1, 109 Stat. 293; Nov. 2, 2002, Pub.L. 107–273, Div. C, Title I, § 11020(b)(2), 116 Stat. 1827.

§ 1392. Defendants or property in different districts in same State

Any civil action, of a local nature, involving property located in different districts in the same State, may be brought in any of such districts. As amended Oct. 1, 1996, Pub.L. 104–220, § 1, 110 Stat. 3023.

§ 1396. Internal revenue taxes

Any civil action for the collection of internal revenue taxes may be brought in the district where the liability for such tax accrues, in the district of the taxpayer's residence, or in the district where the return was filed.

§ 1397. Interpleader

Any civil action of interpleader or in the nature of interpleader under section 1335 of this title may be brought in the judicial district in which one or more of the claimants reside.

§ 1400. Patents and copyrights, mask works, and designs

(a) Civil actions, suits, or proceedings arising under any Act of Congress relating to copyrights or exclusive rights in mask works or designs may be instituted in the district in which the defendant or his agent resides or may be found.

(b) Any civil action for patent infringement may be brought in the judicial district where the defendant resides, or where the defendant has committed acts of infringement and has a regular and established place of business. As amended Nov. 19, 1988, Pub.L. 100–702, Title X, § 1020(a)(5), 102 Stat. 4671; Oct. 28, 1998, Pub.L. 105–304, Title V, § 503(c), 112 Stat. 2917; Aug. 5, 1999, Pub.L. 106–44, § 2(a), 113 Stat. 223.

§ 1401. Stockholder's derivative action

Any civil action by a stockholder on behalf of his corporation may be prosecuted in any judicial district where the corporation might have sued the same defendants.

§ 1402. United States as defendant

(a) Any civil action in a district court against the United States under subsection (a) of section 1346 of this title may be prosecuted only:

(1) Except as provided in paragraph (2), in the judicial district where the plaintiff resides;

(2) In the case of a civil action by a corporation under paragraph (1) of subsection (a) of section 1346, in the judicial district in which is located the principal place of business or principal office or agency of the corporation; or if it has no principal place of business or principal office or agency in any judicial district (A) in the judicial district in which is located the office to which was made the return of the tax in respect of which the claim is made, or (B) if no return was made, in the judicial district in which lies the District of Columbia. Notwithstanding the foregoing provisions of this paragraph a district court, for the convenience of the parties and witnesses, in the interest of justice, may transfer any such action to any other district or division.

(b) Any civil action on a tort claim against the United States under subsection (b) of section 1346 of this title may be prosecuted only in the judicial district where the plaintiff resides or wherein the act or omission complained of occurred.

(c) Any civil action against the United States under subsection (e) of section 1346 of this title may be prosecuted only in the judicial district where the property is situated at the time of levy, or if no levy is made, in the judicial district in which the event occurred which gave rise to the cause of action.

(d) Any civil action under section 2409a to quiet title to an estate or interest in real property in which an interest is claimed by the United States shall be brought in the district court of the district where the property is located or, if located in different districts, in any of such districts. As amended Sept. 2, 1958, Pub.L. 85–920, 72 Stat. 1770; Nov. 2, 1966, Pub.L. 89–719, Title II, § 202(b), 80 Stat. 1149; Oct. 25, 1972, Pub.L. 92–562, § 2, 86 Stat. 1176; Apr. 2, 1982, Pub.L. 97–164, Title I, § 131, 96 Stat. 39.

§ 1404. Change of venue

(a) For the convenience of parties and witnesses, in the interest of justice, a district court may transfer any civil action to any other district or division where it might have been brought.

(b) Upon motion, consent or stipulation of all parties, any action, suit or proceeding of a civil nature or any motion of hearing thereof, may be transferred, in the discretion of the court, from the division in which pending to any other division in the same district. Transfer of proceedings in rem brought by or on behalf of the United States may be transferred under this section without the consent of the United States where all other parties request transfer.

(c) A district court may order any civil action to be tried at any place within the division in which it is pending.

(d) As used in this section, the term "district court" includes the District Court of Guam, the District Court for the Northern Mariana Islands, and the District Court of the Virgin Islands, and the term "district" includes the territorial jurisdiction of each such court. As amended Oct. 18, 1962, Pub.L. 87–845, § 9, 76A Stat. 699; Oct. 19, 1996, Pub.L. 104–317, Title VI, § 610(a), 110 Stat. 3860.

§ 1406. Cure or waiver of defects

(a) The district court of a district in which is filed a case laying venue in the wrong division or district shall dismiss, or if it be in the interest of justice, transfer such case to any district or division in which it could have been brought.

(b) Nothing in this chapter shall impair the jurisdiction of a district court of any matter involving a party who does not interpose timely and sufficient objection to the venue.

(c) As used in this section, the term "district court" includes the District Court of Guam, the District Court for the Northern Mariana Islands, and the District Court of the Virgin Islands, and the term "district" includes the territorial jurisdiction of each such court. As amended May 24, 1949, c. 139, § 81, 63 Stat. 101; Sept. 13, 1960, Pub.L. 86–770, § 1, 74 Stat. 912; Oct. 18, 1962, Pub.L. 87–845, § 10, 76A Stat. 699; Apr. 2, 1982, Pub.L. 97–164, Title I, § 132, 96 Stat. 39; Oct. 19, 1996, Pub.L. 104–317, Title VI, § 610(b), 110 Stat. 3860.

§ 1407. Multidistrict litigation

(a) When civil actions involving one or more common questions of fact are pending in different districts, such actions may be transferred to any district for coordinated or consolidated pretrial proceedings. Such transfers shall be made by the judicial panel on multidistrict litigation authorized by this section upon its determination that transfers for such proceedings will be for the convenience of parties and witnesses and will promote the just and efficient conduct of such actions. Each action so transferred shall be remanded by the panel at or before the conclusion of such pretrial proceedings to the district from which it was transferred unless it shall have been previously terminated: *Provided, however,* That the panel may separate any claim, cross-claim, counter-claim, or third-party claim and remand any of such claims before the remainder of the action is remanded.

(b) Such coordinated or consolidated pretrial proceedings shall be conducted by a judge or judges to whom such actions are assigned by the judicial panel on multidistrict litigation. For this purpose, upon request of the panel, a circuit judge or a district judge may be designated and assigned temporarily for service in the transferee district by the Chief Justice of the United States or the chief judge of the circuit, as may be required, in accordance with the provisions of chapter 13 of this title. With the consent of the transferee district court, such actions may be assigned by the panel to a judge or judges of such district. The judge or judges to whom such actions are assigned, the members of the judicial panel on multidistrict litigation, and other circuit and district judges designated when needed by the panel may exercise the powers of a district judge in any district for the purpose of conducting pretrial depositions in such coordinated or consolidated pretrial proceedings.

(c) Proceedings for the transfer of an action under this section may be initiated by—

(i) the judicial panel on multidistrict litigation upon its own initiative, or

(ii) motion filed with the panel by a party in any action in which transfer for coordinated or consolidated pretrial proceedings under this section may be appropriate. A copy of such motion shall be filed in the district court in which the moving party's action is pending.

The panel shall give notice to the parties in all actions in which transfers for coordinated or consolidated pretrial proceedings are contemplated, and such notice shall specify the time and place of any hearing to determine whether such transfer shall be made. Orders of the panel to set a hearing and other orders of the panel issued prior to the order either directing or denying transfer shall be filed in the office of the clerk of the district court in which a transfer hearing is to be or has been held. The panel's order of transfer shall be based upon a record of such hearing at which material evidence may be offered by any party to an action pending in any district that would be affected by the proceedings under this section, and shall be supported by findings of fact and conclusions of law based upon such record. Orders of transfer and such other orders as the panel may make thereafter shall be filed in the office of the clerk of the district court of the transferee district and shall be effective when thus filed. The clerk of the transferee district court shall forthwith transmit a certified copy of the panel's order to transfer to the clerk of the district court from which the action is being transferred. An order denying transfer shall be filed in each district wherein there is a case pending in which the motion for transfer has been made.

(d) The judicial panel on multidistrict litigation shall consist of seven circuit and district judges designated from time to time by the Chief Justice of the United States, no two of whom shall be from the same circuit. The concurrence of four members shall be necessary to any action by the panel.

(e) No proceedings for review of any order of the panel may be permitted except by extraordinary writ pursuant to the provisions of title 28, section 1651, United States Code. Petitions for an extraordinary writ to review an order of the panel to set a transfer hearing and other orders of the panel issued prior to the order either directing or denying transfer shall be filed only in the court of appeals having jurisdiction over the district in which a hearing is to be or has been held. Petitions for an extraordinary writ to review an order to transfer or orders subsequent to transfer shall be filed only in the court of appeals having jurisdiction over the transferee district. There shall be no appeal or review of an order of the panel denying a motion to transfer for consolidated or coordinated proceedings.

(f) The panel may prescribe rules for the conduct of its business not inconsistent with Acts of Congress and the Federal Rules of Civil Procedure.

(g) Nothing in this section shall apply to any action in which the United States is a complainant arising under the antitrust laws. "Antitrust laws" as used herein include those acts referred to in the Act of October 15, 1914, as amended (38 Stat. 730; 15 U.S.C. 12), and also include the Act of June 19, 1936 (49 Stat. 1526; 15 U.S.C. 13, 13a, and 13b) and the Act of September 26, 1914, as added March 21, 1938 (52 Stat. 116, 117; 15 U.S.C. 56); but shall not include section 4A of the Act of October 15, 1914, as added July 7, 1955 (69 Stat. 282; 15 U.S.C. 15a).

(h) Notwithstanding the provisions of section 1404 or subsection (f) of this section, the judicial panel on multidistrict litigation may consolidate and transfer with or without the consent of the parties, for both pretrial purposes and for trial, any action brought under section 4C of the Clayton Act. Added Apr. 29, 1968, Pub.L. 90–296, § 1, 82 Stat. 109; as amended Sept. 30, 1976, Pub.L. 94–435, Title III, § 303, 90 Stat. 1396.

§ 1408. Venue of cases under title 11

Except as provided in section 1410 of this title, a case under title 11 may be commenced in the district court for the district—

(1) in which the domicile, residence, principal place of business in the United States, or principal assets in the United States, of the person or entity that is the subject of such case have been located for the one hundred and eighty days immediately preceding such com-

mencement, or for a longer portion of such one-hundred-and-eighty-day period than the domicile, residence, or principal place of business, in the United States, or principal assets in the United States, of such person were located in any other district; or

(2) in which there is pending a case under title 11 concerning such person's affiliate, general partner, or partnership. Added July 10, 1984, Pub.L. 98–353, Title I, § 102(a), 98 Stat. 334.

§ 1409. Venue of proceedings arising under title 11 or arising in or related to cases under title 11

(a) Except as otherwise provided in subsections (b) and (d), a proceeding arising under title 11 or arising in or related to a case under title 11 may be commenced in the district court in which such case is pending.

(b) Except as provided in subsection (d) of this section, a trustee in a case under title 11 may commence a proceeding arising in or related to such case to recover a money judgement of or property worth less than $1,000 or a consumer debt of less than $5,000 only in the district court for the district in which the defendant resides.

(c) Except as provided in subsection (b) of this section, a trustee in a case under title 11 may commence a proceeding arising in or related to such case as statutory successor to the debtor or creditors under section 541 or 544(b) of title 11 in the district court for the district where the State or Federal court sits in which, under applicable nonbankruptcy venue provisions, the debtor or creditors, as the case may be, may have commenced an action on which such proceeding is based if the case under title 11 had not been commenced.

(d) A trustee may commence a proceeding arising under title 11 or arising in or related to a case under title 11 based on a claim arising after the commencement of such case from the operation of the business of the debtor only in the district court for the district where a State or Federal court sits in which, under applicable nonbankruptcy venue provisions, an action on such claim may have been brought.

(e) A proceeding arising under title 11 or arising in or related to a case under title 11, based on a claim arising after the commencement of such case from the operation of the business of the debtor, may be commenced against the representative of the estate in such case in the district court for the district where the State or Federal courts sits in which the party commencing such proceeding may, under applicable nonbankruptcy venue provisions, have brought an action on such claim, or in the district court in which such case is pending. Added July 10, 1984, Pub.L. 98–353, Title I, § 102(a), 98 Stat. 334.

§ 1410. Venue of cases ancillary to foreign proceedings

(a) A case under section 304 of title 11 to enjoin the commencement or continuation of an action or proceeding in a State or Federal court, or the enforcement of a judgment, may be commenced only in the district court for the district where the State or Federal court sits in which is pending the action or proceeding against which the injunction is sought.

(b) A case under section 304 of title 11 to enjoin the enforcement of a lien against a property, or to require the turnover of property of an estate, may be commenced only in the district court for the district in which such property is found.

(c) A case under section 304 of title 11, other than a case specified in subsection (a) or (b) of this section, may be commenced only in the district court for the district in which is located the principal place of business in the United States, or the principal assets in the United States, of the estate that is the subject of such case. Added July 10, 1984, Pub.L. 98–353, Title I, § 102(a), 98 Stat. 335.

§ 1411. Jury trials

(a) Except as provided in subsection (b) of this section, this chapter and title 11 do not affect any right to trial by jury that an individual has under applicable nonbankruptcy law with regard to a personal injury or wrongful death tort claim.

(b) The district court may order the issues arising under section 303 of title 11 to be tried without a jury. Added July 10, 1984, Pub.L. 98–353, Title I, § 102(a), 98 Stat. 335.

§ 1412. Change of venue

A district court may transfer a case or proceeding under title 11 to a district court for another district, in the interest of justice or for the convenience of the parties. Added July 10, 1984, Pub.L. 98–353, Title I, § 102(a), 98 Stat. 335.

§ 1441. Actions removable generally

(a) Except as otherwise expressly provided by Act of Congress, any civil action brought in a State court of which the district courts of the United States have original jurisdiction, may be removed by the defendant or the defendants, to the district court of the United States for the district and division embracing the place where such action is pending. For purposes of removal under this chapter, the citizenship of defendants sued under fictitious names shall be disregarded.

(b) Any civil action of which the district courts have original jurisdiction founded on a claim or right arising under the Constitution, treaties or laws of the United States shall be removable without regard to the citizenship or residence of the parties. Any other such action shall be removable only if none of the parties in interest properly joined and served as defendants is a citizen of the State in which such action is brought.

(c) Whenever a separate and independent claim or cause of action within the jurisdiction conferred by section 1331 of this title is joined with one or more otherwise non-removable claims or causes of action, the entire case may be removed and the district court may determine all issues therein, or, in its discretion, may remand all matters in which State law predominates.

(d) Any civil action brought in a State court against a foreign state as defined in section 1603(a) of this title may be removed by the foreign state to the district court of the United States for the district and division embracing the place where such action is pending. Upon removal the action shall be tried by the court without jury. Where removal is based upon this subsection, the time limitations of section 1446(b) of this chapter may be enlarged at any time for cause shown.

(e)(1) Notwithstanding the provisions of subsection (b) of this section, a defendant in a civil action in a State court may remove the action to the district court of the United States for the district and division embracing the place where the action is pending if—

(A) the action could have been brought in a United States district court under section 1369 of this title; or

(B) the defendant is a party to an action which is or could have been brought, in whole or in part, under section 1369 in a United States district court and arises from the same accident as the action in State court, even if the action to be removed could not have been brought in a district court as an original matter.

The removal of an action under this subsection shall be made in accordance with section 1446 of this title, except that a notice of removal may also be filed before trial of the action in State court within 30 days after the date on which the defendant first becomes a party to an action under section 1369 in a United States district court that arises from the same accident as the action in State court, or at a later time with leave of the district court.

(2) Whenever an action is removed under this subsection and the district court to which it is removed or transferred under section 1407(j) has made a liability determination requiring further proceedings as to damages, the district court shall remand the action to the State court from which it had been removed for the determination of damages, unless the court finds that, for the convenience of parties and witnesses and in the interest of justice, the action should be retained for the determination of damages.

(3) Any remand under paragraph (2) shall not be effective until 60 days after the district court has issued an order determining liability and has certified its intention to remand the removed action for the determination of damages. An appeal with respect to the liability determination of the district court may be taken during that 60–day period to the court of appeals with appellate jurisdiction over the district court. In the event a party files such an appeal, the remand shall not be effective until the appeal has been finally disposed of. Once the remand has become effective, the liability determination shall not be subject to further review by appeal or otherwise.

(4) Any decision under this subsection concerning remand for the determination of damages shall not be reviewable by appeal or otherwise.

(5) An action removed under this subsection shall be deemed to be an action under section 1369 and an action in which jurisdiction is based on section 1369 of this title for purposes of this section and sections 1407, 1697, and 1785 of this title.

(6) Nothing in this subsection shall restrict the authority of the district court to transfer or dismiss an action on the ground of inconvenient forum.

(f) The court to which a civil action is removed under this section is not precluded from hearing and determining any claim in such civil action because the State court from which such civil action is removed did not have jurisdiction over that claim. As amended Oct. 21, 1976, Pub.L. 94–583, § 6, 90 Stat. 2898; June 19, 1986, Pub.L. 99–336, § 3, 100 Stat. 637; Nov. 19, 1988, Pub.L. 100–702, Title X, § 1016(a), 102 Stat. 4669; Dec. 1, 1990, Pub.L. 101–650, Title III, § 312, 104 Stat. 5114; Dec. 9, 1991, Pub.L. 102–198, § 4, 105 Stat. 1623; Nov. 2, 2002, Pub.L. 107–273, Div. C, Title I, § 11020(b)(3), 116 Stat. 1827.

§ 1442. Federal officers or agencies sued or prosecuted

(a) A civil action or criminal prosecution commenced in a State court against any of the following may be removed by them to the district court of the United States for the district and division embracing the place wherein it is pending:

(1) The United States or any agency thereof or any officer (or any person acting under that officer) of the United States or of any agency thereof, sued in an official or individual capacity for any act under color of such office or on account of any right, title or authority claimed under any Act of Congress for the apprehension or punishment of criminals or the collection of the revenue.

(2) A property holder whose title is derived from any such officer, where such action or prosecution affects the validity of any law of the United States.

(3) Any officer of the courts of the United States, for any Act under color of office or in the performance of his duties;

(4) Any officer of either House of Congress, for any act in the discharge of his official duty under an order of such House.

(b) A personal action commenced in any State court by an alien against any citizen of a State who is, or at the time the alleged action accrued was, a civil officer of the United States and is a nonresident of such State, wherein jurisdiction is obtained by the State court by personal service of process, may be removed by the defendant to the district court of the United States for the district and division in which the defendant was served with process. As amended Oct. 19, 1996, Pub.L. 104–317, Title II, § 206, 110 Stat. 3850.

§ 1442a. Members of armed forces sued or prosecuted

A civil or criminal prosecution in a court of a State of the United States against a member of the armed forces of the United States on account of an act done under color of his office or status, or in respect to which he claims any right, title, or authority under a law of the United States respecting the armed forces thereof, or under the law of war, may at any time before the trial or final hearing thereof be removed for trial into the district court of the United States for the district where it is pending in the manner prescribed by law, and it shall thereupon be entered on the docket of the district court, which shall proceed as if the cause had been originally commenced therein and shall have full power to hear and determine the cause. Added Aug. 10, 1956, c. 1041, § 19(a), 70A Stat. 626.

§ 1443. Civil rights cases

Any of the following civil actions or criminal prosecutions, commenced in a State court may be removed by the defendant to the district court of the United States for the district and division embracing the place wherein it is pending:

(1) Against any person who is denied or cannot enforce in the courts of such State a right under any law providing for the equal civil rights of citizens of the United States, or of all persons within the jurisdiction thereof;

(2) For any act under color of authority derived from any law providing for equal rights, or for refusing to do any act on the ground that it would be inconsistent with such law.

§ 1445. Nonremovable actions

(a) A civil action in any State court against a railroad or its receivers or trustees, arising under sections 1–4 and 5–10 of the Act of April 22, 1908 (45 U.S.C. 51–54, 55–60), may not be removed to any district court of the United States.

(b) A civil action in any State court against a carrier or its receivers or trustees to recover damages for delay, loss, or injury of shipments, arising under section 11706 or 14706 of Title 49, may not be removed to any district court of the United States unless the matter in controversy exceeds $10,000, exclusive of interest and costs.

(c) A civil action in any State court arising under the workmen's compensation laws of such State may not be removed to any district court of the United States.

(d) A civil action in any State court arising under section 40302 of the Violence Against Women Act of 1994 may not be removed to any district court of the United States. As amended July 25, 1958, Pub.L. 85–554, § 5, 72 Stat. 415; Oct. 17, 1978, Pub.L. 95–473, § 2(a)(3)(A), 92 Stat. 1465; Oct. 20, 1978, Pub.L. 95–486, § 9(b), 92 Stat. 1634; Sept. 13, 1994, Pub.L. 103–322, Title IV, § 40302(e)(5), 108 Stat. 1942; Dec. 29, 1995, Pub.L. 104–88, Title III, § 305(b), 109 Stat. 944; Oct. 11, 1996, Pub.L. 104–287, § 3, 110 Stat. 3388.

§ 1446. Procedure for removal

(a) A defendant or defendants desiring to remove any civil action or criminal prosecution from a State court shall file in the district court of the United States for the district and division within which such action is pending a notice of removal signed pursuant to Rule 11 of the Federal Rules of Civil Procedure and containing a short and plain statement of the grounds for removal, together with a copy of all process, pleadings, and orders served upon such defendant or defendants in such action.

(b) The notice of removal of a civil action or proceeding shall be filed within thirty days after the receipt by the defendant, through service or otherwise, of a copy of the initial pleading setting forth the claim for relief upon which such action or proceeding is based, or within thirty days after the service of summons upon the defendant if such initial pleading has then been filed in court and is not required to be served on the defendant, whichever period is shorter.

If the case stated by the initial pleading is not removable, a notice of removal may be filed within thirty days after receipt by the defendant, through service or otherwise, of a copy of an amended pleading, motion, order or other paper from which it may first be ascertained that the case is one which is or has become removable, except that a case may not be removed on the basis of jurisdiction conferred by section 1332 of this title more than 1 year after commencement of the action.

(c)(1) A notice of removal of a criminal prosecution shall be filed not later than thirty days after the arraignment in the State court, or at any time before trial, whichever is earlier, except that for good cause shown the United States district court may enter an order granting the defendant or defendants leave to file the notice at a later time.

(2) A notice of removal of a criminal prosecution shall include all grounds for such removal. A failure to state grounds which exist at the time of the filing of the notice shall constitute a waiver of such grounds, and a second notice may be filed only on grounds not existing at the time of the original notice. For good cause shown, the United States district court may grant relief from the limitations of this paragraph.

(3) The filing of a notice of removal of a criminal prosecution shall not prevent the State court in which such prosecution is pending from proceeding further, except that a judgment of conviction shall not be entered unless the prosecution is first remanded.

(4) The United States district court in which such notice is filed shall examine the notice promptly. If it clearly appears on the face of the notice and any exhibits annexed thereto that removal should not be permitted, the court shall make an order for summary remand.

(5) If the United States district court does not order the summary remand of such prosecution, it shall order an evidentiary hearing to be held promptly and after such hearing shall make such disposition of the prosecution as justice shall require. If the United States district court determines that removal shall be permitted, it shall so notify the State court in which prosecution is pending, which shall proceed no further.

(d) Promptly after the filing of such notice of removal of a civil action the defendant or defendants shall give written notice thereof to all adverse parties and shall file a copy of the notice with the clerk of such State court, which shall effect removal and the State court shall proceed no further unless and until the case is remanded.

(e) If the defendant or defendants are in actual custody on process issued by the State court, the district court shall issue its writ of habeas corpus, and the marshal shall thereupon take such defendant or defendants into his custody and deliver a copy of the writ to the clerk of such State court.

(f) With respect to any counterclaim removed to a district court pursuant to section 337(c) of the Tariff Act of 1930, the district court shall resolve such counterclaim in the same manner as an original complaint under the Federal Rules of Civil Procedure, except that the payment of a filing fee shall not be required in such cases and the counterclaim shall relate back to the date of the original complaint in the proceeding before the International Trade Commission under section 337 of that Act. As amended May 24, 1949, c. 139, § 83, 63 Stat. 101; Sept. 29, 1965, Pub.L. 89–215, 79 Stat. 887; July 30, 1977, Pub.L. 95–78, § 3, 91 Stat. 321; Nov. 19, 1988, Pub.L. 100–702, Title X, § 1016(b), 102 Stat. 4669; Dec. 9, 1991, Pub.L. 102–198, § 10(a), 105 Stat. 1626; Dec. 12, 1994, Pub.L. 103–465, Title III, § 321(b)(2), 108 Stat. 4946; Oct. 19, 1996, Pub.L. 104–317, Title VI, § 603, 110 Stat. 3857.

§ 1447. Procedure after removal generally

(a) In any case removed from a State court, the district court may issue all necessary orders and process to bring before it all proper parties whether served by process issued by the State court or otherwise.

(b) It may require the removing party to file with its clerk copies of all records and proceedings in such State court or may cause the same to be brought before it by writ of certiorari issued to such State court.

(c) A motion to remand the case on the basis of any defect other than lack of subject matter jurisdiction must be made within 30 days after the filing of the notice of removal under section 1446(a). If at any time before final judgment it appears that the district court lacks subject matter jurisdiction, the case shall be remanded. An order remanding the case may require payment of just costs and any actual expenses, including attorney fees, incurred as a result of the removal. A certified copy of the order of remand shall be mailed by the clerk to the clerk of the State court. The State court may thereupon proceed with such case.

(d) An order remanding a case to the State court from which it was removed is not reviewable on appeal or otherwise, except that an order remanding a case to the State court from which it was removed pursuant to section 1443 of this title shall be reviewable by appeal or otherwise.

(e) If after removal the plaintiff seeks to join additional defendants whose joinder would destroy subject matter jurisdiction, the court may deny joinder, or permit joinder and remand the action to the State court.

As amended May 24, 1949, c. 139, § 84, 63 Stat. 102; July 2, 1964, Pub.L. 88–352, Title IX, § 901, 78 Stat. 266; Nov. 19, 1988, Pub.L. 100–702, Title X, § 1016(c), 102 Stat. 4670; Dec. 9, 1991, Pub.L. 102–198, § 10(b), 105 Stat. 1626; Oct. 1, 1996, Pub.L. 104–219, § 1, 110 Stat. 3022.

§ 1448. Process after removal

In all cases removed from any State court to any district court of the United States in which any one or more of the defendants has not been served with process or in which the service has not been perfected prior to removal, or in which process served proves to be defective, such process or service may be completed or new process issued in the same manner as in cases originally filed in such district court.

This section shall not deprive any defendant upon whom process is served after removal of his right to move to remand the case.

§ 1449. State court record supplied

Where a party is entitled to copies of the records and proceedings in any suit or prosecution in a State court, to be used in any district court of the United States, and the clerk of such State court, upon demand, and the payment or tender of the legal fees, fails to deliver certified copies, the district court may, on affidavit reciting such facts, direct such record to be supplied by affidavit or otherwise. Thereupon such proceedings, trial, and judgment may be had in such district court, and all such process awarded, as if certified copies had been filed in the district court. As amended May 24, 1949, c. 139, § 85, 63 Stat. 102.

§ 1450. Attachment or sequestration; securities

Whenever any action is removed from a State court to a district court of the United States, any attachment or sequestration of the goods or estate of the defendant in such action in the State court shall hold the goods or estate to answer the final judgment or decree in the same manner as they would have been held to answer final judgment or decree had it been rendered by the State court.

All bonds, undertakings, or security given by either party in such action prior to its removal shall remain valid and effectual notwithstanding such removal.

All injunctions, orders, and other proceedings had in such action prior to its removal shall remain in full force and effect until dissolved or modified by the district court.

§ 1451. Definitions

For purposes of this chapter—

(1) The term "State court" includes the Superior Court of the District of Columbia.

(2) The term "State" includes the District of Columbia. Added July 29, 1970, Pub.L. 91–358, Title I, § 172(d)(1), 84 Stat. 591.

§ 1452. Removal of claims related to bankruptcy cases

(a) A party may remove any claim or cause of action in a civil action other than a proceeding before the United States Tax Court or a civil action by a governmental unit to enforce such governmental unit's police or regulatory power, to the district court for the district where such civil action is pending, if such district court has jurisdiction of such claim or cause of action under section 1334 of this title.

(b) The court to which such claim or cause of action is removed may remand such claim or cause of action on any equitable ground. An order entered under this subsection remanding a claim or cause of action, or a decision to not remand, is not reviewable by appeal or otherwise by the court of appeals under section 158(d), 1291, or 1292 of this title or by the Supreme Court of the United States under section 1254 of this title. Added July 10, 1984, Pub.L. 98–353, Title I, § 103(a), 98 Stat. 335; as amended Dec. 1, 1990, Pub.L. 101–650, Title III, § 309(c), 104 Stat. 5113.

§ 1602. Findings and declaration of purpose

The Congress finds that the determination by United States courts of the claims of foreign states to immunity from the jurisdiction of such courts would serve the interests of justice and would protect the rights of both foreign states and litigants in United States courts. Under international law, states are not immune from the jurisdiction of foreign courts insofar as their commercial activities are concerned, and their commercial property may be levied upon for the satisfaction of judgments rendered against them in connection with their commercial activities. Claims of foreign states to immunity should henceforth be decided by courts of the United States and of the States in conformity with the principles set forth in this chapter. Added Oct. 21, 1976, Pub.L. 94–583, § 4(a), 90 Stat. 2892.

§ 1603. Definitions

For purposes of this chapter—

(a) A "foreign state", except as used in section 1608 of this title, includes a political subdivision of a foreign state or an agency or instrumentality of a foreign state as defined in subsection (b).

(b) An "agency or instrumentality of a foreign state" means any entity—

(1) which is a separate legal person, corporate or otherwise, and

(2) which is an organ of a foreign state or political subdivision thereof, or a majority of whose shares or other ownership interest is owned by a foreign state or political subdivision thereof, and

(3) which is neither a citizen of a State of the United States as defined in section 1332(c) and (d) of this title, nor created under the laws of any third country.

(c) The "United States" includes all territory and waters, continental or insular, subject to the jurisdiction of the United States.

(d) A "commercial activity" means either a regular course of commercial conduct or a particular commercial transaction or act. The commercial character of an activity shall be determined by reference to the nature of the course of conduct or particular transaction or act, rather than by reference to its purpose.

(e) A "commercial activity carried on in the United States by a foreign state" means commercial activity carried on by such state and having substantial contact with the United States. Added Oct. 21, 1976, Pub.L. 94–583, § 4(a), 90 Stat. 2892.

§ 1604. Immunity of a foreign state from jurisdiction

Subject to existing international agreements to which the United States is a party at the time of enactment of this Act a foreign state shall be immune from the jurisdiction of the courts of the United States and of the States except as provided in sections 1605 to 1607 of this chapter. Added Oct. 21, 1976, Pub.L. 94–583, § 4(a), 90 Stat. 2892.

§ 1605. General exceptions to the jurisdictional immunity of a foreign state

(a) A foreign state shall not be immune from the jurisdiction of courts of the United States or of the States in any case—

(1) in which the foreign state has waived its immunity either explicitly or by implication, notwithstanding any withdrawal of the waiver which the foreign state may purport to effect except in accordance with the terms of the waiver;

(2) in which the action is based upon a commercial activity carried on in the United States by the foreign state; or upon an act performed in the United States in connection with a commercial activity of the foreign state elsewhere; or upon an act outside the territory of the United States in connection with a commercial activity of the foreign state elsewhere and that act causes a direct effect in the United States;

(3) in which rights in property taken in violation of international law are in issue and that property or any property exchanged for such property is present in the United States in connection with a commercial activity carried on in the United States by the foreign state; or that property or any property exchanged for such property is owned or operated by an agency or instrumentality of the foreign state and that agency or instrumentality is engaged in a commercial activity in the United States;

(4) in which rights in property in the United States acquired by succession or gift or rights in immovable property situated in the United States are in issue;

(5) not otherwise encompassed in paragraph (2) above, in which money damages are sought against a foreign state for personal injury or death, or damage to or loss of property, occurring in the United States and caused by the tortious act or omission of that foreign state or of any official or employee of that foreign state while acting within

the scope of his office or employment; except this paragraph shall not apply to—

(A) any claim based upon the exercise or performance or the failure to exercise or perform a discretionary function regardless of whether the discretion be abused, or

(B) any claim arising out of malicious prosecution, abuse of process, libel, slander, misrepresentation, deceit, or interference with contract rights;

(6) in which the action is brought, either to enforce an agreement made by the foreign state with or for the benefit of a private party to submit to arbitration all or any differences which have arisen or which may arise between the parties with respect to a defined legal relationship, whether contractual or not, concerning a subject matter capable of settlement by arbitration under the laws of the United States, or to confirm an award made pursuant to such an agreement to arbitrate, if (A) the arbitration takes place or is intended to take place in the United States, (B) the agreement or award is or may be governed by a treaty or other international agreement in force for the United States calling for the recognition and enforcement of arbitral awards, (C) the underlying claim, save for the agreement to arbitrate, could have been brought in a United States court under this section or section 1607, or (D) paragraph (1) of this subsection is otherwise applicable; or

(7) not otherwise covered by paragraph (2), in which money damages are sought against a foreign state for personal injury or death that was caused by an act of torture, extrajudicial killing, aircraft sabotage, hostage taking, or the provision of material support or resources (as defined in section 2339A of title 18) for such an act if such act or provision of material support is engaged in by an official, employee, or agent of such foreign state while acting within the scope of his or her office, employment, or agency, except that the court shall decline to hear a claim under this paragraph—

(A) if the foreign state was not designated as a state sponsor of terrorism under section 6(j) of the Export Administration Act of 1979 (50 U.S.C. App. 2405(j)) or section 620A of the Foreign Assistance Act of 1961 (22 U.S.C. 2371) at the time the act occurred, unless later so designated as a result of such act or the act is related to Case Number 1:00CV03110(EGS) in the United States District Court for the District of Columbia; and

(B) even if the foreign state is or was so designated, if—

(i) the act occurred in the foreign state against which the claim has been brought and the claimant has not afforded the foreign state a reasonable opportunity to arbitrate the claim in accordance with accepted international rules of arbitration; or

(ii) neither the claimant nor the victim was a national of the United States (as that term is defined in section

101(a)(22) of the Immigration and Nationality Act) when the act upon which the claim is based occurred.

(b) A foreign state shall not be immune from the jurisdiction of the courts of the United States in any case in which a suit in admiralty is brought to enforce a maritime lien against a vessel or cargo of the foreign state, which maritime lien is based upon a commercial activity of the foreign state: *Provided,* That—

(1) notice of the suit is given by delivery of a copy of the summons and of the complaint to the person, or his agent, having possession of the vessel or cargo against which the maritime lien is asserted; and if the vessel or cargo is arrested pursuant to process obtained on behalf of the party bringing the suit, the service of process of arrest shall be deemed to constitute valid delivery of such notice, but the party bringing the suit shall be liable for any damages sustained by the foreign state as a result of the arrest if the party bringing the suit had actual or constructive knowledge that the vessel or cargo of a foreign state was involved; and

(2) notice to the foreign state of the commencement of suit as provided in section 1608 of this title is initiated within ten days either of the delivery of notice as provided in paragraph (1) of this subsection or, in the case of a party who was unaware that the vessel or cargo of a foreign state was involved, of the date such party determined the existence of the foreign state's interest.

(c) Whenever notice is delivered under subsection (b)(1), the suit to enforce a maritime lien shall thereafter proceed and shall be heard and determined according to the principles of law and rules of practice of suits in rem whenever it appears that, had the vessel been privately owned and possessed, a suit in rem might have been maintained. A decree against the foreign state may include costs of the suit and, if the decree is for a money judgment, interest as ordered by the court, except that the court may not award judgment against the foreign state in an amount greater than the value of the vessel or cargo upon which the maritime lien arose. Such value shall be determined as of the time notice is served under subsection (b)(1). Decrees shall be subject to appeal and revision as provided in other cases of admiralty and maritime jurisdiction. Nothing shall preclude the plaintiff in any proper case from seeking relief in personam in the same action brought to enforce a maritime lien as provided in this section.

(d) A foreign state shall not be immune from the jurisdiction of the courts of the United States in any action brought to foreclose a preferred mortgage, as defined in the Ship Mortgage Act, 1920 (46 U.S.C. 911 and following). Such action shall be brought, heard, and determined in accordance with the provisions of that Act and in accordance with the principles of law and rules of practice of suits in rem, whenever it appears that had the vessel been privately owned and possessed a suit in rem might have been maintained.

(e) For the purposes of paragraph (7) of subsection (a)—

(1) the terms "torture" and "extrajudicial killing" have the meaning given those terms in section 3 of the Torture Victim Protection Act of 1991;

(2) the term "hostage taking" has the meaning given that term in Article 1 of the International Convention Against the Taking of Hostages; and

(3) the term "aircraft sabotage" has the meaning given that term in Article 1 of the Convention for the Suppression of Unlawful Acts Against the Safety of Civil Aviation.

(f) No action shall be maintained under subsection (a)(7) unless the action is commenced not later than 10 years after the date on which the cause of action arose. All principles of equitable tolling, including the period during which the foreign state was immune from suit, shall apply in calculating this limitation period.

(g) Limitation on Discovery.—

(1) In General.—(A) Subject to paragraph (2), if an action is filed that would otherwise be barred by section 1604, but for subsection (a)(7), the court, upon request of the Attorney General, shall stay any request, demand, or order for discovery on the United States that the Attorney General certifies would significantly interfere with a criminal investigation or prosecution, or a national security operation, related to the incident that gave rise to the cause of action, until such time as the Attorney General advises the court that such request, demand, or order will no longer so interfere.

(B) A stay under this paragraph shall be in effect during the 12–month period beginning on the date on which the court issues the order to stay discovery. The court shall renew the order to stay discovery for additional 12–month periods upon motion by the United States if the Attorney General certifies that discovery would significantly interfere with a criminal investigation or prosecution, or a national security operation, related to the incident that gave rise to the cause of action.

(2) Sunset.—(A) Subject to subparagraph (B), no stay shall be granted or continued in effect under paragraph (1) after the date that is 10 years after the date on which the incident that gave rise to the cause of action occurred.

(B) After the period referred to in subparagraph (A), the court, upon request of the Attorney General, may stay any request, demand, or order for discovery on the United States that the court finds a substantial likelihood would—

(i) create a serious threat of death or serious bodily injury to any person;

(ii) adversely affect the ability of the United States to work in cooperation with foreign and international law enforcement agencies in investigating violations of United States law; or

(iii) obstruct the criminal case related to the incident that gave rise to the cause of action or undermine the potential for a conviction in such case.

(3) Evaluation of Evidence.—The court's evaluation of any request for a stay under this subsection filed by the Attorney General shall be conducted ex parte and in camera.

(4) Bar on Motions to Dismiss.—A stay of discovery under this subsection shall constitute a bar to the granting of a motion to dismiss under rules 12(b)(6) and 56 of the Federal Rules of Civil Procedure.

(5) Construction.—Nothing in this subsection shall prevent the United States from seeking protective orders or asserting privileges ordinarily available to the United States. Added Oct. 21, 1976, Pub.L. 94–583, § 4(a), 90 Stat. 2892; as amended Nov. 9, 1988, Pub.L. 100–640, § 1, 102 Stat. 3333; Nov. 16, 1988, Pub.L. 100–669, § 2, 102 Stat. 3969; Dec. 1, 1990, Pub.L. 101–650, Title III, § 325(b)(8), 104 Stat. 5121; Apr. 24, 1996, Pub.L. 104–132, Title II, § 221(a), 110 Stat. 1241; Apr. 25, 1997, Pub.L. 105–11, 111 Stat. 22; Nov. 28, 2001, Pub.L. 107–77, Title VI, § 626(c), 115 Stat. 803; Jan. 10, 2003, Pub.L. 107–117, Div. B, § 208, 115 Stat. 2299.

§ 1606. Extent of liability

As to any claim for relief with respect to which a foreign state is not entitled to immunity under section 1605 or 1607 of this chapter, the foreign state shall be liable in the same manner and to the same extent as a private individual under like circumstances; but a foreign state except for an agency or instrumentality thereof shall not be liable for punitive damages; if, however, in any case wherein death was caused, the law of the place where the action or omission occurred provides, or has been construed to provide, for damages only punitive in nature, the foreign state shall be liable for actual or compensatory damages measured by the pecuniary injuries resulting from such death which were incurred by the persons for whose benefit the action was brought. Added Oct. 21, 1976, Pub.L. 94–583, § 4(a), 90 Stat. 2894; as amended Oct. 21, 1998, Pub.L. 105–277, Div. A, § 101(h) [Title I, § 117(b)], 112 Stat. 2681–491; Oct. 28, 2000, Pub.L. 106–386, Div. C, § 2002(f)(2), 114 Stat. 1543.

§ 1607. Counterclaims

In any action brought by a foreign state, or in which a foreign state intervenes, in a court of the United States or of a State, the foreign state shall not be accorded immunity with respect to any counterclaim—

(a) for which a foreign state would not be entitled to immunity under section 1605 of this chapter had such claim been brought in a separate action against the foreign state; or

(b) arising out of the transaction or occurrence that is the subject matter of the claim of the foreign state; or

(c) to the extent that the counterclaim does not seek relief exceeding in amount or differing in kind from that sought by the foreign state. Added Oct. 21, 1976, Pub.L. 94–583, § 4(a), 90 Stat. 2894.

§ 1608. Service; time to answer; default

(a) Service in the courts of the United States and of the States shall be made upon a foreign state or political subdivision of a foreign state:

(1) by delivery of a copy of the summons and complaint in accordance with any special arrangement for service between the plaintiff and the foreign state or political subdivision; or

(2) if no special arrangement exists, by delivery of a copy of the summons and complaint in accordance with an applicable international convention on service of judicial documents; or

(3) if service cannot be made under paragraphs (1) or (2), by sending a copy of the summons and complaint and a notice of suit, together with a translation of each into the official language of the foreign state, by any form of mail requiring a signed receipt, to be addressed and dispatched by the clerk of the court to the head of the ministry of foreign affairs of the foreign state concerned, or

(4) if service cannot be made within 30 days under paragraph (3), by sending two copies of the summons and complaint and a notice of suit, together with a translation of each into the official language of the foreign state, by any form of mail requiring a signed receipt, to be addressed and dispatched by the clerk of the court to the Secretary of State in Washington, District of Columbia, to the attention of the Director of Special Consular Services—and the Secretary shall transmit one copy of the papers through diplomatic channels to the foreign state and shall send to the clerk of the court a certified copy of the diplomatic note indicating when the papers were transmitted.

As used in this subsection, a "notice of suit" shall mean a notice addressed to a foreign state and in a form prescribed by the Secretary of State by regulation.

(b) Service in the courts of the United States and of the States shall be made upon an agency or instrumentality of a foreign state:

(1) by delivery of a copy of the summons and complaint in accordance with any special arrangement for service between the plaintiff and the agency or instrumentality; or

(2) if no special arrangement exists, by delivery of a copy of the summons and complaint either to an officer, a managing or general agent, or to any other agent authorized by appointment or by law to receive service of process in the United States; or in accordance with an applicable international convention on service of judicial documents; or

(3) if service cannot be made under paragraphs (1) or (2), and if reasonably calculated to give actual notice, by delivery of a copy of the

summons and complaint, together with a translation of each into the official language of the foreign state—

(A) as directed by an authority of the foreign state or political subdivision in response to a letter rogatory or request or

(B) by any form of mail requiring a signed receipt, to be addressed and dispatched by the clerk of the court to the agency or instrumentality to be served, or

(C) as directed by order of the court consistent with the law of the place where service is to be made.

(c) Service shall be deemed to have been made—

(1) in the case of service under subsection (a)(4), as of the date of transmittal indicated in the certified copy of the diplomatic note; and

(2) in any other case under this section, as of the date of receipt indicated in the certification, signed and returned postal receipt, or other proof of service applicable to the method of service employed.

(d) In any action brought in a court of the United States or of a State, a foreign state, a political subdivision thereof, or an agency or instrumentality of a foreign state shall serve an answer or other responsive pleading to the complaint within sixty days after service has been made under this section.

(e) No judgment by default shall be entered by a court of the United States or of a State against a foreign state, a political subdivision thereof, or an agency or instrumentality of a foreign state, unless the claimant establishes his claim or right to relief by evidence satisfactory to the court. A copy of any such default judgment shall be sent to the foreign state or political subdivision in the manner prescribed for service in this section.
Added Oct. 21, 1976, Pub.L. 94–583, § 4(a), 90 Stat. 2894.

§ 1609. Immunity from attachment and execution of property of a foreign state

Subject to existing international agreements to which the United States is a party at the time of enactment of this Act the property in the United States of a foreign state shall be immune from attachment arrest and execution except as provided in sections 1610 and 1611 of this chapter.
Added Oct. 21, 1976, Pub.L. 94–583, § 4(a), 90 Stat. 2895.

§ 1610. Exceptions to the immunity from attachment or execution

(a) The property in the United States of a foreign state, as defined in section 1603(a) of this chapter, used for a commercial activity in the United States, shall not be immune from attachment in aid of execution, or from execution, upon a judgment entered by a court of the United States or of a State after the effective date of this Act, if—

(1) the foreign state has waived its immunity from attachment in aid of execution or from execution either explicitly or by implication,

notwithstanding any withdrawal of the waiver the foreign state may purport to effect except in accordance with the terms of the waiver, or

(2) the property is or was used for the commercial activity upon which the claim is based, or

(3) the execution relates to a judgment establishing rights in property which has been taken in violation of international law or which has been exchanged for property taken in violation of international law, or

(4) the execution relates to a judgment establishing rights in property—

(A) which is acquired by succession or gift, or

(B) which is immovable and situated in the United States: *Provided,* That such property is not used for purposes of maintaining a diplomatic or consular mission or the residence of the Chief of such mission, or

(5) the property consists of any contractual obligation or any proceeds from such a contractual obligation to indemnify or hold harmless the foreign state or its employees under a policy of automobile or other liability or casualty insurance covering the claim which merged into the judgment, or

(6) the judgment is based on an order confirming an arbitral award rendered against the foreign state, provided that attachment in aid of execution, or execution, would not be inconsistent with any provision in the arbitral agreement, or

(7) the judgment relates to a claim for which the foreign state is not immune under section 1605(a)(7), regardless of whether the property is or was involved with the act upon which the claim is based.

(b) In addition to subsection (a), any property in the United States of an agency or instrumentality of a foreign state engaged in commercial activity in the United States shall not be immune from attachment in aid of execution, or from execution, upon a judgment entered by a court of the United States or of a State after the effective date of this Act, if—

(1) the agency or instrumentality has waived its immunity from attachment in aid of execution or from execution either explicitly or implicitly, notwithstanding any withdrawal of the waiver the agency or instrumentality may purport to effect except in accordance with the terms of the waiver, or

(2) the judgment relates to a claim for which the agency or instrumentality is not immune by virtue of section 1605(a)(2), (3), (5), or (7), or 1605(b) of this chapter, regardless of whether the property is or was involved in the act upon which the claim is based.

(c) No attachment or execution referred to in subsections (a) and (b) of this section shall be permitted until the court has ordered such attachment and execution after having determined that a reasonable period of time has elapsed following the entry of judgment and the giving of any notice required under section 1608(e) of this chapter.

(d) The property of a foreign state, as defined in section 1603(a) of this chapter, used for a commercial activity in the United States, shall not be immune from attachment prior to the entry of judgment in any action brought in a court of the United States or of a State, or prior to the elapse of the period of time provided in subsection (c) of this section, if—

(1) the foreign state has explicitly waived its immunity from attachment prior to judgment, notwithstanding any withdrawal of the waiver the foreign state may purport to effect except in accordance with the terms of the waiver, and

(2) the purpose of the attachment is to secure satisfaction of a judgment that has been or may ultimately be entered against the foreign state, and not to obtain jurisdiction.

(e) The vessels of a foreign state shall not be immune from arrest in rem, interlocutory sale, and execution in actions brought to foreclose a preferred mortgage as provided in section 1605(d).

(f)(1)(A) Notwithstanding any other provision of law, including but not limited to section 208(f) of the Foreign Missions Act (22 U.S.C. 4308(f)), and except as provided in subparagraph (B), any property with respect to which financial transactions are prohibited or regulated pursuant to section 5(b) of the Trading with the Enemy Act (50 U.S.C. App. 5(b)), section 620(a) of the Foreign Assistance Act of 1961 (22 U.S.C. 2370(a)), sections 202 and 203 of the International Emergency Economic Powers Act (50 U.S.C. 1701–1702), or any other proclamation, order, regulation, or license issued pursuant thereto, shall be subject to execution or attachment in aid of execution of any judgment relating to a claim for which a foreign state (including any agency or instrumentality or such state) claiming such property is not immune under section 1605(a)(7).

(B) Subparagraph (A) shall not apply if, at the time the property is expropriated or seized by the foreign state, the property has been held in title by a natural person or, if held in trust, has been held for the benefit of a natural person or persons.

(2)(A) At the request of any party in whose favor a judgment has been issued with respect to a claim for which the foreign state is not immune under section 1605(a)(7), the Secretary of the Treasury and the Secretary of State should make every effort to fully, promptly, and effectively assist any judgment creditor or any court that has issued any such judgment in identifying, locating, and executing against the property of that foreign state or any agency or instrumentality of such state.

(B) In providing such assistance, the Secretaries—

(i) may provide such information to the court under seal; and

(ii) should make every effort to provide the information in a manner sufficient to allow the court to direct the United States Marshall's office to promptly and effectively execute against that property.

(3) Waiver.—The President may waive any provision of paragraph (1) in the interest of national security. Added Oct. 21, 1976, Pub.L. 94–583, § 4(a), 90 Stat. 2896; as amended Nov. 9, 1988, Pub.L. 100–640, § 2, 102 Stat. 3333; Nov. 16, 1988, Pub.L. 100–669, § 3, 102 Stat. 3969; Dec. 1, 1990, Pub.L. 101–650, Title III, § 325(b)(9), 104 Stat. 5121; Apr. 24, 1996, Pub.L. 104–132, Title II, § 221(b), 110 Stat. 1242; Oct 21, 1998, Pub.L. 105–277, Div. A, § 101(h) [Title I, § 117(a)], 112 Stat. 2681–491; Oct. 28, 2000, Pub.L. 106–386, Div. C, § 2002(f)(1), 114 Stat. 1543.

§ 1611. Certain types of property immune from execution

(a) Notwithstanding the provisions of section 1610 of this chapter, the property of those organizations designated by the President as being entitled to enjoy the privileges, exemptions, and immunities provided by the International Organizations Immunities Act shall not be subject to attachment or any other judicial process impeding the disbursement of funds to, or on the order of, a foreign state as the result of an action brought in the courts of the United States or of the States.

(b) Notwithstanding the provisions of section 1610 of this chapter, the property of a foreign state shall be immune from attachment and from execution, if—

(1) the property is that of a foreign central bank or monetary authority held for its own account, unless such bank or authority, or its parent foreign government, has explicitly waived its immunity from attachment in aid of execution, or from execution, notwithstanding any withdrawal of the waiver which the bank, authority or government may purport to effect except in accordance with the terms of the waiver; or

(2) the property is, or is intended to be, used in connection with a military activity and

(A) is of a military character, or

(B) is under the control of a military authority or defense agency.

(c) Notwithstanding the provisions of section 1610 of this chapter, the property of a foreign state shall be immune from attachment and from execution in an action brought under section 302 of the Cuban Liberty and Democratic Solidarity (LIBERTAD) Act of 1996 to the extent that the property is a facility or installation used by an accredited diplomatic mission for official purposes. Added Oct. 21, 1976, Pub.L. 94–583, § 4(a), 90 Stat. 2897; as amended March 12, 1996, Pub.L. 104–114, Title III, § 302(e), 110 Stat. 818.

§ 1631. Transfer to cure want of jurisdiction

Whenever a civil action is filed in a court as defined in section 610 of this title or an appeal, including a petition for review of administrative action, is noticed for or filed with such a court and that court finds that there is a want of jurisdiction, the court shall, if it is in the interest of justice, transfer such action or appeal to any other such court in which the action or appeal could have been brought at the time it was filed or noticed, and the action or appeal shall proceed as if it had been filed in or noticed for the court to which it is transferred on the date upon which it was actually filed in or noticed for the court from which it is transferred. Added Apr. 2, 1982, Pub.L. 97–164, Title III, § 301(a), 96 Stat. 55.

§ 1651. Writs

(a) The Supreme Court and all courts established by Act of Congress may issue all writs necessary or appropriate in aid of their respective jurisdictions and agreeable to the usages and principles of law.

(b) An alternative writ or rule nisi may be issued by a justice or judge of a court which has jurisdiction. As amended May 24, 1949, c. 139, § 90, 63 Stat. 102.

§ 1652. State laws as rules of decision

The laws of the several states, except where the Constitution or treaties of the United States or Acts of Congress otherwise require or provide, shall be regarded as rules of decision in civil actions in the courts of the United States, in cases where they apply.

§ 1653. Amendment of pleadings to show jurisdiction

Defective allegations of jurisdiction may be amended, upon terms, in the trial or appellate courts.

§ 1654. Appearance personally or by counsel

In all courts of the United States the parties may plead and conduct their own cases personally or by counsel as, by the rules of such courts, respectively, are permitted to manage and conduct causes therein. As amended May 24, 1949, c. 139, § 91, 63 Stat. 103.

§ 1655. Lien enforcement; absent defendants

In an action in a district court to enforce any lien upon or claim to, or to remove any incumbrance or lien or cloud upon the title to, real or personal property within the district, where any defendant cannot be served within the State, or does not voluntarily appear, the court may order the absent defendant to appear or plead by a day certain.

Such order shall be served on the absent defendant personally if practicable, wherever found, and also upon the person or persons in possession or charge of such property, if any. Where personal service is not practicable, the order shall be published as the court may direct, not less than once a week for six consecutive weeks.

If an absent defendant does not appear or plead within the time allowed, the court may proceed as if the absent defendant had been served with process within the State, but any adjudication shall, as regards the absent defendant without appearance, affect only the property which is the subject of the action. When a part of the property is within another district, but within the same state, such action may be brought in either district.

Any defendant not so personally notified may, at any time within one year after final judgment, enter his appearance, and thereupon the court shall set aside the judgment and permit such defendant to plead on payment of such costs as the court deems just.

§ 1657. Priority of civil actions

(a) Notwithstanding any other provision of law, each court of the United States shall determine the order in which civil actions are heard and determined, except that the court shall expedite the consideration of any action brought under chapter 153 or section 1826 of this title, any action for temporary or preliminary injunctive relief, or any other action if good cause therefor is shown. For purposes of this subsection, "good cause" is shown if a right under the Constitution of the United States or a Federal Statute (including rights under section 552 of title 5) would be maintained in a factual context that indicates that a request for expedited consideration has merit.

(b) The Judicial Conference of the United States may modify the rules adopted by the courts to determine the order in which civil actions are heard and determined, in order to establish consistency among the judicial circuits. Added Nov. 8, 1984, Pub.L. 98–620, Title IV, § 401(a), 98 Stat. 3356.

§ 1658. Time limitations on the commencement of civil actions arising under Acts of Congress

(a) Except as otherwise provided by law, a civil action arising under an Act of Congress enacted after the date of the enactment of this section may not be commenced later than 4 years after the cause of action accrues.

(b) Notwithstanding subsection (a), a private right of action that involves a claim of fraud, deceit, manipulation, or contrivance in contravention of a regulatory requirement concerning the securities laws, as defined in section 3(a)(47) of the Securities Exchange Act of 1934 (15 U.S.C. 78c(a)(47)), may be brought not later than the earlier of—

(1) 2 years after the discovery of the facts constituting the violation; or

(2) 5 years after such violation. Added Dec. 1, 1990, Pub.L. 101–650, Title III, § 313(a), 104 Stat. 5114; as amended July 30, 2002, Pub.L. 107–204, Title VIII, § 804(a), 116 Stat. 801.

§ 1693. Place of arrest in civil action

Except as otherwise provided by Act of Congress, no person shall be arrested in one district for trial in another in any civil action in a district court.

§ 1694. Patent infringement action

In a patent infringement action commenced in a district where the defendant is not a resident but has a regular and established place of business, service of process, summons or subpoena upon such defendant may be made upon his agent or agents conducting such business.

§ 1695. Stockholder's derivative action

Process in a stockholder's action in behalf of his corporation may be served upon such corporation in any district where it is organized or licensed to do business or is doing business.

§ 1696. Service in foreign and international litigation

(a) The district court of the district in which a person resides or is found may order service upon him of any document issued in connection with a proceeding in a foreign or international tribunal. The order may be made pursuant to a letter rogatory issued, or request made, by a foreign or international tribunal or upon application of any interested person and shall direct the manner of service. Service pursuant to this subsection does not, of itself, require the recognition or enforcement in the United States of a judgment, decree, or order rendered by a foreign or international tribunal.

(b) This section does not preclude service of such a document without an order of court. Added Oct. 3, 1964, Pub.L. 88–619, § 4(a), 78 Stat. 995.

§ 1697. Service in multiparty, multiforum actions

When the jurisdiction of the district court is based in whole or in part upon section 1369 of this title, process, other than subpoenas, may be served at any place within the United States, or anywhere outside the United States if otherwise permitted by law. Added Nov. 2, 2002, Pub.L. 107–273, Div. C, Title I, § 11020(b)(4)(A), 116 Stat. 1828.

§ 1738. State and Territorial statutes and judicial proceedings; full faith and credit

The Acts of the legislature of any State, Territory, or Possession of the United States, or copies thereof, shall be authenticated by affixing the seal of such State, Territory or Possession thereto.

The records and judicial proceedings of any court of any such State, Territory or Possession, or copies thereof, shall be proved or admitted in other courts within the United States and its Territories and Possessions by the attestation of the clerk and seal of the court annexed, if a seal exists, together with a certificate of a judge of the court that the said attestation is in proper form.

Such Acts, records and judicial proceedings or copies thereof, so authenticated, shall have the same full faith and credit in every court within the United States and its Territories and Possessions as they have by law or usage in the courts of such State, Territory or Possession from which they are taken.

§ 1738A. Full faith and credit given to child custody determinations

(a) The appropriate authorities of every State shall enforce according to its terms, and shall not modify except as provided in subsections (f), (g), and (h) of this section, any custody determination or visitation determination made consistently with the provisions of this section by a court of another State.

(b) As used in this section, the term—

(1) "child" means a person under the age of eighteen;

(2) "contestant" means a person, including a parent or grandparent, who claims a right to custody or visitation of a child;

(3) "custody determination" means a judgment, decree, or other order of a court providing for the custody of a child, and includes permanent and temporary orders, and initial orders and modifications;

(4) "home State" means the State in which, immediately preceding the time involved, the child lived with his parents, a parent, or a person acting as parent, for at least six consecutive months, and in the case of a child less than six months old, the State in which the child lived from birth with any of such persons. Periods of temporary absence of any of such persons are counted as part of the six-month or other period;

(5) "modification" and "modify" refer to a custody or visitation determination which modifies, replaces, supersedes, or otherwise is made subsequent to, a prior custody or visitation determination concerning the same child, whether made by the same court or not;

(6) "person acting as a parent" means a person, other than a parent, who has physical custody of a child and who has either been awarded custody by a court or claims a right to custody;

(7) "physical custody" means actual possession and control of a child;

(8) "State" means a State of the United States, the District of Columbia, the Commonwealth of Puerto Rico, or a territory or possession of the United States; and

(9) "visitation determination" means a judgment, decree, or other order of a court providing for the visitation of a child and includes permanent and temporary orders and initial orders and modifications.

(c) A child custody or visitation determination made by a court of a State is consistent with the provisions of this section only if—

(1) such court has jurisdiction under the law of such State; and

(2) one of the following conditions is met:

(A) such State (i) is the home State of the child on the date of the commencement of the proceeding, or (ii) had been the child's home State within six months before the date of the commencement of the proceeding and the child is absent from such State because of his removal or retention by a contestant or for other reasons, and a contestant continues to live in such State;

(B)(i) it appears that no other State would have jurisdiction under subparagraph (A), and (ii) it is in the best interest of the child that a court of such State assume jurisdiction because (I) the child and his parents, or the child and at least one contestant, have a significant connection with such State other than mere physical presence in such State, and (II) there is available in such State substantial evidence concerning the child's present or future care, protection, training, and personal relationships;

(C) the child is physically present in such State and (i) the child has been abandoned, or (ii) it is necessary in an emergency to protect the child because the child, a sibling, or parent of the child has been subjected to or threatened with mistreatment or abuse;

(D)(i) it appears that no other State would have jurisdiction under subparagraph (A), (B), (C), or (E), or another State has declined to exercise jurisdiction on the ground that the State whose jurisdiction is in issue is the more appropriate forum to determine the custody or visitation of the child, and (ii) it is in the best interest of the child that such court assume jurisdiction; or

(E) the court has continuing jurisdiction pursuant to subsection (d) of this section.

(d) The jurisdiction of a court of a State which has made a child custody or visitation determination consistently with the provisions of this section continues as long as the requirement of subsection (c)(1) of this section continues to be met and such State remains the residence of the child or of any contestant.

(e) Before a child custody or visitation determination is made, reasonable notice and opportunity to be heard shall be given to the contestants, any parent whose parental rights have not been previously terminated and any person who has physical custody of a child.

(f) A court of a State may modify a determination of the custody of the same child made by a court of another State, if—

(1) it has jurisdiction to make such a child custody determination; and

(2) the court of the other State no longer has jurisdiction, or it has declined to exercise such jurisdiction to modify such determination.

(g) A court of a State shall not exercise jurisdiction in any proceeding for a custody or visitation determination commenced during the pendency of a proceeding in a court of another State where such court of that other State is exercising jurisdiction consistently with the provisions of this section to make a custody or visitation determination.

(h) A court of a State may not modify a visitation determination made by a court of another State unless the court of the other State no longer has jurisdiction to modify such determination or has declined to exercise jurisdiction to modify such determination. Added Dec. 28, 1980, Pub.L. 96–611, § 8(a), 94 Stat. 3569; as amended Nov. 12, 1998, Pub.L. 105–374, § 1, 112 Stat. 3383; Oct. 28, 2000, Pub.L. 106–386, Div. B, Title III, § 1303(d), 114 Stat. 1512.

§ 1738B. Full faith and credit for child support orders

(a) General Rule.—The appropriate authorities of each State—

(1) shall enforce according to its terms a child support order made consistently with this section by a court of another State; and

(2) shall not seek or make a modification of such an order except in accordance with subsections (e), (f), and (i).

(b) Definitions.—In this section:

"child" means—

(A) a person under 18 years of age; and

(B) a person 18 or more years of age with respect to whom a child support order has been issued pursuant to the laws of a State.

"child's State" means the State in which a child resides.

"child's home State" means the State in which a child lived with a parent or a person acting as parent for at least 6 consecutive months immediately preceding the time of filing of a petition or comparable pleading for support and, if a child is less than 6 months old, the State in which the child lived from birth with any of them. A period of temporary absence of any of them is counted as part of the 6–month period.

"child support" means a payment of money, continuing support, or arrearages or the provision of a benefit (including payment of health insurance, child care, and educational expenses) for the support of a child.

"child support order"—

(A) means a judgment, decree, or order of a court requiring the payment of child support in periodic amounts or in a lump sum; and

(B) includes—

(i) a permanent or temporary order; and

(ii) an initial order or a modification of an order.

"contestant" means—

(A) a person (including a parent) who—

(i) claims a right to receive child support;

(ii) is a party to a proceeding that may result in the issuance of a child support order; or

(iii) is under a child support order; and

(B) a State or political subdivision of a State to which the right to obtain child support has been assigned.

"court" means a court or administrative agency of a State that is authorized by State law to establish the amount of child support payable by a contestant or make a modification of a child support order.

"modification" means a change in a child support order that affects the amount, scope, or duration of the order and modifies, replaces, supersedes, or otherwise is made subsequent to the child support order.

"State" means a State of the United States, the District of Columbia, the Commonwealth of Puerto Rico, the territories and possessions of the United States, and Indian country (as defined in section 1151 of title 18).

(c) Requirements of Child Support Orders.—A child support order made by a court of a State is made consistently with this section if—

(1) a court that makes the order, pursuant to the laws of the State in which the court is located and subsections (e), (f), and (g)—

(A) has subject matter jurisdiction to hear the matter and enter such an order; and

(B) has personal jurisdiction over the contestants; and

(2) reasonable notice and opportunity to be heard is given to the contestants.

(d) Continuing Jurisdiction.—A court of a State that has made a child support order consistently with this section has continuing, exclusive jurisdiction over the order if the State is the child's State or the residence of any individual contestant unless the court of another State, acting in accordance with subsections (e) and (f), has made a modification of the order.

(e) Authority to Modify Orders.—A court of a State may modify a child support order issued by a court of another State if—

(1) the court has jurisdiction to make such a child support order pursuant to subsection (i); and

(2)(A) the court of the other State no longer has continuing, exclusive jurisdiction of the child support order because that State no longer is the child's State or the residence of any individual contestant; or

(B) each individual contestant has filed written consent with the State of continuing, exclusive jurisdiction for a court of another State to modify the order and assume continuing, exclusive jurisdiction over the order.

(f) Recognition of Child Support Orders.—If 1 or more child support orders have been issued with regard to an obligor and a child, a court shall apply the following rules in determining which order to recognize for purposes of continuing, exclusive jurisdiction and enforcement:

(1) If only 1 court has issued a child support order, the order of that court must be recognized.

(2) If 2 or more courts have issued child support orders the same obligor and child, and only 1 of the courts would have continuing, exclusive jurisdiction under this section, the order of that court must be recognized.

(3) If 2 or more courts have issued child support orders for the same obligor and child, and more than 1 of the courts would have continuing, exclusive jurisdiction under this section, an order issued by a court in the current home State of the child must be recognized but if an order has not been issued in the current home State of the child, the order most recently issued must be recognized.

(4) If 2 or more courts have issued child support orders for the same obligor and child, and none of the courts would have continuing, exclusive jurisdiction under this section, a court having jurisdiction over the parties shall issue a child support order, which must be recognized.

(5) The court that has issued an order recognized under this subsection is the court having continuing, exclusive jurisdiction under subsection (d).

(g) Enforcement of Modified Orders.—A court of a State that no longer has continuing, exclusive jurisdiction of a child support order may enforce the order with respect to nonmodifiable obligations and unsatisfied obligations that accrued before the date on which a modification of the order is made under subsections (e) and (f).

(h) Choice of Law.—

(1) In general.—In a proceeding to establish, modify, or enforce a child support order, the forum State's law shall apply except as provided in paragraphs (2) and (3).

(2) Law of state of issuance of order.—In interpreting a child support order including the duration of current payments and other obligations of support, a court shall apply the law of the State of the court that issued the order.

(3) Period of limitation.—In an action to enforce arrears under a child support order, a court shall apply the statute of limitation of the forum State or the State of the court that issued the order, whichever statute provides the longer period of limitation.

(i) Registration for Modification.—If there is no individual contestant or child residing in the issuing State, the party or support enforcement agency seeking to modify, or to modify and enforce, a child support order issued in another State shall register that order in a State with jurisdiction over the nonmovant for the purpose of modification. Added Oct. 20, 1994, Pub.L. 103–383, § 3(a), 108 Stat. 4064; Aug. 22, 1996, Pub.L. 104–193,

Title III, § 322, 110 Stat. 2221; Aug. 5, 1997, Pub.L. 105–33, Title V, § 5554, 111 Stat. 636.

§ 1738C. Certain acts, records, and proceedings and the effect thereof

No State, territory, or possession of the United States, or Indian tribe, shall be required to give effect to any public act, record, or judicial proceeding of any other State, territory, possession, or tribe respecting a relationship between persons of the same sex that is treated as a marriage under the laws of such other State, territory, possession, or tribe, or a right or claim arising from such relationship. Added Sept. 21, 1996, Pub.L. 104–199, § 2, 110 Stat. 2419.

§ 1739. State and Territorial nonjudicial records; full faith and credit

All nonjudicial records or books kept in any public office of any State, Territory, or Possession of the United States, or copies thereof, shall be proved or admitted in any court or office in any other State, Territory, or Possession by the attestation of the custodian of such records or books, and the seal of his office annexed, if there be a seal, together with a certificate of a judge of a court of record of the county, parish, or district in which such office may be kept, or of the Governor, or secretary of state, the chancellor or keeper of the great seal, of the State, Territory, or Possession that the said attestation is in due form and by the proper officers.

If the certificate is given by a judge, it shall be further authenticated by the clerk or prothonotary of the court, who shall certify, under his hand and the seal of his office, that such judge is duly commissioned and qualified; or, if given by such Governor, secretary, chancellor, or keeper of the great seal, it shall be under the great seal of the State, Territory, or Possession in which it is made.

Such records or books, or copies thereof, so authenticated, shall have the same full faith and credit in every court and office within the United States and its Territories and Possessions as they have by law or usage in the courts or offices of the State, Territory, or Possession from which they are taken.

§ 1746. Unsworn declarations under penalty of perjury

Wherever, under any law of the United States or under any rule, regulation, order, or requirement made pursuant to law, any matter is required or permitted to be supported, evidenced, established, or proved by the sworn declaration, verification, certificate, statement, oath, or affidavit, in writing of the person making the same (other than a deposition, or an oath of office, or an oath required to be taken before a specified official other than a notary public), such matter may, with like force and effect, be supported, evidenced, established, or proved by the unsworn declaration, certificate, verification, or statement, in writing of such person which is subscribed by him, as true under penalty of perjury, and dated, in substantially the following form:

(1) If executed without the United States: "I declare (or certify, verify, or state) under penalty of perjury under the laws of the United States of America that the foregoing is true and correct. Executed on (date).

(Signature)".

(2) If executed within the United States, its territories, possessions, or commonwealths: "I declare (or certify, verify, or state) under penalty of perjury that the foregoing is true and correct. Executed on (date).

(Signature)".

Added Oct. 18, 1976, Pub.L. 94–550, § 1(a), 90 Stat. 2534.

§ 1785. Subpoenas in multiparty, multiforum actions

When the jurisdiction of the district court is based in whole or in part upon section 1369 of this title, a subpoena for attendance at a hearing or trial may, if authorized by the court upon motion for good cause shown, and upon such terms and conditions as the court may impose, be served at any place within the United States, or anywhere outside the United States if otherwise permitted by law. Added Nov. 2, 2002, Pub.L. 107–273, Div. C, Title I, § 11020(b)(4)(B), 116 Stat. 1828.

§ 1861. Declaration of policy

It is the policy of the United States that all litigants in Federal courts entitled to trial by jury shall have the right to grand and petit juries selected at random from a fair cross section of the community in the district or division wherein the court convenes. It is further the policy of the United States that all citizens shall have the opportunity to be considered for service on grand and petit juries in the district courts of the United States, and shall have an obligation to serve as jurors when summoned for that purpose. As amended Sept. 9, 1957, Pub.L. 85–315, Part V, § 152, 71 Stat. 638; Mar. 27, 1968, Pub.L. 90–274, § 101, 82 Stat. 53.

§ 1870. Challenges

In civil cases, each party shall be entitled to three peremptory challenges. Several defendants or several plaintiffs may be considered as a single party for the purposes of making challenges, or the court may allow additional peremptory challenges and permit them to be exercised separately or jointly.

All challenges for cause or favor, whether to the array or panel or to individual jurors, shall be determined by the court. As amended Sept. 16, 1959, Pub.L. 86–282, 73 Stat. 565.

§ 1873. Admiralty and maritime cases

In any case of admiralty and maritime jurisdiction relating to any matter of contract or tort arising upon or concerning any vessel of twenty tons or upward, enrolled and licensed for the coasting trade, and employed in the business of commerce and navigation between places in different states upon the lakes and navigable waters connecting said lakes, the trial of all issues of fact shall be by jury if either party demands it.

§ 1914. District court; filing and miscellaneous fees; rules of court

(a) The clerk of each district court shall require the parties instituting any civil action, suit or proceeding in such court, whether by original process, removal or otherwise, to pay a filing fee of $150, except that on application for a writ of habeas corpus the filing fee shall be $5.

(b) The clerk shall collect from the parties such additional fees only as are prescribed by the Judicial Conference of the United States.

(c) Each district court by rule or standing order may require advance payment of fees. As amended Nov. 6, 1978, Pub.L. 95–598, Title II, § 244, 92 Stat. 2671; June 19, 1986, Pub.L. 99–336, § 4(a), 100 Stat. 637; Oct. 18, 1986, Pub.L. 99–500, Title I, § 101(b) [Title IV, § 407(a)], 100 Stat. 1783–64; Oct. 30, 1986, Pub.L. 99–591, Title I, § 101(b) [Title IV, § 407(a)], 100 Stat. 3341–64; Oct. 19, 1996, Pub.L. 104–317, Title IV, § 401(a), 110 Stat. 3853.

§ 1915. Proceedings in forma pauperis

(a)(1) Subject to subsection (b), any court of the United States may authorize the commencement, prosecution or defense of any suit, action or proceeding, civil or criminal, or appeal therein, without prepayment of fees or security therefor, by a person who submits an affidavit that includes a statement of all assets such prisoner possesses that the person is unable to pay such fees or give security therefor. Such affidavit shall state the nature of the action, defense or appeal and affiant's belief that the person is entitled to redress.

(2) A prisoner seeking to bring a civil action or appeal a judgment in a civil action or proceeding without prepayment of fees or security therefor, in addition to filing the affidavit filed under paragraph (1), shall submit a certified copy of the trust fund account statement (or institutional equivalent) for the prisoner for the 6–month period immediately preceding the filing of the complaint or notice of the appeal, obtained from the appropriate official of each prison at which the prisoner is or was confined.

(3) An appeal may not be taken in forma pauperis if the trial court certifies in writing that it is not taken in good faith.

(b)(1) Notwithstanding subsection (a), if a prisoner brings a civil action or files an appeal in forma pauperis, the prisoner shall be required to pay the full amount of a filing fee. The court shall assess and, when funds exist, collect, as a partial payment of any court fees required by law, an initial partial filing fee of 20 percent of the greater of—

(A) the average monthly deposits to the prisoner's account; or

(B) the average monthly balance in the prisoner's account for the 6–month period immediately preceding the filing of the complaint or notice of appeal.

(2) After payment of the initial partial filing fee, the prisoner shall be required to make monthly payments of 20 percent of the preceding month's income credited to the prisoner's account. The agency having custody of the prisoner shall forward payments from the prisoner's account to the clerk of the court each time the amount in the account exceeds $10 until the filing fees are paid.

(3) In no event shall the filing fee collected exceed the amount of fees permitted by statute for the commencement of a civil action or an appeal of a civil action or criminal judgment.

(4) In no event shall a prisoner be prohibited from bringing a civil action or appealing a civil or criminal judgment for the reason that the prisoner has no assets and no means by which to pay the initial partial filing fee.

(c) Upon the filing of an affidavit in accordance with subsections (a) and (b) and the prepayment of any partial filing fee as may be required under subsection (b), the court may direct payment by the United States of the expenses of (1) printing the record on appeal in any civil or criminal case, if such printing is required by the appellate court; (2) preparing a transcript of proceedings before a United States magistrate in any civil or criminal case, if such transcript is required by the district court, in the case of proceedings conducted under section 636(b) of this title or under section 3401(b) of title 18, United States Code; and (3) printing the record on appeal of such printing is required by the appellate court, in the case of proceedings conducted pursuant to section 636(c) of this title. Such expenses shall be paid when authorized by the Director of the Administrative Office of the United States Courts.

(d) The officers of the court shall issue and serve all process, and perform all duties in such cases. Witnesses shall attend as in other cases, and the same remedies shall be available as are provided for by law in other cases.

(e)(1) The court may request an attorney to represent any person unable to afford counsel.

(2) Notwithstanding any filing fee, or any portion thereof, that may have been paid, the court shall dismiss the case at any time if the court determines that—

(A) the allegation of poverty is untrue; or

(B) the action or appeal—

(i) is frivolous or malicious;

(ii) fails to state a claim on which relief may be granted; or

(iii) seeks monetary relief against a defendant who is immune from such relief.

(f)(1) Judgment may be rendered for costs at the conclusion of the suit or action as in other proceedings, but the United States shall not be liable for any of the costs thus incurred. If the United States has paid the cost of a stenographic transcript or printed record for the prevailing party, the same shall be taxed in favor of the United States.

(2)(A) If the judgment against a prisoner includes the payment of costs under this subsection, the prisoner shall be required to pay the full amount of the costs ordered.

(B) The prisoner shall be required to make payments for costs under this subsection in the same manner as is provided for filing fees under subsection (a)(2).

(C) In no event shall the costs collected exceed the amount of the costs ordered by the court.

(g) In no event shall a prisoner bring a civil action or appeal a judgment in a civil action or proceeding under this section if the prisoner has, on 3 or more prior occasions, while incarcerated or detained in any facility, brought an action or appeal in a court of the United States that was dismissed on the grounds that it is frivolous, malicious, or fails to state a claim upon which relief may be granted, unless the prisoner is under imminent danger of serious physical injury.

(h) As used in this section, the term "prisoner" means any person incarcerated or detained in any facility who is accused of, convicted of, sentenced for, or adjudicated delinquent for, violations of criminal law or the terms and conditions of parole, probation, pretrial release, or diversionary program. As amended May 24, 1949, c. 139, § 98, 63 Stat. 104; Oct. 31, 1951, c. 655, § 51(b, c), 65 Stat. 727; Sept. 21, 1959, Pub.L. 86–320, 73 Stat. 590; Oct. 10, 1979, Pub.L. 96–82, § 6, 93 Stat. 645; Apr. 26, 1996, Pub.L. 104–134, Title I, § 804, 110 Stat. 1321–73.

§ 1915A. Screening

(a) Screening.—The court shall review, before docketing, if feasible or, in any event, as soon as practicable after docketing, a complaint in a civil action in which a prisoner seeks redress from a governmental entity or officer or employee of a governmental entity.

(b) Grounds for Dismissal.—On review, the court shall identify cognizable claims or dismiss the complaint, or any portion of the complaint, if the complaint—

(1) is frivolous, malicious, or fails to state a claim upon which relief may be granted; or

(2) seeks monetary relief from a defendant who is immune from such relief.

(c) Definition.—As used in this section, the term "prisoner" means any person incarcerated or detained in any facility who is accused of, convicted of, sentenced for, or adjudicated delinquent for, violations of criminal law or the terms and conditions of parole, probation, pretrial release, or diversionary program. Added Apr. 26, 1996, Pub.L. 104–134, Title I, § 805, 110 Stat. 1321–75.

§ 1919. Dismissal for lack of jurisdiction

Whenever any action or suit is dismissed in any district court, the Court of International Trade, or the Court of Federal Claims for want of jurisdiction, such court may order the payment of just costs. As amended Oct. 10, 1980, Pub.L. 96–417, Title V, § 510, 94 Stat. 1743; Oct. 29, 1992, Pub.L. 102–572, Title IX, § 908, 106 Stat. 4519.

§ 1920. Taxation of costs

A judge or clerk of any court of the United States may tax as costs the following:

(1) Fees of the clerk and marshal;

(2) Fees of the court reporter for all or any part of the stenographic transcript necessarily obtained for use in the case;

(3) Fees and disbursements for printing and witnesses;

(4) Fees for exemplification and copies of papers necessarily obtained for use in the case;

(5) Docket fees under section 1923 of this title;

(6) Compensation of court appointed experts, compensation of interpreters, and salaries, fees, expenses, and costs of special interpretation services under section 1828 of this title.

A bill of costs shall be filed in the case and, upon allowance, included in the judgment or decree. As amended Oct. 28, 1978, Pub.L. 95–539, § 7, 92 Stat. 2044.

§ 1924. Verification of bill of costs

Before any bill of costs is taxed, the party claiming any item of cost or disbursement shall attach thereto an affidavit, made by himself or by his duly authorized attorney or agent having knowledge of the facts, that such item is correct and has been necessarily incurred in the case and that the services for which fees have been charged were actually and necessarily performed.

§ 1927. Counsel's liability for excessive costs

Any attorney or other person admitted to conduct cases in any court of the United States or any Territory thereof who so multiplies the proceedings in any case unreasonably and vexatiously may be required by the court to satisfy personally the excess costs, expenses, and attorneys' fees reasonably incurred because of such conduct. As amended Sept. 12, 1980, Pub.L. 96–349, § 3, 94 Stat. 1156.

§ 1961. Interest

(a) Interest shall be allowed on any money judgment in a civil case recovered in a district court. Execution therefor may be levied by the marshal, in any case where, by the law of the State in which such court is held, execution may be levied for interest on judgments recovered in the courts of the State. Such interest shall be calculated from the date of the entry of the judgment, at a rate equal to the weekly average 1-year constant maturity Treasury yield, as published by the Board of Governors of the Federal Reserve System, for the calendar week preceding the date of the judgment. The Director of the Administrative Office of the United States Courts shall distribute notice of that rate and any changes in it to all Federal judges.

(b) Interest shall be computed daily to the date of payment except as provided in section 2516(b) of this title and section 1304(b) of title 31, and shall be compounded annually.

(c)(1) This section shall not apply in any judgment of any court with respect to any internal revenue tax case. Interest shall be allowed in such cases at the underpayment rate or overpayment rate (whichever is appropriate) established under section 6621 of the Internal Revenue Code of 1954.

(2) Except as otherwise provided in paragraph (1) of this subsection, interest shall be allowed on all final judgments against the United States in the United States Court of Appeals for the Federal circuit, at the rate provided in subsection (a) and as provided in subsection (b).

(3) Interest shall be allowed, computed, and paid on judgments of the United States Court of Federal Claims only as provided in paragraph (1) of this subsection or in any other provision of law.

(4) This section shall not be construed to affect the interest on any judgment of any court not specified in this section. As amended Apr. 2, 1982, Pub.L. 97–164, Title III, § 302(a), 96 Stat. 55; Sept. 13, 1982, Pub.L. 97–258, § 2(m)(1), 96 Stat. 1062; Jan. 12, 1983, Pub.L. 97–452, § 2(d)(1), 96 Stat. 2478; Oct. 22, 1986, Pub.L. 99–514, Title XV, § 1511(c)(17), 100 Stat. 2745; Oct. 29, 1992, Pub.L. 102–572, Title IX, § 902(b)(1), 106 Stat. 4516; Dec. 21, 2000, Pub.L. 106–554, § 1(a)(7)[307(d)(1)], 114 Stat. 2763A–636.

§ 1963. Registration of judgments for enforcement in other districts

A judgment in an action for the recovery of money or property entered in any court of appeals, district court, bankruptcy court, or in the Court of International Trade may be registered by filing a certified copy of the judgment in any other district or, with respect to the Court of International Trade, in any judicial district, when the judgment has become final by appeal or expiration of the time for appeal or when ordered by the court that entered the judgment for good cause shown. Such a judgment entered in favor of the United States may be so registered any time after judgment is entered. A judgment so registered shall have the same effect as a judgment of the district court of the district where registered and may be enforced in like manner.

A certified copy of the satisfaction of any judgment in whole or in part may be registered in like manner in any district in which the judgment is a lien.

The procedure prescribed under this section is in addition to other procedures provided by law for the enforcement of judgments. As amended Aug. 23, 1954, c. 837, 68 Stat. 772; July 7, 1958, Pub.L. 85–508, § 12(*o*), 72 Stat. 349; Nov. 19, 1988, Pub.L. 100–702, Title X, § 1002, 102 Stat. 4664; Nov. 29, 1990, Pub.L. 101–647, Title XXXVI, § 3628, 104 Stat. 4965; Oct. 19, 1996, Pub.L. 104–317, Title II, § 203, 110 Stat. 3849.

§ 1964. Constructive notice of pending actions

Where the law of a State requires a notice of an action concerning real property pending in a court of the State to be registered, recorded, docketed, or indexed in a particular manner, or in a certain office or county or parish in order to give constructive notice of the action as it relates to the real property, and such law authorizes a notice of an action concerning real property pending in a United States district court to be registered, recorded, docketed, or indexed in the same manner, or in the same place, those requirements of the State law must be complied with in order to give constructive notice of such an action pending in a United States district court as it relates to real property in such State. Added Aug. 20, 1958, Pub.L. 85–689, § 1(a), 72 Stat. 683.

§ 2071. Rule-making power generally

(a) The Supreme Court and all courts established by Act of Congress may from time to time prescribe rules for the conduct of their business. Such rules shall be consistent with Acts of Congress and rules of practice and procedure prescribed under section 2072 of this title.

(b) Any rule prescribed by a court, other than the Supreme Court, under subsection (a) shall be prescribed only after giving appropriate public notice and an opportunity for comment. Such rule shall take effect upon the date specified by the prescribing court and shall have such effect on pending proceedings as the prescribing court may order.

(c)(1) A rule of a district court prescribed under subsection (a) shall remain in effect unless modified or abrogated by the judicial council of the relevant circuit.

(2) Any other rule prescribed by a court other than the Supreme Court under subsection (a) shall remain in effect unless modified or abrogated by the Judicial Conference.

(d) Copies of rules prescribed under subsection (a) by a district court shall be furnished to the judicial council, and copies of all rules prescribed by a court other than the Supreme Court under subsection (a) shall be furnished to the Director of the Administrative Office of the United States Courts and made available to the public.

(e) If the prescribing court determines that there is an immediate need for a rule, such court may proceed under this section without public notice and opportunity for comment, but such court shall promptly thereafter afford such notice and opportunity for comment.

(f) No rule may be prescribed by a district court other than under this section. As amended May 24, 1949, c. 139, § 102, 63 Stat. 104; Nov. 19, 1988, Pub.L. 100–702, Title IV, § 403(a)(1), 102 Stat. 4650.

§ 2072. Rules of procedure and evidence; power to prescribe

(a) The Supreme Court shall have the power to prescribe general rules of practice and procedure and rules of evidence for cases in the United States district courts (including proceedings before magistrates thereof) and courts of appeals.

(b) Such rules shall not abridge, enlarge or modify any substantive right. All laws in conflict with such rules shall be of no further force or effect after such rules have taken effect.

(c) Such rules may define when a ruling of a district court is final for the purposes of appeal under section 1291 of this title. As amended May 24, 1949, c. 139, § 103, 63 Stat. 104; July 18, 1949, c. 343, § 2, 63 Stat. 446; May 10, 1950, c. 174, § 2, 64 Stat. 158; July 7, 1958, Pub.L. 85–508, § 12(m), 72 Stat. 348; Nov. 6, 1966, Pub.L. 89–773, § 1, 80 Stat. 1323; Nov. 19, 1988, Pub.L. 100–702, Title IV, § 401(a), 102 Stat. 4648; Dec. 1, 1990, Pub.L. 101–650, Title III, § 315, 104 Stat. 5115.

§ 2073. Rules of procedure and evidence; method of prescribing

(a)(1) The Judicial Conference shall prescribe and publish the procedures for the consideration of proposed rules under this section.

(2) The Judicial Conference may authorize the appointment of committees to assist the Conference by recommending rules to be prescribed under sections 2072 and 2075 of this title. Each such committee shall consist of members of the bench and the professional bar, and trial and appellate judges.

(b) The Judicial Conference shall authorize the appointment of a standing committee on rules of practice, procedure, and evidence under subsection (a) of this section. Such standing committee shall review each recommendation of any other committees so appointed and recommend to the Judicial Conference rules of practice, procedure, and evidence and such changes in rules proposed by a committee appointed under subsection (a)(2) of this section as may be necessary to maintain consistency and otherwise promote the interest of justice.

(c)(1) Each meeting for the transaction of business under this chapter by any committee appointed under this section shall be open to the public, except when the committee so meeting, in open session and with a majority present, determines that it is in the public interest that all or part of the remainder of the meeting on that day shall be closed to the public, and states the reason for so closing the meeting. Minutes of each meeting for the transaction of business under this chapter shall be maintained by the committee and made available to the public, except that any portion of such minutes, relating to a closed meeting and made available to the public, may contain such deletions as may be necessary to avoid frustrating the purposes of closing the meeting.

(2) Any meeting for the transaction of business under this chapter, by a committee appointed under this section, shall be preceded by sufficient notice to enable all interested persons to attend.

(d) In making a recommendation under this section or under section 2072 or 2075, the body making that recommendation shall provide a proposed rule, an explanatory note on the rule, and a written report explaining the body's action, including any minority or other separate views.

(e) Failure to comply with this section does not invalidate a rule prescribed under section 2072 or 2075 of this title. Added Nov. 19, 1988, Pub.L. 100–702, Title IV, § 401(a), 102 Stat. 4648; as amended Oct. 22, 1994, Pub.L. 103–394, Title I, § 104(e), 108 Stat. 4110.

§ 2074. Rules of procedure and evidence; submission to Congress; effective date

(a) The Supreme Court shall transmit to the Congress not later than May 1 of the year in which a rule prescribed under section 2072 is to become effective a copy of the proposed rule. Such rule shall take effect no earlier than December 1 of the year in which such rule is so transmitted unless otherwise provided by law. The Supreme Court may fix the extent such rule shall apply to proceedings then pending, except that the Supreme Court shall not require the application of such rule to further proceedings then pending to the extent that, in the opinion of the court in which such proceedings are pending, the application of such rule in such proceedings would not be feasible or would work injustice, in which event the former rule applies.

(b) Any such rule creating, abolishing, or modifying an evidentiary privilege shall have no force or effect unless approved by Act of Congress. Added Nov. 19, 1988, Pub.L. 100–702, Title IV, § 401(a), 102 Stat. 4648.

§ 2075. Bankruptcy rules

The Supreme Court shall have the power to prescribe by general rules, the forms of process, writs, pleadings, and motions, and the practice and procedure in cases under title 11.

Such rules shall not abridge, enlarge, or modify any substantive right.

The Supreme Court shall transmit to Congress not later than May 1 of the year in which a rule prescribed under this section is to become effective a copy of the proposed rule. The rule shall take effect no earlier than December 1 of the year in which it is transmitted to Congress unless otherwise provided by law. Added Oct. 3, 1964, Pub.L. 88–623, § 1, 78 Stat. 1001; as amended Nov. 6, 1978, Pub.L. 95–598, Title II, § 247, 92 Stat. 2672; Oct. 22, 1994, Pub.L. 103–394, Title I, § 104(f), 108 Stat. 4110.

§ 2077. Publication of rules; advisory committees

(a) The rules for the conduct of the business of each court of appeals, including the operating procedures of such court, shall be published. Each court of appeals shall print or cause to be printed necessary copies of the rules. The Judicial Conference shall prescribe the fees for sales of copies under section 1913 of this title, but the Judicial Conference may provide for free distribution of copies to members of the bar of each court and to other interested persons.

(b) Each court, except the Supreme Court, that is authorized to prescribe rules of the conduct of such court's business under section 2071 of this title shall appoint an advisory committee for the study of the rules of practice and internal operating procedures of such court and, in the case of an advisory committee appointed by a court of appeals, of the rules of the judicial council of the circuit. The advisory committee shall make recommendations to the court concerning such rules and procedures. Members of the committee shall serve without compensation, but the Director may pay travel and transportation expenses in accordance with section 5703 of title 5. Added Apr. 2, 1982, Pub.L. 97–164, Title II, § 208(a), 96 Stat. 54; as amended Nov. 19, 1988, Pub.L. 100–702, Title IV, § 401(b), 102 Stat. 4650; Dec. 1, 1990, Pub.L. 101–650, Title IV, § 406, 104 Stat. 5124.

§ 2101. Supreme Court; time for appeal or certiorari; docketing; stay

(a) A direct appeal to the Supreme Court from any decision under section 1253 of this title, holding unconstitutional in whole or in part, any Act of Congress, shall be taken within thirty days after the entry of the interlocutory or final order, judgment or decree. The record shall be made up and the case docketed within sixty days from the time such appeal is taken under rules prescribed by the Supreme Court.

(b) Any other direct appeal to the Supreme Court which is authorized by law, from a decision of a district court in any civil action, suit or proceeding, shall be taken within thirty days from the judgment, order or decree, appealed from, if interlocutory, and within sixty days if final.

(c) Any other appeal or any writ of certiorari intended to bring any judgment or decree in a civil action, suit or proceeding before the Supreme Court for review shall be taken or applied for within ninety days after the entry of such judgment or decree. A justice of the Supreme Court, for good cause shown, may extend the time for applying for a writ of certiorari for a period not exceeding sixty days.

(d) The time for appeal or application for a writ of certiorari to review the judgment of a State court in a criminal case shall be as prescribed by rules of the Supreme Court.

(e) An application to the Supreme Court for a writ of certiorari to review a case before judgment has been rendered in the court of appeals may be made at any time before judgment.

(f) In any case in which the final judgment or decree of any court is subject to review by the Supreme Court on writ of certiorari, the execution and enforcement of such judgment or decree may be stayed for a reasonable time to enable the party aggrieved to obtain a writ of certiorari from the Supreme Court. The stay may be granted by a judge of the court rendering the judgment or decree or by a justice of the Supreme Court, and may be conditioned on the giving of security, approved by such judge or justice, that if the aggrieved party fails to make application for such writ within the period allotted therefor, or fails to obtain an order granting his application, or fails to make his plea good in the Supreme Court, he shall answer for all damages and costs which the other party may sustain by reason of the stay.

(g) The time for application for a writ of certiorari to review a decision of the United States Court of Appeals for the Armed Forces shall be as prescribed by rules of the Supreme Court. As amended May 24, 1949, c. 139, § 106, 63 Stat. 104; Dec. 6, 1983, Pub.L. 98–209, § 10(b), 97 Stat. 1406; June 27, 1988, Pub.L. 100–352, § 5(b), 102 Stat. 663; Oct. 5, 1994, Pub.L. 103–337, Div. A, Title IX, § 924(d)(1)(C), 108 Stat. 2832.

§ 2102. Priority of criminal case on appeal from State court

Criminal cases on review from State courts shall have priority, on the docket of the Supreme Court, over all cases except cases to which the United States is a party and such other cases as the court may decide to be of public importance.

§ 2104. Reviews of State court decisions

A review by the Supreme Court of a judgment or decree of a State court shall be conducted in the same manner and under the same regulations, and shall have the same effect, as if the judgment or decree reviewed had been rendered in a court of the United States. As amended June 27, 1988, Pub.L. 100–352, § 5(d)(1), 102 Stat. 663.

§ 2105. Scope of review; abatement

There shall be no reversal in the Supreme Court or a court of appeals for error in ruling upon matters in abatement which do not involve jurisdiction.

§ 2106. Determination

The Supreme Court or any other court of appellate jurisdiction may affirm, modify, vacate, set aside or reverse any judgment, decree, or order of a court lawfully brought before it for review, and may remand the cause and direct the entry of such appropriate judgment, decree, or order, or require such further proceedings to be had as may be just under the circumstances.

§ 2107. Time for appeal to court of appeals

(a) Except as otherwise provided in this section, no appeal shall bring any judgment, order or decree in an action, suit or proceeding of a civil nature before a court of appeals for review unless notice of appeal is filed, within thirty days after the entry of such judgment, order or decree.

(b) In any such action, suit or proceeding in which the United States or an officer or agency thereof is a party, the time as to all parties shall be sixty days from such entry.

(c) The district court may, upon motion filed not later than 30 days after the expiration of the time otherwise set for bringing appeal, extend the time for appeal upon a showing of excusable neglect or good cause. In addition, if the district court finds—

(1) that a party entitled to notice of the entry of a judgment or order did not receive such notice from the clerk or any party within 21 days of its entry, and

(2) that no party would be prejudiced,

the district court may, upon motion filed within 180 days after entry of the judgment or order or within 7 days after receipt of such notice, whichever is earlier, reopen the time for appeal for a period of 14 days from the date of entry of the order reopening the time for appeal.

(d) This section shall not apply to bankruptcy matters or other proceedings under Title 11. As amended May 24, 1949, c. 139, §§ 107, 108, 63 Stat. 104; Dec. 9, 1991, Pub.L. 102–198, § 12, 105 Stat. 1627.

§ 2108. Proof of amount in controversy

Where the power of any court of appeals to review a case depends upon the amount or value in controversy, such amount or value, if not otherwise satisfactorily disclosed upon the record, may be shown and ascertained by the oath of a party to the case or by other competent evidence.

§ 2109. Quorum of Supreme Court justices absent

If a case brought to the Supreme Court by direct appeal from a district court cannot be heard and determined because of the absence of a quorum of qualified justices, the Chief Justice of the United States may order it remitted to the court of appeals for the circuit including the district in which the case arose, to be heard and determined by that court either sitting in banc or specially constituted and composed of the three circuit judges senior in commission who are able to sit, as such order may direct. The decision of such court shall be final and conclusive. In the event of the disqualification or disability of one or more of such circuit judges, such court shall be filled as provided in chapter 15 of this title.

In any other case brought to the Supreme Court for review, which cannot be heard and determined because of the absence of a quorum of qualified justices, if a majority of the qualified justices shall be of opinion that the case cannot be heard and determined at the next ensuing term, the court shall enter its order affirming the judgment of the court from which the case was brought for review with the same effect as upon affirmance by an equally divided court.

§ 2111. Harmless error

On the hearing of any appeal or writ of certiorari in any case, the court shall give judgment after an examination of the record without regard to errors or defects which do not affect the substantial rights of the parties. Added May 24, 1949, c. 139, § 110, 63 Stat. 105.

§ 2113. Definition

For purposes of this chapter, the terms "State court", "State courts", and "highest court of a State" include the District of Columbia Court of Appeals. Added July 29, 1970, Pub.L. 91–358, Title I, § 172(a)(2)(A), 84 Stat. 590.

§ 2201. Creation of remedy

(a) In a case of actual controversy within its jurisdiction, except with respect to Federal taxes other than actions brought under section 7428 of the Internal Revenue Code of 1986, a proceeding under section 505 or 1146 of title 11, or in any civil action involving an antidumping or countervailing duty proceeding regarding a class or kind of merchandise of a free trade area country (as defined in section 516A(f)(10) of the Tariff Act of 1930), as determined by the administering authority, any court of the United States, upon the filing of an appropriate pleading, may declare the rights and other legal relations of any interested party seeking such declaration, whether or not further relief is or could be sought. Any such declaration shall have the force and effect of a final judgment or decree and shall be reviewable as such.

(b) For limitations on actions brought with respect to drug patents see section 505 or 512 of the Federal Food, Drug, and Cosmetic Act. As amended May 24, 1949, c. 139, § 111, 63 Stat. 105; Aug. 28, 1954, c. 1033, 68 Stat. 890; July 7, 1958, Pub.L. 85–508, § 12(p), 72 Stat. 349; Oct. 4, 1976, Pub.L. 94–455, Title XIII, § 1306(b)(8), 90 Stat. 1719; Nov. 6, 1978, Pub.L. 95–598, Title II, § 249, 92 Stat. 2672; Sept. 24, 1984, Pub.L. 98–417, Title I, § 106, 98 Stat. 1597; Sept. 28, 1988, Pub.L. 100–449, Title IV, § 402(c), 102 Stat. 1884; Nov. 16, 1988, Pub.L. 100–670, Title I, § 107(b), 102 Stat. 3984; Dec. 8, 1993, Pub.L. 103–182, Title IV, § 414(b), 107 Stat. 2147.

§ 2202. Further relief

Further necessary or proper relief based on a declaratory judgment or decree may be granted, after reasonable notice and hearing, against any adverse party whose rights have been determined by such judgment.

§ 2241. Power to grant writ

(a) Writs of habeas corpus may be granted by the Supreme Court, any justice thereof, the district courts and any circuit judge within their respective jurisdictions. The order of a circuit judge shall be entered in the records of the district court of the district wherein the restraint complained of is had.

(b) The Supreme Court, any justice thereof, and any circuit judge may decline to entertain an application for a writ of habeas corpus and may transfer the application for hearing and determination to the district court having jurisdiction to entertain it.

(c) The writ of habeas corpus shall not extend to a prisoner unless—

(1) He is in custody under or by color of the authority of the United States or is committed for trial before some court thereof; or

(2) He is in custody for an act done or omitted in pursuance of an Act of Congress, or an order, process, judgment or decree of a court or judge of the United States; or

(3) He is in custody in violation of the Constitution or laws or treaties of the United States; or

(4) He, being a citizen of a foreign state and domiciled therein is in custody for an act done or omitted under any alleged right, title, authority, privilege, protection, or exemption claimed under the commission, order or sanction of any foreign state, or under color thereof, the validity and effect of which depend upon the law of nations; or

(5) It is necessary to bring him into court to testify or for trial.

(d) Where an application for a writ of habeas corpus is made by a person in custody under the judgment and sentence of a State court of a State which contains two or more Federal judicial districts, the application may be filed in the district court for the district wherein such person is in custody or in the district court for the district within which the State court was held which convicted and sentenced him and each of such district courts shall have concurrent jurisdiction to entertain the application. The district court for the district wherein such an application is filed in the exercise of its discretion and in furtherance of justice may transfer the application to the other district court for hearing and determination. As amended May 24, 1949, c. 139, § 112, 63 Stat. 105; Sept. 19, 1966, Pub.L. 89–590, 80 Stat. 811.

§ 2242. Application

Application for a writ of habeas corpus shall be in writing signed and verified by the person for whose relief it is intended or by someone acting in his behalf.

It shall allege the facts concerning the applicant's commitment or detention, the name of the person who has custody over him and by virtue of what claim or authority, if known.

It may be amended or supplemented as provided in the rules of procedure applicable to civil actions.

If addressed to the Supreme Court, a justice thereof or a circuit judge it shall state the reasons for not making application to the district court of the district in which the applicant is held.

§ 2243. Issuance of writ; return; hearing; decision

A court, justice or judge entertaining an application for a writ of habeas corpus shall forthwith award the writ or issue an order directing the respondent to show cause why the writ should not be granted, unless it appears from the application that the applicant or person detained is not entitled thereto.

The writ, or order to show cause shall be directed to the person having custody of the person detained. It shall be returned within three days unless for good cause additional time, not exceeding twenty days, is allowed.

The person to whom the writ or order is directed shall make a return certifying the true cause of the detention.

When the writ or order is returned a day shall be set for hearing, not more than five days after the return unless for good cause additional time is allowed.

Unless the application for the writ and the return present only issues of law the person to whom the writ is directed shall be required to produce at the hearing the body of the person detained.

The applicant or the person detained may, under oath, deny any of the facts set forth in the return or allege any other material facts.

The return and all suggestions made against it may be amended, by leave of court, before or after being filed.

The court shall summarily hear and determine the facts, and dispose of the matter as law and justice require.

§ 2244. Finality of determination

(a) No circuit or district judge shall be required to entertain an application for a writ of habeas corpus to inquire into the detention of a person pursuant to a judgment of a court of the United States if it appears that the legality of such detention has been determined by a judge or court of the United States on a prior application for a writ of habeas corpus, except as provided in section 2255.

(b)(1) A claim presented in a second or successive habeas corpus application under section 2254 that was presented in a prior application shall be dismissed.

(2) A claim presented in a second or successive habeas corpus application under section 2254 that was not presented in a prior application shall be dismissed unless—

(A) the applicant shows that the claim relies on a new rule of constitutional law, made retroactive to cases on collateral review by the Supreme Court, that was previously unavailable; or

(B)(i) the factual predicate for the claim could not have been discovered previously through the exercise of due diligence; and

(ii) the facts underlying the claim, if proven and viewed in light of the evidence as a whole, would be sufficient to establish by clear and convincing evidence that, but for constitutional error, no reasonable factfinder would have found the applicant guilty of the underlying offense.

(3)(A) Before a second or successive application permitted by this section is filed in the district court, the applicant shall move in the appropriate court of appeals for an order authorizing the district court to consider the application.

(B) A motion in the court of appeals for an order authorizing the district court to consider a second or successive application shall be determined by a three-judge panel of the court of appeals.

(C) The court of appeals may authorize the filing of a second or successive application only if it determines that the application makes a prima facie showing that the application satisfies the requirements of this subsection.

(D) The court of appeals shall grant or deny the authorization to file a second or successive application not later than 30 days after the filing of the motion.

(E) The grant or denial of an authorization by a court of appeals to file a second or successive application shall not be appealable and shall not be the subject of a petition for rehearing or for a writ of certiorari.

(4) A district court shall dismiss any claim presented in a second or successive application that the court of appeals has authorized to be filed unless the applicant shows that the claim satisfies the requirements of this section.

(c) In a habeas corpus proceeding brought in behalf of a person in custody pursuant to the judgment of a State court, a prior judgment of the Supreme Court of the United States on an appeal or review by a writ of certiorari at the instance of the prisoner of the decision of such State court, shall be conclusive as to all issues of fact or law with respect to an asserted denial of a Federal right which constitutes ground for discharge in a habeas corpus proceeding, actually adjudicated by the Supreme Court therein, unless the applicant for the writ of habeas corpus shall plead and the court shall find the existence of a material and controlling fact which did not appear in the record of the proceeding in the Supreme Court and the court shall further find that the applicant for the writ of habeas corpus could not have caused such fact to appear in such record by the exercise of reasonable diligence.

(d)(1) A 1-year period of limitation shall apply to an application for a writ of habeas corpus by a person in custody pursuant to the judgment of a State court. The limitation period shall run from the latest of—

(A) the date on which the judgment became final by the conclusion of direct review or the expiration of the time for seeking such review;

(B) the date on which the impediment to filing an application created by State action in violation of the Constitution or laws of the

United States is removed, if the applicant was prevented from filing by such State action;

(C) the date on which the constitutional right asserted was initially recognized by the Supreme Court, if the right has been newly recognized by the Supreme Court and made retroactively applicable to cases on collateral review; or

(D) the date on which the factual predicate of the claim or claims presented could have been discovered through the exercise of due diligence.

(2) The time during which a properly filed application for State post-conviction or other collateral review with respect to the pertinent judgment or claim is pending shall not be counted toward any period of limitation under this subsection. As amended Nov. 2, 1966, Pub.L. 89–711, § 1, 80 Stat. 1104; Apr. 24, 1996, Pub.L. 104–132, Title I, §§ 101, 106, 110 Stat. 1217, 1220.

§ 2254. State custody; remedies in Federal courts

(a) The Supreme Court, a Justice thereof, a circuit judge, or a district court shall entertain an application for a writ of habeas corpus in behalf of a person in custody pursuant to the judgment of a State court only on the ground that he is in custody in violation of the Constitution or laws or treaties of the United States.

(b)(1) An application for a writ of habeas corpus on behalf of a person in custody pursuant to the judgment of a State court shall not be granted unless it appears that—

(A) the applicant has exhausted the remedies available in the courts of the State; or

(B)(i) there is an absence of available State corrective process; or

(ii) circumstances exist that render such process ineffective to protect the rights of the applicant.

(2) An application for a writ of habeas corpus may be denied on the merits, notwithstanding the failure of the applicant to exhaust the remedies available in the courts of the State.

(3) A State shall not be deemed to have waived the exhaustion requirement or be estopped from reliance upon the requirement unless the State, through counsel, expressly waives the requirement.

(c) An applicant shall not be deemed to have exhausted the remedies available in the courts of the State, within the meaning of this section, if he has the right under the law of the State to raise, by any available procedure, the question presented.

(d) An application for a writ of habeas corpus on behalf of a person in custody pursuant to the judgment of a State court shall not be granted with respect to any claim that was adjudicated on the merits in State court proceedings unless the adjudication of the claim—

(1) resulted in a decision that was contrary to, or involved an unreasonable application of, clearly established Federal law, as determined by the Supreme Court of the United States; or

(2) resulted in a decision that was based on an unreasonable determination of the facts in light of the evidence presented in the State court proceeding.

(e)(1) In a proceeding instituted by an application for a writ of habeas corpus by a person in custody pursuant to the judgment of a State court, a determination of a factual issue made by a State court shall be presumed to be correct. The applicant shall have the burden of rebutting the presumption of correctness by clear and convincing evidence.

(2) If the applicant has failed to develop the factual basis of a claim in State court proceedings, the court shall not hold an evidentiary hearing on the claim unless the applicant shows that—

(A) the claim relies on—

(i) a new rule of constitutional law, made retroactive to cases on collateral review by the Supreme Court, that was previously unavailable; or

(ii) a factual predicate that could not have been previously discovered through the exercise of due diligence; and

(B) the facts underlying the claim would be sufficient to establish by clear and convincing evidence that but for constitutional error, no reasonable factfinder would have found the applicant guilty of the underlying offense.

(f) If the applicant challenges the sufficiency of the evidence adduced in such State court proceeding to support the State court's determination of a factual issue made therein, the applicant, if able, shall produce that part of the record pertinent to a determination of the sufficiency of the evidence to support such determination. If the applicant, because of indigency or other reason is unable to produce such part of the record, then the State shall produce such part of the record and the Federal court shall direct the State to do so by order directed to an appropriate State official. If the State cannot provide such pertinent part of the record, then the court shall determine under the existing facts and circumstances what weight shall be given to the State court's factual determination.

(g) A copy of the official records of the State court, duly certified by the clerk of such court to be a true and correct copy of a finding, judicial opinion, or other reliable written indicia showing such a factual determination by the State court shall be admissible in the Federal court proceeding.

(h) Except as provided in section 408 of the Controlled Substances Act, in all proceedings brought under this section, and any subsequent proceedings on review, the court may appoint counsel for an applicant who is or becomes financially unable financially unable to afford counsel, except as provided by a rule promulgated by the Supreme Court pursuant to statutory authority. Appointment of counsel under this section shall be governed by section 3006A of title 18.

(i) The ineffectiveness or incompetence of counsel during Federal or State collateral post-conviction proceedings shall not be a ground for relief in a proceeding arising under section 2254. As amended Nov. 2, 1966, Pub.L. 89–711, § 2, 80 Stat. 1105; Apr. 24, 1996, Pub.L. 104–132, Title I, § 104, 110 Stat. 1218.

§ 2255. Federal custody; remedies on motion attacking sentence

A prisoner in custody under sentence of a court established by Act of Congress claiming the right to be released upon the ground that the sentence was imposed in violation of the Constitution or laws of the United States, or that the court was without jurisdiction to impose such sentence, or that the sentence was in excess of the maximum authorized by law, or is otherwise subject to collateral attack, may move the court which imposed the sentence to vacate, set aside or correct the sentence.

Unless the motion and the files and records of the case conclusively show that the prisoner is entitled to no relief, the court shall cause notice thereof to be served upon the United States attorney, grant a prompt hearing thereon, determine the issues and make findings of fact and conclusions of law with respect thereto. If the court finds that the judgment was rendered without jurisdiction, or that the sentence imposed was not authorized by law or otherwise open to collateral attack, or that there has been such a denial or infringement of the constitutional rights of the prisoner as to render the judgment vulnerable to collateral attack, the court shall vacate and set the judgment aside and shall discharge the prisoner or resentence him or grant a new trial or correct the sentence as may appear appropriate.

A court may entertain and determine such motion without requiring the production of the prisoner at the hearing.

An appeal may be taken to the court of appeals from the order entered on the motion as from a final judgment on application for a writ of habeas corpus.

An application for a writ of habeas corpus in behalf of a prisoner who is authorized to apply for relief by motion pursuant to this section, shall not be entertained if it appears that the applicant has failed to apply for relief, by motion, to the court which sentenced him, or that such court has denied him relief, unless it also appears that the remedy by motion is inadequate or ineffective to test the legality of his detention.

A 1-year period of limitation shall apply to a motion under this section. The limitation period shall run from the latest of—

(1) the date on which the judgment of conviction becomes final;

(2) the date on which the impediment to making a motion created by governmental action in violation of the Constitution or laws of the United States is removed, if the movant was prevented from making a motion by such governmental action;

(3) the date on which the right asserted was initially recognized by the Supreme Court, if that right has been newly recognized by the

Supreme Court and made retroactively applicable to cases on collateral review; or

(4) the date on which the facts supporting the claim or claims presented could have been discovered through the exercise of due diligence.

Except as provided in section 408 of the Controlled Substances Act, in all proceedings brought under this section, and any subsequent proceedings on review, the court may appoint counsel, except as provided by a rule promulgated by the Supreme Court pursuant to statutory authority. Appointment of counsel under this section shall be governed by section 3006A of title 18.

A second or successive motion must be certified as provided in section 2244 by a panel of the appropriate court of appeals to contain—

(1) newly discovered evidence that, if proven and viewed in light of the evidence as a whole, would be sufficient to establish by clear and convincing evidence that no reasonable factfinder would have found the movant guilty of the offense; or

(2) a new rule of constitutional law, made retroactive to cases on collateral review by the Supreme Court, that was previously unavailable. As amended May 24, 1949, c. 139, § 114, 63 Stat. 105; Apr. 24, 1996, Pub.L. 104–132, Title I, § 105, 110 Stat. 1220.

§ 2283. Stay of State court proceedings

A court of the United States may not grant an injunction to stay proceedings in a State court except as expressly authorized by Act of Congress, or where necessary in aid of its jurisdiction, or to protect or effectuate its judgments.

§ 2284. Three-judge court; when required; composition; procedure

(a) A district court of three judges shall be convened when otherwise required by Act of Congress, or when an action is filed challenging the constitutionality of the apportionment of congressional districts or the apportionment of any statewide legislative body.

(b) In any action required to be heard and determined by a district court of three judges under subsection (a) of this section, the composition and procedure of the court shall be as follows:

(1) Upon the filing of a request for three judges, the judge to whom the request is presented shall, unless he determines that three judges are not required, immediately notify the chief judge of the circuit, who shall designate two other judges, at least one of whom shall be a circuit judge. The judges so designated, and the judge to whom the request was presented, shall serve as members of the court to hear and determine the action or proceeding.

(2) If the action is against a State, or officer or agency thereof, at least five days' notice of hearing of the action shall be given by registered or certified mail to the Governor and attorney general of the State.

(3) A single judge may conduct all proceedings except the trial, and enter all orders permitted by the rules of civil procedure except as provided in this subsection. He may grant a temporary restraining order on a specific finding, based on evidence submitted, that specified irreparable damage will result if the order is not granted, which order, unless previously revoked by the district judge, shall remain in force only until the hearing and determination by the district court of three judges of an application for a preliminary injunction. A single judge shall not appoint a master, or order a reference, or hear and determine any application for a preliminary or permanent injunction or motion to vacate such an injunction, or enter judgment on the merits. Any action of a single judge may be reviewed by the full court at any time before final judgment. As amended June 11, 1960, Pub.L. 86–507, § 1(19), 74 Stat. 201; Aug. 12, 1976, Pub.L. 94–381, § 3, 90 Stat. 1119; Nov. 8, 1984, Pub.L. 98–620, Title IV, § 402(29)(E), 98 Stat. 3359.

§ 2361. Process and procedure

In any civil action of interpleader or in the nature of interpleader under section 1335 of this title, a district court may issue its process for all claimants and enter its order restraining them from instituting or prosecuting any proceeding in any State or United States court affecting the property, instrument or obligation involved in the interpleader action until further order of the court. Such process and order shall be returnable at such time as the court or judge thereof directs, and shall be addressed to and served by the United States marshals for the respective districts where the claimants reside or may be found.

Such district court shall hear and determine the case, and may discharge the plaintiff from further liability, make the injunction permanent, and make all appropriate orders to enforce its judgment. As amended May 24, 1949, c. 139, § 117, 63 Stat. 105.

§ 2401. Time for commencing action against United States

(a) Except as provided by the Contract Disputes Act of 1978, every civil action commenced against the United States shall be barred unless the complaint is filed within six years after the right of action first accrues. The action of any person under legal disability or beyond the seas at the time the claim accrues may be commenced within three years after the disability ceases.

(b) A tort claim against the United States shall be forever barred unless it is presented in writing to the appropriate Federal agency within two years after such claim accrues or unless action is begun within six months after the date of mailing, by certified or registered mail, of notice of final denial of the claim by the agency to which it was presented. As amended Apr. 25, 1949, c. 92, § 1, 63 Stat. 62; Sept. 8, 1959, Pub.L.

86–238, § 1(3), 73 Stat. 472; July 18, 1966, Pub.L. 89–506, § 7, 80 Stat. 307; Nov. 1, 1978, Pub.L. 95–563, § 14(b), 92 Stat. 2389.

§ 2402. Jury trial in actions against United States

Subject to chapter 179 of this title, any action against the United States under section 1346 shall be tried by the court without a jury, except that any action against the United States under section 1346(a)(1) shall, at the request of either party to such action, be tried by the court with a jury. As amended July 30, 1954, c. 648, § 2(a), 68 Stat. 589; Oct. 26, 1996, Pub.L. 104–331, § 3(b)(3), 110 Stat. 4069.

§ 2403. Intervention by United States or a State; constitutional question

(a) In any action, suit or proceeding in a court of the United States to which the United States or any agency, officer or employee thereof is not a party, wherein the constitutionality of any Act of Congress affecting the public interest is drawn in question, the court shall certify such fact to the Attorney General, and shall permit the United States to intervene for presentation of evidence, if evidence is otherwise admissible in the case, and for argument on the question of constitutionality. The United States shall, subject to the applicable provisions of law, have all the rights of a party and be subject to all liabilities of a party as to court costs to the extent necessary for a proper presentation of the facts and law relating to the question of constitutionality.

(b) In any action, suit, or proceeding in a court of the United States to which a State or any agency, officer, or employee thereof is not a party, wherein the constitutionality of any statute of that State affecting the public interest is drawn in question, the court shall certify such fact to the attorney general of the State, and shall permit the State to intervene for presentation of evidence, if evidence is otherwise admissible in the case, and for argument on the question of constitutionality. The State shall, subject to the applicable provisions of law, have all the rights of a party and be subject to all liabilities of a party as to court costs to the extent necessary for a proper presentation of the facts and law relating to the question of constitutionality. As amended Aug. 12, 1976, Pub.L. 94–381, § 5, 90 Stat. 1120.

§ 2412. Costs and fees

(a)(1) Except as otherwise specifically provided by statute, a judgment for costs, as enumerated in section 1920 of this title, but not including the fees and expenses of attorneys, may be awarded to the prevailing party in any civil action brought by or against the United States or any agency or any official of the United States acting in his or her official capacity in any court having jurisdiction of such action. A judgment for costs when taxed against the United States shall, in an amount established by statute, court rule, or order, be limited to reimbursing in whole or in part the prevailing party for the costs incurred by such party in the litigation.

(2) A judgment for costs, when awarded in favor of the United States in an action brought by the United States, may include an amount equal to the filing fee prescribed under section 1914(a) of this title. The preceding sentence shall not be construed as requiring the United States to pay any filing fee.

(b) Unless expressly prohibited by statute, a court may award reasonable fees and expenses of attorneys, in addition to the costs which may be awarded pursuant to subsection (a), to the prevailing party in any civil action brought by or against the United States or any agency or any official of the United States acting in his or her official capacity in any court having jurisdiction of such action. The United States shall be liable for such fees and expenses to the same extent that any other party would be liable under the common law or under the terms of any statute which specifically provides for such an award.

(c)(1) Any judgment against the United States or any agency and any official of the United States acting in his or her official capacity for costs pursuant to subsection (a) shall be paid as provided in sections 2414 and 2517 of this title and shall be in addition to any relief provided in the judgment.

(2) Any judgment against the United States or any agency and any official of the United States acting in his or her official capacity for fees and expenses of attorneys pursuant to subsection (b) shall be paid as provided in sections 2414 and 2517 of this title, except that if the basis for the award is a finding that the United States acted in bad faith, then the award shall be paid by any agency found to have acted in bad faith and shall be in addition to any relief provided in the judgment.

(d)(1)(A) Except as otherwise specifically provided by statute, a court shall award to a prevailing party other than the United States fees and other expenses, in addition to any costs awarded pursuant to subsection (a), incurred by that party in any civil action (other than cases sounding in tort), including proceedings for judicial review of agency action, brought by or against the United States in any court having jurisdiction of that action, unless the court finds that the position of the United States was substantially justified or that special circumstances make an award unjust.

(B) A party seeking an award of fees and other expenses shall, within thirty days of final judgment in the action, submit to the court an application for fees and other expenses which shows that the party is a prevailing party and is eligible to receive an award under this subsection, and the amount sought, including an itemized statement from any attorney or expert witness representing or appearing in behalf of the party stating the actual time expended and the rate at which fees and other expenses are computed. The party shall also allege that the position of the United States was not substantially justified. Whether or not the position of the United States was substantially justified shall be determined on the basis of the record (including the record with respect to the action or failure to act by the agency upon which the civil action is based) which is made in the civil action for which fees and other expenses are sought.

(C) The court, in its discretion, may reduce the amount to be awarded pursuant to this subsection, or deny an award, to the extent that the prevailing party during the course of the proceedings engaged in conduct which unduly and unreasonably protracted the final resolution of the matter in controversy.

(D) If, in a civil action brought by the United States or a proceeding for judicial review of an adversary adjudication described in section 504(a)(4) of title 5, the demand by the United States is substantially in excess of the judgment finally obtained by the United States and is unreasonable when compared with such judgment, under the facts and circumstances of the case, the court shall award to the party the fees and other expenses related to defending against the excessive demand, unless the party has committed a willful violation of law or otherwise acted in bad faith, or special circumstances make an award unjust. Fees and expenses awarded under this subparagraph shall paid only as a consequence of appropriations provided in advance.

(2) For the purposes of this subsection—

(A) "fees and other expenses" includes the reasonable expenses of expert witnesses, the reasonable cost of any study, analysis, engineering report, test, or project which is found by the court to be necessary for the preparation of the party's case, and reasonable attorney fees (The amount of fees awarded under this subsection shall be based upon prevailing market rates for the kind and quality of the services furnished, except that (i) no expert witness shall be compensated at a rate in excess of the highest rate of compensation for expert witnesses paid by the United States; and (ii) attorney fees shall not be awarded in excess of $125 per hour unless the court determines that an increase in the cost of living or a special factor, such as the limited availability of qualified attorneys for the proceedings involved, justifies a higher fee.);

(B) "party" means (i) an individual whose net worth did not exceed $2,000,000 at the time the civil action was filed, or (ii) any owner of an unincorporated business, or any partnership, corporation, association, unit of local government, or organization, the net worth of which did not exceed $7,000,000 at the time the civil action was filed, and which had not more than 500 employees at the time the civil action was filed; except that an organization described in section 501(c)(3) of the Internal Revenue Code of 1954 (26 U.S.C. 501(c)(3)) exempt from taxation under section 501(a) of such Code, or a cooperative association as defined in section 15(a) of the Agricultural Marketing Act (12 U.S.C. 1141j(a)), may be a party regardless of the net worth of such organization or cooperative association or for purposes of subsection (d)(1)(D), a small entity as defined in section 601 of title 5;

(C) "United States" includes any agency and any official of the United States acting in his or her official capacity;

(D) "position of the United States" means, in addition to the position taken by the United States in the civil action, the action or failure to act by the agency upon which the civil action is based; except that fees and expenses may not be awarded to a party for any portion of the litigation in which the party has unreasonably protracted the proceedings;

(E) "civil action brought by or against the United States" includes an appeal by a party, other than the United States, from a decision of a contracting officer rendered pursuant to a disputes clause in a contract with the Government or pursuant to the Contract Disputes Act of 1978;

(F) "court" includes the United States Court of Federal Claims and the United States Court of Appeals for Veterans Claims;

(G) "final judgment" means a judgment that is final and not appealable, and includes an order of settlement;

(H) "prevailing party", in the case of eminent domain proceedings, means a party who obtains a final judgment (other than by settlement), exclusive of interest, the amount of which is at least as close to the highest valuation of the property involved that is attested to at trial on behalf of the property owner as it is to the highest valuation of the property involved that is attested to at trial on behalf of the Government; and

(I) "demand" means the express demand of the United States which led to the adversary adjudication, but shall not include a recitation of the maximum statutory penalty (i) in the complaint, or (ii) elsewhere when accompanied by an express demand for a lesser amount.

(3) In awarding fees and other expenses under this subsection to a prevailing party in any action for judicial review of an adversary adjudication, as defined in subsection (b)(1)(C) of section 504 of title 5, United States Code, or an adversary adjudication subject to the Contract Disputes Act of 1978, the court shall include in that award fees and other expenses to the same extent authorized in subsection (a) of such section, unless the court finds that during such adversary adjudication the position of the United States was substantially justified, or that special circumstances make an award unjust.

(4) Fees and other expenses awarded under this subsection to a party shall be paid by any agency over which the party prevails from any funds made available to the agency by appropriation or otherwise.

(e) The provisions of this section shall not apply to any costs, fees, and other expenses in connection with any proceeding to which section 7430 of the Internal Revenue Code of 1954 applies (determined without regard to subsections (b) and (f) of such section). Nothing in the preceding sentence shall prevent the awarding under subsection (a) of section 2412 of title 28, United States Code, of costs enumerated in section 1920 of such title (as in effect on October 1, 1981).

(f) If the United States appeals an award of costs or fees and other expenses made against the United States under this section and the award is affirmed in whole or in part, interest shall be paid on the amount of the award as affirmed. Such interest shall be computed at the rate determined under section 1961(a) of this title, and shall run from the date of the award through the day before the date of the mandate of affirmance. As amended July 18, 1966, Pub.L. 89–507, § 1, 80 Stat. 308; Oct. 21, 1980, Pub.L. 96–481, Title II, § 204(a), (c), 94 Stat. 2327, 2329; Sept. 3, 1982, Pub.L. 97–248, Title II, § 292(c), 96 Stat. 574; Aug. 5, 1985, Pub.L. 99–80, §§ 2, 6, 99 Stat. 184, 186; Oct. 29, 1992, Pub.L. 102–572, Title III, § 301(a), Title V, §§ 502(b), 506(a), Title IX, § 902(b)(1), 106 Stat. 4511, 4512, 4513, 4516; Dec. 21, 1995, Pub.L. 104–66, Title I, § 1091(b), 109 Stat. 722; Mar. 29, 1996, Pub.L. 104–121, Title II, § 232, 110 Stat. 863; Nov. 11, 1998, Pub.L. 105–368, Title V, § 512(b)(1)(B), 112 Stat. 3342.

§ 2671. Definitions

As used in this chapter and sections 1346(b) and 2401(b) of this title, the term "Federal agency" includes the executive departments, the judicial and legislative branches, the military departments, independent establishments of the United States, and corporations primarily acting as instrumentalities or agencies of the United States, but does not include any contractor with the United States.

"Employee of the government" includes (1) officers or employees of any federal agency, members of the military or naval forces of the United States, members of the National Guard while engaged in training or duty under section 115, 316, 502, 503, 504, or 505 of title 32, and persons acting on behalf of a federal agency in an official capacity, temporarily or permanently in the service of the United States, whether with or without compensation, and (2) any officer or employee of a Federal public defender organization, except when such officer or employee performs professional services in the course of providing representation under section 3006A of title 18.

"Acting within the scope of his office or employment", in the case of a member of the military or naval forces of the United States or a member of the National Guard as defined in section 101(3) of title 32, means acting in line of duty. As amended May 24, 1949, c. 139, § 124, 63 Stat. 106; July 18, 1966, Pub.L. 89–506, § 8, 80 Stat. 307; Dec. 29, 1981, Pub.L. 97–124, § 1, 95 Stat. 1666; Nov. 18, 1988, Pub.L. 100–694, § 3, 102 Stat. 4564; Oct. 30, 2000, Pub.L. 106–398, § 1[665(b)], 114 Stat. 1654A–169; Nov. 13, 2000, Pub.L. 106–518, Title IV, § 401, 114 Stat. 2421.

§ 2672. Administrative adjustment of claims

The head of each Federal agency or his designee, in accordance with regulations prescribed by the Attorney General, may consider, ascertain, adjust, determine, compromise, and settle any claim for money damages against the United States for injury or loss of property or personal injury or death caused by the negligent or wrongful act or omission of any employee of the agency while acting within the scope of his office or employment, under circumstances where the United States, if a private person, would be liable to the claimant in accordance with the law of the place where the act or omission occurred: *Provided,* That any award, compromise, or settlement in excess of $25,000 shall be effected only with the prior written approval of the Attorney General or his designee.

Subject to the provisions of this title relating to civil actions on tort claims against the United States, any such award, compromise, settlement, or determination shall be final and conclusive on all officers of the Government, except when procured by means of fraud.

Any award, compromise, or settlement in an amount of $2,500 or less made pursuant to this section shall be paid by the head of the Federal agency concerned out of appropriations available to that agency. Payment of any award, compromise, or settlement in an amount in excess of $2,500 made pursuant to this section or made by the Attorney General in any amount pursuant to section 2677 of this title shall be paid in a manner similar to judgments and compromises in like causes and appropriations or funds available for the payment of such judgments and compromises are hereby made available for the payment of awards, compromises, or settlements under this chapter.

The acceptance by the claimant of any such award, compromise, or settlement shall be final and conclusive on the claimant, and shall constitute a complete release of any claim against the United States and against the employee of the government whose act or omission gave rise to the claim, by reason of the same subject matter. As amended Apr. 25, 1949, c. 92, § 2(b), 63 Stat. 62; May 24, 1949, c. 139, § 125, 63 Stat. 106; Sept. 23, 1950, c. 1010, § 9, 64 Stat. 987; Sept. 8, 1959, Pub.L. 86–238, § 1(1), 73 Stat. 471; July 18, 1966, Pub.L. 89–506, §§ 1, 9(a), 80 Stat. 306, 308; Nov. 15, 1990, Pub.L. 101–552, § 8(a), 104 Stat. 2746.

§ 2674. Liability of United States

The United States shall be liable, respecting the provisions of this title relating to tort claims, in the same manner and to the same extent as a private individual under like circumstances, but shall not be liable for interest prior to judgment or for punitive damages.

If, however, in any case wherein death was caused, the law of the place where the act or omission complained of occurred provides, or has been construed to provide, for damages only punitive in nature, the United States shall be liable for actual or compensatory damages, measured by the pecuniary injuries resulting from such death to the persons respectively, for whose benefit the action was brought, in lieu thereof.

With respect to any claim under this chapter, the United States shall be entitled to assert any defense based upon judicial or legislative immunity which otherwise would have been available to the employee of the United States whose act or omission gave rise to the claim, as well as any other defenses to which the United States is entitled.

With respect to any claim to which this section applies, the Tennessee Valley Authority shall be entitled to assert any defense which otherwise would have been available to the employee based upon judicial or legislative immunity, which otherwise would have been available to the employee of the Tennessee Valley Authority whose act or omission gave rise to the claim as well as any other defenses to which the Tennessee Valley Authority is entitled under this chapter. As amended Nov. 18, 1988, Pub.L. 100–694, §§ 4, 9(c), 102 Stat. 4564, 4567.

§ 2675. Disposition by federal agency as prerequisite; evidence

(a) An action shall not be instituted upon a claim against the United States for money damages for injury or loss of property or personal injury or death caused by the negligent or wrongful act or omission of any employee of the Government while acting within the scope of his office or employment, unless the claimant shall have first presented the claim to the appropriate Federal agency and his claim shall have been finally denied by the agency in writing and sent by certified or registered mail. The failure of an agency to make final disposition of a claim within six months after it is filed shall, at the option of the claimant any time thereafter, be deemed a final denial of the claim for purposes of this section. The provisions of this subsection shall not apply to such claims as may be asserted under the Federal Rules of Civil Procedure by third party complaint, cross-claim, or counterclaim.

(b) Action under this section shall not be instituted for any sum in excess of the amount of the claim presented to the federal agency, except where the increased amount is based upon newly discovered evidence not reasonably discoverable at the time of presenting the claim to the federal agency, or upon allegation and proof of intervening facts, relating to the amount of the claim.

(c) Disposition of any claim by the Attorney General or other head of a federal agency shall not be competent evidence of liability or amount of damages. As amended May 24, 1949, c. 139, § 126, 63 Stat. 107; July 18, 1966, Pub.L. 89–506, § 2, 80 Stat. 306.

§ 2676. Judgment as bar

The judgment in an action under section 1346(b) of this title shall constitute a complete bar to any action by the claimant, by reason of the same subject matter, against the employee of the government whose act or omission gave rise to the claim.

§ 2677. Compromise

The Attorney General or his designee may arbitrate, compromise, or settle any claim cognizable under section 1346(b) of this title, after the commencement of an action thereon. As amended July 18, 1966, Pub.L. 89–506, § 3, 80 Stat. 307.

§ 2678. Attorney fees; penalty

No attorney shall charge, demand, receive, or collect for services rendered, fees in excess of 25 per centum of any judgment rendered pursuant to section 1346(b) of this title or any settlement made pursuant to section 2677 of this title, or in excess of 20 per centum of any award, compromise, or settlement made pursuant to section 2672 of this title.

Any attorney who charges, demands, receives, or collects for services rendered in connection with such claim any amount in excess of that allowed under this section, if recovery be had, shall be fined not more than $2,000 or imprisoned not more than one year, or both. As amended July 18, 1966, Pub.L. 89–506, § 4, 80 Stat. 307.

§ 2679. Exclusiveness of remedy

(a) The authority of any federal agency to sue and be sued in its own name shall not be construed to authorize suits against such federal agency on claims which are cognizable under section 1346(b) of this title, and the remedies provided by this title in such cases shall be exclusive.

(b)(1) The remedy against the United States provided by sections 1346(b) and 2672 of this title for injury or loss of property, or personal injury or death arising or resulting from the negligent or wrongful act or omission of any employee of the Government while acting within the scope of his office or employment is exclusive of any other civil action or proceeding for money damages by reason of the same subject matter against the employee whose act or omission gave rise to the claim or against the estate of such employee. Any other civil action or proceeding for money damages arising out of or relating to the same subject matter against the employee or the employee's estate is precluded without regard to when the act or omission occurred.

(2) Paragraph (1) does not extend or apply to a civil action against an employee of the Government—

(A) which is brought for a violation of the Constitution of the United States, or

(B) which is brought for a violation of a statute of the United States under which such action against an individual is otherwise authorized.

(c) The Attorney General shall defend any civil action or proceeding brought in any court against any employee of the Government or his estate for any such damage or injury. The employee against whom such civil action or proceeding is brought shall deliver within such time after date of service or knowledge of service as determined by the Attorney General, all process served upon him or an attested true copy thereof to his immediate superior or to whomever was designated by the head of his department to receive such papers and such person shall promptly furnish copies of the pleadings and process therein to the United States attorney for the district embracing the place wherein the proceeding is brought, to the Attorney General, and to the head of his employing Federal agency.

(d)(1) Upon certification by the Attorney General that the defendant employee was acting within the scope of his office or employment at the time of the incident out of which the claim arose, any civil action or proceeding commenced upon such claim in a United States district court shall be deemed an action against the United States under the provisions of this title and all references thereto, and the United States shall be substituted as the party defendant.

(2) Upon certification by the Attorney General that the defendant employee was acting within the scope of his office or employment at the time of the incident out of which the claim arose, any civil action or proceeding commenced upon such claim in a State court shall be removed without bond at any time before trial by the Attorney General to the district court of the United States for the district and division embracing the place in which the action or proceeding is pending. Such action or proceeding shall be deemed to be an action or proceeding brought against the United States under the provisions of this title and all references thereto, and the United States shall be substituted as the party defendant. This certification of the Attorney General shall conclusively establish scope of office or employment for purposes of removal.

(3) In the event that the Attorney General has refused to certify scope of office or employment under this section, the employee may at any time before trial petition the court to find and certify that the employee was acting within the scope of his office or employment. Upon such certification by the court, such action or proceeding shall be deemed to be an action or proceeding brought against the United States under the provisions of this title and all references thereto, and the United States shall be substituted as the party defendant. A copy of the petition shall be served upon the United States in accordance with the provisions of Rule 4(d)(4) of the Federal Rules of Civil Procedure. In the event the petition is filed in a civil action or proceeding pending in a State court, the action or proceeding may be removed without bond by the Attorney General to the district court of the United States for the district and division embracing the place in which it is pending. If, in considering the petition, the district court determines that the employee was not acting within the scope of his office or employment, the action or proceeding shall be remanded to the State court.

(4) Upon certification, any action or proceeding subject to paragraph (1), (2), or (3) shall proceed in the same manner as any action against the United States filed pursuant to section 1346(b) of this title and shall be subject to the limitations and exceptions applicable to those actions.

(5) Whenever an action or proceeding in which the United States is substituted as the party defendant under this subsection is dismissed for failure first to present a claim pursuant to section 2675(a) of this title, such a claim shall be deemed to be timely presented under section 2401(b) of this title if—

(A) the claim would have been timely had it been filed on the date the underlying civil action was commenced, and

(B) the claim is presented to the appropriate Federal agency within 60 days after dismissal of the civil action.

(e) The Attorney General may compromise or settle any claim asserted in such civil action or proceeding in the manner provided in section 2677, and with the same effect. As amended Sept. 21, 1961, Pub.L. 87–258, § 1,

75 Stat. 539; July 18, 1966, Pub.L. 89–506, § 5(a), 80 Stat. 307; Nov. 18, 1988, Pub.L. 100–694, §§ 5, 6, 102 Stat. 4564.

§ 2680. Exceptions

The provisions of this chapter and section 1346(b) of this title shall not apply to—

(a) Any claim based upon an act or omission of an employee of the Government, exercising due care, in the execution of a statute or regulation, whether or not such statute or regulation be valid, or based upon the exercise or performance or the failure to exercise or perform a discretionary function or duty on the part of a federal agency or an employee of the Government, whether or not the discretion involved be abused.

(b) Any claim arising out of the loss, miscarriage, or negligent transmission of letters or postal matter.

(c) Any claim arising in respect of the assessment or collection of any tax or customs duty, or the detention of any goods, merchandise, or other property by any officer of customs or excise or any other law enforcement officer, except that the provisions of this chapter and section 1346(b) of this title apply to any claim based on injury or loss of goods, merchandise, or other property, while in the possession of any officer of customs or excise or any other law enforcement officer, if—

(1) the property was seized for the purpose of forfeiture under any provision of Federal law providing for the forfeiture of property other than as a sentence imposed upon conviction of a criminal offense;

(2) the interest of the claimant was not forfeited;

(3) the interest of the claimant was not remitted or mitigated (if the property was subject to forfeiture); and

(4) the claimant was not convicted of a crime for which the interest of the claimant in the property was subject to forfeiture under a Federal criminal forfeiture law.

(d) Any claim for which a remedy is provided by sections 741–752, 781–790 of Title 46, relating to claims or suits in admiralty against the United States.

(e) Any claim arising out of an act or omission of any employee of the Government in administering the provisions of sections 1–31 of Title 50, Appendix.

(f) Any claim for damages caused by the imposition or establishment of a quarantine by the United States.

(g) [Repealed.]

(h) Any claim arising out of assault, battery, false imprisonment, false arrest, malicious prosecution, abuse of process, libel, slander, misrepresentation, deceit, or interference with contract rights: *Provid-*

ed, That, with regard to acts or omissions of investigative or law enforcement officers of the United States Government, the provisions of this chapter and section 1346(b) of this title shall apply to any claim arising, on or after the date of the enactment of this proviso, out of assault, battery, false imprisonment, false arrest, abuse of process, or malicious prosecution. For the purpose of this subsection, "investigative or law enforcement officer" means any officer of the United States who is empowered by law to execute searches, to seize evidence, or to make arrests for violations of Federal law.

(i) Any claim for damages caused by the fiscal operations of the Treasury or by the regulation of the monetary system.

(j) Any claim arising out of the combatant activities of the military or naval forces, or the Coast Guard, during time of war.

(k) Any claim arising in a foreign country.

(*l*) Any claim arising from the activities of the Tennessee Valley Authority.

(m) Any claim arising from the activities of the Panama Canal Company.

(n) Any claim arising from the activities of a Federal land bank, a Federal intermediate credit bank, or a bank for cooperatives. As amended July 16, 1949, c. 340, 63 Stat. 444; Sept. 26, 1950, c. 1049, §§ 2(a)(2), 13(5), 64 Stat. 1038, 1043; Aug. 18, 1959, Pub.L. 86–168, Title II, § 202(b), 73 Stat. 389; Mar. 16, 1974, Pub.L. 93–253, § 2, 88 Stat. 50; Apr. 25, 2000, Pub.L. 106–185, § 3(a), 114 Stat. 211.

*

SELECTED PROVISIONS OF OTHER PROCEDURAL STATUTES

TITLE 15, UNITED STATES CODE

§ 4. Jurisdiction of courts; duty of United States attorneys; procedure

The several district courts of the United States are invested with jurisdiction to prevent and restrain violations of sections 1 to 7 [Sherman Antitrust Act] of this title; and it shall be the duty of the several United States attorneys, in their respective districts, under the direction of the Attorney General, to institute proceedings in equity to prevent and restrain such violations. Such proceedings may be by way of petition setting forth the case and praying that such violation shall be enjoined or otherwise prohibited. When the parties complained of shall have been duly notified of such petition the court shall proceed, as soon as may be, to the hearing and determination of the case; and pending such petition and before final decree, the court may at any time make such temporary restraining order or prohibition as shall be deemed just in the premises.

§ 5. Bringing in additional parties

Whenever it shall appear to the court before which any proceeding under section 4 of this title may be pending, that the ends of justice require that other parties should be brought before the court, the court may cause them to be summoned, whether they reside in the district in which the court is held or not; and subpoenas to that end may be served in any district by the marshal thereof.

§ 15. Suits by persons injured

(a) Amount of recovery; prejudgment interest

Except as provided in subsection (b) of this section, any person who shall be injured in his business or property by reason of anything forbidden in the antitrust laws may sue therefor in any district court of the United States in the district in which the defendant resides or is found or has an agent, without respect to the amount in controversy, and shall recover threefold the damages by him sustained, and the cost of suit, including a reasonable attorney's fee. The court may award under this section, pursuant to a motion by such person promptly made, simple interest on actual damages for the period beginning on the date of service of such person's pleading setting forth a claim under the antitrust laws and ending on the date of judgment, or for any shorter period therein, if the court finds that the award of such interest for such period is just in the circumstances. In determining whether an award of interest under this section for any period is just in the circumstances, the court shall consider only—

(1) whether such person or the opposing party, or either party's representative, made motions or asserted claims or defenses so lacking in merit as to show that such party or representative acted intentionally for delay, or otherwise acted in bad faith;

(2) whether, in the course of the action involved, such person or the opposing party, or either party's representative, violated any applicable rule, statute, or court order providing for sanctions for dilatory behavior or otherwise providing for expeditious proceedings; and

(3) whether such person or the opposing party, or either party's representative, engaged in conduct primarily for the purpose of delaying the litigation or increasing the cost thereof.

(b) Amount of damages payable to foreign states and instrumentalities of foreign states

* * *

§ 15a. Suits by United States; amount of recovery; prejudgment interest

Whenever the United States is hereafter injured in its business or property by reason of anything forbidden in the antitrust laws it may sue therefor in the United States district court for the district in which the defendant resides or is found or has an agent, without respect to the amount in controversy, and shall recover threefold the damages by it sustained and the cost of suit. The court may award under this section, pursuant to a motion by the United States promptly made, simple interest on threefold the damages for the period beginning on the date of service of the pleading of the United States setting forth a claim under the antitrust laws and ending on the date of judgment, or for any shorter period therein, if the court finds that the award of such interest for such period is just in the circumstances. In determining whether an award of interest under this section for any period is just in the circumstances, the court shall consider only—

(1) whether the United States or the opposing party, or either party's representative, made motions or asserted claims or defenses so lacking in merit as to show that such party or representative acted intentionally for delay or otherwise acted in bad faith;

(2) whether, in the course of the action involved, the United States or the opposing party, or either party's representative, violated any applicable rule, statute, or court order providing for sanctions for dilatory behavior or otherwise providing for expeditious proceedings;

(3) whether the United States or the opposing party, or either party's representative, engaged in conduct primarily for the purpose of delaying the litigation or increasing the cost thereof; and

(4) whether the award of such interest is necessary to compensate the United States adequately for the injury sustained by the United States.

§ 15b. Limitation of actions

Any action to enforce any cause of action under sections 15, 15a, or 15c of this title shall be forever barred unless commenced within four years after the cause of action accrued. No cause of action barred under existing law on the effective date [1956] of this Act shall be revived by this Act.

§ 15c. Actions by State attorneys general

* * *

§ 16. Judgments

(a) Prima facie evidence; collateral estoppel

A final judgment or decree heretofore or hereafter rendered in any civil or criminal proceeding brought by or on behalf of the United States under the antitrust laws to the effect that a defendant has violated said laws shall be prima facie evidence against such defendant in any action or proceeding brought by any other party against such defendant under said laws as to all matters respecting which said judgment or decree would be an estoppel as between the parties thereto: *Provided,* That this section shall not apply to consent judgments or decrees entered before any testimony has been taken. Nothing contained in this section shall be construed to impose any limitation on the application of collateral estoppel, except that, in any action or proceeding brought under the antitrust laws, collateral estoppel effect shall not be given to any finding made by the Federal Trade Commission under the antitrust laws or under section 45 of this title which could give rise to a claim for relief under the antitrust laws.

* * *

(i) Suspension of limitations

Whenever any civil or criminal proceeding is instituted by the United States to prevent, restrain, or punish violations of any of the antitrust laws, but not including an action under section 15a of this title, the running of the statute of limitations in respect of every private or State right of action arising under said laws and based in whole or in part on any matter complained of in said proceeding shall be suspended during the pendency thereof and for one year thereafter: *Provided, however,* That whenever the running of the statute of limitations in respect of a cause of action arising under section 15 or 15c of this title is suspended hereunder, any action to enforce such cause of action shall be forever barred unless commenced either within the period of suspension or within four years after the cause of action accrued.

§ 22. District in which to sue corporation

Any suit, action, or proceeding under the antitrust laws against a corporation may be brought not only in the judicial district whereof it is an inhabitant, but also in any district wherein it may be found or transacts business; and all process in such cases may be served in the district of which it is an inhabitant, or wherever it may be found.

§ 23. Suits by United States; subpoenas for witnesses

In any suit, action, or proceeding brought by or on behalf of the United States subpoenas for witnesses who are required to attend a court of the United States in any judicial district in any case, civil or criminal, arising under the antitrust laws may run into any other district: *Provided*, That in civil cases no writ of subpoena shall issue for witnesses living out of the district in which the court is held at a greater distance than one hundred miles from the place of holding the same without the permission of the trial court being first had upon proper application and cause shown.

§ 25. Restraining violations; procedure

The several district courts of the United States are invested with jurisdiction to prevent and restrain violations of this [Clayton Antitrust] Act, and it shall be the duty of the several United States attorneys, in their respective districts, under the direction of the Attorney General, to institute proceedings in equity to prevent and restrain such violations. Such proceedings may be by way of petition setting forth the case and praying that such violation shall be enjoined or otherwise prohibited. When the parties complained of shall have been duly notified of such petition, the court shall proceed, as soon as may be, to the hearing and determination of the case; and pending such petition, and before final decree, the court may at any time make such temporary restraining order or prohibition as shall be deemed just in the premises. Whenever it shall appear to the court before which any such proceeding may be pending that the ends of justice require that other parties should be brought before the court, the court may cause them to be summoned whether they reside in the district in which the court is held or not, and subpoenas to that end may be served in any district by the marshal thereof.

§ 26. Injunctive relief for private parties; exception; costs

Any person, firm, corporation, or association shall be entitled to sue for and have injunctive relief, in any court of the United States having jurisdiction over the parties, against threatened loss or damage by a violation of the antitrust laws, including sections 13, 14, 18, and 19 of this title, when and under the same conditions and principles as injunctive relief against threatened conduct that will cause loss or damage is granted by courts of equity, under the rules governing such proceedings, and upon the execution of proper bond against damages for an injunction improvidently granted and a showing that the danger of irreparable loss or damage is immediate, a preliminary injunction may issue: *Provided,* That nothing herein contained shall be construed to entitle any person, firm, corporation, or association, except the United States, to bring suit for injunctive relief against any common carrier subject to the jurisdiction of the Surface Transportation Board under subtitle IV of title 49, United States Code. In any action under this section in which the plaintiff substantially prevails, the court shall award the cost of suit, including a reasonable attorney's fee, to such plaintiff.

TITLE 42, UNITED STATES CODE

§ 1983. Civil action for deprivation of rights

Every person who, under color of any statute, ordinance, regulation, custom, or usage, of any State or Territory or the District of Columbia, subjects, or causes to be subjected, any citizen of the United States or other person within the jurisdiction thereof to the deprivation of any rights, privileges, or immunities secured by the Constitution and laws, shall be liable to the party injured in an action at law, suit in equity, or other proper proceeding for redress, except that in any action brought against a judicial officer for an act or omission taken in such officer's judicial capacity, injunctive relief shall not be granted unless a declaratory decree was violated or declaratory relief was unavailable. For the purposes of this section, any Act of Congress applicable exclusively to the District of Columbia shall be considered to be a statute of the District of Columbia.

§ 1988. Proceedings in vindication of civil rights; attorney's fees; expert fees

(a) Applicability of statutory and common law

The jurisdiction in civil and criminal matters conferred on the district courts by the provisions of this Title, and of Title "CIVIL RIGHTS," and of Title "CRIMES," for the protection of all persons in the United States in their civil rights, and for their vindication, shall be exercised and enforced in conformity with the laws of the United States, so far as such laws are suitable to carry the same into effect; but in all cases where they are not adapted to the object, or are deficient in the provisions necessary to furnish suitable remedies and punish offenses against law, the common law, as modified and changed by the constitution and statutes of the State wherein the court having jurisdiction of such civil or criminal cause is held, so far as the same is not inconsistent with the Constitution and laws of the United States, shall be extended to and govern the said courts in the trial and disposition of the cause, and, if it is of a criminal nature, in the infliction of punishment on the party found guilty.

(b) Attorney's fees

In any action or proceeding to enforce a provision of sections 1981, 1981a, 1982, 1983, 1985, and 1986 of this title, title IX of Public Law 92–318, the Religious Freedom Restoration Act of 1993, the Religious Land Use and Institutionalized Persons Act of 2000, title VI of the Civil Rights Act of 1964, or section 40302 of the Violence Against Women Act of 1994, the court, in its discretion, may allow the prevailing party, other than the United States, a reasonable attorney's fee as part of the costs, except that in any action brought against a judicial officer for an act or omission taken in such officer's judicial capacity such officer shall not be held liable for any costs, including attorney's fees, unless such action was clearly in excess of such officer's jurisdiction.

(c) Expert fees

In awarding an attorney's fee under subsection (b) of this section in any action or proceeding to enforce a provision of section 1981 or 1981a of this title, the court, in its discretion, may include expert fees as part of the attorney's fee.

CALIFORNIA

Code of Civil Procedure

§ 410.10. Basis

A court of this state may exercise jurisdiction on any basis not inconsistent with the Constitution of this state or of the United States.

NEW YORK

Judiciary Law

§ 140–b. General jurisdiction of supreme court

The general jurisdiction in law and equity which the supreme court possesses under the provisions of the constitution [art. VI, § 7] includes all the jurisdiction which was possessed and exercised by the supreme court of the colony of New York at any time, and by the court of chancery in England on the fourth day of July, seventeen hundred seventy-six, with the exceptions, additions and limitations created and imposed by the constitution and laws of the state. Subject to those exceptions and limitations the supreme court of the state has all the powers and authority of each of those courts and may exercise them in like manner.

Civil Practice Law and Rules

Article 2—Limitations of Time

§ 201. Application of article

An action, including one brought in the name or for the benefit of the state, must be commenced within the time specified in this article unless a different time is prescribed by law or a shorter time is prescribed by written agreement. No court shall extend the time limited by law for the commencement of an action.

§ 202. Cause of action accruing without the state

An action based upon a cause of action accruing without the state cannot be commenced after the expiration of the time limited by the laws of either the state or the place without the state where the cause of action accrued, except that where the cause of action accrued in favor of a resident of the state the time limited by the laws of the state shall apply.

§ 203. Method of computing periods of limitation generally

(a) Accrual of cause of action and interposition of claim. The time within which an action must be commenced, except as otherwise expressly prescribed, shall be computed from the time the cause of action accrued to the time the claim is interposed.

(b) Claim in complaint where action commenced by service. In an action which is commenced by service, a claim asserted in the complaint is interposed against the defendant or a co-defendant united in interest with such defendant when:

1. the summons is served upon the defendant; or

2. first publication of the summons against the defendant is made pursuant to an order, and publication is subsequently completed; or

3. an order for a provisional remedy other than attachment is granted, if, within thirty days thereafter, the summons is served upon the defendant or first publication of the summons against the defendant is made pursuant to an order and publication is subsequently completed, or, where the defendant dies within thirty days after the order is granted and before the summons is served upon the defendant or publication is completed, if the summons is served upon the defendant's executor or administrator within sixty days after letters are issued; for this purpose seizure of a chattel in an action to recover a chattel is a provisional remedy; or

4. an order of attachment is granted, if the summons is served in accordance with the provisions of section 6213; or

5. the summons is delivered to the sheriff of that county outside the city of New York or is filed with the clerk of that county within the city of New York in which the defendant resides, is employed or is doing business, or if none of the foregoing is known to the plaintiff after reasonable inquiry, then of the county in which the defendant is known to have last resided, been employed or been engaged in business, or in which the cause of action arose; or if the defendant is a corporation, of a county in which it may be served or in which the cause of action arose; provided that:

(i) the summons is served upon the defendant within sixty days after the period of limitation would have expired but for this provision; or

(ii) first publication of the summons against the defendant is made pursuant to an order within sixty days after the period of limitation would have expired but for this provision and publication is subsequently completed; or

(iii) the summons is served upon the defendant's executor or administrator within sixty days after letters are issued, where the defendant dies within sixty days after the period of limitation would have expired but for this provision and before the summons is served upon the defendant or publication is completed.

6. in an action to be commenced in a court not of record, the summons is delivered for service upon the defendant to any officer author-

ized to serve it in a county, city or town in which the defendant resides, is employed or is doing business, or if none of the foregoing be known to the plaintiff after reasonable inquiry, then in a county, city or town in which defendant is known to have last resided, been employed or been engaged in business, or, where the defendant is a corporation, in a county, city or town in which it may be served, if the summons is served upon the defendant within sixty days after the period of limitation would have expired but for this provision; or, where the defendant dies within sixty days after the period of limitation would have expired but for this provision and before the summons is served upon the defendant, if the summons is served upon his executor or administrator within sixty days after letters are issued.

(c) Claim in complaint where action commenced by filing. In an action which is commenced by filing, a claim asserted in the complaint is interposed against the defendant or a co-defendant united in interest with such defendant when the action is commenced.

(d) Defense or counterclaim. A defense or counterclaim is interposed when a pleading containing it is served. A defense or counterclaim is not barred if it was not barred at the time the claims asserted in the complaint were interposed, except that if the defense or counterclaim arose from the transactions, occurrences, or series of transactions or occurrences, upon which a claim asserted in the complaint depends, it is not barred to the extent of the demand in the complaint notwithstanding that it was barred at the time the claims asserted in the complaint were interposed.

(e) Effect upon defense or counterclaim of termination of action because of death or by dismissal or voluntary discontinuance. Where a defendant has served an answer containing a defense or counterclaim and the action is terminated because of the plaintiff's death or by dismissal or voluntary discontinuance, the time which elapsed between the commencement and termination of the action is not a part of the time within which an action must be commenced to recover upon the claim in the defense or counterclaim or the time within which the defense or counterclaim may be interposed in another action brought by the plaintiff or his successor in interest.

(f) Claim in amended pleading. A claim asserted in an amended pleading is deemed to have been interposed at the time the claims in the original pleading were interposed, unless the original pleading does not give notice of the transactions, occurrences, or series of transactions or occurrences, to be proved pursuant to the amended pleading.

(g) Time computed from actual or imputed discovery of facts. Except as provided in article two of the uniform commercial code or in section two hundred fourteen–a of this chapter, where the time within which an action must be commenced is computed from the time when facts were discovered or from the time when facts could with reasonable diligence have been discovered, or from either of such times, the action must be commenced within two years after such actual or imputed discovery or within the period otherwise provided, computed from the time the cause of action accrued, whichever is longer.

SELECTED PROVISIONS

§ 204. Stay of commencement of action; demand for arbitration

* * *

§ 205. Termination of action

(a) New action by plaintiff. If an action is timely commenced and is terminated in any other manner than by a voluntary discontinuance, a failure to obtain personal jurisdiction over the defendant, a dismissal of the complaint for neglect to prosecute the action, or a final judgment upon the merits, the plaintiff, or, if the plaintiff dies, and the cause of action survives, his or her executor or administrator, may commence a new action upon the same transaction or occurrence or series of transactions or occurrences within six months after the termination provided that the new action would have been timely commenced at the time of commencement of the prior action and that service upon defendant is effected within such six-month period.

(b) Defense or counterclaim. Where the defendant has served an answer and the action is terminated in any manner, and a new action upon the same transaction or occurrence or series of transactions or occurrences is commenced by the plaintiff or his successor in interest, the assertion of any cause of action or defense by the defendant in the new action shall be timely if it was timely asserted in the prior action.

(c) Application. This section also applies to a proceeding brought under the workers' compensation law.

§ 206. Computing periods of limitation in particular actions

[Treatment of actions where a demand is necessary to entitle a person to commence the action and of actions based on misconduct of an agent, on breach of a covenant of seizin or against incumbrances, or on account.]

§ 207. Defendant's absence from state or residence under false name

If, when a cause of action accrues against a person, he is without the state, the time within which the action must be commenced shall be computed from the time he comes into or returns to the state. If, after a cause of action has accrued against a person, that person departs from the state and remains continuously absent therefrom for four months or more, or that person resides within the state under a false name which is unknown to the person entitled to commence the action, the time of his absence or residence within the state under such a false name is not a part of the time within which the action must be commenced. If an action is commenced against a person described above, the time within which service must be made on such person in accordance with subdivisions (a) and (b) of section three hundred six-b of this chapter shall be computed in accordance with this section. This section does not apply:

1. while there is in force a designation, voluntary or involuntary, made pursuant to law, of a person to whom a summons may be delivered within the state with the same effect as if served personally within the state; or

2. while a foreign corporation has one or more officers or other persons in the state on whom a summons against such corporation may be served; or

3. while jurisdiction over the person of the defendant can be obtained without personal delivery of the summons to the defendant within the state.

§ 208. Infancy, insanity

If a person entitled to commence an action is under a disability because of infancy or insanity at the time the cause of action accrues, and the time otherwise limited for commencing the action is three years or more and expires no later than three years after the disability ceases, or the person under the disability dies, the time within which the action must be commenced shall be extended to three years after the disability ceases or the person under the disability dies, whichever event first occurs; if the time otherwise limited is less than three years, the time shall be extended by the period of disability. The time within which the action must be commenced shall not be extended by this provision beyond ten years after the cause of action accrues, except, in any action other than for medical, dental or podiatric malpractice, where the person was under a disability due to infancy. This section shall not apply to an action to recover a penalty or forfeiture, or against a sheriff or other officer for an escape.

§ 209. War

* * *

§ 210. Death of claimant or person liable; cause of action accruing after death and before grant of letters

(a) Death of claimant. Where a person entitled to commence an action dies before the expiration of the time within which the action must be commenced and the cause of action survives, an action may be commenced by his representative within one year after his death.

(b) Death of person liable. The period of eighteen months after the death, within or without the state, of a person against whom a cause of action exists is not a part of the time within which the action must be commenced against his executor or administrator.

(c) Cause of action accruing after death and before grant of letters. In an action by an executor or administrator to recover personal property wrongfully taken after the death and before the issuance of letters, or to recover damages for taking, detaining or injuring personal property within that period, the time within which the action must be commenced shall be computed from the time the letters are issued or from three years after the death, whichever event first occurs. Any distributee, next of kin, legatee or creditor who was under a disability prescribed in section 208 at the time the cause of action accrued, may, within two years after the disability ceases, commence an action to recover such damages or the value of such property as he would have received upon a final distribution of the estate if an action had been timely commenced by the executor or administrator.

§ 211. Actions to be commenced within twenty years

(a) On a bond. An action to recover principal or interest upon a written instrument evidencing an indebtedness of the state of New York or of any person, association or public or private corporation, originally sold by the issuer after publication of an advertisement for bids for the issue in a newspaper of general circulation and secured only by a pledge of the faith and credit of the issuer, regardless of whether a sinking fund is or may be established for its redemption, must be commenced within twenty years after the cause of action accrues. This subdivision does not apply to actions upon written instruments evidencing an indebtedness of any corporation, association or person under the jurisdiction of the public service commission, the commissioner of transportation, the interstate commerce commission, the federal communications commission, the civil aeronautics board, the federal power commission, or any other regulatory commission or board of a state or of the federal government. This subdivision applies to all causes of action, including those barred on April eighteenth, nineteen hundred fifty, by the provisions of the civil practice act then effective.

(b) On a money judgment. A money judgment is presumed to be paid and satisfied after the expiration of twenty years from the time when the party recovering it was first entitled to enforce it. This presumption is conclusive, except as against a person who within the twenty years acknowledges an indebtedness, or makes a payment, of all or part of the amount recovered by the judgment, or his heir or personal representative, or a person whom he otherwise represents. Such an acknowledgment must be in writing and signed by the person to be charged. Property acquired by an enforcement order or by levy upon an execution is a payment, unless the person to be charged shows that it did not include property claimed by him. If such an acknowledgment or payment is made, the judgment is conclusively presumed to be paid and satisfied as against any person after the expiration of twenty years after the last acknowledgment or payment made by him. The presumption created by this subdivision may be availed of under an allegation that the action was not commenced within the time limited.

(c) By state for real property. The state will not sue a person for or with respect to real property, or the rents or profits thereof, by reason of the right or title of the state to the same, unless the cause of action accrued, or the state, or those from whom it claims, have received the rents and profits of the real property or of some part thereof, within twenty years before the commencement of the action.

(d) By grantee of state for real property. An action shall not be commenced for or with respect to real property by a person claiming by virtue of letters patent or a grant from the state, unless it might have been maintained by the state, as prescribed in this section, if the patent or grant had not been issued or made.

(e) For support, alimony or maintenance. An action or proceeding to enforce any temporary order, permanent order or judgment of any court of competent jurisdiction which awards support, alimony or maintenance, regardless of whether or not arrears have been reduced to a money judgment, must be commenced within twenty years from the date of a default in payment. This section shall only apply to orders which have been entered subsequent to the date upon which this section shall become effective.

§ 212. Actions to be commenced within ten years

(a) Possession necessary to recover real property. An action to recover real property or its possession cannot be commenced unless the plaintiff, or his predecessor in interest, was seized or possessed of the premises within ten years before the commencement of the action.

(b) Annulment of letters patent. Where letters patent or a grant of real property, issued or made by the state, are declared void on the ground of fraudulent suggestion or concealment, forfeiture, mistake or ignorance of a material fact, wrongful detaining or defective title, an action to recover the premises may be commenced by the state or by a subsequent patentee or grantee, or his successor in interest, within ten years after the determination is made.

(c) To redeem from a mortgage. An action to redeem real property from a mortgage with or without an account of rents and profits may be commenced by the mortgagor or his successors in interest, against the mortgagee in possession, or against the purchaser of the mortgaged premises at a foreclosure sale in an action in which the mortgagor or his successors in interest were not excluded from their interest in the mortgaged premises, or against a successor in interest of either, unless the mortgagee, purchaser or successor was continuously possessed of the premises for ten years after the breach or non-fulfillment of a condition or covenant of the mortgage, or the date of recording of the deed of the premises to the purchaser.

(d) To recover under an affidavit of support of an alien. An action under section one hundred twenty-two of the social services law to recover amounts paid to or on behalf of an alien for whom an affidavit of support pursuant to section 213A of the immigration and naturalization act has been signed.

§ 213. Actions to be commenced within six years: where not otherwise provided for; on contract; on sealed instrument; on bond or note, and mortgage upon real property; by state based on misappropriation of public property; based on mistake; by corporation against director, officer or stockholder; based on fraud

The following actions must be commenced within six years:

1. an action for which no limitation is specifically prescribed by law;

2. an action upon a contractual obligation or liability, express or implied, except as provided in section two hundred thirteen-a of this article or article 2 of the uniform commercial code or article 36–B of the general business law;

3. an action upon a sealed instrument;

4. an action upon a bond or note, the payment of which is secured by a mortgage upon real property, or upon a bond or note and mortgage so secured, or upon a mortgage of real property, or any interest therein;

5. an action by the state based upon the spoliation or other misappropriation of public property; the time within which the action must be commenced shall be computed from discovery by the state of the facts relied upon;

6. an action based upon mistake;

7. an action by or on behalf of a corporation against a present or former director, officer or stockholder for an accounting, or to procure a judgment on the ground of fraud, or to enforce a liability, penalty or forfeiture, or to recover damages for waste or for an injury to property or for an accounting in conjunction therewith;

8. an action based upon fraud; the time within which the action must be commenced shall be computed from the time the plaintiff or the person under whom he claims discovered the fraud, or could with reasonable diligence have discovered it.

§ 213–a. Actions to be commenced within four years: residential rent overcharge

An action on a residential rent overcharge shall be commenced within four years of the first overcharge alleged and no determination of an overcharge and no award or calculation of an award of the amount of any overcharge may be based upon an overcharge having occurred more than four years before the action is commenced. This section shall preclude examination of the rental history of the housing accommodation prior to the four-year period immediately preceding the commencement of the action.

§ 213–b. Action by a victim of a criminal offense

Notwithstanding any other limitation set forth in this article or in article five of the estates, powers and trusts law, an action by a crime victim, or the representative of a crime victim, as defined in subdivision six of section six hundred twenty-one of the executive law, may be commenced to recover damages from a defendant: (1) convicted of a crime which is the subject of such action, for any injury or loss resulting therefrom within seven years of the date of the crime or (2) convicted of a specified crime as defined in paragraph (e) of subdivision one of section six hundred thirty-two-a of the executive law which is the subject of such action for any injury or loss resulting therefrom within ten years of the date the defendant was convicted of such specified crime.

§ 214. Actions to be commenced within three years: for non-payment of money collected on execution; for penalty created by statute; to recover chattel; for injury to property; for personal injury; for malpractice other than medical, dental or podiatric malpractice; to annul a marriage on the ground of fraud

The following actions must be commenced within three years:

1. an action against a sheriff, constable or other officer for the non-payment of money collected upon an execution;

2. an action to recover upon a liability, penalty or forfeiture created or imposed by statute except as provided in sections 213 and 215;

3. an action to recover a chattel or damages for the taking or detaining of a chattel;

4. an action to recover damages for an injury to property;

5. an action to recover damages for a personal injury except as provided in sections 214–b and 215;

6. an action to recover damages for malpractice, other than medical, dental or podiatric malpractice, regardless of whether the underlying theory is based in contract or tort; and

7. an action to annul a marriage on the ground of fraud; the time within which the action must be commenced shall be computed from the time the plaintiff discovered the facts constituting the fraud, but if the plaintiff is a person other than the spouse whose consent was obtained by fraud, the time within which the action must be commenced shall be computed from the time, if earlier, that that spouse discovered the facts constituting the fraud.

§ 214–a. Action for medical, dental or podiatric malpractice to be commenced within two years and six months; exceptions

An action for medical, dental or podiatric malpractice must be commenced within two years and six months of the act, omission or failure complained of or last treatment where there is continuous treatment for the same illness, injury or condition which gave rise to the said act, omission or failure; provided, however, that where the action is based upon the discovery of a foreign object in the body of the patient, the action may be commenced within one year of the date of such discovery or of the date of discovery of facts which would reasonably lead to such discovery, whichever is earlier. For the purpose of this section the term "continuous treatment" shall not include examinations undertaken at the request of the patient for the sole purpose of ascertaining the state of the patient's condition. For the purpose of this section the term "foreign object" shall not include a chemical compound, fixation device or prosthetic aid or device.

§ 214–b. Action to recover damages for personal injury caused by contact with or exposure to phenoxy herbicides

Notwithstanding any provision of law to the contrary, an action to recover damages for personal injury caused by contact with or exposure to phenoxy herbicides while serving as a member of the armed forces of the United States in Indo-China from January first, nineteen hundred sixty-two through May seventh, nineteen hundred seventy-five, may be commenced within two years from the date of the discovery of such injury, or within two years from the date when through the exercise of reasonable diligence the cause of such injury should have been discovered, whichever is later.

§ 214–c. Certain actions to be commenced within three years of discovery

1. In this section: "exposure" means direct or indirect exposure by absorption, contact, ingestion, inhalation, implantation or injection.

2. Notwithstanding the provisions of section 214, the three year period within which an action to recover damages for personal injury or injury to property caused by the latent effects of exposure to any substance or combination of substances, in any form, upon or within the body or upon or within property must be commenced shall be computed from the date of discovery of the injury by the plaintiff or from the date when through the exercise of reasonable diligence such injury should have been discovered by the plaintiff, whichever is earlier.

3. For the purposes of sections fifty-e and fifty-i of the general municipal law, section thirty-eight hundred thirteen of the education law and the provisions of any general, special or local law or charter requiring as a condition precedent to commencement of an action or special proceeding that a notice of claim be filed or presented within a specified period of time after the claim or action accrued, a claim or action for personal injury or injury to property caused by the latent effects of exposure to any substance or combination of substances, in any form, upon or within the body or upon or within property shall be deemed to have accrued on the date of discovery of the injury by the plaintiff or on the date when through the exercise of reasonable diligence the injury should have been discovered, whichever is earlier.

4. Notwithstanding the provisions of subdivisions two and three of this section, where the discovery of the cause of the injury is alleged to have occurred less than five years after discovery of the injury or when with reasonable diligence such injury should have been discovered, whichever is earlier, an action may be commenced or a claim filed within one year of such discovery of the cause of the injury; provided, however, if any such action is commenced or claim filed after the period in which it would otherwise have been authorized pursuant to subdivision two or three of this section the plaintiff or claimant shall be required to allege and prove that technical, scientific or medical knowledge and information sufficient to ascertain the cause of his injury had not been discovered, identified or determined prior to the expiration of the period within which the action or claim would have been authorized and that he has otherwise satisfied the requirements of subdivisions two and three of this section.

5. This section shall not be applicable to any action for medical or dental malpractice.

6. This section shall be applicable to acts, omissions or failures occurring prior to, on or after July first, nineteen hundred eighty-six, except that this section shall not be applicable to any act, omission or failure:

(a) which occurred prior to July first, nineteen hundred eighty-six, and

(b) which caused or contributed to an injury that either was discovered or through the exercise of reasonable diligence should have been discovered prior to such date, and

(c) an action for which was or would have been barred because the applicable period of limitation had expired prior to such date.

§ 214–d. Limitations on certain actions against licensed engineers and architects

* * *

§ 214–e. Action to recover damages for personal injury caused by the infusion of such blood products which result in the contraction of the human immunodeficiency virus (HIV) and/or AIDS

Notwithstanding any provision of law to the contrary, any cause of action for an injury or death against a proprietary manufacturer of blood products for damages involving the infusion of such blood products which resulted in the contraction of the human immunodeficiency virus (HIV) and/or AIDS which is barred as of the effective date of this section because the applicable period of limitation has expired is hereby revived, and an action thereon may be commenced and prosecuted provided such action is commenced within two years of the effective date of this section. The provisions of this section shall be inapplicable to any civil action governed by the statute of limitations of another jurisdiction.

§ 215. Actions to be commenced within one year: against sheriff, coroner or constable; for escape of prisoner; for assault, battery, false imprisonment, malicious prosecution, libel or slander; for violation of right of privacy; for penalty given to informer; on arbitration award

The following actions shall be commenced within one year:

1. an action against a sheriff, coroner or constable, upon a liability incurred by him by doing an act in his official capacity or by omission of an official duty, except the non-payment of money collected upon an execution;

2. an action against an officer for the escape of a prisoner arrested or imprisoned by virtue of a civil mandate;

3. an action to recover damages for assault, battery, false imprisonment, malicious prosecution, libel, slander, false words causing special damages, or a violation of the right of privacy under section fifty-one of the civil rights law;

4. an action to enforce a penalty or forfeiture created by statute and given wholly or partly to any person who will prosecute; if the action is not commenced within the year by a private person, it may be commenced on behalf of the state, within three years after the commission of the offense, by the attorney-general or the district attorney of the county where the offense was committed; and

5. an action upon an arbitration award.

6. An action to recover any overcharge of interest or to enforce a penalty for such overcharge.

7. an action by a tenant pursuant to subdivision three of section two hundred twenty-three-b of the real property law.

8. Whenever it is shown that a criminal action against the same defendant has been commenced with respect to the event or occurrence from which a claim governed by this section arises, the plaintiff shall have at least one year from the termination of the criminal action as defined in section 1.20 of the criminal procedure law in which to commence the civil action, notwithstanding that the time in which to commence such action has already expired or has less than a year remaining.

§ 217. Proceeding against body or officer; actions complaining about conduct that would constitute a union's breach of its duty of fair representation; four months

1. Unless a shorter time is provided in the law authorizing the proceeding, a proceeding against a body or officer must be commenced within four months after the determination to be reviewed becomes final and binding upon the petitioner or the person whom he represents in law or in fact, or after the respondent's refusal, upon the demand of the petitioner or the person whom he represents, to perform its duty; or with leave of the court where the petitioner or the person whom he represents, at the time such determination became final and binding upon him or at the time of such refusal, was under a disability specified in section 208, within two years after such time.

2. (a) Any action or proceeding against an employee organization subject to article fourteen of the civil service law or article twenty of the labor law which complains that such employee organization has breached its duty of fair representation regarding someone to whom such employee organization has a duty shall be commenced within four months of the date the employee or former employee knew or should have known that the breach has occurred, or within four months of the date the employee or former employee suffers actual harm, whichever is later.

(b) Any action or proceeding by an employee or former employee against an employer subject to article fourteen of the civil service law or article twenty of the labor law, an essential element of which is that an employee organization breached its duty of fair representation to the person making the complaint, shall be commenced within four months of the date the employee or former employee knew or should have known that the breach has occurred, or within four months of the date the employee or former employee suffers actual harm, whichever is later.

Article 3—Jurisdiction and Service, Appearance and Choice of Court

§ 301. Jurisdiction over persons, property or status

A court may exercise such jurisdiction over persons, property, or status as might have been exercised heretofore.

§ 302. Personal jurisdiction by acts of non-domiciliaries

(a) Acts which are the basis of jurisdiction. As to a cause of action arising from any of the acts enumerated in this section, a court may exercise personal jurisdiction over any non-domiciliary, or his executor or administrator, who in person or through an agent:

1. transacts any business within the state or contracts anywhere to supply goods or services in the state; or

2. commits a tortious act within the state, except as to a cause of action for defamation of character arising from the act; or

3. commits a tortious act without the state causing injury to person or property within the state, except as to a cause of action for defamation of character arising from the act, if he

(i) regularly does or solicits business, or engages in any other persistent course of conduct, or derives substantial revenue from goods used or consumed or services rendered, in the state, or

(ii) expects or should reasonably expect the act to have consequences in the state and derives substantial revenue from interstate or international commerce; or

4. owns, uses or possesses any real property situated within the state.

(b) Personal jurisdiction over non-resident defendant in matrimonial actions or family court proceedings. A court in any matrimonial action or family court proceeding involving a demand for support, alimony, maintenance, distributive awards or special relief in matrimonial actions may exercise personal jurisdiction over the respondent or defendant notwithstanding the fact that he or she no longer is a resident or domiciliary of this state, or over his or her executor or administrator, if the party seeking support is a resident of or domiciled in this state at the time such demand is made, provided that this state was the matrimonial domicile of the parties before their separation, or the defendant abandoned the plaintiff in this state, or the claim for support, alimony, maintenance, distributive awards or special relief in matrimonial actions accrued under the laws of this state or under an agreement executed in this state. The family court may exercise personal jurisdiction over a non-resident respondent to the extent provided in sections one hundred fifty-four and one thousand thirty-six of the family court act.

(c) Effect of appearance. Where personal jurisdiction is based solely upon this section, an appearance does not confer such jurisdiction with respect to causes of action not arising from an act enumerated in this section.

§ 303. Designation of attorney as agent for service

The commencement of an action in the state by a person not subject to personal jurisdiction is a designation by him of his attorney appearing in the action or of the clerk of the court if no attorney appears, as agent, during the pendency of the action, for service of a summons pursuant to section 308, in any separate action in which such a person is a defendant and another party to the action is a plaintiff if such separate action would have been permitted as a counterclaim had the action been brought in the supreme court.

§ 307. Personal service upon the state

* * *

§ 308. Personal service upon a natural person

Personal service upon a natural person shall be made by any of the following methods:

1. by delivering the summons within the state to the person to be served; or

2. by delivering the summons within the state to a person of suitable age and discretion at the actual place of business, dwelling place or usual place of abode of the person to be served and by either mailing the summons to the person to be served at his or her last known residence or by mailing the summons by first class mail to the person to be served at his or her actual place of business in an envelope bearing the legend "personal and confidential" and not indicating on the outside thereof, by return address or otherwise, that the communication is from an attorney or concerns an action against the person to be served, such delivery and mailing to be effected within twenty days of each other; proof of such service shall be filed with the clerk of the court designated in the summons within twenty days of either such delivery or mailing, whichever is effected later; service shall be complete ten days after such filing; proof of service shall identify such person of suitable age and discretion and state the date, time and place of service, except in matrimonial actions where service hereunder may be made pursuant to an order made in accordance with the provisions of subdivision a of section two hundred thirty-two of the domestic relations law; or

3. by delivering the summons within the state to the agent for service of the person to be served as designated under rule 318, except in matrimonial actions where service hereunder may be made pursuant to an order made in accordance with the provisions of subdivision a of section two hundred thirty-two of the domestic relations law;

4. where service under paragraphs one and two cannot be made with due diligence, by affixing the summons to the door of either the actual place of business, dwelling place or usual place of abode within the state of the person to be served and by either mailing the summons to such person at his or her last known residence or by mailing the summons by first class mail to the person to be served at his or her actual place of business in an envelope bearing the legend "personal and confidential" and not indicating on the outside thereof, by return address or otherwise, that the communication is from an attorney or concerns an action against the person to be served, such affixing and mailing to be effected within twenty days of each other; proof of such service shall be filed with the clerk of the court designated in the summons within twenty days of either such affixing or mailing, whichever is effected later; service shall be complete ten days after such filing, except in matrimonial actions where service hereunder may be made pursuant to an order made in accordance with the provisions

of subdivision a of section two hundred thirty-two of the domestic relations law;

5. in such manner as the court, upon motion without notice, directs, if service is impracticable under paragraphs one, two and four of this section.

6. For purposes of this section, "actual place of business" shall include any location that the defendant, through regular solicitation or advertisement, has held out as its place of business.

§ 309. Personal service upon an infant, incompetent or conservatee

* * *

§ 310. Personal service upon a partnership

* * *

§ 311. Personal service upon a corporation or governmental subdivision

(a) Personal service upon a corporation or governmental subdivision shall be made by delivering the summons as follows:

1. upon any domestic or foreign corporation, to an officer, director, managing or general agent, or cashier or assistant cashier or to any other agent authorized by appointment or by law to receive service. A business corporation may also be served pursuant to section three hundred six or three hundred seven of the business corporation law. A not-for-profit corporation may also be served pursuant to section three hundred six or three hundred seven of the not-for-profit corporation law;

* * *

§ 312. Personal service upon a court, board or commission

* * *

§ 312–a. Personal service by mail

(a) Service. As an alternative to the methods of personal service authorized by section 307, 308, 310, 311 or 312 of this article, a summons and complaint, or summons and notice, or notice of petition and petition may be served by the plaintiff or any other person by mailing to the person or entity to be served, by first class mail, postage prepaid, a copy of the summons and complaint, or summons and notice or notice of petition and petition, together with two copies of a statement of service by mail and acknowledgement of receipt in the form set forth in subdivision (d) of this section, with a return envelope, postage prepaid, addressed to the sender.

(b) Completion of service and time to answer.

1. The defendant, an authorized employee of the defendant, defendant's attorney or an employee of the attorney must complete the acknowledgement of receipt and mail or deliver one copy of it within thirty (30)

days from the date of receipt. Service is complete on the date the signed acknowledgement of receipt is mailed or delivered to the sender. The signed acknowledgement of receipt shall constitute proof of service.

2. Where a complaint or petition is served with the summons or notice of petition, the defendant shall serve an answer within twenty (20) days after the date the signed acknowledgement of receipt is mailed or delivered to the sender.

(c) Affirmation. The acknowledgement of receipt of service shall be subscribed and affirmed as true under penalties of perjury and shall have the same force and effect as an affidavit.

(d) Form. The statement of service by mail and the acknowledgement of receipt of such service shall be in substantially the following form:

Statement of Service by Mail and
Acknowledgement of Receipt by Mail of
Summons and Complaint or Summons and Notice
or Notice of Petition and Petition

A. STATEMENT OF SERVICE BY MAIL

To: (Insert the name and address of the person or entity to be served.) The enclosed summons and complaint, or summons and notice, or notice of petition and petition (strike out inapplicable terms) are served pursuant to section 312–a of the Civil Practice Law and Rules.

To avoid being charged with the expense of service upon you, you must sign, date and complete the acknowledgement part of this form and mail or deliver one copy of the completed form to the sender within thirty (30) days from the date you receive it. You should keep a copy for your records or your attorney. If you wish to consult an attorney, you should do so as soon as possible before the thirty (30) days expire.

If you do not complete and return the form to the sender within thirty (30) days, you (or the party on whose behalf you are being served) will be required to pay expenses incurred in serving the summons and complaint, or summons and notice, or notice of petition and petition in any other manner permitted by law, and the cost of such service as permitted by law will be entered as a judgment against you.

If you have received a complaint or petition with this statement, the return of this statement and acknowledgement does not relieve you of the necessity to answer the complaint or petition. The time to answer expires twenty (20) days after the day you mail or deliver this form to the sender. If you wish to consult with an attorney, you should do so as soon as possible before the twenty (20) days expire.

If you are served on behalf of a corporation, unincorporated association, partnership or other entity, you must indicate under your signature your relationship to the entity. If you are served on behalf of another person and you are authorized to receive process, you must indicate under your signature your authority.

It is a crime to forge a signature or to make a false entry on this statement or on the acknowledgement.

B. ACKNOWLEDGEMENT OF RECEIPT OF SUMMONS AND COMPLAINT OR SUMMONS AND NOTICE OR NOTICE OF PETITION AND PETITION

I received a summons and complaint, or summons and notice, or notice of petition and petition (strike out inapplicable terms) in the above-captioned matter at (insert address). PLEASE CHECK ONE OF THE FOLLOWING;

IF 2 IS CHECKED, COMPLETE AS INDICATED:

1. / /I am not in military service.

2. / /I am in military service, and my rank, serial number and branch of service are as follows:

Rank:

____

Serial number:

____

Branch of Service:

____

TO BE COMPLETED REGARDLESS OF MILITARY STATUS:

Date:

____

(Date this Acknowledgement is executed)

I affirm the above as true under penalty of perjury.

____

Signature

____

Print name

____

Name of Defendant for which acting

____

Position with Defendant for which acting (i.e., officer, attorney, etc.)

PLEASE COMPLETE ALL BLANKS INCLUDING DATES

(e) Subsequent service. Where a duly executed acknowledgement is not returned, upon the subsequent service of process in another manner permitted by law, the summons or notice of petition or paper served with the summons or notice of petition shall indicate that an attempt previously was made to effect service pursuant to this section.

(f) Disbursements. Where the signed acknowledgement of receipt is not returned within thirty (30) days after receipt of the documents mailed pursuant to subdivision (a) of this section, the reasonable expense of serving process by an alternative method shall be taxed by the court on notice pursuant to section 8402 of this chapter as a disbursement to the party serving process, and the court shall direct immediate judgment in that amount.

§ 313. Service without the state giving personal jurisdiction

A person domiciled in the state or subject to the jurisdiction of the courts of the state under section 301 or 302, or his executor or administrator, may be served with the summons without the state, in the same manner as service is made within the state, by any person authorized to make service within the state who is a resident of the state or by any person authorized to make service by the laws of the state, territory, possession or country in which service is made or by any duly qualified attorney, solicitor, barrister, or equivalent in such jurisdiction.

§ 314. Service without the state not giving personal jurisdiction in certain actions

Service may be made without the state by any person authorized by section 313 in the same manner as service is made within the state:

1. in a matrimonial action; or

2. where a judgment is demanded that the person to be served be excluded from a vested or contingent interest in or lien upon specific real or personal property within the state; or that such an interest or lien in favor of either party be enforced, regulated, defined or limited; or otherwise affecting the title to such property, including an action of interpleader or defensive interpleader; or

3. where a levy upon property of the person to be served has been made within the state pursuant to an order of attachment or a chattel of such person has been seized in an action to recover a chattel.

§ 315. Service by publication authorized

The court, upon motion without notice, shall order service of a summons by publication in an action described in section 314 if service cannot be made by another prescribed method with due diligence.

Rule 316. Service by publication [method]

* * *

§ 317. Defense by person to whom summons not personally delivered

A person served with a summons other than by personal delivery to him or to his agent for service designated under rule 318, within or without the state, who does not appear may be allowed to defend the action within one year after he obtains knowledge of entry of the judgment, but in no event more than five years after such entry, upon a finding of the court that he did not personally receive notice of the summons in time to defend and has a meritorious defense. If the defense is successful, the court may direct and enforce restitution in the same manner and subject to the same conditions as where a judgment is reversed or modified on appeal. This section does not apply to an action for divorce, annulment or partition.

Rule 318. Designation of agent for service

A person may be designated by a natural person, corporation or partnership as an agent for service in a writing, executed and acknowledged in the same manner as a deed, with the consent of the agent endorsed thereon. The writing shall be filed in the office of the clerk of the county in which the principal to be served resides or has its principal office. The designation shall remain in effect for three years from such filing unless it has been revoked by the filing of a revocation, or by the death, judicial declaration of incompetency or legal termination of the agent or principal.

Rule 320. Defendant's appearance

(a) Requirement of appearance. The defendant appears by serving an answer or a notice of appearance, or by making a motion which has the effect of extending the time to answer. An appearance shall be made within twenty days after service of the summons, except that if the summons was served on the defendant by delivering it to an official of the state authorized to receive service in his behalf or if it was served pursuant to section 303, subdivision two, three, four or five of section 308, or sections 313, 314 or 315, the appearance shall be made within thirty days after service is complete. If the complaint is not served with the summons, the time to appear may be extended as provided in subdivision (b) of section 3012.

(b) When appearance confers personal jurisdiction, generally. Subject to the provisions of subdivision (c), an appearance of the defendant is equivalent to personal service of the summons upon him, unless an objection to jurisdiction under paragraph eight of subdivision (a) of rule 3211 is asserted by motion or in the answer as provided in rule 3211.

(c) When appearance confers personal jurisdiction, in certain actions; limited appearance. When the court's jurisdiction is not based upon personal service on the defendant, an appearance is not equivalent to personal service upon the defendant:

1. in a case specified in subdivision (3) of section 314, if jurisdiction is based solely upon a levy on defendant's property within the state pursuant to an order of attachment; or

2. in any other case specified in section 314, if an objection to jurisdiction under paragraphs eight [personal jurisdiction] or nine [nonpersonal jurisdiction] of subdivision (a) of rule 3211, or both, is asserted by motion or in the answer as provided in rule 3211, unless the defendant proceeds with the defense after asserting the objection to jurisdiction and the objection is not ultimately sustained.

(d) Appearance after first publication. Where the defendant appears during the period of publication of a summons against him, the service by publication shall be deemed completed by the appearance.

SELECTED PROVISIONS

Rule 327. Inconvenient forum

(a) When the court finds that in the interest of substantial justice the action should be heard in another forum, the court, on the motion of any party, may stay or dismiss the action in whole or in part on any conditions that may be just. The domicile or residence in this state of any party to the action shall not preclude the court from staying or dismissing the action.

(b) Notwithstanding the provisions of subdivision (a) of this rule, the court shall not stay or dismiss any action on the ground of inconvenient forum, where the action arises out of or relates to a [big commercial] contract, agreement or undertaking to which section 5–1402 of the general obligations law applies, and the parties to the contract have agreed that the law of this state shall govern their rights or duties in whole or in part.

Article 5—Venue

§ 501. Contractual provisions fixing venue

Subject to the provisions of subdivision two of section 510, written agreement fixing place of trial, made before an action is commenced, shall be enforced upon a motion for change of place of trial.

§ 502. Conflicting venue provisions

Where, because of joinder of claims or parties, there is a conflict of provisions under this article, the court, upon motion, shall order as the place of trial one proper under this article as to at least one of the parties or claims.

§ 503. Venue based on residence

(a) Generally. Except where otherwise prescribed by law, the place of trial shall be in the county in which one of the parties resided when it was commenced; or, if none of the parties then resided in the state, in any county designated by the plaintiff. A party resident in more than one county shall be deemed a resident of each such county.

(b) Executor, administrator, trustee, committee, conservator, general or testamentary guardian, or receiver. An executor, administrator, trustee, committee, conservator, general or testamentary guardian, or receiver shall be deemed a resident of the county of his appointment as well as the county in which he actually resides.

(c) Corporation. A domestic corporation, or a foreign corporation authorized to transact business in the state, shall be deemed a resident of the county in which its principal office is located; except that such a corporation, if a railroad or other common carrier, shall also be deemed a resident of the county where the cause of action arose.

(d) Unincorporated association, partnership, or individually-owned business. A president or treasurer of an unincorporated association, suing or being sued on behalf of the association, shall be deemed a resident of any county in which the association has its principal office, as well as the county in which he actually resides. A partnership or an individually-owned business shall be deemed a resident of any county in which it has its principal office, as well as the county in which the partner or individual owner suing or being sued actually resides.

(e) Assignee. In an action for a sum of money only, brought by an assignee other than an assignee for the benefit of creditors or a holder in due course of a negotiable instrument, the assignee's residence shall be deemed the same as that of the original assignor at the time of the original assignment.

(f) Consumer credit transaction. In an action arising out of a consumer credit transaction where a purchaser, borrower or debtor is a defendant, the place of trial shall be the residence of a defendant, if one resides within the state or the county where such transaction took place, if it is within the state, or, in other cases, as set forth in subdivision (a).

§ 504. Actions against counties, cities, towns, villages, school districts and district corporations

* * *

§ 505. Actions involving public authorities

* * *

§ 506. Where special proceeding commenced

* * *

§ 507. Real property actions

The place of trial of an action in which the judgment demanded would affect the title to, or the possession, use or enjoyment of, real property shall be in the county in which any part of the subject of the action is situated.

§ 508. Actions to recover a chattel

The place of trial of an action to recover a chattel may be in the county in which any part of the subject of the action is situated at the time of the commencement of the action.

§ 509. Venue in county designated

Notwithstanding any provision of this article, the place of trial of an action shall be in the county designated by the plaintiff, unless the place of trial is changed to another county by order upon motion, or by consent as provided in subdivision (b) of rule 511.

§ 510. Grounds for change of place of trial

The court, upon motion, may change the place of trial of an action where:

1. the county designated for that purpose is not a proper county; or

2. there is reason to believe that an impartial trial cannot be had in the proper county; or

3. the convenience of material witnesses and the ends of justice will be promoted by the change.

Rule 511. Change of place of trial

(a) Time for motion or demand. A demand under subdivision (b) for change of place of trial on the ground that the county designated for that purpose is not a proper county shall be served with the answer or before the answer is served. A motion for change of place of trial on any other ground shall be made within a reasonable time after commencement of the action.

(b) Demand for change of place of trial upon ground of improper venue, where motion made. The defendant shall serve a written demand that the action be tried in a county he specifies as proper. Thereafter, the defendant may move to change the place of trial within fifteen days after service of the demand, unless within five days after such service plaintiff serves a written consent to change the place of trial to that specified by the defendant. Defendant may notice such motion to be heard as if the action were pending in the county he specified, unless plaintiff within five days after service of the demand serves an affidavit showing either that the county specified by the defendant is not proper or that the county designated by him is proper.

(c) Stay of proceedings. No order to stay proceedings for the purpose of changing the place of trial shall be granted unless it appears from the papers that the change is sought with due diligence.

(d) Order, subsequent proceedings and appeal. Upon filing of consent by the plaintiff or entry of an order changing the place of trial by the clerk of the county from which it is changed, the clerk shall forthwith deliver to the clerk of the county to which it is changed all papers filed in the action and certified copies of all minutes and entries, which shall be filed, entered or recorded, as the case requires, in the office of the latter clerk. Subsequent proceedings shall be had in the county to which the change is made as if it had been designated originally as the place of trial, except as otherwise directed by the court. An appeal from an order changing the place of trial shall be taken in the department in which the motion for the order was heard and determined.

*

FEDERAL RULES OF EVIDENCE

TABLE OF CONTENTS

RULES OF EVIDENCE

Article IX. Authentication and Identification:

Rule

(1) Domestic public documents under seal
(2) Domestic public documents not under seal
(3) Foreign public documents
(4) Certified copies of public records
(5) Official publications
(6) Newspapers and periodicals
(7) Trade inscriptions and the like
(8) Acknowledged documents
(9) Commercial paper and related documents
(10) Presumptions under Acts of Congress
(11) Certified domestic records of regularly conducted activity
(12) Certified foreign records of regularly conducted activity
903. Subscribing witness' testimony unnecessary

Article X. Contents of Writings, Recordings, and Photographs:

Rule

1001. Definitions:
(1) Writings and recordings
(2) Photographs
(3) Original
(4) Duplicate
1002. Requirement of original
1003. Admissibility of duplicates
1004. Admissibility of other evidence of contents:
(1) Originals lost or destroyed
(2) Original not obtainable
(3) Original in possession of opponent
(4) Collateral matters
1005. Public records
1006. Summaries
1007. Testimony or written admission of party
1008. Functions of court and jury

Article XI. Miscellaneous Rules:

Rule

1101. Applicability of rules:
(a) Courts and judges
(b) Proceedings generally
(c) Rule of privilege
(d) Rules inapplicable:
(1) Preliminary questions of fact
(2) Grand jury
(3) Miscellaneous proceedings
(e) Rules applicable in part
1102. Amendments
1103. Title

*

FEDERAL RULES OF EVIDENCE

ARTICLE I. GENERAL PROVISIONS

Rule 101.

SCOPE

These rules govern proceedings in the courts of the United States and before United States bankruptcy judges and United States magistrate judges, to the extent and with the exceptions stated in rule 1101.

As amended 1987, 1988, 1993.

Rule 102.

PURPOSE AND CONSTRUCTION

These rules shall be construed to secure fairness in administration, elimination of unjustifiable expense and delay, and promotion of growth and development of the law of evidence to the end that the truth may be ascertained and proceedings justly determined.

Rule 103.

RULINGS ON EVIDENCE

(a) Effect of erroneous ruling. Error may not be predicated upon a ruling which admits or excludes evidence unless a substantial right of the party is affected, and

(1) *Objection.* In case the ruling is one admitting evidence a timely objection or motion to strike appears of record, stating the specific ground of objection if the specific ground was not apparent from the context; or

(2) *Offer of proof.* In case the ruling is one excluding evidence, the substance of the evidence was made known to the court by offer or was apparent from the context within which questions were asked.

Once the court makes a definitive ruling on the record admitting or excluding evidence, either at or before trial, a party need not renew an objection or offer of proof to preserve a claim of error for appeal.

(b) Record of offer and ruling. The court may add any other or further statement which shows the character of the evidence, the form in which it was offered, the objection made, and the ruling thereon. It may direct the making of an offer in question and answer form.

(c) Hearing of jury. In jury cases, proceedings shall be conducted, to the extent practicable, so as to prevent inadmissible evidence from being suggested to the jury by any means, such as making statements or offers of proof or asking questions in the hearing of the jury.

(d) Plain error. Nothing in this rule precludes taking notice of plain errors affecting substantial rights although they were not brought to the attention of the court.

As amended 2000.

Rule 104.

PRELIMINARY QUESTIONS

(a) Questions of admissibility generally. Preliminary questions concerning the qualification of a person to be a witness, the existence of a privilege, or the admissibility of evidence shall be determined by the court, subject to the provisions of subdivision (b). In making its determination it is not bound by the rules of evidence except those with respect to privileges.

(b) Relevancy conditioned on fact. When the relevancy of evidence depends upon the fulfillment of a condition of fact, the court shall admit it upon, or subject to, the introduction of evidence sufficient to support a finding of the fulfillment of the condition.

(c) Hearing of jury. Hearings on the admissibility of confessions shall in all cases be conducted out of the hearing of the jury. Hearings on other preliminary matters shall be so conducted when the interests of justice require, or when an accused is a witness and so requests.

(d) Testimony by accused. The accused does not, by testifying upon a preliminary matter, become subject to cross-examination as to other issues in the case.

(e) Weight and credibility. This rule does not limit the right of a party to introduce before the jury evidence relevant to weight or credibility.

As amended 1987.

Rule 105.

LIMITED ADMISSIBILITY

When evidence which is admissible as to one party or for one purpose but not admissible as to another party or for another purpose is admitted, the court, upon request, shall restrict the evidence to its proper scope and instruct the jury accordingly.

Rule 106.

REMAINDER OF OR RELATED WRITINGS OR RECORDED STATEMENTS

When a writing or recorded statement or part thereof is introduced by a party, an adverse party may require the introduction at that time of any other part or any other writing or recorded statement which ought in fairness to be considered contemporaneously with it.

As amended 1987.

ARTICLE II. JUDICIAL NOTICE

Rule 201.

JUDICIAL NOTICE OF ADJUDICATIVE FACTS

(a) Scope of rule. This rule governs only judicial notice of adjudicative facts.

(b) Kinds of facts. A judicially noticed fact must be one not subject to reasonable dispute in that it is either (1) generally known within the territorial jurisdiction of the trial court or (2) capable of accurate and ready determination by resort to sources whose accuracy cannot reasonably be questioned.

(c) When discretionary. A court may take judicial notice, whether requested or not.

(d) When mandatory. A court shall take judicial notice if requested by a party and supplied with the necessary information.

(e) Opportunity to be heard. A party is entitled upon timely request to an opportunity to be heard as to the propriety of taking judicial notice and the tenor of the matter noticed. In the absence of prior notification, the request may be made after judicial notice has been taken.

(f) Time of taking notice. Judicial notice may be taken at any stage of the proceeding.

(g) Instructing jury. In a civil action or proceeding, the court shall instruct the jury to accept as conclusive any fact judicially noticed. In a criminal case, the court shall instruct the jury that it may, but is not required to, accept as conclusive any fact judicially noticed.

ARTICLE III. PRESUMPTIONS IN CIVIL ACTIONS AND PROCEEDINGS

Rule 301.

PRESUMPTIONS IN GENERAL IN CIVIL ACTIONS AND PROCEEDINGS

In all civil actions and proceedings not otherwise provided for by Act of Congress or by these rules, a presumption imposes on the party against whom it is directed the burden of going forward with evidence to rebut or meet the presumption, but does not shift to such party the burden of proof in the sense of the risk of nonpersuasion, which remains throughout the trial upon the party on whom it was originally cast.

Rule 302.

APPLICABILITY OF STATE LAW IN CIVIL ACTIONS AND PROCEEDINGS

In civil actions and proceedings, the effect of a presumption respecting a fact which is an element of a claim or defense as to which State law supplies the rule of decision is determined in accordance with State law.

ARTICLE IV. RELEVANCY AND ITS LIMITS

Rule 401.

DEFINITION OF "RELEVANT EVIDENCE"

"Relevant evidence" means evidence having any tendency to make the existence of any fact that is of consequence to the determination of the action more probable or less probable than it would be without the evidence.

Rule 402.

RELEVANT EVIDENCE GENERALLY ADMISSIBLE; IRRELEVANT EVIDENCE INADMISSIBLE

All relevant evidence is admissible, except as otherwise provided by the Constitution of the United States, by Act of Congress, by these rules, or by other rules prescribed by the Supreme Court pursuant to statutory authority. Evidence which is not relevant is not admissible.

Rule 403.

EXCLUSION OF RELEVANT EVIDENCE ON GROUNDS OF PREJUDICE, CONFUSION, OR WASTE OF TIME

Although relevant, evidence may be excluded if its probative value is substantially outweighed by the danger of unfair prejudice, confusion of the issues, or misleading the jury, or by considerations of undue delay, waste of time, or needless presentation of cumulative evidence.

Rule 404.

CHARACTER EVIDENCE NOT ADMISSIBLE TO PROVE CONDUCT; EXCEPTIONS; OTHER CRIMES

(a) Character evidence generally. Evidence of a person's character or a trait of character is not admissible for the purpose of proving action in conformity therewith on a particular occasion, except:

(1) *Character of accused.* Evidence of a pertinent trait of character offered by an accused, or by the prosecution to rebut the same, or if evidence of a trait of character of the alleged victim of the crime is offered by an accused and admitted under Rule 404(a)(2), evidence of the same trait of character of the accused offered by the prosecution;

(2) *Character of alleged victim.* Evidence of a pertinent trait of character of the alleged victim of the crime offered by an accused, or by the prosecution to rebut the same, or evidence of a character trait of peacefulness of the alleged victim offered by the prosecution in a homicide case to rebut evidence that the alleged victim was the first aggressor;

(3) *Character of witness.* Evidence of the character of a witness, as provided in rules 607, 608, and 609.

(b) Other crimes, wrongs, or acts. Evidence of other crimes, wrongs, or acts is not admissible to prove the character of a person in order to show action in conformity therewith. It may, however, be admissible for other purposes, such as proof of motive, opportunity, intent, preparation, plan, knowledge, identity, or absence of mistake or accident, provided that upon request by the accused, the prosecution in a criminal case shall provide reasonable notice in advance of trial, or during trial if the court excuses pretrial notice on good cause shown, of the general nature of any such evidence it intends to introduce at trial.

As amended 1987, 1991, 2000.

Rule 405.

METHODS OF PROVING CHARACTER

(a) Reputation or opinion. In all cases in which evidence of character or a trait of character of a person is admissible, proof may be made by testimony as to reputation or by testimony in the form of an opinion. On cross-examination, inquiry is allowable into relevant specific instances of conduct.

(b) Specific instances of conduct. In cases in which character or a trait of character of a person is an essential element of a charge, claim, or defense, proof may also be made of specific instances of that person's conduct.

As amended 1987.

Rule 406.

HABIT; ROUTINE PRACTICE

Evidence of the habit of a person or of the routine practice of an organization, whether corroborated or not and regardless of the presence of eyewitnesses, is relevant to prove that the conduct of the person or organization on a particular occasion was in conformity with the habit or routine practice.

Rule 407.

SUBSEQUENT REMEDIAL MEASURES

When, after an injury or harm allegedly caused by an event, measures are taken that, if taken previously, would have made the injury or harm less likely to occur, evidence of the subsequent measures is not admissible to prove negligence, culpable conduct, a defect in a product, a defect in a product's design, or a need for a warning or instruction. This rule does not require the exclusion of evidence of subsequent measures when offered for another purpose, such as proving ownership, control, or feasibility of precautionary measures, if controverted, or impeachment.

As amended 1997.

Rule 408.

COMPROMISE AND OFFERS TO COMPROMISE

Evidence of (1) furnishing or offering or promising to furnish, or (2) accepting or offering or promising to accept, a valuable consideration in compromising or attempting to compromise a claim which was disputed as to either validity or amount, is not admissible to prove liability for or invalidity of the claim or its amount. Evidence of conduct or statements made in compromise negotiations is likewise not admissible. This rule does not require the exclusion of any evidence otherwise discoverable merely because it is presented in the course of compromise negotiations. This rule also does not require exclusion when the evidence is offered for another purpose, such as proving bias or prejudice of a witness, negativing a contention of undue delay, or proving an effort to obstruct a criminal investigation or prosecution.

Rule 409.

PAYMENT OF MEDICAL AND SIMILAR EXPENSES

Evidence of furnishing or offering or promising to pay medical, hospital, or similar expenses occasioned by an injury is not admissible to prove liability for the injury.

Rule 410.

INADMISSIBILITY OF PLEAS, PLEA DISCUSSIONS, AND RELATED STATEMENTS

Except as otherwise provided in this rule, evidence of the following is not, in any civil or criminal proceeding, admissible against the defendant who made the plea or was a participant in the plea discussions:

(1) a plea of guilty which was later withdrawn;

(2) a plea of nolo contendere;

(3) any statement made in the course of any proceedings under Rule 11 of the Federal Rules of Criminal Procedure or comparable state procedure regarding either of the foregoing pleas; or

(4) any statement made in the course of plea discussions with an attorney for the prosecuting authority which do not result in a plea of guilty or which result in a plea of guilty later withdrawn.

However, such a statement is admissible (i) in any proceeding wherein another statement made in the course of the same plea or plea discussions has been introduced and the statement ought in fairness be considered contemporaneously with it, or (ii) in a criminal proceeding for perjury or false statement if the statement was made by the defendant under oath, on the record and in the presence of counsel.

As amended 1975, 1980.

Rule 411.

LIABILITY INSURANCE

Evidence that a person was or was not insured against liability is not admissible upon the issue whether the person acted negligently or otherwise wrongfully. This rule does not require the exclusion of evidence of insurance against liability when offered for another purpose, such as proof of agency, ownership, or control, or bias or prejudice of a witness.

As amended 1987.

Rule 412.

SEX OFFENSE CASES; RELEVANCE OF ALLEGED VICTIM'S PAST SEXUAL BEHAVIOR OR ALLEGED SEXUAL PREDISPOSITION

(a) Evidence generally inadmissible. The following evidence is not admissible in any civil or criminal proceeding involving alleged sexual misconduct except as provided in subdivisions (b) and (c):

(1) Evidence offered to prove that any alleged victim engaged in other sexual behavior.

(2) Evidence offered to prove any alleged victim's sexual predisposition.

(b) Exceptions.

(1) In a criminal case, the following evidence is admissible, if otherwise admissible under these rules:

(A) evidence of specific instances of sexual behavior by the alleged victim offered to prove that a person other than the accused was the source of semen, injury or other physical evidence;

(B) evidence of specific instances of sexual behavior by the alleged victim with respect to the person accused of the sexual misconduct offered by the accused to prove consent or by the prosecution; and

(C) evidence the exclusion of which would violate the constitutional rights of the defendant.

(2) In a civil case, evidence offered to prove the sexual behavior or sexual predisposition of any alleged victim is admissible if it is otherwise admissible under these rules and its probative value substantially outweighs the danger of harm to any victim and of unfair prejudice to any party. Evidence of an alleged victim's reputation is admissible only if it has been placed in controversy by the alleged victim.

(c) Procedure to determine admissibility.

(1) A party intending to offer evidence under subdivision (b) must—

(A) file a written motion at least 14 days before trial specifically describing the evidence and stating the purpose for which it is offered unless the court, for good cause requires a different time for filing or permits filing during trial; and

(B) serve the motion on all parties and notify the alleged victim or, when appropriate, the alleged victim's guardian or representative.

(2) Before admitting evidence under this rule the court must conduct a hearing in camera and afford the victim and parties a right to attend and be heard. The motion, related papers, and the record of the hearing must be sealed and remain under seal unless the court orders otherwise.

Added 1978; as amended 1988, 1994.

Rule 413.

EVIDENCE OF SIMILAR CRIMES IN SEXUAL ASSAULT CASES

(a) In a criminal case in which the defendant is accused of an offense of sexual assault, evidence of the defendant's commission of another offense or offenses of sexual assault is admissible, and may be considered for its bearing on any matter to which it is relevant.

(b) In a case in which the Government intends to offer evidence under this rule, the attorney for the Government shall disclose the evidence to the defendant, including statements of witnesses or a summary of the substance of any testimony that is expected to be offered, at least fifteen days before the scheduled date of trial or at such later time as the court may allow for good cause.

(c) This rule shall not be construed to limit the admission or consideration of evidence under any other rule.

(d) For purposes of this rule and Rule 415, "offense of sexual assault" means a crime under Federal law or the law of a State (as defined in section 513 of title 18, United States Code) that involved—

(1) any conduct proscribed by chapter 109A of title 18, United States Code;

(2) contact, without consent, between any part of the defendant's body or an object and the genitals or anus of another person;

(3) contact, without consent, between the genitals or anus of the defendant and any part of another person's body;

(4) deriving sexual pleasure or gratification from the infliction of death, bodily injury, or physical pain on another person; or

(5) an attempt or conspiracy to engage in conduct described in paragraphs (1)–(4).

Added 1995.

Rule 414.

EVIDENCE OF SIMILAR CRIMES IN CHILD MOLESTATION CASES

(a) In a criminal case in which the defendant is accused of an offense of child molestation, evidence of the defendant's commission of another offense or offenses of child molestation is admissible, and may be considered for its bearing on any matter to which it is relevant.

(b) In a case in which the Government intends to offer evidence under this rule, the attorney for the Government shall disclose the evidence to the defendant, including statements of witnesses or a summary of the substance of any testimony that is expected to be offered, at least fifteen days before the scheduled date of trial or at such later time as the court may allow for good cause.

(c) This rule shall not be construed to limit the admission or consideration of evidence under any other rule.

(d) For purposes of this rule and Rule 415, "child" means a person below the age of fourteen, and "offense of child molestation" means a crime under Federal law or the law of a State (as defined in section 513 of title 18, United States Code) that involved—

(1) any conduct proscribed by chapter 109A of title 18, United States Code, that was committed in relation to a child;

(2) any conduct proscribed by chapter 110 of title 18, United States Code;

(3) contact between any part of the defendant's body or an object and the genitals or anus of a child;

(4) contact between the genitals or anus of the defendant and any part of the body of a child;

(5) deriving sexual pleasure or gratification from the infliction of death, bodily injury, or physical pain on a child; or

(6) an attempt or conspiracy to engage in conduct described in paragraphs (1)–(5).

Added 1995.

Rule 415.

EVIDENCE OF SIMILAR ACTS IN CIVIL CASES CONCERNING SEXUAL ASSAULT OR CHILD MOLESTATION

(a) In a civil case in which a claim for damages or other relief is predicated on a party's alleged commission of conduct constituting an offense of sexual assault or child molestation, evidence of that party's commission of another offense or offenses of sexual assault or child molestation is admissible and may be considered as provided in Rule 413 and Rule 414 of these rules.

(b) A party who intends to offer evidence under this Rule shall disclose the evidence to the party against whom it will be offered, including statements of witnesses or a summary of the substance of any testimony that is expected to be offered, at least fifteen days before the scheduled date of trial or at such later time as the court may allow for good cause.

(c) This rule shall not be construed to limit the admission or consideration of evidence under any other rule.

Added 1995.

ARTICLE V. PRIVILEGES

Rule 501.

GENERAL RULE

Except as otherwise required by the Constitution of the United States or provided by Act of Congress or in rules prescribed by the Supreme Court pursuant to statutory authority, the privilege of a witness, person, government, State, or political subdivision thereof shall be governed by the principles of the common law as they may be interpreted by the courts of the United States in the light of reason and experience. However, in civil actions and proceedings, with respect to an element of a claim or defense as to which State law supplies the rule of decision, the privilege of a witness, person, government, State, or political subdivision thereof shall be determined in accordance with State law.

ARTICLE VI. WITNESSES

Rule 601.

GENERAL RULE OF COMPETENCY

Every person is competent to be a witness except as otherwise provided in these rules. However, in civil actions and proceedings, with respect to an element of a claim or defense as to which State law supplies the rule of decision, the competency of a witness shall be determined in accordance with State law.

Rule 602.

LACK OF PERSONAL KNOWLEDGE

A witness may not testify to a matter unless evidence is introduced sufficient to support a finding that the witness has personal knowledge of the matter. Evidence to prove personal knowledge may, but need not, consist of the witness' own testimony. This rule is subject to the provisions of rule 703, relating to opinion testimony by expert witnesses.

As amended 1987, 1988.

Rule 603.

OATH OR AFFIRMATION

Before testifying, every witness shall be required to declare that the witness will testify truthfully, by oath or affirmation administered in a form calculated to awaken the witness' conscience and impress the witness' mind with the duty to do so.

As amended 1987.

Rule 604.

INTERPRETERS

An interpreter is subject to the provisions of these rules relating to qualification as an expert and the administration of an oath or affirmation to make a true translation.

As amended 1987.

Rule 605.

COMPETENCY OF JUDGE AS WITNESS

The judge presiding at the trial may not testify in that trial as a witness. No objection need be made in order to preserve the point.

Rule 606.

COMPETENCY OF JUROR AS WITNESS

(a) At the trial. A member of the jury may not testify as a witness before that jury in the trial of the case in which the juror is sitting. If the juror is called so to testify, the opposing party shall be afforded an opportunity to object out of the presence of the jury.

(b) Inquiry into validity of verdict or indictment. Upon an inquiry into the validity of a verdict or indictment, a juror may not testify as to any matter or statement occurring during the course of the jury's deliberations or to the effect of anything upon that or any other juror's mind or emotions as influencing the juror to assent to or dissent from the verdict or indictment or concerning the juror's mental processes in connection therewith, except that a juror may testify on the question whether extraneous prejudicial information was improperly brought to the jury's attention or whether any outside influence was improperly brought to bear upon any juror. Nor may a juror's affidavit or evidence of any statement by the juror concerning a matter about which the juror would be precluded from testifying be received for these purposes.

As amended 1975, 1987.

Rule 607.

WHO MAY IMPEACH

The credibility of a witness may be attacked by any party, including the party calling the witness.

As amended 1987.

Rule 608.

EVIDENCE OF CHARACTER AND CONDUCT OF WITNESS

(a) Opinion and reputation evidence of character. The credibility of a witness may be attacked or supported by evidence in the form of opinion or reputation, but subject to these limitations:

(1) the evidence may refer only to character for truthfulness or untruthfulness, and (2) evidence of truthful character is admissible only after the character of the witness for truthfulness has been attacked by opinion or reputation evidence or otherwise.

(b) Specific instances of conduct. Specific instances of the conduct of a witness, for the purpose of attacking or supporting the witness' character for truthfulness, other than conviction of crime as provided in rule 609, may not be proved by extrinsic evidence. They may, however, in the discretion of the court, if probative of truthfulness or untruthfulness, be inquired into on cross-examination of the witness (1) concerning the witness' character for truthfulness or untruthfulness, or (2) concerning the character for truthfulness or untruthfulness of another witness as to which character the witness being cross-examined has testified.

The giving of testimony, whether by an accused or by any other witness, does not operate as a waiver of the accused's or the witness' privilege against self-incrimination when examined with respect to matters that relate only to character for truthfulness.

As amended 1987, 1988, 2003.

Rule 609.

IMPEACHMENT BY EVIDENCE OF CONVICTION OF CRIME

(a) General rule. For the purpose of attacking the credibility of a witness,

(1) evidence that a witness other than an accused has been convicted of a crime shall be admitted, subject to Rule 403, if the crime was punishable by death or imprisonment in excess of one year under the law under which the witness was convicted, and evidence that an accused has been convicted of such a crime shall be admitted if the court determines that the probative value of admitting this evidence outweighs its prejudicial effect to the accused; and

(2) evidence that any witness has been convicted of a crime shall be admitted if it involved dishonesty or false statement, regardless of the punishment.

(b) Time limit. Evidence of a conviction under this rule is not admissible if a period of more than ten years has elapsed since the date of the conviction or of the release of the witness from the confinement imposed for that conviction, whichever is the later date, unless the court determines, in the interests of justice, that the probative value of the conviction supported by specific facts and circumstances substantially outweighs its prejudicial effect. However, evidence of a conviction more than 10 years old as calculated herein, is not admissible unless the proponent gives to the adverse party sufficient advance written notice of intent to use such evidence to provide the adverse party with a fair opportunity to contest the use of such evidence.

(c) Effect of pardon, annulment, or certificate of rehabilitation. Evidence of a conviction is not admissible under this rule if (1) the conviction has been the subject of a pardon, annulment, certificate of rehabilitation, or other equivalent procedure based on a finding of the rehabilitation of the person convicted, and that person has not been convicted of a subsequent crime which was punishable by death or imprisonment in excess of one year, or (2) the conviction has been the subject of a pardon, annulment, or other equivalent procedure based on a finding of innocence.

(d) Juvenile adjudications. Evidence of juvenile adjudications is generally not admissible under this rule. The court may, however, in a criminal case allow evidence of a juvenile adjudication of a witness other than the accused if conviction of the offense would be admissible to attack the credibility of an adult and the court is satisfied that admission in evidence is necessary for a fair determination of the issue of guilt or innocence.

(e) Pendency of appeal. The pendency of an appeal therefrom does not render evidence of a conviction inadmissible. Evidence of the pendency of an appeal is admissible.

As amended 1987, 1990.

Rule 610.

RELIGIOUS BELIEFS OR OPINIONS

Evidence of the beliefs or opinions of a witness on matters of religion is not admissible for the purpose of showing that by reason of their nature the witness' credibility is impaired or enhanced.

As amended 1987.

Rule 611.

MODE AND ORDER OF INTERROGATION AND PRESENTATION

(a) Control by court. The court shall exercise reasonable control over the mode and order of interrogating witnesses and presenting evidence so as to (1) make the interrogation and presentation effective for the ascertainment of the truth, (2) avoid needless consumption of time, and (3) protect witnesses from harassment or undue embarrassment.

(b) Scope of cross-examination. Cross-examination should be limited to the subject matter of the direct examination and matters affecting the credibility of the witness. The court may, in the exercise of discretion, permit inquiry into additional matters as if on direct examination.

(c) Leading questions. Leading questions should not be used on the direct examination of a witness except as may be necessary to develop the witness' testimony. Ordinarily leading questions should be permitted on cross-examination. When a party calls a hostile witness, an adverse party, or a witness identified with an adverse party, interrogation may be by leading questions.

As amended 1987.

Rule 612.

WRITING USED TO REFRESH MEMORY

Except as otherwise provided in criminal proceedings by section 3500 of title 18, United States Code, if a witness uses a writing to refresh memory for the purpose of testifying, either—

(1) while testifying, or

(2) before testifying, if the court in its discretion determines it is necessary in the interests of justice,

an adverse party is entitled to have the writing produced at the hearing, to inspect it, to cross-examine the witness thereon, and to introduce in evidence those portions which relate to the testimony of the witness. If it is claimed that the writing contains matters not related to the subject matter of the testimony the court shall examine the writing in camera, excise any portions not so related, and order delivery of the remainder to the party entitled thereto. Any portion withheld over objections shall be preserved and made available to the appellate court in the event of an appeal. If a writing is not produced or delivered pursuant to order under this rule, the court shall make any order justice requires, except that in criminal cases when the prosecution elects not to comply, the order shall be one striking the testimony or, if the court in its discretion determines that the interests of justice so require, declaring a mistrial.

As amended 1987.

Rule 613.

PRIOR STATEMENTS OF WITNESSES

(a) Examining witness concerning prior statement. In examining a witness concerning a prior statement made by the witness, whether written or not, the statement need not be shown nor its contents disclosed to the witness at that time, but on request the same shall be shown or disclosed to opposing counsel.

(b) Extrinsic evidence of prior inconsistent statement of witness. Extrinsic evidence of a prior inconsistent statement by a witness is not admissible unless the witness is afforded an opportunity to explain or deny the same and the opposite party is afforded an opportunity to interrogate the witness thereon, or the interests of justice otherwise require. This provision does not apply to admissions of a party-opponent as defined in rule 801(d)(2).

As amended 1987, 1988.

Rule 614.

CALLING AND INTERROGATION OF WITNESSES BY COURT

(a) Calling by court. The court may, on its own motion or at the suggestion of a party, call witnesses, and all parties are entitled to cross-examine witnesses thus called.

(b) Interrogation by court. The court may interrogate witnesses, whether called by itself or by a party.

(c) Objections. Objections to the calling of witnesses by the court or to interrogation by it may be made at the time or at the next available opportunity when the jury is not present.

Rule 615.

EXCLUSION OF WITNESSES

At the request of a party the court shall order witnesses excluded so that they cannot hear the testimony of other witnesses, and it may make the order of its own motion. This rule does not authorize exclusion of (1) a party who is a natural person, or (2) an officer or employee of a party which is not a natural person designated as its representative by its attorney, or (3) a person whose presence is shown by a party to be essential to the presentation of the party's cause, or (4) a person authorized by statute to be present.

As amended 1987, 1988, 1998.

ARTICLE VII. OPINIONS AND EXPERT TESTIMONY

Rule 701.

OPINION TESTIMONY BY LAY WITNESSES

If the witness is not testifying as an expert, the witness' testimony in the form of opinions or inferences is limited to those opinions or inferences which are (a) rationally based on the perception of the witness, (b) helpful to a clear understanding of the witness' testimony or the determination of a fact in issue, and (c) not based on scientific, technical, or other specialized knowledge within the scope of Rule 702.

As amended 1987, 2000.

Rule 702.

TESTIMONY BY EXPERTS

If scientific, technical, or other specialized knowledge will assist the trier of fact to understand the evidence or to determine a fact in issue, a witness qualified as an expert by knowledge, skill, experience, training, or education, may testify thereto in the form of an opinion or otherwise, if (1) the testimony is based upon sufficient facts or data, (2) the testimony is the product of reliable principles and methods, and (3) the witness has applied the principles and methods reliably to the facts of the case.

As amended 2000.

Rule 703.

BASES OF OPINION TESTIMONY BY EXPERTS

The facts or data in the particular case upon which an expert bases an opinion or inference may be those perceived by or made known to the expert at or before the hearing. If of a type reasonably relied upon by experts in the particular field in forming opinions or inferences upon the subject, the facts or data need not be admissible in evidence in order for the opinion or inference to be admitted. Facts or data that are otherwise inadmissible shall not be disclosed to the jury by the proponent of the opinion or inference unless the court determines that their probative value in assisting the jury to evaluate the expert's opinion substantially outweighs their prejudicial effect.

As amended 1987, 2000.

Rule 704.

OPINION ON ULTIMATE ISSUE

(a) Except as provided in subdivision (b), testimony in the form of an opinion or inference otherwise admissible is not objectionable because it embraces an ultimate issue to be decided by the trier of fact.

(b) No expert witness testifying with respect to the mental state or condition of a defendant in a criminal case may state an opinion or inference as to whether the defendant did or did not have the mental state or condition constituting an element of the crime charged or of a defense thereto. Such ultimate issues are matters for the trier of fact alone.

As amended 1984.

Rule 705.

DISCLOSURE OF FACTS OR DATA UNDERLYING EXPERT OPINION

The expert may testify in terms of opinion or inference and give reasons therefor without first testifying to the underlying facts or data, unless the court requires otherwise. The expert may in any event be required to disclose the underlying facts or data on cross-examination.

As amended 1987, 1993.

Rule 706.

COURT APPOINTED EXPERTS

(a) Appointment. The court may on its own motion or on the motion of any party enter an order to show cause why expert witnesses should not be appointed, and may request the parties to submit nominations. The court may appoint any expert witnesses agreed upon by the parties, and may appoint expert witnesses of its own selection. An expert witness shall not be appointed by the court unless the witness consents to act. A witness so appointed shall be informed of the witness' duties by the court in writing, a copy of which shall be filed with the clerk, or at a conference in which the parties shall have opportunity to participate. A witness so appointed shall advise the parties of the witness' findings, if any; the witness' deposition may be taken by any party; and the witness may be called to testify by the court or any party. The witness shall be subject to cross-examination by each party, including a party calling the witness.

(b) Compensation. Expert witnesses so appointed are entitled to reasonable compensation in whatever sum the court may allow. The compensation thus fixed is payable from funds which may be provided by law in criminal cases and civil actions and proceedings involving just compensation under the fifth amendment. In other civil actions and proceedings the compensation shall be paid by the parties in such proportion and at such time as the court directs, and thereafter charged in like manner as other costs.

(c) Disclosure of appointment. In the exercise of its discretion, the court may authorize disclosure to the jury of the fact that the court appointed the expert witness.

(d) Parties' experts of own selection. Nothing in this rule limits the parties in calling expert witnesses of their own selection.

As amended 1987.

ARTICLE VIII. HEARSAY

Rule 801.

DEFINITIONS

The following definitions apply under this article:

(a) Statement. A "statement" is (1) an oral or written assertion or (2) nonverbal conduct of a person, if it is intended by the person as an assertion.

(b) Declarant. A "declarant" is a person who makes a statement.

(c) Hearsay. "Hearsay" is a statement, other than one made by the declarant while testifying at the trial or hearing, offered in evidence to prove the truth of the matter asserted.

(d) Statements which are not hearsay. A statement is not hearsay if—

(1) *Prior statement by witness.* The declarant testifies at the trial or hearing and is subject to cross-examination concerning the statement, and the statement is (A) inconsistent with the declarant's testimony, and was given under oath subject to the penalty of perjury at a trial, hearing, or other proceeding, or in a deposition, or (B) consistent with the declarant's testimony and is offered to rebut an express or implied charge against the declarant of recent fabrication or improper influence or motive, or (C) one of identification of a person made after perceiving the person; or

(2) *Admission by party-opponent.* The statement is offered against a party and is (A) the party's own statement, in either an

individual or a representative capacity or (B) a statement of which the party has manifested an adoption or belief in its truth, or (C) a statement by a person authorized by the party to make a statement concerning the subject, or (D) a statement by the party's agent or servant concerning a matter within the scope of the agency or employment, made during the existence of the relationship, or (E) a statement by a coconspirator of a party during the course and in furtherance of the conspiracy. The contents of the statement shall be considered but are not alone sufficient to establish the declarant's authority under subdivision (C), the agency or employment relationship and scope thereof under subdivision (D), or the existence of the conspiracy and the participation therein of the declarant and the party against whom the statement is offered under subdivision (E).

As amended 1975, 1987, 1997.

Rule 802.

HEARSAY RULE

Hearsay is not admissible except as provided by these rules or by other rules prescribed by the Supreme Court pursuant to statutory authority or by Act of Congress.

Rule 803.

HEARSAY EXCEPTIONS; AVAILABILITY OF DECLARANT IMMATERIAL

The following are not excluded by the hearsay rule, even though the declarant is available as a witness:

(1) Present sense impression. A statement describing or explaining an event or condition made while the declarant was perceiving the event or condition, or immediately thereafter.

(2) Excited utterance. A statement relating to a startling event or condition made while the declarant was under the stress of excitement caused by the event or condition.

(3) Then existing mental, emotional, or physical condition. A statement of the declarant's then existing state of mind, emotion, sensation, or physical condition (such as intent, plan, motive, design, mental feeling, pain, and bodily health), but not including a statement of memory or belief to prove the fact remembered or believed unless it relates to the execution, revocation, identification, or terms of declarant's will.

(4) Statements for purposes of medical diagnosis or treatment. Statements made for purposes of medical diagnosis or treatment and describing medical history, or past or present symptoms, pain, or sensations, or the inception or general character of the cause or external source thereof insofar as reasonably pertinent to diagnosis or treatment.

(5) Recorded recollection. A memorandum or record concerning a matter about which a witness once had knowledge but now has insufficient recollection to enable the witness to testify fully and accurately, shown to have been made or adopted by the witness when the matter was fresh in the witness' memory and to reflect that knowledge correctly. If admitted, the memorandum or record may be read into evidence but may not itself be received as an exhibit unless offered by an adverse party.

(6) Records of regularly conducted activity. A memorandum, report, record, or data compilation, in any form, of acts, events, conditions, opinions, or diagnoses, made at or near the time by, or from information transmitted by, a person with knowledge, if kept in the course of a regularly conducted business activity and if it was the regular practice of that business activity to make the memorandum, report, record, or data compilation, all as shown by the testimony of the custodian or other qualified witness, or by certification that complies with Rule 902(11), Rule 902(12), or a statute permitting certification, unless the source of information or the method or circumstances of preparation indicate lack of trustworthiness. The term "business" as used in this paragraph includes business, institution, association, profession, occupation, and calling of every kind, whether or not conducted for profit.

(7) Absence of entry in records kept in accordance with the provisions of paragraph (6). Evidence that a matter is not included in the memoranda reports, records, or data compilations, in any form, kept in accordance with the provisions of paragraph (6), to prove the nonoccurrence or nonexistence of the matter, if the matter was of a kind of which a memorandum, report, record, or data compilation was regularly made and preserved, unless the sources of information or other circumstances indicate lack of trustworthiness.

(8) Public records and reports. Records, reports, statements, or data compilations, in any form, of public offices or agencies, setting forth (A) the activities of the office or agency, or (B) matters observed pursuant to duty imposed by law as to which matters there was a duty to report, excluding, however, in criminal cases matters observed by police officers and other law enforcement personnel, or (C) in civil actions and proceedings and against the Government in criminal cases, factual findings resulting from an investigation made pursuant to authority granted by law, unless the sources of information or other circumstances indicate lack of trustworthiness.

(9) Records of vital statistics. Records or data compilations, in any form, of births, fetal deaths, deaths, or marriages, if the report thereof was made to a public office pursuant to requirements of law.

(10) Absence of public record or entry. To prove the absence of a record, report, statement, or data compilation, in any form, or the nonoccurrence or nonexistence of a matter of which a record, report, statement, or data compilation, in any form, was regularly made and preserved by a public office or agency, evidence in the form of a certification in accordance with rule 902, or testimony, that diligent search failed to disclose the record, report, statement, or data compilation, or entry.

(11) Records of religious organizations. Statements of births, marriages, divorces, deaths, legitimacy, ancestry, relationship by blood or marriage, or other similar facts of personal or family history, contained in a regularly kept record of a religious organization.

(12) Marriage, baptismal, and similar certificates. Statements of fact contained in a certificate that the maker performed a marriage or other ceremony or administered a sacrament, made by a clergyman, public official, or other person authorized by the rules or practices of a religious organization or by law to perform the act certified, and purporting to have been issued at the time of the act or within a reasonable time thereafter.

(13) Family records. Statements of fact concerning personal or family history contained in family Bibles, genealogies, charts, engravings on rings, inscriptions on family portraits, engravings on urns, crypts, or tombstones, or the like.

(14) Records of documents affecting an interest in property. The record of a document purporting to establish or affect an interest in property, as proof of the content of the original recorded document and its execution and delivery by each person by whom it purports to have been executed, if the record is a record of a public office and an applicable statute authorizes the recording of documents of that kind in that office.

(15) Statements in documents affecting an interest in property. A statement contained in a document purporting to establish or affect an interest in property if the matter stated was relevant to the purpose of the document, unless dealings with the property since the document was made have been inconsistent with the truth of the statement or the purport of the document.

(16) Statements in ancient documents. Statements in a document in existence twenty years or more the authenticity of which is established.

(17) Market reports, commercial publications. Market quotations, tabulations, lists, directories, or other published compilations, generally used and relied upon by the public or by persons in particular occupations.

(18) Learned treatises. To the extent called to the attention of an expert witness upon cross-examination or relied upon by the expert witness in direct examination, statements contained in published treatises, periodicals, or pamphlets on a subject of history, medicine, or other science or art, established as a reliable authority by the testimony or admission of the witness or by other expert testimony or by judicial notice. If admitted, the statements may be read into evidence but may not be received as exhibits.

(19) Reputation concerning personal or family history. Reputation among members of a person's family by blood, adoption, or marriage, or among a person's associates, or in the community, concerning a person's birth, adoption, marriage, divorce, death, legitimacy, relationship by blood, adoption, or marriage, ancestry, or other similar fact of personal or family history.

(20) Reputation concerning boundaries or general history. Reputation in a community, arising before the controversy, as to boundaries of or customs affecting lands in the community, and reputation as to events of general history important to the community or State or nation in which located.

(21) Reputation as to character. Reputation of a person's character among associates or in the community.

(22) Judgment of previous conviction. Evidence of a final judgment, entered after a trial or upon a plea of guilty (but not upon a plea of nolo contendere), adjudging a person guilty of a crime punishable by death or imprisonment in excess of one year, to prove any fact essential to sustain the judgment, but not including, when offered by the Government in a criminal prosecution for purposes other than impeachment, judgments against persons other than the accused. The pendency of an appeal may be shown but does not affect admissibility.

(23) Judgment as to personal, family, or general history, or boundaries. Judgments as proof of matters of personal, family or general history, or boundaries, essential to the judgment, if the same would be provable by evidence of reputation.

(24) [Transferred to Rule 807]

As amended 1975, 1987, 1997, 2000.

Rule 804.

HEARSAY EXCEPTIONS; DECLARANT UNAVAILABLE

(a) Definition of unavailability. "Unavailability as a witness" includes situations in which the declarant—

(1) is exempted by ruling of the court on the ground of privilege from testifying concerning the subject matter of the declarant's statement; or

(2) persists in refusing to testify concerning the subject matter of the declarant's statement despite an order of the court to do so; or

(3) testifies to a lack of memory of the subject matter of the declarant's statement; or

(4) is unable to be present or to testify at the hearing because of death or then existing physical or mental illness or infirmity; or

(5) is absent from the hearing and the proponent of a statement has been unable to procure the declarant's attendance (or in the case of a hearsay exception under subdivision (b)(2), (3), or (4), the declarant's attendance or testimony) by process or other reasonable means.

A declarant is not unavailable as a witness if exemption, refusal, claim of lack of memory, inability, or absence is due to the procurement or wrongdoing of the proponent of a statement for the purpose of preventing the witness from attending or testifying.

(b) Hearsay exceptions. The following are not excluded by the hearsay rule if the declarant is unavailable as a witness:

(1) *Former testimony.* Testimony given as a witness at another hearing of the same or a different proceeding, or in a deposition taken in compliance with law in the course of the same or another proceeding, if the party against whom the testimony is now offered, or, in a civil action or proceeding, a predecessor in interest, had an opportunity and similar motive to develop the testimony by direct, cross, or redirect examination.

(2) *Statement under belief of impending death.* In a prosecution for homicide or in a civil action or proceeding, a statement made by a declarant while believing that the declarant's death was imminent, concerning the cause or circumstances of what the declarant believed to be impending death.

(3) *Statement against interest.* A statement which was at the time of its making so far contrary to the declarant's pecuniary or proprietary interest, or so far tended to subject

the declarant to civil or criminal liability, or to render invalid a claim by the declarant against another, that a reasonable person in the declarant's position would not have made the statement unless believing it to be true. A statement tending to expose the declarant to criminal liability and offered to exculpate the accused is not admissible unless corroborating circumstances clearly indicate the trustworthiness of the statement.

(4) *Statement of personal or family history.* (A) A statement concerning the declarant's own birth, adoption, marriage, divorce, legitimacy, relationship by blood, adoption, or marriage, ancestry, or other similar fact of personal or family history, even though declarant had no means of acquiring personal knowledge of the matter stated; or (B) a statement concerning the foregoing matters, and death also, of another person, if the declarant was related to the other by blood, adoption, or marriage or was so intimately associated with the other's family as to be likely to have accurate information concerning the matter declared.

(5) [Transferred to Rule 807]

(6) *Forfeiture by wrongdoing.* A statement offered against a party that has engaged or acquiesced in wrongdoing that was intended to, and did, procure the unavailability of the declarant as a witness.

As amended 1975, 1987, 1988, 1997.

Rule 805.

HEARSAY WITHIN HEARSAY

Hearsay included within hearsay is not excluded under the hearsay rule if each part of the combined statements conforms with an exception to the hearsay rule provided in these rules.

Rule 806.

ATTACKING AND SUPPORTING CREDIBILITY OF DECLARANT

When a hearsay statement, or a statement defined in Rule 801(d)(2)(C), (D), or (E), has been admitted in evidence, the credibility of the declarant may be attacked, and if attacked may be supported, by any evidence which would be admissible for those purposes if declarant had testified as a witness. Evidence of a statement or conduct by the declarant at any time, inconsistent with the declarant's hearsay statement, is not subject to any requirement that the declarant may have been afforded an opportunity to deny or explain. If the party against whom a hearsay statement has been admitted calls the declarant as a witness, the party is entitled to examine the declarant on the statement as if under cross-examination.

As amended 1987, 1997.

Rule 807.

RESIDUAL EXCEPTION

A statement not specifically covered by Rule 803 or 804 but having equivalent circumstantial guarantees of trustworthiness, is not excluded by the hearsay rule, if the court determines that (A) the statement is offered as evidence of a material fact; (B) the statement is more probative on the point for which it is offered than any other evidence which the proponent can procure through reasonable efforts; and (C) the general purposes of these rules and the interests of justice will best be served by admission of the statement into evidence. However, a statement may not be admitted under this exception unless the proponent of it makes known to the adverse party sufficiently in advance of the trial or hearing to provide the adverse party with a fair opportunity to prepare to meet it, the proponent's intention to offer the statement and the particulars of it, including the name and address of the declarant.

Added 1997.

ARTICLE IX. AUTHENTICATION AND IDENTIFICATION

Rule 901.

REQUIREMENT OF AUTHENTICATION OR IDENTIFICATION

(a) General provision. The requirement of authentication or identification as a condition precedent to admissibility is satisfied by evidence sufficient to support a finding that the matter in question is what its proponent claims.

(b) Illustrations. By way of illustration only, and not by way of limitation, the following are examples of authentication or identification conforming with the requirements of this rule:

(1) Testimony of witness with knowledge. Testimony that a matter is what it is claimed to be.

(2) Nonexpert opinion on handwriting. Nonexpert opinion as to the genuineness of handwriting, based upon familiarity not acquired for purposes of the litigation.

(3) Comparison by trier or expert witness. Comparison by the trier of fact or by expert witnesses with specimens which have been authenticated.

(4) Distinctive characteristics and the like. Appearance, contents, substance, internal patterns, or other distinctive characteristics, taken in conjunction with circumstances.

(5) Voice identification. Identification of a voice, whether heard firsthand or through mechanical or electronic transmission or recording, by opinion based upon hearing the voice at any time under circumstances connecting it with the alleged speaker.

(6) Telephone conversations. Telephone conversations, by evidence that a call was made to the number assigned at the time by the telephone company to a particular person or business, if (A) in the case of a person, circumstances, including self-identification, show the person answering to be the one called, or (B) in the case of a business, the call was made to a place of business and the conversation related to business reasonably transacted over the telephone.

(7) Public records or reports. Evidence that a writing authorized by law to be recorded or filed and in fact recorded or filed in a public office, or a purported public record, report, statement, or data compilation, in any form, is from the public office where items of this nature are kept.

(8) Ancient documents or data compilation. Evidence that a document or data compilation, in any form, (A) is in such condition as to create no suspicion concerning its authenticity, (B) was in a place where it, if authentic, would likely be, and (C) has been in existence 20 years or more at the time it is offered.

(9) Process or system. Evidence describing a process or system used to produce a result and showing that the process or system produces an accurate result.

(10) Methods provided by statute or rule. Any method of authentication or identification provided by Act of Congress or by other rules prescribed by the Supreme Court pursuant to statutory authority.

Rule 902.

SELF-AUTHENTICATION

Extrinsic evidence of authenticity as a condition precedent to admissibility is not required with respect to the following:

(1) Domestic public documents under seal. A document bearing a seal purporting to be that of the United States, or of any

State, district, Commonwealth, territory, or insular possession thereof, or the Panama Canal Zone, or the Trust Territory of the Pacific Islands, or of a political subdivision, department, officer, or agency thereof, and a signature purporting to be an attestation or execution.

(2) Domestic public documents not under seal. A document purporting to bear the signature in the official capacity of an officer or employee of any entity included in paragraph (1) hereof, having no seal, if a public officer having a seal and having official duties in the district or political subdivision of the officer or employee certifies under seal that the signer has the official capacity and that the signature is genuine.

(3) Foreign public documents. A document purporting to be executed or attested in an official capacity by a person authorized by the laws of a foreign country to make the execution or attestation, and accompanied by a final certification as to the genuineness of the signature and official position (A) of the executing or attesting person, or (B) of any foreign official whose certificate of genuineness of signature and official position relates to the execution or attestation or is in a chain of certificates of genuineness of signature and official position relating to the execution or attestation. A final certification may be made by a secretary of an embassy or legation, consul general, consul, vice consul, or consular agent of the United States, or a diplomatic or consular official of the foreign country assigned or accredited to the United States. If reasonable opportunity has been given to all parties to investigate the authenticity and accuracy of official documents, the court may, for good cause shown, order that they be treated as presumptively authentic without final certification or permit them to be evidenced by an attested summary with or without final certification.

(4) Certified copies of public records. A copy of an official record or report or entry therein, or of a document authorized by law to be recorded or filed and actually recorded or filed in a public office, including data compilations in any form, certified as correct by the custodian or other person authorized to make the certification, by certificate complying with paragraph (1), (2), or (3) of this rule or complying with any Act of Congress or rule prescribed by the Supreme Court pursuant to statutory authority.

(5) Official publications. Books, pamphlets, or other publications purporting to be issued by public authority.

(6) Newspapers and periodicals. Printed materials purporting to be newspapers or periodicals.

(7) Trade inscriptions and the like. Inscriptions, signs, tags, or labels purporting to have been affixed in the course of business and indicating ownership, control, or origin.

(8) Acknowledged documents. Documents accompanied by a certificate of acknowledgment executed in the manner provided by law by a notary public or other officer authorized by law to take acknowledgments.

(9) Commercial paper and related documents. Commercial paper, signatures thereon, and documents relating thereto to the extent provided by general commercial law.

(10) Presumptions under Acts of Congress. Any signature, document, or other matter declared by Act of Congress to be presumptively or prima facie genuine or authentic.

(11) Certified domestic records of regularly conducted activity. The original or a duplicate of a domestic record of regularly conducted activity that would be admissible under Rule 803(6) if accompanied by a written declaration of its custodian or other qualified person, in a manner complying with any Act of Congress or rule prescribed by the Supreme Court pursuant to statutory authority, certifying that the record—

(A) was made at or near the time of the occurrence of the matters set forth by, or from information transmitted by, a person with knowledge of those matters;

(B) was kept in the course of the regularly conducted activity; and

(C) was made by the regularly conducted activity as a regular practice.

A party intending to offer a record into evidence under this paragraph must provide written notice of that intention to all adverse parties, and must make the record and declaration available for inspection sufficiently in advance of their offer into evidence to provide an adverse party with a fair opportunity to challenge them.

(12) Certified foreign records of regularly conducted activity. In a civil case, the original or a duplicate of a foreign record of regularly conducted activity that would be admissible under Rule 803(6) if accompanied by a written declaration by its custodian or other qualified person certifying that the record—

(A) was made at or near the time of the occurrence of the matters set forth by, or from information transmitted by, a person with knowledge of those matters;

(B) was kept in the course of the regularly conducted activity; and

(C) was made by the regularly conducted activity as a regular practice.

The declaration must be signed in a manner that, if falsely made, would subject the maker to criminal penalty under the laws of the country where the declaration is signed. A party intending to offer a record into evidence under this paragraph must provide written notice of that intention to all adverse parties, and must make the record and declaration available for inspection sufficiently in advance of their offer into evidence to provide an adverse party with a fair opportunity to challenge them.

As amended 1987, 1988, 2000.

Rule 903.

SUBSCRIBING WITNESS' TESTIMONY UNNECESSARY

The testimony of a subscribing witness is not necessary to authenticate a writing unless required by the laws of the jurisdiction whose laws govern the validity of the writing.

ARTICLE X. CONTENTS OF WRITINGS, RECORDINGS, AND PHOTOGRAPHS

Rule 1001.

DEFINITIONS

For purposes of this article the following definitions are applicable:

(1) Writings and recordings. "Writings" and "recordings" consist of letters, words, or numbers, or their equivalent, set down by handwriting, typewriting, printing, photostating, photographing, magnetic impulse, mechanical or electronic recording, or other form of data compilation.

(2) Photographs. "Photographs" include still photographs, X-ray films, video tapes, and motion pictures.

(3) Original. An "original" of a writing or recording is the writing or recording itself or any counterpart intended to have the same effect by a person executing or issuing it. An "original" of a photograph includes the negative or any print therefrom. If data are stored in a computer or similar device, any printout or other output readable by sight, shown to reflect the data accurately, is an "original."

(4) Duplicate. A "duplicate" is a counterpart produced by the same impression as the original, or from the same matrix, or by means of photography, including enlargements and miniatures, or by mechanical or electronic re-recording, or by chemical reproduction, or by other equivalent techniques which accurately reproduces the original.

Rule 1002.

REQUIREMENT OF ORIGINAL

To prove the content of a writing, recording, or photograph, the original writing, recording, or photograph is required, except as otherwise provided in these rules or by Act of Congress.

Rule 1003.

ADMISSIBILITY OF DUPLICATES

A duplicate is admissible to the same extent as an original unless (1) a genuine question is raised as to the authenticity of the original or (2) in the circumstances it would be unfair to admit the duplicate in lieu of the original.

Rule 1004.

ADMISSIBILITY OF OTHER EVIDENCE OF CONTENTS

The original is not required, and other evidence of the contents of a writing, recording, or photograph is admissible if—

(1) Originals lost or destroyed. All originals are lost or have been destroyed, unless the proponent lost or destroyed them in bad faith; or

(2) Original not obtainable. No original can be obtained by any available judicial process or procedure; or

(3) Original in possession of opponent. At a time when an original was under the control of the party against whom offered, that party was put on notice, by the pleadings or otherwise, that the contents would be a subject of proof at the hearing, and that party does not produce the original at the hearing; or

(4) Collateral matters. The writing, recording, or photograph is not closely related to a controlling issue.

As amended 1987.

Rule 1005.

PUBLIC RECORDS

The contents of an official record, or of a document authorized to be recorded or filed and actually recorded or filed, including data compilations in any form, if otherwise admissible, may be proved by copy, certified as correct in accordance with rule 902 or testified to be correct by a witness who has compared it with the original. If a copy which complies with the foregoing cannot be obtained by the exercise of reasonable diligence, then other evidence of the contents may be given.

Rule 1006.

SUMMARIES

The contents of voluminous writings, recordings, or photographs which cannot conveniently be examined in court may be presented in the form of a chart, summary, or calculation. The originals, or duplicates, shall be made available for examination or copying, or both, by other parties at reasonable time and place. The court may order that they be produced in court.

Rule 1007.

TESTIMONY OR WRITTEN ADMISSION OF PARTY

Contents of writings, recordings, or photographs may be proved by the testimony or deposition of the party against whom offered or by that party's written admission, without accounting for the nonproduction of the original.

As amended 1987.

Rule 1008.

FUNCTIONS OF COURT AND JURY

When the admissibility of other evidence of contents of writings, recordings, or photographs under these rules depends upon the fulfillment of a condition of fact, the question whether the condition has been fulfilled is ordinarily for the court to determine in accordance with the provisions of rule 104. However, when an issue is raised (a) whether the asserted writing ever existed, or (b) whether another writing, recording, or photograph produced at the trial is the original, or (c) whether other evidence of contents correctly reflects the contents, the issue is for the trier of fact to determine as in the case of other issues of fact.

ARTICLE XI. MISCELLANEOUS RULES

Rule 1101.

APPLICABILITY OF RULES

(a) Courts and judges. These rules apply to the United States district courts, the District Court of Guam, the District Court of the Virgin Islands, the District Court for the Northern

Mariana Islands, the United States courts of appeals, the United States Claims Court, and to United States bankruptcy judges and United States magistrate judges, in the actions, cases, and proceedings and to the extent hereinafter set forth. The terms "judge" and "court" in these rules include United States bankruptcy judges and United States magistrate judges.

(b) Proceedings generally. These rules apply generally to civil actions and proceedings, including admiralty and maritime cases, to criminal cases and proceedings, to contempt proceedings except those in which the court may act summarily, and to proceedings and cases under title 11, United States Code.

(c) Rule of privilege. The rule with respect to privileges applies at all stages of all actions, cases, and proceedings.

(d) Rules inapplicable. The rules (other than with respect to privileges) do not apply in the following situations:

(1) *Preliminary questions of fact.* The determination of questions of fact preliminary to admissibility of evidence when the issue is to be determined by the court under rule 104.

(2) *Grand jury.* Proceedings before grand juries.

(3) *Miscellaneous proceedings.* Proceedings for extradition or rendition; preliminary examinations in criminal cases; sentencing, or granting or revoking probation; issuance of warrants for arrest, criminal summonses, and search warrants; and proceedings with respect to release on bail or otherwise.

(e) Rules applicable in part. In the following proceedings these rules apply to the extent that matters of evidence are not provided for in the statutes which govern procedure therein or in other rules prescribed by the Supreme Court pursuant to statutory authority: the trial of misdemeanors and other petty offenses before United States magistrate judges; review of agency actions when the facts are subject to trial de novo under section 706(2)(F) of title 5, United States Code; review of orders of the Secretary of Agriculture under section 2 of the Act entitled "An Act to authorize association of producers of agricultural products" approved February 18, 1922 (7 U.S.C. 292), and under sections 6 and 7(c) of the Perishable Agricultural Commodities Act, 1930 (7 U.S.C. 499f, 499g(c)); naturalization and revocation of naturalization under sections 310–318 of the Immigration and Nationality Act (8 U.S.C. 1421–1429); prize proceedings in admiralty under sections 7651–7681 of title 10, United States Code; review of orders of the Secretary of the Interior under section 2 of the Act entitled "An Act authorizing associations of producers of aquatic products" approved June 25, 1934 (15 U.S.C. 522); review of orders of petroleum control boards under section 5 of the Act entitled "An Act to regulate interstate and foreign commerce in petroleum and its products by prohibiting the shipment in such commerce of petroleum and its products produced in violation of State law, and for other purposes", approved February 22, 1935 (15 U.S.C. 715d); actions for fines, penalties, or forfeitures under part V of title IV of the Tariff Act of 1930 (19 U.S.C. 1581–1624), or under the Anti-Smuggling Act (19 U.S.C. 1701–1711); criminal libel for condemnation, exclusion of imports, or other proceedings under the Federal Food, Drug, and Cosmetic Act (21 U.S.C. 301–392); disputes between seamen under sections 4079, 4080, and 4081 of the Revised Statutes (22 U.S.C. 256–258); habeas corpus under sections 2241–2254 of title 28, United States Code; motions to vacate, set aside or correct sentence under section 2255 of title 28, United States Code; actions for penalties for refusal to transport destitute seamen under section 4578 of the Revised Statutes (46 U.S.C. 679); actions against the United States under the Act entitled "An Act authorizing suits against the United States in admiralty for damage caused by and salvage service rendered to public vessels belonging to the United States, and for other purposes", approved March 3, 1925 (46 U.S.C. 781–790), as implemented by section 7730 of title 10, United States Code.

As amended 1975, 1979, 1982, 1987, 1988, 1993.

Rule 1102.

AMENDMENTS

Amendments to the Federal Rules of Evidence may be made as provided in section 2072 of title 28 of the United States Code.

As amended 1991.

Rule 1103.

TITLE

These rules may be known and cited as the Federal Rules of Evidence.

[The Act of Congress of January 2, 1975, Pub.L. 93–595, § 1, 88 Stat. 1926, stated that the rules therein set forth, to be known as the Federal Rules of Evidence, "shall take effect on the one hundred and eightieth day beginning after the date of the enactment of this Act. These rules apply to actions, cases, and proceedings brought after the rules take effect. These rules also apply to further procedure in actions, cases, and proceedings then pending, except to the extent that application of the rules would not be feasible, or would work injustice, in which event former evidentiary principles apply." The Rules became effective July 1, 1975. For legislative history, see Michael H. Graham, Handbook of Federal Evidence.]

[Rule 801(d) was amended October 16, 1975, Pub.L. 94–113, § 1, 89 Stat. 576, to be effective October 31, 1975.]

[Technical corrections to Rules 606(b), 803(23), 804(b), and 1101(e), and an amendment to Rule 410, were made December 12, 1975, Pub.L. 94–149, § 1, 89 Stat. 805.]

[Rule 412 was added October 28, 1978, Pub.L. 95–540, § 2, 92 Stat. 2046, to be effective November 28, 1978.]

[Rule 1101(a) and (b) was amended November 6, 1978, Pub.L. 95–598, Title II, § 251, 92 Stat. 2673, to be effective October 1, 1979.]

[Rule 410 was amended by the order of the Supreme Court of April 30, 1979. 441 U.S. 1005. The effective date of this amendment was delayed by Congress July 31, 1979, Pub.L. 96–42, 93 Stat. 326, until December 1, 1980.]

[Rule 1101(a) was amended April 2, 1982, Pub.L. 97–164, Title I, § 142, 96 Stat. 45, to be effective October 1, 1982.]

[Rule 704 was amended October 12, 1984, Pub.L. 98–473, Title II, § 406, 98 Stat. 2067.]

[Rules 101 and 1101(a) were amended, and gender-specific language was neutralized in numerous Rules, by the order of the Supreme Court of March 2, 1987, to be effective October 1, 1987. 480 U.S. 1023.]

[Technical corrections to Rules 101, 602, 608(b), 613(b), 615, 902(3), and 1101(a) and (e) were made by the order of the Supreme Court of April 25, 1988, to be effective November 1, 1988. 485 U.S. 1049.]

[Rules 412, 804(a), and 1101(a) were amended November 18, 1988, Pub.L. 100–690, Title VII, §§ 7046, 7075, 102 Stat. 4400, 4405.]

[Rule 609(a) was amended by the order of the Supreme Court of January 26, 1990, to be effective December 1, 1990. 493 U.S. 1173.]

[Rules 404(b) and 1102 were amended by the order of the Supreme Court of April 30, 1991, to be effective December 1, 1991. 500 U.S. 1001.]

[Rules 101, 705, and 1101(a) and (e) were amended by the order of the Supreme Court of April 22, 1993, to be effective December 1, 1993. 507 U.S. 1187.]

[Rule 412 was amended September 13, 1994, Pub.L. 103–322, Title IV, § 40141(b), 108 Stat. 1919, to be effective December 1, 1994.]

[Rules 413, 414, and 415 were added September 13, 1994, Pub.L. 103–322, Title XXXII, § 320935(a), 108 Stat. 2135, to be effective July 9, 1995.]

[Rules 407, 801(d), 803(24), 804(b), and 806 were amended, and Rule 807 added, by the order of the Supreme Court of April 11, 1997, to be effective December 1, 1997. 520 U.S. 1323.]

[Rule 615 was amended by the order of the Supreme Court of April 24, 1998, to be effective December 1, 1998. 523 U.S. 1235.]

[Rules 103(a), 404(a), 701, 702, 703, 803(6), and 902 were amended by the order of the Supreme Court of April 17, 2000, to be effective December 1, 2000. 529 U.S. 1189.]

[Rule 608(b) was amended by the order of the Supreme Court of March 27, 2003, to be effective December 1, 2003. ___ U.S. ___.]

LOCAL RULES OF PRACTICE FOR THE UNITED STATES DISTRICT COURT FOR THE NORTHERN DISTRICT OF NEW YORK

SECTION I. SCOPE OF THE RULES— ONE FORM OF ACTION

1.1 Scope of the Rules

(a) Title and Citation. These are the Local Rules of Practice for the United States District Court for the Northern District of New York. They shall be cited as "L.R. . . . "

(b) Effective Date; Transitional Provision. These Rules became effective on **January 1, 2004**. Recent amendments are noted with the phrase.

(c) Scope of the Rules; Construction. These Rules supplement the Federal Rules of Civil and Criminal Procedure. They shall be construed so as to be consistent with those Rules and to promote the just, efficient and economical determination of every action and proceeding.

(d) Sanctions and Penalties for Noncompliance. Failure of an attorney or of a party to comply with any provision of these Rules, General Orders of this District, Orders of the Court, or the Federal Rules of Civil or Criminal Procedure shall be a ground for imposition of sanctions.

(e) Definitions.

1. The word "court," except where the context otherwise requires, refers to the United States District Court for the Northern District of New York.

2. The word "judge" refers either to a United States District Judge or to a United States Magistrate Judge, where appropriate.

3. The words "assigned judge," except where the context otherwise requires, refer to the United States District Judge or United States Magistrate Judge exercising jurisdiction with respect to a particular action or proceeding.

4. The words "Chief Judge" refer to the Chief Judge or a judge temporarily performing the duties of Chief Judge under 28 U.S.C. § 136(e).

5. The word "clerk" refers to the Clerk of the Court or to a deputy clerk whom the Clerk designates to perform services of the general class provided for in Fed. R. Civ. P. 77.

6. The word "marshal" refers to the United States Marshal of this district and includes deputy marshals.

7. The word "party" shall include a party's representative.

8. Reference in these Rules to an attorney for a party is in no way intended to preclude a party from appearing pro se, in which case reference to attorney applies to the pro se litigant.

9. Where appropriate the "singular" shall include the "plural" and vice versa.

1.2 Availability of the Local Rules

Copies of these Rules are available from the Clerk's office or at the Court's webpage at "www.nynd.uscourts.gov."

2.1 One Form of Action

[Reserved.]

SECTION II. COMMENCEMENT OF ACTION; SERVICE OF PROCESS, PLEADINGS, MOTIONS AND ORDERS

3.1 Civil Cover Sheet

A completed civil cover sheet on a form available from the Clerk shall be submitted with every complaint, notice of removal, or other document initiating a civil action. This requirement is solely for administrative purposes, and matters appearing on the civil cover sheet have no legal effect in the action.

3.2 Venue

Venue for civil cases filed in the Northern District of New York shall be controlled by the Court's Civil Case Assignment Plan.

3.3 Complex and Multi-district Litigation

(a) If the judge presiding over a case determines, in his or her discretion, that the case is of such a complex nature that it cannot reasonably be trial ready within eighteen months from the date the complaint is filed, the judge may design and issue a particularized case management order which will move the case to trial as quickly as the complexity of the case allows.

(b) The parties shall promptly notify the Court in writing if any action commenced is appropriate for multi-district litigation.

4.1 Service of Process

(a) Service shall be made in the manner specified in the Federal Rules of Civil Procedure or as required or permitted by statute. The party seeking service of papers shall be responsible for arranging the service. The Clerk is authorized to sign orders appointing persons to serve process.

(b) Upon the filing of a complaint, the Clerk shall issue to the plaintiff General Order 25 which requires, among other things, service of process upon all defendants within sixty (60) days of the filing of the complaint. This expedited service requirement is necessary to ensure adequate time for pretrial discovery and motion practice. In no event shall service of process be completed after the time specified in Fed. R. Civ. P. 4.

(c) At the time the complaint or notice of removal is served, the party seeking to invoke the jurisdiction of this Court shall also serve on all parties the following materials:

1. Judicial Case Assignment Form;
2. Joint Civil Case Management Plan Containing Notice of Initial Pretrial Conference;
3. Notice and Consent Form to Proceed Before a United States Magistrate Judge; and
4. Notice and Consent Form for the Court Sponsored Alternative Dispute Resolution Procedures.

The Clerk shall furnish these material to the party seeking to invoke the jurisdiction of this Court at the time the complaint or notice of removal is filed.

5.1 Service and Filing of Papers

(a) All pleadings and other papers shall be served and filed in accordance with the Federal Rules of Civil Procedure and shall be in the form prescribed by L.R. 10.1. The party or its designee shall declare, by affidavit or certification, that they have provided all other parties in the action with all documents they have filed with the Court. See also L.R. 26.2 (discovery material).

(b) In civil actions where the Court has directed a party to submit an order or judgment, that party shall file all such orders or judgments in duplicate, and the Clerk's entry of such duplicate in the proper record book shall be deemed in compliance with Fed. R. Civ. P. 79(b). Such party shall also furnish the Clerk with a sufficient number of additional copies for each party to the action, which the Clerk shall mail with notice of entry in accordance with Fed. R. Civ. P. 77(d).

(c) In a civil action, on filing a notice of appeal, the appellant shall furnish the Clerk with a sufficient number of copies for mailing in accordance with Fed. R. App. P. 3(d).

(d) On filing of a motion pursuant to Fed. R. Civ. P. 65.1, the moving party shall furnish the Clerk with a sufficient number of copies of the motion and notice of the motion in compliance with the mailing provision of that rule.

(e) No paper on file in the Clerk's office shall be removed except pursuant to the Court's order.

(f) All civil complaints submitted to the Clerk for filing shall be accompanied by a summons or, if electing to serve by mail, the approved service by mail forms, together with sufficient copies of the complaint for service on each of the named defendants.

(g) Every summons shall be served by a private process server, except as otherwise required by statute or rule or as the Court directs for good cause shown. A private process server is any person authorized to serve process in an action brought in the New York State Supreme Court or in the court of general jurisdiction of the State in which service is made.

(h) In the case of a prisoner's civil rights action, or any action where a party has been granted leave to proceed in forma pauperis, the Marshal shall serve the summons and complaint by regular mail pursuant to Fed. R. Civ. P. 4(c)(2). The Marshal shall file the return or other acknowledgment of service with the Court. The return shall constitute prima facie evidence of the service of process. If no acknowledgment of service is filed with the Court, the Marshal shall notify the plaintiff and, if requested by the plaintiff, shall make personal service as provided in Fed. R. Civ. P. 4.

5.1.2 Electronic Case Filing

All cases filed in this Court may be assigned to the Electronic Case Files System ("ECF") in accordance with the Procedural Order on Electronic Case Filing (General Order #22), the provisions of which are incorporated herein by reference, and which the Court may amend from time to time. Copies of General Order #22 are available at the Clerk's office or at the Court's webpage at "www.nynd.uscourts.gov."

5.2 Prepayment of Fees

(a) Filing Fees. A party commencing an action or removing an action from a state court must pay to the Clerk the statutory filing fee before the case will be docketed and process issued. In forma pauperis proceedings are governed by Title 28 U.S.C. § 1915 and L. R. 5.4.

(b) Miscellaneous Fees. The Clerk shall not be required to render any service for which a fee is prescribed by statute or by the Judicial Conference of the United States unless the fee for the service is paid in advance.

5.3 Schedule of Fees

Fee schedules are available at the Clerk's office or at the Court's webpage at "www.nynd.uscourts.gov."

5.4 Civil Actions Filed In Forma Pauperis; Applications for Leave to Proceed In Forma Pauperis

(a) On receipt of a complaint or petition and an application to proceed in forma pauperis, and supporting documentation as required for prisoner litigants, the Clerk shall promptly file the complaint or petition without the payment of fees and assign the action in accordance with L.R. 40.1. The complaint, application, and supporting documentation then shall be forwarded to the assigned Magistrate Judge for a determination of whether the applicant will be granted leave to proceed in forma pauperis and whether the complaint or petition shall be served by the Marshal. Prior to service of process by the Marshal pursuant to 28 U.S.C. § 1915(d) and L.R. 5.1(h), the Court shall review all actions filed pursuant to 28 U.S.C. § 1915 to determine whether sua sponte dismissal is appropriate. The granting of an in forma pauperis application shall in no way relieve the party of the obligation to pay all other fees for which such party is responsible regarding such action, including, but not limited to, copying and/or witness fees.

(b) Whenever a fee is due for a civil action subject to the Prison Litigation Reform Act ("PLRA"), the prisoner must comply with the following procedure:

1.(A) Submit a signed, fully completed and properly certified in forma pauperis application; and

(B) Submit the authorization form issued by the Clerk's office.

2.(A)(i) If the prisoner **has not** fully complied with the requirements set forth in paragraph 1 above, and the action is not subject to sua sponte dismissal, a judicial officer shall, by Court order, inform the prisoner as to what must be submitted in order to proceed with such action in this District ("Order").

(ii) The Order shall afford the prisoner **thirty (30) days** in which to comply with the terms of same. If the prisoner fails to fully comply with the terms of such Order within such period of time, the action shall be dismissed.

(B) If the prisoner **has** fully complied with the requirements set forth in paragraph 1 above, and the action is not subject to sua sponte dismissal, the judicial officer shall review the in forma pauperis application. The granting of the application shall in no way relieve the prisoner of the obligation to pay the full amount of the filing fee.

3. After being notified of the filing of the civil action, the agency having custody of the prisoner shall comply with the provisions of 28 U.S.C. § 1915(b) regarding the filing fee due concerning the action.

5.5 Filing by Facsimile

The Clerk's office shall *not* accept any facsimile transmission unless the Court gives prior approval.

5.6 Service of the Writ in Exclusion and Deportation Cases

(a) After delivery of an alien for deportation to the master of a ship or the commanding officer of an airplane, the writ shall be addressed to, and served on, the master or commanding officer only. Notice to the respondent of the allowance or issuance of the writ shall not be recognized as binding without proper service. Service shall be made by delivery of the original writ to the respondent while the alien is in custody. Service shall not be made on a master after a ship has cast off her moorings.

(b) In case the writ is served on the master of a ship or on the commanding officer of an airplane, such person may deliver the alien at once to the officer from whom such person received the alien for custody until the return day. In such case, the writ shall be deemed returnable promptly; and the custody of the officer receiving the alien shall be deemed that of the respondent, pending disposition of the writ.

5.7 Documents to Be Provided to the Clerk

All pretrial and settlement conference statements shall be provided to the Clerk but not filed. These documents are not for public view. Forms for preparation of pretrial and settlement conference statements are available from the Clerk's office or at the Court's webpage at "www.nynd.uscourts.gov."

6.1 Calculation of Time Periods

[Reserved.]

SECTION III. PLEADINGS AND MOTIONS

7.1 Motion Practice

Introduction—Motion Dates and Times. Unless the Court directs otherwise, motions shall be made returnable at the **next regularly scheduled motion date at least thirty-one days from the date the motion is filed and served**. The moving party shall select a return date in accordance with the procedures set forth in subdivision (b). If the return date selected is not the next regularly scheduled motion date, or if no return date is selected, the Clerk will set the proper return date and notify the parties.

Information regarding motion dates and times is specified on the case assignment form provided to the parties at the commencement of the litigation or may be obtained from the Clerk's office or at the Court's webpage at "www.nynd.uscourts.gov."

(a) Papers Required. Except as otherwise provided in this paragraph, all motions and opposition to motions require a memorandum of law, supporting affidavit, and proof of service on all the parties. See L.R. 5.1(a). Additional requirements for specific types of motions, including cross-motions, See L.R. 7.1(c), are set forth in this rule.

1. *Memorandum of Law.* No party shall file or serve a memorandum of law that exceeds twenty-five (25) pages in length, unless leave of the judge hearing the motion is obtained prior to filing. All memoranda of law shall contain a table of contents and, wherever possible, parallel citations. Memoranda of law that contain citations to decisions exclusively reported on computerized databases (e.g., Westlaw, Lexis, Juris, etc.) shall be accompanied by copies of the decisions.

When making a motion based upon a rule or statute, the moving papers must specify the rule or statute upon which the motion is predicated.

A memorandum of law is required for all motions except the following:

(A) a motion pursuant to Fed. R. Civ. P. 15 to amend or supplement a pleading;

(B) a motion pursuant to Fed. R. Civ. P. 12(e) for a more definite statement;

(C) a motion pursuant to Fed. R. Civ. P. 17 to appoint next friend or guardian ad litem;

(D) a motion pursuant to Fed. R. Civ. P. 25 for substitution of parties; and

(E) a motion pursuant to Fed. R. Civ. P. 37 to compel discovery.

2. *Affidavit.* An affidavit must not contain legal arguments but must contain factual and procedural background as appropriate for the motion being made.

An affidavit is required for all motions except the following:

(A) a motion pursuant to Fed. R. Civ. P. 12(b)(6) for failure to state a claim upon which relief can be granted;

(B) a motion pursuant to Fed. R. Civ. P. 12(c) for judgment on the pleadings; and

(C) a motion pursuant to Fed. R. Civ. P. 12(f) to strike a portion of a pleading.

3. *Summary Judgment Motions.* Any motion for summary judgment shall contain a Statement of Material Facts. The Statement of Material Facts shall set forth, in numbered paragraphs, each material fact about which the moving party contends there exists no genuine issue. Each fact listed shall set forth a specific citation to the record where the fact is established. The record for purposes of the Statement of Material Facts includes the pleadings, depositions, answers to interrogatories, admissions and affidavits. It does not, however, include attorney's affidavits. *Failure of the moving party to submit an accurate and complete Statement of Material Facts shall result in a denial of the motion.*

The opposing party shall file a response to the Statement of Material Facts. The non-movant's response shall mirror the movant's Statement of Material Facts by admitting and/or denying each of the movant's assertions in matching numbered paragraphs. Each denial shall set forth a specific citation to the record where the factual issue arises. The non-movant's response may also set forth any additional material facts that the non-movant contends are in dispute in separately numbered paragraphs. *Any facts set forth in the Statement of Material Facts shall be deemed admitted unless specifically controverted by the opposing party.*

4. *Motions to Amend or Supplement Pleadings or for Joinder or Interpleader.* An unsigned copy of the proposed amended pleading must be attached to a motion brought under Fed. R. Civ. P. 14, 15, 19–22. Except as provided by leave of Court, the proposed amended pleading must be a complete pleading, which will supersede the original pleading in all

respects. No portion of the prior pleading shall be incorporated into the proposed amended pleading by reference.

The motion must set forth specifically the proposed amendments and identify the amendments in the proposed pleading, either through the submission of a red-lined version of the original pleading or other equivalent means.

Where leave to supplement a pleading is sought under Fed. R. Civ. P. 15(d), the proposed supplemental pleading must be limited to acts that occurred subsequent to the filing of the original pleading. The paragraphs in the proposed pleading must be numbered consecutively to the paragraphs contained in the pleading that is to be supplemented.

Caveat: The granting of the motion does not constitute the filing of the amended pleading. After leave is given, unless otherwise ordered, the moving party must file and serve the original signed amended pleading within ten (10) days of the Order granting the motion.

(b) Motions.

1. *Dispositive Motions.* All motion papers must be filed with the Court and served upon the other parties not less than THIRTY–ONE DAYS prior to the return date of the motion. The Notice of Motion must state the return date which has been selected by the moving party.

Opposing papers must be filed with the Court and served upon the other parties not less than SEVENTEEN DAYS prior to the return date of the motion.

Reply papers must be filed with the Court and served upon the other parties not less than ELEVEN DAYS prior to the return date of the motion.

A surreply is not permitted.

All original motion papers, including memoranda of law and supporting affidavits, if any, shall be filed in accordance with the Administrative Procedures for Electronic Case Filing (General Order #22) and/or the case assignment form provided to the parties at the commencement of the litigation. The assigned judge may request that the parties provide a courtesy copy of the motion papers.

2. *Non-Dispositive Motions.* Prior to making any non-dispositive motion before the assigned Magistrate Judge, the parties must make **good faith efforts among themselves to resolve or reduce all differences relating to the non-dispositive issue**. If, after conferring, the parties are unable to arrive at a mutually satisfactory resolution, the party seeking relief must then request a court conference with the assigned Magistrate Judge.

A court conference is a prerequisite to filing a non-dispositive motion before the assigned Magistrate Judge. Within the notice of motion, the moving party is required to set forth the date that the court conference with the Magistrate Judge was held regarding the issues being presented in the motion. Failure to include this information within the notice of motion may result in the rejection of the motion papers.

Actions which involve an incarcerated, pro se party are not subject to the requirement that a court conference be held prior to filing a non-dispositive motion.

Unless the Court orders otherwise, all motion papers must be filed with the Court and served upon the other parties not less than THIRTY–ONE DAYS prior to the return date of the motion.

Opposing papers must be filed with the Court and served upon the other parties not less than SEVENTEEN DAYS prior to the return date of the motion.

Reply papers are not permitted without the Court's prior permission.

3. *Failure to Timely File or Comply.* Any papers required under this Rule that are not timely filed or are otherwise not in compliance with this Rule shall not be considered unless good cause is shown. Where a properly filed motion is unopposed and the Court determines that the moving party has met its burden to demonstrate entitlement to the relief requested therein, the non-moving party's failure to file or serve any papers as required by this Rule shall be deemed as consent to the granting or denial of the motion, as the case may be, unless good cause is shown.

Any party who does not intend to oppose a motion, or a movant who does not intend to pursue a motion, shall promptly notify the Court and the other parties of such intention. Notice should be provided at the earliest practicable date, but in any event no less than SEVEN CALENDAR DAYS prior to the scheduled return date of the motion, unless for good cause shown. **Failure to comply with this Rule may result in the Court imposing sanctions.**

(c) Cross–Motions. A cross-motion may be filed and served at the time opposition papers to the original motion are filed and served (not less than SEVENTEEN DAYS prior to the return date of the motion). If a cross-motion is made, the cross-motion brief must be joined with the opposition brief and may not exceed twenty-five (25) pages in length, exclusive of exhibits. A separate brief in opposition to the original motion is not permissible.

The original moving party may reply in further support of the original motion and in opposition to the cross-motion with a reply/opposition brief that does not exceed twenty-five (25) pages in length, exclusive of exhibits. The reply/opposition papers must be filed with the Court and served on the other parties not less than ELEVEN DAYS prior to the return date of the original motion.

The cross-moving party may not reply in further support of its cross-motion without the Court's prior permission.

(d) Discovery Motions. The following steps are required prior to making any discovery motion pursuant to Rules 26 through 37 of the Federal Rules of Civil Procedure.

1. Parties must make good faith efforts among themselves to resolve or reduce all differences relating to discovery prior to seeking court intervention.

2. The moving party must confer in detail with the opposing party concerning the discovery issues between them in a good faith effort to eliminate or reduce the area of controversy and to arrive at a mutually satisfactory resolution. Failure to do so may result in denial of a motion to compel discovery and/or imposition of sanctions.

3. If the parties' conference does not fully resolve the discovery issues, the party seeking relief must then request a court conference with the assigned Magistrate Judge. Incarcerated, pro se parties are not subject to the court conference requirement prior to filing a motion to compel discovery. The assigned Magistrate Judge may direct the party making the request for a court conference to file an affidavit setting forth the date(s) and mode(s) of the consultation(s) with the opposing party and a letter that concisely sets forth the nature of the dispute and a specific listing of each of the items of discovery sought or opposed. Immediately following each disputed item, the party must set forth the reason why the item should be allowed or disallowed.

4. Following a request for a discovery conference, the Court may schedule a conference and advise all parties of a date and time. The discovery conference may be conducted by telephone conference call, initiated by the party making the request for the conference, by video conference, or by personal appearance, as directed by the assigned Magistrate Judge.

5. Following a discovery conference, the Court may direct the prevailing party to submit a proposed order, on notice to the other parties.

6. If a party fails or refuses to confer in good faith with the requesting party, thus requiring the request for a discovery conference, at the Court's discretion, the resisting party will be subject to the sanction of the imposition of costs, including the

attorneys' fees of opposing counsel in accordance with Fed. R. Civ. P. 37.

7. A party claiming privilege with respect to a communication or other item must specifically identify the privilege and the grounds for the privilege claimed. No generalized claims of privilege may be made.

8. Any motion to compel discovery authorized by these Rules shall be filed no later than TEN CALENDAR DAYS after the discovery cut-off date. See L.R. 16.2.

(e) Order to Show Cause. All motions brought by Order to Show Cause shall conform with the requirements set forth in L. R. 7.1(a)(1) and (2). **Immediately after filing an Order to Show Cause, the moving party must telephone the Chambers of the presiding judicial officer and inform Chambers staff that they have filed an Order to Show Cause.** Telephone numbers for all Chambers may be obtained from the Clerk's office or at the Court's webpage at "www.nynd.uscourts.gov." The Court shall determine the briefing schedule and return date applicable to motions brought by Order to Show Cause.

In addition to the requirements set forth in Local Rule 7.1(a)(1) and (2), a motion brought by Order to Show Cause must include an affidavit clearly and specifically showing good and sufficient cause why the standard Notice of Motion procedure cannot be used. Reasonable advance notice of the application for an Order to Show Cause must be given to the other parties, except in those circumstances where the movant can demonstrate, in a detailed and specific affidavit, good cause and substantial prejudice that would result from the requirement of reasonable notice.

An Order to Show Cause must contain a space for the assigned judge to set forth (a) the deadline for supporting papers to be filed and served, (b) the deadline for opposing papers to be filed and served, and (c) the date and time for the hearing.

(f) Temporary Restraining Order. A temporary restraining order may be sought by Notice of Motion or Order to Show Cause, as appropriate. Filing procedures and requirements for supporting documents are the same as set forth in this Rule for other motions. Any application for a temporary restraining order must be served on all other parties unless otherwise permitted by Fed. R. Civ. P. 65. Motions for injunctive relief, other than those brought by Order to Show Cause, are governed by L.R. 7.1(b)(2). Motions brought by Order to Show Cause are governed by L.R. 7.1(e).

(g) Motion for Reconsideration. Motions for reconsideration or reargument, unless otherwise governed by Fed. R. Civ. P. 60, may be filed and served no later than TEN CALENDAR DAYS after the entry of the challenged judgment, order, or decree. All motions for reconsideration shall conform with the requirements set forth in L.R. 7.1(a)(1) and (2). The briefing schedule and return date applicable to motions for reconsideration shall conform to L.R. 7.1(b)(2). Motions for reconsideration or reargument will be decided on submission of the papers, without oral argument, unless the Court directs otherwise.

(h) Oral Argument. On all motions made to a district court judge, except motions for reconsideration, the parties shall appear for oral argument on the scheduled return date of the motion. In the discretion of the district court judge, or on consideration of a request of any party, a motion returnable before a district court judge may be disposed of without oral argument. Thus, the parties should be prepared to have their motion papers serve as the sole method of argument on the motion.

On all motions made to a magistrate judge, the parties shall not appear for oral argument on the scheduled return date of the motion unless the Magistrate Judge sua sponte directs or grants the request of any party for oral argument.

(i) Sanctions for Vexatious or Frivolous Motions or Failure to Comply with this Rule. A party who presents vexatious or frivolous motion papers or fails to comply with this Rule is subject to discipline as the Court deems appropriate, including sanctions and the imposition of costs and attorneys' fees to opposing counsel.

(j) Adjournments. Adjournment of motions is in the Court's discretion. Any party seeking an adjournment from the court must first contact the opposing party. No motion under this Rule will be adjourned more than two times unless the party seeking the adjournment has satisfied the Court that a further adjournment is necessary. In no event shall an adjournment last longer than four months. The party requesting the adjournment is responsible for renoticing the motion. Any motion not renoticed within four months from the initial adjournment will be deemed withdrawn.

8.1 Personal Privacy Protection

Parties shall refrain from including, or shall redact where inclusion is necessary, the following personal identifiers from all pleadings filed with the Court, including exhibits thereto, whether filed electronically or in paper form, unless the Court orders otherwise.

1. *Social security numbers*. If an individual's social security number must be included in a document, use only the last four digits of that number.

2. *Names of minor children.* If the involvement of a minor child must be mentioned, use only the initials of that child.

3. *Dates of birth.* If an individual's date of birth must be included in a document, use only the year.

4. *Financial account numbers.* If financial account numbers are relevant, use only the last four digits of those numbers.

5. *Home Addresses.* If a home address must be used, use only the City and State.

In addition, caution shall be exercised when filing documents that contain the following:

1) personal identifying number, such as a driver's license number;

2) medical records, treatment and diagnosis;

3) employment history;

4) individual financial information; and

5) proprietary or trade secret information.

In compliance with the E–Government Act of 2002, a party wishing to file a document containing the personal data identifiers specified above may file an unredacted document under seal. The Court shall retain this document as part of the record. The Court may, however, still require the party to file a redacted copy for the public. Counsel is strongly urged to discuss this issue with all their clients so that an informed decision about the inclusion of certain information may be made. The responsibility for redacting these personal identifiers **rests solely with counsel and the parties**. The Clerk will not review each pleading for compliance with this Rule. Counsel and the parties are cautioned that failure to redact these personal identifiers may subject them to the Court's full disciplinary power.

Exception: Transcripts of the administrative record in social security proceedings and state court records relating to a habeas corpus petitions are exempt from this requirement.

9.1 Request for Three–Judge Court

Whenever a party believes that the relief requested in a lawsuit is such that it may be granted only by a three-judge court, the words "Three–Judge Court," or the equivalent, shall be included immediately following the title of the first pleading in which the cause of action requesting a three-judge court is asserted. Unless the basis for the request is apparent from the pleading, it shall be set forth in the pleading or in an attached statement. On the convening of a three-judge court, in addition to the original papers on file, the following shall be made available to the clerk for distribution: three copies of the pleadings, three copies of the motion papers, and three copies of all memoranda of law.

9.2 Requirement to File a Civil RICO Statement

In any action in which a party asserts a claim under the Racketeer Influenced and Corrupt Organizations Act ("RICO"), 18 U.S.C. § 1961 et seq., the party asserting such a claim shall file, within thirty (30) days of the filing of the pleading containing such claim, a RICO statement. This statement shall conform to the format that the Court has adopted and shall be entitled "RICO Statement." Copies of General Order #14—CIVIL RICO STATEMENT FILING REQUIREMENTS may be obtained from the Clerk's office or at the Court's webpage at "www.nynd.uscourts.gov." This statement shall state in detail and with specificity the information requested in the RICO Statement. The Court shall construe the RICO Statement as an amendment to the pleadings.

10.1 Form of Papers

(a) Form Generally. All pleadings, motions, and other documents presented for filing shall be in the following form:

- 8 ½ x 11 inch white paper of good quality,
- plainly and legibly written, typewritten, printed or reproduced,
- without erasures or interlineation materially defacing them,
- in black ink,
- pages fastened,
- text in minimum 12 point type; footnotes minimum 10 point type,
- text double-spaced
- block quotation and footnotes may be single-spaced,
- extensive footnotes may not be used to circumvent page limitations,
- compacted or other compressed printing features are prohibited,
- 3 inch top margin on first page,
- typed matter not exceeding 6–1/2 x 9–1/2 inches on subsequent pages,
- pages consecutively numbered,
- punched with two (2) holes approximately 1/4 inch in diameter, centered 2–3/4 inches apart, ½ to 5/8 inch from top edge of document,

- the Court may order electronic submission in a WordPerfect-compatible format.

Documents that do not comply with the requirements listed above may be rejected upon order of the Court.

(b) Information required. The following information must appear on each document filed:

1. A caption, which must include the title of the Court, the title of the action, the civil action number of the case, the initials of the assigned judges, and the name or nature of the paper in sufficient detail for identification. **Affidavits and declarations must be separately captioned and *must not* be physically attached to the Notice of Motion or Memorandum of Law.**

2. Each document must identify the person filing the document. This identification must include an original signature of the attorney or pro se litigant; the typewritten name of that person; the address of a pro se litigant; and the bar roll number, office address, telephone number, e-mail address and fax number of the attorney. **All attorneys of record and pro se litigants must immediately notify the Court of any change of address.** The notice of change of address is to be filed with the Clerk and served on all other parties to the action. The notice must identify each and every action for which the notice shall apply.

Attorneys shall also file a new registration statement within ten days of a change of address, firm name, telephone number, e-mail address and fax number. Attorney registration forms may be obtained at the Court's webpage at "www.nynd.uscourts.gov;" see also L.R. 41.2(b); L.R. 83.1(e).

(c) The record on hearings, unless ordered printed, shall be plainly typewritten and bound in book form, paged and indexed.

(d) All documents including exhibits must be in the English language or be accompanied by an English translation.

11.1 Signing of Pleadings, Motions, and Other Papers; Sanctions

[Reserved.]

12.1 Defenses and Objections—How Presented

[Reserved.]

13.1 Counterclaims and Cross-claims

[Reserved.]

14.1 Impleader

See L.R. 7.1(a)(4).

15.1 Form of a Motion to Amend and Its Supporting Documentation

See L.R. 7.1(a)(4).

16.1 Civil Case Management

This Court has found that the interests of justice are most effectively served by adopting a systematic, differential case management system that tailors the level of individualized and case-specific management to such criteria as case complexity, time required to prepare a case for trial, and availability of judicial and other resources.

(a) Filing of Complaint/Service of Process. Upon the filing of a complaint, the Clerk shall issue to the plaintiff General Order 25, which requires, among other things, service of process upon all defendants within sixty (60) days of the filing of the complaint. This expedited service requirement is necessary to ensure adequate time for pretrial discovery and motion practice.

(b) Assignment of District Judge/Magistrate Judge. Upon filing of a complaint, the Clerk shall assign a district judge and a magistrate judge to preside over each case. The assignment shall be made in accordance with the provisions of the case assignment plan. Once assigned, either judicial officer shall have authority to design and issue a case management order.

(c) Initial Pretrial Conference. Except for cases excluded under section II of General Order 25, an initial pretrial conference pursuant to Fed. R. Civ. P. 16 shall be held within 120 days after the filing of the complaint. The Clerk shall set the date of this conference upon the filing of the complaint. The purpose of this conference will be to prepare and adopt a case-specific management plan which will be memorialized in a case management order. See subsection (d) below. In order to facilitate the adoption of such a plan, prior to the scheduled conference, counsel for all parties shall confer among themselves as required by Fed. R. Civ. P. 26(f) and shall use the Civil Case Management Plan form contained in the General Order 25 filing packet. The parties' jointly-proposed plan, or if consensus cannot be reached, each party's proposed plan, shall be filed with the Clerk at least ten (10) business days prior to the scheduled pretrial conference.

(d) Subject Matter of Initial Pretrial Conference. At the initial pretrial conference, the Court shall consider, and the parties shall be prepared to discuss, the following:

1. Deadlines for joinder of parties, amendment of pleadings, completion of discovery, and filing of dispositive motions;
2. Trial date;
3. Requests for jury trial;

4. Subject matter and personal jurisdiction;

5. Factual and legal bases for claims and defenses;

6. Factual and legal issues in dispute;

7. Factual and legal issues that can be agreed upon or which can be narrowed through motions and which will expedite resolution of the dispute;

8. Specific relief requested, including method for computing damages;

9. Intended discovery and proposed methods to limit and/or decrease time and expense thereof;

10. Suitability of case for voluntary arbitration;

11. Measures for reducing length of trial;

12. Related cases pending before this or other U.S. District Courts;

13. Procedures for certifying class actions, if appropriate;

14. Settlement prospects; and

15. If the case is in the ADR track, choice of ADR method and estimated time for completion of ADR.

(e) Uniform Pretrial Scheduling Order. Upon completion of the initial pretrial conference, the presiding judge may issue a Uniform Pretrial Scheduling Order setting forth deadlines for joinder of parties, amendment of pleadings, production of expert reports, completion of discovery, and filing of motions; a trial ready date; the requirements for all trial submissions; and if an ADR track case, the ADR method to be used and the deadline for completion of ADR.

(f) Enforcement of Deadlines. Deadlines that the Court institutes in any case management order shall be strictly enforced and shall not be modified by the Court, even upon stipulation of the parties, except upon a showing of good cause.

16.2 Discovery Cut–Off

The "discovery cut-off" is that date by which all responses to written discovery shall be due according to the Federal Rules of Civil Procedure and by which all depositions shall be concluded. Counsel are advised to initiate discovery requests and notice depositions sufficiently in advance of the cut-off date to comply with this Rule. Discovery requests that call for responses or scheduled depositions after the discovery cut-off will not be enforceable except by order of the court for good cause shown. Motions to compel discovery shall be filed and served no later than ten (10) days after the discovery cut-off. See L.R. 7.1(d)(8).

SECTION IV. PARTIES

17.1 Actions by or on Behalf of Infants and/or Incompetents

(a) An action by or on behalf of an infant or incompetent shall not be settled or compromised, or voluntarily discontinued, dismissed or terminated, without leave of the Court embodied in an order, judgment or decree. The proceedings on an application to settle or compromise such an action shall conform to the New York State statutes and rules; but the Court, for good cause shown, may dispense with any New York State requirement.

(b) The Court shall authorize payment of a reasonable attorneys' fee and proper disbursements from the amount recovered in such an action, whether realized by settlement, execution or otherwise, and shall determine the fee and disbursements, after due inquiry as to all charges against the amount recovered.

(c) The Court shall order the balance of the proceeds of the recovery or settlement to be distributed as it deems will best protect the interest of the infant or incompetent.

18.1 Joinder of Claims and Remedies

See L.R. 7.1(a)(4).

19.1 Joinder of Persons Necessary for Just Adjudication

See L.R. 7.1(a)(4).

20.1 Permissive Joinder of Parties

See L.R. 7.1(a)(4).

21.1 Misjoinder and Nonjoinder of Parties

See L.R. 7.1(a)(4).

22.1 Interpleader

[Reserved.]

23.1 Designation of "Class Action" in the Caption

(a) In any case sought to be maintained as a class action pursuant to Fed. R. Civ. P. 23, the complaint or other pleading asserting a class action shall include next to its caption the words "Class Action."

(b) The plaintiff also shall check the appropriate box on the Civil Cover Sheet at the time of filing the action.

23.2 Certification of a Class Action

As soon as practicable after the commencement of an action designated as a "Class Action," the plaintiff shall file a motion, with the assigned district judge, seeking an order of the court determining that the action may be maintained as a class action.

24.1 Intervention

[Reserved.]

25.1 Substitution of Parties

[Reserved.]

SECTION V. DEPOSITIONS AND DISCOVERY

26.1 Form of Certain Discovery Documents

The parties shall number each interrogatory or request sequentially, regardless of the number of sets of interrogatories or requests. In answering or objecting to interrogatories, requests for admission, or requests to produce or inspect, the responding party shall first state verbatim the propounded interrogatory or request and immediately thereafter the answer or objection.

26.2 Filing Discovery

Parties shall not file notices to take depositions, transcripts of depositions, interrogatories, requests for documents, requests for admissions, disclosures, and answers and responses to these notices and requests unless the Court orders otherwise; provided, however, that discovery material to be used at trial or in support of any motion, including a motion to compel or for summary judgment, shall be filed with the Court prior to the trial or motion. Any motion pursuant to Fed. R. Civ. P. 37 shall be accompanied by the discovery materials to which the motion relates if those materials have not previously been filed with the Court.

26.3 Production of Expert Witness Information

There shall be binding disclosure of the identity of expert witnesses. Such disclosure, including a curriculum vitae and, unless waived by the other parties, service of the expert's written report pursuant to Fed. R. Civ. P. 26(a)(2)(B), must be made before the completion of discovery in accordance with the deadlines contained in the Uniform Pretrial Scheduling Order or any other Court order. Failure to comply with these deadlines may result in the imposition of sanctions, including the preclusion of testimony, pursuant to Fed. R. Civ. P. 16(f).

If a treating physician is expected to be called as a witness, he or she must be identified in accordance with the timetable provided in the Uniform Pretrial Scheduling Order or other Court order.

26.4 Timing of Discovery

Fed. R. Civ. P. 26(d), which prohibits discovery prior to a meeting and conference between the parties, and Fed. R. Civ. P. 26(f), which directs parties to meet and confer with each other relative to the nature and basis of claims and defenses to a lawsuit, shall not apply to any action in which a party is incarcerated.

27.1 Depositions Before Action or Pending Appeal

[Reserved.]

28.1 Persons Before Whom Depositions Shall Be Taken

[Reserved.]

29.1 Discovery Stipulations

See L.R. 16.1(f); 16.2.

30.1 Depositions

Unless the Court orders otherwise pursuant to Fed. R. Civ. P. 5(d) and 26(c), transcripts of depositions when received and filed by the Clerk, shall then be opened by the Clerk who shall affix the filing stamp to the cover page of the transcripts. See L.R. 26.2.

31.1 Depositions on Written Questions

[Reserved.]

32.1 Use of Depositions in Court Proceedings

[Reserved.]

33.1 Interrogatories

[Reserved.]

34.1 Production of Documents and Things

[Reserved.]

35.1 Physical and Mental Examination of Persons

[Reserved.]

36.1 Requests for Admission

[Reserved.]

37.1 Form of Discovery Motions

See L.R. 7.1(d).

SECTION VI. TRIALS

38.1 Notation of "Jury Demand" in the Pleading

(a) If a party demands a jury trial as permitted by Fed. R. Civ. P. 38(b), the party shall place a notation on the front page of the initial pleading signed by the party stating "Demand for Jury

Trial'' or an equivalent statement. This notation shall serve as a sufficient demand under Fed. R. Civ. P. 38(b).

(b) In cases removed from state court, a party may file a ''Demand for Jury Trial'' that is separate from the initial pleading. See Fed. R. Civ. P. 81.3; L.R. 81.3.

39.1 Opening Statements and Closing Arguments

The Court will determine the time to be allotted for opening and closing arguments.

39.2 Submission of Pretrial Papers

All pretrial submissions are to be filed in accordance with the requirements of the Uniform Pretrial Scheduling Order unless the Court orders otherwise.

40.1 Case Assignment System

Immediately upon the filing of a civil action or proceeding, the Clerk shall assign to such action or proceeding a district judge and magistrate judge pursuant to the Court's Assignment Plan. See General Order #12.

40.2 Preferences

Only the following causes shall be entitled to preferences:

1. Issues in bankruptcy framed by an answer to a bankruptcy petition which are triable by a jury;

2. Causes entitled to a preference under any statute of the United States;

3. Causes restored to the calendar for a new trial by the setting aside of a former verdict, by reversal of a former judgment, or after a mistrial;

4. Causes to which a receiver appointed by any court or a trustee or debtor-in-possession in a bankruptcy proceeding is a party;

5. Causes which, in the discretion of the assigned judge, are entitled to a preference for meritorious reasons.

Preferences shall be obtained only by order of the Court on two-days notice of the application.

40.3 Trial Calendar

The trial calendar number shall be the same as the docket number. No note of issue is required. Each judge shall dispose of cases as required by law and the effective administration of justice.

41.1 Settlements, Apportionments and Allowances in Wrongful Death Actions

In an action for wrongful death

1. The Court shall apportion the proceeds of the action only where required by statute;

2. The Court shall approve a settlement only in a case covered by subdivision 1; and

3. The Court shall approve an attorneys' fee only upon application in accordance with the provisions of the Judiciary Law of the State of New York.

41.2 Dismissal of Actions

(a) Each judge shall from time to time notice for hearing on a dismissal calendar such actions or proceedings assigned to that judge which appear not to have been diligently prosecuted. Whenever it appears that the plaintiff has failed to prosecute an action or proceeding diligently, the assigned judge shall order it dismissed. In the absence of an order by the assigned judge or magistrate judge setting any date for any pretrial proceeding or for trial, the plaintiff's failure to take action for four (4) months shall be presumptive evidence of lack of prosecution. Unless otherwise ordered by the assigned judge or magistrate judge, each party shall, not less than ten (10) days prior to the noticed hearing date, serve and file a certificate setting forth the status of the action or proceeding and whether good cause exists to dismiss it for failure to prosecute. The parties need not appear in person. No explanations communicated in person, over the telephone, or by letter shall be acceptable. If a party fails to respond as required by this Rule, the Court shall issue a written order dismissing the case for failure to prosecute or providing for sanctions or making other directives to the parties as justice requires. Nothing in this Rule shall preclude any party from filing a motion to dismiss an action or proceeding for failure to prosecute under Fed. R. Civ. P. 41(b).

(b) Failure to notify the Court of a change of address in accordance with L.R. 10.1(b) may result in the dismissal of any pending action.

41.3 Actions Dismissed by Stipulation

Stipulations of dismissal shall be signed by each attorney and/or pro se litigant appearing in the action. Any action which is submitted for dismissal by stipulation of the parties shall contain the following language, if applicable: "That no party hereto is an infant or incompetent." For actions involving an infant or incompetent. See L.R. 17.1.

42.1 Separation of Issues in Civil Suits

[Reserved.]

43.1 Examination of Witnesses

[Reserved.]

44.1 Official Records

[Reserved.]

45.1 Subpoenas

See Fed. R. Civ. P. 45.

46.1 Exceptions to Rulings

[Reserved.]

47.1 Grand and Petit Jurors

Grand and petit jurors to serve at stated and special sessions of the Court shall be summoned pursuant to the Jury Selection and Service Act of 1968, as amended, codified in Title 28 of the United States Code, and the Plan adopted and approved by the judges of this Court and approved by the Judicial Council for the Court of Appeals for the Second Circuit. The selection of grand and petit jurors is made by random selection from voter registration lists and supplemented by, if available, lists of licensed drivers from the New York State Department of Motor Vehicles. Court sessions, pursuant to 28 U.S.C. § 112, are designated to be held in the Northern District of New York in the cities of Albany, Auburn, Binghamton, Malone, Syracuse, Utica and Watertown. For jury selection purposes under § 1869(c) of the Act, this district is divided into divisions from which jurors are selected for the particular place where jury sessions are to be held. The divisions are as follows:

1. ALBANY DIVISION: Albany, Clinton, Columbia, Essex, Greene, Rensselaer, Saratoga, Schenectady, Schoharie, Ulster, Warren and Washington Counties.

2. AUBURN DIVISION: Cayuga, Cortland and Tompkins Counties.

3. BINGHAMTON DIVISION: Broome, Chenango, Delaware, Otsego and Tioga Counties.

4. SYRACUSE DIVISION: Madison, Onondaga and Oswego Counties.

5. UTICA DIVISION: Fulton, Hamilton, Herkimer, Montgomery and Oneida Counties.

6. WATERTOWN–MALONE DIVISION: Franklin, Jefferson, Lewis and St. Lawrence Counties.

A copy of the Plan for the NDNY for Random Selection of Grand and Petit Jurors, is available upon request at the Clerk's office or on the Court's webpage at "www.nynd.uscourts.gov."

47.2 Jury Selection

(a) Voir Dire. Voir dire examination shall be conducted by the Court, by the attorneys, or by both, as the Court shall determine. Within the sound discretion of the Court, the attorneys' examination shall be limited by time and subject matter.

(b) Impanelment of the Jury. Unless otherwise ordered, the jury shall be impaneled by use of the "Strike" or "Jury Box" selection method at the discretion of the Court.

(c) Peremptory Challenges. Unless otherwise provided, peremptory challenges shall be exercised alternately by all parties.

(d) Waiver of Peremptory Challenges. Except when using the strike method, to pass or refuse to exercise a peremptory challenge shall constitute a waiver of the right to exercise the challenge.

47.3 Assessment of Juror Costs

Whenever any civil action scheduled for jury trial is postponed, settled or otherwise disposed of in advance of the actual trial, then, except for good cause shown, all juror costs, including marshal's fees, mileage and per diem, shall be assessed against the parties and/or their attorneys as the Court directs, unless the Court and the Clerk's office are notified at least one full business day prior to the day on which the action is scheduled for trial, in time to advise the jurors that it shall not be necessary for them to attend. The parties shall receive an advance estimation of costs upon request to the Clerk.

47.4 Jury Deliberation

Availability of Attorneys During Jury Deliberations. Attorneys shall be available on short notice during jury deliberations in the event of a verdict or a question by the jury. The Clerk shall be kept informed as to where attorneys will be at all times when the jury is deliberating. Attorneys should not leave the building without the prior approval of the presiding judge.

47.5 Jury Contact Prohibition

The following rules apply in connection with contact between attorneys or parties and jurors:

1. At any time after the Court has called a jury panel from which jurors shall be selected to try cases for a term of Court fixed by the presiding judge or otherwise impaneled, no

party or attorney, or anyone associated with the party or the attorney, shall have any communication or contact by any means or manner with any juror until such time as the panel of jurors has been excused and the term of court ended.

2. This prohibition is designed to prevent all unauthorized contact between attorneys or parties and jurors and does not apply when authorized by the judge while court is in session or when otherwise authorized by the presiding judge.

48.1 Number of Jurors

In civil cases the Court shall determine the number of jurors, which shall not be less than six nor more than twelve.

49.1 Special Verdicts and Interrogatories

[Reserved.]

50.1 Judgment as a Matter of Law in Actions Tried by Jury; Alternative Motion for New Trial; Conditional Rulings

[Reserved.]

51.1 Instructions to the Jury

When Submitted and Served. See Uniform Pretrial Scheduling Order issued by the court following the initial pretrial conference. See L.R. 16.1(e).

52.1 Proposed Findings in Civil Cases

(a) In civil non-jury trials, each party shall submit proposed findings of fact and conclusions of law sufficiently detailed that, if adopted by the Court, would form an adequate factual basis, supported by anticipated evidence, for the resolution of the case and the entry of judgment.

(b) When Submitted and Served. See Uniform Pretrial Scheduling Order issued by the Court following the initial pretrial conference. See L.R. 16.1(e).

53.1 Masters

[Reserved]

53.2 Master's Fees

The Court, in its discretion, shall fix the compensation of masters. Factors the Court shall consider include expended hours, disbursements, the relative complexity of the matter, and whether the parties have previously consented to a reasonable rate of compensation. The compensation and disbursements shall be paid and taxed as costs in the manner and amounts that the Court directs unless the parties stipulate otherwise.

53.3 Oath of Master, Commissioner, etc.

Every person appointed master, special master, commissioner, special commissioner, referee, assessor or appraiser (collectively referred to as "master") shall take and subscribe an oath, which, except as otherwise prescribed by statute or rule, shall be to the effect that said duties shall be faithfully and impartially discharged. The oath shall be taken before any federal or state officer authorized by federal law to administer oaths and shall be filed in the Clerk's office.

SECTION VII. JUDGMENTS

54.1 Taxation of Costs

(a) Procedure for Taxation in Civil Cases. The party entitled to recover costs shall file, within thirty (30) days after entry of judgment, a verified bill of costs on the forms that the Clerk provides. The verified bill of costs shall include the date on which the party shall appear before the Clerk for taxation of the costs and proof of service of a copy on the party liable for the costs. Post-trial motions shall not serve to extend the time within which a party may file a verified bill of costs as provided by this Rule, except on an order extending the time. Forms for the preparation of a bill of costs are available from the Clerk's office or at the Court's webpage at "www.nynd.uscourts.gov."

(b) To Whom Payable. Except in criminal cases, suits for civil penalties for violations of criminal statutes, and government cases not handled by the Department of Justice, all costs taxed are payable directly to the party entitled thereto and not to the Clerk, unless the Court orders otherwise.

(c) Waiver of Costs. Failure to file a bill of costs within the time provided for in this Rule shall constitute a waiver of the taxable costs.

54.2 Jury Cost Assessment

See L.R. 47.3.

54.3 Award of Attorneys' Fees

[Reserved]

54.4 Allowances to Attorneys and Receivers

Every attorney and receiver requesting an allowance for services rendered in a civil action where a receiver has been appointed shall, on filing the receiver's report with the Clerk, file a detailed statement of the services and the amount claimed, with a statement of any partial allowance previously made, together with an affidavit of the applicants, stating that no agreement has been made, directly or indirectly, and that no understanding exists for a division of fees between the attorney and the receiver. The petition shall be heard and allowance made on notice as the Court shall direct.

55.1 Certificate of Entry of Default

A party applying for a certificate of entry of default by the Clerk pursuant to Fed. R. Civ. P. 55(a) shall submit an affidavit showing that (1) a party against whom a judgement for affirmative relief is sought has failed to plead or otherwise defend the action as provided by the Federal Rules of Civil Procedure and (2) the pleading to which no response has been made was properly served.

55.2 Default Judgment

(a) By the Clerk. When a party is entitled to have the Clerk enter a default judgment pursuant to Fed. R. Civ. P. 55(b)(1), the party shall submit, with the form of judgment, **the Clerk's certificate of entry of default**, a statement showing the principal amount due, not to exceed the amount demanded in the complaint, giving credit for any payments, and showing the amounts and dates of payment, a computation of the interest to the day of judgment, a per diem rate of interest, and the costs and taxable disbursements claimed. An affidavit of the party or the party's attorney shall be appended to the statement showing that

1. The party against whom judgment is sought is not an infant or an incompetent person;

2. The party against whom judgment is sought is not in the military service, or if unable to set forth this fact, the affidavit shall state that the party against whom judgment is sought by default is in the military service or that the party seeking a default judgment is not able to determine whether or not the party against whom judgment by default is sought is in the military service;

3. The party has defaulted in appearance in the action;

4. Service was properly effectuated under Fed. R. Civ. P. 4;

5. The amount shown by the statement is justly due and owing and that no part has been paid except as set forth in the statement required by this Rule; and

6. The disbursements sought to be taxed have been made in the action or will necessarily be made or incurred.

The Clerk shall then enter judgment for principal, interest and costs. If, however, the Clerk determines, for whatever reason, that it is not proper for a default judgment to be entered, the Clerk shall forward the documents submitted in accordance with L.R. 55.2(a) to the assigned district judge for review. The assigned district judge shall then promptly notify the Clerk as to whether the Clerk shall properly enter a default judgment under this L.R. 55.2(a).

(b) By the Court. A motion to the Court for the entry of a default judgment, pursuant to Fed. R. Civ. P. 55(b)(2), shall be accompanied by a **clerk's certificate of entry of default** in accordance with Fed. R. Civ. P. 55(a), a **proposed form of default judgment**, and by a copy of the pleading to which no response has been made. The application also shall be accompanied by an affidavit of the party or the party's attorney setting forth facts as required by L.R. 55.2(a).

56.1 Summary Judgment Procedure

See L.R. 7.1 (a)(3).

56.2 Notice to Pro Se Litigants of the Consequences of Failing to Respond to a Summary Judgment Motion

When moving for summary judgment against a pro se litigant, the moving party shall inform the pro se litigant of the consequences of failing to respond to the summary judgment motion. Counsel for the moving party shall send a notice to the pro se litigant that a motion for summary judgment seeks dismissal of some or all of the claims or defenses asserted in their complaint or answer and that their failure to respond to the motion may result in judgment being entered against them. A sample notice can be obtained from the Court's webpage at "www.nynd.uscourts.gov."

57.1 Declaratory Judgment

[Reserved.]

58.1 Entry of Judgment

(a) On the verdict of a jury or the decision by the Court, a separate document which shall constitute the judgment shall be signed by the Clerk and entered. The judgment shall contain no recitals other than a recital of the verdict or any direction by the Court on which the judgment is entered. Unless the Court specifically directs otherwise, the Clerk shall promptly prepare the judgment. The Clerk shall promptly sign and enter it, except that where the Court's approval is required by Fed. R. Civ. P. 58, the Clerk shall first submit the judgment to the Court, which shall manifest approval by signing it or noting approval on the margin. The notation of the judgment in the appropriate docket shall constitute the entry of judgment.

(b) The attorney causing the entry of an order or judgment shall append to, or endorse on, it a list of the names of the parties entitled to be notified of the entry and the names and addresses of their respective attorneys if known.

58.2 Entering Satisfaction of Judgment or Decree

The Clerk shall enter satisfaction of a money judgment recovered or registered in the district as follows:

(a) Upon the payment into Court of the amount, plus applicable interest, and the payment of the marshal's fees, if any;

(b) Upon the filing of a satisfaction-piece executed and acknowledged by:

1. The judgment-creditor; or

2. The judgment-creditor's legal representative or assigns, with evidence of the representative's authority; or

3. The judgment-creditor's attorney or proctor, if within two years of the entry of the judgment or decree.

(c) If the judgment-creditor is the United States, upon filing of a satisfaction-piece executed by the United States Attorney.

(d) In admiralty, pursuant to an order of satisfaction; but an order shall not be made on the consent of the proctors only, unless consent is given within two years from the entry of the decree to be satisfied.

(e) Upon the registration of a certified copy of a satisfaction entered in another district.

59.1 New Trial; Amendment of Judgment

See L.R. 7.1(g) (Motions for Reconsideration).

60.1 Relief from Judgment or Order

[Reserved.]

61.1 Harmless Error

[Reserved.]

62.1 Stay of Proceedings

[Reserved.]

62.2 Supersedeas Bond

See L.R. 67.1.

63.1 Disability of a Judge

[Reserved.]

SECTION VIII. PROVISIONAL AND FINAL REMEDIES AND SPECIAL PROCEEDINGS

64.1 Seizure of Person or Property

The Court has adopted a Uniform Procedure for Civil Forfeiture Cases which is available from the Clerk's office or at the Court's webpage at "www.nynd.uscourts.gov."

65.1 Injunctions

See L.R. 7.1(f).

65.1.1 Sureties

(a) Whenever a bond, undertaking or stipulation is required, it shall be sufficient, except in bankruptcy or criminal cases, or as otherwise prescribed by law, if the instrument is executed by the surety or sureties only.

(b) Except as otherwise provided by law, every bond, undertaking or stipulation shall be secured by the deposit of cash or government bonds in the amount of the bond, undertaking or stipulation; or be secured by the undertaking or guaranty of a corporate surety holding a certificate of authority from the Secretary of the Treasury; or the undertaking or guaranty of two individual residents of the Northern District of New York, each of whom owns real or personal property within the district worth double the amount of the bond, undertaking or stipulation, over all the debts and liabilities of each of the residents, and over all obligations assumed by each of the residents on other bonds, undertakings or stipulations, and exclusive of all legal exemptions.

(c) In the case of a bond or undertaking, or stipulation executed by individual sureties, each surety shall attach an affidavit of justification, giving full name, occupation, residence and business address and showing that the surety is qualified as an individual surety under subdivision (b) of this Rule.

(d) Members of the bar, administrative officers or employees of this Court, the Marshal, or the Marshal's deputies or assistants shall not act as sureties in any suit, action or proceeding pending in this Court. See L.R. 67.3.

65.2 Temporary Restraining Orders

See L.R. 7.1(f).

66.1 Receiverships

[Reserved.]

67.1 Deposits in Court

(a) A supersedeas bond, where the judgment is for a sum of money only, shall be in the amount of the judgment plus 11% to cover interest and any damage for delay as may be awarded, plus $250 to cover costs.

When a stay shall be effected solely by the giving of the supersedeas bond, but the judgment or order is not solely for a sum of money, the Court, on notice, shall fix the amount of the bond. In all other cases, the Court shall, on notice, grant a stay on the terms it deems proper.

On approval, a supersedeas bond shall be filed with the Clerk, and a copy thereof, with notice of filing, shall promptly be served upon all parties affected thereby. If the appellee raises objections to the form of the bond or to the sufficiency of the surety, the Court shall provide prompt notice of a hearing on such objections.

(b) Order Directing the Investment of Funds. Any order directing the Clerk to invest funds deposited with the registry account of the Court pursuant to 28 U.S.C. § 2041 shall include the following:

1. The amount to be invested; and
2. The type of interest-bearing account in which the funds are to be invested.

(c) Time for Investing Funds. The Clerk shall take all reasonable steps to invest the funds within ten (10) days of the filing date of the order.

(d) Fee. Unless the Court orders otherwise, the Clerk, at the time the income becomes available, shall deduct from the income earned on the investment a fee as authorized by the Judicial Conference of the United States and set out by the Director of the Administrative Office.

67.2 Withdrawal of a Deposit Pursuant to Fed. R. Civ. P. 67

Any person seeking withdrawal of money deposited in the Court pursuant to Fed. R. Civ. P. 67 and subsequently deposited into an interest-bearing account or instrument as required by Fed. R. Civ. P. 67 shall provide a completed Internal Revenue Service Form W–9 with the motion papers seeking withdrawal of the funds.

67.3 Bonds and Other Sureties

(a) General Requirements. Unless the Court expressly directs otherwise pursuant to the provisions of 18 U.S.C. § 3146 in the supervision of a criminal matter, every bond, recognizance or other undertaking required by law or court order in any proceeding shall be executed by the principal obligor and by one or more sureties qualified as provided by this Rule.

(b) Unacceptable Sureties. An attorney or the attorney's employee, a party to an action, or the spouse of a party to an action or of an attorney shall not be accepted as surety on a cost bond, bail bond, appeal bond, or any other bond.

(c) Corporate Surety. A corporate surety on any undertaking in which the United States is the obligee shall be qualified in accordance with the provisions of 6 U.S.C. §§ 6–13, and approved thereunder by the Secretary of the Treasury of the United States. In all other instances, a corporate surety qualified to write bonds in the State of New York shall be an acceptable surety. In all actions, a power of attorney showing authority of the agent signing the bond shall be attached to the bond.

(d) Personal Surety. Persons competent to convey real property who own real property in the State of New York of an unencumbered value of at least the stated penalty of the bond shall obtain consideration for qualification as surety thereon by attaching thereto a duly acknowledged justification showing (1) the legal description of the real property; (2) a complete list of all encumbrances and liens thereon; (3) its market value based upon recent sales of like property; (4) a waiver of inchoate rights of any character and certification that the real property is not exempt from execution; and (5) certification as to the aggregate amount of penalties of all other existing undertakings, if any, assured by the bondsperson as of that date. The Court will review the justifications and certifications for approval or disapproval of the surety.

(e) Cost Bonds. The Court on motion, or upon its own initiative, may order any party to file an original bond for costs or additional security for costs in such an amount and so conditioned as the court by its order shall designate.

(f) Cash Bonds. Cash bonds shall be deposited into the Court's registry only upon execution and filing of a written bond sufficient as to form and setting forth the conditions of the bond. Withdrawal of cash bonds so deposited shall not be made except upon the Court's written order.

(g) Insufficiency—Remedy. An opposing party may raise objections to a bond's form or timeliness or the sufficiency of the surety. If the bond is found to be insufficient, the Court shall order that a sufficient bond be filed within a stated time. If the order is not complied with, the case shall be dismissed for want of prosecution or the Court shall take other appropriate action as justice requires.

68.1 Settlement Conferences

See L.R. 16.1.

68.2 Settlement Procedures

(a) On notice to the Court or the Clerk that an action has been settled, and upon confirmation by all parties, the Court may issue a judgment dismissing the action by reason of settlement. The order shall be issued without prejudice to the right to secure reinstatement of the case within thirty (30) days after the date of judgment by making a showing that the settlement was not, in fact, consummated.

(b) If the Court decides not to follow the procedures set forth in L.R. 68.2(a), the parties shall file within thirty (30) days of the notification to the Court, unless otherwise directed by written order, such pleadings as are necessary to terminate the action. If the required documents are not filed within the thirty (30) day period, the Clerk shall place the action on the dismissal calendar.

See also L.R. 17.1 (Actions involving infants and/or incompetents).

69.1 Execution

[Reserved.]

70.1 Judgment for Specific Acts; Vesting Title

[Reserved.]

71.1 Process in Behalf of and Against Persons Not Parties

[Reserved.]

71A.1 Condemnation Cases

[Reserved.]

72.1 Authority of Magistrate Judges

(a) A full-time Magistrate Judge is authorized to exercise all powers and perform all duties permitted by 28 U.S.C. § 636(a), (b), and (c) and any additional duties that are consistent with the Constitution and laws of the United States. Part-time Magistrate Judges are authorized to exercise all of those duties, except that only Magistrate Judges specifically designated by the Court are authorized to perform duties allowed under 28 U.S.C. § 636(c) and any additional duty consistent with the Constitution and laws of the United States.

(b) Any party may file objections to a Magistrate Judge's determination of a non-dispositive matter by filing with the Clerk and serving upon all parties their objections. The objections must be filed and served within ten (10) days after being served with the Magistrate Judge's order, must state a return date in accordance with L.R. 7.1(b)(2) and must specifically designate the order or part of the order from which they seek relief and the basis for the objection. All supporting and opposition papers must be filed in accordance with L.R. 7.1(b)(2). The supporting papers shall include the following documents:

1. A designation of the contents of the record on appeal, including the documents, exhibits and other materials to be considered; and

2. A memorandum of law.

Opposition papers shall also include a memorandum of law responsive to the appellant's arguments. Appeals will be decided on submission of the papers without oral argument unless the Court directs otherwise.

(c) Any party may object to a Magistrate Judge's proposed findings, recommendations, or report issued pursuant to 28 U.S.C. § 636(b)(1)(B) and (C) within ten (10) days after being served with a copy of the Magistrate Judge's recommendation. The party must file with the Clerk and serve upon all parties written objections which specifically identify the portions of the proposed findings, recommendations, or report to which objection is made and the basis for the objection. The party shall file with the Clerk a transcript of the specific portions of any evidentiary proceedings to which objection is made. Objections may not exceed twenty-five (25) pages without the Court's prior approval. Response to the objections may be filed and served within ten (10) days after being served with a copy of the objections. Replies by the objecting party are not permitted. The Court will proceed in accordance with Fed. R. Civ. P. 72(b) or Rule 8(b) of the Rules Governing Section 2254 Petitions, as applicable.

72.2 Duties of Magistrate Judges

(a) In all civil cases, in accordance with Fed. R. Civ. P. 16, the Magistrate Judge assigned pursuant to L.R. 40.1 is authorized to hold conferences before trial, enter scheduling orders, and modify scheduling orders. The scheduling order may limit the time to join parties, amend pleadings, file and hear motions, and complete discovery. It may also include dates for a final pretrial conference and other conferences, a trial ready date, a trial date, and any other matters appropriate under the circumstances of the case. A schedule cannot be modified except by order of the Court. The Magistrate Judge may explore the possibility of settlement and hold settlement conferences.

(b) The following procedure will be followed regarding consent of the parties and designation of a Magistrate Judge to exercise civil trial jurisdiction under 28 U.S.C. § 636(c):

1. Upon the filing of a complaint or petition for removal, the Clerk shall promptly provide to the plaintiff, or the plaintiff's attorney, a notice, as approved by the Court, informing the parties of their right to consent to have the full-time Magistrate Judge conduct all proceedings in the case. Proceedings in the case include hearing and determining all pretrial and post-trial motions, including dispositive motions; conducting a jury or non-jury trial; and ordering the entry of a final judgment. Copies of the notice shall be attached to the copies of the complaint and summons when served. Additional copies of the notice shall be furnished to the parties at later stages of the proceedings and shall be included with pretrial notices and instructions. The consent form will state that any appeal lies directly with the Court of Appeals for the Second Circuit.

2. If the parties agree to consent, the attorney for each party or the party, if pro se, must execute the consent form. Executed consent forms shall be filed directly with the Clerk. No consent form shall be made available, nor shall its contents be made known, to any District Judge or Magistrate Judge, unless all of the parties have executed the consent form. No judge or other court official shall attempt to persuade or induce any party to consent to the reference of any matter to a Magistrate Judge. A District Judge, Magistrate Judge, or other court official may again inform or remind the parties that they have the option of referring the case to a Magistrate Judge. In reminding the parties about the availability of consent to a Magistrate Judge, the parties must be informed that they are free to withhold consent without adverse substantive consequences. The parties may agree to a Magistrate Judge's exercise of civil jurisdiction at any time prior to trial, subject to the approval of the District Judge.

3. When all of the parties have executed and filed the consent forms, the Clerk shall then transmit them along with the file to the assigned District Judge for approval and referral of the case to a Magistrate Judge. If the District Judge assigns the case to a Magistrate Judge on consent, authority vests in the Magistrate Judge to conduct all proceedings and to direct the Clerk to enter a final judgment in the same manner as if a District Judge presided over the case.

4. The Clerk shall notify any parties added to an action after consent and reference to a Magistrate Judge of their right to consent to the exercise of jurisdiction by the Magistrate Judge. If an added party does not consent to the Magistrate Judge's jurisdiction, the action shall be returned to the referring District Judge for further proceedings.

(c) Assignment of Magistrate Judges to Serve as Special Masters. A Magistrate Judge shall serve as a special master subject to the procedures and limitations of 28 U.S.C. § 636(b)(2) and Fed. R. Civ. P. 53. Where the parties consent, a Magistrate Judge shall serve as a special master in any civil case without regard to the provisions of Fed. R. Civ. P. 53(b).

(d) Other Duties in Civil Actions. A magistrate judge is also authorized to:

1. Conduct proceedings for the collection of civil penalties of not more than $200 assessed under the Federal Boat Safety Act of 1971, as amended, in accordance with 46 U.S.C. § 4311(d), 12309(c);

2. Conduct examinations of judgment debtors in accordance with Fed. R. Civ. P. 69;

3. Review petitions in civil commitment proceedings under Title III of the Narcotic Rehabilitation Act;

4. Supervise proceedings conducted pursuant to letters rogatory in accordance with 28 U.S.C. § 1782;

5. Exercise general supervision of the Court's civil calendar, conduct calendar and status calls, and determine motions to expedite or postpone the trial of cases for the judges; and

6. Administer oaths and affirmations and take acknowledgments, affidavits, and depositions.

72.3 Assignment of Duties to Magistrate Judges

(a) Upon filing of the complaint, the Clerk shall assign the case to a District Judge and a Magistrate Judge. See L.R. 40.1.

(b) All civil cases in which consent forms have been executed and filed pursuant to 28 U.S.C. § 636(c) and L.R. 72.2(b) shall be transmitted to the judge to whom the case has been assigned for approval and referral of the case to a Magistrate Judge, who shall then have the authority to conduct all proceedings and to direct the Clerk to enter a final judgment. See L.R. 72.2(b)(3).

(c) Prisoner Cases. Proceedings commenced by an unrepresented prisoner shall, unless the Court orders otherwise, be referred to a Magistrate Judge for the purpose of reviewing applications, petitions and motions in accordance with these Rules and 28 U.S.C. § 636.

(d) Social Security Appeal Cases. Upon the filing of the complaint, social security appeal cases shall be assigned in rotation to the active district judges. These cases shall be referred immediately in rotation to a full-time magistrate judge for the purpose of review and submission of a report-recommendation relative to the complaint or, if the Magistrate Judge has been assigned to the case pursuant to 28 U.S.C. § 636(c) and L.R. 72.2(b), for final judgment.

(e) Federal Debt Collection Act Cases.

1. Any action brought pursuant to the Federal Debt Collection Act, 28 U.S.C. § 3001 et seq., shall be handled on an expedited basis and brought before a Magistrate Judge in Syracuse, New York, or to a District Judge if no Magistrate Judge is available, for an initial determination.

2. If appropriate, an order shall be issued directing the Clerk to issue the writ being sought, except that an application under 28 U.S.C. § 3203 for a writ of execution in a post-judgment proceeding shall not require an order of the Court.

3. Thereafter, the Clerk is directed to assign geographically a Magistrate Judge if none was previously assigned in accordance with General Order #12.

4. The assigned Magistrate Judge shall conduct any hearing that may be requested, decide all non-dispositive issues, and issue a report-recommendation on any and all dispositive issues.

5. The parties shall file written objections to the report-recommendation within twenty (20) days of the filing of same. Without oral argument, the assigned District Judge shall review the report-recommendation along with any objections that have been filed.

6. On the request for a hearing, the Clerk shall make a good faith effort to schedule the hearing within five (5) days of the receipt of the request or "as soon after that as possible," pursuant to 28 U.S.C. § 3101(d)(1).

72.4 Habeas Corpus

(a) Petitions under 28 U.S.C. §§ 2241, 2254 and 2255 shall be filed pursuant to the Rules Governing § 2254 Cases in the United States District Courts and the Rules Governing § 2255 Proceedings in the United States District Courts.

(b) Subject to the requirement of subsection (c), the original verified petition shall be filed with the Clerk at Syracuse, New York. Applications for a writ of habeas corpus made by persons in custody shall be filed, heard and determined in the district court for the district within which they were convicted and sentenced provided, however, that if the convenience of the parties and witnesses requires a hearing in a different district, such application shall be transferred to any district that the assigned judge finds or determines to be more convenient.

(c) Before a second or successive application is filed in this Court, the applicant shall move in the Second Circuit Court of

Appeals for an order authorizing the district court to consider the application.

(d) If state court records are to be submitted with respondent's answer to the petition, the records must be properly identified in the answer and arranged in chronological order. The pages of the state court records must be sequentially numbered so that citations to those records will identify the exact location where the information appears. If documents are separately bound and the citation to the documents is easily identifiable, the documents need not be repaginated.

72.5 Habeas Corpus Petitions Involving the Death Penalty; Special Requirements

(a) Applicability. This Rule shall govern the procedures for a first petition for a writ of habeas corpus filed pursuant to 28 U.S.C. § 2254 in which a petitioner seeks relief from a judgment imposing the penalty of death. A subsequent filing relating to a particular petition may be deemed a first petition under this Rule if the original filing was not dismissed on the merits. The District Judge or Magistrate Judge to whom the petition is assigned may modify the application of this Rule. This Rule shall supplement the Rules Governing § 2254 Cases and does not in any regard alter or supplant those rules.

(b) Notices from Office of the Attorney General for the State of New York. The Office of the Attorney General for the State of New York ("Attorney General") shall send to the Clerk (1) prompt notice whenever the New York State Court of Appeals affirms a sentence of death; (2) at least once a month, a list of scheduled executions; and (3) at least once a month, a list of the death penalty appeals pending before the New York State Court of Appeals.

(c) Notice from Petitioner's Counsel. Whenever counsel determines that a petition will be filed in this Court, counsel shall promptly file with the Clerk and serve on the Attorney General a written notice of counsel's intention to file a petition. The notice shall state the name of the petitioner, the district in which the petitioner was convicted, the place of the petitioner's incarceration, the status of the petitioner's state court proceedings and the scheduled date of execution. The notice is for the Court's information only and the failure to file the notice shall not preclude the filing of the petition.

(d) Counsel.

1. *Appointment of Counsel.* Each indigent petitioner shall be represented by counsel unless petitioner has clearly elected to proceed pro se and the Court is satisfied, after a hearing, that

petitioner's election is intelligent, competent, and voluntary. Where counsel is to be appointed, such appointment shall be made at the earliest practicable time. A panel of attorneys qualified for appointment in death penalty cases ("qualified panel") will be certified by the active judges of this district.

If state appellate counsel is available to continue representation into the federal courts and counsel is deemed qualified to do so by the assigned District Judge, there is a presumption in favor of continued representation except when state appellate counsel was also counsel at trial. In light of this presumption, it is expected that appointed counsel who is willing to continue representation and who has been certified by the assigned District Judge as qualified to do so, would ordinarily file a motion for appointment of counsel on behalf of his or her client together with the client's federal habeas corpus petition. If, however, counsel for any reason wishes to confirm appointment before preparing the petition, counsel may move for appointment as described above before filing the petition.

If state appellate counsel is not available to represent the petitioner on federal habeas corpus or if appointment of state appellate counsel would be inappropriate for any reason, the Court may appoint counsel upon application of the petitioner. The Clerk shall have available forms for such application. Counsel may be appointed from the qualified panel. The assigned District Judge may suggest one or more counsel for appointment. If application for appointed counsel is made before a petition is filed, the application shall be assigned to a District Judge and Magistrate Judge in the same manner that a non-capital petition would be assigned. The District Judge and Magistrate Judge so assigned shall be the District Judge and Magistrate Judge assigned when counsel files a petition for writ of habeas corpus.

2. *Second Counsel.* Appointment and compensation of second counsel shall be governed by the Guide to Judiciary Policies and Procedures, Appointment of Counsel in Criminal Cases.

(e) Filing.

1. *General requirement.* Petitions as to which venue lies in this district shall be filed in accordance with the applicable Local Rules. Petitions shall be filled in by printing or typewriting. In the alternative, the petition may be in a legible typewritten or written form which contains all of the information required by that form. All petitions shall (1) state whether the petitioner has previously sought relief arising out of the same matter from this Court or any other federal court, together with the ruling and reasons given for denial of relief; (2) set forth any scheduled execution date; and (3) contain the wording in full caps and underscored "Death Penalty Case" directly under the case number on each pleading. Counsel for

petitioner shall file an original and three (3) copies of the petition. A pro se petitioner need file only the original.

The Clerk will immediately notify the Attorney General's office when a petition is filed.

When a petitioner who was convicted outside of this district files a petition, the Court will immediately advise the clerk of the district in which the petitioner was convicted.

2. *Emergency motions or applications.* Emergency motions or applications shall be filed with the Clerk. If time does not permit the filing of a motion or application in person or by mail, counsel may communicate with the Clerk and obtain the Clerk's permission to file the motion by facsimile. Counsel should communicate with the Clerk by telephone as soon as it becomes evident that emergency relief will be sought from this Court. The motion or application shall contain a brief account of the prior actions, if any, of this Court and the name of the judge or judges involved in the prior actions.

(f) Assignment to Judicial Officers. Notwithstanding the Court's case assignment plan, petitions shall be assigned to judges of the Court as follows: (1) the Clerk shall establish a separate category for these petitions, to be designated with the title "Capital Case"; (2) all active judges of this Court shall participate in the assignments; (3) the Clerk shall assign petitions in the Capital Case category randomly to each of the available active judges of the Court; (4) if a petitioner has previously sought relief in this Court with respect to the same conviction, the petition shall, when practical, be assigned to the judicial officers who were assigned to the prior proceeding; and (5) pursuant to 28 U.S.C. § 636(b)(1)(B), and consistent with law, the Court may designate Magistrate Judges to perform all duties under this Rule, including evidentiary hearings.

(g) Transfer of Venue. Subject to the provisions of 28 U.S.C. § 2241(d), it is the Court's policy that a petition should be heard in the district in which the petitioner was convicted rather than in the district of the petitioner's present confinement. See L.R. 72.4(b). If an order for the transfer of venue is made, the Court will order a stay of execution which shall continue until such time as the transferee court acts upon the petition or the order of stay.

(h) Stays of Execution.

1. *Stay Pending Final Disposition.* Upon the filing of a habeas corpus petition, unless the petition is patently frivolous, the Court shall issue a stay of execution pending final disposition of the matter. Notwithstanding any provision of this paragraph (h), stays of execution shall not be granted, or maintained, except in accor-

dance with law. Thus, the provisions of this paragraph (h) for a stay shall be ineffective in any case in which the stay would be inconsistent with the limitations of 28 U.S.C. § 2262 or any other governing statute.

2. *Temporary Stay for Appointment of Counsel.* Where counsel in state court proceedings withdraws at the conclusion of the state court proceedings or is otherwise not available or qualified to proceed, the Court may designate an attorney who will assist an indigent petitioner in filing pro se applications for appointment of counsel and for a temporary stay of execution. Upon the filing of this application, the Court shall issue a temporary stay of execution and appoint counsel. The temporary stay will remain in effect for forty-five (45) days unless the Court extends this time.

3. *Temporary Stay for Preparation of the Petition.* Where counsel new to the case is appointed, upon counsel's application for a temporary stay of execution accompanied by a specification of nonfrivolous issues to be raised in the petition, the Court shall issue a temporary stay of execution unless no nonfrivolous issues are presented. The temporary stay will remain in effect for one hundred twenty (120) days to allow newly appointed counsel to prepare and file the petition. The Court may extend the temporary stay upon a subsequent showing of good cause.

4. *Temporary Stay for Transfer of Venue.* See paragraph (g).

5. *Temporary Stay for Unexhausted Claims.* If the petition indicates that there are unexhausted claims for which a state court remedy is still available, the petitioner will be granted a sixty (60) day stay of execution in which to seek a further stay from the state court in order to litigate the unexhausted claims in state court. During the proceedings in state court, the proceedings on the petition will be stayed. After the state court proceedings have been completed, the petitioner may amend the petition with respect to the newly exhausted claims.

6. *Stay Pending Appeal.* If the petition is denied and a certificate of appealability for appeal is issued, the Court will grant a stay of execution which will continue in effect until the court of appeals acts upon the appeal or the order of stay.

7. *Notice of Stay.* Upon the granting of any stay of execution, the Clerk will immediately notify the appropriate prison superintendent and the Attorney General. The Attorney General shall ensure that the Clerk has a twenty-four (24) hour telephone number for the superintendent.

(i) Procedures for Considering the Petition. Unless the Court summarily dismisses the petition as patently frivolous, the following schedule and procedures shall apply subject to modification by the court. Requests for enlargement of any time period in this Rule shall comply with these Local Rules.

1. Respondent shall, as soon as practicable, but in any event on or before twenty (20) days from the date of service of the petition, file with the Court the following:

(A) Transcripts of the state trial court proceedings;

(B) Appellant's and respondent's briefs on direct appeal to the Court of Appeals, and the opinion or orders of that Court;

(C) Petitioner's and respondent's briefs in any state court habeas corpus proceedings, and all opinions, orders and transcripts of such proceedings;

(D) Copies of all pleadings, opinions and orders in any previous federal habeas corpus proceeding filed by petitioner which arose from the same conviction; and

(E) An index of all materials described in paragraphs (A) through (D) above.

The materials are to be marked and numbered so that they can be uniformly cited. Respondent shall serve this index upon counsel for petitioner or the petitioner pro se. If time does not permit, the answer may be filed without attachments (A) through (D) above, but the respondent shall file the necessary copies as soon as possible. If any items identified in paragraphs (A) through (D) above are not available, respondent shall state when, if at all, such missing material can be filed.

2. If counsel for petitioner claims that respondent has not complied with the requirements of paragraph (1), or if counsel for petitioner does not have copies of all the documents filed with the court by respondent, counsel for petitioner shall immediately notify the Court in writing, with a copy to respondent. The Court will provide copies of any missing documents to the petitioner's counsel.

3. Respondent shall file an answer to the petition with accompanying points and authorities within thirty (30) days from the date of service of the petition. Respondent shall attach any other relevant documents not already filed.

4. Within thirty (30) days after respondent has filed the answer, petitioner may file a traverse.

5. There shall be no discovery without leave of the Court.

6. Any request for an evidentiary hearing by either party shall be made within fifteen (15) days from the filing of the traverse or within fifteen (15) days from the expiration of the time for filing the traverse. The request shall include a specifi-

cation of which factual issues require a hearing and a summary of what evidence petitioner proposes to offer. Any opposition to the request for an evidentiary hearing shall be made within fifteen (15) days from the filing of the request. The Court will then give due consideration to whether an evidentiary hearing will be held.

(j) Evidentiary Hearing. If an evidentiary hearing is held, the Court will order the preparation of a transcript of the hearing, which is to be immediately provided to petitioner and respondent for use in briefing and argument. Upon the preparation of the transcript, the Court may establish a reasonable schedule for further briefing and argument of the issues considered at the hearing.

(k) Rulings. The Court's rulings may be in the form of a written opinion, which will be filed, or in the form of an oral opinion on the record in open court, which shall be promptly transcribed and filed. The Clerk will immediately notify the appropriate prison superintendent and the Attorney General whenever relief is granted on a petition. The Clerk will immediately notify the clerk of the United States Court of Appeals for the Second Circuit by telephone of (1) the issuance of a final order denying or dismissing a petition without a certificate of probable cause for appeal or (2) the denial of a stay of execution. When a notice of appeal is filed, the Clerk will transmit the appropriate documents to the United States Court of Appeals for the Second Circuit immediately.

73.1 Magistrate Judges: Trial by Consent

Upon the consent of the parties, a Magistrate Judge shall conduct all proceedings in any civil case, including a jury or nonjury trial and shall order the entry of a final judgment, in accordance with 28 U.S.C. § 636(c). See L.R. 72.2(b)(2).

74.1 Method of Appeal to District Judge in Consent Cases

[Reserved.]

75.1 Proceedings on Appeal from Magistrate Judge to District Judge under Rule 73(d)

[Reserved.]

76.1 Bankruptcy Cases

(a) Reference to Bankruptcy Court. All cases under Title 11 of the United States Code, and all proceedings arising under Title 11, or arising in, or related to, a case under Title 11, are referred to the bankruptcy court of this district pursuant to Title 28 U.S.C. § 157.

76.2 Bankruptcy Appeals

(a) When a notice of appeal is filed with the bankruptcy court clerk, and the notice is not timely filed in accordance with Fed. R. Bankr. P. 8002(a), and no motion for extension of time has been filed in accordance with Fed. R. Bankr. P. 8002(c), the bankruptcy court clerk shall forward the notice of appeal together with a "Certification of Noncompliance" to the Clerk without assembling the record as provided for in Fed. R. Bankr. P. 8007(b). The notice and certificate shall be filed, assigned a civil action number, and forwarded to a District Judge for a determination as to whether the notice of appeal was timely filed or the appeal is to be dismissed as untimely. If the District Judge makes a determination that the appeal was timely filed or should otherwise be perfected, the bankruptcy court clerk shall be notified to complete the record promptly in accordance with Fed. R. Bankr. P. 8007(b).

(b) The Clerk shall issue a standard bankruptcy appeal scheduling order at the time of the filing of the record on appeal, a copy of which shall be provided to the parties, the bankruptcy judge from whom the appeal was taken, and the bankruptcy court clerk.

(c) Appeals from a decision of the bankruptcy court shall be in accordance with 28 U.S.C. § 158 and applicable bankruptcy rules. Fed. R. Bankr. P. 8009 respecting the filing of briefs shall not be applicable, and briefs shall be filed in accordance with the scheduling order of this Court.

76.3 Bankruptcy Record of Transmittal, Certificate of Facts, and Proposed Findings Pursuant to Title 11, Section 110(i)

(a) Upon direction of the bankruptcy judge, the bankruptcy court clerk shall cause to be filed with the Clerk the designated record of transmittal, which shall consist of certified copies of the Memorandum–Decision, Findings of Fact, Conclusions of Law, bankruptcy docket, and transcript of proceedings which relate to the bankruptcy judge's findings. The bankruptcy court clerk shall also provide the Clerk with a list of those individuals to whom the notice of filing shall be given.

(b) Upon receipt of the above, the Clerk shall assign a civil action number, assign a District Judge and issue a scheduling order for the filing of motions pursuant to Title 11, Section 110(i)(1). Copies of the scheduling order shall be served upon those individuals designated by the bankruptcy court clerk.

Upon the filing of any motion(s), the Clerk shall schedule and notice all concerned parties of a hearing date. Failure to file motions within the time ordered will be deemed a waiver of the provisions of Title 11, Section 110(i)(1). The Clerk shall prepare and present to the assigned District Judge a proposed order pursuant to the provisions of L. R. 41.2.

SECTION IX. DISTRICT COURT AND CLERKS

77.1 Hours of Court

[Reserved.]

77.2 Orders

(a) With these exceptions, all orders, whether by consent or otherwise, shall be presented for approval and execution to the assigned judge. The Clerk may sign without submission to the assigned judge the following orders:

1. Orders specifically appointing persons to serve process in accordance with Fed. R. Civ. P. 4;

2. Orders on consent for the substitution of attorneys in civil cases where the trial of the action has not been set. See also L.R. 83.2;

3. Orders restoring an action to the court docket after the filing of a demand for trial de novo pursuant to L.R. 83.7–7 (Consensual Arbitration Program);

4. Orders on consent satisfying decrees and orders on consent canceling stipulations and bonds.

(b) If instructed to do so by the assigned judge, the prevailing party shall submit a proposed order which has been approved by the opposing party and which contains the endorsement of the opposing party: "Approved as to form."

When the parties are unable to agree as to the form of the proposed order, the prevailing party shall, on three (3) days notice to all other parties, submit a proposed order and a written explanation for the form of that order. Costs and attorneys' fees may be awarded against a party whose unreasonable conduct is deemed to have required the bringing of the motion. The provisions of L.R. 7.1 shall not apply to such motion and oral argument shall not be heard.

77.3 Sessions of Court

The Court shall be in continuous session in Albany, Binghamton, Syracuse, and Utica. Sessions shall from time to time be held in Auburn, Malone and Watertown, or such other place as the Court shall, by order, deem appropriate. Jurors shall serve as the Court directs.

77.4 Court Library

The district court libraries are not open for use by the public.

77.5 Official Newspapers

All process, notices, and orders required to be published shall be published in the proper county in an official newspaper. The Court shall direct the publication of process, notices, and orders in any other newspaper, upon proper showing, as it shall deem advisable. The following are designated as official newspapers:

County	Newspaper	City
Albany	Times Union (D)	Albany, NY
Broome	Binghamton Press/ Sun Bulletin (D)	Binghamton, NY
Cayuga	The Citizen (D)	Auburn, NY
Clinton	Press–Republican (D)	Plattsburgh, NY
Chenango	Evening Sun (D)	Norwich, NY
Columbia	Register Star (D)	Hudson, NY
	The Independent (W)	Hillsdale, NY
Cortland	Cortland Standard (D)	Cortland, NY
Delaware	Walton Reporter (W)	Walton, NY
Essex	Lake Placid News (W)	Lake Placid, NY
Franklin	Adirondack Enterprise (D)	Saranac Lake, NY
Fulton	Leader Herald (D)	Gloversville, NY
Greene	Catskill Daily Mail (D)	Catskill, NY
Hamilton	Post Star (D)	Glens Falls, NY
Herkimer	Telegram (D)	Herkimer, NY
	The Evening Times (D)	Little Falls, NY
Jefferson	Watertown Times (D)	Watertown, NY
	Thousand Island Sun (W)	Alexandria Bay, NY
Lewis	Journal Republican (W)	Lowville, NY
Madison	Oneida Dispatch (D)	Oneida, NY
Montgomery	The Recorder (D)	Amsterdam, NY
Oneida	Utica Observer Dispatch (D)	Utica, NY
	Rome Sentinal (D)	Rome, NY
Onondaga	Post Standard (D)	Syracuse, NY
Oswego	Palladium Times (D)	Oswego, NY
Otsego	The Daily Star	Oneonta, NY
Rensselaer	Times Record (D)	Troy, NY
St. Lawrence	Ogdensburg Journal (D)	Ogdensburg, NY
	Tribune Press (W)	Gouverneur, NY
	Daily Courier Observer (D)	Massena, NY
Saratoga	Saratogian–Tri City News (D)	Saratoga Springs, NY
Schenectady	Schenectady Gazette (D)	Schenectady, NY
Schoharie	Times Journal (W)	Cobleskill, NY
Tioga	Owego Pennysaver (W)	Owego, NY
Tompkins	Ithaca Journal (D)	Ithaca, NY
Ulster	The Daily Freeman (D)	Kingston, NY
Warren	Post Star (D)	Glen Falls, NY
	Times (D)	Glen Falls, NY
Washington	Whitehall Times (W)	Whitehall, NY
(D) = Daily	(W) = Weekly	

77.6 Release of Information

All court personnel, including but not limited to marshals, deputy clerks, court clerks, bailiffs, court reporters, law clerks, secretaries, and probation officers, shall not disclose to any person, without the Court's authorization, information divulged in arguments and hearings held in chambers or otherwise outside the presence of the public or any information relating to a pending case that is not part of the Court's public records.

77.7 Official Station of the Clerk

The Clerk's official station shall be Syracuse. The Clerk shall appoint deputy clerks in such number as are necessary and shall be stationed at Albany, Binghamton, Utica, Syracuse and Watertown.

78.1 Motion Days

Listings of the regularly scheduled motion days for all judges shall be available at each Clerk's office and are available on the Court's webpage at "www.nynd.uscourts.gov." Notice of the regular motion days for all judges shall be provided at the time an action is commenced.

79.1 Custody of Exhibits and Transcripts

(a) Unless the Court orders otherwise, exhibits and transcripts shall not be filed with the Clerk. Rather, they shall be retained in the custody of the attorney who produced them in court.

(b) In the case of an appeal or other review by an appellate court, the parties are encouraged to agree with respect to which exhibits and transcripts are necessary for the determination of the appeal. In the absence of agreement and except as provided in this Rule, a party, upon written request of any other party or by Court order, shall make available at the Clerk's office all the original exhibits in the party's possession, or true copies, to enable such other party to prepare the record on appeal. At the same time and place, such other party also shall make available all the original exhibits in that party's possession. All exhibits made available at the Clerk's office, which are designated by any party as part of the record on appeal, shall be filed with the Clerk, who shall transmit them together with the record on appeal to the clerk of the Second Circuit Court of Appeals. Exhibits and transcripts not so designated shall remain in the custody of the respective attorneys who shall have the responsibility of promptly forwarding them to the clerk of the Second Circuit Court of Appeals on request.

(c) Documents of unusual bulk or weight and physical exhibits, other than documents, shall remain in the custody of the attorney producing them, who shall permit their inspection by any party for the purpose of preparing the record on appeal and who shall be charged with the responsibility for their safekeeping and transportation to the Second Circuit Court of Appeals.

(d) Exhibits and transcripts which have been filed with the Clerk shall be removed by the party responsible for them (1) if no appeal is taken, within ninety (90) days after a final decision is rendered or (2) if an appeal has been taken, within thirty (30) days after the mandate of the final reviewing court is filed. The Clerk shall notify the parties that fail to comply with this Rule to remove their exhibits. Upon their failure to do so within thirty (30) days, the Clerk shall dispose of them as the Clerk sees fit.

79.2 Books and Records of the Clerk

[Reserved.]

80.1 Stenographic Transcript: Court Reporting Fees

Subject to the provisions of Fed. R. Civ. P. 54(d), the expense of any party in obtaining all or any part of a transcript for the Court's use when the Court so orders and the expense of any party in obtaining all or any part of a transcript for the purposes of a new trial or for amended findings or for appeals shall be a taxable cost against the unsuccessful party. A fee schedule of transcript rates is available on the Court's webpage at "www.nynd.uscourts.gov."

81.1 Removal Bonds

[Reserved.]

81.2 Copies of State Court Proceedings in Removed Actions

[Reserved.]

81.3 Removed Cases, Demand for Jury Trial

In an action removed from a state court, a party entitled to trial by jury under Fed. R. Civ. P. 38 shall be accorded a jury trial if a demand is filed and served in accordance with the provisions of Fed. R. Civ. P. 81 and L.R. 38.1.

81.4 Actions Removed Pursuant to 28 U.S.C. § 1452

If removal is based upon 28 U.S.C. § 1452 (Removal of claims related to bankruptcy cases), the removing party shall specifically identify in its Notice of Removal which claims or causes of action it is removing and which of the parties in the state court action are parties to the removed claims or causes of action.

82.1 Jurisdiction and Venue Unaffected

[Reserved.]

83.1 Admission to the Bar

(a) Permanent Admission. A member in good standing of the bar of the State of New York or of the bar of any United States

District Court, whose professional character is good, may be permanently admitted to practice in this court on motion of a member of the bar of this Court in compliance with the requirements of this Rule. **An admission packet containing all the required forms is available from the Clerk's office and on the Court's webpage at "www.nynd.uscourts.gov."**

Each applicant for permanent admission must file, at least ten (10) days prior to the scheduled hearing (unless, for good cause shown, the Court shortens the time), documentation for admission as set forth below. Ordinarily, the Court entertains applications for admission only on regularly scheduled motion days. Documentation required for permanent admission includes:

1. *A verified petition for admission* stating the following:

- place of residence and office address;
- the date(s) when and court(s) where previously admitted;
- legal training and trial experience;
- whether the applicant has ever been held in contempt of court, censured, suspended or disbarred by any court and, if so, the facts and circumstances connected therewith; and
- that the applicant is familiar with the provisions of the Judicial Code (Title 28 U.S.C.), which pertain to the jurisdiction of, and practice in, the United States District Courts; the Federal Rules of Civil Procedure and the Federal Rules of Evidence for the District Courts; the Federal Rules of Criminal Procedure for the District Courts; the Local Rules of the District Court for the Northern District of New York; and the N.Y.S. Lawyer's Code of Professional Responsibility. The applicant shall further affirm faithful adherence to these Rules and responsibilities.

2. *Affidavit of Sponsor.* The sponsor must be a member in good standing of the bar of the Northern District of New York who has personal knowledge of the petitioner's background and character. A form Affidavit of Sponsor is available from the Clerk's office.

3. *Attorney Registration Form.* The Registration Form must be in the form prescribed by the Clerk, which sets forth the attorney's current residence; office addresses; telephone and fax number(s), if any, and e-mail address; and the bars of all states, territories, districts, commonwealths or possessions or other courts of the United States to which the attorney is admitted and the dates of admission. A copy of the Attorney Registration Form is available on the Court's webpage at

"www.nynd.uscourts.gov." See subdivision (e) for requirements when information on the Registration Form changes.

4. *Certificate of Good Standing.* The certificate of good standing must be dated within six (6) months of the date of admission.

5. *The Required Fee.* As prescribed by and pursuant to the Judicial Conference of the United States and the Rules of this Court, the fee for admission to the bar is $80.00 ($50.00 and an additional fee of $30.00).

In addition to the initial admission fee, there shall be a $30.00 biennial registration fee. This fee shall be due and owning on June 1st, 2001 and every two years thereafter unless deferred by the Board of Judges. Failure to remit this fee will result in the removal of the non-paying attorney from the court's bar roll. Should the payment of this biennial fee present a significant financial hardship, an attorney may request, via an application to the Chief Judge, that the biennial registration fee be waived.

The Clerk shall deposit the additional $30.00 fee required for admission to the bar and the $30.00 biennial registration fee into the District Court Fund. The Clerk shall be the trustee of the Fund, and the monies deposited in the Fund shall be used only for the benefit of the bench and bar in the administration of justice. All withdrawals from the Fund require the approval of the Chief Judge or a judge designated by the Chief Judge to authorize the withdrawals.

The admission fees and biennial registration fees are waived for all attorneys in the employ of the United States Government.

The biennial registration fees **only** are waived for all attorneys employed by state and local public sector entities.

6. *Oath on Admission.* An applicant must swear or affirm that as an attorney and counselor of this Court the applicant will conduct himself or herself uprightly and according to law, and that he or she will support the Constitution of the United States. The Oath on Admission, form AO 153, is signed in court at the time of the admission.

(b) Applicants who are not admitted to another United States District Court in New York State must appear with their sponsor for formal admission unless such appearance is waived in the exercise of judicial discretion. If the applicant is admitted to practice in New York State, the Certificate of Good Standing submitted with the application for admission must be from the appropriate

New York State Appellate Division. All requirements of subdivision (a) apply.

If the applicant is from outside New York State, the Certificate of Good Standing may be from the highest court of the state or from a United States District Court. All requirements of subdivision (a) apply. Out-of-state applicants must maintain an office in the state in which the applicant is admitted. Upon ceasing to maintain an office in that state, the attorney automatically ceases to be a member of the bar of this Court.

(c) Applicants who are members in good standing of a United States District Court for the Eastern, Western, or Southern District of New York need not appear for formal admission. The applicant must submit a Certificate of Good Standing from the United States District Court where the applicant is a member and a proposed order granting the admission. A sponsor's affidavit is not required. All other requirements of subdivision (a) apply.

(d) Pro Hac Vice Admission. A member in good standing of the bar of any state, or of any United States District Court, may be admitted pro hac vice to argue or try a particular case in whole or in part. In addition to the requirements of L.R. 83.1(a)(1)(3) and (4), a Motion for Pro Hac Vice Admission must be made, which includes the case caption of the particular case for which the admission is being sought. See L.R. 10.1(b). In lieu of a written motion for admission, an oral motion may be made by the sponsoring attorney in open court on the record. In that case, the attorney must immediately complete and file the required documents as set forth above.

The pro hac vice admission fee is $30.00. The Clerk deposits all pro hac vice admission fees into the District Court Fund. See L.R. 83.1(a)(5). While an attorney may be admitted pro hac vice in connection with a particular case, only an attorney permanently admitted to practice in this Court may enter appearances for parties, sign stipulations, or receive payments on judgments, decrees or orders. An attorney admitted pro hac vice must file a written notice of appearance in the case for which the attorney was admitted in accordance with L.R. 83.2.

(e) Registration Form Changes. Every attorney must file a supplemental statement setting forth any change in the information on the Registration Form within ten (10) days of the change. This supplemental statement should be made by filing a new Registration Form which reflects the new information and which identifies which information changed. Failure to timely file a supplemental Registration Form may result in inability to notify that attorney of developments in the case or other sanctions in the Court's discretion. See L.R. 41.2(b). A copy of the Attorney Registration Form is available on the Court's webpage at "www.nynd.uscourts.gov."

(f) Pro Bono Service. Every member of the bar of this Court shall be available upon the Court's request for appointment to represent or assist in the representation of indigent parties. Appointments under this Rule shall be made in a manner such that no attorney shall be requested to accept more than one appointment during any twelve-month period.

(g) United States Attorney's Office. An attorney appointed by the United States Attorney General as a United States Attorney, an assistant United States attorney, or as a special assistant United States attorney under 28 U.S.C. §§ 541–543, who has been admitted to practice before any United States District Court, shall be admitted to practice in this Court upon motion of a member of the bar of this Court. Thereafter, the attorney may appear before this Court on any matter on behalf of the United States.

83.2 Appearance and Withdrawal of Attorney

(a) Appearance. An attorney appearing for a party in a civil case shall promptly file with the Clerk a written notice of appearance, however no notice of appearance needs to be filed if the party that would be filing the notice of appearance is the same individual that has signed the complaint, notice of removal, pre-answer motion, or answer.

(b) Withdrawal. An attorney who has appeared may withdraw only upon notice to the client and all parties to the case and an order of the Court, upon a finding of good cause, granting leave to withdraw. If leave to withdraw is granted, the withdrawing attorney must serve a copy of the order upon the affected party and file an affidavit of service.

Unless the Court orders otherwise, withdrawal of counsel shall not result in the extension of any of the deadlines contained in any case management orders, including the Uniform Pretrial Scheduling Order, see L.R. 16.1(e), or the adjournment of a trial ready or trial date.

83.3 Pro Bono Panel

(a) Description of Panel. In recognition of the need for representation of indigent parties in civil actions, this Court has established the Pro Bono Panel ("Panel") of the Northern District of New York.

1. The Panel shall include those members of the Criminal Assigned Counsel Panel in this Court. Any other attorney admitted to practice in this Court shall also be expected to

participate in periodic training as offered by the Court and to accept no more than one pro bono assignment per year.

2. The Court shall maintain a list of Panel members, which shall include the information deemed necessary for the effective administration and assignment of Panel attorneys.

3. The Court shall select Panel members for assignment upon its determination that the appointment of an attorney is warranted. The Court shall select from the Panel a member who has not received an appointment from the Court during the past year and (i) has attended a training seminar sponsored by this Court, (ii) has adequate prior experience closely related to the matter assigned, or (iii) has accepted criminal (CJA) assignments from the Court.

4. Where a pro se party has one or more other cases pending before this Court in which an attorney has been appointed, the Court may determine it to be appropriate that the attorney appointed in the other case or cases be appointed to represent the pro se party in the case before the Court.

5. Where the Court finds that the nature of the case requires specific expertise, and among the Panel members available for appointment there are some with the required expertise, the attorney may be selected from among those included in the group or the Court may designate a specific member of the Panel.

6. Where the Court finds that the nature of the case requires specific expertise and none of the Panel members available for appointment has indicated that expertise, the Court may appoint an attorney with the required expertise who is not on the Panel.

(b) Application for Appointment of Attorney.

1. Any application for the appointment of an attorney by a party appearing pro se shall include a form of affidavit stating the party's efforts to obtain an attorney by means other than appointment and indicating any prior pro bono appointments of an attorney to represent the party in cases brought in this Court, including both pending and terminated actions.

2. Failure of a party to make a written application for an appointed attorney shall not preclude appointment.

3. Where a pro se litigant, who was ineligible for an appointed attorney at the time of initial or subsequent requests, later becomes eligible by reason of changed circumstances, a subsequent application may be entertained, using the procedures specified above, within a reasonable time after the change in circumstances has occurred.

(c) Factors Used in Determining Whether to Appoint Counsel. On receipt of an application for the appointment of an attorney, the Court shall determine whether an attorney is to be appointed to represent the pro se party. That determination shall be made within a reasonable time after the application is made. Factors to be taken into account in making the determination are as follows:

1. The potential merit of the claims as set forth in the pleading;

2. The nature and complexity of the action, both factual and legal, including the need for factual investigation;

3. The presence of conflicting testimony calling for an attorney's presentation of evidence and cross-examination;

4. The capability of the pro se party to present the case;

5. The inability of the pro se party to retain an attorney by other means;

6. The degree to which the interests of justice shall be served by appointment of an attorney, including the benefit the Court shall derive from the assistance of an appointed attorney;

7. Any other factors the Court deems appropriate.

(d) Order of Appointment. Whenever the Court concludes that the appointment of an attorney is warranted, the Court shall issue an order directing the appointment of an attorney to represent the pro se party. The order shall be transmitted promptly to the Clerk. If service of the summons and complaint has not yet been made, an order directing service by the United States Marshal or by other appropriate method of service shall accompany the appointment order.

(e) Notification of Appointment. After an attorney has been selected, the Clerk shall send the attorney a copy of the order of appointment. Copies of the pleadings filed to date, relevant correspondence, and all other relevant documents shall be forwarded to the Clerk's office nearest to the attorney and made available for immediate review and copying of the necessary papers without charge. In addition to notifying the attorney, the Clerk shall also notify all of the parties to the action of the appointment, together with the name, address and telephone number of the appointed attorney.

(f) Duties and Responsibilities of Appointed Counsel. On receiving notice of the appointment, the attorney shall promptly file an appearance in the action to which the appointment applies unless precluded from acting in the action or appeal, in which event the attorney shall promptly notify the Court and the putative client. Promptly following the filing of an appearance, the attorney shall communicate with the newly-represented party concerning the action. In addition to a full discussion of the merits of the dispute, the attorney shall explore with the party any possibilities of resolving the dispute in other forums, including but not limited to administrative forums. If after consultation with the attorney the party decides to prosecute or defend the action, the attorney shall proceed to represent the party in the action unless or until the attorney-client relationship is terminated as provided by these Rules. In the Court's discretion, stand-by counsel may be appointed to act in an advisory capacity. "Stand-by counsel" is not the party's representative; rather, the role of stand-by counsel is to provide assistance to the litigant and the Court where appropriate. The Court may in its discretion appoint counsel for other purposes.

(g) Reimbursement for Expenses. Pro Bono attorneys who are appointed pursuant to this Rule may seek reimbursement for expenses incident to representation of indigent clients by application to the Court. Reimbursement or advances shall be permitted to the extent possible in light of available resources and, absent extraordinary circumstances, shall not exceed $1,200.00. Any expenses in excess of $300.00 should receive the Court's prior approval. If good cause is shown, the Court may approve additional expenses. Request for reimbursement should be submitted on the Pro Bono Fund Voucher and Request for Reimbursement Form and be accompanied by detailed documentation. Counsel are advised that vouchers submitted in excess of $1,200.00, absent the Court's prior approval, may be reduced or denied. All reimbursements made by withdrawal from the District Fund shall require the approval of the Chief Judge or a judge designated by the Chief Judge to authorize withdrawals. **To the extent that appointed counsel seeks reimbursement for expenses that are recoverable as costs to a prevailing party under Fed R. Civ. P. 54, the appointed attorney must submit a verified bill of costs on the form provided by the Clerk for reimbursement of such expenses.**

(h) Grounds for Relief from Appointment. After appointment, an attorney may apply to be relieved of an order of appointment only on one or more of the following grounds, or on such other grounds as the appointing judge finds adequate for good cause shown:

1. some conflict of interest precludes the attorney from accepting the responsibilities of representing the party in the action;

2. the attorney does not feel competent to represent the party in the particular type of action assigned;

3. some personal incompatibility exists between the attorney and the party or a substantial disagreement exists between the attorney and the party concerning litigation strategy; or

4. in the attorney's opinion the party is proceeding for purposes of harassment or malicious injury or the party's claims or defenses are not warranted under existing law and cannot be supported by a good faith argument for extension, modification or reversal of existing law.

(i) Application for Relief from Appointment. Any application by an appointed attorney for relief from an order of appointment on any of the grounds set forth in this Rule shall be made to the Court promptly after the attorney becomes aware of the existence of such grounds or within such additional period as the Court may permit for good cause shown.

(j) Order Granting Relief from Appointment. If an application for relief from an order of appointment is granted, the Court shall issue an order directing the appointment of another attorney to represent the party. Where the application for relief from appointment identifies an attorney affiliated with the moving attorney who is able to represent the party, the order shall direct appointment of the affiliated attorney with the consent of the affiliated attorney. Any other appointment shall be made in accordance with the procedures set forth in these Rules. Alternatively, the Court shall have the discretion not to issue a further order of appointment, in which case the party shall be permitted to prosecute or defend the action pro se.

83.4 Discipline of Attorneys

(a) The Chief Judge shall have charge of all matters relating to discipline of members of the bar of this Court.

(b) Any member of the bar of this Court who is convicted of a felony in any State, Territory, other District, Commonwealth, or Possession shall be suspended from practice before this Court and, upon the judgment of conviction becoming final, shall cease to be a member of the bar of this Court.

1. On the presentation to the Court of a certified or exemplified copy of a judgment of conviction, the attorney shall be suspended from practicing before this Court and, on presentation of proof that judgment of conviction is final, the name of the attorney convicted shall, by order of the Court, be struck from the roll of members of the bar of this Court.

(c) Any member of the bar of the Northern District of New York who shall resign from the bar of any State, Territory, other District, Commonwealth or Possession while an investigation into allegations of misconduct is pending shall cease to be a member of the bar of this Court.

On the presentation to the Court of a certified or exemplified copy of an order accepting resignation, the name of the attorney resigning shall, by order of the Court, be struck from the roll of members of the bar of this Court.

(d) Any member of the bar of the Northern District of New York who shall be disciplined by a court in any State, Territory, other District, Commonwealth, or Possession shall be disciplined to the same extent by this Court unless an examination of the record resulting in the discipline discloses

1. that the procedure was so lacking in notice or opportunity to be heard as to constitute a deprivation of due process;

2. that there was such an infirmity of proof establishing the misconduct as to give rise to the clear conviction that this court should not accept as final the conclusion on that subject;

3. that the imposition of the same discipline by this Court would result in grave injustice; or

4. that the misconduct has been held by this Court to warrant substantially different discipline.

On the filing of a certified or exemplified copy of an order imposing discipline, the attorney shall, by order of the Court, be disciplined to the same extent by this court. It is provided, however, that within thirty (30) days of service on the attorney of the order of discipline imposed by the Northern District of New York, either the attorney or a bar association designated by the Chief Judge in the order imposing discipline shall apply to the Chief Judge for an order to show cause why the discipline imposed in the Northern District of New York should not be modified on the basis of one or more of the grounds set forth in this Rule. The term "bar association" as used in this Rule shall mean the following: The New York State Bar Association or any city or county bar association.

(e) Any member of the bar of this Court who is convicted of a misdemeanor in any State, Territory, other District, Commonwealth, or Possession, upon such conviction, may be disbarred, suspended, or censured.

Upon the filing of a certified or exemplified copy of a judgment of conviction, the Chief Judge may designate a bar association to prosecute a proceeding against the attorney. The bar association shall obtain an order requiring the attorney to show cause within thirty (30) days after service, personally or by mail, why the attorney should not be disciplined. The Chief Judge may, for good cause, temporarily suspend the attorney pending the determination of the proceeding. On the attorney's answer to the order to show cause, the Chief Judge may set the matter for prompt hearing before a court of one or more judges or shall appoint a master to hear and to report findings and a recommendation. After a hearing and report, or if no timely answer is made by the attorney or the answer raises no issue requiring a hearing, the Court shall take action as justice requires. In all proceedings, a certificate of conviction shall constitute conclusive proof of the attorney's guilt of the conduct for which the attorney was convicted.

(f) Any attorney who has been disbarred from the bar of a state in which the attorney was admitted to practice shall have their name stricken from the roll of attorneys of this Court or, if suspended from practice for a period at such bar, shall be suspended automatically for a like period from practice in this Court.

(g) In addition to any other sanctions imposed in any particular case under these Rules, any person admitted to practice in this Court may be disbarred or otherwise disciplined, for cause, after hearing, and as the court may direct. The Chief Judge may appoint a Magistrate Judge or attorney(s) to investigate, advise or assist as to grievances or complaints from any source and as to applications by attorneys for relief from discipline. Other than provided by subsection (b) of this Rule, no censure, suspension, disbarment, or other attorney discipline shall be applied without both notice and an opportunity to be heard and the approval of a majority of the judges of the Court in active service, except that any judge of this Court may for cause revoke an admission pro hac vice previously granted by that judge. Complaints or grievances, and any files based on them, shall be treated as confidential. Discipline shall be imposed only upon suitable order of the Court, which shall or shall not be made available to the public, or published or circulated, as the Court shall determine in its discretion.

(h) A visiting attorney permitted to argue or try a particular cause in accordance with L.R. 83.1 who is found guilty of misconduct shall be precluded from again appearing in this Court. On entry of an order of preclusion, the Clerk shall transmit to the court of the State, Territory, District, Commonwealth, or Possession where the attorney was admitted to practice a certified copy of the order and of the Court's opinion.

(i) Unless the Court orders otherwise, no action shall be taken pursuant to L.R. 83.4 (e) and (f) in any case in which disciplinary proceedings against the attorney have been instituted in the State.

(j) The Court shall enforce the N.Y.S. Lawyer's Code of Professional Responsibilities, as adopted from time to time by the Appellate Division of the State of New York and as interpreted and applied by the United States Court of Appeals for the Second Circuit.

(k) Nothing in this Rule shall limit the Court's power to punish contempts or to sanction counsel in accordance with the Federal Rules of Civil or Criminal Procedure or the Court's inherent authority to enforce its rules and orders.

83.5 Contempt

(a) A proceeding to adjudicate a person in civil contempt of court, including a case provided for in Fed. R. Civ. P. 37(b)(2)(D), shall be commenced by the service of a notice of motion or order to show cause.

The affidavit on which the notice of motion or order to show cause is based shall set out with particularity the misconduct complained of, the claim, if any, for resulting damages, and evidence as to the amount of damages that is available to the moving party. A reasonable attorneys' fee, necessitated by the contempt proceeding, may be included as an item of damages. Where the alleged contemnor has appeared in the action by an attorney, the notice of motion or order to show cause and the papers on which it is based shall be served on the contemnor's attorney; otherwise service shall be made personally in the manner provided for by the Federal Rules of Civil Procedure for the service of summons. If an order to show cause is sought, the order may, on necessity shown, embody a direction to the United States Marshal to arrest and hold the alleged contemnor in bail in an amount fixed by the order, conditioned upon appearance at the hearing and further conditioned upon the alleged contemnor's amenability to all orders of the Court for surrender.

(b) If the alleged contemnor puts in issue the alleged misconduct or the resulting damages, the alleged contemnor shall, on demand, be entitled to have oral evidence taken either before the Court or before a master appointed by the Court. When by law the alleged contemnor is entitled to a trial by jury, a written demand shall be made on or before the return day or adjourned day of the application; otherwise the alleged contemnor shall be deemed to have waived a trial by jury.

(c) If the alleged contemnor is found to be in contempt of the Court, an order shall be made and entered

1. Reciting or referring to the verdict or findings of fact on which the adjudication is based;

2. Setting forth the amount of the damages to which the complainant is entitled;

3. Fixing the fine, if any, imposed by the Court, which fine shall include the damages found and naming the person to whom the fine shall be payable;

4. Stating any other conditions, the performance of which shall operate to purge the contempt;

5. Directing, in the Court's discretion, the arrest and confinement of the contemnor by the United States Marshal until the performance of the condition fixed in the order and payment of the fine or until the contemnor is otherwise discharged pursuant to law. The order shall specify the place of confinement. No party shall be required to pay or to advance to the Marshal any expenses for the upkeep of the prisoner. On an order of contempt, no person shall be detained in prison by reason of the non-payment of the fine for a period exceeding six months. A certified copy of the order committing the contemnor shall be sufficient warrant to the Marshal for the arrest and confinement. The aggrieved party shall also have the same remedies against the property of the contemnor as if the order awarding the fine were a final judgment.

(d) If the alleged contemnor is found not guilty of the charges, the contemnor shall be discharged from the proceeding and, in the discretion of the Court, shall have judgment against the complainant for costs, disbursements and a reasonable attorneys' fee.

83.6 Transfer of Cases to Another District

In a case ordered transferred from this district, the Clerk, unless otherwise ordered, shall, upon the expiration of ten (10) days, mail to the court to which the case is transferred

1. Certified copies of the Court's opinion and order compelling the transfer and of the docket entries in the case; and

2. The originals of all papers on file in the case except for the opinion ordering the transfer of the action.

SECTION X. ALTERNATE DISPUTE RESOLUTION AND GENERAL PROVISIONS

83.7-1 Scope and Effectiveness of Rule

This Rule governs the consensual arbitration program for referral of civil actions to court-annexed arbitration. It may remain in effect until further order of the Court. Its purpose is to establish a less formal procedure for the just, efficient and economical resolution of disputes, while preserving the right to a full trial on demand.

83.7-2 Actions Subject to this Rule

The Clerk shall notify the parties in all civil cases, except as otherwise directed by these Rules, that they may consent to non-binding arbitration under this Rule. The notice shall be furnished to the parties at pretrial/scheduling conferences or shall be included with pretrial conference notices and instructions. Consent to arbitration under this Rule shall be discussed at the pretrial/scheduling conference. No party or attorney shall be prejudiced for refusing to participate in arbitration. The Court shall allow the referral of any civil action pending before it to the arbitration process if the parties consent. The plaintiff shall be responsible for securing the execution of a consent form by the parties and for filing the form with the Clerk within ten (10) days after receipt of the form by the parties. Consent shall be freely and knowingly entered into.

83.7-3 Referral to Arbitration

(a) Time for Referral. The Clerk shall refer every action subject to this Rule to arbitration in accordance with the procedures under this Rule twenty (20) days after the filing of the last responsive pleading or within twenty (20) days of the filing of a stipulated consent order referring the action to arbitration, whichever event occurs last, except as otherwise provided. If any party notices a motion to dismiss under the provisions of Fed. R. Civ. P. 12(a) and/or (b), or a motion to join necessary parties pursuant to the Federal Rules of Civil Procedure prior to the expiration of the twenty (20) day period, the motion shall be heard by the assigned judge and further proceedings under this Rule shall be deferred pending decision on the motion. If the action is not dismissed on the motion, it shall be referred to arbitration twenty (20) days after the filing of the decision.

Motions for summary judgment pursuant to Fed. R. Civ. P. 56 shall be filed and served within twenty (20) days following the close of discovery. The filing of a Rule 56 motion shall defer further proceedings under this Rule pending decision on the motion.

(b) Authority of Assigned Judge. Notwithstanding any provision of this Rule, every action subject to this Rule shall be assigned to a judge upon filing in the normal course, in accordance with the Court's Assignment Plan. The assigned judge shall have authority to conduct status and settlement conferences, hear motions and in all other respects supervise the action in accordance with these Rules notwithstanding its referral by consent to arbitration.

(c) Relief from Referral. Any party shall request relief from the operation of this Rule by filing with the Court a motion for the relief within twenty (20) days after entry of the initial stipulated consent order which refers the case for arbitration. The assigned judge shall, sua sponte, exempt an action from the application of this Rule where the objectives of arbitration would not be realized because (1) the case involves complex or novel legal issues, (2) legal issues predominate over factual issues, or (3) for other good cause.

83.7-4 Selection and Compensation of Arbitrator

(a) Selection of Arbitrators. The Clerk shall maintain a roster of arbitrators qualified to hear and determine actions under this Rule. The Court shall select arbitrators from time to time from applications submitted by or on behalf of attorneys willing to serve. To be eligible for selection, an attorney (1) shall have been admitted to practice for not less than five (5) years; (2) shall be a member of the bar of this Court or a member of the New York bar and reside within the Northern District of New York; and (3) shall either (i) for not less than five (5) years have devoted 50% or more of the attorney's professional time to matters involving litigation, or (ii) have substantial experience serving as a "neutral" in dispute resolution proceedings, or (iii) have substantial experience negotiating consensual resolutions to complex problems. Each attorney shall, upon selection, take the oath or affirmation prescribed in 28 U.S.C. § 453 and shall complete any training that the Court requires.

(b) Selection of the Panel. Whenever an action has been referred to arbitration through consent of the parties pursuant to this Rule, the parties shall nominate the arbitrator or arbitrators whom they select to serve as an arbitrator(s) in full compliance with L.R. 83-7-4 (a), or the Clerk shall promptly furnish to each party a list of arbitrators whose names shall have been drawn at random from the roster for the division in which the case is pending. If the parties have elected to proceed with a **single** arbitrator, the Clerk shall provide five (5) names for the selection process. If the parties have elected to proceed with a panel of **three** (3) arbitrators, the Clerk shall provide seven (7) names for the selection process.

1. Each side shall be entitled to strike two names from the list. The list shall be signed by all parties and returned to the Clerk within ten (10) days of receipt. Failure of the parties to timely notify the Clerk of strikes shall result in the Clerk's selection of the panel.

2. The Clerk shall promptly notify the person or persons whose names are not stricken. If the parties have elected to proceed with a single arbitrator, and the arbitrator selected is unable or unwilling to serve, the process of selection under this Rule shall begin anew. If the parties have elected to proceed with a panel of arbitrators and any person selected is unable or unwilling to serve, the Clerk shall select an additional name at

random who shall constitute the third member of the panel. If the Clerk is still unable to form a panel of three arbitrators for any reason, the process of selection under this Rule shall begin anew. When a single arbitrator, or when three of the selected arbitrators have agreed to serve, the Clerk shall promptly send written notice of the membership of the panel to each arbitrator and the parties.

(c) Disqualification. No person shall serve as an arbitrator in an action in which any of the circumstances specified in 28 U.S.C. § 455 (conflict of interest) exist or in good faith shall be believed to exist.

(d) Withdrawal by Arbitrator. Any person whose name appears on the roster maintained in the Clerk's office may ask at any time to have their name removed or, if selected to serve on a panel, decline to serve but remain on the roster.

(e) Compensation and Reimbursement. Arbitrators shall be paid $250.00 per day or portion of each day of hearing in which they participate serving as a single arbitrator or $100.00 for each day or portion of a day if serving as a member of a panel of three (3). Compensation for an arbitrator's services outside of the hearing shall be supported by an affidavit setting forth in detail the time required for pre- and post-hearing matters. When the arbitrators file their decision, each shall submit a voucher, on the form prescribed by the Clerk, for payment by the Administrative Office of the United States Courts of compensation and out-of-pocket expenses necessarily incurred in the performance of their duties under this Rule. No reimbursement shall be made for the cost of office or other space for the hearing.

83.7–5 Arbitration Hearings

(a) Hearing Date. After an answer is filed in a case in which the parties have consented to arbitration and the Court has approved the consent and on completion of the parties' selection of the panel, the arbitration clerk shall send a notice to the attorney setting forth the date, time and location for the arbitration hearing. The date of the arbitration hearing set forth in the notice shall be approximately five (5) months, but in no event later than 180 days, from the date the answer was filed, except that the arbitration proceeding shall not, in the absence of the parties' consent, commence until thirty (30) days after the disposition by the Court of any motion to dismiss the complaint, motion for judgment on the pleadings, or motion to join necessary parties if such a motion was filed and served within twenty (20) days after the filing of the last responsive pleading. Motions for summary judgment pursuant to Fed. R. Civ. P. 56 shall be filed in accordance with 83.7–3(a). The Court may modify the 180–day and twenty (20) day periods specified in L.R. 83.7 for good cause shown. The notice shall also advise the attorneys that they may agree to an earlier date for the arbitration hearing provided the arbitration clerk is notified within thirty (30) days of the date of the notice.

The notice shall also advise the attorneys that they have 120 days to complete discovery unless the Court orders a shorter or longer period for discovery. If a third party has been brought into the action, this notice shall not be sent until the third party has filed an answer.

(b) Upon entry of the order designating the arbitrator(s), the arbitration clerk shall send to each arbitrator a copy of the order designating the arbitrator, a copy of the court docket sheet and a copy of the guidelines for arbitrators. On receipt of the notice scheduling the case to proceed to arbitration and appointing an arbitrator, the plaintiff's attorney shall promptly forward to the arbitrator copies of all pleadings, including any counterclaim or third party complaint and respective answer. Thereafter, and at least ten (10) days prior to the arbitration hearing, each attorney shall deliver to the arbitrator and to the adverse attorney pre-marked copies of all exhibits, including expert reports and all portions of depositions and interrogatories to which reference shall be made at the hearing (but not including documents intended solely for impeachment).

(c) Default of a Party. The arbitration hearing shall proceed in the absence of any party who, after notice, fails to be present. If a party fails to participate in the arbitration process in a meaningful manner, the arbitrator(s) shall make that determination and shall support it with specific written findings filed with the Clerk. The Court shall then conduct a hearing, on notice to all attorneys and personal notice to any party adversely affected by the arbitrator's determination, and may impose any appropriate sanctions, including, but not limited to, the striking of any demand for a trial de novo filed by that party.

(d) Conduct of Hearing. The arbitrator is authorized to administer oaths and affirmations and all testimony shall be given under oath or affirmation. Each party shall have the right to cross-examine witnesses, except as otherwise provided. In receiving evidence, the arbitrator shall be guided by the Federal Rules of Evidence. These rules, however, shall not preclude the arbitrator from receiving evidence which the arbitrator considers to be relevant and trustworthy and which is not privileged. A party desiring to offer a document, otherwise subject to hearsay objections, at the hearing shall serve a copy on the adverse party not less than ten (10) days in advance of the hearing, indicating intent to offer it as an exhibit. Unless the adverse party gives written notice in advance of the hearing of intent to cross-examine the author of the document, any hearsay objection to the document shall be deemed waived. Attendance of witnesses and production of documents shall be compelled in accordance with Fed. R. Civ. P. 45.

(e) Transcript or Recording. A party may cause a transcript or recording to be made of the proceedings at its expense but shall, at the request of the opposing party, make a copy available to the party at no charge, unless the parties have otherwise agreed. Except as provided in L.R. 83.7–7(c), no transcript of the proceeding shall be admissible in evidence at any subsequent de novo trial of the action.

(f) Place of Hearing. Hearings shall be held at any location within the Northern District of New York designated by the arbitrator. Hearings may be held in any courtroom or other room in any federal courthouse made available to the arbitrator by the Clerk's office. When no room is available, the hearing shall be held at any suitable location selected by the arbitrator. In selecting a hearing location, the arbitrator shall consider the convenience of the panel, the parties and the witnesses. The date for the hearing shall not be continued except for extreme and unanticipated emergencies.

(g) Time of Hearing. Unless the parties agree otherwise, hearings shall be held during normal business hours.

(h) Authority of Arbitrator. The arbitrator shall be authorized to make reasonable rules and issue orders necessary for the fair and efficient conduct of the hearing before the arbitrator. Any two members of a panel shall constitute a quorum; but, unless the parties stipulate otherwise, the concurrence of a majority of the entire panel shall be required for any action or decision by the panel.

(i) Ex Parte Communication. There shall be no ex parte communication between an arbitrator and any attorney or party on any matter touching the action except for purposes of scheduling or continuing the hearing.

83.7–6 Award and Judgment

(a) Filing of Award. The arbitrator shall file the award with the Clerk promptly following the close of the hearing and in any event not more than ten (10) days following the close of the hearing. As soon as the award is filed, the Clerk shall serve copies on the parties.

(b) Form of Award. The award shall state clearly and concisely the name or names of the prevailing party or parties, the party or parties against which it is rendered, and the precise amount of money and other relief, if any, awarded. It shall be in writing and, unless the parties stipulate otherwise, be signed by the arbitrator or by at least two members of a panel. No panel member shall participate in the award without having attended the hearing.

(c) Entry of Judgment on Award. Unless a party has filed a demand for a trial de novo (or a notice of appeal which shall be treated as a demand for trial de novo) within thirty (30) days of the filing of the arbitration award, the Clerk shall enter judgment on the arbitration award in accordance with Fed. R. Civ. P. 58. A judgment so entered shall be subject to the same provisions of law and shall have the same force and effect as a judgment of the Court in a civil action, except that the judgment shall not be subject to review in any other court by appeal or otherwise.

(d) Sealing of Arbitration Awards. The contents of any arbitration award made under this Rule shall not be made known to any judicial officer who might be assigned to preside at the trial of the case or to rule on potentially dispositive motions

1. Until the district court has entered final judgment in the action or the action has been otherwise terminated;
2. Except for purposes of preparing the report required by section 903(b) of the Judicial Improvements and Access to Justice Act; or
3. Except as necessary for the Court to determine whether to assess costs or attorneys' fees under 28 U.S.C. § 655.

83.7-7 Trial De Novo

(a) Time for Demand. If either party files and serves a written demand for a trial de novo within thirty (30) days of entry of judgment on the award, the Clerk shall immediately vacate the judgement and the action shall proceed in the normal manner before the assigned judge.

(b) Restoration to Court Docket. On a demand for a trial de novo, the action shall be restored to the Court's docket, trial ready, and treated for all purposes as if it had not been referred to arbitration. In such a case, any right of trial by jury that a party otherwise would have had, as well as any place on the Court calendar which is no later than that which a party otherwise would have had, is preserved.

(c) Limitation on Admission of Evidence. At the trial de novo, the Court shall not admit any evidence that an arbitration proceeding has occurred, the nature or amount of any award, or any other matter concerning the conduct of the arbitration proceeding unless

1. The evidence would otherwise be admissible in the Court under the Federal Rules of Evidence; or

2. The parties have stipulated otherwise.

(d) Arbitrator's Costs. The party requesting a trial de novo shall deposit the cost of the arbitrator's services as a prerequisite to the trial. If the requesting party fails to obtain judgment in an amount which, exclusive of interest and costs, is more favorable to that party, such funds so paid shall be retained by the Clerk. However, if that party is successful in obtaining a more favorable result, the prepaid costs shall be reimbursed.

(e) Opposing Party's Costs. If a party has rejected an award and the action proceeds to trial, that party shall pay the opposing party's actual costs unless the verdict is more favorable to the rejecting party than the arbitrator's award on that claim. If the opposing party has also rejected that award, however, a party is entitled to costs only if the verdict is more favorable to that party than the arbitrator's award:

1. Actual costs include those costs and fees taxable in any civil action and attorneys' fees for each day of trial not to exceed $500.00.

2. For good cause shown, the Court shall order relief from payment of any or all costs.

3. The provisions of L.R. 83.7–7 (d) and (e) shall not apply to claims to which the United States or one of its agencies is a party.

83.7–8 Cases Pending Prior to the Implementation of Arbitration

Notwithstanding the provisions of the Rules set forth above, each district judge shall select cases from the docket currently in process and notify the attorneys involved of the availability of the consensual arbitration program. A case shall qualify for referral to arbitration if it complies with the provisions of this Rule.

83.8 Number of Experts in Patent Cases

On the trial of a patent case, whether in open court or by deposition, or partly in each way, only one expert witness shall be allowed to each side, unless leave for additional experts has been obtained from the Court on motion made and cause shown.

83.9 Commission to Take Testimony

(a) Except as otherwise provided by law, in all actions or proceedings where the taking of depositions of witnesses or of parties is authorized, the procedure for obtaining and using the depositions shall be as provided in the Federal Rules of Civil Procedure. The party seeking the deposition shall furnish the officer to whom the commission is issued with a copy of the Federal Rules of Civil Procedure pertaining to discovery.

(b) Upon receipt of a deposition, the Clerk, unless otherwise ordered, shall open and file it promptly.

83.10 Student Practice

General Order #13 pertains to the rules regarding student practice in this district. A copy of General Order #13 may be obtained from the Clerk's office or on the Court's webpage at "www.nynd.uscourts.gov."

83.11-1 Mediation

(a) Purpose. The purpose of this Rule is to provide a supplementary procedure to the court's existing alternative dispute resolution procedures. It provides for an earlier resolution of civil disputes resulting in savings of time and cost to litigants and the court without sacrificing the quality of justice rendered or the right of litigants to a full trial on all issues not resolved through mediation.

(b) Definitions. Mediation is a process by which an impartial person, the mediator, facilitates communication between disputing parties to promote understanding, reconciliation and settlement. The mediator is an advocate for settlement and uses the mediation process to help the parties fully explore any potential area of agreement. The mediator does not serve as a judge or arbitrator and has no authority to render any decision on any disputed issue or to force a settlement. The parties themselves are responsible for negotiating any resolution(s) to their dispute.

83.11-2 Designation and Qualifications of Mediators

(a) Designation of Mediators. The judges of this Court may authorize those persons who are eligible and qualified to serve as mediators under this Rule in such numbers as the court shall deem appropriate. The Court may withdraw such designation of any mediator at any time. Applications for designation as an ADR panel member are available at the Clerk's office.

(b) List of Mediators. The Alternative Dispute Resolution clerk (ADR clerk) shall maintain a list of court-approved mediators that shall be made available to counsel and the public upon request.

(c) Required Qualifications of Mediators.

1. An individual may be designated as a mediator if he or she (1) has practiced law for at least five (5) years; and (2) is a member in good standing of the bar of this court or of the New York bar and resides within the Northern District of New York; or (3)is a professional mediator who would otherwise qualify as a special master or is determined by the Court to be competent to perform the duties of the mediator and has completed appropriate training

in the process of mediation as the Court may from time to time determine and direct; (4) shall attend and complete a mediation training course sponsored by the Court. Upon Court approval as a mediator, every mediator shall take the oath prescribed by 28 U.S.C.§ 453.

2. No person shall serve as a mediator in an action in which any of the circumstances specified in 28 U.S.C. § 455 exist, or may in good faith be believed to exist. Additionally, any mediator may be disqualified for bias or prejudice as provided in 28 U.S.C. § 144. Furthermore, the mediator has a continuing obligation to disclose any information that may cause a party or the court to believe, in good faith, that such mediator should be disqualified.

(d) Removal from the Panel. Membership in the ADR Panel is a privilege, not a right, which may be terminated at any time by the Board of Judges, as they, in their sole discretion may determine.

(e) Service to the Bar and Court Provided by Mediators. The individuals serving as mediators in the Northern District of New York perform their mediation duties as a pro bono service for the Court, litigants and the bar.

83.11-3 Actions Subject to Mediation

(a) The Court may refer any civil action (or any portion thereof) to mediation under this Rule

1. By order of referral; or
2. On the motion of any party; or
3. By consent of the parties.

(b) Any civil action or claim referred to mediation pursuant to this Rule may be withdrawn from mediation by application to the assigned judge at least ten (10) days prior to the scheduled mediation session.

(c) Notwithstanding the provisions of the Rules set forth above, each judge shall select cases from the docket currently pending and notify the attorneys involved of the availability of the mediation program.

83.11-4 Procedures for Referral, Selecting the Mediator, and Scheduling the Mediation Session

(a) The possibility and appropriateness of mediation under this Rule shall be discussed at the initial status/scheduling conference of the case that is held in accordance with the provisions of General Order #25.

(b) In every case in which the Court determines that referral to mediation is appropriate pursuant to 83.11-3 of this Rule, the

Court shall enter an order of reference, which shall define the period of time during which the mediation session shall be conducted. The Court intends that mediation under this Rule occur at the earliest practical time in an effort to encourage earlier, less costly resolutions of disputes. Referral to mediation under this Rule shall not delay or stay other proceedings, including but not limited to discovery, unless the Court so orders.

(c) Within ten (10) days of the order of reference, parties are to select a mediator of their choice from a list of mediators available from the Court and submit the selection to the ADR clerk in the Clerk's office. If no such selection is made in a timely manner or if the parties cannot agree upon the mediator, the ADR clerk shall make the selection for them. The ADR clerk shall work with the selected mediator and counsel of record to set a mutually agreeable date for the mediation within the time prescribed by the order of reference.

(d) Mediation sessions under this Rule may be held in any available court space or in any other suitable location agreeable to the mediator and the parties. Consideration shall be given to the convenience of the parties and to the cost and time of travel involved.

(e) There shall be no continuance of a mediation session beyond the time set in the referral order except by order of this Court upon a showing of good cause. If any rescheduling occurs within the prescribed time, the ADR clerk must be notified and the location of the rescheduled hearing must be selected.

(f) Any settlement prior to the scheduled mediation shall be promptly reported to the mediator and to the ADR clerk.

83.11-5 The Mediation Session

(a) Memorandum for Mediation. At least two days prior to the mediation session, each party shall provide to the mediator and all other such parties a "memorandum for mediation." This memo shall:

1. State the name and role of each person expected to attend;
2. Identify each person with full settlement authority;
3. Include a concise summary of the parties' claims or defenses;
4. Discuss liability and damages; and
5. State the relief sought by such party.

The summary shall not exceed five pages and shall not be filed in the case or otherwise made part of the court file.

(b) Attendance Required. The attorney who is expected to try the case for each party shall appear and shall be accompanied by an individual with authority to settle the lawsuit. The latter shall be the parties (if natural persons) or representatives of parties, that are not natural persons. This latter party may not be counsel (except in-house counsel). Attorneys for the parties shall notify other interested parties such as insurers or indemnitors who shall attend and are subject to the provisions of this Rule. Only the assigned judge may excuse attendance of any attorney, party, or party's representative. Any such request must be made in writing to the presiding judge a minimum of forty-eight (48) hours in advance of the mediation session.

(c) Good Faith Participation in the Process. Parties and counsel shall participate in good faith, without any time constraints, and put forth their best efforts toward settlement. Typically, the mediator will meet initially with all parties to the dispute and their counsel in a joint session and thereafter separately with each party and their representative. This process permits the mediator and the parties to explore the needs and interests underlying their respective positions, generate and evaluate alternative settlement proposals or potential solutions, and consider interests that may be outside the scope of the stated controversy including matters that may not be addressed by the Court. The parties will participate in crafting a resolution of the dispute.

(d) Confidentiality. Mediation is regarded as a settlement procedure and is confidential and private. No participant may disclose, without consent of the other parties, any confidential information acquired during mediation. There shall be no stenographic or electronic record, e.g., audio or video, of the mediation process.

1. All written and oral communications made in connection with or during the mediation session are confidential.

2. No communication made in connection with or during any mediation session may be disclosed or used for any purpose in any pending or future proceeding in the U.S. District Court for the Northern District of New York.

3. Privileged and confidential status is afforded all communications made in connection with the mediation session, including matters emanating from parties and counsel as well as mediators' comments, assessments, and recommendations concerning case development, discovery, and motions. Except for communication between the assigned judge and the mediator regarding noncompliance with program procedures (as set forth in this Rule), *there will be no communications between the Court and the mediator regarding a case that has been desig-*

nated for mediation. The parties will be asked to sign an agreement of confidentiality at the beginning of the mediation session.

4. Parties, counsel and mediators may respond to inquiries from authorized court staff which are made for the purpose of program evaluation. Such responses will be kept in strict confidence.

5. The mediator may not be required to testify in any proceeding relating to or arising out of the matter in dispute. Nor may the mediator be subject to process requiring disclosure of information or data relating to or arising out of the matter in dispute.

6. *Immunity.* A mediator, as well as the Mediation Administrator, shall be immune from claims arising out of acts or omissions incident to service as a court appointee in this mediation. See e.g. Wagshal v. Foster, 28 F.3d 1249 (D.C. Cir. 1994).

7. *Default.* Subject to mediator's approval, the mediation session may proceed in the absence of a party, who, after due notice, fails to be present. The Court may impose sanctions on any party who, absent good cause shown, fails to attend or participate in the mediation session in good faith in accordance with this Rule.

8. *Conclusion of the Mediation Session.* The mediation shall be concluded:

a. By resolution and settlement of the dispute by the parties;

b. By adjournment for future mediation by agreement of the parties and the mediator; or

c. Upon declaration of impasse by the mediator that future efforts to resolve the dispute are no longer worthwhile.

Unless the Court authorizes otherwise, mediation sessions shall be concluded at least ten (10) days prior to any final pretrial conference scheduled by the Court.

If the mediation is adjourned by agreement for further mediation, the additional session shall be concluded within the time the Court orders.

83.11-6 Mediation Report; Notice of Settlement or Trial

(a) Immediately upon conclusion of the mediation, the mediator shall file a mediation report with the ADR clerk, indicating only whether the case settled, settled in part, or did not settle.

(b) In the event the parties reach an agreement to settle the case, the representatives for each party shall promptly notify the ADR clerk and promptly prepare and file the appropriate stipulation of dismissal.

(c) If the parties reach a partial agreement to narrow, withdraw or settle some but not all claims, they shall file a stipulation concisely setting forth the resolved claims with the ADR clerk within five (5) days of the mediation. The parties shall be bound by the stipulation.

(d) If the mediation session does not conclude in settlement of all the issues in the case, the case will proceed toward trial pursuant to the scheduling orders entered in the case.

83.12-1 Early Neutral Evaluation

The ENE Process. Early neutral evaluation (ENE) is a process in which parties obtain from an experienced neutral (an "evaluator") a nonbinding, reasoned, oral evaluation of the merits of the case. The first step in the ENE process involves the Court appointing an evaluator who has expertise in the area of law in the case. After essential information and position statements are exchanged early in the pretrial period (usually within 150 to 200 days after a complaint has been filed), the evaluator convenes an ENE session that typically lasts about two hours. At the ENE meeting, each side briefly presents the factual and legal basis of its position. The evaluator may ask questions of the parties and help them identify the main issues in dispute and also areas of agreement. He or she may also help the parties explore options for settlement. If settlement does not occur, the evaluator then offers his or her opinion as to the settlement value of the case, including the likelihood of liability and the likely range of damages. With the benefit of this assessment, the parties are again encouraged to discuss settlement, with or without the evaluator's assistance. They may also explore ways of narrowing the issues in dispute, exchanging information about the case or otherwise preparing efficiently for trial.

The evaluator has no power to impose a settlement or to dictate any agreement regarding the pretrial management of the case. The ENE process, whether or not it results in settlement, is confidential.

83.12-2 Designation and Qualifications of Evaluators

(a) Designation of Evaluators. The judges of this Court may authorize those persons who are eligible and qualified to serve as evaluators under this rule in such numbers as the Court shall deem appropriate. The Court may withdraw such designation of any evaluator at any time. Applications for designation as an ADR panel member are available at the Clerk's office.

(b) List of Evaluators. The ADR clerk shall maintain a list of court-approved evaluators that shall be made available to counsel and the public upon request.

(c) Required Qualifications of Evaluators.

1. An individual may be designated as an Early Neutral Evaluator if he or she (1) has practiced law for at least fifteen years; and (2) is a member in good standing of the bar of this court or of the New York bar and resides within the Northern District of New York; or (3) is a professional who is determined by the Court to be competent to perform the duties of the evaluator and has completed appropriate training in the process of Early Neutral Evaluation as the Court may from time to time determine and direct. Upon Court approval as an evaluator, every evaluator shall take the oath prescribed by 28 U.S.C. § 453.

2. No person shall serve as an evaluator in an action in which any of the circumstances specified in 28 U.S.C. § 455 exist or may in good faith be believed to exist. Additionally any evaluator may be disqualified for bias or prejudice as provided in 28 U.S.C. § 144. Furthermore, the evaluator has a continuing obligation to disclose any information which may cause a party or the Court to believe in good faith that such evaluator should be disqualified.

(d) Removal from the Panel. Membership in the ADR Panel is a privilege, not a right, which may be terminated at any time by the Board of Judges, as they, in their sole discretion may determine.

(e) Service to the Bar and Court Provided by Evaluators. The individuals serving as evaluators in the Northern District of New York perform their duties as a pro bono service to the Court, litigants, and the bar.

83.12-3 Actions Subject to Early Neutral Evaluation

(a) The Court may refer any civil action (or any portion thereof) to Early Neutral Evaluation under this Rule

1. By order of referral;
2. On the motion of any party; or
3. By consent of the parties.

(b) Any civil action or claim referred to the Early Neutral Evaluation Process pursuant to this Rule may be withdrawn from the program by application to the assigned judge at least ten (10) days before the scheduled evaluation session.

(c) Notwithstanding the provisions of the rules set forth above, each judge shall select cases from the docket currently pending and notify the attorneys involved of the availability of the Early Neutral Evaluation Process.

(d) When a case is designated for ENE, the ADR clerk will provide counsel with copies of the judge's designation order, a listing by division of the available early neutral evaluators, and a copy of the ENE procedure guide.

83.12-4 Administrative Procedures and Requirements

(a) In most cases, the ENE order will be issued early enough in the pretrial period to allow the ENE session to be held between 150 and 200 days from the filing of the complaint.

(b) When the ADR clerk receives a copy of a judicial order designating a case for ENE, the parties will be given a date by which they must choose an evaluator from the list provided to counsel. If selection of an evaluator is not made by the designated date, the ADR clerk will assign an evaluator with expertise in the subject matter of the lawsuit and notify counsel.

(c) The evaluator will contact all attorneys and set the date and place of the evaluation session. Whenever possible, the ENE session shall be held within 150 to 200 days of the filing of the complaint and within forty-five days of the date the ADR clerk notifies counsel of the identity of the evaluator.

(d) The ADR clerk and evaluators shall schedule ENE proceedings in a manner that does not interfere in any way with the management of case processing or actions of the referring judge. *No party may avoid or postpone any obligation imposed by the order of reference on any ground related to the ENE process.*

83.12-5 Evaluation Statements

(a) No later than ten (10) calendar days prior to the ENE session, each party shall submit directly to the evaluator, and shall serve on all other parties, a written evaluation statement not to exceed ten (10) pages *excluding exhibits and attachments*.

Such statements must

1. Identify person(s), in addition to counsel, who will attend the ENE session and who have decision-making authority;

2. Address whether the case involves legal or factual issues the early resolution of which might reduce the scope of the dispute or contribute significantly to settlement negotiations; and

3. Identify the discovery that will contribute most to meaningful settlement negotiations.

(b) Parties may also identify persons whose presence at the ENE session might improve significantly the productivity of the session.

(c) Parties shall attach to the evaluation statements, copies of key documents out of which the suit arose (e.g., contracts) or materials that might advance the purposes of the ENE session (e.g., medical reports).

Written evaluation statements are NOT to be filed with the Court. Evaluation statements are considered confidential between the parties and the evaluator.

83.12–6 Attendance at ENE Sessions

(a) The Court requires parties to attend evaluation sessions. The main purposes of an ENE session are to give litigants the opportunity (1) to present their positions; (2) to hear their opponents' view of the issues in dispute; and (3) to hear a neutral assessment of the strengths of each side's case.

(b) When a party to a case is not a natural person (e.g. a corporation), a person *other than the outside counsel* who has authority to enter stipulations and to bind the party in a settlement must attend.

(c) In cases involving insurance carriers, company representatives with settlement authority shall attend.

(d) When a party is a unit of the federal government, an agency representative and counsel from the U.S. Attorney's Office, must attend the ENE session.

(e) An attorney for each party who has primary responsibility for handling the trial of the matter must attend the ENE session.

(f) A party or attorney may be excused from attending an ENE session only after petitioning the referring judge in writing no fewer than ten (10) calendar days before the scheduled ENE session. Such a petition must show that attendance at the ENE session would impose an extraordinary or unjustifiable hardship.

(g) Default. Subject to the approval of the evaluator, the evaluation session may proceed in the absence of a party, who, after due notice, fails to be present. The Court may impose sanctions on any party who, absent good cause shown, fails to attend or participate in the evaluation session in good faith in accordance with this Rule.

83.12-7 Procedures at ENE Sessions

(a) The evaluator has broad discretion to structure the ENE session. She or he will decide the time and place of the session and will structure the session and any follow-up sessions. Rules of evidence shall not apply and there is no formal examination or cross-examination of witnesses.

(b) The evaluator shall:

1. Permit each party, or counsel, to make an oral presentation of its position;

2. Help parties identify areas of agreement and enter stipulations, wherever feasible;

3. Assess the relative strengths and weaknesses of the parties' positions and explain the reasons for the assessments;

4. Help parties explore settlement;

5. Estimate, where possible, the likelihood of liability and the range of damages;

6. Help parties develop an information-sharing or discovery plan to expedite settlement discussions or to position the case for disposition by other means; and

7. Determine what, if any, follow-up measures will contribute to case development or settlement (e.g. written reports; telephone reports; additional ENE sessions; or other forms of ADR, such as arbitration; mediation; settlement conference; or consent before a Magistrate Judge).

(c) When an evaluator completes work on a case, she or he will, *regardless of case outcome*, submit an evaluator assessment form to the ADR clerk.

83.12-8 Confidentiality

Early Neutral Evaluation is regarded as a settlement procedure and is confidential and private. No participant may disclose, without consent of the other parties, any confidential information acquired during the ENE session. There shall be no stenographic or electronic record, e.g., audio or video, of the ENE process.

(a) All written and oral communications made in connection with or during any ENE sessions are confidential.

(b) No communication made in connection with or during any ENE sessions may be disclosed or used for any purpose in any pending or future proceeding in this Court.

(c) Privileged and confidential status is afforded all communications made in connection with ENE sessions, including matters emanating from parties and counsel as well as evaluators' comments, assessments, and recommendations concerning case development, discovery and motions. Except for communication between the assigned judge and the evaluator regarding noncompliance with program procedures as set forth in this Rule, *there will be no communications between the Court and the evaluator regarding a case that has been designated for evaluation*. The parties will be asked to sign an agreement of confidentiality at the beginning of the evaluation session.

(d) Parties, counsel, and evaluators may respond to inquiries from authorized court staff which are made for the purposes of program evaluation. Such responses will be kept in strict confidence.

(e) The evaluator may not be required to testify in any proceeding relating to or arising out of the matter in dispute. Nor may the evaluator be subject to process requiring disclosure of information or data relating to or arising out of the matter in dispute.

83.12–9 Role of Evaluators

(a) Evaluators may not compel parties or counsel to conduct or respond to discovery or to file motions.

(b) Evaluators may not determine the issues in a case or impose limits on pretrial activities.

(c) Evaluators, and any parties who encounter a problem during the ENE session and have discussed such problem with the evaluator without obtaining a satisfactory resolution of the matter, shall report to the assigned judge any instances of noncompliance with ENE procedures that, in their view, may disrupt the evaluation process or threaten the integrity of the ENE program.

(d) Immunity. An evaluator, as well as the Clerk, shall be immune from claims arising out of acts or omissions incident to service as a court appointee in this Early Neutral Evaluation Program.

83.12–10 Early Neutral Evaluation Report

(a) Immediately upon conclusion of the evaluation session, the evaluator shall file a report with the ADR clerk indicating only whether the case settled, settled in part, or did not settle.

(b) In the event the parties reach an agreement to settle the case, the representatives for each party shall promptly notify the ADR clerk and promptly prepare and file the appropriate stipulation of dismissal.

(c) If the parties reach a partial agreement to narrow, withdraw, or settle some but not all claims, they shall file a stipulation concisely setting forth the resolved claims with the ADR clerk within five (5) days of the evaluation session. The parties shall be bound by the stipulation.

(d) If the Early Neutral Evaluation Session does not conclude in settlement of all the issues in the case, the case will proceed toward trial pursuant to the scheduling orders entered in the case.

83.13 Sealed Matters

Cases may be sealed in their entirety, or only as to certain parties or documents, when they are initiated, or at various stages of the proceedings. The Court may on its own motion enter an order directing that a document, party or entire case be sealed. A party seeking to have a document, party or entire case sealed shall submit an application, under seal, setting forth the reason(s) why the document, party or entire case should be sealed, together with a proposed order for approval by the assigned judge. The proposed order shall include language in the "ORDERED" paragraph stating the referenced document(s) to be sealed and should include the phrase "including this sealing order." Upon the assigned judge's approval of the sealing order, the Clerk shall seal the document(s) and the sealing order. A complaint presented for filing with a motion to seal and a proposed order shall be treated as a sealed case, pending approval of the order. Once a document or case is sealed by court order, it shall remain under seal until a subsequent order, upon the Court's own motion or in response to the motion of a party, is entered directing that the document or case be unsealed.

84.1 Forms

[Reserved.]

85.1 Title

[Reserved.]

86.1 Effective Date

See L.R. 1.1(b).

SECTION XI. CRIMINAL PROCEDURE

[Omitted.]

SECTION XII. LOCAL RULES OF PROCEDURE FOR ADMIRALTY AND MARITIME CASES

[Omitted.]

INDEX

References are to Federal Rule of Civil Procedure (C), Federal Rule of Appellate Procedure (A), Section of 28 U.S.C. (§), or Federal Rule of Evidence (E)

INDEX

†